CRIMINAL EVIDENCE

CRIMINAL EVIDENCE

Second Edition

PAUL ROBERTS

Professor of Criminal Jurisprudence,
University of Nottingham

ADRIAN ZUCKERMAN

Professor of Civil Procedure &
Fellow of University College, Oxford

OXFORD
UNIVERSITY PRESS

OXFORD

UNIVERSITY PRESS

Great Clarendon Street, Oxford OX2 6DP
United Kingdom

Oxford University Press is a department of the University of Oxford.
It furthers the University's objective of excellence in research, scholarship,
and education by publishing worldwide. Oxford is a registered trade mark of
Oxford University Press in the UK and in certain other countries

First published 2004
This edition 2010
Reprinted 2012

British Library Cataloguing in Publication Data
Data available

Library of Congress Cataloging in Publication Data
Data available

ISBN 978-0-19-923164-5

Printed and bound by CPI Group (UK) Ltd, Croydon, CR0 4YY

FOREWORD

The Right Hon Sir Robin Auld

The second edition of this scholarly work is welcome and timely. There has been much legislative, judicial and academic attention to the law of evidence in criminal proceedings since publication of the first edition following the 2003 Act. As the authors acknowledge, they did not intend the work as a conventional legal text book. It is one to which legislators, judges, legal practitioners, academics, and students should all have ready recourse. It continues usefully to bridge principles and practice of the strange common law construct, rules of admissibility – or inadmissibility as Professor J.C. Smith preferred – of evidence in criminal proceedings.

Would that we could do without rules of evidence altogether in criminal proceedings, and rely on fact-finders to give relevant evidence, in whatever form, the weight it deserves – a Utopian ideal provocatively aired by Jeremy Bentham, Sir Rupert Cross and, more recently, William Twining. But, as this new edition so powerfully demonstrates, rules of evidence are inextricably bound up with our historic and constantly evolving adversarial procedural law and practice. In recent years there have been wide and far-reaching changes in procedure flowing from a surge in prominence of fundamental notions of fairness and due process. In the result there is more uncharted territory out there – more unknowns for which legislation, judge-made law, or established practice provide no ready answer. Both practitioners and scholars now have greater encouragement and need than formerly to resort to principle for assistance.

The dramatically changed scene is justification in itself for this new edition. Among the notable and fundamental changes are reforms of the hearsay rule and as to character introduced by the 2003 Act, the respective effects of which are admirably treated in new Chapters 9 and 14. Chapter 9, read with Chapter 7, is right on cue in its examination of recent rulings of our highest court in *Davis* as to the long-term significance of the right to confrontation as a consideration of fairness in individual cases, and in *Horncastle* as to the potential determinative strength of hearsay. Chapter 14 deals with the far-reaching transformation by the 2003 Act of the law of character evidence in the substitution of a comprehensive framework of admissibility for the pre-existing mix of common law and statutory provisions, in particular the introduction of a broad range of meanings of evidence of 'bad character' and identification of 'gateways' for its admissibility.

In those and many other respects, the authors' presentation is an attractive blend of manageable scholarship and practical analysis. I also commend their diligence and responsiveness to comments on the well-received first edition in their editing and substantial re-structuring of the work.

Robin Auld
Cambridge
2nd July 2010

PREFACE TO THE SECOND EDITION

The first edition of this book was gratifyingly well-received. In addition to a string of complimentary reviews,[1] it was honoured with a special symposium issue of the *International Commentary on Evidence*.[2] Student opinion was admittedly more divided. One exasperated undergraduate *Amazon* reviewer bemoaned 'pages and pages of abstract analysis, theoretical waffle and social policy [and].... very little emphasis on cases'. To which another replied: 'I do not understand how anyone can write a negative review about this book. I am reaching the end of my final year of a Law degree, and this book is one of the best that I have read. It is clear, it is well written, and it explains all of the key areas in sufficient detail. There are lots of cases and statutory provisions mentioned... It offers critical comment in appropriate areas, and summarises the opinions of other academics in the field. It can be best described as "the Bible of Criminal Evidence"'.

Whilst we hope to cater for students of criminal evidence at all levels who are willing to be challenged intellectually and are open to all that this fascinating subject has to offer, this is not intended to be 'a law textbook' in the conventional, expository, sense. In the style of a monograph, the book develops a programmatic argument for a particular conception of the discipline of Criminal Evidence and its jurisprudential foundations. Although each chapter is more or less freestanding in its treatment of particular topics, the work as a whole is intended to be read from start to finish. It is a book with a strong theoretical orientation rather than a book about theory; and one that attempts to place criminal trial procedure in its broader epistemological, normative, and socio-legal contexts rather than a book which focuses on context at the expense of doctrinal analysis. We have tried to encompass the substance of the law of criminal evidence in sufficient detail to make the book relevant and useful for judges and lawyers involved in criminal litigation. Thanks to judges in Canada, Hong Kong, and Northern Ireland,[3] we now have some concrete evidence that this aspiration is not completely delusional.

We are truly grateful to everybody who has taken the time to engage with the book's arguments and content and provide critical feedback on the first edition. In writing a book condensing the labours of lifetimes, one incurs more intellectual debts than can be acknowledged in a preface. To our certain knowledge, the following made helpful contributions on this occasion (and we must trust that those unjustly omitted will not draw a mistaken of inference of ingratitude form the fallibilities of human memory): Ron Allen, Christine Boyle, Craig Callen, Debbie Cooper, Antony Duff, Peter Duff, Lindsay Farmer,

---

[1] See [2005] Crim LR 505; (2006) 10 E & P 327; (2005) 50 *Criminal Law Quarterly* 349.

[2] Craig Callen and John Jackson (eds.), *Special Issue: Commentaries on Roberts and Zuckerman's* Criminal Evidence (2005) 2(2) *International Commentary on Evidence*, www.bepress.com/ice/vol2/iss2/. And in reply see Paul Roberts, 'Roberts and Zuckerman's *Criminal Evidence*: (Un)grateful Comments on Six Commentaries' (2007) 5(2) *International Commentary on Evidence*, Article 2, www.bepress.com/ice/vol5/iss2/art2/.

[3] See *R v Khela* [2009] SCC 4, [29] (Fish J); *Re An Application by JA for Judicial Review* [2007] NIQB 64, [17] (Kerr LCJ); *HKSAR v Hung Chan Wa* [2005] HKCA 232, [62] (Stock JA); *R v Lafrance* [2004] ONCJ 302, 66 WCB (2d) 603, [82] (Renaud J).

Jim Fraser, David Hamer, Laura Hoyano, Jill Hunter, John Jackson, Penney Lewis, Andrew Ligertwood, Larry Laudan, Jenny McEwan, Sandra Marshall, Joelle Moreno, Jesse Nyman, Amit Pundik, Mike Redmayne, Gilles Renaud, Candida Saunders, Daniel Seidmann, John Spencer, Alex Stein, Victor Tadros, Peter Tillers, William Twining, and Tony Ward. This new edition has also benefitted greatly from being used in our own teaching: there is surely no better litmus of what works in a text, and what needs reworking, than hearing oneself try to reproduce it in a lecture and reading the reactions in the faces of the audience. In tackling the second edition, we were under no illusions about the scale of remedial work that needed to be undertaken on the original text.

For this edition, the book has been substantially restructured and rewritten, partly to accommodate the welter of new cases, legislation, research, and commentary which have poured forth since 2004, but also to improve the clarity of the exposition and to give greater emphasis to underlying principles. We have expanded the number of chapters from 12 to 16 with only a modest increase in overall length. The original chapter on witness evidence proved unwieldy, and has now been split into three. Likewise for ease of reference, discussion of the privilege against self-incrimination and the law of confessions has been disaggregated into separate chapters. The material on basic definitions and concepts of evidence, proof, and fact-finding has been reordered and consolidated into two consecutive chapters. To round off, there is a new concluding chapter retracing the book's central themes and venturing some tentative remarks on future disciplinary directions.

An impression of the scale of necessary up-dating may be gleaned from the number of times a year after 2003 appears in the table of cases. Whilst every topic discussed in the book has attracted new cases or legislation in the intervening years, the burgeoning case-law interpreting the hearsay and bad character provisions of the Criminal Justice Act 2003 is a particularly notable development since the first edition. Amongst the other case-law landmarks of the last six years, the eye is drawn to *A v Home Secretary (No 2)*[4] on the inadmissibility of torture evidence, *R v Davis*[5] on the right of confrontation, and – handed down just as the manuscript was being finalised – the decision of the UK Supreme Court in *R v Horncastle*[6] on the hearsay evidence of absent witnesses, which is required reading for human rights lawyers and constitutional scholars as much as for students of criminal evidence. New legislation has also continued to appear virtually annually, most recently in the form of the Coroners and Justice Act 2009 (the criminal procedure provisions are mostly not yet in force at the time of writing). Another pivotal legislative development post-2004 is the Criminal Procedure Rules, already in their second, 2010 iteration. In addition to all of these substantive changes, stylistic and other presentational improvements have been made throughout the entire text, which has effectively been rewritten line by line.

A large number of people is involved in turning a manuscript into a book and marketing it to the world, and we should like to record our thanks, also, to all at OUP for their customary professionalism and dedication to this project. Our long-suffering publishing

---

[4] *A v Secretary of State for the Home Department (No 2)* [2006] 2 AC 221, [2005] UKHL 71, discussed in Chapter 5.

[5] *R v Davis* [2008] 1 AC 1128, [2008] UKHL 36, discussed in Chapter 7.

[6] *R v Horncastle* [2009] UKSC 14, [2010] 2 WLR 47, discussed in Chapter 9.

editor Tom Young deserves special mention for his unfailing support and patience in dealing with authors incapable of grasping the concept of a deadline.

We have tried to state the law of England and Wales on 1 January 2010; but more importantly, to elucidate the underlying principles of common law criminal evidence which have developed over the preceding several centuries.

P.R.   A.Z.
Heathrow Terminal 4,   The Bahamas
Ash Wednesday, 2010.

TABLE OF CONTENTS

TABLE OF LEGISLATION

TABLE OF CASES

TABLE OF STATUTORY INSTRUMENTS

TABLE OF INTERNATIONAL & COMPARATIVE MATERIALS

1

PRINCIPLES OF CRIMINAL EVIDENCE

1.1 AN INVITATION TO CRIMINAL EVIDENCE

This book aims to provide an accessible but rigorous and reasonably comprehensive critical introduction to the principles of criminal evidence. On the face of it, *criminal* evidence represents only one half of the Law of Evidence[1] as it is traditionally conceived in common law jurisdictions. Why is our focus so selective, and in particular, why does evidence in civil proceedings not receive equal billing and the same careful attention in the following pages? The next fifteen chapters can be read as an extended answer to these questions, and ultimately stand as their own justification. However, we should say a little more by way of introduction about this book's distinctive focus and methodology. Whilst concentrating exclusively on criminal adjudication admittedly narrows down our focus in one dimension, in virtually every other respect this book adopts a broader, more inclusive, and contextualized approach to evidence and proof than conventional legal treatments of the subject. Orthodox conceptions of the Law of Evidence will serve as a foil for illustrating the distinctive features of our approach.

What, exactly, *is* the Law of Evidence as common lawyers understand it? If that question sounds strange, or if one is tempted to assume that its answer must be obvious, that is only because elementary questions about the scope and content of traditional legal subjects tend not to receive the reflective attention they deserve. It was *not* ever thus in the Law of Evidence. The American legal scholar James Bradley Thayer, who has as good a claim as anyone else to be regarded as the founding father of modern Anglo-American evidence scholarship, took time to reflect on the subject's disciplinary parameters, form, and function.[2] Though they might strike contemporary readers as unusual, such inquiries are neither idle nor abstruse. For the fruits of any investigation are always partly determined – or prejudiced – by its initial parameters and foundational assumptions: spotlights illuminate and microscopes magnify only where they are deliberately directed. The Law of Evidence

---

[1] 'Law of Evidence' (sometimes shortened simply to 'Evidence', or transformed into 'Criminal Evidence') will be capitalized when referring to the legal discipline as a proper noun.

[2] James Bradley Thayer, *A Preliminary Treatise on Evidence at the Common Law* (Little, Brown & Co, 1898), esp. chs 6 and 12. Also see William Twining, *Rethinking Evidence: Exploratory Essays* (CUP, 2nd edn. 2006), ch 7. For discussion of Thayer's influence on the historical evolution of the Law of Evidence, see William Twining, *Theories of Evidence: Bentham and Wigmore* (Weidenfeld & Nicolson, 1985), chs 3–4 and appendix; Eleanor Swift, 'One Hundred Years of Evidence Law Reform: Thayer's Triumph' (2000) 88 *California LR* 2437; Jay Hook, 'A Brief Life of James Bradley Thayer' (1993) 88 *Northwestern University LR* 1.

as a self-conscious discipline is barely more than a century old,[3] so its traditional format can hardly lay claim to eternal preordination. Yet, the twenty-first century English Law of Evidence still retains most of the basic structure, and much of the content and terminology, fashioned by its nineteenth and early twentieth century architects. The time is surely ripe for a measure of rethinking.[4]

The Law of Evidence is conventionally characterized as 'adjectival' as opposed to 'substantive' law, a branch of legal doctrine pertaining to secondary issues of procedure rather than primary legal rights and duties. A more informative (albeit revisionist) working definition might be that the Law of Evidence regulates the generation, collection, organization, presentation, and evaluation of information ('evidence') for the purpose of resolving disputes about past events in legal adjudication. Less technically, we might say in broad terms that the Law of Evidence governs fact-finding in legal proceedings. Fact-finding is a

---

[3] Any statement about the genesis of the Law of Evidence is bound to be contentious. However, it is difficult to see any developments prior to the latter part of the nineteenth century, and certainly not before the mid-nineteenth century statutory reforms of criminal procedure, as heralding anything resembling a self-conscious discipline in the modern sense; though this may be linked more generally to the contemporaneous development of university law teaching and the rise of the 'textbook tradition' from the second half of the nineteenth century, as much as reflecting factors peculiar to the Law of Evidence: cf. David Sugarman, 'Legal Theory, the Common Law Mind and the Making of the Textbook Tradition', in William Twining (ed.), *Legal Theory and Common Law* (Blackwell, 1986). The first notable treatise on the *Law of Evidence* was written by Lord Chief Baron Gilbert during the 1720s, and published in 1754, and there were further key contributions to the evolution of the discipline during the course of the nineteenth century from the likes of Bentham, Starkie, Taylor, and James Fitzjames Stephen: see William Twining, *Theories of Evidence*, 1–5; Stephan Landsman, 'From Gilbert to Bentham: The Reconceptualization of Evidence Theory' (1990) 36 *Wayne Law Review* 1149. However, the earlier of these works were primarily wide-ranging philosophical treatments of problems of proof or, in Bentham's case, a blueprint for systematic reform of procedural law in accordance with his Principle of Utility: see Twining, *Theories of Evidence*, ch 2. The forerunners of modern textbooks really began with the Victorians. On the other hand, if greater emphasis is placed on legal practice as opposed to legal scholarship, the favoured date of origin is the later part of the eighteenth century, certainly after 1750: see John H. Langbein, 'Historical Foundations of the Law of Evidence: A View from the Ryder Sources' (1996) 96 *Columbia LR* 1168. Of course, human societies have been discussing problems of evidence and proof in more general terms since antiquity, and beyond into prehistory: see, for example, Tony Honoré, 'The Primacy of Oral Evidence?' in C. F. H. Tapper (ed.), *Crime, Proof and Punishment* (Butterworths, 1981) (discussing the Roman law of evidence 100–300AD); James Franklin, *The Science of Conjecture* (Johns Hopkins UP, 2001), ch 1 (tracing 'the Ancient Law of Proof' back as far as an Egyptian court document of 2200BC, stated to be 'one of the earliest records of human thought').

[4] See further, Paul Roberts and Mike Redmayne (eds.), *Innovations in Evidence and Proof: Integrating Theory, Research and Teaching* (Hart, 2007); William Twining, *Rethinking Evidence: Exploratory Essays* (CUP, 2nd edn. 2006); Roger C. Park and Michael J. Saks, 'Evidence Scholarship Reconsidered: Results of the Interdisciplinary Turn' (2006) 47 *Boston College LR* 94; Alex Stein, *Foundations of Evidence Law* (OUP, 2005); Mary Childs and Louise Ellison (eds.), *Feminist Perspectives on Evidence* (Cavendish, 2000); W Twining, 'Recent Trends in Evidence Scholarship', in J. F. Nijboer and J. M. Reijntjes (eds.), *Proceedings of the First World Conference on New Trends in Criminal Investigation and Evidence* (Lelystad, 1997); Alex Stein, 'The Refoundation of Evidence Law' (1996) 9 *Canadian Journal of Law and Jurisprudence* 279; John D. Jackson, 'Analysing the New Evidence Scholarship: Towards a New Conception of the Law of Evidence' (1996) 16 *OJLS* 309; Jill Hunter and Kathryn Cronin, *Evidence, Advocacy and Ethical Practice: A Criminal Trial Commentary* (Butterworths, Sydney, 1995); Roger C. Park, 'Evidence Scholarship, Old and New' (1991) 75 *Minnesota LR* 849; William Twining, 'Hot Air in the Redwoods, A Sequel to the Wind in the Willows' (1988) 86 *Michigan LR* 1523, responding to Kenneth W. Graham Jr, ' "There'll Always be an England": The Instrumental Ideology of Evidence' (1987) 85 *Michigan LR* 1204; Richard Lempert, 'The New Evidence Scholarship: Analyzing the Process of Proof' (1986) 66 *Boston University LR* 439.

topic within the field of epistemology (the philosophy of knowledge),[5] and legal adjudication is, amongst other things, an epistemic social practice.

(a) BASIC EPISTEMOLOGY

Anglo-American legal adjudication traditionally adopts an 'adversarial' format, in which fact-finding is structured around competing versions of events advanced by the parties to the litigation. When a court of law sets out to decide whether a contested event took place as party *A* asserts or, to the contrary, in the way that party *B* contends, the court is trying to get at the truth of the matter in dispute. In this general sense, legal or 'forensic'[6] proceedings share much in common with non-forensic processes. The doctor, the scientist, the journalist, and the historian, for example, are also interested in discovering the truth about facts relevant to their professional interests. All of these practices can be brought under the capacious umbrella of social epistemology.[7] Yet each type of investigator adopts a different truth-finding procedure, which poses the question why such variation should occur.

The simple answer is that truth-finding procedures are adapted to suit the purposes of particular types of investigation and the conditions and constraints under which they operate. Consider, for instance, the journalistic enterprise. If a news reporter's overriding objective is to produce an article for tomorrow's papers, there is unlikely to be much opportunity for in-depth background research or even rigorous checking of primary facts, hence journalists tend to rely heavily on informants and easily accessible sources of information (including previous journalism).[8] The daily news journalistic approach to truth-finding is relatively cursory and superficial. This contrasts sharply with the more rigorous, painstaking methods of the professional historian, whose time-scale and objectives are markedly different, albeit that the historian shares with the journalist a serious interest in 'getting at the truth'. The more concerted inquiries of the investigative journalist fall somewhere on the continuum of inquisitorial effort between the copy-deadlined *paparazzo* and the meticulous professional historian.

Although adjectives like 'superficial' and 'rigorous' might appear to load the dice in favour of historical research, one must be wary of jumping to the conclusion that the historian's methods are necessarily and for all purposes superior to the journalist's. In fact, the success or failure of any truth-seeking enterprise must be judged contextually, taking proper account of the objectives and circumstances of the type of inquiry in

---

[5] Paul K. Moser (ed.), *The Oxford Handbook of Epistemology* (OUP, 2002); Ernest Sosa and Jaegwon Kim (eds.), *Epistemology: An Anthology* (Blackwell, 2000).

[6] The word 'forensic' is nowadays commonly used as a shortened form of 'forensic science evidence' (see Chapter 11) but its original meaning is much broader. Deriving from the Roman *forum* where legal and other business was transacted, 'forensic' literally means 'pertaining to legal proceedings' (thus, 'forensic science' and 'forensic medicine' are science and medicine applied to the administration of justice). The broader meaning is intended here, and throughout this book.

[7] Alvin I. Goldman, *Knowledge in A Social World* (OUP, 1999); Alvin I. Goldman, *Pathways to Knowledge: Private and Public* (OUP, 2002). And see Larry Laudan, *Truth, Error, and Criminal Law: An Essay in Legal Epistemology* (CUP, 2006).

[8] Thus, researchers have found that '[t]he first item of the day's business in every TV and radio newsroom is the reading of the newspapers': Canadian Royal Commission on Newspapers, quoted by Richard V. Ericson *et al*, *Visualizing Deviance* (Open UP, 1987), 189.

question. If a journalist makes a factual error it would rarely be appropriate to criticize her for not conducting her investigations with the same fastidiousness and intensity as an historian might have done. The journalist can only afford a level of factual accuracy compatible with meeting her copy deadline: more truth is no use to her, if it will already be old news by the time the facts can be ascertained. This is not to say, of course, that journalists are free from any obligation whatsoever to factual accuracy. A journalist might properly be taken to task for failing to abide by accepted journalistic standards or for flouting her professional code of conduct. We could even take the matter further by enquiring whether the prevailing standards of the journalistic profession are satisfactory. But in this regard, too, the fact that these standards are different from the historian's is not, in and of itself, a reason for disapproval. An historian, on the other hand, might be criticized for adopting journalistic methods even if his facts were correct. Branding scholarship 'journalism' is regarded in academic circles as almost defamatory.

Forensic fact-finding is no exception to these general propositions. Like any procedure for determining the truth about past events, the legal process has to be evaluated contextually, by reference to its objectives, values, institutional resources, and practical constraints. The aims and context of legal inquiry are obviously different from those pertaining to journalism or historical research, though all these modes of enquiry share a central concern with truth-finding. Unique features of legal adjudication generate their own particular requirements, such as the need for fair procedures to assist litigants to obtain and marshal evidence in support of their cases, to present information to the fact-finder and test its accuracy and reliability, and to distribute the risks of factually erroneous verdicts. These are the types of procedural mechanism examined in this book. Law, no less than journalism or history, presents a unique fact-finding environment demanding context-specific analysis and evaluation.

(b) PRINCIPLED DISCIPLINARY TAXONOMY

It might be possible to compile a kind of Encyclopaedia of Evidence listing every one of the many hundreds of evidentiary rules, with their countless exceptions and qualifications, and the literally thousands of decided cases on points of English evidence law. But the usefulness of such a survey would be very limited.[9] Quite apart from the problem of information-overload (which only grows more acute in the age of the internet), a blizzard of technical legal learning or bewildering profusion of single-instances would do little to illuminate what the Law of Evidence *stood for* on any deeper philosophical, moral, or jurisprudential level. It would not tell us, for example, how to organize evidentiary materials into a coherent whole, or how to rank the values embedded in legal rules in order of priority. Nor would it help us to resolve conflicts of value within the law, or indicate how established rules should be developed to fill gaps in existing legal coverage or extended to meet the exigencies of novel situations. These are every bit practical as well as theoretical concerns. Legal practitioners and the courts are, for example, constantly being confronted with novel legal problems thrown up by

---

[9] Cf. Maxwell Barrett, *Blackstone's Law of Evidence Index: Case Precedents 1900–1997* (Blackstone, 1998) critically reviewed by Roberts (1999) 3 *E & P* 138.

technological advances and the human genius for innovation, in committing crimes as in everything else.

To meet these demands, we need to develop a framework of principle, to make normative sense of procedural law as a developing corpus of norms and practices with a distinctive institutional character and tradition. The modern law of evidence is increasingly subject to legislative intervention in direct pursuit of multifarious and not necessarily well-coordinated policy objectives. Nonetheless, having been moulded by a unique professional legal culture, criminal evidence still manages to retain a distinctive identity with a more-or-less predictable trajectory of evolution. Those practitioners and theorists seeking to understand procedural law as more than a ragbag collection of rules at any given point in time must look beyond the technical minutiae of particular doctrines and free their minds from the tyranny of the latest case. Conceived as part of a tradition of justice, the law of evidence represents a reasonably intelligible and enduring commitment to certain values and principles. A logical first step towards understanding and evaluating forensic fact-finding must therefore be to identify the general principles underpinning the rules and practices which courts follow when resolving legal disputes. This is the ambitious challenge that this book takes up.

Evidentiary principles are not simply prefabricated and awaiting collection: rather, they have to be reconstructed from the relevant institutional materials. Case-law precedent, in the form of judicial rulings in decided cases, has traditionally been the most productive source of evidentiary principle. In modern times, however, the common law has been significantly modified and augmented by major statutory reforms. Further important subsidiary sources include judicial practice and the norms of professional legal culture, informal regulation through delegated legislation and 'soft law' instruments (Practice Directions, Codes of Practice, Home Office circulars, and the like), reports of official bodies (including, especially, the Law Commission), and scholarly commentary. The advent of the Human Rights Act 1998 was a key juncture in the on-going development of English evidence law, about which there will be much more to say later in this chapter and throughout the book. More recently, criminal litigation has been remoulded by the Criminal Procedure Rules (CrimPR) 2005 and 2010[10] and the Specimen Directions for trial judges issued by the Judicial Studies Board (JSB).[11] Only once we have extracted the general principles to be gleaned from these diverse materials will we be in a position to evaluate the courts' effectiveness in promoting evidence law's most cherished values and objectives, and, indeed, to judge whether these values and objectives are themselves defensible or call for reconsideration.

As soon as one begins to enquire into the aims and principles governing legal factfinding, it becomes obvious that there is not just one legal procedure for determining facts, but many. Legal adjudication in England and Wales adopts a plurality of procedural forms and techniques. The primary division is conventionally drawn between criminal and civil procedure. Criminal proceedings are further divided into jury trials and trials before magistrates. Civil disputes are tried principally in the High Court, which sits in the

---

[10] www.justice.gov.uk/criminal/procrules_fin/rulesmenu.htm. The CrimPR are drafted by the Criminal Procedure Rule Committee, which was created pursuant to the Courts Act 2003, ss.69–73, and is chaired by the Lord Chief Justice. Consolidated Rules were first issued in 2005 (SI 2005/384). Following a succession of piecemeal amendments, a newly consolidated CrimPR 2010 entered into force on 5 April 2010 (SI 2010/60).

[11] www.jsboard.co.uk/criminal_law/cbb/index.htm.

Royal Courts of Justice in London, and the County Court, which is organized into local courts located throughout the country.[12] Magistrates' courts also retain some jurisdiction in certain civil matters, including family law work.[13] In addition, to a plethora of specialist courts and tribunals devoted to commercial and other matters, there are also various professional disciplinary tribunals, which call errant doctors, lawyers, and police officers, amongst others, to account. Each forensic procedure has distinctive features reflecting a particular underlying philosophy of dispute resolution and the applicable substantive law.

The Law of Evidence is usually described as applying only to criminal and civil proceedings in the higher courts and before magistrates. It is widely acknowledged that fact-finding by other tribunals is governed by different, typically simplified and more informal, procedures. However, even if we restrict our attention to courtrooms and ignore the still greater diversity of pre-trial process, it is obvious that an undifferentiated Law of Evidence cannot be applied to legal disputes in the High Court, Crown Court, and magistrates' courts without major adaptations to accommodate different kinds of cases. The common lawyer's Law of Evidence is exposed as a doctrinal fiction. To make better sense of procedural law and practice, it is necessary, at a minimum, to distinguish between criminal and civil proceedings.

Let us briefly rehearse the considerations making this conclusion irresistible. In England and Wales serious criminal cases are tried by a judge and lay jury, whereas the vast majority of civil disputes, however serious, are tried by a professional judge sitting alone.[14] In criminal litigation the prosecution must prove its case beyond reasonable doubt; civil actions are determined on the balance of probabilities. The presumption of innocence[15] and the privilege against self-incrimination[16] are prominent features of the criminal process, in which confessions[17] often occupy a central position: civil proceedings rarely, if ever, raise such issues in the same way. Important rules of criminal litigation are concerned with the propriety of investigations carried out by the police and other state officials,[18] matters which are usually irrelevant in civil law disputes; and where, unusually, such issues are relevant they are handled differently.[19] Criminal trials are structured by rules about the past conduct and character of the accused which have limited application in civil proceedings.[20] The hearsay rule still applies with much of its original vigour in criminal cases,[21] but has been reduced to a mere shadow of its former self in modern civil litigation, where hearsay evidence is routinely admitted *in lieu* of the parties' evidence in-chief, even where the maker of the statement does not testify at all.[22] Rules for witness 'corroboration' and supporting evidence are individually tailored to the particular requirements of criminal and civil litigation, respectively.[23] Criminal trials raise important issues about the treatment of certain classes of witness, including especially vulnerable victims of crime,[24] which are

---

[12] The web-site of the Court Service is a very useful source of information: www.courtservice.gov.uk.

[13] For a general overview, see Michael Zander, *Cases and Materials on the English Legal System* (CUP, 10th edn. 2007), ch 1.

[14] Magistrates' courts have jurisdiction both over less serious criminal offences and over certain civil matters. However, even where the mode of trial is similar in civil and criminal proceedings, the applicable rules of procedure and evidence differ markedly. The procedural framework of English criminal adjudication is described more fully in Chapter 2.   [15] See Chapter 6.

[16] See Chapter 13.   [17] See Chapter 12.   [18] See, in particular, Chapter 5 on 'Fair Trial'.

[19] See *Zuckerman on Civil Procedure*, §21.72; *Jones* v *University of Warwick* [2003] 1 WLR 954, [2003] EWCA Civ 151.   [20] See Chapter 14.

[21] See Chapter 9.   [22] See *Zuckerman on Civil Procedure*, §21.101.   [23] See Chapter 15.

[24] See Chapter 10.

hardly ever thrown up by civil trial proceedings. Over time these differences have become more firmly institutionalized through the development of separate bodies of law to regulate civil and criminal trials. As we explore each of these topics in later chapters, the distinctiveness of fact-finding in criminal proceedings will become progressively more self-evident.

The evidentiary dimension of civil litigation, meanwhile, has centred on the parties' right of access to evidence, especially the means of securing evidence in the hands of an opponent.[25] Rules of discovery and injunctive relief, traditionally conceived as procedural mechanisms rather than rules of evidence in the strict sense, have lately been reinforced by search orders,[26] confirming the trend towards procedural diversity and specialization. In criminal trials, the prosecution's right of access to information in the possession of the accused is limited by the privilege against self-incrimination (itself now curtailed by statutory provisions which, again, pertain exclusively to criminal proceedings).[27] Even those rules that might be thought to bridge the criminal–civil divide typically undergo contextual adaptations. Thus, in criminal proceedings, public interest immunity potentially trenches on the accused's weighty interest in establishing his innocence.[28] The common law principle that 'he who avers must prove'[29] collides with the presumption of innocence in criminal proceedings, as can be seen in the flurry of recent cases assessing the legitimacy of 'reverse onus clauses' purporting to impose burdens of proof on the accused.[30] Similarly, the effect of common law presumptions, such as the presumption of legitimacy,[31] is modified by the criminal standard of proof beyond reasonable doubt,[32] reflecting the unique balance of interests at stake in criminal trials.

It would patently overstate the case to suggest that criminal and civil adjudication have absolutely nothing in common. Quite apart from their shared epistemic ambitions, both types of procedure bear the hallmarks of the Anglo-American 'adversarial' approach to proving disputed facts in court. In the adversarial model of adjudication truth is expected to emerge from a contest between opposing parties who champion alternative versions of events before an impartial fact-finder.[33] English civil litigation has also traditionally

---

[25] See *Zuckerman on Civil Procedure*, §2.188 and ch 14.

[26] Orders designed to secure evidence from destruction or suppression by an opponent: see *Zuckerman on Civil Procedure*, §14.175.

[27] Criminal Justice and Public Order Act 1994, ss.34–38; Criminal Procedure and Investigations Act 1996: see Chapter 13.   [28] See §7.5.

[29] According to the old civil law maxims, *ei incumbit probatio qui dicit, non qui negat; actori incumbit onus probandi*: the onus of proof lies on the party asserting a proposition, not on the one who denies it. See, e.g., *Oil Property Investment Ltd* v *Olympia & York Canary Wharf Ltd* (1994) 68 P & CR 451, 456, HC (Ch), *per* Harman J: 'It is of course a natural view that "he who avers must prove"'. And see *Wierzbicki* v *Poland* (2004) 38 EHRR 38, [21].

[30] See Paul Roberts, 'Criminal Procedure, the Presumption of Innocence and Judicial Reasoning under the Human Rights Act', in Helen Fenwick, Gavin Phillipson, and Roger Masterman (eds.), *Judicial Reasoning under the UK Human Rights Act* (CUP, 2007). See further, §6.5(c).

[31] The operation of the 'presumption of legitimacy' in civil proceedings is now governed by s.26 of the Family Law Reform Act 1969, replacing the old common law rule that the presumption could be rebutted only by proof beyond reasonable doubt: see *In re H (Minors) (Sexual Abuse: Standard of Proof)* [1996] AC 563, HL; cf. *R* v *Luffe* (1807) 8 East 193, 207, *per* Lord Ellenborough CJ: 'upon the ground of improbability, however strong, I should not venture to proceed.... for the general presumption will prevail, except a case of plain natural impossibility is shewn'.

[32] Cf. *R* v *Hemmings* [1939] 1 All ER 417, CCA (presumption of legitimacy operating in favour of the accused).   [33] The adversarial structure of English criminal proceedings is further explored in §2.2.

shared with its criminal law counterpart a commitment to the values of orality and publicity. In the liberal common law tradition evidence and argument were to be presented orally in proceedings open to the public, not by written proofs assembled in secret in a manner harking back to the despised and discredited *modus operandi* of the medieval Inquisition. Yet even this common denominator is fast diminishing. Considerations of economy and efficiency have eroded the orality of civil trials,[34] whilst – thus far – the impact of these imperatives in criminal litigation, where questions of guilt and innocence are at issue, has been more muted.

Procedural differentiation between criminal and civil proceedings has not always been so marked. Juries used to determine facts in both criminal and civil cases, and many evidentiary rules were of general application. However, criminal proceedings have, in reality, been set on their own distinctive course more or less since the modern form of trial first began to crystallize in the late eighteenth century.[35] Whatever disciplinary taxonomies might have been appropriate in previous centuries, it has become increasingly problematic to treat the Law of Evidence as a single, unified, and coherent body of rules and principles, subject only to limited variations between criminal and civil proceedings.[36] Any serious attempt to catalogue and explain these variations would soon discover that the supposed 'exceptions' have mutated into a different rule.

Residual elements of a shared procedural tradition should not distract attention from the major theoretical and practical differences today distinguishing criminal from civil litigation. Modern trial procedures have grown apart organically rather than following any preordained master-plan,[37] but the trajectory of their development is far from random. Institutional design, procedural forms, and evidentiary techniques reflect particular constellations of objectives and values bisecting orthodox conceptions of the Law of Evidence. The Continental/civilian procedural tradition has always appreciated more clearly than the English common law[38] that criminal evidence has a unique mission, distinctive form and structure, and a coherent foundation of principle which merit, and even require, greater emphasis and wider recognition. The remainder of this introductory chapter will amplify these assertions, and the balance of the book will substantiate them.

---

[34] *Zuckerman on Civil Procedure,* §2.107.

[35] See John H. Langbein, *The Origins of Adversary Criminal Trial* (OUP, 2003); David J. A. Cairns, *Advocacy and the Making of the Adversarial Criminal Trial 1800–1865* (OUP, 1999); John H. Langbein, 'The Criminal Trial Before the Lawyers' (1978) 45 *University of Chicago LR* 263.

[36] In fact, our argument goes 'back to the future'. Langbein, *The Origins of Adversary Criminal Trial,* 178, observes that at their inception rules of criminal evidence 'coalesced into a body of law that for a time was thought of as a distinct field'.

[37] On criminal procedure as 'grown' not 'made', see Ronald J. Allen, 'The Simpson Affair, Reform of the Criminal Justice Process, and Magic Bullets' (1996) 67 *University of Colorado LR* 989, Part I.

[38] Cf. Mirjan Damaška, *Evidence Law Adrift* (Yale UP, 1997), 110, 111: 'In the common law culture of the late eighteenth and nineteenth centuries, the conflict-solving image of adjudication exercised a powerful hold on the legal imagination. The image still insinuates itself in thinking about all kinds of lawsuits, so that the ultimate objective of all adjudicative proceedings is thought to be the just settlement of controversies. Criminal justice too is imagined as an engagement in dispute resolution … In the Continental legal culture, on the other hand, the opinion that civil and criminal proceedings serve widely different goals has a long pedigree.'

1.2 CRIMINAL PROCEDURE AND RETRIBUTIVE JUSTICE

The key to the institutional form and function of English criminal procedure lies in the distinctive brand of justice dispensed by criminal adjudication. Whilst civil trials may be characterized as a mechanism for resolving disputes between the parties' symmetrically competing claims,[39] criminal trials are organized around a state-sponsored examination of an accused's alleged criminal wrongdoing. Once the significance of this fundamental distinction is appreciated, procedural differentiation is only to be expected. Three features of criminal proceedings might be singled out as primary, formative, influences on rules and principles of criminal evidence: (a) the distinctive ideal of retributive justice, explaining the gravity of criminal conviction and punishment; (b) the identity of the parties to criminal litigation; and (c) the importance of maintaining public confidence in the administration of criminal justice.

(a) RETRIBUTIVE JUSTICE AS STRUCTURING IDEAL

The objectives of penal law and policy have been fiercely debated for as long as human beings have fiercely debated anything, and the controversy surrounding the subject has, if anything, increased rather than diminished in modern times. Philosophical justifications for criminal conviction and punishment divide broadly into two camps.[40]

Consequentialist justifications propose that criminal punishment is justified to the extent that, on balance, it brings about good consequences. In this context, 'good consequences' usually means a reduction in crime, and hence these justifications are also sometimes labelled 'reductivist' theories of punishment. The standard means of reducing crime are deterrence, both of the population in general ('general deterrence') and of individual offenders in particular ('special deterrence'); rehabilitation; and incapacitation.[41] Consequentialists argue that criminal punishment is justified if the harm done to the offender through punishment and the loss of freedom suffered by society at large (e.g. through extra police surveillance or random stop and search) are offset by the greater social benefit of crime prevention through deterrence, rehabilitation, or incapacitation of would-be offenders. On a straightforward cost–benefit analysis, the pains associated with enforcing the criminal law through policing, trials, and punishment are worth enduring only insofar as greater harms of criminal victimization are consequently prevented.[42]

---

[39] Dedicated procedures have evolved to deal with asymmetric civil claims, as where, for example, a party seeks special forms of relief against organs of government in administrative proceedings.

[40] Generally, see R. A. Duff, *Punishment, Communication and Community* (OUP, 2001), intro and ch 1; Andrew Ashworth, *Sentencing & Criminal Justice* (CUP, 5th edn. 2010), ch 3; Barbara A. Hudson, *Understanding Justice* (Open UP, 2nd edn. 2003); Antony Duff and David Garland (eds.), *A Reader on Punishment* (OUP, 1994); Nicola Lacey, *State Punishment* (Routledge, 1988); C. L. Ten, *Crime, Guilt and Punishment* (OUP, 1987), chs 2–4.

[41] See Andrew von Hirsch, Andrew Ashworth, and Julian Roberts (eds.), *Principled Sentencing: Readings on Theory & Policy* (Hart Publishing, 3rd edn. 2009), chs 1–3.

[42] In Bentham's pithy formula: 'All punishment is mischief: all punishment in itself is evil. Upon the principle of utility if it ought to be admitted at all, it must only be admitted in so far as it promises to exclude

A second set of justifications for punishment are known as 'deontological', duty-based, or rights-orientated theories.[43] Fully-specified deontological theories are at least as diverse as the many variations on consequentialist arguments, but they all stem from the same fertile intuition that every person is a being of inherent worth and dignity whose rights demand respect, from the state as much as from other individuals. Whereas consequentialist theories typically involve 'head-counting' calculations in which aggregate communal interests take precedence over the rights of individual citizens, deontological theorists view this approach as an illegitimate form of 'human sacrifice', whereby the rights of the one are rendered worthless by the priority of the interests of the many.[44] It does not follow, of course, that citizens are immune from state coercion on the deontological view, because rights are not unlimited, and they must sometimes give way to countervailing rights and interests. Significantly, if a person breaches somebody else's rights he may properly be held liable to criminal conviction and punishment. On some versions of deontological retributivism, the political community acting through its official representatives is *duty-bound* to punish criminal wrongdoers.[45] However, the deontological theorist would insist that an offender may be punished only after he has been found guilty in a fair procedure respecting rights of due process, and only in proportion to his 'just deserts'.[46]

One should be wary of over-exaggerating the practical differences between consequentialist and deontological theories of criminal justice. It is possible to combine aspects of consequentialist and deontological approaches into 'mixed theories' of punishment,[47] and in many of the extreme hypothetical scenarios beloved of moral philosophers, consequentialist and deontological theories produce superficially similar

some greater evil': Jeremy Bentham, *An Introduction to the Principles of Morals and Legislation* (J. H. Burns and H. L. A. Hart (eds.): OUP, 1995 [1789]). In fact, there is nothing 'straightforward' about undertaking such cost-benefit analyses in practice, but that has not prevented modern theorists from attempting to reduce criminal law enforcement to quasi-economic calculations: cf. Richard A. Posner, 'An Economic Theory of the Criminal Law' (1985) 85 *Columbia LR* 1193.

[43] A very readable general introduction to this style of analysis in moral and political philosophy is David S. Oderberg, *Moral Theory: A Non-Consequentialist Approach* (Blackwell, 2000).

[44] The difference in approach is nicely brought out by variations on the well-worn 'sheriff's dilemma' hypothetical, which is also suggested by Harper Lee's classic *To Kill a Mockingbird*. You are the sheriff of a small 'Wild West' town, standing guard over a prisoner accused of some heinous crime. Outside the jail-house a mob is calling for you to hand over the prisoner and allow vigilante 'justice' to take its course. What do you do? Does it make any difference if you believe the prisoner is, or may be, innocent? What if the mob threatens to take the prisoner by force if you refuse to co-operate? What if the mob threatens to lynch you too? The power of the hypothetical resides not so much in the choices one would make in such extreme circumstances, but in the *reasons* one would give for choosing a particular course of action. For further discussion, see Roger Crisp, *Mill on Utilitarianism* (Routledge, 1997), 118–19.

[45] So-called 'positive retributivism' develops the Kantian thought that punishment of wrongdoers is a 'categorical imperative'. See, e.g., Michael S. Moore, *Placing Blame* (OUP, 1997), ch 4.

[46] See Andrew von Hirsch, *Censure and Sanctions* (OUP, 1993), chs 2, 4, and 5; Andrew von Hirsch and Andrew Ashworth, *Proportionate Sentencing* (OUP, 2005); Andrew von Hirsch, *Past or Future Crimes: Deservedness and Dangerousness in the Sentencing of Criminals* (Manchester UP, 1986).

[47] The most celebrated 'mixed theory' was developed by H. L. A. Hart, *Punishment and Responsibility* (OUP, 1968; 2nd edn. Gardner ed., 2008), chs 1–2. Also see Barbara Hudson, *Understanding Justice* (Open UP, 2nd edn. 2003), ch 4; C. L. Ten, *Crime, Guilt and Punishment* (OUP, 1987), ch 4; Nigel Walker, *Why Punish?* (OUP, 1991), chs 15–17; Hyman Gross, *A Theory of Criminal Justice* (OUP, 1979), chs 9–10; Herbert L. Packer, *The Limits of the Criminal Sanction* (Stanford UP, 1968), chs 2–4.

conclusions.[48] Nonetheless, the differences between thoroughgoing consequentialism and deontological retributivism are real and practically significant. Ultimately, they reflect rival philosophical conceptions of the value of human life. A pithy way of summarizing the difference is to say that, whilst consequentialism is 'no respecter of persons' in always prioritizing aggregate social welfare over individuals' personal interests,[49] only deontological theories 'take rights seriously'.[50]

Without attempting here to develop a comprehensive theory of punishment or to take sides on the many enduring controversies in penal theory, we maintain that any plausible account of criminal procedure in England and Wales must contain a substantial deontological component. To be a serious contender as a description or justification of current criminal justice practice, such a theory must accommodate the inherent dignity and separateness of persons, or, in short, must take rights seriously. Any eligible theory must, in addition, be capable of distinguishing criminal proceedings from other forms of state coercion or regulation, in terms of a distinctive ideal of criminal, penal, or 'retributive' justice. The special legal, moral, and social functions of criminal law demand special treatment. Criminal punishment should not be collapsed into other, non-penal processes for righting wrongs (corrective justice) or into general questions of public welfare (distributive justice), for criminal proceedings serve the unique function of blaming wrongdoers according to their just deserts.[51] The right theory of punishment for English criminal proceedings must therefore be some version of deontological retributive justice.[52]

State punishment of crime is, and is intended to be, a grave matter, whereby offenders are called to account and, if found guilty, suffer the consequences of their serious wrongdoing.[53] Punishment in modern western societies involves public denunciation or 'censure' of criminal conduct, backed up by the deliberate infliction of suffering through

---

[48] In fact the similarity is only skin-deep, because the nature of human conduct is partly determined by the *reasons* motivating one's actions, and deontologists and consequentialists by definition act for different reasons. The subtleties of this distinction are brought out, for example, in Michael Moore's highly illuminating discussion of when, if ever, it would be permissible to torture a suspect in order to procure criminal intelligence: see Michael S. Moore, 'Torture and the Balance of Evils' (1989) 23 *Israel LR* 280; reprinted in Moore, *Placing Blame* (OUP, 1997), ch 17. The distinction is also forcefully stated by R. A. Duff, 'In Defence of One Type of Retributivism: A Reply to Bagaric and Amarasekara' (2000) 24 *Melbourne University LR* 411.

[49] Cf. John Rawls, *A Theory of Justice* (OUP, 1972), 29, 187: '[O]ne cannot arrive at a principle of social choice merely by extending the principle of rational prudence to the system of desires constructed by the impartial spectator. To do this is not to take seriously the plurality and distinctiveness of individuals… [C]lassical utilitarianism fails to take seriously the distinction between persons.'

[50] Ronald Dworkin, *Taking Rights Seriously* (Duckworth, new impression 1978), esp. chs 7 and 12.

[51] Which is why all economic theories of penal law are bound to fall short: see Jules L. Coleman, 'Crimes, Kickers and Transaction Structures', reprinted in Coleman, *Markets, Morals and the Law* (CUP, 1988).

[52] On the moral significance of retributive justice, see Michael S. Moore, 'The Moral Worth of Retribution', in Ferdinand Schoeman (ed.), *Responsibility, Character and the Emotions* (CUP, 1987), reprinted in Moore, *Placing Blame: A Theory of the Criminal Law* (OUP, 1997), ch 3; Jeffrie G Murphy and Jean Hampton, *Forgiveness and Mercy* (CUP, 1988); Morris J. Fish, 'An Eye for an Eye: Proportionality as a Moral Principle of Punishment' (2008) 28 *OJLS* 57; William Ian Miller, *Eye for an Eye* (CUP, 2006).

[53] Antony Duff has developed a comprehensive theory of criminal law and criminal adjudication from the core intuition that criminal wrongdoers should be called to account in a public trial: see R. A. Duff, *Answering for Crime: Responsibility and Liability in the Criminal Law* (Hart, 2007); Antony Duff, Lindsay Farmer, Sandra Marshall, and Victor Tadros, *The Trial on Trial Volume Three: Towards a Normative Theory of the Criminal Trial* (Hart, 2007).

state-sanctioned 'hard treatment' of varying types and intensities.[54] Hard treatment is imposed through a variety of familiar criminal penalties including fines, probation, community service, electronic monitoring, home detention curfews, compulsory involvement in treatment or education programmes, and, of course, imprisonment (plus in many jurisdictions, though not in Britain since 1965, the ultimate sanction of the death penalty). But, in terms of a general unit of penal currency, offenders can be said to 'pay' for their crimes through their partial and (usually) temporary loss of liberty.[55] This is obvious in the case of imprisonment, which involves a quite comprehensive and relatively indiscriminate restriction on a person's autonomy. Locking up an offender is an effective way of radically cutting down his options, at least for the period in which he remains incarcerated. However, most other forms of punishment also impinge on liberty and personal autonomy, generally to a lesser degree than imprisonment but often to a greater extent than is commonly recognized. Depriving citizens of their liberty would normally be regarded as seriously abusive in any other context. Indeed, such restrictions on autonomy are themselves normally proscribed by the criminal law, constituting such offences as assault, kidnapping, harassment, theft, blackmail, etc. Hard treatment plainly requires careful scrutiny and cogent justification when inflicted as criminal punishment.

Yet hard treatment *per se*, however severe, is only half the story. Any account of criminal adjudication would be seriously incomplete without reference to the message of blame which penal hard treatment is meant to convey. It is precisely the denunciatory, 'censuring' quality of punishment which distinguishes the penal voice of retributive justice from other modalities of state coercion, like taxation or civil penalties.[56] Whilst governments may routinely impose all manner of constraints on their citizens' liberty and personal autonomy, including even forced confinement of the dangerously mentally ill or carriers of infectious diseases,[57] only criminal proceedings involve judgments of moral wrongdoing for which an accused is publicly called to account and, if found guilty, solemnly condemned in the name of the community.[58]

---

[54] See further, Andrew von Hirsch and Andrew Ashworth, *Proportionate Sentencing: Exploring the Principles* (OUP, 2005), chs 5–7 and 9; Andrew von Hirsch, *Censure and Sanctions* (OUP, 1993); Uma Narayan, 'Appropriate Responses and Preventive Benefits: Justifying Censure and Hard Treatment in Legal Punishment' (1993) 13 *OJLS* 166; John Kleinig, 'Punishment and Moral Seriousness' (1991) 25 *Israel LR* 401; Joel Feinberg 'The Expressive Function of Punishment', reprinted in Antony Duff and David Garland (eds.) *A Reader on Punishment* (OUP, 1994).

[55] Cf. Andrew von Hirsch, 'Intermediate Sanctions', in von Hirsch, *Censure and Sanctions* (OUP, 1993), ch 7; Martin Wasik and Andrew von Hirsch, 'Non-Custodial Penalties and the Principles of Desert' [1988] *Crim LR* 555.

[56] Which is not to deny the existence of troublesome borderline cases, or the blurring effects of recent British penal policy. For further discussion and examples, see Andrew von Hirsch and A. P. Simester (eds.), *Incivilities: Regulating Offensive Behaviour* (Hart, 2006); Andrew Ashworth, 'Social Control and "Anti-Social Behaviour": The Subversion of Human Rights' (2004) 120 *LQR* 263; Andrew Ashworth, 'Is the Criminal Law a Lost Cause?' (2000) 116 *LQR* 225; Andrew von Hirsch and Martin Wasik, 'Civil Disqualifications Attending Conviction: A Suggested Conceptual Framework' (1997) 56 *Cambridge Law Journal* 599; Andrew Ashworth, John Gardner, Rod Morgan, A. T. H. Smith, Andrew von Hirsh, and Martin Wasik, 'Overtaking on the Right' (1995) 145 *New LJ* 9333; and 'Neighbouring on the Oppressive' (1998) 16 *Criminal Justice* 7.

[57] T. M. Wilkinson, 'Contagious Disease and Self-Defence' (2007) 13 *Res Publica* 339.

[58] Cf. S. E. Marshall and R. A. Duff, 'Criminalization and Sharing Wrongs' (1998) 11 *Canadian Journal of Law and Jurisprudence* 7.

Retributive punishment is the appropriate official response to criminal wrongdoing. Offenders should be encouraged to feel guilt and remorse for their actions,[59] whilst the rights of victims are vindicated and, if at all possible, their wellbeing restored[60] through the conviction and punishment of those who have wronged them. The symbolic sting of censure may be more painful to an offender than any hard treatment meted out to him as tangible punishment. In some cases moral condemnation may inflict lasting injury on a convict's self-respect and standing in the community, the effects of which endure long after a fine has been paid or a prison sentence served. Conversely, an innocent person wrongfully convicted and condemned for something he did not do will naturally consider himself the victim of a grave miscarriage of justice,[61] not only because he suffers undeserved hard treatment, but the more so because his public denunciation as a criminal wrongdoer represents a kind of state-sanctioned defamation of his moral character.[62] Small wonder, when contemplated in this light, that those who are wrongly convicted of criminal offences frequently go to such remarkable lengths in order to 'clear their name' and 'set the record straight'.[63]

Beyond the subjective responses of particular offenders and victims, the issue becomes one of governmental competence, rectitude, and integrity in the administration of criminal justice. Accuracy and sound judgment are at a premium in criminal adjudication. False attributions of guilt – tantamount to defamatory official lies – should be avoided at all reasonable cost. English law has long operated on the assumption that the worst kinds of official error involve convicting the innocent, or excessively punishing the guilty. This is not to deny that it is also regrettable whenever offenders escape their just deserts. Occasionally, officials are directly at fault for such failures of justice and ought to be brought to book.[64] However, the state's responsibility for catching and punishing criminals is more attenuated than its direct implication in wrongful convictions

---

[59] See R. A. Duff, *Punishment, Communication and Community* (OUP, 2001), chs 2–3; Stephen P. Garvey, 'Punishment as Atonement' (1999) 46 *UCLA LR* 1801; John Braithwaite, 'Shame and Modernity' (1993) 33 *British Journal of Criminology* 1; John Braithwaite, *Crime, Shame and Reintegration* (CUP, 1989).

[60] The rather disparate collection of ideas and penal practices known as 'Restorative Justice' has been influential with theorists and policy-makers over the last two decades: see Andrew von Hirsch, Andrew Ashworth, and Julian Roberts (eds.), *Principled Sentencing: Readings on Theory & Policy* (Hart Publishing, 3rd edn. 2009), ch 5; Barbara Hudson, *Understanding Justice* (Open UP, 2nd edn. 2003), ch 5; Andrew von Hirsch *et al* (eds.), *Restorative Justice and Criminal Justice: Competing or Reconcilable Paradigms?* (Hart, 2003); Carolyn Hoyle and Richard Young, 'Restorative Justice: Assessing the Prospects and Pitfalls', in Mike McConville and Geoffrey Wilson (eds.), *The Handbook of the Criminal Justice Process* (OUP, 2002); John Braithwaite, 'Restorative Justice: Assessing Optimistic and Pessimistic Accounts' (1999) 25 *Crime & Justice* 1; Richard Young and Benjamin Goold, 'Restorative Police Cautioning in Aylesbury – From Degrading to Reintegrative Shaming Ceremonies?' [1999] *Crim LR* 126.

[61] Also see Ronald Dworkin, 'Principle, Policy, Procedure', in C. F. H. Tapper (ed.), *Crime, Proof and Punishment* (Butterworths, 1981) (discussing the 'moral harm' of wrongful conviction).

[62] In Scotland, revealingly, a criminal charge is formally known as a 'libel': cf. Criminal Procedure (Scotland) Act 1995, s.81.

[63] Convicts have been known to refuse parole and defiantly remain in prison if freedom means admitting an offence they continue to deny, and families have campaigned to rehabilitate the reputations of their long-dead relatives. Timothy Evans and Derek Bentley are well-known examples of post-mortem rehabilitation: see Ludovic Kennedy, *10 Rillington Place* (Grafton, 1971 [1961]); *R v Derek William Bentley (Deceased)* [2001] 1 Cr App R 307, CA. But cf. *R v Hanratty (Deceased)* [2002] EWCA Crim 1141; [2002] 2 Cr App R 419.

[64] Perhaps this is sometimes true in those appalling cases of child murder or prolonged physical or sexual abuse in which the state fails to rescue vulnerable victims from the wickedness of their parents or carers.

or excessive punishment.[65] In modern liberal democracies, the state is rarely directly to blame when offenders evade detection or, if detected, avoid conviction.[66] But when the innocent are wrongly convicted, the state is the immediate agent of their misfortune. Mistakes of such moral magnitude reflect badly on any political community, whatever the individuals directly concerned might think. Lies are wrong even when they are not harmful,[67] but official lies about criminal culpability are almost invariably very harmful as well. In a properly functioning democracy, criminal censure and punishment are imposed in the name of the people, and all citizens are morally implicated in the truth, or falsehood, of official determinations of guilt. Government should always strive to gets its facts straight before publicly condemning any citizen as a moral wrongdoer who deserves to be punished for an appropriately specified criminal offence.[68]

This thumbnail sketch of a retributive theory of criminal justice begins to formalize the widely-held intuition that a finding of guilt leading to the imposition of criminal sanctions is always a very serious matter, even where the offence is comparatively minor and penal hard treatment relatively light. None of these considerations affects civil litigation, where compensation, rather than blame and punishment, is the principal currency of redress. It follows from this analysis that, in order to respect citizens' liberty, personal autonomy, and related rights to security of person and property, criminal sanctions should not be triggered unless exacting procedural standards have been satisfied, minimizing the risk of error. There must, in short, be appropriately robust safeguards against wrongful conviction and punishment of the innocent. This principle is elucidated below in §1.3, and throughout the remainder of the book.

(b) THE PARTIES TO CRIMINAL PROCEEDINGS

A second formative structural influence on the law of evidence in criminal proceedings is the identity of the 'parties'. Civil litigants are typically – though by no means always – private persons of roughly equal resources.[69] In criminal proceedings, however, the adversarial expectation of 'equality of arms' between the parties is hardly ever more than a transparent, and potentially pernicious, fiction.

---

[65] Human rights law now imposes certain duties of investigation and prosecution on state officials: see Alastair Mowbray, *The Development of Positive Obligations under the European Convention on Human Rights by the European Court of Human Rights* (Hart, 2004).

[66] The situation is obviously very different where state officials are themselves corrupt, or worse. When so inclined, governments and other political authorities can be the biggest criminals of all, hence genocide is the ultimate crime.

[67] Hence, the significance of the legend that George Washington could *never* tell a lie. Apparent counter-examples, as where the Nazi storm-trooper is deceived in order to protect Jewish refugees hiding in the attic, in fact demonstrate that lying, though always wrong, is sometimes justifiable as the lesser of two evils.

[68] Legitimate criminal prohibitions must satisfy certain formal criteria in accordance with the rule of law, including: generality of application, specificity in naming and tracking a particular moral wrong, definitional clarity, conceptual continence, and prospectivity. If substantive criminal prohibitions are drafted excessively broadly the probative burdens on the prosecution are normally considerably reduced. Also see ECHR Article 7.

[69] This is, of course, a generalization which fails to do justice to the variety to be found in civil litigation. The assumption of equality is reflected in practice where, for example, one company sues another of comparable size and wealth, but not where a multinational giant sues its minnow contractor or a private, 'one-shot' personal injury claimant takes on 'repeat players' like insurance companies. But such power differentials are nonetheless even more marked and systematic in criminal proceedings.

In criminal proceedings one 'party' is in reality the state (in England represented by the Crown, and hence denoted *R* v *Accused*),[70] pressing charges against a private individual or, more rarely, a company or other corporate legal personality. A profound imbalance between the parties to criminal litigation is an inevitable corollary of the huge material and structural advantages available to the prosecution. We might think of this as 'the adversarial deficit'. Law enforcement agencies are involved in the criminal process not only as representatives of the state at trial but also as pre-trial investigators equipped with a range of powers and associated opportunities to collect evidence. In particular, the authorities may arrest, detain, and question criminal suspects in the hope of securing a confession.[71] The accused may even be detained on remand – i.e. held in prison – pending trial. This clearly adds up to a situation in which the state party to criminal litigation enjoys considerable practical advantages in building up – or 'constructing'[72] – a case against the accused, which in turn are likely to influence, where they do not virtually predetermine, the outcome of any subsequent trial. Corrective institutional measures are consequently required to ensure that individual suspects and accused are not over-exposed to abuses of state power or unacceptable risks of adjudicative error.

One of the principal functions of the law of criminal evidence is to ameliorate the more pronounced and potentially deleterious effects of the adversarial deficit. Criminal procedure's most celebrated corrective mechanisms include the presumption of innocence[73] and the privilege against self-incrimination.[74] Although the traditional position has been eroded through a series of statutory reforms demanding more active defence participation, it remains broadly true to say that an accused is not obliged to account for his actions either in police interview or at trial. He is entitled to put the prosecution to proof of any allegation against him, and to walk free, without calling any evidence or testifying in his own defence, if the prosecution fails to satisfy the exacting standard of proof beyond reasonable doubt. Indeed the privilege against *self*-incrimination is reinforced by the procedural prohibition on compelling the accused's spouse to testify for the prosecution (with some limited, though important, exceptions, to be discussed in due course).[75] Many of the detailed evidentiary rules and doctrines examined in this book were designed, or have evolved, to promote accurate fact-finding and safeguard procedural propriety partly in recognition of the pronounced adversarial deficit dictating the fortunes of notionally equal, but in reality extremely unequal, parties to criminal litigation.

---

[70] *R* is shorthand for *Regina* or *Rex*, depending on whether the reigning monarch is a queen or a king. Common law jurisdictions which are not constitutional monarchies like the UK instead employ variations on *People* v *Accused* or *State* v *Accused*, etc. Whatever the preferred terminology, the same point is being made: criminal trials are public proceedings brought in the name of the political community rather than private disputes between individual litigants.

[71] See Chapter 12. For an overview of police investigative powers, see Paul Roberts, 'Law and Criminal Investigation', in Tim Newburn, Tom Williamson, and Alan Wright (eds.), *Handbook of Criminal Investigation* (Willan, 2007).

[72] On the 'construction' of criminal cases, see Mike McConville, Andrew Sanders, and Roger Leng, *The Case for the Prosecution* (Routledge, 1991); Mike Redmayne, *Expert Evidence and Criminal Justice* (OUP, 2001), ch 2; Gary Edmond, 'Azaria's Accessories: the Social (Legal-Scientific) Construction of the Chamberlains' *Guilt* and *Innocence*' (1998) 22 *Melbourne University LR* 396; Paul Roberts, 'Science in the Criminal Process' (1994) 14 *OJLS* 469; A. A. S. Zuckerman, 'Miscarriage of Justice – A Root Treatment' [1992] *Crim LR* 323; Andrew Sanders, 'Constructing the Case for the Prosecution' (1987) 14 *Journal of Law and Society* 229.　　　　　　　　　　　　　　　　　　　　　　[73] See Chapter 6.

[74] See Chapter 13.　　　　[75] See §7.4(b).

(c) PUBLIC CONFIDENCE IN THE ADMINISTRATION OF CRIMINAL JUSTICE

A third structuring influence on the law of criminal evidence is the need to respond appropriately to criminal victimization and to resolve disputed allegations of criminality in a way that commands public approval and fosters respect for the law. These aspirations animate the well-known, but not necessarily well-understood, aphorism that justice must not only be done, but must manifestly be *seen to be* done. As Lord Atkinson once explained:

The hearing of a case in public may be, and often is ... painful, humiliating, or deterrent both to parties and witnesses, and in many cases, especially those of a criminal nature, the details may be so indecent as to tend to injure public morals, but all this is tolerated and endured, because it is felt that in public trial is to be found, on the whole, the best security for the pure, impartial and efficient administration of justice, the best means for winning for it public confidence and respect.[76]

Common lawyers tend to believe that sunlight is the best disinfectant.[77] There is, however, no external audit or authoritative validation of verdicts in criminal cases, beyond the process itself. The disputed past, like all histories, is 'another country' which can be reconstructed only in imagination through the eyes of the present. Litigated events cannot literally be replayed for the purpose of checking conformity between the facts as they happened and as they appear to the court. Trials are only 'action-replays' in a derivative, figurative sense. In this regard forensic fact-finding is no different to any other historical inquiry. The ultimate ground of epistemic validation is internal to the process itself, representing a social investment in trusted methodologies of inquiry and the persuasive power of the narratives which the process is able to re-construct.[78] In other words, public confidence in criminal verdicts has to be generated and sustained by confidence in the criminal trial process. The jury system, and to a somewhat lesser extent lay magistrates, have an important role to play as direct representatives of the community's beliefs and values. The space preserved for lay fact-finders in modern criminal adjudication is meant to ensure that factual determinations, as well as some important normative judgments, are in touch with prevailing community sentiment. We will return to this theme in the next chapter.

---

[76] *Scott* v *Scott* [1913] AC 417, 463, HL. More recently, see *In re S* [2005] 1 AC 593, [30], *per* Lord Steyn: 'A criminal trial is a public event. The principle of open justice puts, as has often been said, the judge and all who participate in the trial under intense scrutiny. The glare of contemporaneous publicity ensures that trials are properly conducted. It is a valuable check on the criminal process. Moreover, the public interest may be as much involved in the circumstances of a remarkable acquittal as in a surprising conviction. Informed public debate is necessary about all such matters. Full contemporaneous reporting of criminal trials in progress promotes public confidence in the administration of justice. It promotes the values of the rule of law.'

[77] Cf. *McCartan Turkington Breen* v *Times Newspapers* [2001] 2 AC 277, 297, HL, *per* Lord Steyn, quoting a celebrated extra-judicial *dictum* of US Supreme Court Justice Louis Brandeis, *Other People's Money* (National Home Library Foundation, 1933), 62: 'Publicity is justly commended as a remedy for social and industrial diseases. Sunlight is said to be the best of disinfectants; electric light the most efficient policeman.'

[78] Legal discourses of 'guilt' and 'innocence' interact in complex ways with media and political discourses surrounding crime control, punishment, miscarriages of justice, etc. Although legal discourse is influenced by what is said and done in other discursive realms, the courts remain the ultimate arbiters *as a matter of law* of forensically contested facts. In the terminology of autopoiesis, law is 'cognitively open, but normatively closed': see Richard Nobles and David Schiff, *Understanding Miscarriages of Justice: Law, the Media, and the Inevitability of Crisis* (OUP, 2000), critically reviewed by Roberts (2001) 117 *LQR* 503; Walker (2000) 20 *Legal Studies* 615; and Jackson (2001) 28 *Journal of Law and Society* 324.

Rules of evidence also play their part in maintaining public confidence in the administration of justice by demonstrating the integrity of the criminal process, for example when courts refuse to act on prosecution evidence which has been obtained unlawfully or unfairly.[79] In the modern democratic *Rechtsstaat* – the political community characterized by its respect for rights and adherence to the rule of law – it is essential that the state and its agents are seen to be bound by the laws they enforce, rather than cynically exploiting legal duties for partisan advantage whilst themselves remaining above the law. Criminal justice is intimately related to political virtue, since assessing criminal responsibility and inflicting punishment through criminal adjudication is a thoroughly moral enterprise. It follows that a wicked or dissolute political regime which flouts the basic precepts of the rule of law may forfeit the moral authority to call suspected offenders to account and to punish the guilty. Ethical standards for evidence-gathering and proof of guilt at trial should reassure the public that lawful state authority is not being exceeded and that the risk of wrongful conviction has been reduced to a tolerable level – accepting that the risk of convicting the innocent can never be eliminated entirely, given the fallibility of all human endeavours.

At the same time, public confidence in the administration of criminal justice hinges on the state's ability to provide citizens with adequate protection from criminal wrongdoing and to bring offenders to justice. Although crime control has traditionally received little direct acknowledgement in discussions of particular evidentiary rules and doctrines, criminal procedure is undeniably calibrated to facilitate effective law enforcement. A crime control imperative is at work in the various inclusionary exceptions discussed later in this book which operate to rescue incriminating evidence from exclusion at trial, as well as in the default assumption that all relevant evidence, much of which is evidence of guilt, should be placed before the fact-finder. There is an important and rather fundamental sense in which convicting the guilty is prior to acquitting the innocent, since the latter need never be an issue if the former were not paramount amongst the state's duties of justice.

In demanding *both* effective conviction of the guilty *and* solicitous protection of the innocent from wrongful conviction, as well as high standards of moral integrity on the part of institutions and officials, public confidence is a stern taskmaster with exacting, and potentially contradictory, expectations of the administration of justice. These tensions rise to the surface at moments of public anxiety. A much-debated comparative illustration might be the US criminal trial of American football star O. J. Simpson, who was charged with the murder of his wife Nicole and her lover Ronald Goldman.[80] Simpson was acquitted, despite considerable circumstantial evidence of his guilt, after it emerged at trial that the prosecution had botched the collection of physical evidence. It also appeared to be significant that, at one of several moments of high courtroom drama, an LAPD officer was exposed in the witness-box as a racist and perjurer. Yet public confidence in the American criminal justice system was far from restored. Indeed, the American public's reaction to the verdict, which seemed to split along essentially racial lines, calls into question the very notion of a single entity – 'the public' – whose confidence can be won or lost.

---

[79] See Chapter 5.
[80] See George Fisher, 'The O.J. Simpson Corpus' (1997) 49 *Stanford LR* 971 (and further references therein).

High-profile trials like O. J. Simpson's remind us that the pursuit of criminal justice is influenced by contextual factors extending far beyond the institutions and processes of criminal adjudication, including social trust in policing and authority more generally, socio-economic distributions of wealth and opportunity, the impact of media and 'celebrity culture', and racial harmony in multi-cultural societies. Criminal procedure has a role to play in contributing to social stability, peace, prosperity, and individual wellbeing, but its influence is limited. Penal law can only function successfully as part of the broader remit of effective governance. Contrary to what certain politicians or newspapers might have us believe, punishing criminals can never be an all-purpose solution to society's discontents. At all events, these questions of state and society seem very far-removed from the regular fare of civil proceedings. Where the aim is essentially to settle disputes between citizens, such questions rarely arise and are never so acute.[81] Civil litigation does not require procedural mechanisms to protect the innocent from wrongful conviction and punishment or to satisfy the community's need for security and protection from criminal predation.

1.3 FIVE FOUNDATIONAL PRINCIPLES OF CRIMINAL EVIDENCE

Principles of criminal evidence might be conceptualized and elucidated at different levels of generality. They come in various shapes and sizes. The more finely-drawn principles embedded in particular evidentiary rules and doctrines will be examined as we proceed. We begin by painting on a larger canvas and in broader brushstrokes. Five general principles can be distilled from the relevant institutional materials and treated as foundational. Together, these five principles provide the structural framework and serve as moral touchstones for the many other, more particularized, principles of criminal evidence that will be encountered in the following pages.

(a) THE FOUNDATIONAL FIVE DEFINED

We have already emphasized evidence law's epistemic preoccupations. The aspiration that judicial verdicts should conform as nearly as possible with the truth, not surprisingly, merits pride of place as the first principle of criminal evidence. Criminal adjudication is supposed to determine who did what, to whom, when, and why. The fact-finder is meant to get the facts straight. Buttressing the first principle of promoting factual accuracy, English criminal procedure treats four further principles as foundational: (2) the principle of protecting the innocent from wrongful conviction; (3) the principle of liberty, or minimum

---

[81] On the aims and values of civil justice, see *Zuckerman on Civil Procedure*, ch 1; Adrian A. S. Zuckerman (ed.), *Civil Justice in Crisis: Comparative Perspectives of Civil Procedure* (Oxford, 1999); Adrian A. S. Zuckerman, 'Quality and Economy in Civil Procedure: The Case for Commuting Correct Judgments for Timely Judgments' (1994) 14 *OJLS* 353; Sir Jack Jacob, *The Fabric of English Civil Justice* (1987), ch 1; K. E. Scott, 'Two Models of the Civil Process' (1974–5) 27 *Stanford LR* 937 (distinguishing between the 'conflict solving' and 'behaviour modification' functions of legal process).

state intervention; (4) the principle of humane treatment; and (5) the principle of maintaining high standards of propriety in the criminal process. Most of the relevant concepts have already been mentioned, and can now be further elucidated.

(1) Accurate fact-finding in criminal proceedings serves an instrumental and intensely practical objective. In order to do justice in individual cases and to protect the community from crime, the right people – offenders, and only them – have to be caught, tried, and punished. The principle of accurate fact-finding is the ultimate golden thread tying criminal proceedings to the public interest. It must never be allowed to become too badly frayed or torn,[82] for criminal process unconcerned with the truth is the instrument, not of justice, but of despotism. No legal right of any description can be vindicated through recourse to law unless it is possible to make the factual determinations on which the existence of particular vested legal rights and duties depends. A claimant can sue on a contract, for example, only if she can prove that a contract was actually made and that the defendant has breached its terms. A consumer can sue for a defective product only if he can prove that the product *is* defective and that he bought it from the defendant. An accident victim can recover in tort only if she can prove actionable damage caused by the defendant's negligence. And so on. Common lawyers have traditionally conceived rights as being parasitic on remedies or causes of action, rather than the other way around: *ubi remedium, ibi jus.*

In global terms, factual accuracy in adjudication is the cornerstone of the rule of law. In the specific context of criminal adjudication, verdicts of guilt and innocence would be purely formal legal classifications unless they expressed, as they are surely intended to express, substantive evaluations of moral culpability for actual, factual, wrongdoing. The importance of factual accuracy in criminal adjudication cannot be overstated (though on occasion it may be overvalued relative to countervailing considerations). The centrality of ascertaining the truth of disputed allegations to the whole enterprise of criminal adjudication makes it appropriate to characterize the pursuit of factual accuracy as a foundational principle of criminal evidence, and not merely as one of evidence law's ubiquitous objectives.

(2) Conceived merely as the alter ego of convicting the guilty, protecting the innocent from wrongful conviction might be viewed simply as a logical implication of accurate fact-finding. However, English law goes significantly beyond the imperatives of logic, to protect the possibly innocent from criminal conviction and punishment even at the risk of allowing significant numbers of the probably guilty to escape their just deserts. The pro-innocence bias in English criminal procedure, its 'principled asymmetry' of wrongful convictions and acquittals,[83] is encapsulated in Blackstone's famous boast that

---

[82] The connection between criminal procedure and truth-finding is a cornerstone of what Twining has dubbed 'the rationalist tradition' of Evidence scholarship: see William Twining, *Theories of Evidence: Bentham & Wigmore* (Weidenfeld and Nicolson, 1985), ch 1. Twining's position is critically reviewed by Donald Nicolson, 'Truth, Reason and Justice: Epistemology and Politics in Evidence Discourse' (1994) 57 *MLR* 726. For more general discussion, see Michael S. Pardo, 'The Field of Knowledge and the Field of Evidence' (2005) 24 *Law and Philosophy* 321; Ronald J. Allen and Brian Leiter, 'Naturalized Epistemology and the Law of Evidence' (2001) 87 *Virginia LR* 1491; John D. Jackson, 'Theories of Truth Finding in Criminal Procedure: An Evolutionary Approach' (1988) 10 *Cardozo LR* 475. Epistemological issues are further explored in Chapter 4.

[83] See Paul Roberts, 'Double Jeopardy Law Reform: A Criminal Justice Commentary' (2002) 65 *MLR* 393, 402–4.

English law considers it better to let ten guilty men go free than to convict one single innocent.[84] As we will see in later chapters, it resonates through various other legal rules which operate to exclude relevant evidence from a criminal trial, particularly evidence which may create unfair prejudice against the accused, as well as sounding directly in the allocation to the prosecution of the steeply asymmetrical criminal standard of proof.[85]

(3) A third foundational principle might be characterized as 'the principle of minimum intervention'. It is an extension of the liberal state's general respect for the liberty and personal autonomy[86] of individual citizens. The state should not interfere in people's life choices any more than is necessary for the purposes of good government and public peace. This general precept of liberal democracy applies with particular force to criminal proceedings. State power is here experienced at its most nakedly coercive, and the result of conviction in terms of hard treatment and penal censure, as we have already noted, may be radically corrosive of personal autonomy. The implications of the principle of minimum intervention for substantive criminal law have been elaborated by Andrew Ashworth under the rubric of 'the principle of minimum criminalization'.[87] In its procedural guise, minimum intervention is the principle underpinning many of the guarantees for suspects written into the Police and Criminal Evidence Act (PACE) 1984.[88] Later in the process, minimum intervention stands behind both the prosecutor's 'realistic prospect of conviction' test,[89] designed to weed evidentially weak cases out of the process before they reach trial, and the judicial power to direct an acquittal without hearing from the defence where there is 'no case to answer'.[90] In more strictly evidentiary terms, the principle of minimum intervention is closely related to the presumption of innocence[91] and the privilege against self-incrimination.[92] Somewhat less tangibly, minimum intervention explains

[84] Blackstone shared the conventional view that it is 'better to let ten guilty men go free than to convict one innocent', though ratios of five-to-one (Hale), twenty-to-one (Fortescue), 100-to-1 (Bentham), and even 1,000-to-1 (Lord Stafford) can be found in the older literature: see §6.3(b). [85] See §6.3.

[86] For further elaboration, see Joseph Raz, *The Morality of Freedom* (OUP, 1986), Parts III–V; Paul Roberts, 'Privacy, Autonomy and Criminal Justice Rights: Philosophical Preliminaries', in Peter Alldridge and Chrisje Brants (eds.), *Personal Autonomy, The Private Sphere and Criminal Law: A Comparative Study* (Hart, 2001).

[87] Andrew Ashworth, *Principles of Criminal Law* (OUP, 5th edn. 2009), 31–3, 53. And see Doug Husak, *Overcriminalization: The Limits of the Criminal Law* (OUP, 2008).

[88] Including requirements for 'reasonable suspicion' to effect particular kinds of police stop, search or arrest, limitations on the duration of detention without charge, provisions for bail, and so forth. Generally, see Andrew Sanders and Richard Young, *Criminal Justice* (OUP, 3rd edn. 2007), chs 2–6, Satnam Choongh, 'Police Investigative Powers' and Mike Maguire, 'Regulating the Police Station: The Case of the Police and Criminal Evidence Act 1984,' both in Mike McConville and Geoffrey Wilson (eds.), *The Handbook of the Criminal Justice Process* (OUP, 2002); David Feldman, *Civil Liberties and Human Rights in England and Wales* (OUP, 2002), chs 6 and 10; Michael Zander, *The Police and Criminal Evidence Act 1984* (Sweet & Maxwell, 5th edn. 2006).

[89] Crown Prosecutors have an on-going duty to ensure that there is a 'realistic prospect of conviction' in any case brought to trial: *Code for Crown Prosecutors* (Feb 2010 revision), Part 4, www.cps.gov.uk/ Publications/docs/code2010english.pdf. Where there is no realistic prospect of conviction, proceedings must be discontinued under s.23 of the Prosecution of Offences Act 1985. For discussion, see Andrew Ashworth and Mike Redmayne, *The Criminal Process* (OUP, 3rd edn. 2005), ch 7; Glanville Williams, 'Letting off the Guilty and Prosecuting the Innocent' [1985] *Crim LR* 115; Peter Warboys, 'Convicting the Right Person on the Right Evidence' [1985] *Crim LR* 764. [90] See §2.5(c).

[91] See Chapter 6. [92] See Chapter 13.

whatever force appeals to 'privacy' may have in the formulation and application of rules governing the admissibility of evidence at trial.[93]

(4) The related principle of humane treatment likewise expresses respect for personal autonomy and citizens' wellbeing. This fourth principle of criminal evidence states that government in all its forms should respect the inherent dignity and exhibit appropriate regard for the welfare of every person over whom it exercises jurisdiction, an idea closely associated with the eighteenth century idealist philosophy of Immanuel Kant. In Kant's classic formulation:

Every human being has a legitimate claim to respect from his fellow human beings and is *in turn* bound to respect every other. Humanity itself is a dignity; for a human being cannot be used merely as a means by any human being (either by others or even by himself) but must always be used at the same time as an end. It is just in this that his dignity (personality) consists...[94]

The principle of humane treatment exerts an important constraint on the administration of criminal justice, a state-run process which has the potential to do very great harm to anybody who becomes caught up in its snares. Suspects and the accused are the ones most obviously in jeopardy. Procedural rules contribute to suspects' humane treatment by protecting them from physical abuse or excessive psychological pressure at the hands of state officials,[95] and by providing them with legal advice and assistance to prepare and present their cases in court.[96] Rules of evidence perform a similar function by affording accused persons fair opportunity to answer the charges against them, whilst at the same time respecting their right to remain silent if they choose to keep their counsel and put the prosecution to proof. These and other rules of criminal evidence and procedure treat the accused as thinking, feeling, human subjects of official concern and respect, who are entitled to be given the opportunity to play an active part in procedures with a direct and possibly catastrophic impact on their welfare, rather than as objects of state control to be manipulated for the greater good (or some less worthy objective).

Yet suspects and the accused are not the only actors in the criminal trial whose wellbeing may be imperilled by their involvement in criminal adjudication. There has been growing recognition in recent years that witnesses testifying in court have sometimes been subjected to avoidably distressing and unacceptably shabby treatment at the hands of legal professionals.[97] Concerns have crystallized around especially vulnerable witnesses and those required to testify about very traumatic events in their lives, such as victims of child abuse and adult complainants of rape or sexual assault. Rules of evidence and procedure which place additional restrictions on the cross-examination of vulnerable witnesses, or which in other ways ameliorate the trauma of testifying in court, are in partial fulfilment

---

[93] On privacy and criminal justice generally, see Paul Roberts, 'Privacy, Autonomy and Criminal Justice Rights: Philosophical Preliminaries,' in Peter Alldridge and Chrisje Brants (eds.), *Personal Autonomy, The Private Sphere and Criminal Law: A Comparative Study* (Hart, 2001).

[94] Immanuel Kant, *The Metaphysics of Morals* ([1797] Mary Gregor (ed.), CUP, 1996), 209.

[95] The contextual pressures leading to confessions are discussed in Chapter 12.   [96] See §2.2.

[97] On the general penological context of 'victims' rights' and their growing political significance, see Carolyn Hoyle and Lucia Zedner, 'Victims, Victimization and Criminal Justice', in Mike Maguire, Rod Morgan, and Robert Reiner (eds.), *The Oxford Handbook of Criminology* (OUP, 4th edn. 2007); Tim Newburn, *Criminology* (Willan, 2007), ch 17; Helen Fenwick, 'Procedural "Rights" of Victims of Crime: Public or Private Ordering of the Criminal Justice Process?' (1997) 60 *MLR* 317.

of the principle of humane treatment. Nonetheless, when we come to examine these issues in more detail in Chapter 10, we will find both deficiencies in the practical implementation of novel 'special measures', and deeper underlying conflicts of interest between a witness's right to humane treatment and the accused's right to a fair trial.

(5) Our fifth foundational principle is concerned with upholding standards of moral propriety in criminal adjudication. The basic idea is captured by Ian Dennis' useful concept of the 'legitimacy of the verdict'.[98] The imperatives of legitimacy find clear expression in judicial supervision of custodial detention and confessions in the police station.[99] Moral integrity also inspires the courts' attitude towards evidence obtained in breach of legal rules governing police surveillance, arrest, search, and seizure.[100] As Dennis elaborates:

a verdict which is derived from a disregard for the core principle [we would say, *principles*] of criminal law is self-contradictory. It cannot function as an expressive message that the criminal law incorporates values which it is necessary to uphold while appearing to be based itself on a deliberate flouting of those values. This must inevitably lead to a loss of respect both for the trial process and for the criminal law itself.[101]

We might see this as a modern restatement and concrete application of Kant's precept that justice cannot be achieved by an unjust intervention. To pursue justice through injustice is a contradiction in terms,[102] since two wrongs do not make a right, in the administration of criminal justice any more than in the school playground. Righting wrongs, in fulfilment of a requirement of justice, can be achieved only through action which is itself just and otherwise in conformity with relevant ethical standards. Maintaining such standards in service of the legitimacy of the verdict, and in accordance with the basic precepts of retributive justice, is a fifth foundational principle of the law of criminal evidence.[103]

(b) PRINCIPLES IN PRACTICE: AN ILLUSTRATION

Our five foundational principles establish a normative framework which structures criminal adjudication and informs the more detailed evidentiary principles, rules, and

---

[98] I. H. Dennis, 'Reconstructing the Law of Criminal Evidence' [1989] *Current Legal Problems* 21, 35ff. And see Adrian A. S. Zuckerman 'Illegally-Obtained Evidence – Discretion as a Guardian of Legitimacy' [1987] *CLP* 55, 59, invoking 'the principle of judicial integrity or the principle of legitimacy'.

[99] See Chapter 12.   [100] See Chapter 5.

[101] Dennis, 'Reconstructing the Law of Criminal Evidence', 37.

[102] Cf. Bostjan Zupancic, 'The Crown and the Criminal: The Privilege Against Self-Incrimination – Towards General Principles of Criminal Procedure' (1996) 5 *Nottingham Law Journal* 32, 50, (grandiloquently exposing 'the pristine Kafkaesque absurd in which the State uses the fraudulent semblance of the legal process to conceal law's precise opposite – the instant regression to anti-law').

[103] For further explorations of the normative foundations of criminal adjudication, see Paul Roberts, 'Theorising Procedural Tradition: Subjects, Objects and Values in Criminal Adjudication', in Antony Duff, Lindsay Farmer, Sandra Marshall, and Victor Tadros (eds.), *The Trial on Trial Volume Two: Judgment and Calling to Account* (Hart, 2006); Antony Duff, Lindsay Farmer, Sandra Marshall, and Victor Tadros, *The Trial on Trial Volume Three: Towards a Normative Theory of the Criminal Trial* (Hart, 2007); Hock Lai Ho, *A Philosophy of Evidence Law – Justice in the Search for Truth* (OUP, 2008).

doctrines which are discussed throughout this book. Although the foundational principles will rapidly become familiar with continual acquaintance, it might be helpful at this point to provide a more vivid illustration of what has thus far been a fairly schematic and abstract discussion of general principles.

It sometimes happens in the course of a trial that facts emerge, or allegations are made, about past misconduct of the accused which does not figure explicitly as part of the formal charges against him. In English law, the accused cannot be convicted of any additional offences arising out of such misconduct, at least not without first instituting fresh proceedings.[104] At common law, information about extraneous misconduct could not generally be used as evidence to prove any offence with which the accused *was* properly charged, either. Although, as we will see in Chapter 14, the law of bad character has recently undergone extensive statutory reform, it remains true to say that evidence of the accused's extraneous misconduct is subject to an enhanced standard of admissibility over and above threshold relevance. Restricting the trial to formally charged offences, and further restricting the evidence to direct proof of just those charges, can be seen to implement our five foundational principles in the following, mutually reinforcing, ways.

First, these restrictions promote accuracy in fact-finding, because they confine the court's verdict to matters which should have been properly investigated before the case was brought to court, and to which evidence-gathering and testimony at trial have been directed. Unsubstantiated and uninvestigated allegations arising more or less incidentally during the course of the trial would be an unreliable basis on which to pronounce public judgments of guilt and are consequently circumscribed and often excluded.

Secondly, and by extension, the rule protects the innocent from wrongful conviction, by shielding the accused from unsubstantiated rumour, half-truths, or diffuse animosity which repugnant conduct or character traits might stir up in the fact-finder. It is not a criminal offence to have an unsympathetic personality or an unpopular lifestyle, and it would be a blatant miscarriage of justice for an accused to be convicted purely because a jury takes a visceral objection to him – to say nothing of the unacceptability of verdicts based on racial, gender, or other insidious forms of prejudice. As a general proposition, potentially prejudicial prosecution evidence must normally be excluded from the trial unless its probative value outweighs its prejudicial effect (in shorthand, PV > PE). Whilst this formula is too narrowly technical to qualify as a foundational principle of criminal evidence in its own right, PV > PE has been worked up through legal argument and judicial rulings into specific evidentiary rules and principles, as we shall see.[105]

Thirdly, confining verdicts to the charges in the indictment serves the principle of minimum intervention by protecting the accused from an untrammelled and far-reaching public examination of his moral character. Those accused of criminal offences in England and Wales are placed on trial only to answer particularized allegations of wrongdoing. If there is to be a more general moral accounting of their lives as a whole, this is deferred to the wider currents of media speculation and public opinion – or, failing that, to the

---

[104] Criminal trials can proceed only on the basis of a properly drawn-up indictment or information charging offences known to the law, otherwise the court lacks jurisdiction: see John Sprack, *A Practical Approach to Criminal Procedure* (Blackstone, 12th edn 2008), chs 10 and 15.

[105] Especially in §2.5(a), §5.2, and §14.4(a).

spiritual jurisdiction of a higher authority. The temporal authority of liberal states, at all events, is limited to ensuring that everybody lives by the social and moral rules necessary for peaceful coexistence and the enjoyment of maximum equal liberty for all, in contra-distinction to more rigorously 'perfectionist' styles of government which strive to develop excellence of character in all citizens, by coercion if necessary.[106]

Rules limiting the scope of the charges and the evidence might also be said, fourthly, to fulfil the state's duty of humane treatment, albeit that this principle is not as promi-nent as the other four in relation to this particular illustration. Restrictions on the use of extraneous misconduct evidence are, at least, consistent with respecting the accused's privacy. Viewed as part of the normative apparatus for fairly determining the extent of an accused's moral and legal responsibility for his past conduct, they might also be regarded as an extension of the law's respect for human dignity. Treating an offender as a moral agent, rather than as a tiresome social inconvenience or a pest requiring control, might involve making certain allowances for human frailties and shortcomings, especially in relation to the follies of youth. Calling somebody to account for every minor infraction or incivility in their dim and distant past does not seem very respectful of human dignity, since it implies that a person can never learn from their mistakes, move on, turn over a new leaf, or improve themselves.

Be that as it may, the principle of humane treatment assumes greatest prominence in relation to the experiences of complainants and other witnesses testifying in court. As Chapter 10 recounts, English law is currently in the throes of a major programme of reform aimed at correcting past failures to discharge the state's duty of humanity towards witnesses who come forward to testify in criminal proceedings. If it is too prejudicial to expose the jury to information about the accused's bad character which is only margin-ally relevant to the issues in the case, complainants and other witnesses deserve similar protection from gratuitous character assassination in the witness-box. In the sphere of bad character evidence, in other words, what is sauce for the goose should also be sauce for the gander. Although it is often a mistake to assume that rules of criminal proce-dure apply without differentiation to both prosecution and defence, the argument for equality of treatment does retain a measure of plausibility in relation to bad character evidence.[107]

Finally, fifth, the moral integrity of the proceedings and the legitimacy of the verdict are promoted by procedural rules which give the accused fair warning of the allegations he must answer, and a reasonable opportunity to mount a defence, if he has one, in reply. Were the prosecution allowed to ambush an accused with fresh allegations, or overwhelm

---

[106] It should be added that the debate between 'perfectionists' and 'anti-perfectionists' in moral and political philosophy cuts across divisions between liberals and their opponents. Thus, whilst most liberals are anti-perfectionists, Joseph Raz has made the case for liberal perfectionism. See Joseph Raz, *The Morality of Freedom* (OUP, 1986), Part II; Stephen Mulhall and Adam Swift, *Liberals and Communitarians* (Blackwell, 2nd edn. 1996), ch 10; Jeremy Waldron, 'Autonomy and Perfectionism in Raz's *Morality of Freedom*' (1989) 62 *Southern California LR* 1098; Robert P. George, *Making Men Moral: Civil Liberties and Public Morality* (OUP, 1993); Gerard V. Bradley, 'Pluaralistic Perfectionism: A Review Essay of Making Men Moral' (1996) 71 *Notre Dame LR* 671.

[107] Thus, the Law Commission decided to extend its original project re-examining the accused's extrane-ous misconduct to bad character evidence in general: see Law Com No 273, *Evidence of Bad Character in Criminal Proceedings* Cm 5257 (TSO, 2001); cf. LCCP No 141, *Evidence in Criminal Proceedings: Previous Misconduct of a Defendant* (HMSO, 1996).

him with prejudicial evidence of dubious probative value, any resulting conviction could hardly inspire public confidence, particularly in view of the profound imbalance of power between the accused and his state accuser. If the prosecutor has to resort to chicanery or mud-slinging it is only natural to wonder whether the state has enough concrete evidence to secure a conviction; and without evidence, how can we be confident that the accused is truly guilty? Such procedural abuses are the hallmark of political oppression, which may all-too-easily slide into totalitarianism.

Doctrines of criminal evidence and procedure, like the rules on charging and those limiting the admissibility of bad character evidence, thus reinforce political legitimacy and provide some measure of protection for individual rights and basic freedoms. By providing the accused with a fair opportunity of answering the charges against him they also promote the principles of accuracy in fact-finding, protection of the innocent, and respect for the accused as an active, decision-making participant in his own trial. This is consistent with respect for privacy and humane treatment, which benefits crime victims and witnesses as well as alleged offenders, and the whole procedural package conduces to criminal proceedings capable of delivering legitimate and trustworthy verdicts. Legitimacy is secured not merely in the sociological sense that verdicts are in fact trusted and command social authority, but in the normative sense that public trust is epistemically and morally warranted, or in other words *justified*. In this way, liberal states seek to accommodate their duty to secure retributive justice with their foundational moral and political commitments to pluralism, equality, and personal autonomy.[108]

1.4 PRINCIPLES, RULES, AND DISCRETION

The foundational principles of criminal evidence are today widely acknowledged as important procedural standards, albeit not always quite so explicitly or formulated in exactly the same terms as the principles elucidated in the previous section. However, the impact of foundational principles on the day-to-day practice of the courts has been blunted by common lawyers' excessive preoccupation with technical legal definitions. The traditional textbook treatment of the Law of Evidence may allude to the rationale underpinning particular rules, but discussion then tends to proceed as though it can be assumed that the rules are either self-actuating, internally coherent, and exhaustive, or else inexplicably self-contradictory. No further reference to deeper rationalization or justification is thought necessary.

In reality, court practice frequently departs from formal legal definitions, belying an excessively rule-bound (and hidebound) approach to the law of criminal evidence. Many contemporary evidentiary rules evolved from flexible 'rules of practice' which in former times trial judges moulded to the exigencies of the instant case without too much compunction for technical distinctions. This heritage is revived when lawyers and judges in modern criminal litigation invoke, apply, and develop *principles* to govern the reception and evaluation of evidence at trial. Indeed, there is no choice but to appeal to broader

---

[108] On the integration of liberalism and retributive justice, see Paul Butler, 'Retribution, For Liberals' (1999) 46 *UCLA LR* 1873; Jean Hampton, 'How You Can Be Both a Liberal and a Retributivist' (1995) 37 *Arizona LR* 105; Jeffrie G. Murphy, 'Legal Moralism and Liberalism' (1995) 37 *Arizona LR* 73.

underlying principles when the applicable legal rules are vague, incomplete, or apparently in conflict – as rules of criminal procedure not infrequently are.

Trial judges and appellate courts continually strive to negotiate the tensions and competing demands arising from the foundational principles of criminal evidence. Protecting the innocent from wrongful conviction, for example, prompts measures which are liable to frustrate the public interest in punishing offenders. The standard of proof in criminal trials exemplifies this conflict of interests very clearly: the more stringent the requirements of proof of guilt, the more likely it is that some guilty persons will escape the censure and punishment they deserve.[109] Similar conflicts are pervasive in pre-trial criminal process. Rules governing street stops, arrest, search and seizure, police surveillance, the use of informants or databases, and so on,[110] may all impede the detection of crime and the collection of evidence. Again, the desire to treat witnesses with compassion in conformity with the duty of humane treatment may be at odds with legal process objectives, first, to secure a potential witness's evidence, and later at trial, to test that evidence thoroughly and effectively. These deep-seated normative tensions cannot be resolved simply by enumerating foundational evidentiary principles. But specifying the competing principles implicated by the design of criminal procedure and its practical implementation at least serves to clarify the interests at stake and may point the way to arbitrating between them successfully. Principles have differing priority and weight. Doctrinal legal rules, by contrast, simply either apply – or not – to the situation at hand. A rule's contribution to legal analysis and decision-making is exhausted once the scope of its application has been ascertained.

(a) THE LIMITS OF RULES

Confined to their technical definitions, rules of evidence only ever represent part of a complex and differentiated picture. According to the hearsay rule, for example, out-of-court statements adduced for their truth are inadmissible irrespective of the reliability of such statements.[111] However, although the common law rule against hearsay sometimes operated in this inflexible way, its net effect could not be appreciated without taking full account of the many exceptions to hearsay exclusion. In fact, hearsay was frequently admitted at common law, either by utilizing one of several relatively open-ended exceptions to the exclusionary rule or through imaginative judicial interpretation of the rule itself. Admissibility then becomes a function of probative value,[112] rather than being dictated by any peremptory legal definition. Reform of the law of hearsay by the Criminal Justice Act 2003 has served only to reinforce the significance of judicial discretion in assessing the admissibility of probative hearsay, as we will see in Chapter 9.

A similarly contextual approach is required when assessing the admissibility of illegally or otherwise improperly obtained evidence. The lawfulness and propriety of criminal investigations are governed by a plethora of legal standards, but it does not follow that evidence secured in breach of these standards should automatically be inadmissible in court. Once evidence of guilt has actually come to light and is in the possession of the authorities,

---

[109] See §6.3(b).   [110] See §§5.4–5.5.   [111] See Chapter 9.

[112] Probative value can be defined as comprising reliability and weight. Reliability concerns the truth-value of the evidence: how confident are we that it states the truth? Weight is the measure of the contribution of a piece of evidence to proving a fact in issue: to what extent does this evidence prove the contested fact, assuming that it is true? However, lawyers often use 'weight' and 'probative value' interchangeably. Basic concepts of the law of criminal evidence are further analysed in Chapter 3.

the apple of knowledge cannot be unbitten. Especially in serious cases where the stakes are particularly high, there is naturally strong resistance to the suggestion of simply ignoring apparently reliable and cogent evidence of guilt. In these circumstances, the courts are confronted with an age-old dilemma: why should the guilty walk free, evading just punishment and set at liberty to re-offend, merely because a police officer has blundered or misbehaved?[113] This question is taken up again in Chapter 5.

Orthodox expositions of the Law of Evidence perpetuate an unhelpfully rigid dichotomy between rules and discretion. Many of the most important rules of evidence do not in fact provide fixed and determinate standards defining acceptable and unacceptable practices, but rather lay down broad guidelines for decision-makers to follow. Indeed, this has long been recognized in relation to certain pockets of doctrine.[114] By accepting that rules of evidence are circumscribed by discretion one comes close to conceding the centrality of discretionary standards. If the aim is to reach a sensible and just solution to a practical problem, it may be preferable in many circumstances to identify the broad aims and principles that a judge must observe, leaving the details of rule-application in particular cases to the sound judgment of trial judges. The Court of Appeal is increasingly coming around to this way of thinking. In *Renda*, a case concerned with the admissibility of bad character evidence,[115] Sir Igor Judge announced:

The circumstances in which this court would interfere with the exercise of a judicial discretion are limited. The principles need no repetition. However we emphasise that the same general approach will be adopted when the court is being invited to interfere with what in reality is a fact-specific judgment... [T]he trial judge's 'feel' for the case is usually the critical ingredient of the decision at first instance which this court lacks. Context therefore is vital. The creation and subsequent citation from a vast body of so-called 'authority', in reality representing no more than observations on a fact-specific decision of the judge in the Crown Court, is unnecessary and may well be counter-productive.[116]

To those who say that our judges cannot be trusted to discharge the duties of their office, the answer is to provide trial judges with better training and guidance or, failing that, to appoint better judges. There is certainly no mileage in placing inflated demands on procedural rules which, no matter how well-crafted, are bound to disappoint unreasonable expectations.

The significance of discretion in English criminal adjudication is not confined to exclusionary rules of evidence. Adversarial trial procedure affords both prosecution and defence considerable freedom to select the issues to be litigated and the evidence adduced to prove them.[117] However, such freedom must be kept within reasonable bounds to prevent abuses by partisan litigants. Accordingly the courts have evolved procedural standards for curtailing adversarial licence by, for example, limiting opportunities

---

[113] Cf. *People* v *Defore* 242 NY 13, 21, 24–5 (1926), *per* Cardozo J: 'There has been no blinking the consequences. The criminal is to go free because the constable has blundered.... The question is whether protection for the individual would not be gained at a disproportionate loss of protection for society. On the one side is the social need that crime shall be repressed. On the other, the social need that law shall not be flouted by the insolence of office. There are dangers in any choice.'

[114] For a comprehensive albeit now dated survey, see Rosemary Pattenden, *Judicial Discretion and Criminal Litigation* (OUP, 2nd edn. 1990).   [115] See Chapter 14.

[116] *R* v *Renda* [2006] 1 WLR 2948, [2005] EWCA Crim 2826, [3].

[117] The procedural framework of adversarial criminal trials is set out in Chapter 2.

for deliberately creating confusion or prejudice by extending the scope of the dispute beyond the offences charged in the indictment. Yet trial judges are not provided with exhaustive legal definitions of what should qualify as abusive conduct by the parties. They must instead fall back on general principles and refined intuitions to guide their exercise of judgment. In this regard, too, the judicial task is demanding, and trial judges are often called upon to make difficult choices between competing considerations. Resort to procedural principles will rarely carry decision-makers all the way to their required juridical destination. However, our five foundational principles of criminal evidence and their more fine-grained derivatives and concrete applications will usually provide helpful signposts for most of the journey.

Whilst rules of admissibility routinely attract the lion's share of attention, the evidentiary significance of judicial instructions to the jury tends to be overlooked.[118] For reasons already briefly alluded to in this chapter and to be discussed more fully in Chapters 2 and 4, the involvement of ordinary people in criminal adjudication fulfils important social and political functions by injecting broader experiences of the world and popular moral standards into the fact-finding and law-applying processes. However, lay involvement in criminal trials also poses certain difficulties for maintaining the law's advertised epistemic and ethical standards. With this in mind, an expanding corpus of evidentiary rules is concerned with how trial judges, in summing-up, should direct juries in relation to particular types of evidence or inference. Rather than determining admissibility, these 'forensic reasoning rules' address the probative value of admissible evidence.

As Chapter 15 will describe in detail, the judge is obliged to warn the jury about forms of evidence which have come to be viewed, through judicial scruple or experience, as inherently unreliable or prone to misinterpretation. Of course it is difficult to gauge whether juries truly appreciate the significance of such warnings, and there is no way of ensuring that judicial guidance is actually followed in the secrecy of the juryroom. In view of these institutional constraints, we should concentrate on improving the clarity, reasonableness, and comprehensibility of judicial warnings. Where the jury's output is difficult to regulate it is all the more important to refine judicial inputs into the jury's deliberations. Unfortunately, a tendency to divorce evidentiary rules from their procedural context and underlying rationales has sometimes proved counterproductive. On occasion, judges have felt obliged by sterile precedents to repeat boilerplate incantations that are more likely to confuse and perplex a jury than to provide a genuinely helping hand.

Effective judicial warnings, capable of persuading the jury to approach its deliberations in a certain way, must be both intelligible and appealing to the sensibilities and intuitions of ordinary people. Jurors will probably be disinclined to follow a judicial instruction that they consider foolish or perverse, even when the instruction is perfectly clear and well-understood. But here again, preoccupation with the formal wording of judicial warnings, rather than with their underlying values and objectives or the procedural context in which they operate, has deflected academic commentary and undermined judicial efforts to implement legal rules and principles effectively. Trial judges must be entrusted with the discretion to adapt general warnings to the richly-specified facts of the instant case.

---

[118] There are honourable exceptions: cf. Philip McNamara, 'The Canons of Evidence: Rules of Exclusion or Rules of Use?' (1986) 10 *Adelaide LR* 341.

(b) DISCRETION AS JUDGMENT[119]

All this talk of discretion may be apt to foster common misapprehensions which we should take a moment to dispel. To say that a trial judge has 'discretion' to admit or exclude particular evidence, such as hearsay, bad character, or potentially incriminating evidence procured through an unlawful search, does not imply that the judge has *carte blanche* to do whatever he likes as the fancy takes him. That would be the kind of unlimited power Hart dubbed 'scorer's discretion',[120] absolute freedom to make up the rules of the game as one goes along. Judges have discretion in a significantly weaker sense, to use their *judgment* to identify and assess the force of various competing factors and to reach a decision in accordance with that assessment. This requirement is expressed in the oft-repeated *dictum* that 'discretion must be exercised judicially',[121] on the basis of sound factual determinations and according to principle. Once the relevant factors have been identified and analysed to produce a definitive conclusion, it must be implemented. Thus, 'what is loosely described as the discretion...is in fact the judgment of the trial judge'.[122] The juridical distinction between 'questions of law' in the strict sense and decisions calling for the exercise of 'judicial discretion' is itself a question of contextual judicial interpretation with blurred edges occasionally giving rise to hard cases and arbitrary distinctions. Courts sometimes cast around for conceptual hybrids in an effort to indicate particular points on the continuum between near-automatic rule application and highly discretionary judgments tailored to the facts of particular cases.[123] In reality, nothing of importance turns on these classifications. Expectations of conceptual purity need to be scaled down to accommodate the practical complexities of criminal adjudication. The main point for our purposes is that a trial judge's 'discretion' is never at large and untrammelled. It must always be exercised in accordance with evidentiary principle.

In extolling the virtues of discretion, one must not downplay the need to protect rights and promote legal certainty in accordance with the dictates of the rule of law.[124] However, it is a mistake to assume that inflexible rules are always superior to discretion in either respect. Supposedly strict and binding legal definitions will not in practice protect the rights of the accused or guarantee the propriety of criminal investigations if judges come to perceive them as technical fetters on the pursuit of justice. Unless rules of evidence

[119] For further illuminating conceptual analysis, see D. J. Galligan, *Discretionary Powers: A Legal Study of Official Discretion* (OUP, 1986), esp. chs 1–2; Ronald Dworkin, *Taking Rights Seriously* (Duckworth, new impression 1978), 31–9.

[120] H. L. A. Hart, *The Concept of Law* (OUP, 1961), 139ff.

[121] See e.g. *R v Hubbard* [2002] EWCA Crim 1159, [10]; *R v Drew* [1985] 1 WLR 914, 921, CA.

[122] *R v Millard* [2003] EWCA Crim 3629, [15], *per* Judge LJ. And see *R v Davis* [2009] 2 Cr App R 17, [2008] EWCA Crim 1156, [40]: 'The admission of evidence was not a matter of judicial discretion, but more properly an exercise of judgment').

[123] Cf. *R v Gledhill* [2007] EWCA Crim 1183, [20]: 'the trial judge is in the best position to decide what is or is not desirable. He is not, strictly speaking, exercising a discretion but in considering any such decision this court should treat it in much the same way and only disagree with it if it is obviously wrong'; *R v Doherty* [2006] EWCA Crim 2716, [28]: 'The exercise which the judge was required to perform was a balancing exercise: broadly the risk of unfairness to the defence because the evidence could not be challenged, as against risk of unfairness to the prosecution because it could not put before the jury all the available evidence. This is not strictly the exercise of a discretion but something similar to it. It is evaluative and fact sensitive and the sort of exercise which the trial judge is in the best position to perform. This court will therefore only interfere if it is satisfied that the judge's conclusion is obviously wrong, or "perverse or unreasonable".'

[124] Cf. Colin Tapper, 'The Law of Evidence and the Rule of Law' (2009) 68 *Cambridge Law Journal* 67.

retain sufficient flexibility to meet the evolving demands on criminal adjudication, courts will find ways to circumvent or ignore them. Creative judicial interpretation deployed to outflank inconvenient procedural rules is part of the unofficial history of common law evidence. Judicial pragmatism was especially prevalent in relation to 'similar fact evidence'[125] and hearsay, where it even acquired its own ironic terminology – the 'hearsay-fiddle'.[126] On other occasions hard-and-fast rules are capable of increasing the risks of wrongful conviction and undermining standards of procedural propriety, where they entrench legal wrong-turnings as common law precedents or allow judges to take refuge in refined technical distinctions divorced from their underlying rationales.

In short, the familiar objection that by emphasizing the discretionary quality of procedural standards one will inevitably undermine certainty and predictability in criminal proceedings is misconceived. Indeed, experience in criminal litigation stands that complaint on its head. Rules which appear clear and settled on their face, but which in practice are frequently circumvented without warning or explanation, produce only the illusion of certainty and predictability. When the role of discretion is candidly acknowledged, the full range of normative considerations influencing judicial decisions must be articulated and justified. This should facilitate appellate scrutiny and lend impetus to the rational development of evidentiary standards and informed legal debate. Renewed focus on discretion-as-judgment would afford a more realistic basis for understanding and evaluating admissibility determinations, and establish a surer footing for enacting legislative reforms in sympathy with the evolutionary development of common law procedural standards.

1.5 SOURCES OF CRIMINAL EVIDENCE

The Law of Evidence is traditionally viewed as a quintessentially case-law subject. For most of common law evidence's formative years, statutory provisions were relatively few and they were mostly concerned with supplementary or residual issues. Statutory provisions were quite naturally and almost instinctively regarded as exotic interlopers in common law territory. One of the great transformations of English procedural law over the last several decades has been the emergence and gradual predominance of legislation, in the broadest sense. This certainly includes an expanding corpus of primary legislation but it also embraces a diverse range of secondary, delegated, or 'soft law' sources whose direct and growing influence on the day-to-day conduct of criminal litigation utterly belies their modest legal status.

In retrospect, the Police and Criminal Evidence Act (PACE) 1984 can be recognized as the first in a long line of statutes which has progressively, albeit haltingly and unevenly, recast and modernized English criminal procedure law. Since PACE 1984, evidence lawyers have had to get to grips with a welter of further legislative provisions, in particular

---

[125] That is, evidence of the accused's extraneous misconduct adduced in-chief: see §14.1.

[126] D. J. Birch, 'Hearsay-logic and Hearsay-fiddles: *Blastland* Revisited', in Peter Smith (ed.) *Criminal Law: Essays in Honour of JC Smith* (1987), 25: 'The overall picture of the hearsay rule in criminal cases is one of hidden tension between the apparently inexorable hearsay-logic and the judicially unacknowledged but ever-present hearsay-fiddle.'

those contained in the Criminal Justice Act 1988, the Criminal Justice and Public Order Act 1994, the Criminal Procedure and Investigations Act 1996, the Youth Justice and Criminal Evidence Act 1999, the Criminal Justice Act 2003, and the Coroners and Justice Act 2009. These are only the main pieces of legislation that will figure prominently in the following pages. PACE 1984 also pioneered the technique of employing delegated legislation to flesh out the operational details of criminal proceedings, through its Codes of Practice – which originally numbered four and have since expanded to eight. The PACE Codes of Practice have important evidentiary implications, particularly PACE Code C concerning detention, treatment, and questioning of suspects at the police station, and PACE Code D governing identification procedures. However, in terms of their day-to-day impact on criminal litigation up and down the land, by far the most influential secondary legislative instruments are the Criminal Procedure Rules 2010 and the Specimen Directions for trial judges issued by the Judicial Studies Board (JSB). These are now the criminal trial judge's constant companions and guiding lights, and they will crop up repeatedly in the following pages.

The proliferation and diversification of legislative sources with a bearing on criminal evidence and procedure does not imply that case-law ceases to have any importance. In fact, there is now more case-law than ever: not least because electronic databases like Westlaw, LexisNexis, and BAILII[127] have effectively obliterated the distinction between 'reported' and 'unreported' cases. But the hierarchy of evidentiary legal sources needs to be rethought. Much case-law now more closely resembles commentary on statutory provisions rather than primary legal precedents as traditionally understood. At the same time, procedural materials are being claimed by ostensibly more elevated legal categories like 'human rights' and 'constitutional law'. In this jurisprudential maelstrom, where cases and statutes come and go with almost bewildering rapidity, evidentiary principle supplies the only reliable and enduring fixed points of reference.

(a) HUMAN RIGHTS AND CONSTITUTIONAL LAW

The extent to which the law of criminal evidence is developing into a branch of constitutional criminal jurisprudence is one highly significant variable in its current stage of evolution. The specifically constitutional dimensions of criminal procedure are well-recognized in other jurisdictions,[128] and could foreseeably exert progressively greater influence on the way the subject of criminal evidence is conceived, practised, and taught in England and Wales. Pivotal in such developments is the impact on criminal procedure and evidence of the Human Rights Act 1998.

The Human Rights Act (HRA) came into force on 2 October 2000, with the object of making the European Convention on Human Rights (ECHR) and its associated jurisprudence – primarily the decisions of the European Court of Human Rights (ECtHR) – a source of rights and duties in English legal proceedings, including criminal proceedings.[129] The 1998

[127] British and Irish Legal Information Institute (BAILII): www.bailii.org/.

[128] Notably, in the USA: see, Akhil Reed Amar, *The Constitution and Criminal Procedure: First Principles* (Yale UP, 1997); Carol S. Steiker, '"First Principles" of Constitutional Criminal Procedure: A Mistake?' (1999) 112 *Harvard LR* 680; Donald Dripps 'Akhil Amar on Criminal Procedure and Constitutional Law: "Here I Go Down that Wrong Road Again"' (1996) 74 *North Carolina LR* 1559.

[129] See John Wadham, Helen Mountfield, Caoilfhionn Gallagher, and Elizabeth Prochaska, *Blackstone's Guide to the Human Rights Act 1998* (OUP, 5th edn 2009); Ben Emmerson, Andrew Ashworth, and Alison

Act does not entrench the ECHR, or even strictly speaking 'incorporate' it into English law. The Act, instead, strikes a rather subtle constitutional balance, under which all of the ECHR's substantive rights are re-enacted as unique provisions of English law, known as 'Convention rights'. English judges are directed to have regard to the jurisprudence of the ECtHR,[130] without formally affecting the absolute sovereignty of Parliament. Section 3 of the Act creates a strong presumption that English law is Convention-compliant by impos-ing on judges a muscular interpretative obligation to 'read down' English statutory provi-sions in conformity with Convention rights:

Section 3(1)
So far as it is possible to do so, primary legislation and subordinate legislation must be read and given effect in a way which is compatible with the Convention rights...

The House of Lords promptly announced that section 3 authorizes senior judges to read into Acts of Parliament words that are plainly not there, and which some might think actually defeat Parliament's intentions (though the courts themselves could never openly admit it consistently with their orthodox constitutional function).[131] However, language is not infinitely elastic. There will come a point where judicial legislation cannot be passed off as statutory interpretation, and the conclusion that UK legislation is not fully compatible with the ECHR cannot be avoided.

Where it was clearly Parliament's intention to derogate from a Convention right, or where it is otherwise impossible for a judge in good faith to interpret primary legisla-tion compatibly with Convention rights, the Human Rights Acts unequivocally states that Parliament's will must prevail and the right is overridden. As John Spencer wryly mused in anticipation:

What could a UK court do when confronted with a convicted prisoner if a future Parliament, tiring of legislation to safeguard human rights, had re-enacted the Act for the Boiling of Prisoners [22 Hen VIII ch 9, 1530]? Surprisingly, perhaps, the answer seems to be that the court would have to sentence the prisoner to be boiled. If there is one matter of principle on which British politicians of all shades of opinion seem invariably to agree, it is the impor-tance of preserving the sovereignty of Parliament.[132]

The only domestic remedy available to a person whose Convention rights have been delib-erately infringed or curtailed is that the higher courts are empowered, by section 4 of the HRA 1998, to enter a 'declaration of incompatibility'. This is exactly what it says: a

---

Macdonald, *Human Rights and Criminal Justice* (Sweet & Maxwell, 2nd edn. 2007), chs 1–2; Helen Fenwick, Gavin Phillipson, and Roger Masterman (eds.), *Judicial Reasoning under the UK Human Rights Act* (CUP, 2007); David Feldman, 'The Human Rights Act 1998 and Constitutional Principles' (1999) 19 *Legal Studies* 165; A. T. H. Smith, 'The Human Rights Act and the Criminal Lawyer: The Constitutional Context' [1999] *Crim LR* 251.

[130] Section 2 of the HRA 1998 provides that: 'A court or tribunal determining a question which has arisen in connection with a Convention right must take into account any: (a) judgment, decision, declaration or advisory opinion of the European Court of Human Rights; (b) opinion of the Commission ... (c) decision of the Commission ..., or (d) decision of the Committee of Ministers ... whenever made or given, so far as, in the opinion of the court or tribunal, it is relevant to the proceedings in which that question has arisen.'

[131] See *R v A (No 2)* [2002] 1 AC 45, [2001] UKHL 25, discussed in §10.2.

[132] J. R. Spencer, 'English Criminal Procedure and the Human Rights Act 1998' (1999) 33 *Israel LR* 664, 668.

declaration that English law does not conform with the ECHR in some material particular, intended to serve as a warning to the relevant minister of state that the UK is to that extent in breach of its international legal obligations. But such breaches of public international law are not justiciable in domestic British courts. An aggrieved litigant can only hope that the minister will be galvanized by a declaration of incompatibility into rectifying the situation through the political process, ultimately by sponsoring a corrective Act of Parliament. Meanwhile, the victim of a breach of Convention rights always has the option of taking his complaint directly to the ECtHR in Strasbourg, provided that he has access to funds and is not in too much of a hurry. Applications to Strasbourg frequently take five years or more to reach judgment.

Despite evident sensitivity to traditional notions of parliamentary supremacy, the constitutional significance of the Human Rights Act cannot be overstated. Section 2 of the Act requires British courts to take account of the relevant judgments, declarations and opinions of the ECtHR and other Strasbourg institutions in any case in which questions involving Convention rights arise. ECtHR decisions do not have the binding force of precedent in England and Wales; nor is the Strasbourg court itself formally bound by its own previous decisions, to which the common law doctrine of *stare decisis* does not apply. Strasbourg jurisprudence is nonetheless highly influential, and would normally be followed by English courts. In an early decision Lord Slynn observed:

Although the [HRA] 1998 Act does not provide that a national court is bound by these decisions it is obliged to take account of them so far as they are relevant. In the absence of some special circumstances it seems to me that the court should follow any clear and constant jurisprudence of the European Court of Human Rights. If it does not do so there is at least a possibility that the case will go to that court which is likely in the ordinary case to follow its own constant jurisprudence.[133]

This interpretative policy was subsequently firmed up by Lord Bingham in *Ullah*:

[A] national court subject to a duty such as that imposed by section 2 should not without strong reason dilute or weaken the effect of the Strasbourg case law...since the meaning of the Convention should be uniform throughout the states party to it. The duty of national courts is to keep pace with the Strasbourg jurisprudence as it evolves over time: no more, but certainly no less.[134]

It must follow that English courts are no longer bound by common law precedents, to the extent that English law is superseded by decisions of the ECtHR, now or in the future.[135] However, Lord Phillips, President of the new UK Supreme Court, added the following very significant rider in *Horncastle*:

The requirement to 'take into account' the Strasbourg jurisprudence will normally result in the domestic court applying principles that are clearly established by the Strasbourg court. There will, however, be rare occasions where the domestic court has concerns as to whether a decision of the Strasbourg court sufficiently appreciates or accommodates particular aspects

---

[133] *R (on the application of Alconbury Developments Ltd) v Secretary of State for the Environment* [2001] 2 All ER 929, 969, HL.

[134] *R (Ullah) v Special Adjudicator* [2004] 2 AC 323, [2004] UKHL 26, [20].

[135] Also see *Ashworth Hospital Authority v MGN* [2001] 1 WLR 1081, HL; I. Leigh and L. Lustgarten 'Making Rights Real: The Courts, Remedies, and the Human Rights Act' [1999] *CLJ* 509.

of our domestic process. In such circumstances it is open to the domestic court to decline to follow the Strasbourg decision, giving reasons for adopting this course. This is likely to give the Strasbourg court the opportunity to reconsider the particular aspect of the decision that is in issue, so that there takes place what may prove to be a valuable dialogue between the domestic court and the Strasbourg court.[136]

It was predictable from the outset that the Human Rights Act would have a major impact on the law of criminal evidence,[137] and so it has proved. ECHR-inspired arguments on points of criminal procedure were being urged on the courts even before the Human Rights Act had entered fully into force.[138] Further developments have come thick and fast since October 2000,[139] as the frequent references to Convention jurisprudence in subsequent chapters will confirm. Several Convention rights have direct implications for procedural law, including those transposing ECHR Article 3 (prohibition on torture), Article 5 (freedom from unlawful deprivation of liberty), Article 7 (non-retroactivity of penal law), and Article 8 (right to respect for private life). Above all, however, Article 6's 'right to a fair trial' has become a prominent feature of English criminal litigation over the last decade. It merits extensive quotation:

Article 6 – Right to a fair trial

1 In the determination of his civil rights and obligations or of any criminal charge against him, everyone is entitled to a fair and public hearing within a reasonable time by an independent and impartial tribunal established by law...

2 Everyone charged with a criminal offence shall be presumed innocent until proved guilty according to law.

3 Everyone charged with a criminal offence has the following minimum rights:

   (a) to be informed promptly, in a language which he understands and in detail, of the nature and cause of the accusation against him;

   (b) to have adequate time and facilities for the preparation of his defence;

   (c) to defend himself in person or through legal assistance of his own choosing or, if he has not sufficient means to pay for legal assistance, to be given it free when the interests of justice so require;

---

[136] *R v Horncastle* [2009] UKSC 14, [2010] 2 WLR 94, [11].

[137] On the pre-Human Rights Act significance of the ECHR, see Andrew Ashworth, 'Article 6 and the Fairness of Trials' [1999] *Crim LR* 261; Sybil D. Sharpe, 'Article 6 and the Disclosure of Evidence in Criminal Trials' [1999] *Crim LR* 273; Bert Swart, 'The European Convention as an Invigorator of Domestic Law in the Netherlands' (1999) 26 *JLS* 38; Sybil Sharpe, 'The European Convention: A Suspects' Charter?' [1997] *Crim LR* 848.

[138] See in particular, *R v DPP, ex p. Kebilene* [2000] AC 326, HL, discussed by Paul Roberts, 'The Presumption of Innocence Brought Home? *Kebilene* Deconstructed' (2002) 118 *LQR* 41.

[139] See, for example, Ben Emmerson, Andrew Ashworth, and Alison Macdonald, *Human Rights and Criminal Justice* (Sweet & Maxwell, 2nd edn. 2007); Andrew L.T. Choo and Susan Nash, 'Evidence Law in England and Wales: The Impact of the Human Rights Act 1998' (2003) 7 *E & P* 31; Paul Roberts, 'Drug Dealing and the Presumption of Innocence: The Human Rights Act (Almost) Bites' (2002) 6 *E & P* 17; Laura C. H. Hoyano, 'Striking a Balance Between the Rights of Defendants and Vulnerable Witnesses: Will Special Measures Directions Contravene Guarantees of a Fair Trial?' [2001] *Crim LR* 948; Andrew Ashworth, 'Criminal Proceedings After the Human Rights Act: The First Year' [2001] *Crim LR* 855; Anthony Jennings, Andrew Ashworth and Ben Emmerson, 'Silence and Safety: The Impact of Human Rights Law' [2000] *Crim LR* 879.

(d) to examine or have examined witnesses against him and to obtain the attendance and examination of witnesses on his behalf under the same conditions as witnesses against him;

(e) to have the free assistance of an interpreter if he cannot understand or speak the language used in court.

The specific rights enumerated in Article 6(2) and (3), as well as the general concept of a fair trial, are being woven into the fabric of criminal procedure law in England and Wales. Whilst its influence is generally speaking positive and welcome, the impact of human rights law on English criminal litigation is not without on-going controversy, as we shall see.[140]

Re-examining criminal proceedings through the lens of human rights helps to bring into focus the specifically *constitutional* dimensions of criminal evidence. This is a difficult topic for common lawyers: we are not used to thinking primarily in terms of rights, let alone constitutional rights. The genius and blight of the common law derives from its pragmatic emphasis on remedies before rights: *ubi remedium, ibi ius*. For all that, criminal procedure plainly addresses constitutional issues regarding the fundamental rights of the citizen and the limits of state power. The Human Rights Act makes this undeniable fact harder to ignore. It is helping to consolidate a jurisprudential development which actually began prior to the HRA 1998 but which may flourish under its aegis, whereby senior judges go out of their way to declare that a particular procedural norm is *not merely a rule of evidence* but should be recognized, in terms, as a constitutional principle. An important example is the categorical exclusion of evidence that may have been procured through torture of any person, which is discussed in Chapter 5.[141] Several others will be encountered in subsequent chapters.[142]

Although the handful of relevant decisions rendered to-date might reasonably be regarded as rather isolated and equivocal auguries, the progressive constitutionalization of criminal evidence has potentially profound implications for British law and politics. The broad direction of travel is very much in keeping with the historic creation in October 2009 of a UK Supreme Court to replace the House of Lords as the final court of appeal *inter alia* for criminal proceedings in England and Wales. Constitutional law and human rights law (to the extent that these juridical siblings can realistically be distinguished) are concerned primarily with enduring principles of political morality rather than with the changing fashions of subsisting positive law. Their growing influence on criminal procedure can only serve to foster the development of Criminal Evidence as a discrete disciplinary field devoted, first and foremost to the elucidation of legal principles.

(b) HARD-WORKING SOFT LAW

The Criminal Procedure Rules (CrimPR) 2005 and 2010 were drafted and are updated on a rolling basis by the Criminal Procedure Rule Committee chaired by the Lord Chief Justice, under delegated statutory authority. They were designed to gather together, clarify, and

---

[140] In particular (at the time of writing), see *Al-Khawaja and Tahery* v *UK* (2009) 49 EHRR 1, discussed in §9.2(b); and by Ian Dennis [2009] *Crim LR* 311; and Andrew Ashworth [2009] *Crim LR* 353.

[141] See §5.4(c), discussing *A* v *Secretary of State for the Home Department (No 2)* [2006] 2 AC 221, [2005] UKHL 71.

[142] See, e.g., §7.3 (compulsory process); §7.4(c) (legal professional privilege); §9.2(b) (confrontation).

systematize disparate rules of court and judicial practice directions pertaining to criminal litigation. Although the bulk of the Rules is devoted to detailed operational matters of criminal procedure and trial management, Part 1 opens with an eye-catching and ambitiously sweeping restatement of the 'overriding objective' of criminal adjudication:

1.1. The overriding objective

(1) The overriding objective of this new code is that criminal cases be dealt with justly.

(2) Dealing with a criminal case justly includes—

    (a) acquitting the innocent and convicting the guilty;

    (b) dealing with the prosecution and the defence fairly;

    (c) recognising the rights of a defendant, particularly those under Article 6 of the European Convention on Human Rights;

    (d) respecting the interests of witnesses, victims and jurors and keeping them informed of the progress of the case;

    (e) dealing with the case efficiently and expeditiously;

    (f) ensuring that appropriate information is available to the court when bail and sentence are considered; and

    (g) dealing with the case in ways that take into account—

        (i) the gravity of the offence alleged,

        (ii) the complexity of what is in issue,

        (iii) the severity of the consequences for the defendant and others affected, and

        (iv) the needs of other cases.

Strikingly from our perspective, the 'overriding objective' encompasses each of our five foundational principles of criminal evidence, describing several of them in almost identical language. Paragraph (2)(a) makes acquitting the innocent the first explicit criterion of dealing with criminal cases justly. Paragraph 2(d) restates our principle of humane treatment. The principle of procedural propriety and upholding the legitimacy of the verdict are clearly reflected in paragraphs 2(b) and (c). Our first foundational principle of accurate fact-finding is expounded in relation to trial verdicts by paragraph 2(a) and extended to bail and sentencing hearings by paragraph 2(f). The principle of minimum state intervention is most clearly echoed by paragraph 2(g), which effectively contains a general principle of proportionality, but it is also implicit in paragraph 2(c)'s regard for procedural rights and in paragraph 2(e)'s demand for efficiency and expedition, which are general criteria of effective public administration.

It should be noted that Rule 1.1's overriding objective makes fact-finding subservient to justice ('criminal cases [must] be dealt with justly'). This is entirely in keeping with our account.[143] Although we have characterized accurate fact-finding as the first principle of criminal evidence, in recognition of evidence law's strong epistemological associations, this must not be taken to imply that all the other principles are merely extras in an essentially epistemic production. Indeed, it should have been obvious from the proceeding discussion that the other four principles sometimes constrain fact-finding in the name of retributive justice. Legal fact-finding is meant to serve justice, as the CrimPR 2010 clearly imply, not the other way around. But it is not enough to say that the other principles (and

---

[143] Also see Paul Roberts, 'Roberts and Zuckerman's *Criminal Evidence*: (Un)grateful Comments on Six Commentaries' (2007) 5(2) *International Commentary on Evidence*, Article 2, Part 1 (on-line www.bepress. com/ice/vol5/iss2/art2/).

additional considerations such as those specified by Part 1.1 of the CrimPR) operate as side-constraints on fact-finding. We should instead regard all five principles as constitutive of the whole, each principle independently and irreducibly contributing vital threads to be woven into the incrementally embroidered tapestry of justice.

Taken out of context, the CrimPR 2010 might easily be read as a comprehensive code of criminal procedure – which it is not. Appellate courts have occasionally had to remind first instance judges that they cannot use the CrimPR, and in particular the sweeping language of Part 1.1 or the case management powers conferred by Part 3, to disregard vested procedural rights or outflank evidentiary rules unambiguously stated in statutes or enshrined in the common law.[144] Delegated legislation must be kept *intra vires*. Allowed completely free rein, open-ended soft law standards might imperil the development of criminal evidence's nascent constitutional and human rights dimensions noted in the previous section. But these risks must be kept in proportion and balanced against tangible benefits. Notwithstanding some unavoidable scope for overreaching, Rule 1.1 of the CrimPR supplies trial judges with significant normative resources for exercising their extensive discretion in accordance with fundamental principles of criminal evidence.

The formal legal authority of the JSB's Specimen Directions is considerably more attenuated even than delegated legislation like the CrimPR, but their practical authority is immense. The JSB is a statutory body run by the judges themselves to deliver continuing professional education to the judiciary. Strictly speaking, its Specimen Directions are nothing more than informal guidance to trial judges on how to direct criminal juries in relation to various evidentiary topics. In reality, new and recently appointed trial judges, many of whom have little or no previous experience of criminal litigation as advocates, rely implicitly on the JSB's Specimens, which are even officially described as 'the Crown Court Bench Book'. Carefully following the applicable Specimen Directions is the trial judge's best strategy for avoiding criticism or reversal on appeal. Their widespread influence on criminal trial practice is also clearly signalled by the fact that the Court of Appeal sometimes finds it necessary to criticize particular aspects of a Specimen Direction and to call for its revision. More proximately than Shelley's poets, the JSB through its Specimen Directions is a *de facto* worldly legislator of criminal procedure.[145]

References to the JSB's Specimen Directions, the CrimPR 2010, and the PACE Codes of Practice pepper the following exposition. The proliferation of these hard-working secondary and soft law sources of criminal evidence contributes to all of the major disciplinary trends identified in this introductory chapter. Criminal litigation is increasingly governed by dedicated legal norms that do not apply to civil proceedings. These norms predominantly derive from legislation (broadly conceived), in contrast to English evidence law's judicially-fashioned heritage. Secondary legal sources contain open-ended general principles as well as elaborately specified procedural rules with fine-grained contextual applications, and every normative variation in-between. Whatever their degree of particularity, however, evidentiary rules are implemented against a background of extensive judicial discretion to achieve justice according to principle.

---

[144] Cf. *R (Kelly)* v *Warley Magistrates' Court* [2008] 1 WLR 2001; [2007] EWHC 1836 (Admin).

[145] For further discussion, see Roderick Munday, 'Judicial Studies Board Specimen Directions and the Enforcement of Orthodoxy: a Modest Case Study' (2002) 66 *Journal of Criminal Law* 158; Roderick Munday, 'The Bench Books: Can the Judiciary Keep a Secret?' [1996] *Crim LR* 296.

1.6 UNDERSTANDING CRIMINAL EVIDENCE

It is high time that Criminal Evidence was recognized as a discrete field of legal practice, teaching, and scholarship, characterized by the principled elucidation of judicial discretion. The pervasive role of discretion in criminal adjudication has major implications for how all lawyers should understand and participate in the institutionally-structured processes of evidence and proof, whether as academic researchers and commentators, teachers or students of evidence law, practitioners preparing for trial or arguing cases in court, or judges making evidentiary rulings. Rather than conceptualizing the law of criminal evidence as a system of formal rules from which judges freely if somewhat hypocritically deviate in practice, our energies should be concentrated on expounding the principles that ought to structure and inform legitimate exercises of judicial discretion.

(a) PRINCIPLED JUDICIAL DISCRETION

It should not be necessary for judges to cast around for any convenient doctrinal peg on which to hang their inclination to admit contested evidence, exercising *de facto* discretion in the pretence of following a rule. Trial judges should instead evaluate the interests of the accused and complainants and weigh the public interest in the administration of justice in a more direct, transparent, and accountable fashion within an explicit – and increasingly legislated – framework of principle.

Let us be absolutely clear. This is not an argument for abandoning rigid procedural rules altogether. Nobody is suggesting that judges should be at liberty to remake the law of criminal evidence on a whim. To the extent that evidentiary rules are increasingly prescribed by legislation, courts should naturally accord due deference to the will of Parliament. The Human Rights Act 1998 further entrenches procedural principles. Common law procedural doctrines, too, form part of English law's constitutional heritage that judges are duty-bound to preserve. Thus, the judges could not simply declare that in future the prosecution need only prove its case on the balance of probabilities, that suspects will be forced to speak at trial, that there will be no restrictions on adducing evidence of the accused's bad character, or that all hearsay will henceforth be admissible – even though, according to the traditional theory of unlimited sovereignty, Parliament could do any or all of these things. Justice demands fidelity to settled and sometimes unbending rules to this extent.[146] However, the point at which determinate rules should give way to discretionary standards is itself a context-dependent question calling for sound judgment rather than blind rule-following.

Discretion is the oil in the procedural machine, criminal justice's liquid engineering which prevents the system's working parts binding and grinding together or seizing up entirely. Its vital properties ought to be studied, appreciated, and cultivated. Unfortunately, common lawyers' preoccupation with evidentiary rules has obscured the extent and importance of judicial discretion in criminal adjudication, not least from trial judges themselves.

---

[146] On the structural properties of rules and rule-following see Joseph Raz, *The Morality of Freedom* (OUP, 1986), chs 2 and 3; Frederick Schauer, *Playing by the Rules: A Philosophical Examination of Rule-Based Decision-Making in Law and Life* (OUP, 1991).

Rule-worship distracts attention from the general principles which ought to guide judicial decision-making and, perversely, breeds inconsistency, uncertainty, and injustice. Some trial judges will be knowledgeable and skilled in the dark arts of rule-bending and rule-avoidance, others less so. Judging then muddles along as an inarticulate mystery with no systematic attempt to develop judicial intuitions into more refined and reflective trial practice. Far from diverting litigation from truth-finding, weakening the protection of the innocent, or diluting standards of procedural propriety, refocusing trial judges' training and trial management on the principled exercise of judicial discretion should serve to clarify, promote, and reinforce the foundational principles of criminal evidence.

(b) DISCIPLINING CRIMINAL EVIDENCE

Abandoning an artificially rigid dichotomy between rules and discretion should also produce a correspondingly simplified account of evidentiary standards in criminal proceedings, an account which does not overwhelm students or their teachers with an avalanche of undigested – and indigestible – detail. Genuine understanding, as opposed to mere encyclopaedic recitation of authorities, implies being able to see the wood for the trees. From the perspective of principle, vast swathes of case-law can be understood as contextual applications of general principles to particular fact situations, rather than extensions or refinements of rules, and exceptions to rules, and parasitic rules about rules and their rule-bound exceptions, etc. Most fine-grained judgments of relevance, admissibility determinations balancing prejudicial effect against probative value, and tailored evidentiary warnings should be treated as exemplars of the evidentiary method rather than formal legal precedents in the strict common law sense.

The law of criminal evidence is by now sufficiently well-developed for it to be elucidated without exhaustive reference to the entire corpus of appellate decisions. Indeed, the sheer bulk of procedural law has already expanded beyond the point at which any aspiration to comprehensiveness is at odds with genuine comprehension. Lord Hoffmann, writing extra-judicially, once ascribed to the Law of Evidence an evolutionary tendency which Sir Peter Medawar had identified in the natural sciences:

The factual burden of a science varies inversely with its degree of maturity. As a science advances, particular facts are comprehended within, and therefore in a sense annihilated by, general statements of steadily increasing explanatory power and compass – whereupon the facts need no longer be known explicitly, i.e. spelled out and kept in mind. In all sciences we are being progressively relieved of the burden of singular instances, the tyranny of the particular. We need no longer record the fall of every apple.[147]

The law of criminal evidence has attained sufficient maturity to insist on a more selective harvest of principle, whilst some old chestnuts are overdue for the fire.

This book presents our best account of the principles of criminal evidence motivated by the observations and methodological commitments rehearsed in this chapter. It should already be evident from these introductory remarks that criminal evidence has significant institutional, epistemic, and normative dimensions which we need to try to bring together into an integrated conception of the subject. Chapter 2 begins to take up this challenge by

---

[147] Reviewing *Phipson on Evidence* (12th edn. 1976) (1978) 94 *LQR* 457, 459.

providing an overview of the institutional procedural framework of adversarial jury trial and its theoretical underpinnings. This is followed in Chapter 3 by detailed analysis of the core concept of 'admissible evidence'. We discuss both the conceptual structure of legal admissibility and the evidentiary standards the law applies, starting with the threshold criterion of relevance. This chapter also introduces different categories of evidence and investigates the range of sources of information in criminal litigation, which turn out to be considerably more diverse and diffuse than technical conceptions of 'evidence' tend to imply.

In Chapter 4 our attention turns to the closely related topics of fact-finding and proof. Having first clarified the kinds of 'facts' which must be determined in criminal adjudication, we consider how fact-finders are able to arrive at legally significant conclusions, for example by drawing inductive inferences from the evidence or employing probabilistic reasoning. The epistemic techniques and reasoning processes typically utilized by jurors in arriving at their verdicts have direct implications for how – if at all – common sense fact-finding should be regulated by procedural law. Chapters 3 and 4 complete the groundwork for the epistemological explorations of evidence and proof undertaken in the remainder of the book.

Chapter 5 brings us back to more overtly normative questions, by elucidating the concept of 'fair trial' and identifying its institutional manifestations in English law. Emblematic of modern cosmopolitan criminal jurisprudence, our discussion weaves together common law precedents, modern legislation, and international human rights principles. Chapter 6 then examines burdens of proof and the presumption of innocence, a topic which self-evidently combines all three of Criminal Evidence's core institutional, epistemic, and normative elements.

Chapters 7–11 are concerned with various aspects of witness testimony. A central theme of the exposition will be a critical appraisal of the 'principle of orality' and the extent to which recent procedural reforms represent problematic departures form it. Having first introduced the principle of orality and explained its normative salience, Chapter 7 sequentially reviews the law of witness competence, compellability, privilege, and public interest immunity (PII). The procedural rules governing examination-in-chief and cross-examination are subjected to detailed critical scrutiny in Chapter 8, before Chapter 9 tackles the major topic of hearsay which has lately undergone extensive statutory reform. Chapter 10 examines the 'special measures' which have been adopted to ease the plight of vulnerable and intimidated witnesses and secure their best evidence for criminal proceedings, whilst Chapter 11 considers the somewhat different opportunities and challenges for criminal adjudication posed by scientific and other expert witness testimony.

Chapters 12–14 address different evidentiary implications of the special, and especially vulnerable, position of the accused in criminal proceedings. Chapter 12 places confession evidence in its institutional, regulatory, and socio-legal context. This discussion provides the backdrop for Chapter 13's exploration of the related topics of the right to silence and the privilege against self-incrimination. Chapter 14 is concerned with evidence of the accused's extraneous misconduct or 'bad character', a stalwart of evidentiary doctrine which (like hearsay) has been transformed by the Criminal Justice Act 2003. We will need to consider whether the new statutory framework, as interpreted in the first wave of appellate decisions, embodies the foundational principles of criminal evidence or threatens their erosion.

Chapter 15 describes the evolution of judicial warnings from the old inflexible law of corroboration to modern 'post-quantitative' evidentiary standards and forensic reasoning rules. This topic revolves around the division of forensic labour between judge and jury and reprises one of this book's overarching themes, the ubiquity of judicial discretion in criminal adjudication and the urgent need to develop normative standards for its principled exercise. In conclusion, Chapter 16 reiterates the central arguments presaged in this introduction, summarizes the main principles of criminal evidence discussed in each chapter, and ventures some tentative speculations on our subject's emergent trends and future prospects.

2

THE PROCEDURAL
FRAMEWORK OF
ADVERSARIAL JURY TRIAL

2.1 CRIMINAL EVIDENCE IN PROCEDURAL
CONTEXT

Fact-finding and the application of rules of evidence in criminal proceedings do not proceed in hypothetical, disembodied abstraction. Criminal adjudication takes place in particular procedural environments comprised of rules, institutions, processes, routine working practices, and professional cultures, all of which, in combination, stamp their influence on the unique character of fact-finding in English criminal trials and mould the nature and significance of the evidentiary rules and doctrines applied in court. Stripped of this procedural context, the law of evidence might seem like an abstruse and highly stylized legal parlour game, complete with an excess of fiendishly complicated rules. But the law of evidence is neither mental chewing gum for idle legal minds nor a special kind of aptitude test for law students, but a practical, living, body of rules and doctrines, part designed and part evolved, to facilitate forensic fact-finding and serve the ends of criminal justice.

The rules and principles of criminal evidence can barely even be understood, or their significance appreciated, without taking proper account of the procedural environments in which they operate. In practice, the rules are influenced by cultural, ethical, pragmatic, and tactical considerations which cannot be gleaned from the dry letter of the law. Studying the rules in isolation would produce, at best, only a skewed and superficial understanding of the law of criminal evidence, and much that makes sense in procedural context would remain obscure.

This book takes for its paradigm of criminal adjudication one particular procedural environment: adversarial jury trial on indictment in the Crown Court. Jury trial is, of course, a mainstay of Britain's – still largely unwritten – constitution, a fundamental right of 'all natural born Englishmen',[1] and a contemporary cultural icon. The triangular relationship between the parties, the judge, and the jury has been instrumental in shaping the style and content of modern rules of evidence, prompting the great American Evidence

---

[1] A notion supposedly derived from Magna Carta, but the historical lineage is contorted: see §2.4, below.

scholar James Bradley Thayer to declare that evidence law was 'a child of the jury'.[2] Our discussion of relevance and fact-finding in the next two chapters, in particular, shows that Thayer's remark overstates the case, since an important and often neglected dimension of evidentiary theory and practice concerns the logic of fact-finding under conditions of uncertainty about past events. This ubiquitous logic is relatively independent of the nature and composition of the fact-finder in particular types of legal proceeding. Fact-finding by judges and magistrates, whether sitting alone or in panels of two or three, must obey the same formal logic of factual adjudication, just as fact-finding by a jury must dance to its tune. But Thayer was still making an important point: *some* of the rules and doctrines of Evidence are only explicable in terms of the orthodox division of labour in English criminal proceedings, whereby the trial judge is responsible for settling issues of law whilst the jury is called upon to determine questions of fact. (We will later need to refine this simplified dichotomy between 'facts' and 'law',[3] but the distinction is clear enough to be going along with.)

Trials on indictment in the Crown Court, generally speaking, deal with the most serious offences and allegations. Legal representation is almost universal, counsel should be relatively[4] well-prepared, trial judges are experienced lawyers, and trials usually take significantly longer, sometimes *much* longer, than summary trials of roughly comparable[5] cases in the magistrates' courts. Crown Court trial is precisely the procedural environment in which one would expect issues of evidence and procedure to receive their most sustained and careful attention; which is not to say that mistakes, even mistakes of a fundamental or elementary nature, are not routinely made. Observers have often contrasted the thoroughness of trials on indictment with the comparative haste and inattention to finer points of procedural detail which appear characteristic of British summary justice, as dispensed in the magistrates' courts.[6] For over a century, furthermore, the greatest aggregate contribution to developing common law evidence has been made by the Court of Appeal

---

[2] See Eleanor Swift, 'One Hundred Years of Evidence Law Reform: Thayer's Triumph' (2000) 88 *California LR* 2437, 2449–50, discussing James Bradley Thayer, *A Preliminary Treatise on Evidence at the Common Law* (Little, Brown & Co, 1898), esp. 180–1, 508–9. Colin Tapper, *Cross and Tapper on Evidence* (10th edn. 2004), 189, plausibly suggested that '[h]istorically, the separation of the functions of the judge and jury has left so deep a mark upon English jurisprudence that the rules and habits of juristic thought, which it has engendered, are scarcely touched by the current decline of jury trial. Even if jury trial is ever abolished, many of these rules and conceptions will remain so long as the common law system itself subsists.' Also see Frederick Schauer, 'On the Supposed Jury-Dependence of Evidence Law' (2006) 155 *University of Pennsylvania LR* 165.   [3] See §4.2.

[4] Notwithstanding the notorious problem of 'returned briefs', whereby the barrister scheduled to conduct a case becomes unavailable at the eleventh hour – typically because another trial is lasting longer than anticipated – obliging counsel to 'return the brief', usually to a more junior, and almost inevitably less well-prepared, colleague to undertake the trial.

[5] The most serious offences are triable *only* on indictment, but the magistrates' courts deal with matters roughly analogous to most crimes tried on indictment: murder and manslaughter, for example, are triable only on indictment, but endangerment offences risking death, such as breaches of the factories legislation or a failure to control dangerous substances, may be tried by the magistrates if charged as a summary 'regulatory' offence.

[6] Spending less public money to resolve criminal cases of lower gravity is neither irrational nor necessarily unjust, but the details of expenditure and quality of process in summary proceedings are controversial. For empirical accounts of the *summary* nature of magistrates' courts proceedings, see Michael McConville, Jacqueline Hodgson, Lee Bridges, and Anita Pavlovic, *Standing Accused* (OUP, 1994), chs 8–9; Doreen McBarnet, *Conviction* (Macmillan, 1981).

(Criminal Division)[7] in appeals against conviction by a jury after Crown Court trial. Most of the law typically found in books on Evidence, in other words, has both derived from, and been devised for, trial by judge and jury in the Crown Court.

There are good reasons, then, for the student of Evidence to treat trial by judge and jury as the paradigmatic form of criminal adjudication. But this choice must itself be placed in procedural context to avoid misunderstanding. In recent years some commentators have taken exception to what they regard as an unhealthy preoccupation with jury trial, pointing out that the vast majority of criminal cases in England and Wales – some 95%[8] – are conducted in the magistrates' courts where there are no juries and, it would seem, only limited respect for the formal laws of evidence. For these critics, focusing on jury trial diverts attention away from where most of the real action takes place in practice.[9] The criticism might, indeed, be extended to any trial-centred analysis, since very few accused persons actually contest the allegations against them at any level of criminal process. Both in magistrates' courts proceedings and in indictable proceedings in the Crown Court, most accused plead guilty to some or all of the charges brought against them. Contested trials are very much the exception in a system that operates, and pragmatically speaking *must* operate in a context of constrained resources, on the assumption that the question of guilt will in the overwhelming preponderance of cases be settled on the accused's plea.[10]

It is appropriate to be reminded of the broader context of criminal proceedings in order to keep our discussion of the law of evidence in its proper perspective. But this merely qualifies, without displacing, the centrality of adversarial jury trial to a study of criminal evidence. Even if one were to assume, with an excess of caution, that the rules of evidence only really matter in contested trials on indictment of the most serious crimes, like homicide, grievous bodily harm, wounding, armed robbery, rape, arson, and aggravated burglary, these rules would surely still be worthy of serious examination, analysis, and critical re-evaluation, as an indispensable component of public decision-making in matters of the first legal, political, and ethical importance. If the law of criminal evidence were coterminous with adversarial jury trial, it might be necessary to concede that the contribution of the law of evidence to the overall attainment of criminal justice in England and Wales is more modest than is sometimes supposed. Yet, in reality, the influence of rules and principles of evidence is much more extensive, not least because evidence law impacts on the pre-trial conduct of criminal proceedings, as well as directly shaping the outcome of trials.

---

[7]　The Court of Appeal (Criminal Division) was created by the Criminal Appeal Act 1968. Its predecessor was called the Court of Criminal Appeal, which was established by the Criminal Appeal Act 1907. See §2.5(e), below.

[8]　Estimates generally range between about 92% and 98%, depending on the source of the statistics and the finer details of the comparison being made. According to the most authoritative source, 1.64 million defendants were proceeded against at magistrates 'courts in 2008 compared with 88,500 accused prosecuted on indictment in the Crown Court: Ministry of Justice, *Criminal Statistics: England and Wales 2008* (2010). This crude statistical comparison awards nearly 95% of criminal business to magistrates' courts.

[9]　See, for example, Penny Darbyshire, 'Previous Misconduct and Magistrates' Courts – Some Tales from the Real World' [1997] *Crim LR* 105; and 'An Essay on the Importance and Neglect of the Magistracy' [1997] *Crim LR* 627.

[10]　See Mike McConville, 'Plea Bargaining', in Mike McConville and Geoffrey Wilson (eds.), *The Handbook of the Criminal Justice Process* (OUP, 2002). For critical evaluation, see Mike McConville and Chester Mirsky, 'Guilty Plea Courts: A Social Disciplinary Model of Criminal Justice' (1995) 42 *Social Problems* 216; and McConville and Mirsky, 'Looking Through the Guilty Plea Glass: The Structural Framework of English and American State Courts' (1993) 2 *Social and Legal Studies* 173.

Evidence law moulds the conduct of criminal investigations by regulating, for example, the procedures by which confessions[11] and identification evidence[12] must be elicited in order to be admissible at trial. Rules of evidence influence prosecutors' decisions to prosecute or discontinue a case, and are factored into decisions of the accused to plead guilty or go to trial. And beyond these more tangible impacts, evidentiary rules and principles exert further diffuse and subtle influences on the progress of criminal proceedings, and on the quality of justice dispensed in them, because the substance of rules and principles, and the examples set by their implementation or non-enforcement, symbolize the values and objectives to which the justice system subscribes. Procedural law is a standing advertisement, good or bad, for the quality of justice dispensed in British courts which is broadcast before any particular evidentiary rule is invoked, or for that matter ignored, in individual cases.

Focusing more narrowly on criminal *trials* only reinforces this conclusion. Magistrates' courts process more than one-and-a-half million cases every year, whilst about 94,000 criminal defendants enter a plea in the Crown Court. Of those tried on indictment, some 70% plead guilty to all charges and a further 13% are discharged or acquitted at the judge's direction.[13] This leaves just short of 16,000 accused actually tried by juries annually. To be sure, 16,000 accused do not sound so many when pitted against 150 times more magistrates' courts cases, but it is the seriousness of the allegations, and the severity of the censure and punishment following conviction,[14] rather than the size of its caseload, that distinguishes the work of the Crown Court. Moreover, it seriously underplays the practical significance of jury trial to concentrate only on those accused who actually receive one. All 94,000 accused who entered a plea in the Crown Court in 2008 were given *the option* of trial by jury, as were the 450,000 defendants charged with indictable 'either way' offences who opted for summary trial in the magistrates' courts.[15] Being offered something regarded as valuable, and knowing that it is available should one wish to take advantage of it, now or in the future, is not a trivial matter even when one declines the offer on this occasion. A better quantitative measure of the practical significance of jury trial in English criminal proceedings (quite apart from its symbolic dimensions), therefore, would be the over half a million accused to whom it is offered annually rather than the 16,000 actual recipients of a lay jury's verdict following contested criminal trials.

It is right to acknowledge at the outset that Crown Court trials are not the only forum in which criminal adjudication takes place in England and Wales. It might even be true that the conscious invocation and direct application of formal evidence law is a peculiar preoccupation of Crown Court trials. But what follows if these concessions are made? Certainly not that something that 'only' happens to 16,000 accused (and involves countless thousands more complainants and witnesses) and is offered to more than half a million people every year cannot be significant, or even crucial, to the administration of criminal justice in England and Wales. To infer from comparative caseload statistics that Crown Court trials or, by extension, rules of criminal evidence are uninteresting or unimportant would be like refusing to conduct medical research on bowel cancer or coronary disease because flu, myopia, and in-growing toenails are more commonly experienced ailments.

---

[11] Chapter 12.   [12] Chapter 15.
[13] Ministry of Justice, *Judicial and Court Statistics 2008*, Cm. 7697 (rvsd Jan 2010), 124.
[14] §1.2(a).   [15] Ministry of Justice, *Judicial and Court Statistics 2008*, 137–8.

In sketching out the procedural framework in which the modern law of criminal evidence has been developed and continues to operate, this chapter identifies key themes and issues that recur and are explored further throughout this book. In particular, the adversarial structure of courtroom proceedings and the relationship between trial judge and jury will emerge as formative influences on evidentiary rules and principles. These characteristic features of Crown Court trial merit closer attention.

2.2 ADVERSARIAL TRADITIONS

English criminal proceedings are 'adversarial', meaning that they are organized around what continental lawyers call the 'Anglo-Saxon' model, and what British and American lawyers called the 'Anglo-American' or 'common law' model, of legal process. These different labels have intriguing further implications, but it is enough for our purposes to observe that adversarial process is a central structural pillar of English legal heritage,[16] later transported through conquest and colonialism to north America, Australasia, the Indian subcontinent, and significant parts of Africa and the Pacific Rim.

Intense fascination for news and stories about criminal trials and punishments is a long-standing British preoccupation, extending back at least as far as the pre-literate oral tradition of eighteenth century Tyburn ballads,[17] and doubtless much earlier. In modern times, adversarial criminal process, along with trial by a lay jury of twelve, has been celebrated in countless books, films, and plays, and is a subject of perennial interest in factual news-reporting. Yet most of the images of criminal trials today eagerly consumed by the British public are glitzy fantasy combinations of Hollywood dramas, *CSI*, and *Ally McBeal*. Such fictional portrayals are scarcely a reliable guide to the reality of contemporary criminal proceedings in England and Wales – a reality perhaps all the more mysterious and misunderstood for appearing to be familiar. The risk of being led astray by popular misconceptions reinforces the wisdom of undertaking some preliminary clarification of concepts and methodology.

(a) MODELS AND METHOD

Three essential methodological points must be stressed at the outset. First, the terms 'adversarial' system or process, and its almost-inevitable point of comparison in the 'inquisitorial' (a.k.a. 'civilian' or 'continental') system, are ideal-typical models constructed for explanatory purposes.[18] They are valuable tools because they simplify

---

[16] Note, however, that inquisitorial proceedings are not unknown in English legal history. Coroners' courts, which can be traced back to the early twelfth century, are the best surviving modern example: see Paul Matthews, *Jervis on Coroners* (Sweet & Maxwell, 12th edn. 2006). H. Patrick Glenn, *Legal Traditions of the World* (OUP, 3rd edn. 2007) situates the origins of common law systems in the broader context of rival and overlapping legal traditions.

[17] V. A. C. Gatrell, *The Hanging Tree: Execution and the English People 1770–1868* (OUP, 1994), ch 4.

[18] It has even been suggested that the 'inquisitorial model' is largely a phantom of the common lawyer's imagination which few continental scholars would find genuinely illuminating. J. F. Nijboer, 'Common Law Tradition in Evidence Scholarship Observed from a Continental Perspective' (1993) 41 *American Journal of Comparative Law* 299, 301, 334–5, insists that 'the differences between the European countries as to the

complex processes and emphasize their characteristic features. But precisely because these models are substantial, and occasionally gross, simplifications we should not expect any real, functioning criminal process to match up exactly with any theoretical model. Criminal procedures currently in operation in particular jurisdictions are in fact amalgams of different ideal-types, and their inclusion in one or more 'families' of criminal process is really a matter of degree. If the 'adversarial' and 'inquisitorial' models are conceived as opposite ends on the procedural spectrum, particular criminal justice systems might be arranged along a continuum according to their affinity with either pole. Rather than pigeon-holing systems within a rigid, and misleading, adversarial–inquisitorial dichotomy, we might then speak of criminal process as *more or less* adversarial and *more or less* inquisitorial.

When drawing comparisons between 'adversarial' and 'inquisitorial' systems, common lawyers typically have in mind, on the inquisitorial side of the equation, something akin to the Francophone model of criminal procedure, which derives originally from Napoleon's criminal procedure code of 1808, and still defines the basic contours of French criminal procedure today.[19] It makes sense to treat this conception as representative of the inquisitorial tradition more generally, to the extent that the Napoleonic system was transported in France's nineteenth and early twentieth century colonial caravan and implanted in countries as near as Belgium and the Netherlands,[20] and as far afield as Ivory Coast, Cameroon, Niger, Cambodia, and Vietnam.[21] Moreover, the Francophone model tends to facilitate the most sharply-drawn comparisons with Anglo-American process, and is therefore a very useful, not to say tempting, analytical device. On the other hand, it must be admitted that proceeding in this fashion does run the risk of misrepresenting the German, Scandinavian, and (post-)Soviet systems of criminal procedure, most of which are also, of

subject of the law of evidence are really huge. They are much larger than the differences between the several countries belonging to the "Common Law Family".… The very concept of the adversarial system and the adversary process is often used in Anglo-American-Australian literature…It is not easy to find counter examples on the European continent referring to its system as "inquisitorial".… Seen from the European side, the concept of inquisitorial or even the contrast between inquisitorial and adversarial does not cover the major differences in styles on the continent.'

[19] There is an expanding corpus of English-language analysis of French criminal procedure law. See, e.g., Valérie Dervieux, 'The French System', in Mireille Delmas-Marty and J. R. Spencer (eds.), *European Criminal Procedures* (CUP, 2002); Bron McKillop, 'Anatomy of a French Murder Case' (1997) 45 *American Journal of Comparative Law* 527; Helen Trouille, 'A Look at French Criminal Procedure' [1994] *Crim LR* 735; Edward A. Tomlinson, 'The Saga of Wiretapping in France: What it Tells us About the French Criminal Justice System' (1993) 53 *Louisiana LR* 1091; Richard S. Frase, 'Comparative Criminal Justice as a Guide to American Law Reform: How Do The French Do It, How Can We Find Out, And Why Should We Care?' (1990) 78 *California LR* 539. For illuminating socio-legal description, see Jacqueline Hodgson, *French Criminal Justice* (Hart, 2005); Jacqueline Hodgson, 'Hierarchy, Bureaucracy and Ideology in French Criminal Justice: Some Empirical Observations' (2002) 29 *Journal of Law and Society* 227.

[20] See Alexis A. Aronowitz, 'The Netherlands', in *The World Factbook of Criminal Justice Systems* (US Dept of Justice, 1993), www.ojp.usdoj.gov/bjs/abstract/wfcj.htm#V; Stewart Field, Peter Alldridge, and Nico Jörg, 'Prosecutors, Examining Judges, and Control of Police Investigations', in Phil Fennell, Christopher Harding, Nico Jörg and Bert Swart (eds.), *Criminal Justice in Europe: A Comparative Study* (OUP, 1995): cf. J. F. Nijboer, 'Common Law Tradition in Evidence Scholarship Observed from a Continental Perspective' (1993) 41 *American Journal of Comparative Law* 299 (arguing for the distinctiveness of Dutch legal culture, and doubting the value of 'inquisitorial' generalizations).

[21] A useful source of background information on these lesser-known legal systems is the US Library of Congress' Global Legal Information Network, on-line at www.loc.gov/law/guide/nations.html.

course, European continental systems, but which differ from the Francophone tradition, notably in their greater emphasis on securing the formal rights of the accused through more active legal representation. It also fails to account for countries, such as Italy,[22] which have latterly grafted an adversarial procedural superstructure onto their inquisitorial legal cultural heritage.

A second methodological caveat is a refinement of the first. So far we have made several casual references to criminal 'process' or 'systems' in the round, but it is often helpful, and common in practice, to split up criminal proceedings into various stages, which might include some or all of the following: investigation; arrest; interrogation; prosecution; arraignment; trial; verdict; sentence; and punishment. Another common, aggregated distinction is between 'pre-trial', 'trial', and 'post-conviction' processes. Dividing criminal proceedings into their component stages allows us to deploy the standard models of criminal process with greater precision and refinement. A particular system might, for example, resemble the adversarial model in some of its stages or attributes, but follow the inquisitorial pattern in others. This is not merely a theoretical possibility. With growing awareness of the procedures adopted in other European countries, many UK-based scholars now recognize that modern European systems of criminal procedure typically follow a 'mixed model' of criminal process, in which an inquisitorial pre-trial investigation is followed by an essentially adversary trial. It is unnecessary, moreover, to invoke comparative examples to make this point. For even in the heartlands of adversarialism it is perfectly clear that the earlier stages of criminal process, including police investigation and custodial interviews, are towards the 'inquisitorial' pole of the continuum. This obvious but frequently overlooked feature of 'adversarial' process has even received belated statutory acknowledgement in England and Wales.[23]

The third caveat to be borne in mind when approaching adversarialism concerns the distinction between conceptual linkage and coincidental historical association. Prominent aspects of criminal proceedings in England (and in America and other common law jurisdictions), which are often unreflectively assumed to be conceptual outgrowths of adversarial process, are actually more or less contingent features of the historical development of criminal adjudication in particular countries. Two important examples which we explore at greater length later in the chapter are (1) the public nature of trials; and (2) fact-finding by lay jury. Neither of these familiar features of English criminal trials is *conceptually* implied by adversary process; though both of them do have a looser political and cultural affinity with adversarialism.

---

[22] See Elisabetta Grande, 'Italian Criminal Justice: Borrowing and Resistance' (2000) 48 *American Journal of Comparative Law* 227; Stephen P. Freccero, 'An Introduction to the New Italian Criminal Procedure' (1994) 21 *American Journal of Criminal Law* 345.

[23] Criminal Procedure and Investigations Act 1996, s.23(1)(a), provides that the Code of Practice governing police investigations must contain provisions ensuring 'that where a criminal investigation is conducted all reasonable steps are taken for the purposes of the investigation and, in particular, all reasonable lines of inquiry are pursued'. This is a reasonably explicit declaration of the duty to undertake a full investigation of the facts, as opposed to constructing an adversarial case against a suspect, not too far removed from the principle guiding the continental *juge d'instruction* (investigating magistrate), who investigates *à charge et à décharge*, that is, with a view to identifying exculpatory evidence and dismissing the charges as much as in the quest for inculpatory evidence to support a prosecution.

(b) CONCEPTS AND CONTINGENCIES

The concept of adversary process can be boiled right down to just one, basically simple and familiar idea: that legal proceedings should be arranged as a kind of debate or contest between two (or more) parties disputing their legal rights and duties. At the conclusion of the trial contest, an impartial adjudicator renders judgment in favour of one party or the other on the basis of the evidence adduced to support the parties' respective contentions. Thus defined, adversary process is equally compatible with civil and criminal proceedings, and this is exactly what we should expect, since legal systems in the common law family have traditionally extended adversary process to civil as well as criminal disputes. There are, however, important distinctions to be made between criminal and civil proceedings, as we have been at pains to stress in these first two introductory chapters. In criminal proceedings one of the parties is the state, which prosecutes in the name of the political community.[24] The involvement of the state is not, then, an essential feature of *adversary process*, but follows rather from modern conceptions of adversary *criminal* process. As we noted in Chapter 1, state involvement *as a party* distinguishes criminal proceedings from civil litigation aimed at resolving legal disputes between private citizens.[25] Because the accused in criminal proceedings is called upon to answer charges levelled against him or her by the state, adversary criminal process is sometimes also referred to as 'accusatorial', being organized around a formal accusation. However, this terminology is at once both superfluous and potentially misleading.[26] Legal proceedings may be accusatorial, implying an institutional division of labour between prosecutors who accuse and adjudicators who judge, without necessarily also being adversarial – which requires (at least) two parties in addition to an impartial adjudicator.

Neither publicity nor jury trial is logically implied by the concept of adversary process. That trials should take place in public under the media spotlight, so that the symbolic message of the verdict can be communicated effectively to the populace and the proceedings opened up to external scrutiny and evaluation,[27] has come to be accepted as an essential part of legitimate legal process in all modern democratic states regardless of their local procedural traditions. Article 6(1) of the European Convention on Human Rights (ECHR) declares that everyone facing criminal charges 'is entitled to a fair *and public* hearing within a reasonable time by an independent and impartial tribunal established by law'. In purely formal terms a kind of adversarial proceeding could be conducted in secret – as Kafka's dystopian images of *The Trial* memorably insinuate.[28] Publicity gradually became

---

[24] §1.2(b).

[25] This is admittedly a very short way with a long question, but sustained investigation of the philosophical foundations of criminal justice would take us too far beyond the central concerns of this book.

[26] Thus, Richard Vogler *A World View of Criminal Justice* (Ashgate, 2005), 129, warns against the 'accusatorial fallacy': 'The terms are not, as is often supposed, interchangeable. Adversariality as a form of trial has almost nothing to do with the ancient accusatorial tradition and was instead a radical new procedure developed in England in the 18th century'.   [27] §1.2(c).

[28] Franz Kafka, *The Trial* (Penguin, 1953 [1925]), 46–57. On first appearance before the Examining Magistrate, K. infers that his case is the subject of some kind of debate between rival factions in the courtroom: 'a slender path was kept free after all, possibly separating two different factions... K. saw scarcely one face looking his way, but only the backs of people who were addressing their words and gestures to the members of their own party'. Although the procedure in the room is a closed book to K., things initially seem to go well for him, as at least one faction appears to warm to his defiant attitude towards the Magistrate: 'A burst of applause followed, once more from the right side of the hall. "These people are easy to win over", thought

associated with adversarial process because ordinary criminal trials[29] in England have traditionally been conducted in open court, in contrast to the old and despised Roman-Canon model of secret investigation, interrogation, and torture which held sway over continental Europe during the bloody decades of the Inquisition[30] (and also in contrast to the not-too-dissimilar methods of the English Star Chamber operative in the seventeenth century). But this association is historical coincidence rather than conceptual linkage. If publicity is an important aspect of modern criminal trials – as it surely is – its justification must be sought in the principles of open justice, democratic accountability, and effective adjudication, rather than in the concept of adversary process.

Jury trial, likewise, is analytically separate from adversarialism. The modern adversarial trial, which emerged in the late eighteenth century,[31] incorporated the pre-existing institution of the lay jury which dates back to the thirteenth century or earlier. For reasons not altogether clear, and on the basis of arguments not altogether convincing, trial by a jury of twelve ordinary men and women has come to be lauded in the popular imagination as a keystone of British justice, whilst in the United States it has been elevated to the status of a constitutional right.[32] However, adversary process, which requires only that adjudicators make an impartial and independent decision on the merits, is indifferent to lay involvement in adjudication, and quite compatible with none at all. The classic model of inquisitorial process, as much as the adversarial trial model, requires an impartial and independent decision on the merits, and this is now a fundamental 'fair trial' norm applicable right across Europe.[33]

Modern adversary criminal trials can be found in traditionally civilian jurisdictions like the Netherlands where adjudication is the sole province of professional magistrates, common law jurisdictions such as Israel that never adopted the lay jury, and common law systems where the jury has lately been abolished (Singapore)[34] or suspended for particular types of case (Northern Ireland).[35] Where a lay element is retained, the standard model in

K., disturbed only by the silence in the left half of the room...' But K. soon has cause to reappraise the situation: 'Now he stood eye to eye with the crowd. Had he been mistaken in these people? Had he over-estimated the effectiveness of his speech? Had they been disguising their real opinions while he spoke... They all wore these badges, so far as he could see. They were all colleagues these ostensible parties of the Right and the Left, and as he turned round suddenly he saw the same badges on the coat-collar of the Examining Magistrate... "So!" cried K.... "every man jack of you is an official, I see, you are yourselves the corrupt agents of whom I have been speaking".'

[29] Note, however, that criminal *investigations* have traditionally progressed in secret. Modern efforts towards opening up pre-trial process to greater judicial scrutiny and public accountability have only partially ameliorated the situation.

[30] Mirjan Damaška, 'The Death of Legal Torture' (1978) 87 *Yale LJ* 860.

[31] John H. Langbein, *The Origins of Adversary Criminal Trial* (OUP, 2003); David J. A. Cairns, *Advocacy and the Making of the Adversarial Criminal Trial 1800–1865* (OUP, 1999).

[32] The Sixth Amendment to the US Constitution guarantees that '[i]n all criminal prosecutions, the accused shall enjoy the right to a speedy and public trial, by an impartial jury of the State and district wherein the crime shall have been committed, which district shall have been previously ascertained by law...'

[33] Article 6(1) of the ECHR, to which there are now forty-seven states parties stretching from Ireland to Armenia, guarantees that: 'In the determination of his civil rights and obligations or of any criminal charge against him, everyone is entitled to a fair and public hearing within a reasonable time by an independent and impartial tribunal established by law...'

[34] Until 1960 all Singaporean High Court cases were tried by jury. There followed a period of gradual erosion, until jury trials were finally abolished by the Criminal Procedure (Amendment) Act 1969.

[35] See John Jackson and Sean Doran, *Judge Without Jury* (OUP, 1995).

continental jurisdictions is the 'mixed panel' made up of professional judges and layper-
sons, who deliberate and decide together. Mixed panels are used, for example, in France
and Germany, both of which follow adversarial process at the trial stage of their criminal
proceedings.[36] Indeed, whilst adversarial trial has become the norm in the criminal justice
systems of modern western democracies, lay juries are predominantly[37] a peculiarity of
British, Commonwealth, and American legal proceedings. So this much is clear: if the lay
jury can withstand critical scrutiny and should remain at least one permissible variation
on criminal adjudication in a modern liberal democracy, it must do so on its own merits.
The normative considerations promoting trial by lay jury will be examined later.[38] For now
we may conclude that jury trial has no inherent, conceptual, connection with adversary
process.

(c) EPISTEMIC AND NORMATIVE FOUNDATIONS

Adversarialism is underpinned by overlapping epistemological advantages and normative considerations of political morality. From the perspective of marshalling cognitive
and investigative resources effectively, scholars have proposed that the two-way adversary
dialogue is a remarkably efficient way of organizing legal disputes.[39] Any official inquiry
is always confronted with potentially interminable problems of how to define the parameters of an investigation, how to choose its focus, and where best to target finite – and
often frankly inadequate – investigative resources. In adversary proceedings, by contrast,
the parties generally know what is important to them in the matters in dispute, and are
well-motivated to present their 'best case' to the fact-finder. Whilst it is true that the parties might also be motivated to lie and cheat in their own cause,[40] on balance the claim
that adversarial argument is the most efficient way of getting to the bottom of a dispute
retains its plausibility. Indeed, it is conceivable that human beings are only capable of collecting, organizing, and evaluating information in narrative 'story' form,[41] in which case
the supposedly 'inquisitorial' investigation must in reality be operating with the same
information-processing heuristic as the openly adversarial proceeding – the only difference being that in inquisitorial approaches all the stories in play are generated by state
officials.

[36] But note the criticism (quoted by Rod Morgan, 'Magistrates: The Future According to Auld' (2002) 29
Journal of Law and Society 308, 322) that lay assessors may behave like 'decorative flowerpots', merely following the lead of the professional judge and consequently adding nothing more constructive to the bench's
deliberations than their pleasing appearance (if such it be).

[37] The qualification is necessary because lay juries on the English model can also be found in Belgium
and Denmark, and are being reinstated in Spain and Russia for a limited range of offences: see Stephen C.
Thaman, 'Europe's New Jury Systems: The Cases of Spain and Russia', in Neil Vidmar (ed.), *World Jury
Systems* (OUP, 2000). It is notable, however, that in these European jurisdictions the unreasoned jury verdict
does not have the exalted status it commands in England and Wales.   [38] See §2.4, below.

[39] See, e.g., Craig R. Callen, 'Othello Could Not Optimize: Economics, Hearsay and Less Adversary
Systems' (2001) 22 *Cardozo LR* 1791; Ronald J. Allen and Brian Leiter, 'Naturalized Epistemology and the
Law of Evidence' (2001) 87 *Virginia LR* 1491; Ronald J. Allen, 'Factual Ambiguity and A Theory of Evidence'
(1994) 88 *Northwestern University LR* 604.

[40] This is part of the standard critique of adversarialism as antithetical to truth-finding: see, e.g., Gordon
van Kessel, 'Adversary Excesses in the American Criminal Trial' (1992) 67 *Notre Dame LR* 403, 435ff; Marvin
E. Frankel, 'The Search for Truth: An Umpireal View' (1975) 123 *University of Pennsylvania LR* 1031.

[41] See further, §4.6.

Whether or not story-construction is the *exclusive* human method of information-management, it is certainly a prominent feature of virtually all historical or forensic investigations, and this immediately poses the deeply political question as to whose stories will be told and heard. There may be some political cultures in which state officials would be implicitly trusted by citizens to conduct a thorough and systematic investigation of every conceivably pertinent story bearing on a legal dispute, and to adjudicate only after each and every such story has been fairly tested and evaluated. But British political culture does not conform to this paradigm. Our distrust of state – especially executive or administrative – power is well-represented in established legal doctrines facilitating judicial review of executive action. In the criminal justice context, judicial review extends to the decision-making of magistrates' courts and the non-trial functions of the Crown Court,[42] as well as to the exercise of discretion by police and prosecutors. After half a century of the welfare state, one would not generally find in England and Wales the same degree of distrust of state power which is said sometimes to characterize American attitudes towards the US federal government. But British instincts in such matters nonetheless generally tend towards the liberal, individualist pole of the continuum between sceptical self-reliance and social trust in state institutions, bureaucracy, and officialdom.

This being so, it is inconceivable that British citizens would be prepared to embrace an official inquiry into alleged criminal wrongdoing in exchange for their existing adversarial rights of defence and the accused's 'day in court'. Independent-minded, liberty-cherishing, self-reliant people like to feel that their destiny is in their own hands: and this is what adversary process promises to given them, albeit that the promise may frequently prove hollow in practice. The British cultural attachment to adversarialism therefore runs deep. So much more than a convenient, or even necessary, mechanism for processing information, it is a culturally embedded popular expectation, simultaneously both reflecting and reaffirming the collective character of a nation.

2.3   ADVERSARIAL TRIAL PROCEDURE IN ENGLAND AND WALES[43]

Four prominent structural features of English adversary trials can usefully be characterized as the essential 'incidents of adversarial trial', at least in the form in which adversarialism is practised in England and Wales. On the traditional English model: (a) the parties dominate the conduct of proceedings, with the judge playing a relatively passive role; (b) trials are continuous, oral, and public events; (c) the imbalance of power between the state and the accused is ameliorated by rules and principles reducing 'inequality of arms'; and (d) the overriding objective of criminal trials is to achieve a legitimate verdict resolving the disputed issues in the case – in other words, to dispense justice.

---

[42] See Supreme Court Act 1981, s.29(3); discussed, e.g., in *R v DPP, ex p. Kebilene* [2000] 2 AC 326, HL.

[43] Generally, see Mirjan R. Damaška, *Evidence Law Adrift* (Yale UP, 1997), ch 4; John Jackson and Sean Doran, *Judge Without Jury* (OUP, 1995), ch 3.

(a) PARTY-DOMINATED PROCEEDINGS;
RELATIVELY PASSIVE JUDGE

Extensive party control over the conduct of criminal proceedings is a distinctive feature of English adversary process. To an extent that foreign observers find almost incomprehensible, the parties to criminal litigation in England and Wales have a great deal of discretion in their choice of litigation strategy. Prosecutors choose the charge(s) in the indictment[44] and the accused is free to admit or contest them as he sees fit. If the prosecutor decides to alter the charges, or the accused wishes to plead guilty to some or all of the indictment, in its original or amended from, the parties are free to do so with minimal judicial supervision[45] or prospect of intervention by the court; unless either side complains directly to the judge. In cases that proceed all the way to a contested trial, counsel for the parties choose which witnesses to call, which arguments to make, how to cross-examine witnesses for the other side, and generally determine the course, and therefore strongly influence the outcome, of the trial. The parties, we might say, are free to choose the terrain on which to fight out their legal battle and to select their forensic weapons. They are equally free to surrender if and when they choose to do so.[46] This is all in marked contrast to received learning in continental jurisdictions. Orthodox inquisitorial theory rejects unsupervised pleas of guilty,[47] let alone the various forms of negotiation and 'plea-bargaining' known to be prevalent in England[48] and, more overtly, in the USA.

The corollary of party-dominated criminal process is a relatively passive, non-interventionist judge. The idealized common law judge has been likened to an umpire in a sporting contest, who exercises general oversight to ensure 'fair play' but does not become involved in 'scoring points' himself. As Frankel observed, in a classic restatement of the judge's 'umpireal' role, judicial passivity is written into the basic architecture of Anglo-American criminal procedure:

The fact is that our system does not allow much room for effective or just intervention by the trial judge in the adversary fight about the facts. The judge views the case from a peak of Olympian ignorance. His intrusions will in too many cases result from partial or skewed

---

[44] Primary responsibility for initial charging was transferred from the police to the CPS by the Criminal Justice Act 2003: see Ian D. Brownlee, 'The Statutory Charging Scheme in England and Wales: Towards a Unified Prosecution System?' [2004] *Crim LR* 896.

[45] Before accepting the accused's plea of guilty the court must be satisfied that the plea is voluntary and properly informed. For a review of general principles relating to pleas of guilty, see *R v Chalkley* [1998] QB 848, CA.

[46] Martial metaphors are difficult to escape in discussions of adversarial trial. They are harmless enough in themselves, provided that we always remember that criminal proceedings are neither a gladiatorial contest nor any kind of game, but a solemn procedure for adjudicating serious allegations of wrongdoing.

[47] Cf. Thomas Weigend, 'The Decay of the Inquisitorial Ideal: Plea Bargaining Invades German Criminal Procedure', in John Jackson, Maximo Langer, and Peter Tillers (eds.), *Crime, Procedure and Evidence in a Comparative and International Context* (Hart, 2008); Stefano Maffei, 'Negotiations "On Evidence" and Negotiations "On Sentence": Adversarial Experiments in Italian Criminal Procedure' (2004) 2 *Journal of International Criminal Justice* 1050.

[48] *R v Goodyear* [2005] 2 Cr App R 20; [2005] EWCA Crim 888. For comparative discussion of plea-bargaining in US criminal proceedings, see Nick Vamos, 'Please Don't Call it "Plea Bargaining"' [2009] *Crim LR* 617; Jacqueline E. Ross, 'The Entrenched Position of Plea Bargaining in United States Legal Practice' (2006) 54 *American Journal of Comparative Law* 717; Jennifer L. Mnookin, 'Uncertain Bargains: The Rise of Plea Bargaining in America' (2005) 57 *Stanford Law Review* 1721.

insights. He may expose the secrets one side chooses to keep while never becoming aware of the other's. He runs a good chance of pursuing inspirations that better informed counsel have considered, explored, and abandoned after fuller study. He risks at a minimum the supplying of more confusion than guidance by his sporadic intrusions. The ignorance and unpreparedness of the judge are intended axioms of the system.... As a result, his interruptions are just that – interruptions; occasional, unexpected, sporadic, unprogrammed, and unduly dramatic because they are dissonant and out of character.... Within the confines of the adversary framework, the trial judge probably serves best as a relatively passive moderator.[49]

The umpireal model of judging reinforces the common law judge's impartiality and independence, which have already been identified as essential attributes of sound adjudication on any model of trial. Judges in the continental tradition, where the parties play second fiddle, strike a correspondingly activist and interventionist pose. The continental judge calls witnesses of fact, conducts the lion's share of their courtroom examination, organizes the production of any scientific evidence that might be required, and generally dominates the proceedings. In some jurisdictions the parties and their lawyers are effectively relegated to supporting actors, where their common law counterparts take the leading roles.[50]

Although most western European and north American jurisdictions have by now incorporated adversary trials into their criminal procedure, it cannot be reiterated too often that there remains considerable variation in law and practice across these jurisdictions, both within and between the major procedural families. An adversary trial with a passive, non-interventionist judge on the Anglo-American model will differ significantly from the standard continental adversary trial, with its distinctive tradition of activist judging. Moreover, these procedural and cultural variations are reflected in the detailed rules of evidence and procedure to be found in any given jurisdiction. Even within a single process 'family' there are important differences of detail.

Judges in England and Wales, for example, have always been moderately interventionist in certain respects, whereas many American trial judges conform more closely to the 'pure' adversary ideal of judicial passivity. English judges sometimes put questions to witnesses, and frequently comment on the strength of the evidence in summing-up at the close of the trial.[51] Interventionist judging in English criminal proceedings is now expressly encouraged by the Criminal Procedure Rules (CrimPR 2010) which promote active pre-trial judicial case management, as we noted in the previous chapter.[52]

(b) CONTINUOUS, ORAL, AND PUBLIC ADJUDICATION

Common law trial process is 'continuous' in the sense that all the evidence is presented to an unprepared fact-finder in one, unbroken hearing – subject, of course, to short meal-breaks and overnight adjournments for trials lasting several days. (That jurors may

---

[49] Marvin E. Frankel, 'The Search for Truth: An Umpireal View' (1975) 123 *University of Pennsylvania LR* 1031, 1042–3. (Frankel goes on to criticize adversary process, and to argue for reforms, partly inspired by continental procedural traditions and practices, emphasizing truth-finding as litigation's primary objective.) Also see John Jackson and Sean Doran, *Judge Without Jury* (OUP, 1995), ch 5.

[50] Jacqueline Hodgson, 'Constructing the Pre-Trial Role of the Defence in French Criminal Procedure: An Adversarial Outsider in an Inquisitorial Process?' (2002) 6 *E & P* 1.   [51] See §2.5, below.

[52] §1.5(b).

be sequestered in a hotel overnight in order to protect the decision-making process from contaminating influences emphasizes the fact that the trial is still on-going even when the court is not actually sitting.) The full narrative of evidence is laid before the court without assuming that either the judge or the jury has any specialist knowledge relating to the case. An accused who pleads not guilty is entitled to his 'day in court', which might, in fact, stretch out over several days or even months in serious or complex cases.

The desire to present fact-finders with all the evidence in a single continuous trial gives rise to numerous procedural challenges. How, for example, should the system cope with evidence from witnesses who are not available to testify at the trial? Perhaps they have emigrated overseas, or cannot now be traced, or have died before the hearing commences. What about witnesses who refuse to testify, perhaps from fear of intimidation or through party-bias? Then there will be those who have forgotten their evidence, or who contradict what they have previously said. There will usually be a delay of several months between a criminal trial and the incident precipitating it, and in some cases the delay will be very much longer: memories inevitably fade. What if the maker of an oral or written statement cannot even be ascertained, as in the case of much 'hearsay' evidence? English law has devised a raft of technical rules to deal with these and many other situations giving rise to familiar evidential difficulties. There is, as we shall see, much room for debate about the relative success of these endeavours.

Continental criminal process is 'continuous' in a different sense. Once an official investigation is opened against a suspect the prosecutor or examining magistrate builds up a file of evidence – the *dossier* – generated at discrete moments in the process, which might include, for example, the evidential fruits of searches or covert surveillance, interviews with the suspect, statements from witnesses of fact, and expert scientific reports. The trial stage of the process often consists primarily in checking the contents of the file, since most of the work of evidence collection and collation, and even some fact-finding, has already been completed.[53] Continental proceedings amount to a continuous *criminal process* with the trial as its culmination, in contrast to Anglo-American practice, which differentiates more sharply between the trial and pre-trial phases of criminal proceedings and conceives *the trial* as a discrete and continuous event. The advantage of continental process is that evidence can be 'frozen' in the file long before trial, which dispenses with the need for many of the technical rules of evidence found in common law jurisdictions, such as the hearsay rule[54] and the convoluted doctrines governing the production of witness evidence.[55] At the same time, however, continental process is vulnerable to due process objections: it may be argued, for example, that proof-taking is insufficiently open to external scrutiny, and that accused persons are afforded insufficient opportunity to contest the state's evidence.[56] No procedural model supplies a panacea infallibly guaranteeing justice in action. The detailed rules of criminal evidence and procedure adopted in each particular jurisdiction

---

[53] This is more characteristic of the Francophone systems, regarding which it is sometimes said that the purpose of the trial is to try the *dossier*, rather than the accused. For accounts of the extreme brevity of many French trials, see Bron McKillop, 'Readings and Hearings in French Criminal Justice: Five Cases in the *Tribunal Correctionnel*' (1998) 46 *American Journal of Comparative Law* 757. But for related criticisms of German trials, see George P. Fletcher, 'A Trial in Germany' (1999) 18 *Criminal Justice Ethics* 3.

[54] See Chapter 9.   [55] Chapter 8.

[56] Cf. *Al-Khawaja and Tahery v United Kingdom* (2009) 49 EHRR 1; *R v Davis* [2008] 1 AC 1128, [2008] UKHL 36. See further, §9.2(b).

must be examined in terms of the values, objectives, and pragmatic constraints informing their underlying rationales. Chapter 1 described the foundational principles of criminal evidence structuring and animating criminal adjudication in England and Wales,[57] and subsequent chapters will build upon these normative foundations.

Orality is another characteristic feature of common law criminal trials closely related to their continuity. Although documentary evidence is an increasingly familiar feature of modern criminal proceedings in England and Wales,[58] the traditional expectation is that witnesses give their evidence orally and in person during the trial. We will refer to this precept as 'the principle of orality'. As Chapter 8 will explain in detail, evidence is led in answer to questions posed by the parties or their legal representatives, first in examination-in-chief conducted by counsel for the party calling the witness, and then under cross-examination by counsel for the other side. Notwithstanding recent procedural innovations, including expanding use of 'live-link' CCTV and pre-recorded video testimony,[59] the oral tradition retains a strong practical and ideological influence on contemporary trial proceedings. Numerous evidentiary rules governing witness examination and restricting the use of documentary evidence bear the hallmark of orality. A strong preference for oral evidence distinguishes common law criminal proceedings from continental process, in which the investigative file plays such a central role and trials, in jurisdictions such as France, have traditionally been conducted more or less 'on the papers'.[60] The modern democratic expectation of adversary trials has, however, injected a greater degree of orality into civilian criminal adjudication. The 'principle of immediacy' increasingly obliges continental jurisdictions to get to grips with evidentiary issues more characteristic of common law procedural systems, whilst English law has progressively relaxed many of its traditional restrictions on documentary proof. Trial procedure is one area of transnational legal reform tending to support the hypothesis of increasing 'convergence' between common law and continental criminal proceedings.[61]

As well as being continuous and oral, English criminal trials are held in public. Although publicity is not conceptually mandated by adversarialism, as we have said,[62] adversary process, as practised in Anglophone jurisdictions, requires a certain degree of publicity about the nature of the investigation, and the evidence it has brought to light, to allow the parties and their lawyers a meaningful opportunity to participate in the proceedings. How could the parties perform the active roles expected of them in a party-dominated process, marshalling evidence and calling witnesses in support

---

[57] §1.3.   [58] See, in particular, §9.5(b).   [59] §10.4.

[60] See, e.g., Bron McKillop, 'Anatomy of A French Murder Case' (1997) 45 *American Journal of Comparative Law* 527.

[61] The 'convergence thesis' has generated lively debate. For a range of diagnoses and perspectives, see Nico Jorg, Stewart Field, and Chrisje Brants, 'Are Inquisitorial and Adversarial Systems Converging?' in Fennell, Harding, Jorg, and Swart (eds.), *Criminal Justice in Europe: A Comparative Study* (OUP, 1995); Abraham S. Goldstein, 'Converging Criminal Justice Systems: Guilty Pleas and the Public Interest' (1997) 31 *Israel Law Review* 169; Máximo Langer, 'From Legal Transplants to Legal Translations: The Globalization of Plea Bargaining and the Americanization Thesis in Criminal Procedure' (2004) 45 *Harvard International Law Journal* 1; John D. Jackson, 'The Effect of Human Rights on Criminal Evidentiary Processes: Towards Convergence, Divergence or Realignment?' (2005) 68 *MLR* 737; P.J. Schwikkard, 'Convergence, Appropriate Fit and Value in Criminal Process', in Paul Roberts and Mike Redmayne (eds.), *Innovations in Evidence and Proof* (Hart, 2007); Sarah J. Summers, *Fair Trials: The European Criminal Procedural Tradition and the European Court of Human Rights* (Hart, 2007).   [62] §2.2(b), above.

of their cases, without an open exchange of arguments and information at every significant stage of the litigation? In criminal proceedings the issue basically resolves itself into participation rights for the accused and their legal advisers, because the presumption of innocence[63] and the privilege against self-incrimination[64] insulate the defence from demands for information by the prosecution. An accused, meanwhile, cannot even begin to respond to the state's accusations until the charges and evidence against him are clearly laid out.[65] This is done openly at trial when the prosecution presents its case in-chief. However, if the accused is to have a proper opportunity to conduct his own investigations, identify and interview potential witnesses, or arrange for further scientific tests or expert reports, he must be fully informed about the nature of the prosecution's case well in advance of trial. This entails opening up to some measure of scrutiny, and potential challenge, the process by which the prosecution's case is constructed[66] in the pre-trial phases of proceedings, at least to the extent of informing the accused and his legal advisers about the conduct of the investigation and the prosecution. Thus, in England and Wales the prosecutor is obliged to make extensive pre-trial disclosure to the defence,[67] and then to lead in-chief at trial the entirety of the prosecution's evidence.[68] Prosecution 'ambushes' are not permitted.[69]

A comprehensive survey of the values served by open justice would link public criminal trials to the requirements of penal censure and to the democratic accountability of powerful state institutions.[70] The argument sketched here is confined to explaining the apparent affinity between adversary process and public trials. Party-control of proceedings turns out to provide some conceptual linkage, because the degree of participation required of the accused in English criminal adjudication is incompatible with investigation or prosecution, let alone trials, conducted in secret. An official inquiry might treat the accused as its unenlightened object, but the defendant must be an informed *participant* in an adversarial criminal trial. This explains another major defect in Kafka's *Trial*, from an adversarial perspective. Since the entire proceedings were arranged to remain utterly opaque to the accused, *K* was shut out from that active participation[71] which respect for human dignity demands and which is, by extension, essential to the procedural integrity and legitimacy of criminal adjudication.[72]

---

[63] See Chapter 6.   [64] See Chapter 13.   [65] Cf. ECHR Article 6(3)(d).

[66] On the 'construction' of prosecution cases, see Mike McConville, Andrew Sanders, and Roger Leng, *The Case for the Prosecution: Police Suspects and the Construction of Criminality* (Routledge, 1991); Paul Roberts, 'Science in the Criminal Process' (1994) 14 *OJLS* 469; Mike Redmayne, *Expert Evidence and Criminal Justice* (OUP, 2001), ch 2.

[67] Criminal Procedure and Investigations Act 1996, s.3; *Attorney General's Guidelines on Disclosure*, on-line at: www.attorneygeneral.gov.uk/attachments/disclosure.doc; *Disclosure: A Protocol for the Control and Management of Unused Material in the Crown Court* (2006), on-line at: http://www.attorneygeneral. gov.uk/Publications/Documents/disclosure.doc.pdf.   [68] *R v Phillipson* (1989) 91 Cr App R 226, CA.

[69] Which is not, of course, to say that they never happen. Rules are sometimes broken, and sometimes the precise requirements of the rule are unclear. Inadequate prosecution disclosure has been a recurrent feature of notorious miscarriages of justice, as we discuss below: §2.3(c)(ii).   [70] §1.2.

[71] R. A. Duff, 'Law, Language and Community: Some Preconditions of Criminal Liability' (1998) 18 *OJLS* 189; John D. Jackson, 'The Effect of Human Rights on Criminal Evidentiary Processes: Towards Convergence, Divergence or Realignment?' (2005) 68 *MLR* 737.

[72] For further exploration of the significance of human dignity for criminal procedure, see Paul Roberts, 'Theorising Procedural Tradition: Subjects, Objects and Values in Criminal Adjudication', in Antony Duff *et al* (eds.), *The Trial on Trial Volume Two – Judgment and Calling to Account* (Hart, 2006).

(c) RULES AND PRINCIPLES TO REDUCE 'INEQUALITY OF ARMS'

A third characteristic feature of Anglophone adversary process is directed towards successfully translating adversarial theory into criminal justice practice. To do so one must look beyond the formal equality implied by the image of two equally-matched parties contending for their respective cases before an independent adjudicator, since one of these 'parties' is the state, with vastly superior financial, institutional, and informational resources at its disposal. Whilst not everybody facing criminal charges lacks the wherewithal to mount a robust defence – large corporations may have significant funds at their disposal, for example – the majority of criminal accused are drawn from the most disadvantaged sections of society, and even those at the wealthier end of the scale would soon find their resources depleted if required to defend themselves in protracted criminal proceedings. When the state is a party to adversary process, as it always is in criminal proceedings, there is an ever-present and very tangible risk that the criminal contest celebrated in adversarial theory will turn out in practice to be an extreme mismatch, with the result virtually a foregone conclusion.

Two sorts of failings are threatened by this structural 'inequality of arms' between the parties, both of which strike at the heart of the adversary ideal. First, the adversarial theory of truth-finding supposes that adjudicators will infer the truth (in accordance with the first principle of criminal evidence) by choosing between the most compelling evidence and strongest arguments that each party can muster in its own cause. But the truth would not emerge from a grossly uneven contest, in which only one party had a genuine opportunity to prepare and develop its case before the fact-finder. If the state's superior resources guaranteed such an enormous evidential advantage, even the strongest proof of innocence might struggle in vain for recognition. Trials would cease to be genuine inquiries into past events, where truth and liberty hang in the balance of justice, and would instead become cynical exercises in rubber-stamping the exercise of state power. They would be 'show trials' in the most pejorative sense.[73] Without a genuine commitment to effective fact-finding, adversary process would fail to satisfy one of the most fundamental criteria of justice, that the innocent should not be wrongly convicted and punished for crimes they did not commit. Nor will the guilty reliably be brought to justice if the processes of proof systematically misfire.

As well as subverting the adversary theory of truth-finding, a gross adversarial mismatch would also strike most people as intrinsically unfair. Adversary process is generally regarded as a commendably fair model of procedure, even by those who doubt its truth-finding efficacy. Adversarial contest facilitates, and indeed demands, a high degree of active participation by the accused (usually through legal representatives), affording generous opportunities to test and challenge the state's allegations, and to develop alternative arguments and scenarios before the fact-finder. Hearing both sides to a dispute is one of the twin-pillars of the common law conception of natural justice: *audi alteram*

---

[73] Cf. Martti Koskenniemi, 'Between Impunity and Show Trials' (2002) 6 *Max Planck Yearbook of United Nations Law* 1; Jacek R. Kubiak, 'The Secret Criminal Trials in Poland during the Stalinist Period, as Illustrated by the Secret Section of the Warsaw Court during 1950–54', in V. Gessner, A. Hoeland, and C. Varga (eds.), *European Legal Cultures* (Dartmouth, 1996); Peter H. Solomon, Jr, *Soviet Criminal Justice Under Stalin* (CUP, 1996), ch 7.

partem.[74] However, the vaunted fairness of adversarial proceedings can be sustained in reality only for as long as the accused have sufficient resources to secure their meaningful participation in criminal litigation. Retaining the cosmetic trappings of party-dominated adversarial process where grossly unequal resources have effectively gutted genuine adversary contest would only add insult to injury. At least in 'inquisitorial' systems of criminal justice organized around an official inquiry the judge usually retains formal responsibility for safeguarding the interests of the accused. But adversary trial conceived as no-holds-barred party contest threatens to degenerate from a principle of limited government and self-reliance into a callous official rationalization for abandoning the powerless to their fate.

It is becoming common, in continental as much as in common law jurisdictions, to speak of securing 'equality of arms' between the parties. This concept is also regularly invoked by the European Court of Human Rights.[75] The martial metaphor fittingly extends the core adversary idea of party contest, and resonates with the powerful image of a modern-day 'trial by battle'. However, the seductive image of 'equality of arms' is apt to mislead, inasmuch as it implies that genuine parity of resources between the parties is the desired objective. In reality, the bulk of criminal accused could never be equipped with sufficient resources to match the state apparatus of criminal investigation and prosecution, and nor should they be. The real objective imperfectly expressed by the 'equality of arms' slogan is to find ways of mitigating the unavoidable strategic imbalance between prosecution and defence, to enable the practical realities of adversarial trial procedure to approximate sufficiently closely to the theory of adversarialism so that the epistemic and normative credentials remain intact.

In order to neutralize the worst effects of inequality of arms on the fairness and efficacy of adversarial criminal trial, English law has developed a range of procedural techniques and evidentiary devices which compensate for the inevitable imbalance of resources between prosecution and defence. Four such procedural mechanisms merit emphasis as being integral to the conception of adversarial criminal procedure adopted in England and Wales. These features are not necessarily replicated in other – common law or non-common law – adversary trials, and they may not be evident to the casual observer.

(i) Burden and standard of proof

The burden and criminal standard of proof are mainstays of the English law of evidence. As we will see in Chapter 6, the principal function of these institutional manifestations of

---

[74] The second pillar of common law natural justice, impartial adjudication (*nemo judex in sua causa*), is also fully incorporated into the basic adversary model. Cf. *Kanda v Government of Malaya* [1962] AC 322, 337, HL, *per* Lord Denning: 'The rule against bias is one thing. The right to be heard is another. Those two rules are the essential characteristics of what is often called natural justice. They are the twin pillars supporting it. The Romans put them in the two maxims: *Nemo judex in causa sua*: and *Audi alteram partem*. They have recently been put in the two words, Impartiality and Fairness.'

[75] The European Court of Human Rights (EctHR) has developed a standardized articulation of the principle. See, e.g., *Salov v Ukraine* (app. no. 65518/01), ECtHR Judgment 6 September 2005, [87]: '[T]he principle of equality of arms is only one feature of the wider concept of a fair trial, which also includes the fundamental right that proceedings should be adversarial... Furthermore, the principle of equality of arms – in the sense of a "fair balance" between the parties – requires that each party should be afforded a reasonable opportunity to present his case under conditions that do not place him at a substantial disadvantage vis-à-vis his opponent... The right to adversarial proceedings means that each party must be given the opportunity to have knowledge of and comment on the observations filed or evidence adduced by the other party...'

the presumption of innocence is to allocate the risk of non-persuasion – i.e., the risk that a party will fail to persuade the fact-finder that truth and justice are on her side. From the perspective of ameliorating inequality of arms, the burden and standard of proof also incidentally structure criminal proceedings so that the prosecution is obliged to make all the running in gathering, organizing, and presenting evidence of crime.[76] In the investigative and pre-trial stages, the accused is not obliged to assist the police or the prosecution to assemble their case, though he may be detained for interview for an initial period (usually not more than twenty-four hours[77]) and then possibly held 'on remand' if there is sufficient evidence to constitute a *prima facie* case against him. At trial, the state is required to present convincing evidence proving its case to an exacting standard, whilst the accused is entitled to sit back and say nothing, safe in the knowledge that he will enjoy the benefit of any reasonable doubt.

Whilst some charges are obviously going to be harder to prove than others, the task facing the prosecution should not be underestimated. Prosecutorial resources, though impressive in major investigations, are not unlimited. Meanwhile, offenders can be counted on to attempt to conceal evidence of their crimes and to evade detection and apprehension for as long as they can. By insisting that the police and prosecution must overcome these considerable practical obstacles to detecting and prosecuting crime, without any active assistance from suspects or the accused, the state demonstrates its commitment to individual liberty and the protection of innocence, even at the cost of some loss of security for its citizens. Set against this background, the accused's comparatively puny resources no longer appear to pose such a serious threat to justice, since the job of defending oneself against criminal charges, generally speaking, requires fewer resources than proof of guilt.

(ii) Prosecution disclosure

English law has traditionally imposed extensive duties of pre-trial disclosure on the prosecution, with very much lighter reciprocal burdens on the defence. As the position developed at common law, the prosecutor was obliged to disclose, not only all the evidence and witness statements to be adduced by the prosecution at trial, but also any 'unused material' in the prosecutor's possession that might possibly have assisted the defence.[78] The accused, meanwhile, could sit back, refuse to co-operate with the investigation in any way, and put the prosecution to its proof. The only minor exceptions were created by statute: the accused was obliged to provide pre-trial notification of alibi witnesses[79] and of expert evidence[80] to be adduced at trial.

---

[76] Paul Roberts, 'Taking the Burden of Proof Seriously' [1995] *Crim LR* 783.

[77] This is the initial period of detention without charge authorized by PACE 1984 s.41, which can be extended by a senior police officer for a further twelve hours (s.42), and thereafter by a magistrate up to an absolute maximum of ninety-six hours (ss.43–44). The legal framework and practical context of custodial detention are further elucidated in §12.2.

[78] *R v Ward* (1993) 96 Cr App R 1, CA; *Attorney General's Guidelines for the Disclosure of 'Unused Material' to the Defence* (1982) 74 Cr App R 302; *Dallison v Caffery* [1965] 1 QB 348, CA (*per* Lord Denning MR). Cf. *R v Bryant and Dickson* (1946) 31 Cr App R 146, CCA. The mature common law position is summarized by John Niblett, *Disclosure in Criminal Proceedings* (Blackstone, 1997).

[79] Criminal Justice Act 1967, s.11, now superseded by the Criminal Procedure and Investigations Act 1996, s.5.

[80] CrimPR 2010 Rule 33.4, replacing the Crown Court (Advance Notice of Expert Evidence) Rules 1987 made pursuant to PACE 1984 s.81.

Incomplete or otherwise inadequate pre-trial disclosure by the prosecution was a recurrent feature of the high profile miscarriages of justice which came to light in the 1980s and 1990s and precipitated the wide-ranging review of criminal proceedings undertaken by the Runciman Royal Commission on Criminal Justice. A new disclosure regime was introduced by the Criminal Procedure and Investigations Act (CPIA) 1996, partly to address failures by the prosecution but also to limit the extent to which the defence could burden the prosecutor with requests for further information without indicating what they hoped to find. There was some concern in police and prosecution circles that the common law allowed the defence to embark on 'fishing trips', resulting in lengthy and expensive inquiries by the prosecution, without accepting any reciprocal disclosure obligations. The two-stage disclosure process created by the CPIA 1996 was widely regarded as unsatisfactory,[81] and was subsequently realigned by the Criminal Justice Act 2003. The CPIA 1996, as amended, underscores the prosecutor's duty to disclose the entire prosecution case and any 'unused material' that might assist the defence case, but it also requires the accused to produce a 'defence statement' clearly indicating those parts of the prosecution's case, if any, with which the defence intends to take issue in the event of a contested trial.[82] This is very much in keeping with the now ascendant prevailing procedural philosophy of active judicial trial management and encouraging timely guilty pleas, as reflected in the CrimPR 2010.

Whether, and to what extent, the defence in criminal proceedings should be required to disclose its case, or significant parts of it, prior to the commencement of a trial remain controversial questions. It has also been doubted whether the police and prosecution can be relied upon to disclose material information in every case, in view of the partial perspective and institutional and cultural biases almost inevitably associated with adversarial systems of justice.[83] These are large themes in the institutional design of criminal proceedings. For our purposes, two somewhat narrower conclusions may be drawn. First, the form of adversarialism practised in English criminal litigation involves a significant, and progressively growing, element of 'cards-on-the-table' pre-trial disclosure in contrast to the 'cards-to-chest' style of legal contest often associated with the common law adversarial model in which the parties are permitted, and even expected, to 'keep their powder dry' for the main-event trial. Secondly, although the defence has lately been forced to shoulder more onerous reciprocal duties of advance disclosure, the prosecutor's corresponding duties remain *much* more extensive and the procedural repercussions of breaching them, in terms of prosecutions irretrievably derailed and convictions quashed on appeal, are also likely to be more serious than any sanctions for non-compliance imposed on the defence. Steeply asymmetric obligations of pre-trial disclosure therefore continue to function as important procedural correctives to inequality of arms, notwithstanding a more generalized drift towards cards-on-the-table litigation affecting the defence as well as the prosecution in English criminal proceedings.

---

[81] See David Ormerod, 'Improving the Disclosure Regime' (2003) 7 *E & P* 102; Roger Leng, 'The Exchange of Information and Disclosure', in Mike McConville and Geoffrey Wilson (eds.), *The Handbook of the Criminal Justice Process* (OUP, 2002); John Sprack, 'The Criminal Procedure and Investigations Act 1996: (1) The Duty of Disclosure' [1997] *Crim LR* 308.   [82] CPIA 1996, ss.5–6E.

[83] Hannah Quirk, 'The Significance of Culture in Criminal Procedure Reform: Why the Revised Disclosure Scheme Cannot Work' (2006) 10 *E & P* 42.

(iii) Free legal advice and representation

In order to participate fully and effectively in criminal proceedings, the accused need to be able to secure advice and assistance in the preparation and conduct of their cases from lawyers and other professionals such as medical experts and forensic scientists. One of the most direct ways in which the state can mitigate the imbalance of resources between prosecution and defence is to pay for legal services from the public purse, at least where individual accused lack the means to bear the cost themselves. The European Convention on Human Rights lists free legal representation as one of the minimum rights of the accused.[84]

In England and Wales the vast majority of criminal cases tried in the Crown Court is funded by legal aid at the state's expense. This does not mean that the provision of legal services to the accused is beyond criticism: to the contrary, the size of the legal aid budget, mechanisms for recruiting and funding 'service-providers' (lawyers), and the quality of the legal services supplied are topics of almost permanent controversy amongst English lawyers and public policymakers.[85] But the availability of state funds to allow the accused to instruct a solicitor to provide pre-trial advice, and then to secure the services of a barrister to conduct the defence case in court, represents an impressive commitment to reducing inequality of arms in adversarial criminal trials. Few other states around the world would be inclined, or even financially able, to match this level of commitment to publicly-funded legal services.

(iv) Criminal justice ethics

Occupational cultures and professional ethics exert more subtle normative influences on criminal proceedings than explicit rules and principles of law, but their significance should not be underestimated. Informal working rules are sometimes expounded in written texts – the Bar's *Code of Conduct* is an important example[86] – and, whether or not formally committed to paper, they are pivotal in mediating between the law as it is written in the books and the law as it is interpreted and applied (or, quite often, not applied) in police investigations and interviews, solicitors' offices, and courtrooms.

Without undertaking detailed consideration of the working cultures and ethics of criminal justice professionals,[87] it is worth noting that prosecutors in England and Wales are generally regarded as having special ethical responsibilities which defence counsel do not share. Prosecutors have a dual role as adversarial party and 'minister of justice'.[88]

---

[84] ECHR Article 6(3)(c): 'Everyone charged with a criminal offence has the following minimum rights: … to defend himself in person through legal assistance or his own choosing or, if he has not sufficient means to pay for legal assistance, to be given it free when the interests of justice so require.'

[85] For discussion, see Ed Cape, 'The Rise (and Fall?) of a Criminal Defence Profession' [2004] *Crim LR* 401; Lee Bridges, 'The Right To Representation and Legal Aid', in Mike McConville and Geoffrey Wilson (eds.), *The Handbook of the Criminal Justice Process* (OUP, 2002); Richard Young and David Wall (eds.), *Access to Criminal Justice: Legal Aid, Lawyers and the Defence of Liberty* (Blackstone, 1996).

[86] *Code of Conduct of the Bar of England & Wales* (Bar Standards Board, 8th edn. 2004), www.barstandardsboard.org.uk/standardsandguidance/codeofconduct/. Also see the *Solicitor's Code of Conduct* (SRA, 2007), www.sra.org.uk/rules/.

[87] For general discussion see Meredith Blake and Andrew Ashworth, 'Some Ethical Issues in Prosecuting and Defending Criminal Cases' [1998] *Crim LR* 16; Christmas Humphreys, 'The Duties of Prosecuting Counsel' [1955] *Crim LR* 739.

[88] '[A] prosecutor is a minister of justice and frequently calls a witness, or tenders a witness for cross-examination at the request of the defence and in their interests': *Lobban* v *R* [1995] 1 WLR 877, 887, PC (Lord Steyn).

Whilst both parties to criminal litigation are expected to develop their best arguments before the jury, in accordance with the adversary model of trial-as-contest, the prosecutor is expected to conduct her case with temperance and restraint (encapsulated in the aphorism that prosecutors should 'prosecute, not persecute'), whereas defence counsel is afforded greater leeway to press for an acquittal by engaging the passions and sympathies of the jury. The general expectation of prosecutorial restraint can be traced into particular procedural norms, including the rule that English prosecutors never address the court on what the appropriate sentence should be in the event of conviction. This is contrary to the practice in just about every other modern criminal justice system,[89] and both reflects and reinforces the importance of ethical professionalism in reducing inequalities of arms in English criminal proceedings.

Prosecutorial restraint has generally been viewed by lawyers as promoting the interests of justice. It would be entirely inappropriate, after all, for prosecutors to pursue the goal of conviction at any cost, regardless of proper standards of decorum and making no allowances for the fact that the accused is entitled to be treated as innocent unless and until proven otherwise. Greater attention to the rights and interests of victims of crime has complicated this picture more recently. Prosecution counsel have been taken to task for failing to represent the claims of victims with sufficient vigour. Yet such criticisms may underestimate the difficulty of combining in a single individual the roles of responsible state prosecutor and zealous victims' advocate, within the overarching framework of an adversarial system of justice.[90]

(d) LEGITIMATE DISPUTE RESOLUTION AS THE OVERRIDING OBJECTIVE

Building on Damaška's ground-breaking work of the 1970s and 80s,[91] it has become conventional in discussions of procedural models to contrast truth-finding with conflict-resolution as the overriding objective of legal proceedings. Accurate fact-finding as a basis for the rational implementation of criminal policy is said to be the primary objective of 'inquisitorial' procedure on the continental model, leading to a comparatively authoritarian and bureaucratic criminal process structured around an official inquiry (inquisition) into past events. Fact-finding and law application are closely supervised within a pyramidal structure of judicial hierarchy in which the older, more experienced judges staffing appellate tribunals oversee the work of their more junior, trial-level colleagues.

Common law adversary process, by contrast, is understood to be primarily orientated towards providing an authoritative resolution to disputes or conflicts which is, broadly

---

[89] The role of Dutch and German prosecutors in recommending sentences to the court is discussed by Julia Fionda, *Public Prosecutors and Discretion: A Comparative Study* (OUP, 1995), 103–6, 148. This is one respect in which Scottish criminal procedure is more common law than continental: ibid. 87–9.

[90] For discussion, see Matthew Hall, 'The Relationship between Victims and Prosecutors: Defending Victims' Rights' [2010] *Crim LR* 31; Dan Jones and Josie Brown, 'The Relationship between Victims and Prosecutors: Defending Victims' Rights? A CPS Response' [2010] *Crim LR* 212.

[91] Mirjan R. Damaška, *The Faces of Justice and State Authority: A Comparative Approach to the Legal Process* (Yale UP, 1986); Damaška, 'Evidentiary Barriers to Conviction and Two Models of Criminal Procedure: A Comparative Study' (1973) 121 *University of Pennsylvania LR* 506; Damaška, 'Structures of Authority and Comparative Criminal Procedure' (1975) 84 *Yale LJ* 480.

speaking, acceptable to the parties and viewed as legitimate by society at large. The vision is one of individualized justice on the merits dispensed through relatively decentralized and democratic adjudicative processes, as opposed to systematic policy implementation through a national bureaucracy. English trial judges, though subject to appellate review,[92] generally have greater autonomy than their continental counterparts. Many Crown Court judges are older and more experienced in criminal litigation than the members of the Court of Appeal who are their nominal superiors and (as we explore in the next two sections) they try cases in partnership with lay juries to which appellate tribunals routinely defer on questions of fact. The trial judge in adversarial proceedings has more opportunity to exercise discretion and to stamp his personality on 'his' (or, less frequently 'her') courtroom than the members of a continental-style judicial bureaucracy. The adversarial conception of adjudicative authority, in Damaška's terminology, is coordinate rather than hierarchical.

Damaška's models are abstract ideal-types which, like all sweeping generalizations, must be approached with care. So long as they are handled sensitively, however, they have considerable explanatory power.[93] Adversary process as dispute resolution goes a long way to explaining the remarkable degree of party autonomy in Anglo-American criminal proceedings. A decentralized and highly participative process seems well-suited to resolving conflicts on terms that the parties can strongly influence, and are therefore more likely to accept; though it is possibly less well-adapted to criminal policy-implementation or reliable truth-finding. The prominence of dispute resolution as a goal of adjudication can likewise be seen to structure the relationship between trials and appeals in adversarial systems of criminal procedure. One might think of the adversarial goal of dispute resolution as another way of interpreting the CrimPR's 'overriding objective' of 'dealing with criminal cases justly'.[94] Of course, the contrast between resolving disputes and finding facts should not be overdrawn. Promoting factual accuracy in adjudication has already been identified as the first foundational principle of criminal evidence;[95] and it is implausible to think that disputes would ever be resolved satisfactorily unless adjudicative mechanisms are trusted to arrive at factually accurate verdicts at least most of the time. One should also bear in mind the important distinction between peace and justice. Resolving disputes in a way that satisfies the most proximately interested parties may (sometimes) end conflict, but it does not necessarily achieve justice for all concerned – including, in criminal proceedings, society at large ('the public interest').

The basic adversary idea of party-contest ultimately infuses every level of English criminal proceedings, from the grand design of procedural blueprints to the micro-detail of evidentiary rules, doctrines, and principles. Damaška's illuminating models help us to see that distinctive procedural choices and traditions can be traced deep into the fabric of a nation's political character and culture. Though such attenuated linkages tend to reveal themselves only in half-light, these suggestive connections between ideals, institutions,

---

[92] See §2.5(e), below.

[93] See further, Paul Roberts, 'Faces of Justice Adrift? Damaška's Comparative Method and the Future of Common Law Evidence', in John Jackson, Maximo Langer, and Peter Tillers (eds.), *Crime, Procedure and Evidence in a Comparative and International Context* (Hart, 2008); Inga Markovits, 'Playing the Opposites Game: On Mirjan Damaška's *The Faces of Justice and State Authority*' (1989) 41 *Stanford Law Review* 1313.

[94] §1.5(b).   [95] §1.3.

and cultures alert us to our society's deeper psychological, sociological, and normative investments in criminal evidence and procedure. The venerable British institution of trial by jury provides an especially rich and revealing illustration of a procedural mechanism that cannot truly be appreciated without taking account of its broader political and cultural significance.

2.4 SCOPE AND FUNCTION OF THE COMMON LAW JURY

People who know nothing else of Magna Carta 'know'[96] that it guarantees ordinary people charged with criminal offences the opportunity to be judged by a randomly selected jury of twelve ordinary people like themselves. In reality, as Lord Justice Auld's *Review of the Criminal Courts* forcefully reminded us, the formal legal position is more equivocal:

In England and Wales there is no constitutional or indeed any form of general right to trial by judge and jury, only a general obligation to submit to it in indictable cases... Certainly, Magna Carta is no basis for jury trial as we know it today.[97]

More recently, the Lord Chief Justice declared that '[i]n this country trial by jury is a hallowed principle of the administration of criminal justice... deeply entrenched in our constitution'.[98] In any event, the significance of trial by jury for criminal adjudication in England and Wales is far from exhausted by its debateable constitutional status (bearing in mind that just about every aspect of the UK's largely conventional constitution is debateable).

(a) THE PROVINCE OF THE JURY

Common law criminal trials conventionally parcel out questions of fact to the jury and questions of law to the judge. However, the law-fact distinction is not clear-cut. In reality,

---

[96] In fact, the position is complex. Magna Carta does declare that 'No free man shall be seized or imprisoned, or stripped of his rights or possessions, or outlawed or exiled, or deprived of his standing in any other way, nor will we proceed with force against him, or send others to do so, except by the lawful judgement of his equals or by the law of the land', and makes numerous other references to 'judgement of their/his equals': see G. R. C. Davis, *Magna Carta* (British Library, 1989, www.bl.uk/treasures/magnacarta/index.html, clauses 39, 52, 56, 57, and 59). On the other hand, King John cannot have been referring to juries in the modern sense, since they did not emerge until, at the earliest, the fifteenth century; and despite promising 'To all free men of our kingdom we have also granted, for us and our heirs for ever, all the liberties written out below', Magna Carta was essentially conceived as a settlement of grievances between King John and his noblemen. Even those portions of Magna Carta dealing with criminal justice related issues (as opposed to the feudal levies and dues that are its central preoccupation) bear a rather uneven relation to modern conceptions of due process (compare cl 40: 'To no one will we sell, to no one deny or delay right or justice' with cl 54: 'No one shall be arrested or imprisoned on the appeal of a woman for the death of any person except her husband'). Magna Carta today is predominantly of antiquarian interest, but for an argument asserting its continuing constitutional significance, see Lord Irvine of Lairg, 'The Spirit of Magna Carta Continues to Resonate in Modern Law' (2003) 119 *LQR* 227.

[97] Lord Justice Auld, *Review of the Criminal Courts of England and Wales* (TSO, October 2001), para.7.

[98] *R v Twomey* [2009] 2 Cr App R 25, [2009] EWCA Crim 1035, [10], [16] (Lord Judge CJ).

the jury retains jurisdiction over many questions of classification and interpretation extending beyond brute empirical fact-finding.[99] Previous generations of judges recognized that the jury exerts power over the law. Lord Mansfield wrote that 'by means of a general verdict [the jury] are entrusted with a power of blending law and fact, and following the prejudices of their affections or passions'.[100] The interweaving of fact and law in a multitude of statutory and judge-made legal tests entrusts modern juries with the power to pass moral judgment on the conduct of the accused, as part of the process of deciding 'what happened' in relation to the matters in dispute.

A second consideration reinforcing the jury's ability to make binding non-factual judgments is the finality of acquittals. In England, the United States, and most commonwealth jurisdictions, there is traditionally no prosecution appeal against a jury's verdict of acquittal.[101] In 1724 Pratt CJ declared: 'It was never yet known that a verdict was set aside by which the defendant was acquitted in any case whatsoever, upon a criminal prosecution.'[102] This unequivocal statement requires modification to the extent that English law now permits acquittals to be quashed where they were tainted by an offence against the administration of justice[103] or in response to newly discovered 'compelling evidence' of guilt.[104] However, these controversial departures from the traditional finality of acquittals are regarded as highly exceptional expedients reserved for unusual circumstances.[105] It remains true to say that a jury acquittal is dispositive and irrevocable in English criminal proceedings in virtually every case.

The general jury verdict of 'guilty' or 'not guilty' makes it difficult to disentangle factual from non-factual determinations in criminal adjudication. The jury responds to allegations in the round, rather than stating particularized conclusions in relation to each individual factual element of the offence(s) charged. Vaughan CJ explained the common law approach to fact-finding in the celebrated seventeenth century *Bushell's case*:

That *decantatum* in our books, *ad quaestionem facti non respondent judices, ad quaestionem legis non respondent juratores*, literally taken is true: for if it be demanded, what is the fact? the judge cannot answer it: if it be asked, what is the law in the case, the jury cannot answer

---

[99] See W. R. Cornish, *The Jury* (Allen Lane, 1968), 102. Judges occasionally acknowledge that the law–fact distinction fails adequately to describe the limits of the jury's jurisdiction: see *DPP* v *Stonehouse* [1977] 2 All ER 909, 918 (Lord Diplock). The point is also discussed by Thayer, *A Preliminary Treatise on Evidence at the Common Law*, ch 5.

[100] *R* v *Shiply* (1784) 4 Douglas 73, 163, discussed by Patrick Devlin, *The Judge* (OUP, 1981), 117ff.

[101] In Canada the prosecutor can appeal an acquittal, but only on a pure point of law. See Canadian Criminal Code § 676(1): 'The Attorney General or counsel instructed by him for the purpose may appeal to the court of appeal (a) against a judgment or verdict of acquittal or a verdict of not criminally responsible on account of mental disorder of a trial court in proceedings by indictment on any ground of appeal that involves a question of law alone…'

[102] *King* v *Jones* (1725) 8 Mod 201, 208. For the historical background, see James B. Thayer, ' "Law and Fact" in Jury Trials' (1890) 4 *Harvard LR* 147; W. R. Cornish, *The Jury* (Allen Lane, 1968), 116ff.; Devlin, *The Judge*, ch. 5. See also Mortimer R. Kadish and Sanford H. Kadish, *Discretion to Disobey: A Study of Lawful Departures from Legal Rules* (Stanford UP, 1973), 162. It is noteworthy that no such principle existed in favour of the verdict of a civil jury, which could be overturned if contrary to law: see Patrick Devlin, *Trial by Jury* (Stevens, 1956), 89–91; Alan W. Scheflin and Jon M. Van Dyke, 'Jury Nullification: the Contours of a Controversy' (1980) 43 *Law and Contemporary Problems* 5.

[103] CPIA 1996, ss.54–57. These provisions have apparently never been invoked.

[104] CJA 2003, Part 10; *R* v *Dunlop* [2007] 1 Cr App R 8, [2006] EWCA Crim 1354.

[105] See §2.5(f), below.

it ... In special verdicts the jury inform the naked fact, and the Court deliver the law.... But upon all general issues ... the jury... resolve both law and fact complicately... so though they answer not singly to the question what is the law, yet they determine the law in all matters where issue is joyn'd, and tryed in the principal case....[106]

The general jury verdict, implementing a particular division of adjudicative labour between trial judges and lay juries, is preserved in the modern law. As Lord Devlin succinctly expressed it, the 'principle [is] that no man is guilty unless he is so found, not upon this or that issue but upon the *whole crime*'.[107]

Many normative standards of criminal liability call upon the jury to make moral evaluations of the accused's alleged conduct, despite their nominal classification as questions of law rather than questions of fact. For example, the general test for 'dishonesty' applicable to offences of theft and fraud in English criminal law requires jurors to determine whether the accused's conduct was dishonest by the ordinary standards of reasonable and honest people (and then to infer whether the accused must have realized that he was being dishonest by those standards).[108] This is clearly a normative test of dishonesty. Another important example relates to offences requiring proof of intention (so-called 'specific intent' crimes). After much to-ing and fro-ing and several trips to the House of Lords the meaning of intention has been fixed as 'an ordinary English word' on which the jury will usually require no further judicial guidance.[109] Yet the intention with which death is caused is what separates murder from manslaughter in English law; and this is as much a question of legal classification as a simple question of fact. Likewise, English law defines 'gross negligence' in the crime of manslaughter as negligence going beyond ordinary civil liability to compensate injury (corrective justice), amounting to a crime against the state and conduct deserving of punishment (retributive justice) – in other words, a normative test of criminal culpability.[110]

It is sometimes thought, mistakenly, that the legal tests for intention and gross negligence are viciously circular or tautologous. In fact, the purpose of such tests is precisely to allow the jury to determine the scope of criminal liability by resolving certain, carefully circumscribed normative issues. When the jury decides whether the accused was 'dishonest' or whether he 'intended' to produce a prohibited result or whether his carelessness was bad enough to amount to 'gross negligence' and so forth, jurors are not merely deciding 'what happened'. They are simultaneously evaluating whether the accused's past conduct ought to be condemned as criminal wrongdoing deserving state censure and punishment.[111] We may conclude that, in the English system of criminal adjudication, fact-finding and interpretation of law are so interwoven that it is sometimes difficult to discern where fact determination ends and legal or moral reasoning begin.

---

[106] (1670) Vaughan 135, 143.

[107] Devlin, *The Judge*, 143. General verdicts are not obligatory but special verdicts upon individual issues are discouraged. For historical discussion see S. F. C. Milsom, 'Law and Fact in Legal Development' (1967) 17 *University of Toronto LJ* 1.

[108] *R v Ghosh* [1982] QB 1053, CA. See A. P. Simester and G. R. Sullivan, *Criminal Law Theory and Doctrine* (Hart, 3rd edn. 2007), 492–5; Andrew Ashworth, *Principles of Criminal Law* (OUP, 6th edn. 2009), 376–9.

[109] *R v Woollin* [1999] AC 92, HL; *R v Hancock and Shankland* [1986] AC 455, HL. See Simester and Sullivan, *Criminal Law Theory and Doctrine*, §5.1; Ashworth, *Principles of Criminal Law*, 170–7.

[110] *R v Adomako* [1995] 1 AC 171, HL; *Andrews v DPP* [1937] AC 576, HL. See Simester and Sullivan, *Criminal Law Theory and Doctrine*, §5.5; Ashworth, *Principles of Criminal Law*, 185–88, 276–9.

[111] §1.2.

(b) MORAL AND SOCIAL FUNCTIONS OF THE JURY'S VERDICT

An important distinction needs to be drawn between what the jury has the power to do, and what it ought – legally and morally – to do. The fact that a jury acquittal cannot normally be reversed does not necessarily imply that every jury acquittal is justified regardless of how or why it was reached. There are occasions when we might still insist: the jury has acquitted, its verdict is final, but it decided wrongly, or for the wrong reasons.[112]

Nobody believes that a jury may acquit for absolutely any reason whatsoever, say, out of racial solidarity with the accused,[113] or owing to sexual discrimination against the complainant, or because the case is boring and the jurors want to be rid of it as quickly as possible. In practice, however, the general, unreasoned, jury verdict makes it difficult to distinguish legitimate from illegitimate acquittals. Sometimes it is evident that a jury has acquitted in the teeth of overwhelming proof that the accused committed the offence charged. Juries occasionally choose to exercise their 'equity' to disregard the law, presumably because they perceive the law, or the particular prosecution brought under it, to be unjust. Isolated instances of 'jury equity' make the headlines from time to time, the most celebrated example of recent decades being the acquittal of Clive Ponting, a senior civil servant who leaked classified documents to a Member of Parliament concerning the sinking of the Argentinian battleship *General Belgrano* during the Falklands conflict. Ponting's actions constituted a clear breach of section 2(1) of the Official Secrets Act 1911.[114] The jury nonetheless acquitted him, seemingly because Ponting had acted in the best traditions of parliamentary democracy by blowing the whistle on an official cover-up, albeit that he had 'technically' broken the law in order to do so.

How should we characterize such verdicts? Jurors swear an oath to 'faithfully try the defendant and give a true verdict according to the evidence'.[115] Should we say that jurors behave improperly whenever they do not abide by the letter of their oath? Sometimes we would certainly condemn their verdict, as in the case of a racist jury ignoring clear evidence of guilt in order to acquit a white supremacist charged with racially-motivated crimes. Yet on other occasions an acquittal contrary to the evidence might meet with public approval because it reflects moral condemnation of an unjust law or distaste for an oppressive prosecution. Though the verdict might be described as *legally* wrong, because the jury broke its oath, we might still want to say that the jury has been a conscientious representative of broader community expectations and standards of justice.

From a strictly logical point of view, one might think that there is simply no room in a rational modern system of law for lay jurors to take it upon themselves to disobey their oath. Either the jury applies the law, or we tolerate a kind of anarchy in criminal verdicts.

---

[112] There may be reasons of policy or justice, rooted in the finality of verdicts and the democratic accountability of public institutions, why we should not interfere with a verdict of acquittal even where the jury has breached its legal duty. But now see §2.5(f), below.

[113] Cf. Paul Butler, 'Racially Based Jury Nullification: Black Power in the Criminal Justice System' (1995) 105 *Yale Law Journal* 677.

[114] Indeed, the trial judge was minded to direct the jury to convict, but was (rightly – see §2.5(d), below) prevented from doing so by the authority of *DPP* v *Stonehouse* [1977] 3 WLR 143: see *R* v *Ponting* [1985] Crim LR 318, Central Criminal Court.

[115] *The Consolidated Criminal Practice Direction* [2002] 2 Cr App R 533, para.42.4.

This position was emphatically reiterated by Lord Justice Auld in his *Review of the Criminal Courts*:

I regard the ability of jurors to acquit, and it also follows, convict, in defiance of the law and in disregard of their oaths, as more than illogicality. It is a blatant affront to the legal process and the main purpose of the criminal justice system – the control of crime – of which they are so important a part.... Their role is to find the facts and, applying the law to those facts, to determine guilt or no. They are not there to substitute their view of the propriety of the law for that of Parliament or its enforcement for that of its appointed Executive, still less on what may be irrational, secret and unchallengeable grounds.[116]

We venture to suggest, however, that the matter is not nearly so cut-and-dried. It certainly does *not* follow from the fact that jurors may be entitled to acquit against the evidence, that they also have legitimate authority to convict the accused in the absence of proof beyond reasonable doubt.

The idea of 'jury equity' (or 'nullification', as it is generally known in the USA) is at the heart of modern rationales for trial by jury. It does not rest on any claim to technical legal expertise. Lay jurors are not better qualified than professional lawyers and judges to interpret the law correctly. It cannot even be said that juries possess special qualities making them uniquely suited to discovering the truth, compared to the obvious alternatives of fact-finding by professional judges or panels of lay magistrates.[117] Staunch supporters of jury trial, like the late Lord Devlin, instead champion the ability of juries to do justice 'on the merits' and not merely according to the law.[118] It is considered advantageous that the jury's verdict should be open to what are, strictly speaking, legally irrelevant influences, and even that the jury should sometimes exercise its power to disregard the law altogether.[119]

The principal reason for assigning this pivotal role in adjudication to a randomly chosen group of twelve ordinary citizens is the need to secure public confidence in criminal verdicts. In the absence of any superior external mechanism for re-checking or authenticating the accuracy of fact-finding in criminal trials, confidence must be vested directly in the institution responsible for determining issues of guilt and innocence. There is a reciprocal relationship of interdependence between confidence in the accuracy of fact-finding and trust in the independence, wisdom, and good faith of the fact-finder.[120]

---

[116] Lord Justice Auld, *Review of the Criminal Courts of England and Wales* (TSO, October 2001), para.105

[117] For general surveys of the role and performance of juries, see Cheryl Thomas, *Are Juries Fair?* Ministry of Justice Research Series 1/10 (2010); Sean Doran, 'Trial by Jury', in Mike McConville and Geoffrey Wilson (eds.), *The Handbook of the Criminal Justice Process* (OUP, 2002); Penny Darbyshire, Andy Maughan, and Angus Stewart, *What Can the English Legal System Learn from Jury Research Published up to 2001?* on-line via www.criminal-courts-review.org.uk/ (summarized at [2001] *Crim LR* 970); New Zealand Law Commission Report 69, *Juries in Criminal Trials* (2001); Michael Hill and David Winkler, 'Juries: How do They Work? Do We Want Them?' (2000) 11 *Criminal Law Forum* 397; Zander and Henderson, *Crown Court Study* RCCJ Research Study No 19 (1993), ch 6; Baldwin and McConville, *Jury Trials* (1979); Kalven and Zeisel, *The American Jury* (1971).

[118] Devlin, *Trial by Jury* (1956), 151–8; Devlin, *The Judge* (1981), 84ff; Damaška, *The Faces of Justice and State Authority* (1986), ch 1.

[119] For empirical inquiries into nullification, see Kalven and Zeisel, *The American Jury* (1966), ch 15; Richard O. Lempert, 'Uncovering "Non-discernible" Differences: Empirical Research and the Jury-size Cases' (1975) 73 *Michigan LR* 643.

[120] On generating confidence in criminal verdicts, see Charles Nesson, 'The Evidence or the Event? On Judicial Proof and the Acceptability of Verdicts' (1985) 98 *Harvard LR* 1357; W. H. Simon, 'The Ideology of

Trial by jury secures public confidence in the legitimacy of criminal adjudication in several, mutually reinforcing, respects. First, as Lord Devlin observed:

the jury is the means by which the people play a direct part in the application of the law.... Constitutionally it is an invaluable achievement that popular consent should be at the root not only of the making but also of the application of the law. It is one of the significant causes of our political stability.[121]

Secondly, by involving ordinary citizens in the criminal trial we make the community's own standards of justice and morality an arbiter of legal guilt and innocence. To quote Lord Devlin again:

It is not a perverse acquittal that an innocent man is looking for when he asks for trial by jury, but a trial by men and women of his own sort. A professional man accused of a professional offence is not said to be seeking a perverse acquittal when he demands to be tried by men of his own profession. He is invoking the obverse of the right which enables the ordinary man charged with an ordinary offence to demand trial by ordinary men and not by a professional. Each is seeking the application to his case of a set of standards which he believes will be better understood and applied by one tribunal as by the other.[122]

The jury system ensures that English criminal trials remain sensitive to popular perceptions of right and wrong, and in this way criminal proceedings cultivate that public support which is essential to the effective administration of justice. Conversely, when public confidence in some aspect of criminal justice is shaken – as it periodically has been, for example, in the wake of high-profile miscarriages of justice – legal practitioners report that juries have a tendency to become hyper-sceptical of the prosecution's case, and will frequently refuse to convict solely on the basis of a confession or other police-generated evidence. An unpopular law is likewise liable to receive short-shrift from lay jurors, and this realization may concentrate policymakers' minds and provide some measure of insulation form executive over-reaching. Empirical research findings have long suggested that 'a provision of which juries will not approve is unlikely to be regularly enforced'.[123]

The celebrated 1957 trial of Dr John Bodkin Adams nicely illustrates how jury trial may operate to calibrate legal with moral conceptions of guilt and innocence. Bodkin Adams was a medical practitioner accused of murdering his patient, Mrs Morrell. Before and during the trial rumours widely circulated that the accused had murdered many of his other patients for personal gain. Additional murder charges were initially preferred against him, but abandoned prior to trial. The trial was presided over by Lord Devlin, who later, in an extra-judicial memoir, drew parallels between Bodkin Adams' prosecution and the old

Advocacy' [1978] *Wisconsin LR* 29; H. M. Hart and J. T. McNaughton, 'Evidence and Inference in the Law', in D. Lerner (ed.), *Evidence and Inference* (Free Press, 1958), 48, 52.

[121] Devlin, *The Judge*, 127.

[122] ibid. 141–2. And see E. P. Thompson, 'Subduing the Jury', *London Review of Books*, 4 and 18 December 1986; Cornish, *The Jury*, 126.

[123] Cornish, *The Jury*, 116. Lord Goff recalled, with apparent approval, juries refusing to convict of murder, despite indisputable evidence of the accused's intention to cause grievous bodily harm, on the basis of a common sense reluctance to equate 'implied malice' with an intention to kill: Robert Goff, 'The Mental Element in the Crime of Murder' (1988) 104 *LQR* 30, 49. Cf. the Supreme Court of Canada's stern disapproval of an express invitation to a jury to ignore the law: *R* v *Morgentaler* (1988) 62 CR (3d) 1.

forms of trial by ordeal.[124] For this latter-day 'trial by battle', Devlin suggested, the Crown selected its champion in the form of a single specimen charge relating to the death of Mrs Morrell. With the accused's acquittal this champion was formally defeated. Yet the accused was not entirely exonerated in the 'court' of public opinion because he declined to enter the witness-box to dispel widespread suspicions surrounding his conduct towards his patients. Lord Devlin likened Bodkin Adams' insistence on his right to silence in this case as a partial failure of the accused to subject himself to the full 'ordeal' of criminal trial:

As for the ordeal, the accused declined it. The only way in which he could have challenged his invisible foes [public rumours and suspicions] was by going into the witness-box and submitting to cross-examination... The result of the test would have depended not so much upon the content of his answers as upon his demeanour and what he showed of himself to the public. Certainly he had something to explain in the Morrell case and his explanations would have had to have been plausible. If they were and if he had been acquitted, the British public would have acquitted him of all else because he had faced the music. Refusal of the ordeal left him with a verdict of Non-Proven on all that was rumoured or alleged and untried as well as in the trial itself.[125]

To be believed by a jury seems, at least in some cases, tantamount to receiving a special kind of moral dispensation. Yet such dispensation can be won only by an accused who enters the witness-box and thereby exposes his moral character to searching examination. An accused who declines to submit to the modern trial ordeal prevents the jury from undertaking a more thoroughly extensive evaluation of his conduct on the occasions in question.

Now, there are obvious potential risks and drawbacks to investing the trial process generally, and the jury's verdict in particular, with this kind of symbolic significance. The necessary corollary of a jury's freedom to indulge in moral evaluation of the accused's general character is the possibility that criminal verdicts will be infected by unfair prejudice, stereotyping, discrimination, or other forms of irrationality. This is why the common law took such great pains, over the course of more than a century, to prevent prosecutors or prosecution witnesses from mentioning the accused's extraneous misconduct ('bad character') to the jury, unless for some reason such information was especially probative.[126] It is a plausible assumption that the idiosyncratic preferences of individual jurors will more or less 'cancel each other out' in the process of arriving at a group decision (in turn underlining the importance of ensuring large and reasonably representative jury panels),[127] but this still leaves open the possibility of verdicts being tainted by systematic biases and misperceptions.

It must be emphasized that Lord Devlin was describing the broader social and political significance of criminal trials rather than their formal legal implications. Bodkin Adams was perfectly entitled to remain silent and put the prosecution to its proof, and his acquittal was in no way tainted, in the eyes of the law, by his refusal to testify in his own defence.

---

[124] Patrick Devlin, *Easing The Passing: The Trial of Doctor John Bodkin Adams* (1985), 197.

[125] ibid.

[126] The law of character evidence was extensively reformed by the CJA 2003, as explained in Chapter 14.

[127] Renewed efforts have been made to ensure that everybody called for jury service who is eligible and capable should actually perform their civic duty: see Cheryl Thomas, 'Exposing the Myths of Jury Service' [2008] *Crim LR* 415.

The presumption of innocence absolutely forbids the application of any official criminal censure, punishment, sanction, or other legal disability to a person who has not been convicted of an offence, either because he was never prosecuted in the first place or because he was acquitted after a contested trial.[128]

The 'court of public opinion' operates in a less constrained normative environment, with a more free-ranging, roving commission. One might choose, for example, not to be friendly with a person who has been acquitted of a serious crime of violence, or one might refuse to transact business with a person acquitted of commercial fraud, on the basis that, despite the absence of formal proof beyond reasonable doubt, sufficiently disturbing evidence of wrongdoing was presented in their trials to warrant keeping such people at arm's length. Unlike the state, which must be even-handed and abjure unfair discrimination, private citizens can pick and choose their friends and business associates without, in general, having to justify their personal preferences and predilections. Through its impact on these broader realms of personal conduct, social interaction, and moral judgments, trial by jury makes a profound, albeit diffuse, contribution to the maintenance of social trust in and beyond criminal proceedings, at least in high-profile cases attracting widespread publicity. Bodkin Adams remained a free man after his trial (subject to any further civil or disciplinary proceedings that might be brought against him), but his social standing may have been irreparably compromised by his failure to undergo, in Lord Devlin's terms, the full ordeal of trial.

Criminal litigation, as an extension of criminal justice policy more generally, is riven by the tension between justice and security: between punishing and deterring crime, on the one hand, and protecting the innocent both form victimization by crime and from erroneous conviction by a criminal court, on the other. Entrusting criminal adjudication to a lay jury of twelve ordinary men and women ensures that trade-offs between competing policy choices in individual cases remain responsive to popular opinion and promotes democratic accountability. But that is far from saying that the jury does, or should, enjoy free rein in determining an accused's guilt or innocence, for then responsiveness to popular opinion might descend into a 'tyranny of the majority' in which the capricious whims of the 'gang of twelve' could defeat the ends of justice. Within its delineated sphere of responsibility and discretion the jury is king, but its powers are carefully circumscribed and regulated by a complex institutional structure of legal rules, principles, and professional practices. These are the institutional mechanisms, to which we now turn, which define the practical meaning of 'trial by judge and jury' in English criminal proceedings.

2.5 TRIAL BY JUDGE AND JURY IN ENGLAND AND WALES

English juries deliberate in secret without any direct judicial participation at that stage, and ultimately deliver an unreasoned peremptory general verdict. Nonetheless, judges in English criminal proceedings have at their disposal numerous ways of influencing trial

---

[128] All forms of preventive regulation are suspect from the perspective of traditional conceptions of the presumption of innocence: see Chapter 6.

outcomes, especially before, but also to some extent after, the jury has spoken. This section provides an overview of the five most important judicial techniques for controlling or influencing the jury's decision-making, namely: (a) rulings on the admissibility of evidence advanced by the parties; (b) judicial stays of proceedings for abuse of process; (c) rulings on defence submissions of 'no case to answer'; (d) judicial comment and summing-up at the close of trial proceedings; and (e) appellate review of convictions. It also briefly notes a recent related procedural innovation: (f) the Court of Appeal's power to quash acquittals.

(a) TRIAL RULINGS GOVERNING THE ADMISSIBILITY OF EVIDENCE

One of the trial judge's principal functions is to filter the information presented to the jury by ruling on its legal admissibility. Evidence proffered by any party to the proceedings must 'pass the judge' in order to be admitted into the trial. Under the influence of Thayer,[129] common law Evidence has traditionally been viewed as a collection of exclusionary rules qualifying the general principle that all relevant evidence should be presented to the fact-finder. Although we advocate a more expansive conception of our subject, as Chapter 1 explained from the outset,[130] we do not deny that exclusionary rules remain a significant feature of the broader disciplinary landscape of evidence and proof in criminal adjudication. The following chapters contain detailed exegesis on many exclusionary rules and principles. Here it will suffice to offer some preliminary generalizations.

Judicial filtering of evidence is governed by a mixture of pragmatic, instrumental, and intrinsic moral considerations. Evidence which is irrelevant, in the sense that it does not tend to prove or disprove any fact in issue, should naturally be excluded, since – by definition – it bears no logical relation to the facts in issue.[131] But technically relevant evidence should also be excluded if its probative contribution is likely to be negligible when set against the time and effort that may be wasted by its admission. Even Jeremy Bentham, that scourge of technical legal rules of inadmissibility, agreed that evidence should be excluded if its production would involve disproportionate 'vexation, expense, or delay'.[132] Some relevant evidence is simply more trouble than it is worth, given that the overriding objective is to deal with cases justly rather than, say, adding to the store or human knowledge or promoting cosmic understanding.

Certain principles of admissibility have hardened, through sedimentary judicial practice, into well-defined exclusionary rules, like the hearsay prohibition discussed in Chapter 9. Others, including the old 'best evidence' rule that used to be very prominent, have faded into the background and been replaced by flexible tests of evidential sufficiency.[133] In order to determine legal admissibility, trial judges often have to assess the likelihood that relevant evidence might generate unfair prejudice against the accused. Generally speaking, potentially prejudicial prosecution evidence will be admitted only if its weight, or 'probative value', is likely to exceed its prejudicial effect (PV > PE). Thus, at common law, judges

---

[129] James Bradley Thayer, *A Preliminary Treatise on Evidence at the Common Law* (Little, Brown & Co, 1898).
[130] §1.1.   [131] Legal conceptions of relevance are explored in §3.2.
[132] William Twining, *Theories of Evidence: Bentham & Wigmore* (Weidenfeld, 1985), 28ff.
[133] See *Garton v Hunter* [1969] 2 QB 37, CA; *Kajala v Noble* (1982) 75 Cr App R 149, DC; *R v Wayte* (1983) 76 Cr App R 110, CA.

would prevent the jury from learning about the accused's previous crimes or other dis-creditable conduct extraneous to the offences charged, unless the probative value of the evidence was sufficient to compel its admission.[134] The same general PV > PE test applies, in parallel with other legal standards, to regulate the admissibility of evidence tainted by investigative impropriety.[135] At common law, the trial judge retains an inherent discre-tion to ensure that the proceedings are 'fair' and conducted according to law. A classic statement of this principle was delivered by Lord Reading in the pre-Great War case of *Christie*:

There are exceptions to the law regulating the admissibility of evidence which apply only to criminal trials, and which have acquired their force by the constant and invariable practice of judges when presiding at criminal trials. They are rules of prudence and discretion, and have become so integral a part of the administration of the criminal law as almost to have acquired the full force of law.... Such practice has found its place in the administration of the criminal law because judges are aware from their experience that in order to ensure a fair trial for the accused, and to prevent the operation of indirect but not the less serious prejudice to his interests, it is desirable in certain circumstances to relax the strict applica-tion of the law of evidence. Nowadays, it is the constant practice for the judge who presides at the trial to indicate his opinion to counsel for the prosecution that *evidence which, although admissible in law, has little value in its direct bearing upon the case, and might indirectly oper-ate seriously to prejudice the accused, should not be given against him*, and speaking generally counsel accepts the suggestion and does not press for the admission of the evidence, unless he has good reason for it.[136]

This common law discretion has largely been superseded by a statutory provision, sec-tion 78 of PACE 1984, which will be examined in Chapter 5. However, it continues to be invoked intermittently in modern times, having been expressly preserved by section 82(3) of PACE 1984. What is sometimes referred to as the '*Sang* discretion'[137] endures, as it were, in the normative background, infrequently relied upon but always available to trial judges as an endlessly malleable juridical resource for ensuring the fairness of trials.

Where the admissibility of evidence turns on some disputed fact, the court may need to conduct its own factual inquiry.[138] For instance, it is for the judge to decide whether to receive the evidence of a witness whose competence has been challenged by the oppos-ing party.[139] Similarly, before admitting an accused's extra-judicial confession the judge has to determine whether the circumstances in which the admission was allegedly made render it anadmissible as confession evidence.[140] Both inquiries – Is the witness compe-tent? Was the confession obtained in circumstances liable to render it unreliable? – raise preliminary questions of fact which must be resolved before the admissibility of evidence

---

[134] The statutory regime now applicable to evidence of the accused's extraneous misconduct is set out in Chapter 14.   [135] See Chapter 5.

[136] *R v Christie* [1914] AC 545, 564–5, HL (emphasis supplied).

[137] Cf. *R v Sang* [1980] AC 402, 434, HL, *per* Lord Diplock: 'I would hold that there has now developed a general rule of practice whereby in a trial by jury the judge has a discretion to exclude evidence which, though technically admissible, would probably have a prejudicial influence on the minds of the jury, which would be out of proportion to its true evidential value.'

[138] For systematic analysis, see Rosemary Pattenden, 'Pre-verdict Judicial Fact-finding in Criminal Trials with Juries' (2009) 29 *OJLS* 1.   [139] §7.2.

[140] §12.3.

can be determined. Such questions are frequently litigated prior to the commencement of the trial, to the extent that admissibility issues are predictable in advance.[141] Alternatively, the point may arise whilst the trial is already in progress, in which case the jury is sent out of the courtroom until the issue of admissibility is resolved. These judicial inquiries are known as *voir dire* hearings; or more colloquially, as a 'trial within a trial'. If the evidence turns out to be admissible, then the party seeking to adduce it may proceed to do so when the jury is called back into court and the trial proper resumes. However, if the judge rules the evidence inadmissible the jury will never be allowed to hear it.[142]

Exclusionary rules are as many and varied as the diverse range of values, objectives, and policies they encapsulate and promote. One must consequently be wary of over-generalization. Although it may seem paradoxical that the law should strive to promote truth-seeking by *withholding* information from the jury, this strategy makes sense if certain forms of evidence have a particular propensity to confuse, mislead, or otherwise divert jurors from their task. Other exclusionary rules rest on explicitly normative foundations that have nothing to do with fact-finding accuracy, and sometimes patently conflict with criminal adjudication's epistemic aspirations. Rules of privilege, for example, protect relationships founded on mutual trust and confidence between husband and wife, client and legal adviser, etc. even at the cost of depriving the fact-finder of relevant information.[143]

In general terms, judicial regulation of the admissibility of evidence might be regarded as serving three core objectives. First, the jury is spared distraction by trivial and unhelpful evidence and can concentrate its attention on the most significant evidential aspects of the case. Secondly, the judge is in a position to limit the scope of the jury's discretion to return questionable verdicts by excluding unreliable or unfairly prejudicial evidence, which might otherwise lead the jury astray and thus undermine the factual accuracy of criminal adjudication. The third function of rules of admissibility is to implement and reinforce the law's intrinsic normative commitments, not only to the fundamental policy of protecting the innocent, but also to a broader range of values and policies considered important in liberal societies, including fairness to the parties, due process, humane treatment, non-discrimination, and integrity in the administration of criminal justice.[144] The political morality of criminal procedure has assumed greater prominence in recent years, especially under the rubric of 'fair trial rights'[145] but also through the medium of a revitalized judicial jurisdiction to stay proceedings for abuse of process. English law is increasingly (albeit somewhat unevenly) coming round to the view that criminal adjudication must be *fair* as well as accurate in its pursuit of justice, so that even highly probative and reliable evidence may have to be excluded if it was produced or acquired through unconscionable official conduct. Occasionally, investigative impropriety may be judged so egregious that the entire prosecution must be stopped in its tracks.

---

[141] This process has been refined through more active judicial case management within the framework of the CrimPR 2010, and more particularly by the innovation of interlocutory appeals on evidentiary rulings: CPIA 1996, ss.35–36; CJA 2003, ss.57–61 (and s.62, which is still not in force at the time of writing); *R v Y* [2008] 1 WLR 1683, [2008] EWCA Crim 10. For discussion, see David Ormerod, Adrian Waterman, and Rudi Fortson, 'Prosecution Appeals – Too Much of a Good Thing?' [2010] *Crim LR* 169.

[142] Unless for some reason the proponent of the evidence is able to make a renewed, and ultimately successful, application for its admission. It sometimes happens that evidence inadmissible for one purpose is admissible for another, or evidence inadmissible in chief becomes admissible in rebuttal of the opponent's evidence. These issues are explored in Chapter 8.   [143] See §7.4.

[144] §1.3.   [145] See Chapter 5.

(b) JUDICIAL STAYS FOR ABUSE OF PROCESS

At common law, all criminal tribunals, including the Crown Court and magistrates' courts,[146] claim inherent jurisdiction to control their own proceedings in the interests of justice. Whilst procedural fairness is now promoted by a host of particularized evidentiary standards, trial judges – as we have just seen – retain a residual, background, jurisdiction to ensure that trial proceedings are conducted fairly.[147] This is the deep, if under-cultivated, soil in which the doctrine of abuse of process took root, and subsequently blossomed.

A judicial stay of proceedings for abuse of process is a jurisdictional remedy which operates irrespective of the substantive merits of the case. It authorizes a judge to 'stay', that is stop or suspend, a prosecution indefinitely where the judge decides that a fair trial cannot take place, either because of something that has already happened in the course of the proceedings or in anticipation of circumstances likely to prevail at any future trial. An example of the former would be a case where the police or prosecutor has behaved so indefensibly – e.g. by torturing suspects or joining a criminal conspiracy, to give extreme illustrations – that the integrity of the proceedings is fatally compromised, *even though the accused may well be guilty of the crime charged*. An example of the latter would be a case where an accused has attracted such unfairly prejudicial pre-trial publicity that his right to receive a fair trial by unbiased jurors is seriously jeopardized.

In entering a stay, the judge effectively declares the prosecution so flawed or tainted or precarious that it is not possible to be confident that the accused will receive a fair trial. Such irremediably defective proceedings must therefore be halted without even examining the evidence on the substantive charge. A stay is not the legal equivalent of an acquittal, nor even strictly speaking a final determination of the case. But it operates in practice to terminate proceedings without any real possibility of their ever being recommenced – subject to appellate review if the prosecutor challenges the judge's ruling.[148] Indeed, it would probably be a further abuse of process, absent some material change of circumstances, for a prosecutor to attempt to resurrect an indictment previously stayed for abuse of process.

The doctrine of abuse of process is more than a century old, but its application to modern criminal proceedings really begins with the House of Lords' landmark decision in *Connelly* v *DPP*.[149] The question in *Connelly* was whether the accused could be prosecuted and convicted of robbery when he had already been acquitted of a murder arising out of the same underlying incident, an armed robbery of the Mitcham Co-op. Although it was concluded that a second prosecution was permissible in these particular circumstances, at least three of their Lordships affirmed the existence of a general jurisdiction, extending beyond the narrow ambit of the formal 'double jeopardy' pleas in bar *autrefois convict* and *autrefois acquit*, that would prevent vexatious or otherwise unfair repeat prosecutions of

---

[146] Magistrates should resort to this power only very sparingly: *R* v *Oxford City JJ, ex p. Smith* (1982) 75 Cr App R 200, 204, DC; *R* v *Horsham JJ, ex p. Reeves* (1982) 75 Cr App R 236, 241, DC (Ackner LJ); *King* v *Kucharz* [1989] COD 469, DC; *R* v *Telford JJ, ex p. Badhan* [1991] 2 QB 78, DC.

[147] *R* v *Christie* [1914] AC 545, HL; *R* v *Sang* [1980] AC 402, HL.

[148] Provision for the prosecution to appeal against a trial judge's rulings 'in relation to a trial on indictment' was made by CJA 2003, ss.57–61. If the appeal succeeds, the proceedings are resumed, but if the appeal fails the accused is formally acquitted. Also see Law Com No 267, *Double Jeopardy and Prosecution Appeals*, Cm 5048 (TSO, 2001); Rosemary Pattenden, 'Prosecution Appeals Against Judges' Rulings' [2000] *Crim LR* 971.

[149] *Connelly* v *DPP* [1964] AC 1254, HL.

technically different, but circumstantially related, offences. Lord Morris explicitly invoked the court's inherent control over the integrity of its own process:

There can be no doubt that a court which is endowed with a particular jurisdiction has powers which are necessary to enable it to act effectively within such jurisdiction. I would regard them as powers which are inherent in its jurisdiction. A court must enjoy such powers in order to enforce its rules of practice and to suppress any abuses of its process and to defeat any attempted thwarting of its process.... The power (which is inherent in a court's jurisdiction) to prevent abuses of its process and to control its own procedure must in a criminal court include a power to safeguard an accused person from oppression or prejudice.[150]

Though the power of judicial stay recognized in *Connelly* was expressed in apparently sweeping terms, its development over the next three decades was modest and gradual.[151] Stays appeared to be available only in certain exceptional and quite narrowly circumscribed situations involving:[152] (1) prosecution manipulation or misuse of procedure; (2) undue delay;[153] or (3) police impropriety in the conduct of criminal investigations. These general headings of abusive process can be further broken down into identifiable sub-categories, including unfair repeat prosecutions ('double jeopardy'),[154] breach of a promise made to the accused by police or prosecutors,[155] prosecutions in bad faith, and illegal or irregular extradition. Stays may also be entered on account of adverse pre-trial publicity, though this last head of abuse is apparently very difficult to satisfy in practice.[156] In 1993, the House of Lords made a second major stride forward in developing a modern abuse of process jurisprudence in *ex parte Bennett*.[157]

Bennett was a New Zealand national who was wanted for offences in England connected with his allegedly fraudulent acquisition of a helicopter. He had fled to South Africa beyond the reach of then-existing extradition regimes. So, it would appear,[158] the British and South African police (apparently with the blessing of the CPS) colluded to have Bennett deported from South Africa to New Zealand via London Heathrow Airport, where he could be apprehended *en route* by the British police whilst supposedly transiting between flights. The plan seemed to have worked flawlessly. But when the British authorities tried to bring Bennett to trial, he raised the threshold jurisdictional objection that he

---

[150] ibid. 1301–2. Also see *Mills v Cooper* [1967] 2 QB 459, 467, DC, *per* Lord Parker CJ: 'every court has undoubtedly a right in its discretion to decline to hear proceedings on the ground that they are oppressive and an abuse of the process of the court'.

[151] Generally, see Andrew L.-T. Choo, *Abuse of Process and Judicial Stays of Criminal Proceedings* (OUP, 2nd edn. 2008), chs 1–4; Andrew L.-T. Choo, 'Halting Criminal Prosecutions: The Abuse of Process Doctrine Revisited' [1995] Crim LR 864.

[152] *R v Derby Crown Court, ex p. Brooks* (1984) 80 Cr App R 164, DC.

[153] *Attorney General's Reference (No 2 of 2001)* [2004] 2 AC 72, [2003] UKHL 68. For a detailed comparative case-study, see Penney Lewis, *Delayed Prosecution for Childhood Sexual Abuse* (OUP, 2006), ch 3.

[154] *R v Beedie* [1998] QB 356, CA.   [155] *R v Croydon Justices, ex p. Dean* [1993] QB 769, DC.

[156] *R v Taylor and Taylor* (1994) 98 Cr App R 361, CA; cf. *R v West* [1996] 2 Cr App R 374, CA (stay refused despite very extensive and patently prejudicial pre-trial media coverage of the notorious crimes of Fred and Rose West. Lord Taylor CJ stated: 'The question raised on behalf of the defence is whether a fair trial could be held after such intensive publicity adverse to the accused. In our view it could. To hold otherwise would mean that if allegations of murder are sufficiently horrendous so as inevitably to shock the nation, the accused cannot be tried. That would be absurd').

[157] *R v Horseferry Road Magistrates' Court, ex p. Bennett* [1994] 1 AC 42, HL.

[158] The police maintained that Bennett's arrival at Heathrow was merely serendipitous, but it was assumed for the purposes of the appeal that the British and South African authorities had been in cahoots.

had been brought into the UK by unlawful means, effectively amounting (he contended) to official kidnap. Departing from earlier authority to the effect that it is no business of the courts to inquire into the manner in which a person properly charged with a criminal offence was brought within the jurisdiction,[159] the House of Lords held that the proceedings against Bennett would have to be stayed for abuse of process if the British and South African authorities had in fact colluded in the way alleged. Lord Griffiths announced:

[I]t is the function of the High Court to ensure that executive action is exercised responsibly and as Parliament intended. So also should it be in the field of criminal law and if it comes to the attention of the court that there has been a serious abuse of power it should, in my view, express its disapproval by refusing to act upon it.... The courts, of course, have no power to apply direct discipline to the police or the prosecuting authorities, but they can refuse to allow them to take advantage of abuse of power by regarding their behaviour as an abuse of process and thus preventing a prosecution.[160]

Lord Lowry added the following important statement of principle:

[T]he court, in order to protect its own process from being degraded and misused, must have the power to stay proceedings which have come before it and have only been made possible by acts which offend the court's conscience as being contrary to the rule of law. Those acts by providing a morally unacceptable foundation for the exercise of jurisdiction over the suspect taint the proposed trial and, if tolerated, will mean that the court's process has been abused. Therefore, although the power of the court is rightly confined to its inherent power to protect itself against the abuse of its own process, I respectfully cannot agree that the facts relied on in cases such as the present case (as alleged) 'have nothing to do with that process' just because they are not part of the process. They are the indispensable foundation for the holding of the trial.... I regard it as essential to the rule of law that the court should not have to make available its process and thereby endorse (on what I am confident will be a very few occasions) unworthy conduct when it is proved against the executive or its agents, however humble in rank.[161]

The jurisprudential significance of the House of Lords' *Bennett* ruling resonates far beyond the immediate context of extradition cases.[162] The idea of the court's conscience as a litmus-test for the moral legitimacy of criminal prosecutions, so clearly articulated in the speech of Lord Lowry, was subsequently extended to cases concerned with the propriety of undercover police operations and the vexed question of 'entrapment'.[163] Generalizing from these specific applications, moral integrity emerges as a new 'golden-thread'[164] running through each discrete chapter of the law of criminal evidence and procedure.[165] So

---

[159] *R v Plymouth Justices, ex p. Driver* [1986] QB 95, DC. Also see *US v Alvarez-Machain* 119 L Ed 2d 441 (1992), in which the US Supreme Court reaffirmed the long-standing rule of federal law that official kidnap is no barrier to fair trial.   [160] *ex p. Bennett*, 62.

[161] ibid. 76, 77.

[162] But also see *R v Mullen* [2002] QB 520, CA. See Laura Davidson, 'Quashing Convictions for Pre-Trial Abuse of Process: Breaching Public International Law and Human Rights' [1999] *CLJ* 466.

[163] *R v Looseley; Attorney-General's Reference (No 3 of 2000)* [2001] 1 WLR 2060, [2001] UKHL, discussed in §5.5.

[164] The original 'golden thread' being the presumption of innocence, famously reaffirmed in *Woolmington v DPP* [1935] AC 462, HL: see Chapter 6.

[165] Cf. Andrew L.-T. Choo and Susan Nash, 'What's the Matter with Section 78?' [1999] *Crim LR* 929 (arguing that judicial applications of PACE 1984 s.78, in affording insufficient weight to the moral integrity of criminal proceedings, are inconsistent with the abuse of process authorities).

far as the institutional framework of criminal adjudication is concerned, stays for abuse of process are now a well-established procedural mechanism through which judges can control the flow of cases to the jury – albeit that trial judges will not lightly resort to the 'nuclear option' of stopping a prosecution dead in its tracks. The High Court has indicated that 'this residual (and discretionary) power of any court to stay criminal proceedings as an abuse of its process is one which ought only to be employed in exceptional circumstances, whatever the reasons submitted for invoking it'.[166] There would need to be clear evidence of serious investigative or prosecutorial impropriety or compelling reason to think that the accused could not get a fair trial before proceedings would be stayed, irrevocably, as an abuse of process.[167]

(c) SUBMISSIONS OF 'NO CASE TO ANSWER'

Even after a trial commences, the judge's regulatory function is not confined to determining the admissibility of individual pieces of evidence. There are two intermediate stages, between the prosecution's opening statement and the judge's summing-up, at which the judge may have to decide whether the cumulative weight of the prosecution's evidence is sufficient to warrant submitting the case to the jury's consideration.

At the end of the prosecution's case, and before being called upon to mount a positive defence, the accused may submit that there is no case to answer. This 'half-time motion' asserts that the prosecution's evidence, taken at its highest, could not be regarded by any reasonable jury as constituting proof beyond reasonable doubt of any charge on the indictment. If the submission succeeds, the judge must 'direct an acquittal'. In formal terms, the jury acquits, but in reality the decision has been taken by the judge. The jury has no say in the matter. Juries bringing in directed verdicts of acquittal do not retire to deliberate over the evidence presented in the trial and cannot disobey the judge's instruction.

In an indictment charging multiple offences, a submission of no case to answer may succeed with regard to all of the offences charged, or only in relation to certain counts. Where a 'no case' submission is only partly successful, the judge will withdraw the unsupported charges from the jury's consideration and proceed to trial on the remainder.[168]

Later, after both parties have presented their cases but before the judge sums up to the jury, an equivalent test of evidential sufficiency may be applied to the entire body of evidence. Again, if a 'no case to answer' submission succeeds at this stage, a directed verdict follows automatically. Defence counsel will frequently chance their arm with a 'half-time' or 'full-time' submission of 'no case' whenever the prosecution's evidence seems dubiously thin. But the judge does not necessarily have to wait to be asked. Rather, the court itself is under a continuing duty to withdraw any case (or particular charges) from the jury if the judge decides that the prosecution's evidence, taken at its highest, would be insufficient to justify a conviction.[169]

---

[166] *R (Ebrahim)* v *Feltham Magistrates' Court* [2001] 1 WLR 1293, [2001] EWHC Admin 130, [17] (Brooke LJ).

[167] One high-profile example is *R* v *Colin Stagg*, 14 September 1994 (Central Criminal Court), discussed in §5.5.

[168] Just as, conversely, the judge should withdraw from the jury's consideration any issue on which the defence has failed to satisfy an evidential burden of production: see §6.2(a).

[169] *R* v *Brown (Davina)* [2002] 1 Cr App R 46, [2001] EWCA Crim 961.

In the frequently criticized but still authoritative case of *Galbraith*, Lord Lane CJ set out the test to be applied by trial judges in ruling on defence submissions of no case to answer:

How then should the judge approach a submission of 'no case'? (1) If there is no evidence that the crime alleged has been committed by the defendant, there is no difficulty. The judge will of course stop the case. (2) The difficulty arises where there is some evidence but it is of a tenuous character, for example because of inherent weakness or vagueness or because it is inconsistent with other evidence. (a) Where the judge comes to the conclusion that the prosecution evidence, taken at its highest, is such that a jury properly directed could not properly convict upon it, it is his duty, upon a submission being made, to stop the case. (b) Where however the prosecution evidence is such that its strength or weakness depends on the view to be taken of a witness's reliability, or other matters which are generally speaking within the province of the jury and where on one possible view of the facts there is evidence upon which a jury could properly come to the conclusion that the defendant is guilty, then the judge should allow the matter to be tried by the jury.[170]

Accordingly, the prosecution must adduce evidence capable of making an ordinary person sure that the accused is guilty.[171] If the prosecutor fails to adduce *any* evidence to prove an element of the offence, or adduces only evidence so weak or equivocal as to be incapable of supporting a guilty verdict, there is no case to answer and the accused is entitled to be acquitted by operation of law, on the judge's direction.

The first limb of the *Galbraith* test restates a logical proposition: if there is an evidential gap in the prosecution's case, the onus of proof resting on the prosecutor cannot possibly be discharged. *Galbraith's* second limb is more debateable. It is sometimes said that a judge should not weigh evidence or assess the credibility of witnesses when ruling on a submission of no case to answer,[172] but in reality this is sometimes unavoidable. Suppose, for example, that the prosecution's case rests entirely on the testimony of a single eyewitness who, by turns, asserts and then denies that he saw the accused commit the offence. In these circumstances, the trial judge might readily accede to a defence submission of 'no case to answer', on the basis that no reasonable jury could possibly convict on such patently unreliable evidence. But it is not possible to arrive at this judicial determination without making some threshold assessment of the witness's reliability and testimonial credibility.

The second limb of the rule in *Galbraith* attempts to strike a balance between the demands of rationality in adjudication (which in turn promotes the ends of justice and protects the innocent from wrongful conviction), and the almost equally compelling policy of reserving questions of fact in criminal adjudication to the jury. In most cases, the policy of judicial deference to lay fact-finding prevails. The judge should not intervene, for

---

[170] *R v Galbraith* [1981] 1 WLR 1039, 1042, CA.

[171] J. C. Wood, 'The Submission of No Case to Answer In Criminal Trials – the Quantum of Proof' (1961) 77 *LQR* 491.

[172] Cf. *R v Barker (Note)* (1975) 65 Cr App R 287, 288, *per* Lord Widgery CJ: 'even if the judge has taken the view that the evidence could not support a conviction because of the inconsistencies, he should nevertheless have left the matter to the jury. It cannot be too clearly stated that the judge's obligation to stop the case is an obligation which is concerned primarily with those cases where the necessary minimum evidence to establish the facts of the crime has not been called. It is not the judge's job to weigh the evidence, decide who is telling the truth, and to stop the case merely because he thinks the witness is lying. To do that is to usurp the function of the jury...'

example, just because he personally finds a witness unconvincing.[173] But submissions of 'no case' do succeed in a substantial minority of trials,[174] in accordance with the demands of rational adjudication and the fundamental normative expectation that criminal guilt must be proved beyond reasonable doubt by admissible evidence. Furthermore, the Court of Appeal will quash the conviction of an accused whose 'no case' submission was erroneously rejected by the trial judge, even though the jury has, by definition, proceeded to find the accused guilty beyond reasonable doubt on the evidence presented at trial.[175]

Allowing the accused's appeal in such circumstances might appear to reflect an unreasonably narrow, legalistic approach, since, after all, the accused has been convicted by a jury on the evidence.[176] Yet, it would inevitably compromise the rule of law and the moral integrity of criminal proceedings if his conviction were allowed to stand. The accused must either have been convicted on the basis of evidence insufficient in law to satisfy the prosecutor's burden of proof, or, alternatively, on the basis of defence evidence that he should never have been required to give. In the first scenario, the conviction is an affront to rational adjudication and a threat to innocence; in the second, the conviction was undeniably procured in breach of due process and the rights of the accused and possibly contrary to the presumption of innocence.[177]

Whether the rule of law and the maintenance of moral integrity in criminal proceedings would *always* require a conviction to be quashed where the trial judge has erroneously rejected a submission of no case to answer may, however, be doubted. These are questions of degree in which every relevant circumstance must be taken into account, and reasonable minds may beg to differ. If, for example, compelling evidence of guilt of a very serious offence were to emerge from the accused's own testimony, the Court of Appeal might feel constrained to uphold the conviction, even whilst regretting the trial judge's mistake in allowing the accused, effectively, to talk himself into being convicted.[178] Short of such extremes, however, quashing the conviction gives practical effect to English law's fundamental commitments to due process, moral integrity, and protection of the innocent.

The *Galbraith* test has frequently been criticized for being *too* deferential to jury factfinding. Critics object that *Galbraith* is narrower than the test applied by the Court of

---

[173] R v *Siddique* [1995] Crim LR 875, CA.

[174] In the Runciman Royal Commission's Crown Court Study 'no case' submissions were made in approximately one third of all cases in the sample, and were successful on about one third of the occasions on which they were made – a success rate of about 10% of all Crown Court prosecutions: Michael Zander and Paul Henderson, *Crown Court Study*, RCCJ Research Report No 19 (HMSO, 1993), para.4.9.

[175] R v *Smith (Patrick Joseph)* [1999] 2 Cr App R 238, [2000] 1 All ER 263, CA; R v *Broadhead* [2006] EWCA Crim 1705. Earlier, conflicting, authorities were reviewed by A. A. S. Zuckerman, *The Principles of Criminal Evidence* (OUP, 1989), 54–5. Also see Rosemary Pattenden, 'The Submission of No Case – Some Recent Developments' [1982] *Crim LR* 558.

[176] Victor Tunkel, 'When Safe Convictions are Unsafely Quashed' (1999) 149 *NLJ* 1089.

[177] If 'the presumption of innocence' is not equated reductively with the burden and standard of proof: see Chapter 6.

[178] But cf. R v *Smith (Patrick Joseph)* [1999] 2 Cr App R 238, 242, where Mantell LJ mused: 'What if a submission is wrongly rejected but the defendant is cross-examined into admitting his guilt? Should the conviction be said to be unsafe? We think it should. The defendant was entitled to be acquitted after the evidence against him had been heard. To allow the trial to continue beyond the end of the prosecution case would be an abuse of process and fundamentally unfair. So even in the extreme case, the conviction should be regarded as unsafe.'

Appeal when quashing a conviction on the basis of insufficiency of evidence.[179] So why should the law put off until tomorrow what it could do more fairly and efficiently today? Rather than putting the accused through the ordeal of trial and conviction only to be released on appeal, it might seem logical to authorize the trial judge to pre-empt wasteful and arguably oppressive appellate proceedings by upholding a submission of no case to answer at trial.[180] The Runciman Commission recommended *Galbraith's* replacement with a rule permitting the trial judge to 'stop any case if he or she takes the view that the prosecution evidence is demonstrably unsafe or unsatisfactory or too weak to be allowed to go to the jury'.[181]

Interestingly, Lord Lane CJ explicitly considered and rejected this argument in *Galbraith* itself, observing that '[t]he fact that the Court of Appeal have power to quash a conviction on these grounds is a slender basis for giving the trial judge similar powers at the close of the prosecution case'.[182] A purely formalistic distinction between the powers of the trial judge to withdraw a case from the jury, and the jurisdiction of the Court of Appeal to quash a conviction after the jury has spoken, cannot be expected to hold much water with reformers keen to pre-empt what they regard as miscarriages of justice and avoidable waste of precious resources. *Galbraith's* longevity might, however, owe more to the symbolic significance of criminal trials and to the social and moral authority of jury verdicts than reformers' strictly logical analysis is able to credit. For although it is perfectly true that the judge has had the advantage of hearing the witnesses at first-hand, and that the Court of Appeal is generally very reluctant to uphold an appeal purely on the basis of evidential insufficiency, it is, in the final analysis, the jury and not the judge that is the trier of fact in English criminal trials. In this procedural environment, judicial deference to lay fact-finding is the default-setting.

(d) JUDICIAL COMMENT AND SUMMING-UP

By ruling evidence inadmissible, and still more by withdrawing particular charges or even the whole case from the jury, the judge exerts direct, peremptory, control over the jury's responsibility for fact-finding in criminal litigation. More subtle influence is brought to bear by the judge's power to comment on the evidence, either whilst questioning witnesses during the course of the trial, or, more routinely, in summing-up the evidence at the close of trial proceedings and directing the jury on the applicable law. In adversarial trials, the primary responsibility for calling and questioning witnesses lies with the parties, but the judge is permitted to ask supplementary questions, provided that he does not 'descend into the arena' and compromise his impartiality by usurping the function of the prosecution or defence advocate.[183] Judicial questioning of witnesses contradicts the adversarial

---

[179] See, e.g., Royal Commission on Criminal Justice, *Report*, Cm 2263 (1993), paras.41–42.

[180] Compare the legislative technique adopted by CJA 2003, s.107, which instructs the trial judge to withdraw a case from the jury which appears to rest on unsafe bad character evidence: see §14.3(c).

[181] Royal Commission on Criminal Justice, *Report*, para.42.

[182] *R v Galbraith* [1981] 1 WLR 1039, 1041, CA.

[183] See Rosemary Pattenden, *Judicial Discretion and Criminal Litigation* (OUP, 2nd edn. 1990), 98–102. In *R v Fixou* [1998] Crim LR 352, CA, the Recorder who presided at trial was found to have gone too far, but only because his 106 interventions were made in a 'hostile' and 'sarcastic' tone. The sheer number of questions and comments did not necessarily constitute inappropriate judicial behaviour in the circumstances.

archetype of 'umpireal' judging[184] and may not be a routine feature of English criminal litigation, though its frequency doubtless depends on the personal style and experience of individual judges. Be that as it may, the judge is obliged to sum-up on the evidence and direct the jury on the law in every case that proceeds to a verdict.

Reports of appeal decisions conventionally recite that the accused 'was tried by Judge So-and-So and a Jury at Such-and-Such Crown Court', and this description of joint responsibility is no mere empty legal formalism or *pro forma* genuflection to judicial authority. Criminal adjudication in England and Wales really is a kind of partnership between judge and jury. Unlike many of their continental counterparts, English judges do not deliberate with jurors after they have retired to consider their verdict. Instead, English trial judges exert indirect influence over jurors' deliberations through their comments and summing-up in the course of the trial. A standard summing-up sets out the elements of the offence charged and the facts which need to be proved and explains the prosecutor's burden and standard of proof. Approved formulations of the most commonly applicable legal tests and evidentiary rules are collected together in the JSB's Specimen Directions, portentously presented as 'the Crown Court Bench Book'.[185] Despite official protestations to the contrary, the JSB's Specimens seem to be hardening into prescriptive rules of practice.[186]

So far as judicial comment on the facts of the case is concerned, the summing-up should include:

a succinct but accurate summary of the issues of fact as to which a decision is required, a correct but concise summary of the evidence and the arguments on both sides and a correct statement of the inferences which the jury are entitled to draw from their particular conclusions about the primary facts.[187]

The summing-up is meant to assist the jury to arrive at a just, epistemically warranted, and properly reasoned verdict. In most cases this aspiration is doubtless fulfilled. Jurors benefit from judicial guidance, not only regarding the doctrinal intricacies of substantive criminal law, but also on practical points of criminal process and procedure. As experienced professional adjudicators, trial judges can help lay jurors to structure the evidence they have heard, in terms of the formal requirements of criminal charges, and to approach the fact-finding task in a systematic, logical fashion. But there are inevitable risks, as well as clear benefits, in this arrangement. It is well-established that during the summing-up the trial judge must emphasize to members of the jury that fact-finding is entirely a matter for them. The jury is the fact-finder in English criminal adjudication, and the judge's opinion on questions of fact carries no formal weight.[188] Yet jurors are very likely to be swayed by

---

[184] See §2.3(a), above.   [185] www.jsboard.co.uk/criminal_law/cbb/index.htm.

[186] As noted, with misgivings, by Roderick Munday, 'Judicial Studies Board Specimen Directions and the Enforcement of Orthodoxy: A Modest Case Study' (2002) 66 *Journal of Criminal Law* 158.

[187] *R* v *Lawrence* [1982] AC 510, 519, HL (Lord Hailsham LC).

[188] Cf. Judicial Studies Board Specimen Direction No 1: 'Our functions in this trial have been and remain quite different. Throughout this trial the law has been my area of responsibility, and I must now give you directions as to the law which applies in this case. When I do so, you must accept those directions and follow them. I must also remind you of the prominent features of the evidence. However, it has always been your responsibility to judge the evidence and decide all the relevant facts of this case, and when you come to consider your verdict you, and you alone, must do that….. Equally, if in the course of my review of the evidence, I appear to express any views concerning the facts, or emphasise a particular aspect of the evidence, do not adopt those views unless you agree with them; and if I do not mention something which you think is

hints and intimations from judicial authority figures, in all the pomp of their wigs and robes. Trial judges, for their part, have occasionally courted controversy by expressing strong opinions about the state of the evidence and its probative value.

The limits of judicial comment on the evidence were identified over a century ago by Channell J in *Cohen and Bateman*:

[A] judge is not only entitled, but ought, to give the jury some assistance on questions of fact as well as on questions of law. Of course, questions of fact are for the jury and not for the judge, yet the judge has experience on the bearing of evidence, and in dealing with the relevancy of questions of fact, and it is therefore right that the jury should have the assistance of the judge. It is not wrong for the judge to give confident opinions upon questions of fact. It is impossible for him to deal with doubtful points of fact unless he can state some of the facts confidently to the jury. It is necessary for him sometimes to express extremely confident opinions. The mere finding, therefore, of very confident expressions in the summing up does not show that it is an improper one. When one is considering the effect of a summing up, one must give credit to the jury for intelligence, and for the knowledge that they are not bound by the expressions of the judge upon questions of fact.[189]

The general rule clearly entrusts trial judges with considerable discretion in commenting on the evidence. However, this is probably an inevitable consequence of the infinitely variable factual permutations thrown up by criminal litigation, and there is no reason to believe that English judges systematically fail to exercise this discretion wisely, or without appropriate restraint.

Difficulties have occasionally arisen where trial judges have apparently concluded that the prosecution case is overwhelming, and have communicated their assessment to the jury in no uncertain terms. This is sometimes described, pejoratively, as 'summing-up for a conviction'. In the posthumous appeal of Derek Bentley, for example, the Court of Appeal concluded 'with genuine diffidence' that Lord Goddard CJ's summing-up in the original 1952 trial had been so one-sided as to 'deny to the appellant that fair trial which is the birthright of every British citizen'.[190] Bridge J's summing-up in the 1975 trial of the Birmingham Six trial has attracted similar criticism for failing to present a balanced overview of the scientific evidence on which the convictions of the accused were substantially based.[191] This criticism is borne out to the extent that, with the benefit of hindsight, we can now say that the prosecution's scientific evidence was not nearly as conclusive as Bridge J made it seem to the jury in his summing-up.[192]

In contrast to the British practice, many US state jurisdictions prohibit judicial comment on the evidence altogether, fearing over-weaning influence by trial judges trespassing on the jury's fact-finding province. This has been criticized as an over-reaction, which leaves juries having to puzzle out for themselves the meaning and forensic implications of

important, you should have regard to it, and give it such weight as you think fit. When it comes to the facts of this case, it is your judgement alone that counts.'

[189] *R v Cohen and Bateman* (1909) 2 Cr App R 197, 208, CCA.

[190] *R v Derek William Bentley (Deceased)* [2001] 1 Cr App R 307, CA, [68] (Lord Bingham CJ).

[191] See James Wood, 'Appendix: Extracts from the Transcript of the Trial of the Birmingham Six, Lancaster, June 1975', in Clive Walker and Keir Starmer (eds.), *Justice in Error* (Blackstone, 1993).

[192] See Mike Redmayne, 'Expert Evidence and Scientific Disagreement' (1997) 30 *UC Davis LR* 1027; Gary Edmond, 'Whigs in Court: Historiographical Problems with Expert Evidence' (2002) 14 *Yale Journal of Law and the Humanities* 123, Part III.

complex directions of law without the benefit of the judge's contextualizing explanations or illustrative applications to the facts of the case.[193] Judicial reticence in commenting on the facts is likely to impair rational adjudication, yet the lay jury's fact-finding autonomy is not meaningfully bolstered by casting them adrift in a sea of confusion. The English approach, trusting to the sound judgment of the trial judge (with the Court of Appeal as the ultimate longstop), seems preferable even if the danger of excessive judicial influence cannot be eliminated entirely. A trial judge's latitude to comment on the evidence is generous, but not unlimited. It stops well short of directing a verdict of guilty, which is emphatically prohibited.[194] Nor, at the other extreme, may the judge inform the jury that the case has not been proved before the prosecutor has even had a chance to lead her evidence.[195]

Over the years, the effectiveness of judicial comment and directions in summing-up has probably been retarded by traditional evidentiary doctrines which appear to rest on unrealistic conceptions of the jury's approach to reasoning about facts and arriving at its verdict. Some rules of criminal procedure, such as the orthodox theory of 'refreshing memory' from out-of-court statements,[196] instruct juries to make highly dubious assumptions seemingly contradicting common sense. Other rules require trial judges to tell juries that they may use evidence for one purpose but not for another – for example, that bad character impacts on the accused's credibility as a witness but cannot be considered in relation to the main issue of guilt or innocence.[197] Yet the efficacy of such instructions is doubtful where, from a common sense perspective, the evidence appears highly probative in relation to the legally prohibited use. Juries will predictably do exactly what they are empanelled to do, which is to arrive at a verdict according to ordinary, everyday understandings and expectations of proof and justice.[198]

Bentham clearly saw, two centuries ago, that rules of law cutting across ordinary epistemic standards are likely to be counterproductive.[199] One can order a person to act in a certain way, but one cannot order – or even coerce – a belief,[200] and hence an instruction to discount the believable will be just as ineffective as an instruction to believe the unbelievable.[201] As Bentham explained, mandatory instructions can be addressed effectively to the will ('Do this or that') but not to the understanding ('Believe this or that').[202] Trying to railroad a jury

[193] Ronald J. Allen, 'Structuring Jury Decisionmaking in Criminal Cases: A Unified Constitutional Approach to Evidentiary Devices' (1980) 94 *Harvard LR* 321, 365, advocates 'eliminating the irrationality of uninformative instructions on inferences and presumptions in favour of accurate judicial comment on the evidence'.

[194] '[T]here are no circumstances in which a judge is entitled to direct a jury to return a verdict of guilty.... [N]o matter how inescapable a judge may consider a conclusion to be, in the sense that any other conclusion would be perverse, it remains his duty to leave that decision to the jury and not to dictate... what that verdict should be': *R v Wang* [2005] 2 Cr App R 8, [2005] UKHL 9, [18], [13] (Lord Bingham). Also see *R v Martin* (1973) 57 Cr App R 279, CA; Edward Griew, 'Directions to Convict' [1972] *Crim LR* 204; M. J. McConville, 'Directions to Convict – A Reply' [1973] *Crim LR* 164.

[195] *Attorney General's Reference (No2 of 2000)* [2001] 1 Cr App R 503, CA.   [196] §8.2(b).

[197] §14.3(b).

[198] The logic and pitfalls of 'common sense' reasoning are more fully explored in Chapter 4.

[199] Bentham, *Rationale of Judicial Evidence* (1827), vol. 3, 219ff.

[200] Forms of psychological torture or indoctrination may be exceptions to this proposition, but are hardly pertinent in the context of the present discussion. It is safe to assume that the rules would be abandoned before the judges went to such extreme lengths to enforce them!

[201] Jurors might be instructed to proceed *as if* they held a certain belief, but the efficacy of such an instruction is very doubtful.

[202] *Rationale of Judicial Evidence* (1827), vol. 6, 151–2. Also see William Twining, *Theories of Evidence: Bentham and Wigmore* (Weidenfeld & Nicolson, 1985), 67.

by issuing peremptory judicial commands is bound to be less effective than clearly explaining legal requirements and seeking to encourage jurors' positive allegiance to the rules of criminal procedure and the values for which they stand. A more measured, collaborative approach to criminal adjudication also requires sensitivity to the subtle ways in which non-factual judgments bear on forensic fact-finding, as we explained in the previous section. Public debate surrounding the right to jury trial has always openly celebrated the infusion of common sense morality and prevailing social standards into criminal adjudication.[203]

It is hardly the fault of jurors if they cannot grasp or implement judicial directions which seem to defy reason or would require extraordinary feats of mental agility or self-deception. For several decades now there has been growing recognition amongst legislators and the senior judiciary that it is pointless to issue judicial directions requiring 'the jury to indulge in the kind of mental gymnastics which even a judge might find difficult to perform, for very little, if any, benefit'.[204] Changes are being implemented,[205] but the process of recasting the law of criminal evidence in conformity with modern expectations is a gradual and still unfinished project. It is further complicated by the need to structure jurors' common sense reasoning in accordance with the dictates of justice. For although lay jurors are the embodiment of ordinary community standards, the responsibilities of criminal adjudication often require them to concentrate and think harder and more carefully than is necessary in most aspects of their everyday lives. Judicial directions establish a framework of law and principle to facilitate jury fact-finding and keep it on track.

(e) APPELLATE REVIEW

We have so far been considering institutional mechanisms of 'input control', that is, ways in which the trial judge may regulate the flow of cases and information to the jury or seek to influence its deliberations before the jury retires to consider its verdict. A further opportunity for judicial control over jury decision-making arises where the accused is granted leave[206] to appeal against conviction to the Court of Appeal (Criminal

---

[203] See, e.g., E. P. Thompson, 'Subduing the Jury', *London Review of Books*, 4 and 18 December 1986; A. Nicol, 'Official Secrets and Jury Vetting' [1979] Crim LR 284; D. Wolchover, 'The Right to Jury Trial' (1986) 136 *NLJ* 530. Cf. *R v Crown Court at Sheffield, ex p. Brownlow* [1980] 2 All ER 444, 452–4, 455–6, where the Court of Appeal described as unconstitutional the practice of investigating the criminal records of prospective jurors with a view to excluding them from the jury panel, except in limited circumstances. Also see *R v Mason* (1980) 71 Cr App R 157; *Attorney General's Guidelines on Jury Checks* [1980] 2 All ER 457.

[204] *R v Robinson* [2006] 1 Cr App R 32, [2005] EWCA Crim 3233, [54]. Also see, e.g., *R v Watts* (1983) 77 Cr App R 126, 129–30, CA ('This in many cases requires the jury to perform difficult feats of intellectual acrobatics... The direction was, of itself, sound in law, but in the circumstances of this case it would have been extremely difficult, if not practically impossible, for the jury to have done what the learned judge was suggesting'); *DPP v Boardman* [1975] AC 421, 459, HL (Lord Cross). The more general trend is indicated by *R v H* [1995] 2 AC 596, 613, HL, *per* Lord Griffiths: 'In the past when jurors were often uneducated and illiterate and the penal laws were of harsh severity, when children could be transported, and men were hanged for stealing a shilling and could not be heard in their own defence, the judges began to fashion rules of evidence to protect the accused from a conviction that they feared might be based on emotion or prejudice rather than a fair evaluation of the facts of the case against him. The judges did not trust the jury to evaluate all the relevant material and evolved many restrictive rules which they deemed necessary to ensure that the accused had a fair trial in the climate of those times. Today with better educated and more literate juries the value of those old restrictive rules of evidence is being re-evaluated and many are being discarded or modified.... This seems to me to be a wholly desirable development of law.'   [205] See esp. §8.6.

[206] A trial judge may grant a certificate that the case is fit for appeal; otherwise an accused who wishes to appeal against conviction must apply to judges of the Court of Appeal for leave to appeal: Criminal Appeal Act 1968, s.1.

Division). This is 'output control' exercised after the jury has already delivered its verdict of guilty.

Ever since the Court of Appeal's predecessor, the Court of Criminal Appeal, was created in 1907,[207] reformers concerned to avoid or correct miscarriages of justice have argued that the Court of Appeal's jurisdiction is too limited and that appellate judges are too conservative and deferential to first instance verdicts. It is almost as if the work of the Court and criticism of its performance are inextricably interwoven. Reform of the Court's powers is rarely off the policy agenda and yet reformers' aspirations seem fated to be permanently disappointed.[208] The most significant institutional innovation of recent years was the creation of the Criminal Cases Review Commission (CCRC),[209] pursuant to recommendations of the Runciman Royal Commission.[210] The CCRC opened for business in March 1997 with the mandate to review, and where necessary re-investigate, alleged miscarriages of justice, and to refer appropriate cases back to the Court of Appeal for reconsideration.[211] The CCRC provides a 'last line of defence' in cases of alleged miscarriage of justice in which routine appeal rights are already exhausted or out of time. Despite some teething troubles (under-funding being not the least of them), the Commission appears to have found its footing and is regularly making referrals back to the Court of Appeal.[212] However, only an eternal optimist would expect this to be the last word on the subject of criminal appeals and post-conviction review, following well over a century of fierce debate on miscarriages of justice and their correction. The fundamental enigma remains: how can alleged defects in a criminal trial be corrected by *a different kind* of appellate process without turning the appeal into a re-run of the trial? If the appeal were to become a second trial, would the

---

[207] On the historical development of defence appeal rights, see Rosemary Pattenden, *English Criminal Appeals 1844–1994* (OUP, 1996).

[208] A theoretically sophisticated explanation for this cycle of reform and disappointed expectations is developed by Richard Nobles and David Schiff, *Understanding Miscarriages of Justice* (OUP, 2000), and summarized in Nobles and Schiff, 'The Never Ending Story: Disguising Tragic Choices in Criminal Justice' (1997) 60 *MLR* 293. But for some doubts, see Roberts (2001) 117 *LQR* 503; and Walker (2000) 20 *Legal Studies* 615.

[209] www.ccrc.gov.uk/. The CCRC serves England, Wales, and Northern Ireland. Scotland has its own – part-time – Commission: www.sccrc.org.uk/home.aspx.

[210] Royal Commission on Criminal Justice, *Report*, Cm 2263 (HMSO, 1993), ch 11.

[211] The Commission assumed this responsibility from the much-criticized C3 Unit of the Home Office, which formerly undertook the task of advising the Home Secretary of the day about which cases of alleged miscarriage of justice might be suitable for a referral to the Court of Appeal under s.17 of the Criminal Appeal Act 1968. See, further, Nick Taylor and Mike Mansfield, 'Post-Conviction Procedures', in Clive Walker and Keir Starmer (eds.), *Miscarriages of Justice: A Review of Justice in Error* (Blackstone, 1999); Kate Malleson, 'The Criminal Cases Review Commission: How Will it Work?' [1995] *Crim LR* 929.

[212] To 28 February 2010 the Commission had made a total of 447 referrals, 290 of which resulted in the conviction being quashed. For generally positive assessments of the CCRC, see Peter Duff, 'Straddling Two Worlds: Reflections of a Retired Criminal Cases Review Commissioner' (2009) 72 *MLR* 693; Graham Zellick, 'The Criminal Cases Review Commission and the Court of Appeal: The Commission's Perspective' [2005] *Crim LR* 937; Clive Walker, 'Miscarriages of Justice and the Correction of Error', in Mike McConville and Geoffrey Wilson (eds.), *The Handbook of the Criminal Justice Process* (OUP, 2002); Peter Duff, 'Criminal Cases Review Commissions and "Deference" to the Courts: The Evaluation of Evidence and Evidentiary Rules' [2001] *Crim LR* 341; Annabelle James, Nick Taylor, and Clive Walker, 'The Criminal Cases Review Commission: Economy, Effectiveness and Justice' [2000] *Crim LR* 140. More critically, see Michael Naughton (ed.), *The Criminal Cases Review Commission: Hope for the Innocent?* (Palgrave, 2010); Richard Nobles and David Schiff, 'The Criminal Cases Review Commission: Establishing a Workable Relationship with the Court of Appeal' [2005] *Crim LR* 173 and 'A Reply to Graham Zellick' [2005] Crim LR 951; David Schiff and Richard Nobles, 'Criminal Appeal Act 1995: The Semantics of Jurisdiction' (1996) 59 *MLR* 573.

first trial not then be downgraded to a prelude to the appeal, which all convicted appellants would presumably claim as their right?[213] One might as well proceed directly to the appeal/second trial. But then would it not be necessary to make provision for a further appeal from that appeal/trial? The intensely practical challenge of restricting the flow of criminal appeals against conviction to a manageable level hovers above the quicksand of this profound theoretical conundrum.[214]

It will be observed, in any event, that the CCRC acts as an investigator and referral agency rather than a final arbiter of justice. The ultimate decision to allow or dismiss a referred appeal remains with the Court of Appeal, so that the Court's legal powers, and its exercise of them, are no less significant than they were before the CCRC's creation. The basic test applied by the Court of Appeal in determining an appeal against conviction is contained in section 2(1) of the Criminal Appeal Act 1968. Section 2 was redrafted by the Criminal Appeal Act 1995 in terms of a single consolidated criterion, the 'safety' of the conviction:

Criminal Appeal Act 1968, section 2 (as amended)
   (1) ...the Court of Appeal –
       (a) shall allow an appeal against conviction if they think that the conviction is unsafe; and
       (b) shall dismiss such an appeal in any other case.

The old version of section 2 stated three grounds for allowing an appeal: (a) that the conviction was 'unsafe or unsatisfactory'; (b) owing to 'a wrong decision of any question of law'; or (c) 'that there was a material irregularity in the course of the trial'.[215] The new, unified test of 'safety' was explicitly introduced into Parliament as a consolidation measure having no bearing on the substance of the test to be applied.[216] In *Chalkley*,[217] however, the Court of Appeal seemed to equate 'safety' with factual guilt, observing that '[t]he court has no power under the substituted section 2(1) to allow an appeal if it does not think the conviction unsafe but is dissatisfied in some way with what went on at the trial... [we agree] that it is an important change... particularly in those cases where, although the court is of the view that justice has not been seen to be done, it is satisfied that it has been done – that is, that the conviction is safe'.[218] The clear implication was that the Court of Appeal no longer had the power to do justice by quashing a conviction obtained after an unfair trial, unless the type of unfairness involved happened, in the circumstances of particular cases, to cast doubt on the factual basis – the 'safety', narrowly construed – of the conviction.

---

[213] The International Covenant on Civil and Political Rights, Art 14(5) states: 'Everyone convicted of a crime shall have the right to his conviction and sentence being reviewed by a higher tribunal according to law.' For discussion of the right to appeal as one component of the right to a fair trial, see Stefan Trechsel with Sarah J Summers, *Human Rights in Criminal Proceedings* (OUP, 2005), ch 14.

[214] Richard Nobles and David Schiff, 'The Right to Appeal and Workable Systems of Justice' (2002) 65 *MLR* 676.

[215] The three grounds were subject to 'the proviso': 'Provided that the court may, notwithstanding that they are of opinion that the point raised in the appeal might be decided in favour of the appellant, dismiss the appeal if they consider that no miscarriage of justice has actually occurred.'

[216] On the legislative background, see J. C. Smith, 'The Criminal Appeal Act 1995: (1) Appeals Against Conviction' [1995] *Crim LR* 920.   [217] *R v Chalkley* [1998] QB 848, CA.

[218] ibid. 868.

Fortunately, the *Chalkley* interpretation of section 2(1) was short-lived (and anyway expressly stated to be subject to the Human Rights Act's coming into force). In subsequent decisions the Court of Appeal preferred a broader interpretation of section 2(1), assimilating 'safety' to the concept of 'fair trial' employed in Article 6 of the ECHR,[219] and this approach was soon endorsed by the House of Lords.[220] The settled position was succinctly summarized by Lord Woolf CJ in *Hanratty*:

[A] conviction can be unsafe for two distinct reasons that may, but do not necessarily, overlap. The first reason being that there is doubt as to the safety of the conviction and the second being that the trial was materially flawed. The second reason can be independent of guilt because of the fundamental constitutional requirement that even a guilty defendant is entitled, before being found guilty, to have a trial which conforms with at least the minimum standards of what is regarded in this jurisdiction as being an acceptable criminal trial. These standards include those that safeguard a defendant from serious procedural, but not technical, unfairness. A technical flaw is excluded because it is wrong to elevate the procedural rules that govern a trial to a level where they become an obstacle as opposed to an aid to achieving justice.[221]

The distinction invoked by the Lord Chief Justice between mere 'technical flaws' and serious procedural defects is further explored in Chapter 5's discussion of 'fair trials'. For the purposes of understanding the procedural framework in which the English law of criminal evidence currently operates, it is sufficient to know that appellate review of the 'safety' of convictions extends beyond their factual accuracy to an examination of procedural rectitude. One might say – though the Court itself has never used this terminology – that convictions must be *morally* as well as factually safe, meaning that the guilt of the accused must have been proved, by admissible evidence, to the requisite standard in fair trial proceedings and by due process of law. This interpretation brings the test applied by the Court of Appeal under section 2(1) of the CAA 1968 broadly into line with the European Court of Human Rights' fair trial jurisprudence and also with the domestic English law doctrine of abuse of process.[222] The possibility of introducing further legislation to restrict the powers of the Court of Appeal to allow appeals against conviction on, broadly speaking, 'due process' grounds, has been mooted in policy circles,[223] but credible proposals have not thus far been produced. It would cut against the grain of modern developments and contradict our fifth foundational principle of criminal evidence (as well as conflicting with numerous specific evidentiary doctrines discussed in later chapters) to require the Court of Appeal to uphold a conviction that, although probably factually accurate, was produced by a trial tainted by major rights violations, pronounced procedural unfairness, or serious official impropriety.

In relation to findings of fact, the Court of Appeal's general approach is characterized by deference to the trial court. The general, unreasoned, verdict of guilty, combined with

---

[219] *R* v *Togher, Doran and Parsons* [2001] 1 Cr App R 457, CA.

[220] *R* v *Forbes* [2001] 1 Cr App R 430, HL, [30] (Lord Bingham).

[221] *R* v *Hanratty (Deceased)* [2002] EWCA Crim 1141, [2002] 2 Cr App R 419, CA, [95].

[222] §2.5(b), above.

[223] Office for Criminal Justice Reform, *Quashing Convictions – Report of A Review by the Home Secretary, Lord Chancellor and Attorney General* (September 2006); the shortcomings of which are mercilessly exposed by J. R. Spencer, 'Quashing Convictions for Procedural Irregularities' [2007] *Crim LR* 835.

procedural mechanisms designed to ensure that the jury's private deliberations remain forever secret,[224] make it very difficult in practice for the Court of Appeal rationally to second-guess the jury's assessment of the evidence. Even in cases which appear less than compelling on paper, the Court of Appeal is inclined to say that it will not interfere with the jury's verdict because the jury is far better placed than an appellate tribunal to assess witness credibility, having had the benefit of seeing witnesses testify in person and observing their demeanour. As Lord Widgery CJ observed in *R v Cooper*:

It has been said over and over again throughout the years that this court must recognise the advantage which a jury has in seeing and hearing the witnesses, and if all the material was before the jury and the summing-up was impeccable, this court should not lightly interfere.[225]

The English Court of Appeal does not have a general power to review the evidential sufficiency of convictions similar to that exercised by some American courts.[226] Nonetheless, as Lord Widgery proceeded to elaborate in *Cooper*, the Court of Appeal may allow the accused's appeal where, despite the formal propriety of a conviction, the court harbours a 'lurking doubt' about its safety:

[I]n cases of this kind the court must in the end ask itself a subjective question, whether we are content to let the matter stand as it is, or whether there is not some lurking doubt in our minds which makes us wonder whether an injustice has been done. This is a reaction which may not be based strictly on the evidence as such; it is a reaction which can be produced by the general feel of the case as the court experiences it.[227]

The 'lurking doubt' test has been criticized, for its subjectivity and vagueness as well as for the infrequency with which it is employed in practice. There are very few reported cases. Coupled with the permissive *Galbraith* standard, which allows cases to go forward to a jury's verdict even where the judge thinks that the prosecution's evidence is too weak to constitute proof beyond reasonable doubt, this rather undemanding standard of judicial oversight and regulation might be thought to expose the accused to inflated risks of wrongful conviction. The justification for appellate deference towards first-instance fact-finding is further assailed by extensive behavioural science research questioning the supposed link between witness demeanour and credibility.[228]

---

[224] It is a contempt of court, punishable by a substantial fine or imprisonment, for a juror to divulge any information regarding what took place in the juryroom (other than in the course of returning a verdict in the case), or for any other person to attempt to solicit such disclosures from a juror: Contempt of Court Act 1981, s.8. [225] *R v Cooper* [1969] 1 QB 267, 271, CA.

[226] As occurred in the keenly observed 'British nanny' case, in which Louise Woodward's conviction of murdering baby Matthew Eappen was, somewhat controversially, substituted with a conviction of manslaughter by order of the trial judge. Judge Hiller Zobel concluded that 'after having heard *all* the evidence and considered the interests of justice' this 'sad scenario' was 'most fairly characterized as manslaughter, not mandatory-life-sentence murder. I view the evidence as disclosing confusion, fright, and bad judgment, rather than rage or malice': *Commonwealth v Woodward* 7 Mass L Rptr 449 (10 November 1997) (Mass. Superior Court), affirmed 694 N E 2d 1277 (1998) (Mass. Supreme Judicial Court). Note, however, that the power invoked by Judge Zobel in this case – Massachusetts Rule of Criminal Procedure 25(b)(2) (reduction in verdict) – extends beyond mere evidential insufficiency to permit judges to substitute a just verdict for the jury's original determination, taking account of all the circumstances of the case.

[227] *R v Cooper* [1969] 1 QB 267, 271, CA. Also see *Stafford v DPP* [1974] AC 878, HL; *R v B (Brian S)* [2003] 2 Cr App R 197, [2003] EWCA Crim 319, CA. [228] §7.1(c).

Whilst these criticisms may be warranted to some extent, they probably underestimate the practical and symbolic significance of jury trial in sustaining public confidence in criminal adjudication and conferring legitimacy on trial outcomes in England and Wales. The criminal trial is a unique and essentially unrepeatable public event. Guilty verdicts conveying moral censure and imposing serious penalties (up to and including loss of liberty) are authenticated by the lay jury's seal of approval after the proper order of process has been observed. Appellate tribunals cannot recreate the events of a trial. If a serious procedural irregularity has occurred, or the accused's rights have been seriously infringed, then the Court of Appeal may be prepared to quash the conviction and, in effect, declare the trial a nullity on procedural grounds. The Court has doubtless been more willing to do so since its powers to order retrials were significantly expanded by the Criminal Justice Act 1988.[229] But even a retrial, though often clearly preferable to abandoning particular proceedings entirely, is only an opportunity for a re-run. It does not recreate the original, unique, trial event. The judges' intuitive grasp of the deeper significance of the criminal trial – which may be characterized as a pivotal moment in which a community forges its moral and political identity[230] – may be part of the explanation for appellate court deference to jury verdicts, rather than self-abnegating submission to lay fact-finding or misplaced faith in witness demeanour as the authentic barometer of credibility.

(f) QUASHING ACQUITTALS

Permitting the defence to appeal against conviction is one thing; allowing the prosecutor to appeal an acquittal quite another. For most of the history of the common law, the jury's acquittal has been final. Those who have stood their trial have been insulted from the 'double jeopardy' of repeat prosecution, in formal legal terms by the 'pleas in bar' *autrefois acquit* and, for those previously convicted, *autrefois convict*. The pleas in bar, which are strictly confined to repeat prosecutions for *the same* offence, are supplemented by the somewhat broader jurisdiction to stay unfair prosecutions as an abuse of process where fresh charges arise out of previously litigated facts, as we have already seen.[231]

English law now permits jury acquittals to be set aside on two discrete grounds. First, an acquittal may be quashed if it is shown to have been procured through an offence against the administration of justice such as witness intimidation or jury tampering.[232] This can be rationalized in accordance with traditional principles by saying that an accused who sets out to cheat the system has not genuinely stood his trial and submitted to the judgement

---

[229] Section 7(1) of the Criminal Appeal Act 1968, as amended, provides that '[w]here the Court of Appeal allow an appeal against conviction and it appears to the court that the interests of justice so require, they may order the appellant to be retried'. Prior to the 1988 Act's amendment the power to order a retrial was limited to cases involving fresh evidence, which constitute only a tiny proportion of appeals heard by the Court.

[230] Cf. Sherman J. Clark, 'The Courage of Our Convictions' (1999) 97 *Michigan LR* 2381, 2382 ('the way in which we go about performing certain difficult societal tasks says something about what we stand for, what kind of people we are, and what sort of community we want to be. I suggest that the passing of judgment on our fellow citizens is just such a task. How we do it may be as important to us as what we do'); Robert P. Burns, 'Some Realism (and Idealism) about the Trial' (1997) 31 *Georgia LR* 715, 763–4 ('The trier's judgment in a particular case is an act of self-definition: a judgment about the meaning of this case is a determination of political and moral identity.... In common sense terms, it inevitably says as much about who the trier is as about "what happened"').   [231] §2.5(b), above.

[232] CPIA 1996, ss.54–57. These provisions have apparently never been invoked.

of his peers in the first place. His formal acquittal was a mere sham, and setting it aside so that fresh proceedings may be commenced does no more than formalize a subsisting legal nullity.[233] The second basis for quashing an acquittal, introduced by the Criminal Justice Act 2003, is the post-trial discovery of 'new and compelling evidence'.[234] This is a far more controversial reform, which appears to mark a significant departure from traditional principles of common law criminal procedure.[235] It extends only to serious offences and is subject to demanding judicial safeguards. The Director of Public Prosecutions must apply to the Court of Appeal for an order quashing the acquittal, which will be granted only where new and compelling evidence of the accused's guilt is adduced and granting the order would serve the interests of justice. Even if the acquittal is quashed it does not necessarily follow that a retrial will be possible.[236] It is conceivable, for example, that adverse pre-trial publicity[237] would lead to fresh proceedings being stayed as an abuse of process. It must be stressed that the procedure for quashing acquittals is an exceptional post-verdict remedy, quite distinct from the normal appellate process. An acquittal can be quashed only if the Court of Appeal is satisfied that there is *new* and *compelling* evidence of guilt. There is no jurisdiction to quash an acquittal where, for example, the Court of Appeal thinks that the accused is probably guilty but the new evidence is insufficiently probative to constitute compelling proof of his guilt.

To-date, only a tiny number of acquittals has been quashed.[238] But this does not mean that curtailment[239] of the ancient double jeopardy prohibition is 'merely symbolic'. The finality of *all* acquittals of serious offences in England and Wales has been compromised, to the extent that *any* such acquittal could conceivably be reopened on the discovery of

---

[233] The issue is complicated where the accused himself is not responsible for witness tampering or any similar major procedural defect in the trial. One might say that exactly the same analysis applies: if the trial was a nullity the accused was never properly acquitted, there was no 'trial' in the technical sense (only a flawed procedure resembling a trial), and the accused can be prosecuted again like any other person who has yet to stand their trial. On the other hand, it is possible to imagine scenarios in which applying the strict logic of procedural nullity might seem hard on an accused who has ostensibly already been tried and acquitted. At the very least, the argument for retrial is far stronger where the logic of nullity is reinforced by the moral and legal precept that nobody should profit through their own wrongdoing.

[234] CJA 2003, Part 10: see Ian Dennis, 'The Criminal Justice Act 2003: Prosecution Appeals and Retrial for Serious Offences' [2004] *Crim LR* 619.

[235] See Paul Roberts, 'Double Jeopardy Law Reform: A Criminal Justice Commentary' (2002) 65 *MLR* 393; Paul Roberts, 'Justice for All? Two Bad Arguments (and Several Good Suggestions) for Resisting Double Jeopardy Reform' (2002) 6 *E & P* 197; David S. Rudstein, 'Retrying the Acquitted in England, Part I: The Exception to the Rule Against Double Jeopardy for 'New and Compelling Evidence'' (2007) 8 *San Diego International Law Journal* 387. Cf. Ian Dennis, 'Rethinking Double Jeopardy: Justice and Finality in Criminal Process' [2000] *Crim LR* 933; David Hamer, 'The Expectation of Incorrect Acquittals and the "New and Compelling Evidence" Exception to Double Jeopardy' [2009] *Crim LR* 63.

[236] *R v Andrews* [2009] 1 Cr App R 26, [2008] EWCA Crim 2908, [42], *per* Lord Judge CJ: 'It is ultimately for the court to examine the interests of justice, and the interests of justice cannot be served by a retrial of an acquitted defendant unless the prospects of conviction at the retrial are very good. That is not resuscitating the rule against double jeopardy. It simply represents the practical application of the statutory requirements that an individual who has been acquitted should not be unduly harassed by a second set of proceedings, with all the complications and difficulty and interference with his ordinary life which this would inevitably entail, when the proposed case for the prosecution is nevertheless already irremediably flawed.'

[237] CJA 2003, s.82, authorizes further reporting restrictions *in relation to the application for quashing an acquittal*. But this will not necessarily cure any adverse publicity following the original acquittal itself.

[238] The first case was *R v Dunlop* [2007] 1 Cr App R 8, [2006] EWCA Crim 1354.

[239] Cf. *R v Andrews* [2009] 1 Cr App R 26, [2008] EWCA Crim 2908, [41], *per* Lord Judge CJ: 'Double jeopardy as a prohibition against a second trial following an acquittal was abolished by the Act.'

new evidence. It is also conceivable that the police and prosecution might in future pursue orders quashing acquittals more energetically,[240] although the Court of Appeal has already indicated that 'compelling' evidence is a tough standard that it intends to police rigorously.[241] At this juncture, we may conclude that a jury's 'not guilty' verdict is not, in formal terms, quite as final as it used to be in England and Wales, but for the foreseeable future the trial jury's verdict will continue to be the last word in the vast majority of cases resulting in an acquittal.

2.6 THE INSTITUTIONAL CONTEXT OF CRIMINAL EVIDENCE

Rules and principles of criminal evidence must be understood in terms of the institutional context in which they operate. For England and Wales, the paradigmatic model of criminal adjudication is adversarial jury trial. To be sure, modern British adversarialism is far removed from the archetypal no-holds-barred legal contest mimicking trial by battle; and the rise of managerial judging within the framework of the CrimPR 2010 is gradually eroding adversarial tendencies even further. It is also fair to point out that juries actually hear comparatively few cases. Nor do successive governments seemingly ever tire of finding new ways to limit access to trial by jury. Downgrading offences to 'summary only' is a tried-and-tested tactic.[242] Long-standing discussion of judge-only trials in serious or complex fraud cases[243] has recently borne fruit,[244] alongside provision for non-jury bench trials where there is 'a real and present danger' of jury tampering.[245] To the extent that sweeping historical generalizations are ever valid, it is plausible to contend that both adversary process[246] and trial by jury[247] are in decline in modern criminal adjudication.

Yet there are counter-tendencies, the picture is mixed, and progress (or decay, depending on one's perspective) is uneven. ECHR jurisprudence notably reinforces many fea-

---

[240] As advocated by David Hamer, 'The Expectation of Incorrect Acquittals and the "New and Compelling Evidence" Exception to Double Jeopardy' [2009] *Crim LR* 63.

[241] Applications were rejected in *R v B(J)* [2009] EWCA Crim 1036; and *R v G(G) and B(S)* [2009] EWCA Crim 1207.

[242] Thus, common assault was reclassified as 'summary only' by the Criminal Justice Act 1988, s.39. But note that successive attempts to remove offences of theft and dishonesty, however apparently trivial, from the jury's purview have been strenuously resisted, on the basis that anyone at risk of receiving such a serious stain on their moral character is entitled, if they so choose, to be judged by their peers.

[243] See Fraud Trials Committee (Chairman: Lord Roskill), *Report* (HMSO, 1986); Michael Levi, *The Investigation, Prosecution and Trial of Serious Fraud*, RCCJ Research Study No 14 (HMSO, 1993, ch 5; Mr Justice Henry, 'Serious Fraud, Long Trials and Criminal Justice' [1992] *Denning LJ* 75.

[244] CJA 2003, s.43 (not yet in force).

[245] CJA 2003, s.44, which came into force on 24 July 2006 and was applied in *R v Twomey* [2009] 2 Cr App R 25, [2009] EWCA Crim 1035. However, the government's additional proposal to allow the accused to elect judge-only 'bench trial' was defeated. For general discussion, see Lord Justice Auld, Review of the Criminal Courts of England and Wales (TSO, 2001), 177–81; Sean Doran and John Jackson, 'The Case for Jury Waiver' [1997] *Crim LR* 155; Sean Doran, John D. Jackson, and Michael L. Seigel, 'Rethinking Adversariness in Nonjury Criminal Trials' (1995) 23 *American Journal of Criminal Law* 1.

[246] Mirjan R. Damaška, *Evidence Law Adrift* (Yale UP, 1997), chs 4–5.

[247] Sally Lloyd-Bostock and Cheryl Thomas, 'The Continuing Decline of the English Jury', in Neil Vidmar (ed.), *World Jury Systems* (OUP, 2000).

tures of adversarialism but may one day challenge trial by jury. Article 6 fair trial rights assume a broadly adversarial structure to criminal proceedings, in which the rights of the defence must be respected by the police and prosecuting authorities, and vindicated by the judges. Observing how the ECHR has fostered adversary process in jurisdictions with an 'inquisitorial' procedural heritage, English law is unlikely to foreswear the adversarial trial at just the time when our continental neighbours are being persuaded of its merits. However, another strand of Article 6 jurisprudence requiring fully-reasoned fact-finding in criminal cases could be on a collision course with common law practice. In those few continental jurisdictions making use of lay juries, the problem of stating the reasons for a jury's decision has been solved, either by requiring the jury to respond to specific questions with particularized answers (the English 'special verdict') or by having professional judges deliberate together with lay jurors and take responsibility for writing a reasoned verdict on their collective behalf. Yet one only has to state these 'solutions' to appreciate how radically they depart from the traditional British conception of jury trial, implying an unreasoned general verdict by a lay tribunal with no professional legal involvement in its deliberations. Thus far, the Strasbourg court's pronouncements on the reasoning of English juries have been relatively modest and unthreatening.[248] However, the demands of Article 6, as interpreted by European judges for whom a reasoned verdict is an axiomatic pre-condition of fair trial, could conceivably become more onerous, sooner or later. Whether such demands could be accommodated without affecting the essential character of trial by jury, as understood and practised in England and Wales, only time will tell.[249] This issue has all the makings of an instructive test-case which might in due course shed light on the extent to which universalistic human rights standards can be integrated with talismanic domestic procedural traditions in a time of cosmopolitan legality.

The administration of criminal justice is almost perpetually in the grip of one 'crisis' or another, and yet jury trial, by any measure, remains very popular and highly-rated: as an abstract symbol of justice, but also in more practical currency by citizens who serve on juries and criminal justice professionals and researchers who evaluate their performance.[250] Notwithstanding its – by now, very well-rehearsed – drawbacks and limitations,[251]

---

[248] *Sander* v *UK* (2001) 31 EHRR 44, upholding an Article 6 complaint on the basis of a juror's suspected racial bias, marks the limit of the Strasbourg court's ambitions in this regard to-date, but even that went too far for some: cf. Michael Zander, 'The Complaining Juror' (2000) 150 *NLJ* 723 (19 May), suggesting that 'the Strasbourg court does not sufficiently understand or value the jury system'. For further discussion, see Pamela R. Ferguson, 'The Criminal Jury in England and Scotland: the Confidentiality Principle and the Investigation of Impropriety' (2006) 10 *E & P* 180; Gillian Daly and Rosemary Pattenden, 'Racial Bias and the English Criminal Trial Jury' (2005) 64 *Cambridge Law Journal* 678; Katie Quinn, 'Jury Bias and the European Convention on Human Rights: A Well-Kept Secret?' [2004] *Crim LR* 998.

[249] For a thoughtful discussion suggesting some room for manoeuvre, see John D. Jackson, 'Making Juries Accountable' (2002) 50 *American Journal of Comparative Law* 477. Cf. J. C. Smith, 'Is Ignorance Bliss? Could Jury Trial Survive Investigation' (1998) 38 *Medicine, Science and the Law* 98, 98, 105: 'An error actually made in the jury room cannot be of less significance than a potential error which may have been induced by a mistake in summing up or in the admission of evidence. But we do not know about it – and we do not want to know. Ignorance is bliss … If we are to keep jury trial – and there is an overwhelming sentiment in favour of doing so – it is perhaps better not to know'.

[250] Most recently, Cheryl Thomas, *Are Juries Fair?* Ministry of Justice Research Series 1/10 (2010).

[251] Cf. Penny Darbyshire's broadside warning against 'sentimental attachment to the symbol of the jury … an anti-democratic, irrational and haphazard legislator, whose erratic and secret decisions run counter to the rule of law': 'The Lamp that Shows that Freedom Lives – Is it Worth the Candle?' [1991] *Crim LR* 740, 741, 750.

the institution of the lay jury still inspires implicit trust and remarkable loyalty in all sectors of society. 'Useless Jury Allows Dangerous Criminal to Walk Free' is one banner headline lambasting ineffective criminal justice policy or institutional incompetence that the tabloids never seem to run (perhaps because implying that one's readers are gullible or stupid is not likely to sell many newspapers). Even a Government with a massive Commons majority can be defeated on jury reform, since few causes are more calculated to rouse the passions of parliamentarians than (in the time-honoured phrase) the ancient right of freeborn Englishmen to trial by jury.[252] Bolstered by the inherent cultural conservatism and institutional stasis characteristic of criminal proceedings, these powerful forces can be expected to insulate adversarial jury trial from potentially destructive winds of change.

One can insist that rules and principles of criminal evidence have been moulded by their institutional context without falling into the trap of thinking that common law evidence was sired by the jury. Rules of admissibility, to be sure, but also procedural doctrines of abuse of process, no case to answer, the trial judge's summing-up, appellate review, and – the most recent addition – exceptions to the double jeopardy prohibition are all pieces of the broader institutional framework specifying the terms of the partnership between judge and jury in English criminal trials. The orthodox division of adjudicative labour, according to which the jury finds facts and the judge determines the law, is only a rough approximation of actual trial practice. Judges are often required to make factual determinations and juries routinely make normative judgements. Since the law of criminal procedure is central to the allocation of judges' and jurors' respective fact-finding and law-applying responsibilities, the competing objectives, values, and policies shaping the procedural mechanisms examined in this chapter will naturally be encountered time and again, in new but still instantly recognizable configurations, as we explore detailed rules and principles of criminal evidence in the following pages.

---

[252] Twice in 2000 Home Secretary Jack Straw attempted to abolish the accused's right to elect jury trial in cases 'triable either way'. He encountered a storm of public protest and his two Mode of Trial Bills suffered humiliating defeats in the House of Lords: see Sean Enright, '"A Silly and Dangerous Bill"' (2000) 150 *NLJ* 12 (14 January); David Wolchover and Anthony Heaton-Armstrong, 'The Right to Jury Trial' (2000) 150 *NLJ* 158 (11 February); Michael Zander, 'Why Jack Straw's Jury Reform Has Lost the Plot' (2000) 150 *NLJ* 366 (10 March); Lee Bridges, 'Welcome Conversion' (Letter) (2000) 150 *NLJ* 380 (17 March); Jack Straw, 'Changes to Mode of Trial' (2000) 150 *NLJ* 670 (12 May); Sean Enright, 'Facts, Not Assertions' (2000) 150 *NLJ* 724 (19 May) and 'A Graceful Withdrawal?' (2000) 150 *NLJ* 1560 (27 October). Cf. Peter Duff, 'The Defendant's Right to Trial by Jury: A Neighbour's View' [2000] *Crim LR* 85.

3

ADMISSIBLE EVIDENCE

3.1 THE LEGAL FRAMEWORK OF ADMISSIBILITY

Chapter 1 introduced the ideals, objectives, and foundational principles of criminal evidence. These are the raw normative materials shaping our discipline. Chapter 2 then sketched out the rules, principles, institutions, and practices forming the procedural context of criminal adjudication. In this chapter we examine the concept of 'evidence'. Broadly understood as an ordinary English word, 'evidence' simply means information. We pick out particular pieces of information and designate them 'evidence' when they are believed to be interesting or useful for some purpose, typically for the purpose of learning new facts about the world and acting on them. This is a fundamentally epistemic and intensely practical enterprise.

Evidence can be classified and differentiated adjectively. 'Judicial evidence', 'legal evidence', and – in its original, literal sense – 'forensic evidence' are all serviceable synonyms for information in the litigation context. Evidence is the hard currency of proof. Criminal charges are proved by pertinent information sufficient to persuade the trier of fact to form a belief that the accused is guilty to some specified standard of certainty, traditionally expressed in criminal proceedings as 'proof beyond reasonable doubt'.[1] Evidence might also prove innocence, of course, but English criminal proceedings are not structured to assess whether the accused is actually innocent of the charges brought against him. Unless the accused is proved guilty by admissible evidence he is entitled to be acquitted, innocent or otherwise.[2] As in most other contexts in which questions of evidence arise, information in criminal litigation is culled from a variety of sources and may be classified in different ways. Later in the chapter we will review the principal classifications of judicial or forensic evidence and suggest that the sources of information in criminal litigation are actually more diverse, interesting, and potentially problematic, than orthodox accounts of the Law of Evidence typically acknowledge. Before reconsidering taxonomies of evidence, however, we need to elucidate the elementary proposition, introduced in general terms in the previous chapter, that evidence presented to the fact-finder must be legally admissible.

The law of admissibility regulates whether a particular piece of evidence should be received – or 'admitted' – into the trial. The question, 'Is e (some item of evidence) admissible?' is shorthand for asking: 'Should the fact-finder be informed about e and given the opportunity of taking e into account in arriving at its verdict?' As we saw in the previous

---

[1] Burdens and standards of proof are explained in Chapter 6.   [2] §2.3(c)(i); §6.1.

chapter,[3] questions of admissibility are always questions of law for the judge even though they frequently involve a preliminary assessment of factual issues. In this way, judges regulate the informational resources available to the fact-finder. The judicial role is limited to discarding unhelpful or inappropriate information – a filtering exercise – whereas the jury is charged with drawing factual inferences and arriving at conclusions based on the entirety of the evidence presented at trial. This summary, broadly speaking, encapsulates the institutional division of fact-finding labour in English criminal adjudication.

The overarching admissibility inquiry can be conceptualized and structured in different ways. The simplest and conceptually most elegant approach would be to say that evidence is admissible just insofar as it satisfies the principles of criminal evidence and appropriate evidentiary standards. The task for a book like this one would then be to elucidate those principles and provide illustrations of their concrete application. Much of the following exposition does precisely that. It is our aspiration to get away from the rule-fixated approach of orthodox treatments of common law evidence in order to focus on general principles. However, it cannot be denied that courts and legal practitioners, as well as many Evidence teachers and scholars, still think of common law evidence in terms of a series of technical rules and their exceptions. Getting to grips with this disciplinary orthodoxy presents certain pedagogical challenges. For this reason only, it is convenient to regard the admissibility inquiry as involving three discrete stages or 'hurdles to admissibility'. These stages/hurdles correspond to a series of questions that trial judges (or anybody else interested in assessing evidentiary admissibility) must ask themselves in order to determine whether a particular item of evidence should be admitted or excluded in the proceedings:

1. Is the evidence relevant?

2. Is the evidence subject to any exclusionary rule(s)?

3. Is the evidence subject to any inclusionary exceptions to the applicable exclusionary rule(s)?

Assessments of legal admissibility can be fitted into this simple tripartite structure in every case. The questions are cumulative. Only if the first, relevancy, question is answered in the affirmative is it necessary to consider the second question. Irrelevant evidence is conclusively inadmissible for all purposes. However, relevant evidence which successfully surmounts the first hurdle to admissibility may still be rendered inadmissible by the application of an exclusionary rule, such as the hearsay prohibition, rules regulating the examination of witnesses, or constraints on the admissibility of bad character evidence. Relevance is always a necessary, but never a sufficient condition, of legal admissibility.

If the evidence is relevant and there are no applicable exclusionary rules it is admissible: there is, in other words, no legal objection to adducing it in the trial if the tendering party wishes to do so. On the other hand, evidence caught by an exclusionary rule is not necessarily conclusively inadmissible. At the third stage of the inquiry one needs to ask whether there are any applicable inclusionary exceptions that can rescue the evidence from presumptive inadmissibility. As we will see in subsequent chapters, it turns out that English law's rules of exclusion are riddled with exceptions applicable to particular types

[3] §2.5(a).

of evidence. There is consequently usually a decent chance that evidence rendered presumptively inadmissible by the application of an exclusionary rule at the second stage of the admissibility inquiry can be brought under the protective wing of an inclusionary exception at the third and final stage of the analysis.

The basic structure of legal admissibility is depicted graphically by the flowchart presented in Figure 3.1. This is the best way to approach questions of admissibility in a logical and systematic fashion, avoiding technical errors or material omissions – provided that the structure itself is not taken too seriously. It should not be reified or fetishized. Regardless of how the admissibility inquiry is conceptualized, the only issue of any practical significance is whether the evidence in question is fit to be placed before the fact-finder. Put another way, is there any reason why the fact-finder should *not* be told about the evidence? Each of the principal exclusionary rules listed on the left-hand side of the flowchart, all of which purport to answer this question affirmatively for certain kinds of evidence, is examined in detail in later chapters. Note that the general criteria of admissibility apply to questions asked of witnesses in cross-examination as well as to evidence adduced in-chief. The practical significance of this stricture will become clear in Chapter 8 where the procedural rules governing witness testimony are reviewed and critically evaluated.

Relevance is a principle of logic which the law merely adopts and adapts to its own purposes. Irrespective of their local legal colour and doctrinal peculiarities, all legal systems – just like every other type of factual inquiry – aspire to conform with principles of relevance. Whatever the matters under investigation happen to be, it would be irrational to seek out irrelevant information or to be swayed by it in drawing conclusions. As Thayer put it, '[t]here is a principle – not so much a rule of evidence as a proposition involved in the very conception of a rational system of evidence, as contrasted with the old formal mechanical systems – which forbids receiving anything irrelevant, not logically probative'.[4] Conversely, it would be presumptively irrational to ignore relevant information, *unless there are good epistemic or normative reasons for ignoring or discounting it.*

To insist that relevancy is a precondition of logical inquiry is not yet to define concrete standards or criteria of relevance. Although English law claims to take 'logic and common sense' as its guiding lights, we will see in the next section that concepts of 'legal relevance' are not entirely straightforward or uncontroversial. Chapter 4 will explore ways in which 'common sense' is itself a complex and sometimes problematical notion.

Exclusionary rules of evidence might be conceptualized as evidentiary standards purporting to encapsulate – or at least to serve as durable proxies for – good epistemic or normative reasons for ignoring relevant information in criminal adjudication. Later chapters will identify, for particular exclusionary doctrines, what these reasons are conventionally said to be. We will also try to assess whether these rationales are truly good enough to warrant withholding from the fact-finder information which *ex hypothesi* is relevant to resolving disputed questions of fact.

---

[4] James Bradley Thayer, *A Preliminary Treatise on Evidence at the Common Law* (Little, Brown & Co, 1898), 264. Also see J. L. Montrose, 'Basic Concepts of the Law of Evidence' (1954) 70 *LQR* 527; *Wigmore on Evidence* (Tillers revision), vol. 1A, §37.

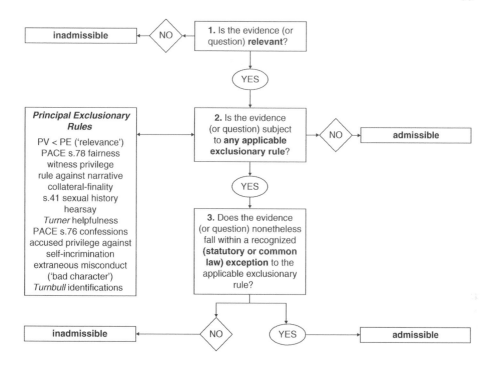

Fig. 3.1 Admissibility Flowchart

NB: The test of legal admissibility must be applied to both (a) evidence adduced in-chief; and (b) questions put in cross-examination of an opposing witness.

Lawyers frequently refer to the judicial 'discretion' to exclude evidence,[5] but this usage can be misleading. Admissibility standards vary in the extent to which they call for an exercise of 'discretionary' judgment in their application. The effect of some rules is almost automatic, once the conditions for their application have been found to exist, whilst others leave trial judges with much greater room for manoeuvre in deciding whether to admit or exclude contested evidence. The difference, however, is a matter of degree, inadequately expressed by a categorical distinction between *rules* of admissibility and judicial *discretion*. Provided that it is understood that rules come in different shapes and sizes and require more or less fine-grained contextual applications to the facts of the instant case, there is no need to insist on a further, superfluous, subdivision of admissibility standards.

3.2 RELEVANCE

Relevance describes a relationship such that one fact, *x*, has some material bearing on another fact, *y*. The contours and content of this relationship are defined by the aims and methods of the overarching enterprise. Expressed more colloquially, relevance is a function of what you want to know and why you want to know it. The enterprise of criminal

---

[5] §1.4. For a comprehensive, if dated, survey, see Rosemary Pattenden, *Judicial Discretion and Criminal Litigation* (OUP, 1990).

adjudication, we have said, is centrally concerned with the proof of disputed allegations of criminal conduct. Information relevant to this type of inquiry must be capable of shedding light on the truth of past events in order to assist the fact-finder to arrive at an accurate and just verdict. In simple terms, x is relevant to y for our purposes if x contributes towards proving or disproving y.

(a) THE LOGIC OF RELEVANCE

James Fitzjames Stephen proposed that 'relevance' connotes that:

any two facts to which it is applied are so related to each other that according to the common course of events one either taken by itself or in connection with other facts proves or renders probable the past, present or future existence or non-existence of the other.[6]

Stephen's classic formulation incorporates several important features of the legal conception of relevance meriting emphasis. First, the relevance of fact x to fact y may be judged in isolation 'or in connection with other facts'. This flags up the contextual and dynamic nature of relevance. In cases where the relevance of a particular piece of evidence may be doubtful or contested, it is incumbent on counsel to make imaginative arguments to persuade the judge that the evidence should be admitted. Counsel must seek to elaborate probative connections with other evidence in the case and to frame the disputed evidence in contextual webs of meaning and significance for the fact-finder. Evidence rejected on one 'theory of relevance' (or 'story' about the disputed facts), may yet be admissible when re-presented as part of an alternative theory or story that the judge finds more persuasive. A host of further examples will be encountered in later chapters, but here is one simple illustration. A witness's assertion that the moon is made of green cheese would clearly be irrelevant (and consequently inadmissible) on the question of the molecular composition of the moon. However, this nursery rhyme declaration could be both relevant and admissible to prove that the witness has the power of speech or can speak English, if for some reason either of *those* issues was contested in the trial.

Relevance is as much a function of the arguments made by lawyers and judges, as it is an inherent quality of pieces of information. Grasping from the outset the dynamic nature of judgments of relevance, as they appear refracted through the tactical demands of adversarial litigation, will equip the student of criminal evidence to avoid treacherous forensic quicksands that from time to time ensnare even experienced criminal practitioners.

A second illuminating feature of Stephen's definition is his reference to 'proves or renders probable', which – contrary to superficial first impressions – is not merely redundant repetition. For fact x to *prove* fact y, x must establish y's existence to some accepted normative standard of proof, such as 'beyond reasonable doubt' or 'on the balance of probabilities'. But relevance does *not* require proof, but only that the existence of y be rendered more or (Stephen should have added) less probable by x. To the question 'How much more (un)likely must x render y for x to be judged relevant to y?', the logically correct response

---

[6] James Fitzjames Stephen, *A Digest of the Law of Evidence* (Stevens, 12th edn. 1948), Art. 1. Cf. US Federal Rules of Evidence, Rule 401: '"Relevant evidence" means evidence having any tendency to make the existence of any fact that is of consequence to the determination of the action more probable or less probable than it would be without the evidence.'

must be 'any at all'. If the probability of *y* is one-in-ten-million ($p(y) = 0.0000001$) and proof of *x* increases that probability by the minuscule amount of another one-in-ten-million, to $p(y) = 0.0000002$, *x* is relevant to *y*.[7] Relevance is binary and, as it were, one-dimensional: *x* is either relevant to *y*, or it is irrelevant. Relevance, like physical presence and pregnancy, conforms to the precept of the excluded middle: one cannot be only partly present in the room, or just a little bit pregnant. Put another way, there is no quantum of relevance. The question '*How* relevant is *x* to *y*?' simply makes no sense from a logical point of view, like asking how many cats make Christmas. We will see in a moment that this conceptually neat orthodoxy has rather been bent out of shape by judicial practice. But the essential point to appreciate is that relevance denotes a relationship of probability, not a relationship of proof. In practical legal terms, this means that the test of relevance is relatively undemanding and, generally speaking, easily satisfied. When one encounters loose phrases in common usage like 'very relevant', 'highly relevant', 'strongly relevant', etc., the speaker is almost invariably referring to something else – the weight of the evidence or its 'probative value' – rather than invoking *relevance* in the strict logical sense.

Thirdly, in drawing attention to 'the common course of events', Stephen's definition highlights an enduring truth about the source of substantive criteria of relevance, which was most famously restated by Thayer:

The law furnishes no test of relevancy. For this, it tacitly refers to logic and general experience – assuming that the principles of reasoning are known to its judges and ministers, just as a vast multitude of other things are assumed as already sufficiently known to them.... To the hungry furnace of the reasoning faculty the law of evidence is but a stoker.[8]

Having located the test for relevance in ordinary everyday processes of inquiry, inference and fact-finding, Thayer insisted that the forensic criteria of relevance are logic and common sense reasoning, rather than artificial rules of evidence. There is high English authority to the same effect,[9] though the meaning and significance of relevance are today so widely taken-for-granted that judges rarely pause to articulate such 'elementary' propositions. On this view, the lawyer's concept of relevance is exhausted by the canons of logical reasoning and the naturalistic epistemology of common sense inference and fact-finding. The meaning and implications of these assumptions will be scrutinized in Chapter 4. Thereafter, their pervasive influence will be seen in the application of particular legal rules and principles examined in subsequent chapters.

The test of relevance actually utilized by the courts is somewhat more complex than a strictly logical approach would dictate. Any system of inquiry, be it legal or otherwise, is bound to be affected by the conditions under which fact-finding is conducted, by the competence and skills of the people involved, and by the objectives of the inquiry. Whilst the overarching aim of criminal proceedings is to settle disputes and administer just

---

[7] For further mathematical approaches, see the classic treatment by Richard O. Lempert, 'Modeling Relevance' (1977) 75 *Michigan LR* 1021.

[8] Thayer, *A Preliminary Treatise on Evidence at the Common Law*, 265, 271.

[9] The modern *locus classicus* is *DPP* v *Kilbourne* [1973] AC 729, 756, HL, *per* Lord Simon: 'Evidence is relevant if it is logically probative or disprobative of some matter which requires proof.... [R]elevant (i.e. logically probative or disprobative) evidence is evidence which makes the matter which requires proof more or less probable.' Also see *R* v *A* [2002] 1 AC 45, [2001] UKHL 25, [31] *per* Lord Steyn: 'Relevance and sufficiency of proof are different things.... After all, to be relevant the evidence need merely have some tendency in logic and common sense to advance the proposition in issue.'

penal censure to offenders,[10] these are significant practical constraints on the attainment of these objectives.

(b) RELEVANCE IN LAW: A QUESTION OF RESOURCES

Resource considerations shape the entire process of fact-finding in criminal adjudication. Individual cases cannot be allowed to exhaust disproportionate shares of the courts' time and attention, because that would deny access to justice to other victims and accused persons waiting in the wings. Wealthy accused must not be allowed to procrastinate, filibuster, or unreasonably burden the public finances. Timely administration of justice – 'speedy trial' – is necessary if wrongs are to be remedied effectively, social tensions defused, and crime policy successfully implemented.[11] Excessive delay may lead to loss of evidence and failed prosecutions, disappointed expectations, and diminishing faith in the competence of government to combat crime and safeguard citizens' security.

A practical constraint of a different kind is imposed by the limitations of the human mind. There are finite limits to the amount of information that any person, however experienced or talented, can digest. Human beings have limited cognitive competence. Piling up more and more evidence, even evidence that is indubitably relevant to the task in hand, will eventually produce mental saturation, a point beyond which any additional information is likely to diminish, rather than enhance, the accuracy of the final determination. Cumulating evidence beyond the computational capacities of the average juror may be worse than a useless waste of resources. It might actually be counterproductive in confusing jurors and burying the truth under a mass of superfluous distractions.

Information-overload is a function not only of the quantity of evidence presented at trial, but also of the mechanisms and techniques that are to be employed for its evaluation. Serious criminal cases in England and Wales are tried before a judge and twelve lay jurors. This arrangement implies that the evidence must be presented in such a way that it is comprehensible to ordinary people without legal training. Trials must adopt a format and timetable compatible with the average citizen's powers of perception and concentration. And the prosecution's case and supporting evidence must be such that ordinary jurors are able to assess and debate its merits during the course of their deliberations and arrive at a collective verdict[12] on rationally defensible grounds. These institutional factors place further constraints on the type and quantity of information that can be regarded as 'relevant'

---

[10] §2.3(d); §1.2.

[11] See *Zuckerman on Civil Procedure*, ch 1; Adrian A. S. Zuckerman, 'Quality and Economy in Civil Procedure: The Case for Commuting Correct Judgments for Timely Judgments' (1994) 14 *OJLS* 353; Lon L. Fuller, 'The Forms and Limits of Adjudication' (1978) 92 *Harvard LR* 353; Melvin Aron Eisenberg, 'Participation, Responsiveness and the Consultative Process: An Essay for Lon Fuller' (1978) 92 *Harvard LR* 410; Kenneth E. Scott, 'Two Models of the Civil Process' (1975) 27 *Stanford LR* 937.

[12] Majority verdicts of 11-1 or 10-2 were introduced in England and Wales by the Criminal Justice Act 1967, owing to fears of 'jury nobbling' by organized crime gangs. Unanimity is still sought in the first instance, but the trial judge may indicate that a majority verdict would be acceptable after the jury has deliberated for a substantial period (relative to the complexity of the case) without achieving unanimous agreement. Now see Juries Act 1974, s.17; *R v Watson* [1988] QB 690, (1988) 87 Cr App R 1, CA; and Judicial Studies Board (JSB) Specimen Direction No 57: 'I ask you once more to retire and to continue to try to reach a unanimous verdict; but if you cannot, I will accept a majority verdict. This is a verdict with which at least ten of you agree.'

to criminal adjudication. As Baron Rolfe B once observed, '[i]f we lived for a thousand years instead of about sixty or seventy, and every case was of sufficient importance, it might be possible, and perhaps proper... to raise every possible inquiry as to the truth of statements made... In fact mankind finds it to be impossible.'[13]

The availability and design of forensic procedures for testing witnesses' accuracy, recall, and credibility are additional variables with significant implications for relevancy.[14] Suppose that the only eyewitness to an assault testifies for the prosecution that the accused struck the first blow. The reliability of this witness is obviously crucial to the outcome of the case. If a month earlier that witness had made a mistake in observing some other event from a similar distance, the accused would want to use this information to challenge the witness's record for accuracy. This tactic seems logical and reasonable, from a common sense point of view, since people who have been mistaken before might be prone to making the same mistake again. Such 'impeachment of credibility' is a strategy frequently employed during cross-examination in criminal trials, where there is admissible information to hand that might prompt the fact-finder to doubt the reliability of a witness's testimony.[15] Notice, however, that impeachment opens up a new dispute over what happened on the previous occasion, necessitating an inquiry into questions of fact which are otherwise entirely unrelated to the instant case. Such 'collateral' issues might themselves generate further argument, threatening an infinite regress of disputed facts recursively more distant from the trial's central focus. Alert trial judges will not tolerate major diversions of proceedings up blind alleys leading to evidential cul-de-sacs.[16] Well short of such deviations, the more side issues that the parties are permitted to raise, the more likely it becomes that the trier of fact will be distracted from focusing squarely on the main issues.[17] And with wandering concentration and a loss of 20–20 vision come heightened risk of adjudicative error.[18]

(c) RELEVANCE AND 'LEGAL RELEVANCE'

If it is accepted that judges ought to shield the fact-finder from probatively trivial, misleading, or needlessly cumulative evidence, the question becomes one of identifying the best procedural mechanism to achieve this objective. Thayer's pupil, Wigmore, promoted 'legal

[13] *A-G* v *Hitchcock* (1847) 1 Exch 91, 105. Generally, see Jeremy Bentham, *Rationale of Judicial Evidence* (1827) vol 4, 477; Jerome Michael and Mortimer J. Adler, 'The Trial of an Issue of Fact I & II' (1934) 34 *Columbia LR* 1224 & 1462; L. H. Hoffmann, 'Similar Facts after *Boardman*' (1975) 91 *LQR* 193, 204–5.

[14] See §6.1.   [15] See §8.4.

[16] Cf. *Hollingham* v *Head* (1858) 4 CB (NS) 388, 391; 140 ER 1135, 1137 *per* Willes J: 'It is not easy in all cases to draw the line, and to define with accuracy where probability ceases and speculation begins: but we are bound to lay down the rule to the best of our ability. No doubt, the rule as to confining the evidence to that which is relevant and pertinent to the issue, is one of great importance, not only as regards the particular case, but also with reference to saving the time of the court, and preventing the minds of the jury from being drawn away from the real point they have to decide.'

[17] This is the key to appreciating the logic, and limitations, of the 'collateral-finality rule': see §8.5.

[18] Cf. Rule 403 of the US Federal Rules of Evidence 1975, entitled 'Exclusion of Relevant Evidence on Grounds of Prejudice, Confusion, or Waste of Time': 'Although relevant, evidence may be excluded if its probative value is substantially outweighed by the danger of unfair prejudice, confusion of the issues, or misleading the jury, or by considerations of undue delay, waste of time, or needless presentation of cumulative evidence.' Bentham insisted that rectitude of decision be tempered by utility in the ascertainment of truth: *Rationale of Judicial Evidence* (1827), vol. 1, 31ff; William Twining, *Theories of Evidence*, 91.

relevance' as a technical juridical concept extending beyond the ordinary meaning of logical, common sense relevance. On this view, the first (relevance) hurdle to admissibility must be broken down into two stages. Having initially determined that the evidence bears a logical relationship to an issue in the trial, the judge must additionally satisfy himself that the evidence is sufficiently probative, in the light of the other evidence in the case, to justify the extra time and trouble involved in its reception. The Wigmorean standard of 'legal relevance' requires, not merely a determination that the evidence affects the probability of some fact in issue, but also that the evidence has sufficient weight, or 'probative value', to be worthy of admission.

Legal relevance is therefore a 'two-dimensional' concept, introducing the dimension of quantum which merely logical relevance lacks.[19] Treating relevance as a legal term of art incorporating a sufficiency requirement makes sense to some commentators.[20] Furthermore, English judges intermittently refer to 'degrees' of relevance,[21] apparently endorsing and perpetuating Wigmore's concept (albeit that this implicit conceptual preference is almost never consciously articulated let alone explained or defended). There is no doubt that judges can, and sometimes do, utilize the concept of legal relevance to filter out distorting or superfluous information from the trial, and in doing so successfully promote accurate fact-finding, at least on some occasions. From the point of view of logical relevance, however, the idea of a variable relevancy standard is doctrinally heretical as well as conceptually muddled. The starting point for legal analysis should be the same concept of logical relevance applicable to any factual inquiry.

On the Wigmorean conception of relevance, our first hurdle to admissibility would be satisfied only by evidence with a probative 'plus-value', over and above logical relevance. If this were merely a question of conceptual purity it would hardly matter which conception of relevance, legal or logical, the courts chose to adopt. However, the legally-inflated conception is hobbled by a debilitating Achilles' Heel with serious practical implications. By cloaking rejected evidence with blanket pronouncements of 'irrelevance', Wigmore's approach tends to obscure the reasons supposedly justifying inadmissibility in any particular case. Legal relevance, in other words, lacks transparency as a standard of admissibility. Moreover, in departing from common sense judgments of relevance,[22] it may imperil

[19] It might be said that weight is integral to the concept of relevance. Evidence is relevant because it is capable of affecting judgments of probability. The amount by which evidence affects probability is its weight. We might say, therefore, that evidence is relevant because it has quantifiable weight. However, the two propositions – (1) evidence is relevant because it has weight and (2) evidence is relevant if it has sufficient weight – are not equivalent. From the point of view of logical relevance, weight is merely a minimum threshold for the recognition of relevance, in the same way that a straight line is considered one-dimensional even though it must in fact have some minuscule width, as well as length, in order to be visible to the human eye.

[20] See, e.g., Richard D. Friedman, 'Irrelevance, Minimal Relevance, and Meta-Relevance' (1997) 34 *Houston LR* 55; L. H. Hoffmann, 'Similar facts after *Boardman*' (1975) 91 *LQR* 193, 205: 'The degree of relevance needed to qualify for admissibility is not a fixed standard, like a point on some mathematical scale of persuasiveness. It is a *variable* standard, the probative value of the evidence being balanced against the disadvantages of receiving it such as taking up a lot of time or causing confusion.'

[21] See, e.g., *R v A* [2002] 1 AC 45, HL, [46] (Lord Steyn invoking the test that evidence may be '*so relevant* to the issue of consent that to exclude it would endanger the fairness of the trial'); and [55] (Lord Hope referring to 'evidence about the complainant's sexual behaviour which is *not directly* relevant to the offence charged') (emphases supplied).

[22] Friedman, 'Irrelevance, Minimal Relevance, and Meta-Relevance', 62–7, wants to retain a common sense, intuitive sense of relevance that would satisfy the reasonable juror, but he does not explain how

the legitimacy and public acceptability of criminal verdicts. These difficulties are nicely illustrated by the well-known case of *Blastland*.[23]

Blastland was charged with the buggery and murder of twelve-year-old Karl Fletcher. He admitted to paying Karl for consensual intercourse, but claimed that he had left him (otherwise) unharmed. It was the defence case that Karl had been murdered by another man, Mark, whom the accused accurately described to the police. This counter-allegation was lent credence by the fact that Mark had come home on the day of the murder, in a dishevelled and agitated state, and had told a women with whom he was living that 'a young boy had been murdered' before the murder was public knowledge. However, Blastland's counsel was not permitted[24] to reveal these facts to the jury at the trial, and Blastland's appeal against conviction was rejected, ultimately, by the House of Lords. Lord Bridge justified the exclusion of Mark's apparently incriminating knowledge on the basis that it lacked 'direct and immediate relevance'[25] to the issues in the case. His Lordship reasoned that Mark could have come by his intimate knowledge of the murder in any one of a number of ways – some innocent, others at least partly incriminating – but the jury would have been in no position to judge how Mark knew so much. Better in these circumstances, concluded the House of Lords, that these unnecessarily complicating and ultimately inconclusive 'speculations' should be kept from the jury altogether.

Lord Bridge's invocation of 'direct and immediate relevance' was a variation on the Wigmorean concept of legal relevance.[26] There is no other general exclusionary rule dictating the inadmissibility of evidence that is only indirectly and distantly relevant, much less is there any residual exclusionary discretion applicable to *defence* evidence.[27] Yet it seems manifestly unsatisfactory to dismiss Mark's knowledge as 'irrelevant' to the issue of Blastland's guilt or innocence. Most people intuitively grasp the logic of the connection. If Mark was somehow involved in the murder, the prosecution's case identifying Blastland as the sole assailant is weakened. Anyone imagining themselves to be a juror in the case would consequently want to know about the evidence implicating Mark, if only to rule out the possibility of Mark's involvement (as the police and prosecution had obviously done). Indeed, defence counsel clearly wanted the jury to engage in precisely the kinds of 'speculation' that Lord Bridge considered an unprofitable diversion. *Sed cui bono?* Judicial exclusion of evidence nearly always impacts unevenly on adversarial litigants, disadvantaging

---

predicating admissibility on 'substantial' probative value would square with ordinary usage. Surely, if evidence is being excluded, not because it is literally irrelevant but because the nuisance value of the evidence makes it more trouble than it is worth, it would be better to say so directly, rather than camouflaging the cost-benefit calculation in conclusory pronouncements of 'irrelevance'.

[23] *R v Blastland* [1986] 1 AC 41, HL. See Mike Redmayne, 'Analysing Evidence Case Law', in Paul Roberts and Mike Redmayne (eds.), *Innovations in Evidence and Proof* (Hart, 2007); Andrew L.-T. Choo, 'The Notion of Relevance and Defence Evidence' [1993] *Crim LR* 114.

[24] There may have been practical difficulties in securing this evidence. Certainly, Mark would have been an unreliable witness for the defence (the proper approach would have been to have Mark called by the prosecution and tendered for cross-examination by the defence), but there were other witnesses who had given relevant statements to the police and who, if necessary, could have been required under *sub poena* to testify: see §7.3.   [25] *R v Blastland* [1986] 1 AC 41, 54.

[26] Lord Bridge's casual reference to 'the degree of relevance', ibid. 62, confirms that his Lordship was working with a concept of relevance incorporating a criterion of quantum or weight, which is another tell-tale sign that 'relevance' is being employed as a legal term of art rather than with its logical, everyday meaning.

[27] Cf. PACE 1984, s.78, which is expressly restricted to prosecution evidence: see Chapter 5.

one side as it favours the other. On reflection, the pre-empted speculations look suspiciously like the precursors of reasonable doubt, which the defence might have developed before the jury as grounds for Blastland's acquittal, rather than irrelevant distractions that could only hamper jurors in arriving at a true verdict.

Blastland is a particularly troubling decision because it is hard to shake the lingering impression that evidence of Mark's knowledge ought to have been admitted, after all. But even supposing that the evidence was rightly excluded, it hardly makes for transparency in judicial decision-making to label the evidence 'irrelevant', since its relevance can hardly be doubted from a common sense point of view. *Blastland* stands for the paradoxical proposition that obviously relevant information was (legally) irrelevant. It would have been preferable to say that the evidence, though relevant, was going to be excluded because the trouble it would create in generating collateral issues and imponderable speculation more than outweighed its marginal probative value. The problem with this candid rationalization, from the courts' perspective, is that English law does not recognize any exclusionary rule applicable to potentially exculpatory defence evidence – nor should it. How could such a rule be squared with the foundational principle of protecting the innocent from wrongful conviction? Perhaps this only goes to show that the evidence in *Blastland* should never have been excluded in the first place; and the purist conception of logical relevance, far from being undermined by such a conclusion, seems rather to grow in stature.

There is a cautionary historical precedent warning against over-expansive conceptions of relevance. Misconstruing 'relevance' as the ultimate criterion of admissibility to which all other evidentiary standards could be reduced, James Fitzjames Stephen set about reonceptualizing every ground of inadmissibility as a function of relevance: hearsay was excluded because it was unreliable and therefore 'irrelevant'; bad character evidence, in tending unreasonably to prejudice the jury against the accused, was 'irrelevant'; 'opinion evidence' likewise 'irrelevant'; and so on. In fact, bringing independent exclusionary rules under the overarching rubric of 'relevance' adds nothing to the underlying rationales for exclusion in each case, and can only serve to overcomplicate, confuse, and mislead. As superfluous ornamentation to self-sustaining rules and principles of admissibility, the concept of relevance should be cut away by Ockham's Razor[28] to leave the operative justifications for exclusion clearly visible and available for inspection and evaluation. Restricted to its appropriate sphere of application, logical relevance continues to provide a powerful lens through which to analyse admissibility rulings when English judges, forsaking conceptual purity, fail to articulate their motivations for excluding evidence.

The importance of clarity and transparency in admissibility determinations is underscored by the fact that trial judges making evidentiary rulings are frequently required to make finely-balanced judgments which are beyond the effective reach of appellate review.[29]

---

[28] *OED* (2nd edn. 1989): 'Occam's (also Ockham's) razor, the leading principle of the nominalism of William of Occam…, that for purposes of explanation things not known to exist should not, unless it is absolutely necessary, be postulated as existing; usually called the Law of Parsimony.'

[29] §2.5(e). Thayer, *A Preliminary Treatise on Evidence at the Common Law*, 516, contended that admissible evidence, 'must not unnecessarily complicate the case, or too much tend to confuse, mislead or tire… the jury, or to withdraw their attention too much from the real issues of the case. Now in the application of such standards as these, the chief appeal is made to sound judgment; to what our lawyers have called, for six or seven centuries at least, the discretion of the judge. Decisions on such subjects are not readily open to revision; and, when revised, they have to be judged of in a large way; this is expressed by saying that the question is whether the discretion has been unreasonably exercised, has been abused.'

On some occasions the probative value of evidence, such as the testimony of an eyewitness to the disputed event, is immediately apparent. At other times the significance of evidence only emerges in the context of other pieces of evidence or known facts. The probative value of Mark's knowledge in *Blastland*, for example, is not immediately obvious. It is only in light of the fact that information about the murder had not yet been released to the general public that the incriminating nature of Mark's inside-knowledge becomes apparent. If the judge is in doubt about the relevance of an isolated piece of evidence, the tendering party can be asked to explain how it relates to the rest of the evidence he plans to adduce. Evidence or questioning in cross-examination is sometimes admitted on trust – *de bene esse* – that its relevance will be demonstrated as the party's case unfolds.[30] If the party fails to make good on his assurances, the jury will be directed to ignore the evidence. With the benefit of hindsight, the evidence turned out to be irrelevant, and irrelevant evidence is categorically inadmissible. It falls at the first hurdle of admissibility.

Certain admissibility standards, including the common law PV > PE test applicable to all prosecution evidence,[31] overtly require the trial judge to make determinations of probative value. Extrapolating from the basic test of relevance, questions of probative value are likewise matters of logic and common sense. The law cannot prescribe detailed rules to determine whether a piece of evidence has sufficient probative potential to justify its reception.[32] The self-same piece of evidence in support of the self-same proposition may be sufficient in one set of circumstances, but insufficient in others. Legal precedent cannot substitute for a case-by-case assessment of evidential sufficiency. Past decisions may nonetheless serve as useful guides for implementing evidentiary goals and policies, such as avoiding confusion, forestalling proliferation of side-issues, and minimizing costs in the administration of justice.

Whenever trial judges make determinations of evidentiary sufficiency, either in the application of discrete exclusionary rules or under the supposed authority of an expanded conception of legal relevance, the overriding consideration is that they should clearly justify their admissibility rulings in terms of the authentic rules and principles of criminal evidence. Legal relevance should not become a conveniently capacious conceptual dustbin into which rejected evidence can be tossed without any further explanation for its exclusion from the trial. If there is good reason for excluding relevant evidence tendered by the parties, the judge should say in plain terms what the fatal defect is, opening up admissibility rulings to further adversarial argument and the possibility of appellate review. This is

---

[30] 'In its long established meaning...*de bene esse* means "to allow or accept for the present till it comes to be more fully examined, and then to stand or fall according to the merit of the thing in its own nature". More succinctly, as Burton J has explained (see *In the case of AFP Berry* [2002] EWHC 1718 (Admin), [3]; and *R (on the application of Murray)* v *Hampshire CC (No.1)* [2002] EWHC 1401 (Admin), [2003] JP L 224, [3]), it means "under reserve" or, as another modern authority puts it (see Gray, *Lawyers' Latin – A Vade Mecum* (2006), 46) "provisionally" or "for what it is worth"': *Butland* v *Powys CC* [2009] EWHC 151 (Admin), [45] (Munby J). [31] §2.5(a).

[32] Theoretically, it would be possible to translate considerations of time and confusion into fixed rules of law. We might, for example, adopt a rule that no trial should last more than two days or that no party should call more than four witnesses. Although such rules would save time, they are obviously inappropriate, being rigidly inflexible and totally insensitive to the infinitely variable, contextualized challenges of effective fact-finding in particular cases. For the view that the law sometimes does lay down rules of this type, see *Wigmore on Evidence* (Little, Brown & Co, 3rd edn. 1940), vol. 1, §12, 298. For commentary see, Twining, *Theories of Evidence*, 154; *Wigmore on Evidence* (Tillers Revision, 1983), vol. 1, §§11–12.

now a legislative requirement in relation to certain kinds of evidence,[33] but also a general principle of fair and effective adjudication. Conversely, pretending that evidence is 'irrelevant' when any fair-minded person, looking at all the circumstances of the case, would regard it as capable of properly influencing the fact-finder's decision is no way to serve the rule of law or to foster public confidence in criminal verdicts.

(d) MATERIALITY

It is sometimes said that admissible evidence must be *material* as well as relevant.[34] Materiality is meant to encapsulate the thought that a relationship of relevance between x and y must, in addition, have some bearing on – must be *material to* – the issues in the case if information concerning x is to be legally admissible. Thus, evidence of x is material and (subject to any applicable exclusionary rules) legally admissible only if y is a disputed issue in the proceedings. Conversely, evidence establishing a logical relationship of relevancy is not necessarily material. It is relevant to setting fires that the air contains oxygen, for example, but this elementary fact about the physical universe may have no material bearing whatever on – it may be *immaterial to* – the accused's trial for arson.

Materiality picks out an undeniably important quality of judicial evidence. However, there is no real need to employ a separate concept for this purpose.[35] For it is usually already implicit in the language of relevance employed in forensic contexts that we mean *relevant to the facts in issue in this particular trial*, rather than describing an acontextual relationship between two abstract factual propositions. Criminal adjudication is concerned only with those facts which applicable substantive law, rules of criminal procedure, and the contours of the factual dispute between the parties qualify as relevant. No other facts may be the subject of a criminal trial,[36] and if the evidence tendered by either party is not – directly or indirectly –relevant to one of those facts, it should be excluded as irrelevant.[37]

It is still necessary to pay close attention to the myriad ways in which the law's relevancy standards may be satisfied, or not, on the facts of particular cases. Relevance is as variable as human experience, and sometimes just as unexpected. Even the existence of

---

[33] See, e.g., Criminal Justice Act (CJA), 2003, s.110 (bad character); Youth Justice and Criminal Evidence Act 1999, s.43 (complainant's previous sexual history).

[34] George F. James, 'Relevancy, Probability and the Law' (1941) 29 *California LR* 689; J. L. Montrose, 'Basic Concepts of the Law of Evidence' (1954) 70 *LQR* 527: cf. *Wigmore on Evidence* (3rd edn. 1940), vol. 1, §12, 296.

[35] If 'materiality' involves ascertaining which factual elements are required by the substantive law for any legal result, then the issue is one of interpretation of the substantive law, and not a question of evidence. Likewise, the critical variation of this argument, which contends that criminal responsibility should be judged in the light of broad moral, political, socio-economic, and cultural considerations (such as a history of discrimination or 'rotten social background') really boils down to a set of arguments about the substantive grounds of criminal liability with no specifically *evidentiary* purchase: cf. Andrew E. Taslitz, 'Abuse Excuses and the Logic and Politics of Expert Relevance' (1998) 49 *Hastings LJ* 1039.

[36] Generally speaking, the courts will not adjudicate on hypothetical scenarios that might never arise: *Re Barnato* [1949] Ch 258, CA.

[37] *R v Byrne* [2002] Crim LR 487, CA, provides a striking illustration. The Court of Appeal held that the wife of the deceased should not have been allowed to testify that B had been a principal instigator of her husband's murder. The prosecution had argued its case explicitly on the basis that B was guilty of manslaughter, not murder. Consequently, evidence tending to show that B was a murderer was strictly irrelevant and should have been excluded from the trial.

oxygen in the air could conceivably be a relevant fact in criminal adjudication – as where the accused is charged with committing arson in a chemistry laboratory and claims that he believed he was lighting the match in a vacuum where the fire could not take hold. Some general characteristics of relevant evidence are explored further in the remainder of this chapter, and will be expounded in relation to fact-finding and proof in the next. In terms of basic concepts, references to 'material' evidence are usually harmless but super-fluous. We can describe the basic legal framework for receiving evidence in criminal trials perfectly adequately in terms of (logical) relevance and admissibility. Whilst materiality could safely be dispensed with, however, the concept of legal relevance is more tenacious and troublesome. In the teeth of principled objections to allowing unacknowledged nor-mative and pragmatic considerations to distort common sense fact-finding, Wigmorean 'legal relevance' will retain some heuristic value for as long as judges persist in speaking of 'degrees' of relevance, and in using 'relevance' as a catch-all repository for reasons to exclude logically relevant evidence of marginal or contested probative value.

3.3 TYPOLOGIES OF EVIDENCE

Lawyers classify evidence in various ways employing somewhat specialist terminology. There is no juridical magic in these classifications. Some of the concepts and language are not even especially well chosen, but lawyers frequently slip into using them as convenient shorthand. Students and practitioners of criminal evidence must therefore become famil-iar with the following basic classifications and should grasp their probative significance: (a) direct evidence; (b) circumstantial evidence; (c) real evidence; (d) collateral evidence; and (e) testimonial and non-testimonial evidence.

To the extent that they influence the way in which legal issues are conceived and tackled in criminal litigation, lawyers' classifications are themselves important material for schol-arly analysis, criticism, and possible re-classification. A useful starting point in constructing any typology of judicial evidence is the contrast between direct and circumstantial evidence.

(a) DIRECT EVIDENCE

Direct evidence goes to prove a fact in issue directly. Paradigmatic illustrations include the testimony of the complainant of a criminal assault, the evidence of an eyewitness who observed the crime in progress, and the voluntary confession of the accused to having committed the offence charged. Direct evidence is not necessarily conclusive, because it might be incomplete or disbelieved by the fact-finder. Perhaps the complainant has made a false allegations, or the eyewitness has poor eyesight, or the confession was coerced or a misguided attempt to protect the real culprit. However, the purported relevance and pro-bative value of direct evidence are usually tolerably clear. If believed, such evidence will often suffice to determine particular facts in issue. Depending on its factual content and the nature of the charge, direct evidence might be sufficient to dispose of the entire case by proving the accused's guilt beyond reasonable doubt.[38]

---

[38] There is no general corroboration requirement in English law: see Chapter 15.

(b) CIRCUMSTANTIAL EVIDENCE

Circumstantial evidence is an indirect form of proof. Opportunity, motive, previous conduct, possession of incriminating articles, and physical proof of identity (including fingerprints and DNA samples) are all standard forms of circumstantial evidence. Circumstantial evidence must of course be relevant to cross the first hurdle to admissibility,[39] but its probative value is highly variable. One might expect indirect circumstantial evidence to be less probative than direct evidence of guilt, and this is often so. A confession or eyewitness account, if believed, is conclusive of the facts narrated, whilst such things as motive or opportunity, though probative, may be very equivocal. Nearly every reader of this book will have the opportunity to commit theft or fraud in the next seven days, and motives like greed, selfishness, jealousy, and anger are human vices from which hardly anybody is completely immune. But opportunity and motive do not make us all thieves. That the accused had the opportunity and the motive to commit the offence might not, in the circumstances of particular cases, be proof of very much at all. However, it would be an elementary mistake to conclude from such examples that circumstantial evidence is always probatively weak. In fact, circumstantial evidence can sometimes amount to overwhelming proof of guilt, as where the accused had the opportunity to commit a burglary, *and* items taken from the burgled house are found in his lock-up garage, *and* a fingerprint recovered from the window forced by the burglar matches the accused's fingerprints, *and* the accused is a career burglar with fifty previous convictions for housebreaking. Circumstantial evidence could be sufficient to prove murder even in the absence of a body or any eyewitness account.[40]

Yet even overwhelming circumstantial evidence is never irrefutable proof of guilt. Lord Normand cautioned in *Teper v R*:

Circumstantial evidence may sometimes be conclusive, but it must always be narrowly examined, if only because evidence of this kind may be fabricated to cast suspicion on another. Joseph commanded the steward of his house 'put my cup, the silver cup, in the sack's "mouth of the youngest",' and when the cup was found there Benjamin's brethren too hastily assumed that he must have stolen it. It is also necessary before drawing the inference of the accused's guilt from circumstantial evidence to be sure that there are no other co-existing circumstances which would weaken or destroy the inference.[41]

Litigation-hardened lawyers tend to treat the 'open-and-shut case' much like the unicorn, as a creature of fiction.[42] It is *possible*, for example, that the accused has moved into another line of criminal activity. Perhaps, though innocent of this particular burglary, the accused is 'fencing' stolen items for burglars, hence his possession of the burgled items; and the fingerprint could have been planted by a police detective who, thinking that the current offence was obviously the work of the local professional burglar, took it upon himself to 'gild the lily' in order to ensure that the accused, whom the detective 'knows' is guilty, will

---

[39] §3.1, above.

[40] As in *R v Athwal* [2009] 1 WLR 2430, [2009] EWCA Crim 789, where the deceased was taken to a family wedding in India and never seen or heard of again.   [41] *Teper v R* [1952] AC 480, 489, PC.

[42] 'As everybody who has anything to do with the law well knows, the path of the law is strewn with examples of open and shut cases which, somehow, were not; of unanswerable charges which, in the event, were completely answered; of inexplicable conduct which was fully explained; of fixed and unalterable determinations that, by discussion, suffered a change': *John v Rees* [1970] Ch 345, 402 (Megarry J).

not evade conviction. These may be remote possibilities, which might never spontaneously occur to a fact-finder – though that would depend on the relative cynicism of individual jurors, and possibly also on their personal experiences of policing and crime. But if the evidence in the trial betrayed any hint of such possibilities, jurors would need to apply their minds to assessing whether the accused just might be innocent. Every realistic prospects of innocence must be eliminated before arriving at a verdict of guilty.

There is, in short, an inferential gap between even very persuasive evidence and conclusive knowledge of guilt. This may account for a certain residual sense of uneasiness about convictions based exclusively on circumstantial evidence, even forms of circumstantial evidence like fingerprints or DNA profiles which are almost universally recognized as highly probative. It is almost as if, when there is direct evidence, a measure of the responsibility for convicting the accused can be shifted to somebody else: to the eyewitness who says she is sure that the accused was the burglar, or to the accused himself who has confessed guilt from his own mouth. But circumstantial evidence does not literally 'speak for itself', and blood samples, fingerprints, or even a smoking gun do not take moral responsibility for penal censure. When the prosecution's case rests entirely on circumstantial evidence, there is no hiding from the fact that responsibility for criminal adjudication rests four-square on the shoulders of the jury and, by extension, with the political community whom serving jurors represent.[43]

(c) REAL EVIDENCE (EXHIBITS)

By long-sanctified tradition, physical objects like seized drugs, contraband or stolen goods, housebreaking tools, murder weapons, video-recordings, and fingerprints are known as 'real evidence'.[44] This label is hardly illuminating, since other kinds of evidence – including witness testimony – are no less 'real' than those corporeal, physical, means of proof designated 'real evidence'. But the label has stuck.

Objects and documents, if relevant and not rendered inadmissible by any applicable exclusionary rule,[45] may be adduced in the trial as 'exhibits' for the jury's inspection. The jury is normally able to retire with an exhibit,[46] whereas jurors may not generally take transcripts of witness testimony with them into the juryroom for fear that this evidence

---

[43] Cf. James Q. Whitman, *The Origins of Reasonable Doubt: Theological Roots of the Criminal Trial* (Yale UP, 2008) (exploring the deep historical roots of the notion that fact-finders take personal responsibility for criminal verdicts).

[44] '[R]eal evidence ... is conveniently defined in *Cockle's Cases and Statutes on Evidence* (10th edn. 1963), 348: "Real evidence is the evidence afforded by the production of physical objects for inspection or other examination by the court"': *The Statue of Liberty* [1968] 1 WLR 739, 740.

[45] Strictly speaking, there is a further pre-condition to admissibility: as a practical matter, an item of real evidence must physically exist before it can be produced for the jury's inspection. Hence, dogs and horses can be real evidence, but not unicorns (as opposed – recalling Magritte's instructive meditation, *ceci n'est pas une pipe* – to artistic representations of unicorns, which *can* be real evidence). This thought suggests that 'real evidence' might more usefully be conceptualized as *corporeal* evidence. The relevant distinction is, then, not between real and unreal evidence, but between physically tangible and intangible evidence. However, it is difficult to see how the distinction between tangible and intangible evidence maps on to any useful generalization about probative value, since intangible evidence – like eyewitness testimony – is often, but by no means always, more probative than tangible, (corpo)real evidence.

[46] Cf. *R v Lowry* [2004] EWCA Crim 555, where the issue of improper juror experimentation with exhibits – a knife used in an assault – arose.

would exert a disproportionate influence on the jury's deliberations relative to other evidence and testimony not contained in the transcript.[47] The party tendering real evidence must prove its discovery and demonstrate an unbroken chain of custody as a pre-condition of admissibility, in order to establish that the evidence is authentic and has not been tampered with.[48]

(d) COLLATERAL EVIDENCE

Another convenient distinction frequently drawn by common lawyers contrasts evidence going directly to a fact in issue with evidence on 'collateral' matters. The dividing line tends to blur in practice, but in theory any proffered evidence not relating directly to the facts constituting an offence[49] or to eligible criminal law defences is collateral.

For example, in a burglary trial evidence that the accused entered the victim's home uninvited goes directly to an issue in the case, since trespass is a constitutive fact of burglary. The fact that the accused had ham and eggs for dinner is not directly in issue in a burglary prosecution, and would normally be irrelevant and therefore inadmissible. But suppose that the accused says that he always needs to sleep for two hours after a heavy dinner of ham and eggs, and that he consequently cannot have committed burglary on the night in question because, at the material time, he was sleeping off the after-effects of dining on ham and eggs. Improbably enough, the accused's dinner menu now becomes a relevant issue in the trial, as does the further question whether the accused really needs to sleep for two hours after every meal of ham and eggs. *Any* proposition of fact could in principle be relevant in a criminal trial. But this still does not qualify the contents of the accused's dinner-plate or his postprandial sleeping habits as matters *directly* in issue on a charge of burglary. Rather, these are collateral issues, which derive their relevance to the case from their implications for a further collateral question, *viz.* the credibility of the accused's gastronomic alibi.

The distinction between evidence going directly to the issue and evidence on collateral matters is sometimes doctrinally significant and must be reflected in judicial directions to the jury, but its practical significance is more difficult to assess. The success of rules of evidence instructing juries to use information for one purpose but not for another has already been called into question.[50] Conceptual and doctrinal purity is especially difficult to sustain in trials where the factual dispute effectively boils down to one person's word against another's. Questions of witness credibility are always notionally collateral.[51] But in a direct credibility battle, supposedly collateral matters assume centre-stage. As Henry J once remarked in relation to allegations of sexual assault, 'where the disputed issue is a sexual one between two persons in private the difference between questions going to credit and questions going to the issue is reduced to vanishing point'.[52]

[47] But exceptionally the jury may be permitted to retire with a transcript of video-recorded testimony if the process is carefully managed and appropriate judicial directions are given: *R* v *Welstead* [1996] 1 Cr App R 59, CA; cf. *R* v *SW* [2004] EWCA Crim 2979; *R* v *McQuiston* [1998] 1 Cr App R 139, CA;

[48] Rosemary Pattenden, 'Authenticating "Things" in English Law: Principles for Adducing Tangible Evidence in Common Law Jury Trials' (2008) 12 *E & P* 273.   [49] On 'constitutive facts' see §4.2.

[50] §2.5(d).

[51] Except in exceptional circumstances where a witness's credibility is directly in issue, e.g. on a charge of perjury.   [52] *R* v *Funderburk* [1990] 1 WLR 587, 597, CA.

(e) TESTIMONIAL AND NON-TESTIMONIAL EVIDENCE

Cutting across the distinction between direct and circumstantial evidence is another doctrinally significant dichotomy differentiating 'testimonial' from 'non-testimonial' evidence. Testimonial evidence is paradigmatically the evidence of a witness testifying orally and in person at trial. If an eyewitness comes to court and narrates what she saw to the fact-finder, in answer to counsel's questions, this is direct testimonial evidence by a witness in the trial. Circumstantial evidence can also be testimonial evidence, as where a witness at trial testifies to the accused's motive, or supports or undermines his alibi (bearing on opportunity). Physical objects and other forms of real evidence, like fingerprints or hair samples, exemplify non-testimonial evidence. Physical objects, though *ex hypothesi* relevant to the proceedings, do not literally *testify* as human witnesses do, and are therefore aptly described as 'non-testimonial' evidence.

The neat dichotomy between testimonial and non-testimonial evidence is complicated by various nuances and exceptions. It is vital to grasp that a single piece of information may perform a multiplicity of evidential functions. Documents and reported speech, in particular, may have testimonial as well as non-testimonial significance, and are sometimes used in both ways simultaneously.[53] Everything depends on the *purpose or purposes* for which the evidence is adduced or employed in the trial. Documentary evidence is the prime instance, because documents are both physical things in themselves which can be adduced as real evidence, and written communications with a content and meaning that can be relied on *testimonially*, as (direct or circumstantial) proof of a fact in issue. If, for example, the existence of a will is contested in legal proceedings, the relevant piece of paper bearing the testator's signature might be produced in court as real evidence proving that a will was validly executed. But if a party wished to rely on the content of the will, say as evidence of the testator's feelings towards those named as beneficiaries, then it would be adduced, as it were, 'testimonially', as direct or circumstantial evidence of some further fact in issue. Where both aspects of the will have become live issues in the trial, the same piece of paper could take on a double life, being employed first as real evidence of the will's physical existence, and subsequently – for example – as direct proof of the testator's affections.[54]

The same duality of purpose and function can attend reported, out-of-court, speech. Sometimes the very fact that particular words were spoken is itself relevant in criminal proceedings, as where the accused is alleged to have made a threat to kill or perpetrated fraud or blackmail.[55] The victim to whom a criminal threat was addressed, or a bystander who overheard it, may be able to give direct, testimonial evidence in court that a particular threat was made. So far, so good: direct testimonial evidence of a fact in issue is straightforwardly admissible. But on other occasions, a party may wish to rely upon the content of an out-of-court statement as proof of some fact asserted in the statement, as where the out-of-court statement names the accused as the perpetrator of a crime. In this case, as in

---

[53] This duality frequently gives rise to difficulties in applying the hearsay prohibition: see Chapter 9.

[54] Cf. *Wright* v *Tatham* (1837) 7 Ad & Ell 313; 112 ER 488, Ex Cham; *R* v *Lydon (Sean)* (1987) 85 Cr App R 221, CA.   [55] So-called 'legally operative words': see §9.4(a).

the previous example of the dual-purpose will, lawyers might say that the party is seeking to use the statement 'testimonially'.[56] A reported statement is not literally oral testimony, whether contained in a document or in the form of reported speech conveyed to the court by another witness – a witness to the statement, rather than a witness to any fact directly in issue. However, the party's intention is to use the statement *as though it were* courtroom testimony, hence the adverbial *testimonially* is apt.

We will see in Chapter 9 that out-of-court statements relied on testimonially may be admissible by way of an exception to the hearsay prohibition.[57] For now, the essential point to grasp is that the probative significance of judicial evidence is not simply a property of the quality of objects, documents, or spoken words adduced at trial. Rather, the relevance and probative value of evidence adduced in criminal proceedings are circumscribed by the uses to which particular items of evidence are put. This is decided in the first instance by the party tendering the evidence. Once evidence has been adduced, however, the trial judge's summing-up may influence its evaluation and the matter is ultimately settled by the jury. To the extent that legally authorized uses of evidence are dictated by judgments of logical relevance rather than legal technicalities, there is no reason why jurors should refuse to follow the trial judge's directions, provided that they are able to appreciate the sense and legitimacy of the distinctions being made.

Further complications arise from entrenched linguistic conventions, which often exert a profound and tenacious hold over legal theory and lawyers' consciousness out of all proportion to their usefulness. The accused's out-of-court confession is one of the oldest exceptions to the hearsay rule, and involves the testimonial use of an out-of-court statement just as surely as any of the examples given in the preceding paragraphs. But lawyers would not generally think of the accused's confession as 'testimonial' evidence. Meanwhile, new forms of evidence, like the pre-recorded video testimony of children and other 'vulnerable' witnesses which is discussed in Chapter 10, are extending the boundaries of traditional conceptions of 'testimonial' evidence. A pre-recorded video is not live oral witness testimony in the traditional sense, but it is much closer to the paradigm than (merely) testimonial uses of out-of-court statements. One might say that modern technologies, allied to contemporary political campaigns driving procedural reform, are expanding the concept of 'a trial' beyond its traditional temporal parameters.[58] The vocabulary of Criminal Evidence must constantly adapt and evolve to meet the new challenges of the times.

3.4 SOURCES OF INFORMATION IN CRIMINAL LITIGATION

The intellectual discipline of classifying evidence as direct, circumstantial, real, collateral, or testimonial emphasizes the dynamic relationship between evidence and proof. It focuses on the nature and strength of the inference form the evidence to a pertinent

---

[56] *R* v *Kearley* [1992] 2 AC 228, 241, 284, 287, HL. Also see *Ritz Hotel* v *Charles of the Ritz Ltd* [1989] RPC 333, 350, Sup Ct of NSW ('The effect of the hearsay rule is to preclude an extra-judicial assertion being used testimonially').   [57] Also see Michael S. Pardo, 'Testimony' (2007) 82 *Tulane LR* 119.

[58] The temporal expansion of criminal proceedings is also noted by John D. Jackson, 'Silence and Proof: Extending the Boundaries of Criminal Proceedings in the United Kingdom' (2001) 5 *E & P* 145.

factual conclusion. An alternative way of classifying evidence is by source. This exercise usefully demonstrates the highly acculturated nature of what common lawyers conventionally regard as 'evidence'. Information formally adduced in the trial as 'evidence' by no means exhausts all of the jury's informational resources. In the interests of a more comprehensive survey, we should consider 'information in criminal litigation' as an inclusive concept covering both evidence as an ordinary English word[59] and 'evidence' in the common lawyer's narrower technical sense.

Notwithstanding some conceptual blurring at the edges, the distinction between testimonial and non-testimonial evidence remains central to the theory and practice of criminal litigation. Live oral witness testimony is still the paradigmatic source of evidence in English criminal trials. Chapters 7–10 are devoted to detailed analysis of the procedural rules and principles governing the presentation of witness testimony and its cross-examination. A central theme of this discussion will be the extent to which recent evidentiary reforms are compatible with English law's traditional 'principle of orality'.

Scientific and other expert evidence is a second important source of information in contemporary criminal litigation. Expert evidence may be adduced through the oral testimony of an expert witness testifying live in court, or in the form of a documentary expert report presented at trial.[60] Irrespective of the mechanism by which it is communicated to the court, however, expert evidence commands special epistemic authority, because it purports to supply the fact-finder with recondite information beyond the ken of the ordinary lay juror. Chapter 11 reconsiders the rules of evidence regulating the admissibility and interpretation of expert evidence, drawing attention to their broader social, procedural, and epistemic implications.

In addition to witness testimony, experts, documents, and exhibits, there is a variety of other sources of information in criminal litigation which are typically relegated to a residual 'miscellaneous' category by the textbook writers, if deemed worthy of mention at all. This section considers four neglected evidentiary sources: (a) formalities; (b) agreed evidence; (c) views and demonstrations; and (d) informal evidence. Each of these subsidiary sources of information is of greater theoretical and practical significance than is commonly appreciated. Formalities and agreed evidence, in particular, are relied on very frequently in criminal adjudication; and what we are calling 'informal evidence' is pervasive, as we shall see. Moreover, all four subsidiary evidentiary sources exemplify issues of principle. It is difficult to see how a taxonomy of criminal evidence could be considered satisfactory, let alone comprehensive, if it fails to incorporate sources of information that routinely affect the outcome of criminal trials and are potentially dispositive.

(a) FORMALITIES

Parliament has passed a miscellany of statutes declaring that specified matters may be proved in a formal way, typically by producing a certificate or authenticated copy issued by an appropriate authority. Such statutory authorizations build upon a venerable heritage of common law precedents, established at a time when the judges were much more inclined

---

[59] 'An appearance from which inferences may be drawn; an indication, mark, sign, token, trace': *OED* (2nd edn. 1989).   [60] CJA 1988, s.30; Crim PR 2010, Part 33.

to improvise procedural law than they are today.[61] Statutes sometimes also operate by way of evidentiary 'presumption', a technique discussed later in conjunction with burdens of proof.[62] Here, we are primarily concerned with direct proof by parliamentary or common law authorization, whereby it is declared that 'x may be proved by y' (or words to that effect) for the purposes of the proceedings.

Unsurprisingly, proof by formalities is by and large confined to relatively uncontroversial matters that would not generally be viewed as making significant inroads into the accused's presumption of innocence. The main constituents of this category of information are public records, including judicial documents, which by statute may be proved by the certificate of an authorized official. Formal proof is permitted for such matters as the dates on which statutory instruments[63] and byelaws[64] were validly made, records of legal proceedings,[65] certified plans or drawings of a place or object,[66] matters recorded in public registers likes births, marriages, and deaths,[67] professional qualifications,[68] and information pertaining to the registration and membership of publicly-listed companies.[69] Similar statutory authorizations have been extended to certain classes of private document, notably records of banking transactions under the Bankers' Books Evidence Act 1879, as amended. There are long-established catch-all provisions permitting the admission of certified copies of admissible documents,[70] more recently updated to authorize the production of microfilm copies.[71]

Formalities of proof have accumulated piecemeal over the years in response to the practical exigencies of litigation. For the most part, these statutory authorizations represent either sensible short-cuts to proof of matters for which no better evidence is likely to be found, or convenient alternative mechanisms for settling issues that might otherwise necessitate protracted investigation out of all proportion to their significance in the litigation. In relation to proof of such matters as births, marriages, and deaths by reference to public registers and the courts' reliance on respected reference works and histories,[72] both rationales apply.

---

[61] See, e.g., *Read* v *The Bishop of Lincoln* [1892] AC 644, PC (historical works recording 'ancient facts of a public nature'); *Doe d Wollaston* v *Barnes* (1834) 1 M & Rob 386, 174 ER 133 (parish registers); *R* v *Milton (Inhabitants of)* (1843) 1 Car & M 58; 174 ER 711 (ancient maps); *R* v *Mawhey* (1796) 6 T R 619; 101 ER 736 (magistrate's certificate concerning the repair of a highway; also, *per* Lawrence J ibid. 637 & 746, certificates of bishops with respect to marriages, and the customs of London certified by the Recorder); *R* v *Mothersell* (1718) 1 Str 93; 93 ER 405 (entries in corporation books).   [62] §6.2(b).

[63] Statutory Instruments Act 1946, s.3(1).   [64] Local Government Act 1972, s.238.

[65] Senior Courts Act 1981, s.132 (all documents bearing the seal or stamp of the Senior Courts to be admissible without further proof of their authenticity); PACE 1984 ss.73–75 (proof of convictions and acquittals in criminal proceedings); Criminal Procedure Rules (CrimPR) 2010, Rule 5.7 (an extract of the register of a magistrates' court, certified as true by the magistrates' court officer, is admissible as evidence of proceedings of the court).   [66] Criminal Justice Act 1948, s.41.

[67] But see Births and Deaths Registration Act 1953, s.34, for further formalities that must be observed before entries in the relevant registers can be taken as proof of the facts they purport to record.

[68] See, for example, Medical Act 1983, s.34A; Veterinary Surgeons Act 1966, ss.2 and 9; Dentists Act 1984, s.14; the Opticians Act 1989, s.11; the Osteopaths Act 1993, s.9(4) and (5).

[69] Companies Act 2006, s.15(4); Companies Clauses Consolidation Act 1845, s.28; Open-Ended Investment Companies Regulations, SI 2001/1228, sch.3, para.2.

[70] Evidence Act 1851, s.14. Now also see CJA 2003, s.133.   [71] PACE 1984 ss.71–72.

[72] Thus in *Read* v *The Bishop of Lincoln* [1892] AC 644, 652–3, PC, where a prosecution of ecclesiastical offences raised questions about the practices of the Primitive Church and the correct form of holy communion, Lord Halsbury LC observed that 'if our law were to exclude all such historical investigation . . . and

Notwithstanding their sound pragmatic justification and generally low-profile in discussions of criminal evidence, however, it would be a mistake to infer that proof by formalities is invariably uncontroversial. The potential scope for unanticipated difficulties is well-illustrated by the courts' experience with the formalities provisions of PACE 1984.

Sections 73–75 of PACE were designed to facilitate proof of previous convictions and acquittals and to restrict the scope for questioning the factual accuracy of criminal convictions. At common law, a trial court's verdict was treated as a mere 'opinion' about the underlying facts with no binding force in subsequent proceedings involving different parties.[73] This could be highly inconvenient for the prosecution where, for example, in order to prove a charge of handling stolen goods it was necessary to show that the goods in question were in fact stolen. If the thief had already been convicted of stealing those goods in an earlier trial, both the prosecutor's probative burden and the public expense of trials could be lessened considerably by allowing the prosecution to adduce evidence of the thief's conviction in the earlier proceedings to prove that the goods were stolen in the subsequent trial of the alleged handler. This is the type of situation in which section 74(1) renders the previous conviction admissible.[74] Section 74 also comes into its own in cases of group participation in public order offences like affray, and in prosecutions involving conspiracy[75] or accessorial liability.[76] Section 74(2) goes on to provide that: 'In any proceedings in which by virtue of this section a person other than the accused is proved to have been convicted of an offence by or before any court... he shall be taken to have committed that offence unless the contrary is proved'. Subsection (3) extends a similar authorization and presumption to *the accused's* previous convictions as evidence of guilt, again 'unless the contrary is proved'. Thus, section 74 renders a previous conviction both admissible in evidence *and* presumptively sufficient proof of the underlying facts.

Sections 73 and 75 specify the types of documents that may be adduced in proof of a conviction or acquittal which is admissible independently of these formalities provisions. These are formal rules of *proof* rather than criteria of admissibility. Whenever the fact of an acquittal or conviction is relevant in the proceedings and not caught by an applicable exclusionary rule, section 73 authorizes its proof by 'a certificate, signed by the proper officer of the court where the conviction or acquittal took place, giving the substance and effect (omitting the formal parts) of the indictment and of the conviction or acquittal'.[77] Finally, section 75 provides that the underlying facts of a conviction admitted under

---

questions of ritual and ecclesiastical practice could only be investigated by the light of the words of an Act of Parliament some centuries old, and by the testimony of living witnesses, it would disclose a very unreasonable and unsatisfactory state of the law. Who can doubt that contemporaneous usage would be of incalculable value in forming a judgment on such subjects as are indicated above? And if no historical investigation can be permitted as to what was the contemporaneous usage, one source of light upon doubtful questions would be excluded.'

[73] *Hollington* v *F. Hewthorn & Co Ltd* [1943] KB 587, CA. So far as the original parties themselves are concerned, the trial court's verdict is binding *res judicata*, once any appeal rights have been exhausted.

[74] And see *R* v *Pigram* [1995] Crim LR 808, CA, extending this illustration to the conviction of another handler.   [75] *R* v *Robertson* [1987] QB 920, CA.

[76] *R* v *Turner* [1991] Crim LR 57, CA.

[77] s.73(2)(a). For summary proceedings, proof is by 'a copy of the conviction or of the dismissal of the information, signed by the proper officer of the court where the conviction or acquittal took place or by the proper officer of the court, if any, to which a memorandum of the conviction or acquittal was sent': s.73(2)(b).

section 74 may be proved by '(a) the contents of any document which is admissible as evidence of the conviction; and (b) the contents of the information, complaint, indictment or charge-sheet on which the person in question was convicted'.

Apart from their relative complexity, sections 73–75 are typical formalities provisions that might appear unexceptional. However, they have presented trial courts with difficulties on several fronts. Section 74, facilitating the admission of evidence of the accused's extraneous misconduct, has created most problems. As Chapter 14 will elucidate, the admission of such 'bad character' evidence always risks exposing the accused to unfair prejudice, and the risk is so much the greater when the prosecution can rely on formal proof of the accused's bad character in the shape of a previous conviction. Where the previous conviction was entered after a guilty plea the underlying facts will never have been investigated at trial. Nor is it unknown for innocent people to plead guilty, and for a host of reasons ranging from a desire to protect the real culprits (whether motivated by fear or affection) to pragmatic calculations of personal advantage. A tactical plea may seen especially attractive where the accused stands in peril of being convicted on the available evidence if he tries to contest the charge, whereas a 'bargained' plea of guilty might save him from a custodial sentence.[78] In the worst case scenario, a past miscarriage of justice might be recycled to contribute to further wrongful convictions. To their credit, the courts have responded positively to this risk through a creative application of section 78 of PACE.[79] Thus, a prior conviction rendered admissible by section 74 can still be excluded under section 78, if the trial judge determines that fairness demands its exclusion.[80]

A related problem, shared by sections 73 and 75, concerns the scope and details of the information that may be adduced by the prosecution in proof of a conviction.[81] A court clerk's certificate stating 'the substance and effect... of the indictment and of the conviction or acquittal' under section 73, and 'the contents of the information, complaint, indictment or charge-sheet' admissible under section 75, could conceivably include material of dubious relevance to the current proceedings, or material which is likely to be prejudicial to the accused. In *Hacker*[82] the House of Lords confirmed that section 73(2) means what it says: a certificate of conviction can include details of the surrounding circumstances, beyond the bare fact, of the previous conviction. Thus in *Hacker*, where the accused was charged with handling the stolen body-shell of a Ford Escort RS Turbo, evidence of the accused's previous conviction of handling – admitted under section 27(3) of the Theft Act 1968[83] in conjunction with PACE section 73 – informed the jury, not only that the accused

---

[78] See CJA 2003, s.144 (Reduction in sentences for guilty pleas); *R v Goodyear* [2005] 2 Cr App R 20, [2005] EWCA Crim 888.   [79] See Chapter 5.

[80] See *R v Robertson* [1987] QB 920, CA; *R v Curry* [1988] Crim LR 527, CA; *R v Kempster* [1989] 1 WLR 1125, CA; *R v Skinner* [1995] Crim LR 805, CA.

[81] Or in proof of an acquittal under s.73, though this arises less frequently in practice. For illustrations demonstrating how the circumstances of a prior acquittal might become relevant in later proceedings, see *R v Ollis* [1900] 2 QB 758, CCR; *Sambasivam v Public Prosecutor, Federation of Malaya* [1950] AC 458, PC; *Jones v DPP* [1962] AC 635, HL; *R v H* (1989) 90 Cr App R 440, CA; *R v Y* [1992] Crim LR 436, CA. As a matter of law, however, these cases must now be read in the light of *R v Z (Prior Acquittal)* [2000] 2 AC 483, HL.

[82] *R v Hacker* [1994] 1 WLR 1659, HL.

[83] Section 27(3) provides that: 'Where a person is being proceeded against for handling stolen goods (but not for any offence other than handling stolen goods), then at any stage of the proceedings, if evidence has been given of his having or arranging to have in his possession the goods the subject of the charge, or of

already had a previous handling conviction, but also that the vehicle in question on that occasion had been a Ford Escort RS Turbo as well. Notwithstanding the formal strictures on the use of evidence admitted under section 27, which is supposed to be confined to proving that the alleged handler knew or believed that the goods in question were stolen, the clear implication was that the accused was a serial handler of supercharged Ford Escorts. Yet these incriminating details would probably have been inadmissible at common law.[84]

The ever-present risk of exposing the jury to irrelevant or prejudicial information is accentuated to the extent that formalities relieve the prosecution of the need to satisfy normal expectations of proof by admissible evidence. Yet, somewhat ironically, formal proof of a previous conviction (or acquittal) may be no less prejudicial if it comes packaged with *too little* contextualizing information. The problem here is that the jury in a later trial may form a misleading impression of the true nature of the conduct leading to conviction (or acquittal) in the earlier proceedings. When from time to time criminal litigation throws up such practical conundrums, the courts have sensibly looked for pragmatic solutions. Judicial approaches are sometimes difficult to reconcile with formal rules of evidence, but trial judges' overriding concern must be to strive for a fair balance between prosecution and defence in all the circumstances of the trial.[85]

Sections 73–75 of PACE have not resulted in a flood of appeals, nor have they confronted trial judges with difficulties that cannot be accommodated by an imaginative exercise of judicial discretion. It must be remembered that section 73 merely facilitates proof of a conviction or acquittal that is otherwise independently relevant and admissible. Section 74, by contrast, extends the scope of statutory formalities by enabling a previous conviction to constitute proof of the underlying conduct. The position is ameliorated by the fact that previous convictions admitted under section 74 are not *conclusive* proof of previous criminality:[86] the inference can be rebutted by evidence establishing that the previous conviction was mistaken.[87] Nonetheless, this brief survey of the problems thrown up by sec-

---

his undertaking or assisting in, or arranging to undertake or assist in, their retention, removal, disposal or realization, the following evidence shall be admissible for the purpose of proving that he knew or believed the goods to be stolen goods: (a) evidence that he has had in his possession, or has undertaken or assisted in the retention, removal, disposal or realization of, stolen goods from any theft taking place not earlier than 12 months before the offence charged; and (b) (provided that seven days' notice in writing has been given to him of the intention to prove the conviction) evidence that he has within the five years preceding the date of the offence charged been convicted of theft or of handling stolen goods'. Section 27(3)(b), operating in conjunction with PACE 1984 s.73(3), can be thought of as a localized statutory formality designed to give the prosecutor a helping hand in overcoming a particular problem of proof, *viz* establishing the accused's knowledge or belief at the material time.

[84] Under the so-called 'similar facts' doctrine, discussed in Chapter 14.

[85] *R v Doosti* (1986) 82 Cr App R 181, CA, discussed in §8.5(b), provides a good illustration of the residual judicial discretion to achieve fairness in all the circumstances of the trial.

[86] Cf. *R v Dixon* [2001] Crim LR 126, CA, where the trial judge erroneously informed the jury that evidence of an accomplice's conviction admitted under s.74 was conclusive proof of the underlying burglary. The accused's conviction was quashed on appeal.

[87] *R v Z (Prior Acquittal)* [2000] 2 AC 483, HL, reaffirmed the mirror-image proposition (disavowing the 'rule in *Sambasivam*'), that previous acquittals are not conclusive proof of innocence, either. For discussion, see Paul Roberts, 'Acquitted Misconduct Evidence and Double Jeopardy Principles, From *Sambasivam* to *Z*' [2000] *Crim LR* 952, and other commentaries by Birch [2001] *Crim LR* 222, Munday [2000] CLJ 468, Tapper (2001) 117 *LQR* 1, and Mirfield (2001) 117 *LQR* 194.

tions 73–75 belies the innocuous appearance of these provisions, and may serve as a general warning against the complacent assumption that formal proof by statutory authorization is always 'a mere formality'.[88]

(b) AGREED EVIDENCE

In an adversarial system, the parties are officially the primary provider and conduit of information placed before the fact-finder. The prosecution and defence in criminal proceedings assemble their own evidence and call witnesses at trial from whom they expect to elicit favourable testimony (though, of course, counsel's expectations may be disappointed by what a chosen witness actually tells the court when he or she goes into the witness-box). The powerful image of an adversarial contest must not, however, lead one to overlook the fact that a significant amount of information presented to juries in criminal trials is actually agreed by the parties in advance and stipulated to be true for the purposes of the proceedings.

Section 10(1) of the Criminal Justice Act 1967 provides that 'any fact of which oral evidence may be given in any criminal proceedings may be admitted for the purpose of those proceedings by or on behalf of the prosecutor or defendant, and the admission by any party of any such fact under this section shall as against that party be conclusive evidence in those proceedings of the fact admitted'. If formal admissions are made out of court they must be signed in writing, and are subject to counsel's approval.[89] As well as binding the parties in the current trial, a formal admission is operative in any 'subsequent criminal proceedings relating to that matter (including any appeal or retrial)',[90] though an admission may be vacated at any time with the leave of the court.[91] Formal admissions under section 10 are clearly stated to be limited to matters which could otherwise be proved by admissible oral testimony.[92] However, section 9 of the 1967 Act effectively authorizes the parties by agreement to circumvent the hearsay rule to the extent of adducing a signed witness statement 'as evidence to the like extent as oral evidence to the like effect by that person'. The cumulative effect of sections 9 and 10 of the Criminal Justice Act 1967 is to allow the parties to adduce written witness statements as agreed evidence at trial, provided that the content of the statement would have been admissible as oral testimony. It is difficult to know how much evidence is routinely presented to the jury in this consensual fashion, but the practice is probably endemic – just as guilty pleas and directed acquittals, rather than contested trials, are the humdrum reality of the greater part of criminal litigation.[93]

'Section 9 witness statements' and formal admissions under section 10 reflect the pragmatic imperatives of expediting trial proceedings and minimizing avoidable costs, considerations which appear especially compelling where there is no material dispute between

---

[88] Further probative complications arise where the previous conviction (or acquittal) in question was produced by a foreign court. This is an increasingly likely scenario within a borderless Europe: cf. *R v Kordasinksi* [2007] 1 Cr App R 17, [2006] EWCA Crim 2984.   [89] s.10(2).

[90] s.10(3).   [91] s.10(4).

[92] Cf. *R v Coulson* [1997] Crim LR 886, CA (police officer's hearsay-based suspicions that a third party was a 'known drugs user' cannot be the subject of a s.10 admission).

[93] In the Royal Commission's *Crown Court Study*, counsel attempted to settle evidence in advance of trial in 27% of cases, and were successful in securing formal admissions in around 80% of such cases: Michael Zander and Paul Henderson, *Crown Court Study* RCCJ Research Study No 19 (HMSO, 1993), 73.

the parties about a particular matter. Moreover, paring down the issues should help the jury to get to the heart of the matter and concentrate its fact-finding energies on the main points in dispute.[94] Restricting the jury's focus to a limited number of disputed facts might therefore conceivably be in everybody's best interests, though this is by no means inevitable. A guilty accused with no real defence may prefer to see the fact-finder confused and diverted away from a clear-headed appraisal of the evidence, for example, whilst prosecutors also sometimes have tactical reasons for seeking to open up or close down particular lines of inquiry.

The adversarial structure of English criminal procedure suggests a deeper rationale for permitting agreed evidence. It is a hallmark of an adversarial system, in which the parties enjoy substantial freedom to define the parameters of the litigation contest, that disputable issues can be resolved peremptorily by agreement between the parties. This follows from the notion that dispute resolution – a.k.a. achieving justice[95] – is the overriding objective of adversarial adjudication.[96] Points on which the prosecution and defence are agreed at trial can be regarded as settled and require no further scrutiny by judge or jury. Indeed, formal admissions are not always necessary to achieve this. A similar type of closure around specified issues or evidence can be implemented by a sort of 'gentleman's agreement' or tacit understanding between the parties' lawyers that their respective clients' mutual self-interest will be better served by keeping the jury selectively uninformed and in the dark. Party-autonomy is thereby promoted, but potentially at the expense of truth-finding. Critics of adversarialism might view such forensic tactics as a truth-defeating conspiracy of silence.[97] Though ostensibly routine and innocuous, agreed evidence provisions, like sections 9 and 10 of the Criminal Justice Act 1967, are therefore part-and-parcel of broader debates surrounding the merits of adversarial criminal procedure.

(c) VIEWS AND DEMONSTRATIONS

The 'view' is an interesting variation on the production of real evidence and exhibits at trial. If the evidence cannot conveniently be brought to the jurors, Mohammed must go to the mountain. It is occasionally decided, on the application of any party or of the court's own motion, that jurors would be assisted in their assessment of the evidence by being taken to see the scene of the crime or some other relevant location or object. A 'view' then technically becomes a 'demonstration' if the jury is invited to observe more than an inert *locus in quo*. Where, for example, an eyewitness is present and explains that 'I stood about

---

[94] *R* v *Greenwood* [2005] 1 Cr App R 7, CA.   [95] Cf. CrimPR 2010, Rule 1.1.   [96] §2.3(d).

[97] The majority of continental jurists, steeped in a tradition of extending judicial scrutiny to all significant factual determinations, would tend to agree. The contrast in approach is strongest in relation to guilty pleas, which civilian lawyers typically regard with great suspicion. For further discussion, see Thomas Weigend, 'The Decay of the Inquisitorial Ideal: Plea Bargaining Invades German Criminal Procedure', in John Jackson, Maximo Langer, and Peter Tillers (eds.), *Crime, Procedure and Evidence in a Comparative and International Context* (Hart, 2008); Abraham S. Goldstein, 'Converging Criminal Justice Systems: Guilty Pleas and the Public Interest' (1997) 31 *Israel LR* 169; Bert Swart, 'Settling Criminal Cases Without a Trial' (1997) 31 *Israel LR* 223; Joachim Herrmann, 'Bargaining Justice – A Bargain for German Criminal Justice?' (1992) 53 *University of Pittsburgh LR* 755; John H. Langbein, 'Torture and Plea Bargaining' (1978) 46 *University of Chicago LR* 3.

here, and looked in this direction', we have a demonstration in both the literal and the legal-technical sense.[98]

The potential benefits of views and demonstrations are obvious. Where a case turns on the testimony of a key eyewitness, for example, it might be helpful for jurors in assessing the reliability of the witness's testimony to observe the scene for themselves and try to imagine how the events in question must have appeared to the witness at the time. Is there a clear line of sight, or do natural or man-made obstacles obscure the observer's vision? What would the lighting conditions have been like at the material time? Is the witness tall enough to be able to see over that wall, as he claims? Or again, the cause of a road accident might more easily be gauged by direct inspection of a blind bend or concealed entrance. It sometimes helps to concretize a disputed question of fact by being able to see a physical location for oneself, rather than merely having it depicted by proxy. If a picture is worth a thousand words, how much more valuable a direct viewing of the real thing?

On the downside, conducting a view is time-consuming and expensive, and its probative value may be equivocal. Visiting the locus might serve only to mislead or to induce a false sense of confidence in jurors who, after all, have no formal training in crime scene examination. And there is always the risk that jurors will be exposed to unauthorized and potentially prejudicial information in the relatively uncontrolled environment of an on-site view. On balance, regular juror 'away-days' seem unlikely to be conducive to the efficient administration of justice, and this doubtless accounts for the rarity of extra-curial views and demonstrations. A high-profile prosecution under the War Crimes Act 1991 provides a striking illustration of potential difficulties. In *Sawoniuk*,[99] the jury and a substantial entourage of court personnel and media hangers-on traipsed all the way to Belarus to inspect the site of alleged World War II atrocities. The merits of this 'view' – which was instigated by the defence – are far from self-evident.[100] The utility of inspecting the locus in quo over fifty years after the events in question took place may be doubted, whilst touring sites of Nazi war crimes may have evoked powerful – and potentially prejudicial – emotional responses from the jurors. With the benefit of hindsight, photographs might have been just as helpful, less risky, and far cheaper.

Expert evidence will often be a viable alternative to conducting a view in the majority of cases. The relevant information may be provided by a scenes of crime examiner (SOCO) or police photographer, for example. Courts have occasionally received video-recorded reconstructions of the alleged offence itself, produced by police investigators with the co-operation of the accused.[101] There is also the possibility of computer-aided courtroom simulations, the scope for which is constantly expanding with the development of

---

[98] Cf. *M v DPP* [2009] EWHC 752, [2009] Crim LR 658, DC (magistrates parking their car in the place where the victim's car had suffered criminal damage did not turn a view into a demonstration).

[99] *R v Sawoniuk* [2000] 2 Cr App R 220, [2000] Crim LR 506, CA.

[100] David Ormerod, 'A Prejudicial View?' [2000] Crim LR 452.

[101] *Li Shu-ling v R* [1989] AC 270, PC. Cf. *R v Quinn* [1962] 2 QB 245, 257, CCA, where Ashworth J. said: 'demonstrations are altogether different in character from a reconstruction of an entire scene, a reconstruction which has been brought into existence in private for the purpose of constituting evidence at a trial. It is obvious that to allow such a reconstruction would be introducing a method of proof which would be most unsatisfactory for the reason that it would be almost impossible to analyse motion by motion those slight differences which may in the totality result in a scene of quite a different character from [the original events] .... [T]his objection goes not only to weight, as was argued, but to admissibility: it is not the best evidence.'

new technologies. Video film reconstructions and computer-generated simulations can be classified as 'demonstrative evidence', together with such tried-and-tested, lower-tech alternatives as models, graphs, and charts.[102]

(d) INFORMAL EVIDENCE

A further set of more intangible evidential sources is hardly ever mentioned in cases, textbooks, or academic commentary on the Law of Evidence. What (for the want of a better label) we will call 'informal evidence' comprises information which is imparted informally to the jury during the course of the proceedings, by the words or behaviour of counsel, from the reactions of the public gallery, through media reporting of the on-going proceedings, or from informal courtroom interactions between jurors, witnesses, and legal professionals. The most important source of such information is the accused himself, as he sits through the trial proceedings, readily observable and frequently scrutinized by jurors. Significantly, in English criminal trials, the accused sits isolated in the dock, the physical geography of the courtroom accentuating his transitional moral status as a person called upon to answer charges of criminal wrongdoing. Does the accused sit impassively throughout? Or is there a nod, a shake of the head, a smile, or some other meaningful reaction to the unfolding evidence? How does the accused appear to respond to the complainant's testimony? Does he appear remorseful or defiant, stare off into space, listen intently, or apparently sit and sneer?

The accused's reactions will obviously be equivocal on many occasions, and how, if at all, they affect a jury's evaluation of a particular witness, or of the case as a whole, can only be the subject of speculation, at least for as long as serving jurors remain off-limits to researchers.[103] Yet we would be overlooking a significant aspect of the criminal trial's 'spectacular performance' if we failed to register the potential impact of such informal influences on a jury's deliberations. Our inquiry must therefore extend beyond those sources of information dignified by doctrinal orthodoxy as 'evidence', to embrace the totality of informational resources in criminal adjudication. This expanded vision implies an ambitious research agenda which to-date has barely even been fully formulated by Evidence scholars, much less systematically implemented. For now we must content ourselves with drawing attention to anecdotal examples as a basis for further and better-informed speculation and future research. The US trial of the British *au pair* Louise Woodward provides one suggestive illustration.

Louise Woodward was convicted of the second-degree murder of baby Matthew Eappen, one of two Eappen children in her care, who died from a pronounced skull fracture which

---

[102] For further discussion and many more illustrations, see Peter Tillers (ed.), 'Graphic and Visual Representations of Evidence and Inference in Legal Settings' (2007) 6 *Law, Probability & Risk*, Special Issue; H. Wayne Gardner, 'Explanations and Illustrations: Demonstrative Evidence in the Criminal Court-room' (1996) 38 *Criminal Law Quarterly* 425.

[103] It is a contempt of court both for jurors themselves to divulge information about their deliberations or votes in the juryroom, and for anybody else to encourage them to do so: Contempt of Court Act 1981, s.8. However, this does not preclude research with mock jurors, which is increasingly sophisticated and illuminating: see, e.g., Cheryl Thomas, *Are Juries Fair?* Ministry of Justice Research Series 1/10 (2010); Louise Ellison and Vanessa Munro, 'Getting to (Not) Guilty: Examining Jurors' Deliberative Processes in, and Beyond, the Context of a Mock Rape Trial' (2010) 30 *Legal Studies* 74; Emily Finch and Vanessa E. Munro, 'Juror Stereotypes and Blame Attribution in Rape Cases Involving Intoxicants: The Findings of a Pilot Study' (2005) 45 *British Journal of Criminology* 25.

the prosecution said could only have been inflicted by a deliberate blow. It was suggested at the time that American jurors must have drawn negative impressions from Woodward's demeanour in the witness-box, which was widely described as cold and unemotional. This fitted with the prosecution's depiction of Woodward as a sophomore Lady Macbeth, who had battered baby Matthew's brains out in a fit of temper and then lied to cover her tracks. However, Woodward's extraordinary emotional outburst in reaction to the jury's guilty verdict may have immediately sown fresh doubt, not only in the minds of jurors, but also with the viewing millions around the world who had watched enthralled, via live satellite broadcast, as the trial unfolded. Observers remarked on the sharp contrast between the sincerity of Woodward's spontaneous violent sobbing after she had been convicted and the apparently scripted performance of the accused and her defence team during the trial, which in all probability had alienated the jury against them:

[C]onfidence emanated from the defence table, and it ricocheted around the courtroom. Which was exactly the problem with their case. Right from the start, they were over-confident. And if there is one thing juries like less than an over-technical trial, it is an over-confident, cocky defendant.... Then there was the time she started laughing in the witness box. Yes, she was nervous, but it never looked like nervous laughter. Coached relentlessly by her defence team, she started to snigger when Andrew Good, her own attorney, tearfully asked her if she had ever shaken or hurt Matthew. 'No, I did not', she said, smiling broadly as if laughing at a friend who was behaving strangely. Then she bit her lip and tried to stop herself. To stop her laughing in court again, her lawyers instructed her to keep drinking water – which she did, non-stop, during the cross-examination.[104]

Of course it was too late for the jury to change its mind, once a verdict of guilty had been formally pronounced. Perhaps if Woodward had broken down before rather than after the jury's retirement the verdict might have been different. Irrespective of *Woodward*'s ultimate denouement,[105] criminal trials as dramatic and topical as this remind us that trials are 'staged' public events in their own right, which are designed to function as a rich, multi-layered source of information addressed to the fact-finder, and beyond to the public gallery – both literal and figurative. The jury is surely influenced in arriving at its verdict, both consciously and unconsciously, by the myriad subtle interactions and meaningful exchanges which together constitute the drama of the trial.

The *Woodward* case nicely illustrates the cultural variability of evaluating human conduct.[106] Americans weaned on Oprah and Jerry Springer stereotypically expect truthful witnesses to be emotional and demonstrative, whereas the British preference is supposedly

---

[104] Joanna Coles and Ed Vulliamy, 'The Conviction of Louise Woodward', *The Observer*, 2 November 1997 (WL 13000335). Also see Pamela Ferdinand, 'Mass. Jury Finds Au Pair Guilty in Baby's Death; English Teenager Faces Life for Second-Degree Murder,' *Washington Post*, 31 October 1997 (WL 14710435); Diane Purkiss, 'The Children of Medea: Euripides, Louise Woodward, and Deborah Eappen' (1999) 11 *Cardozo Studies in Law and Literature* 53.

[105] In the event, Woodward's murder conviction was set aside by the trial judge, in exercise of a broadly-worded discretion not available to English judges to vacate jury verdicts in order to rectify a failure of justice. Woodward was re-sentenced to time-served for manslaughter, and released: see Daniel P. Barry, 'Commonwealth v Woodward, A Failure of Justice Averted' (1999) 4 *Suffolk Journal of Trial and Appellate Advocacy* 295.

[106] Another memorable example is the Greek plane-spotting case, discussed by Paul Roberts, 'Why International Criminal Evidence?' in Paul Roberts and Mike Redmayne (eds.), *Innovations in Evidence and Proof* (Hart, 2007), 371–2.

for self-discipline, reserve, and the stiff upper lip.[107] In these culturally-scripted ways, criminal trials may be said to encapsulate in microcosm, and for better or worse, the peculiarities of national character. These themes are explored further in the next chapter's discussion of 'common sense' fact-finding.

3.5 CONCEPTIONS OF EVIDENCE AND PRINCIPLES OF JUSTICE

The modern criminal trial process evolved for the express purpose of communicating information to the fact-finder and testing its reliability. Witness testimony, documents, and real evidence are the principal sources of information in criminal litigation which, understandably, attract the lion's share of attention in Evidence texts, including this one. Yet trials routinely expose jurors to a range of more subtle informational cues and resources. Regrettably, these have often slipped below the radar of traditional evidentiary concerns, and remain relatively unregulated by the formal law of evidence Recognizing the full range and diversity of sources of information in criminal litigation has important theoretical and practical implications. As well as recasting doctrinal issues and highlighting practical problems for modern litigation, an expanded conception of informational resources prompts reconsideration of the foundational objectives, values, and presuppositions of criminal trials.

The right to be heard, enshrined in Article 6(1) of the European Convention on Human Rights as the right to a 'fair and public hearing', is one of the most basic rights of a person accused of crime. To deny an accused person the opportunity of challenging the evidence or factual assumptions underpinning his conviction would usually be considered an elementary failure of justice. The right to be heard shares a common root with the right of compulsory process compelling the testimony of material witnesses.[108] Together these procedural principles ensure that the parties are afforded a fair opportunity to participate in the proceedings and to contest any evidence that might turn out to be adverse to their interests. In accordance with these principles, the formal legal position is that issues of fact must be decided only upon evidence that the litigants have placed before the court.[109]

---

[107] As one contemporary US commentator put it, 'Where was the emotion, some Americans wanted to know, where were the signs of inner turmoil and the anguish, the tortured features, the tears, the sobs of an unjustly accused woman or, depending on the viewer's opinion, the wrenching of deep regret for a horrible crime? Or, if not that, then the paralysis and vacuous blankness of someone who cannot face what she did or her fate, at least? No, what they got was a composed young woman who spoke in carefully parsed and always complete sentences. To some, she seemed calculated, cold. The only time she broke down was when the jury's verdict was read and she said out loud, "How could they do this to me!" and buried her head in her hands. That was more like it, but it didn't last very long.... [J]udging from my experiences in Britain you are much more likely to see full frontal nudity on British television than the sort of emotional outbursts and revelations of inner conflicts that we are exposed to routinely in American daytime television talk shows': Adrian Peracchio, 'Yo! The Mother Tongue is Spoken Differently Here', *Newsday*, 13 November 1997 (WL 2717966). [108] §7.3.

[109] This is the modern expectation. At one time, however, jurors served as 'compurgators' who were expected to resolve disputes on the basis of their own first-hand knowledge of the parties and the events in question: see James Q. Whitman, *The Origins of Reasonable Doubt* (Yale UP, 2008), ch 5; George Fisher, 'The Jury's Rise as Lie Detector' (1997) 107 *Yale LJ* 575; Sir William Holdsworth, *A History of English Law*, vol. 1 (Methuen, 7th edn. 1956), 317; Colin Manchester, 'Judicial Notice and Personal Knowledge' (1979)

Adjudication is supposedly based on evidence in the lawyer's narrow technical sense, meaning admissible evidence formally adduced at trial. Yet the institutional realities of evidence-taking and fact-finding complicate this picture.

Formal legal doctrine has for the most part chosen to ignore the significance of the courtroom drama as a source of information in criminal litigation, and consequently has made little constructive contribution to its analysis or regulation.[110] Fortunately, the potential of other routine features of criminal litigation to strain or warp legal principle is more widely appreciated. Trial judges instruct jurors that '[t]he evidence is what you hear in court and nowhere else; and it is for you, the jury – and no one else – to assess it'.[111] Jurors are specifically warned against speaking to anybody else – 'that includes your family and friends' – about the case and implored not to 'try to obtain information elsewhere (e.g. on the internet) about the case in general or about other matters that are raised during the trial'. It is explained that 'if you were, unknown to the prosecution and defence, to research your own sources of information they would not be in a position to comment on or otherwise deal with it and that would not be fair'. Yet if jurors are supposed to confine their attention to evidence formally presented in the trial, how can this be squared with their reliance on personal background knowledge and frequent recourse to common sense factual inferences in arriving at their verdict? Whilst evidence adduced in court is subjected to the 'quality control' of rules of admissibility, the fact-finder's unarticulated general knowledge obviously evades this safeguard. How, then, can procedural law guarantee the integrity of the evidential basis of criminal adjudication? A third issue concerns the institutional division of labour between judge and jury, which we began to explore in the previous chapter. Is the judge legally entitled to bind the parties and instruct the jury to accept certain facts as given, when it is normally for the parties to adduce evidence and for the jury to determine the facts? We will see in the next chapter that English law has sought to resolve these tensions in its time-honoured evolutionary fashion, through pragmatic accommodation between the dictates of principle and the practical exigencies of criminal litigation.

---

42 MLR 22; Edward Jenks, 'According to the Evidence', in G. G. Alexander (ed.), *Cambridge Legal Essays* (Heffer, 1926), 191.

[110] Certain rules of evidence and procedure do, however, implicitly venture onto this terrain. The list includes judicial directions on the presumption of innocence (see Chapter 6) and on dock identifications of the perpetrator (see Chapter 15). There is also the important procedural rule that nothing said by an advocate should be treated as evidence: only the witness's – verbal or non-verbal – responses to an advocate's questions are formally regarded as evidence in the trial: see, e.g., *R v Hussain (Tariq)* [2007] EWCA Crim 1918, [16]; *R v Lovelock* [2007] EWCA Crim 476.

[111] JSB Specimen Direction No. 55a – Initial Remarks to the Jury.

4

FACT-FINDING AND PROOF

4.1 TAKING FACTS SERIOUSLY

Evidence texts and treatises typically organize their subject matter around the exposition of rules, and in this respect scholarship reflects common usage. Lawyers speak generally of the 'rules of evidence'. Familiar evidentiary doctrines such as the 'rule against hearsay' and the 'rule against narrative'[1] are commonly presented in the language of rules, and referred to collectively as rules of admissibility. Many of this book's chapters resemble the traditional format in being taken up with discussions of these various legal rules. However, it follows from what was said in the previous chapter about the significance of (logical) relevance that legal rules cannot be *the sole* preoccupation of juridical evidence and proof. Doctrinal points of procedural law frequently arise in criminal trials and regularly form the basis of appeals. Disputes about the substantive criminal law are less routine, but perfectly familiar and potentially of great significance when they do arise. Yet by far the greater share of time and effort in litigation is devoted, not to wrangles over legal rules of either substance or procedure, but to collecting, presenting, testing, challenging, and evaluating 'the evidence'; devoted, that is to say, to 'the facts', rather than the law.

The apparent mismatch between Evidence treatises' preoccupation with rules, and the reality of legal practice which is dominated by fact-finding, has become a commonplace of modern scholarship. William Twining summed up the situation in two memorable similes.[2] The rule-based conception of the Law of Evidence, he suggested, resembles a slice of Gruyère, with more empty holes than cheese; or is reminiscent of the Cheshire Cat in *Alice in Wonderland*, 'who keeps appearing and disappearing and fading away, so that sometimes one could see the whole body, sometimes only a head, sometimes only a vague outline and sometimes nothing at all, so that Alice was never sure whether or not he was there or, indeed, whether he existed at all'.[3] Both similes are apt. Today the hearsay prohibition,[4] the very epitome of common law exclusionary rules, is riddled with exceptions to the point where the holes in the rule are more extensive than its residual coverage. And rules on such topics as character evidence,[5] witness credibility, and the privilege against self-incrimination have an elusive and amorphous quality not unlike the enigmatic Cheshire Cat.[6]

---

[1] §8.3.

[2] William Twining, 'What is the Law of Evidence?' in *Rethinking Evidence: Exploratory Essays* (CUP, 2nd edn. 2006), ch 6.　　　　　　　　　　　　　　　　　　　　[3] ibid. 211–12.

[4] See Chapter 9.　　　[5] See Chapter 14.

[6] Also see Christine Boyle, 'A Principled Approach to Relevance: The Cheshire Cat in Canada', in Paul Roberts and Mike Redmayne (eds.), *Innovations in Evidence and Proof* (Hart, 2007).

Twining draws programmatic conclusions from his critique of the excessive concentration on exclusionary rules, arguing for a 'total process' view of litigation which would extend the domain of Evidence to incorporate proof and fact-finding, and would have appropriate regard to the varied contexts in which adjudication takes place. Other writers have drawn attention to the significance of 'narrative construction' – the formulation and elaboration of 'stories' – in litigation generally, and in the courtroom in particular.[7] What stories do the parties, through their lawyers, narrate to the fact-finder? In a murder trial, for example, the accused might be presented by the prosecutor as a vicious and calculating harridan who took the opportunity to despatch her husband as punishment for his fecklessness. The defence, in response, might tell an altogether different story, perhaps of a long-abused wife lashing out in desperation at the onset of yet another violent and unprovoked assault by her brute of a husband, a case of self-defence rather than culpable homicide. Story-telling is an integral and essential feature of legal proceedings, which involves – as this example well demonstrates – social, political, and ethical choices which may be exceedingly controversial.[8] Some commentators argue that lawyers' preoccupation with rules serves to obscure these value choices at the heart of litigation. It is said that Evidence books and curricula require radical overhaul, to incorporate candid recognition of the politics of legal proceedings,[9] as well as to make university teaching more useful for intending practitioners who will find, when they actually come to try criminal cases, that most of their energies are consumed by fact-management.[10] The busy trial lawyer has little time and even less occasion to grapple with those paper rules which are the mainstays of criminal appeals and undergraduate legal education but only infrequently crop up in legal practice.

This is the argument for 'taking facts seriously'.[11] To achieve a rounded view of the law of evidence it is necessary to know something about the nature of the holes in the cheese,

---

[7] See Nancy Pennington and Reid Hastie, 'The Story Model For Juror Decision Making', in Reid Hastie (ed.), *Inside the Juror: The Psychology of Juror Decision-Making* (CUP, 1993); Michael S. Pardo and Ronald J. Allen, 'Juridical Proof and the Best Explanation' (2008) 27 *Law and Philosophy* 223; Terence Anderson, David Schum, and William Twining, *Analysis of Evidence* (CUP, 2nd edn. 2005), ch 6; William Twining, *Rethinking Evidence*, chs 9–10.

[8] See §4.6, below. Further examples illuminating the moral and political dimensions of forensic story-telling, and their broader social implications, include: David Hirsch, 'The Trial of Andrei Sawoniuk: Holocaust Testimony Under Cross-Examination' (2001) 10 *Social and Legal Studies* 529; Tony Jefferson, 'The Tyson Rape Trial: The Law, Feminism and Emotional "Truth"' (1997) 6 *Social and Legal Studies* 281; Christine Bell and Marie Fox, 'Telling Stories of Women Who Kill' (1996) 5 *Social and Legal Studies* 471; Keith Soothill and Debbie Soothill, 'Prosecuting the Victim? A Study of the Reporting of Barristers' Comments in Rape Cases' (1993) 32 *Howard Journal of Criminal Justice* 12; Anne Worrall, *Offending Women: Female Lawbreakers and the Criminal Justice System* (1990), ch 6.

[9] Donald Nicolson, 'Truth, Reason and Justice: Epistemology and Politics in Evidence Discourse' (1994) 57 *Modern Law Review* 726; Kenneth W. Graham Jr, '"There'll Always be an England": The Instrumental Ideology of Evidence' (1987) 85 *Michigan Law Review* 1204 (and the withering riposte by William Twining, 'Hot Air in the Redwoods, A Sequel to the Wind in the Willows' (1988) 86 *Michigan Law Review* 1523).

[10] See Anderson, Schum, and Twining, *Analysis of Evidence*, ch 1; Donald Nicolson, 'Facing Facts: The Teaching of Fact Construction in University Law Schools' (1997) 1 *E & P* 132.

[11] cf. Twining, 'Taking Facts Seriously', in N. Gold (ed.), *Essays on Legal Education* (Toronto, Butterworths, 1982) (reprinted (1984) 34 *Journal of Legal Education* 22); and Twining, *Rethinking Evidence*, ch 2; Twining, 'Taking Facts Seriously – Again', in Paul Roberts and Mike Redmayne (eds.), *Innovations in Evidence and Proof* (Hart, 2007); and Nicolson, 'Truth Reason and Justice', 741: 'Universities need, therefore, to start "taking facts seriously". And, unless other courses are to be devoted to the factual side of lawyering, the subject of Evidence needs to be reconceptualised.'

and to be better prepared for the Cheshire Cat's disappearing act. We begin our inquiry into fact-finding by looking more carefully at the type of 'facts' which must be found in criminal adjudication, building on Chapter 2's discussion of the jury's role in developing and applying normative standards. This conceptual analysis is rounded off by a section exploring the supposed distinction between facts and 'opinions'. It turns out that these are points on a continuum rather than sharply differentiated categories.

The remainder of the chapter examines the relationship between fact-finding and proof. We will see that forensic fact-finding generally adopts the ordinary canons of 'common sense' logical inference which are perfectly familiar from everyday life. Probability, too, frequently crops up in litigation. Mathematical theorems are naturally just as valid in the courtroom as they are anywhere else, though formalized probabilistic reasoning may pose particular problems for a system of criminal adjudication predicated on lay fact-finding. This largely explains why English judges have been hostile to certain attempted uses of mathematical formulae and probabilistic reasoning.

The final two sections of the chapter explore the extent to which the law deems it possible and desirable to regulate common sense fact-finding and actively manage the process of inference. The doctrine of 'judicial notice' empowers the trial judge to remove particular issues from adversarial dispute and substitute his or her own common sense for the fact-finder's. Properly confined, judicial notice is an expedient technique for promoting efficient adjudication, but the potential for controversial applications and judicial overreaching is obvious. The conceptual incontinence of 'judicial notice' in English law has not assisted trial judges to exercise their powers of trial management in accordance with evidentiary principle.

Chapter 2 described the formal procedural mechanisms through which trial judges can seek to influence the jury's deliberations.[12] Setting aside peremptory interventions such as stays for abuse of process and directed acquittals, the trial judge's main tools for filleting the information available to jurors and influencing how they use it are admissibility determinations and directions issued as part of the summing-up. However, both of these procedural devices mainly target judicial 'evidence' in the narrow sense, particularized items of information proffered or adduced in evidence by the parties. To what extent are trial judges willing and able to regulate the full range of sources of information in criminal litigation identified in the last chapter? To what extent should they do so?

4.2 FINDING FACTS[13]

The jurisprudential distinction between law and fact has important procedural ramifications in English legal proceedings. Received legal wisdom has it that litigants must plead only facts, not law; that the jury decides questions of fact, leaving questions of law for the

[12] §2.5.
[13] Generally, see Hock Lai Ho, *A Philosophy of Evidence Law – Justice in the Search for Truth* (OUP, 2008), ch 1; Ronald J. Allen and Michael S. Pardo, 'Facts in Law and Facts of Law' (2003) 7 *E & P* 153; A. A. S. Zuckerman, 'Law, Fact or Justice?' (1986) 66 *Boston University LR* 487; John Jackson, 'Questions of Fact and Questions of Law', in William Twining (ed.), *Facts in Law* (Franz Steiner, 1983), and essays by Ockelton, White, and Summers, ibid.

judge; that decisions on the law give rise to binding precedent, whereas factual determinations do not; and that appeals (as opposed to retrial *de novo*) are, generally speaking, on points of law, not fact.

The classificatory distinction between fact and law is meant to track a substantive distinction between questions about past events (or occasionally predictions about the future)[14] and questions about their legal consequences. Common lawyers differentiate 'questions of law' from 'questions of fact'.[15] Legal rules specify the rights, duties, and liabilities which crystallize in particular scenarios, whilst the underlying facts of particular cases are assumed to exist independently of legal definitions and categories. On a plain view of the matter, legal process serves the instrumental function of discovering the truth of disputed facts – finding out 'what really happened' – so that the appropriate legal consequences may follow. Most people – lawyers and laymen alike – regard fact-finding as a process of historical enquiry, sharply differentiated from the normative enterprise of identifying, applying and, where necessary, developing the law. To ascertain the facts in legal adjudication, it is said, one need only employ the familiar reasoning processes utilized in any factual inquiry.[16]

In reality, there is no clear or determinate boundary separating the descriptive realm of fact from the normative realm of law. Chapter 2 introduced the idea that decision-making by juries is not confined to the straightforwardly factual, but also extends to determining normative moral issues, like the meaning of dishonesty in theft and the ambit of 'gross negligence' in manslaughter.[17] This suggests an overlap or blurring between the spheres of 'law' and 'fact', which legal theory has traditionally conceived as distinct, autonomous realms. Forensic fact-finding is consequently more complex, and inevitably more controversial, than any simplistic fact-law dichotomy might encourage one to believe.

(a) CONSTITUTIVE FACTS AND EVIDENTIAL FACTS

The first stage in moving beyond rigid and simplistic dichotomies is to appreciate that 'facts' play different roles in legal adjudication. An important analytical distinction for our purposes is the contrast between facts established directly by the evidence before the court (testimony, documents, objects, etc.) and derivative factual inferences and conclusions drawn from that evidence. For example, a witness might testify to the fact that the burglar had brown hair, from which the jury infers the further fact that the accused, who also has brown hair, committed the burglary. Even this simple contrived example indicates that 'facts' in legal proceedings are of differing types and qualities. The jury can

---

[14] Certain litigated questions concern future events, such as a tort victim's loss of future earnings or prospects for recovery: cf. *Gary Smith v Ben Collett* [2009] EWCA Civ 583 (court awarded £3.85 million damages in lost future earnings to Manchester United trainee footballer whose career was cut short by a dangerously high tackle). Assessing the risks of future offending posed by particular offenders has become a routine feature of sentencing hearings in England and Wales: see, e.g., *R v Bennett* [2008] 1 Cr App R (S) 11, [2007] EWCA Crim 1093 (applying CJA 2003, s.225).

[15] 'Questions of "law" and questions of "fact" may be combined in a question of "mixed law and fact" but the judicial process of dealing with any of these three classes of question is different in kind from the judicial process of exercising a discretion conferred by law': *Mohindar Singh v R* [1950] AC 345, 355, PC. Cf. *Farmer v Cotton's Trustees* [1915] AC 922, 932, HL ('it is not always easy to distinguish between questions of fact and questions of law').   [16] Thayer, *A Preliminary Treatise on Evidence at the Common Law*, 265.

[17] §2.3.

see for itself that the accused has brown hair, whereas jurors need to rely on the witness's word for the fact that the offender also had brown hair. The fact that the accused is guilty of the burglary is of a different kind again. So to speak, there are facts and there are facts. Unfortunately, these important distinctions tend to become obscured in legal theory and practice. Part of the reason for their obscurity is the inherent strangeness of reflecting seriously on something – common sense factual reasoning – that we all do every day and normally take for granted. However, the difficulty is exacerbated by Evidence scholars' lack of a standard conceptual notation for differentiating types of fact.

Analytical work on concepts of facts was previously undertaken by an American legal philosopher, Wesley Newcomb Hohfeld, writing in the 1920s. Hohfeld proposed distinguishing between 'evidential' and 'constitutive' facts, in the following way:

An evidential fact is one which, on being ascertained, affords some logical basis – not conclusive – for inferring some other facts. The latter may be either a constitutive fact or an intermediate evidential fact.[18]

Hohfeld's 'constitutive facts' are variously known to lawyers as 'ultimate', 'material', 'operative', or 'dispositive' facts, or simply as 'the facts in issue'. These are facts to which the law attaches specified legal consequences. Thus, in English law a sane adult who intentionally kills another person in the absence of any recognized justification or excuse is guilty of murder. The facts corresponding to each element of the offence definition – the fact of a killing by a sane adult; the fact that the victim was a person; the fact that the killing was done intentionally; and the fact that the killing was neither justified nor excused[19] – are constitutive of the crime of murder. Courts are only invited to adjudicate on factual disputes affecting legal rights, duties, or other cognizable causes of action. In Hohfeldian terminology, the epistemic objective of legal proceedings is to ascertain the constitutive facts designated by substantive law.[20]

---

[18] Wesley Newcomb Hohfeld, *Fundamental Legal Conceptions as Applied in Judicial Reasoning* (Yale UP, 1923), 34. A minor correction is that sometimes evidential facts *do* have necessary implications, though these are seldom of great practical significance. For example, from the fact that *V* is clinically dead it follows by necessary implication that he is not breathing, that he will not get up, that he is not reading this book, etc. Hohfeld should have said 'not *necessarily* conclusive'.

[19] Anticipating complexities discussed later in this section, it is of course controversial whether the moral standards incorporated into legal justifications and excuses are properly described as '(moral) facts'. Certainly, according to one ontological position – moral realism – moral standards *are* matters of fact: see Michael S. Moore, 'Moral Reality Revisited' (1992) 90 *Michigan LR* 2424. But one need not insist on any strong ontological commitment, since concrete examples of justification and excuse always refer to conduct or states of affairs that are indubitably matters of fact. For example, it is possible to inquire whether, *in fact*, *D* had a genuine belief in the need for self-defensive force, without prejudicing the issue as to whether such a belief is exculpatory in either law or morals, and certainly without implying any ontological thesis. Only the most hard-bitten fact-sceptic would contest that proposition, and there are none too many of them: cf. William Twining, 'Some Scepticism about Some Scepticisms' (1984) 11 *British Journal of Law and Society* 137. At the other end of the ontological spectrum, a reflective moral realist might want to bring (i) *D*'s actual beliefs, (ii) pertinent legal doctrine, *and* (iii) the moral truth about justifications and excuses all under the umbrella of constitutive facts.

[20] As Thayer, *A Preliminary Treatise on Evidence at the Common Law*, 197, put it: 'When it is said that a fact is for the jury, the fact intended … is that which is in issue, the ultimate fact, that to which the law directly annexes consequences.' Being designated by substantive law, constitutive facts are often couched in the language of legal rules and concepts, such as 'grievous bodily harm', 'deception', or 'trespass', and are frequently only intelligible in these terms.

Hohfeld's 'evidential facts' designate facts presented to the tribunal for the purpose of establishing a constitutive fact. This can be achieved either directly, or indirectly via intermediate evidential facts from which constitutive facts may ultimately be inferred. Finding the accused's fingerprints on the murder weapon, for example, might – through a sequence of successive, 'cascaded' inferences – authorize the penultimate[21] inference that the accused was the killer. This example is representative of the greater part of fact-finding in litigation, in that it involves a number of discrete inferential steps, which can be broken down for analytical purposes allowing each individual step to be examined. A police officer produces a gun in court and testifies that he found it at the scene of the crime. A forensic scientist testifies that the gun bore a single fingerprint, which belonged to the accused. The gun and the testimony establishing its provenance and physical condition supply evidential facts, e.g. that the gun presented in court is the same one that was found at the crime scene; that it fired the fatal shot, etc. So does the expert's testimony that the fingerprint found on the gun was created by the accused's finger. From these evidential facts the jury may infer further, intermediate evidential facts: that the accused has indeed handled the gun, that the gun was the murder weapon, and that the accused fired the gun. Finally, the jury is able to determine a constitutive fact: that the accused shot and killed the victim. When combined with other constitutive facts constituting the offence, this factual conclusion may authorize the ultimate inference that the accused is guilty of murder.

Hohfeld insisted that the constitutive facts stated in a criminal charge are not merely *proved* by extra-legal events; rather, he emphasized, these events, properly characterized, *are* the constitutive facts. Thus, on a charge of burglary, the fact that the accused put his arm through the window (where we know this *for a fact*) is not proof of a felonious entry or 'trespass', as a witness's testimony that the accused put his arm through the window would be evidence adduced as proof of that fact. Rather, the fact of the accused's having put his arm through the window is itself the entry, the constitutive fact. Fingerprints on the window frame, or eyewitness testimony that a figure was seen disappearing through the window, would be evidential facts from which the constitutive fact of entry might be inferred. Evidential facts warrant further inferences, whereas constitutive facts are legally significant conclusions bringing the chain of inference to an end, so far as that fact is concerned. But herein lurks a further puzzle. To move from the statement '*X* put his arm through the window' to the conclusion '*X* entered the building' or even, more ambitiously, '*X* trespassed' appears to require some further judgment in ascribing meaning to conduct, an inferential leap beyond self-evident factual generalizations about the material world. It would appear on close examination that constitutive facts – legally relevant conclusions – cannot simply be 'read-off' from brute empirical reality. This puzzle crystallizes the problem of understanding how facts are found in law.

Hohfeld's analysis points to the necessity of developing a better appreciation of how the techniques for establishing evidential facts differ from the process of inferring constitutive facts from them. The completed inferential process, from raw data to legally significant conclusion, involves two significant moves. The first move, which takes us from the witness's testimony or other evidence presented in the trial, to the conclusion that something was 'in fact' the case, is governed by what Thayer called 'logic and general experience'[22]

---

[21] The *ultimate* inference would be that as well as being a killer the accused is a murderer.

[22] Thayer, *A Preliminary Treatise on Evidence at the Common Law*, 265.

or simply 'common sense' inferences and reasoning. In other words, the relation of an evidential fact (the witness's statement) to the fact it tends to prove (that X put his arm through the window) is a function of relevance and probative value. But the second move, from 'X put his arm through the window' to 'X entered the building', requires more. The accused can be convicted of burglary only if putting his arm through the window amounts to the constitutive fact of 'entry'. Definitions of English criminal offences are full of familiar-sounding words and concepts like 'entry', such as 'bodily harm', 'property', 'intention', 'threatening', 'knowingly', 'wounding', and so forth. Oue challenge is to identify the legal rules and linguistic conventions governing the inferential leap from evidential facts to these constitutive facts.

(b) NORMATIVE FACTS

Elizabeth Anscombe once invoked the undeniably mundane example of 'supplying a quarter of potatoes' to illustrate that *every* factual description is *always* under-specified and non-exhaustive, and consequently potentially ambiguous.[23] Anscombe pointed out that a literal 'supplying' of vegetables would not necessarily constitute what would normally be thought of as a potato delivery, as where the potatoes were gone over to seed, or where the potatoes were immediately taken away again, or where they actually belonged to somebody else, etc. She concluded:

There can be no such thing as an exhaustive description of *all* the circumstances which theoretically could impair the description of an action of leaving a quarter of potatoes in my house as 'supplying me with a quarter of potatoes'. If there were such an exhaustive description, one would say that 'Supplying me with a quarter of potatoes' *means* leaving them at my house, together with the absence of any of those circumstances. As things are, we could only say 'It means leaving them... together with the absence of any of the circumstances which would impair the description of that action as an action of supplying me with potatoes'; which is hardly an explanation.

Anscombe's conclusion is germane to the question of whether our alleged burglar 'entered' the building when he put his arm through the window. The point is that this question cannot be definitively settled empirically. Rather, the practical tasks of interpreting and applying legal definitions and managing linguistic ambiguity in litigation are essentially problems of *classification*. Deploying its traditional dichotomy between questions of law and questions of fact, English law has developed three basic strategies for this purpose.

First, the legal meaning of terms sometimes conforms to ordinary usage, that is to say, to the fact-finder's understanding of the way a word or phrase is used in common parlance. The richness and subtlety of ordinary language is indeed a powerful resource for turning evidential generalizations into constitutive facts. On the other hand, reliance on prevailing linguistic practice suffers from the informality and lack of conceptual rigour, not to mention frequent lapses of logic and coherence, which are characteristic of our everyday speech. Common usage is silent or equivocal on the meaning of many constitutive facts, particularly those incorporating quasi-technical expressions such as 'trespass',

---

[23] G. E. M. Anscombe, 'On Brute Facts' (1958) 18 *Analysis* 69.

'appropriation', or 'recklessness'.[24] Ordinary language may fail to match up to the law's extraordinary requirements.

Alternatively, and mindful of the special demands placed on legal definitions, the law might deliberately engineer linguistic closure, by coining legal terms of art defining constitutive facts. For example, a burglary statute might specifically provide that putting one's arm through a window *shall* constitute 'entering' for the purposes of the offence. Legal stipulation can be a neat and effective solution to definitional problems. By increasing the transparency and predictability of adjudication stipulation promotes the formal values of legality.[25] Yet, for the very reason demonstrated by Anscombe's meditations on potato deliveries, it is impossible to formulate exhaustive stipulations of constitutive facts. There will always be significant gaps, and therefore uncertainty, in legal standards because, as J. L. Austin quipped, 'fact is richer than diction'. Quite apart from this threshold philosophical constraint, maximum certainty is not even a desirable objective. Flexibility to modify or depart from fixed general standards is sometimes more important than certainty. It would also frequently be counterproductive to render legal meaning as determinate, certain, and exhaustive as humanly possible. Elaborate definitions quickly become unwieldy. Over-complexity in the law is itself a vice, which tends to generate additional cost, delay, errors, and confusion, and therefore, paradoxically, greater uncertainty.

A third possibility is to invite the trier of fact to settle the meaning of terms for legal, institutional purposes. We saw in Chapter 2 that this is English criminal law's chosen strategy in relation to the *Andrews/Adomako* test for gross negligence manslaughter[26] and the *Feely/Ghosh* test for dishonesty in theft and related offences.[27] On a charge of manslaughter, the jury is invited to determine whether the accused's conduct fell so far below the standard of reasonable care to be expected of a person in the accused's situation that criminal punishment, over and above liability to civil compensation, is warranted. When trying theft offences, the jury must determine whether the accused realized that his conduct was dishonest according to the standards of ordinary decent people.[28] In both scenarios the jury is presented with a radically indeterminate standard of liability and asked to follow its own moral lights, eliding the traditional distinction between applying the law and making it. In Hohfeldian terms, the gap between evidential and constitutive facts is bridged by the jury's

---

[24] In *R* v *Caldwell* [1982] AC 341, HL, Lord Diplock infamously attempted to derive the meaning of the statutory concept of 'recklessness' from its ordinary (Eighth Century Middle English!) etymology: cf. *R* v *Lawrence* [1982] AC 510, 520–1, HL, *per* Lord Hailsham. The troubled career and unlamented demise of 'Caldwell recklessness' in English law stands as an object lesson in the perils of treating common usage as the litmus of statutory interpretation. Lord Edmund-Davies, dissenting ibid. 357, replied: 'The law in action compiles its own dictionary. In time, what was originally the common coinage of speech acquires a different value in the pocket of the lawyer than when in the layman's purse'. Now see *R* v *G* [2004] 1 AC 1034, [2003] UKHL 50.

[25] The ability to predict the legal consequences of one's conduct with a reasonable level of confidence is essential to any future-orientated activity, and therefore one of the pre-conditions for an autonomous life in a modern regulatory state. Personal autonomy is diminished to the extent that legal standards are left open to be determined, and applied retrospectively, by *ad hoc* fact-finders. As Lord Diplock explained in *Black-Clawson International Ltd* v *Papierwerke Waldhof-Aschaffenberg AG* [1975] AC 591, 638, HL: 'The acceptance of the rule of law as a constitutional principle requires that a citizen, before committing himself to any course of action, should be able to know in advance what are the legal consequences that will flow from it.'

[26] *Andrews* v *DPP* [1937] AC 576, HL; *R* v *Adomako* [1995] 1 AC 171, HL.

[27] *R* v *Feely* [1973] QB 530, CA; *R* v *Ghosh* [1982] QB 1053, CA.

[28] These formulations are not tautologies, as some have supposed, but rather serve to assign to the jury responsibility for applying open-textured legal standards to particular fact situations: see §2.4(a).

evaluative judgment. By deciding which conduct should be censured as grossly negligent a jury literally lays down the law on manslaughter. The question of dishonesty is notionally more nuanced, since jurors are formally required to hold the accused to ordinary standards of decency, not to indulge their own, possibly idiosyncratic or deviant, moral preferences. But how are jurors supposed to decide what ordinary standards of decency entail? Chiefly, it is safe to assume, by imagining that their own preferences and ordinary decency coincide. So once again, in practice if not in strict legal doctrine, the fact-finder's normative commitments facilitate the inferential leap from proof to conclusive judgment, that is, from evidential to constitutive facts.

All three of the standard juridical techniques for managing linguistic latitude and fixing legal meanings rest on a shared premiss: constitutive facts are never established simply by reference to 'what happened' as a purely empirical matter. Philosophers would not regard this as a novel thesis. Positivist fantasies of a realm of pristine facts hermetically sealed off against the corrupting influence of evaluation have been debunked many times,[29] and the traditional dichotomy between facts and law in criminal procedure is doomed for essentially the same reasons. Values inevitably pervade fact-finding, just as fact-finding is sometimes a kind of law-making. Herein lies the truth of the assertion that facts are *made*, as much as found, in legal process. Detailed empirical studies have painstakingly documented the social construction of facts in criminal proceedings.[30] However, the socially constructed nature of reality must not be confused with radical epistemological scepticism.[31] In particular, it does not imply that we can never really know anything or that fact-finding in criminal trials must be 'just made up', a set of stories or narratives with no foundation in empirical reality. Of course, the full facts are not always discovered in criminal proceedings, and this for a host of reasons: the inherent fallibility of criminal adjudication is hardly newsworthy. We simply insist that 'fact-finding' in criminal trials is a function of conceptual classification and normative evaluation *as well as* being a process of discovering the truth about historical events. Hohfeld's distinction between evidential and constitutive facts helps to tease out how and why forensic fact-finding is to that extent more complex and controversial, but also more interesting, than is often appreciated.

---

[29] 'The totality of our so-called knowledge or beliefs, from the most casual matters of geography and history to the profoundest laws of atomic physics or even of pure mathematics and logic, is a man-made fabric which impinges on experience only along the edges.... [I]n point of epistemological footing the physical objects and the gods differ only in degree and not in kind. Both sorts of entities enter our conception only as cultural posits': Willard van Orman Quine, *From A Logical Point of View* (Harvard UP, 2nd revsd. edn. 1980), 42, 44. Also see, e.g., Charles Taylor, *Philosophy and the Human Sciences: Philosophical Papers 2* (CUP, 1985), Part 1; Richard Rorty, *Objectivity, Relativism and Truth: Philosophical Papers Volume 1* (CUP, 1991); Tom Sorell, *Scientism: Philosophy and the Infatuation with Science* (Routledge, 1991); Wayne Morrison, *Theoretical Criminology: Form Modernity to Postmodernism* (Cavendish, 1995), esp. chs 6–9; Ian Taylor, Paul Walton, and Jock Young, *The New Criminology* (Routledge, 1973), chs 1–2.

[30] Mike McConville, Andrew Sanders, and Roger Leng, *The Case for the Prosecution* (Routledge, 1991); Andrew Sanders, 'Constructing the Case for the Prosecution' (1987) 14 *Journal of Law and Society*, 229; Paul Roberts, 'Science in the Criminal Process' (1994) 14 *OJLS*, 469; Carol A. G. Jones, *Expert Witnesses: Science, Medicine and the Practice of Law* (OUP, 1994), chs 8–10. For further illuminating discussion, see Mike Redmayne, *Expert Evidence and Criminal Justice* (OUP, 2001), ch 2; Gary Edmond, 'Azaria's Accessories: the Social (Legal-Scientific) Construction of the Chamberlains' *Guilt* and *Innocence*' (1998) 22 *Melbourne University LR* 396; A. A. S. Zuckerman, 'Miscarriage of Justice – A Root Treatment' [1992] *Crim LR* 323; Roger Smith, 'Forensic Pathology, Scientific Expertise and the Criminal Law', in Roger Smith and Brian Wynne (eds.), *Expert Evidence: Interpreting Science in the Law* (Routledge, 1989).

[31] For illuminating further discussion see Ian Hacking, *The Social Construction of What?* (Harvard UP, 1999); Joseph Raz, *Engaging Reason* (OUP, 1999), chs 6–10.

(c) JURIDICAL CLASSIFICATIONS

Issues of classification typically become apparent at the end of a chain of inferential reasoning, and usually concern constitutive facts. The question of whether the accused's act amounted to entry, for example, has to be answered only once we have inferred from the evidence that the accused did indeed put his arm through the window. Likewise, it might be contentious in particular proceedings whether leaving potatoes at X's house should qualify as supplying potatoes to X, but this does not become a live issue for the purposes of litigation until it is established that the potatoes were in fact left at X's house. The classificatory question of the meaning of 'supply' arises only after it has been decided that the potatoes were actually deposited on X's doorstep.

However, questions of classification can also arise during the course of the inferential process, in relation to evidentiary facts. Suppose that part of the evidence against our burglar is that a witness, since deceased (and therefore unavailable for further questioning), told the police that he saw a tall man outside the relevant window. A question now arises as to whether this statement can apply to the accused, who – let us say – measures five feet ten inches. Whether putting one's arm through a window amounts to burglarious entry is obviously a different type of question to asking whether people measuring five feet ten inches are 'tall'. Both questions are framed by the open-texture of language, but the interpretational standards and criteria needed to answer them are located in different places. The scope of burglarious entry – a legally constitutive fact – is ultimately referable to normative principles of criminalization which should determine the proper ambit of the criminal law. Tallness, by contrast, is an ordinary everyday notion understood in the light of prevailing linguistic usage and any relevant attributes of the speaker. For example, if the deceased witness happened to be six feet in height, he is unlikely to have described someone more than two inches shorter than himself as 'tall'. Stature considered 'tall' for a women would not necessarily be 'tall' for a man, and standards for assessing tall children or tall buildings would be different again.

Criteria for settling issues of classification pertaining to evidential facts naturally differ from those required to determine constitutive facts. Practical issues before the court often blend aspects of factual inference and juridical classification, as where the trier of fact has to decide whether the accused has inflicted 'grievous bodily harm' or has done an act which is sufficiently proximate to the commission of an offence for it to constitute a criminal attempt.[32] Further examples that have cropped up in litigation include the definition of activity as 'trade',[33] the meaning of 'insulting behaviour',[34] and the identification of 'immoral purposes'.[35] Lawyers and courts generally lump such issues together as 'questions of fact', but this classification obscures the crucial distinction between evidential

[32] Criminal Attempts Act 1981, s.1.

[33] *Edwards* v *Bairstow* [1956] AC 14, 33, *per* Lord Radcliffe: 'All these cases in which the facts warrant a determination either way can be described as questions of degree and, therefore, as questions of fact'. The same view was expressed by Lord Hailsham LC in *Cole Bros Ltd* v *Phillips* [1982] 2 All ER 247, 253. Accordingly, questions permitting only one answer are characterized as questions of law, which turns the traditional conception of a fact-law dichotomy on its head. On that view, facts either existed or they did not, whereas legal standards can be developed in different ways. For further discussion, see W. A. Wilson, 'Questions of Degree' (1969) 32 *MLR* 361.

[34] *Brutus* v *Cozens* [1973] AC 854, HL, held that this is also a question of fact for the jury.

[35] *R* v *Gray* (1982) 74 Cr App R 324, CA.

facts which must be proved through evidence, and constitutive facts which must be determined in the process of rendering judgment. As we have seen, judgments of gross negligence and dishonesty, amongst many others, require moral reasoning as well as factual inquiry. English law sometimes reserves classificatory issues to the judge, to be resolved as problems of legal interpretation, whilst at other times they are treated as part of the jury's law-applying function.[36]

There is no context-free way of understanding or evaluating legal classifications of law and fact. Each classificatory judgment must instead be considered in its particular juridical context, and in light of the values and interests it affects. 'Particular fact situations,' Herbert Hart wrote, 'do not await us already marked off from each other, and labelled as instances of the general rule, the application of which is in question; nor can the rule itself step forward to claim its own instances'.[37] Definitions of criminal offences, in common with most other rules of law, are open-textured, allowing 'at the point of actual application, a fresh choice between open alternatives'.[38] When such questions are delegated to lay triers of fact, as they frequently are, jurors and magistrates are not only being asked to establish the truth of past events, but to determine the legal consequences of the facts they find. They are, so far as the instant case is concerned, a kind of local law-giver.[39] Classification in constitutive fact-finding contributes a strong normative dimension to adjudicators' historical inquiries.

(d) THE INSTITUTIONAL MORALITY OF FACT-FINDING

That fact-finders should become arbiters of normative legal standards is not simply an inevitable consequence of the open texture of legal rules. Legal rules and practices which classify particular questions as 'law' or 'fact' are no more self-actuating than definitions of criminal offences. These classifications, too, represent value-choices embedded in the law, and are consequently only as good as the normative arguments supporting them. It is possible to envisage a form of criminal trial procedure very different to our own, in which the jury was confined to determining what happened, without any element of evaluative interpretation. For this imaginary trial procedure to function as intended, it would be necessary to devise a mechanism for isolating the disputed factual issues prior to their being presented to the trier of fact.

Now, it would certainly be possible to submit to a jury a single, isolated, factual issue or menu of such issues, devoid of any contextualizing information about the nature of the charge or the surrounding circumstances. Suppose that in a murder trial the only live issue is whether the accused was at the scene of the crime at the material time: if he was there, he is guilty as charged, but otherwise he is innocent. Unlike real English juries trying murder

---

[36] Discussed by Etienne Mureinik, 'The Application of Rules: Law or Fact?' (1982) 98 *LQR* 587; Edward Griew, 'Directions to Convict' [1972] *Crim LR* 204; M. J. McConville, 'Directions to Convict – A Reply' [1973] *Crim LR* 164; Glanville Williams, 'Law and Fact' [1976] *Crim LR* 472.

[37] H. L. A. Hart, *The Concept of Law* (OUP, 1961), 123.   [38] ibid. 125.

[39] Whether such determinations properly constitute 'law' poses the jurisprudential problem of subsumption: see J. W. Harris, 'Kelsen and Normative Consistency', in R. Tur and W. Twining (eds.), *Essays on Kelsen* (OUP, 1986). Not many contemporary (or past!) writers accept Kelsen's view that they *are* law, but this point of conceptual scruple is not our present concern. The important point for us is that constitutive fact-finding requires normative moral reasoning as well as empirical inquiry.

cases, our imaginary, single-issue jury would have no role in applying the law to the facts. It would not decide, for example, whether the accused's conduct in despatching the victim was justified in all the circumstances of the case, or should be excused on some ground of mitigation such as provocation or diminished responsibility. Our fictional jury would not even know what the accused was on trial *for*. The question of the accused's presence at the scene of the crime would be presented for the jury's completely acontextual determination. Was the accused at such-and-such a place on a specified occasion, or not? These jurors would also be insulated from many potential sources of bias which might otherwise threaten the purity of their factual inquiry, such as information about the accused's virtuous character, previous criminal record, or odious habits, to which real juries are regularly exposed.[40]

This strange hypothetical fact-finding procedure stretches the limits of credence on at least two fronts. First, it is readily apparent that no feasible, let alone desirable, process of adjudication could sustain a strict separation of fact from value. How, for example, would jurors go about deciding the single issue of the accused's presence at the scene? They would need to draw inferences form pieces of evidence, including witness testimony. And how would they do this? Only by drawing upon the stock of common sense generalizations about human behaviour, the physical environment, indicia of truthfulness, and so on, which are composed of evaluative, as well as descriptive, beliefs, experiences, preconceptions and prejudice. Fact-finding could only be purified of value by filleting the process to such an extent – e.g. by reducing it to a series of logical operations with mathematical formulae – that it would no longer be of any use to a system for adjudicating practical disputes in the real world.

Secondly, even if feasible procedural arrangements could be devised to allow a single-issue jury to resolve disputed factual issues free from all evaluative influences, the resulting trial system would hardly be appealing. The point is that *we want fact-finders to make moral judgments*. After all *somebody* has to make normative choices at some point in the process, if not during the trial proceedings themselves, then in conducting the investigation (which may involve deciding who was the injured party and who the aggressor), generating relevant evidence, and framing the issues for the jury's determination. There are cogent considerations of factual accuracy,[41] community participation, democratic accountability, and procedural legitimacy for ensuring that at least some of these decisions remain open to non-professional appraisal.[42] A filleted and decontextualized trial of single issues would be ill-suited to the task of legitimizing criminal adjudication as the authoritative, official resolution of – often emotionally-charged – disputes concerning liability, redress, and punishment.[43] The moral force of a criminal verdict, in generating popular acceptance of particular decisions and maintaining public confidence in the institutions

---

[40] The Runciman Royal Commission's *Crown Court Study* found that information about the accused's antecedents was made known to the jury in around 20% of cases in which the accused had previous convictions (such cases being 77% of the total sample): Michael Zander and Paul Henderson, *Crown Court Study*, RCCJ Research Study No.19 (HMSO, 1993), para.4.6. Character evidence is discussed in Chapter 14.

[41] See §§4.4 and 4.6, below.   [42] §2.4.

[43] It is doubtful whether such a model of adjudication would appeal to the public even if it would verifiably improve the accuracy of verdicts over the long run of cases. Verdicts based on purely factual information and rendered in blissful ignorance of their consequences are unlikely to fulfil the social functions performed by judicial decisions. For general discussion, see Charles Nesson, 'The Evidence or the Event? On Judicial Proof and the Acceptability of Verdicts' (1985) 98 *Harvard LR* 1357.

of law enforcement, rests on more than mere historical accuracy.[44] It is expected that jurors will understand the gravity of the charges brought against the accused, and appreciate the consequences of their verdict if they find him guilty. This expectation generates pressure for jurors to be *better* informed about the contextual details and surrounding circumstances of the cases they try – even more so than at present. The current trend in criminal justice policy, driven in large measure by fear of crime and the desire to see more offenders convicted, is towards providing the fact-finder with more information, not less.

4.3 A MATTER OF OPINION?

Another legally significant classification purports to distinguish 'facts' from 'opinions'. According to the traditional common law 'rule against stating opinions' or more simply 'the opinion rule', ordinary witnesses are permitted to testify to facts but must not express any of their opinions. Testimony is supposed to supply the unvarnished facts without editorial commentary. It is for the jury to draw its own inferences from factual testimony, whilst witnesses must confine themselves to recounting what happened. 'The concept of evidence,' Schiemann LJ observed, 'is used in two different ways: factual evidence and opinion evidence. Factual evidence is apposite when the question is: "What are the facts?" And even in certain circumstances when the question is: "What are the facts likely to be?", factual evidence may well be a prerequisite for opinion evidence.'[45]

In reality, 'opinion' is difficult to disentangle from 'fact'. There is an elementary sense in which virtually all factual reports also express opinions. Suppose that, glimpsing the back of a person crossing the road, you decide that it is your friend Jim who walks with a limp and wears a distinctive, wide-brimmed hat. If you were later to testify in court that you saw Jim crossing the road you would not simply be reporting visual sense-data. You would also be stating your 'opinion' (inferential conclusion) about the meaning of what you saw, in this case that a limping man wearing a wide-brimmed hat was your friend Jim. Nineteenth century judgments sometimes make this very point.[46] As Thayer observed, '[i]n a sense all testimony to matter of fact is opinion evidence; i.e. it is a conclusion formed from phenomena and mental impressions'.[47] Of course, the so-called opinion rule notwithstanding, the law will not exclude your testimony. You are only giving garden variety identification testimony that courts up and down the country routinely receive into evidence. In the absence of any robust legal conception of 'opinion', the admissibility of a witness's testimony cannot really be made to turn on the application of a rigid, formalistic, dichotomy between

---

[44] Even in civil litigation there is a tendency to fashion legal principles as closely as possible to their factual context; hence judges' reluctance to determine important points of legal principle as preliminary issues on assumed facts.　　　　[45] *R v Leominster DC* (1998) 76 P & C R 346, 355 CA (Civ).

[46] See, e.g., *Beaumont v Perkins* (1809) 1 Phillimore 78, 82; 161 ER 919, 922 ('It has been truly said that all evidence of hand-writing is evidence of opinion; if a person has seen another write twenty years ago, he can only form his belief as to his writing by a comparison with what he once saw: what is this but evidence of opinion?').

[47] Thayer, *A Preliminary Treatise on Evidence at the Common Law*, 524. Also see *Wigmore on Evidence* (Chadbourn revision), vol. 7, §1978; Jack B. Weinstein, 'Some Difficulties in Devising Rules for Determining Truth in Judicial Trials' (1966) 66 *Columbia LR* 223, 231: '[T]he testimony of any witness describes the combination of himself and the event.'

'facts' and 'opinions'; though this does not stop courts and commentators talking as if it did. The highest claim made for the so-called 'opinion rule' in modern times is that it appears to work because it is 'laxly applied'.[48]

On closer examination, hardly any decision will be found to turn exclusively on the fact–opinion distinction. When judges in earlier times rejected opinion evidence they did so, Wigmore pointed out, because they regarded the statement of opinion as a mere guess or groundless assertion devoid of probative value. They did not disparage statements of opinion resting on 'an inference or conclusion from personally observed data'.[49] Then as now, opinion evidence is excluded from criminal trials either because it makes an insufficient probative contribution or because the matter in question should be left to the judge or jury, possibly aided by an appropriately qualified expert.[50] The principled basis for a 'rule' excluding opinions is to be found in a preference for 'the more concrete description to the less concrete, the direct form of statement to the inferential'.[51] Where the rule operates, the process of drawing more refined inferences is reserved to the court.

To illustrate: suppose that on a charge of causing the death of a pedestrian by dangerous driving a witness testifies that she was present at the scene and that the accused was responsible for the accident. No reasonable adjudicator would return a verdict solely on the basis of this testimony because it is expressed in such general terms that we cannot be sure of its true meaning or value. If the witness adds that the accused drove dangerously, her statement becomes a little less vague, inasmuch as it explicitly appeals to a normative standard of conduct. But this does not take matters much further, because, as yet, we have no way of judging how the witness assesses appropriate driving; nor has she explained her grounds for believing that the accused was driving dangerously. If the witness then goes on to say that the accused drove too fast, she informs us of the factual basis for her assessment. But this is still an inadequate amount of information to judge what happened, since we do not know, in concrete terms, how fast the accused was driving. How are we to tell what driving speed this witness considers 'too fast'? It is only when the witness give her assessment of the accused's actual speed that the court can form its own view about the event in question.

Notice, however, that the final statement is no more one of pure fact, shorn of all 'opinions', than the first. Clearly, the witness's view of the speed at which the accused drove relies on conscious and unconscious inferences, extending beyond the report of brute physical sensations. The progression is not from opinion to fact, but from higher levels of generality to progressively more particularized assertions. Greater specificity facilitates the trier of fact's evaluation of the evidence, by exposing the assumptions embedded in the witness's testimony and indicating which faculties of perception are being relied on and need to be tested. Testimonial specificity is also desirable to the extent that it discourages witnesses from volunteering their views about the appropriateness of the accused's conduct. Witnesses' opinions on such matters should have no bearing on the outcome of litigation; it is the court's exclusive prerogative to judge the appropriateness of the accused's conduct by interpreting standards of legal liability and applying them to the facts of the instant case.

---

[48] Zelman Cowen and P. B. Carter, *Essays on the Law of Evidence* (OUP, 1956), 164. See also J. D. Heydon, *Evidence, Cases and Materials* (Butterworths, 2nd edn. 1984), 367.

[49] *Wigmore on Evidence* (Chadbourn revision), vol. 7, 5.   [50] See Chapter 11.

[51] *McCormick on Evidence* (West Publishing, 3rd edn. 1984), 30.

Recognizing that human perceptions of events can be reported at different levels of generality, and from the point of view of different interests, witnesses in court should be encouraged to testify to specific facts unclouded by their personal interpretations or speculations. However, there comes a point beyond which it is both impractical and undesirable to insist on further specificity. A report of visual identification, for example, consists of a final inference drawn from countless minute perceptions which it is not easy, and rarely instructive, to attempt to individuate. Even if an eyewitness were capable of describing the minutiae of her impressions, detailing the offender's height, weight, eye and hair colour, complexion, clothing, speech, facial expressions, gait, mannerisms, etc., this exhaustive inventory would rarely be more helpful or informative than a simple composite identification, such as 'The man I saw was Jim' or pointing at the accused and saying, 'He is the man I saw'.[52] To maximize its usefulness in criminal adjudication, testimony should narrate facts at a level of generality which is neither over-refined (concealing witnesses' interpretational biases) nor too unrefined (swamping fact-finders with undigested raw sense-data). Particular aspects of perception, such as the offender's hair colour or height, can be isolated and scrutinized microscopically just insofar as they become contested issues in particular trials.[53]

It is not possible to formulate general rules prescribing the optimal degree of testimonial specificity for every type of evidence in every type of case. As Wigmore observed:

We are dealing merely with a broad principle that, whenever the point is reached at which the tribunal is being told that which it is itself entirely equipped to determine without the witness' aid on this point, his testimony is superfluous and is to be dispensed with.[54]

English law has reached its own accommodation with the 'opinion rule' along similar lines. A witness may state opinions provided that this is only a 'compendious means of conveying facts perceived by him'.[55] For example, evidence that the accused 'appeared surprised, shocked and distressed' by a significant revelation is treated as factual evidence rather than evidence of opinion.[56] This pragmatic compromise is a neat way of allowing witnesses to give their evidence in its most helpful form, whilst paying lip-service to doctrinal orthodoxy's insistence on a strict dichotomy between facts and opinions. Conversely, the

---

[52] See, e.g., *R v Ali (Faraz)* [2008] EWCA Crim 1522; [2009] Crim LR 40; and cf. *R v Breddick* [2001] EWCA Crim 984. The same analysis applies *mutatis mutandis* to testimony purporting to identify an individual from his or her voice: see *R v Flynn and St John* [2008] 2 Cr App R 20, [2008] EWCA Crim 970, [13]–[14] (distinguishing 'lay listener' testimony from expert evidence of voice identification); *R v Robb* [1991] 93 Cr App R 161, 168, CA ('the policemen did not purport to identify the appellant's voice on the disputed tapes as experts giving evidence of opinion. They testified, as witnesses of fact, that they recognised the voice on the disputed tapes as that of the man they had talked to in the car. That is crucially different'); cf. *R v Crouch* (1850) 4 Cox CC, 163, 164.

[53] Cf. *Huggins v R* [2004] UKPC 7 (conflict between eyewitness testimony and expert ballistic evidence considered immaterial to resolving the contested issues).

[54] *Wigmore on Evidence* (Chadbourn revision), vol. 7, §1918, 11–12. Cf. Rule 701 of the US Federal Rules of Evidence: 'If the witness is not testifying as an expert, his testimony in the form of opinions or inferences is limited to those opinions or inferences which are (a) rationally based on the perception of the witness and (b) helpful to clear understanding of his testimony or the determination of a fact in issue.' A similar attitude is evident in Canadian decisions such as *Graat v R* (1982) 144 DLR (3d) 267; [1982] 2 SCR 819.

[55] *Blackstone's Criminal Practice* 2010, F10.2. Cf. Civil Evidence Act 1972, s.3(2), providing that 'where a person is called as a witness in any civil proceedings, a statement of opinion by him on any relevant matter on which he is not qualified to give expert evidence, if made as a way of conveying relevant facts personally perceived by him, is admissible as evidence of what he perceived'.

[56] *R v Woodall* [2003] EWCA Crim 2345, [43], [46].

Court of Appeal has expressed its 'doubts whether a modern jury would be assisted by evidence of opinion by a witness the basis of which is not in any way particularised'.[57] So far as ordinary witnesses are concerned, there are few authorities and the issue does not appear to cause significant problems in practice. The one major application of the 'opinion rule' is, ironically, stated as an exception to it. As we will see in Chapter 11, expert witnesses *are* allowed to state their opinion on matters within the scope of their expertise.[58] Indeed, such is the affinity between experts and opinion evidence that common lawyers often describe as expert 'opinion' testimony that can only sensibly be regarded as factual (on any robust and defensible classification of 'fact' and 'opinion').[59] The so-called opinion rule in reality is only a rough proxy for the two important evidentiary principles that lie at its foundation: the principle that witness evidence should be presented in a form calculated to maximize its probative utility, and the principle that the accused's conduct and potential criminal liability should, as far as practicable, be assessed by the court and not by the witness. These principles will reappear, in various guises, as our exploration of criminal evidence proceeds.

4.4 COMMON SENSE FACT-FINDING

There is nothing at all unusual or mysterious about the process of drawing factual inferences from evidence. People draw such inferences every day. Occasionally factual inferences relate to momentous topics or decisions, but much more often they are prosaic and mundane. In going about our ordinary affairs we draw countless inferences from known facts. These inferences contribute to the stock of an individual's knowledge,[60] beliefs, and assumptions, and are continuously put to work by each of us in deciding what to think and how to act. The human facility for inference-drawing is crucial in making the most basic existential decisions, let alone to the continuance of any kind of social group existence. At the very most basic and unsophisticated level of individual survival, inferences generalized from experience tell us, for example, not to jump head-first from great heights onto concrete floors, not to eat razor blades or rat poison, not to run in front of moving vehicles, and so on. We know all this and much more, we say, as a matter of ordinary *common sense*.

---

[57]   *R* v *Colwill* [2002] EWCA Crim 1320, [12] (referring specifically to evidence of reputation). Also see *R* v *Del-Valle* [2004] EWCA Crim 1013.

[58]   'Evidence of opinion is not ordinarily admissible. Opinion based upon identifiable expertise outside the experience of the jury is one exception': *R* v *Atkins* [2010] 1 Cr App R 8, [2009] EWCA Crim 1876, [9]. The same common law principle has always applied in civil litigation, too: 'When looking at evidence sought to be adduced on matters of opinion, one must start from the position that opinion evidence is not generally admissible. However, by way of exception the opinion of an expert may be admissible. The general principle is that evidence of opinion, that is conclusions drawn from received facts, is not admissible but an expert called as a witness in civil proceedings can give evidence of his opinion upon relevant matters': *Re Oakfame Construction Ltd* [1996] BCC 67, 68, Ch (Companies Court).

[59]   Cf. *Crossland* v *DPP* [1988] RTR 417, DC (testimony reporting readings from stop watches, electronic speed traps, and similar devices states facts rather than opinion). Also see *R* v *McGuire* (1985) 81 Cr App R 323, CA.

[60]   Knowledge is constituted by warranted beliefs. On the standard account, beliefs are warranted when they are *true* and *justified*. There are various theoretical complications which need not detain us here: see Hock Lai Ho, *A Philosophy of Evidence Law – Justice in the Search for Truth* (OUP, 2008), ch 3; Paul K. Moser (ed.), *The Oxford Handbook of Epistemology* (OUP, 2002); Ernest Sosa and Jaegwon Kim (eds.), *Epistemology: An Anthology* (Blackwell, 2000).

Suppose that one needs to take the train from Nottingham to Oxford to arrive in time for dinner at 7.00pm. How can this simple aim be achieved? A quick internet search reveals that a train departs Nottingham station at 4.00pm, to meet a connecting service from Birmingham at 5.30pm, which arrives in Oxford at 6.45pm. From this piece of information a number of factual inferences may be drawn: (i) a train will arrive at Nottingham station at 4.00pm; (ii) it will be a passenger service (on-line customer information would not be giving out details of freight trains!); (iii) its destination will be Birmingham; (iv) it will arrive there in time to allow passengers to alight, change platforms (if necessary), and board the 5.30pm to Oxford; (v) another train will depart Birmingham station for Oxford at 5.30pm; (vi) it will, again, be a passenger service; and (vii) it will arrive at Oxford station at 6.45pm. Further, possibly less secure, inferences might also be drawn, such as (viii) there will be seats available on the train, because these trains are rarely full; and (ix) no advance bookings are necessary, since it is not usually necessary to book in advance on British trains. (This last inference, in particular, demonstrates the cultural specificity of inferential logic: advance-bookings *are* typically required for inter-city train journeys in continental Europe.) Finally, a little more 'common sense' knowledge is needed to complete the inferential web. On the assumption that it is no more than a fifteen-minute walk from Oxford station to one's dinner venue, the final inference is: (x) the 4.00pm Nottingham train will meet one's requirements. Alternatively, the final inference might be that, since Oxford trains always run at least fifteen minutes late, (x*) you will miss dinner if you take the 4.00pm from Nottingham.

Articulating some of the inferences that might be drawn in undertaking a simple and familiar operation like planning a train journey serves to demonstrate that the process of inference-drawing is ubiquitous in everyday life. It also begins to bring home the mind-boggling speed and complexity of human rationality. We would never usually spell out each step in the inferential process, since the type of operation modelled here is achieved by fully-functioning human adults in a trice. Moreover, as inferences (viii)–(x) hint, by adding in further pieces of common sense knowledge to the equation the number of possible inferences that might be drawn could be multiplied, literally, to infinity. Yet still the human mind is undaunted. Mental operations of staggering subtlety and complexity are bound up in even the most mundane and apparently simple features of modern social existence.

The same logical reasoning process is employed in any form of practical inquiry into facts, including fact-finding in criminal adjudication. To help us explore this proposition further, a useful analytical distinction may be drawn between two forms of reasoning about facts, 'deduction' and 'induction'.[61]

(a) FORENSIC INDUCTION

Deductive inferences are *deduced* – that is to say, they follow by logical necessity – from given premises. Here is the classical illustration of a 'deductive syllogism':

Major premiss: all men are mortal
Minor premiss: Socrates is a man
ergo
Deduction: Socrates is mortal

---

[61] See further, *Wigmore on Evidence* (Tillers Revision, 1983), vol. 1A, §30.

Criminal investigation and the proof of criminal charges at trial are linked in the popular imagination with deductive logic, which is celebrated in the achievements of fictional sleuths like Sherlock Holmes who unravelled even the most tangled of criminal plots by the rigorous application of 'elementary' deductions. All the clues necessary to solve the puzzle are already in evidence, and it only needs somebody with adequate powers of perception and analysis to put them together in the right way – to join up the dots, as we might say – in order to deduce the appropriate conclusions. After Holmes has narrated the final *denouement*, my dear Doctor Watson – and Conan Doyle's readers – are left wondering why they had not already worked it out for themselves. The syllogistic form clarifies that a deductive inference contains no new information. Rather, it only spells out in a useful way the information already contained in its premises. To affirm the premises yet deny the conclusion would entail self-contradiction. It would be illogical.

However, most reasoning about facts, in law as in life, takes a different form. Deductive reasoning works well in mathematics, where certain axioms are beyond serious contention, and in some scientific applications, where an hypothesis is assumed to be true, at least for the purpose of an experiment. Such axioms or hypotheses then constitute the major premisses in deductive syllogisms. But the reality with which the forensic process must grapple is altogether more messy and uncertain. The vast majority of issues arising in court cannot be resolved by appealing to the analytical truths of mathematics, or by assuming the truth of any given hypothesis. In other words, we do not usually have access to premises from which conclusions may be deduced with logical certainty. That is why forensic reasoning must routinely be *in*ductive rather than *de*ductive. A sub-variant of inductive reasoning with important forensic applications is *ab*duction. This refers to the imaginative process of generating new hypotheses from which further deductive syllogisms and inductive inferences may be derived and tested against the available evidence.[62]

Inductive reasoning involves drawing non-deductive inferences which rest on assessments of probability rather than being dictated by the irresistible force of logic. Suppose the question is whether a certain student is reading law, and the evidence is that this student was spotted using the university library. If that were all we knew, no inference could be drawn either way. The student could be reading any subject on which the library holds books. But suppose we also know that 90% of the people using that particular library are law students; in fact, it turns out that this is the law library. On the basis of the information now available to us, we can say that there is a 90% chance that the mystery student studies law.[63] Inductive reasoning employs probabilistic inferences which may be based on quantified frequencies of past events, where known. In our example, let us say that a survey of law library users found that nine out of ten students were studying law (the rest just found the working environment congenial). This empirically ascertained frequency – nine out of every ten library users are law students – supports a robust probabilistic inference regarding our mystery student's course of study.

---

[62] The term abduction is attributable to the early twentieth century American philosopher Charles Sanders Peirce. Generally, see Michael S. Pardo and Ronald J. Allen, 'Juridical Proof and the Best Explanation' (2008) 27 *Law and Philosophy* 223; Burkhard Schafer, Jeroen Keppens, and Qiang Shen, 'Thinking With and Outside the Box: Developing Computer Support for Evidence Teaching', in Paul Roberts and Mike Redmayne (eds.), *Innovations in Evidence and Proof* (Hart, 2007); David A. Schum, *The Evidential Foundations of Probabilistic Reasoning* (Northwestern UP, 1994), ch 9; Anderson, Schum and Twining, *Analysis of Evidence*, 56–60.

[63] The role of probability in adjudication is addressed more systematically in §4.5, below.

Whilst it is justifiable to conclude that the person seen in the library is very probably a law student, she might of course turn out to belong to the 10% (one in ten) minority of non-law students. The possibility of error in no way precludes us from drawing a reasonable inference or, in appropriate cases, from acting upon it. Factual uncertainty is a chronic condition of human existence. Since omniscience is denied to human beings, all fact-finders can ever do is extrapolate from current knowledge and past experience to produce probabilistic conclusions. Some degree of uncertainty is always inherent in factual reasoning, but we still form beliefs and act on them, as we must if life is to go on. Many decisions have to be taken quickly on the basis of whatever information is to hand at the time, and few important matters can be delayed indefinitely. Keynes quipped that in the very long run we are all dead. Indecision may be a greater enemy of the good than the wrong decision. Prevarication and paralysis in the face of uncertainty are rarely attractive, laudable, or even plausible options. People persevere, as they should, in reasoning about facts under conditions of uncertainty, to make the best decisions and choices they can, given the cognitive and motivational limitations under which we all must labour. Crucially, much also turns on what is at stake in drawing or acting upon any particular inference.

The nature of the interests at stake determines how reasonable it would be to rely on probabilistic inferences. Most people think it reasonable to risk small amounts of stake money on the National Lottery each week even though the odds against winning the jackpot are many millions to one against. By contrast – and excluding highly unusual and unfortunate circumstances – it would not be reasonable to accept a 50–50 chance of blowing one's brains out playing Russian Roulette. Generally speaking, for the more important decisions in life, such as changing jobs or getting married, it will be desirable to gather as much information as possible before committing oneself to action, but even the most life-altering decisions have to be made on the basis of limited information; if any decisions are to be taken at all. At the trivial end of the spectrum meanwhile, decision-making can be a relatively care-free exercise. Even small probabilities might provide sufficient warrant for belief or action where little is being risked either way. If you need to locate the *Criminal Appeal Reports* in an unfamiliar library, and you know that 90% of library users are law students, it is perfectly rational to stop and ask directions from the first student you meet. You have a 90% chance of stopping a law student,[64] and no real harm will be done if, against the odds, you happen to encounter a non-law student at the first attempt. You can simply apologize for stopping the wrong person, and repeat your request to the very next student you come across. You are bound to meet a law student very soon (the chances of consecutively stopping two non-law students are one in hundred; three non-law students, one in a thousand, etc.), but it hardly matters if you do not succeed at the first few attempts.

The empirical generalizations underpinning a factual inference are always based on incomplete information. Particular inferences may also rest on flawed data. If the generalization that 90% of library users are law students was based on a single poll undertaken in the week before law examinations, it might reflect an unusually high concentration of law students in the library at that time. Skewed sampling is just one type of methodological defect that may undermine the reliability of inferences drawn from survey data. Conversely, such inferences may be made with much greater confidence where data collection is more

---

[64] Assuming, perhaps irrationally, that any law student would know where the *Criminal Appeal Reports* are housed in the law library.

sophisticated; where, for example, data are drawn from a larger sampling frame with a methodology controlling for material variations in the circumstances affecting the issues under investigation. Similarly, inferences are usually robust when they are drawn from experimental or experiential generalizations that have stood the test of time, e.g. that licensed taxi drivers with 'the knowledge' are able to navigate their way around London, that real property is a sound long-term investment, or that peace without justice is unlikely to be permanent.

(b) COMMON SENSE GENERALIZATIONS[65]

Factual generalizations are imported into the trial arena as the accumulated 'common sense' of the jury or magistrates. But there are also additional, supplementary sources of inductive factual inference. Some factual generalizations may be introduced by expert witnesses instructed by the parties,[66] others by counsel in their questioning of witnesses or in their opening or closing speeches in court, and still others by the judge when taking 'judicial notice' of supposedly self-evident truths[67] or in summing-up the case to the jury. Whatever the source of factual generalizations in legal proceedings, they share the same range of functions. Common sense generalizations supplement the evidence formally adduced by the parties, fill gaps in trial narratives, warrant inferential jumps to salient conclusions on constitutive facts,[68] and assist fact-finders to assess the comparative plausibility of the parties' contentions.

One familiar common sense generalization is that running away from the scene of the crime is suspicious conduct amounting to suggestive, albeit inconclusive, evidence of guilt. Similarly, silence in the face of an accusation is often regarded as being tantamount to an admission. It was widely assumed that people who behave in these ways have something to hide and nothing to say for themselves. When called upon to evaluate oral testimony, the trier of fact likewise draws upon prevailing wisdom about the visible signs of veracity and falsehood.[69] Does the witness speak confidently, with certainty and without self-contradiction, or does she hesitate, seem unsure and equivocate over important details? Is the witness an impartial and independent source of information about past events, or an interested party whose evidence may be self-serving or tainted with bias? Examples could be endlessly multiplied. Fact-finders inevitably bring to the task of adjudication their individual and collective stores of beliefs and assumptions about the world, some of which will have been acquired through experience or formal education, whilst the rest – perhaps the greater part – are absorbed more or less unconsciously from their social and cultural *milieux*. And here it bears repeating that people acquire their knowledge, beliefs, assumptions, stereotypes, fears, and prejudices about crime and criminal justice from news media and fictional portrayals on television and film, as much as from personal or even second-hand experience.

Common sense, it turns out, is highly acculturated and differentially distributed. Only a limited number of factual generalizations are truly common to the bulk of humanity,

---

[65] See Twining, *Rethinking Evidence*, ch 11; Anderson, Schum, and Twining, *Analysis of Evidence*, ch 10; Terence J. Anderson, 'On Generalizations I: A Preliminary Exploration' (1999) 40 *South Texas LR* 455.

[66] The epistemology of expertise is explored in §11.2.   [67] See §4.7, below.   [68] §4.2, above.

[69] Received wisdom, in this as in just about everything else, is open to challenge: see §7.1(c).

and even within smaller communities 'common sense' may be contested terrain. At the consensual end of the spectrum, the basic laws of physics and Newton's theory of gravity supply generalizations that nearly everybody accepts and which are normally a sound basis for adjudicative fact-finding. Jurors in criminal trials are justified in assuming that at normal gravity, and absent the application of some external force, heavy objects fall down, not up. Other generalizations are more sensitive to time and place. When we say that 'everybody knows' that during rush hours central London commuters are packed into underground trains like sardines, we mean that people like us with experience of London commuting know this. Whilst these generalizations happen to be true, others are far less reliable, or even demonstrably false – creatures of ignorance, propaganda, superstition, or prejudice.[70]

Personal experience, and the beliefs which go with it, are moulded by all of the major psycho-sociological variables: class, sex/gender, age, ethnicity, nationality, and religion. There is consequently much variation between differently-situated groups and individuals, and this has important implications for some of the generalizations available to fact-finders in legal proceedings. Whilst running away from the police might look like an admission of guilt to some people (e.g. white, suburban middle class, 'law-abiding' adults), others (e.g. black, inner-city, 'underclass', youth) might perceive it as nothing more than a sensible act of self-preservation[71] with no bearing whatever on an individual's involvement in crime. Needless to say, the existence of competing generalizations, rooted in different experiences of life, gives rise to the possibility that conduct will be *mis*interpreted, with the attendant risks that an innocent person will suffer wrongful conviction and punishment or a guilty person be mistakenly acquitted. Try to imagine which generalizations and assumptions an all white, middle class jury might attach to the fact that, when challenged by the police, the black suspect tried to make a run for it. Now repeat the exercise for an all-black, working class jury and a white middle class suspect.[72] This simple thought-experiment crystallizes the realization that 'common sense' factual inferences, in litigation as elsewhere, are an interpretative *achievement* of particular groups of interpreters with a shared language and cultural reference points.[73]

[70] For further analysis of the epistemic credentials and forensic uses of common sense generalizations, see Ronald J. Allen, 'Common Sense, Rationality, and the Legal Process' (2001) 22 *Cardozo LR* 1417; Ann Althouse, 'Beyond King Solomon's Harlots: Women in Evidence' (1992) 65 *Southern California LR* 1265; Christine L. Boyle and Jesse Nyman, 'Finding Facts Fairly in Roberts and Zuckerman's *Criminal Evidence*' (2005) 2(2) ICE Article 3, www.bepress.com/ice/vol2/iss2/; Marilyn MacCrimmon, 'What is "Common" About Common Sense?: Cautionary Tales for Travelers Crossing Disciplinary Boundaries' (2001) 22 *Cardozo LR* 1433; J. L. Mackie, *The Cement of the Universe* (OUP, 1974), ch 3; P.-O. Ekelof, 'Free Evaluation of Evidence' (1964) 8 *Scandinavian Studies in Law* 47. On generalizations as the basis of rule-based social practices (including language), see Frederick Schauer, *Playing by the Rules: A Philosophical Examination of Rule-Based Decision-Making in Law and in Life* (OUP, 1991).

[71] Whether such beliefs are justified is entirely beside the point. (In some places they are, in others not). We are concerned here with *perceptions*, and their implications for the correct interpretation of conduct, rather than with the question of whether such perceptions are factually sound.

[72] A further complication: what colour did you imagine the police officers to be? Why? Does it matter? Cf. Andrew E. Taslitz, 'An African-American Sense of Fact: The OJ Trial and Black Judges on Justice' (1998) 7 *Boston University Public Interest Law Journal* 219; Sheri Lynn Johnson, 'The Color of Truth: Race and the Assessment of Credibility' (1996) 1 *Michigan Journal of Race and Law* 261.

[73] This is not an argument for racial quotas on juries, which raises a host of further complications. English law has always resisted the suggestion: *R v Smith (Lance Percival)* [2003] 1 WLR 2229, [2003] EWCA Crim 283; *R v Ford* [1989] QB 868, CA. Also see Cheryl Thomas, *Are Juries Fair?* Ministry of Justice Research

The quality of adjudication turns crucially on the soundness of the empirical generalizations relied on by fact-finders. The factual generalization that people cannot be in two places at once is entirely sound, and reliably supports the inference that if the accused was at home all evening watching television with his parents he cannot simultaneously have been stealing a car in another part of town. The generalization that people who run away from the police have something to hide, though far from groundless, is much more equivocal – just like the generalization that silence in the face of an accusation betokens guilt.[74] Non-co-operation with the police does not always warrant the negative inferences that jurors may be predisposed to draw, in light of their personal experiences, beliefs, and values.

4.5 PROBABILITY AND STATISTICS

Whilst common sense generalizations, for all their familiarity, are never simple, nor yet is forensic fact-finding simply a matter of common sense. Probability is another important dimension of modern legal proceedings. Lawyers are not known for their mathematical competence,[75] and parts of the very substantial literature surrounding issues of probability, inference, and fact-finding in legal and extra-legal contexts may appear daunting to those lacking any post-16 formal education in mathematics or statistics. However, there is no excuse for not making an effort to grasp the basics which every practising lawyer needs to cope with the demands of modern litigation.[76]

It is well-known that statistical and probabilistic evidence is being adduced with increasing frequency in criminal trials, a development associated with new technologies of proof – most notably, DNA profiling evidence – and ever greater reliance on expert witness testimony. These developments pose very practical questions for criminal adjudication. How should the parties marshal, present, and test statistical evidence? How should the trial judge direct the jury in relation to it? To what extent can jurors be expected to interpret probabilistic evidence or even to employ formal models of probabilistic reasoning in their deliberations? In one sense, criminal adjudication is blindingly obviously about probability and always has been, because legal standards of proof express a level of epistemic warrant necessarily less than absolute 100% certainty. This is just another way of saying that forensic fact-finding is probabilistic. On the other hand, some of the more abstruse mathematics of probability seem a long way removed from ordinary common sense reasoning. But is that a weakness or a strength? As well as thinking about the uses of probability *in* criminal litigation, it is also worth considering whether theorems and concepts of probability might be useful explanatory devices for improving our general understanding of criminal evidence and proof.

Series 1/10 (2010) (finding no evidence of racial bias amongst mock jurors and concluding that 'one stage in the criminal justice system where BME groups do not face persistent disproportionality is when a jury reaches a verdict').

[74] See further, §13.3(b).

[75] Cf. Peter Hawkins and Anne Hawkins, 'Lawyers' Probability Misconceptions and the Implications for Legal Education' (1998) 18 *Legal Studies* 316.

[76] Generally, see Bernard Robertson and G. A. Vignaux, *Interpreting Evidence: Evaluating Forensic Science in the Courtroom* (Wiley, 1995); Mike Redmayne, *Expert Evidence and Criminal Justice* (OUP, 2001), chs 3–4.

(a) CLASSICAL CONCEPTS AND NOTATIONS[77]

In mathematical notation, probabilities are conventionally quantified as numerical values between 0 and 1, with 1 designating absolute certainty ('x is definitely true'; 'x is certain to happen') and 0 its negation ('x is definitely false'; 'x is certain not to happen'). If there was one offender and 1,000 suspects, and we knew nothing else about the evidence, the probability that a suspect picked at random is the offender is p(G) = 1/1000, or 0.001. The probability of innocence is the complement of the probability of guilt, i.e. p(I) = 1 – p(G) = 1 – 0.001 = 0.999. We can verify the result of this simple illustration intuitively, because we know that 999 of the 1,000 suspects are innocent, i.e. p(I) = 999/1,000 = 0.999. Alternatively, forensic probabilities can be expressed as odds ratios. A fifty-fifty chance – p(x) = 0.5 – would give odds of 1:1; a one-in-four chance (p(x) = 0.25) expressed as in the language of odds is 3:1 against. The odds of picking the offender at random from our 1,000 suspects are 999:1 against.

It is convenient to assign notional mathematical probabilities for analytical purposes, as in our previous hypothetical illustration involving a 0.9 probability that any student stopped at random in the law library will be a law student. Quantified probabilities like this one rarely figure in real cases, however, for the simple reason that we do not have statistical frequencies for most of the events disputed in criminal trials. We do not know, for example, how frequently instances of flowerpots falling into the street are caused by recklessness, how often drunks intend to inflict GBH when they throw a punch, or what proportion of people in possession of jemmies have used them to crack safes. Even where the relevant databases exist, moreover – as they now do, for example, as a consequence of new advances in DNA technology[78] – it is far from clear how this statistical information should be combined with more traditional forms of evidence and inference.

Different types of probability need to be distinguished.[79] The *a priori* theory or 'classical doctrine of chances' applies only to situations involving a predetermined number of equally probable outcomes, such as rolling dice, selecting playing cards from a deck, or drawing coloured balls from a bag containing a known number of balls of particular colours. These probabilities are axiomatic and objective, part of 'the furniture of the universe'. Thus, we know that the chances of rolling a '6' on an unbiased six-sided die are 1/6. This is always true; even if, by some fluke, one were to roll a die a thousand times without ever landing on a 6. However, criminal trials only very infrequently raise such neat, discrete, issues of probability.[80]

A second kind of probability is variously known as 'frequentist', 'empirical', 'statistical', or (loosely) 'classical'. These labels all refer to the same basic idea of calculating

---

[77] For accessible introductions, see C. G. G. Aitken and F. Taroni, 'Fundamentals of Statistical Evidence – A Primer for Legal Professionals' (2008) 12 *E & P* 181; Richard Eggleston, *Evidence, Proof and Probability* (Butterworths, 2nd edn. 1983), ch 2; Philip Dawid, 'Appendix: Probability and Proof', in Terrence Anderson and William Twining, *Analysis of Evidence* (Weidenfeld and Nicolson, 1991).

[78] Mike Redmayne, 'Doubts and Burdens: DNA Evidence, Probability and the Courts' [1995] *Crim LR* 464.

[79] Generally, see Anderson, Schum and Twining, *Analysis of Evidence*, ch 9; Richard Eggleston, *Evidence, Proof and Probability*, esp. chs 2 & 3; William Twining, 'Debating Probabilities' (1980) II *Liverpool Law Review* 51; David A. Schum, *The Evidential Foundations of Probabilistic Reasoning* (Northwestern UP, 1994), 34–54.

[80] Eggleston, *Evidence, Proof and Probability*, 9, cites the example of a case under the Betting and Gaming Act 1960 in which a question arose as to the fairness of the odds being offered in particular wagers.

probabilities by observing events of interest over a sequence of trials, experiments, or surveys. The question is: how frequently does *x* occur? One might investigate, for example, how often seatbelts fail, or the success rate of a medical cure, or (to return to a previous illustration) patterns of law library usage. Frequentist probability obeys powerful mathematical axioms, including the conjunction (or multiplication) rule, according to which the probability of two independent events both occurring is equal to the compound probability of each individual event multiplied together $[p(x + y) = p(x).p(y)]$. Observed frequencies can be plotted diagrammatically as the function of $p(x)$ and modelled against various contingencies. They are widely employed in public policy development and implementation, financial planning, disaster management, etc. For example, the frequency with which unusually high temperatures are recorded might be used to calculate the probability of experiencing catastrophic weather events like hurricanes or tsunamis resulting from climate change.

Frequentist probabilities provide an objective empirical foundation for predicting the future which is generally more reliable than pure guesswork. If the relevant past history of prior frequencies is long, and if thorough investigation has failed to turn up any causally potent changes in circumstances over that period, frequentist probability should be a reliable basis for future planning, or, at all events, will be a sounder bet than any other basis for projection.[81] However, specifying the predictive strengths of frequentist probability simultaneously exposes its limited forensic applications. Criminal trials are one-shot, unique investigations into past events. Except in certain special instances, they are not concerned with predicting the future,[82] nor are they part of any sequence of similar events from which a statistical frequency could be derived. We know, both intuitively *a priori* and as a matter of empirical observation, that tossing a fair coin will produce the same number of 'heads' and 'tails' over a long trial (mathematically, $p(heads) = 0.5$; $p(tails) = 0.5$). Likewise, the probability of drawing a red card from a playing deck is 1/2 ($p(red) = 0.5$), of drawing a king is 4/52 = 1/13, and of drawing any named cared is 1/52, etc. But what is the probability that the accused is guilty if he pleads not guilty? Or the probability of guilt if the accused retracts a confession? Or if there is an eyewitness? Or if there are three, but one is near-sighted? These questions, and a literally infinite number like them, are not *in principle* directly amenable to empirical testing since trials necessarily take place under conditions of uncertainty, and the uncertainty persists even after the accused has been acquitted or, as the case may be, convicted and punished.

This is a very important point which is not always grasped by policy-makers: the processes of fact-finding or the outcomes of decided cases are dubious data from which to construct frequentist probabilities for use in future proceedings, because those earlier inferences and decisions are never themselves subjected to independent verification. We simply have no reliable statistical base rates for criminal trials, which are events not even remotely akin to cutting a deck of cards or tossing a coin. Another, particularly striking, way of expressing the same point is to say that if we already had access to reliable base rates for criminal trials we would not need to have any trials, since, by definition, we would

---

[81] It may still be advisable to hedge against highly unlikely contingencies with catastrophic potential: cf. Nassim Nicholas Taleb, *The Black Swan: The Impact of the Highly Improbable* (Allen Lane, 2007).

[82] With some important exceptions, such as the predictions of future dangerousness necessary in imposing certain sentences on convicted offenders: cf. CJA 2003, s.225; *R v Bennett* [2008] 1 Cr App R (S) 11, [2007] EWCA Crim 1093.

already know – as much as we can ever know – whether particular defendants were inno-cent or guilty. A verified base rate would be the best information it is possible to have and trials in individual cases would be epistemically superfluous (except as further data for up-dating the base rate).

(b) BACONIAN 'PROBABILITY' AND NAKED STATISTICS

The widely and strongly held intuition that proof of guilt in criminal cases requires indi-vidualized evidence pertaining specifically to *this* accused can be tested through vari-ous 'paradoxes of proof' exploring the probative limits of so-called 'naked statistical evidence'.[83] It is vital not to confuse legal standards of admissibility with assessments of the sufficiency of proof. There is no threshold objection to statistical information being given in a statistical form if it is available and otherwise relevant and admissible.[84] For example, an expert witness might testify that a crime-scene sample matching glass frag-ments found on the accused's clothing has a refractive index appearing in only 1% of glass in the United Kingdom; or that the probability of the accused's DNA matching a blood sample recovered from the crime scene purely by chance is a billion to one against. But how should a jury approach the task of assessing the significance of such frequencies?

Imagine a sporting event watched by 1,000 spectators. Suppose we know that only 499 have paid for their tickets; the other 501 gatecrashed by climbing over the fence. The pro-moter naturally wants to recover the ticket price from the gatecrashers. On the basis of this naked statistical evidence, the probability that a spectator picked at random is a gate-crasher is 501/1,000, or p(crasher) = 0.501. Now, the standard of proof in civil proceedings is 'the balance of probabilities', and p(crasher) > 0.5. So the promoter should win his case. But if this analysis is correct, the promoter would win in every such case against a ran-domly chosen spectator. He could recover the price of the ticket from all 1,000 spectators, even though we know for a fact that 499 have already paid! Moreover, a slight change in the hypothetical scenario produces a radically different result. If we knew that 500 specta-tors had paid, rather than 499, the promoter could not win his case against *any* randomly chosen spectator. In the revised scenario, p(crasher) = 0.5, which means that the promoter cannot discharge the burden of proof in any case. All he can show is that p(crasher) = p(not crasher) = 0.5, and this is insufficient to tilt the probabilities in his favour. The promoter recovers nothing, even though we know for a fact that 500 spectators owe him the price of the ticket. There appears to be something puzzling if not strictly speaking paradoxical

[83] See Mike Redmayne, 'Exploring the Proof Paradoxes' (2008) 14 *Legal Theory* 281; Richard Lempert, 'The New Evidence Scholarship: Analyzing the Process of Proof' (1986) 66 *Boston University LR* 439, Part III; Stephen E. Feinberg, 'Gatecrashers, Blue Buses, and the Bayesian Representation of Legal Evidence' Proof' (1986) 66 *Boston University LR* 693; D. H. Kaye, 'The Paradox of the Gate-Crasher and Other Stories' [1979] *Arizona State LJ* 101; David T. Wasserman, 'The Morality of Statistical Proof and the Risk of Mistaken Liability' (1991) 13 *Cardozo Law Review* 935; Amit Pundik, 'Statistical Evidence and Individual Litigants: A Reconsideration of Wasserman's Argument from Autonomy' (2008) 12 *E & P* 303; and further discussion in §6.4(b).

[84] It has been suggested that purely 'normative' statistical data are inadmissible in a criminal trial on the ground that '[t]o exclude reasonable doubt as to the guilt of an individual, and to reach the required level of probability, positive data are required': David H. Sheldon and Malcolm D. MacLeod, 'From Normative to Positive Data: Expert Psychological Evidence Re-Examined' [1991] *Crim LR* 811, 814. However, this argu-ment confuses criteria of admissibility with questions of sufficiency of proof.

about naked statistical evidence. And yet everything we have said conforms with the axioms of classical probability theory.

This type of puzzle prompted Jonathan Cohen, in an original and provocative work, to suggest that probabilistic reasoning in legal and other naturalistic settings is a special non-mathematical variety of probability, and not, as others had assumed, merely a flawed practical corruption of classical probability.[85] Cohen argued for a naturalized (as opposed to logical or mathematical), inductive (not deductive), 'Baconian' (rather than 'Pascalian') type of probability which, he claimed, was exactly the right kind of probability for human decision-making based on necessarily less than perfect information. Those who sought the mathematical style of quantifiable probabilities in legal decision-making were consequently bound to be disappointed, like members of a polar bear-watching expedition to the Antarctic.

Cohen's thesis provoked a strong critical reaction and extensive discussion. The case for Baconian probability seems to have encountered two principal stumbling blocks. First, the technical and logical objections levelled by Cohen against classical probability theory have been answered,[86] at least in such a way that any still-unexplained weaknesses of Pascalian probabilities also infect the Baconian variety. Secondly, critics pointed to the apparent circularity of Cohen's justificatory argument. Jurors reason inductively, we are told, and *therefore* they *should* reason inductively without regard for the axioms of mathematical probability. The very fact that jurors *do* reason inductively (which is verified by empirical observation and chimes with our own intuitions) is also supposed to supply the justification for common habits of thought and reasoning, presented as a distinct and peculiarly well-adapted species of probabilistic evaluation of evidence. The strong suspicion here is that 'Baconian probability' amounts to nothing more than a fancy-sounding way of dignifying 'common sense' jury reasoning, however conducted. A sceptic might call Baconian probability plain old-fashioned prejudice or irrationality; and even an admirer of the reasoning processes Cohen describes might wonder in what sense they are 'probabilistic', beyond the truism that they involve reasoning under uncertainty

In an influential article, Tribe questioned the wisdom of even attempting to quantify concepts such as 'beyond reasonable doubt' which are invested with symbolic meaning, as well as serving instrumental functions.[87] For example, the beyond reasonable doubt standard might embody a commitment to withholding judgments of criminal guilt until every scintilla of doubt has been dispelled, knowing full well, in our heart of hearts, that absolute certainty always eludes mortal comprehension. Perhaps, as some have argued, we should not say all we know. Quantifying the error rate threatens to destroy the delicate balance of that cognitive dissonance which allows us to keep faith with normative aspirations like avoiding miscarriages of justice 'at all costs,' despite those aspirations being logically incompatible with hard-headed realism ('to err is human'). Laying the facts bare with quantified naked statistics seems, on one view, like a distasteful display of consequentialist calculation, as though it were our boast for criminal proceedings that jurors

---

[85] L. Jonathan Cohen, *The Probable and the Provable* (OUP, 1977).

[86] See Bernard Robertson and G. A. Vignaux, *Interpreting Evidence: Evaluating Forensic Science in the Courtroom* (Wiley, 1995); Richard D. Friedman, 'Assessing Evidence' (1996) *Michigan LR* 1810; David Kaye, 'The Laws of Probability and the Law of the Land' (1979) 47 *University of Chicago LR* 34.

[87] Laurence H. Tribe, 'Trial by Mathematics: Precision and Ritual in the Legal Process' (1971) 84 *Harvard LR* 1329.

have to be (only) 90% sure in order to convict, when that ought really to be our shameful confession.[88]

(c) BAYES' THEOREM

Bayesian probability is a sub-genre or application of classical, mathematical probability, with one important twist. In contrast to the *a priori* and frequentist conceptions of probability which aspire to objectivity and employ deduction, forensic applications of Bayes' Theorem are nearly always subjectivist. What counts for Bayes' Theorem are the subjective beliefs of the person making an assessment of probability, as opposed to any empirically verifiable frequency or logical mathematical deduction. Bayesian analysis consequently has greater forensic potential.

Bayes' Theorem is named after the eighteenth century parson who is credited with discovering it.[89] It is not a self-sufficient, comprehensive, theory of probability, but rather – as its name suggests – a particular theorem within the general demesne of classical-mathematical probability. In technical terms, Bayes' Theorem is a mathematical formula for transposing the conditional. That is to say, it allows one to move from a 'prior probability', such as the probability of finding a particular piece of evidence if the accused were guilty – conventionally denoted, $p(E|G)$ – to a 'posterior probability', specifically the probability that the accused is guilty given that evidence, $p(G|E)$.[90] Moreover, the process can be repeated over and over, taking each successive posterior probability as a new

---

[88] It should be stressed, however, that standards of proof are (subjective) measures of fact-finder confidence, rather than (objective) measures of verdict accuracy. Thus, it does *not* follow, as Glanville Williams once argued, that '[u]sing numbers has the advantage of making one face the unpleasant fact that convicting in a criminal case on a probability of 0.95, high though that may seem at first sight, involves convicting one innocent person in 20': Glanville Williams, 'The Mathematics of Proof I' [1979] *Crim LR* 297, 305–6. In fact, far from criminal trials being random events like tossing a coin, a significant majority of those accused are probably guilty – were that not so, the police and the CPS would be doing a poor job of investigating and prosecuting crimes. It follows that even a much lower 0.5 balance of probabilities standard of proof ought to produce a smaller percentage of wrongful convictions than the 1 in 20 hypothesized by Williams.

[89] The now-celebrated 'Essay Toward Solving a Problem in the Doctrine of Chances' was discovered amongst the papers of the Reverend Thomas Bayes (1702–1761), and published posthumously by the Royal Society in 1763: see David A. Schum, *The Evidential Foundations of Probabilistic Reasoning* (Northwestern UP, 1994), 47–52. For a clear, critical introduction to Bayes' Theorem in forensic contexts, see Mike Redmayne, 'Bayesianism and Proof', in Michael Freeman and Helen Reece (eds.), *Science in Court* (Ashgate, 1998).

[90] More formally, in its forensic application Bayes' Theorem holds that the posterior probability of guilt is equal to the prior probability of guilt, $p(G)$, multiplied by the likelihood ratio given by the probability that the evidence (E) would have been found were the accused guilty (G), divided by the probability that the evidence would have been found in any case, even were the accused innocent. In symbolic notation: $p(G|E) = p(G) \times p(E|G)/ p(E)$. Suppose a prior probability of $p(G) = 0.5$ (or 1:1 even odds, because $p(I) = p(1-G) = p(1-0.5) = 0.5$), and DNA evidence with a match probability of one-in-one-thousand, i.e. one in every thousand tests would produce a match, or $p(E) = 0.001$. On the (unrealistic) assumptions that the DNA database is comprehensive and that no testing errors occurred, $p(E|G) = 1$, i.e. the accused's DNA is certain to be found to match the crime sample. These figures give, as a posterior probability of guilt, $p(G) \times p(E|G)/p(E) = 0.5 \times 1/0.001 = 500$. The value of $p(G)$ has been increased by a factor of 1,000. Expressed as an odds ratio, Bayes Theorem gives: $p(G|E)/p(I|E) = p(G)/p(I) \times p(E|G)/p(E|I)$. On our example, the DNA evidence increases the odds on guilt from evens to 1,000-to-1 on, or $p(G) = 0.999$, that the accused is in fact guilty, in light of all the evidence. This is a highly stylized example using simplifying assumptions that do not hold in the real world (databases are *not* comprehensive; testing errors *do* occur), but nonetheless serves to indicate how powerful DNA evidence really is, given that the chances of an adventitious match (random false positive) are actually in the order of a billion-to-one against.

prior probability which is then up-dated by factoring an additional piece of evidence into the calculation, until a final posterior probability is ultimately produced, taking account of all the evidence in the case. The final posterior probability is the probability that the accused is guilty of the offence charged. Its complement is the probability of innocence, i.e. $p(I) = 1 - p(G)$. A mathematical formula capable of turning individual pieces of evidence into a quantified probability of guilt ought to be worth its weight in gold to adjudicators. The question is: does Bayes' Theorem yield genuine bullion, or only the alchemist's fool's gold? Evidence scholars have been sharply divided on the issue.

Advocates for Bayes' Theorem argue that its forensic application involves nothing more, and nothing less, than a necessary extension of the principles of logic and reason to the fact-finding process. A typically Bayesian claim, as formulated by two well-known enthusiasts, Bernard Robertson and Tony Vignaux, is that '[t]he axioms of probability follow from the fundamentals of rationality, logic and common sense'.[91] For them, there is only one form of probability, and that is the classical-mathematical kind: and the logic of that form of probability is also 'the logic of the law'. Other supporters are more guarded, arguing that Bayes' Theorem is useful for some forensic-related purposes but not others. Richard Lempert, for example, has stressed the pedagogic and educational virtues of Bayes Theorem but doubts its utility in the courtroom,[92] whilst Mike Redmayne, one of the leading British scholars working in the area of probability and theories of proof, has only been prepared to describe himself as 'a conservative fan of Bayesian reasoning'.[93]

The claims of Bayesian enthusiasts have been fiercely contested by a rival group of scholars dubbed 'Bayesioskeptics'.[94] Some of the arguments become rather technical and convoluted, but in broad outline the Bayesioskeptics take issue with every stage in the forensic application of Bayes' Theorem. In order to apply the Theorem, it is first necessary to calculate the 'prior odds' of guilt, the odds prior to the target piece of evidence being factored into the equation. The sceptics have several worries about these 'priors'. First, as we observed in relation to frequentist probabilities, there are no base rates for evaluating the strength of evidence at any particular point in a trial. Where is the algorithm to tell jurors that two eyewitness accounts, one somewhat dubious alibi, and a 'no comment' police interview equate, say, to a 0.7 probability of guilt? Jurors are basically expected to guess what an appropriate 'prior' would be in the light of their personal experiences

---

[91] Bernard Robertson and G. A. Vignaux, 'Probability – The Logic of the Law' (1993) 13 *OJLS* 457, 462. The argument is elucidated in Bernard Robertson and G. A. Vignaux, *Interpreting Evidence: Evaluating Forensic Science in the Courtroom* (Wiley, 1995).

[92] Richard Lempert, 'The New Evidence Scholarship: Analyzing the Process of Proof' (1986) 66 *Boston University LR* 439; Richard O. Lempert, 'Analyzing Relevance' (1977) 75 *Michigan LR* 1021.

[93] Mike Redmayne, 'Bayesianism and *Apriorism*' (1998) 1(1) ICE, Article 6, www.bepress.com/ice/vol1/iss1/art6/. And see Mike Redmayne, 'Presenting Probabilities in Court: The DNA Experience' (1997) 1 *E & P* 187, 213 (arguing that 'it would be wrong to forbid the use of Bayes' theorem as an educative tool in court').

[94] The 'skeptics' include Ron Allen, 'Rationality, Algorithms, and Juridical Proof: A Preliminary Inquiry' (1997) 1 *E & P* 254; Alex Stein, 'Judicial Fact-finding and the Bayesian Method: The Case for Deeper Scepticism about their Combination' (1996) 1 *E & P* 25; Craig R. Callen, 'Notes on a Grand Illusion: Some Limits on the Use of Bayesian Theory in Evidence Law' (1982) 57 *Indiana LJ* 1. For rejoinders, see Richard D. Friedman, 'Answering the Bayesioskeptical Challenge' (1997) 1 *E & P* 276; Peter Donnelly, 'Approximation, Comparison, and Bayesian Reasoning in Juridical Proof' (1997) 1 *E & P* 304; Richard Lempert, 'Of Flutes, Oboes and the *As If* World of Evidence Law' (1997) 1 *E & P* 316; Michael O. Finkelstein and William B. Fairly, 'A Comment on "Trial by Mathematics"' (1971) 84 *Harvard LR* 1801.

and the evidence adduced up to that point in the trial. This is, as it were, the dark side of subjectivist probability, since jurors' subjective assessments may be radically at odds with the (objective) truth of the matter. All twelve jurors might each adopt their own idiosyncratic estimate or prior probability with no reliable means of calibrating – much less integrating – their subjective probabilities into a single coherent assessment. Bayesioskeptics worry that the forensic application of Bayes' Theorem is nothing more than an elaborate intellectual smokescreen shrouding decisions arrived at through non-probabilistic reasoning in the beguiling raiment of mathematical deduction. Bayes' Theorem would then obscure the true basis for public decision-making.[95] Another objection is that inviting jurors to formulate a 'prior' probability of guilt appears inconsistent with the presumption of innocence.[96] It also cuts against the usual rule, solemnly imparted by trial judges, that jurors should keep an open mind about the case until they have heard all the evidence.[97]

The second stage of the Bayesian calculation involves updating the prior odds by factoring in a new piece of evidence. We now need to know the probability of finding that piece of evidence if the accused were guilty. For some types of evidence this will already be a quantified probability. Thus, for example, an expert presenting DNA profiling evidence would be able to say that the probability of the accused's DNA matching the crime sample, on the assumption that the accused is guilty, is very high indeed; there is only the remotest possibility of a 'false negative' elimination of a guilty suspect, such that the probability of a match *on the assumption of guilt* is effectively $p(E|G) = 1$. In the light of advances in DNA technology, 'false positive' identifications of suspects who are *not* the source of the crime-stain sample are also very remote probabilities. Assuming that the suspect pool does not include close relatives, the random match probability – the probability of a match *assuming innocence* – is conventionally stated to be one in a billion,[98] or $p(E|I) = 1/1,000,000,000 = 0.000000001$. This gives us the likelihood ratio $p(E|G)/p(E|I)$,[99] on which Bayes' Theorem then works its transpositional magic to produce a figure for the probability of guilt in light of all the evidence ($p(E|G)$) – the posterior odds. Comparing

[95] cf. Callen's warning that Bayesian calculations 'may simply provide false reassurance about what we already think we know': Craig R. Callen, '*Adams* and the Person in the Locked Room' (1998) 1(1) ICE, Article 3, www.bepress.com/ice/vol1/iss1/art3/, 7.

[96] Laurence H. Tribe, 'Trial by Mathematics: Precision and Ritual in the Legal Process' (1971) 84 *Harvard LR* 1329. The answer is that jurors should begin the trial with a very low prior probability of guilt (it being mathematically impossible that the prior odds of guilt should be zero) that can only be overcome by convincing prosecution evidence excluding any real possibility of innocence. However, this assumption is actually counter-intuitive – the accused has not been picked out and put on trial at random! – and might be hard to sustain in practice. See Richard D. Friedman, 'A Presumption of Innocence, Not of Even Odds' (2000) 52 *Stanford LR* 873.

[97] See Judicial Studies Board Specimen Direction No 55a, Further Remarks (v): 'The jury should avoid reaching concluded views about the case until they have heard all the evidence'. For an example of such a direction, see *R v Robinson* [2002] EWCA Crim 2489, [36] (quoting HHJ David Smith QC at first instance): 'But I just remind you of the vital importance of keeping an open mind and not coming to a conclusion until you have heard all the evidence, and the speeches and the summing-up. That is the time when you can validly come to a conclusion in accordance with your oath, because you have sworn an oath to try the case in accordance with the evidence and that means in accordance with all the evidence, and, although it does not say so, it really means in accordance not just with the evidence but what people say to us about it, and then, when you have given it mature reflection, you can conscientiously, in accordance with your oath, return a verdict.'   [98] *R v Bates* [2006] EWCA Crim 1395, [22].

[99] i.e., the probability of the evidence assuming guilt, divided by the probability of the evidence assuming innocence.

the prior odds with the posterior odds produces a quantified figure for the probative value of the additional piece of evidence.

The sceptics' objection to this stage of the Bayesian calculation is, bluntly, that it cannot be performed successfully, certainly not by human beings, and probably not by any being conceivable, except perhaps God. (And God, being omniscient and therefore never having to make decisions under conditions of uncertainty, would anyway have no use for Bayes' Theorem!) There are several versions and numerous strands to this argument, but at its kernel is the image of human beings with limited brain power ('computational capacity') struggling to get to grips with the (literally) infinite variety of evidential possibilities thrown up by any realistic trial scenario. Ron Allen, perhaps the most cheerfully combative of all the Bayesioskeptics, spells out the astonishing implications of this objection:

If there is any conflict in the testimony or the objects, anything at all may be deduced from the evidence, and the conflict need not centre on a fact crucial to liability; it need merely exist. *Any logical inconsistency permits any inference at all to be deduced.* Thus, only if the propositional and physical evidence contains no inconsistencies can deduction lead to a conclusion about liability, a possible but relatively uninteresting case (Why would such a case be tried?)[100]

The endless potential for new and conflicting interpretations of any body of evidence seems to imply that the Bayesian calculation should be repeated indefinitely for every conceivable evidential variation, each with its own 'prior odds'. This reasoning process is evidently viciously regressive – not merely absolutely impracticable, but literally impossible. Allen once more has a nice turn of phrase:

Even if a coherent Bayesian structural theory [of proof] can be offered, humans lack the computational capacity to implement it. So, too, do the fastest supercomputers in existence, thus leaving a supernatural being as the only possible juror under the Bayesian structural argument.[101]

'The key to success in human problem-solving', Craig Callen advises, 'is not raw mental power, but rather the ability to use one's limited cognitive resources efficiently'.[102]

Cutting short this foray into the outer reaches of human cognition and epistemology, Bayesioskeptical objections to the third and final stage of Bayes' Theorem's forensic application bring us back to the local demands of criminal adjudication. At the third stage of

---

[100]   Ronald J. Allen, 'Factual Ambiguity and A Theory of Evidence' (1994) 88 *Northwestern University LR* 606, 617 (footnote omitted, emphasis supplied). The radical indeterminacy of empirical propositions which precludes the possibility of an entirely formal system of proof can also be expressed in terms of the notorious 'reference class problem': see Ronald J. Allen and Michael Pardo, 'The Problematic Value of Mathematical Models of Evidence' (2007) 36 *Journal of Legal Studies* 107; Ron Allen and Paul Roberts (eds.), *Special Issue on the Reference Class Problem* (2007) 11(4) *E & P* 243; Peter Tillers, 'If Wishes Were Horses: Discursive Comments on Attempts to Prevent Individuals form being Unfairly Burdened by their Reference Class' (2005) 4 *Law, Probability & Risk* 33.   [101]   Allen, 'Factual Ambiguity and A Theory of Evidence', 607.

[102]   Callen demonstrates that human reasoning cannot be reduced to any formal logico-deductive system, irrespective of the complexity issue. In other words, Bayes' Theorem would still be incomplete even if human computational capacity were unlimited: Craig R. Callen, '*Adams* and the Person in the Locked Room', 3. This thought is often ascribed to Willard van Orman Quine, *From A Logical Point of View* (Harvard UP, 2nd revsd edn. 1980), 45: 'Total science, mathematical and natural and human, is similarly underdetermined by experience. The edge of the system must be kept squared with experience; the rest, with all its elaborate myths or fictions, has as its objective the simplicity of laws.'

the Bayesian procedure fact-finders are meant to be able to re-evaluate the overall strength of the case, in the light of any given new piece of evidence, after the Theorem has done its work in transposing the conditional into an up-dated probability of guilt. The problem here, say Bayesioskeptics, is that jurors will be none the wiser at the end of this improbable calculus because they will not know how to interpret a quantified measure of guilt. Suppose that the prior odds of guilt are 3 to 1 against, that is, $p(G) = 1/(3 + 1) = 0.25$. Now imagine that Bayes' Theorem shows that a new piece of evidence produces posterior odds of 2 to 1 in favour of guilt, or $p(G) = 2/3 = 0.66$. We can now be confident in saying certain things about the new piece of evidence. Firstly, it is certainly relevant to the issues in the case, having made an impact on a probabilistic assessment of the evidence.[103] Second, it is clear that the evidence favours guilt and, more than this, third, it is evidence of guilt with substantial probative value, having converted a weak case, perhaps amounting to no more than *prima facie* suspicion, into an easily better than evens chance of guilt. But what, precisely, does this add up to in a criminal case? Should the verdict be guilty, or not guilty?

The Bayesioskeptics' argument here boils down to the objection that the standard of proof in criminal proceedings is unquantified. Indeed, some would go further by insisting that it is unquantifiable. Our example is an easy case, since few would be prepared to argue that a probability as low as 0.66 is sufficient to satisfy the criminal standard.[104] The figure is conventionally placed somewhere in the range $p(G) = 0.9 - 0.99$. But these standards are hardly precise, and they appear more dubious still when it is recalled that the original probabilities factored into Bayesian calculations are themselves subjective guesstimates possibly plucked out of thin air.[105] Bayesioskeptics want to know what jurors are supposed to do with these numbers once they have them, and for whatever they might be worth.

After several decades of heated debate between Bayesians and sceptics, a measure of consensus has emerged around core propositions.[106] One significant point of agreement is that Bayes' Theorem is not an empirical-descriptive model of how jurors in fact reach their verdicts in criminal cases. In some ways this is a ludicrously obvious point: after all, most people reading this book are eligible for jury service, but few readers will even have heard of Bayes' Theorem before reading about it in this chapter, much less would they have been tempted to reach for their calculators in the juryroom! Most Bayes enthusiasts now concede that ordinary people are not natural Bayesian reasoners. In fact, a substantial body of work in social psychology demonstrates that human reasoning is constructed around narratives or 'stories' rather than through any form of probabilistic inference or logical deduction.[107] In the legal context, jurors typically reconstruct competing narratives from

---

[103] This confirms the explicitly probabilistic language of classic legal definitions of relevance, such as Stephen's: see §3.2(a); and generally, Richard O. Lempert, 'Modeling Relevance' (1977) 75 *Michigan LR* 1021.

[104] But cf. Lawrence M. Solan, 'Refocusing the Burden of Proof in Criminal Cases: Some Doubt about Reasonable Doubt' (1999) 78 *Texas LR* 105, and further discussion in §6.4(a).

[105] The difficulty of identifying appropriate priors is nicely encapsulated by one judge's account of his good faith attempt to perform this task. He confesses 'I had to cheat': see David Hodgson, 'Probability: The Logic of the Law – A Response' (1995) 15 *OJLS* 51, 56.

[106] Richard Lempert, 'Of Flutes, Oboes and the *As If* World of Evidence Law' (1997) 1 *E & P* 316; John A. Michon, 'The Time Has Come to Put this Debate Aside and Move on to Other Matters' (1997) 1 *E & P* 331; Richard D. Friedman, 'Towards a (Bayesian) Convergence?' (1997) 1 *E & P* 348.

[107] Nancy Pennington and Reid Hastie, 'The Story Model for Juror Decision Making', in Reid Hastie (ed.), *Inside the Juror: The Psychology of Juror Decision-Making* (CUP, 1993). For further discussion, see Anderson, Schum and Twining, *Analysis of Evidence*, ch 6; Twining, *Rethinking Evidence*, chs 9–10; Michael

the evidential material presented to them combined with their own personal stock of common sense generalizations[108] and other 'informal' sources of information in litigation.[109] If they are following the judge's instructions properly, jurors will base their decision on the legal consequences of the narrative they find most plausible and satisfying after each side's case is closed.[110]

Many sceptics, for their part, now accept that Bayesian analysis can contribute positively to various aspects of criminal litigation in theory and practice. Whether or not they share Lempert's enthusiasm for Bayes' Theorem as a teaching tool,[111] Bayesioskeptics must accept that probabilistic methods underpin important forms of physical evidence, including forensic (science) evidence routinely admitted in criminal proceedings, such as glass fragment or fibre analysis and blood typing.[112] Moreover, the most influential and rapidly expanding forensic technology of the day – DNA profiling – has a statistical foundation in population genetics.[113] Mathematics come as part and parcel of these sciences and, whether it is openly acknowledged in court or not, the maths cannot be rejected without casting out the evidence as well. Needless to add, Luddite renunciation of the best modern forensic science techniques is not on the Bayesioskeptical agenda.

Bayesian reasoning might also make important contributions to criminal investigations and the production of evidence in the earlier stages of criminal proceedings. A major strength of the Bayesian approach is that it formalizes the conditionality of evidence, the fact that it is always predicated on certain *assumptions* which ought to be spelt out. Bayes' Theorem requires the relevance and probative value of any item of evidence to be assessed comparatively, as a ratio of competing propositions. The likelihood ratio is the probability of the evidence assuming guilt, divided by the probability of the evidence assuming innocence: $p(E|G) / p(E|I)$. The practical significance of approaching the task of evidence analysis through comparative conditionalities is that this reasoning protocol helps investigators and forensic scientists to guard against confirmation bias. Suppose that $p(E|G) = 0.9$, meaning that *on the assumption that the accused is guilty* the probability of finding the evidence is 0.9. Would finding such evidence constitute strong proof of guilt? The Bayesian answer is that *it is categorically impossible to say either way* until one has considered the competing conditionality, $p(E|I)$. Where $p(E|I) > 0.9$, E is probative of innocence rather than guilt! This is not a fanciful illustration. It is almost certainly true, for example, that

S. Pardo and Ronald J. Allen, 'Juridical Proof and the Best Explanation' (2008) 27 *Law and Philosophy* 223; Michael S. Pardo, 'Juridical Proof, Evidence, and Pragmatic Meaning: Toward Evidentiary Holism' (2000) 95 *Northwestern University LR* 399.

[108] §4.4, above.   [109] §3.4(d).

[110] D. N. MacCormick, 'The Coherence of a Case and the Reasonableness of Doubt' (1980) II *Liverpool LR* 45; Ronald. J Allen, 'Factual Ambiguity and a Theory of Evidence' (1994) 88 *Northwestern University LR* 604.

[111] Richard O. Lempert, 'Modeling Relevance' (1977) 75 *Michigan LR* 1021; Richard Lempert, 'The New Evidence Scholarship: Analyzing the Process of Proof' (1986) 66 *Boston University LR* 439.

[112] For a very readable exposition, see Robertson and Vignaux, *Interpreting Evidence*, chs 7–9.

[113] See Nation Research Council, *Strengthening Forensic Science in the United States: A Path Forward* (National Academy Press, 2009), ch 4; Michael J. Saks and Jonathan J. Koehler, 'The Coming Paradigm Shift in Forensic Identification Science' (2005) 309 *Science* 892; NRC, *The Evaluation of Forensic DNA Evidence* (National Academy Press, 1996), 25–30 and ch 4; Peter Donnelly and Richard D. Friedman, 'DNA Database Searches and the Legal Consumption of Scientific Evidence' (1999) 97 *Michigan LR* 931; Mike Redmayne, 'Doubts and Burdens: DNA Evidence, Probability and the Courts' [1995] *Crim LR* 464; Richard Lempert, 'Some Caveats Concerning DNA as Criminal Identification Evidence: With Thanks to the Reverend Bayes' (1991) 13 *Cardozo LR* 303.

the unexpected and unrelated deaths of two or more infants in the same family is more frequently evidence of serial cot death than multiple infant murder.[114] Employing the Bayesian reasoning procedure may help investigators and forensic scientists (and prosecutors and judges) to resist the temptation of jumping to premature conclusions about the meaning and strength of particular items of evidence.

By insisting on the practical impossibility of Bayesian calculations (limited computational capacity, the 'blizzard of evidence',[115] infinite regress, and the reference class problem, etc.) the sceptics are in danger of sawing off the branch of the tree of knowledge on which they themselves perch, inasmuch as their critique can be extrapolated into a general assault on the possibility of rationality in fact-finding. For if logic is beyond human competence, what is there to deliver us from our 'irrational' intuitions? Bayesian enthusiasts may answer as follows. One can accept that Bayes' Theorem is a demanding rubric, even one demanding beyond human endeavour, and yet insist, pragmatically, that we should strive to come as near as possible to the unattainable ideal. Employing techniques such as 'batching' similar scenarios together has been shown to reduce complexity to a manageable level at which simplified calculations can be performed.[116] Even quite rough-and-ready calculations are arguably superior, in certain appropriately well-defined contexts, to brute guesswork and intuition.[117] Once the equally untenable extremes, of uncompromising Bayesianism and its unqualified rejection, no longer divert our attention, we can concentrate on the real issues of practical significance: when, and how, should Bayesian analysis enter into the forensic arena, either as a reasoning strategy or a tool of analysis?

(d) THE ADAMS FAMILY: BAYES THEOREM ON TRIAL

In a trilogy of cases involving DNA profiling evidence, all coincidentally with an accused called Adams, the Court of Appeal issued guidance on the presentation of DNA evidence to the jury and expressly rejected a controversial use of Bayes' Theorem in the courtroom. The 'Adams family' is best approached out of chronological sequence, starting with the conjoined appeals of *Doheny and Adams*[118] (which is actually the second case in the trilogy).

In *Doheny* the Court of Appeal endorsed a notably cautious approach. Experts were instructed that they should confine their testimony to stating 'the random occurrence ratio', more commonly known to mathematicians as the random match probability. The Court of Appeal insisted that a scientist 'should not be asked his opinion on the likelihood that it was the defendant who left the crime stain, nor when giving evidence should he use terminology which may lead the jury to believe that he is expressing such an opinion'.[119] Expert testimony confined to the random occurrence (a.k.a. 'random match') ratio would enable the trial judge to direct the jury along the following lines:

Members of the jury, if you accept the scientific evidence called by the Crown, this indicates that there are probably only four or five white males in the United Kingdom from whom that

---

[114] Cf. *R v Clark* [2003] EWCA Crim 1020, discussed in §11.4(b).

[115] Ronald J. Allen, 'The Nature of Juridical Proof' (1991) 13 *Cardozo LR* 373.

[116] Richard D. Friedman, 'Assessing Evidence' (1996) 94 *Michigan LR* 1810.

[117] Peter Donnelly, 'Approximation, Comparison, and Bayesian Reasoning in Juridical Proof' (1997) 1 *E & P* 304; Richard D. Friedman, 'Towards a (Bayesian) Convergence?' (1997) 1 *E & P* 348.

[118] *R v Doheny and Adams* [1997] 1 Cr App R 369, CA.   [119] ibid. 374.

[crime] stain could have come. The defendant is one of them. If that is the position, the decision you have to reach, on all the evidence, is whether you are sure that it was the defendant who left that stain or whether it is possible that it was one of that other small group of men who share the same DNA characteristics.[120]

Why is the expert not even allowed to say that DNA evidence places the accused at the scene of the crime with a quantifiably very high degree of probability? The answer is that the courts are striving to protect jurors from drawing faulty inferences, and in particular to prevent them from slipping into the notorious 'prosecutor's fallacy'.[121] The prosecutor's fallacy can be formulated in various ways. This is the version suggested by the Court of Appeal in *Doheny*:

1. Only one person in a million will have a DNA profile which matches that of the crime stain.

2. The defendant has a DNA profile which matches the crime stain.

3. Ergo there is a million to one probability that the defendant left the crime stain and is guilty of the crime.[122]

Attractive though this line of reasoning might at first sight appear to be, it is clearly fallacious. If the relevant potential suspect population includes, say, four million people, then fully four of these individuals would be expected to have DNA profiles matching the crime stain. Taken in isolation, this is only a 1-in-4 (25%) chance of guilt, or odds of 1:3 – a very long way away from the one-in-a-million chance of *innocence* proposed by the prosecutor's fallacy. Furthermore, as the Court's hypothetical deduction (3) correctly implies, a random match probability should not even be equated with the probability that the accused left the crime stain, let alone that he is guilty of the crime charged. It is impossible to calculate the probability that the accused left the crime stain without first trying to estimate the size of the suspect population, which, taking account of all the other evidence in the case, could be just a handful of suspects, or might be more in the order of every male in a radius of 100 miles. Allowances should also be made for confounding factors such as the possibility of sample contamination or laboratory testing error.

The Court of Appeal found that versions of the prosecutor's fallacy had been committed by the forensic scientists, and then repeated by the judges in summing-up their evidence to the jury, in the trials of both Doheny and Adams. However, in neither case was the error held to be fatal to the safety of the accused's conviction, principally because the mild version of the fallacy (equating the random occurrence ratio with the probability that the accused left the crime-stain) is essentially harmless when the random occurrence ratio is very small. As the forensic scientist who testified at Adams' trial explained, 'there probably are only 27 million male people in the whole of the United Kingdom so a figure of 1 in 27 million does tend to imply that it is extremely likely there is only really one man in the whole of the United Kingdom who has this DNA profile'.[123]

---

[120] ibid. 375. There might be 'four or five white males in the United Kingdom from whom that [crime] stain could have come' because DNA profiling was less discriminating in 1997 than it is today.

[121] See David J. Balding and Peter Donnelly, 'The Prosecutor's Fallacy and DNA Evidence' [1994] *Crim LR* 711.   [122] *R v Doheny and Adams* [1997] 1 Cr App R 369, 372–3.

[123] ibid. 384. Doheny's appeal was still allowed, notwithstanding this convenient neutralization of the prosecutor's fallacy, because the forensic scientist had also perpetrated the elementary statistical error of

The other two *Adams* cases both involved the same defendant. Denis Adams was convicted of rape exclusively on the basis of DNA evidence. He successfully appealed against this conviction,[124] but was convicted again at a retrial. Adams then launched a second, this time unsuccessful, appeal.[125] At both trials a prosecution expert witness testified that Adams' DNA matched the assailant's, and that the odds against achieving such a match purely by chance were (at that time) over 200 million to 1 against. Fearing, with good reason, that this kind of statistic would prove fatal to the accused's chances of securing an acquittal, the defence attempted a novel forensic strategy by instructing an expert statistician to apply Bayes' Theorem to the evidence as the defence saw it. By assigning probability estimates to the hypothesis that the rapist would have been a local man, and to the complainant's failure to pick out Adams at an identity parade, and making several other estimates and assumptions, the defence expert purported to demonstrate that the impact of the DNA evidence was far less dramatic than the prosecution's statistic implied. According to the defence expert's assumptions and calculations, the prosecution's case favoured guilt by a ratio of 55 to 1, or to a probability of a little over $p(G) = 0.98$.[126] This is still a very high probability of guilt, of course, but $p(I) = 0.02$ chance of innocence is better odds than one chance in 200 million, ostensibly[127] equating to $p(G) = 0.9999995$.

With evident reluctance, the Court of Appeal allowed Adams' first appeal against conviction on the ground that the judge had failed to give an adequate direction to the jury on the correct approach to evaluating probabilistic evidence. However, the Court dropped heavy hints that it was not at all impressed by Bayes' Theorem. Lord Justice Rose intoned:

[W]hatever the merits or demerits of the Bayes Theorem in mathematical or statistical assessments of probability, it seems to us that it is not appropriate for use in jury trials, or as a means to assist the jury in their task.... [T]he attempt to determine guilt or innocence on the basis of a mathematical formula, applied to each separate piece of evidence, is simply inappropriate to the jury's task. Jurors evaluate evidence and reach a conclusion not by means of a formula, mathematical or otherwise, but by the joint application of their individual common sense and knowledge of the world to the evidence before them.[128]

The defence decided not to take the hint. At Adams' retrial, they went further than before, presenting a Bayesian analysis of the evidence in meticulous detail, and even providing jurors with a questionnaire outlining each stage of the Bayesian approach so that, if they accepted defence counsel's invitation to adopt that style of reasoning themselves, jurors could perform their own calculations in the juryroom. Rejecting Adams' second appeal against conviction, which once again complained of inadequacies in the judge's summing up, the Court of Appeal in *Adams (No 2)* reiterated its dissatisfaction

---

multiplying together two random occurrence ratios, to produce a composite ratio of 1 in 40 million, without first ensuring that the two ratios were truly independent of each other. The same error was exposed in *R v Sally Clark* [2003] EWCA Crim 1020.

[124] *R v Adams* [1996] 2 Cr App R 467, CA.   [125] *R v Adams (No.2)* [1998] 1 Cr App R 377, CA.

[126] Because 55:1 = 55/56 = 0.9821428.

[127] Note that treating the '200 million to 1' figure as a probability of guilt unambiguously commits the prosecutor's fallacy. The mischief is, fortunately, mitigated in practice because, as the Court of Appeal recognised in *R v Doheny and Adams* [1997] 1 Cr App R 369, 384–5, the computational error is trivial when the probability of an adventitious match is sufficiently remote and the facts of the case are such that evidence of identity is conclusive proof of guilt.   [128] [1996] 2 Cr App R 467, 481.

with probabilistic approaches to non-statistical evidence, and spelt out the evidentiary ramifications:

[W]e regard the reliance on evidence of this kind…as a recipe for confusion, misunderstanding and misjudgment, possibly even among counsel, but very probably among judges and, as we conclude, almost certainly among jurors. It would seem to us that this was a case properly approached by the jury along conventional lines … We do not consider that [juries] will be assisted in their task by reference to a very complex approach which they are unlikely to understand fully and even more unlikely to apply accurately, which we judge to be likely to confuse them and distract them from their consideration of the real questions on which they should seek to reach a unanimous conclusion. We are very clearly of opinion that in cases such as this, lacking special features absent here, expert evidence should not be admitted to induce juries to attach mathematical values to probabilities arising from non-scientific evidence adduced at the trial.[129]

The Court of Appeal's anxious response to the introduction of Bayes' Theorem in the *Adams* litigation illuminates the traditional Anglo-American approach to forensic fact-finding. Juries and magistrates are expected to utilize ordinary everyday fact-finding strategies that have stood the test of (evolutionary?) time, drawing on relevant generalizations from their own knowledge and experience. This is thought to contribute towards producing legitimate verdicts generating social trust and popular allegiance.[130] What occurred at Adams' retrial was qualitatively different from the routine exposure of juries to scientific evidence couched in the language of probability. Whilst statistical and probabilistic evidence might be regarded as presenting special difficulties of juror comprehension,[131] it is routinely adduced in criminal proceedings without objection. The troubling feature of *Adams*, however, was not probabilistic *evidence*, but the defence expert's invitation to jurors to engage in formalized probabilistic *reasoning*.

Set aside the very real risk of error as jurors struggled to get to grips with an unfamiliar technical and possibly quite confusing probabilistic formula.[132] A more profound objection is that inviting jurors to apply an artificial mathematical theorem, in which they must first be tutored and practised, defeats the entire object of submitting the determination of facts in litigation to ordinary common sense judgment. Lay juries are valued precisely because they are not panels of experts; or, perhaps we might say, they are experts in ordinary common sense. If juries should ever be thought to need expert instruction, not on specialist matters of science or law, but on how to draw factual inferences and arrive at conclusions regarding constitutive facts, the traditional rationales for jury trial will have been forgotten or subverted. The Court of Appeal in *Adams* signalled that this day has not

---

[129] [1998] 1 Cr App R 377, 384, 385.   [130] §2.4.

[131] Expert witness testimony raises a host of further issues explored in Chapter 11.

[132] Whilst the magnitude of the risk would depend on each individual juror's level of numeracy and educational background, as well as on the dynamics of group decision-making, empirical studies provide ample grounds for concern: see, e.g., Jonathan L. Koehler, 'The Psychology of Numbers in the Courtroom: How to Make DNA-Match Statistics Seem Impressive or Insufficient' (2001) 74 *Southern California LR* 1275, reporting jurors' generally 'abysmal' performance in interpreting the meaning of statistics. And for discussion of standard fallacies of statistical reasoning, see Bernard Robertson and G. A. Vignaux, *Interpreting Evidence: Evaluating Forensic Science in the Courtroom* (Wiley, 1995), ch 6; David J. Balding and Peter Donnelly, 'The Prosecutor's Fallacy and DNA Evidence' [1994] *Crim LR* 711; Laurence H. Tribe, 'Trial by Mathematics: Precision and Ritual in the Legal Process' (1971) 84 *Harvard LR* 1329.

yet arrived, and, keeping faith with evidentiary orthodoxy, reaffirmed the primacy of the jury's common sense reasoning.

4.6 JUST INFERENCES?

We have seen that jury fact-finding in criminal adjudication proceeds on the basis of largely unarticulated 'common sense' inferences. The scope for formalizing the inferential process through deductive syllogisms or probabilistic calculations is limited and frowned on if overtly attempted in the courtroom. Jury deliberations are conducted in secret and the general verdict precludes *ex post facto* scrutiny of the jury's inferential reasoning.[133] Unarticulated assumptions cannot therefore be challenged or tested by the parties during the trial proceedings. Coupled with the jury's exposure to a range of informal sources of information of varying quality,[134] these procedural arrangements inevitably pose questions about the justice of fact-finding in English criminal trials. Are particular common sense inferences sound and free from prejudice? Are verdicts epistemically warranted? Could jurors be better informed or advised? To make progress on these and related questions one must try to subject the inferential process to greater analytical rigour.

We observed in the previous section that ordinary people in their daily lives organize and interpret information in terms of stories or narratives (what behavioural scientists call 'schemas'). If this is a rational epistemic foundation for adjudicating criminal cases, it behoves us to try to say something more illuminating about the inferential process than simply that jurors, for unknown or inscrutable reasons, intuitively prefer certain stories rather than others and pronounce their peremptory verdicts on that obscure basis. The extent to which fact-finding is or can become more transparent is a significant variable in assessing the legitimacy of criminal proceedings and the scope for further institutional reform. We can hope to make analytical progress in deconstructing common sense inferential reasoning without assuming that the motivations of adjudicative fact-finding can ever be rendered *completely* intelligible, even to fact-finders themselves.

(a) DECONSTRUCTING INFERENCES

Our quest for greater analytical clarity may begin with a simple hypothetical. Suppose that *D* is charged with *V*'s murder, and the prosecution proves that *V* has previously insulted *D*. The insult goes to prove *D*'s motive (revenge), which is usually an issue of central importance for fact-finders. Although some crimes are 'motiveless', as we might say when referring to 'mindless' violence or vandalism, most human conduct, including offending, is done for reasons that the actor took to be good enough to perform the action in question. In looking for an alleged offender's motive the fact-finder is seeking to identify the reasons which supplied the motivation for the offender's conduct. The inquiry calls for a judicious, multi-layered, blend of logical analysis, and empathetic imagination.

Attribution of probative weight to the insult in our example can be broken down into a number of stages. Here is one way of characterizing the situation (there is no single

---

[133] §2.4(a).   [134] §3.4(d).

definitive account, because empirical matters can be brought under an infinite variety of descriptions – as we saw in §4.2's analysis of 'finding facts'). First, in the absence of anything to indicate a joke or prank, it may be inferred that *V*'s insult genuinely offended *D*. Next, the offence he experienced must have caused *D* to harbour lasting ill-feeling towards *V*. The final step in the inferential process is to say that, given this ill-feeling, *D* is more likely to have committed the murder. Clearly, none of these inferential steps is inevitable. Individuals' tendency to take offence varies greatly, as do the sources of indignation and the duration of emotional disturbance when offence is taken. Most significantly, the vast majority of people who take offence and harbour ill-feeling do not seek murderous revenge. The probative value commonly attributed to generalizations about motive is thus obviously debatable, the more so once the explicit chain of inference is laid bare to inspection.

Thayer was one of the first Evidence scholars to draw attention to the hidden complexities and subtleties of forensic reasoning and proof. He observed:

In conducting a process of judicial reasoning, as of other reasoning, not a step can be taken without assuming something which has not been proved; and the capacity to do this, with competent judgment and efficiency, is imputed to judges and juries as part of their necessary mental outfit.[135]

Assumptions made by the fact-finder in the course of a trial are often subconscious, particularly in relation to the truthfulness of witnesses. Jurors assess veracity from a witness's demeanour,[136] amongst other considerations. But generalizations about the significance of this or that behavioural trait or conduct will often remain hidden, not only from the parties but even from jurors themselves. In the final analysis, the decision to credit or to disbelieve a particular witness may not be fully susceptible to rational explanation. Jerome Frank mused that legal adjudication, 'like the artistic process, involves feelings that words cannot ensnare'.[137]

The relationship between unstated assumptions and inferences from evidence is further complicated by moral judgments, or immoral prejudices, which can also be more-or-less hidden, unconscious, or unexamined. Whilst similar evaluative judgments routinely insinuate themselves into criminal adjudication, famous historical trials are a particularly good source of illustrations. Innocent of twenty-first century conceits and mores, commentaries on the trials of yesteryear unselfconsciously narrate the 'common sense' assumptions of their day.

Alma Rattenbury and George Stoner stood trial in 1935 for the murder of Alma Rattenbury's husband.[138] Alma, aged thirty-eight, had taken the eighteen-year-old George as her lover. From the outset, Alma was made to appear as the principal guilty party, both because the sin of a wife in adultery must be greater than her lover's and also

---

[135] Thayer, *A Preliminary Treatise on Evidence at the Common Law*, 279–80.   [136] §7.1(c).

[137] Jerome Frank, *Courts on Trial* (Princeton UP, 1949), 173. There is an analogy to legal reasoning: cf. Joseph C. Hutcheson Jr, 'The Judgment Intuitive: the Function of the "Hunch" in Judicial Decisions' (1929) 14 *Cornell Law Quarterly* 274; Charles L. Zelden, 'The Judge Intuitive: The Life and Judicial Philosophy of Joseph C. Hutcheson Jr.' (1998) 39 *South Texas LR* 905.

[138] F. Tennyson Jesse's account of the trial is reproduced by John Mortimer *et al* (eds.), *Famous Trials* (Penguin, 1984), 15.

because the difference in their ages meant that Alma must have been the dominant influence. It was further assumed in the trial that an adulterous wife would want to find a way of marrying her lover, and hence that Alma needed to get her existing husband out of the way.[139]

To twenty-first century eyes, it is obvious that none of these assumptions can withstand scrutiny. The idea that older women always dominate younger men in relationships is risible as a general proposition, then as now,[140] and only marginally less sexist than automatically blaming wives for adultery. Contemporary assumptions about marriage were also wide of the mark in this case. Alma was allowed considerable freedom by her husband to conduct extra-marital affairs. In Alma's personal circumstances, there was little to be gained by marrying a young man twenty years her junior with no money, and much to be lost.[141] But sexist stereotyping and moral condemnation were pervasive features of twentieth century criminal trials, permitting English courts 'to animadvert upon the moral qualities, or lack of them in a person accused of crime'.[142] Today, overtly discriminatory assumptions and prejudices are no longer socially acceptable in polite society, but that does not necessarily mean that moral stereotyping has ceased to influence fact-finding in criminal adjudication. Discrimination may be all the more insidious for being concealed under a veneer of outward respectability.

William Twining sounds an appropriately cautious note about the currency of factual generalizations:

In respect of any… generalization one should not assume too readily that there is in fact a 'cognitive consensus' on the matter. The stock of knowledge in any society varies from group to group, from individual to individual and from time to time. Even when there is a widespread consensus, what passes as 'conventional knowledge' may be untrue, speculative or otherwise defective; moreover, 'common-sense generalizations' tend not to be 'purely factual' – they often contain a strong mixture of evaluation and prejudice, as is illustrated by various kinds of social, national and racial stereotypes.[143]

It can hardly be doubted that many of the regularities we attribute to the world around us, especially those concerned with human conduct and intentions, are not always securely rooted in empirical observation and experience. Such generalizations at times betray visceral emotions and possibly a measure of irrationality.

[139] Similar assumptions were plainly at work in the 1922 trial of Fredrick Bywaters and Edith Thompson: see René Weis, *Criminal Justice: The True Story of Edith Thompson* (Penguin, 2001); Anderson, Schum, and Twining, *Analysis of Evidence*, ch 7; Twining, *Rethinking Evidence*, ch 12. One may wonder to what extent similar fact patterns and prejudices have influenced juries in modern decisions. See, for instance, *R v May (Susan)* [2001] EWCA Crim 2788, where the accused, who was convicted of murdering her elderly aunt, had both a secret toy-boy lover and massive gambling debts. Both facts were ostensibly irrelevant to the facts in issue in the case, but it is hard to imagine that the accused's lifestyle would have endeared her to a jury.

[140] F. Tennyson Jesse, in Mortimer *et al.* (eds.), *Famous Trials*, 25, asserted that 'there is no woman so under the dominion of her lover as the elderly mistress of a very much younger man', a contention that works better as a demonstration of the contestability of 'common sense' factual assumptions than as a profound truth about the balance of power in relationships.   [141] ibid. 47.

[142] ibid. 49.

[143] Twining, *Theories of Evidence*, 146. See also Jack B. Weinstein, 'Some Difficulties in Devising Rules for Determining Truth in Judicial Trials' (1966) 66 *Columbia LR* 223, 232.

(b) WIGMOREAN CHARTING

It was Wigmore's aspiration to minimize the risk of ill-founded generalizations infecting forensic fact-finding and skewing the outcome of trials. He conceptualized the problem in this way:

What is wanted is simple enough in purpose – namely, some method which will enable us to lift into consciousness and to state in words the reasons why a total mass of evidence does or should persuade us to a given conclusion, and why our conclusion would or should have been different or identical if some part of that total mass of evidence had been different. The mind is moved; then can we not explain why it is moved? If we can set down and work out a mathematical equation, why can we not set down and work out a mental probative equation?[144]

The question is perfectly valid and well motivated. However, the analogy to a 'mathematical equation' is problematic and its solution has proved considerably more elusive than Wigmore anticipated. After a long period when Wigmore's research agenda was virtually forgotten, renewed enthusiasm has been brought to it by later generations of scholars, working across a diverse range of disciplines of which Law is only one, but united in their interest in the uses of information as a basis for rational fact-finding and practical decision-making.[145] In theoretical terms, genuine progress is being made in laying bare the logical structure and method of factual inference, but the labour is painstaking and not always easily translated into litigation practice.[146]

Wigmore was a pioneer in this field. He set out to devise a system by which every single move from evidence through inference to conclusion would be formalized, recorded and rendered transparent to analysis. The most straightforward approaches to this task are variations on the 'narrative method' by which, Wigmore explained, one may arrange 'all evidential data under some scheme of logical sequence, narrating at each point the related evidential facts, and at each fact noting the subordinate evidence on which it depends; concluding with a narrative summary'.[147] However, narrative did not satisfy Wigmore's aspirations for rigour and analytical clarity, and he soon abandoned it in favour of a more effective and rigorous style of analysis, his trademark 'chart method'.[148]

The chart method allows the Wigmorean analyst to plot networks of inferences drawn from mixed masses of evidence. This exercise produces a formal model of the probative tasks confronting legal professionals in preparing for and conducting criminal trials, and

---

[144] John Henry Wigmore, *The Science of Judicial Proof* (Little, Brown & Co, 1937), 8. This was the third edition of a book originally titled *The Principles of Judicial Proof, As Given by Logic, Psychology, and General Experience and illustrated in Judicial Trials* (1913).

[145] For historical descriptions and modern reinterpretations of Wigmore's project, see Anderson, Schum and Twining, *Analysis of Evidence*, chs 4–5; William Twining, *Theories of Evidence*, chs 3–4 and Appendix; Peter Tillers and David Schum, 'Charting New Territory in Judicial Proof: Beyond Wigmore' (1988) 9 *Cardozo LR* 907; Kola Abimbola, 'Questions and Answers: The Logic of Preliminary Fact Investigation' (2002) 29 *Journal of Law and Society* 533.

[146] In addition to the trail-blazing work of Twining and Anderson, see e.g., David A. Schum, *The Evidential Foundations of Probabilistic Reasoning* (John Wiley & Sons, 1994); Peter Tillers and David Schum, 'A Theory of Preliminary Fact Investigation' (1991) 24 *UC Davis LR* 813. But cf. Robert P. Burns, 'Some Realism (and Idealism) About the Trial' (1997) 31 *Georgia LR* 715.

[147] Wigmore, *The Science of Judicial Proof* (1937), 7.

[148] The chart method was first presented in Wigmore, 'The Problem of Proof' (1913) 8 *Illinois LR* 77.

which also maps out the epistemic possibilities open to fact-finders. Wigmorean charts employ a bespoke vocabulary of special symbols to designate the relations between each item of evidence, with further notation linking up the chains of evidence and inference to the issues they go to prove. The immediate analytical objective is to bring out all the tacit underlying assumptions which are employed to sustain inferential connections and conclusions in adjudication. In addition to its theoretical and pedagogical value, a completed chart could in principle have a range of practical applications in criminal litigation, from helping investigators to identify any weak links in their existing evidence, through assisting lawyers to prepare their cases for trial, to playing a role in the fact-finder's deliberations.

However, modelling even relatively simple cases with the chart method involves long and quite complex chains of notation. Just reading, let alone constructing, such a chart presents a considerable challenge to anybody who has not had some instruction and practice in articulating their thoughts in this artificial way. Wigmorean chart analysis is therefore unlikely to be suitable for use by lay jurors in traditional criminal trials. In this regard, it shares some of the deficiencies of Bayes' Theorem discussed in the previous section. Jurors lack both the training and, as the law stands, the opportunity to engage in Wigmorean charting.[149] Yet, generally speaking, reasoned fact-finding improves both the quality and the transparency of forensic decision-making. Reason-giving is thus a standard feature of the 'fair trial' ideal developed in European Convention on Human Rights jurisprudence and elsewhere.[150] But in this context we seemingly must choose between trial by professional judges, who can be instructed to give comprehensive reasons for their verdicts, and lay juries which do not give reasons for their decisions, and probably could not do so; certainly not with the facility and precision attained by an experienced judge, to say nothing of an expert in Wigmorean chart analysis.

Given that any assessment of evidence is bound to be influenced by the fact-finder's predispositions, general knowledge and experience, there is much to be said for deferring to the judgments of lay juries, reflecting the experiences and attitudes of broad cross-sections of society. A professional judiciary, on the other hand, will usually represent a narrower social outlook. Even if judges were not drawn predominantly from an unrepresentative segment of society (as judges in England and Wales have been), the institutional demands of the judicial role would tend to produce a narrowing of vision, as Damaška observed:

Long terms of office create the space for routinization and specialization of tasks. Routinization of activity implies that issues that come before the official are no longer apprehended as representing a unique constellation of circumstances calling for 'individualized justice'. Choices are narrowed: while there may be many ways to go about solving a problem, only one emerges as habitual. A considerable degree of emotional disengagement also becomes possible. Specialization implies, of course, that only certain factors – those within a narrow realm – play a part in decision making. As a consequence of habitualization and

---

[149] Jurors are not provided with a transcript of the evidence and they are forbidden from seeking outside advice in their deliberations. Until recently, most judges even prevented jurors from taking notes during the trial, in the belief that note-taking would distract jurors' attention from carefully observing witnesses giving their evidence. The balance of modern opinion favours providing jurors with the opportunity for modest note-taking, but a consensus of judicial practice is difficult to sustain in the face of continued controversy.

[150] Generally, see Stefan Trechsel, 'Why Must Trials be Fair?' (1997) 31 *Israel LR* 94; H. L. Ho, 'The Judicial Duty to Give Reasons' (2000) 20 *Legal Studies* 42.

specialization, a professional's official and personal reactions part company: he acquires the capacity of anesthetizing his heart, if necessary, and of making decisions in his official capacity that he might never make as an individual.[151]

The effects of bureaucratization and 'case-hardening' need to be factored into the equation. Though professional judges might be better equipped than an untrained juror to articulate the assumptions underpinning inferences of fact in adjudication, any advantage for justice would probably be outweighed by the loss of pluralism in social outlook and diversity of experience which a lay jury contributes to fact-finding in English criminal trials.

In the past, even professional judges have exhibited reluctance to provide detailed accounts of their factual reasoning, perhaps reflecting a degree of scepticism about the value of such exercises.[152] The Human Rights Act now lends additional weight to the pressure for reasoned verdicts. Practice in the magistrates' courts quickly fell into step,[153] whilst the unreasoned jury verdict has thus far remained relatively impervious to similar demands.[154] In *McKerry* v *Teesdale and Wear Valley Justices* Lord Bingham observed:

It is not usual for magistrates to give detailed reasons; nor is it usual for juries, who make very important decisions affecting human rights, to give any reasons at all. If an aggrieved party wishes to obtain more detailed reasons from a magistrates' court, then a request can be made to state a case, as was done here, and the justices have given their reasons at somewhat greater length.[155]

It is noteworthy that what currently passes for 'giving reasons' falls far short of providing anything nearly so elaborate as a comprehensive account of the inferential process leading to a verdict.[156] Nor is this necessarily grounds for criticism. A reconstructed account of evidence and inferences with anything approaching Wigmorean particularity would be a ludicrously time-consuming undertaking if it were required in each and every case. It is far from clear when – if ever – the benefits, in terms of greater transparency and marginal improvements in the quality of decision-making, would justify the additional delay and expense inevitably involved. The jurisprudence of the European Court of Human Rights is consistent with a flexible, context-specific, and relatively undemanding approach to reasoned verdicts.[157]

---

[151] Mirjan Damaška, *The Faces of Justice and State Authority* (Yale UP, 1986), 19.

[152] In *Varndell* v *Kearney & Trecker Marwin Ltd* [1983] ICR 683, 693, CA, Eveleigh LJ opined that, in the absence of an appeal on findings of fact, 'a detailed recitation of the evidence' would be otiose. Similarly, in *Union of Construction Allied Trades and Technicians* v *Brain* [1981] ICR 542, 551, Donaldson LJ said that 'it would be a thousand pities if... reasons [for decisions of fact] began to be subjected to detailed analysis and appeals were to be brought based upon such analysis'. Also see *Morris* v *London Iron and Steel Co* [1988] QB 493, CA. Judicial attitudes have softened in the post-Human Rights Act era.

[153] *R* v *Brent Justices, ex p. McGowan* [2001] EWHC Admin 814, [2002] Crim LR 412.

[154] For further discussion, see John D. Jackson, 'Making Juries Accountable' (2002) 50 *American Journal of Comparative Law* 477; J. R. Spencer 'Inscrutable Verdicts, the Duty to Give Reasons and Article 6 of the European Convention on Human Rights' [2001] 1 *Archbold News* 5–8.

[155] *McKerry* v *Teesdale and Wear Valley Justices* [2001] EMLR 5, [2000] Crim LR 594, DC, [23].

[156] 'Justices do not have to state their reasons in the form of a judgment – reciting the charges, the evidence they have heard and all their findings of fact. The essence of the exercise in a criminal case such as this is to inform the Defendant why he has been found guilty. That can usually be done in a few simple sentences': *R* v *Brent Justices, ex p. McGowan* [2001] EWHC Admin 814, [18] (Tuckey LJ).

[157] See *Sanchez Cardenas* v *Norway* (2009) 49 EHRR 6, [49]: 'Although Article 6(1) obliges courts to give reasons for their decisions, it cannot be understood as requiring a detailed answer to every argument. Thus,

4.7 JUDICIAL NOTICE

Judicial notice may be conceptualized as an alternative, and strikingly different, procedural mechanism for managing the inferential process. Common law judges are empowered to take 'judicial notice' of certain facts. These noticed facts are then treated as settled for all purposes. Authorizing judges to decide factual issues by judicial fiat would pose issues of procedural fairness, transparency, and epistemic reasonableness in any system of adjudication. It is an especially surprising way of resolving factual issues in an adversarial system in which proof through party evidence is the norm. The traditional rationalization is that noticed facts are too obvious and indisputable to require explicit proof, which would be an unnecessary and time-wasting formality.[158]

Sensible as this sounds taken at face-value, it remains deeply puzzling that facts could be so indisputable that they require no proof. If a fact is truly beyond argument, why does the judge need to step in and remove it from the forensic contest by formally 'noticing' it? The suspicion must be that, at least on occasion, the parties *would* contest a notionally indisputable fact if they were given the opportunity to do so. Reported appeals bear out the prediction that judicial notice is sometimes extended beyond its legitimate remit to promote efficient adjudication. The picture is further complicated because the concept and language of judicial notice are frequently applied to decision-making that, whilst properly the responsibility of the trial judge, has nothing whatever to do with fact-finding or proof.

(a) NORMATIVE LIMITS OF INDISPUTABILITY

In theory, the doctrine of judicial notice answers all of the standard objections to settling questions of fact by judicial fiat. When a genuinely indisputable fact is taken for granted, it cannot be said that either party has been deprived of a fair opportunity to advance his case. Not even *the appearance* of unfairness is given, since *ex hypothesi* there is no real dispute to be had. Nor is there need for matters beyond dispute to be regulated by admissibility requirements, at least to the extent that rules of admissibility are designed to minimize time-wasting, confusion or misapprehension.[159] And the test of indisputability also pre-empts jurisdictional qualms regarding potential judicial encroachments into the

---

in dismissing an appeal an appellate court may, in principle, simply endorse the reasons for the lower court's decision. A lower court or authority in turn must give such reasons as to enable the parties to make effective use of any existing right of appeal'; and *Helle v Finland* (1998) 26 EHRR 159, [55]: 'The extent to which the duty to give reasons applies may vary according to the nature of the decision at issue. It is moreover necessary to take into account, *inter alia*, the diversity of the submissions that a litigant may bring before the courts and the differences existing in the Contracting States with regard to statutory provisions, customary rules, legal opinion and the presentation and drafting of judgments. That is why the question whether a court has failed to fulfil the obligation to state reasons, deriving from Article 6 of the Convention, can only be determined in the light of the circumstances of the case.'

[158] See, e.g., *Hughes v DPP* [2004] Env LR 28, [2003] EWHC Admin 2470, [13]: 'the magistrates would have been entitled to take judicial notice of the fact that birds as common as goldfinches are "ordinarily resident in or visitors to Great Britain". That they are so is notorious and indisputable.'

[159] Even indisputable facts may be highly prejudicial, however. This should immediately raise a suspicion that matters are never as straightforward as legal orthodoxy would have us suppose.

jury's fact-finding territory. In the absence of a genuine dispute for the jury's determination, there can be no objection to settling factual questions on the trial judge's direction. Conversely, it would be gratuitous to insist on a full trial of fact in such circumstances.[160] Requiring a party to prove a matter which is patently a foregone conclusion would saddle him with an excessive and unnecessary burden.

The test of indisputability is therefore the key to identifying when a judge may properly dispense with the normal requirements of proof. However, 'indisputability' can be understood in two different senses. The first sense corresponds to facts that 'everybody knows'. For example, judicial notice has been taken of the fact that human gestation takes longer than two weeks,[161] that the University of Oxford exists for the advancement of learning,[162] and that a postcard is likely to be read by people other than the addressee.[163] Indisputability in a second sense covers facts that can be ascertained definitively without necessarily being universally, or even widely, known. Verification by reference to indisputable sources occurs where, for example, the court needs to know the day of the week on which 1 January 2010 fell,[164] or to ascertain historical facts, such as the date on which the USA declared war on Japan,[165] or geographical locations. For the purpose of informing itself of such matters the court may have access not only to reliable documentary sources but also to experts.[166] To summarize, facts may be indisputable either because they are generally accepted by the community at large or because they may be ascertained by consulting reliable and trusted sources.[167]

The theoretically strict test of indisputability in practice has proved ambiguous and malleable, precipitating judicial over-reaching. It seems plausible enough, in this day and age, that a court might take judicial notice of 'the widespread knowledge that computer use can be reconstructed from the hard drive, even after files have been wiped off the computer'[168] and that passengers flying economy 'have to accept relatively cramped conditions which bring them into close proximity with their neighbours'.[169] It may even be indisputable in certain social *milieux* that 'by mid 1996 the style of restaurants in London had greatly changed. Apart from a few established and very traditional restaurants such as Simpsons and perhaps Rules the era of minimalist decorations and almost minimalist cuisine had begun.'[170] For the purposes of taking judicial notice, 'general knowledge'

---

[160] Though of course evidence will still have to be called if the judge happens to be ignorant of an indisputable fact. In *Ingram* v *Percival* [1969] 1 QB 548, DC, Lord Parker CJ approved of a decision by magistrates to take judicial notice of local tides, but added that, where particular justices did not have the requisite knowledge, the matter must be proved by evidence.   [161] *R* v *Luffe* (1807) 8 East 193, 103 ER 316, KB.

[162] *Re Oxford Poor Rate Case* (1857) 8 E & B 184.   [163] *Huth* v *Huth* (1915) 3 KB 32, CA.

[164] New Year's Day fell on Friday that year.

[165] The USA declared war on Japan on 8 December 1941, following the Japanese air attack on the US Pacific fleet at Pearl Harbor, Hawaii, the previous day.

[166] For example, to ascertain professional conventions and practices: *Davey* v *Harrow Corp* [1958] 1 QB 60, CA; *Re Rosher* (1884) 26 Ch D 801. Also see *McQuaker* v *Goddard* [1940] 1 KB 687, CA.

[167] 'Judicial notice refers to facts, which a Judge can be called upon to receive and to act upon, either from his general knowledge of them, or from inquiries to be made by himself for his own information from sources to which it is proper for him to refer': *Commonwealth Shipping Representative* v *Peninsular and Oriental Branch Services* [1923] AC 191, 212 (Lord Sumner). For discussion, see Edmund Morgan, 'Judicial Notice' (1944) 57 *Harvard LR* 269.   [168] *Daly* v *Sheikh* [2004] EWCA Civ 119, [46].

[169] *Morris* v *KLM Royal Dutch Airlines* [2001] EWCA Civ 790, [2001] 3 All ER 126, [29], *per* Lord Phillips MR, adding that '[j]udges do not travel exclusively in first-class seats'.

[170] *Campbell* v *Crabtree*, Ch Div (Transcript), 6 July 2001 (Patten J).

may be assessed by reference to a particular locality[171] or specialist group of litigants.[172] Proceeding by way of judicial notice is unobjectionable provided that the noticed facts are truly indisputable *between the parties* and everybody knows where they stand. In certain cases, however, judges have purported to 'notice' facts which were far from indisputable, including facts which were actually disputed in the proceedings.[173] In these scenarios judicial notice becomes an illegitimate pretext for short-circuiting adversarial argument and proof.

A different, even more troubling, type of judicial overreaching occurs when adjudicators rely on their personal knowledge to supplement the evidence and settle factual issues contested in the trial. In *Wetherall* v *Harrison*[174] the prosecution's medical expert testified that the accused had no good clinical reason for refusing to give a blood sample. Relying on the knowledge of one of their number who happened to be a doctor, the magistrates concluded to the contrary that the accused might well have had a good medical reason for refusing. Lord Widgery CJ rationalized this manoeuvre by saying that, whilst magistrates may not contradict factual evidence given in court, individual magistrates are permitted to draw on their personal knowledge when assessing the evidence in order to arrive at factual conclusions, as the doctor-magistrate had done in this case. Unfortunately, Lord Widgery's suggested distinction between supplying and evaluating evidence is insufficiently determinate and robust to keep judicial notice within acceptable bounds.

Suppose that the accused disputes the prosecution's evidence that he was in Piccadilly at the material time. A juror would not be permitted to settle this issue against the accused on the basis that, as luck would have it, the juror himself happened to spot the accused in Piccadilly at just that moment. Although the juror would only be drawing upon his personal knowledge to evaluate, and reject, the accused's testimony, it would clearly be inappropriate for a juror to rely on his personal knowledge in such circumstances. If this were permitted the accused would be denied any opportunity to hear or contest pivotal evidence adversely affecting his case. By parity of reasoning, if the magistrates in *Wetherall* v *Harrison* were in possession of information bearing on the issue, fairness demanded that the prosecution should be notified and afforded the opportunity of challenging it. The

---

[171] *Dennis* v *A J White & Co* [1917] AC 479, 492, HL; *Ingram* v *Percival* [1969] 1 QB 548, DC; *Keane* v *Mount Vernon Colliery Co* [1933] AC 309, HL.

[172] Cf. *Haberman* v *Comptroller General of the Patent Office* [2003] EWHC 430 (Pat), [2004] RPC 414, [2] – [3] *per* Peter Prescott QC: 'Mrs Mandy Haberman is a well known inventor. She is best known for her "Anywayup" trainer cup (baby feeding cup). It will not dribble Ribena on the carpet when a child holds it upside down. It may not sound like rocket science but for parents of small children it is far more important. For inventing this cup she received the British Female Inventor of the Year award (2000) and a gold medal at the Salon International des Inventions. From small beginnings, she has become a successful entrepreneur. Millions of trainer cups made to her design have been sold. See, for example, the website of the World Intellectual Property Organisation, which has chosen Mrs Haberman as a case study, precisely in order to show what a private inventor can achieve. Mrs Haberman is also recognised for her efforts as a campaigner. She is in favour of a patent system which should be truly accessible to persons such as herself, that is so say, the small entrepreneur and innovator. Her opinions have achieved respect. So much so, that she has been invited to sit on various government committees which address that topic. (I take judicial notice of the foregoing facts since they are well known or readily accessible to those who practise in this branch of the law.)'

[173] Cf. *R* v *Panesar* [2008] EWCA Crim 1526, [13] (judge took judicial notice that '[t]axi driving is a cash business and … people operating cash businesses, reprehensibly, do not always declare their full income for the purpose of taxation'); *DPP* v *King* [2008] EWHC 447 (Admin) (mini-motors are not used on the highway). *Hughes* v *DPP* [2004] Env LR 28, [2003] EWHC Admin 2470, might be regarded as a borderline case.

[174] [1976] QB 773, DC.

Divisional Court was seemingly led astray by a meaningless distinction between information received as evidence and information used for assessing evidence.

The indisputability principle implies, conversely, that adjudicators should notify the parties of their intention to rely on information in the adjudicator's possession whenever that information is neither incontestable nor widely known. In *Blick*,[175] for example, the accused tried to account for his presence at the scene of a robbery by saying that he was visiting a nearby public lavatory. A juror happened to know that the lavatory in question was actually closed at the time, and reported this fact to the judge. In contrast to *Wetherall* v *Harrison*, the trial judge then invited the prosecution to call evidence to establish the point in open court so that the juror's information might be properly investigated and tested by the parties.[176]

Whether or not a fact can be regarded as indisputable depends on the state of knowledge at the time and place of the trial. What may reasonably be disputed today may cease to be controversial as time and progress march on. It follows that a decision to take judicial notice of a certain fact cannot conclude the matter once and for all.[177] If it did, judicial notice of fact X would effectively create an irrebuttable legal presumption[178] that X is the case. Only Creationists or members of the Flat Earth Society could endorse such an inflexible fetter on forensic fact-finding, which would saddle contemporary trial proceedings with the outmoded beliefs and superstitions of yesteryear.

As long as a fact is genuinely indisputable, on the other hand, it should be noticed consistently by different courts in successive proceedings. Indeed, it may verge on abuse of process for a party to attempt to re-litigate a previously noticed matter which is not reasonably open to dispute. This still of course leaves open the possibility that scientific or other advances will continuously reconfigure the shifting boundary between what is, and what is not, reasonably open to dispute in criminal litigation.

(b) REDUNDANT NOTICE

Judges have sometimes declared themselves to be taking notice of matters which, on more careful examination, have nothing whatever to do either with factual indisputability or an appropriately circumscribed doctrine of judicial notice. Thus, it is said that judicial notice is taken of the law of the land or – a close analogue – that courts are presumed to know the law, dispensing, in either case, with the need for proof in accordance with the ordinary

---

[175]   *R v Blick* (1966) 50 Cr App R 280, CCA.

[176]   To similar effect are *R v Fricker* (1999) 96(30) LSG 29, CA; and *Hammington v Berker Sportcraft Ltd* [1980] 1 ICR 248, 252, EAT, where it was emphasized that the trier of fact must not produce from his personal knowledge evidence 'with which the parties have not had an opportunity of dealing'. And see John D. Jackson, 'Expertise or Evidence?' (1982) 98 *LQR* 192.

[177]   Chapter 2 introduced the orthodox legal division of labour according to which the judge decides questions of law, leaving questions of fact to the jury. It might appear to follow that, in taking judicial notice of a certain fact, the court would be creating a binding precedent on a question of law. But this reasoning involves an elementary *non sequitur*, because the judge makes many decisions that bind the parties without creating legal precedents. For example, judges are called upon to make conclusive assessments of relevance during the course of a trial, and these binding rulings are typically purely factual determinations devoid of precedential significance.

[178]   On presumptions, see §6.2(b).

rules of evidence.[179] But this is to confuse matters of evidence and proof with judicial interpretation and development of the law. Legal *argument* may need to be addressed to disputable points of law, but judicial notice, as a proxy for proof by admissible evidence, is confined to indisputable questions of fact.

When the Court of Appeal declared in *Simpson*[180] that a flick-knife qualifies as an offensive weapon within the legislative definition,[181] and that future courts may take judicial notice of this fact, the court was stretching the concept of notice beyond the point at which it ceases to be useful. These are issues of classification similar to those discussed earlier in the chapter.[182] Whereas jurors make normative choices as part of their fact-finding responsibilities, however, judicial classifications settle questions of law.[183] When courts are engaged in law-making[184] they are not noticing facts, or concerning themselves with any other aspect of evidence or proof, but simply discharging their constitutional mandate to maintain and, where necessary, develop and repair the law. Judicial law-making should be openly acknowledged for what it is, free from confused and confusing appeals

---

[179] Cf. *Cross on Evidence* (Butterworths, 5th edn. 1979), 155. However, foreign law is a question of fact in English criminal proceedings, and therefore potentially a proper object of judicial notice: *Saxby* v *Fulton* [1909] 2 KB 208, CA (judicial notice taken of the fact that gambling is lawful in Monte Carlo); but cf. *R* v *Ofori and Tackie (No 2)* (1994) 99 Cr App R 223, CA (where a technical point of foreign law is crucial to the prosecution's case, this must be proved by admissible evidence and cannot simply be established by judicial notice). This ruling was applied in *R* v *Okolie*, CA Trans 99/6570/Y5, 15 May 2000, [11], where Henry LJ said: 'Foreign law must be proved strictly. It should be proved, as the case *Ofori* makes clear, by calling a properly qualified expert in that law, who will give evidence himself unless his testimony is agreed or no issue is taken.... [I]n criminal cases foreign law cannot be the subject of judicial notice, and it is not possible to rely on any rebuttable presumption that it is the same as our law.'

[180] *R* v *Simpson* [1983] 1 WLR 1494, CA. Extended to butterfly knives in *DPP* v *Hynde* [1998] 1 WLR 1222, DC, applying Lord Lane CJ's *Simpson* dictum that '[b]y their very design...they betray the purpose for which they were made'. Consequently, 'the stipendiary magistrate could and should have taken judicial notice of that fact'. This is tantamount to saying that, by definition, butterfly knives constitute offensive weapons in English law. [181] Prevention of Crime Act 1953, s.1.

[182] §4.2, above.

[183] Cf. the distinction between 'adjudicative facts' and 'legislative facts' suggested by Kenneth Culp Davis, 'An Approach to Problems of Evidence in the Administrative Process' (1942) 55 *Harvard LR* 364; 'Judicial Notice' (1955) 55 *Columbia LR* 945; and 'Facts in Lawmaking' (1980) 80 *Columbia LR* 931. According to this taxonomy, adjudicative facts relate to a particular event in litigation, e.g. the date on which an offence took place, whereas legislative facts concern general states of affairs relevant to interpreting and developing the law. In determining whether flick-knives are offensive weapons, for example, it is relevant to know how often flick-knives are used offensively and whether they might have other legitimate uses, etc.

[184] According to an old common law conceit, judges only ever 'find' and declare and never *make* law. Nobody seriously believes this today, not even Law Lords: 'The common law develops as circumstances change and the balance of legal, social and economic needs changes. New concepts come into play; new statutes influence the non-statutory law. The strength of the common law is its ability to develop and evolve. All this carries with it the inevitable need to recognise that decisions may change. What was previously thought to be the law is open to challenge and review; if the challenge is successful, a new statement of the law will take the place of the old statement': *R* v *Governor of Brockhill Prison* [2001] 2 AC 19, 48, HL (Lord Hobhouse). The writing was already on the wall three decades earlier when Lord Reid told an SPTL lecture audience: 'There was a time when it was thought almost indecent to suggest that judges make law – they only declare it. Those with a taste for fairy tales seem to have thought that in some Aladdin's cave there is hidden the Common Law in all its splendour and that on a judge's appointment there descends on him knowledge of the magic words Open Sesame. Bad decisions are given when the judge has muddled the password and the wrong door opens. But we do not believe in fairy tales any more. So we must accept the fact that for better or for worse judges do make law, and tackle the question how do they approach their task and how should they approach it': (1972) 12 *Journal of the Society of Public Teachers of Law* 220.

to evidentiary doctrines. To bring this activity under the umbrella of judicial notice serves only to obscure the test of indisputability and imperil the values of open justice and fair procedure which that test aims to preserve. Judges are not the only culprits. The term 'judicial notice' appears in a number of English statutes in the over-extended sense in which it was used in *Simpson*.[185]

Political questions of state policy are a second pretext for conceptual disfigurement. In *Duff Development Co* v *Government of Kelantan*,[186] where the independence of Kelantan was in dispute, the House of Lords stated that the proper way of proceeding was 'to take judicial notice of the sovereignty of a State, and for that purpose ... to seek information from a Secretary of State; and when information is obtained the court does not permit it to be questioned by the parties'.[187] The courts have proceeded in similar fashion regarding the duration of the Second World War,[188] diplomatic status,[189] and the UK's recognition of other foreign states.[190]

Factual indisputability is not at issue in any of these cases. Judicial deference to ministerial guidance is a feature of the constitutional division of authority between executive and judiciary; it has nothing to do with the expediency of accepting indisputable facts. The principle accepted in English courts is that it is for the government, and not for judges, to settle questions of foreign relations, even for the purpose of litigation. This raises no less important, but legally and conceptually distinct, issues about the constitutional propriety of allowing executive officers, rather than the courts, to pronounce on matters within the sphere of Public International Law for the purposes of domestic litigation. Constitutional orthodoxy is especially troubling in the context of criminal proceedings, where government might appear to be acting as judge in its own cause (albeit that foreign affairs and domestic criminal prosecutions are generally handled by different government departments). However this tension between diplomacy and trial fairness ought to be resolved, neither the test of indisputability nor the doctrine of judicial notice can be expected to provide answers to what are essentially constitutional questions.

(c) NOTICE AND PROOF

Having restricted judicial notice to genuinely indisputable propositions of fact, a further doctrinal issue arises: is a judicially noticed fact incontrovertible for the purposes of the litigation, or may the opposing party adduce evidence in rebuttal? Thayer and Wigmore considered rebuttal evidence admissible, but a later generation of American Evidence scholars, led by Morgan and Maguire, denied it.[191] The apparent disagreement is resolved by clarifying two different purposes for which rebuttal evidence might be adduced.

Logically, a fact is either open to dispute amongst reasonable people, or it is not. If not, then (by hypothesis) no dispute can arise once that fact has been judicially noticed and rebuttal evidence is precluded. If, on the other hand, the point can reasonably be disputed, the test for judicial notice is not satisfied and the matter remains open to proof by admissible

---

[185] Statutes sometimes provide that the court is to take judicial notice of certain official acts. The true effect is to lay down substantive rules of law: cf. Interpretation Act 1978, s.3; European Communities Act 1972, s. 3(2); Civil Jurisdiction and Judgments Act 1982, s.2.   [186] [1924] AC 797, HL.
[187] ibid. 805–6.   [188] *R* v *Botrill, ex p. Kuechenmeister* [1947] KB 41, CA.
[189] *Engelke* v *Musmann* [1928] AC 433, HL.
[190] *Carl Zeiss Stiftung* v *Rayner and Keeler (No 2)* [1967] 1 AC 853, HL.
[191] The controversy is recounted in *McCormick on Evidence* (3rd edn. 1984), 930–4.

evidence in the ordinary way. Argument should therefore concentrate on whether a particular fact is amenable to being noticed, and once *that* question is settled there is no room for further evidence to unseat noticed facts – though, of course, the nature of any further inferences that might be drawn from a noticed fact remains fully contestable.

Though rebuttal evidence cannot be adduced to dispute a noticed fact, it remains entirely legitimate for the opposing party to adduce evidence to show that particular facts *are not indisputable* and consequently are not amenable to judicial notice in the first place. Suppose that the timing of tidal flows at a particular coastal location on a certain day becomes relevant in a criminal trial. The approximate times of high and low tide are not really disputable, and judicial notice may be taken. For that purpose the trial judge would normally consult a tide-table or receive expert advice. But what if the parties want to challenge the authenticity of the table or the reliability of the expert? Authenticity and reliability are clearly questions of fact. However, the parties' objection is not to an already noticed fact, but goes to the prior question of whether notice should be taken in reliance on those particular sources of information. Only if that collateral question[192] can be answered satisfactorily, in our hypothetical by evidence or agreement that a certain tide-table or expert is authoritative, may judicial notice be taken.[193] But at that point the noticed fact is conclusively settled for the purposes of the trial.

Where the conditions for judicial notice are properly satisfied, an issue of proof normally within the province of the jury is transmuted by the rules of criminal procedure into a matter for judicial determination, in the name of fair and efficient trial process. The distinctive function of judicial notice is to make explicit those assumptions about the world which both merit special attention, and are capable of receiving it. Some judicially noticed facts may be indisputable but relatively inaccessible, such as a well-established but obscure piece of technical or scientific information. At other times judicial notice simply identifies the source of indisputable information, in a calendar, almanac, tide-table or similar work of reference. These are indubitably valuable, if limited, functions. However, judicial notice must be strictly delimited by the test of indisputability, for the reasons we have seen.

It is clearly not the function of judicial notice to draw attention to every factual assumption supporting a criminal verdict. Rather, as things are, the fact-finding process proceeds against the backdrop of countless unstated, and therefore largely unexamined and untested, 'common sense' assumptions. One might almost speak of an implicit doctrine of 'juror notice', whereby the law tacitly permits lay fact-finders to draw freely on whatever informational resources individual jurors bring with them to the task of criminal adjudication. But unlike judicially noticed facts, being tacit and implicit, juror notice almost invariably operates without explicit articulation, let alone judicial filtering, of its factual content or epistemic adequacy.

---

[192] The status of information about tidal flows is not itself directly in issue in the trial, making this a collateral question in the sense explained in §3.3(d).

[193] In the process of attempting to identify an authoritative source, it may become apparent that the facts in question are not really indisputable after all, in which case they must be proved in the ordinary way by the party bearing the probative burden. If it transpires that different tide-tables give conflicting information, for example, the time of the relevant tide will have to be settled without resort to the short-cut of judicial notice.

5

FAIR TRIAL

5.1 SOURCES OF PROCEDURAL FAIRNESS

The concept of 'fair trial' plays an expansive, and expanding, role in English criminal litigation. Contemporary English fair trial jurisprudence is a blend of common law principles and international human rights law, more particularly in the form of Article 6 of the European Convention on Human Rights (ECHR) and local judicial innovation under the Human Rights Act. However, the key provision facilitating the recent development of English evidentiary rules on the fairness of trials has been a modest, and initially rather unpromising, statutory provision.

Section 78 was a late addition to the Bill that became PACE 1984,[1] and at the time few commentators entertained much hope for it.[2] The section, as enacted, is drafted in broad (if not entirely grammatical) language:

In any proceedings the court may refuse to allow evidence on which the prosecution proposes to rely to be given if it appears to the court that, having regard to all the circumstances, including the circumstances in which the evidence was obtained, the admission of the evidence would have such an adverse effect on the fairness of the proceedings that the court ought not to admit it.

On its face, section 78 appears to invite trial judges to undertake wide-ranging scrutiny of the circumstances in which prosecution evidence was obtained, and to utilize their discretion to exclude any evidence which might have a seriously detrimental impact on the fairness of the proceedings. Commentators' initially doubted whether section 78 would really turn out in practice to mean what it apparently seems to say. Their scepticism was informed by the common law's ancient hostility towards the exclusion of evidence purely on grounds of unfairness, impropriety, or illegality.

5.2 THE PRE-HISTORY OF SECTION 78

The traditional common law rule, stretching back at least to the mid-eighteenth century, is that the admissibility of evidence at trial is wholly unaffected by the circumstances in which it was obtained.[3] Where the police breached a citizen's rights, for example by

---

[1] The legislative history is summarized by Sybil Sharpe, *Judicial Discretion and Criminal Investigation* (Sweet & Maxwell, 1998), 81–5. The story is updated by David Ormerod and Di Birch, 'The Evolution of the Discretionary Exclusion of Evidence' [2004] *Crim LR* 767.

[2] See, e.g., see Adrian A. S. Zuckerman 'Illegally-Obtained Evidence – Discretion as a Guardian of Legitimacy' [1987] *CLP* 55.

[3] Classic early authorities include: *R v Warwickshall* (1783) 1 Leach 263; *R v Griffin* (1809) Russ & Ry 151; *R v Gould* (1840) 9 C & P 364; *R v Leatham* (1861) 8 Cox CC 498; *R v Berriman* (1854) 6 Cox CC 388.

conducting an unlawful arrest, search, or seizure, a remedy might lie in a private law tort action against the individual officers concerned or against their superiors, but the admissibility in criminal proceedings of evidence resulting from police illegality would be unaffected. Some nineteenth century authorities went so far as to say that even if evidence were *stolen* it would remain admissible at trial,[4] provided, of course, that the evidence was relevant and not excluded by any other applicable exclusionary doctrine. By the third quarter of the twentieth century, the only real hint of an exclusionary discretion regulating improperly obtained evidence at common law concerned evidence procured in circumstances tantamount to compulsory self-incrimination. This was a modest outgrowth of the common law rule excluding 'involuntary' confessions.[5] But even in this respect the authorities were few, and difficult to reconcile.[6] In particular, the nascent PV > PE rule, the common law roots of which can be traced at least as far back as early twentieth century cases like *Christie*,[7] has continued to exert little direct influence on the admissibility of improperly obtained evidence.

This state of affairs was the result of a narrow legal formalism, by the 1980s already fast becoming an exclusive conceit of English common lawyers, dictating that major issues of moral principle should receive the same interpretative treatment as technical provisions of company law or taxation. The well-known case of *Sang*[8] is a classic illustration. Invited to assess the admissibility of evidence obtained by an *agent provocateur,* five Law Lords devoted their entire energies to reconciling conflicting *dicta* in previous cases, while leaving untouched the essential question of fundamental principle: should the law provide for such an exclusionary discretion and, if so, what were its ambit and rationale? Despite some suggestive passages in their Lordships' speeches, the narrowly-reasoned decision in *Sang* tended to cast doubt on the viability of any judicial discretion to exclude unlawfully or unfairly obtained evidence.[9]

Another exemplar of the common law approach is *Fox* v *Chief Constable of Gwent*,[10] which was decided shortly before section 78 entered into force. In the aftermath of a road traffic accident involving the accused, police officers unlawfully entered the accused's home and asked him to provide a specimen of breath. When he refused, the accused was arrested, taken to a police station and forced to comply with the officers' request. His breath specimen duly showed that he had exceeded the prescribed limit for the consumption of alcohol. At trial this evidence was instrumental in securing the accused's convictions, first, of failing to provide a breath specimen and, secondly, of driving under the influence of an intoxicant. The first conviction was subsequently quashed on appeal because, following *Morris* v *Beardmore*,[11] the policemen's request for a breath specimen could not have been legally valid whilst officers were trespassing on the accused's property. As regards the drunk-driving conviction, however, the House of Lords was not prepared to accept that a

---

[4] *R v Leatham* (1861) 8 Cox CC 498.   [5] See Chapter 12.

[6] Especially the delphic *dictum* of Lord Goddard CJ in *Kuruma v R* [1955] AC 197, 204, PC, to the effect that 'in a criminal case the judge always has a discretion to disallow evidence if the strict rules of admissibility would operate unfairly against an accused . . . If, for instance, some admission of some piece of evidence, e.g. a document, had been obtained from a defendant by a trick, no doubt the judge might properly rule it out.' This *dictum* must, however, be read in light of the actual decision in the case, which was that real evidence (live ammunition) procured from about the accused's person by an unlawful police search was nonetheless properly admitted at his trial.   [7] *R v Christie* [1914] AC 545, HL, discussed in §2.5(a).

[8] *R v Sang* [1980] AC 402, HL.

[9] See P. G. Polyviou, 'Illegally-obtained Evidence and *R v Sang*' in C. F. H. Tapper (ed.), *Crime Proof and Punishment* (Butterworths, 1981), 175.   [10] [1986] 1 AC 281, HL.

[11] [1981] AC 446, HL.

breath specimen obtained after a wrongful arrest should have been excluded in exercise of the trial judge's discretion. Rejecting this argument, Lord Fraser said:

the Divisional Court was... right in treating the fact that the appellant was in the police station because he had been unlawfully arrested merely as a historical fact, with which the court was not concerned. The duty of the court is to decide whether the appellant has committed the offence with which he is charged, and not to discipline the police for exceeding their powers.... [T]here were several reasons any one of which might have accounted for the appellant's being in the police station perfectly lawfully. He might have been there because he had been lawfully arrested. Or he might have gone there voluntarily, to report the accident. Or he might have been there because, without having been arrested, he had been required... to provide a specimen and the constable making the requirement had thought fit to require him to provide it at the police station.[12]

It did not seem to matter that none of these hypothetical scenarios actually accounted for the accused's presence in the police station in this particular case. Police illegality was simply deemed irrelevant to the admissibility of subsequently procured real evidence.

Given that it is almost always possible to postulate circumstances in which improperly obtained evidence *might* have been procured without impropriety, the distinction invoked by Lord Fraser between 'mere historical facts' and live issues before the court seems distinctly dubious.[13] Hinting at deeper concerns for the proper administration of justice, Lord Fraser did add that, '[o]f course, if the appellant had been lured to the police station by some trick or deception, or if the police officers had behaved oppressively towards the appellant, the justices' jurisdiction to exclude otherwise admissible evidence... might have come into play'.[14] Such apparent after-thoughts, at that time, rang rather hollow. One might wonder why, if the accused was induced to go to the police station by being told, falsely as it turned out, that he was under lawful arrest, this did not amount to deception? And why did false imprisonment not constitute oppression? These were the substantive issues of legal and moral principle which the formalistic approach to investigative improprieties, exemplified by *Fox* and *Sang*, failed to address.

The law of criminal evidence has undergone a major transformation since these cases were decided. Legislation enacted since the mid-1980s, subsequently reinforced by human rights principles, have recast the common law's excessively indulgent traditional attitude towards improperly obtained evidence. Before describing and attempting to evaluate the development of an exclusionary discretion under section 78 of PACE 1984, it is worth pausing to consider the basic underlying rationales which might legitimate, or even require, the exclusion of evidence tainted by impropriety.

---

[12] [1986] 1 AC 281, 292.

[13] Why not, after all, draw an 'historical' divide between the unlawful entry and subsequent request for a specimen, and thus uphold the initial police request as valid? Indeed, this merely restates the very argument that the House of Lords in *Morris* v *Beardmore* refused to accept. The prosecution in that case tried to downplay the constables' illegal entry, claiming that the circumstances of their presence in the accused's home should have no bearing on their demand for a breath sample. But Lord Diplock was unimpressed by this logic-chopping: 'I find it quite impossible to suppose that Parliament intended that a person whose common law right to keep his home free from unauthorized intruders had been violated in this way should be bound under penal sanctions to comply with a demand which only the violation of that common law right had enabled the constable to make to him': [1981] AC 446, 456.   [14] [1986] 1 AC 281, 293.

5.3 RATIONALES FOR EXCLUSION

We have already alluded to the four principal rationales for excluding improperly obtained evidence: (a) reliability, (b) rights protection, (c) deterrence ('disciplining the police'), and (d) moral integrity and the legitimacy of the verdict. Whilst particular theorists and legal practitioners may advocate different combinations and detailed variations on these themes, these are the four core ideas – the basic building blocks of more sophisticated theories. This section examines each rationale in turn. Having canvassed their respective merits, the significance of the fourth idea – moral integrity – will be underscored. To begin with, however, we should acknowledge that the common law's traditional preference for blanket admissibility has not lacked distinguished defenders and apologists.

(a) RELIABILITY

Jeremy Bentham is regularly invoked as a standard-bearer by the proponents of admissibility, though in fact Bentham believed that evidence should be excluded if it was superfluous or likely to produce unjustifiable 'vexation, expense or delay'.[15] Wigmore, too, was a stanch critic of excluding evidence on grounds of procedural impropriety.[16] More recently, the philosopher Larry Laudan has renewed the assault against exclusionary doctrines, contending that '[i]f we take seriously the notion...that the trier of fact should see relevant evidence, then the requirement that evidence must be excluded if it was illegally obtained should be abandoned'.[17] Laudan's neo-Benthamite first premise is that criminal trials aspire to do justice by seeking the truth of disputed past events:

whatever else it is, a criminal trial is first and foremost an *epistemic* engine, a tool for ferreting out the truth from what will often initially be a confusing array of clues and indicators. To say that we are committed to error reduction in trials is just another way of saying that we are earnest about seeking the truth.[18]

There is nothing in this first premise which rules out the exclusion of *unreliable* evidence, since unreliable evidence – or at least that which can reliably be flagged as unreliable *ex ante* – is not conducive to truth-finding or the minimization of errors in adjudication. However, theorists and commentators in this camp tend to think that only confession evidence poses serious risks of unreliability,[19] whereas circumstantially incriminating real evidence should always, or virtually always, be admitted. Deferring consideration of the important topic of confession evidence until Chapter 12, our present concerns are more generic. Can unreliability be the only rationale for justifiably excluding improperly obtained evidence?

It is sometimes said or implied that relevant and reliable evidence must always be admissible irrespective of its provenance. As Lord Goddard CJ once pithily stated: 'the

---

[15] See William Twining, *Theories of Evidence: Bentham & Wigmore* (Weidenfeld, 1985), 28ff.

[16] *Wigmore on Evidence* (3rd edn. 1940), vol. 8, §2183.

[17] Larry Laudan, *Truth, Error, and Criminal Law: An Essay in Legal Epistemology* (CUP, 2006), 187.

[18] ibid. 2.

[19] Laudan insists on drawing a distinction between genuine, will-sapping coercion – 'situations in which someone is being subjected to some form or other of police brutality' – and the merely technical, expansive sense of 'coercion' utilized by the law: ibid. 174–5.

test to be applied in considering whether evidence is admissible is whether it is relevant to the matters in issue. If it is, it is admissible and the court is not concerned with how the evidence was obtained.'[20] Such sweeping statements (if they rest on any defensible rationale at all), implicitly appeal to Laudan's neo-Benthamite premiss that the objectives of criminal adjudication are fundamentally epistemic. If truth-finding is the overriding objective and evidence is the only rational means of proof, all relevant and reliable evidence must be received, since – accepting the premiss – 'to exclude evidence is to exclude justice'.[21] There is a great deal of truth in these contentions, but the argument is seriously incomplete as it stands. The normative conception of criminal adjudication sketched in Chapter 1 placed accurate fact-finding on a roster of five foundational values. Notwithstanding the undoubted importance of accurate fact-finding, reflected in its position at the top of our list, it should not be assumed that factual accuracy always and in every context enjoys lexical priority over the other four values we singled out for foundational status. A pluralistic account of criminal adjudication allows for the possibility that, for example, considerations of humane treatment or protection of the innocent from wrongful conviction will predominate over factual accuracy in particular circumstances. More fundamentally, the Benthamite premiss reverses the order of priority between fact-finding and justice, or perhaps collapses the distinction between them. It asserts or assumes that accurate fact-finding *just is* doing justice, whereas the account we elaborated in Chapter 1 is faithful to English law in proposing that (retributive) justice is the overriding ideal which accurate fact-finding must be fashioned to serve. Whilst justice could never require conviction of the innocent, there are circumstances in which justice might require acquittal of the guilty or, *a fortiori*, exclusion of tainted evidence incriminating the guilty. English law contains many rules of evidence which operate to exclude relevant evidence, and it remains to be seen whether these positive legal doctrines are normatively defensible. Later chapters take up this challenge for particular exclusionary doctrines. The question for present purposes is precisely whether 'unfairness', interpreted in ways yet to be clarified, should ground its own distinctive exclusionary rule. Bare appeals to relevance, which merely restate the puzzle without attempting to resolve it, are therefore transparently inadequate to justify a comprehensively inclusionary policy towards improperly obtained evidence.

A different argument was popularized by Wigmore, and remains influential with contemporary critics of evidentiary exclusion. It is objected that criminal proceedings are an unwieldy instrument for judging, *en passant*, alleged violations of legal rules only tangentially connected with the issues at trial. Contested allegations of police illegality or other abuses by officials might require thorough and prolonged judicial examination, but in the context of a criminal trial this would tend to distract the fact-finder and delay adjudication on the main issue. In Wigmore's colourful analogy:

a judge does not hold court in a street-car to do summary justice upon a fellow-passenger who fraudulently evades payment of his fare; and, upon the same principle, he does not attempt, in the course of a specific litigation, to investigate and punish all offences which incidentally cross the path of that litigation. Such a practice might be consistent with the

---

[20] *Kuruma* v *R* [1955] AC 197, 203, PC.

[21] Jeremy Bentham, *Rationale of Judicial Evidence* (1827), bk 9, ch 3, 490; quoted (with apparent approval) by Larry Laudan, *Truth, Error, and Criminal Law: An Essay in Legal Epistemology* (CUP, 2006), 171.

primitive system of justice under an Arabian sheik; but it does not comport with our own system of law.[22]

Just like the assumption that evidentiary reliability is the sole and overriding objective of criminal adjudication, this argument is radically question-begging. It assumes, without explanation, that investigative impropriety has no direct bearing on the nature or quality of criminal adjudication, and consequently should be shunted off to collateral proceedings where it cannot interfere with the matters in hand. Such compartmentalized thinking betrays an abstract, de-contextualized approach to improperly obtained evidence, as though illegality were a technical problem of the Law of Evidence straddling civil and criminal proceedings without distinction. In fact it is necessary both to look beyond technical legal rules, and to take the special character of *criminal* trials more seriously, in order to get properly to grips with improperly obtained evidence.

Beyond appeals to (un)reliability, two further rationales have featured prominently in debates surrounding the common law exclusionary rule. The first might be termed the 'vindication' or 'remedial theory', according to which evidence must be excluded in order to uphold or *vindicate* rights that have been breached. The thought here is that the real value of citizens' rights would depreciate if rights violations went unchecked and, further, that it is inappropriate for the state to benefit from the wrongdoing of its own officials. When prosecution evidence procured through police illegality is admitted at trial it might appear to breach the general moral precept that 'no-one should profit by their own wrongdoing'. A second rationale, commonly referred to as the 'deterrence theory', postulates that exclusion of evidence will deter investigators and prosecutors from repeating their unlawful conduct in the future. If judges, through routine exclusion of improperly obtained evidence, send a clear message to state officials that there is no advantage to be gained by breaking the law, then (the argument runs) the motivation for official law-breaking is removed and actual violations should accordingly decrease. In other words, deterring official law-breaking is valued instrumentally as a way of securing greater respect for rights in future criminal investigations.

Rights protection and deterrence have both enjoyed widespread currency as rationales for excluding improperly obtained evidence, especially in the United States where evidentiary exclusion is fiercely contested in the long-running dispute between supporters and critics of the Fourth Amendment (search and seizure) exclusionary rule.[23] However, neither rationale considered in isolation satisfactorily explains or justifies fairness-based exclusion as it has evolved and been consolidated in England and Wales. For a fuller explanation, we must have regard to the moral integrity of criminal proceedings and its implications for the legitimacy of decision-making in criminal adjudication.

(b) VINDICATING RIGHTS: THE REMEDIAL THEORY[24]

The remedial theory begins by reaffirming the value of liberty under the rule of law. Citizens enjoy the law's protection from illegal searches of their person or property, from

---

[22] *Wigmore on Evidence*, (3rd edn. 1940), 5. In *Fox v Chief Constable of Gwent* [1986] 1 AC 281, 292, the argument is reduced to a simpler form: it is not the courts' function to discipline the police.

[23] For an overview of US doctrine and debates, see Joshua Dressler and Alan C. Micheals, *Understanding Criminal Procedure* (Matthew Bender, 4th edn. 2005).

[24] The classic discussion is A. J. Ashworth, 'Excluding Evidence as Protecting Rights' [1977] *Crim LR* 723.

illegal seizures of their possessions, and from unlawful arrest or detention. Rights to liberty, security, and freedom of movement were first established at common law[25] and later underpinned by statute. They are now reinforced by the Human Rights Act 1998.[26] Covert surveillance and monitoring are also closely regulated by domestic legislation and delimited by international human rights law, as the serious threats to privacy posed by digital and other technologies have come to be more widely appreciated.[27] According to the remedial theory, by announcing these standards and formally enshrining them in law, the state has implicitly staked out the boundaries for lawful access to evidence. It follows that beyond these limits the state is willing to forego potentially material evidence of crime in deference to personal autonomy and freedom from state intrusion. Consequently, it is said, exclusion of evidence secured through illegal searches, seizures, or arrests puts the prosecution in exactly the position that Parliament envisaged: deprived of evidence that could only be obtained by infringing legally-protected rights. In the USA, with its written federal constitution incorporating a Bill of Rights, the exclusionary rule for a time was elevated to a constitutionally-mandated remedy for the violation of an accused person's legal rights,[28] though its status was subsequently somewhat downgraded.[29]

Despite the appealing moral symmetry of treating anything discovered in consequence of a rights violation as contaminated 'fruit of the poisoned tree' with which the courts should not soil their hands, and reinstating the evidential *status quo ante* the breach for the purposes of the trial, the remedial theory suffers from fatal weaknesses. Chief amongst them is its failure to register the moral salience of having discovered evidence incriminating a suspect, which once known cannot simply be erased from memory in order to vindicate rights. In general, we can agree, it is better for law enforcement officials to respect the law they themselves uphold. But it does not necessarily follow that the state should ignore cogent evidence of guilt once such evidence has been procured, albeit by improper means, or even that the state should never under any circumstances condone official law-breaking.

Suppose, to take an extreme but by no means entirely fanciful example, a police officer considers it necessary to threaten a suspect with violence in order to discover the

[25] See, e.g., the celebrated case of *Entick* v *Carrington* (1765) 19 State Tr 1029.

[26] See, in particular, Article 5 of the ECHR, providing that: 'Everyone has the right to liberty and security of person. No one shall be deprived of his liberty save [by lawful arrest or detention] and in accordance with a procedure prescribed by law.'

[27] A useful resource for more information on this topic is the website of the Office of Surveillance Commissioners, www.surveillancecommissioners.gov.uk/.

[28] In its landmark *Mapp* v *Ohio*, 367 US 643 (1961) decision, the Supreme Court, building on *Weeks* v *US*, 232 US 383 (1914), ruled that all evidence obtained by unconstitutional search or seizure was inadmissible in a criminal trial. The main source of pertinent constitutional rights is the Fourth Amendment, protecting: 'The right of people to be secure in their persons, houses, papers, and effects, against unreasonable searches and seizures, shall not be violated, and no warrants shall issue, but upon probable cause, supported by oath or affirmation, and particularly describing the place to be searched, and the persons or things to be seized.'

[29] *US* v *Calandra*, 414 US 338, 348 (1974) held that 'the rule is a judicially created remedy designed to safeguard Fourth Amendment rights generally through its deterrent effect, rather than a personal constitutional right of the party aggrieved.' The Fourth Amendment itself 'contains no provision expressly precluding the use of evidence obtained in violation of its commands': *Arizona* v *Evans*, 514 US 1, 10 (1995). The unmistakable trend of US Supreme Court jurisprudence since the *Mapp* era has been to narrow down the scope of the exclusionary rule: see, e.g., *Herring* v *US*, 129 S Ct 695 (2009); *US* v *Leon*, 468 US 897 (1984); *Stone* v *Powell*, 96 S Ct 3037 (1976). The Court now maintains that exclusion 'has always been our last resort, not our first impulse': *Hudson* v *Michigan*, 547 US 586, 591 (2006).

whereabouts of a terrorist bomb, which is primed to detonate in the city centre and will certainly wreak murder and mayhem unless the authorities can defuse it in time. What can this celebrated 'ticking bomb' hypothetical teach us about the morality of relying on improperly obtained evidence in a criminal trial?[30]

First, the officer might well have acted morally in threatening violence, not simply because he has subordinated the rights of one person to the interests of many (a simple consequentialist rationalization), but because he has perpetrated a moderately serious rights violation against an individual who is (we can assume for these hypothetical purposes) largely responsible for his own predicament in order to save innocent persons from much more serious violations of their rights to life, security, and bodily integrity. The officer, in other words, has chosen the lesser of two evils, and this is exactly what morality advocates in zero-sum situations where some rights are going to be infringed, and the only questions are, whose and by how much?

Secondly, and on the assumption that the officer acted morally, must it follow from the prohibition on using violence against suspects that our hypothetical terrorist's confession of the whereabouts of the bomb must be excluded at his subsequent trial for conspiracy to cause explosions? It surely does not. There is no inconsistency in maintaining a general rule against threatening suspects with violence, whilst condoning selective departures from the rule to cover extreme and unusual circumstances. Moreover, thirdly, even if the officer had acted immorally – say, in torturing a suspect in order to induce him to confess to murder – it does not necessarily follow that the state should always turn its back on cogent evidence of serious criminality. There would be no inconsistency in charging the officer with assault whilst simultaneously using reliable evidence procured by the officer through torture to prosecute and convict a murderer.

Once evidence has been discovered, no matter on this score *how* it was discovered, our knowledge of the world has changed forever and moral evaluation must take account of the realities of the situation. No one would suggest, for example, that the officer must not act on the information to save lives by defusing the bomb or evacuating the detonation site if he can. The intuition in favour of saving lives seems secure *almost irrespective of how the information in question was obtained*. Time and events have marched on, and the informational *status quo ante* can never, in reality, be retrieved once epistemic innocence is lost. Simple versions of the vindication theory are flawed because they fail to see that the discovery of cogent evidence of crime engages the state's crime control responsibilities in new ways once an evidence-producing rights-violation has already occurred. Nothing in heaven or earth can literally undo the violation, which at the point of decision is what economists call a 'sunk cost'. The state cannot simply pretend that it does not know that the suspect is probably a dangerous murderer, when it knows this full well, since the illegality of officials is not to be equated with official ignorance.

Careful readers will have noticed that our thumbnail sketch of the 'ticking bomb' hypothetical is founded on contestable assumptions and hedged about with qualifications and conditions. In real life things are never so simple, because, for example, the police will usually only suspect – they cannot know – that their detainee is a bomber; threats of violence

---

[30] For further, philosophically-informed discussion, see: Bob Brecher, *Torture and the Ticking Bomb* (Blackwell, 2007); Michael S. Moore, 'Torture and the Balance of Evils' (1989) 23 *Israel Law Review* 280. Also see *A v Home Secretary (No 2)* [2006] 2 AC 221, HL, discussed below, §5.4(c).

may produce false confessions; even truthful confessions appear suspect if they are procured outside the regime of procedural guarantees designed to ensure their trustworthiness; and so forth. In reality, moral accounting must factor in all the fine-grained details of particular circumstances (an injunction which will re-emerge in our analysis of recent case-law later in the chapter). Above all, a political community might rationally decide that it should never tempt police officers into unwarranted violence against suspects by appearing to condone official torture in any way whatsoever. The reason for considering hypothetical scenarios involving terrorists and torture, however, is to isolate and test moral intuitions, and this process of reflection has so far yielded two significant conclusions: (1) not all official illegality is morally proscribed; and (2) even where official illegality is immoral, it does not follow that cogent evidence of serious criminality procured by official law-breaking must always be ignored by the state. The remedy of exclusion, in other words, might be wholly disproportionate or otherwise inappropriate to the nature or gravity of particular rights violations by state officials.

This is not to say that victims of rights violations should be left without any remedy. Indeed, the common law has traditionally inverted that relationship and made remedies the foundation of rights: *ubi remedium, ibi jus*. Trespass, trespass to the person, assault, wrongful arrest, false imprisonment, and malicious prosecution are the principal torts (civil wrongs) for which citizens can claim damages against police officers or prosecutors if they consider themselves to have been victims of an illegal search, seizure, arrest, or prosecution.[31] These is also a dedicated system for handling complaints against the police, recently rebranded and re-launched as the Independent Police Complaints Commission (IPCC),[32] which can investigate allegations of police wrongdoing and impose disciplinary sanctions on serving officers where complaints are upheld.[33] Now it is right to add that both sources of redress have attracted searching criticism. Private law tort remedies tend to be accessible only to well-informed, financially secure, and determined complainants, raising the thorny issue of access to justice for economically disadvantaged citizens, whilst the system for handling police complaints has not always inspired public confidence in its motivations or impartiality.[34] These debates roam far beyond the scope of this book. For present purposes we need only say that if existing remedies are deficient, they should be reformed, and possibly expanded. In the USA, the Civil Rights Act of 1964 provides a direct remedy, including money damages, for those who suffer infringement of their constitutional rights. A similar remedial mechanism might be fashioned in the UK through judicial development of the Human Rights Act.[35] At all events, there is nothing in the proposition that rights violations require some remedy which requires that remedy to take the particular form of evidentiary exclusion. Evidence discovered as a consequence

[31] Andrew Sanders and Richard Young, *Criminal Justice* (Butterworths, 3rd edn. 2007), 604–12; Simon Deakin, Angus Johnston, and Basil Markesinis, *Markesinis and Deakin's Tort Law* (OUP, 6th edn. 2007), chs 8–9.   [32] Pursuant to Part 2 of the Police Reform Act 2002. See www.ipcc.gov.uk/.
[33] Sanders and Young, *Criminal Justice*, 612–30.
[34] Sanders and Young, ibid. 624, summarize: 'Despite several major changes in the system over the past 30 years or so, the complaints system is still unsatisfactory – except as a way of preserving the freedom of the police to follow their own informal norms.'
[35] HRA 1998, s.8(1) provides that 'In relation to any act (or proposed act) of a public authority which the court finds is (or would be) unlawful, it may grant such relief or remedy, or make such order, within its powers as it considers just and appropriate.'

of a rights violation might be rendered inadmissible, but not solely in order to vindicate a substantive right.

Two further criticisms are regularly levelled against the remedial theory. First, it has been objected that the remedy of evidentiary exclusion assists only those who are factually guilty – or, more accurately, those against whom there is sufficient evidence to sustain a prosecution. An entirely innocent person whose rights are breached in the course of a criminal investigation, but who is not subsequently prosecuted, derives no benefit from the exclusionary rule. Likewise, a person who is acquitted at trial – whether factually guilty or innocent – will not be helped by the exclusionary rule unless (apparently) incriminating information was obtained through that violation of his rights. Whilst the guilty no less than the innocent are entitled to have their rights respected, the remedial theory seems committed to the perverse contention that *only* the guilty (along with a few innocents who appear guilty) should enjoy a special remedy for the violation of their rights. Secondly, US critics argue that excluding unlawfully obtained evidence is directly counterproductive in producing, in the aggregate, *less* respect for individual rights and personal freedom than would be secured by routinely admitting improperly obtained evidence. This strategy is self-defeating when, in order to avoid the evidentiary implications of the exclusionary rule, courts are tempted into narrowing down the scope of the substantive right – the temptation being all the greater because defendants with the most to gain from exclusion will be those who are most obviously guilty. Consequently, 'liberals ought to hate the exclusionary rule'.[36]

These further criticisms both rest on contingencies, since securing the rights of the guilty need not leave the innocent remediless (if there is adequate civil law provision, for example), and judges are not bound to respond to an exclusionary rule by seeking to evade it through liberty-eroding interpretations of substantive law rights. But where and to the extent that either contingency is satisfied, these further considerations reinforce the basic objection that pretending not to know what – for better or worse – we now already know in virtue of investigative impropriety is, on the face of it, an odd way to vindicate rights.

(c) DISCIPLINING THE POLICE: THE DETERRENT THEORY

In view of the remedial theory's evident shortcomings, the argument for excluding improperly obtained evidence might shift to new ground: that exclusion is necessary, not so much to vindicate the accused's rights, as to deter the police from operating outside the law and thereby secure citizens' future peace, privacy, and security from official harassment. This is the deterrent theory of exclusion.

Deterrence is a future-orientated, instrumental, aggregated rationale for the exclusionary rule, where vindication is an essentially backward-looking, deontological (rights-based), individualized justification. Whilst the remedial theory is concerned with righting a particular wrong in the instant case, deterrence is concerned only with the conduct of future cases. By definition, the police were not deterred from violating the accused's rights in the instant case. However, if the police are deprived of the evidential fruits of their

---

[36] Guido Calabresi, 'The Exclusionary Rule' (2003) 26 *Harvard Journal of Law and Public Policy* 111, 112. Also see Christopher Slobogin, 'Why Liberals Should Chuck the Exclusionary Rule' [1999] *University of Illinois Law Review* 363.

illegality in the instant case (so the theory goes), they will think twice before depriving a suspect of his rights in future investigations. If the incentive to violate a right is withdrawn, rights-violations should logically diminish, because calculated illegality will no longer be worth the candle. In addition, officers might exercise greater care to avoid accidental rights-violations if a careless legal slip threatens the loss of crucial evidence.

On the deterrent rationale for excluding improperly obtained evidence, the accused on trial is the beneficiary of undeserved good fortune. Evidence is not excluded to protect any right of the accused, but rather in furtherance of instrumental objectives entirely unrelated to the merits of the instant case. For an accused who is guilty, this lucky break may turn into a windfall jackpot, where depriving the prosecution of material evidence leads to his unexpected acquittal. Deterrence theorists do not seek to justify unmerited acquittals of the guilty *per se*. Rather, they argue that this is a regrettable side-effect which must be endured in order to promote the overriding policy of deterring official misconduct and protecting citizens' rights in future criminal investigations.

The deterrent theory must confront an objection of principle implicit in our previous analysis of rights vindication. For if, as we observed, it is sometimes morally permissible or even morally obligatory for law enforcers to breach rights, why ever would we want to deter them from doing so on such occasions? Even with regard to those potential rights violations that we *do* want to deter, moreover, it will often seem perverse to employ an exclusionary remedy in the name of enhancing citizens' freedom and security. It is hard to believe that citizens will sleep safer in their beds if, for example, known rapists are freed in order to deter the police from conducting unlawful bag searches (albeit that this calculus of competing security interests is not as straightforward as it can be made to sound[37]). Legally authorized police powers themselves curb citizens' rights and liberties in furtherance of effective crime control,[38] and one would expect similar crime control considerations to carry over into the development and application of evidentiary standards.

It might be retorted that known offenders will *not* in fact go free, because an efficient system of deterrence will pre-empt illegalities in the first place, so that evidence tainted by rights violation will never, or at least hardly ever, come to light. Notice, however, that this argumentative gambit is premised on *successful* deterrence, and here, as a practical matter, the deterrent theory is at its weakest.[39] To assume that rights violations are

---

[37] If, for example, corrupt police routinely searched people's bags in order to plant incriminating evidence and then extorted bribes on pain of prosecution on trumped up charges, people might well feel more secure, on balance, if the courts insisted on a rigid exclusionary rule. Though many police forces around the world are riddled with corruption, the British police – notwithstanding periodic scandals – are relatively disciplined, trustworthy, and popular. Nonetheless, there are communities in England and Wales whose relationship with the police is characterized by mutual suspicion and hostility. It must therefore be an open question whether, for example, the denizens of a council estate in London or Liverpool would benefit from a rigid exclusionary policy, even at the cost of known offenders escaping justice.

[38] For example, PACE 1984, s.24(1), authorizes a police constable to arrest without warrant '(a) anyone who is about to commit an offence; (b) anyone who is in the act of committing an offence; (c) anyone whom he has reasonable grounds for suspecting to be about to commit an offence; (d) anyone whom he has reasonable grounds for suspecting to be committing an offence'. In other words, it is lawful to arrest a completely innocent person where there are reasonable grounds for, wrongly as it turns out, suspecting his guilt. This is just one illustration of police powers limiting every citizen's freedom in the name of crime control.

[39] For further – mostly critical – discussion of the deterrent rationale, see L. Timothy Perrin, H. Mitchell Caldwell, Carol A. Chase, and Ronald W. Fagan, 'If It's Broken, Fix It: Moving Beyond the Exclusionary Rule' (1998) 83 *Iowa LR* 669; Christine M. D'Elia, 'The Exclusionary Rule: Who Does it Punish?' (1995) 5 *Seton Hall*

always incidental to criminal investigations leading to formal prosecution and trial is to adopt a naïve view of contemporary policing. In fact, there is a rich sociological literature documenting how much policing is orientated towards order maintenance, intelligence-gathering, and summary conflict resolution.[40] To the extent that rights violations are incidental to these functions and objectives (and they are),[41] the exclusionary rule will have no deterrent effect whatever.

Even where policing leads to prosecution, moreover, the vast majority of cases are concluded by guilty plea without a contested trial, which means that the legality of police conduct is never scrutinized, much less tested, in court. Police officers who are motivated to break the law, doubtless, usually, for what the officers themselves take to be good reasons in the 'fight against crime', could rationally calculate that more often than not they will get away with breaking the rules and still secure a conviction. An occasional judicial rebuke and the loss of evidence in isolated cases will not deter law enforcers from adopting practices that succeed in the majority of investigations. From the police perspective, the exclusionary rule is at best a remote and uncertain sanction, whereas the expectations of peers and supervisors and public pressure to catch criminals (not to mention terrorists) are immediate influences on their daily working lives. It cannot be assumed that front line officers are fully appraised of the nuances of criminal procedure law; and even if their legal knowledge is accurate and up-to-date, there must be a real possibility that police officers who knowingly break the law are sufficiently circumspect to cover their tracks.

This last remark hints at a broader concern, much discussed by US commentators, that the exclusionary rule indirectly encourages police perjury and so-called 'testilying'[42] – as where officers falsely claim to have witnessed facts that would have supplied probable cause for a lawful search, in order to pre-empt evidentiary exclusion. This is a parallel objection to the idea, discussed above, that the exclusionary rule may prompt judges to give substantive rights restrictively narrow interpretations in order to be able to conclude that the right has not been breached on the instant facts, thereby pre-empting exclusion. It invites a parallel response: rather than pandering to guerrilla action by criminal justice professionals, we should demand that police officers and judges discharge their duties in accordance with the spirit of the law and not in an effort to subvert it. The response is satisfyingly purist, but not entirely realistic. In the real world, it must count against a legal norm that it cannot be explained and commended to criminal justice professionals in such a way as to engage their committed allegiance to its faithful implementation. If this were indeed how police (and/or judges) regarded the exclusionary rule, the prospects for sustaining an entirely consequentialist deterrence-based rationale would seem doubtful

Constitutional LJ 563; Randy E. Barnett, 'Resolving the Dilemma of the Exclusionary Rule: An Application of Restitutive Principles of Justice' (1983) 32 *Emory LJ* 937; Dallin H. Oakes, 'Studying the Exclusionary Rule in Search and Seizure' (1970) 37 *University of Chicago LR* 665.

[40] See, e.g., Tim Newburn, *Criminology* (Willan, 2007), ch 25; Carolyn Hoyle, *Negotiating Domestic Violence: Police, Criminal Justice and Victims* (OUP, 1998); Satnam Choongh, *Policing as Social Discipline* (OUP, 1997); Richard V. Ericson and Kevin D. Haggerty, *Policing the Risk Society* (OUP, 1997).

[41] For systematic comparative analysis, see David Dixon, *Law in Policing: Legal Regulation and Police Practices* (OUP, 1997).

[42] Christopher Slobogin, 'Testilying: Police Perjury and What to Do About It' (1996) 67 *University of Colorado LR* 1037.

in the extreme. Deterrence is nonetheless the prevailing orthodoxy in the USA,[43] which possibly explains why the exclusionary rule has fallen into (terminal?) decline in that federal jurisdiction. In the absence of systematic empirical data, we can only speculate about police and judicial attitudes in England and Wales.

All in all, the exclusionary rule appears to be an astonishingly inept tool for deterring official misconduct, even on the contestable assumption that the police should always be deterred from breaking the law. This brings us to our fourth and final rationale, elaborating on the relatively neglected themes of moral integrity in criminal proceedings and the legitimacy of the verdict.

(d) MORAL INTEGRITY AND THE LEGITIMACY OF THE VERDICT

A central contention of this book, introduced in Chapter 1, is that criminal proceedings have a distinctive moral dimension, which sets them apart from civil litigation and, indeed, from every other social institution for defining, upholding, and reinforcing standards of conduct. Criminal trials apportion moral blame, which in turn justifies the infliction of suffering and public censure, in addition to a formal determination of legal liability. Underpinning a system of penal law is a claim to moral legitimacy and public acceptance which cannot be sustained – expect by deception or force, and even then, history teaches us, not for very long – unless the system itself exhibits moral integrity. Amongst the many factors contributing to the moral integrity of criminal proceedings (independent judiciary; open, public justice; respect for citizens' rights; proof by reliable evidence, etc.), the attitude of the judiciary towards official impropriety is a significant consideration.

If judges routinely winked at rights violations by state investigators and prosecutors, criminal proceedings would be tainted by the appearance of double standards, and the public would probably quickly lose respect for a system of law apparently announcing 'do as we say, not as we do'. More to the (moral) point, a system of law predicated on such double standards *would not merit* public confidence and respect. Its legitimacy to legislate and enforce criminal laws would be seriously compromised, essentially for the reason articulated by Aquinas when he posed his celebrated rhetorical question: what are states without justice, but robber-bands enlarged? In a liberal constitutional democracy under the rule of law all state officials, including even monarchs and prime ministers, are subjects of the law, not its masters. Judges are bound to take official rule-breaking seriously, because to fail to do so is to betray the liberal democratic ideal of 'rule by law, not by men'. Beyond identifiable instances of illegality, moreover, judges are charged with the general responsibility of upholding high standards of moral integrity in criminal proceedings, because a system of law that purports to teach moral lessons to others must itself at least aspire to be beyond moral criticism. As US Supreme Court Justices Holmes and Brandeis once memorably wrote: 'Our government is the potent, the omnipresent teacher. For good or for ill, it

---

[43] The Supreme Court in *Stone v Powell*, 428 US 465, 486 (1976) authoritatively stated that: 'The primary justification for the exclusionary rule … is the deterrence of police conduct that violates Fourth Amendment rights. Post-*Mapp* decisions have established that the rule is not a personal constitutional right. It is not calculated to redress the injury to the privacy of the victim of the search or seizure, for any "[r]eparation comes too late": *Linkletter v Walker*, 381 US 618, 637 (1965). Instead, "the rule is a judicially created remedy designed to safeguard Fourth Amendment rights generally through its deterrent effect": *United States v Calandra*, 414 US 338, 348 (1974).'

teaches... by its example... If the government becomes a law breaker, it breeds contempt for law; it invites every man to become a law unto himself; it invites anarchy.'[44]

Although the core idea of procedural moral integrity supplies a robust normative standard, it application to the problem of improperly obtained evidence is not always straightforward. For one thing, some procedural irregularities are, relatively speaking, too trivial to derail the important business of doing justice by punishing criminality. Another significant consideration is that the state is not automatically tainted by every procedural breach or illegality bearing on criminal litigation.[45] To ascertain the ambit of official responsibility it is necessary to develop principles of attribution specifying the circumstances in which the state is properly answerable for the activities of its servants and agents. These principles should reflect the realities of political administration, which vary according to time and place. Judges in nineteenth century criminal proceedings, for example, might have been justified in divorcing evidentiary admissibility from investigative illegality. At that time the trial process might have been regarded as so detached from police investigations as to be insulated from pre-trial illegalities occurring in police stations and other extra-judicial settings. But this proposition is no longer tenable with respect to modern regulatory states and their governments in twenty-first century western democracies. As Justice Brennan put it in a leading US authority on 'the exclusionary rule' (such is the perceived importance of Fourth Amendment jurisprudence that it comes to stand for an entire evidentiary technique), 'police and the courts cannot be regarded as constitutional strangers to each other; because the evidence-gathering role of the police is directly linked to the evidence-admitting function of the courts, and individuals' Fourth Amendment rights may be undermined as completely by the one as by the other'.[46]

Moral integrity is neither an ethereal nor an isolated dimension of legitimate criminal process; it is an urgent practical demand, taking its place alongside, and sometimes competing with, the full gamut of moral values, policy objectives, and pragmatic constraints in the administration of criminal justice. Procedural integrity and moral legitimacy together constitute a more expansive rationale for evidentiary exclusion than the remedial theory, for the simple reason that not all immorality violates rights. This is significant, because certain official conduct – e.g. forms of race, class, or gender bias – may harm the integrity of criminal proceedings without actually breaching any identifiable rights. From the perspective of upholding the integrity of the administration of criminal justice, therefore, the remedial theory is too narrowly focused on rights violations, and simultaneously too broad in its apparent implication that any and every rights violation by law enforcement officials should automatically lead to the exclusion of evidence.

However, citizens also demand effective protection from the depredations of criminality and a reasonable measure of security to go about their lawful business unmolested. A government incapable of meeting these basic needs would lose the respect and support of

---

[44] Dissenting in *Olmstead* v *US*, 277 US 438, 484–5 (1928).

[45] The admissibility of illegally obtained evidence in civil litigation, where the transgressors are private citizens and the state is neither responsible for rights violations nor in any sense a beneficiary of them, provides an illustrative contrast: see *Calcraft* v *Guest* [1898] 1 QB 759, CA; *Ashburton* v *Pape* [1913] 2 Ch 469, CA. Criminal cases involving 'private entrapment' – e.g. by a private investigator or journalist – pose more difficult issues, since in these cases the state makes use of the evidential fruits despite having had no hand in their original cultivation. For general discussion, see Kate Hofmeyr, 'The Problem of Private Entrapment' [2006] *Crim LR* 319.   [46] *US* v *Leon*, 468 US 897, 938 (1984).

the people, just as surely – and probably much more quickly – than a government indifferent to official law-breaking. The lesson of modern day 'failed states' is that security, law, and order are necessary pre-conditions for any form of legitimate governance. In the stylized dust-up between advocates of 'due process' and their 'crime control' sparring partners,[47] neither side has a monopoly interest in public confidence. If courts invariably admitted illegally obtained evidence, it would be difficult to resist the cynical conclusion that routine malpractice by law enforcement agencies is condoned by the judiciary. This would be a serious failing of justice and a betrayal of the rule of law. Yet a blanket rule of exclusion might leave citizens at the mercy of vicious criminals 'let off an a technicality.' Since the topic of improperly obtained evidence lies in tension between these two poles, one might suspect from the outset that an inflexible rule, either of exclusion or of admissibility, is bound to be inadequate. But, at least until quite recently, English courts have been disinclined to engage in the kind of reasoning and analysis which are necessary to make headway in bringing the admissibility of evidence into conformity with the dictates of moral integrity and legal principle.

The strategy of incorporating procedural integrity and moral legitimacy into standards of admissibility has been criticized for its supposed indeterminacy and lack of clarity, especially in the United States where the fortunes of these and related ideas have ebbed and flowed for over a century. Behind these reheated objections one can often still discern Bentham's fulminations against 'nonsense on stilts'.[48] Committed utilitarians are never going to be convinced by appeals to intrinsic moral values. Bentham, and modern-day evidentiary Benthamites like Larry Laudan,[49] simply fail to credit the non-instrumental values of evidentiary rules and principles that other commentators, including us, regard as foundational. Other critics seem to be hankering after a level of deductive moral certainty to which the complexities of the moral universe are resolutely impervious. The merits of admitting or excluding improperly obtained evidence are frankly too complex, circumstantial, and uncertain to be reduced to any simple, algorithmic, all-purpose rule. In its 'liberal' heyday the US Supreme Court experimented with an inflexible rule of exclusion,[50] but soon found itself back-pedalling (and has been in reverse-gear more or less ever

---

[47] See Andrew Sanders and Richard Young, *Criminal Justice* (OUP, 3rd edn. 2007), 19–27; Andrew Ashworth, *The Criminal Process: An Evaluative Study* (OUP, 2nd edn. 1998), 3–29; Stuart Macdonald, 'Constructing A Framework for Criminal Justice Research: Learning from Packer's Mistakes' (2008) 11 *New Criminal Law Review* 257; David J. Smith, 'Case Construction and the Goals of the Criminal Process' (1997) 37 *British Journal of Criminology* 319; Mike McConville, Andrew Sanders and Roger Leng, 'Descriptive or Critical Sociology? The Choice is Yours' (1997) 37 *British Journal of Criminology* 347; Doreen McBarnet, *Conviction: Law, the State and the Construction of Justice* (MacMillan, 1981), ch 8. The *fons et origo* is, of course, Herbert L. Packer, 'Two Models of the Criminal Process' (1964) 113 *University of Pennsylvania LR* 1; Packer, *The Limits of the Criminal Sanction* (Stanford UP, 1968), chs 8–10.

[48] For critical discussion of Bentham's hostility towards moral rights, see Hugo Adam Bedau, '"Anarchical Fallacies": Bentham's Attack on Human Rights' (2000) 22 *Human Rights Quarterly* 261.

[49] Laudan is especially dismissive of the moral integrity rationale for exclusion, branding it 'the most common, but perhaps most disingenuous, justification of all for the warped character of so many exclusionary rules': Larry Laudan, *Truth, Error, and Criminal Law: An Essay in Legal Epistemology* (CUP, 2006), 226. In fact, Laudan's big guns are trained on the details of US constitutional criminal procedure law rather than on the underlying moral theory (which makes the claim that moral integrity is 'the most common' rationale for Fourth Amendment exclusion rather puzzling, since most US commentators appear to favour instrumental rationalizations or reject the exclusionary rule on instrumental grounds).

[50] *Mapp v Ohio*, 367 US 643 (1961); *Weeks v US*, 232 US 383 (1914).

since).[51] So whatever one may think of English judges' admissibility decisions in particular cases, a corpus of law to which we now turn, our courts' contextual, microscopically fact-based approach to discretionary exclusion under section 78 is fundamentally sound. We would always want the police officer to defuse the bomb or clear the area, for example, but whether evidence could legitimately be adduced at the trial of the bomber might depend on what was done to him to get it. When properly structured by a framework of principle, case-by-case analysis betokens, not confusion or lack of integrity, but a mature engagement with the moral and practical complexities of improperly obtained evidence.

5.4 THE JURISPRUDENCE OF SECTION 78

Despite an unpropitious legislative history and its deliberate departure from entrenched common law traditions, it soon became clear, after PACE was fully implemented on 1 January 1986, that appellate judges were not going to treat section 78 as a mere rhetorical fig-leaf. A landmark of the early jurisprudence is *Mason*,[52] in which the accused confessed to having participated in arson after the police told him, falsely, that his fingerprint had been recovered from a glass fragment found at the scene of the crime. The question on appeal was whether the accused's admission to the police had been properly admitted at trial, given that it had been procured by deliberate police deception. The trial judge had previously rejected defence submissions that the evidence be excluded under section 78 or section 76 of PACE,[53] on the basis that the accused had had the benefit of independent legal advice and had freely chosen to answer police questions. This was an unexceptional ruling by the standards of the day.

The Court of Appeal, however, took a markedly different view of the matter. First, it was stated that the general words of section 78 should be given their natural, broad meaning, so that, in particular, the section applied to confessions and admissions as well as to non-confessional evidence. This was a significant ruling, since it might have been anticipated, on the basis of the parliamentary history and the general scheme of PACE, that section 78 was intended to cover only evidence falling outside the ambit of section 76, which addresses confession evidence directly. But the courts rejected such a constrained reading, crediting section 78 with a 'roving brief' to monitor and check the fairness of *all* prosecution evidence. Moreover, Watkins LJ went on to castigate the police tactics employed in this case in quite remarkable language:

It is obvious from the undisputed evidence that the police practised a deceit not only upon the appellant, which is bad enough, but also upon the solicitor whose duty it was to advise him. In effect, they hoodwinked both solicitor and client. That was a most reprehensible thing to do.... This is not the place to discipline the police. That has been made clear here on a number of previous occasions. We are concerned with the application of the proper law.... [T]he only question to be answered by this court is whether, having regard to the

---

[51] See the cases cited in n.29, above. Revisionism was eminently predictable: Judge Cardozo, amongst others, had highlighted the moral problem decades before *Mapp* in *People* v *Defore*, 242 NY 13, 150 NE 585 (1926). [52] *R* v *Mason* [1988] 1 WLR 139, CA.

[53] PACE 1984, s.76 governs the admissibility of confessions or, more technically, 'admissions': see Chapter 12.

way the police behaved, the judge exercised that discretion correctly. In our judgment he did not. He omitted a vital factor from his consideration, namely, the deceit practised upon the appellant's solicitor.[54]

Since the only evidence against the accused was his confession, and since it now transpired that that confession should have been excluded, the Court of Appeal was obliged to allow the appeal and quash the accused's conviction. And for good measure Watkins LJ fired off this parting shot, with the clear intention that the Court's meaning should not be mistaken:

Before parting with this case, despite what I have said about the role of the court in relation to disciplining the police, we think we ought to say that we hope never again to hear of deceit such as this being practised upon an accused person, and more particularly possibly on a solicitor whose duty it is to advise him unfettered by false information from the police.[55]

Mason raised more questions than it answered. It is significant, in retrospect, that the Court seemed more offended by the deception practised on the accused's solicitor (thereby engaging issues of access to effective legal advice and representation[56]) than by the underlying grievance, that the accused's confession had been procured by police trickery. Subsequent case-law has established, and repeatedly confirmed, that police deception *per se* does not, without more, trigger section 78 exclusion. Evidence remains admissible where, for example, the police lawfully arrest a suspect for one offence in order to investigate other, more serious offences ('pre-textual arrest');[57] or prime an informant to secretly record his conversations with a suspect;[58] or even fool accomplices into making incriminating statements to each other by pretending that they have been placed in the same (bugged) police cell contrary to the officers' wishes owing to shortage of space.[59] The Court of Appeal has been unmoved by complaints of police deception ('charade, trick, device, deceit, subterfuge – call it what one will'), especially where 'very serious crimes have been committed – and committed by men who have not themselves shrunk from trickery and a good deal worse – and where there has never been the least suggestion that their covertly taped confessions were oppressively obtained or other than wholly reliable'.[60] *Mason* nonetheless represented a decisive and unequivocal break with the traditional common law attitude, that, so far as questions of admissibility are concerned, the judges take no notice of what goes on outside the doors of the courtroom. It could no longer be said, after

---

[54] *R v Mason* [1988] 1 WLR 139, 144, CA.   [55] ibid.

[56] Access to custodial legal advice is part of the right to a fair trial, as specified by ECHR, Art 6(1) and (3)(c). The European Court of Human Rights has said that 'in order for the right to a fair trial to remain sufficiently "practical and effective" Article 6(1) requires that, as a rule, access to a lawyer should be provided as from the first interrogation of a suspect by the police, unless it is demonstrated in the light of the particular circumstances of each case that there are compelling reasons to restrict this right. Even where compelling reasons may exceptionally justify denial of access to a lawyer, such restriction—whatever its justification— must not unduly prejudice the rights of the accused under Article 6... The rights of the defence will in principle be irretrievably prejudiced when incriminating statements made during police interrogation without access to a lawyer are used for a conviction': *Salduz v Turkey* (2009) 49 EHRR 19, [55].

[57] *R v Chalkley* [1998] QB 848, CA; *R v Mason* [2002] 2 Cr App R 38, [2002] EWCA Crim 385.

[58] *R v Jelen and Katz* (1990) 90 Cr App R 456, CA; *R v Winter* [2007] EWCA Crim 3493. A more high-tech deception was practised in *R v Jones (Ian)* [2008] QB 460, [2007] EWCA Crim 1118, utilizing text-messaging.   [59] *R v Bailey and Smith* (1993) 97 Cr App R 365, CA.

[60] ibid. 368, 375.

Mason, that police or prosecutorial impropriety is conceptually divorced from the fairness of the trial and the admissibility of evidence.

Once the judges had been entrusted with (or, according to one's reading of the legislative history, once they had successfully enlarged) this discretionary power and responsibility, many new questions regarding the nature and extent of the exclusionary jurisdiction conferred by section 78 were opened up. The boundaries of section 78 to this day remain fluid and controversial, not least because there has never been a settled, authoritative position on the section's underlying rationale (although judicial pronouncements over the last several years have provided rich material from which such a rationale might be reconstructed). Notice how Watkins LJ vacillates in *Mason*, first saying the Court did not mean to discipline the police by excluding the evidence, but then proceeding to given them a dressing-down anyway. Section 78 jurisprudence has never really extricated itself from this type of double-think. In some respects it is easier to be confident in saying what section 78 does *not* stand for, than to give a positive account of its legal effect.

(a) 'SIGNIFICANT AND SUBSTANTIAL' ILLEGALITY

One possible reading of section 78 is that evidence should automatically be excluded every time the police or prosecution infringe somebody's rights or break a rule of criminal procedure. That interpretation would be preposterous, however, and it has been unequivocally rejected. PACE 1984 and its associated Codes of Practice[61] contain literally hundreds of detailed rules governing such matters as stop and search,[62] search and seizure,[63] detention and questioning,[64] identification parades,[65] the tape-recording of interviews,[66] and the procedures to be followed when making an arrest.[67] All these rules serve useful

---

[61] Issued pursuant to PACE 1984 ss.60(1)(a), 66, and 67. Section 67(10) provides that, 'A failure on the part...of a police officer to comply with any provision of such a code...shall not of itself render him liable to any criminal or civil proceedings'. However, by subsection (11): 'In all criminal and civil proceedings any such code shall be admissible in evidence; and if any provision of such a code appears to the court or tribunal conducting the proceedings to be relevant to any question arising in the proceedings it shall be taken into account in determining that question'.

[62] PACE Code A, *Code of Practice for the Exercise by: Police Officers of Statutory Powers of Stop and Search; Police Officers and Police Staff of Requirements to Record Public Encounter* (2008 edn.): see www.police. homeoffice.gov.uk/operational-policing/powers-pace-codes/.

[63] PACE Code B, *Code of Practice for Searches of Premises by Police Officers and the Seizure of Property Found by Police Officers on Persons or Premises* (2008 edn.).

[64] PACE Code C, *Code of Practice for the Detention, Treatment and Questioning of Persons by Police Officers* (2008 edn.). Also see PACE Code H, *Code of Practice in Connection with the Detention, Treatment and Questioning by Police Officers of Persons under Section 41 of, and Schedule 8 to, the Terrorism Act 2000* (2006).

[65] PACE Code D, *Code of Practice for the Identification of Persons by Police Officers* (2008 edn.).

[66] PACE Code E, *Code of Practice on Audio Recording Interviews with Suspects* (2008 edn.). With limited exceptions, it is mandatory to record interviews with suspects in relation to indictable offences triable in the Crown Court, whilst interviews relating to summary offences may be recorded at investigators' discretion: paras.3.1 and 3.3 and Note for Guidance 3A. Interviews with terrorist suspects detained pursuant to s.41 or sch.7 of the Terrorism Act 2000 are governed by a separate Code of Practice. Also see PACE Code F, *Code of Practice on Visual Recording with Sound of Interviews with Suspects* (2005 edn.), extending Code E *mutatis mutandis* to video-recording.

[67] PACE Code G, *Code of Practice for the Statutory Power of Arrest by Police Officers* (2005 edn.).

purposes – if any do not, they are superfluous and should be dispensed with – but taken in isolation many individual requirements are relatively trivial.

Paragraph 8.6 of Code C on 'Detention, Treatment and Questioning,' for example, provides that '[a]t least two light meals and one main meal shall be offered [to police station detainees] in any period of 24 hours'. Paragraph 9.3 adds that '[d]etainees shall be visited at least every hour' whilst those 'suspected of being intoxicated through drink or drugs or have swallowed drugs must...be visited and roused at least every half hour'. The purpose of these directives is clear enough. It would be intolerable for the police to deprive detainees, who are to be treated as innocent unless and until proven otherwise,[68] of basic sustenance – to say nothing of effectively trying to starve suspects into confessing. Likewise, it would be grossly irresponsible to leave detainees unsupervised for long periods when they are likely to be disorientated, if not fright-ened, agitated, confused, and vulnerable, and possibly in some cases at risk of chok-ing to death or committing suicide. But suppose that, for reasons good or bad, police officers breach these provisions, by restricting a suspect to three light meals a day or by only checking up on him every ninety minutes instead of every hour. We might possibly want to consider taking disciplinary action against the responsible offic-ers or their superiors, though that would depend on the reasons for the breach. But nobody seriously contends that minor breaches of this nature should render inadmis-sible a detainee's subsequent voluntary confession to a major crime, like murder, rape, robbery, or wounding. A peremptory evidentiary rule of exclusion would surely be a wholly disproportionate response if it were applied automatically to each and every rule infringement, no matter how minor or excusable, or even justified, any breach might have been in the circumstances.

When the Court of Appeal squarely confronted this issue in *Keenan*,[69] Hodgson J. artic-ulated a pithy and flexible formula to ensure that trials are reasonably fair and untainted by police impropriety, whilst at the same time maintaining some sensible relationship of proportionality between the seriousness of a rule violation and the implications for justice and public safety of excluding evidence obtained consequent to the breach:

It is clear that not every breach or combination of breaches of the codes will justify the exclu-sion of interview evidence under section 76 or section 78... They must be significant and substantial. If this were not the case, the courts would be undertaking a task which is no part of their duty: as Lord Lane CJ said in *R v Delaney, The Times*, 30 August 1988: 'It is no part of the duty of the court to rule a statement inadmissible simply in order to punish the police for failure to observe the Codes of Practice'. But if the breaches are 'significant and substantial', we think it makes good sense to exclude them.... If the rest of the evidence is strong, then it may make no difference to the eventual result if [the trial judge] excludes the evidence. In cases where the rest of the evidence is weak or non-existent, that is just the situation where the temptation to do what the provisions are aimed to prevent is greatest, and the protection of the rules is most needed.[70]

In *Keenan* the accused was convicted of possessing an offensive weapon, after the police recovered a home-made spear ('a two-foot pole with a six-inch knife blade attached to the

---

[68] The presumption of innocence is examined in Chapter 6.   [69] *R v Keenan* [1990] 2 QB 54, CA.
[70] ibid. 69–70.

end') from the accused's car. The police alleged that Keenan had admitted in interview that he knew the spear was there, but tried to explain it away by saying that the car was new and that the spear did not belong to him. The admissibility of this statement was later contested because the police had failed, in contravention of PACE Code C, to make a contemporaneous record of the interview and to give the accused an opportunity to read and sign it as accurate or indicate any points of disagreement.[71] There was no record that Keenan had actually seen the spear. Indeed, at trial the defence case was that no interview ever took place at all: the accused had only just acquired the car, he said, and had no knowledge whatever of any 'spear.'

Notwithstanding these admitted breaches of Code of C, the assistant recorder presiding at trial allowed the prosecution to lead evidence of the alleged interview, apparently[72] on the basis that it was open to the accused to go into the witness-box and contest the police officers' evidence if he chose to do so. But the Court of Appeal could not accept this approach. The whole point of the PACE reforms relating to confessions had been to open up the interview room to judicial scrutiny in order to put an end to suspects' allegations of fabricated confessions and phantom interrogations – so-called 'verballing'. As the Court reiterated in *Keenan*,[73] Code C was meant to be an even-handed ally of honesty, since it both protects suspects from actual verballing (a practice of uncertain extent, but certainly not a mere figment of suspects' imagination) while simultaneously protecting police officers from wild and unsubstantiated allegations of impropriety. In bypassing Code C's provisions for accurate, contemporaneous record-keeping of interviews with suspects, the police officers in *Keenan* had effectively short-circuited the scrutiny mechanism created by PACE. Nor was it good enough to say, as the recorder had held, that the accused could always put his version of events to the jury by testifying in his own defence, since this would deprive the accused of his right to remain silent whilst putting the prosecution to proof at trial[74] and expose him to the perils of entering the witness-box. The only fair way for trial judges to proceed in the face of significant and substantial breaches of the Codes of Practice, and without knowing whether the accused intended to testify or what he would say if he did, was to invoke section 78 to exclude evidence obtained in consequence of the breach. It followed that the Court of Appeal was compelled to allow Keenan's appeal and to quash his conviction. And as in *Mason*, the Court went out of its way to condemn lax police practices. Hodgson J. considered it 'appalling' that the police officers in this case claimed to be ignorant of the Code C provisions they had breached, more than two years after PACE had been activated.[75] Indeed, one officer expressed the belief, under cross-examination, that *none* of his colleagues were familiar with all the relevant provisions of Code C! Since those heady early days when PACE was apparently experienced as something of a shock to the traditional policing system, English criminal procedure law has become much more sophisticated and detailed operational knowledge of it is now essential for keeping criminal investigations on the right side of the law.

---

[71] Now see PACE Code C, paras.11.7 and 11.11 and Note for Guidance 11E.

[72] The Court of Appeal later confessed to difficulty in identifying the precise basis for the recorder's ruling: *R v Keenan* [1990] 2 QB 54, 60.   [73] ibid. 63.

[74] Incidental to the presumption of innocence: see Chapter 6.   [75] *R v Keenan* [1990] 2 QB 54, 59.

(b) A UBIQUITOUS STANDARD OF PROCEDURAL FAIRNESS

The concept of 'significant and substantial'[76] breaches is a flexible formula for the application of section 78's jurisdiction to exclude 'unfair' evidence. There are scores of detailed
procedural rules governing criminal investigations and prosecutions that are, taken in isolation, too trivial or insufficiently associated with the production of evidence to be capable
of triggering section 78 exclusion. However, this still leaves a large number of procedural
requirements that *are* capable, on their own or in combination with other improprieties, of
prompting a trial judge to exclude evidence procured in consequence of the breach.

For example, the right to 'consult a solicitor privately at any time' during custodial
detention was thought important enough by the drafters of PACE 1984 (in the light of
recent miscarriages of justice) to incorporate it into primary legislation, as section 58 of the
1984 Act. The Court of Appeal in *Samuel*[77] described the right to custodial legal advice as
'one of the most important and fundamental rights of a citizen',[78] and proceeded to quash
the appellant's conviction where S had been improperly denied that right through deliberate police obstruction. The Court added, however, that it was 'undesirable to attempt
any general guidance as to the way in which a judge's discretion under section 78 or his
inherent powers should be exercised. Circumstances vary infinitely.'[79] The truth of this
statement was soon confirmed by *Alladice*,[80] in which the accused knew his rights and
consequently – so it was held – suffered no material disadvantage through the police officers' inadvertent breach of section 58. On this occasion, the Court of Appeal concluded that
this was 'a case where a clear breach of section 58 nevertheless does not require the Court
to rule inadmissible subsequent statements made by the defendant'.[81] Notwithstanding
their contrasting outcomes, this pair of decisions on the combined effect of PACE 1984,
ss.58 and 78 concurred in holding that, whilst good faith error will not necessarily insulate
police investigators from evidentiary exclusion, deliberate violations by them are *pro tanto*
liable to provoke it.[82]

Section 78, as we have already seen, can be invoked to exclude prosecution evidence
obtained in breach of provisions contained in subsidiary legislation, such as the PACE
Codes of Practice, as well as in response to violations of statutory rights. The argument
sometimes develops in unexpected ways. In *Forbes*,[83] for example, the House of Lords contemplated that a failure to hold an identification parade, in accordance with the procedures
set out in PACE Code D, might in principle require exclusion, under section 78, of other
identification evidence (albeit not on the facts of the instant case, where 'there were in effect
two informal identifications' which were regarded as reliable). Although an identification

---

[76] The phrase may have been first coined, in this context, by Bingham LJ in *R v Absolam* (1988) 88 Cr App
R 332, CA.   [77] *R v Samuel* [1988] QB 615, CA.

[78] ibid. 630; endorsed by *R v James (David)* [2008] EWCA Crim 1869, [35]–[36].

[79] *R v Samuel* [1988] QB 615, 630, CA.   [80] *R v Alladice* (1988) 87 Cr App R 380, CA.

[81] ibid. 387.

[82] 'If the police have acted in bad faith, the court will have little difficulty in ruling any confession inadmissible under section 78, if not under section 76. If the police, albeit in good faith, have nevertheless fallen
foul of section 58, it is still necessary for the Court to decide whether to admit the evidence would adversely
affect the fairness of the proceedings, and would do so to such an extent that the confession ought to be
excluded ... It is not possible to say in advance what would or would not be fair': *R v Alladice* (1988) 87 Cr App
R 380, 386, CA. Absence of bad faith is likewise relevant to parallel common law powers to exclude evidence
which is more prejudicial than probative or to stay proceedings as an abuse of process: *R v Mason* [2002] 2
Cr App R 38, [85].   [83] *R v Forbes* [2001] 1 AC 473, HL.

parade often serves to strengthen the prosecution's case, Lord Bingham observed, it 'may also protect the suspect against the risk of mistaken identification, and a suspect should not save in circumstances which are specified or exceptional be denied his *prima facie* right to such protection on the decision of a police officer'.[84] In other words, an identification parade could be advantageous to the accused, if the witness fails to recognize him or picks out somebody else form the line-up, and the accused should not be denied any reasonable opportunity of putting an eyewitness to the test in the circumstances anticipated by Code D. It is not hard to imagine scenarios in which exclusion might follow, e.g. if the police deliberately kept a witness away from an identification parade because it was feared that the witness would not be able to replicate his informal street identification of the suspect.[85]

PACE 1984 might fairly be described as the first truly modern piece of criminal procedure legislation in England and Wales. The ensuing three decades have brought a slew of further enactments to regulate different aspects of criminal investigation, prosecution, and trial procedure, often in minute detail. (Compliance with human rights standards, demanding that law enforcement should be conducted 'in accordance with the [written] law', has supplied much of the impetus for systematic procedural reform.) Primary enactments are regularly accompanied by expository Codes of Practice, on the PACE model. Thus, the interception of telecommunications ('telephone-tapping') is now governed by a combination of Part III of the Police Act 1997, Part I of the Regulation of Investigatory Powers Act (RIPA) 2000, and the Code of Practice on the Interception of Communications.[86] For the time being, telephone tap evidence (as opposed to telephone conversations covertly recorded by one of the parties to the conversation) is not admissible in England and Wales,[87] although this evidential constraint on law enforcement is widely denounced and has been subjected to almost perpetual official review in recent years.[88] There are further RIPA Codes on covert surveillance (including so-called 'bugging and burgling' operations)[89] and the use of informants (known by the faintly Orwellian acronym 'CHIS', covert human intelligence sources).[90] A separate Code of Practice on criminal investigations was issued pursuant to the Criminal Procedure and Investigations Act (CPIA) 1996,[91] which mainly governs pre-trial disclosure of evidence, in conjunction with an expanding array of supplementary official guidance and soft law instruments.[92] The range of 'special measures' for vulnerable or intimidated witnesses contained in Part II

---

[84] ibid. [30].

[85] It was mentioned in *Forbes* that 'no accusation of bad faith was made against the police investigating officer in this case': ibid. [31].

[86] Issued pursuant to RIPA 2000, s.71, and in force from 1 July 2002. RIPA and its associated Codes of Practice are available on-line, via a dedicated webpage (a tacit admission of the complexity and piecemeal nature of this legislation?): http://security.homeoffice.gov.uk/ripa/.

[87] RIPA 2000, s.17.

[88] Most recently, see *Privy Council Review of Intercept as Evidence – Report* Cm. 7324 (TSO, 2008), on-line at: www.official-documents.gov.uk/document/cm73/7324/7324.pdf.

[89] See RIPA 2000, Part II, and the Code of Practice on Covert Surveillance (in force 1 August 2002) issued pursuant to s.71 of the Act. For discussion linking the RIPA provisions to s.78 exclusion, see Peter Mirfield, 'Regulation of Investigatory Powers Act 2000 (2): Evidential Aspects' [2001] *Crim LR* 91.

[90] See the Code of Practice on Covert Human Intelligence Sources, issued pursuant to RIPA 2000, s.71 (in force 1 August 2002).

[91] Code of Practice issued under Part II of the Criminal Procedure and Investigations Act 1996.

[92] See, e.g., *Attorney General's Guidelines on Disclosure*, on-line at: http://www.attorneygeneral.gov.uk/Publications/Documents/disclosure.doc.pdf; *Disclosure: A Protocol for the Control and Management*

of the Youth Justice and Criminal Evidence Act 1999, which will be described in detail in Chapter 10, are accompanied by voluminous guidance for practitioners,[93] governing such matters as video-recorded investigative interviews with children and other vulnerable witnesses. Prosecutors are subject to the general Code for Crown Prosecutors, introduced by the Prosecution of Offences Act 1985, and to more task-specific guidelines and codes of practice, for example in relation to their new (non-statutory) power to conduct pre-trial interviews with complainants and other potential prosecution witnesses.[94] This is by no means a comprehensive survey of relevant legislation, Codes of Practice, and supplementary legal instruments, but we should at least mention in passing the Criminal Procedure Rules[95] and the *Consolidated Criminal Practice Direction*.[96] Criminal procedure law has undergone nothing short of a reformist revolution since the enactment of PACE 1984, rendering the legality of criminal investigations and prosecutions something of a moving target.

The salient point for present purposes is that section 78's exclusionary empire is constantly being expanded, as the law of criminal procedure becomes ever more detailed and complex. Each new statute or Code of Practice introduces further layers of normative due process standards potentially triggering the exclusion of any evidence obtained in consequence of their breach, courtesy of section 78's all-purpose remedy. Some statutory provisions expressly invoke section 78 as a residual guarantor of procedural fairness,[97] but even where the statute is silent the courts will tend to assume that section 78 applies to prosecution evidence of any kind and automatically 'read it in', unless the statute specifically ousts it. The inevitable consequence is that section 78 jurisprudence is growing at a fantastic rate. By December 2009, Westlaw catalogued 856 cases citing section 78, an increase of about 75 citations within the previous twelve months. The thousandth case milestone will certainly be passed before the third edition of this book is printed.

'Fairness' is a flexible standard, and this partly accounts for the ubiquity of section 78 as a free-floating procedural remedy. The concomitants of flexibility are generality, and some measure of uncertainty and inconsistency, and this is where the role of the appellate courts in developing a framework of principle to guide and structure the decision-making of trial judges is paramount. The precise contours of a 'significant and substantial' breach obviously remain to be fleshed out as the test is applied to the facts of particular cases. We have already explained that 'unfairness' is a broader concept than, and should not reductively be equated with, breaches of individuals' due process rights. Section 78 nonetheless plays a pivotal role in allowing the courts to address rights violations – the more so when the rights in question enjoy the elevated constitutional status of 'human rights', as defined by European human rights law and elaborated by British courts under the Human Rights Act 1998.

---

of Unused Material in the Crown Court (2006), on line at: www.judiciary.gov.uk/judgment_guidance/protocols/crown_unused_material.htm.

[93] CJS, *Achieving Best Evidence in Criminal Proceedings* (2007 revision), on-line at: www.cps.gov.uk/publications/docs/achieving_best_evidence_final.pdf.

[94] Paul Roberts and Candida Saunders, 'Introducing Pre-Trial Witness Interviews – A Flexible New Fixture in the Crown Prosecutor's Toolkit' [2008] *Crim LR* 831.

[95] www.justice.gov.uk/criminal/procrules_fin/rulesmenu.htm.

[96] www.justice.gov.uk/criminal/procrules_fin/contents/practice_direction/pd_consolidated.htm.

[97] e.g. CJA 2003, s.126.

(c) CONSTITUTIONAL FAIRNESS UNDER THE HUMAN RIGHTS ACT

The Human Rights Act introduced a new dimension to the operation of section 78, as part of the broader process of 'constitutionalization' of the law of criminal evidence referred to in Chapter 1. Certain features of criminal procedure are coming to be viewed as essential components in the basic complex of rights and duties defining the relationship between citizens and the state. In a liberal democracy the state and all its agencies are meant to respect the rule of law, and this in turn has direct implications for judicial approaches to improperly obtained evidence. If the police, prosecutors, or other state officials were permitted – let alone encouraged – to break the law of the land with impunity, the state would be setting itself above the law and betraying its liberal democratic credentials. Whilst this fundamental point of constitutional principle is by now widely recognized, the Human Rights Act has given judges direct access to a new set of juridical tools – European human rights law, principles, doctrines, concepts, ideas, and arguments – with which to work through the evidentiary implications of defending and upholding a modern British constitution in the twenty-first century.

Article 6 of the European Convention on Human Rights (ECHR) was set out in full in Chapter 1. Article 6(1) provides that 'everyone is entitled to a fair and public hearing within a reasonable time by an independent and impartial tribunal established by law', whilst Articles 6(2) and 6(3) proceed to enumerate further aspects of 'fair trial' in criminal proceedings, including the presumption of innocence, access to legal advice and representation, and the right to call and examine witnesses. Although the concept of 'fair trial' under the ECHR remains somewhat imprecise,[98] the European Court of Human Rights has handed down hundreds of judgments applying Article 6, from which a patchwork of interlocking and overlapping rules and principles can be derived. One of the European Court's guiding precepts is that 'the admissibility of evidence is primarily a matter for regulation by national law and as a general rule it is for the national courts to assess the evidence before them. The Court's task under the Convention is… to ascertain whether the proceedings as a whole, including the way in which evidence was taken, were fair.'[99] In ECHR terminology, rules of evidence fall with the 'margin appreciation' allowed to all states parties to adapt their domestic legal practices to comply with the minimum requirements demanded by the Convention. However, this apparent self-restraint cannot be taken at face-value. True enough, the European Court of Human Rights (ECtHR) always

---

[98] cf. the remarks of Judge Martens, dissenting in *Borgers* v *Belgium* (1993) 15 EHRR 92: 'the concept of "fair trial"… calls for careful handling. To begin with the concept is vague and "open-ended". It needs "filling in". This gradually occurs as case-law develops more specific rules. The Court, however, has a tendency always to rule *in concreto*, taking into account the specific features of the case at hand. Thus elaborating the notion of "fair trial" is not without risks: the rules that emerge from such a case-law develop a momentum of their own and a tendency to engender specific new rules. These new rules may overstrain a concept which, after all, refers to very basic principles of procedure. As long as it has not elaborated a more comprehensive analytical view of the notion of "fair trial" the Court should be aware of these risks.'

[99] *Teixeira de Castro* v *Portugal* (1998) 28 EHRR 101, [34]. Also see *Schenk* v *Switzerland*, (A/140) (1991) 13 EHRR 242, [46]: 'While Article 6 of the Convention guarantees the right to a fair trial, it does not lay down any rules on the admissibility of evidence as such, which is therefore primarily a matter for regulation under national law. The Court therefore cannot exclude as a matter of principle and in the abstract that unlawfully obtained evidence… may be admissible.'

ties its rulings down to the facts of the instant case, and avoids propounding general rules of admissibility in the abstract. Nonetheless, the Court has made numerous pronouncements on evidentiary topics, with direct implications for the post-Human Rights Act English law of criminal evidence.

The leading Strasbourg decision bearing on section 78 of PACE, like so many of the English cases to be discussed in the next section, concerned alleged 'entrapment'. In *Teixeira de Castro*[100] Portuguese undercover police officers invited VS, a known hashish user and small-time dealer, to put them in touch with somebody who could supply heroin. After much inconclusive negotiation, VS introduced the officers to the accused, who duly procured heroin from an acquaintance and sold it on to the officers. The accused's conviction and six-year sentence for drug-dealing were upheld by the Portuguese Supreme Court, which took the view that sacrifices of individual freedom are sometimes justified in order to pursue legitimate law enforcement objectives like tackling the scourge of illegal drug distribution and all its associated misery.

The ECtHR, however, upheld the accused's complaint that he had been denied a fair trial in contravention of Article 6, characterizing the undercover officers' conduct as impermissible 'incitement', which created a crime that would not otherwise have been committed. The operation was further compromised, in the European Court's eyes, because it was not conducted by properly authorized drugs-squad officers, nor was it subject to judicial supervision by a magistrate. According to the Court:

> The necessary inference from these circumstances is that the two police officers did not confine themselves to investigating Mr Teixeira de Castro's criminal activity in an essentially passive manner, but exercised an influence such as to incite the commission of the offence.... [T]he Court concludes that the two police officers' actions went beyond those of undercover agents because they instigated the offence and there is nothing to suggest that without their intervention it would have been committed. That intervention and its use in the impugned criminal proceedings meant that, right from the outset, the applicant was definitively deprived of a fair trial.[101]

The European Court's judgment in *Teixeira* is, not uncharacteristically, vulnerable to criticism on both legal and factual grounds. The Court's suggested tests of incitement and instigation are under-elaborated and possibly unhelpful, and some of its inferences of fact are decidedly shaky.[102] But *Teixeira* was nonetheless a pivotal decision, because it unequivocally established that the concept of 'fair trial' within Article 6 of the ECHR extends to evaluating the propriety of *pre*-trial proceedings, including police investigations. Just as section 78 of PACE is concerned with how evidence was obtained, as well as with its proposed use as prosecution evidence at trial, under the Convention system an accused may be deprived of a fair trial 'right from the outset' if law enforcement officers have violated his rights during the course of their investigations. The principles established in *Teixeira*

---

[100] *Teixeira de Castro* v *Portugal* (1998) 28 EHRR 101.   [101] ibid. [38], [39].

[102] As Judge Butkevych points out, in his dissenting opinion, there was evidence to suggest that Teixeira was regularly dealing in heroin, albeit that he was obliged to arrange for the undercover officers to be supplied from a third party. Furthermore, the Portuguese courts had found as a fact that the undercover officers did *not* behave as *agents provocateurs*. For sustained criticism of the decision, see David Ormerod and Andrew Roberts, 'The Trouble with *Teixeira*: Developing a Principled Approach to Entrapment' (2002) 6 *E & P* 38.

have consistently been reaffirmed in the Strasbourg Court's subsequent case-law, not only in relation to undercover investigations of suspected drug-dealers,[103] but even in one case where a prosecutor was apparently bribed to get a criminal defendant acquitted.[104]

Prior to the advent of the Human Rights Act the attitude of the English courts towards the ECHR was at best lukewarm. Some senior judges made no secret of their impatience with arguments founded on breaches of Convention rights. In *Khan*,[105] for example, the police had attached a covert listening device to the exterior of a residential property. The operation involved trespass and minor damage to the dwelling, in addition to being an obvious intrusion on the privacy of its occupants. Khan, a visitor to the premises, was caught on audio-tape admitting his involvement in narcotics smuggling, and was duly convicted of serious drug trafficking offences. In the course of upholding his conviction, the House of Lords went out of its way to emphasize that Khan's Article 8 right to respect for private life would still not have availed him, even if the Convention had then been enforceable in English law.[106] Like the Portuguese courts in *Teixiera de Castro*, the House of Lords insisted that individual rights sometimes have to defer to important public policies like catching and deterring drug smugglers. All domestic remedies having been exhausted, Khan took his case to Strasbourg, where an Article 8 complaint ultimately prevailed before the European Court.[107]

The United Kingdom attempted to justify its breach of Khan's Article 8(1) rights to respect for his private life by invoking Article 8(2), which permits state interference which is 'in accordance with the law and is necessary in a democratic society in the interests of national security, public safety or the economic well-being of the country, for the prevention of disorder or crime, for the protection of health or morals, or for the protection of the rights and freedoms of others'. It was contended that covert bugging of residential premises was a necessary and proportionate measure of crime control in a democratic society. This submission was rebuffed, but only on the relatively narrow technical ground that the police surveillance operation conducted in *Khan* had not been 'in accordance with the law'.[108] Such operations were governed at the time merely by Home

---

[103] e.g. *V v Finland*, App No 40412/98, ECtHR Judgment, 24 April 2007; *Vanyan v Russia*, App No 53203/99, ECtHR Judgment 15 December 2005.

[104] *Ramanauskas v Lithuania*, App No 74420/01, ECtHR Judgment, 5 February 2008; [2008] Crim LR 639.

[105] *R v Khan (Sultan)* [1997] AC 558, HL.

[106] Thus, Lord Nolan states, ibid. 580 and 582, that '[t]he question whether there was a breach, and if so what the consequences should be, is solely one for the European Court of Human Rights. That is not to say that the principles reflected in the Convention on Human Rights are irrelevant to the exercise of the section 78 power. They could hardly be irrelevant, because they embody so many of the familiar principles of our own law and of our concept of justice.... [I]f the behaviour of the police in the particular case amounts to an apparent or probable breach of some relevant law or convention, common sense dictates that this is a consideration which may be taken into account for what it is worth. Its significance, however, will normally be determined not so much by its apparent unlawfulness or irregularity as upon its effect, taken as a whole, upon the fairness or unfairness of the proceedings. The fact that the behaviour in question constitutes a breach of the Convention or of a foreign law can plainly be of no greater significance per se than if it constituted a breach of English law. Upon the facts of the present case...I consider that the judge was fully entitled to hold that the circumstances in which the relevant evidence was obtained, even if they constituted a breach of Article 8, were not such as to require the exclusion of the evidence.'

[107] *Khan v UK* (2001) 31 EHRR 45.

[108] Note, however, that the entire Convention system is predicated on the foundational assumption that liberal democracies are *rechtsstaaten* which subject public power to the rule of law. The Preamble to the Convention rehearses that 'the governments of European countries...have a common heritage of political

Office Guidelines,[109] which the Court felt were neither sufficiently binding nor adequately publicized to qualify as an acceptable legal basis for trenching on privacy interests protected by the Convention. Interestingly, and rather disappointingly for human rights enthusiasts,[110] the Court went on to hold that even though Khan's incriminating statements had been obtained in breach of Article 8 it did not necessarily follow that their admission at his trial contravened Article 6 of the ECHR. In the present circumstances, where the accused had pleaded guilty and the domestic courts had considered the argument for excluding his admissions under section 78 of PACE, the European Court found that Khan's trial had been fair, notwithstanding that his conviction was based entirely on evidence procured through a violation of his right to respect for private life.

Since the Human Rights Act (HRA) 1998 became fully operational in October 2000, Convention rights have acquired a firmer and more explicit legal foundation in English law. British judges are specifically directed by section 2 of the HRA 1998 to have regard to the jurisprudence of the Strasbourg court in elaborating Convention rights under the Act,[111] and the House of Lords has said that 'a national court subject to a duty such as that imposed by section 2 should not without strong reason dilute or weaken the effect of the Strasbourg case law...since the meaning of the Convention should be uniform throughout the states party to it. The duty of national courts is to keep pace with the Strasbourg jurisprudence as it evolves over time: no more, but certainly no less.'[112] The scope and contextual application of PACE 1984, section 78, have been clarified by post-HRA 1998 decisions in three significant ways meriting further brief elaboration.

First of all, recent cases have addressed the underlying rationale(s) for evidentiary exclusion. The most important decision to-date is not, strictly speaking, a criminal case or one directly concerned with section 78, though it arose out of the government's post 9/11 anti-terrorism legislation and policy – a topic with obvious and multiple connections to the criminal law – and explicitly concerned the normative justifications for excluding relevant evidence. *A v Home Secretary (No 2)*[113] involved conjoined appeals by ten individuals who had been certified as threats to national security by the Home Secretary and detained without charge pursuant to Part 4 of the Anti-Terrorism, Crime and Security Act 2001.[114] A person so certified could appeal to 'SIAC' – the Special Immigration Appeals

---

traditions, ideals, freedom and the rule of law'. Consequently the 'technical' violation in this case arguably has more profound resonances.

[109] Now see RIPA 2000, Part II (covert surveillance generally); and the Police Act 1997, Part III (regarding surveillance devices that can only be installed by trespass, criminal damage or interference with wireless telegraphy). For a critical overview, see Yaman Akdeniz, Nick Taylor, and Clive Walker, 'Regulation of Investigatory Powers Act 2000 (1): Bigbrother.gov.uk: State Surveillance in the Age of Information and Rights' [2001] *Crim LR* 73.

[110] Andrew Ashworth described *Khan*, with characteristic diplomacy, as 'one of the least impressive examples of Strasbourg jurisprudence': [2000] *Crim LR* 684.

[111] HRA 1998, s.2(1): 'A court or tribunal determining a question which has arisen in connection with a Convention right must take into account any – (a) judgment, decision, declaration or advisory opinion of the European Court of Human Rights...'

[112] *R (Ullah) v Special Adjudicator* [2004] 2 AC 323, [2004] UKHL 26, [20] (Lord Bingham). But also see *R v Horncastle* [2009] UKSC 14, [2010] 2 WLR 94, [11], quoted in §1.5(a).

[113] *A v Secretary of State for the Home Department (No 2)* [2006] 2 AC 221, [2005] UKHL 71.

[114] By the time of these proceedings Part 4 of the 2001 Act had in fact been repealed and replaced by the Prevention of Terrorism Act 2005, but the appellants' rights of appeal had plainly survived the demise of the 2001 legislation and jurisdiction was not challenged.

Commission, established by the Special Immigration Appeals Commission Act 1997. The question for their Lordships was whether SIAC was entitled in the course of its deliberations to rely on what we may call 'third-party foreign torture evidence', that is to say, evidence elicited from somebody who was not an applicant in the proceedings which had, or might have been, procured by torture perpetrated overseas by a foreign power neither at the behest nor with the encouragement or connivance of the British authorities.[115] These facts presented a strong test-case for the admissibility of torture evidence in English legal proceedings. General rules regulating the admissibility of confessions did not apply, because the applicants themselves had not been coerced. The alleged torture had taken place overseas, and the British authorities were not responsible for it. Assuming that the evidence in question was not utterly discredited by the circumstances in which it had allegedly been obtained, was there any basis on which this presumptively material evidence could or should be excluded?

SIAC elected to hear the evidence, and the Court of Appeal (by a majority) confirmed that this was the correct approach. On further appeal to the House of Lords, an enlarged panel of seven Law Lords unanimously contradicted the lower courts' conclusions, anathematizing all evidence procured by torture as categorically inadmissible – even the attenuated 'third-party foreign' variety at issue in the current proceedings. The reasons given for this ruling are illuminating. Concerns about the potential unreliability of information procured by torture were canvassed, but very much down-played compared with moral objections to the inherent wickedness and intolerability of torture. Lord Nicholls simply stated, 'torture is not acceptable. This is a bedrock moral principle in this country.'[116] Lord Hope branded torture 'one of the most evil practices known to man'.[117] Taking his cue from Blackstone, Lord Hoffmann spoke of dishonour, corruption, degradation, and the censure of enlightened opinion:

The use of torture is dishonourable. It corrupts and degrades the state which uses it and the legal system which accepts it. When judicial torture was routine all over Europe, its rejection by the common law was a source of national pride and the admiration of enlightened foreign writers such as Voltaire and Beccaria.[118]

Lord Brown called torture 'an unqualified evidence. It can never be justified. Rather it must always be punished.'[119] The style of reasoning employed to substantiate these propositions in law was no less significant than the conclusion itself. Lord Bingham's speech presents a *tour de force* of constitutional history, common law authority, and cosmopolitan jurisprudence. Observing that 'from its very earliest days the common law of England set its face firmly against the use of torture',[120] Lord Bingham drew freely on international law texts and treaties, the judgments of international criminal tribunals, and the decisions of domestic courts in both Commonwealth and civilian jurisdictions to corroborate and sanctify the common law's absolute prohibition on the reception of torture evidence in legal proceedings. Although the clarity of its message became clouded by a dispute between their Lordships over the appropriate standard of proof,[121] on the primary

---

[115] It was accepted for the purposes of the litigation that the British authorities were in no way responsible for the alleged maltreatment of the third-party witness.   [116] *A v Home Secretary (No 2)*, [64].

[117] ibid. [101].   [118] ibid. [82].   [119] ibid. [160].   [120] ibid. [11].

[121] A narrow majority comprising Lords Hope, Rodger, Carswell, and Brown held that alleged foreign torture evidence could be received by SIAC unless it had been established, on the balance of probabilities,

question of admissibility *A v Home Secretary (No 2)* supplies a model illustration of the fourth, intrinsic, rationale for evidentiary exclusion identified earlier in this chapter, emphasizing procedural integrity and the legitimacy of the verdict. Viewed in broader theoretical terms, the case exemplifies a discernible trend to relocate evidentiary doctrine within a rights-based framework of 'constitutional' criminal jurisprudence, underwritten by the Human Rights Act 1998 and the ECHR. 'It trivialises the issue before the House', declared Lord Bingham, 'to treat it as an argument about the law of evidence. The issue is one of constitutional principle.'[122]

A second significant feature of post-HRA 1998 jurisprudence on section 78 concerns the interactions between discrete procedural rights and their potentially cumulative impact on the admissibility of evidence. We have seen that evidence is not automatically excluded whenever the police engage in subterfuge or perpetrate deliberate deceptions. However, the legal position may be transformed if investigative tactics *also* undermine significant due process rights. In retrospect, the early decision in *Mason*[123] can be seen as the prototype of this analysis. There, it will be recalled, the Court of Appeal favoured exclusion where police deception effectively undermined the suspect's right of access to custodial legal advice. More recent decisions of the ECtHR demonstrate that the accused's Article 6 rights may come to be infringed in two broadly differing ways. In one type of case, the police undercover operation becomes so persistent, intrusive, or insidious that it is regarded as incompatible with suspects' privilege against self-incrimination.[124] This was found to be the situation in *Allan v UK*,[125] where, after repeated 'no comment' interviews, the police had placed an informant in the accused's remand cell in an effort to catch him out in damaging admissions whilst his guard was down. In a second type of scenario, illustrated by *Edwards and Lewis v UK*,[126] it is inadequate prosecution disclosure regarding the details of undercover operations which constitutes the breach of Article 6. The argument here is not that the police investigation breached the standards of investigative propriety demanded by *Teixeira*, but rather the preliminary objection that the accused is deprived of a fair opportunity of demonstrating police overreaching if crucial operational details are withheld from the defence. Both types of breaches of Article 6 are capable of turning otherwise unexceptional police deception into a human rights violation potentially requiring exclusion of any evidence obtained in consequence of the breach.

The third noteworthy feature of section 78 jurisprudence post-HRA 1998 is a direct outgrowth of the second. Inadmissibility of evidence is never *directly* mandated by Article 6 of the ECHR: the issue is whether the trial was fair, but sometimes evidence is so seriously tainted by the way in which it was obtained that fairness would be fatally compromised unless that evidence is excluded. This rather refined distinction between the direct requirements of Article 6 and the contingencies of satisfying them in the instant case is vitally important, because it opens up the possibility that some way might be found to cure, if not to condone, investigative impropriety without having to exclude the evidence.

---

that the information was tainted by torture. The minority, which notably comprised the three most senior Law Lords, Lord Bingham, Lord Nicholls, and Lord Hoffmann, insisted that SIAC should reject information alleged to be the fruits of torture unless the suspicion of torture could be disproved on the balance of probabilities.

[122] *A v Home Secretary (No 2)*, [51].   [123] *R v Mason* [1988] 1 WLR 139, CA.
[124] See Chapter 13.   [125] *Allan v United Kingdom* (2003) 36 EHRR 143, ECtHR.
[126] *Edwards and Lewis v United Kingdom* (2005) 40 EHRR 24, ECtHR (Grand Chamber).

The European Court of Human Rights propounds the general principle that, 'in order to ensure that the accused receives a fair trial, any difficulties caused to the defence by a limitation on its rights must be sufficiently counterbalanced by the procedures followed by the judicial authorities'.[127] One notable procedural innovation that has been proposed as a 'counterbalancing' measure in English criminal proceedings is the provision of 'special counsel' to represent the accused's interests in relation to undisclosed evidence. We will return to this intriguing development when we address the topic of public interest immunity in Chapter 7. Suffice it here to observe that part of the impetus for experimenting with new procedural mechanisms like 'special counsel'[128] arises from the need to comply with the accused's Article 6 fair trial rights, which might otherwise be violated because the accused is deprived of information relevant to arguing a case for excluding prosecution evidence under section 78 of PACE 1984.

Rights violations, then, may trigger section 78 exclusion where police deception, plain and simple, would not be regarded as exceeding the boundaries of investigative propriety. But just how far should police subterfuges be allowed to go before they call into question the integrity of criminal censure and punishment, whether or not identifiable due process rights have been breached? What if the offence in question would not have been committed at all without official enticement or facilitation? Cases of alleged 'entrapment' by undercover police officers or other law enforcement officials supply further rich material through which to trace the development of a principled jurisprudence of exclusion under section 78.[129] As well as providing another testing ground for concepts of procedural fairness, the moral and legal limits of undercover police-work are of vital importance in their own right in the modern era of proactive, intelligence-led policing.[130]

5.5 ENTRAPMENT

Modern discussions of entrapment begin with the pre-PACE decision in *Sang*,[131] in which the House of Lords delivered an authoritative ruling on two related aspects of the topic. It was held, first, that there is no substantive defence of 'entrapment' in English criminal law; and secondly, that evidence procured by entrapment remains in principle admissible, for to exclude it would effectively reintroduce a defence of entrapment 'through the back door' of criminal procedure when the decision had already been taken, as a matter of substantive law, to pull up the drawbridge against admitting the defence. Undercover police operations involving 'entrapment' tactics are conducted precisely in order to secure evidence of crime or, more controversially, to induce suspected repeat offenders to commit fresh

---

[127] ibid. [53].   [128] §7.5(c).

[129] Generally, see Andrew L.-T. Choo, *Abuse of Process and Judicial Stays of Criminal Proceedings* (OUP, 2nd edn. 2008), ch 5; Simon Bronitt and Declan Roche, 'Between Rhetoric and Reality: Sociolegal and Republican Perspectives on Entrapment' (2000) 4 *E & P* 77; John Kleinig, *The Ethics of Policing* (CUP, 1996), ch 8; Diane Birch, 'Excluding Evidence from Entrapment: What is a "Fair Cop"?' (1994) 67 *Current Legal Problems* 73; Geoffrey Robertson, 'Entrapment Evidence: Manna from Heaven, or Fruit of the Poisoned Tree? [1994] *Crim LR* 805 (referring to a 'season of the "sting"').

[130] Jerry Ratcliffe, *Intelligence-Led Policing* (Willan, 2008); Tim John and Mike Maguire, 'Criminal Intelligence and the National Intelligence Model', in Tim Newburn, Tom Williamson, and Alan Wright (eds.), *Handbook of Criminal Investigation* (Willan, 2007).   [131] *R v Sang* [1980] AC 402, HL.

crimes. In either case, the enterprise would be pointless if the prosecution were unable to utilize the fruits of undercover operations as evidence with which to secure convictions at trial. These practical considerations reinforced the House of Lords' conviction that there is no common law objection to the admissibility of entrapment evidence. *Sang* was entirely in keeping with the common law's traditional lack of concern for the fairness or legality of the means by which evidence is obtained.

The enactment of section 78, of course, had no bearing on the first question of substantive criminal law, on which *Sang* remains a leading authority. But it did precipitate reconsideration of the evidentiary issue. For if entrapment evidence might sometimes have been procured in circumstances rendering its use in a criminal trial unfair, section 78 seemed to give trial judges the authority to exclude it. The Court of Appeal returned to this issue on a number of occasions during the 1990s, supplying trial judges with important – if not always unequivocal – guidance on the correct approach to defence submissions urging the exclusion of entrapment evidence under section 78. This jurisprudence now bears the imprimatur of the House of Lords.[132]

Christou and Wright[133] concerned the propriety of a 'honey trap' operation in which the police set up a fake jewellers' shop in Tottenham, London – 'Stardust Jewellers' – and let it be known that they were interested in 'shady' dealing. The object of this 'unorthodox stratagem'[134] was to flush out thieves, burglars, and handlers of stolen goods who were suspected of operating in the area. Sure enough, some thirty local villains, including the accused, took the bait. When attempting to sell stolen property to Stardust, customers were quizzed by the undercover police officers posing as shop assistants as to whether there were any areas of London in which it would be unwise to resell the merchandise. This euphemistic inquiry was said to mimic the standard dialogue between thieves and their semi-respectable 'fences' (handlers), who would naturally want to minimize the chances of the real owner spotting their stolen property advertised for sale in the fence's shop window. The whole transaction was captured on videotape by a hidden camera, providing conclusive evidence that the 'customers' were not only in possession of stolen goods, but also knew them to be stolen, thus satisfying the *mens rea* element of the handling offence under section 22 of the Theft Act 1968.

On appeal it was contended for Christou and Wright that all of the evidence against them should have been excluded, under section 78, on the basis that the entire Stardust Jewellers operation was irremediably unfair. More specifically, it was contended that the undercover operation had deprived the accused of the privilege against self-incrimination, and had involved a catalogue of breaches of PACE Code C, including the important requirement that suspects must be cautioned ('read their rights') prior to commencing an interview with a police officer. The Court of Appeal rejected every one of these submissions and upheld the convictions. To begin with, Lord Taylor CJ explained, the very fact that the accused had been tricked into giving themselves up did not make the undercover operation 'unfair,' much less did it render all of the evidence produced by the operation inadmissible:

[T]he trick was not applied to the appellants; they voluntarily applied the trick to themselves. It is not every trick producing evidence against an accused which results in unfairness.

---

[132] *R v Looseley; Attorney-General's Reference (No 3 of 2000)* [2001] 1 WLR 2060, [2001] UKHL 53.
[133] *R v Christou and Wright* (1992) 95 Cr App R 264, CA.   [134] ibid. 266.

There are, in criminal investigations, a number of situations in which the police adopt ruses or tricks in the public interest to obtain evidence.[135]

Lord Taylor next held that objections to breaches of Code C were entirely misconceived, because the Code was never intended to apply, and did not apply, to undercover operations such as that in the present case. This must surely be right. If the undercover officers had been obliged to caution potential 'customers' before proceeding with their transactions the officers' cover would have been blown, the customers would have beaten a hasty retreat, and the whole exercise would have been fruitless and pointless. So long as the officers were doing no more than was required to maintain the outward authenticity of their assumed roles as jewellers' shop counter-staff, the operation could not be denounced as an elaborate ruse concocted merely to circumvent the protections for suspects built into the PACE regime governing formal police interviews. As Lord Taylor concluded '[t]he appellants were not being questioned by police officers acting as such. Conversation was on equal terms. There could be no question of pressure or intimidation.'[136]

This is not to say that fear of PACE safeguards being outflanked by police tactics is entirely unfounded. After the new PACE regime had bedded-down and turned police station interview rooms into quite tightly regulated environments open to effective external scrutiny, there was some evidence that suspects were more frequently being conveyed to police stations 'via the scenic route', leading to unregulated, but supposedly spontaneous, confessions in police vans and the like.[137] Such practices threaten the integrity of the PACE system in exactly the same way as the breaches of recording requirements that were castigated by Hodgson J. in *Keenan*. It is therefore crucial that trial judges restrict the indulgence shown in *Christou and Wright* to genuine undercover operations, and then only to the extent strictly necessary to facilitate the operation. Admittedly, however, the line between legitimate undercover conversations and cynical PACE-cheating interviews may be rather fine and difficult to draw, especially for appellate judges a long way removed from operational realities and their detailed forensic dissection at trial.

Lord Taylor CJ nonetheless determined that the line had been crossed in *Bryce*,[138] in which a police officer posed as a potential buyer of a stolen Saab motorcar. According to the undercover officer's evidence, the accused had intimated that he knew the car was stolen and admitted having paid only £1,800 for it in the knowledge that the car's true market value was nearer £23,000. Allowing the appeal and quashing the accused's conviction of handling stolen goods, Lord Taylor distinguished these circumstances from *Christou and Wright* on two main grounds. First, there was no audio record of the accused's alleged admissions during the operation, or, indeed, of the accused's subsequent interrogation at a police station. Secondly, in putting direct questions to the accused calculated to probe his knowledge of the car's provenance, the undercover officer had gone beyond what was necessary to maintain his cover. He had, in effect, begun a covert interview in order to secure incriminating admissions from the accused. This went too far in circumventing PACE protections, and the evidence ought to have been excluded under section 78. The Court of Appeal's analysis and ruling in *Bryce* thus provide an instructive counterpoint

---

[135] ibid. 269.   [136] ibid. 271.

[137] Cf. the discussion of 'informal questioning' by Andrew Sanders and Richard Young, *Criminal Justice* (OUP, 3rd edn. 2007), 259–63 (commenting that informal questioning 'subverts the PACE framework of rules designed to protect the suspect').   [138] *R v Bryce* (1992) 95 Cr App R 320, CA.

to *Christou and Wright*. In addition, *Bryce* exemplifies the principle that cumulative breaches – here, non-recording *and* excessively intrusive questioning – may lead to exclusion where individual breaches taken in isolation might possibly have been condoned.

Another significant dimension of *Christou and Wright* is brought out in contrast with the situation confronting the Divisional Court in *Williams and O'Hare* v *DPP*.[139] In *Christou and Wright* (and also in *Bryce*) the offences with which the accused were charged had already been committed prior to the commencement of the undercover operation. The police were only trying to recover evidence of consummated crimes. In *Williams and O'Hare*, by contrast, 'Operation Rover' sailed perilously close to official incitement of criminality. An insecure and apparently unattended Ford Transit van was left in a busy shopping area known to suffer from a high rate of vehicle crime. The van's rear shutter was left partly ajar to reveal what appeared to be a valuable cargo of cigarette cartons inside. The police laid in wait until passers-by, like the accused, attempted to make off with the cigarettes, whereupon the would-be thieves were apprehended and duly convicted of interfering with a motor vehicle with intent to steal.[140] The objection that the police had behaved as *agents provocateurs* in entrapping the accused, so that the evidence against them should have been excluded under section 78, received short shrift from the Divisional Court, and their convictions were upheld.

One may entertain mixed feelings about Operation Rover and the courts' satisfaction with the convictions it produced. On the one hand, it is undeniable that Williams and O'Hare should have kept their sticky fingers out of other people's property. As Mr Justice Wright summarized the Divisional Court's reasoning:

[A]n ordinary honest person would not be tempted to take, or take, some of the contents of the van, but both appellants intended to steal cigarettes, were acting dishonestly and knew what they were doing was wrong. The appellants therefore incriminated themselves, not through any trick but by their dishonesty.... The police officers did nothing to force, persuade, encourage or coerce the appellants to do what they did. The appellants did the acts complained of voluntarily of their own free will, in the absence of any pressure and with full understanding of their own dishonesty.[141]

And yet there remains a sense of unease, which springs from the fact that we are all fallible beings with limited powers of self-discipline and moral fibre. Many people who would regard themselves as generally law-abiding might well have followed Williams and O'Hare in helping themselves to 'abandoned' cigarettes that were virtually dangled under their noses. Even the steeliest resolve is prone to buckle in the face of extreme, prolonged, or repeated temptation.

The American case of *Jacobson*[142] represents a rather exaggerated instance. Federal agents, posing as a mail-order firm and as various bogus lobbying organizations committed to libertarian sexual freedom, targeted suspected sex offenders with paedophilic literature and invitations to purchase pictures of young boys engaged in sexual conduct. The accused Jacobson was known previously to have purchased mail-order magazines entitled *Bare Boys I and II*, at a time when receipt of such material was lawful (prior to the introduction

---

[139] *Williams and O'Hare* v *DPP* [1993] 3 All ER 365, DC.   [140] Criminal Attempts Act 1981, s.9(1).

[141] *Williams and O'Hare* v *DPP* [1993] 3 All ER 365, 368, 369.

[142] *Jacobson* v *US*, 503 US 540, 112 S Ct 1535 (1992).

of the federal Child Protection Act of 1984 which criminalized receipt through the mails of sexually explicit depictions of children). After some two and half years' prompting and solicitation, Jacobson finally succumbed and attempted to buy some of what was being offered to him. His conviction of knowingly receiving child pornography was upheld by the US Court of Appeals for the Eighth Circuit, but set aside by a narrow 5–4 majority of the Supreme Court. The majority ruled that '[w]hen the Government's quest for convictions leads to the apprehension of an otherwise law-abiding citizen who, if left to his own devices, likely would have never run afoul of the law, the courts should intervene'.[143] Indeed, the type of targeting involved in *Jacobson*, exploiting the known weaknesses of a person vulnerable to temptation, seems especially objectionable, like forcing a reformed alcoholic to work in a brewery. As well as unfairly pressurizing a person to (re)offend when he might otherwise have stayed out of trouble, such operations consume valuable policing resources that might more profitably be employed in preventing or detecting crime, rather than in procuring or inciting – in effect, *creating* – additional criminal offences.[144]

Operation Rover did not involve the same degree of targeting or solicitation as *Jacobson*. Rather than seeking to exploit particular individuals' criminal propensities, it was more in the nature of randomized virtue testing in a designated locale. But question marks still hang over the propriety of this type of honey trap and, by extension, over the fairness of basing a conviction on the evidence it produced. Suppose that instead of cigarettes in an unlocked van, the police had strategically placed £50 notes along the highway in order to see whether people would pick them up and attempt to keep or spend them. If this seems more dubious than the tactic actually employed in Operation Rover, it is perhaps because the morality of finding money is even more blurred by social convention ('finders keepers, losers weepers') than the morality of taking property from owners who fail to take sensible precautions for its safety. Everybody knows that lost property ought to be surrendered to the police, or to some other repository of safe-keeping, in order that it might be returned to its rightful owner. Yet the common practice of rewarding finders, and especially finders of money, with part of the spoils suggests that returning money or other lost property to its owner, rather than simply pocketing it for oneself, is almost supererogatory – beyond the call of duty – by prevailing moral standards. Operation Rover was not testing virtue to quite this extent, but nor was it confined to detecting habitual thieves going about their routine crooked business, for which a *locked* van might have provided more suitable bait. If the police had been truly concerned about thefts from unlocked vehicles, a crime prevention programme encouraging owners to 'lock it or lose it' might have been more cost-effective than an undercover sting operation liable to trawl mere opportunists into its dragnet.

'Test-purchases' and other covert checks on business and commerce present a somewhat different situation. Proactive policing in a commercial context does not, generally speaking, seem as problematic as undercover operations targeting ordinary members of the public. Consider, for example, a publican or shopkeeper who holds a licence for the sale of alcohol on condition, *inter alia*, that alcoholic beverages must not be sold to minors.

---

[143]   ibid. 553–4 and 1543 (Justice White, joined by Blackmun, Stevens, Souter, and Thomas JJ).

[144]   As the *Jacobson* majority put it, ibid. 548 and 1540: 'there can be no dispute that the Government may use undercover agents to enforce the law.... In their zeal to enforce the law, however, Government agents may not originate a criminal design, implant in an innocent person's mind the disposition to commit a criminal act, and then induce commission of the crime so that the Government may prosecute.'

Even wholly random testing would not necessarily be an unreasonable means of ensuring that the conditions of the licence are being met, provided that licence-holders know that they are subject to random-testing and that the test itself is not conducted unfairly – e.g. by deliberately choosing children who look much older than they really are to undertake test purchases. If a licensee is prepared to sell alcohol to a test-purchasing teenager who is clearly and by a margin under the legal age, the chances are that he is systematically breaching the terms of his licence by selling alcohol to any under-age customer who happens to enter his shop. The test-purchase is not so much crime creation or incitement as a means of proving on-going criminality,[145] and this connection is all the stronger where the 'target' is already suspected on reasonable grounds of breaching the terms of his licence, rather than being chosen at random. English law broadly reflects these morally salient distinctions. Challenges under section 78 to the admissibility of test-purchase evidence have usually been rejected, facilitating the conviction of retailers charged with irregular sales of alcohol, cigarettes, or videotapes[146] and moonlighting mini-cab drivers plying for unlicensed fares.[147]

Drawing together and expanding on the legal and moral distinctions made in previous cases, the Court of Appeal in *Smurthwaite; Gill*[148] endeavoured to lay down general guidelines for determining the admissibility of evidence procured by 'entrapment'. The two appellants independently attempted to enlist the services of a 'hit-man' to murder their respective spouses: S wanted his wife dead because he feared that she was about to divorce him and reveal his financial irregularities to the Inland Revenue; G was no longer prepared to tolerate the antics of her abusive and philandering husband. In fact the person posing as a contract killer in both cases was an undercover police officer, whose illicit conversations with each appellant were secretly recorded. S went so far as to pay over £10,000 to have the contract on his wife carried out. At their respective trials both S and G were convicted of soliciting murder; their cases were subsequently joined at the appellate level before the Court of Appeal.

Having first reaffirmed, following *Sang*, that English law recognizes no substantive defence of entrapment, Lord Taylor CJ proceeded to identify a number of general considerations to which trial judges might have regard when invited by the defence to exclude evidence on grounds of unfairness under section 78:

In exercising his discretion whether to admit the evidence of an undercover officer, some, but not an exhaustive list, of the factors that the judge may take into account are as follows: Was the officer acting as an *agent provocateur* in the sense that he was enticing the defendant to commit an offence he would not otherwise have committed? What was the nature of any entrapment? Does the evidence consist of admissions to a completed offence, or does it consist of the actual commission of an offence? How active or passive was the officer's role in obtaining the evidence? Is there an unassailable record of what occurred, or is it strongly corroborated? .... Beyond mentioning the considerations set out above, it is not possible to

---

[145] Cf. James Chalmers, 'Test Purchasing, Entrapment and Human Rights' (2000) 150 *NLJ* 1444, 1446 (6 October): 'The point of test purchase operations must be to identify persons who are already (one assumes) consistently breaking the law, and not to tempt or trick them into a one-off breach.'

[146] *DPP* v *Marshall* [1988] 3 All ER 683, DC; *Ealing LBC* v *Woolworths plc* [1995] Crim LR 58 (Woolworths employee sold 18-rated video to 11-year-old son of a trading standards officer, posing as a regular customer).   [147] *Nottingham City Council* v *Amin* [2000] 1 Cr App R 426, DC.

[148] *R* v *Smurthwaite; R* v *Gill* (1994) 98 Cr App R 437, CA.

give more general guidance as to how a judge should exercise his discretion under section 78 in this field, since each case must be determined on its own facts.[149]

Both appeals were rejected on the facts. It was emphasized that the undercover officer had played an essentially passive role in his interactions with the appellants, whilst S and G had 'made all the running' in relationships that they, rather than the officer, had instigated. The officer was not in fact an *agent provocateur*, but a reactive foil for the appellants' solicitations. Furthermore, there were audio tapes constituting an 'unassailable record' of what had occurred on all but the first meeting with G. These recordings supplied cogent evidence that S and G had both spontaneously proposed murder without any prompting, and had done so entirely voluntarily. In view of the apparently cordial nature of the recorded conversations, the tapes also contradicted the appellants' claims that they had wanted to back out but were too afraid of this dangerous 'contract killer' whom they soon regretted ever having contacted.

In other cases, the potential unreliability of the evidence has been a key determinant of admissibility decisions under section 78. Perhaps the best illustration remains the unreported ruling by Mr Justice Ognall in *R v Colin Stagg*, delivered at the Central Criminal Court on 14 September 1994. Stagg was (and for a long time afterwards apparently remained) the principal suspect in the police investigation of the brutal murder of Rachel Nickell on Wimbledon Common in July 1992. Under the direction of an eminent forensic psychologist, Paul Britton, who had constructed a 'psychological profile' of the killer, a female police officer assumed the undercover identity of 'Lizzie James' and set about wheedling her way into Stagg's affections and gaining his trust. Their 'relationship' was conducted over a period of 28 weeks, during which time 'Lizzie' encouraged Stagg to share his sexual fantasies with her, in the hope of eliciting damaging admissions that would link Stagg to the murder. In the event, Stagg turned out to be, from the police perspective, disappointingly vague and evasive in his responses to Lizzie's overtures. Nonetheless, at the conclusion of this extended undercover operation, the police and the CPS felt that enough evidence had been gleaned to prosecute Stagg for the murder of Rachel Nickell.

However, Stagg never actually faced a jury, because his trial collapsed when the Lizzie James evidence was successfully challenged by the defence at a pre-trial hearing and excluded under section 78. The prosecution conceded from the outset that Stagg had been tricked into making incriminating statements, but contended that, as in *Christou and Wright*, the accused had 'applied the trick to himself' by freely confessing his deviant sexual fantasies to Lizzie James. Moreover, all Stagg and Lizzie's conversations had been covertly tape-recorded so that the court would have direct access to incontrovertible evidence of exactly what had passed between them. For all that, Ognall J. still found that the Lizzie James evidence flunked the section 78 fairness test, essentially because the 'admissions' procured from Stagg could not be relied upon in all the circumstances of the case. Subsequent events were to vindicate the judge's decisive intervention, but there were many sceptics at the time.[150]

---

[149] ibid. 440, 441.

[150] Duncan Campbell, 'Condon defends Rachel Nickell Murder Inquiry', *The Guardian*, 17 September 1994; Stephen Ward, 'Police and DPP defend Nickell prosecution', *The Independent*, 17 September 1994; 'Stagg lie test "proves nothing"', *Daily Mail*, 19 September 1994. David Mellor, 'These "tinpot gods" who have abused British justice', *Mail on Sunday*, 18 September 1994: 'There is, of course, a terrible implication behind

Paul Britton's psychological profile of the Wimbledon Common murderer included a timetable predicting at what points in a relationship the killer could be expected to start making damaging admissions to a trusted confidante. When the progress of the under-cover operation began to fall behind the hypothesized timetable, Lizzie was instructed to increase the emotional pressure on Stagg by threatening to break off the relationship unless Stagg was more forthcoming about his sexual fantasies. It was later accepted by Ognall J. that Stagg was a lonely, sexually inexperienced man who had been desperate to continue the liaison with Lizzie. In all likelihood he would have been willing to invent any fantasy to please his seductress,[151] yet, despite all this pressure, he never did in fact confess to killing Rachel Nickell, or even make any disclosure that could be considered unequivo-cally incriminating.[152] His Lordship concluded:

A careful appraisal of all the material demonstrates a skilful and sustained enterprise to manipulate the accused. Sometimes subtle, sometimes blatant in its technique, it was designed by deception to manoeuvre and seduce him to reveal fantasies of a suggested incriminating character and additionally, and as it turned out wholly unsuccessfully, to admit the offence.[153]

In excluding all the Lizzie James evidence under section 78 (or, in the alternative, at com-mon law[154]), Ognall J. was notably forthright in his response to the prosecution's con-tention that proactive measures were needed in order to expose the murderer: 'so be it. But if that route involves clear trespass into the territory of impropriety, the Court must stand firm and bar the way.' The case of Rachel Nickell's murder was finally closed on 18 December 2008, when Robert Napper – a sexual psychopathic already detained for life in secure hospital – pleaded guilty to her manslaughter. Sir Harry Ognall reflects, modestly, that any trial judge would have made the same exclusionary ruling,[155] yet it is strongly suspected that it took '16 years for [Napper] to be brought to justice for the death of Ms Nickell, because police believed that Colin Stagg was guilty'.[156]

We will see in Chapter 12 that reliability is one of two key factors determining the admissibility of all confession evidence.[157] Ognall J.'s ruling in *Stagg* demonstrates that reliability is also amongst the factors that a judge should take into account, in appropriate circumstances, in responding to a defence application for the exclusion of 'unfair' prosecu-tion evidence under section 78. Conversely, and as predicated by the reliability rationale canvassed earlier in the chapter,[158] the courts are generally disposed to admit apparently

[Metropolitan Police Commissioner, Sir] Paul Condon's refusal to apologise to Colin Stagg that anyone who lives in my part of London should be aware of. Since we are entitled to assume that the Commissioner would like to solve the mystery of Rachel's death if he could, the fact he is taking no further steps to do so can mean only one thing. So far as the police are concerned, they still believe they got the right man.'

[151] Mark Wilder, ' "Lizzie": The Yard's undercover love-bait', *Daily Mail*, 15 September 1994.

[152] Stephen Ward, 'Promise of Sex Failed to Win Confession', *The Independent*, 15 September 1994.

[153] *R v Stagg*, at H of the Transcript.

[154] The *Christie/Sang* exclusionary discretion is belatedly being given freer rein by some judges, but its resuscitation may be largely academic now that s.78 has filled the vacuum which previously existed at com-mon law.

[155] Sir Harry Ognall, 'Any judge would do the same. The case against Colin Stagg was based on a single rotten plank', *The Times*, 19 December 2008.

[156] Sean O'Neill and Adam Fresco, 'Rachel Nickell's killer is linked to 109 sex crimes', *The Times*, 19 December 2008.   [157] Under PACE 1984, s.76(2): see §12.3(d).

[158] §5.3(a), above.

reliable physical evidence, even where it has been obtained unlawfully[159] or is the product of an inadmissible confession.[160]

The leading English case on entrapment is now the House of Lords' judgment in *Looseley; Attorney General's Reference (No 3 of 2000)*,[161] which developed and consolidated the admissibility criteria identified by the Court of Appeal in *Smurthwaite; Gill* and confirmed their post-Human Rights Act 1998 compatibility with ECHR Article 6. The two conjoined appeals in *Looseley; Attorney General's Reference (No 3 of 2000)* arose out of separate incidents in which undercover police officers had been supplied with quantities of heroin by the accused. In the first case, L was identified as a drug dealer during a surveillance operation centred on the Wooden Bridge public house, which was strongly suspected of being a key distribution point for drugs supply in the local area. Officers 'put out the word' that they were after drugs and were given L's name by pub regulars. They then made direct contact with L and asked if he could supply them with 'brown'. L apparently needed little prompting to sell heroin to the undercover officers on three separate occasions. In the second case, the accused agreed to supply undercover officers with heroin only after the officers had first ingratiated themselves with the accused by plying him with cartons of cheap cigarettes, and then only after the officers had made repeated requests for drugs, fifteen such requests in all. The accused disclaimed any interest in drug-dealing, but said that he would supply the undercover officers with heroin on the reciprocal basis of 'a favour for a favour'. The trial judge felt that the officers had gone too far in soliciting the offence, and ordered that the proceedings be stayed as an abuse of process. However, the Court of Appeal disagreed: the accused had voluntarily supplied drugs to the officers, and his previous convictions for supplying cannabis constituted (it was said) clear evidence of his propensity to supply heroin to all-comers. The stage was then set for a further appeal to the House of Lords, which delivered the most authoritative ruling on cases of entrapment since *Sang*.

In upholding L's conviction but allowing the defence appeal in the second case, the House of Lords issued some of its strongest ever statements reiterating the foundational importance of preserving moral integrity in criminal proceedings. Lord Nicholls, for example, declared that:

[E]very court has an inherent power and duty to prevent abuse of its process. This is a fundamental principle of the rule of law. By recourse to this principle courts ensure that executive agents of the State do not misuse the coercive, law enforcement functions of the courts and thereby oppress citizens of the state.... It is simply not acceptable that the State through its agents should lure its citizens into committing acts forbidden by the law and then seek to prosecute them for doing so. That would be entrapment. That would be a misuse of state power, and an abuse of the process of the court.... The role of the courts is to stand between the state and its citizens and make sure this does not happen.... Police conduct which brings about, to use the catch-phrase, state-created crime is unacceptable and improper. To prosecute in such circumstances would be an affront to the public

---

[159] *R v Apicella* (1985) 82 Cr App R 295, CA; *Attorney-General's Reference (No 3 of 1999)* [2001] 2 AC 91, HL.

[160] The common law rule is given statutory form by PACE 1984, s.76(4). The evidence must be relevant *per se*, since no reference may be made to an inadmissible confession as the source of the evidence: cf. *Lam Chi-ming v R* [1991] 2 AC 212, PC.

[161] *R v Looseley; Attorney-General's Reference (No 3 of 2000)* [2001] 1 WLR 2060, [2001] UKHL 53, HL. See Andrew Ashworth, 'Re-drawing the Boundaries of Entrapment' [2002] *Crim LR* 161.

conscience…Ultimately the overall consideration is always whether the conduct of the police or other law enforcement agency was so seriously improper as to bring the administration of justice into disrepute. Lord Steyn's formulation [in *R* v *Latif and Shahzad* [1996] 1 WLR 104, 112] of a prosecution which would affront the public conscience is substantially to the same effect.[162]

Their Lordships agreed that a stay of proceedings for abuse of process was the only appropriate remedy in circumstances of egregious entrapment, though it was added that section 78 of PACE might still have a residual role to play in cases where tainted evidence could be excluded from the trial without necessarily undermining the entire prosecution. On the facts of the two appeals in *Looseley*, a clear distinction could be drawn between L's willing supply of heroin to undercover officers, who had behaved like any ordinary 'punter' requesting drugs from their regular dealer, and the campaign of repeated instigation and blandishments directed towards the accused by the undercover officers in *Attorney General's Reference (No 3 of 2000)*. The former was unexceptional undercover police-work aimed at catching active criminals; the latter went too far in testing the susceptibilities of ordinary citizens.

The well-established precept that each case must be decided on its particular facts was also reaffirmed. Building on the guidance to trial judges previously laid down in *Smurthwaite; Gill* and other section 78 authorities, Lord Hoffmann canvassed five general criteria of admissibility. His Lordship began with the proposition that '[t]he test of whether the law enforcement officer behaved like an ordinary member of the public works well and is likely to be decisive in many cases of regulatory offences committed with ordinary members of the public'.[163] However, this simple rule-of-thumb, ideal in cases of test-purchases, would clearly need to be adapted to situations in which the standards of 'ordinary members of the public' seem inapposite, in confronting criminal transactions from underworld drug deals to hiring hit-men. So far as these types of clandestine activity are concerned, it was stressed that the police should be acting on reasonable suspicion, of particular locations or specific individuals, rather than trawling for offences on spec. The seriousness of the offence does not automatically justify resorting to undercover tactics involving an element of police procurement or facilitation. On the other hand, officers must be allowed to behave in ways normal for their assumed identities, and this might mean, for example, making repeated requests for drugs – since drug dealers are reputed to be reluctant to supply drugs to strangers before they have stuck up at least a passing acquaintance. Finally, the concept of '*agent provocateur*' and the test of offender 'predisposition,' both of which were invoked by the European Court in *Teixeira de Castro*, were rejected as unhelpful[164] and a potential source of injustice. If 'predisposition' were a relevant consideration, the police might be tempted to target undercover operations on offenders with previous convictions, individuals who might well be 'particularly vulnerable to unfair pressures'.[165] English law

---

[162]   *R* v *Looseley; Attorney-General's Reference (No 3 of 2000)* [2001] 1 WLR 2060, [1], [19], [25].

[163]   ibid. [55].

[164]   The concept of *agent provocateur* was summarily dispatched by Lord Hoffmann in *Looseley*, ibid. [49]: 'Limited assistance can…be gained from distinctions which restate the question rather than provide a criterion for answering it. For example, it has been said that a policeman or paid informer should not act as an *agent provocateur*; an expression used to signify practices employed by foreigners unacquainted with English notions of decency and fair play…But what exactly is an *agent provocateur*?'

[165]   ibid. [68].

was nonetheless unanimously held to be in conformity with the principles enshrined in Article 6 of the ECHR, as elaborated in *Teixeira*.

Subsequent case-law has explored the contextual application of *Looseley's* 'unexceptional opportunity' test in a diverse range of scenarios. In *Jones*, it was held to be acceptable for a policewoman to pretend to be a twelve-year old girl in text-messages sent to a suspected paedophile.[166] The accused had left messages, including his telephone number, soliciting young girls aged 8–13 years for paid sex in various locations at railway stations and on trains. The Court of Appeal concluded that:

> Far from instigating the offence, the police officer's conduct provided only the opportunity for the defendant to attempt to commit a similar offence and provide the evidence necessary for a conviction. The police officer's response to the invitation in the graffiti by pretending to be a child was a necessary pretence to that end; the pretence did not go beyond providing the necessary opportunity for the defendant to attempt to commit the offence by inciting a person whom he believed to be under the age of 13 to engage in penetrative sex. The police officer's replies thereafter to the text messages were entirely acceptable in a covert operation of this kind, as otherwise the nature of her actions would have increased the suspicions of the defendant. It was the defendant who, after he had been told of the person's age, continued and went on to incite penetrative sexual activity on more than one occasion on the days that followed.[167]

In another case in which the accused tried to solicit his wife's murder, the fact that an undercover officer and a participating informant had together offered to provide the accused with an alibi did not taint the subsequent prosecution and conviction. The plan was already well-advanced by this point, and the Court of Appeal considered it 'quite clear from the transcript that whether or not the appellant had a driver to provide an alibi he was going to commit the offence. There is no suggestion that he could not or would not do it without a driver.... In short it did not cross the boundary of what was acceptable and what was unacceptable and amounted to state created crime.'[168]

However, the appeal against conviction succeeded in *Moon*, where an undercover officer conducting 'test purchases' in a well-known drug-dealing locale was found to have exceeded the bounds of reasonable solicitation when posing as a vulnerable, homeless addict thrown out by her boyfriend and desperate for 'a fix'.[169] Reversing the ruling at first instance, the Court of Appeal emphasized that, so far as the prosecution's evidence had shown, Moon herself might merely have been another drug user tempted to help out a fellow addict with a hard-luck story. At any rate, she had not been proved to be the type of hardened drug-dealer against whom undercover operations might appropriately be targeted:

> [W]hether the matter is looked [at] through the lens of the proper safeguards of authorisation, or through the lens of the appellant's absence of predisposition or antecedents, or through the lens of the actual nature of the police activities in relation to this appellant, the conclusion to which we are driven is that this appellant was lured into crime or was entrapped, and that it was a case of causing crime rather than merely providing an opportunity for it, and

---

[166] *R v Jones (Ian)* [2008] QB 460, [2007] EWCA Crim 1118. Also see Kate Beaumont, 'Text Tactics in Rape Investigation – An Interview with Fred Ferguson' (2008) 172 *JP* 112.   [167] ibid. [23].
[168] *R v Winter* [2007] EWCA Crim 3493, [30], [33].   [169] *R v Moon* [2004] EWCA Crim 2872.

ultimately that it would be unfair for the State to prosecute her for this offending. In these circumstances, the application to stay for abuse should, we think, have been accepted.[170]

The factual scenario confronting the Administrative Court in *Jenkins* v *USA*[171] also involved drug-dealing, but the circumstances could not have been further removed from the street-level user-dealing prosecuted in *Moon*. Jenkins and his associate Benbow were contesting their extradition to the USA. B had been caught in a sting operation attempting to sell Russian-sourced radioactive material valued at $220m to undercover DEA agents. The agents suggested that payment be made in drugs, prompting B to bring J into the conspiracy as the representative of an English crime syndicate willing to convert the drugs into cash. The Administrative Court ruled that nothing had been done which would have rendered the agents' evidence inadmissible in English criminal proceedings. The sting might have amounted to entrapment, Sedley LJ explained, '[i]f Benbow had been offering to sell, say, a stolen television set . . . because there might have been no appreciable connection between the two offers: the offer of drugs might in other words have been regarded as an inducement to commit a crime outside the offender's league'. But on the actual facts of the case, the applicants were 'engaged of [their] own volition in a covert international trade in which payment might as readily be made in drugs as in cash. For the authorities to respond with an offer to pay in drugs was not . . . to initiate drug dealing by someone who there was otherwise no reason to suppose would get involved in it. It was to enter into the class of transaction which Benbow was putting on offer.'[172] Clearly, what passes as 'normal practice' amongst organized crime groups trafficking black-market nuclear material is a world away from the culture of selling £10 wraps of heroin to the homeless in the bus stations of provincial English towns. Comparing *Moon* and *Jenkins* graphically illustrates that when applying section 78, as elucidated in *Looseley*, to cases of alleged entrapment, circumstances can radically alter cases.

5.6 FAIR TRIAL AS CONSTITUTIONAL PRINCIPLE AND THE DESTINY OF SECTION 78

Section 78 of PACE 1984 has come a remarkably long way in a comparatively short space of time. What began life as a legislative afterthought at odds with the grain of English common law, a quarter century later has become a ubiquitous admissibility standard with a roving brief covering a massively expanded (and still expanding) law of criminal procedure, the subject of hundreds of reported appellate decisions and – presumably – thousands of first-instance applications and admissibility contests on the *voir dire*. But section 78's importance is far from exhausted by its ubiquity in litigation practice.

Many of the cases addressing section 78 (and its procedural counterpart, judicial stays for abuse of process) considered in this chapter have made signal contributions to the general development of the English law of criminal evidence, in particular to its emergence as a subject with self-consciously constitutional dimensions, overlapping with international human rights law and cosmopolitan in its sources. Fair trial is the conceptual, ethical, and

---

[170] ibid. [51].   [171] *Jenkins* v *USA*; *Benbow* v *USA* [2005] EWHC 1051 (Admin).
[172] ibid. [20].

legal-doctrinal point of rendezvous on which all of these forces converge. Thus, in the act of setting forth a framework of principle to guide trial judges' decision-making in particular cases, the House of Lords in *Looseley; Attorney General's Reference (No 3 of 2000)* was also engaged in the historic judicial project of moulding section 78 into a primary bulwark of fairness and moral integrity in English criminal proceedings. Several of their Lordships looked to the case-law of jurisdictions with greater experience of a justiciable bill of rights, and in particular drew upon the judgment of the Supreme Court of Canada in *Mack*,[173] in working through their approaches to entrapment evidence. This cosmopolitan conception of juridical resources was taken several steps further by Lord Bingham in *A v Home Secretary (No 2)*, who made a point of saying that English common law's condemnation of torture evidence 'is more aptly categorized as a constitutional principle than as a rule of evidence'.[174] It is now hardly possible to talk about the fairness of proactive policing, covert surveillance, undercover agents, entrapment, and the rest, without detailed reference to the European Court of Human Rights' burgeoning jurisprudence on Articles 6 and 8; and many of the cases discussed in this chapter might just as easily be included in a text on European human rights law.[175] The gradual constitutionalization of English criminal procedure law and its foundation in the law of human rights underwrite the claims of 'fair trial' to be included, alongside admissibility and relevance, in the modern canon of basic evidentiary concepts.

Two related points about fairness as a test of admissibility, which clearly emerge from the selective survey of section 78 cases presented in this chapter, merit emphasis by way of conclusion. First, the discretion conferred on trial judges by section 78 is highly contextual, particularistic, and fact-sensitive. It is possible to formulate general guidelines for its exercise, such as those principles applicable to entrapment cases consolidated and reissued by the House of Lords in *Looseley*, but the final decision to admit or exclude contested evidence must necessarily be a function of the unique facts of individual cases, for which no appellate blueprint or juridical algorithm can be given. It follows, secondly, that the success – or otherwise – of section 78, as an arbiter of the tension between proof and justice, turns substantially on the moral intuitions, forensic expertise and good judgement of trial judges. In view of the fact that much Evidence scholarship has been preoccupied with formal legal rules, reflecting legal scholarship generally, it is worth underlining the point that translating the aspirations of criminal justice into practical decision-making in criminal adjudication depends as much on the quality, experience, and training of the judiciary and lay magistracy, as it does on the choice and design of procedural legislation and general normative standards.

Indeterminate objectives and uncertainty in application are, for some commentators, the epitome of 'what's wrong with section 78'.[176] It is undeniable that the open-ended nature of the enquiry which trial judges are required to undertake generates a measure of uncertainty, and creates real risks of inconsistency, in first instance applications of section 78. In *Roberts*[177] the accused was convicted of robbery and firearms offences, and sentenced to a total of fifteen years' imprisonment, partly on the basis of admissions made to a fellow

---

[173] *R v Mack* [1988] 2 SCR 903, SCC.   [174] [2006] 2 AC 221, [12].

[175] Cf. D. J. Harris, M. O'Boyle, E. P. Bates, and C. M. Buckley, *Law of the European Convention on Human Rights* (OUP, 2nd edn. 2009), 256–65.

[176] Cf. Andrew L.-T. Choo and Susan Nash, 'What's the Matter with Section 78?' [1999] *Crim LR* 929; Birch, 'Excluding Evidence From Entrapment', 98–9.   [177] *R v Roberts* [1997] 1 Cr App R 217, CA.

detainee in a police cell that had been bugged. On appeal it was argued for the accused that his cell-mate had been a police stooge primed to pump him for incriminating information. Rejecting this contention and upholding the trial judge's decision to admit the evidence, the Court of Appeal was at pains to stress its circumscribed role in reviewing the exercise of a trial court's discretion. The Court of Appeal pointedly refused to substitute its own speculations for the trial judge's determinations of fact:

[T]he true test is whether, having regard to the circumstances of the case as whole, the conduct of the police, either wittingly or unwittingly, led to unfairness or injustice: and we consider that the proper adjudicator of this question is the trial judge himself, who has seen the witness, and who has a wide margin of discretion under section 78 which should only be disturbed in this Court if it can be shown that he erred in principle or was plainly wrong.[178]

The Court of Appeal is in no position to second-guess every finding of fact by the trial judge. But there is a fine line in appellate supervision between reasonable deference and unhealthy distance, which lazy phrases like 'wide margin of discretion' are liable to leave hostage to subjective interpretations. An excessively 'hands-off' approach by the Court of Appeal should provoke unease. In *Roberts*, the judge found as a fact that no stooge was ever enlisted or primed to secure admissions, yet the alleged 'plant' was never himself charged with any offence even though an eyewitness placed him at the scene of the robbery. Too many unanswered questions may impact adversely on the fairness of the proceedings and imperil the legitimacy of the verdict, just as surely as too much unexplained variation in trial judges' decisions on the admissibility of disputed evidence.

Much of what the Court of Appeal has had to say about section 78 provides little or no concrete guidance for trial judges. Take, for example, the distinction which recurs through the cases on entrapment between deliberately tricking a suspect and the suspect's supposedly 'applying the trick to himself'. This is really just a poetic way of restating a conclusion about whether contested investigative techniques satisfy section 78's fairness test, or not. The active/passive trick metaphor discloses no concrete criteria of fairness, and is consequently vacuous as a *test* of admissibility. Decisions to admit or exclude evidence must be based, not around easy slogans,[179] but on fine-grained evaluations of the legitimacy of particular techniques in the circumstances of particular investigations. Many of the cases we have considered in this chapter, for example, call for contextual evaluations of the moral and legal boundaries of justifiable deception in law enforcement.[180] Yet, for all the doubts that may linger, the House of Lords in *Looseley* and the Court of Appeal in *Smurthwaite; Gill* and in *Roberts* were right to insist that the rules, principles, and general guidance formulated by appellate tribunals can never be an all-purpose substitute for contextual applications of an open-ended standard of fairness. There is, in other words, an indispensable,

---

[178] ibid. 232.

[179] The analogous distinction between 'active' and 'passive' conduct by undercover law enforcement officers is similarly rejected as a test of admissibility by Andrew Ashworth, 'Re-drawing the Boundaries of Entrapment' [2002] *Crim LR* 161, 165. Also see the incisive remarks of Lord Hoffmann in *R v Looseley* [2001] UKHL 53, [49]: 'Limited assistance can ... be gained from distinctions which restate the question rather than provide a criterion for answering it. For example, it has been said that a policeman or paid informer should not act as an *agent provocateur*; an expression used to signify practices employed by foreigners unacquainted with English notions of decency and fair play ... But what exactly is an *agent provocateur*?'

[180] See Andrew Ashworth, 'Should the Police be Allowed to Use Deceptive Practices?' (1998) 114 *LQR* 108; John Kleinig, *The Ethics of Policing* (CUP, 1996), ch 7.

irreducible role for trial judges' good faith reasoning and judgment in the exercise of their 'discretion' to exclude unfair prosecution evidence under section 78.

A final question remains: are there any types of evidence, or forms of investigative conduct (possibly involving rights violations), that are so inherently abhorrent and inconsistent with the moral integrity of criminal proceedings that an exclusionary remedy must be applied automatically in (virtually) every case? We have seen that English law gives an affirmative answer in relation to one type of evidence, that procured by torture of any degree or description.[181] Are there any other forms of evidence or investigative tactics that also fit this model? Several national jurisdictions, including South Africa,[182] Italy,[183] and Greece,[184] have elevated the exclusion of unlawfully obtained evidence to the status of a constitutional principle, which – at least sometimes – appears to operate more or less automatically. In addition to these comparative illustrations, it is also worth noting Article 69(7) of the Statute of the International Criminal Court, which provides that: 'Evidence obtained by means of a violation of this Statute or internationally recognized human rights shall not be admissible if: (a) The violation casts substantial doubt on the reliability of the evidence; or (b) The admission of the evidence would be antithetical to and would seriously damage the integrity of the proceedings'. Whether this formulation will encourage the ICC to treat certain kinds of evidence as automatically inadmissible remains to be seen. Within the common law world, a contextualised 'balancing' approach continues to predominate,[185] and New Zealand has even expressly renounced its weak *prima facie* presumption in favour of excluding improperly obtained evidence.[186] With the notable but eminently distinguishable exception of torture, English law, for the time being at least, remains wedded to a similarly contextual approach to judging whether fairness demands the exclusion of tainted evidence pursuant to PACE 1984, section 78, or at common law, interpreted in the light of ECHR Article 6 and the evolving jurisprudence of human rights.

---

[181] *A v Secretary of State for the Home Department (No 2)* [2006] 2 AC 221, [2005] UKHL 71.

[182] S. E. Van der Merwe, 'The "Good Faith" of the Police and the Exclusion of Unconstitutionally Obtained Evidence' (1998) 11 *South African Journal of Criminal Justice* 462.

[183] Ennio Amodio, 'The Accusatorial System Lost and Regained: Reforming Criminal Procedure in Italy' (2004) 52 *American Journal of Comparative Law* 489.

[184] Dimitrios Giannoulopoulos, 'The Exclusion of Improperly Obtained Evidence in Greece: Putting Constitutional Rights First' (2007) 11 *E & P* 181.

[185] Andrew L.-T. Choo and Susan Nash, 'Improperly Obtained Evidence in the Commonwealth: Lessons for England and Wales?' (2007) 11 *E & P* 75; Peter Duff, 'Irregularly Obtained Real Evidence: The Scottish Solution?' (2004) 8 *E & P* 77.

[186] The New Zealand equivalent of PACE 1984, s.78, is now Evidence Act 2006, s.30. The *prima facie* rule mandating exclusion of evidence obtained in breach of the New Zealand Bill of Rights Act 1990 was rejected in *R v Shaheed* [2002] 2 NZLR 377 (NZCA). See Chris Gallavin, *Evidence* (LexisNexis, 2008), 48–58; Richard Mahoney, 'Abolition of New Zealand's *Prima Facie* Exclusionary Rule' [2003] *Crim LR* 607.

6

BURDENS OF PROOF AND THE
PRESUMPTION OF INNOCENCE

6.1 BURDENS AND PRESUMPTIONS

Previous chapters have considered the nature and varieties of admissible evidence;[1] the matters requiring proof in criminal adjudication;[2] the procedural context[3] and epistemological resources of 'common sense' fact-finding;[4] and the jurisprudence and philosophical foundations of fair trials.[5] This chapter addresses a topic which is intimately connected with everything we have discussed so far, and one which can be regarded as encapsulating in microcosm the theoretical evolution and contemporary practical challenges of our entire subject of Criminal Evidence. There is no neutral name for this topic. Orthodox doctrinal conceptions of the Law of Evidence refer to 'burdens of proof' and evidentiary 'presumptions'. Revisionists accounts of Criminal Evidence might instead begin with the idea of 'the presumption of innocence' as a human right with (proto-)constitutional status in English law. This chapter will attempt to weave both strands of analysis into a coherent vision, extracting the complementary strengths of orthodox and revisionist approaches and thereby, we hope, providing more illumination than any single, monocular perspective.

Narrowly conceived, our topic concerns the distribution of probative burdens. In other words, the primary question is: *who* is required to prove what? *To whom* are burdens of proof allocated, and on what basis? There is extensive doctrinal learning on burdens of proof in English law. Legal-definitional questions to be addressed in this chapter include: What is a burden of proof? Are there different kinds? (Yes.) What is the standard of proof? Are there multiple standards? (Yes, again.) What is the relationship between burdens and standards of proof? How is a burden of proof discharged? How should judges direct juries on burdens and standards of proof? What are the forensic consequences of discharging a burden of proof, or of failing to do so? Do burdens of proof ever shift? (No, never!) We will argue that burdens of proof are procedural devices for allocating the risk of error in criminal adjudication. The allocation of probative burdens must therefore be explained in terms of the relative badness (or 'disutility') of factually erroneous acquittals of the guilty and wrongful convictions of the innocent. In performing this allocative function, burdens of proof

---

[1] Chapters 1 and 3.   [2] Chapter 4.   [3] Chapters 1 and 2.   [4] Chapters 1 and 4.
[5] Chapter 1 and 5.

are indispensable keystones in the architecture of adversarial criminal procedure. However, their structural role only becomes fully apparent after stripping out some of the more baroque accretions that have disfigured English law. It will be crucial, in particular, to clarify (and to some extent stipulate) terminology before genuine progress can be made.

Legal presumptions of fact are a second, subsidiary, procedural device for allocating risks of error in criminal adjudication. Presumptions have attracted even more technical doctrinal learning than burdens of proof, but this has not been conducive to clarity of understanding or ease of application – quite the reverse. The American evidence scholar Edmund Morgan famously remarked that 'every writer of sufficient intelligence to appreciate the difficulties of the subject matter has approached the topic of presumptions with a sense of hopelessness, and has left it with a feeling of despair'.[6] In fact the case is far from desperate let alone hopeless. We will show that it is possible to make perfectly good sense of evidentiary presumptions as devices for allocating the risks of forensic error. Nonetheless, judicial and academic references to 'presumptions' should be treated with circumspection. There is no settled terminology or generally accepted analysis of evidentiary presumptions, and much avoidable confusion has been generated through loose definitions, convoluted conceptualizations, and inconsistent usage. This situation calls for a prescriptive and unsentimental approach to defining legal presumptions. We will extract a useful and workable concept from the previous efforts of scholars and judges, and unceremoniously junk the rest.

Orthodox conceptions of the Law of Evidence might rest content with disentangling the conceptual foundations of legal doctrine pertaining to burdens and standards of proof and presumptions and exploring their judicial applications. Important – and challenging – though this work undoubtedly is, a doctrinal approach does not really begin to get to grips with the full significance of burdens and presumptions in modern criminal adjudication. It fails to grapple, more specifically, with the presumption of innocence as a human right enjoying constitutional protection in many domestic legal systems, including (we will suggest) England and Wales. Only by exploring the political morality of the presumption of innocence can its true jurisprudential significance be appreciated. Traditional legal language and habits of thought have tended to induce a relatively narrow doctrinalism. English lawyers and judges have generally been preoccupied with prosaic rules of evidence specifying the burden and standard of proof,[7] with infrequent explicit reference to the more elevated presumption of innocence. By recovering the constitutional, human rights, and philosophical dimensions of this topic, this chapter attempts for the presumption of innocence what the book as a whole is trying to achieve for Criminal Evidence.

The 'presumption of innocence' is an integral component of the 'fair trial' rights contained in international human rights treaties, including the European Convention on Human

---

[6] Edmund Morgan, 'Presumptions' (1937) 12 *Washington LR* 255.

[7] Historical context is supplied by Barbara J. Shapiro, *Beyond Reasonable Doubt and Probable Cause: Historical Perspectives on the Anglo-American Law of Evidence* (California UP, 1991); Barbara J. Shapiro, '"To a Moral Certainty": Theories of Knowledge and Anglo-American Juries 1600–1850' (1986) 38 *Hastings LJ* 153; Theodore Waldman, 'Origins of the Legal Doctrine of Reasonable Doubt' (1959) 20 *Journal of the History of Ideas* 299.

Rights (ECHR) and the International Covenant on Civil and Political Rights (ICCPR).[8] It is also frequently elevated to the status of a constitutional guarantee in jurisdictions with written Bills of Rights.[9] Article 6(2) of the ECHR provides that:

Everyone charged with a criminal offence shall be presumed innocent until proved guilty according to law.

However, the presumption of innocence was a cherished part of English legal heritage long before the Human Rights Act 1998 made the ECHR a formal source of law in English criminal proceedings. Viscount Sankey LC's 'golden thread' speech in *Woolmington* v *DPP*, extolling the merits of the presumption, is one of the most famous and frequently quoted passages in English criminal jurisprudence:[10]

Throughout the web of the English Criminal Law one golden thread is always to be seen, that it is the duty of the prosecution to prove the prisoner's guilt subject... to the defence of insanity and subject also to any statutory exception. If, at the end of and on the whole of the case, there is a reasonable doubt, created by the evidence given by either the prosecution or the prisoner... the prosecution has not made out the case and the prisoner is entitled to an acquittal. No matter what the charge or where the trial, the principle that the prosecution must prove the guilt of the prisoner is part of the common law of England and no attempt to whittle it down can be entertained.

It does not seem extravagant to describe 'the golden thread' as a 'constitutional' principle of English criminal law, albeit that the precise contents of Britain's unwritten constitution are inevitably matters of contentious speculation. It is instructive to compare parallel developments in American common law. Pre-dating modern constitutional instruments, the US Constitution betrays its eighteenth century provenance by referring expressly neither to the presumption of innocence nor to the burden of proof. But the US Supreme Court nevertheless found, in its celebrated *In re Winship* opinion, that the requirement of proof beyond reasonable doubt is mandated by the Due Process Clause of the Fourteenth Amendment. Justice Brennan explained:[11]

The reasonable-doubt standard plays a vital role in the American scheme of criminal procedure. It is the prime instrument for reducing the risk of convictions resting on factual error. The standard provides concrete substance for the presumption of innocence – that

---

[8] ICCPR Article 14(2) provides in almost identical terms to ECHR Article 6(2) that: 'Everyone charged with a criminal offence shall have the right to be presumed innocent until proved guilty according to law'. And see the Charter of Fundamental Rights of the European Union (2007/C 3003/01), Article 48: Presumption of innocence and right of defence.

[9] For a useful survey, see M. Cherif Bassiouni, 'Human Rights in the Context of Criminal Justice: Identifying International Procedural Protections and Equivalent Protections in National Constitutions' (1993) 3 *Duke Journal of Comparative and International Law* 235.

[10] [1935] AC 462, 481–2, HL. Viscount Sankey makes explicit reference to the 'presumption of innocence' only once, and almost in passing, near the end of his speech. For the history of doctrinal developments preceding *Woolmington* see J. C. Smith, 'The Presumption of Innocence' (1987) 38 *Northern Ireland Legal Quarterly* 223.

[11] *In re Winship*, 397 US 358, 363 (1970), quoting *Coffin* v *US*, 156 US 432, 453 (1896). See further, Donald A. Dripps, 'The Constitutional Status of the Reasonable Doubt Rule' (1987) 75 *California LR* 1665; Ronald J. Allen, 'Structuring Jury Decision-making in Criminal Cases: A Unified Constitutional Approach to Evidentiary Devices' (1980) 94 *Harvard LR* 321.

bedrock 'axiomatic and elementary' principle whose 'enforcement lies at the foundation of the administration of our criminal law.'

A 'presumption of innocence' is only truly valuable if it carries robust implications for criminal procedure generally,[12] and for the burden and standard of proof in particular. In order to merit its reputation as a fundamental constitutional guarantee, the presumption must be reasonably extensive and not too easily defeated. Imagine, by contrast, a very weak formal presumption which the state could rebut simply by establishing that the accused had the *opportunity* of committing a crime, effectively requiring accused persons to prove their innocence whenever this minimal requirement had been met. The presumption of innocence would hardly be much to boast about unless, at the least, it required the state to prove every element of a criminal offence to an appropriately exacting standard. The related notions of the presumption of innocence and the burden and standard of proof are intimately bound up with a third idea: the right of the innocent not to suffer criminal conviction and punishment, which was identified as a foundational principle of criminal evidence in Chapter 1.[13] Protection of the innocent from wrongful conviction is, we propose, a key constitutional right at English common law as much as in American constitutional criminal jurisprudence, though it has seldom been formulated explicitly or openly discussed in these terms on this side of the Atlantic.

In light of the confusion surrounding the terminology of 'presumptions' and 'burdens of proof' in English legal theory, to which reference has already been made, it should come as no surprise that there is no settled meaning of 'presumption of innocence'. References in legal scholarship to the presumption of innocence are sometimes shorthand for the duty of the state to prove the accused's guilt beyond reasonable doubt. On other occasions the presumption stands for the proposition that fact-finders must determine a criminal charge without any predisposition towards finding guilt. From a broader, political theory or philosophical perspective, one might expect the presumption of innocence to say something important about the relationship between the state and the individual, as reflected, perhaps, in the scope and drafting of criminal legislation or the enforcement of criminal prohibitions. Explicating the philosophical and juridical foundations of the presumption of innocence, and their translation into English criminal procedure, will be a major task for this chapter.

Equipped with a normative conception of the presumption of innocence, we may then set about evaluating the performance of English law judged against this normative ideal. Alas, it turns out that *Woolmington's* fine-sounding phrases often amount to no more than a rhetorical commitment to the presumption of innocence. The celebrated golden thread is badly frayed in places – especially where a burden of proof is placed on the accused by a statutory 'reverse onus clause'. This legislative technique is utilized far more frequently than would ever be guessed, and the courts have been, one might think disturbingly,

---

[12] In addition to its specifically evidentiary functions, the presumption of innocence can also be regarded as reinforcing a more general principle of liberty in the enforcement of criminal law. This is manifested, for example, by legal restrictions on police powers of stop, search, arrest, and pre-trial detention. Also see Roderick Munday, 'Name Suppression: An Adjunct to the Presumption of Innocence and to Mitigation of Sentence' [1991] *Crim LR* 680 and 753. But for the contrary argument, that the presumption of innocence should be given a narrower interpretation restricted to the burden and standard of proof, see P. J. Schwikkard, 'The Presumption of Innocence: What is It?' (1998) 11 *South African Journal of Criminal Justice* 396.

[13] §1.3.

sanguine about it. English judges have not, generally speaking, apprehended *Woolmington* as a call to arms in defence of a cherished principle. The advent of the Human Rights Act 1998, however, precipitated an unprecedented number of appeals on this issue. Within the space of a decade, the House of Lords was called upon to reconsider the compatibility of contested reverse onus clauses with ECHR Article 6(2) on no fewer than five separate occasions. Whilst authoritative interpretations of particular statutory provisions have been issued, there is no sign of the wider legal controversy having yet exhausted itself. Even if English courts were able to achieve doctrinal equilibrium on the legality of reverse onus clauses, there is no guarantee that Strasbourg would rubber-stamp the domestic consensus. And even if English and European judges arrived at shared understandings of the requirements of European human rights law, parliamentarians and policy-makers would still need to address broader philosophical questions concerning the meaning of the presumption of innocence and its implications for criminal procedure law in general, for the burden and standard of proof in criminal adjudication more particularly, and for the legitimacy of reverse onus clauses at the 'retail' end of legislative drafting.

6.2 PROCEDURAL TECHNIQUES OF RISK-ALLOCATION[14]

The key to understanding burdens of proof and presumptions, on the orthodox account, is to appreciate their assigned roles within the broader framework of adversarial criminal procedure. Recall that, in comparison to the continental model of active judicial investigation, adjudication in common law adversarial proceedings is relatively passive.[15] The trier of fact approaches the factual dispute with an open mind, leaving it to the parties to marshal and present their evidence, each attempting to persuade the court of the merits of their respective cases. The adversary model requires a procedure for determining what should happen in the event of 'a tie', where a litigant fails to persuade the court of a fact essential to that party's case. What should a fact-finder do if, having heard all the evidence, an essential fact remains in doubt, neither party having proved or disproved the issue either way? The burden of proof breaks the logjam and overcomes the stalemate in such situations. The law of evidence determines which litigant must prove particular constitutive facts, and the degree of probability which such proof must attain. Another way of expressing this is to say that evidentiary rules allocate the risk of losing the case should a party fail to prove a constitutive fact.

The juridical technique of risk-allocation is most straightforwardly illustrated by considering a simple factual dispute in the context of civil litigation. The law of contract lays down that a person who lends money to another, under a legally binding agreement that it should be repaid, is entitled to repayment of the loan. *A* lends *B* £100, but later claims

---

[14] Generally, see *Wigmore on Evidence* (3rd edn. 1940), vol 9, §§2485ff; J. Stone, 'Burden of Proof and the Judicial Process: A Comment on *Joseph Constantine Steamship line Ltd v Imperial Corporation Ltd*' (1944) 60 *LQR* 262; A. T. Denning, 'Presumptions and Burdens' (1945) 61 *LQR* 379; Nigel Bridge, 'Presumptions and Burdens' (1949) 12 *MLR* 273; Glanville Williams, *Criminal Law: the General Part* (2nd edn. 1961), ch 23; Ariel Porat and Alex Stein, *Tort Liability Under Uncertainty* (OUP, 2001).

[15] See §2.2(c)(i), and in particular, the classic discussion of Marvin E. Frankel, 'The Search for Truth: An Umpireal View' (1975) 123 *University of Pennsylvania LR* 1031.

that *B* has defaulted on the loan and sues for repayment. *B* counter-claims that the money was never actually paid over to him in the first place. Suppose that at the end of the trial the court is left in doubt as to whether *B* ever received or repaid the £100 allegedly lent to him by *A*. There is now a choice to be made: award judgment either to the claimant or to the defendant, or else follow King Solomon's principle[16] by dividing the disputed amount equally between the parties, each to receive £50 in this case.

All three options clearly involve some risk of error, since handing down a factually erroneous judgment will deprive one of the parties of at least part of his legal right, whilst the other will scoop an unmerited windfall. If we say, as we generally do, that the claimant wins if he proves his case on the balance of probabilities (which for the sake of argument we may regard as 51% probability), it follows that we are prepared to accept a certain degree of risk that the decision against the defendant in that case will be wrong. It is a common mistake to conclude that the risk of error in this scenario must therefore be 49%, leading to the extraordinary conclusion that 49 out of every 100 civil judgments are in error. If that were the case, the accuracy of civil litigation would be no better than tossing a coin! Fortunately, that disturbing conclusion is only valid if the chances of a civil action being meritorious or not were equi-probable, or, put another way, that 50 out of every 100 civil suits are ill-founded. In fact there are good reasons to believe that a far higher proportion of claims is meritorious. Litigation is expensive and time-consuming, and the courts are primed to strike-out vexatious or hopeless claims.[17] Cases that go all the way to trial have already been rigorously pre-selected by checks and balances built into the system of litigation, enhancing the accuracy of litigation outcomes over the aggregate total of civil disputes taken to law.

In any event, the '51%' standard is a measure of the fact-finder's (subjective) confidence in the result, not a measure of the (objective) accuracy of outcomes.[18] The empirical relationship between confidence and accuracy is complex. Very confident, and even widely-shared, subjective judgments can be systematically wrong – like the ancient conviction that the Earth is the centre of the universe, or the medieval belief in witchcraft,[19] for

---

[16] According to the Biblical tale (Old Testament, 1 Kings 3), when confronted with two women each claiming to be the mother of a newborn, King Solomon offered to have the baby cut down the middle so that both claimant mothers could have half a baby each. The woman who reacted to this awful prospect by saying that, if that would otherwise be the verdict, her rival must take the baby to spare its life, was adjudged by Solomon to be the true mother, and awarded custody of the infant. The story is generally taken to demonstrate 'the Wisdom of Solomon': 'When all Israel heard the verdict the king had given, they held the king in awe, because they saw that he had wisdom from God to administer justice'. For discussion, see L. H. LaRue, 'Solomon's Judgment: A Short Essay on Proof' (2004) 3 *Law, Probability & Risk* 13; Ann Althouse, 'Beyond King Solomon's Harlots: Women in Evidence' (1992) 65 *Southern California LR* 1265.

[17] Observe, further, that in many civil cases the claimant achieves more than a preponderance of probabilities, quite likely even proof beyond reasonable doubt. In other cases claimants may achieve, say, 80% or 70% probabilities. The overall rate of erroneous determinations in civil litigation should therefore be much lower than 49%, as one would hope.

[18] For instructive discussion, see Mike Redmayne, 'Standards of Proof in Civil Litigation' (1999) 62 *MLR* 167; D. H. Kaye, 'Clarifying the Burden of Persuasion: What Bayesian Decision Rules Do and Do Not Do' (1999) 3 *E & P* 1; Ronald J. Allen, 'Clarifying the Burden of Persuasion and Bayesian Decision Rules: A Response to Professor Kaye' (2000) 4 *E & P* 246; D. H. Kaye, 'Bayes, Burdens and Base Rates' (2000) 4 *E & P* 260.

[19] See, for example, Stuart Clark, *Thinking with Demons: The Idea of Witchcraft in Early Modern Europe* (OUP, 1997) (demonstrating the power and coherence of medieval beliefs in witchcraft, even amongst intellectuals).

example. Nonetheless, provided that meritorious actions are routinely supported by reliable evidence, whereas weak or speculative claims generally lack convincing proof, litigation should do rather better than coin-tossing in establishing the facts and vindicating litigants' rights. Once the logical fallacy of equating fact-finders' subjective confidence with the accuracy of trial verdicts has been exposed and neutralized, confidence levels framed in percentage terms can continue to serve as useful and vivid reminders of the real, albeit empirically unquantifiable, risks of error in litigation.

(a) VARIETIES OF PROBATIVE BURDEN

The simplest device for allocating the risk of error in litigation is a decision-rule providing that the court will vindicate and enforce a claimant's right only if constitutive facts are proved by the claimant, to a specified degree of probability. English law works with the rule of thumb that the proponent on any issues bears the burden of proof.[20] This risk allocation device is variously known as the 'legal' or 'persuasive' or 'probative' burden. The first term reflects the dependence of the burden of proof on substantive law to specify the parties' respective legal rights and entitlements, while the other two emphasize the burden on the proponent to adduce enough evidence to produce a certain degree of assurance in the mind of the fact-finder. There is no consistent usage, either in precedents or commentary. For the avoidance of doubt, the burden requiring the proponent to prove his case to a specified degree of probability is generally referred to throughout this book as the probative burden, though we also sometimes speak of 'the burden of persuasion' where that better suits the context.

A belief in the truth of a proposition can be held with varying degrees of confidence. Legal rules are therefore needed to establish, not only the allocation of the probative burden, but also the requisite *standard* of proof, that is to say, the level of confidence which the evidence has to produce in the trier of fact.[21] Since assessments of probabilities in everyday naturalistic contexts – including criminal trials – cannot be expressed in precise numerical terms, the law is obliged to work with fairly rough-and-ready estimates of confidence levels. English law classically adopts two basic standards: proof on the balance of probabilities, and proof beyond reasonable doubt. Proof 'on the balance of probabilities' means (assuming no third possibility)[22] that the probability of the proponent's contention being

---

[20] The *in dubio pro reo* or *contra proferentem* principle: see *Amos* v *Hughes* (1835) 1 Mood & R 464, 174 ER 160; *Soward* v *Leggatt* (1836) 7 C & P 613, 615, where Lord Abinger emphasized that it was the substance of the issue, rather than the form of pleadings, that settled the incidence of the probative burden: '[W]e should consider what is the substantive fact to be made out, and on whom it lies to make it out. It is not so much the form of the issue which ought to be considered, as the substance and effect of it. In many cases, a party, by a little difference in the drawing of his pleadings might make it either affirmative or negative, as he pleased.'

[21] Forensic evaluation of evidence can be described as 'subjective', in the sense that decisions are made on the basis of jurors' personal evaluations of the evidence, rather than on some more objective criterion of proof: J. P. McBaine, 'Burden of Proof: Degrees of Belief' (1944) 32 *California LR* 242; D. H. Kaye, 'The Paradox of the Gate-Crasher and Other Stories' [1979] *Arizona State LJ* 101. Various forms of probabilistic reasoning in forensic contexts were discussed in §4.5.

[22] The fact-finder in an adversarial trial is typically invited to select between the competing contentions or narratives advanced by the parties: see §2.3. However, it is conceivable that the fact-finder might regard neither contention as more likely than not; perhaps neither party's case is at all plausible. When this 'none of the above' conclusion occasionally arises in practice the party bearing the probative burden inevitably loses his case: cf. *Rhesa Shipping Co. SA* v *Edmunds* ('*The Popi M*') [1985] 1 WLR 948, 955–6, HL, *per*

true is at least marginally greater than the probability of the opponent's counter-claim being true; or, more simply, that a proposition is established if it is *more likely than not* to be true. This is conventionally denoted mathematically as a '51% probability', though, strictly speaking, proof on the balance of probabilities would be satisfied by any probability greater than 0.5 or 50%, even if less than 51%. 'Proof beyond reasonable doubt' connotes a level of confidence in a conclusion that could be doubted only unreasonably. Whether it makes sense to try to quantify this level of persuasion mathematically, and even whether it is sensible to continue to employ the time-honoured phrase 'beyond reasonable doubt', are questions that will need to be confronted later in the chapter.

In traditional evidentiary theory the probative burden relates in the first instance to particular issues or facts, and only by extension to the ultimate issue in criminal proceedings: whether the accused is guilty or innocent. Failure to discharge the probative burden results in the proponent losing on that particular issue. This might, or might not, mean losing the case as a whole, depending on the type of claim and the nature of the issue. If a contract-debt claimant fails to prove on the balance of probabilities that he handed over any money to the defendant, he obviously loses outright. But suppose the defendant, in addition to denying receipt of the money, also claims that he was coerced into signing an agreement to repay. On the issue of coercion the defendant is the proponent, and the probative burden lies with him. In these circumstances, the defendant's failure to convince the court on the balance of probabilities that he was coerced into signing is *not* fatal to his defence, since the claimant could still fail to prove that the defendant received the money in the first place, which would be fatal to the claimant's suit. This illustration demonstrates the significance of terminological precision in relating probative burdens to particular issues or facts. In criminal proceedings the prosecution bears the ultimate probative burden of proving its case beyond reasonable doubt, but this is – at least conceptually – consistent with the accused shouldering probative burdens on certain issues. We will have much more to say about these 'reverse onus clauses' in the concluding sections of this chapter.

A second familiar risk-allocation technique is commonly referred to as the 'evidential burden', though it is more accurately described as the burden of adducing evidence or, better still in the context of criminal trials on indictment,[23] the duty to 'pass the judge'. To combine the two descriptions into 'evidential burden of production' would be accurate but long-winded; we will generally settle for 'burden of production'. The burden of production imposes a lesser obligation, to adduce sufficient evidence to make any given contention a live issue in the trial. In contrast to the probative burden, the burden of production does not require the proponent to establish any particular degree of confidence in the

Lord Brandon: 'the judge is not bound always to make a finding one way or the other with regard to the facts averred by the parties. He has open to him the third alternative of saying that the party on whom the burden of proof lies in relation to any averment made by him has failed to discharge that burden.... [T]he legal concept of proof of a case on a balance of probabilities must be applied with common sense. It requires a judge of first instance, before he finds that a particular event occurred, to be satisfied on the evidence that it is more likely to have occurred than not. If such a judge concludes, on a whole series of cogent grounds, that the occurrence of an event is extremely improbable, a finding by him that it is nevertheless more likely to have occurred than not, does not accord with common sense. This is especially so when it is open to the judge to say simply that the evidence leaves him in doubt whether the event occurred or not, and that the party on whom the burden of proving that the event occurred lies has therefore failed to discharge such burden.'

[23] This is another respect in which the language and concepts of criminal evidence diverge from civil procedure.

adjudicator's mind. The proponent simply has to persuade the adjudicator that the issue is worth considering in arriving at judgment; hence the notion of 'passing the judge' on a particular issue. A further procedural consequence of satisfying the burden of production in criminal proceedings is that, once an issue has been successfully introduced into the trial, the judge is usually obliged to deal with it during his summing-up to the jury at the close of proceedings[24] – another sense in which the successful proponent has 'passed the judge' in relation to a particular issue.

The 'evidential burden of proof' of popular imagination is, strictly speaking, a solecism, because the evidential burden does not require the proponent actually to *prove* anything in the sense of convincing the fact-finder of the truth of any fact in issue.[25] At a stretch, conventional usage can be rescued if 'proof' is understood somewhat archaically, connot- ing verb rather than noun, referring to the evidentiary labours of the parties in *proving* (adducing, establishing) particular facts. The 'evidential burden' does impose a burden of 'proving' facts in this secondary sense, to a minimal threshold standard. It might also be contended that the weight of evidence required to discharge the burden of production should be greater where the proponent simultaneously bears the probative burden, since it would be pointless to allow a party to raise an issue in these circumstances unless he could also demonstrate some reasonable prospect of discharging his probative burden in due course. Why allow a party to raise an issue he is bound to lose at the end of the day? There would be no need for these elaborate rationalizations, or for the equivocal language of 'evidential burdens', if everybody referred instead to the 'burden of production'. It must be admitted, however, that judicial usage is inconsistent, and some lawyers regard 'evidential burden' as perfectly serviceable terminology.[26]

It is commonplace, though by no means invariable, for the probative and evidential burdens to go together. In criminal proceedings the prosecution must normally adduce evidence capable of proving each and every ingredient of the offence(s) charged on the indictment to the criminal standard, beyond reasonable doubt.[27] On a charge of mur- der, for example, the prosecution must present evidence which, if believed, is sufficient to entitle a reasonable jury to conclude that the accused caused the victim's death with malice aforethought.[28] If this onus cannot be discharged, the prosecution fails to meet an essential threshold requirement of pursuing its case to judgment, and the accused will not even be called upon to answer the charge. A defence submission of 'no case to answer' would succeed in this scenario.[29] Where probative and production burdens go together,

---

[24] The evidential significance of the judge's summing-up to the jury is discussed throughout this book, but see in particular §2.4(4) and Chapter 15.

[25] Thus in *Sheldrake v DPP; Attorney General's Reference (No 4 of 2002)* [2005] 1 AC 264, [2004] UKHL 43, [1], Lord Bingham remarked: 'An evidential burden is not a burden of proof. It is a burden of raising, on the evidence in the case, an issue as to the matter in question fit for consideration by the tribunal of fact. If an issue is properly raised, it is for the prosecutor to prove, beyond reasonable doubt, that that ground of exoneration does not avail the defendant.'

[26] Cf. *Sheldrake v DPP* [2003] 2 Cr App R 206, [2003] EWHC Admin 273, [47], where Clarke LJ stated: 'There has been some criticism of the use of the expression evidential burden...However...it is to my mind sensible to continue to use it provided that it is recognised that all that is required to discharge the burden is to identify evidence raising the issue.'   [27] *Woolmington v DPP* [1935] AC 462, HL.

[28] Which is the definition of murder in English criminal law: see A. P. Simester and G. R. Sullivan, *Criminal Law Theory and Doctrine* (Hart, 3rd edn. 2007), ch 10; David Ormerod, *Smith and Hogan Criminal Law* (OUP, 12th edn. 2008), ch 14.   [29] §2.4(3).

the effect is to relieve the opponent of the need to defend himself until sufficient evidence to engage the probative burden has been adduced. In these circumstances, the probative burden effectively subsumes the lesser evidential burden of production.

Suppose now that, in answer to a murder charge, the accused claims that she killed in lawful self-defence. On this issue, the production and probative burdens diverge. The burden of making self-defence an issue in the case lies with the accused. But the probative burden to dispel any reasonable doubt of guilt remains at all times with prosecuting counsel. The accused must adduce or at least identify[30] some evidential basis for a claim of self-defence, or the judge will not even mention the possibility of that defence to the jury. Once self-defence is before the jury, however, the prosecution's task of proving beyond reasonable doubt that the killing was unlawful is enlarged, to include disproving the possibility of lawful self-defence.[31] Since the accused does not bear the probative burden on this issue, she need only produce evidence which could, if believed, create a reasonable doubt that she might have acted in self-defence. In this practical sense, the burden of adducing evidence – the burden of production – may vary in magnitude according to whether the proponent also shoulders the probative burden, and also according to the relevant standard of proof.

The reason for separating the burden of proof from the burden of production on any issue is to avoid troubling the other party and the trier of fact with claims that are wholly unsupported by evidence. In the last example, the trier of fact need not give any thought to self-defence unless there is material evidence to consider, whilst the prosecution is spared the difficult and time-consuming task of trying to disprove from the outset every conceivable defence that the accused might possibly raise. As Lord Morris once explained, '[t]he "golden" rule of the English criminal law that it is the duty of the prosecution to prove an accused person's guilt…does not involve that the prosecution must speculate as to and specifically anticipate every conceivable explanation that an accused person might offer'.[32] In this way burdens of production make an important contribution to the efficiency of litigation, but it cannot be denied that efficiency comes at a price. The fact that the accused is unable to discharge the burden of adducing evidence to support a particular defence conclusively settles that issue against the accused for the purposes of the proceedings, but is inconclusive in a broader sense. Perhaps the accused acted in self-defence, after all, but lacks any evidence to prove it.[33] Situations where the accused has a genuine defence but cannot discharge a threshold burden of production are probably rare; and in many cases the defendant has the option of going into the witness-box and testifying to the relevant facts himself (though this might not strike the accused or his lawyer as a particularly attractive option). It is undeniable, nonetheless, that burdens of production in respect

---

[30] A burden of production can be satisfied in several different ways, e.g. by eliciting favourable responses in cross-examination of a prosecution witness. It is not always necessary for a party to adduce evidence in order to discharge a burden of production.

[31] *R v Lobell* [1957] 1 QB 547, CCA. Also see *R v Stripp* (1979) 69 Cr App R 318, 323, CA, in relation to a plea of automatism: 'once a proper foundation for such a defence has been laid, the burden, which is always on the prosecution, to prove that the acts were voluntary, becomes an active burden and it is for the prosecution to satisfy the jury at the end of the day that the actions were voluntary in the sense that they were fully conscious'.   [32] *Bratty* v *Attorney General of Northern Ireland* [1963] AC 386, 416, HL.

[33] An example, albeit rarely encountered, is where the accused claims to be suffering from amnesia: see, e.g., *R v O'Brien* [2004] EWCA Crim 2900; cf. *R v Critchley* [1982] Crim LR 524, CA.

of self-defence and other affirmative defences, like duress and provocation,[34] inevitably transfer to the accused some additional risk of wrongful conviction, however small and unquantifiable.

In addition to (legal) burdens of proof and (evidential) burdens of production, commentators occasionally also refer to the *provisional* or *tactical* burden. These terms are sometimes synonyms for the burden of production, but they are also occasionally invoked in a looser sense, to refer to the tactical balance of advantage in litigation. Suppose that on a charge of murder the prosecution adduces uncontradicted testimony from an eyewitness who maintains that he saw the accused deliver the fatal blow. In so doing, the prosecution has apparently discharged its burden of proving the cause of *V*'s death at *D*'s hands: certainly, the prosecution would have 'passed the judge' on the issue of the cause of death, and should be able to pre-empt any defence submission of 'no case to answer'. However, it is impossible to determine at this stage whether the prosecution's overall probative burden, of satisfying the jury beyond reasonable doubt that *D* killed *V* with malice aforethought, has conclusively been discharged. The accused could sit tight, decline to make any reply or to adduce any evidence to the contrary, and hope that the jury will disbelieve the prosecution's witness – or, expressed more precisely, that the jury will not accept the witness's evidence as proof beyond reasonable doubt of the accused's guilt.

An accused who adopts this tactic clearly runs the risk that the jury will in fact believe the witness and convict him. This type of scenario is sometimes, misleadingly, described as imposing a provisional or tactical burden on the accused. Worse, one may fall into the habit of thinking and saying that in these circumstances the tactical burden 'shifts' to the accused.[35] But so-called tactical burdens are not true *burdens of proof*, and, in any case, burdens of proof never shift between the parties in the course of proceedings. What is being described in such cases are merely the practical exigencies of litigation, for which special evidentiary concepts and terminology are unnecessary. So-called tactical burdens are not formal techniques of risk allocation, which is the definitive quality of genuine burdens of proof (and an incidental feature of burdens of production). To avoid confusion, it is better to speak of the tactical *necessity*, rather than the 'burden', of responding to the proponent's evidence. And whilst the balance of advantage in litigation may shift to and fro as the evidence unfolds, burdens of proof remain at all times with the party to whom they are initially allocated.[36] Burdens are either discharged successfully, or the proponent

---

[34] Section 3 of the Homicide Act 1957 has, however, been interpreted to require the judge to direct the jury on provocation whenever relevant evidence has emerged in the trial, even where the defendant is *not* claiming to have been provoked to kill: *R v Cambridge* (1994) 99 Cr App R 142, CA; *R v Acott* [1997] 2 Cr App R 94, HL. Lord Steyn explained in *Acott*, ibid. 102: 'What is sufficient evidence in the particular context is not a question of law. Where the line is to be drawn depends on a judgment involving logic and common sense. The assessment of matters of degree and intense focus on the circumstances of the particular case. It is unwise to generalise on such matters. It is a subject best left to the good sense of trial judges.' Compare in this regard, *R v Serrano* [2006] EWCA Crim 3182; [2007] Crim LR 569, with *Burnett v Trinidad and Tobago* [2009] UKPC 42.

[35] This is a bad habit that many lawyers unfortunately seem unable to resist: for recent examples, cf. *R v Zafar* [2008] QB 810 [2008], EWCA Crim 184, [15] (Lord Phillips CJ); *Grayson v United Kingdom* (2009) 48 EHRR 30, [23] (ECtHR); *Islington LBC v Ladele* [2009] ICR 387, EAT, [40] (Elias J); *DPP v Parker* [2006] RTR 26, [2006] EWHC 1270 (Admin), [10] (Leveson J).

[36] The only context in which it is not an abuse of language to speak of shifting burdens is the legislative. Parliament can fairly be said to 'shift' the burden of proof to the accused when it enacts reverse onus clauses;

loses on that issue. Nothing more can usefully be said, or needs to be added, by way of general conceptual analysis.[37]

(b) PRESUMPTIONS AS TECHNIQUES OF RISK ALLOCATION[38]

In addition to utilizing burdens and standards of proof, the law of evidence allocates forensic risks by employing the device of presumption. We need here to repeat our previous warning about the severe terminological difficulties attending the use of this concept. The word 'presumption' is applied to a disparate range of distinctive legal techniques and doctrines, and to make any headway at all it is necessary to be prescriptive. When thinking about presumptions as techniques for the allocation of risks of error in adjudication, we mean, specifically: (1) rules of evidence which (2) permit the fact-finder to draw specified factual inferences which (3) would not otherwise be warranted by the information available to the fact-finder. For reasons that will become clearer as we proceed, we will call these rules of inference (true) *legal presumptions of fact*. These presumptions are dubbed 'legal' because they work by operation of law, rather than according to the ordinary canons of common sense inferential reasoning; but they are presumptions 'of fact' because they authorize factual conclusions rather than propositions of law. A presumption *of law* is not a true evidentiary presumption on this account. Neither is a legal rule purporting to authorize fact-finders to arrive at conclusions which are anyway logically open to them on the evidence, and for which they consequently require no additional legal authorization beyond their initial appointment as jurors or magistrates.

Part of the definitional problem is simply that 'presumptions' arise in different law-related contexts, where the word can means different things, terminology may be ill-defined, and usage lax. We have already hinted at competing interpretations of the 'presumption of innocence'. The following sections of this chapter will explain why the presumption of innocence is best regarded as a complex legal and political doctrine rather than simply as a rule of evidence. Again, common lawyers sometimes refer to the 'presumption of sanity',[39] which is really just a roundabout way of saying that the accused bears the burden of proving an insanity defence (as *Woolmington* itself acknowledged).[40] Neither of these examples uses 'presumption' in our stipulated sense.

---

on which, see §6.5 and §6.6, below. But the idea of shifting burdens is so troublesome that it is usually better avoided altogether.

[37] To similar effect, see *Snell* v *Farrell* (1990) 72 DLR 4th 289, 301, where Sopinka J said: 'Whether an inference is or is not drawn is a matter of weighing evidence. The defendant runs the risk of an adverse inference in the absence of evidence to the contrary. This is sometimes referred to as imposing on the defendant a provisional or tactical burden...In my opinion, this is not a true burden of proof, and the use of an additional label to describe what is an ordinary step in the fact finding process is unwarranted'; quoted with approval by Toulson LJ in *Drake* v *Harbour* [2008] EWCA Civ 25, [26].

[38] For philosophical analysis, see Edna Ullmann-Margalit, 'On Presumption' (1983) 80 *Journal of Philosophy* 143.

[39] See, e.g., *Bratty* v *Attorney General of Northern Ireland* [1963] AC 386, HL (also referring to a 'presumption of mental capacity'); *R* v *Dickie* [1984] 1 WLR 1031, 1036, CA.

[40] 'Every man is assumed to be sane at the time of an alleged offence, and accordingly the burden is on the defendant to establish insanity at the time of the commission of the offence on the balance of probabilities': *DPP* v *Harper* [1997] 1 WLR 1406, 1409, DC.

Legal doctrine, more pointedly, does not obey our linguistic stipulations: in fact, it openly flouts them. According to what might be regarded as the 'classical' taxonomy,[41] presumptions are divided into three groups – only the third of which is a true legal presumption on the conception we have stipulated. First, so-called *presumptions of fact* arise where the court may draw a particular factual inference from the existence of a certain set of facts. On a charge of handling stolen goods, for example, if the accused fails to provide a credible explanation for his possession of recently stolen goods, a presumption of guilty knowledge is said to arise.[42] Such alleged 'presumptions' merely restate the normal inferential process, articulating what the jury might, as a matter of ordinary logic and common sense, infer from the accused's possession of recently stolen goods. Presumptions of fact link circumstances which commonly occur in conjunction. Fact *B* may be inferred from fact *A* because *A* and *B* usually occur together; and the inference is even stronger where *A* seldom occurs without *B*. The so-called 'presumption of continuance', permitting the trier of fact to 'presume' the existence of a state of affairs from its existence at an earlier point in time, is another common sense inference of this type. Thus, it may be inferred that *V* was still alive at the relevant time if a witness saw *V* hale and healthy a short time before.[43] Such 'presumptions of fact' do not involve any formal distribution of risk of error. Indeed, since factual inferences remain to be drawn in the normal way, talk of presumptions in this context is completely redundant.[44]

The second classical category of presumptions consists of *irrebuttable presumptions of law*. This type of presumption entails that, upon proof of certain basic facts, the court is duty-bound to find the existence of another fact or facts, irrespective of the availability of evidence indicating the true state of affairs, and possibly contradicting the presumed fact. A well-known irrebuttable presumption is that all persons know the law.[45] Another is that children under ten years-of-age lack 'mischievous direction', i.e. the capacity to be held criminally responsible for their wrongful acts. In substance, however, these are not procedural rules allocating the distribution of probative risk in adjudication, but substantive rules of criminal liability. The first is a corruption of the maxim that 'ignorance of the law is no excuse' (*ignorantia juris non excusat*),[46] whilst the second rule establishes ten years-of-age as the minimum threshold of criminal liability.[47] In these

---

[41] Cf. *Al-Amoudi v Brisard* [2007] 1 WLR 113, [2006] EWHC 1062 (QB), [29], endorsing the orthodox tripartite classification presented in *Phipson on Evidence* (Sweet & Maxwell, 16th edn. 2005).

[42] See, for example, *R v Pieterson* [1995] 1 WLR 293, CA; *R v Raviraj* (1987) 85 Cr App R 93, CA; *R v Ball and Winning* (1983) 77 Cr App R 131, CA; *R v Langmead* (1864) L & C 427; *R v Partridge* (1836) 7 C & P 551; *R v Adams* (1829) 3 C & P 600.

[43] See *R v Lumley* (1869) LR 1 CCR 196; *R v Tolson* (1889) 23 QBD 168, CCR.

[44] Another (archaic) example of this redundancy is characterizing the tendency of proven facts to support a certain conclusion as giving rise to 'a presumption' in favour of that conclusion: cf. *In Re White's Charities* [1898] 1 Ch 659, 665; *The Laurel* (1863) Brown. & Lush. 191, 198; 167 ER 330, 335.

[45] 'A man is presumed to know the law': *Burrows v Rhodes* [1899] 1 QB 816, 829.

[46] 'The rule is not, that a man is always presumed to know the law, but that no man shall be excused for an unlawful act from his ignorance of the law': *R v Bentley* (1850) 4 Cox CC 408, 410 (Talfourd J), quoted with approval by Rose LJ in *R v Lee* [2001] 1 Cr App R 293, CA, [12]. And see *Evans v Bartlam* [1937] AC 473, 479 *per* Lord Atkin: 'The fact is that there is not and never has been a presumption that every one knows the law. There is the rule that ignorance of the law does not excuse, a maxim of very different scope and application.'

[47] The minimum age of criminal responsibility has been placed on a statutory footing: Children and Young Persons Act 1933, s.50 (as amended). For the legislative history, see *R v JTB* [2009] UKHL 20, [2009] 2 Cr App R 13.

and other analogous cases, it is more convenient and transparent simply to state the relevant positive rule of criminal law, avoiding the terminology of presumption altogether. Parliament nonetheless still chooses to employ the circumlocutory formula of 'irrebuttable presumption'.[48]

Only the third classical category, *rebuttable presumptions of law*, corresponds to our central stipulated case of the risk-allocating evidentiary presumption. These rules permit or require presumed facts to be established *by operation of law*, on proof of a basic or triggering fact or facts, without the necessity of adducing evidence in the normal way. We will later complicate the picture slightly by differentiating between permissive and mandatory risk-allocating presumptions. But for the remainder of this section we can greatly simplify matters by dispensing with the conceptual language of the classical taxonomy and reserving the term 'presumption' to our stipulated meaning, *legal presumptions of fact*.

English criminal law makes extensive use of evidential presumptions as a technique of risk-allocation in adjudication. Only some of these devices are couched in the explicit language of presumption; in other instances the same effect is achieved through a variety of standard linguistic formulations. In the modern law, the most important presumptions are statutory, but there is also a residual stock of common law presumptions which occasionally feature in criminal litigation. These presumptions serve diverse substantive and evidentiary policies.[49] For example, the common law presumes that a person who disappears for seven years and is never seen or heard of during that time despite diligent inquiry must be dead.[50] This is a genuine legal presumption of fact: absence for seven years does not *prove* death as a matter of logic and common sense, though it might raise suspicions and concern. The legal presumption operates to resolve quickly and conclusively an issue frequently contested in litigation (e.g. regarding matters of probate and succession) where prolonged uncertainty would be unacceptably disruptive for legal entitlements and duties. Another well-known common law presumption, usually associated with civil negligence claims rather than criminal prosecutions,[51] is *res ipsa loquitur* – 'the matter speaks for itself'.[52] This presumption typically assists a claimant

---

[48] An important recent example is Sexual Offences Act 2003, s.76, creating 'conclusive presumption about consent'. See *R v Jheeta* [2008] 1 WLR 2582, [2007] EWCA Crim 1699.

[49] A presumption might reflect the perceived probative significance of the basic fact but, in the case of true presumptions, there has to be a reason for wishing to give legal support to inferences that would otherwise in any event follow from the probative force of the basic fact.

[50] *Thomas v Thomas* (1864) 2 Drewry and Smale 298; 62 ER 635. 'One of the well known presumptions of law is the presumption of death presumed after evidence of seven years' absence': *Campbell v Wallsend Slipway and Engineering Co. Ltd.* [1978] ICR 1015, 1025, QBD (Eveleigh J). The common law presumption was written into English criminal law as a 'proviso' defence to bigamy in the Offences Against the Person Act 1861, s.57: see *R v Taylor* [1950] 2 KB 368, CCA; *R v Tolson* (1889) LR 23 QBD 168, CCR. A related example can be found in Law of Property Act 1925, s.184, providing that, where two or more persons have died in circumstances rendering the order of their demise uncertain, it shall be assumed that they died in order of seniority, eldest to youngest.

[51] But cf. *Penny v Hanson* (1887) LR 18, QBD 478, where, on a charge of 'pretending or professing to tell fortunes', Denman J. peremptorily dismissed a claim of a genuine belief in supernatural powers: 'In this case *res ipsa loquitur*. It is absurd to suggest that this man could have believed in his ability to predict the fortunes of another by knowing the hour and place of his birth and the aspect of the stars at such time. We do not live in times when any sane man believes in such a power.'

[52] *Scott v London and St Katherine Docks Co* (1865) 3 H & C 596.

in proving causation, where it is felt that it would be unfair to require full proof in the circumstances (e.g. because an accident has been caused by a process or machinery over which the defendant has control and the claimant cannot be expected to know exactly what went wrong).[53] Claims of *res ipsa loquitur* hover around the borderline separating genuine evidentiary presumptions and mere descriptions of the normal inferential process.[54] Other (so-called) presumptions are designed to ensure that one party does not enjoy an unfair or politically unacceptable probative advantage in litigation. The 'presumption of sanity' in criminal cases, for instance, is intended to prevent the accused from faking mental illness and exploiting a plea of insanity to evade his just deserts.[55] Since the rationales for presumptions are as numerous and open-ended as the rules and policies of substantive law they are designed to promote, the quest for a 'unified theory' of presumptions capable of reducing all legal presumptions to a conceptual formula is a fool's errand. Presumptions are found in family law, matrimonial law, the law of succession, land law, torts and contracts, as well as in criminal jurisprudence. It would be very surprising if a single set of *evidentiary* doctrines and concepts could classify and rationalize this great diversity, and there is no reason to believe that any such comprehensive theory could be constructed. To the contrary, a history of failed attempts confirms the folly of the exercise.

Whilst common law presumptions sometimes arise in criminal proceedings, the most frequently encountered presumptions are those attached by Parliament to particular statutory offences. By way of concrete illustration, Figure 6.1 provides three examples of provisions relating to statutory offences expressly creating evidentiary presumptions. They follow a familiar pattern. In each case, once certain triggering fact(s) have been established – a dangerous dog is seen in public; being the parent of a child who has not attended school; intimidating a witness or juror, etc. – further fact(s) are treated as established 'unless the contrary is proved' (or 'shown', etc). The typical effect, as in these three examples, is to relieve the prosecution of the burden of proving offence elements which are likely to be especially inconvenient or difficult to prove, whether *actus reus* elements such as the breed of an apparently dangerous dog or a child's age on a particular day, or *mens rea* elements such as motive or ulterior intent. At the same time as the prosecution is relieved of its burden, a corresponding probative burden is placed on the accused to rebut the presumption, on the balance of probabilities.

---

[53] 'Where the thing is shown to be under the management of the defendant or his servants and the accident is such as in the ordinary course of things does not happen if those who have the management use proper care, it affords reasonable evidence, in the absence of explanation by the defendants that the accident arose from want of care': ibid. 601, *per* Earl CJ. Also see *Barkway* v *South Wales Transport Company Limited* [1950] 1 All ER 392, HL.

[54] Thus, in *Lloyd* v *West Midlands Gas Board* [1971] 1 WLR 749, 755, McGaw LJ remarked: 'I doubt whether it is right to describe *res ipsa loquitur* as a "doctrine". I think that it is no more than an exotic, although convenient, phrase to describe what is in essence no more than a common sense approach, not limited by technical rules, to the assessment of the effect of evidence in certain circumstances. It means that a plaintiff *prima facie* establishes negligence where: (i) it is not possible for him to prove precisely what was the relevant act or omission which set in train the events leading to the accident; but (ii) on the evidence as it stands at the relevant time it is more likely than not that the effective cause of the accident was some act or omission of the defendant or of someone for whom the defendant is responsible, which act or omission constitutes a failure to take proper care for the plaintiff's safety.'

[55] Though it is questionable whether it is justified to impose a burden of persuasion on an accused to prove lack of sanity: see §6.6, below.

Fig. 6.1 Statutory Presumptions (emphasis supplied in each case).

1. **Dangerous Dogs Act 1991, s.5 (seizure, entry of premises and evidence)**
   (1)   A constable or an officer of a local authority authorised by it to exercise the powers conferred by this subsection may seize—
   - (a)   any dog which appears to him to be a [pit bull terrier or other designated fighting breed] and which is in a public place—
     - (i)   after the time when possession or custody of it has become unlawful by virtue of that section; or
     - (ii)   before that time, without being muzzled and kept on a lead;
   - (b)   any dog in a public place which appears to him to be a dog to which an order under section 2 above applies [other dangerous breeds] and in respect of which an offence against the order has been or is being committed; and
   - (c)   any dog in a public place (whether or not one to which that section or such an order applies) which appears to him to be dangerously out of control…

   (5)   If in any proceedings it is alleged by the prosecution that a dog is one to which section 1or an order under section 2 above applies it *shall be presumed* that it is such a dog unless the contrary is shown by the accused by such evidence as the court considers sufficient…

2. **Education Act 1996, s.445 (presumption of age in relation to truancy)**
   (1)   This section applies for the purposes of any proceedings for an offence under section 443 or 444 [liability of parent for child's failure to attend compulsory schooling or breach of an attendance order]

   (2)   In so far as it is material, the child in question *shall be presumed* to have been of compulsory school age at any time unless the parent proves the contrary.

3. **Criminal Justice and Public Order Act 1994, s.51 (interfering with justice by intimidating a witness or juror)**
   (1)   A person who does to another person–
   - (a)   an act which intimidates, and is intended to intimidate, that other person;
   - (b)   knowing or believing that the other person is assisting in the investigation of an offence or is a witness or potential witness or a juror or potential juror in proceedings for an offence; and
   - (c)   intending thereby to cause the investigation or the course of justice to be obstructed, perverted or interfered with,
   commits an offence.

   (2)   A person who does or threatens to do to another person–
   - (a)   an act which harms or would harm, and is intended to harm, that other person;
   - (b)   knowing or believing that the other person, or some other person, has assisted in an investigation into an offence or has given evidence or particular evidence in proceedings for an offence, or has acted as a juror or concurred in a particular verdict in proceedings for an offence; and
   - (c)   does or threatens to do the act because of what (within paragraph (b)) he knows or believes,
   commits an offence...

   (7)   If, in proceedings against a person for an offence under subsection (1) above, it is proved that he did an act falling within paragraph (a) with the knowledge or belief required by paragraph (b), he *shall be presumed*, unless the contrary is proved, to have done the act with the intention required by paragraph (c) of that subsection.

   (8)   If, in proceedings against a person for an offence under subsection (2) above, it is proved that he did or threatened to do an act falling within paragraph (a) within the relevant period with the knowledge or belief required by paragraph (b), he *shall be presumed*, unless the contrary is proved, to have done the act with the motive required by paragraph (c) of that subsection.

Statutory presumptions can also be created through the equivalent language of 'deeming', as section 2 of the Prevention of Corruption Act 1916, set out in Figure 6.2, shows:

Fig. 6.2 Presumption by 'deeming' (emphasis supplied)

Prevention of Corruption Act 1916, s.2 – corruption in the award of governmental contracts

Where in any proceedings against a person for an offence under the Prevention of Corruption Act 1906, or the Public Bodies Corrupt Practices Act 1889, it is proved that any money, gift, or other consideration has been paid or given to or received by a person in the employment of His Majesty or any Government Department or a public body by or from a person, or agent of a person, holding or seeking to obtain a contract from His Majesty or any Government Department or public body, the money, gift, or consideration *shall be deemed* to have been paid or given and received corruptly as such inducement or reward as is mentioned in such Act unless the contrary is proved.

Although section 2 of the 1916 does not expressly say that anything 'shall be presumed', the legislative technique of 'deeming' (in this context) achieves exactly the same effect. The element of 'corruption' is plainly a vital part of the offence of giving or receiving corrupt payments, yet the prosecution need not prove it. One it is shown that payments have passed between contractors and public officials, corruption is *presumed* 'unless the contrary is proved'. The rationale for reversing the onus here is not difficult to reconstruct (and is related to the thinking behind the reverse onus clauses in the Sexual Offences Act 2003 discussed below). Corrupt payments are clandestine, difficult to detect, and easily camouflaged or explained away on some pretext or other if they do happen to be discovered. If the prosecution were required to prove the existence of a corrupt motive beyond reasonable doubt many offenders might evade justice, so Parliament has decided that those who make or receive such payments must affirmatively prove their *bona fides* and thereby displace the presumption of corruption. This is how and why section 2's presumption operates: whether such reverse onus clauses can be regarded as *legitimate* derogations from the presumption of innocence is a question we will tackle later in the chapter.

Presumptions are also regularly employed in conjunction with formalities provisions. A good example is section 74 of PACE 1984, regarding the proof of previous offending, which we encountered in Chapter 3.[56] Subsection 74(2) provides that: 'In any proceedings in which by virtue of this section a person other than the accused is proved to have been convicted of an offence by or before any court in the United Kingdom or by a Service court outside the United Kingdom, *he shall be taken to have committed that offence* unless the contrary is proved'. Subsection (3) establishes a parallel presumption in relation to *the accused's* previous convictions as evidence of guilt 'in so far as that evidence is relevant to any matter in issue in the proceedings for a reason other than a tendency to show in the

---

[56] §3.4(a).

accused a disposition to commit the kind of offence with which he is charged'. As well as supplying several examples of statutory presumptions concerned with the formalities of proof, PACE section 74 also demonstrates another form of words that can be used to create presumptions. The 'shall be taken' formulation is an alternative mode of 'deeming' facts proved by statutory mandate.

The presumptions considered thus far are accompanied by probative burdens, requiring an accused to rebut the presumed fact on the balance of probabilities. However, the technique of presumption may also be used to distribute the burden of adducing evidence – the burden of production.[57] Suppose that in a civil action the claimant's case requires him to prove that a certain person public official was duly appointed. General principles would normally dictate that the burden of proving an authorized appointment in the legally prescribed form would rest with the claimant, who is the proponent on that issue. However, there is a common law presumption of regularity – *omnia praesumuntur rite esse acta*[58] – which would operate to relieve the claimant from adducing evidence to prove proper authorization in the first instance. If he shows that the person in question purported to act in the requisite capacity, the court will proceed on the basis that the official was duly appointed, unless and until another litigant produces evidence to the contrary. Only after an opponent has produced sufficient evidence of lack of authority to 'pass the judge' would the proponent be required to prove every aspect of a valid appointment to the requisite standard (i.e. the balance of probabilities in civil litigation). Sufficient evidence means, in this context, evidence from which an irregularity in the officer's appointment might reasonably be inferred. Section 76 of PACE, which governs the admissibility of confession evidence, has a similar structure.[59] Confessions are rendered *prima facie* admissible by section 76(1). But if an accused adduces evidence that the confession might have been obtained by oppression or in circumstances conducive to unreliability (an evidential burden), the prosecution is obliged to disprove the allegation of oppression or unreliability beyond reasonable doubt – a probative burden. Another important recent example of a presumption adopting the 'shall be taken' formulation imposing only a burden of production is set out in Figure 6.3.

The practical significance of presumptions is dictated by the procedural contexts in which they operate. In criminal proceedings, fact-finders' assessment of evidence is holistic, not sequential or piecemeal, and takes place only when the parties have concluded their cases. Criminal trials are not interrupted midstream in order to determine whether the proponent has discharged his burden in respect of a particular triggering fact or whether, if so, his opponent has nonetheless succeeded in producing sufficient evidence to rebut

---

[57] Glanville Williams distinguished 'evidential presumptions' and 'persuasive presumptions', whilst Lord Denning dubbed the latter 'compelling presumptions': see Glanville Williams, *Criminal Law: The General Part* (Stevens, 2nd edn. 1961), ch 23; A. T. Denning, 'Presumptions and Burdens' (1945) 61 *LQR* 379; *Edwards v The Minister of Pensions* [1947] KB 564, KBD. Also see Nigel Bridge, 'Presumptions and Burdens' (1949) 12 *MLR* 273. Specialist terminology to differentiate types of onus-reversing presumption never caught on; and for the sake of clarity it is always advisable – for legislators and judges, as much as for legal commentators – to spell out the consequences of any particular presumption.

[58] All deeds are presumed to have been done in accordance with the requisite formalities, absent proof to the contrary. This is a venerable common law maxim: see, for example, *R v Gordon* (1789) 1 Leach 515; *R v Rees* (1834) 6 C & P 606. For modern applications, see *Standard Commercial Property Securities Ltd v Glasgow City Council (No 2)* [2006] UKHL 50, [74] (Lord Brown); *Campbell v Wallsend Shipway and Engineering Co Ltd* [1977] Crim LR 351, DC.   [59] See Chapter 12.

Fig. 6.3 Presumption by 'is to be taken' imposing burden of production (emphasis supplied).

Sexual Offences Act 2003, s. 75 – Evidential presumptions about consent
(1) If in proceedings for an offence to which this section applies it is proved–
    (a) that the defendant did the relevant act,
    (b) that any of the circumstances specified in subsection (2) existed, and
    (c) that the defendant knew that those circumstances existed,

the complainant *is to be taken* not to have consented to the relevant act unless sufficient evidence is adduced to raise an issue as to whether he consented, and the defendant *is to be taken* not to have reasonably believed that the complainant consented unless sufficient evidence is adduced to raise an issue as to whether he reasonably believed it.

(2) The circumstances are that–
    (a) any person was, at the time of the relevant act or immediately before it began, using violence against the complainant or causing the complainant to fear that immediate violence would be used against him;
    (b) any person was, at the time of the relevant act or immediately before it began, causing the complainant to fear that violence was being used, or that immediate violence would be used, against another person;
    (c) the complainant was, and the defendant was not, unlawfully detained at the time of the relevant act;
    (d) the complainant was asleep or otherwise unconscious at the time of the relevant act;
    (e) because of the complainant's physical disability, the complainant would not have been able at the time of the relevant act to communicate to the defendant whether the complainant consented;
    (f) any person had administered to or caused to be taken by the complainant, without the complainant's consent, a substance which, having regard to when it was administered or taken, was capable of causing or enabling the complainant to be stupefied or overpowered at the time of the relevant act ...

---

the presumed fact. There is no 'time out' to see whether a party has discharged his burden of adducing evidence on an isolated issue, and no 'running commentary' on the 'state of play'. Whereas parties to civil proceedings are nowadays generally quite well-informed about the nature of each other's claims and evidence through extensive pre-trial disclosure and mutual service of witness statements,[60] cards-to-chest secrecy has traditionally been the default setting in criminal proceedings (albeit that recent years have witnessed major departures from the traditional philosophy).[61] The prosecution must make a more-or-less educated guess about the accused's next move, on the basis of patchy and limited pre-trial disclosure (including the defence statement)[62] and whatever evidence has emerged thus far in the course of the trial. This relative uncertainty reduces the practical utility of presumptions in criminal trials, as well as making their operation more difficult for the theorist to

---

[60] See *Zuckerman on Civil Procedure* (Sweet & Maxwell, 2nd edn. 2006), esp. chs 1 and 14.
[61] §2.3(c)(ii).   [62] CPIA 1996, ss.5–6E.

observe. It would be imprudent for either party to bank on benefiting from a presumption when there is no telling how a fact-finder will evaluate the evidence presented in the trial. To be on the safe side, prosecution and defence alike will try, if they can, to strengthen their respective cases by adducing positive evidence to supplant the need for presumptions.

The practical utility of a presumption is further diminished to the extent that the pre-conditional 'triggering' fact or facts are themselves open to challenge. To continue with the examples of statutory presumptions given in Figures 6.1 to 6.3: instead of attempting to rebut the presumption of consent, the accused could deny sexual contact; instead of quibbling about their child's age, parents might claim that their child was not absent from school on the days in question, or was absent for legitimate reasons (such as illness); rather than seeking to dislodge the presumption of intent to pervert the course of justice, the accused might deny outright any allegation of intimidating a witness or juror; and rather than, or in addition to, denying a corrupt motive, the accused might contest the proof that he ever received any gift. Section 74 of PACE 1984 is deliberately constructed to reduce the scope for challenging a certificate of conviction,[63] but even here it is possible – if unlikely – that a challenge to the form of the certificate could succeed. Tactical decisions have to be made in the light of all the circumstances of particular cases. It will often serve a party's interests to contest the issue on both fronts, by attacking the underlying basic fact and simultaneously seeking to rebut the fact that would otherwise be presumed against him if the basic fact is proved to the tribunal's satisfaction.

The statutory presumptions set out in Figures 6.1–6.3 can all be described as *mandatory* (legal) presumptions (of fact). Mandatory presumptions require that a court *shall* draw the directed inference, normally adding 'unless the contrary is proved' or words to that effect. Other statutory presumptions, by contrast, are merely *permissive*: they permit, but do not require, the specified inference(s) to be drawn. Permissive presumptions can be genuine (legal) presumptions satisfying our stipulated definition provided that they authorize factual conclusions going beyond the realms of ordinary common sense inferences. A recent illustration can be found in section 57 of the Terrorism Act 2000, which makes it an offence to possess ordinary, everyday articles in circumstances giving rise to a reasonable suspicion that they are possessed for a terrorist purpose. Section 57 is set out in Figure 6.4.

This is a textbook permissive presumption. Subsection 57(3) permits – but does not require – the court to infer that the accused had possession of articles merely from his physical proximity to them or from their discovery on his property. Although the court is allowed to choose whether or not to draw the inference, section 57(3) nonetheless facilitates a genuine presumption, allowing facts to be presumed against the accused that have not otherwise been proved by evidence to the criminal standard, and thereby imposing on the accused the onus of disproving possession. This hallmark legal effect distinguishes the operation of section 57(3) from the so-called factual presumptions, the first category of the

---

[63] PACE s.75(1) renders admissible '(a) the contents of any document which is admissible as evidence of the conviction; and (b) the contents of the information, complaint, indictment or charge-sheet on which the person in question was convicted.' Subsection (2) goes on to provide that:

Where in any proceedings the contents of any document are admissible in evidence by virtue of subsection (1) above, a copy of that document, or of the material part of it, purporting to be certified or otherwise authenticated by or on behalf of the court or authority having custody of that document shall be admissible in evidence and shall be taken to be a true copy of that document or part unless the contrary is shown.

This section, in other words, creates a presumption of authenticity to establish the factual trigger for a presumption of rightful conviction!

Fig. 6.4 Permissive statutory presumption (emphasis supplied)

Terrorism Act 2000, s.57 – Possession for terrorist purposes
(1) A person commits an offence if he possesses an article in circumstances which give rise to a reasonable suspicion that his possession is for a purpose connected with the commission, preparation or instigation of an act of terrorism.

(2) It is a defence for a person charged with an offence under this section to prove that his possession of the article was not for a purpose connected with the commission, preparation or instigation of an act of terrorism.

(3) In proceedings for an offence under this section, if it is proved that an article–
    (a) was on any premises at the same time as the accused, or
    (b) was on premises of which the accused was the occupier or which he habitually
        used otherwise than as a member of the public,
the court may assume that the accused possessed the article, unless he proves that he did not know of its presence on the premises or that he had no control over it.

classical trichotomy, which merely (and entirely superfluously) purport to authorize the normal inferential process. It is precisely because 'possession' often *cannot* be inferred, as a straightforward common sense conclusion, from mere physical proximity to one's person or property – at least not to the requisite standard of proof, beyond reasonable doubt – that Parliament saw fit to arm prosecutors in terrorist cases with an auxiliary evidentiary presumption. Section 57(3) is a standing invitation to treat mere proximity as the equivalent of possession; albeit that, since the presumption is permissive ('may assume') rather than mandatory, it must be necessary to consider the surrounding factual circumstances in order to decide whether to invoke the presumption in any particular case. This train of thought is in danger of collapsing into ordinary inferential reasoning – or perhaps that is its salvation. Section 57's reverse onus clause is especially controversial, because – where it operates – the presumption serves to lessen an already exceptionally light probative burden in prosecutions of the relevant offences. Reverse onus clauses merit extended discussion, and we return to them in §6.5 below.

6.3 PHILOSOPHICAL FOUNDATIONS OF THE PRESUMPTION OF INNOCENCE – THE POLITICAL MORALITY OF *WOOLMINGTON*

The conceptual analysis undertaken in the last section clarifies how probative burdens, burdens of production, and evidentiary presumptions allocate the risk of error in litigation. It is now time to extract the important moral and political principles embedded in these evidentiary techniques of risk-allocation.

The protection of the innocent from conviction was identified in Chapter 1 as a foundational principle of criminal evidence.[64] Its significance derives directly from the

---

[64] §1.3.

neo-Kantian, deontological requirement that, at least in broadly liberal societies, the interests of individual citizens must be afforded high priority in government policy and administration, sometimes at the expense of maximizing aggregate social welfare. Liberal societies, as the political philosopher John Rawls pithily summarized in a brilliant turn of phrase, 'take seriously the distinction between persons'.[65] A major implication of the idea of 'taking persons seriously' is that governments and political communities (should) have appropriate regard for personal autonomy and other fundamental interests of individual citizens. People have a profound interest in not being publicly censured and punished for crimes of which they are innocent, or, at least, for which they cannot be held fully responsible. Chapter 1's thumbnail sketch of retributive justice indicates why this is not simply a question of misapplying the material deprivations of penal hard-treatment, like fines, community service, or imprisonment; though that is certainly a relevant consideration. More fundamentally, to resent wrongful censure is a psychologically basic, characteristically human trait, which goes to the very core of personhood and identity. The moral parameters of doing, deserving, and being are intimately related in the evaluation of human activity, and their dynamic configurations are a potent force in all our public and private lives.

A trivial, though probably widely recognizable and therefore telling, illustration of how deeply we resent even small injustices is to notice how minor grievances suffered as a child – e.g. being blamed by one's parents for the misbehaviour of a sibling; or a teacher's unfair rebuke for lack of application to one's schoolwork – can be nursed long into adulthood. Closer to our present subject matter, those tireless public campaigns to reverse 'miscarriages of justice' are another, more pronounced, manifestation of the indomitable human desire to have the public slander of unjustified censure expunged. People think it worthwhile 'fighting to clear their name' even after they have been released from prison, and campaigns 'for justice' are continued beyond the grave by relatives and friends seeking to rehabilitate the reputation of a deceased loved one. The posthumous victories won for Timothy Evans and Derek Bentley, both of whom were hanged for murder and later exonerated, are cases in point.[66] Perhaps the most powerful illustrations, however, are those cases in which a prisoner would be eligible for parole if he admitted guilt, yet steadfastly continues to protest his innocence at the price of remaining in custody.[67] The lengths to which people are prepared to go in order to erase the stain of unjustified censure graphically demonstrate the strength of feeling which a miscarriage of justice evokes. A legal

---

[65] John Rawls, *A Theory of Justice* (OUP, revd. edn. 1999 [1971]), 24.

[66] See Ludovic Kennedy, *10 Rillington Place* (Grafton, 1971 [1961]); *R v Derek William Bentley (Deceased)* [2001] 1 Cr App R 307, CA.

[67] As in the case of Stephen Downing, released after spending an additional ten years in prison, on top of his seventeen-year tariff for murder, because he continued to assert his innocence. Downing is reported as saying: 'they told me I could go to a nice warm prison if only I would admit murder, that I should stop causing trouble for them and myself.... They denied me my right to have a parole hearing because they said I was "in denial." During my whole 27 years in prison, the staff would try to persuade me to confess. It seems as if they were having some sort of competition to see who could be the one that made me finally admit it. It was always pressure, pressure, pressure. But I was optimistic that we would win in the end. It was hard work, but I believed in myself. I wanted to clear my name': Jeevan Vasagar, 'Downing Tells of Pressure to Admit Killing', *The Guardian*, 12 February 2001. Downing's murder conviction was finally quashed by the Court of Appeal on 15 January 2002: see Vasagar, 'End of a Nightmare' *The Guardian*, 16 January 2002; *R v Stephen Lesley Downing* [2002] EWCA Crim 263.

process systematically prone to inflicting such serious wrongs, so that – as the nineteenth century reformer Romilly graphically put it – 'each wretch that goes to the scaffold may be an innocent victim',[68] would not only fail to inspire public confidence.[69] It would also flunk the more fundamental liberal litmus-test of taking individuals, and their rights and interests, seriously.

Unfortunately, of course, the pristine ideal eludes practical realization. As a human and therefore fallible set of institutions and processes, criminal proceedings carry an unavoidable risk of error: some people who are truly guilty are going to be acquitted or, more likely, never detected or prosecuted in the first place,[70] and some poor unfortunates who are innocent – at least of the instant charge – will be wrongly convicted and punished. Institutional error and bad practice account for a certain percentage of mistakes. Criminal process is exceedingly complex, and many different things can go wrong in any particular case.[71] For example: police officers may overlook potentially exculpatory evidence or otherwise present a distorted picture of reality in their 'construction' of the case for the prosecution; prosecutors may fail to disclose crucial information to the defence; the accused may receive poor quality legal advice and representation; the judge might present a skewed summary of the facts to the jury, or give an erroneous direction of law; and jurors might make reasoning errors leading them to return verdicts not supported by the evidence. Such institutional errors are in principle remediable, and a society committed to liberty and justice should strive to remedy them as best it can. Procedural law reform is an essential component of this project, though here, as elsewhere, one must steadfastly resist the simplistic notion that the world can be made a better place *simply* by designing a better set of rules. As we explained in Chapters 3 and 4, attitudes, beliefs, preferences, and 'common sense' knowledge are also crucial determinants of fact-finding in criminal proceedings, and these features of adjudication cannot be dictated by legal doctrine. But legal rules *can* make a difference, by expressing official value-choices and structuring the process of fact-finding. So it is important that rules of evidence and procedure should be refined to the best of our abilities, even though procedural reform can only ever be one dimension of doing justice in practical settings.

Other types of probative error are still less amenable to conscious correction. Eyewitness identification evidence, for example, is notoriously unreliable, but it is also an indispensable

[68] Sir Samuel Romilly, *Observations on the Criminal Law of England* (T. Cadell and W. Davies, 1810), Note D, quoted in T. B. Howell, 7 State Trials (32 Charles II, 1680), 1529.

[69] Cf. Justice Brennan's observation that the 'use of the reasonable doubt standard is indispensable to command the respect and the confidence of the community in its applications of the criminal law. It is critical that the moral force of the criminal law not be diluted by a standard of proof that leaves people in doubt whether innocent men are being condemned': *In re Winship*, 397 US 358, 364 (1970).

[70] Detection rates vary dramatically by offence type, but are currently estimated to be in the region of 28% on average: Alison Walker, John Flatley, Chris Kershaw, and Debbie Moon (eds.), *Crime in England and Wales 2008/09*, Home Office Statistical Bulletin 11/09 (RDS, July 2009), ch 6. Only a small proportion of police detentions results in a conviction or caution. Formerly, the Home Office's best guess has been that approximately 3% of all offences are successfully investigated and prosecuted or cautioned, but there are strong methodological grounds for considering this a substantial *over*estimate: Home Office, *Digest 4: Information on the Criminal Justice System in England and Wales* (RDS, October 1999), 29.

[71] On the causes of 'miscarriages of justice', see Clive Walker, 'Miscarriages of Justice and the Correction of Error', in Mike McConville and Geoffrey Wilson (eds.), *The Handbook of the Criminal Justice Process* (OUP, 2002); Clive Walker and Keir Starmer (eds.), *Miscarriages of Justice: A Review of Justice in Error* (Blackstone, 1999).

source of proof. Short of excluding identification evidence altogether, it is impossible to be sure that an apparently confident, truthful, and persuasive eyewitness account will not lead to a wrongful conviction.[72] Equally, the law can only go so far in vouchsafing the reliability of confession evidence.[73] For example, if people with undetected personality disorders are intent on giving apparently plausible, albeit false, confessions to crimes they did not commit,[74] it is likely that some of them will be convicted without anyone being any the wiser. But for all that, it is insufficient answer to the criticism of miscarriage of justice that no particular criminal process agency or professional can be singled out as individually at fault for making a mistake. Criminal verdicts are measured against the external, real-world standard of guilt and innocence, not merely in terms of procedural propriety.[75] Without this stabilizing anchorage in external truths, criminal procedure cannot serve its function of apportioning blame for criminal wrongdoing whilst safeguarding rights under the rule of law.[76] In criminal proceedings, in short, getting *the right result* is no less important than maintaining due process of law. Hence, as Chapter 1 stated, accurate fact-finding should be regarded as the first foundational principle of criminal evidence.[77] If it later transpires that the result was erroneous criminal adjudication will be judged to have miscarried, even though procedural rectitude might have been observed to the letter in arriving at the original verdict. To borrow Nesson's handy slogan, criminal proceedings are first and foremost concerned with 'the event, not the evidence'.[78]

The only sure-fire, fool-proof way of avoiding wrongful conviction of the innocent would be to abandon criminal proceedings altogether. But that certainly would *not* promote criminal justice, which mandates justified censure and punishment of wrongdoers and deterrence of future criminality. Liberal respect for persons and the ideal of retributive justice, sketched in Chapter 1,[79] combine to reinforce the state's responsibility to formulate and implement effective criminal justice policies. Whilst the harmfulness of some crimes is open to doubt,[80] it is clear that much criminal activity threatens individuals' fundamental interests in life, liberty, bodily security, freedom of movement, and the quiet

---

[72] Eyewitness identification evidence is discussed in §15.4.   [73] See Chapter 12.

[74] As did Judith Ward, who served 17 years for the M62 coach bomb murders (though in that case Ward's own fantasizing was compounded by a catalogue of official errors and impropriety): *R v Ward* [1993] 1 WLR 619, CA.

[75] Some of the complexities of mediating between legal fact-finding and social conceptions of 'the truth' are explored by Richard Nobles and David Schiff, *Understanding Miscarriages of Justice* (OUP, 2000).

[76] This is a fundamental point of agreement amongst otherwise divergent conceptions of the law of evidence: see, e.g., Larry Laudan, *Truth, Error, and Criminal Law: An Essay in Legal Epistemology* (CUP, 2006); Hock Lai Ho, *A Philosophy of Evidence Law: Justice in the Search for Truth* (OUP, 2008), chs 2–3.

[77] §1.3.

[78] Cf. Charles Nesson, 'The Evidence or the Event? On Judicial Proof and the Acceptability of Verdicts' (1985) 98 *Harvard LR* 1357, 1358, 1361: 'The judicial process must somehow accomplish an inductive leap from the evidence presented to a statement about a past event. Only then can the public accept the verdict and the judicial sanction as exemplifying the legal rule and affirming its behavioural message.' Our position builds on Nesson's insight, but goes further in insisting that criminal adjudication must be worthy of public confidence as well as actually securing it. This is not simply a question of conveying a 'behavioural message' effectively, as Nesson seems to suggest. Also see Hock Lai Ho, *A Philosophy of Evidence Law* (OUP, 2008), 60.   [79] §1.2.

[80] As on-going debates surrounding the (de)criminalization of cannabis possession and other 'harmless' or minor infringements of regulatory norms well illustrate: see Richard B. Macrory, *Regulatory Justice: Making Sanctions Effective – Final Report* (Better Regulation Executive, 2006), www.berr.gov.uk/files/file44593.pdf; Lord Justice Auld, *Review of the Criminal Courts of England and Wales* (TSO, 2001), ch 9.

enjoyment of property. Punishing and deterring such attacks on individual interests is not only compatible with liberal philosophy, but positively demanded by it. Liberal governments respect persons by helping to protect their citizens' vital interests, not by leaving people to fend for themselves, so that only the strongest and fittest survive, with open season to victimize the rest.

The liberal state is subject to these competing claims and pressures. On the one hand, it must establish an effective criminal process to punish and deter wrongdoing in order to protect citizens' vital interests and deliver justice. Yet, at the same time, all human beings have a fundamental right not to be subjected to the profound harm of wrongful conviction and punishment. The presumption of innocence and the evidentiary rules allocating the burden and standard of proof are part of the normative machinery by which the state seeks to mediate this fundamental tension. Allocation of the probative burden to the prosecution, and the criminal standard of proof beyond reasonable doubt, are the twin evidentiary pillars of the presumption of innocence encapsulated in English law's 'Woolmington principle'. We will now consider the theoretical significance of each of these twin pillars, as a prelude to examining the status of the Woolmington principle in contemporary criminal adjudication.

(a) THE BURDEN OF PROOF AS A BULWARK OF LIBERTY

Requiring the prosecution to prove all the primary elements of a criminal charge directly promotes the liberty, security, and privacy of each and every citizen. All of us are at risk of being falsely or wrongly accused of committing a crime. Allocating the probative burden to the prosecution entails that the state must make all the initial running. The accused has no duty to account for himself or his actions: he is entitled to sit back and – as lawyers say – 'put the prosecution to proof', by insisting that the prosecution prove its case against him with minimal co-operation from the defence.[81]

In evidentiary terms, the first limb of Woolmington implies that, in addition to the probative burden of proving guilt, the prosecutor also shoulders a burden of production to 'pass the judge' in respect of each element of the offence(s) charged. Unless the prosecution can adduce sufficient evidence to enable a reasonable jury to infer guilt beyond reasonable doubt, there is not even a prima facie case to answer, and the accused will be acquitted without ever being called upon to respond to the charges brought against him. The duties of citizenship arguably imply that the accused should not be entirely absolved of all evidential labour, however. A mixture of pragmatic and moral considerations can be advanced in support of requiring the accused to establish certain facts in particular situations. The allocation of evidential burdens of production, and even sometimes of probative burdens of proof, therefore needs to be specified in relation to each particular charge.

As a general rule-of-thumb, the Woolmington principle allocates to the prosecution the evidential and probative burdens in relation to every condition of liability specified in the charges on the indictment. However, indictments are only an incomplete guide to pertinent criteria of criminal liability. In a murder prosecution, for instance, the indictment will state that the accused killed V with malice aforethought, and the prosecution's task

---

[81] This is the point of contact between the presumption of innocence and the privilege against self-incrimination: the latter is discussed in Chapter 13.

is to adduce evidence proving both that the accused is causally responsible for V's death, and that he had the requisite state of mind – 'malice aforethought' – when he killed V. But murder indictments are not required to spell out[82] a range of potentially relevant exculpatory factors, such as killing in self-defence or under provocation, and the prosecutor is not obliged to adduce evidence on such matters in the first instance. Most criminal charges are likewise subject to a range of general and specific 'defences' (broadly conceived),[83] which prosecutors are not required to rebut unless the accused, or occasionally the court of its own motion, makes them an issue in the case.

This procedural balance represents a trade-off between the accused's interests in liberty and privacy, and citizens' interests (including the accused's interest *qua* citizen) in a workable and reasonably efficient system of justice. If the prosecution were obliged to adduce evidence to rebut every single exculpatory argument which might conceivably be relied upon by the accused, much time and money would be wasted in proving matters which were not really in dispute,[84] and some guilty offenders would escape just condemnation and punishment simply because the prosecution was unable to disprove wholly fanciful claims of excuse or justification for which there was not one shred of substantiation. The purpose of imposing a burden of production on the accused is to avoid such inefficiency and potential injustice. Over the years, burdens of production have been allocated to the accused on an *ad hoc* basis, essentially as a matter of precedent.[85]

Whilst the accused is obliged to raise any issue on which the defence bears the burden of production, affirmative evidence is not always required to discharge it. It is sometimes enough for the accused to point to aspects of the prosecution's evidence from which a jury might infer pertinent exculpatory facts, or at least entertain a reasonable doubt about them.[86] Once the accused successfully passes the judge on any such issue, of course, it remains the duty of the prosecution to prove beyond reasonable doubt that the accused did not act in self-defence, under provocation, and so forth.[87] We are discussing the allocation of burdens of production to the accused; the *Woolmington* principle definitively allocates the underlying probative burden to the prosecution, in accordance with the presumption of innocence.

If an accused implies a ground of defence, for example by putting questions to a prosecution witness in cross-examination, but fails to discharge the evidential burden on that

---

[82] It can be said that the common law definition of murder as *unlawful* killing makes oblique reference to potentially relevant justifications, including self-defence, necessity, and the prevention of crime.

[83] Notoriously, some pleas generally known as 'defences' are in fact negations of an essential ingredient of the *actus reus*, and therefore amount to a denial of wrongdoing rather than constituting an affirmative defence in the strict sense. For general discussion, see John Gardner, *Offences and Defences* (OUP, 2007), chs 4–7; R. A. Duff, *Answering For Crime: Responsibility and Liability in the Criminal Law* (Hart, 2007), chs 9 and 11; Jeremy Horder, *Excusing Crime* (OUP, 2004); Paul H. Robinson, 'Criminal Law Defenses: A Systematic Analysis' (1982) 82 *Columbia LR* 199.

[84] See Sir Francis Boyd Adams, *Criminal Onus and Exculpations* (Sweet & Maxwell, NZ, 1968), para.3; and Glanville Williams, 'The Evidential Burden: Some Common Misapprehensions' (1977) 127 *NLJ* 156.

[85] In addition to issues of self-defence, an evidential burden has been imposed on the accused in relation to such general defences as automatism: *Bratty* v *A-G for Northern Ireland* [1963] AC 386, HL(NI); necessity/duress of circumstances: *R* v *Pommell* [1995] 2 Cr App R 607, CA; *R* v *Trim* [1943] VLR 109, VSC; and duress: *R* v *Gill* [1963] 1 WLR 841, CCA; and also in relation to offence-specific arguments, for example a claim of mechanical defect on a charge of dangerous driving: *R* v *Spurge* [1961] 2 QB 205, CCA.

[86] *R* v *Hamand* (1986) 82 Cr App R 65, CA.

[87] *R* v *Lobell* [1957] 1 QB 547, CCA; *R* v *Gill* [1963] 1 WLR 841, CCA.

issue, the judge must instruct jurors to ignore that particular line of defence. They should put it out of their heads entirely and not allow it to influence their deliberations in any way. Although this is the orthodox analysis, there is a discernable trend in modern times to require the judge to direct the jury on any defence that is suggested by the evidence, even if neither party has made any argument about it during the course of the trial. On a charge of murder, for example, the Court of Appeal has said that the judge must always leave provocation to the jury whenever there is evidence that the accused was provoked to kill, even where the accused is arguing something entirely different, such as self-defence or even alibi or mistaken identity.[88] This development might be regarded as welcome judicial encouragement to the jury to consider every plausible avenue of exculpation. But the matter is complicated by the structural framework of adversary trial, organized around party-dominated proceedings[89] and a split tribunal of fact and law,[90] in which the judge is expected to be a neutral and essentially reactive umpire, rather than an active seeker of truth. This is a pressure point in adversarial theory: should the trial judge actively strive to assist the find-finder in arriving at the truth or passively defer to the parties' litigation strategies? Common law expectations of judicial neutrality are now underwritten by Article 6(1) of the ECHR, which specifies that all trials must be conducted by 'an independent and impartial tribunal established by law'. This general European standard is inevitably inflected by common law perspectives in English criminal proceedings.

Quite part from its implications for judicial neutrality, the 'invisible burden'[91] on the trial judge to sum up on additional defences implied by the evidence, but unargued by the parties, exacerbates the complexity of judicial directions and increases the possibility that the judge will omit to mention something material or make some other kind of appealable mistake. More fundamentally, it cuts across the traditional adversary precept that the judge should remain aloof from the fray and allow the parties considerable latitude to develop their respective cases, within the broad confines of legality and propriety. Consider, for example, the following pair of defence arguments on a charge of murder:

Defence #1: 'The accused cannot have committed the murder, because an alibi witness places him 50 miles away from the scene of the crime at the material time'.

Defence #2: 'The accused cannot have committed the murder, because an alibi witness places him 50 miles away from the scene of the crime at the material time; but if that alibi is rejected, the accused was anyway provoked to kill'.

It is far from clear that Defence #2 is more persuasive than Defence #1, because its second limb tends to undermine the credibility of the first, possibly to the detriment of both in the eyes of the jury. In this scenario, less looks like more. Neither the accused nor his counsel would necessarily thank the judge for turning the simple alibi argument into the more complex, and equivocal, composite of 'alibi or provocation'. Yet the judge is apparently bound to do so. The safest course would be to return the responsibility for developing their cases to the parties and their legal advisers. Rather than blundering into the adversarial contest by raising new defences of the court's own motion, the judge should

---

[88] R v *Cambridge* [1994] 1 WLR 971, CA. This ruling turned in part on the precise wording of s.3 of the Homicide Act 1957.   [89] §2.3(a).

[90] But see §4.2 for more nuanced analysis.

[91] Sean Doran, 'Alternative Defences: the "Invisible Burden" on the Trial Judge' [1991] *Crim LR* 878.

first of all share his thinking and discuss any proposed direction with defence counsel. If the accused's legal team would rather that no mention be made of additional affirmative defences, such as provocation, that might be available on the evidence, the judge should accede to their wishes, since the accused's legal advisers are far better placed than the judge to determine the accused's trial strategy in an adversarial system of justice.

(b) THE STEEPLY ASYMMETRIC CRIMINAL STANDARD OF PROOF

A second major dimension of criminal procedure law's commitment to the presumption of innocence is the adoption of a steeply asymmetrical standard of proof. As everybody knows, the prosecution has to prove its case *beyond reasonable doubt*: this is the second limb of the *Woolmington* principle. Put another way, the accused is not required to prove his innocence, but only needs to establish a reasonable doubt that he *might* be innocent in order to secure an acquittal. This asymmetrical standard is not a natural or inevitable incident of allocating probative burdens; it is, rather, an *additional* commitment, over and above requiring the prosecution to prove guilt, to the presumption of innocence and its animating liberal philosophy of respect for persons. The standard applicable to civil claims and to the accused's probative burdens in criminal proceedings is proof on the balance of probabilities.[92] Care must be exercised when referring to *the* 'criminal standard' of proof: proof beyond reasonable doubt applies only to the prosecution in criminal proceedings. Assuming that 'equality is equity',[93] dividing the risk of adjudicative error equally between the parties is presumptively fair. On this approach, no party's rights are afforded greater legal protection than any other's. The claimant must establish a factual basis for legal intervention to vindicate his rights, otherwise there would be no rational basis for disturbing the status quo. Proof on the balance of probabilities is therefore immediately intuitively appealing. The criminal standard of proof 'beyond reasonable doubt', by contrast, requires further explanation and justification.

Standards of proof correspond to the (subjective) confidence levels of fact-finders. They answer the juror's question: how sure should I be before I decide the case in favour of one party or the other? The appropriate confidence level depends on what is at stake in the proceedings; more specifically, it depends on the relative seriousness (or 'disutility') of a mistake in either direction.

In ordinary affairs we deal with the relative disutility of errors by factoring together the likelihood of making a mistake with the harm that might result by acting on it. For instance, before setting out on a long walk it is prudent to listen to the weather forecast. If the chances of rain are small, one might accept the (remote) risk of being caught in a downpour. The walk will in all probability be precipitation-free; and even if, as (bad) luck would have it, the heavens open, getting soaked to the skin is hardly the end of the world. But suppose a long-standing health problem creates a small, but non-negligible, risk of contracting potentially fatal pneumonia if one is caught in a downpour. In these circumstances, one

---

[92] *R v Hunt* [1987] 1 AC 352, 374, HL, *per* Lord Griffiths: '[I]f a burden of proof is placed on the defendant it is the same burden whether the case be tried summarily or on indictment, namely, a burden that has to be discharged on the balance of probabilities.' Also see *R v Carr-Briant* [1943] KB 607, CCA.

[93] Cf. *Cox v Bankside Members Agency Ltd* [1995] 2 Lloyd's Rep 437, 457, CA (referring to 'the familiar equitable principle that equality is equity').

might at least think twice about running even a remote risk of a soaking, and perhaps one would decide not to embark on the walk after all. The greater the magnitude of harm that might result, the less one would be inclined to take the risk. An increase in the magnitude of harm would at least need to be offset by a corresponding reduction in the probability of its occurrence before the risk might be viewed as acceptable.

Legal procedures should strive to minimize all types of error, by weeding out bad claims and encouraging good ones, facilitating appropriate communication between the parties, securing reliable forms of evidence on which to render judgment, and so on. At the adjudicative stage, however, proof on the balance of probabilities is the appropriate level of fact-finder confidence in civil proceedings, because the relative disutility of error is presumptively in equilibrium. There is no general *a priori* reason to think that erroneously rejecting a good civil law claim is any worse, or any better, than forcing somebody to pay more than they owe or incur other adverse consequences. This being the case, the law refrains from loading the dice either in favour of claimants or against them. The probative burden on the ultimate issue is allocated to claimants in civil proceedings on the basis that a party invoking judicial intervention in support of his asserted rights should at least be required to demonstrate why, on balance, the *status quo* should not be allowed to continue undisturbed. Within this overarching structure, the risks of adjudicative error may be adjusted by allocating probative burdens on particular issues, including affirmative defences, to the defendant.[94]

The steeply asymmetrical criminal standard of proof, by contrast, reflects the widely-held belief that the relative disutility of error tilts strongly against wrongful conviction in criminal trials. Lawyers have long been taught, and most ordinary citizens would probably instinctively agree, that erroneously convicting an innocent person of a crime he or she did not commit is significantly worse than simply failing to catch and convict someone who is guilty. *How much* worse is a contentious matter. According to Blackstone's sanctified formulation, it is better 'to acquit ten guilty persons rather than convict one innocent'.[95] However, various alternative ratios are quoted in the common law's institutional sources. Fortescue, writing in the fifteenth century, preferred twenty-to-one,[96] whilst Lord Stafford, specifically contemplating the death penalty, significantly upped the ante to 1000-to-1.[97] The numbers are unimportant, however, and possibly import a spurious pseudo-mathematical precision. The courts rarely deal with evidence capable of generating quantifiable probabilities of error; and even where quantified probabilities are available (e.g. DNA profiles) the evidence is rarely conclusive taken in isolation.[98] What is really at issue is the strength of different writers' rhetorical commitment to avoiding wrongful conviction of the innocent: the more extravagant the ratio, the stronger that commitment, broadly speaking. Precise quantification is neither necessary nor realistic.

Competing odds ratios, in spite of their numerical discrepancies, share an implicit recognition that every conceivable human system of criminal justice remain error prone.

---

[94] See *Zuckerman on Civil Procedure*, §§21.39–21.43.

[95] Sir William Blackstone, *Commentaries* (Wayne Morrison, ed., Cavendish, 2001), vol 4, 358, who was apparently reverting to the ratio coined by Sir Edward Seymour in 1696, after Hale had suggested a more modest five-to-one: see Glanville Williams, *The Proof of Guilt* (Stevens, 3rd edn. 1963), 186–7.

[96] Sir John Fortescue, *De Laudibus Legum Angliae* (A. Amos ed., 1825), ch. 27.

[97] Howell, 7 State Trials (32 Charles II, 1680) 1529. Also see Sir William Holdsworth, *A History of English Law* (Methuen, 5th edn. 1942), vol. 3, 620.   [98] See §4.5.

Although we can – and should – minimize the risk of wrongful conviction with an appropriately asymmetric standard of proof, it is impossible to say that innocent accused will never be wrongly convicted and punished by mistake. Statistical data and empirical research from England and the USA indicate that miscarriages of justice involving conviction of the innocent occur routinely in both systems,[99] despite proof beyond reasonable doubt being a formal prerequisite to conviction. Confronting this realization prompts two further questions. First, what are the implications for justice and legitimate political authority of the seemingly unavoidable trade-off between successfully convicting and punishing the guilty, on the one hand, and avoiding conviction of the innocent on the other? More particularly, is there a rationale justifying the pragmatic operation of criminal proceedings that is consistent with the foundational liberal principle of respect for persons? Secondly, if an acceptable justification for making such a trade-off can be found, how exactly can an appropriate level of commitment to avoiding conviction of the innocent be identified and translated into workable legal principles, rules and procedures?

The language of 'trade-offs' superficially implies some kind of consequentialist social welfare maximization, whereby the interests of individuals are to be sacrificed in order to promote the aggregate communal good. The subordination of individual to collective interests is characteristic of consequentialist ethics, and is a major theme running through such otherwise disparate philosophical and political traditions as classical utilitarianism, Soviet communism in its heyday, and the national socialism of Hitler's Germany. The eighteenth century social philosopher William Paley seems to have been urging something similar on his Georgian readers when he insisted that judges should not be swayed by the risk of convicting the innocent when the situation called for hard-headed decision-making in the public interest:

When certain rules of adjudication must be pursued, when certain degrees of credibility must be accepted, in order to reach the crimes with which the public are infested, courts of justice should not be deterred from the application of these rules by *every* suspicion of danger, or by the mere possibility of confounding the innocent with the guilty. They ought rather to reflect, that he who falls by a mistaken sentence may be considered as falling for his country.[100]

---

[99] Professional respondents to the Runciman Commission's *Crown Court Study* considered 2% (judges and prosecution counsel) or 17% (defence barristers) of jury convictions to be 'problematic', in the sense of being against the weight of evidence, contrary to law or completely inexplicable. Whilst cautioning about the lack of statistical significance of their sample, the authors comment that the 'grossed up' figures of wrongful conviction for that year (1991) translate into 250 cases on the more conservative judicial/Crown counsel estimate, or over 2,000 cases if defence counsel are nearer the mark: Michael Zander and Paul Henderson, *Crown Court Study*, RCCJ Research Study No 19 (HMSO, 1993), para.6.1.8. For an American perspective, see Daniel Givelber, 'Meaningless Acquittals, Meaningful Convictions: Do We Reliably Acquit the Innocent?' (1997) 49 *Rutgers LR* 1317. An expanded conception of 'miscarriage of justice' naturally (and controversially) inflates the count: cf. Michael Naughton, *Rethinking Miscarriages of Justice: Beyond the Tip of The Iceberg* (Palgrave, 2007).

[100] William Paley, *Principles of Moral and Political Philosophy* (Alexander Chalmers, ed., F. C. & J. Rivington, 1817), vol 6, 428. Along similar lines, Lenin mused: 'which is better, to put in prison several tens or hundreds of instigators, guilty or innocent, or to lose thousands of workers and Army men. The first is better. The interest of workers...must win out': quoted by Mirjan R Damaška, *The Faces of Justice and State Authority* (Yale UP, 1986), 121, n.41. See also Glanville Williams, *The Proof of Guilt* (Stevens, 3rd edn. 1963), 187.

This 'unwilling hero' or martyr conception of wrongful conviction was famously attacked by Paley's adversary, the parliamentarian and renowned anti-capital punishment campaigner Sir Samuel Romilly.[101] Indeed, Paley's analogy seems disingenuous, for whereas real war heroes are awarded posthumous medals, Remembrance Day, and dependants' war pensions, the wrongfully convicted are punished and condemned as criminals and neither they nor their families can expect any sympathy – let alone gratitude – for their 'sacrifice' unless and until their innocence is later discovered. Doubts about the legitimacy of punishing the innocent nonetheless resurface towards the end of the nineteenth century, for example in the influential writing of James Fitzjames Stephen:

[I]t is by no means true that under all circumstances it is better that ten guilty men should escape than that one innocent man should suffer. Everything depends on what the guilty men have been doing, and something depends on the way in which the innocent man came to be suspected.[102]

Statements such as this are, however, open to a range of possible interpretations. Stephen might have been proposing a situationally-flexible standard of proof, rather than arguing for a lower level of fact-finder confidence across the board.

At any rate, it is a serious, if regrettably common, misapprehension to suppose that any attempt to balance individuals' interests, or to make trade-offs between them, must necessarily collapse into crude social welfare maximization, whereby the interests of the one must be sacrificed for the benefit of the many. In fact, balance and trade-off are inescapable, in our individual lives as much as at the aggregate level of penal policy-making, because interests often compete and sometimes openly and directly conflict. Where it is not possible to have, or to be, everything one wants to have or to be in everyday life, choices must be made from the range of eligible options. One cannot simultaneously be a nun and a mother; students cannot party every night and do well in Finals; you can't have your cake and eat it. Governments confront structurally identical choices and dilemmas. In order to guarantee a high level of personal autonomy and security to its citizens, for example, governments and citizens alike must accept some risk of wrongful conviction, given the practical constraints of human fallibility in decision-making and limited knowledge of what goes on in the world.

This is not a straightforward matter of balancing A's security interest against B's right not to be wrongfully convicted, because B has just as much of an interest in personal security as A, and A is (let us assume) no less at risk of wrongful conviction than B. It would egregiously misrepresent the efforts of the liberal state to manage this conflict, in part

---

[101] Romilly, *Observations on the Criminal Law of England* (1810), Note D, quoted in Howell, 7 State Trials, (32 Charles II, 1680), 1529. For further discussion of the celebrated Paley-Romilly debate and its historical context, see David J. A. Cairns, *Advocacy and the Making of the Adversarial Criminal Trial 1800–1865* (OUP, 1998), 21–3 and ch 3; William Twining *Theories of Evidence: Bentham and Wigmore* (Weidenfeld & Nicolson, 1985), 96.

[102] Sir James Fitzjames Stephen, *History of the Criminal Law of England* (Macmillan, 1883), vol 1, 438. It might, conceivably, be justified to harm some innocent people for the greater good under conditions of complete breakdown in the rule of law, as where anarchy has broken out and a policy of shooting curfew breakers on sight is necessary for the purpose of restoring order. But it is inconceivable that a society in which the rule of law obtains should subscribe to a systematic policy of inflicting harm on the innocent for the greater good. The consequentialist's purported rationale for routinely torturing suspects fails for essentially the same reasons: see §5.3(d) and §5.4(c).

through an asymmetrical standard of proof, to say that the state has resolved to sacrifice individual interests on the altar of public welfare. In trying to afford appropriate legal recognition to a range of conflicting individual and collective interests, the liberal state does its best in an imperfect world to respect the humanity, dignity, and rights of every person under its jurisdiction. This conscientious weighting of partly incommensurable interests contrasts starkly with the consequentialist approach to social policy-making, which reduces all values and interests to a single metric of aggregate preference satisfaction and, in calculating the balance of advantage without any regard for the moral quality of registered preferences, contemplates sacrifice of the innocent without compunction or regret. A liberal might, for example, think it acceptable to tax A, who has two good eyes, in order to provide a measure of social assistance to B, who is blind. Consequentialists, uninhibited by any principled respect for persons or their physical integrity, might contemplate going much further. On the (eminently plausible) assumption that aggregate social welfare would be maximized if both A and B could see, and supposing medical feasibility, the obvious consequentialist solution would be to rip out one of A's good eyes and give it to B.

Contemporary moral and political philosophy and penal theory supply the conceptual and normative resources needed to grasp the deeper significance of proof beyond reasonable doubt in criminal adjudication. Chapter 1 drew attention to the fact that criminal justice systems pursue a range of objectives and promote multiple values.[103] According to principles of retributive justice, criminal proceedings are meant to censure wrongdoing and give offenders their just deserts by imposing proportionate punishment. The standard of proof in criminal adjudication is steeply asymmetrical because, from this perspective, the 'disutility' – that is to say, the injury and wrongfulness – of wrongful conviction of the innocent significantly outweighs the countervailing immorality of mistaken acquittal of the guilty. Wrongful censure and punishment of the innocent constitute profound moral harms which, moreover, are inflicted by the state in the name, and on the authority, of each and every member of the political community. Every citizen is therefore implicated in a miscarriage of justice, as its symbolic author. A liberal state built on respect for persons will never knowingly convict an innocent, but the risk of mistaken conviction can never be eliminated entirely. For the liberal state is simultaneously duty-bound to safeguard the autonomy and security of its citizens – especially society's weakest members, who are least able to protect themselves – by detecting and investigating crime, convicting and punishing the guilty, and reducing the risk of future offending utilizing the range of deterrent, incapacitation, and rehabilitative techniques at its disposal. The most that coherently can be demanded of the liberal state, in discharging its duties of security and justice, is that it also makes an unequivocal commitment to the importance of avoiding wrongful conviction. Proof beyond reasonable doubt is the juridical symbol, and practical evidentiary manifestation, of that commitment. Even in the knowledge that innocents will inevitably be convicted when unavoidable error strikes, if the state at all times is striving to satisfy the contradictory demands of respect for persons, its liberal credentials remain intact.

Nor yet does the liberal state exhibit disrespect for victims of crime, simply because the asymmetrical standard of proof means, without doubt, that more criminals will

[103] §1.3.

evade justice than if a lower standard of proof were adopted. Failure to convict the guilty must be viewed in practical and procedural context. Policing, prosecution, legal aid, courts, prisons, probation, and the whole panoply of criminal justice machinery consumes an enormous amount of taxpayers' money, and yet only a small percentage of offences results in a conviction (or even any broadly defined 'sanction detection').[104] The reality, however unpalatable it may be to swallow, is that the greater majority of offending is always going to escape public censure, primarily because most crime goes unreported or undetected. Against a backdrop of extensive attrition in the early stages of criminal proceedings, it is safe to assume that only a small fraction of potential convictions are lost because criminal charges cannot be proved beyond reasonable doubt in court.[105]

Absent official abuse or culpable error, the state is not in any sense *to blame* because offenders are wily or lucky enough to cheat justice. It would require a massive and manifestly unjustifiable reallocation of public money, away from hospitals and schools and pensions and the like, to make any noticeable impact on the criminal justice system's overall success rate. Although fear of crime has become an increasingly prominent issue of public concern since the 1990s and into the twenty-first century, no British government has ever had an electoral mandate to become obsessively preoccupied with punishing offenders at the expense of its other major responsibilities to safeguard national security, manage the economy effectively, organize the full range of social welfare provision, health care, and education, and preserve the cultural wellbeing of the nation; to say nothing of fundamental objections of principle to over-criminalization[106] and penal excess.[107] Surely, if an appropriate proportion of tax revenue is already being devoted to crime prevention and punishment, and public officials are doing their level best to bring offenders to justice (consistent with discharging the state's other duties in the penal context, including maintaining proper commitment to avoiding wrongful conviction of the innocent), it is fatuous to charge the state with 'disrespect' for victims of crime or to equate its limited competence in crime-fighting with the betrayal of liberal principles.

---

[104] See n.70, above.

[105] Though it should be added that a certain fraction of cases might be lost in the early stages of proceedings precisely because the police or prosecutors predict that proof beyond reasonable doubt is not going to be achieved in a particular case. A 'feedback loop' effect of the criminal standard of proof on criminal justice professionals' pre-trial decision-making is both plausible and difficult to quantify, but it seems unlikely to figure in decisions of the general public whether to report an offence in the first instance – and this is the point where the attrition curve is at its steepest.

[106] Over-criminalization breaches the 'principle of minimum intervention' discussed in §1.3. For general discussion, see Doug Husak, *Overcriminalization: The Limits of the Criminal Law* (OUP, 2008); Andrew von Hirsch and A. P. Simester (eds.), *Incivilities: Regulating Offensive Behaviour* (Hart, 2006); Joel Feinberg, *The Moral Limits of the Criminal Law*, vols I–IV (OUP, 1984–1988); Andrew Ashworth, 'Is The Criminal Law A Lost Cause?' (2000) 116 *LQR* 225; Jonathan Schonsheck, *On Criminalization: An Essay in the Philosophy of the Criminal Law* (Kluwer, 1994); Paul Roberts, 'Consent and the Criminal Law: Philosophical Foundations', in LCCP No 139, *Consent in the Criminal Law* (HMSO, 1995), Appendix C; Herbert L. Packer, *The Limits of the Criminal Sanction* (Stanford UP, 1969), Part III.

[107] For cogent arguments explaining the significance of proportionality in criminal punishment, see Andrew von Hirsch, *Censure and Sanctions* (OUP, 1993), chs 2 and 4; Andrew von Hirsch and Andrew Ashworth, *Proportionate Sentencing: Exploring the Principles* (OUP, 2005).

6.4 PROOF BEYOND REASONABLE DOUBT IN THEORY AND PRACTICE

Discussion to this point has proceeded as though proof 'beyond reasonable doubt' were a transparent standard with a settled meaning and function in criminal trials. Having explored the deeper moral and political significance of a steeply asymmetrical standard of proof, we must now investigate the practical dimensions of proof beyond reasonable doubt more closely. The criminal standard of proof has generated much controversy, and far more appellate attention, than such an apparently innocuous and familiar phrase might be expected to draw to itself. Although the period of greatest judicial agitation seems now to have passed, and many previously contested points appear settled for the time being, proof beyond reasonable doubt remains a troubled and troubling notion that must be handled with care.

(a) THE MEANING OF PROOF BEYOND REASONABLE DOUBT

Notwithstanding its revered legal status and popular resonance, the meaning of the phrase 'proof beyond reasonable doubt' is far from self-evident or universally agreed. Several modern judges, including notably Lord Denning in the following well-known passage, have maintained that proof beyond reasonable doubt denotes neither a single nor an inflexible standard:

It is of course true that by our law a higher standard of proof is required in criminal cases than in civil cases. But this is subject to the qualification that there is no absolute standard in either case. In criminal cases the charge must be proved beyond reasonable doubt, but there may be degrees of proof within that standard. As...great judges have said, 'in proportion as the crime is enormous, so ought the proof to be clear'.[108]

The implication appears to be that proof beyond reasonable doubt is a contextually flexible standard, envisaging a sliding-scale of fact-finder confidence levels corresponding to the facts and circumstances of particular cases. Proof leaving no doubt whatsoever of the accused's guilt would be the most exacting standard. Further sub-standards of proof might correspond to progressively less-stringent evidential requirements; though we are left guessing as to the minimum threshold of fact-finder confidence at the lower end of the scale. The idea of proof requirements varying with the seriousness of the charge has had a long and somewhat chequered career in English law, but it is currently out of favour. Lord Brown recently doubted the common law maxim, noting that if a tribunal found a matter proved against A on the balance of probabilities it 'would be quite wrong for that tribunal to decide the question in A's favour merely to save him from the serious consequences of a finding against him – for example, to save a bank manager from a finding of dishonesty'.[109] As his Lordship rightly cautioned, there is an important difference between certain serious

---

[108] *Bater* v *Bater* [1951] P 35, 36–7, CA; and see *Blyth* v *Blyth* [1966] AC 643, 669, HL. Lord Denning's view was later endorsed in the House of Lords in *Khawaja* v *Secretary of State for the Home Office* [1984] AC 74, 112–13 (Lord Scarman).

[109] *In re D* [2009] 1 AC 11, [2008] UKHL 33, [45], [47] (Lord Brown; Lord Neuberger agreeing).

things being inherently unlikely – like being mauled by a tiger in Hyde Park – and any serious matter requiring a higher level of proof just in virtue of its being serious.

In his understanding of the variability of standards of proof, as in so much else, Denning was unorthodox. Generally speaking, the judges have got themselves into hot water whenever they have attempted to expound the meaning of proof 'beyond reasonable doubt' for the benefit of the jury. In another oft-quoted *dictum*, Lord Denning gave the following elaboration of the criminal standard:

It need not reach certainty, but it must carry a high degree of probability. Proof beyond reasonable doubt does not mean proof beyond the shadow of doubt. The law would fail to protect the community if it admitted fanciful possibilities to deflect the course of justice. If the evidence is so strong against a man as to leave only a remote possibility in his favour which can be dismissed with the sentence 'of course it is possible, but not in the least probable', the case is proved beyond reasonable doubt, but nothing short of that will suffice.[110]

Alternative formulations, which attempted to give the requisite standard of proof a more accessible and popular meaning, turned out to have a limited shelf-life. In a handful of cases the Court of Appeal instructed trial judges to translate 'reasonable doubt' as uncertainty that would make jurors hesitate in the conduct of personal business, that it was 'the sort of doubt which may affect the mind of a person in the conduct of important affairs.'[111] But this approach, it quickly came to be appreciated, makes the standard unacceptably subjective and relative to individual jurors' experience. The notion of 'important affairs' means different things to different people: Getting married? Alleviating world poverty? Being promoted at work? Whether Sheffield Wednesday avoid relegation? With the benefit of hindsight, it was plainly unsatisfactory to define 'reasonable doubt' in criminal adjudication by reference to risk-taking in other contexts, when different people have different levels of enthusiasm for, and aversion to, risk and there are no uniform standards of acceptable risk-taking applicable across diverse spheres of human activity.[112]

Despairing of definitions, Lord Goddard CJ was driven to exclaim that:

When once a judge begins to use the words 'reasonable doubt' and to try to explain what is a reasonable doubt and what is not, he is much more likely to confuse the jury then if he tells them in plain language: 'It is the duty of the prosecution to satisfy you of the man's guilt'.[113]

Unfortunately, telling the jury that they must be 'satisfied' is not wholly instructive, either, and the Lord Chief Justice was soon revisiting this theme. Lord Goddard even suggested (presciently, as it ultimately turned out) that the talismanic words should be abandoned altogether:

If a jury is told that it is their duty to regard the evidence and see that it satisfies them so that they can feel sure when they return a verdict of Guilty, that is much better than using the expression 'reasonable doubt' and I hope in future that that will be done.[114]

---

[110] *Miller* v *Minister of Pensions* [1947] 2 All ER 372, 373–4.

[111] *R* v *Gray* (1974) 58 Cr App R 177, 183, CA. Also, *Walters* v *R* [1969] 2 AC 26, PC; *R* v *Yap Chuan Ching* (1976) 63 Cr App R 7, CA (where the trial judge told the jury that they should be as sure as they would need to be to take out a residential mortgage).

[112] Cf. *R* v *Hepworth and Fearnley* [1955] 2 QB 600, 603, CCA, where Lord Goddard CJ remarked that: 'To tell [jurors] that a reasonable doubt is such a doubt as to cause them to hesitate in their own affairs never seems to me to convey any particular standard…'   [113] *R* v *Kritz* [1950] 1 KB 82, 90, CCA.

[114] *R* v *Summers* [1952] 1 All ER 1059, CCA. Lord Goddard also disapproved of a direction telling the jury that they must be persuaded to 'a high degree of certainty': *R* v *Onufrejczyk* [1955] 1 QB 388, CCA.

A direction that the jury must 'feel sure' was approved in a succession of later cases.[115] But the phraseology of proof beyond reasonable doubt was apparently too well-established in judicial practice and the popular consciousness to be expunged by fiat of the Lord Chief Justice. Certain judges openly signalled their dissatisfaction with the Court of Appeal's revisionist jury directions on the criminal standard of proof.[116] If proof 'beyond reasonable doubt' became freighted with the criminal justice system's foundational rhetorical commitment to respect for persons and its implications for distributing the risks of error in criminal adjudication, as we have argued, its resilience and loyal following amongst the judiciary are more easily comprehended.

When this book's predecessor was published in 1989 trial judges were being advised 'not to volunteer an explanation of this expression'[117] but to satisfy themselves with the 'time honoured formula'[118] of proof beyond reasonable doubt.[119] Since then, the Judicial Studies Board (JSB) has issued the following Specimen Direction, which trial judges are encouraged to adopt:

How does the prosecution succeed in proving the defendant's guilt? The answer is – by making you sure of it. Nothing less than that will do. If after considering all the evidence you are sure that the defendant is guilty, you must return a verdict of 'Guilty.' If you are not sure, your verdict must be 'Not Guilty'.[120]

Judges are further advised that they need not mention the words 'beyond reasonable doubt', but if the phrase has already been used in the trial by counsel, they should add that being 'sure' is the same as proof beyond reasonable doubt.

Although successive linguistic refinements were often short-lived, produced no appreciable advantage over their predecessors and, at times, seemed to lead the law round in circles, judicial attempts to clarify the meaning of 'proof beyond reasonable doubt' are not a trivial distraction. It is difficult to believe that the expression 'beyond reasonable doubt' is self-explanatory in a pluralist liberal society, and it would be naïve to assume that every juror has the same instinctive grasp of its meaning. The notion of being 'sure' may be no less indeterminate and problematic as an expression of the level of fact-finder confidence required to sustain a guilty verdict in criminal proceedings than its renowned but now disfavoured rival.

Such suspicions are fuelled by empirical research conducted with mock jurors, judges and magistrates, and members of the public, in Britain and America. These studies demonstrate considerable variation in participants' willingness to convict in hypothetical scenarios applying the 'beyond reasonable doubt' standard. When invited to quantify

---

[115] *Walters v R* [1969] 2 AC 26, PC; *Ferguson v R* [1979] 1 WLR 94, PC; *R v Bracewell* (1979) 68 Cr App R 44, CA (where a direction containing the following explanation was approved: 'There is no such thing as certainty in this life, absolute certainty. You ask yourselves the simple question upon the whole of the evidence do I feel sure?').

[116] Cf. Lawton LJ's remark in *R v Yap Chuan Ching* (1976) 63 Cr App R 7, 11. CA, that 'if judges stopped trying to define that which is almost impossible to define there would be fewer appeals'.

[117] *Archbold* (42nd edn. 1985), 492.

[118] In *Dawson v R* (1961) 106 CLR 1, 18, HCA, Dixon CJ advised trial judges that 'it is a mistake to depart from the time-honoured formula. It is, I think, used by ordinary people and is understood well enough by the average man in the community. The attempts to substitute other expressions, of which there have been many examples not only here but in England, have never prospered.'

[119] See A. A. S. Zuckerman, *The Principles of Criminal Evidence* (OUP, 1989), 131–2.

[120] JSB Specimen Direction No 2B, www.jsboard.co.uk/criminal_law/cbb/index.htm.

the meaning of beyond reasonable doubt as a percentage, average responses ranged from a remarkable, not to say perplexing, lower threshold of 61.1% in one study, to more reassuring values of 85%–90% in other experimental research.[121] A study testing comprehension of the JSB's 'making you sure of it' direction on the part of magistrates, criminal justice professionals, and members of the public (prospective jurors) recorded considerable, albeit less pronounced, variation in understanding. Some 51% of the prospective jurors, but significantly fewer magistrates (31%) or criminal justice professionals (30%), interpreted 'sure' to mean 100% certain. A clear majority of the whole sample, almost 75%, rated 'sure' as at least 90% certain, but this still leaves one in four who thought that 'sure' meant less than 90% certain, including around 4% who indicated a 70% confidence level.[122] In light of this empirical evidence, the view once expressed by the Privy Council (*per* Lord Diplock) that 'there is safety in numbers, and shared responsibility and the opportunity for discussion after retiring serves to counteract individual idiosyncrasies'[123] might appear complacent.

It is not only for the benefit of juries that we need authoritative elaboration of the criminal standard of proof. The judiciary might also otherwise be prone to dangerous misconceptions. In *Khawaja*[124] the House of Lords had to decide whether proof beyond reasonable doubt or proof on the balance of probabilities was the appropriate standard in applications for habeas corpus. Lord Scarman declared: 'My Lords, I have come to the conclusion that the choice between the two standards is not one of any great moment. It is largely a matter of words.'[125] Echoing Lord Denning's preference for a variable standard, Lord Scarman believed that the cogency of proof should increase in line with the gravity of the issue.

Yet if juries were instructed in terms of a flexible criminal standard they would not necessarily conclude that graver offences demand more convincing proof. A jury might reason, to the contrary, that although the accused's guilt has not been proved beyond reasonable doubt, conviction is the safer option because the offence was serious and the prospect of releasing a dangerous criminal into the community to repeat his offence would present too great a risk.[126] Down this road might a jury wander into consequentialist welfare-maximization, negating the presumption of innocence, and sacrificing the interests of the accused to a majoritarian greater good. The notion that the civil quantum of proof

---

[121] The empirical evidence is helpfully summarized by Lawrence M. Solan, 'Refocusing the Burden of Proof in Criminal Cases: Some Doubt about Reasonable Doubt' (1999) 78 *Texas LR* 105, Part III.

[122] Michael Zander, 'The Criminal Standard of Proof – How Sure is Sure?' (2000) 150 *NLJ* 1517 (20 October). This type of study is highly suggestive, but fundamental methodological doubts remain. Jurors are not in fact called upon to quantify their levels of certainty in criminal trials, so it is difficult to know what their percentage scores would mean in practice. Moreover, respondents give subjective confidence levels that are not reliably calibrated to a shared, objective scale. One hard-nosed person's 70% persuaded might, for example, be quite difficult to achieve in practice, whereas another more accepting person's 90% might be an evidential pushover.

[123] *Walters* v *R* [1969] 2 AC 26, 30, PC. Cases such as *R* v *Gibson* (1983) 77 Cr App R 151, CA, supply further illustrations of apparent juror (and judicial!) confusion regarding the standard of proof in criminal trials.

[124] *Khawaja* v *Secretary of State for the Home Office* [1984] AC 74, HL.

[125] ibid. 112. This view appears to trivialize a major feature of *Woolmington's* golden thread. Yet, Lord Goddard CJ, too, once confessed to having 'some difficulty in understanding how there is or there can be two standards', the criminal and the civil standards of proof: *R* v *Hepworth and Fearnley* [1955] 2 QB 600, 603, CCA.

[126] Cf. John Kaplan, 'Decision Theory and Factfinding Process' (1968) 20 *Stanford LR* 1065, 1074; Harry Kalven Jr. and Hans Zeisel, *The American Jury* (Little, Brown & Co, 1966), ch 14.

is variable, and can even equate to proof beyond reasonable doubt in relation to very serious matters like extradition or the imposition of a sex offender order,[127] might arguably be appropriate for civil proceedings. Were it imported into criminal trials, however, an elastic quantum of proof would threaten to undermine the rigour of the traditional, steeply asymmetric criminal standard to the detriment of the values it instantiates.

It is conceivable that, in establishing certain propositions in criminal adjudication, proof beyond reasonable doubt might be regarded as an inappropriately demanding standard where proof on the balance of probabilities would be unacceptably lax. Might it be possible to devise an intermediate standard? Very precise quantification, seeking to differentiate, say, 90% from 95% certain, is obviously ruled out on pragmatic grounds: such precision could never be achieved in practice, given the inherent subjectivity of individual jurors' confidence levels. Any intermediate test of sufficiency of proof would have to be set at some rough point between the two established standards. In the United States there has been experimentation with intermediate standards in civil cases involving fraud, lost wills, and rectification of contracts. The third standard of sufficiency has variously been described as proof by 'clear and convincing evidence', 'clear, cogent and convincing proof', and 'clear, unequivocal, satisfactory and convincing proof', amongst other formulations.[128] In England and Wales, too, there have been suggestions for a formalized intermediate standard, expressed in terms of 'strong, irrefragable evidence' or 'strong, distinct and satisfactory evidence', or to the effect that the issues be 'clearly and unequivocally proved'.[129] In its latest intervention, however, the House of Lords has emphatically rejected the suggestion that there could be a 'third standard' of proof in English law:

It is indisputable that only two standards are recognised by the common law, proof on the balance of probabilities and proof beyond reasonable doubt. The latter standard is that required by the criminal law and in such areas of dispute as contempt of court or disciplinary proceedings brought against members of a profession. The former is the general standard applicable to all other civil proceedings and means simply, as Lord Nicholls of Birkenhead said in *In re H (Minors) (Sexual Abuse: Standard of Proof)* [1996] AC 563, 586, that 'a court is satisfied an event occurred if the court considers that, on the evidence, the occurrence of the event was more likely than not'.[130]

Reassertion of legal orthodoxy seems right in principle from the perspective of criminal adjudication. Suggested formulations of a third standard imply degrees of latitude in

---

[127] Cf. *B v Chief Constable of Avon and Somerset Constabulary* [2001] 1 WLR 340, [31], DC, where Lord Bingham CJ insisted: '[i]n a serious case such as the present the difference between the two standards is, in truth, largely illusory'. And see *R (on the application of McCann and others) v Crown Court at Manchester* [2001] 1 WLR 1084, [2001] EWCA Civ 281, [65]–[67] (extending Lord Bingham's approach to Anti-Social Behaviour Orders – ASBOs).

[128] See, for example, *McCormick on Evidence* (3rd edn. 1984), 959; Jack B. Weinstein, John H. Mansfield, Norman Abrams, and Margaret A. Berger, *Evidence: Cases and Materials* (Foundation Press, 8th edn. 1988), 1157–8.

[129] *Cross and Tapper on Evidence* (OUP, 11th edn. 2007), 185–6. But judges have been less enthusiastic: see e.g., *Re Cleaver (Deceased), Cleaver v Insley* [1981] 1 WLR 939, 947, Ch; *Dingwall v J Wharton (Shipping) Ltd* [1961] 2 Lloyds Rep 213, 216, HL, *per* Lord Tucker: 'I am quite unable to accede to the proposition that there is some intermediate onus between that which is required in criminal cases and the balance of probability which is sufficient in timeous civil actions.'

[130] *In re D* [2009] 1 AC 11, [2008] 1 WLR 1499, [2008] UKHL 33, [23] (Lord Carswell; Lords Bingham, Scott, and Neuberger agreeing).

fact-finder confidence which are plainly too wide for criminal proceedings. At the lower end of the scale an intermediate standard might be satisfied by a degree of probability scarcely greater than a mere preponderance of probabilities. It is undeniable that the notion of 'proof beyond reasonable doubt' has sometimes created difficulties for trial courts and the Court of Appeal, or that it remains perplexingly enigmatic in the eyes of some. Even after promulgation of the JSB's Specimen Directions on the burden and standard of proof, the flow of appeals, though staunched, has not dried up entirely.[131] Yet it is one thing to query the precise meaning of proof beyond reasonable doubt, quite another to contemplate conviction on little more than the civil standard of proof where a strong possibility of the accused's innocence cannot be discounted. The objection to intermediate standards in criminal trials is not that they are inherently more vague than proof 'beyond reasonable doubt' or being 'sure', but that they evince insufficient commitment to avoiding wrongful conviction of the innocent, and to that extent are incompatible with the foundational principles of criminal evidence.

(b) THE CRIMINAL STANDARD AS REASONING PROCEDURE[132]

Whatever words are chosen to express the criminal standard, the jury must be brought to appreciate its function in protecting the innocent from the profound moral harm of wrongful conviction. Unless this message can be communicated to the fact-finder effectively, the criminal standard could be vulnerable to weak interpretations undermining the law's commitment to the presumption of innocence. Justice and individuals' rights in criminal adjudication would then be at the mercy of *ad hoc* calculations of social advantage and the greater good.

On the traditional legal conception, the jury should approach the task of evaluating evidence by progressively eliminating explanations consistent with the accused's innocence, until guilt is the only eligible and inevitable conclusion. If the evidence in the case does not allow this point to be reached, the accused is entitled to an acquittal. Thus, in a murder trial turning on circumstantial evidence, Alderson B. instructed the jury that a guilty verdict should not be returned unless jurors were 'satisfied that the facts were such as to be inconsistent with any other rational conclusion than that the prisoner was the guilty person'.[133] This type of direction makes explicit what 'proof beyond reasonable doubt' and equivalent phrases merely imply: that the jury may convict only when all explanations of the evidence that are consistent with innocence have been dismissed as untenable. From the fact-finder's perspective, the asymmetrical 'proof beyond reasonable doubt' standard may function, not so much as a subjective measure of confidence in a particular conclusion, but as a procedure for reasoning about evidence.

---

[131] See e.g., *R* v *Majid* [2009] EWCA Crim 2563; *R* v *Stephens* [2002] EWCA Crim 1529.

[132] An interesting version of this perspective is developed by Hock Lai Ho, *A Philosophy of Evidence Law: Justice in the Search for Truth* (OUP, 2008), ch 4. Ho's analysis leads him to the – heretical – conclusion that standards of proof are not fixed. Even if this were true in ideal theory, however, procedural reforms to implement this proposal could not be sustained without considering a range of pragmatic issues affecting the successful transition of theory into practice that Ho does not address.

[133] *R* v *Hodge* (1838) 2 Lew CC 227, 228. cf. *R* v *Bracewell* (1979) 68 Cr App R 44, 49, CA (jurors' rationality is bounded by common sense reasoning; jurors should not, for example, become preoccupied with esoteric scientific possibilities beyond the comprehension of ordinary people); *McGreevy* v *DPP* [1973] 1 WLR 276, HL.

The technical name for this reasoning procedure or 'heuristic' is 'eliminative induction'.[134] Inductively constructed hypotheses[135] are progressively eliminated until the only remaining possibility must be accepted as the truth. In *The Sign of Four* Sir Arthur Conan-Doyle famously has the greatest of all fictional detectives chide his ever-corrigible side-kick Dr Watson: 'You will not apply my precept.... How often have I said to you that when you have eliminated the impossible, whatever remains, *however improbable*, must be the truth?'[136] Earlier in the tale Sherlock Holmes had instructed Dr Watson: 'Eliminate all other factors, and the one which remains must be the truth'.[137] Suppose, for example, that a person is charged with theft and the only evidence against him is the testimony of a witness, who says that he saw the accused snatch a wallet. In order to infer the accused's guilt beyond reasonable doubt the fact-finder has to dismiss every hypothesis that is consistent both with the evidence and with the accused's innocence. The fact-finder must be satisfied, in particular, that the witness is not mistaken in identifying the accused, nor deliberately telling lies. The fact-finder must also be sure that the wallet did not belong to the accused, and that the accused did not have the owner's permission to take it; and so on. The same reasoning process should be adopted in relation to circumstantial evidence.

Eliminative induction was essentially the model of scientific inquiry urged on his scientific peers by Karl Popper, widely known as 'falsificationism'. The theory therefore has heavyweight intellectual credentials outside the law. It nonetheless remains doubtful whether human reasoners ever actually adopt a systematically inductive or falsificationist approach to problem-solving in naturalistic settings like criminal adjudication. Many modern scholars, influenced by behavioural science research, believe that some version of the 'story model' of adjudication, according to which fact-finders choose holistically between competing narrative accounts ('stories') proffered by prosecution and defence, more accurately describes the thought-processes of real jurors in real trials.[138] But even if it is true that people generally think and reason about contested facts in terms of competing stories, it does not follow that the law's orthodox commitment to eliminative induction is necessarily irrational, or even that it is ineffective in practice. Some jurors might be persuaded to adopt a more analytically rigorous style of reasoning for the special purpose of criminal adjudication than they would naturally be inclined to follow in their everyday lives. Failing that, jury instructions commending eliminative induction as the proper approach to fact-finding in criminal trials may serve, in every case, to reinforce the law's rhetorical commitment to the presumption of innocence, and to invite jurors to share that commitment and give it practical purchase in their deliberations.

---

[134] See David A. Schum, *The Evidential Foundations of Probabilistic Reasoning* (Wiley, 1994), 26–30, 245–51.

[135] i.e. hypotheses generated through 'abduction': see §4.4(a). For detailed illustrations see Burkhard Schafer, Jeroen Keppens, and Qiang Shen, 'Thinking With and Outside the Box: Developing Computer Support for Evidence Teaching' in Paul Roberts and Mike Redmayne (eds.), *Innovations in Evidence and Proof* (Hart, 2007).

[136] Sir Arthur Conan Doyle, *The Penguin Complete Sherlock Holmes* (Penguin, 1981 [1930]), 111 (original emphasis).

[137] ibid. 92.

[138] See §4.4–§4.6; and for further discussion: Nancy Pennington and Reid Hastie, 'The Story Model for Juror Decision Making,' in Hastie (ed.), *Inside the Juror: the Psychology of Juror Decision-Making* (CUP, 1993); Ronald J. Allen, 'Factual Ambiguity and a Theory of Evidence' (1994) 88 *Northwestern University LR* 604.

We still need to know how to assess when the process of elimination has been completed successfully. At what point should reasoning about alternative hypotheses come to an end? What are the criteria to be applied? Suppose that a witness testifies that immediately after a 'mugging' (robbery from the person) he saw the accused running away from the scene. A police officer subsequently testifies that she recovered the stolen wallet from the accused's house. The defence accounts for the accused's haste by saying that he was running to catch a train, and the accused denies all knowledge of the wallet and its presence in his house. All reasonable doubt about the accused's guilt in this scenario will have been eliminated only when, Jonathan Cohen informs us, 'every let-out of this nature is eliminated, either by oral, documentary, or other evidence, or by reference to facts that the defence admits or the court is prepared to notice'.[139] But then the question becomes: when can it be said that every 'let-out' (innocent explanation) has been eliminated? When, in other words, is a jury entitled to conclude that only *un*reasonable doubt remains?

Since absolute certainty is unattainable in our world, the highest feasible standard is one that so approximates to certainty as to make no practical difference. Cohen calls this 'full proof'.[140] In the absence of absolute certainty it is always possible that even the most robust hypothesis will turn out to be false. But although one must allow for the theoretical possibility of error, there may be no earthly reason whatever to doubt the truth of a particular hypothesis. The mere theoretical possibility that a well-evidenced hypothesis may be false is, we will say, radically *inert* and cannot figure in practical deliberations about the truth of any proposition in criminal adjudication. Such doubts merely rehearse the trite truth that no inference about the physical world (or anything else, for that matter, including your own existence) is absolutely certain: in other words, that every conceivable inference is prone to error and radical scepticism ultimately eludes rational refutation.[141] The realm of inert doubt forms the background structural (epistemological) context of all reasoning under uncertainty, in contrast to the type of doubt actively at play in the reasoning process itself. Only the second kind of uncertainty is genuinely interesting for our purposes. One must take care in discussing and thinking about forensic reasoning to avoid illegitimate conflation or transgression between these two conceptually distinct realms of doubt, the one active and in principle remediable, the other inert and definitively ineliminable.

In ordinary reasoning one would say that all doubt about the occurrence of fact X is dispelled when, in our terminology, the only residual doubt that X did not occur is inert. The hypothesis that X did not occur is inert when it cannot sensibly be assigned even minimal probative value. When this is the case, the hypothesis that X did not occur no longer figures in our practical deliberation: for all practical purposes, there is no residual scope for entertaining reasonable doubt about the occurrence of X. Note that a normative criterion of reasonableness is inescapable at this level of fact-finding. One could literally believe *anything* if one were determined to be *un*reasonable.[142] In our earlier hypothetical, if the prosecution proves that all trains were cancelled on the day of the mugging, when according

---

[139] *The Probable and the Provable* (OUP, 1977), 249.   [140] ibid. 247.

[141] See e.g., Bryan Frances, *Scepticism Comes Alive* (OUP, 2005); Michael Williams, *Unnatural Doubts: Epistemological Realism and the Basis of Scepticism* (Princeton UP, 1996).

[142] This is not to suggest that beliefs are characteristically 'voluntary': to the contrary, there is an important and perfectly familiar sense in which one cannot help believing what one happens to believe. Nonetheless, people can and sometimes do force themselves to believe certain things, and this may well be a particular accomplishment of the unreasonable.

to the defence the accused was running to catch a train, and if the accused is shown to have paid for goods using credit cards stolen from *V*'s wallet, one may conclude beyond reasonable doubt that the accused is the mugger. Of course it is *possible* that the accused was running for a train in ignorance of the strike, and that he mistook the wallet and the credit cards for his own. But these hypothetical possibilities require further explanation. If, for example, the accused's flight was innocent, why did he claim to have succeeded in catching the train to London? Or again, how could he have mistaken *V*'s wallet for his own, and used credit cards in somebody else's name without noticing the error? Maybe if he was extremely short-sighted or mentally disturbed, but there is no evidence of any such disorientation. Without some evidence of special circumstances, which might lend credence to what is otherwise pure speculation, these theoretical possibilities and their associated doubts are inert – they are things that *can* happen in the world, but there is no reason to believe that they actually *did* happen here.[143] To afford them more than cursory consideration in defiance of compelling evidence of guilt would be unreasonable.

Conveying to the jury that doubt is dispelled if, and only when, the probability of innocence can no longer reasonably be entertained directly promotes the law's commitment to the presumption of innocence. The JSB's 'making you sure of it' standard might be taken to mandate the same process of eliminating explanations consistent with innocence, albeit with somewhat less clarity and assurance. In directing the jury on the burden and standard of proof, the trial judge is not delivering an academic lecture on the requisite quantum of proof to support a guilty verdict, but providing practical instruction on fact-finding. Judicial directions also seek to inoculate jurors against potentially prejudicial contextual information which, left unchallenged, might dilute the practical strength of the presumption of innocence. Darling J once observed, extra-judicially:

The truth is that, although the law pays a prisoner the compliment of supposing him wrongly accused, it nevertheless knows that the probabilities are in favour of the prosecutor's accusation being well founded... No defendant [in civil proceedings] is brought through a hole in the floor; he is not surrounded by a barrier, nor guarded by a keeper of thieves; he is not made to stand up alone while his actions are being judged; and his latest address is not presumably the jail of his county.[144]

Whilst the courtroom procedures (like the language used to describe it) have undergone modernization, the force of Darling J's principal contention remains undiminished by the passage of time. Criminal accused are not plucked at random off the street – even when the police 'round up the usual suspects', particular individuals are targeted precisely because they *are* the usual suspects – and the jury will tend to assume that there is 'no smoke without fire'. If the adverse impression created by the very fact of accusation is to be neutralized, it is imperative that juries should be encouraged to give the

---

[143] In *R v Majid* [2009] EWCA Crim 2563, [12], the jury asked the trial judge the following question: 'If the evidence supports possible but very unlikely scenarios, which themselves would lead to a "not guilty" verdict, does this exclude a "beyond reasonable doubt" conclusion. There are concerns over how to interpret "beyond reasonable doubt" – does this need to exclude *all* possible scenarios associated with "not guilty"?' The Court of Appeal observed: 'The question, we suggest, could have been answered simply by telling the jury to exclude any fanciful possibility and act only on those which were realistic.'

[144] Mr Justice Darling, *Scintillae Juris and Meditations in the Tea Room* (Stevens, 6th edn. 1914), 33–4. The semiotics of courtroom geography and drama were discussed in §3.4(d), under the rubric of 'informal evidence'.

possibility of innocence full and fair consideration. It is neither possible nor desirable to conceal from jurors that they must make their own subjective assessment of the evidence. Naturally, this element of subjectivity leaves room for a measure of flexibility in sufficiency of proof. But jurors should understand that they must be fully convinced, in their own minds, of the accused's guilt to the exclusion of all tangible, 'active', or 'realistic' doubts. The clearer the jury's understanding of its moral,[145] as well as legal, duties in criminal adjudication, the better hope for sustaining a robust and reasonably consistent criminal standard of proof in practice.

The contrast between active, tangible doubts, on the one hand, and inert and intangible (unreasonable) doubt on the other, helps to clarify an old puzzle – or 'paradox'[146] – of statistical proof, popularized by Jonathan Cohen.[147] Here is our version. Suppose that a policeman enters the lounge of a public house where twenty customers are drinking. According to uncontroverted evidence, nineteen of the drinkers – perhaps they are gangland criminals – set upon the policeman and beat him to death. The remaining individual tried, unsuccessfully, to shield the victim from this fatal attack. Suppose now that just one of the twenty is caught and prosecuted for the murder. Are these facts, without more, sufficient to authorize a conviction of murder by joint enterprise? Is the mere ('naked') statistical probability of guilt enough to constitute proof beyond reasonable doubt?

Most lawyers (and many non-lawyers) will instinctively reply that the evidence is not sufficient, but not because a 5% chance of error is poor odds; indeed, for most purposes 95% probability would be considered more than adequate. If the objection were merely to the magnitude of doubt, it could be met by increasing the statistical odds against innocence and in favour of guilt. But in fact, even if the rescuer were one out of a crowd of a hundred possible assailants – or even one in a thousand – the same instinctive aversion to conviction would arise. Yet, in scenarios where the mathematical probability of guilt can be calculated to 0.99, or greater, what is the stumbling block to conviction? This is the puzzle that we need to unravel.

It runs contrary to widely-shared intuitions to convict a person of a criminal offence purely on the basis of 'naked statistical evidence', where there is no other rational means for judging, in terms of Cohen's hypothetical, whether the accused is one of the multitude that murdered the policeman or his brave lone defender. If statistical evidence were sufficient in such circumstances, it would be possible to convict every person present, including the one innocent individual, since the evidence incriminates each of them to exactly the same extent. This is where the puzzle turns paradoxical. For any one of the twenty drinkers chosen at random from Cohen's pub, there is a 95%, or 0.95, probability that he took part in the policeman's murder. Hypotheticals such as this demonstrate that statistical evidence falls short of proof beyond reasonable doubt whenever there is an active

---

[145] The moral foundations of the criminal standard of proof are excavated in a recent historical study: James Q. Whitman, *The Origins of Reasonable Doubt: Theological Roots of the Criminal Trial* (Yale UP, 2008).

[146] This well-known puzzle, commonly known as the 'gate-crasher' or 'rodeo' paradox, was introduced in §4.5(b). See further, Mike Redmayne, 'Exploring the Proof Paradoxes' (2008) 14 *Legal Theory* 281; Richard Lempert, 'The New Evidence Scholarship: Analyzing the Process of Proof' (1986) 66 *Boston University LR* 439, Part III; Stephen E Feinberg, 'Gatecrashers, Blue Buses, and the Bayesian Representation of Legal Evidence' Proof' (1986) 66 *Boston University LR* 693; D. H. Kaye, 'The Paradox of the Gate-Crasher and Other Stories' [1979] *Arizona State LJ* 101.   [147] *The Probable and the Provable*, 74–6.

possibility, which cannot safely be eliminated from practical deliberation, that the accused might be innocent. So long as the evidence leaves room for a tangible and active possibility of innocence, however small, we are morally obliged to withhold criminal censure and punishment, despite well-founded suspicions of guilt. Our instinctive disinclination to convict tracks this moral duty better than any probabilistic calculation.[148]

In practice, of course, statistical evidence is usually accompanied by other forms of proof, which in combination are perfectly capable of dispelling all reasonable doubt. In *Abadom*,[149] for example, four masked men broke into an office, smashed an internal window, and robbed the occupants. The prosecution alleged that the accused was the robber who broke the window. Taking fragments of glass recovered from the accused's shoes, the prosecution was able to establish two pertinent facts by expert evidence: first, that the refractive index of the glass in the shoes matched the glass from the broken window; and second, that only 4% of UK glass had that particular refractive index. In other words, it was highly likely that the glass in the shoes came from the broken window, which strongly supported the further inference that the accused was one of the robbers.

By itself, however, the glass fragment evidence would have been inconclusive. A match to 4% of the glass in domestic and commercial use, equating to an estimated 20,000 to 40,000 tons, left plenty of room for doubt. The accused might conceivably have become contaminated with glass fragments from some alternative, innocent, source. But expert evidence of the distribution of glass in the accused's footwear was available to counter this hypothesis. A number of fragments were found in the upper part of the accused's shoes, further fragments came from inside the shoes, and the remainder were embedded in his soles. This distribution meant that the fragments must have showered down from above when glass shattered in the accused's presence, and were subsequently trodden into the soles of his footwear, which was entirely consistent with Abadom being a robber and inconsistent with coincidental contamination by a different source of glass which just happened to have the same refractive index as the glass from the office robbery.

Abadom was, not surprisingly, convicted. Still, the glass fragment evidence viewed in isolation, even as improved through expert interpretation, would barely be regarded as proof of guilt beyond reasonable doubt. The probability of innocent contamination with glass fragments matching the window at the scene of a robbery is both small and unquantifiable, but it cannot be dismissed out of hand as inconsequential or too unreasonable to influence the jury's deliberations. It is not so rare, after all, for glass to shatter, and when it does the shoes of people in the vicinity might well show a similar pattern of contamination to that found on Abadom. We may speculate (of course, we cannot possibly know) that three further considerations might have led the jury to a confident finding of guilt. First, it is improbable that a man picked out at random would have glass, and of the right sort, in his shoes. The police would not have randomly stopped people in the street on the off-chance that passers-by might be contaminated with glass from a particular robbery. Rather, the finger of suspicion must have pointed to Abadom for

---

[148] Alternatively, one might say that any purely probabilistic inference lacks sufficient epistemic weight or robustness to constitute a satisfactory evidential basis for a criminal conviction, because – given the artificial parameters of the hypothetical – the likelihood of wrongly convicting the innocent is known, quantified, and therefore always 'active' in our sense.   [149] [1983] 1 WLR 126, CA.

a reason, and sure enough, when his involvement was further investigated, glass of the correct specification was discovered. Secondly, no direct[150] evidence was given of previous situations in which footwear has become contaminated with fragments of glass. Jurors were thus deprived of tangible illustrations of innocent contamination. Thirdly, the accused failed to account for the presence of glass in his shoes, leaving the jury without any plausible 'story' of innocence to compete with the prosecution's story of guilt. A jury is entitled to expect that any pertinent innocent explanation will be advanced in evidence. If no such explanation is forthcoming, either from defence witnesses or in cross-examination of the prosecution's evidence, jurors will naturally conclude that there is none to be heard.

Abadom brings out the crucial distinction between reasoning under uncertainty in real criminal cases, and artificially-constructed hypotheticals like those designed to test the probative significance of naked statistical evidence. In Cohen's pub murder, for example, it was established by hypothesis that the crowd contained an innocent person who bears a quantifiable risk of wrongful conviction. There is no reason to make any such assumptions in real criminal trials.[151] Of course, an innocent person might always be charged, or even convicted. But there is invariably more to go on in real life than naked statistics. Innocent people can reasonably be expected to come forward with their exculpatory explanations, if they have any.[152] Meanwhile, the police have a duty to search for exculpatory as well as incriminating evidence,[153] and the CPS should not keep a prosecution going unless there is a realistic prospect of conviction on the evidence.[154] The whole system of criminal procedure is designed to ensure that evidentially weak cases are weeded out of the process long before a case gets to trial (though the extent to which this objective is achieved in practice is a matter of controversy).

Taking proper account of the broader procedural context of criminal adjudication in no way detracts from the presumption of innocence, as we understand it. The presumption is a normative moral and legal standard encapsulating a strong commitment to avoiding wrongful convictions, rather than a detailed specification for drawing factual

---

[150] Such evidence was subsumed within the expert's evidence, inasmuch as his opinion would be derived from statistical generalizations and his own previous experience of glass contamination. However, these previous instances could not figure in the jury's decision-making unless they were specifically highlighted and explained. More commonly, experts assert more-or-less 'black-box' conclusions without explicating the specialist knowledge, data, judgments, or inferential steps which precede and support them: see Chapter 11.

[151] Although the report is silent on the point, the jury which convicted Abadom presumably had no reason to think he had been selected for prosecution at random. Had it been thought that the police conducted random checks and prosecuted the first person to be found with that type of glass in his shoes, it would have been more difficult to dismiss the possibility of there being another person – or several – with equally incriminating evidence in their footwear. The advent of increasingly extensive DNA databases makes this scenario a genuine operational possibility, although – for the time being at least – prosecutions based solely on DNA profiling 'matches' are not generally brought in England and Wales: see CPS, *Guidance on DNA Charging* (2004), on-line via: www.cps.gov.uk/legal/d_to_g/index.html.

[152] On the position of the accused as a source of evidence, see Chapters 12 and 13.

[153] See the Code of Practice issued pursuant to Part II of the Criminal Procedure and Investigations Act 1996, para.3.4 of which provides that: 'In conducting an investigation, the investigator should pursue all reasonable lines of inquiry, whether these point towards or away from the suspect. What is reasonable in each case will depend on the particular circumstances.'

[154] *Code for Crown Prosecutors* (Feb 2010), Part 4.

inferences in criminal adjudication.[155] The presumption of innocence demands that at all stages of criminal proceedings prior to verdict the accused is treated for official purposes *as though he were* innocent, unless and until proven otherwise, and in particular that the jury approaches its task with a firm commitment to affording the accused the benefit of any reasonable doubt. This is entirely consistent with jurors drawing on their common sense to interpret the evidence in the case, which is precisely what juries are empanelled to do.

In the final analysis, the court can only advise and cajole a jury to approach the task of adjudication in the proper spirit, using the law's officially-mandated decision procedures. A trial judge cannot be certain that the jury will even comprehend the instructions issued in his summing-up,[156] let alone being confident that his advice will be taken to heart. But this does not mean that judges entirely lack influence over fact-finding, still less does it imply that judicial directions to the jury lack normative significance in giving official, public, expression to the values embedded in criminal procedure. A trial judge's directions can be more or less accomplished as a restatement of evidentiary principle, and more or less conducive to promoting the jury's understanding and co-operation in translating the principles of criminal evidence into the practice of adjudication. A direction of the sort given by Alderson B., essentially requiring the jury to exclude every active or tangible explanation consistent with innocence, is well-suited to conveying the significance of the criminal standard of proof. It articulates and commends to jurors the reasoning process by which the presumption of innocence should be given concrete expression in criminal trials.

6.5 REVERSING THE ONUS OF PROOF – BEFORE AND AFTER THE HUMAN RIGHTS ACT

For all its ostentatious celebration of 'golden threads', English law by no means evinces an unequivocal commitment to the *Woolmington* principle. The legality of 'reverse onus clauses', purporting to place the (probative) burden of proof in relation to designated 'defences' on the accused, has become one of the hottest evidentiary topics under the Human Rights Act 1998. Before examining recent jurisprudence under the Human Rights Act, however, we first need to review the earlier development of three recognized 'exceptions' to *Woolmington*.

(a) THREE EXCEPTIONS TO *WOOLMINGTON*

The common law concedes only one exception to the requirement that the prosecution must prove the accused's guilt beyond reasonable doubt. This first exception was specifically reserved by *Woolmington* itself: an accused pleading insanity bears the burden of proving it, on the balance of probabilities.[157] This exception, however, is of limited

---

[155] Laurence H. Tribe, 'Trial by Mathematics' (1971) 84 *Harvard LR* 1329, 1371.

[156] Especially where the logic and intelligibility of the directions themselves are seriously open to doubt. For examples and discussion, see §2.5(d), §8.6, §13.3(b), and Chapter 15.

[157] *Woolmington* v *DPP* [1935] AC 462, 481–2, HL.

practical significance. Historically, a finding of 'not guilty by reason of insanity' meant mandatory detention in a secure hospital, for a period of confinement likely to be greater than the average 'time served' by convicted offenders. The Criminal Procedure (Insanity and Unfitness to Plead) Act 1991 subsequently ameliorated the predicament of mentally disturbed accused by providing for an expanded range of sentencing options, including non-custodial disposals. Nonetheless, a plea of insanity remains an unattractive option for most accused, and the defence is seldom raised.[158]

Of far greater importance are various forms of statutory exception. Some of these exceptions have been expressly created by Parliament, whilst others are the outcome of statutory interpretation by the judges. A long, and constantly expanding list of statutes has been held to impose a burden on the accused to disprove an element of a statutory offence, or to establish a particular statutory defence, in order to escape liability.[159] Indeed, it has been estimated that approximately 40% of the indictable offences regularly prosecuted in England and Wales employ some form of reverse onus device.[160] Though manifestly contrary to evidentiary principle, a Diceyan Parliament claiming unlimited sovereignty within its territorial jurisdiction can undoubtedly decree that a person shall be convicted of a criminal offence unless he proves his innocence. Express reverse onus clauses of this type constitute the second group of exceptions to *Woolmington*.

Responsibility for interpreting statutory language rests with the courts, however, and the judges might have declined to derogate from *Woolmington's* fundamental principle unless Parliament expressly directed them to do so. But they did not take such a principled stand. To the contrary, appellate courts have been willing to find breaks and knots in the golden thread even where the relevant statute was silent as to the allocation of burdens of proof. The judges must therefore accept their share of responsibility for weakening the presumption of innocence in English law. Reverse onus clauses implied into statutory offences by judicial interpretation are known as the third class of *Woolmington* exceptions.

Each of the exceptions to *Woolmington* poses two, analytically distinct, doctrinal questions. First, in what circumstances does the burden of proof lie on an accused? Second, when the accused bears the burden, is it a fully probative onus, or merely an evidential

---

[158] The accused is credited with a 'presumption of sanity' which, generally speaking, only the accused him – or herself may put in issue. But the trial judge may have a residual discretion to direct on an insanity verdict in appropriate cases, which would be 'exceptional and very rare': *R v Dickie* [1984] 1 WLR 1031, CA. Since the prosecution is not allowed to prove insanity, the prosecutor's standard of proof in relation to this issue never arises. 'The prosecution has a positive duty to prove if it can the allegation which it makes upon the indictment. It has the power if the issue is raised by the defence to rebut by its own evidence the attempt by the defence to establish insanity. It has the obligation, if it has evidence in its possession of insanity which will assist the defence to establish that the defendant was in that condition when the crime was committed, to make that evidence available to the defence in good time, so that in its discretion it may make proper use of it': ibid. 1037.

[159] In addition to the examples discussed in the text, they include, Sexual Offences Act 2003, s.75 (absence of consent); Homicide Act 1957, ss.2 and 4 (respectively, diminished responsibility and suicide pacts); Criminal Justice Act 1988, s.139 (having object with blade or sharp point in a public place); Public Order Act 1986, s.6 (defence of involuntary intoxication); Protection from Eviction Act 1977 (reasonable belief that occupier has vacated); Misuse of Drugs Act 1971, s.28 (ignorance of identity of drug); Prevention of Corruption Act 1916, s.2 (corrupt intention).

[160] Andrew Ashworth and Meredith Blake, 'The Presumption of Innocence in English Criminal Law' [1996] *Crim LR* 314.

burden of production, that he must discharge? Although these are technically separate questions, they are closely related considerations which in practice often run together. As we will see in section (c), below, the Human Rights Act has introduced a third question, which must now be addressed when the first two have been answered in the affirmative: where a reverse onus clause purports to impose a probative burden on the accused, is this measure compatible with ECHR Article 6(2), or must it instead be 'read down' under section 3 of the Human Rights Act to a merely evidential burden of production?

(b) THE THIRD EXCEPTION AT COMMON LAW: *EDWARDS* AND *HUNT*

In 1974 the Court of Appeal enunciated a doctrine designed to pre-empt any strenuous interpretative effort on the part of trial judges in determining whether a particular statute imposed a burden of proof on the accused. It was held in *Edwards*[161] that, in addition to insanity at common law and express statutory exceptions, English law recognized a third set of exceptions to the *Woolmington* principle comparable in effect to what is now section 101 of the Magistrates' Courts Act 1980. Section 101 provides that:

Where the defendant to any information or complaint relies for his defence on any exception, exemption, proviso, excuse or qualification, whether or not it accompanies the description of the offence or matter of complaint in the enactment creating the offence or on which the complaint is founded, the burden of proving the exception, exemption, proviso, excuse or qualification shall be on him; and this notwithstanding that the information or complaint contains an allegation negativing the exception, exemption, proviso, excuse or qualification.

According to *Edwards*, terms like 'exemption', 'exception', 'proviso', and so forth relate to statutory offences which are designed to prohibit specified conduct save in legislatively-permitted circumstances, or by designated persons with particular qualifications, or with the licence or permission of specified authorities. In such cases, but only in them, it is for the accused to prove that he qualifies for inclusion in the exempted class.

As an attempt to delimit a robust third exception to the *Woolmington* principle, the *Edwards* approach focusing on the concept of 'exception, etc.' is seriously flawed. Consider two alternative formulations of a statutory offence of unlicensed driving:

1. 'It is forbidden for any person to drive without a driving licence';
2. 'It is forbidden for any person to drive, except where such person holds a driving licence'.

The distinction between these two models for drafting criminal prohibitions resides, not in the concept of an exception, but in the subtleties of linguistic emphasis and meaning, which convey further moral and juridical distinctions. Drafting style #1 would be appropriate where certain conditions are being applied to a basically lawful activity. Driving is not inherently wrong. However, taking account of safety, crime prevention, and other relevant considerations, it is wrong to drive without a licence. Drafting style #2 is appropriate

---

[161] *R v Edwards* [1974] 1 QB 27, CA. See A. A. S. Zuckerman, 'The Third Exception to the *Woolmington* Rule' (1976) 92 *LQR* 402.

where the targeted activity is essentially unlawful, but may be undertaken by specified persons or under exceptional circumstances. Thus, for example, supplying controlled drugs is generally prohibited, except when the supplier is a registered medical practitioner, pharmacist, or the like. These distinctions, though linguistically fine, are enormously significant in terms of fair labelling and justified censure of criminal wrongdoing.[162]

The inherent weakness of the *Edwards* exception is not, therefore, that it lacks any deeper rationalization or moral justification, but rather that it is beset by practical difficulties. To begin with, the precise moral significance of language is often illusive at the best of times. The inherent vagueness of language is compounded, secondly, by the fact that substantive moral propositions are contestable and frequently contested. Thirdly, and above all, parliamentary draftsmen have never formulated the wording of offences with the degree of precision or attention to moral nuance that would be required to allow the courts to apply and develop the *Edwards* exception in an appropriately structured and morally rigorous fashion.[163] The inevitable consequence, in practice, has been uncertainty, confusion, and inconsistency in the law – which are regrettable enough on their own account, without recalling that the whole dubious enterprise was undertaken in order to water down a foundational precept of criminal evidence.

This unsatisfactory state of affairs was exacerbated by the theoretical impoverishment of English criminal law theory, the more so in the 1970s and 1980s than today. In particular, the concept of a 'defence' was underdeveloped in English criminal jurisprudence. Thus, self-defence offers a common law escape-route from criminal liability – albeit, one intuitively feels, in a rather different sense from the way in which presenting a driving licence is an answer to a charge of unlicensed driving. Yet it cannot follow that self-defence is to be regarded as a defence or exemption, in the narrow technical sense, for all purposes. It might be sensible to categorize self-defence as a 'defence' for the purpose of drafting indictments, thereby relieving the prosecution of the need to negate self-defence in the initial charge and imposing a corresponding burden of production on the accused to make self-defence an issue in the case if he chooses to do so. At the same time, the law may insist, as *Woolmington* does, that the (probative) burden of disproving self-defence at all times remains with the Crown.[164] It is the prosecution's limited duty to plead its case, not the accused's substantive plea, that is 'exceptional' in this context, and which explains the institutionalized solecism of referring to a plea of lawful force as a 'defence', when it is in fact a blanket denial of wrongdoing – a claim of justification, rather than a plea to be excused. This highly instructive example should provide ample warning of the perils of relying on conventional terminology and definitions – whether found in statute, at common law, or in lawyers' everyday conversation – as the basis for allocating probative burdens of proof. It would be obtuse to think that legislative drafting choices always track salient moral distinctions or that Parliament's intentions hang on the positing of every clause or word.[165]

---

[162] If this should be doubted, imagine a statute that read: 'All sexual intercourse is a serious criminal offence carrying a maximum sentence of life imprisonment, except where both parties consent'. See further, Paul Roberts, 'Strict Liability and the Presumption of Innocence: An Exposé of Functionalist Assumptions', in Andrew Simester (ed.), *Appraising Strict Liability* (OUP, 2005).

[163] See Glanville Williams, 'Offences and Defences' (1982) 2 *Legal Studies* 233.

[164] This fits with the linguistic and moral distinction outlined in the text, to the extent that self-defensive action is justified, or at least permitted, rather than merely excused. That is to say, violence in self-defence is not *wrongful* and does not therefore constitute any offence of *unlawful* assault, wounding, killing, etc.

[165] As Glanville Williams, 'The Logic of "Exceptions"' (1988) 47 *Cambridge LJ* 261, 270, 272, observed, with customary forthrightness: 'Parliamentary draftsmen do not follow strict and publicly proclaimed

Edwards set a dangerous precedent in this respect. Its impact would have been muted if the courts had said that only a burden of production could be imposed on the accused. However, it was universally assumed – adopting the strict meaning of 'burden of proof'[166] – that the accused must shoulder the full probative burden, which indeed is clearly what the Court of Appeal had in mind in *Edwards* itself. This gave licence to the courts to demand that an accused person prove his innocence merely because an element of the offence happened to be contained in a sub-clause employing any of the 'exception'-importing trigger-words. Fortunately, some of the damage was subsequently repaired through revisionist judicial interpretation of *Edwards*.

In *Hunt*[167] the House of Lords drew the sting from the decision in *Edwards* by treating it as no more than a general guide to statutory interpretation in related contexts. Terms like 'exception', 'proviso', and the rest consequently had no automatic effect in allocating the burden of proof,[168] and section 101 of the Magistrates' Courts Act 1980 was likewise inconclusive, requiring particularistic application to individual statutory offences on a case-by-case basis. By taking this line, their Lordships significantly cut down the scope for *ad hoc* departures from *Woolmington*, both in summary proceedings and in trials on indictment. The House was urged by counsel to take matters further by ruling that statutory exceptions to *Woolmington* are limited to provisions that expressly, and not just by implication, impose a burden of proof on the accused. But there was limited authority in favour of that proposition,[169] and several decisions against it.[170] Counsel's submission was accordingly rejected – and the 'third exception' to *Woolmington* became further entrenched.[171]

Their Lordships were invited to place a further restriction on deviations from *Woolmington*, by restricting the accused's burden, whenever it arose, to a burden of production. This was a golden opportunity to reinvigorate the *Woolmington* principle by declaring that an accused should only ever be required to adduce sufficient evidence from which

principles in the wording of offences (they rightly think there is no need to do so). Sometimes they separate the statement of a rule from a statement of what are thought of as exceptions to it, but sometimes combine what might have been stated as exceptions into the sentence stating the rule. When they use the former style of drafting (rule + exception), they do not say why, but the obvious explanation is that it is a mere matter of presentation.... Statutes are often unskilfully drafted, and even if well drafted at the outset they are frequently pulled about during their passage through Parliament. There is no assurance that the order of words represents a considered legislative judgment as to the burden of proof.'

[166] See §6.2(a), above.   [167] *R v Hunt* [1987] AC 352, HL.

[168] See ibid. 375, *per* Lord Griffiths: 'I would prefer to adopt the formula as an excellent guide to construction rather than as an exception to [the *Woolmington*] rule. In the final analysis each case must turn upon the construction of the particular legislation...' And see Lord Ackner, ibid. 386, to similar effect.

[169] Apart from Viscount Sankey LC's speech in *Woolmington*, there is the following *dictum* of Viscount Simon LC in *Mancini v DPP* [1942] AC 1, HL: 'the [*Woolmington*] rule is of general application in all charges under the criminal law. The only exceptions arise, as explained in *Woolmington's* case, in the defence of insanity and in offences where the onus of proof is specially dealt with by statute'. And see *Jayasena v R* [1970] AC 618, 623, PC, further *obiter* remarks.

[170] Numerous older decisions had already interpreted non-express statutory provisions as imposing a burden on the accused: *R v Ewens* [1967] 1 QB 322, CCA; *R v Oliver* [1944] KB 68, CCA; *R v Scott* (1921) 86 JP 69; *Apothecaries' Co v Bentley* (1824) 1 C & P 538; *R v Turner* (1816) 5 M & S 206; 105 ER 1026.

[171] A further difficulty in the way of counsel's argument was that the burden in trials on indictment would then have been different to that dictated by s.101 for summary proceedings. As Lord Griffiths observed in *R v Hunt* [1987] AC 352, 373, the 'law would have developed on absurd lines if in respect of the same offence the burden of proof... differed according to whether the case was heard by the magistrates or on indictment'. The disparity might have been defensible if the magistrates courts and Crown Court had mutually exclusive jurisdiction, but the existence of a large category of offences 'triable either way' presents a seemingly insurmountable anomaly.

a reasonable jury might infer relevant facts in his favour, leaving the prosecution to prove beyond reasonable doubt that the accused did not qualify for any claimed statutory exception once the issue had been raised in the trial.[172] But the House of Lords was unmoved on this occasion: when a statute imposes a burden on the accused, their Lordships said, it is the burden of proving the relevant fact on the balance of probabilities.

This ruling was objectionable on two counts. First, to countenance an accused's conviction, in circumstances where reasonable doubt still remains as to some element of the offence, is a straightforward derogation from the presumption of innocence and its underlying liberal philosophy of respect for persons. This aspect of the decision accounts for academic commentators' largely hostile reaction to *Hunt*.[173] Secondly, if it is appropriate for courts to scrutinize each individual statutory provision to determine whether the legislature intended to impose any burden at all on the accused, why is the court not equally free to ascertain, on a section by section basis, whether an evidential rather than a probative burden was intended?[174] Logical consistency would seem to buttress the *Woolmington* principle in this regard, and yet their Lordships – apparently trying almost too hard – insisted on an interpretation of the law which detracts from the practical value of the presumption of innocence. Had the House of Lords stated unequivocally that there is no 'third exception' to *Woolmington*, responsibility for derogating from the presumption of innocence would have rested fairly and squarely with Parliament. Thereafter, if Parliament were minded to create criminal liability without full proof of each offence element, it would have been obliged to say so clearly and publicly. As it is, we possibly now have more reverse onus provisions than governments would have been brave enough to introduce into Parliament, or powerful enough to force through into legislation.

These missed opportunities must, however, be set against the positive aspects of *Hunt*.[175] Lord Griffiths articulated an important principle to limit the scope for deviation from the presumption of innocence:

Parliament can never lightly be taken to have intended to impose an onerous duty on a defendant to prove his innocence in a criminal case, and a court should be very slow to draw any such inference from the language of a statute.[176]

---

[172] This was the recommendation of the Criminal Law Revision Committee's influential Eleventh Report, *Evidence: General* Cm 4991 (HMSO, 1972), paras.137–42. And see Rupert Cross, 'The Golden Thread of the English Criminal Law', Rede Lecture (1976).

[173] Glanville Williams, 'The Logic of "Exceptions"' (1988) 47 *CLJ* 261; J. C. Smith, 'The Presumption of Innocence' (1987) 38 *NILQ* 223; P. Healy, 'Proof and Policy: No Golden Threads' [1987] *Crim LR* 355; Peter Mirfield, 'The Legacy of *Hunt*' [1988] *Crim LR* 19.

[174] One possible rejoinder is that evidential burdens are not strictly burdens of *proof*, but only burdens of production to adduce evidence, so that Parliament must be taken to intend a probative burden whenever it uses the language of 'proof' and its cognates: see Paul Roberts, 'Drug-Dealing and the Presumption of Innocence: The Human Rights Act (Almost) Bites' (2002) 6 *E & P* 17, 33–5. But that view is still consistent with section by section statutory interpretation, and raises no objection to finding an evidential burden where a particular statutory provision avoids the explicit terminology of 'proof'. It might, however, be said to credit Parliament with an unrealistically acute facility with evidentiary concepts.

[175] For a more positive reading than most, see D. J. Birch, 'Hunting the Snark: The Elusive Statutory Exception' [1988] *Crim LR* 221.

[176] *R v Hunt* [1987] AC 352, 374. And see Lord Ackner, ibid. 379–80, apparently holding that the third exception to *Woolmington* is limited to cases in which Parliament's intention to impose a probative burden on the accused is a 'necessary implication' of the relevant statutory language.

What is more, the House of Lords practised what it preached. Hunt was charged with unlawful possession of morphine contrary to section 5(2) of the Misuse of Drugs Act 1971. Under the Misuse of Drugs Regulations 1973 preparations containing up to 0.2% morphine were exempted from the scope of the offence. The prosecution adduced evidence at trial to prove that the substance found in the accused's possession contained morphine, but led no evidence to establish the concentration of the preparation. The House of Lords held that, in relation to this particular statutory offence, the probative burden rested with the prosecution to prove that the substance found in the accused's possession exceeded the legal limit. In arriving at this conclusion, their Lordships were influenced by the comparative ease with which the prosecution could have proved the contested issue. After all, the police had confiscated Hunt's morphine, so he was no longer in a position to test its concentration; and, in any case, the prosecution generally enjoys far better access to scientific testing equipment than criminal accused. A natural interpretation of section 5(2), read in conjunction with the 1973 Regulations, is that the offence is limited to possessing substances containing more than 0.2% concentrations of morphine. There was therefore no interpretative obstacle to ruling that the concentration of the allegedly controlled substance was a basic offence element which, as the House of Lords held, the prosecution must prove beyond reasonable doubt.

Hunt established, in general terms, that an implied burden of proof could only be found where: first, a statutory offence exempts specified classes of persons or permit-holders from the scope of the general prohibition; and, secondly, it would not be unreasonably onerous to expect an accused to prove that he belongs to the designated class or, as the case may be, possesses the necessary permit, etc. From a practical point of view, allocating a burden of proof to the accused in such circumstances is typically of limited significance. Suppose that a particular activity, like a dangerous industrial process, is prohibited without a special licence to engage in it. Now imagine that, contrary to *Hunt*, the burden of proving that a factory was engaged in dangerous industrial processes without a licence fell entirely on the prosecution, rather than the factory-owner being required to show that he possesses a licence specifically authorizing that line of business. How would the prosecution discharge its burden? In most cases it would surely be sufficient for the prosecution to call evidence that the factory-owner had been challenged to produce his licence and had failed to do so. If the accused cannot produce the licence, or any credible explanation for failing to do so, the prosecution will have gone most of the way towards discharging its burden of persuasion as to the existence of the licence.[177] It is possible that an unusually lenient, or gullible, jury or bench of magistrates might give the accused the benefit of residual doubt in such circumstances. But in most cases the accused would be obliged to do much the same as he must do under the *Hunt* regime, allocating the probative burden to him: produce his licence, or at least a credible explanation for its absence.[178]

---

[177] *Westminster City Council* v *Croyalgrange Ltd* [1986] 1 WLR 674, HL, *per* Lord Bridge.

[178] Cf. *Oxford* v *Lincoln*, *The Times* 1 March 1982, where the Divisional Court found that, as a question of statutory interpretation, s.101 of the Magistrates' Courts Act 1980 did not apply to s.161 of the Licensing Act 1964. In this particular instance, the accused bore only an evidential burden of production. And see Michael Dean, 'Negative Averments and the Burden of Proof' [1966] *Crim LR* 594, criticizing the Court of Criminal Appeal in *R* v *Ewens* [1966] 1 QB 322 for arriving at the opposite conclusion in relation to s.1(1)(a) of the Drugs (Prevention of Misuse) Act 1964.

An appreciation of the limited practical purchase of reverse onus clauses should not lead to the conclusion that little of consequence therefore turns on the allocation of the burden of proof in relation to affirmative defences. To the contrary, pragmatic considerations tend to reinforce principled objections to derogating from the *Woolmington* principle, especially in relation to exceptions of the implied, third kind, where judicial hands are not tied by parliamentary fiat. If allocating an implied probative burden to the accused only has practical significance, generally speaking, in exceptional or marginal cases, the sacrifice of principle in qualifying the presumption of innocence without Parliament's express command seems all the more gratuitous. The advent of the Human Rights Act provided judges with the doctrinal pretext for considering anew these fundamental issues of the scope and meaning of the presumption of innocence in English law.

(c) *WOOLMINGTON* AFTER THE HUMAN RIGHTS ACT

One immediate effect of the Human Rights Act was to increase the doctrinal salience of the concept of 'presumption of innocence', as contained in ECHR Article 6(2), where previously English judges had usually employed the more anodyne terminology of 'burden and standard or proof'.[179] However, Strasbourg jurisprudence specifically addressing the legality of reverse onus clauses is sparse. In *Salabiaku*, the leading European authority on the interpretation of Article 6(2), the Strasbourg court made the following observations:

Presumptions of fact or of law operate in every legal system. Clearly, the Convention does not prohibit such presumptions in principle. It does, however, require the Contracting States to remain within certain limits in this respect as regards criminal law ... Article 6(2) does not therefore regard presumptions of fact or of law provided for in the criminal law with indifference. It requires States to confine them within reasonable limits which take into account the importance of what is at stake and maintain the rights of the defence.[180]

The European Court has thus established two principles, which have to be balanced one against the other: on the one hand, the presumption of innocence is not absolute in European human rights law; but at the same time, on the other hand, the Court insists on maintaining a level of supervision over the use of presumptions in domestic law, otherwise 'the national legislature would be free to strip the trial court of any genuine power of assessment and deprive the presumption of innocence of its substance ...'[181] These remarks

---

[179] The Law Reports from 1865 contain only seven pre-Human Rights Act English criminal cases in which the phrase 'presumption of innocence' appears in the judgment of the court, on no occasion attracting more than a few cursory remarks (Westlaw search for 'presumption of innocence' in LAW-RPTS database, 30 March 2006). As a rough comparator, a search in the same database on the same day for 'burden of proof' scored 1,414 'hits': for discussion, see Paul Roberts, 'Criminal Procedure, the Presumption of Innocence and Judicial Reasoning under the Human Rights Act', in Helen Fenwick, Gavin Phillipson, and Roger Masterman (eds.), *Judicial Reasoning under the UK Human Rights Act* (CUP, 2007).

[180] *Salabiaku* v *France* (1991) 13 EHRR 379, [28], applied in *Pham Hoang* v *France* (A/243) (1993) 16 EHRR 53, ECtHR. The presumption of innocence is also considered to be subsumed within Article 6(1)'s general 'fair trial' provision, and there is an uncertain degree of overlap with the privilege against self incrimination: see *Saunders* v *UK* (1996) 23 EHRR 313, ECtHR, [68]; *Telfner* v *Austria* (2002) 34 EHRR 7, ECtHR; and discussion in §13.2(b).   [181] *Salabiaku*, [28].

have been received by English judges as general statements of principle.[182] In Lord Hope's pithy summary in *Lambert*:

What it means is that, as the article 6(2) right is not absolute and unqualified, the test to be applied is whether the modification or limitation of that right pursues a legitimate aim and whether it satisfies the principle of proportionality...[183]

Whilst this formulation provides a baseline for analysis, proportionality tests are notoriously vague and require careful contextual application. The burning question now became whether the courts would use their newfound latitude to insist on the full vigour of *Woolmington*, or whether they would allow doctrinal flexibility to become a pretext for progressively whittling away at the presumption of innocence, severing the golden thread by a thousand cuts. The story so far suggests an uneasy compromise falling somewhere between these polar opposites.

The flood of new appellate decisions reconsidering the legality of reverse onus clauses began even before the Human Rights Act had entered fully into force,[184] and the early signs might have given proponents of a robust presumption of innocence reason for hope. In *Lambert*[185] the accused was convicted of possessing cocaine with intent to supply, contrary to section 5(3) of the Misuse of Drugs Act 1971. Lambert challenged section 28 of the 1971 Act, which affords a defence if the accused can prove that 'he neither believed nor suspected nor had reason to suspect that the substance or product in question was a controlled drug'.[186] The Court of Appeal[187] rejected this argument without much difficulty, and had even less hesitation in dismissing parallel Article 6(2) arguments challenging the Homicide Act 1957's reverse onus clause governing a plea of diminished responsibility to a charge of murder, which were urged on the court by two other accused in conjoined appeals.[188] Lord Woolf CJ held that there were compelling reasons for reversing the onus of proof in each of these circumstances. Even on the assumption that jurisdictional objections to the application of Article 6(2) in the present proceedings could be overcome (the defendants' convictions having been entered prior to 2 October 2000 when the Human Rights Act came fully into force),[189] neither section 28 of the Misuse of Drugs Act 1971 nor section 2 of the Homicide Act 1957 breached European human rights law.

But a further appeal to the House of Lords produced a surprising reversal of fortune, and a remarkable departure from previous learning. The House of Lords (Lord Hutton

---

[182] See, e.g., *R v Lambert* [2002] 2 AC 545, HL, [34] (Lord Steyn), [87] (Lord Hope), [184] (Lord Hutton); *Attorney General's Reference (No 4 of 2002)* [2003] 2 Cr App R 346, CA, [32]; *Sheldrake v DPP* [2003] 2 Cr App R 206, [2003] EWHC Admin 273, [18]; *L v DPP* [2001] EWHC Admin 882, [2002] 1 Cr App R 420, [10].

[183] *R v Lambert (Steven)* [2002] 2 AC 545, HL, [88].

[184] Also see *R v DPP, ex p. Kebilene* [2000] 2 AC 326, DC and HL, dissected by Paul Roberts, 'The Presumption of Innocence Brought Home?: *Kebeline* Deconstructed' (2002) 118 *LQR* 41.

[185] *R v Lambert (Steven)* [2002] 2 AC 545, HL. See Paul Roberts, 'Drug-Dealing and the Presumption of Innocence: The Human Rights Act (Almost) Bites' (2002) 6 *E & P* 17.

[186] Misuse of Drugs Act 1971, s.28(3)(b)(i).   [187] *R v Lambert; Ali; Jordan* [2001] Cr App R 205, CA.

[188] Homicide Act 1957, s.2(2): '... it shall be for the defence to prove that the person charged is by virtue of this section not liable to be convicted of murder'.

[189] Lord Woolf CJ expressed doubts 'as to whether Parliament could have intended such a result', but was prepared to proceed on the basis that 'we have to approach the safety of any conviction as if the Act had been in force when the judge summed up': [2001] Cr App R 205, [28]. The House of Lords subsequently confirmed Lord Woolf's doubts, and overruled that part of the Court of Appeal's decision, as well.

dissenting) ruled that, contrary to the Court of Appeal's understanding, if section 5(3), in conjunction with section 28, imposed probative burdens on the accused to prove statutory defences to charges of drug-dealing, the 1971 Act would have been in contravention of Article 6(2). Their Lordships further indicated, however, that section 28 should be 'read down', in accordance with the interpretative obligation imposed by section 3 of the Human Rights Act,[190] so that only an *evidential* burden of production would be imposed by the relevant statutory language. In this way, the section 28 defence conceded by the Misuse of Drugs Act 1971 Act could be rendered compatible with Article 6(2) of the ECHR and also, by extension, with the Human Rights Act.

Their Lordships' analysis of Article 6(2) and reverse onus clauses was strictly *obiter*, since Lambert's appeal was determined on the jurisdictional basis that the Human Rights Act has no general retroactive effect.[191] But it is clear that Lords Slynn, Steyn, Hope, and Clyde intended to state binding propositions of law, which lower courts were expected to follow, and have followed.[192] Lord Hope signalled that the same approach might be taken to third-exception implied reverse onus clauses under the *Edwards/Hunt* line of authority. Lord Steyn, meanwhile, endorsed the following passage from the judgment of Dickson CJ in the Canadian Supreme Court:

The real concern is not whether the accused must disprove an element or prove an excuse, but that an accused may be convicted while a reasonable doubt exists. When that possibility exists, there is a breach of the presumption of innocence. The exact characterization of a factor as an essential element, a collateral factor, an excuse, or a defence should not affect the analysis of the presumption of innocence. It is the final effect of a provision on the verdict that is decisive. If an accused is required to prove some fact on the balance of probabilities to avoid conviction, the provision violates the presumption of innocence because it permits a conviction in spite of a reasonable doubt in the mind of the trier of fact as to the guilt of the accused.[193]

Yet this unflinching and admirably clear statement of principle is wholly at odds with the English courts' approach to reverse onus clauses, before and after *Woolmington*. If Dickson CJ's reasoning were adopted without qualification, to impose *any* probative burden on the accused would contravene the presumption of innocence. The Canadian Supreme Court, as good as its word, has held that the common law probative burden in relation to insanity is *prima facie* incompatible with the presumption of innocence, as that concept is

---

[190] See §1.5(a).

[191] Strictly speaking, the *ratio* of *Lambert* was that the Human Rights Act has no retroactive effect, beyond that specifically mandated by s.22(4) of the Act itself. A majority of their Lordships later said in *R v Kansal (No 2)* [2002] 2 AC 69, HL, that *Lambert* had been wrongly decided on this point, but refused to invoke the Practice Direction to overrule *Lambert* on the basis that legal certainty was more important than establishing the best legal rule in this rather unusual context concerning merely transitional provisions.

[192] *R v Lang and Deadman* [2002] EWCA Crim 298; *Sheldrake v DPP* [2003] 2 Cr App R 206 [2003] EWHC 273 Admin, [20], *per* Clarke LJ: 'It may be said that this part of the discussion in the House of Lords in *Lambert* is *obiter* because the House decided that Article 6 of the ECHR had no application because the trial took place before the HRA came into force. However, the reasoning in this part of *Lambert* has since been followed in the Court of Appeal...and in my opinion we should follow it.'

[193] *R v Whyte* (1988) 51 DLR (4th) 481, 493, SCC.

understood in Canada.[194] Could we, then, infer that *M'Naghten*[195] (and *Woolmington*) had been overruled, to the extent that the accused no longer had to *prove* insanity on the balance of probabilities in English law, but only to present enough evidence to make insanity an issue in the trial, which the prosecution must then disprove beyond reasonable doubt? This was one of several pressing questions left unanswered by their Lordships' bold pronouncements in *Lambert*.

Subsequent appeals – of which there have been an extraordinary number, including three further visits to the House of Lords – have dashed early hopes that the Human Rights Act might have inaugurated the renaissance of *Woolmington*. The main doctrinal point to be extracted from this thicket of case-law is that the Article 6(2) compatibility of each reverse onus provision must be assessed on its own individual merits; in other words, a reassertion of the contextual approach to 'third exceptions' propounded by *Hunt*. From a broader socio-legal perspective, the main lesson of this jurisprudence might well be that most reverse onus clauses are judged to the pass the proportionality test, although there are significant exceptions where the courts have insisted on 'reading down' to a burden of production.

Next in the sequence of House of Lords cases after *Lambert* comes *Johnstone*,[196] which concerned alleged trade mark infringement contrary to section 92 of the Trade Marks Act 1994. The presumption of innocence was implicated by section 92(5) which provides 'a defence for a person charged with an offence under this section to show that he believed on reasonable grounds that the use of the sign in the manner in which it was used, or was to be used, was not an infringement of the registered trade mark'. The starting point for Lord Nicholls was that section 92(5) patently contemplated imposing a fully probative burden on the accused, as Parliament must certainly have intended:

I entertain no doubt that, unless this interpretation is incompatible with Article 6(2) of the Convention, s. 92(5) should be interpreted as imposing on the accused person the burden of proving the relevant facts on the balance of probability. Unless he proves these facts he does not make good the defence provided by s. 92(5). The contrary interpretation of s. 92(5) involves a substantial re-writing of the subsection.... [R]aising an issue does not provide the person charged with a defence. It provides him with a defence only if, he having raised an issue, the prosecution then fails to disprove the relevant facts beyond reasonable doubt. I do not believe s. 92(5) can be so read. I do not believe that is what Parliament intended.[197]

This interpretation of subsection 92(5), Lord Nicholls acknowledged, must necessarily entail a *prima facie* breach of Article 6(2) at the next stage of the analysis, since 'this interpretation...sets out facts a defendant must establish if he is to avoid conviction. These

---

[194] *R v Chaulk* [1990] 3 SCR 1303. However, the traditional reverse onus clause in relation to insanity was upheld as a justifiable derogation from the presumption of innocence under the general saving clause afforded by s.1 of the Canadian Charter of Rights and Freedoms. It is noteworthy that there is no comparable provision applicable to Article 6(2) under the ECHR.

[195] *M'Naghten's Case* (1843) 10 C & F 200. Lord Tindal CJ advised Parliament that 'jurors ought to be told in all cases that every man is to be presumed sane...until the contrary be proved to their satisfaction,' which is hardly consistent with a merely evidential onus. For extended critique and argument in favour of introducing the evidential burden, see T. H. Jones, 'Insanity, Automatism, and the Burden of Proof on the Accused' (1995) 111 *LQR* 475.   [196] *R v Johnstone* [2003] 1 WLR 1736, [2003] UKHL 28.

[197] ibid.[46].

facts are presumed against him unless he establishes the contrary.'[198] The determinative question thus becomes whether a particular derogation from the presumption of innocence is justifiable in the terms indicated by the European Court of Human Rights (ECtHR) in *Salabiaku*, and previously elaborated by the House of Lords in *Kebilene* and *Lambert*. Lord Nicholls confessed the difficulty of this task, which appeared to him to involve a paradoxical balancing of 'incommensurables':

In the face of this paradox all that can be said is that for a reverse burden of proof to be acceptable there must be a compelling reason why it is fair and reasonable to deny the accused the protection normally guaranteed by the presumption of innocence.[199]

Derogating from the presumption of innocence in this fashion 'permits a conviction in spite of the fact-finding tribunal having a reasonable doubt as to the guilt of the accused', and this threshold consideration 'should colour one's approach when evaluating the reasons why it is said that, in the absence of a persuasive burden on the accused, the public interest will be prejudiced to an extent which justifies placing a persuasive burden on the accused'.[200] Lord Nicholls then expounded further factors bearing on this determination. Where the punishment on conviction would involve serious hardship, the justification for imposing a probative burden on the accused must be correspondingly weighty. Account should also be taken of the nature and extent of the matters which the prosecution must prove in order to constitute a case to answer and call forth a defence, and the countervailing ease with which the accused might establish facts readily, and perhaps peculiarly, accessible to him.

　　Turning to the circumstances of the present appeal, manufacturing and distributing counterfeit goods have been shown to involve serious criminality with a major detrimental impact on the global economy. Parliament has responded to what it perceives as a growing menace by enacting offences, including those provided by section 92 of the TMA 1994, which 'have rightly been described as offences of "near absolute liability"'.[201] These offences require no proof of intent to infringe a trade mark, yet carry severe maximum penalties of up to ten years' imprisonment and unlimited fines, flanked by swingeing confiscation and civil forfeiture provisions. This unflinching penal regime exemplifies Lord Nicholls' 'paradox',[202] that 'the more serious the crime and the greater the public interest in securing convictions of the guilty, the more important the constitutional protection of the accused becomes'.[203] However, two further factors were regarded by their Lordships as decisive in *Johnstone*. First, traders who deal in branded products are well aware of the risks of piracy and counterfeiting and ought to stick to reputable suppliers: should they choose to peddle goods of dubious provenance, they do so at their own peril. Secondly, international supply chains of counterfeit goods are exceedingly difficult for investigators to detect and unravel. Even if the original suppliers are ever traced, their voluntary participation in criminal investigations and prosecutions is seldom forthcoming. Traders can always claim that they received counterfeit supplies in good faith from a trustworthy source. Without the assistance of a reverse onus clause to lighten its probative load, the prosecution's task of proving that in reality the trader knew his goods were counterfeit,

[198] ibid. [47].　　[199] ibid. [49].　　[200] ibid. [50].　　[201] ibid. [52].
[202] ibid. [220], adopting the analysis of Sachs J in the South African Constitutional Court in *State* v *Coetzee* [1997] 2 LRC 593.　　[203] [2003] 1 WLR 1736, [49].

or that he at any rate lacked reasonable grounds for believing them to be genuine, would be intolerably burdensome in the majority of cases. The constitutional guarantee of the presumption of innocence, their Lordships concluded, must in these circumstances defer to the imperatives of crime control and the practical exigencies of proof:

Given the importance and difficulty of combating counterfeiting, and given the comparative ease with which an accused can raise an issue about his honesty, overall it is fair and reasonable to require a trader, should need arise, to prove on the balance of probability that he honestly and reasonably believed the goods were genuine.[204]

Since, on closer examination, section 92(5) turned out to be compatible with Article 6(2) after all, the question of 'reading down' under section 3 of the Human Rights Act did not arise in this appeal.[205]

The House of Lords' analysis and conclusion in *Johnstone* make for a striking contrast with what their Lordships said in *Lambert* only a few months earlier. There could hardly be any better demonstration of the implications of contextual balancing on the scales of 'proportionality'. Indeed, so great was the contrast that the Court of Appeal initially thought that *Johnstone* had effectively replaced *Lambert*. Speaking for an enlarged five-member Court of Appeal specially convened 'to pull together the authorities so as to identify the relevant principles to be applied' in cases contesting the legality of reverse onus provisions, Lord Chief Justice Woolf's first principle was that '[c]ourts should strongly discourage the citation of authority to them other than the decision of the House of Lords in *Johnstone* and this guidance. *Johnstone* is at present the latest word on the subject.'[206] Not only did the House of Lords in *Sheldrake*[207] promptly reject this reading of the authorities. Astonishingly, their Lordships also instructed trial judges to disregard the Court of Appeal's carefully-constructed general guidance as well. Lord Bingham admonished:

Both *R v Lambert* and *R v Johnstone* are recent decisions of the House, binding on all lower courts for what they decide. Nothing said in *R v Johnstone* suggests an intention to depart from or modify the earlier decision, which should not be treated as superseded or implicitly overruled. Differences of emphasis (and Lord Steyn was not a lone voice in *R v Lambert*) are explicable by the difference in the subject matter of the two cases.[208]

The two conjoined appeals in *Sheldrake*, which can now fairly be regarded as the leading case on reverse onus provisions under the Human Rights Act, further illustrate the flexibility of a proportionality test supposedly capable of accommodating the decisions in both *Lambert* and *Johnstone* without self-contradiction.[209] *Sheldrake* itself concerned the

---

[204] ibid. [53].   [205] ibid. [54].

[206] *Attorney General's Reference (No 1 of 2004)*; *R v Edwards*; *R v Denton and Jackson*; *R v Hendley*; *R v Crowley* [2004] 2 Cr App R 27, [2004] EWCA Crim 1025, [10], [52].

[207] *Sheldrake v DPP; Attorney General's Reference (No 4 of 2002)* [2005] 1 AC 264, [2004] UKHL 43.

[208] ibid. [30].

[209] Cf. Lord Woolf CJ's analysis in *Attorney General's Reference (No 1 of 2004)* [2004] 2 Cr App R 27, [2004] EWCA Crim 1025, [30]–[38], detecting a 'significant difference in emphasis' between, in particular, the speech of Lord Steyn in *Lambert* and the approach of at least four of their Lordships in *Johnstone*. Moreover, the 'views expressed by the other members of the House [in *Lambert*] were not as forceful as those of Lord Steyn', and 'perhaps not sufficient weight had been given to Lord Hutton's [dissenting] views…[I]t may be of assistance to [the House of Lords] to know that in practice our collective experiences are the same as Lord Hutton's.'

relatively prosaic offence of being drunk in charge of a motor vehicle contrary to section 5 of the Road Traffic Act (RTA) 1988. By subsection 5(2) of the 1988 Act:

It is a defence for a person...to prove that at the time he is alleged to have committed the offence the circumstances were such that there was no likelihood of his driving the vehicle whilst the proportion of alcohol in his breath, blood or urine remained likely to exceed the prescribed limit.

Sheldrake was discovered at 10.30pm, asleep and slumped over the steering wheel of his stationery vehicle, having consumed more than four times the legally prescribed limit of alcohol for drivers. He claimed that he had made arrangements with a friend to drive him home, but the friend was nowhere to be seen. Sheldrake was convicted at first instance by the magistrates, but a specially-convened three member Administrative Court allowed Sheldrake's Article 6(2)-based appeal, by a majority of two-to-one (and after the original two-member bench had been deadlocked).[210] The House of Lords unanimously allowed the appeal of the Director of Public Prosecutions against the Administrative Court's ruling and restored Sheldrake's conviction. This conclusion was supported both in terms of the policy imperative of safeguarding society from the death and destruction wreaked by drunk drivers, and by undertaking close textual analysis of section 5 of the RTA 1988 and its legislative precursors. Lord Bingham summarized their Lordships' reasoning:

There is an obvious risk that a person may cause death, injury or damage if he drives or attempts to drive a car when excessive consumption of alcohol has made him unfit (I use that adjective compendiously) to do so. That is why such conduct has been made a criminal offence. There is also an obvious risk that if a person is in control of a car when unfit he may drive it, with the consequent risk of causing death, injury or damage.... The defendant can exonerate himself if he can show that the risk which led to the creation of the offence did not in his case exist. If he fails to establish this ground of exoneration, a possibility (but not a probability) would remain that he would not have been likely to drive. But he would fall squarely within the class of those whose conduct Parliament has, since 1930, legislated to criminalise.... This is not in my view an oppressive outcome, since a person in charge of a car when unfit to drive it may properly be expected to divest himself of the power to do so (as by giving the keys to someone else) or put it out of his power to do so (as by going well away).[211]

Conjoined with the appeal in *Sheldrake* was *Attorney General's Reference (No 4 of 2002)*, a 'war on terror' decision specifically concerned with the offence of belonging to a proscribed (terrorist) organization contrary to section 11 of the Terrorism Act 2000. Subsection 11(2) provides that it shall be 'a defence for a person...to prove (a) that the organization was not proscribed on the last (or only) occasion on which he became a member or began to profess to be a member, and (b) that he has not taken part in the activities of the organization at any time while it was proscribed'. A defence application of 'no case to answer' succeeded at first instance in the proceedings generating *Attorney General's Reference (No 4 of 2002)*, it having been common ground during the trial, for as long as it lasted, that subsection 11(2) imposes only an evidential burden on the accused. The Attorney General subsequently disavowed this concession, and successfully argued before the Court of Appeal

---

[210] *Sheldrake v DPP* [2003] 2 Cr App R 206, [2003] EWHC Admin 273.
[211] [2005] 1 AC 264, [40].

that subsection 11(2) imposes a fully probative burden which, moreover, is nonetheless compatible with Article 6(2).[212] By a narrow three-two majority, however, the House of Lords (Lords Rodger and Carswell dissenting) reversed this holding.

The decision of Lords Bingham, Steyn, and Phillips, comprising the majority in *Attorney General's Reference (No 4 of 2002)*, was all the more notable in the light of recent legislation. The Terrorism Act 2000 deliberately reduces specified reverse onus clauses to burdens of production in order to comply with Article 6(2).[213] Ameliorated criminal prohibitions include the statutory successors of the offences prosecuted in the first Human Rights Act-era challenge to reverse onus clauses to reach the House of Lords in *Kebilene*.[214] However, the offences involving membership in terrorist organizations proscribed by section 11 of the Terrorism Act were, presumably no less deliberately, left unmodified. The inference is irresistible: 'There can be on doubt that Parliament intended s. 11(2) to impose a legal burden on the defendant'.[215] Yet opposing and ultimately countermanding Parliament's clearly expressed intention were weighty considerations of principle which, Lord Bingham concluded, required the language of the section to be 'read-down' pursuant to section 3 of the Human Rights Act in this instance:

[A] person who is innocent of any blameworthy or properly criminal conduct may fall within s. 11(1). There would be a clear breach of the presumption of innocence, and a real risk of unfair conviction, if such persons could exonerate themselves only by establishing the defence provided on the balance of probabilities. It is the clear duty of the courts, entrusted to them by Parliament, to protect defendants against such a risk. It is relevant to note that a defendant who tried and failed to establish a defence under s. 11(2) might in effect be convicted on the basis of conduct which was not criminal at the date of commission.... While a defendant might reasonably be expected to show that the organisation was not proscribed on the last or only occasion on which he became a member or professed to be a member, so as to satisfy subs. (2)(a), it might well be all but impossible for him to show that he had not taken part in the activities of the organisation at any time while it was proscribed, so as to satisfy subs. (2)(b). Terrorist organisations do not generate minutes, records or documents on which he could rely. Other members would for obvious reasons be unlikely to come forward and testify on his behalf... While the defendant himself could assert that he had been inactive, his evidence might well be discounted as unreliable.[216]

It also had to be borne in mind that this was a serious offence, for which a gaol term of up to ten years' imprisonment could be imposed. The fact that the case raised security concerns could not in and of itself justify wholesale derogations from Convention rights, as the European Court of Human Rights has reminded states parties from time to time.[217] The Human Rights Act facilitated this counter-intuitive interpretation of section 11(2) of the 2000 Act because 'the interpretative obligation under section 3 is a very strong and far reaching one, and may require the court to depart from the legislative intention of Parliament'.[218] This approach was calculated to serve parliamentary sovereignty in a deeper, richer sense, by giving effect to Parliament's contextualizing second-order

---

[212] [2003] 2 Cr App R 22, [2003] EWCA Crim 762.   [213] Terrorism Act 2000, s. 118.

[214] *R v DPP, ex p. Kebilene* [2000] 2 AC 326, HL.   [215] [2005] 1 AC 264, [50].   [216] ibid. [51]

[217] e.g. *Aksoy v Turkey* (1997) 23 EHRR 553, [76]–[78]; *Fox, Campbell and Hartley v UK* (1991) 13 EHRR 157, [32]–[36].

[218] [2005] 1 AC 264, [28], reciting *Ghaidan v Godin-Mendoza* [2004] 2 AC 557, [2004] UKHL 30.

directive for broad compliance with the Human Rights Act in all aspects of legislation and law enforcement – including judicial interpretation of Parliament's own first-order legislative intentions.[219]

These illustrations bring out significant implications of employing a flexible proportionality standard to determine the legal effect of reverse onus provisions. First and most obviously, each individual provision must be subjected to detailed critical examination in the light of its own particular objectives, values, policies and practical circumstances. Broad generalizations will have limited utility for the purposes of this exercise: a contextual approach to statutory interpretation necessarily demands close attention to context.[220] However this implies, secondly, that the status of particular reverse onus provisions may be difficult to predict in advance of an authoritative ruling. This is why Article 6(2) has generated so many appeals under the Human Rights Act 1998. If a decision on the effect of one provision (e.g. *Lambert's* ruling on section 28 of the Misuse of Drugs Act 1971) has little bearing on the correct interpretation of a reverse onus provision in a different statute (e.g. *Johnstone's* analysis of section 92 of the Trade Marks Act 1994), it seems that each and every reverse onus clause in English criminal law must be reconsidered on an individual, case-by-case, basis. Given that there are literally scores, if not hundreds, of reverse onus clauses scattered throughout the penal law, this could amount to a daunting schedule of works for the appellate courts.

A third notable feature of these cases is that particular factors, such as the seriousness of the offence or the practical difficulty for one party or the other of discharging the onus, sometimes forms part of the argument for imposing a probative burden on the accused but on other occasions supports the case for 'reading down'. This 'floating' quality of material considerations bearing on proportionality compounds the unpredictability of judicial decisions, and taken together with a fourth characteristic, goes a long way towards explaining why, in addition to the large volume of cases, reverse onus appeals so often produce reversals and dissents. The fourth characteristic is that, insofar as the true constitutional import of the presumption of innocence is perceived by the courts, it can be invoked to legitimate creative judicial interpretations of statutes that seemingly stretch ordinary linguistic usage and rewrite legislative history. Thus in *Attorney General's Reference (No 4 of 2002)* the 'strong and far reaching' interpretative obligation imposed by section 3 induced a majority of the House of Lords to read the word 'prove' as though it meant 'adduce sufficient evidence to raise an issue in the case', knowing full well that this was not Parliament's immediate intention. However, Lord Rodger, dissenting, could detect no infringement of Article 6(2) whatever. Section 11(2) of the TA 2000 served to ameliorate what would otherwise be a strict liability offence in favour of the accused, and the distinction between probative and evidential burdens 'has no direct counterpart in

---

[219] Cf. *R v A (No. 2)* [2002] 1 AC 45, [2001] UKHL 25, [44]: 'Section 3 places a duty on the court to strive to find a possible interpretation compatible with Convention rights. Under ordinary methods of interpretation a court may depart from the language of the statute to avoid absurd consequences: section 3 goes much further…. In accordance with the will of Parliament as reflected in section 3 it will sometimes be necessary to adopt an interpretation which linguistically may appear strained. The techniques to be used will not only involve the reading down of express language in a statute but also the implication of provisions.'

[220] 'Each Statute gives rise to different considerations, so that it is unlikely to be helpful to consider what decisions have been made in different cases under different statutes concerned with different subject matters': *Sheldrake v DPP* [2003] 2 Cr App R 206, [65].

civil law systems and is, of course, not mentioned, one way or the other, in any guarantee in Article 6 of the Convention'.[221] This appeal, for Lord Rodger, raised only local issues of criminal procedure law, in which the European Court of Human Rights itself disavows any material jurisdiction.[222]

If the contextual approach to assessing reverse onus clauses confirmed by the House of Lords in *Sheldrake* has left counsel and trial courts to contend with a blizzard of single instances, it should also be said in partial mitigation that the task of providing provision-specific appellate guidance has proceeded apace. Fully probative reverse onus burdens have been upheld in relation *inter alia* to suicide pacts,[223] racially aggravated harassment,[224] possession of an offensive weapon,[225] road traffic offences involving intoxication by drink or drugs,[226] trade mark offences,[227] immigration offences,[228] and health and safety violations exposing employees to dangerous conditions of work.[229] Several of the earlier decisions in which the Administrative Court or the Court of Appeal, applying *Lambert*, opted for 'reading down' have been reversed – including the first appeal in *Sheldrake*, as we have seen.[230] *Lambert* itself remains authority for 'reading down' reverse onus clauses in the Misuse of Drugs Act 1971 to evidential burdens of production,[231] although Parliament subsequently (in retaliation?) moved to dilute its impact by redrafting section 5.[232] Curiously, one of the few statutory reverse onus provisions to be 'read down' after *Sheldrake* concerns 'exempt hunting' under the Hunting Act 2004.[233]

David Hamer contends that the bulk of the courts' post-Human Rights Act reverse onus jurisprudence can be rationalized in terms of 'weighing the defendant's right to avoid wrongful conviction against the community's interest in law enforcement, having regard

---

[221] [2005] 1 AC 264, [71].

[222] e.g. *Teixeira de Castro* v *Portugal* (1999) 28 EHRR 101, [34]: 'admissibility of evidence is primarily a matter for regulation by national law and as a general rule it is for the national courts to asses the evidence before them'.

[223] Homicide Act 1957, s.4: *R* v *Hendley* [2004] 2 Cr App R 27, [2004] EWCA Crim 1025.

[224] Contrary to s.51 of the Criminal Justice and Public Order Act 1994: *R* v *Crowley* [2004] 2 Cr App R 27, [2004] EWCA Crim 1025.

[225] Contrary to s.139(1) of the Criminal Justice Act 1988: *L* v *DPP* [2001] Cr App R 420, DC.

[226] *Crown Prosecution Service* v *Thompson* [2008] RTR 5; [2007] EWHC 1841 (Admin); *DPP* v *Ellery* [2005] EWHC 2513 (Admin); *DPP* v *Barker* [2006] Crim LR 140, [2004] EWHC 2502 (Admin); *R* v *Drummond* [2002] 2 Cr App R 352, CA.

[227] Contrary to s.92(1) of the Trade Marks Act 1994: *R* v *S (Trademark Defence)* [2003] 1 Cr App R 602, CA; confirmed in *R* v *Johnstone* [2003] 1 WLR 1736, HL.

[228] *R* v *Makuwa* [2006] EWCA Crim 175; *R* v *Navabi*; *R* v *Embaye* [2005] EWCA Crim 2865, *The Times*, 12 May 2005.

[229] Contrary to s.3(1) of the Health and Safety at Work Act 1974: *R* v *Chargot Ltd* [2009] 1 WLR 1, [2008] UKHL 73; *Davies* v *Health and Safety Executive* [2002] EWCA Crim 2949, [2003] ICR 586.

[230] Also *R* v *Carass* [2002] 1 WLR 1714, CA, overruled in *Attorney General's Reference (No 1 of 2004)* [2004] 2 Cr App R 27, [2004] EWCA Crim 1025, [84] ('the decision in *Carass* cannot stand with *Johnstone*, and must be treated as impliedly overruled'); as confirmed in *Sheldrake* v *DPP* [2005] 1 AC 264, [2004] UKHL, [32].   [231] Also see *R* v *Lang and Deadman* [2002] EWCA Crim 298.

[232] Section 2(2) of the Drugs Act 2005 was poised to insert subsections (4A) to (4C) into s.5 of the MDA 1971, by which 'if it is proved that the accused had an amount of a controlled drug in his possession which is not less than the prescribed amount, the court or jury must assume that he had the drug in his possession with the intent to supply it'. However, it now appears that this provision will be repealed without ever being brought into force: Policing and Crime Act 2009, sch.8, Part 13.

[233] *DPP* v *Wright (Anthony)* [2009] 3 All ER 726, [2009] EWHC 105 (Admin).

to the practicalities of proving guilt and innocence'.[234] However, even this avowedly modest attempt at rational reconstruction seems to credit the emerging law with unmerited
coherence. Much of the weight of Hamer's argument falls on the proposition that reverse
onus clauses are most readily justifiable in regulatory contexts,[235] but the decided cases
are recalcitrant to any recognizably principled rationalization even here. Thus, in the fifth
Article 6(2) appeal to reach the House of Lords in less than a decade,[236] their Lordships
were content to uphold a fully probative reverse onus in relation to a 'regulatory' offence,
in this case involving the death of a construction worker, which carries a maximum sentence on conviction on indictment of two years' imprisonment.[237] Yet in *Wright*,[238] the
Administrative Court read down a provision relating to an offence of unlawful hunting
attracting a maximum penalty of a £5,000 fine. '[T]his is not,' the Court insisted, 'mere
regulatory criminality to be equated with minor motoring offences or routine licensing
matters. Although the offences created by the Act are summary only, the subject matter is
of great social and emotional importance to a large number of people, both the proponents
and opponents of the ban on hunting with dogs.'[239] If there is some principled explanation
for these two decisions,[240] it eludes us. Ian Dennis' pessimistic conclusion seems entirely
warranted as a statement of positive law: 'Such is the complexity and controversy that
results from this approach that we might be justified in asking whether the search for
principle should be abandoned'.[241]

6.6 *WOOLMINGTON'S* LEGACY AND THE LIMITS OF THE PRESUMPTION OF INNOCENCE

To avoid Dennis' pessimistic conclusion as a normative proposition, one must return to
first principles. In particular, protection of the innocent from wrongful conviction is a
foundational principles of criminal evidence.[242] This chapter has summarised the historical evolution of the presumption of innocence in English law, from Blackstone's ratio and
Woolmington's golden thread to current controversies surrounding reverse onus clauses
under the Human Rights Act. The orthodox common law conception equates the presumption of innocence with the burden and standard of proof, barely ever mentioning
the presumption by name. We have seen that considerable analytical progress can be

---

[234] David Hamer, 'The Presumption of Innocence and Reverse Burdens: A Balancing Act' (2007) 66
Cambridge Law Journal 143, 150.

[235] 'Pragmatic proof arguments gain the most leverage in relation to regulatory offences. Regulated parties have relatively less at stake than other criminal defendants, and may have a genuine proof advantage
over a resource-strapped regulator. Furthermore, the regulated defendant may be considered to have voluntarily traded in some of his procedural rights for the opportunity to profitably engage in a hazardous
activity': ibid. 160.   [236] *R v Chargot Ltd* [2009] 1 WLR 1, [2008] UKHL 73.

[237] Health and Safety at Work etc. Act 1974, ss.2, 3, 33, and sch.3A. In *Chargot* itself, the penalties were
limited to substantial (£100,000 and £75,000) fines.

[238] *DPP v Wright (Anthony)* [2009] 3 All ER 726, [2009] EWHC 105 (Admin).   [239] ibid. [4].

[240] Hamer does not claim to be able to accommodate *every* decided case within his principled framework. The contrast between *Chargot* and *Wright* is merely an illustration of unprincipled distinctions which,
we say, pervades the Article 6(2) jurisprudence, including cases dealing with so-called 'regulatory crime'.

[241] Ian Dennis, 'Reverse Onuses and the Presumption of Innocence: In Search of Principle' [2005] *Crim
LR* 901, 904.   [242] §1.3.

made in getting to grips with a topic renowned for its terminological incontinence, first by stipulating serviceable definitions of burdens of proof and presumptions, and thereafter conceptualizing them as procedural devices for allocating the risks of error in criminal adjudication. However, conceptual analysis can only take us so far on our journey of discovery. In order to appreciate the deeper significance of the presumption of innocence it is necessary to relocate the foundations of legal doctrines in the political moralities which ultimately sustain them. This is by no means a task reserved exclusively to legal theorists. The project of rediscovering or reconstructing *Woolmington's* philosophical foundations bears directly on the courts' treatment of the presumption of innocence in English law, and in particular on the impact of Article 6(2) of the European Convention on Human Rights, via the Human Rights Act 1998.

As a cherished procedural manifestation of the foundational liberal commitment to respect for persons, the presumption of innocence is a vital legal buttress of individual rights in the service of criminal justice. But that is far from saying that every significant penal value and interest can be subsumed within this single concept, as though 'the presumption of innocence' were synonymous with 'fair trial', or even 'criminal justice' itself. Concepts are useful, when they are, because they pick out some pertinent aspect of a broader field for special focus and attention. If one were to stipulate, as a matter of definition, that the presumption of innocence was equivalent to – that it *meant* – 'fair trial' or some other more general concept, the utility of the presumption as a discrete tool of legal analysis and forensic argument would be lost. This chapter has developed a conceptualization of the presumption of innocence which aims to incorporate but also quite self-consciously extend beyond the common law's traditional preoccupation with the burden and standard of proof. The style of analysis is at once descriptive *and* normative, akin to what Dworkin calls an 'interpretive' approach.[243] It is important to stress in conclusion, however, the perils of *over*extending this style of analysis. There is reason to think that the presumption of innocence in English law might become susceptible to this kind of infection in the next phases of its doctrinal development. A measure of prophylactic inoculation is in order.

This chapter has characterized the presumption of innocence as a core *procedural* component of a fair trial, developed at common law through the *Woolmington* principle and lately finessed by the ECHR system under the Human Rights Act 1998. We might contrast our 'procedural' conception with a rival 'substantive' conception of the presumption of innocence. The rival might be thought to gain a doctrinal toehold in the following remarks of the European Court of Human Rights in *Salabiaku*:

[I]n principle, the Contracting States may, *under certain conditions*, penalise a simple or objective fact as such, irrespective of whether it results from criminal intent or from negligence. Examples of such offences may be found in the laws of the Contracting States.[244]

The precise meaning of this passage is obscure,[245] not least because continental European jurists do not necessarily share common lawyers' understanding of criteria of criminal

---

[243] Ronald Dworkin, *Law's Empire* (Fontana, 1986).

[244] *Salabiaku* v *France* (1991) 13 EHRR 379, [27] (emphasis supplied).

[245] Cf. Lord Hoffmann's trenchant remarks in *R* v *G* [2009] 1 AC 92, [2008] UKHL 37, [5]–[6]: 'No one has yet discovered what this paragraph means but your Lordships were referred to a wealth of academic learning which tries to solve the riddle ... [J]udges and academic writers have picked over the carcass of this

liability such as 'intent' and 'negligence'. One possible interpretation of the italicized clause is that Article 6(2) is applicable whenever elements of strict liability in domestic criminal law are achieved through the mechanism of evidentiary presumptions – i.e. in relation to all express or implied reverse onus clauses. That is unexceptional, and obviously correct. But another reading might suggest that the Court is asserting jurisdiction over the substantive elements of states' parties criminal law, so that, for example, certain strict liability offences might be found to contravene Article 6(2)'s presumption of innocence and derogate from the right to a fair trial, as a matter of European human rights law. This interpretation, which affords to an ostensibly procedural presumption of innocence a degree of corrective supervision over the substantive criminal law, would be novel and controversial. It was considered and expressly rejected by both the Court of Appeal and the House of Lords in G.[246] Yet it also has a seductive of logic, which has impressed some British commentators[247] and judges in their early Human Rights Act jurisprudence.[248] Thus, Tadros and Tierney contend:

If the technical definition of the offence fails properly to recognise that the defendant is to be presumed innocent until proven guilty of conduct which the creation of the offence was intended to deter or control, that offence interferes with the presumption of innocence. And this is so even if the prosecution is required to prove all elements of that offence as technically defined. To that degree, article 6(2), properly interpreted, does not provide the defendant merely with procedural protection, but also affects the substance of the criminal law.[249]

It is instructive to interject a comparative dimension at this point in the discussion. We noted at the start of this chapter that 'proof beyond reasonable doubt' is a constitutionally-mandated aspect of due process in the United States.[250] However, heightened concern for the procedural rights of the accused produces an apparently paradoxical result: it is unconstitutional to impose probative burdens on the defence to prove an element of a criminal offence, yet individual states remain free to create strict liability offences without conceding any such defence whatsoever. For instance, there is no constitutional objection to state legislatures drafting the offence of unlawful sexual intercourse with a minor (USI)

---

unfortunate case so many times in attempts to find some intelligible meat on its bones that the time has come to call a halt. The Strasbourg court, uninhibited by a doctrine of precedent or the need to find a *ratio decidendi*, seems to have ignored it. It is not mentioned in *Z* v *United Kingdom* 34 EHRR 97. I would recommend your Lordships to do likewise.'

[246] 'We do not consider it right to draw this conclusion from the reasoning of the court in *Salabiaku*. An absolute offence may subject a defendant to conviction in circumstances where he has done nothing blameworthy. Prosecution for such an offence and the imposition of sanctions under it may well infringe articles of the Convention other than Article 6. The legislation will not, however, render the trial under which it is enforced unfair, let alone infringe the presumption of innocence under article 6(2)': *R* v *G* [2006] 1 WLR 2052, [2006] EWCA Crim 821, [33] (Lord Phillips CJ); adopted by Lord Hope, *R* v *G* [2009] 1 AC 92, [2008] UKHL 37, [30]. Lord Hoffmann went further, ibid. [6], suggesting that *Salabiaku* was unintelligible and should simply be ignored.

[247] See, in particular, Victor Tadros and Stephen Tierney, 'The Presumption of Innocence and the Human Rights Act' (2004) 67 MLR 402; Victor Tadros, 'Rethinking the Presumption of Innocence' (2007) 1 *Criminal Law & Philosophy* 193.

[248] Also see the European Court's perplexing judgment in *Osman* v *UK* (1998) 29 EHRR 245, regarding the 'substantive right of access to a court' under Article 6(1), which is critically dissected by Conor A. Gearty, 'Unravelling *Osman*' (2001) 64 *MLR* 159.

[249] Victor Tadros and Stephen Tierney, 'The Presumption of Innocence and the Human Rights Act' (2004) 67 *MLR* 402, 413.   [250] *In re Winship*, 397 US 358 (1970).

as an absolute offence regarding the victim's age, so that the accused can be guilty even though he truly believed a willing sexual partner to have attained the age of consent, and had no reason for thinking otherwise.[251] But the Constitution prohibits state legislatures from providing those accused of USI with a reverse onus 'reasonable mistake as to age' defence. A legislature is thus presented with the choice of either making *mens rea* as to the victim's age an element of the offence and requiring the prosecution to prove it, or else doing away with *mens rea* altogether in relation to this issue and making the prohibition one of strict liability to that extent. This stark alternative has created considerable practical difficulty, and commentators have invested much effort and ingenuity into devising credible legal arguments to ameliorate its consequences.[252]

Developments in American procedural jurisprudence thus teach a cautionary lesson: a well-motivated desire to equip the presumption of innocence with sharp legal teeth could prove counterproductive. If reverse onus clauses are liable to be struck down by the courts, legislatures might be encouraged to adopt the defensive strategy of dispensing with affirmative excuse defences altogether. One response would be to encourage courts to be still more adventurous, and undertake substantive judicial review of the legality of statutory criminal prohibitions. The US Supreme Court has repeatedly declined to take this step, however, on the federalist ground that the scope of the substantive criminal law is a matter for individual states to determine. It would be even more surprising if the European Court of Human Rights ventured far down this road. States parties might understandably be alarmed to discover that in committing themselves to the 'right to fair trial' under Article 6 of the Convention they have ceded part of their prescriptive power to define substantive criminal offences to the Strasbourg Court.

Our contention that the presumption of innocence is essentially *procedural* is not a purely *conceptual* claim: concepts can take any stipulated meaning. Rather, the argument is underpinned by moral and political convictions regarding: (1) the proper ambit and function of juridical concepts in criminal procedure; and (2) an appropriate division of responsibility for penal legislation between the UK Parliament, the European Court of Human Rights, and the domestic criminal courts of England and Wales.[253] If it were said that an accused cannot have a fair trial because he has been charged with an 'unfair' offence, Article 6 would become a roving brief for the ECtHR to rewrite states' parties municipal criminal laws.

English judges developing English criminal law under the Human Rights Act are not bound, in the strict precedential sense, by Strasbourg jurisprudence although there is

---

[251] This also used to be the law in England and Wales, under *R v Prince* (1875) LR 2, CCR 154, until the judges decided to reinvigorate the 'presumption of *mens rea*' in *B (A Minor) v DPP* [2000] 2 AC 428, HL.

[252] Donald A. Dripps, 'The Constitutional Status of the Reasonable Doubt Rule' (1987) 75 *California LR* 1665; Ronald J. Allen, 'Structuring Jury Decision-making in Criminal Cases: A Unified Constitutional Approach to Evidentiary Devices' (1980) 94 *Harvard LR* 321 (also criticism by Nesson ibid. 1574, and Allen's rejoinder ibid. 1795); John Calvin Jeffries and Paul B. Stephan III, 'Defences, Presumptions, and the Burden of Proof in the Criminal Law' (1979) 88 *Yale LJ* 1325; Barbara D. Underwood, 'The Thumb on the Scales of Justice: Burdens of Persuasion in Criminal Cases' (1977) 86 *Yale LJ* 1299; Harold A. Ashford and D. Michael Risinger, 'Presumptions, Assumptions and Due Process in Criminal Cases: A Theoretical Overview' (1969) 79 *Yale LJ* 165. And for English perspectives on a similar theme, see Martin Wasik, 'Shifting the Burden of Strict Liability' [1982] *Crim LR* 567; D. J. Birch, 'Hunting the Snark: The Elusive Statutory Exception' [1988] *Crim LR* 221.

[253] See further, Paul Roberts 'The Presumption of Innocence Brought Home? *Kebilene* Deconstructed' (2002) 117 *LQR* 40, Part VIII.

a strong presumption in favour of following the ECtHR's interpretations[254] In particular, English judges are at liberty to develop procedural rights that are *more favourable* to the accused than the minimum human rights guarantees mandated by Strasbourg. Nonetheless, it would be surprising to find English courts infusing Article 6(2) with much if any substantive content under the Human Rights Act. This would be like excluding evidence under section 78 of PACE 1984,[255] not because it suffers from any specifically procedural defect, but because the evidence is being used to prove an excessively broadly-drafted criminal offence *and therefore* it would be unfair for the prosecution to rely on it. This comparison might seem outlandish, yet in *Kebilene*[256] and again in *Lambert* senior judges appeared to adopt an exactly analogous approach to the interpretation of Article 6(2).

Kebilene concerned the blunderbuss offence of possessing articles, innocent in themselves, in circumstances giving rise to reasonable suspicion that such articles were possessed for a terrorist purpose.[257] A very strong Divisional Court said that the offence breached Article 6(2) by assuming intention and imposing a reverse onus on the accused to prove innocent possession.[258] The case was decided on a different point in the House of Lords, but several of their Lordships seemed to incline towards the Divisional Court's analysis of Article 6(2). And in *Lambert*, as we have seen, their Lordships held by a majority of four-to-one that Article 6(2) required section 28 of the Misuse of Drugs Act 1971 to be read as though it imposed merely an evidential burden of production on the accused. The striking feature of both these decisions is that Article 6(2) was extended to the proof of facts *that were not elements of the offence* that the prosecution had to prove to secure a conviction. In *Kebilene* both the Divisional Court and the House of Lords proceeded as if 'terrorist purpose' were an element of the offence, when, on the face of it, the statutory language provides no warrant for requiring any such criterion of criminal liability.[259] *Lambert* is, if anything, an even stronger example. The House of Lords expressly stated that knowledge of the nature of the substance is *not* an element of the offence of possession of a controlled drug with intent to supply,[260] contrary to section 5(3) of the Misuse of Drugs Act 1971, and yet proceeded to find that section 28's reverse onus clauses would breach Article 6(2) unless read-down to impose merely evidential burdens. This analysis involves treating an affirmative defence *as if* it were an element of the offence, for the sole purpose of imputing a legal presumption into the statute imposing a manufactured reverse onus clause, which in turn can be subjected to Article 6(2)'s test of proportionality to a legitimate objective. Notwithstanding these contortions, the net effect of this convoluted argument is clear.

---

[254] The status of Strasbourg jurisprudence in English law was discussed in §1.5.

[255] See Chapter 5.   [256] *R v DPP, ex p.Kebilene* [2000] 2 AC 326; [2000] Crim LR 486, DC and HL.

[257] Prevention of Terrorism (Temporary Provisions) Act 1989, s.16A, substantially re-enacted as Terrorism Act 2000, s.57.

[258] The reverse onus provision was originally s.16A(3) of the 1989 Act, now s.57(2) of the 2000 Act.

[259] The offences created by s.16A(1) were defined as follows: 'A person is guilty of an offence if he has any article in his possession in circumstances giving rise to a reasonable suspicion that the article is in his possession for a purpose connected with the commission, preparation or instigation of acts of terrorism to which this section applies'. For further discussion, see Paul Roberts, 'The Presumption of Innocence Brought Home? *Kebilene* Deconstructed' (2002) 117 *LQR* 40.

[260] e.g. Lord Hope, [2002] 2 AC 545, [61]: 'The mental element involves proof of knowledge that the thing exists and that it is in his possession. Proof of knowledge that the thing is an article of a particular kind, quality or description is not required. It is not necessary for the prosecution to prove that the defendant knew that the thing was a controlled drug which the law makes it an offence to possess'. And see Lord Clyde, ibid. [122], [126], [128], [149].

Article 6(2)'s presumption of innocence is imbued with a measure of substantive content in English law.

And a good thing too, some might and do say. Commenting on the American situation, Jeffries and Stephan contended that:

A constitutional policy to minimize the risk of convicting the 'innocent' must be grounded in a constitutional concern of what may constitute 'guilt'. Otherwise 'guilt' would have to be proved with certainty, but the legislature could define 'guilt' as it pleased, and the grand ideal of individual liberty would be reduced to an empty promise.[261]

Translated to the British context, the worry is that Parliament could always intentionally 'evade the implications of article 6(2) by creating new criminal offences':

In that case, the presumption of innocence would provide citizens with no protection against the state whatsoever. It would be capable of evasion merely by reconstructing the surface of the offence, leaving the underlying evidential requirements unchecked.[262]

These are provocative remarks with far-reaching implications for British constitutional traditions. A Diceyan Parliament presumably can indeed draft any offence it pleases, as a matter of positive law, and English judges are certainly not equipped with powers of substantive judicial review akin to those exercised by Justices of the United States Supreme Court. However, even if the scope and content of criminal prohibitions ought in principle to be amenable to substantive judicial review, it does not follow that evidentiary concepts like the presumption of innocence are the right forensic tools for the job. Indeed, English common law has evolved other legal standards, such as the recently reinvigorated 'presumption' of *mens rea* (really a rule of substantive criminal law),[263] as counterweights to over-extensive criminal liability. To announce that English law usually requires (advertent) *mens rea* as a precondition of criminal culpability is a clear and transparent rule, firmly rooted in the promotion of autonomy and respect for persons, which Parliament knows it must expressly countermand if and when it chooses to do so. Rewriting criminal prohibitions under the aegis of Article 6(2) is neither transparent nor predictable. If courts routinely blur the conceptual distinction between affirmative criminal law defences and onus-reversing evidentiary presumptions, treating both as equally amenable to Article 6(2) analysis, Parliament is unlikely to reform its bad habits of loose drafting or try harder to be more careful in its choice of statutory language. More seriously, if all affirmative defences are rendered vulnerable to Convention-based challenge, Parliament might be tempted to follow the US example, by withdrawing some affirmative defences altogether, and framing new criminal prohibitions in terms of strict liability. As Lord Woolf has rightly said:

It would not assist the individuals who are charged with offences if, because of the approach adopted to 'statutory defences' by the courts, the legislature, in order to avoid the risk of

---

[261] John Calvin Jeffries and Paul B. Stephan III, 'Defences, Presumptions, and the Burden of Proof in the Criminal Law' (1979) 88 *Yale LJ* 1325, 1347.

[262] Victor Tadros and Stephen Tierney, 'The Presumption of Innocence and the Human Rights Act' (2004) 67 *MLR* 402, 413–14.

[263] See *B (A Minor) v DPP* [2000] 2 AC 428, HL; *R v K* [2002] 1 AC 462, HL; *R v Kumar* [2005] 1 WLR 1352, [2004] EWCA Crim 3207; *Sweet v Parsley* [1970] AC 132, HL.

legislation being successfully challenged, did not include in the legislation a statutory defence to a charge.[264]

For theorists who start from a conception of criminal law as justified censure of moral wrongdoing,[265] or who focus on the critical potential of human rights law, these objections may seem like trivial pragmatic quibbles. They are not. What is at stake is a defensible conception of political authority and judicial competence in a pluralistic, multi-level, cosmopolitan world in which the state and state law no longer define the limits of jurisdiction. We can agree that many English criminal offences are excessively overbroad, and that this vice has been taken to extremes in recent criminal legislation.[266] But it does not follow that this vice can be addressed effectively by any juridical concept that happens to be to hand, or that co-opting procedural doctrines to do substantive work will not produce conceptual distortions or prove strategically counterproductive in the long run. Our judgment is that Article 6(2) ECHR, as refracted through the Human Rights Act 1998, is neither doctrinally competent nor jurisprudentially appropriate for the task to which proponents of a substantive conception of the presumption of innocence want to put it. In the most recent cases, senior judges have uniformly endorsed our preference for procedural over substantive conceptions of the presumption of innocence.[267] Lord Hope expressed the position very clearly in *R* v *G*:

Article 6(2), like article 6(3), must be read in the context of article 6(1). The article as a whole is concerned essentially with procedural guarantees to ensure that there is a fair trial, not with the substantive elements of the offence with which the person has been charged. As has been said many times, article 6 does not guarantee any particular content of the individual's civil rights. It is concerned with the procedural fairness of the system for the administration of justice in the contracting states, not with the substantive content of domestic law... [I]t is a matter for the contracting states to define the essential elements of the offence with which the person has been charged. So when article 6(2) uses the words 'innocent' and 'guilty' it is dealing with the burden of proof regarding the elements of the offence and any defences to it. It is not dealing with what those elements are or what defences to the offence ought to be available.

---

[264] *Attorney-General of Hong Kong* v *Lee Kwong-kut* [1993] AC 951, 975, PC.

[265] R. A. Duff, *Answering for Crime: Responsibility and Liability in the Criminal Law* (Hart, 2007).

[266] A point nicely punned by Jacqueline Hodgson and Victor Tadros, 'How to Make A Terrorist Out of Nothing' (2009) 72 *MLR* 984. The general argument is presaged in Paul Roberts, 'The Presumption of Innocence Brought Home? *Kebilene* Deconstructed' (2002) 117 *LQR* 40, 66–7.

[267] In *R* v *Daniel* [2003] 1 Cr App R 99, CA, [34], Auld LJ stated: 'In determining the essentials of an offence, courts should also keep in mind the distinction between the procedural guarantees provided by article 6(2) and the substantive elements of the offence... As Paul Roberts has argued, in an article entitled "The Presumption of Innocence Brought Home? *Kebilene* Deconstructed" (2002) 118 *LQR* 41, 50: "Article 6(2) has no bearing on the reduction or elimination of *mens rea* requirements, and is therefore perfectly compatible with offences of strict or even absolute liability".' This passage was quoted with approval by the Court of Appeal in *R* v *G* [2006] 1 WLR 2052, [2006] EWCA Crim 821, [39] (Lord Phillips CJ). Also see *R* v *G* [2003] 3 All ER 206, [33] *per* Dyson LJ ('The position is quite clear. So far as article 6 is concerned, the fairness of the provisions of the substantive law of the contracting states is not a matter for investigation. The content and interpretation of domestic substantive law is not engaged by article 6'); *Matthews* v *Ministry of Defence* [2003] 1 AC 1163, [3] (Lord Bingham), [30]–[35] (Lord Hoffmann), [142] (Lord Walker); *R (Kehoe)* v *Secretary of State for Work and Pensions* [2006] 1 AC 42, [41]; *Barnfather* v *Islington Education Authority* [2003] 1 WLR 2318, [2003] EWHC 418 (Admin).

One way forward might be found in a planned programme of de-criminalization.[268] Many of the offences to which section 101 of the Magistrates' Court Act 1980 applies are *mala prohibita* regulatory infractions which arguably ought not to be within the province of criminal law at all. This in part may explain why the courts have been relatively sanguine in permitting what, at first blush, appear to be dramatic in-roads on the *Woolmington* principle. If these offences were reinvented as administrative infractions, freed from the taint of criminal censure and punishment, there would be no general principled objection to requiring violators to establish relevant facts in order to avoid the imposition of a penalty, which in effect would be a tax on conduct. Under the existing system of Council Tax in England and Wales, for example, valuation officers make an assessment of the appropriate level ('band') of local council tax based on standardized criteria like location of dwelling, number of rooms, size of plot and so on. Householders have a fixed period to contest this assessment by providing evidence to show why their individual property qualifies for a lower banding. Failure to produce such evidence where it exists is not a criminal offence, nor even *wrong* in any sense, but it does result in liability to higher taxation than is strictly owed. Decriminalized administrative offences might operate on a similar model, where effective regulation and efficient revenue generation take precedence over censuring wrongdoing in the public interest.

A strategy of progressive de-criminalization deserves serious consideration, and not only in order to promote the logic of the law of evidence. There are also, more obviously, significant considerations of liberty, justified censure of wrongdoing and proportionality of hard treatment at stake.[269] But two caveats must be entered. First, it should not be assumed that all strict liability offences are necessarily minor matters involving little or no moral culpability on the part of offenders. Some conduct which has traditionally been viewed as 'mere' regulatory crime is actually very serious, including such matters as widespread environmental pollution, threats to biodiversity, occupational illness, industrial accidents and horrific transport disasters. Culpable omissions on the part of employers or corporate managers to operate safe systems of work, or failures by major commercial retailers to protect consumers from hazardous goods and services, for example, are eminently worthy of criminal censure and punishment in appropriate cases. There is no reason to sanctify the law's traditional underestimation of their seriousness by including such *mala in se* offences within a programme to decriminalize genuinely minor infractions.

The second caveat concerns the attitude of the Strasbourg Court to the conceptual taxonomies woven into the domestic laws of states parties to the European Convention. It is trite learning that the Court ascribes an 'autonomous meaning' to the concept of a 'criminal charge' within Article 6 of the Convention.[270] This entails that the Court has regard to domestic legal definitions of criminal offences, but is not bound by them. It follows that, just because an accused was charged with a non-criminal administrative offence in English law, the Strasbourg Court would not be precluded from deciding, to the contrary,

---

[268] For recent law reform proposals on this theme, see Richard B. Macrory, *Regulatory Justice: Making Sanctions Effective – Final Report* (Better Regulation Executive, 2006), Better Regulation Executive, *Regulatory Justice: Sanctioning in a post-Hampton World – Consultation Document* (Cabinet Office, 2005); Lord Justice Auld, *Review of the Criminal Courts of England and Wales* (TSO, 2001), ch 9.

[269] See further, Andrew Ashworth, 'Is The Criminal Law A Lost Cause?' (2000) 116 *LQR* 225.

[270] See e.g., *R (McCann and others) v Crown Court at Manchester; Clingham v Kensington and Chelsea Royal LBC* [2003] 1 AC 787, HL, applying *Steel v UK* (1998) 28 EHRR 603; and *Benham v UK* (1996) 22 EHRR 293.

that the charge was criminal for Convention purposes and that Article 6(2) consequently applies. Domestic decriminalization cannot therefore be regarded as a failsafe means of insulating reverse onus clauses from Conventional challenge, though the Court's juris-prudence suggests that this strategy would be likely to succeed in the majority of cases, provided that the penalties imposed for an administrative offence are not excessive.

Many significant issues still remain unresolved at this time of rapid doctrinal develop-ment and novel legal interpretation. European human rights law is regarded as a living body of jurisprudential principles that alters its shape and appearance as it evolves over time.[271] Meanwhile, English judges are still feeling their way around a somewhat unfamil-iar post-Human Rights Act legal landscape. The first flush of enthusiasm for rediscovering and reinvigorating the presumption of innocence, exemplified by *Lambert*, seems to have run out, some early gains have been rolled back, and the law has settled down into more predictable patterns. An infinitely malleable proportionality standard results, in practice, in most reverse onus clauses being upheld. There have been notable strategic gains in con-verting particular reverse onus clauses into burdens of production, but a full-scale rein-vigoration of the *Woolmington* principle has not (yet) occurred. It might have been hoped that at least one positive outcome of the Human Rights Act would have been that English lawyers would be forced to develop more sophisticated conceptions of the presumption of innocence than had previously seemed necessary to comprehend and negotiate the com-mon law's traditionally more prosaic preoccupations. But even this keenly anticipated renaissance in conceptual thinking thus far remains in its formative stages.

---

[271] This is a long-standing principle of ECHR law: *Tyrer* v *UK* (1979–80) 2 EHRR 1, [31] ('the Convention is a living instrument which...must be interpreted in the light of present-day conditions.... [T]he Court cannot but be influenced by the developments and commonly accepted standards in the penal policy of the member States of the Council of Europe...'); *Pretty* v *UK* (2002) 35 EHRR 1, [54]: 'While the Court must take a dynamic and flexible approach to the interpretation of the Convention, which is a living instrument, any interpretation must also accord with the fundamental objectives of the Convention and its coherence as a system of human rights protection.'

7

WITNESS TESTIMONY AND
THE PRINCIPLE OF ORALITY

7.1 THE ORAL TRADITION AND ITS
MODERN DISCONTENTS

Live courtroom testimony, delivered orally by witnesses with relevant first-hand knowledge of the matters in issue, is the paradigmatic from of evidence in English criminal trials. In earlier centuries, when criminal adjudication was typically a short, rough-and-ready affair,[1] the prosecution's evidence would often be limited to oral witness testimony from the complainant and any eyewitnesses there might have been (though at that time the accused himself was an even more important source of evidence of his own guilt than he is in modern proceedings).[2] Today, oral witness testimony is frequently supplemented by documentary, physical, or scientific evidence, so it can no longer be assumed that oral testimony is necessarily the primary or most significant source of information for the fact-finder in every case. Certainly, there are some types of prosecution in which oral testimony plays a relatively minor role: consider, for example, a rape case resting chiefly on DNA evidence, or a serious fraud trial based predominantly on documentary evidence of fraudulent transactions.

Oral testimony nonetheless remains paradigmatic in a secondary, symbolic – or iconic – sense. For orality is part and parcel of the English tradition of criminal adjudication in which a mini-drama is played out 'live' and in 'real time' in the courtroom, narrating in the presence of the fact-finder an unfolding evidential story of allegation and denial, claim and counter-claim, damning proof and plausible exculpation. As §2.3 intimated, this conception has taken deep root in the common law psyche, and to this day remains embedded within the legal and broader social conventions underpinning criminal justice.

---

[1] To give just one telling illustration: in December 1678 two Old Bailey juries 'returned verdicts in thirty-two cases involving thirty-six accused in two days. Further, these cases were tried and decided in batches. The Middlesex jury that handled a total of twenty-one cases deliberated only three times. It heard all seven trials on Wednesday morning before deliberating on any of the cases; it then withdrew to formulate verdicts in all seven. It proceeded in like manner with its two Thursday deliberations – the eight morning verdicts together and the six afternoon verdicts in another batch': John H. Langbein, 'The Criminal Trial before the Lawyers' (1978) 45 *University of Chicago LR* 263, 275.

[2] For the modern position, see Chapters 12 and 13. In the period 1675–1735 Langbein reports, ibid. 283, that he failed to find 'a single case in which an accused refused to speak on asserted grounds of privilege...Without counsel to shoulder the nontestimonial aspects of the defence, the accused's privilege would simply have amounted to the right to forfeit all defence, and we do not wonder that he never claimed it.'

We will refer to English law's culturally embedded ideological preference for live witness testimony as 'the principle of orality'.

A trial can only ever be an imperfect re-run of the original 'drama', a simulacrum of the alleged crime that is the subject matter of the charge. However, modern communications technologies are opening up new possibilities for the presentation of evidence beyond the imagination of previous generations. The proliferation of CCTV cameras on motorways and in town centres, car parks, shopping malls, and other types of 'mass private space',[3] means that the fact-finder is sometimes able to watch literal re-runs of crime, video recordings of the offence actually being committed.[4] Further possibilities include video-taped witness statements, which can be recorded close to the time of the incident when the witness's recollections are fresh and her reactions authentic, video-recordings of police interviews and identification parades, and live-link CCTV allowing witness testimony to be 'beamed-in' to the courtroom, whether from a comfortable witness-suite in the curial precincts or from an absent witness located half-way around the world. Nobody should expect an institution as venerable as the criminal law to be at the very cutting-edge of technological development. However, Parliament has acted with perhaps surprising alacrity to make provision for new communications media in criminal adjudication, especially in order to ameliorate the trauma of testifying for vulnerable witnesses. The details and implications of these developments will be examined in Chapter 10. For now, the point to register is that contemporary communications technologies undeniably pose the question whether the traditional means of evidence-taking, which were more or less foisted on our ancestors who lacked any practical alternatives, are still fit to serve the ends of justice in modern society.

This is a complicated and, for many people, highly politically-charged question. We will not be able to provide a completely satisfactory answer to it in this book, partly because the legal reforms and developments in litigation practice we will be describing are still in the process of being implemented and their ultimate shape and implications remain somewhat conjectural. What we can hope to achieve, however, is to provide a reasonably detailed sketch of the considerations that any satisfactory answer would need to address. A major part of this task is descriptive. This and the next three chapters describe the legal rules governing criminal trial procedure which, taken together, constitute the doctrinal manifestations of the principle of orality. This chapter will consider the most basic evidentiary rules regulating access to witness testimony as an informational resource. English law divides this task between the doctrines of competence, compellability (a.k.a. 'the principle of compulsory process'), and testimonial privileges. Chapter 8 will then examine the main procedural rules governing 'the course of the trial', which are principally a set of doctrines governing the presentation of evidence through examination-in-chief and cross-examination. Chapter 9 is devoted to an exposition of the rule against hearsay and its many, often highly technical exceptions. The rule against hearsay can be regarded as the principle of orality's alter-ego: by excluding many out-of-court statements it directly buttresses English law's default preference for live oral witness testimony. We will see,

---

[3] Generally, see Andrew von Hirsch, David Garland, and Alison Wakefield (eds.), *Ethical and Social Perspectives on Situational Crime Prevention* (Hart, 2000).

[4] See, e.g., *R v Campbell (Andre)* [2009] EWCA Crim 50; *R v Lawson* [2007] 1 WLR 1191, [2006] EWCA Crim 2572.

however, that the common law has always permitted recourse to certain kinds of hearsay, and that major reforms introduced by the Criminal Justice Act 2003 have greatly accelerated the drift towards admissibility. If hearsay is today routinely received where formally it would have been excluded at common law, where does this leave English law's orthodox commitment to orality? The question becomes more pointed still when, in Chapter 10, we go on to consider successive reforms introduced to address the plight of especially vulnerable or intimidated witnesses. When we have reviewed the ways in which criminal trial procedure has been modified to ameliorate the experiences of these witnesses, we will be in a much better position to reconsider the strength of English law's on-going commitment to the principle of orality.

This inquiry cannot, however, be entirely descriptive. In order to understand the principle of orality and to assess its current juridical vitality or decline it is necessary to appreciate the values which the principle encapsulates, and also to clarify the values and objectives of its critics and reformers. This requires self-consciously normative analysis. Which values or objectives are in play when we debate the means and forms of presenting witness evidence? Where values or objectives conflict, which should prevail?

If effective communication of evidence to fact-finders were the sole objective of a criminal trial, the normative purchase of the principle of orality would be flimsy and the corresponding prognosis for oral witness testimony would surely be bleak. For on this score the traditional process, whereby a witness is summoned to attend a particular court many months or even years after the incident and invited to speak form unaided memory, seems hopelessly unwieldy and antiquated, if not irrational. Why not rely instead on a video-taped witness statement recorded close to the time of the incident, permitting the fact-finder to observe the witness's (almost) immediate recollections and reactions?[5] And rather than going to all the trouble and expense of flying a witness half-way around the world to testify in person, why not also allow his evidence to be pre-recorded on videotape or, failing that, make provision for him to testify by live-link satellite from his current location? Whilst English law already now accommodates such arrangements in exceptional cases, this line of thought easily leads one to question why the exception should not become the norm. At a time when teenagers use their mobile phones to 'text' and 'tweet' their friends around the globe, do we really still need to require *any* witnesses to undergo the inconvenience of court-attendance, which nearly always means wasted hours waiting, and further difficulties arranging child-care or absence from work? Can we really expect witnesses to provide live testimony in court, which is frequently unpleasant and sometimes even traumatic and harmful for particular witnesses? Is this primitive ritual (as some might see it) past its sell-by date?

The enduring status of live oral testimony in English criminal proceedings is a strong clue that trials are *not* merely mechanisms for conveying information to fact-finders. The traditional model of criminal adjudication must serve significant objectives and values in addition to truth-seeking. These traditional objective and values may be derived through further elucidation of the 'five foundational principles' identified in Chapter 1.[6]

---

[5] Criminal Justice Act (CJA) 2003, s.137, makes provision for the admissibility of video-recorded witness statements, if 'the account was given at a time when…events were fresh in the person's memory' and 'it is in the interests of justice for the recording to be admitted'. Section 137 has not yet been brought into force: see §8.2(b).   [6] §1.3.

One such value is publicity, or 'open justice'. Another is vigorous testing through cross-examination of any testimony which may lead to the public condemnation and punishment of a fellow human being. Here, the principles of accurate fact-finding and of protecting the innocent form wrongful conviction are plainly engaged. In recent decades, however, the traditional procedures for presenting and testing witness testimony in English criminal trials have endured a barrage of criticism from those who doubt their efficacy in promoting the interests of justice.

(a) ORAL TRIAL AND OPEN JUSTICE

The narrative of evidence which unfolds in court is not only laid before the fact-finder, but is also made accessible and transparent to the general public as well. Any citizen (or, indeed, any foreign visitor) can choose to sit in the public gallery of a courtroom and observe the justice process in action. Moreover, proceedings are monitored and reported by a free press. In this way, the state machinery of criminal justice is laid bare to public scrutiny and made accountable to the people. These are essential preconditions for the legitimacy of criminal verdicts.

At first blush the connection between open justice and live oral testimony may not be self-evident. After all, the media and members of the public could still attend and monitor criminal trials if evidence consisted of video-recordings, live-link CCTV transmissions, and the like. Yet, on reflection, it is obvious that such surrogates would provide an inferior from of transparency and accountability compared with live oral testimony. It is already, and perhaps unavoidably, the case that much of the work of evidence-gathering and 'case construction' takes place in locales and institutional settings which are difficult to subject to effective public scrutiny, either at the time or in retrospect. Dispensing with live oral testimony would tend to insinuate this *de facto* insulation from democratic accountability into the procedures by which evidence is presented as well. It would consequently be impossible to dispel legitimate suspicions about what had taken place off-camera before video testimony was recorded.[7] How could we be sure that the witness had not been pressurized or bribed to give their evidence? Is it not possible that a witness testifying from overseas by live-link CCTV is speaking under duress, or even that there is someone just off-camera pointing a gun at her head? The courtroom is by contrast a relatively safe public environment in which a witness should be able to speak freely, at least if she is telling the truth. Moreover, a courtroom witness is available in person to elaborate on her evidence, clear up any confusions or ambiguities in her testimony, and answer further questions

---

[7] It is fair to point out that witnesses can also be primed, bribed, or intimidated before giving oral evidence in court. But at least a witness is free from *immediate* coercion in the trial setting, and has ample opportunity to seek official assistance. There is not the same level of anxiety about 'witness-coaching' in England as there appears to be in the United States (but see *R v Momodou and Limani* [2005] 1 WLR 3442, [2005] EWCA Crim 177), in part because advocates in the higher courts are instructed by solicitors and consequently have limited direct contact with lay witnesses before the trial. There is now a limited power for Crown Prosecutors to interview complainants and other prosecution witnesses prior to their testifying at trial: see Paul Roberts and Candida Saunders, 'Introducing Pre-Trial Witness Interviews – A Flexible New Fixture in the Crown Prosecutor's Toolkit' [2008] *Crim LR* 831; Louise Ellison, 'Witness Preparation and the Prosecution of Rape' (2007) 27 *Legal Studies* 171. Witness intimidation, on the other hand, is a growing concern in England and Wales.

about it. A video or disembodied digital CCTV image is therefore no real substitute for a live witness testifying in public, from the perspective of open justice and 'justice being seen to be done'.[8]

(b) NORMATIVE CRITIQUES OF CROSS-EXAMINATION

Criminal trials are also fundamentally a mechanism for *testing*, as well as for communicating, evidence. Indeed, as we observed in §3.4, criminal trials *generate new evidence*, in the form of the witnesses' demeanour, and also the demeanour of the accused in the dock as he reacts, or remains impassive, to what each witness says in his presence. The time-honoured mechanism for testing witness evidence is, of course, courtroom cross-examination, another iconic feature of English adversary trials.

No barrister's memoirs would be complete without a good sprinkling of anecdotes recounting how through skilful cross-examination the advocate was able to expose his opponent's main witness as a liar, or at least to reveal some crucial gap or inconsistency in the witness's evidence, thus winning the day for his client. Wigmore famously hailed cross-examination as the 'greatest legal engine ever invented for the discovery of truth'.[9] If cross-examination were truly such a magnificent asset to criminal adjudication, the law's reluctance to dispense with live oral testimony, at least for the phases of proceedings in which evidence is *tested* rather than merely conveyed, would be entirely understandable. However, in recent times cross-examination has attracted extensive criticism, to the point where it is now widely regarded as an obstacle, rather than the royal road, to effective forensic fact-finding. These days Wigmore's peroration is more likely to be cited as evidence of the legal profession's collective self-delusion, than as a serious proposition about the best way to discover the truth about past events.

Criticism has rightly focused on abusive cross-examination. Advocates are bound, both in law and by the Bar's professional *Code of Conduct*, to treat witnesses courteously and to restrict their lines of questioning to relevant matters. Such restrictions are in partial fulfilment of the state's universal duty of concern and respect, which is owed to everybody who becomes embroiled in criminal proceedings in accordance with the principle of humane treatment.[10] It is impermissible for an advocate to put wholly unfounded allegations of impropriety to a witness, or otherwise to subject the witness to unreasonably protracted, aggressive, repetitive, or hectoring cross-examination, especially on matters of the witness's general credibility.[11] On the other hand, however, a defence advocate is duty-bound to further his client's legitimate interest in vigorously testing the prosecution's evidence

---

[8] See §1.2(c) and §2.3(b).   [9] *Wigmore on Evidence* (Chadbourn revision), vol. 5, §1367.

[10] §1.3.

[11] The Bar's *Code of Conduct* (8th edn., 2004), §708 provides that a 'barrister when conducting proceedings in Court...(e) must not adduce evidence obtained otherwise than from or through the client or devise facts which will assist in advancing the lay client's case; (f) must not make a submission which he does not consider to be properly arguable; (g) must not make statements or ask questions which are merely scandalous or intended or calculated only to vilify insult or annoy either a witness or some other person;... (j) must not suggest that a victim, witness or other person is guilty of crime, fraud or misconduct or make any defamatory aspersion on the conduct of any other person or attribute to another person the crime or conduct of which his lay client is accused unless such allegations go to a matter in issue (including the credibility of the witness) which is material to the lay client's case and appear to him to be supported by reasonable grounds'.

against him.[12] Furthermore, the advocate will be taken to have accepted on behalf of his client any part of an opposing witness's testimony that is not specifically challenged in cross-examination.[13] The obvious tension between these two sets of considerations leaves counsel with considerable professional discretion to determine how far it is appropriate to go in turning the screw in cross-examination. Key witnesses whose evidence, if accepted by the fact-finder, could settle a disputed issue may confidently anticipate searching scrutiny of their testimony and may experience a relatively rough ride in the witness-box.

Abusive cross-examination has been a subject of judicial concern and public controversy for more than a century. In a 1935 civil case, Lord Sankey LC stated that 'cross-examination becomes indefensible when it is conducted... without restraint and without the courtesy and consideration which a witness is entitled to expect in a Court of law',[14] and proceeded to endorse this *dictum* of Lord Hanworth MR in the court below:

Cross-examination is a powerful and valuable weapon for the purpose of testing the veracity of a witness and the accuracy and completeness of his story. It is entrusted to the hands of counsel in the confidence that it will be used with discretion; and with due regard to the assistance to be rendered by it to the [fact-finder], not forgetting at the same time the burden that is imposed upon the witness.[15]

Implicit in Lord Hanworth MR's remarks are the two main concerns surrounding cross-examination: first, that a witness might be gratuitously abused, damaging the integrity of criminal proceedings and possibly breaching the state's duty of humanity; and secondly, that a truthful and reliable witness might be made to look unsure or even deceitful because she is outmanoeuvred by artful lawyers' trick-questioning. In circumstances where the latter occurs, cross-examination begins to appear as the enemy rather than the servant of truth. A further consequence of both eventualities may be that potential witnesses will in future withhold their willing co-operation from a process that appears to treat them, and their evidence, with contempt.

A recent high-profile example of arguably abusive cross-examination occurred in the trial of the juveniles originally charged with the murder of Damilola Taylor. The case against the two[16] boys accused of this apparently motiveless fatal attack effectively collapsed after the judge directed the jury to disregard the evidence of the prosecution's star witness, a fourteen-year-old girl who claimed to have been an eyewitness to the incident. 'Witness Bromley', as she was known in the proceedings to protect her anonymity, was caught out in various self-contradictions and shown on police video singing 'I'm in the Money', a reference to the £50,000 reward put up for information leading to the successful prosecution of

---

[12] The Bar Council, *Code of Conduct* (8th edn. 2004), §303: 'A barrister... must promote and protect fearlessly and by all proper and lawful means the lay client's best interests and do so without regard to his own interests or to any consequences to himself or to any other person...'

[13] This is actually a sensible rule designed to give the witness an opportunity to respond to any objection that might later be taken to her evidence: *Browne v Dunn* (1894) 6 R 67, HL; The Bar Council, *Code of Conduct* (8th edn. 2004), §708(i).

[14] *Mechanical & General Inventions v Austin Motor Co* [1935] AC 346, 360, HL.   [15] ibid. 359.

[16] At the start of the trial there had been four juvenile accused charged with murder, but evidential developments led the CPS to offer no evidence against one, whilst a second successfully made a plea of 'no case to answer' at the conclusion of the prosecution's case.

Damilola's killers.[17] The trial, which lasted three months before the jury returned verdicts of acquittal on all charges, was branded a travesty in many quarters, partly on account of the way in which, it was said, 'witness "Bromley"… was ripped to shreds by a succession of highly-paid QCs'.[18] A subsequent inquiry into the conduct of the investigation and trial chaired by the Right Reverend John Sentamu, Bishop of Birmingham (as he then was), concluded more even-handedly that Bromley's cross-examination 'was both vigorous and probing, as indeed it had to be in all the circumstances', but added that:

The Panel has reason to believe that Bromley and her family found her treatment at Court to be profoundly disturbing…. The Panel believes that the underlying culture of the judicial process has yet to fully recognize and take account of the emotional and psychological consequences that potentially follow from the experience of a vulnerable witness at court, including the additional trauma that can accrue.[19]

Other voices were more strident in their justification of Witness Bromley's treatment during the course of the trial. Viewed from a more traditional perspective, the outcome of this prosecution might be said to vindicate the potency of cross-examination as an instrument of truth and justice.[20] Four years later, two boys who had not previously been charged or prosecuted (although they had been early suspects) were convicted of Damilola's manslaughter.[21]

Modern scepticism about the merits of cross-examination does not rest exclusively on its susceptibility to abuse by counsel. If that were critics' only concern it might be possible to purge cross-examination of its worst excesses by, for example, tightening up the Bar's self-regulatory *Code of Conduct* (with meaningful sanctions for culpable breaches) and encouraging trial judges to be more actively interventionist in restraining counsel and protecting witnesses from inappropriate questioning. Behavioural scientists and others have levelled a more basic charge with radical implications: that live testimony in general, and cross-examination in particular, are inherently defective techniques for investigating the truth of past events. If these critics are right, the oral tradition of fact-finding embraced in common law jurisdictions rests on a fundamental misconception, and would seem ripe for reappraisal.

(c) BEHAVIOURAL SCIENCE CHALLENGES TO TRADITIONAL TRIAL PROCEDURE

Social psychologists and other behavioural scientists have investigated the conditions most conducive to full and accurate recall by witnesses, and have devised experiments

[17] Nick Hopkins, 'Secrets and Lies of a Far From Expert Witness', *The Guardian*, 28 February 2002; Sandra Laville, 'Lure of Money Tainted Damilola Witness', *The Telegraph*, 28 February 2002.

[18] Leading Article, 'Another Betrayal', *Daily Mail*, 29 April 2002.

[19] Oversight Panel (Chair: The Rt Revd John Sentamu), *The Damilola Taylor Murder Investigation Review* (December 2002), paras.5.4.16, 5.4.30–32, on-line via http://image.guardian.co.uk/sys-files/Guardian/documents/2002/12/09/damilola.pdf.

[20] Cf. John Cooper, 'No Second Chance for the Police', *The Times*, 7 May 2002: 'The 14-year-old girl known as Bromley was not, as the police would like it believed, cross-examined into confusion by "four Oxbridge graduates". Quite the contrary, she was an ill-prepared witness who, by the sensitive but probing techniques of skilled criminal advocacy, was shown to be inconsistent and unreliable.'

[21] Shenai Raif, 'Brothers Convicted for Damilola's Killing', *The Independent*, 9 August 2006.

to test potential jurors' ability to distinguish between reliable and mistaken or lying witnesses. On both sets of criteria, the model of adversary criminal trial currently practised in England and Wales has repeatedly been exposed as deficient.

There is broad consensus amongst researchers that witnesses perform best when they are asked to recount events which are fairly recent in time, in open-ended narrative form with minimal initial prompting, and in a stress-free environment.[22] Memories are apparently *creative and dynamic reconstructions* of past events, rather than snap-shots of reality faithfully recorded and stored away in the mind's permanent archive. Psychologists inform us that information may be lost or distorted at each of the three key stages, of memory acquisition ('encoding'), storage, and retrieval.[23] The danger in delay is that the mind's serial reconstructions will move further and further away from one's original perceptions. The likelihood of embellishment increases every time a witness is asked to recount – or, one might say, *recreate* – the events in question.[24] Moreover, because these mental processes are largely subconscious, even the witness him- or herself may be unaware of any deviation from their initial perceptions.

The science of memory has alarming forensic implications. A scrupulously honest witness could be absolutely unshakeable in her conviction that she is providing an accurate account of events, and yet have incorporated 'facts' into her memory that are in reality fabrications, mere artefacts of other stimuli, suggestion by others,[25] or the endless churning of her own thought processes as events are constantly replayed in the mind's eye. The traditional mechanisms for testing evidence in court, which are meant to detect if a witness is uncertain or lying, are largely impotent when confronted with the honest and confident, yet mistaken, witness.[26] Worse, English criminal proceedings are characterized by long delays, during which time witnesses may be required to repeat their stories over and over to the police, to their lawyers and in pre-trial court hearings. When finally the witness is called upon to address the fact-finder at trial, she must present her evidence through the highly artificial medium of examination-in-chief and then undergo a stressful cross-examination. It is almost as if the architects of adversary proceedings had studied the findings of modern psychological research and then perversely created a trial system founded on diametrically opposite principles. For '[i]f there are two scientific facts about the psychology of human memory which are clear beyond any doubt, one is that memory

---

[22] See J. R. Spencer and Rhona Flin, *The Evidence of Children: the Law and the Psychology* (Blackstone, 2nd edn. 1993), chs 10–13, which in the course of focusing primarily on the child witness, also provides an excellent discussion of the forensic implications of psychological research for witness testimony generally.

[23] Gillian Cohen, 'Human Memory in the Real World', in Anthony Heaton-Armstrong, Eric Shepherd, and David Wolchover (eds.), *Analysing Witness Testimony* (Blackstone, 1999); Gisli Gudjonsson, *The Psychology of Interrogations, Confessions and Testimony* (Wiley, 1992), ch 5.

[24] Cohen, 'Human Memory in the Real World', 15, explains that '[w]hen people are asked to produce the same memory repeatedly it has been shown that their accounts undergo considerable transformation from one occasion to another. Although the core of the memory remains fairly stable, some of the peripheral details tend to drop out and more new details are added'.

[25] Graphically demonstrated by the hotly-debated topic of 'recovered/false memories'. It is reported that '25% of adults will begin to recover "memories" of non-existent events after three sessions devoted to intensive reminiscence': Graham Davies, 'Contamination of Witness Memory', in Anthony Heaton-Armstrong, Eric Shepherd, and David Wolchover (eds.), *Analysing Witness Testimony* (Blackstone, 1999), 26.

[26] Mistaken identifications, in particular, have been a potent source of miscarriages of justice: see §15.4.

for an event fades gradually with time, and the other is that stress beyond a certain level can impair the power of recall'.[27]

Further research findings shed light on the reliability of judgments of witness accuracy and credibility. It is a familiar feature of everyday life that we judge truthfulness not only by what a speaker says to us – some things being inherently more likely to be true than others[28] – but also by how it is said, and by whom. A raft of non-verbal cues, including tone of voice, eye movement, facial gestures, and other aspects of 'body language', are taken to be involuntary physical signs of truth and falsehood. We expect the truth to be spoken coherently and with confidence, whereas dissimulation announces itself in hesitancy, bashfulness, and self-contradiction. The identity of the speaker, if known, is also highly significant. If Bishop has a well-deserved reputation for the utmost veracity and candour in all things, it is probably safe to rely on his assurances; whereas it would be prudent to take anything said by Practical Joker with a pinch of salt. Translated to the forensic context, these familiar expectations and assumptions explain the significance attached to observing a witness's demeanour whilst giving evidence in court, which in turn reinforces English law's traditional preference for live oral testimony.

Behavioural science research confirms that potential jurors are frequently influenced by non-verbal cues of veracity.[29] Indeed, many research subjects consider themselves quite accomplished in distinguishing truthfulness from falsehood on the basis of demeanour. Unfortunately, these same studies show that such confidence is largely misplaced. People are actually quite poor at judging credibility from demeanour.[30] Some experimental subjects' success rate is less than what might be achieved purely by chance: in other words, they would do better simply to toss a coin than to rely on their supposedly well-honed instincts for smelling a rat and seeing through deception! Part of the problem is that observers are more attuned to those body language cues which emit the least reliable signals. Information from the 'leakier' (i.e. more subconscious, less controllable) channels of communication is meanwhile overlooked. Researchers have concluded that the pitch of a speaker's voice and other 'paralinguistic' indicators are the best indicia of deception, yet these tell-tale signs are frequently missed:

Observers commonly assume that people who are being deceptive are uncomfortable, shifty, restless in their seats, and move their heads in all directions so as to avoid an observer's scrutiny. During deception, however, there is in fact a decrease in each of these behaviours. This

---

[27] Spencer and Flin, *The Evidence of Children*, 268.

[28] If a shopkeeper tells you that he is out of bananas this is more likely to be true, all things being equal, than the market-square preacher's prediction that the world is about to end. But overall judgments of credibility also depend on what other information is available. If you can see with your own eyes that the shopkeeper has several bunches of bananas under the counter, he is obviously lying. Either the bananas are already spoken for, or he just does not want you to have them.

[29] Relevant research findings are usefully summarized by Olin Guy Wellborn III, 'Demeanor' (1991) 76 *Cornell LR* 1075. Also see Marcus Stone, 'Instant Lie Detection? Demeanour and Credibility in Criminal Trials' [1991] *Crim LR* 821, 823–4, reporting that: 'sufficient research has been carried out on lying to undermine the claim that demeanour is a key to veracity … [T]here are no specific signs of deceit to indicate lying. Thus, if accepted, these psychological findings destroy any naïve view of demeanour as a simple and crude test of credibility.'

[30] Wellborn concludes from his review of the data that '[a]lthough most people cannot do better than chance in detecting falsehoods, most people confidently believe they can do so': (1991) 76 *Cornell LR* 1075, 1081. Also see Andreas Kapardis, *Psychology and Law* (CUP, 1997), 211–15.

is probably a direct result of the fact that people who are being deceptive know which behaviours result in judgments of deception. If a speaker expects those observing him to interpret postural shifts as signs of deception, he will try to reduce such movement.... Reliance on vocal evidence, however, appears to be more valuable. Most of the behaviours received through the auditory channel that were associated with perceptions of deception were also observed during actual deception: increases in speech hesitations, speech errors, and in the pitch of a speaker's voice.... Since the visual channels of face and body are more controllable than the leakier voice channel, it is easier for a speaker to conceal useful information from an observer who is focusing on visual cues.[31]

Social psychological research findings deliver a 'double-whammy' to the oral tradition. It is bad enough to be told that demeanour is not a reliable guide to veracity, when the law's preference for live oral testimony is partly founded on the opposite assumption. But if jurors simultaneously entertain unwarranted confidence in their demeanour-based judgments of witness credibility, the risk of error in criminal adjudication – including, presumably, wrongful conviction of the innocent – must necessarily be compounded.

A further disturbing implication of psychological research on demeanour arises from the stereotypical nature of observers' expectations. Assessments of credibility are apparently influenced by a range of cultural assumptions and social stereotypes, with class, race, and gender dimensions (amongst others). This poses two, related, difficulties where the witness and the fact-finder do not share similar life experiences, social *milieux*, and cultural assumptions. First, witnesses may be disbelieved because they fail to satisfy mainstream expectations of how a truthful witness should behave. Such a witness, one might say, is being discriminated against (or at least disadvantaged) for nonconformity with social norms. Imagine, for example, that the witness is a rape complainant or victim of some other serious crime of personal violence. If the testimony of such complainants is systematically being discounted on the basis of inappropriate stereotypes,[32] this is tantamount to withdrawing the protection of the criminal law – or some part of it – from certain groups in society, a failing all the more egregious when the groups in question are already socially disadvantaged or marginalized.[33]

Secondly, fact-finders immersed in the dominant culture may be ignorant of the behavioural cues in operation amongst minority groups and communities. Jurors in the grip of such ignorance are especially likely to 'mis-read the signals' of a witness's body language, increasing the risk of adjudicative error and effectively perpetrating a form of indirect discrimination against members of minority groups, whether defined by race, religion, language, class, age, culture, or some other existential attribute. The mental operations leading to culturally-skewed assessments of credibility are barely understood by modern psychology, and will perhaps never be susceptible to conclusive demonstration. The processes at work are subtle and difficult to disentangle from the impact of more straightforward bias and discrimination. However, American commentary on race and credibility,

---

[31] Jeremy A. Blumenthal, 'A Wipe of the Hands, A Lick of the Lips: The Validity of Demeanor Evidence in Assessing Witness Credibility' (1993) 72 *Nebraska LR* 1157, 1194–5 (footnotes omitted).

[32] See further, Mary White Stewart, Shirley A. Dobbin, and Sophia I. Gatowski, '"Real Rapes" and "Real Victims": the Shared Reliance on Common Cultural Definitions of Rape' (1996) IV *Feminist Legal Studies* 159.

[33] This consideration lends impetus to the argument for reforming criminal trial procedure in order to assist particularly vulnerable or intimidated witnesses: see Chapter 10.

to cite one highly-charged illustration, has at the least established a circumstantial case to answer.[34]

This is merely the briefest summary of a substantial corpus of psychological and behavioural science research challenging the foundational assumptions of the oral tradition in criminal trial procedure. It is intended only to indicate the broad themes of this literature and their evident salience for criminal adjudication. When combined with normative critiques of cross-examination and an influential political lobby promoting victims' interests, we have a powerful force for change. Small wonder, then, that recent innovation in the mechanisms for receiving witness testimony has been both swift, relative to the often glacial pace of evidentiary reform, and increasingly radical. Whether these developments presage the complete demise of orality in English criminal trials, or only its timely correction, is a question we will defer to the concluding section of Chapter 10. One thing to bear in mind as we work our way towards that conclusion is the vital distinction between pillorying or demolishing a traditional set of institutional practices and devising something better to replace them. Even if traditional trial procedure is deficient in all or most of the ways in which normative and behavioural science critiques maintain, it should not simply be assumed that any proposed alternativeness are either viable or desirable. To the extent that any blueprints for root-and-branch reform are implicitly on offer, they too must be specified in detail and judged on their merits.

We will not make any real headway with normative analysis without first acquainting ourselves with traditional legal procedures regulating the admissibility and presentation of witness evidence. The meaning of the 'principle of orality' in English law is informed by the answers to prosaic procedural questions. Who is permitted to testify in criminal proceedings? Do witnesses themselves have any say in the matter? Can they choose to withhold particular sorts of information from the court, and if so, what and when? How do established legal doctrines regulate the presentation of oral witness testimony in the course of the trial? What evidentiary restrictions limit the admissibility of witness evidence or the uses to which it may be put by the fact-finder? These are the questions which will occupy us for the remainder of this chapter and for most of the following three, beginning with an assessment of 'competence' – the first legal qualification for appearing as a witness in a criminal trial.

7.2 TESTIMONIAL COMPETENCE

Only witnesses deemed 'competent' at law may testify in legal proceedings. Traditionally, 'competent to testify' meant competent to swear an oath to tell the truth, of the canonical form:

I swear by Almighty God that the evidence which I shall give shall be the truth, the whole truth and nothing but the truth.[35]

---

[34] Sheri Lynn Johnson, 'The Color of Truth: Race and the Assessment of Credibility' (1996) 1 *Michigan Journal of Race and Law* 261, esp. 312–17 and 329–39; Andrew E. Taslitz, 'An African-American Sense of Fact: The OJ Trial and Black Judges on Justice' (1998) 7 *Boston University Public Law Journal* 219.

[35] *David Mildrone's Case* (1786) 1 Leach 412, 168 ER 308. Now see Oaths Act 1978, s.1.

In addition to the 'divine sanction' for deliberately bearing false witness,[36] lying on oath constitutes the temporal crime of perjury for which witnesses can be prosecuted and imprisoned.[37] English criminal law has always laid great store by acquiring reliable witness testimony, but its conceptions of the reliable witness have ebbed and flowed with the times. Two centuries ago English law adopted a very restrictive test of witness competency. The story ever since has been one of gradual liberalization, as each of the old categorical restrictions was in its turn debunked and discarded. The process was only finally completed at the turn of the twenty-first century.

Well into the 1800s, English law was very selective in the witnesses it deemed competent to testify in court. Certain classes of witness were regarded as lacking what Wigmore perceptively described as the 'moral responsibility' to justify the law's reliance on their testimony.[38] Those with a criminal conviction were considered 'incompetent from infamy' and altogether disqualified as potential witnesses.[39] The parties to the dispute were also legally incompetent. It was assumed that they would inevitably lie in their own cause, so that their testimony, if received, would be evidentially worthless. This historical background is essential for contextualizing the fact, amazing to modern eyes, that the accused did not become generally competent as a witness in his own defence until 1898.[40]

Though legal incompetence might be rationalized in terms of the presumptive unreliability of particular kinds of witness, the exclusion of entire classes of witness from English criminal trials also had broader and more sinister connotations. Since the verdict of the court is meant to convey authoritative official censure of moral wrongdoing, the law has reason to take an interest in the moral standing, or supposed moral standing, of the witnesses on whose testimony the factual integrity of adjudication must rest.[41]

At one time non-Christians were completely excluded from testifying in court on account of their inability to swear an oath to tell the truth on the New Testament. In centuries past, when the idea of an established Anglican Church was a more meaningful social and political reality than it is today, the standard mechanism for demonstrating honour, fidelity and veracity in all walks of public life was to swear an oath on the Bible. The oath stood for allegiance to the political authority of church and state, which for Anglicans had became merged into one, at the same time as declaring fidelity to the higher spiritual authority. It is difficult in these more secular, Enlightened times fully to appreciate the very real influence that must have been exerted over the imagination of a seventeenth- or eighteenth-century witness in a criminal trial by a fervent belief that lying on oath might result in eternal damnation. As Abbott CJ colourfully put it in *The Queen's Case*, 'in taking that oath, he has called his God to witness, that what he shall say will be the truth, and that he has imprecated the divine vengeance upon his head, if what he shall afterward say

---

[36] 'Thou shalt not bear false witness against thy neighbour': Exodus 20:16 Also Exodus 23:1; Deuteronomy 5:20 and 19:16, etc. Equivalent prohibitions appears in the Koran, e.g. 2.283: 'do not conceal testimony, and whoever conceals it, his heart is surely sinful; and Allah knows what you do'.

[37] Perjury Act 1911, s.1.   [38] *Wigmore on Evidence*, (3rd edn. 1940), vol. 2, §515.

[39] These disqualifications were abolished by the Civil Rights of Convicts Act 1828 and finally by the Evidence Act 1843.

[40] For an historical account of the serial reverses and ultimate success of reform efforts, see Christopher Allen, *The Law of Evidence in Victorian England* (CUP, 1997), ch 5.

[41] Which ties in with the moral and social functions of jury verdicts, previously discussed in §2.4.

is false'.[42] However, it is evident that the law's commendable aspiration to secure reliable testimony under divine sanction was laced with barely-concealed religious bigotry.[43]

Pedantic religious scruple proved very costly in evidential terms. Much testimony, and many prosecutions and causes of action, are going to be lost if entire cohorts of potential witnesses are rejected out-of-hand on grounds of 'defect of religious principle'. In a landmark case of 1745 it was established that a witness would be competent provided that he professed some version of deistic religion, and could swear an oath to tell the truth on that basis.[44] The oath requirement was later relaxed in favour of Protestant dissenters, such as Quakers who object in principle to oath-taking, in the early decades of the nineteenth century. However, the pragmatic demand for admissible testimony was still not felt sufficiently keenly to permit atheists to affirm, rather than swear an oath, until 1861.[45] By this time incompetence on grounds of interest was also on the wane. Successive pieces of legislation through mid-century removed disqualifications on the parties appearing in court as witnesses on their own behalf.[46] This incremental process of liberalization in favour of interested parties was completed by the Criminal Evidence Act 1898, which for the first time made accused persons in general (as opposed to a selective few charged with designated offences) competent to testify in their own defence.

Two groups whose evidence continued to attract special scrutiny in modern times, and continued (albeit intermittently) to be excluded on a categorical basis, are children and adults suffering from mental disorder or mental illness. However, the last vestiges of class incompetence were finally swept away by the Youth Justice and Criminal Evidence Act 1999. Neither children nor 'persons of defective intellect' are any longer turned away purely on account of their membership in a class of witness deemed inherently incapable of providing reliable testimony.

Prior to the most recent reforms, children were allowed to testify under oath as long as they understood its significance,[47] whilst children 'of tender years' could testify without taking an oath provided they were judged to possess sufficient intelligence to make receiving their testimony worthwhile. Lord Goddard CJ once doubted whether a court should ever receive the evidence of any child under five years-of-age,[48] but that view is contradicted by clinical experience[49] and was ultimately rejected at common law,[50] before Parliament intervened and conclusively settled the issue. Section 53(1) of the Youth Justice and Criminal Evidence Act 1999 now provides that: '[a]t every stage in criminal proceedings all persons are (whatever their age) competent to give evidence'. Younger children

---

[42] (1820) 2 Brod & B 284, 285; 129 ER 976, HL.

[43] Cf. *Clavin's Case* 7 Co 17, cited in W. M. Best, *The Principles of the Law of Evidence* (5th edn. 1870), 192: 'All infidels are in law *perpetui inimici*, perpetual enemies... for between them, as with the devils, whose subjects they are, and the Christians, there is perpetual hostility, and can be no peace.' (Such 'Christian' sentiments, incidentally, remind us that Islam does not have an exclusive historical monopoly on Jihad.)

[44] *Omychund* v *Barker* (1745) 1 Atk 21 discussed by Best, ibid. 196.

[45] The story is fully recounted by Allen, *The Law of Evidence in Victorian England*, ch 3.

[46] Evidence Act 1843; Evidence Act 1851; Evidence Further Amendment Act 1869. See Allen, *The Law of Evidence in Victorian England*, ch 4.

[47] *R* v *Hayes* [1977] 1 WLR 234, CA; *R* v *Brasier* (1779) 1 Leach 199.

[48] *R* v *Wallwork* (1958) 42 Cr App R 153, CCA; applied in *R* v *Wright* (1990) 90 Cr App R 91, CA, to a child of six years.

[49] For a first-hand account of one remarkable instance, see David P. H. Jones, 'The Evidence of a Three-Year-Old Child' [1987] *Crim LR* 677. And see Ray Bull, 'Obtaining Evidence Expertly: The Reliability of Interviews with Child Witnesses' (1992) 1 *Expert Evidence* 5.   [50] *R* v *Z* [1990] 2 QB 355, CA.

under fourteen years-of-age still give unsworn testimony.[51] However, unsworn testimony is to all intents and purposes on a equal evidentiary footing with testimony on oath. Crucially, the test of 'competence' is now set at a minimum standard of intelligibility, as defined by section 53(3) of the 1999 Act:

Section 53(3)
A person is not competent to give evidence in the proceedings if it appears to the court that he is not a person who is able to –
  (a) understand questions put to him as a witness, and
  (b) give answers to them which can be understood.

The Court of Appeal has indicated that section 53(3), 'which is commendably clear in its language', means exactly what it says:

[T]he issue raised by paragraphs (a) and (b) of section 53[3] is one of understanding, that is to say: can the witness understand what is being asked and can the jury understand that witness's answers? . . . . [T]he words 'put to him as a witness' mean the equivalent of being 'asked of him in court'. So, it would be the case that an infant who can only communicate in baby language with its mother would not ordinarily be competent. But a young child . . . who can speak and understand basic English with strangers would be competent.[52]

Moreover, '[q]uestions of credibility and reliability are not relevant to competence. Those matters go to the weight of the evidence and might be considered, if appropriate, at the end of the prosecution case, by way of a submission of no case to answer'.[53] Simply put, 'a child should not be found incompetent on the basis of age alone'.[54] Section 53 essentially reduces the competency standard for all witnesses, including children, to the threshold test of relevance: a child who is not even *intelligible* is literally incapable of communicating relevant information to the fact-finder. Memory loss should not be equated with incompetence if the amnesiac witness is capable of answering questions pertinent to the proceedings.[55] If, however, a particular child were shown to be a pathological liar, or to be radically incapable of distinguishing fact from fantasy, his superficially intelligible testimony would presumably be rejected as incompetent. Besides, the accused must have a fair trial, and this implies amongst other things that the witness's evidence can be fairly and properly tested. Child witnesses have occasionally been declared incompetent under section 53 where background concerns arising from their youth have been compounded by excessive delay in the proceedings[56] or mental disability[57] (and the trial judge did not believe that these deficiencies could be

---

[51] Youth Justice and Criminal Evidence (YJCE) Act 1999, s.55(2), re-enacting Criminal Justice Act (CJA) 1991, s.52(1).

[52] *R v MacPherson* [2006] 1 Cr App R 30, [2005] EWCA Crim 3605, [26]–[27], [29], quoted with approval in *R v M* [2008] EWCA Crim 2751, [14].   [53] *R v MacPherson* [2006] 1 Cr App R 30, [29].

[54] ibid. [31].   [55] *DPP v R* [2007] EWHC 1842 (Admin).

[56] *R v Malicki* [2009] EWCA Crim 365.

[57] *R v M* [2008] EWCA Crim 2751 (complainant was nine-year-old boy, with reading age of five; 'a statement of special educational needs . . . described [him] as presenting with a severe receptive language delay and a severe delay to his attention development. He had a very limited understanding of oral language and interpreting simple instructions. He had difficulties with classroom relationship skills and communication. According to the statement, he was unable to sustain concentration for longer than two to three minutes on any classroom task').

satisfactorily accommodated by the 'special measures' now available to child witnesses, which we discuss in Chapter 10).[58]

Sections 53–55 of the Youth Justice and Criminal Evidence Act 1999 have also super-seded the common law rules governing the reception of testimony from adults with a mental illness or disability. Any witness over thirteen years-of-age may testify on oath if 'he has a sufficient appreciation of the solemnity of the occasion and of the particular responsibility to tell the truth which is involved in taking an oath'. This already flexible and (historically speaking) comparatively generous[59] standard of competence for sworn testimony is underwritten by a rebuttable presumption that all adult witnesses satisfy the test.[60] Furthermore, even if a party's witness is challenged, and the party fails to prove on the balance of probabilities[61] that his witness qualifies to testify on oath, the witness may still provide unsworn evidence provided only that the threshold test of competence laid down by section 53(3) is satisfied. This is a principled approach to the testimony of adults with mental problems affecting their testimonial capacity. If the testimony of a six-year-old child is to be received on the ground that the child would be an intelligible witness, for example, essentially the same criterion should apply to an adult with the mental age and emotional maturity of a six-year-old. So long as the jury is fully appraised of any factors possibly affecting a witness's reliability, there is no principled basis for treating adults with learning difficulties or suffering from cognitive mental disorder any less favourably than children with comparable intellectual abilities.[62]

Today, the law's only surviving *categorical* judgments of incompetence are actually technical incidents of adversary criminal procedure, divorced from considerations of truthfulness and reliability. Strictly speaking, the accused is incompetent to testify for the prosecution,[63] and this makes sense in terms of the structural framework of adversarial proceedings (quite apart from the pragmatic constraint that an accused pleading 'not guilty' would seldom be a suitable witness for the prosecution in any event).[64] It is incon-sistent with the basic premiss of adversarial trial that one of the parties should appear as

---

[58] But note that in *R* v *M* [2008] EWCA Crim 2751, [14], the Court of Appeal observed that, 'on the basis of the material we have seen the members of this court think it very likely that if they have been dealing with the matter at first instance they would have allowed [the complainant] to give evidence so as to see how things worked out in the course of cross-examination before making a final ruling on the issue of compe-tence'. It could not be said, however, that the trial judge had acted unreasonably in coming to the opposite conclusion.

[59] Older common law authorities required the witness to demonstrate basic theological beliefs about God, the afterlife, etc: *R* v *Hill* (1851) 2 Den CC 254. Modern cases required only that the witness appreci-ated the solemnity of a criminal trial and the special responsibility to tell the truth in court, over and above the everyday expectation of veracity: *R* v *Bellamy* (1985) 82 Cr App R 222, CA; *R* v *Dunning* [1965] Crim LR 372, CA.   [60] YJCE Act 1999, subs.55(3).

[61] YJCE Act 1999, subs.55(4).

[62] See, e.g., *R* v *Sed* [2004] 1 WLR 3218, [2004] EWCA Crim 1294 (complainant was an eighty-one-year-old woman suffering from Alzheimer's disease; upholding the trial judge's finding of competency, the Court of Appeal opined that 'depending on the length and the nature of the questioning and the complexity of the matter the subject of it, it may not always require 100%, or near 100%, mutual understanding between questioner and questioned as a precondition of competence').

[63] YJCE Act 1999, s.53(4), preserving the old rule under s.1 of the Criminal Evidence Act 1898. See *R* v *Rhodes* [1899] 1 QB 77, CCR.

[64] Intriguingly, litigants *are* able to compel their opponents to testify in civil proceedings: *Price* v *Manning* (1889) LR 42 Ch D 372, CA. This may reflect a different balancing of interests between civil and criminal litigation, or possibly a slightly different conception of adversarialism.

a witness for his adversary, even voluntarily:[65] if there is no dispute between the parties, what would be the point of having a trial? However, it can be misleading to say, without embellishment, that the accused is an incompetent witness for the prosecution, because the accused's testimony *can* in fact contribute to the prosecution's case against him. An accused who has chosen to testify is duty-bound to answer truthfully all relevant questions put to him by the prosecution, even if his answers would incriminate either the accused himself or a co-accused. In this sense the accused's own testimony may be competent evidence against himself or his co-accused.[66] Once the privilege against self-incrimination has been waived by going into the witness-box, the accused is no longer legally at liberty to withhold information helpful to the prosecution (though many accused persons probably tell lies in their own defence, and sanctions for perjury are seldom imposed).

A second technical restriction is that the accused is incompetent as a prosecution witness against a co-accused.[67] The same adversarial logic applies. However, prosecutors can circumvent this restriction in practice, either by terminating the proceedings against the accused – for example through the Attorney-General's power to enter a *nolle prosequi* – or by first completing the accused's trial before prosecuting his co-accused. In either event the accused ceases to be a co-accused and the legal restriction on the competency of an accused no longer pertains. The prosecutor is thus freed up to broker 'deals' to drop charges against an accomplice in return for the accomplice's testimony against his erstwhile criminal associates.[68] This may be a necessary expedient in the prosecution of certain offences, for example where there were no other witnesses, or where, as in gangland or organized crime, other potential witnesses are too fearful to testify. But the scope for abuse is patent, so that brokerage with accomplices must be carefully monitored to guard against coercion and corruption.[69] The criminal process needs to be equipped with a long, sturdy spoon if it is going to risk supping with the devil.

7.3 COMPELLABILITY – THE PRINCIPLE OF COMPULSORY PROCESS

The primary purpose and effect of replacing the common law's generic categories of incompetence with a general presumption of competency, backed-up by personalized assessments of individual witnesses' capacities, has been to ensure that the flow of relevant information to the fact-finder is not blocked by artificial legal obstacles. However, the law goes considerably further in securing vital informational resources. Generally speaking,

---

[65] It follows from the privilege against self-incrimination that the accused cannot be a compellable witness for the prosecution: see §7.3, below, and Chapter 13.

[66] *R v Rudd* (1948) 32 Cr App R 138, CCA; *R v Paul* [1920] 2 KB 183, CCA.

[67] YJCE Act 1999, subss.53(4) and (5) preserve this longstanding restriction. See *R v Payne* [1950] 1 All ER 102; and discussions by J. D. Heydon, 'Obtaining Evidence versus Protecting the Accused: Two Conflicts' [1971] *Crim LR* 13; and R. N. Gooderson, 'The Evidence of Co-prisoners' (1953) 11 *CLJ* 209.

[68] Also now see Serious Organised Crime and Police Act 2005, ss.71–75 ('offenders assisting investigations and prosecutions').

[69] One way in which the prosecution may sail close to the wind is to adduce the testimony of an accomplice against whom proceedings are still pending: see *R v Pipe* (1966) 51 Cr App R 17, CA; *R v Turner (Bryan James)* (1975) 61 Cr App R 67, CA; *R v Governor of Pentonville Prison, ex p. Schneider* (1981) 73 Cr App R 200, DC.

participation in criminal trials is no more optional for witnesses or even complainants than it is for the accused. Witnesses can be required to attend court and to testify, under penalty of a substantial fine or even imprisonment for contempt of court should they refuse.[70]

English lawyers speak of witnesses being 'compellable' at the instance of the parties or, more rarely, at the behest of the court. The general principle is that all persons competent to give evidence may also lawfully be summoned to testify, and must answer all relevant questions addressed to them in the witness-box. Lord Wilberforce called this a 'constitutional principle underlying our whole system of justice'.[71] In other legal systems this 'principle of compulsory process' is indeed afforded constitutional status. For example, the Sixth Amendment to the US Constitution includes the guarantee that:

In all criminal prosecutions, the accused shall enjoy the right ... to have compulsory process for obtaining witnesses in his favor ...

A similar principle is written into Article 6(3)(d) of the European Convention on Human Rights, specifying that:

Everyone charged with a criminal offence has the following minimum rights: ...
    (d) to examine or have examined witnesses against him and to obtain the attendance and examination of witnesses on his behalf under the same conditions as witnesses against him ...

With the advent of the Human Rights Act 1998, it is not extravagant to describe the principle of compulsory process as a 'constitutional' component of English criminal procedure law in the fullest sense available to a common law constitution.

What is so significant about compulsory process in criminal adjudication? Witnesses are the principal source of information in criminal trials. Given the importance of arriving at the truth in criminal proceedings in order to secure justice, the law rightly imposes a civic duty on every person with relevant information in their possession to testify or to hand over evidence. A criminal court will summon any person in possession of relevant information to divulge it.[72] This is because penal law affords priority to the need to secure information for the purposes of criminal adjudication over the convenience of citizens and their competing interests. A person cannot excuse himself from giving evidence by saying that he is otherwise engaged, or that he has promised not to disclose the sought-after information, or that its disclosure would embarrass him.[73] Reflecting this principle, the

---

[70] In relation to trials on indictment, see Criminal Procedure (Attendance of Witnesses) Act 1965, ss.2–3. Parallel provisions apply to summary proceedings: Magistrates' Courts Act 1980, s.97.

[71] *Hoskyn* v *MPC* [1979] AC 474, 484, HL.

[72] The Criminal Procedure (Attendance of Witnesses) Act 1965 confers on the courts the power to order the attendance of witnesses by means of witness summons. By s.4 the court may, if necessary, enforce its orders by ordering recalcitrant witnesses to be arrested. The witness may be detained even after testifying, if the court thinks that she might have to be recalled at some later point in the proceedings: *R (H)* v *Crown Court at Wood Green* [2007] 1 WLR 1670, [2006] EWHC 2683 (Admin).

[73] *The Countess of Shrewsbury's Trial*, 2 How St Tr 769, 778. This categorical prioritization of forensic over other interests drew Bentham's fire: 'Are men of first rank and consideration – are men high in office – men whose time is not less valuable to the public than to themselves – are such men to be forced to quit their business, their functions, and what is more than all, their pleasure, at the beck of every idle or malicious adversary, to dance attendance upon every petty cause? Yes, as far as it is necessary, they and everybody ... Were the Prince of Wales, the Archbishop of Canterbury, and the Lord High Chancellor, to be passing by

Criminal Procedure (Attendance of Witnesses) Act 1965 lays down that a person served with a witness summons cannot release himself from his duty to attend court unless he satisfies a judge that 'he cannot give any material evidence or... produce any document or thing likely to be material evidence'.[74]

Compulsory process is an effective, if occasionally controversial,[75] judicial tool in the service of justice. However, a witness's duty to provide information to the courts is not absolute or unlimited. Its most important general limitation is the common law principle that a person should not be compelled to be a witness against themselves, *nemo tenetur prodere seipsum*.[76] This is the celebrated (and sometimes vilified) 'privilege against self-incrimination'. The accused in criminal proceedings is never a compellable witness in his own trial, not even at the behest of a co-accused.[77] The privilege against self-incrimination enjoyed by suspects and accused persons merits extended treatment in a chapter of its own.[78] Our present concern is with the testimonial privileges granted to witnesses in general (including complainants), one of which is the (witness) privilege against self-incrimination. Other important privileges attach to the accused's spouse and to his confidential communications with his lawyer. Any privilege to withhold potentially relevant evidence from the fact-finder constitutes a limitation on the constitutional principle of compulsory process which may operate as an obstacle to truth-finding. As such, all testimonial privileges demand careful scrutiny and cogent justification.

Before examining individual privileges in detail, a point of terminology requires clarification. In some contexts witnesses are described as being non-compellable, whereas on other occasions a witness is said to possesses a privilege to refuse to answer certain types of question. For the most part, this conceptual distinction lacks any real substance – as might readily be inferred from lawyers' terminological laxity in referring to the non-compellability of spouses as spousal 'privilege'.[79] The upshot, in either case, is that the fact-finder is deprived of potentially pertinent information. In this fundamental respect, non-compellability and testimonial privilege can be regarded as functional equivalents. The only practical difference is that a non-compellable witness cannot be compelled to go

---

in the same coach, while a chimney-sweeper and a barrow-woman were in dispute about a halfpennyworth of apples, and the chimney-sweeper or the barrow-woman were to think proper to call upon them for their evidence, could they refuse it? No, most certainly': *Works of Jeremy Bentham*, Bowring edn. (1843), vol. 4, 320ff. But a more positive spin can be placed on the peremptory nature of compulsory process: when questions of guilt and innocence, liberty and incarceration, are to be determined, no person – of any rank, first or last – should shirk their duty as a witness in a criminal trial.

[74] Section 2(2). Section 3 continues: '[a]ny person who without just excuse disobeys a witness order or summons requiring him to attend before any court shall be guilty of contempt of that court and may be punished summarily by that court... .'

[75] Judges have occasionally been rather heavy-handed and have even committed complainants to gaol who, whilst technically 'mute of malice,' were apparently too upset or frightened to continue with their evidence. In *R v Thompson* (1977) 64 Cr App R 96, CA, for example, Mr Justice Melford-Stevenson told a complainant in an incest case who was called as a prosecution witness but then refused to testify against her father: 'You won't like it in Holloway [Prison] I assure you. You answer these questions and behave yourself, otherwise you will be in serious trouble. Do you understand that?'

[76] See *R v Sang* [1980] AC 402, 436, HL.

[77] Criminal Evidence Act 1898, s.1(1); Police and Criminal Evidence Act 1984, s. 80(4).

[78] Chapter 13.

[79] e.g. *Rumping v DPP* [1964] AC 814, HL, 833 (Lord Reid) and 862 (Lord Hodson). And see Civil Evidence Act 1968, s.14 ('privilege against self-incrimination of self or spouse').

into the witness-box *at all* – the witness is immune from compulsory process – whereas a compellable witness with a testimonial privilege must go into the witness-box and assert his privilege.[80] One might still insist that this is a theoretical distinction without a difference, because in either case the information sought will not be divulged unless the witness chooses to co-operate. However, it is conceivable that a litigant might want to question a witness in relation to privileged information for tactical reasons. Even if the witness steadfastly refuses to answer, the fact-finder might find this behaviour suspicious and be inclined to draw negative inferences from the witness's assertion of privilege. This tactical ploy cannot be sprung on non-compellable witnesses. In all other respects, whether a witness's immunity from compulsory process is characterized as non-compellability or as privilege is a matter of terminological convention and convenience.

7.4 TESTIMONIAL PRIVILEGES

The common law has not traditionally been as receptive or deferential to testimonial privileges as many continental European jurisdictions, where extensive protection for familial and professional confidences is the norm.[81] English criminal procedure is more sparing in making exceptions to the principle of compulsory process, although doctrines of privilege or non-compellability may be decisive where they apply in individual cases.

There are some relatively esoteric categories of non-compellable witness. The reigning monarch,[82] foreign diplomats and their families and staff,[83] and – it was quite recently held – judges, in relation to their judicial functions,[84] are not compellable at the instance of the parties or the court. More significantly for routine criminal proceedings, the accused's wife or husband was not a compellable witness for the prosecution at common law. Adopting the alternative locution, a witness testifying in a civil or criminal trial is conventionally described as enjoying a 'privilege' to refuse to answer questions that might implicate him or her in criminality. We might just as well say, however, that both spouse and witness are able to choose whether or not to testify on certain matters: a wife is free not to incriminate her husband, for example, and a witness is free to refrain from incriminating himself. Likewise, the privilege attaching to confidential communications between lawyer and client entails that the client cannot be compelled to divulge confidential legal advice.

---

[80] Thus, in a civil (family) law case, *Re X (Children) (Disclosure for Purposes of Criminal Proceedings)* [2008] 3 All ER 958, [2008] EWHC 242 (Fam), [9], Munby J observed: 'even if [the defendant] had the right to refuse to answer a question on the grounds of some privilege that was no answer to his obligation to enter the witness box and be sworn (or affirmed); any claim to privilege could and should be taken after he was sworn and by way of objection to some specific question'.

[81] See, for example, Mirjan Damaška, 'The Uncertain Fate of Evidentiary Transplants: Anglo-American and Continental Experiments' (1997) 45 *American Journal of Comparative Law* 839, 842, 848, observing that '[i]n many countries of continental Europe ... testimonial privileges are much more encompassing than any known in the common law orbit.... [W]itnesses can in many continental countries refuse to answer questions potentially capable of incriminating their close relatives, dishonouring them, or exposing the witness to financial loss.'   [82] *A-G v Radloff* (1854) 10 Exch 84, 94.

[83] The Diplomatic Privileges Act 1964 relieves foreign ambassadors from compulsory process.

[84] *Warren v Warren* [1997] QB 488, CA. Though it was added that judges could normally be relied on to testify voluntarily in appropriate cases. Lay magistrates, apparently, are still compellable.

This section reviews three of the testimonial privileges that most commonly arise in criminal proceedings and critically evaluates their scope and rationales. The three privileges we will discuss have already been mentioned: (a) the witness privilege against self-incrimination; (b) spousal privilege; and (c) legal professional privilege. Consideration of a fourth topic, formerly known as 'Crown Privilege' but today more appropriately labelled 'public interest immunity', is held over to §7.5.

(a) THE WITNESS PRIVILEGE AGAINST SELF-INCRIMINATION

The privilege against self-incrimination confers on citizens the freedom to refuse to divulge information that might incriminate them in a criminal offence. A person called as witness in a criminal or civil trial may refuse 'to answer any question if the answer thereto would, in the opinion of the judge, have a tendency to expose the [witness] to any criminal charge, penalty or forfeiture which the judge regards as reasonably likely to be preferred or sued for'.[85] Protection is limited to potential liability in English law, including EU law,[86] though the judge may in his discretion excuse a witness from answering questions that might expose the witness to criminal liability in a foreign jurisdiction.[87]

This privilege entitles a witness to withhold, not only answers that disclose directly incriminating facts, but also answers that disclose facts which might later be used to prove criminal conduct[88] or which the prosecuting authorities might take into account in deciding whether to initiate proceedings against him.[89] A witness must reassert his privilege every time he is asked a question that might incriminate him[90] (unlike the accused, who can invoke a blanket privilege by remaining silent when interrogated by the police and by staying out of the witness-box at trial). This is a procedural necessity. Neither the witness nor the court – and sometimes not even the party examining him – knows in advance whether particular questions will tend to incriminate the witness. Consequently, before an issue of self-incrimination can arise, specific questions have to be put to the witness.

It is important to appreciate that the privilege belongs to the *witness* and in no way confers any rights on the parties. The witness must actively claim his privilege; though in practice he will often be advised of any impending risk of self-incrimination by the judge.[91] When the privilege has been claimed, the trial judge must determine whether a proposed question does in fact create a material risk of self-incrimination. The court is therefore the final arbiter of the scope of the privilege.[92] The fact that a witness was wrongly obliged to incriminate himself is no ground for quashing the accused's conviction, since this is a matter wholly collateral to the question whether the accused was properly convicted on the evidence.[93] Conversely, wrongfully compelled self-incriminating evidence may *not* be

---

[85] *Blunt* v *Park Lane Hotel Ltd* [1942] 2 KB 253, 257, CA (Goddard LJ). On the relatively esoteric topics of (non-criminal) penalties and forfeiture, see *Cross and Tapper on Evidence*, (11th edn. 2007), 455–9.

[86] *Rio Tinto Zinc Corp* v *Westinghouse Electrical Corp* [1978] AC 547, HL.

[87] *A-G for Gibraltar* v *May* [1999] 1 WLR 998.   [88] *R* v *Slany* (1832) 5 C & P 213.

[89] *A T & T Istel Ltd* v *Tully* [1993] AC 45.   [90] *Allhusen* v *Labouchere* (1878) 3 QBD 654, 660.

[91] *R* v *Coote* (1873) LR 4 PC 599; *Thomas* v *Newton* (1827) 2 C & P 606.

[92] *R* v *Boyes* (1861) 1 B & S 311; *Spokes* v *Grosvenor Hotel Co* [1897] 2 QB 124; *Triplex Safety Glass Co* v *Lancegay Safety Glass* [1939] 2 All ER 613; *Rio Tinto Zinc Corp* v *Westinghouse Electric Corp* [1978] AC 547, HL.

[93] *R* v *Kinglake* (1870) 11 Cox CC 499. It is a theoretical possibility that a breach of the witness privilege against self-incrimination might have such an adverse impact on the integrity of the proceedings that the

used in subsequent proceedings brought against the witness.[94] These two complementary rules demonstrate the essential structure of the privilege, which is designed for the exclusive benefit of the witness. The privilege assists a litigant only contingently and indirectly, by suppressing information that would be useful to his adversary.

In favour of the witness privilege it is said that if people were exposed to answering self-incriminating questions in court they might be reluctant to come forward to testify as witnesses. But it must be doubtful whether anybody with something to hide would anyway be keen to volunteer evidence to the court, irrespective of the testimonial privilege. In the very act of asserting his privilege against self-incrimination the witness is bound to draw attention to himself and alert investigators, whether police or journalists, to his secrets. It seems unlikely that the law would ever have extended the testimonial privilege to a mere witness if it had not already afforded a privilege against self-incrimination to suspects and the accused.

The courts have restricted the scope of the privilege by holding that self-incriminating answers furnished in ignorance, and without the benefit of judicial guidance on the existence and ambit of the privilege, are nonetheless admissible in subsequent proceedings against the witness, as well as being properly received in the current trial.[95] Moreover, Parliament has frequently enacted legislative provisions derogating from the witness privilege, so that particular types of proceedings will not be frustrated by a potential witness's non-co-operation. Some of these measures preserved much of the substance of the privilege by preventing self-incriminating answers from being used against the witness in subsequent proceedings.[96] This may be described as 'use immunity'. In other contexts, however, Parliament moved to abrogate the privilege entirely. In matters as diverse as official secrets, taxation, family law, gambling, and the investigation of serious fraud and financial irregularities, for example, witnesses were not only required to provide self-incriminating information, but such information could for a time be deployed in later proceedings to their detriment.[97]

The use of compelled information in subsequent criminal prosecutions of the witness himself is now subject to scrutiny under the Human Rights Act 1998[98] and the general restrictions imposed by the Youth Justice and Criminal Evidence Act 1999.[99] But this does not protect an ordinary witness from being forced to divulge self-incriminating information in *somebody else's* criminal trial, or from doing so voluntarily in ignorance of his privilege. English law continues to whittle down the scope of the witness privilege against self-incrimination, for the most part unmolested by Strasbourg.

---

accused's conviction could no longer be regarded as (morally) safe. But it is difficult to think of – even hypothetical – illustrations.

[94] *R v Garbett* (1847) 1 Den 236.

[95] *Cross and Tapper on Evidence* (11th edn. 2007), 459, citing *R v Coote* (1873) LR 4 PC 599. Contrast the position of the accused whose spouse testifies against him or her in ignorance of the spousal privilege. In these circumstances the accused's conviction may be quashed: *R v Pitt* [1983] QB 25, CA; *R v Norton and Driver (No 1)* [1987] Crim LR 687, CA.

[96] Theft Act 1968, s 31; Supreme Court Act 1981, s 72. See *Zuckerman on Civil Procedure*, §17.13ff.

[97] *Cross and Tapper on Evidence* (9th edn. 1999), 432–5; J. D. Heydon, 'Statutory Restrictions on the Privilege Against Self-incrimination' (1971) 87 *LQR* 214.   [98] §13.3.

[99] YJCE Act 1999, s.59 and sch.3 operate to restrict the uses of information compelled under specified enactments.

(b) SPOUSAL PRIVILEGE

The non-compellability of spouses, Wigmore observed, has a long history wrapped 'in tantalizing obscurity'.[100] In fact, it was not until 1898 that a husband or wife became *competent* (let alone compellable) to testify against their spouse in a criminal trial.[101] What we will call the 'spousal privilege' is now governed by section 80 of the Police and Criminal Evidence Act 1984 (as amended). Broadly speaking, the accused's spouse is always competent and may elect to testify either for the accused or for the prosecution. However, subject to a number of exceptions, the spouse is not in general a compellable witness either for the prosecution or for a person jointly charged with the accused. Given that competence normally implies compellability in English law, the justification for this blanket exemption from an important civic duty is far from self-evident.

Of the four principal reasons advanced over the years to justify spousal privilege,[102] only one retains contemporary currency. The argument now underpinning section 80 of PACE 1984, and previously propounded by the House of Lords in *Hoskyn*, is that compelled testimony might engender marital discord. In the words of Lord Salmon:

At common law, the wife of a defendant charged with a crime however serious was not, as a general rule, a competent witness for the Crown. If a man were charged with murder, for example, much as it would be in the public interest that justice should be done, his wife, whatever vital evidence she might have been able to give was not at common law a competent, let alone a compellable witness at his trial. This rule seems to me to underline the supreme importance attached by the common law to the special status of marriage and to the unity supposed to exist between husband and wife. It also no doubt recognized the natural repugnance of the public at the prospect of a wife giving evidence against her husband in such circumstances.[103]

In *Hoskyn*, the leading pre-PACE case at common law, the issue was whether a wife could be compelled to testify against her husband where she was the complainant and the husband was charged with assaulting her. Their Lordships ruled that a wife could not be compelled

---

[100] *Wigmore on Evidence*, (3rd edn. 1940), vol. 8, §2227. Wigmore speculated that the origin of a wife's incompetence to testify against her husband might have originated in her semi-servitudinal status.

[101] Criminal Evidence Act 1898, s.1, though the consent of the spouse was required in relation to certain offences: s.4. This general provision was pre-dated by a number of nineteenth century enactments declaring a married person competent, and in some cases also compellable, to testify against their spouse in relation to specified offences.

[102] Other possible rationalizations are that spouses should not be forced to choose between betrayal, perjury, and contempt; and that it is unconscionable for the state to co-opt the accused's own spouse into the state machinery of his prosecution. These arguments are inherently weak counterweights to the moral duty of testifying truthfully in criminal proceedings, and also fail to explain why the privilege should not be extended to other close family members, especially parents and children. For general discussion, see the Criminal Law Revision Committee's Eleventh Report, *Evidence: General*, Cm 4991, paras.143–157. The Committee's analysis was echoed by the House of Lords in *R v Hoskyn* [1979] AC 474, HL, and prefigured s.80.

[103] *R v Hoskyn* [1979] AC 474, 495, HL. And see Lord Wilberforce, ibid. 484–5, noting Coke's contention that spousal compellability 'might be a cause of implacable discord and dissension between the husband and the wife, and a means of great inconvenience', and quoting Gilbert's *Law of Evidence* (1760) to the effect that: 'it would be very hard that a wife should be allowed as evidence against her own husband, when she cannot attest for him; such a law would occasion implacable divisions and quarrels, and destroy the very legal policy of marriage that has so contrived it, that their interest should be but one; which it could never be if wives were admitted to destroy the interest of their husbands, and the peace of families could not easily be maintained, if the law admitted any attestation against the husband'.

to testify against her husband in such circumstances – a seemingly perverse application of the rationale supposedly underpinning the privilege, since marital harmony is presumably already seriously strained in cases of domestic violence. In significant measure, *Hoskyn* was decided on a rather narrow, legalistic basis in deference to some notably superannuated common law authorities.

Section 80 subsequently legislated a general privilege for husbands and wives to refuse to testify for the prosecution or for their accused spouse's co-accused, but also created several exceptions, overruling *Hoskyn* on its facts. The general assumption written into PACE is that if relations between the spouses are poor, a spouse will not require legal compulsion to testify in any event. If, on the other hand, husband and wife remain on good terms, a spouse might legitimately refuse to testify for the prosecution in order to preserve a happy home. Consistent with this logic, sub-section 80(5) of PACE provides that once the marriage is over and there is no longer any marital harmony to preserve, the ex-spouse 'shall be compellable to give evidence as if that person and the accused had never been married'.

Whilst marital harmony is not a trivial consideration, whether it should be allowed to take priority over doing justice in contemporary society is another matter entirely. Lord Reid once confessed himself mystified 'why it was decided to give this privilege to the spouse who is a witness: it means that if that spouse wishes to protect the other he or she will disclose what helps the other spouse but use this privilege to conceal communications if they would be injurious, but on the other hand a spouse who has become unfriendly to the other spouse will use this privilege to disclose communications if they are injurious to the other spouse but conceal them if they are helpful'.[104] Part of the answer may be found in historical social context. When marriage was indissoluble, the souring of relations between spouses would have condemned them to living together in enmity for the rest of their lives or, alternatively, to separation without the prospect of establishing another family. However, there has since been a revolution in attitudes towards marriage, with a diversity of socially acceptable long-term partnerships and easy access to divorce and remarriage for those who want it. In these dramatically changed circumstances it is difficult to believe that the spousal privilege has much bearing on marital harmony or, still less, on the general stability of marriage in modern society.

There are further important considerations to be factored into a cost-benefit analysis of the spousal privilege. First and foremost, spouses who are competent but non-compellable witnesses for the prosecution are presented with a potentially invidious choice between testifying against their husband or wife, or shirking their civic duty in favour of domestic peace. Those who regard it as repugnant to call a wife to testify against her husband (or a husband against his wife) should reflect that the present law may tempt an accused to exert pressure on his or her spouse to refrain from testifying, to say nothing of the threat of reprisals. At least the old common law, for all its defects, spared spouses this dilemma by treating them as incompetent witnesses for the prosecution. Now, if a wife or husband succumbs to pressure from their accused partner, they are in effect made an unwilling accomplice to the offence in assisting their spouse to escape punishment (assuming, of course, that he is guilty). A spouse who thus becomes an instrument of their partner's wrongdoing suffers moral degradation, which itself could undermine the couple's relationship, as well as being detrimental to the innocent spouse.

[104] *Rumping* v *DPP* [1964] AC 814, 833–4, HL.

Even where a spouse freely declines to testify, her choice might be considered morally dubious. One could perhaps rationalize a wife's failure to initiate a complaint on the basis that reporting her husband to the police would be an act of betrayal inconsistent with the maintenance of a marital relationship built on trust. But withholding incriminating evidence from the court, once the accused has already been charged, is morally delinquent, the more so if the crime is especially grave. Even on the assumption that the spousal privilege does buttress marital harmony, why is that a good enough reason to reduce public protection from criminal victimization and to allow the guilty to escape their just deserts?

Section 80 of PACE 1984 reflects some of these considerations by carving out important exceptions to the spousal privilege. In the first place, a husband or wife is virtually always[105] a compellable witness for their accused spouse (but not, generally, for the spouse's co-accused, which could conceivably create difficulties).[106] In addition, a spouse is compellable by the prosecution or a co-accused in relation to a 'specified offence', as defined by section 80(3) of PACE 1984:

PACE 1984, s.80(3)
In relation to the spouse or civil partner[107] of a person charged in any proceedings, an offence is a specified offence... if –
  (a) it involves an assault on, or injury or a threat of injury to, the spouse or civil partner of the accused or a person who was at the material time under the age of 16; or
  (b) it is a sexual offence alleged to have been committed in respect of a person who was at the material time under that age; or
  (c) it consists of attempting or conspiring to commit, or of aiding, abetting, counselling, procuring or inciting the commission of, an offence falling within paragraph (a) or (b) above.

Each of these limitations on the spousal privilege has a clear rationale. Given that offences between spouses are likely to be committed in private, a wife (or husband) would be at the mercy of their partner if spouses were not compellable to testify against a violent companion. The battering relationship would simply be extended into keeping the battered partner too frightened to testify. This was recognized for a time at common law:[108] indeed, a spouse's competence in such circumstances was also thought to imply compellability, until the House of Lords said otherwise in *Hoskyn*.[109]

In signalling that the protection of children should henceforth take priority over marital harmony, PACE broke new ground. As well as constituting a significant development in its own right, the logic of newly-created exceptions to spousal privilege could easily be extended. Children are not the only vulnerable group at risk of criminal victimization. Why must older people, or racial minorities, or the socially and economically deprived, etc., suffer in order to protect their tormentors' relationships with their spouses? This is an area where legal line-drawing seems arbitrary in the strong, pejorative sense, rather

---

[105] Except where the spouse herself is charged in the proceedings. Accused persons are never compellable in their own trials: PACE 1984, s.80(4).   [106] PACE 1984, s.80(2).

[107] The original wording, 'wife or husband', was replaced with 'spouse or civil partner' by the Civil Partnership Act 2004.

[108] *R v Lapworth* [1931] 1 KB 117; CCA; *R v Algar* [1954] 1 QB 279, CCA. This was the principle applied by the Court of Appeal in *Hoskyn*.   [109] Restoring the authority of *Leach v R* [1912] AC 305, HL.

than merely an inevitable feature of living by rules.[110] Once the legislature has conceded that spousal privilege should be balanced against greater public protection from crime, the door is seemingly open to the creation of further exceptions to facilitate the prosecution of serious offences. It would make sense to start at the highest level of gravity, with murder, and possibly even to dismantle the privilege altogether. However, in the ensuing decades Parliament has shown little inclination towards adopting this reformist agenda. Indeed, the most recent legislative intervention actually *extended* the scope of the privilege, to cover those in registered civil partnership pursuant to the Civil Partnership Act 2004. This doubtless had more to do with Parliament's establishing the equality of civil partners and married couples than with any great affinity for spousal privilege, but the contrast with the Court of Appeal's refusal to extend spousal privilege to unmarried cohabitees is nonetheless striking.[111] Another intimation of the Court of Appeal's limited enthusiasm for spousal privilege is that a spouse cannot block the admissibility of statements made to the police which fall into an exception to the hearsay rule, even if the spouse was unaware of her privilege when she spoke and could have refused to co-operate. There is no requirement at common law to provide spouses with any kind of 'privilege warning' akin to cautioning suspects ('reading suspects their rights') prior to being interviewed by the police.[112]

Section 80(2A)(a) of PACE 1984 states that a spouse is compellable to testify on behalf of a person jointly charged with the accused only to the same, limited, extent that a spouse is compellable for the prosecution. It is difficult to comprehend why, for example, a wife should be compellable for her husband's co-accused when both men are jointly charged with child abuse but not in other cases. If the co-accused requires the wife's assistance to prove his innocence, the law should compel her testimony regardless of the impact on the wife's marital harmony; or at least, in the alternative, should sanction separate trials.[113]

The scope for prosecution comment on a spouse's failure to testify is another contentious matter. Section 80A of PACE 1984 now provides that:

The failure of the spouse or civil partner of a person charged in any proceedings to give evidence in the proceedings shall not be made the subject of any comment by the prosecution.[114]

---

[110] cf. *Cross and Tapper on Evidence* (11th edn. 1999), 269: 'the accused's wife is compellable against him if he kissed a 15-year-old... but not if he raped and murdered a 16-year-old'. The CLRC proposed limiting the exception to children living with the accused, on the basis that intra-familial abuse would not ordinarily be witnessed by others. A spouse's testimony should therefore be compellable, in the likely absence of other evidence, in order to protect young members of the family as well as the spouse him- or herself. In justifying this limitation the Committee fell back on the traditional rationalization that 'the law has never, except perhaps in treason, made the seriousness of an offence by itself a ground for compellability': *Eleventh Report*, Cm 4991, para.152.

[111] *R v Pearce* [2002] 1 Cr App R 39, [2001] EWCA Crim 2834 (spousal privilege does not extend to 'common law' wife of nineteen years' cohabitation).

[112] *R v L (R)* [2008] 2 Cr App R 18, [2008] EWCA Crim 973, [31] (Lord Phillips CJ): 'The need to caution a suspect arises from the fundamental principle that a person cannot be required to give evidence that may incriminate himself. The policy against compelling a wife to give evidence against her husband is not the same. To caution a wife before taking evidence from her could inhibit the investigation of crime. We do not think that the policy that prevents a wife from giving evidence against her husband requires such a limitation upon the powers of investigation of the police to be implied.'

[113] Generally, see Peter Creighton, 'Spouse Competence and Compellability' [1990] *Crim LR* 34, 37, remarking that '[i]t seems hard that the co-accused may suffer conviction for a serious offence just to preserve the marital bond between the accused and his wife'.

[114] As inserted by the YJCE Act 1999, re-enacting PACE 1984, s.80(8), with slight modifications.

Contrary to the CLRC's recommendations,[115] prosecution comment is forbidden not only on the fact that the spouse declined to testify for the prosecution, but also that the spouse refused to testify for a co-accused. Thus, the prosecution may not comment on the accused's failure to call his wife to testify even where such testimony would usually be expected in the circumstances of the case: where, for example, the accused sets up the alibi that he was with his wife at the material time. An argument for restricting prosecution comment is that it removes some of the temptation for the accused to pressure his spouse into testifying falsely in his favour.[116] But even if it is possible that the threat of comment might encourage accused persons to solicit perjury from their spouses, it is difficult to imagine that this incentive would appreciably increase the emotional pressure (not to mention threats or coercion) that spouses may already feel to substantiate dubious alibis and the like.

Preventing the prosecutor from commenting on a spouse's failure to testify is not a measure to promote marital harmony: a spouse who refuses to testify is usually doing exactly what her partner wants. Spousal silence does not in itself prove anything, since there are many reasons why a husband or wife might not want to get involved in criminal proceedings irrespective of the strength of the prosecution's case. Still, a blanket prohibition is arguably excessive, insofar as it plays down even contextually legitimate inferences from a spouse's reticence to tell what she knows. The trial judge, however, remains at liberty to pass comment, where particular observations seem appropriate on the facts.[117] This might well be a more even-handed way of drawing the jury's attention to gaps in the evidence left by a spouse's absence from the witness-box; assuming, of course, that the jury has not already spotted the anomaly for itself and needs no extra prompting to draw the common sense inference.[118]

In one respect, finally, the prohibition on prosecution comment *does* potentially contribute to marital harmony. A spouse in possession of incriminating information is given an opportunity of maximizing the accused's prospects of an unmerited acquittal, in which case the couple will remain at liberty to continue enjoying each other's company! But it is safe to assume that this Bonnie and Clyde rationalization played no part in the legislature's decision to enact section 80A.

In summary, the spousal privilege rests on unconvincing rationales and flawed reasoning. Its legal definition and practical scope are consequently bound to be somewhat haphazard. Parliament may yet have to reconsider the balance of policy, having passed up an opportunity to do so when enacting the Youth Justice and Criminal Evidence Act 1999.[119] In civil proceedings spouses are for the most part treated like any other witnesses, and may

---

[115] *Eleventh Report*, para. 154.

[116] Though if that were truly the rationale underpinning s.80A, one might have expected to find similar restrictions on *D2*'s right to comment adversely on the absence of *D1*'s wife from the witness-box. No such restriction exists: *D2* is free to make such comments whenever it suits his case.

[117] The judge should proceed with circumspection if he chooses to mention the accused's spouse's absence from the witness-box in his summing-up: *R v Naudeer* (1985) 80 Cr App R 9, CA; *R v Whitton* [1998] Crim LR 492, CA.

[118] In *R v Marsh* [2008] EWCA Crim 1816, the Court of Appeal upheld M's conviction where prosecuting counsel had commented unfavourably on M's wife's absence from the witness-box, but neither counsel nor trial judge had been aware of PACE 1984, s.80A. The Court of Appeal remarked, somewhat indulgently, that '[t]he existence of that provision was overlooked by everybody. It may be that it is not particularly present to the minds of many people in criminal trials.' However, whilst the safety of the conviction was not affected in the instant case, the Court of Appeal confirmed that *R v Naudeer* (1985) 80 Cr App R 9, CA, remained good law and that breaches of s.80A could in principle result in a conviction being quashed.

[119] See Diane Birch and Roger Leng, *Blackstone's Guide to the Youth Justice and Criminal Evidence Act 1999* (Blackstone, 2000), 145–6.

be called to testify against each other without any limitation. The resulting marital discord may be just as great as it would be in criminal proceedings, and with substantially less justification. PACE 1984 already concedes that the value of marital harmony must defer to the interests of securing convictions and doing justice in cases of child abuse and domestic violence. There will be mounting pressure to extend these categories whenever assertion of the privilege in high-profile cases attracting media attention provokes public outrage. Over time, these pressures may be expected to undermine the credibility of spousal privilege in criminal adjudication, precipitating its ultimate demise.

(c) LEGAL PROFESSIONAL PRIVILEGE[120]

Communications between lawyers and their clients have long been afforded privileged status at common law. Lord Brougham LC declared in *Greenough* v *Gaskell*:

The foundation of this rule is not difficult to discover. It is not (as has sometimes been said) on account of any particular importance which the law attributes to the business of legal professors, or any particular disposition to afford them protection, though certainly it may not be very easy to discover why a like privilege has been refused to others, and especially to medical advisers. But it is out of regard to the interests of justice, which cannot be upholden, and to the administration of justice, which cannot go on without the aid of men skilled in jurisprudence, in the practice of the courts, and in those matters affecting rights and obligations which form the subject of all judicial proceedings. If the privilege did not exist at all, every one would be thrown upon his own legal resources; deprived of all professional assistance, a man would not venture to consult any skilful person, or would only dare to tell his counsellor half his case.[121]

Legal professional privilege, in other words, is regarded as an essential incident of access to legal advice, which in turn is a pre-condition of enforceable legal rights and entitlements under the rule of law. The principal justification for protecting lawyer-client confidentiality with a special privilege is to encourage candour on the part of the client, which in turn assists lawyers in providing useful advice and effective legal representation.[122] Whilst this rationale has always been implicit in the common law authorities, it is only comparatively recently, in the era of the Human Rights Act 1998, that its full constitutional implications have been spelt out. Legal professional privilege is now recognized as a fundamental tenet of access to justice, fair trial, and the rule of law:

[A] man must be able to consult his lawyer in confidence, since otherwise he might hold back half the truth. The client must be sure that what he tells his lawyer in confidence will never be revealed without his consent. Legal professional privilege is thus much more than an ordinary rule of evidence, limited in its application to the facts of a particular case. It is a fundamental condition on which the administration of justice as a whole rests.[123]

---

[120] See *Zuckerman on Civil Procedure*, ch 15; Jonathan Auburn, *Legal Professional Privilege: Law & Theory* (Hart, 2000).

[121] *Greenough* v *Gaskell* (1833) 1 My and K 98, 103. Also see *Holmes* v *Baddeley* (1844) 1 Ph 476, 480–1 (Lord Lyndhurst LC); *Anderson* v *Bank of British Columbia* (1876) 2 Ch D 644, 649 (Sir George Jessel MR); *Re Saxton (decd), Johnson* v *Saxton* [1962] 1 WLR 968, CA; *Re L (a minor) (police investigation: privilege)* [1996] 2 All ER 78, HL.

[122] For extended discussion of the privilege's underlying rationales, see Auburn, *Legal Professional Privilege*, chs 4–5.

[123] *R* v *Derby Magistrates' Court, ex p. B* [1996] 1 AC 487, 507, HL (Lord Taylor CJ).

Warming to this theme, Lord Hoffmann hailed legal professional privilege as 'a fundamental human right long established in the common law'.[124] The intimate connection between fair trial and lawyer–client confidentiality is also well-established in Strasbourg jurisprudence,[125] further cementing the common law privilege under the Human Rights Act 1998.

Legal professional privilege (LPP) has two discrete limbs. The first limb is known as 'advice privilege', and the second-limb as 'litigation privilege'. These labels are apt and literal. 'Litigation privilege', Lord Scott recently observed, 'covers all documents brought into being for the purposes of litigation. Legal advice privilege covers communications between lawyers and their clients whereby legal advice is sought or given'.[126] Giving and receiving legal advice is interpreted expansively, stretching the scope of the privilege.[127] Both limbs of LPP cover confidential lawyer–client communications, but litigation privilege is somewhat broader in extending also to communications between the client's legal advisers and third parties, if made in confidence and for the purpose of pending or contemplated litigation. Material subject to legal professional privilege is generally immune from search and seizure under PACE.[128]

Legal professional privilege is for the benefit of the client, and indirectly for the public interest in promoting access to justice and the efficient resolution of legal disputes, not for the benefit of lawyers. It follows that the client is at liberty to waive his privilege, whereupon the lawyer has no standing to oppose subsequent disclosure or to refuse to answer questions regarding previously privileged matters if called as a witness in a court of law (unless, of course, the lawyer is able to claim a *different* privilege, such as the privilege against self-incrimination).[129] Nor can a lawyer withhold a document in circumstances in which the client would not have been entitled to do so.[130]

---

[124] *R (Morgan Grenfell & Co Ltd) v Special Commissioner of Income Tax* [2002] 3 All ER 1, [7].

[125] *S v Switzerland* (1992) 14 EHRR 670; *Campbell and Fell v UK* (1983) 5 EHRR 207.

[126] *Three Rivers District Council v Bank of England (No 6)* [2005] 1 AC 610, [2004] UKHL 48, [9]. Also see the classic definition given by Sir Rupert Cross in *Cross on Evidence* (5th edn. 1979), 282: 'In civil and criminal cases, confidential communications passing between a client and his legal adviser need not be given in evidence by the client and, without the client's consent, may not be given in evidence by the legal adviser in a judicial proceeding if made either (1) to enable the client to obtain, or the adviser to give, legal advice; or (2) with reference to litigation that is actually taking place or was in the contemplation of the client.' Cf. the precise, if more convoluted, statutory definition of 'items subject to legal privilege' given in PACE 1984 s.10(1).

[127] '[T]he process by which a client seeks and obtains his lawyer's assistance in the presentation of his case for the purposes of any formal inquiry—whether concerned with public law or private law issues, whether adversarial or inquisitorial in form, whether held in public or in private, whether or not directly affecting his rights or liabilities—attracts legal advice privilege. Such assistance to my mind clearly has the character of legal business': *Three Rivers District Council*, [120] (Lord Brown).

[128] Though there are exceptions: see PACE 1984, ss.8–10. For commentary, see David Feldman, *Civil Liberties and Human Rights in England and Wales* (OUP, 2nd edn. 2002), 631–9; R. T. H. Stone, 'PACE: Special Procedures and Legal Privilege' [1988] *Crim LR* 498.

[129] *Wilson v Rastall* (1792) 4 TR 753. One side-effect of the provisions on the accused's pre-trial silence introduced by the Criminal Justice and Public Order Act 1994, ss.34–38, was to open up the possibility that solicitors providing custodial legal advice to suspects will themselves subsequently become witnesses in the case. Where the circumstances surrounding an accused's 'significant silences' are later contested, it may be in the accused's best interests to waive legal professional privilege and instruct another solicitor, so that the original adviser can testify on his behalf as to what transpired in the police station: see Desmond Wright, 'The Solicitor in the Witness Box' [1998] *Crim LR* 44; Ed Cape, 'Sidelining Defence Lawyers: Police Station Advice after *Condron*' (1997) 1 *E & P* 386.

[130] *R v Peterborough Justices, ex p. Hicks* [1977] 1 WLR 1371, DC; *Re Murjani (a bankrupt)* [1996] 1 All ER 65, Ch.

Like the other two privileges we have already considered in this section, legal professional privilege represents a significant, though not quite absolute, constraint on fact-finding in criminal trials. Traditionally, there were two important common law 'exceptions' to legal professional privilege in criminal litigation. First, communications between client and lawyer prior to the commission of an offence are not privileged if the purpose of such communications was to facilitate crime.[131] This remains the law, albeit that the so-called 'fraud/crime exception' might more accurately be regarded as establishing the outer boundaries of privileged communications rather than derogating from the legitimate ambit of legal professional privilege. In whatever way it is conceptualized, legal professional privilege cannot be used as a means of concealing fraudulent transactions. However, a second well-established exception to the privilege, permitting an accused person to secure information to prove his innocence, was – rather unexpectedly – jettisoned by the House of Lords in the *Derby Magistrates* case.[132]

In *Derby Magistrates* the question was whether an accused charged with the murder of a teenage girl could obtain access to communications passing between his stepson and the stepson's lawyer, where the stepson had previously been tried and acquitted of the same murder. The accused had reason to believe that his stepson may have made a confession of murder to his defence solicitor, but the stepson refused to divulge the contents of these communications, which were clearly subject to litigation privilege. Quashing a witness summons demanding compulsory disclosure, the House of Lords held, controversially, that legal professional privilege was 'absolute' and should never be balanced against other interests. According to their Lordships, *ad hoc* balancing would undermine the confidence of all litigants in the sanctity of private legal advice, because nobody could ever be sure that confidential consultations with a lawyer would not later be divulged contrary to their wishes for the purposes of subsequent criminal proceedings. How litigants' notional confidence is supposed to square with other well-recognized limits on the efficacy of legal professional privilege – including the fact that the privilege, as a (procedural) rule of immunity rather than an (evidentiary) rule of inadmissibility, can be surrendered by accident[133] – was not explained.[134]

---

[131] *R v Cox and Railton* (1884) 14 QBD 153. PACE 1984, s.10, preserves the common law rule that documents drawn up or held for a criminal purpose are not protected by legal professional privilege: *Francis & Francis (a firm)* v *Central Criminal Court* [1988] 3 All ER 775, HL. Furthermore, when a privileged document falls into the hands of a third party, a court will not prevent the prosecution from using such a document to prove the accused's guilt: *Butler* v *Board of Trade* [1971] 1 Ch 680, Ch.

[132] *Derby Magistrates' Court, ex p. B* [1996] AC 487, overruling *R v Barton* [1973] 1 WLR 115, CA, and *R v Ataou* [1988] QB 798, CA.

[133] *Calcraft* v *Guest* [1898] 1 QB 759; *R v Tompkins* (1977) 67 Cr App R 181, CA. But if the erstwhile privilege-holder is on his toes, he might be able to persuade a court to grant an equitable injunction restraining the use of formerly privileged material in breach of confidence, depending on the circumstances in which the privilege was lost: *Ashburton* v *Pape* [1913] 2 Ch 469; *Webster* v *James Chapman & Co* [1989] 3 All ER 939, Ch. Compare *Istil Group Inc* v *Zahoor* [2003] 2 All ER 252, [2003] EWHC 165 (Ch), [112], where Lawrence Collins J. found that 'the combination of forgery and misleading evidence make this a case where the equitable jurisdiction to restrain breach of confidence gives way to the public interest in the proper administration of justice'. For the argument that legal professional privilege can provide a 'private and secure place', in fulfilment of its underlying rationale, only if it operates as a rule of inadmissibility and not merely as a rule of immunity, see *Zuckerman on Civil Procedure*, §§15.21ff.

[134] For convincing critique, see Colin Tapper, 'Prosecution and Privilege' (1996) 1 *E & P* 5.

The merits of the *Derby Magistrates* decision are complicated by the fact that the information sought by the accused might have implicated the privilege-holder in a crime of which the latter had already been acquitted. This raises collateral questions of finality in criminal litigation.[135] But the upshot, nonetheless, is that secure access to legal advice has been prioritized over securing proof of innocence. If (as this book argues and seeks to demonstrate) avoiding wrongful conviction of the innocent is a fundamental principle of English criminal procedure law, the decision in *Derby Magistrates* must be regarded as a significant – and somewhat surprising – derogation from traditional priorities. There has been ample opportunity since this case was decided for senior judges to reconsider the House of Lords' weighting of interests in *Derby Magistrates*, but the absolute character of legal professional privilege has been reasserted on every such occasion.[136]

7.5 PUBLIC INTEREST IMMUNITY

A fourth ground on which a party to legal proceedings may object to the disclosure of information is that disclosure would harm the public interest. It used to be said that information in this category was protected by 'Crown Privilege', but that was always a potentially misleading description, both because the scope of protection is not confined to matters of 'high' state policy or national security,[137] and because the protection of such information is not a matter of 'privilege' in any ordinary sense of the word.[138] The modern, more descriptive, concept is 'public interest immunity' (PII).

(a) THE DEVELOPMENT OF PII AT COMMON LAW

In *D v NSPCC*, where the anonymity of reports of suspected child abuse was at issue, it was said that the categories of PII material are never closed.[139] PII can be claimed by anybody, whether or not they are a party to the litigation, and at any stage in the proceedings. The court itself can raise the issue of PII protection of its own motion. Regardless of the way in which PII questions come to be litigated, the court is the final arbiter of what is required, disclosure or secrecy, in the public interest.[140]

---

[135] For further discussion of the value of finality in criminal litigation, see Paul Roberts, 'Double Jeopardy Law Reform: A Criminal Justice Commentary' (2002) 65 *MLR* 393, 405–12; Ian Dennis, 'Rethinking Double Jeopardy: Justice and Finality in Criminal Process' [2000] *Crim LR* 933; Paul Roberts, 'Acquitted Misconduct Evidence and Double Jeopardy Principles, from *Sambasivam* to *Z*' [2000] *Crim LR* 952; Peter Mirfield, 'Shedding A Tear for Issue Estoppel' [1980] *Crim LR* 336.

[136] See, e.g., *McE v Prison Service of Northern Ireland* [2009] 1 AC 908, HL (NI), [2009] UKHL 15; *Three Rivers District Council v Bank of England (No 6)* [2005] 1 AC 610, [2004] UKHL 48; *R (Morgan Grenfell & Co Ltd) v Special Commissioner of Income Tax* [2002] 3 All ER 1, [7].

[137] As it was, e.g., in *Duncan v Cammell Laird & Co* [1942] AC 624, HL.

[138] Cf. *Buttes Gas & Oil Co v Hammer (No 3)* [1981] QB 223, 262, CA, *per* Brightman LJ: 'it is not a matter of privilege and it is not confined to the Crown'.

[139] *D v NSPCC* [1978] AC 171, 230, HL (Lord Hailsham). And see *R v Chief Constable of the West Midlands Police, ex p. Wiley* [1995] 1 AC 274, HL.

[140] Though due deference will be given to ministerial opinions on matters of state policy such as national security: *Council of Civil Service Unions v Minister for the Civil Service* [1984] 3 All ER 935.

In deciding whether to accede to a request for immunity – whether from an organ of the state or from anyone else – the court has to balance two general sets of considerations. On the one hand, there is the public interest in preserving the secrecy of information which might prove damaging if revealed; on the other hand, there are the general interests of the proper administration of justice and the specific interests of the party seeking disclosure.[141] These are also both weighty matters of public interest. In other words, PII requires the court to balance different aspects of the public interest, rather than adjudicating a stand-off between public and (merely) private interests. Only if the balance tilts decisively in favour of secrecy will the court refrain from ordering disclosure, because as Lord Simon observed in *D v NSPCC*:

It is a serious step to exclude evidence relevant to an issue, for it is in the public interest that the search for truth should, in general, be unfettered. Accordingly, any hindrance to its seeker needs to be justified by a convincing demonstration that an even higher public interest requires that only part of the truth should be told.[142]

The test to be applied by the trial judge in determining the proper scope of public interest immunity is flexible and context-sensitive. The strength of a claim to withhold relevant information from the fact-finder depends both on the potential importance of the information to the litigation, and on the damage to the public interest which might result from its disclosure.[143] In striking this balance, criminal courts should recognize and accommodate the accused's overwhelming interest in establishing his innocence. Thus, in *Keane* Lord Taylor CJ said that disclosure must be ordered if 'the disputed material may prove the defendant's innocence or avoid a miscarriage of justice'.[144] Indeed, if a piece of evidence tends to prove the accused's innocence, the balance should be expected to tilt in favour of disclosure almost regardless of the collateral damage to which disclosure might lead.[145] The failure of a PII claim should not *per se* be equated with court-ordered disclosure, because the prosecution could always be abandoned if preserving the secrecy of the information is truly paramount.

Over the course of the twentieth century, Ministers of State have, generally speaking, declined to press their claims for 'Crown privilege'/PII in criminal cases.[146] In recent times, however, there have been flashpoints of controversy. The 'Arms to Iraq' affair investigated by Lord Justice Scott's public inquiry[147] revealed that directors of Matrix Churchill, a firm engaged in the supply of 'dual use' machine tools[148] to Iraq, almost went to gaol for contravening export restrictions on military equipment, until it emerged that material

---

[141] *Conway v Rimmer* [1968] AC 910, HL. See Adrian A. S. Zuckerman, 'Privilege and Public Interest', in C. F. H. Tapper (ed.), *Crime Proof and Punishment* (Butterworths, 1981), 248.

[142] *D v NSPCC* [1978] AC 171, 242, HL.

[143] See, e.g., *Air Canada v Secretary of State for Trade* [1983] 2 AC 394, 435, HL (Lord Fraser).

[144] *R v Keane* (1994) 99 Cr App R 1, 6, CA. Also see *R v Brown (Winston)* [1995] 1 Cr App R 191, CA; *R v Ward* (1993) 96 Cr App R 1, CA.

[145] *R v Richardson* (1863) 3 F & F 693; *R v Brown and Daley* (1988) 87 Cr App R 52, CA; *R v Hardy* [1988] Crim LR 687, CA; *R v Johnson* [1988] Crim LR 831, CA.

[146] 'Crime and Crown Privilege' [1959] *Crim LR* 10.

[147] Sir Richard Scott V-C, *Report of the Inquiry into the Export of Defence Equipment and Dual-Use Goods to Iraq and Related Prosecutions*, HC Paper 115 (Session 1995–96). And see John Andrews, 'Public Interest and Criminal Proceedings' (1988) 104 *LQR* 410.

[148] Ostensibly innocuous civil engineering with potential military applications.

contained in ministerial 'PII certificates' established their innocence. It later transpired that at least one of the accused had all along been working for British Intelligence, but this information had not been passed on to HM Customs and Excise,[149] the relevant prosecuting authority.[150] Following these disturbing revelations, the government promised that it would not in future assert controversial 'class claims' covering whole categories of documents, but would instead restrict any PII application to specified material requiring protection in the public interest. This effectively established a new constitutional convention, though it is not a rule of law in the strict sense and it applies only to central government. Other potential PII applicants, such as police chief constables and local authority social work departments, theoretically remained at liberty to apply for aggregated PII certificates claiming blanket protection for multiple documents in a particular class or category. However, more rigorous judicial scrutiny of PII claims has since largely superseded the discredited practice of making speculative applications to withhold entire categories of information on the basis of blunderbuss 'class claims'.[151]

The reformed procedure for making PII applications was assimilated into the statutory framework governing pre-trial disclosure established by the Criminal Procedure and Investigations Act 1996, but its content was devised by the judges at common law.[152] It is now governed by Part 22 of the Criminal Procedure Rules 2010. In the standard case, the trial judge conducts a pre-trial hearing *inter partes* at which all pertinent submissions can be made, before the judge adjudicates on the claim for PII protection. If disclosure is ordered, this is clearly the end of the matter: once the judge's order has been complied with, the cat is irretrievably out of the bag. If the claim is upheld, on the other hand, the court is obliged to keep the matter under review,[153] and may later elect to order disclosure, after all, if events at trial appear to demand that PII be set aside in the interests of justice.[154]

In certain circumstances, however, the information for which PII protection is claimed may be regarded as too sensitive to debate in an *inter partes* hearing, in which case the judge is obliged to make a ruling without hearing defence submissions in response to the prosecution's *ex parte* application. In cases of the utmost secrecy, where to announce that a PII application was being made might in itself effectively disclose sensitive information that ought to be concealed in the public interest, the accused's legal representatives are not even informed that an *ex parte* PII hearing has taken place. This of course raises the question of how the accused's interests in disclosure can properly be taken into account at a hearing at which the defence is not represented, the more so – in the extreme case – where

---

[149] The predecessor of HM Revenue and Customs.

[150] Alex McLoughlin, 'The Scott Report: Export Control and Customs Issues' (1996) 2 *International Trade Law and Regulation* 144.

[151] See *R v Horseferry Road Magistrates' Court, ex p. Bennett (No 2)* [1994] 1 All ER 289, 293, DC; *R (Mohamed) v Secretary of State for Foreign and Commonwealth Affairs* [2009] 1 WLR 2653, [2009] EWHC 152 (Admin).

[152] *R v Davis, Rowe and Johnson* [1993] 1 WLR 613, CA; *R v Keane* [1994] 1 WLR 746, CA; *R v Davis, Rowe and Johnson (No 2)* [2001] 1 Cr App R 115, CA; *R v Botmeh; R v Alami* [2002] 1 Cr App R 345, [2001] EWCA Crim 2226.

[153] Section 15(3) of the Criminal Procedure and Investigations Act 1996 provides that 'The court must keep under review the question whether at any given time it is still not in the public interest to disclose material affected by its order'.

[154] *R v Chief Constable of the West Midlands Police, ex p. Wiley* [1995] 1 AC 274, HL.

an *ex parte* hearing is held in secret. We will return to this question in the concluding section of the chapter, having first examined the types of information for which PII protection is commonly claimed in criminal proceedings and the procedural strategies for balancing the conflicting interests associated with such claims

(b) PII IN CRIMINAL PROCEEDINGS AND THE PROBLEM OF ANONYMOUS WITNESSES

In routine criminal cases, lacking any international relations dimension or high state policy warranting the assertion of 'Crown Privilege', there is nonetheless a long-established practice of invoking (what we now call) public interest immunity to protect the identities of police informants.[155] Until recently, however, there were few reported cases and the issue apparently generated little controversy, perhaps because anonymity for prosecution witnesses was rarely sought in criminal trials. But this is now changing, as a consequence both of enhanced expectations of full prosecution disclosure, and of increasing resort to 'proactive' policing methods, including extensive use of undercover agents ('plants') conducting covert surveillance and intelligence-gathering operations and co-opted civilian informants.[156] Witness intimidation has also become a matter of increasing concern. In modern times, PII protection has been successfully claimed to conceal the location of undercover observation posts,[157] and to protect the sources of information garnered during police investigations,[158] on a similar footing to the established practice of preserving informants' anonymity.

Where there is a genuine fear that informants or those who provide information or surveillance locations to the police may suffer reprisals if their identities become known to the accused or his associates, the preservation of their anonymity through public interest immunity is a logical measure to promote the administration of justice in the public interest. People are not going to come forward to help the police if their personal safety might be jeopardized by doing so. Equally, there is a strong public interest in retaining the operational usefulness of experienced undercover police investigators by concealing their true identities: once a 'plant' is exposed as a police officer he can no longer successfully infiltrate the sort of highly-evolved criminal organizations whose activities most often call for proactive policing techniques (drug traffickers, football hooligans, people smugglers, race-hate groups, and terrorists). Moreover, the officer's personal safety might easily be compromised.

Yet at the same time it must be recognized that witness anonymity may pose significant problems for the accused trying to establish his innocence. How is the defence advocate supposed to cross-examine a witness on his identification of the accused when the location of the covert surveillance post from which the identification was made is unknown? How

---

155 *Hardy's Case* (1794) 24 St Tr 199; *A-G v Briant* (1846) 15 M & W 169; *Marks v Beyfus* [1890] 25 QBD 494, CA.

156 Known to aficionados of 1970s police dramas as 'snouts', 'snitches', and 'grasses', but more properly described (in the language of the Regulation of Investigatory Powers Act 2000) as 'CHISs' – covert human intelligence sources.   157 *R v Rankine* [1986] QB 861, CA.

158 *Taylor v Anderton*, *The Times*, 21 October 1986, Ch D. But cf. *Norwich Pharmacal Co v Customs and Excise Commissioners* [1974] AC 133, HL (PII does *not* automatically attach to information procured in the course of a criminal investigation).

is an advocate supposed to test the credibility of a key prosecution witness whose identity is kept secret? These questions pack an additional punch in this context, because police informants are often themselves people of bad character who would generally make poor witnesses in court if their true identities were known to the jury and who might well be acting for ulterior motives. Undercover police officers, for their part, are both notoriously difficult to supervise effectively and exceptionally exposed to the temptations of corruption. None of these matters will be properly ventilated in court if the accused and his legal team are kept in the dark about the identity, or even in some cases about the very existence, of a police informant or undercover officer.

The European Court of Human Rights has considered whether witness anonymity is compatible with Article 6(3)(d) of the ECHR on a number of occasions. In *Doorson*,[159] the European Court held that a witness might testify anonymously if the witness's safety might otherwise be placed in jeopardy, where – for example – the witness was testifying against violent drug traffickers. Although Article 6 does not specifically mention witnesses' rights, the general scheme of the ECHR, with its emphasis on individual liberty, security, and privacy, was found to imply that 'principles of fair trial also require that in appropriate cases the interests of the defence are balanced against those of witnesses or victims called upon to testify'.[160] The European Court was careful to acknowledge, however, that witness anonymity *does* disadvantage the defence, requiring compensatory measures to ensure that the accused has a fair trial in accordance with the requirements of Article 6. Moreover, 'even when "counterbalancing" procedures are found to compensate sufficiently the handicaps under which the defence labours, a conviction should not be based either solely or to a decisive extent on anonymous statements'.[161] The limits of anonymous evidence were soon further tested in a second Article 6 complaint taken against the Netherlands. In *Van Mechelen*,[162] as in *Doorson*, the Dutch courts ruled that sufficient measures had been taken to compensate the defence for the anonymity of key prosecution witnesses. In particular, the witnesses had been questioned extensively by an examining magistrate who knew their identities, and also by defence lawyers themselves via an audio-link to the interview-room. Albeit without actually seeing the witnesses in the flesh, defence lawyers had been able to ask the witnesses any questions they liked via the audio-link other than questions likely to reveal the witnesses' identities. This time, however, the European Court held (by a majority of 6 to 3) that there had been a violation of Article 6. One significant point of contrast with the earlier ruling in *Doorson* was that in *Van Mechelen* the anonymous witnesses were serving police officers. As the European Court observed:

[Police officers] owe a general duty of obedience to the State's executive authorities and usually have links with the prosecution; for these reasons alone their use as anonymous witnesses should be resorted to only in exceptional circumstances. In addition, it is in the nature of things that their duties, particularly in the case of arresting officers, may involve giving evidence in open court.[163]

But too much should not be made of this distinction. It was noted in *Van Mechelen* that the officers' families, as well as the officers themselves, were potential targets of intimidation or violence. The case concerned extremely violent robbers armed with submachine guns

---

[159] *Doorson* v *Netherlands* (1996) 22 EHRR 330, ECtHR.   [160] ibid. [70].   [161] ibid. [76].
[162] *Van Mechelen* v *Netherlands* (1997) 25 EHRR 647, ECtHR.   [163] ibid. [56].

who had fired on officers at the scene when attempting to evade capture, wounding several of them. The majority's finding of a violation in *Van Mechelen* seems to have been driven more by considerations of general principle. In the first place, the Court announced a strong presumption that 'all the evidence must normally be produced at a public hearing, in the presence of the accused, with a view to adversarial argument'.[164] Secondly, in view of the exalted 'place that the right to a fair administration of justice holds in a democratic society, any measures restricting the rights of the defence should be strictly necessary'.[165] It follows, third, that '[i]f a less restrictive measure can suffice then that measure should be applied'.[166] In the final analysis, the judges comprising the majority in *Van Mechelen* were not persuaded that the Dutch authorities had reduced the forensic disadvantages imposed on the defence to the unavoidable minimum compatible with respecting the witnesses' interests (e.g. through partial disguise rather than complete anonymity), which is an understandable judgment-call on a close-run question – even if it is not readily apparent how this ruling can be squared with the opposite conclusion in *Doorson*.[167]

Notwithstanding these European decisions and the passage of the Human Rights Act 1998, it was not until a decade later that witness anonymity became a burning issue in English criminal proceedings. The accused in *Davis*[168] was convicted of a double murder at a flat in Hackney, following an all-night New Year's Eve party. The only evidence directly identifying Davis as the gunman came from three witnesses, all of whom were in fear of reprisals. The judge acceded to a prosecution submission that the witnesses should be permitted to testify anonymously, behind screens and with their voices altered. Only the judge and jury could see the witnesses and hear their real voices. Defence counsel was offered the opportunity to view the witnesses giving evidence, but declined to be put in a position of knowing information that he was not permitted to impart to his client. The issue taken on appeal, ultimately to the House of Lords, was whether these arrangements were compatible with the accused's Article 6(3)(d) right 'to examine or have examined witnesses against him'.

In light of the European Court's decisions in *Doorson* and *Van Mechelen*, the procedures adopted in *Davis* might have been expected to pass muster (and the Court of Appeal held that they did). The witnesses whose identities were concealed in *Davis* were civilians, as in *Doorson*, and their fears for their personal safety were accepted as genuine. Furthermore, the witnesses were present in court and gave live testimony, which was entirely transparent to the fact-finder. Only the witnesses' true identities were concealed, and only from the accused and his lawyers. These arrangements could plausibly be described as the least restrictive measures necessary to preserve the witnesses' anonymity, in compliance with the principle announced in *Van Mechelen*. However, the House of Lords unanimously allowed Davis' appeal, and in doing so placed greater emphasis on traditional common law principles than on Article 6 or its expository jurisprudence. Lord Bingham set the tone:

It is a long-established principle of the English common law that, subject to certain exceptions and statutory qualifications, the defendant in a criminal trial should be confronted by his accusers in order that he may cross-examine them and challenge their evidence.[169]

---

164 ibid. [51].   165 ibid. [58].   166 ibid.
167 A criticism developed with considerable cogency in Judge van Dijk's Dissenting Opinion.
168 *R v Davis* [2008] 1 AC 1128, [2008] UKHL 36.   169 ibid. [5].

Their Lordships went on to hold that the concerns for witnesses' safety recognized in the instant case did not constitute legitimate grounds for an exception or statutory qualification to 'the right to be confronted by one's accusers [which] is a right recognized by the common law for centuries'.[170] Witness intimidation was a genuine problem, but it was not a new problem – and the common law had consistently set its face against anonymous evidence as a way of combating it. One must not simply assume that a prosecution witness might be threatened or that the accused must be lying. In *Davis* itself, the accused was claiming that the allegations against him were malicious, but this was not a line of argument that could be developed successfully without knowing the identities of his accusers. As Lord Mance observed:

[I]n all such cases the problem exists that the concealment of identity means that the defendant cannot himself check, investigate or (save by guesswork) give directly any relevant information about the character, motives or reliability of the witness. The defence is to that extent potentially hampered both in cross-examination and in relation to any positive case and evidence which it can adduce. In many cases, particularly cases where credibility is in issue, identification will be essential to effective cross-examination.[171]

European human rights law was regarded by their Lordships as reinforcing their analysis at common law. In particular, it was doubted whether the procedures adopted in *Davis* would satisfy Article 6 since the 'sole or decisive' evidence implicating the accused in the shooting was presented anonymously.[172]

Having (re)stated the position at common law, with considerable emphasis and deliberation,[173] several of their Lordships concluded their speeches in *Davis* by remarking that if the position were regarded as unsatisfactory it would now have to be altered by legislation. In fact, the *Davis* judgment generated minor panic amongst detectives and prosecutors. It was said that scores of criminal convictions and on-going prosecutions of gangland violence, armed robberies, and murders might now be jeopardized owing to their reliance on anonymous witness testimony.[174] Parliament responded with alacrity, in the first instance by immediately enacting temporary legislation,[175] which was subsequently incorporated into the Coroners and Justice Act 2009.[176] The legislation supersedes the common law relating specifically to witness anonymity but

---

[170] ibid. [34] (Lord Bingham).   [171] ibid. [71]–[72].

[172] See, e.g., ibid [59] (Lord Carswell), [95]–[96] (Lord Mance).

[173] Lord Brown, ibid. [66], was particularly forthright: 'the creeping emasculation of the common law principle must be not only halted but reversed. It is the integrity of the judicial process that is at stake here. This must be safeguarded and vindicated whatever the cost.'

[174] See, e.g., Richard Edwards, 'Dozens of trials hit by witness anonymity ban', *Daily Telegraph*, 25 June 2008; Jeff Wells, 'Legal chaos may help free killers', *Western Daily Press*, 25 June 2008; Mike Sullivan, 'Anarchy is unleashed', *The Sun*, 25 June 2008 ('Barmy Law Lords were last night accused of unleashing anarchy by barring anonymous witnesses in court trials.... One angry Scotland Yard detective said: "We cannot over-emphasise how grave the threat to public safety is because of this judgment You will have Zimbabwe UK on the streets. Unless we can guarantee anonymity to witnesses in danger it will lead to terrorist and murder trials collapsing and hundreds of convicted killers walking out of prison on appeal"').

[175] Criminal Evidence (Witness Anonymity) Act 2008. See *R v Mayers* [2009] 1 WLR 1915, [2008] EWCA Crim 2989.

[176] C&JA 2009, ss.86–97, brought into force on 1 January 2010 by s.182(3)(a). The corresponding provisions of the Criminal Evidence (Witness Anonymity) Act 2008 were simultaneously repealed: C&JA 2009, s.96.

has no effect on PII generally.[177] It authorizes judges to make a 'witness anonymity order' directing such measures as withholding a witness's name and address, the use of pseudonyms, screening, and voice modulation,[178] in order to conceal a witness's identity where this is deemed necessary in the interests of justice.[179] Each measure must be justified on a case-by-case basis taking account of specified considerations,[180] which simultaneously vests primary responsibility for making these decisions with trial judges and thereby effectively insulates their decision-making from excessively fussy appellate review. Of course, the ultimate possibility of an application to Strasbourg alleging a breach of Article 6 remains in every case, and so it is unlikely that we have heard the last from the ECtHR on the issue of witness anonymity. In the meantime, the legislative framework now contained in the Coroners and Justice Act 2009 also helps to define the extent to which a witness's identity falls within the scope of PII protection during the pre-trial process.[181] Only those details likely to be covered at trial by a witness anonymity order may be withheld; and such orders will not be granted unless the prosecution has diligently complied with its disclosure obligations in every other respect.[182]

In adjudicating any PII application, as we have seen, trial judges must strive to strike the right balance between competing public interest considerations. However, the special circumstances of criminal proceedings demand that truth-finding and avoiding wrongful convictions should tilt the scales in favour of disclosure. An accused who is denied access to crucial information cannot have a fair trial, either at common law (as *Davis* reiterated) or under Article 6 of the ECHR.[183] In cases where the extreme sensitivity of the information in question is regarded as an absolutely insurmountable obstacle to its public disclosure, the prosecution's ultimate fallback option is to abandon criminal proceedings entirely. This is a distasteful outcome if it means that victims of crime are left without redress and an offender goes unpunished. But it may be the lesser of all evils, where the irresistible force of the accused's right to a fair trial meets the immovable object of public interest immunity.

---

[177] C&JA 2009, s.95.

[178] C&JA 2009, s.86(2); these are merely examples of specified measures: s.86(3). But the judge and jury must be able to see the witness and hear his or her natural voice: s.86(4).   [179] C&JA 2009, s.88.

[180] Including: the general right of criminal defendants to know the identity of witnesses; whether the witness's evidence might be the 'sole or decisive evidence' implicating the accused; whether the witness's credibility is in issue; and whether the witness's evidence can be properly tested without revealing his or her identity: C&JA 2009, s.89(2). An order cannot be made unless 'the effect of the proposed order would be consistent with the defendant receiving a fair trial': s.88(4).

[181] C&JA 2009, s.87(4). In addition, magistrates may issue 'investigation anonymity orders' specifically in relation to homicide with a weapon by youthful gang members (under 30 years of age),: C&JA 2009, ss.76 and 78.

[182] Cf. *R v Mayers* [2009] 1 WLR 1915, [2008] EWCA Crim 2989, [12]: '[T]he Crown must comply with its existing duties in relation to full and frank disclosure (save as expressly permitted by the Act in relation to withholding of information on the basis of public interest immunity). The process as a whole must be fair. Disclosure must be complete...In short, the Crown must be proactive, focusing closely on the credibility of the anonymous witness and the interests of justice.' Whilst these remarks were made in relation to the 2008 Act, it is inconceivable that the courts would interpret the 2009 Act any differently in this respect.

[183] *Rowe and Davis* v *UK* (2000) 30 EHRR 1; Sybil D. Sharpe, 'Article 6 and the Disclosure of Evidence in Criminal Trials' [1999] *Crim LR* 273; Stewart Field and James Young, 'Disclosure, Appeals and Procedural Traditions: *Edwards* v *UK*' [1994] *Crim LR* 264.

(c) FURTHER PROCEDURAL INNOVATION – SPECIAL COUNSEL AS PARTIAL COMPENSATION

One possible answer to the PII conundrum, which satisfied a narrow 9–8 majority of the European Court of Human Rights in *Jasper* v *UK*,[184] is that the judge must do his level best to anticipate the accused's contentions at an *ex parte* hearing. Trial judges will doubtless press prosecutors to supply robust justification of their claims to PII protection and will inspect the material and form a view about its potential significance for themselves. But the idea that the adjudicator must be both referee and striker for the opposing team does not sit well with adversarial philosophy. Besides, how is the judge supposed to represent the accused's interests effectively if he can only guess what challenges and arguments the defence are going to make at trial?

Building on its approach to anonymous witness testimony discussed in the previous section, Strasbourg jurisprudence has developed the following general principles formulated to ensure that non-disclosure of sensitive material does not undermine the fairness of criminal trials:

[T]he entitlement to disclosure of relevant evidence is not an absolute right. In any criminal proceedings there may be competing interests, such as national security or the need to protect witnesses at risk of reprisals or keep secret police methods of investigation of crime, which must be weighed against the rights of the accused. In some cases it may be necessary to withhold certain evidence from the defence so as to preserve the fundamental rights of another individual or to safeguard an important public interest. However, only such measures restricting the rights of the defence which are strictly necessary are permissible under Article 6(1). Moreover, in order to ensure that the accused receives a fair trial, any difficulties caused to the defence by a limitation on its rights must be sufficiently counterbalanced by the procedures followed by the judicial authorities.[185]

With these principles in mind, it is noteworthy that in both *Jasper* and *Fitt* the prosecutor had notified the defence legal teams that *ex parte* PII applications were being made, providing them with advance warning that sensitive aspects of the police surveillance operations conducted in those cases were being suppressed. In other circumstances, the Strasbourg judges have condemned non-disclosure where significant information was withheld from the trial court as well as from the accused.[186] Non-disclosure pursuant to *ex parte* PII hearings of the identities of suspected informants was also a central issue in the two conjoined applications of *Edwards and Lewis* v *UK*,[187] an important decision ultimately endorsed by the ECtHR's Grand Chamber. The Strasbourg judges began by observing that '[i]n cases where evidence has been withheld from the defence on public interest grounds, it is not the role of this Court to decide whether or not such non-disclosure was strictly necessary since, as a general rule, it is for the national courts to assess the evidence before them'. However, the ECtHR *will* intervene if non-disclosure is judged to constitute or contribute decisively towards a violation of Article 6, as it was in both instant cases. Neither applicant's trial had been fair, the Court held, because both Edwards and Lewis had been deprived of information that they needed in order to mount a defence of unfair

---

[184] *Jasper* v *UK* (2000) 30 EHRR 441. And see *Fitt* v *UK* (2000) 30 EHRR 480.
[185] *Fitt* v *UK* (2000) 30 EHRR 480, [45].   [186] *Atlan* v *UK* (2002) 34 EHRR 33.
[187] *Edwards and Lewis* v *UK* (2005) 40 EHRR 24.

'entrapment' contrary to *Looseley* and *Teixeira*.[188] Claiming PII protection for informants' identities was not *per se* a violation of Article 6, but it might become one depending on the nature of any defence arguments and other relevant circumstantial factors.

Which brings us back to the question of 'counterbalancing' measures capable of compensating an accused for any procedural disadvantages created by non-disclosure of PII material. An innovative solution has been proposed specifically to ameliorate the potential unfairness of *ex parte* hearings: the appointment of independent special counsel exclusively to represent the accused's interests in PII proceedings. An approved list of security-cleared special counsel was originally devised in order to regulate the flow of sensitive information in the context of immigration proceedings[189] and was later extended to terrorism cases.[190] However, this novel variation on adversarial procedure has subsequently been adapted to various types of judicial hearing, supplying a flexible mechanism for retaining the traditional two-way adversarial dialogue in circumstances where, for reasons of national security or other public interest, it is deemed inappropriate to include the accused or his legal advisers in the normal way.[191] With special counsel on the scene, all PII applications could be structured as contested *inter partes* hearings, and the system would still operate even where utmost secrecy precluded the bare fact that a hearing had taken place from being divulged. Six of the dissenting ECtHR judges in *Jasper*,[192] who ruled that the procedure adopted in that case breached Article 6, indicated that provision of special ssscounsel at an *ex parte* PII hearing would have been sufficient to guarantee the accused's right to a fair trial. Special counsel were also championed by Lord Justice Auld's *Review of the Criminal Courts*.[193]

However, there may be a tendency to underestimate the practical difficulties involved in the appointment and operation of special counsel. The accused's regular legal team, or the accused himself if he is unrepresented, must ensure that this 'hired-help' is sufficiently well-briefed about broader aspects of the case in general, and fully conversant with defence arguments and tactics in particular, to be able to represent the accused's interests with intelligence and vigour. This may be a lot harder to achieve in practice than it might sound in glib statements of principle. Barristers who have actually appeared as special counsel report that, even if an applicant's lawyers are co-operative, effective communication may be stymied by legal restrictions, especially after the special advocate has accessed sensitive material that must not be disclosed to the accused or his lawyers.[194] It was in deference

---

[188] *Teixeira de Castro* v *Portugal* (1998) 28 EHRR 101; *R* v *Looseley; Attorney General's Reference (No 3 of 2000)* [2001] 1 WLR 2060, [2001] UKHL 53, both discussed in Chapter 5.

[189] Special Immigration Appeals Commission Act 1997, providing for the appointment of special counsel in immigration cases, introduced in response to the ECtHR's rulings in *Chahal* v *UK* (1997) 23 EHRR 413 and *Tinnelly* v *UK* (1999) 27 EHRR 249.

[190] *Secretary of State for the Home Department* v *MB* [2008] 1 AC 440, [2007] UKHL 46; *M* v *Secretary of State for the Home Department* [2004] 2 All ER 863, [2004] EWCA Civ 324.

[191] See, e.g., *Roberts* v *Parole Board* [2005] 2 AC 738, HL; *R* v *Shayler* [2003] 1 AC 247, HL, [34]; *Malik* v *Manchester Crown Court* [2008] 4 All ER 403, [2008] EWHC 1362 (Admin); *Al Rawi* v *Security Service* [2009] EWHC 2959 (QB). For discussion, see John Ip, 'The Rise and Spread of the Special Advocate' [2008] *Public Law* 717.

[192] *Jasper* v *UK* (2000) 30 EHRR 441, Dissenting Opinion of Judges Palm, Fischbach, Vaji, Thomassen, Tsatsa-Nikolovska, and Traja.

[193] Lord Justice Auld, *Review of the Criminal Courts of England and Wales – Report* (TSO, 2001), 477–8.

[194] See Martin Chamberlain, 'Special Advocates and Procedural Fairness in Closed Proceedings' (2009) 28 *Civil Justice Quarterly* 314.

to these practical difficulties, as well as to avoid extra cost and delay, that the House of Lords in *R v H*[195] unequivocally rejected the proposition that special counsel should be appointed routinely in all *ex parte* PII hearings. Whilst conceding that 'novelty is not of itself an objection, and cases will arise in which the appointment of an approved advocate as special counsel is necessary, in the interests of justice, to secure protection of a criminal defendant's right to a fair trial', Lord Bingham admonished that '[s]uch an appointment will always be exceptional, never automatic; a course of last and never first resort. It should not be ordered unless and until the trial judge is satisfied that no other course will adequately meet the overriding requirement of fairness to the defendant.'[196]

The promise of modern adversarial criminal procedure is that *your* lawyer – not just any old lawyer – will provide you with advice and representation, and will do so at state expense if you lack private means, at least when you are charged with a serious criminal offence. Special counsel represent an interesting procedural innovation, which doubtless improves on the default position in which the accused enjoys no dedicated representation whatever in *ex parte* PII hearings. But it still needs to be asked whether the assignment of special counsel constitutes an ingenious way of preserving the adversarial ideal of access to justice, or contributes towards its erosion. One answer is suggested by Lord Bingham's preference for conventional due process over procedural innovation:

Fairness ordinarily requires that any material held by the prosecution which weakens its case or strengthens that of the defendant, if not relied on as part of its formal case against the defendant, should be disclosed to the defence. Bitter experience has shown that miscarriages of justice may occur where such material is withheld from disclosure. The golden rule is that full disclosure of such material should be made . . . [197]

To the extent that the 'golden rule' of full disclosure is followed, resort to procedural expedients like special counsel will be unnecessary.

---

[195] *R v H* [2004] 2 AC 134; [2004] UKHL 3.

[196] ibid. [22]. An example of an 'exceptional' PII hearing in criminal proceedings requiring the appointment of special counsel is *R v Austin* [2009] EWCA Crim 1527. Also see *R v Mayers* [2009] 1 WLR 1915, [2008] EWCA Crim 2989, [10].

[197] *R v H* [2004] 2 AC 134, HL, [14].

8

CRIMINAL TRIAL PROCEDURE –
EXAMINATION-IN-CHIEF AND
CROSS-EXAMINATION

8.1 THE PROCEDURAL COURSE OF THE TRIAL

The previous chapter considered the law governing witness competence, compellability, privilege, and public interest immunity. This set of procedural rules establishes who is eligible to testify in criminal trials and what information they may be compelled to divulge. This chapter examines the rules of law and practice regulating the presentation and critical examination of witness testimony in criminal adjudication. English common law developed an extensive corpus of procedural rules and principles specifying the order and manner in which oral witness testimony – as well as documents and exhibits adduced through witnesses – must be presented to the court. Known prosaically as the rules on 'the course of the trial', common law doctrines have periodically been supplemented by statutory provisions, most recently by several key sections of the Criminal Justice Act 2003.

Despite its sometimes byzantine complexity (which the 2003 Act sought to ameliorate), the law's overriding objective is simply stated: to ensure that the process of fact-finding is conducted fairly, efficiently, and economically, in order to establish the truth and render a just verdict. Or in the pithy language of the Criminal Procedure Rules, '[t]he overriding objective...is that criminal cases be dealt with justly'.[1]

Criminal trial procedure reflects the overarching adversarial structure of English criminal proceedings described in Chapter 2. The trial begins with an opening speech by the prosecutor who then proceeds to present the evidence for the prosecution.[2] In adversarial proceedings, the parties choose which witnesses to call and in what order; these decisions are generally regarded as tactical questions in which the court does not interfere.[3] Although

---

[1] Criminal Procedure Rules (CrimPR) 2010, Part 1.1. The significance of the 'overriding objective', in explicitly linking criminal litigation practice to its underpinning normative rationales, was noted in §1.5(b).

[2] Those who view a trial as a contest between competing 'narratives' (stories) might consider that the defence is disadvantaged by not having an opportunity to fix its story in jurors' minds at the beginning of the trial. Lord Justice Auld confessed to being 'puzzled at the lack of any formal provision for a short opening defence speech at the beginning of a criminal trial and at the general reluctance of defence advocates to make one...[I]n many cases it would be of strategic advantage to the defendant as well as of assistance to the jury for his advocate to balance the prosecution's opening by underlining the nature of his defence at that stage': Lord Justice Auld, *Review of the Criminal Courts of England and Wales: Report* (TSO, 2001), ch 11, para.28.

[3] *Briscoe* v *Briscoe* [1966] 1 All ER 465, HC.

witnesses are called by one or other of the parties, there is said to be 'no property in a witness'.[4] In practical terms, this means that a witness from whom a statement has already been taken can still be approached by any other party to the proceedings, remains free to divulge information to all and sundry,[5] and could be called to testify by any litigant if the case goes to trial. As we saw in the last chapter, witnesses swear an oath (or solemnly affirm) to tell the truth, and this holds whoever is asking the questions. The party calling a witness or his advocate first examines the witness in-chief with a view to eliciting information favourable to the party's case. The witness is then cross-examined by the opposing party or parties, usually in an attempt to discredit his testimony or to extract further information undermining the proponent's case. Cross-examination is by right, and once a witness has gone into the witness-box he or she cannot avoid it.[6] Conversely, any aspect of the witness's evidence which the opposing party intends to challenge must be raised explicitly in cross-examination, to provide the witness with a fair opportunity to expound on, clarify, defend, or resile from their position.[7] Finally, the party calling the witness may be allowed to ask further questions in re-examination, but only for the purpose of clarifying any matter that has arisen out of cross-examination.[8] When the prosecution has closed its case (and assuming there is no successful submission of 'no case to answer'[9]), the accused responds by presenting the case for the defence, adducing witness testimony through the same three-stage process of examination-in-chief by the defence, cross-examination by the prosecution (and any co-accused), and re-examination (if required).

In trials on indictment in the Crown Court the vast majority of accused persons are represented by professional advocates (barristers or solicitors with rights of audience in the higher courts), but the accused is entitled to represent themselves if they prefer. Many do so in the magistrates' courts, where legal aid is not so readily available. If the accused intends to testify, he is normally required to do so before any other defence witness.[10] This is to prevent the accused from 'trimming' his evidence to fit in with whatever other defence witnesses might say. If the accused elects to testify he goes into the witness-box[11] and swears an oath (or affirms) like any other witness. The symbolism is important: the accused appears as a witness of truth – and is subject to the sanction

---

[4] See, e.g., *In Re L (A Minor) (Police Investigation: Privilege)* [1997] AC 16, 34, HL, *per* Lord Nicholls (referring to 'the time honoured aphorism, there is no property in a witness').

[5] On prosecution contact with defence witnesses, see CPS, *Legal Guidance: Interviewing Witnesses for the Other Side* (2007), on-line via www.cps.gov.uk/legal/.

[6] Witnesses in the trial can be cross-examined by every other opposing party, regardless of whether the witness's testimony is contrary to the cross-examiner's interests. For example, if an accused in a multi-handed trial elects to testify in his own defence he can be cross-examined by counsel for a co-accused as well as by the prosecution advocate: *R v Hilton* [1972] 2 QB 421, CA.

[7] This is known as the rule in *Browne v Dunn* (1894) 6 R 67, 72, HL, *per* Lord Herschell LC: 'if you intend to impeach a witness you are bound, whilst he is in the box, to give him an opportunity of making any explanation which is open to him.... [I]t will not do to impeach the credibility of a witness upon a matter on which he has not had any opportunity of giving an explanation by reason of there having been no suggestion whatever in the course of the case that his story is not accepted.'

[8] *Prince v Samo* (1838) 7 LJQB 123, QB; *The Queen's Case* (1820) 2 Brod & B 284, 297 & 129 ER 976, 981, *per* Abbott CJ: 'counsel has a right, upon re-examination, to ask all questions, which may be proper to draw forth an explanation of the sense and meaning of the expressions used by the witness on cross-examination...but, I think, he has no right to go further, and to introduce matter new in itself, and suited to the purpose of explaining either the expressions or the motives of the witness'. For a modern illustration of the scope of re-examination in criminal proceedings, see *R v Doosti* (1986) 82 Cr App R 181, CA.   [9] §2.5(c).

[10] PACE 1984, s. 79.   [11] Criminal Evidence Act 1898, s.1(4).

of perjury, like any other witness – not merely as an accused person pleading his case from the dock. In practice, however, accused persons who testify in their own defence are seldom prosecuted for perjury, even though the clear implication of a guilty verdict is often that their testimony contained lies. After the defence is concluded, the prosecutor has a right to make a closing speech in which he may comment on the evidence as a whole, 'painting a picture' of the prosecution's allegations and the evidence said to support them. The defence then makes its own closing speech, either advancing a counter-narrative according to which the accused is innocent (or guilty only of a lesser charge) or reiterating the accused's denials and asserting that the prosecution has failed to discharge the burden of proof, so that the jury must acquit.[12] Whether or not the defence has called evidence, it always has the right to the last word, before the judge sums up the case, both law and fact, for the benefit of the jury, which then retires to deliberate on its verdict.

The rest of this chapter is divided into main four sections, the first two of which consider legal rules relating specifically to examination-in-chief, followed by two sections exploring doctrines applicable to cross-examination. Section 8.2 considers three procedural doctrines which structure the conduct of examination-in-chief, and whose study will help to clarify the underlying assumptions and aspirations of criminal trial procedure. Section 8.3 describes 'the rule against narrative' and its various exceptions, a particularly characteristic feature of common law evidence. The two sections devoted to cross-examination adopt a broadly parallel approach. Section 8.4 considers the general objectives of cross-examination and the legal limitations placed on attempts to undermine the credibility of opposing witnesses. Section 8.5 then looks in detail at the 'collateral-finality rule' and its various exceptions, which might loosely be regarded as cross-examination's counterpart to the rule against narrative. In conclusion, Section 8.6 picks up a common thread – the progressive erosion of the common law's traditional distinction between evidence or questions 'going directly to the issue' and 'collateral' evidence or questions going only 'to credit' – and highlights some broader implications for the principle of orality.

8.2 PROCEDURAL REGULATION OF EXAMINATION-IN-CHIEF

English criminal trial procedure has been shaped by the fact that witness evidence is generated by interested litigants, rather than by a neutral 'investigating magistrate' or judicial officer[13] as it would be in most continental criminal trials for serious crimes. Party control over evidence gathering is reinforced by the practical difficulties of extending effective judicial scrutiny to criminal investigations and pre-trial proceedings, a feature of criminal litigation in common law jurisdictions which has been ameliorated, but far from entirely

---

[12] There is intermittently expressed concern that advocates' opening and closing speeches are sometimes rambling and long-winded and do nothing to assist the jury in reaching a true and just verdict, but the introduction of artificial time-limits is not generally favoured: see *Auld Review*, ch 11, paras.27 and 40; cf. Royal Commission on Criminal Justice, *Report*, Cm 2263 (HMSO, 1993), ch 8, paras.8 and 19.

[13] Note that prosecutors are regarded as part of the magistracy in francophone jurisdictions.

displaced, by the modern trend towards more proactive judicial case management.[14] For these reasons, common law rules of evidence and procedure partly evolved with an eye to preventing abuses by displaying a sceptical attitude towards the reliability and credibility of witness testimony, at least until it has been thoroughly tested in court.[15]

Whatever else it is, running trials is also an intensely practical task, demanding flexibility to meet the exigencies of the instant case and a healthy dose of common sense. The trial judge presiding in the courtroom, watching the proceedings and the evidence unfold, is the key figure. Appellate courts will tend to defer to the trial judge's assessment of what fairness demanded in the circumstances, provided that there was no manifest breach of law, serious procedural irregularity or '*Wednesbury* unreasonableness'. Procedural doctrines regulating the course of the trial are conventionally expressed in terms of 'rules', but in fact often operate more in the manner of open-ended principles flexibly attuned to the interests of justice. Common law trial procedure should answer to the practical demands of accurate fact-finding rather than falling hostage to technical rule-worship, as Sachs LJ once observed:

> The courts...must take care not to deprive themselves by new, artificial rules of practice of the best chances of learning the truth. The courts are under no compulsion unnecessarily to follow on a matter of practice the lure of the rules of logic in order to produce unreasonable results which would hinder the course of justice.[16]

Truth-finding, as we have seen,[17] is a foundational principle of criminal evidence. It takes its place alongside other foundational principles and the pragmatic demands for speed and economy[18] in constituting the normative framework of criminal trial procedure.

This section considers three procedural doctrines structuring the conduct of examination-in-chief: (a) the rule forbidding leading questions; (b) rules specifying the kinds of documents to which witnesses may refer in order to 'refresh their memory'; and (c) rules regulating the examination of a witness who turns 'hostile'. On closer inspection many of these 'rules' assume a more open-ended, discretionary cast, and the thrust of contemporary reforms has been to nudge procedural rules further in that direction.

(a) LEADING QUESTIONS

The logic of adversarial proceedings is that each party will only call witnesses who are expected to advance the party's case. This is an efficient way of narrowing down the issues and the evidence produced in the trial to focus on the nub of the disagreement between the parties,[19] but it also presents a greater risk that the prosecution or defence will try to induce 'their' witness to say, not so much what the witness believes, as what the instruct-

---

[14] The trend towards proactive judicial trial management, underpinned by the CrimPR 2005 and 2010, was noted in §2.3(a) and further discussed in our concluding chapter: see §16.3(a).

[15] Cf. Edward J. Imwinkelried, 'The Worst Evidence Principle: The Best Hypothesis as to the Logical Structure of Evidence Law' (1992) 46 *University of Miami LR* 1069.

[16] *R v Richardson* [1971] 2 QB 484, 490, CA.   [17] §1.3.

[18] 'Justice delayed is justice denied'; informational quality may degrade over time and its quantity must not exceed fact-finders' cognitive capacities: see §3.2.

[19] Cf. Richard A. Posner, 'An Economic Approach to the Law of Evidence' (1999) 51 *Stanford Law Review* 1477, 1492: 'the adversarial system relies on the market to a much greater extent than the inquisitorial system does, and the market is a more efficient producer of most goods than the government'.

ing party wishes to hear. Notwithstanding the strict legal position, parties will tend to regard witnesses as either 'for' or 'against' them in an adversarial system, and to behave accordingly. This is a reason for curbing the extent to which an advocate is permitted to orchestrate or stage-manage a witness's answers during examination-in-chief, as Best long ago observed:

> [T]he party calling a witness has an advantage over his adversary, in knowing beforehand what the witness will prove, or at least is expected to prove;... if he were allowed to lead, he might interrogate in such a manner as to extract only so much of the knowledge of the witness as would be favourable to his side, or even put a false gloss on the whole.[20]

A leading question is one which suggests to the witness that a specific answer is desired of him, or which implies a fact not already proved in evidence. Thus, if the witness is asked 'You saw the assailant's face very clearly, didn't you?' she is being led. The advocate's 'question' is really just a statement of fact which the witness is being invited to adopt courtesy of the ubiquitous tagline, 'Isn't that the case?' Equally, the question 'What colour was the thief's mask?' is leading if it is yet to be proved in evidence that the thief was wearing any mask, since the question directly invites the witness to assent to a proposition with no evidential foundation. Nothing that counsel says in examining a witness is 'evidence' in law, strictly speaking, even though in practice the question itself, as well as the witness's reaction to it (which *does* constitute evidence *stricto sensu*), may influence the fact-finder.[21] The rule against leading questions is designed to safeguard the integrity of a witness's evidence from the potentially corrupting influences of an adversarial trial process. Counsel must not put words into the witness's mouth.[22]

At times, however, leading questions *are* permitted. Leading is problematic when it concerns disputed issues in the case, but there is no harm in leading with regard to routine information provided to the court, like the witness's name and address, or even when a witness is asked to confirm material facts about which there is no real dispute. A flexible attitude towards leading questions clearly demonstrates that the objection is not to all questions adopting a particular structure – 'questions suggesting an answer' – but to questions directed to an improper end. The real test is whether the question put to the witness is likely to distort the witness's testimony on a disputed fact in issue, in which case the question will be forbidden.[23] But harmless leading is allowed, by concession of the opposing party and with the blessing of the court.[24]

(b) REFRESHING MEMORY

While a party must not put words into the mouth of his witness, witnesses sometimes need help to narrate the events in question. One obvious source of potential assistance would be a document – such as a diary entry, business record, or a previous statement to the police – recording the events in question. But jogging the witness's memory in this way presents an

---

[20] W. M. Best, *Principles of the Law of Evidence* (Sweet & Maxwell, 5th edn. 1870; 12th edn. 1922), 802.

[21] Another source of 'informal evidence': see §3.4(d).

[22] Cf. Keith Evans, *The Golden Rules of Advocacy* (Blackstone, 1993), 29–30: 'Mandatory Rule Number Six: Never Put Words into the Mouth of Your Own Witness'.

[23] *Pratt v Medwin* [2003] EWCA Civ 906, [2003] 2 P & CR DG22. Also see Glanville Williams, *The Proof of Guilt* (Stevens, 3rd edn. 1963), 93.   [24] *Ex p. Bottomley* [1909] 2 KB 14, 20–2, KBD.

obvious risk: the more a witness relies on a document, the more he is being influenced by what he reads, as opposed to what he truly remembers. This is an attempted end-run on the principle of orality. Beyond a certain point the document itself, rather than the witness's testimony, becomes the source of the information.

Wigmore[25] believed that a useful distinction could be drawn between situations where a document triggers a genuine recollection of an event, and other situations where the witness can only say that she believes the content of the document to be true. Documents in the first category, Wigmore thought, should not be subject to any restriction, while documents in the second category should be regarded as hearsay and admitted in evidence only if an established exception to the hearsay rule applied.[26] English law, however, has long held the view that this theoretical distinction is hard to maintain in practice. The common law adopted a typically pragmatic approach, implicitly condoning witnesses' recourse to *aides-mémoire* of genuine probative value whilst striving to close down the main avenues for insinuating information into courtroom testimony for which the witness cannot personally vouch.

The first safeguard is designed to counteract improper preparation of witnesses – 'witness coaching' – before the trial. If, prior to entering the witness-box, a witness has been allowed to consult statements previously made to the police, the prosecution must notify the defence.[27] The defence advocate is then put on notice to test through cross-examination the extent to which a witness speaks from his own recollection, as opposed merely to repeating what the witness has just read in his police statement. The Court of Appeal has recently deprecated in the strongest terms any attempt to 'coach' a witness through pre-trial rehearsals of their evidence.[28] Allowing witnesses to read over their police statements prior to going into the witness-box is not thought to contravene the injunction against improper witness preparation, though it may reflect a rather simplistic conception of the psychology of memory.[29] At all events, it is difficult to see how a strict legal ban on witnesses, as it were, informally 'revising' from previous statements could be policed effectively outside the courtroom. In court, the situation is entirely different. The common law imposed strict limitations on previous writings to which a witness could refer during the course of his or her testimony. Only written records that had been made at, or close to, the time of the events in question, and which were written by the witness himself or under his supervision, could qualify in formal terms as memory-refreshing documents.[30]

---

[25] *Wigmore on Evidence* (Chadbourn revision), vol. 3, §§754, 754A.

[26] Chapter 9 examines the hearsay rule and its principal exceptions.

[27] *R v Richardson* [1971] 2 QB 484, CA; *R v Westwell* [1976] 2 All ER 812, CA. Note that there is no requirement that documents consulted by a witness prior to entering the witness-box should be contemporaneous records of the events in question.

[28] *R v Momodou and Limani* [2005] 1 WLR 3442, [2005] EWCA Crim 177, [61], *per* Judge LJ: 'Training or coaching for witnesses in criminal proceedings (whether for prosecution or defence) is not permitted.... The witness should give his or her own evidence, so far as practicable uninfluenced by what anyone else has said, whether in formal discussions or informal conversations. The rule reduces, indeed hopefully avoids any possibility, that one witness may tailor his evidence in the light of what anyone else said, and equally, avoids any unfounded perception that he may have done so.'

[29] See §7.1(c).

[30] *Attorney General's Reference (No 3 of 1979)* (1979) 69 Cr App R 411, CA. *R v Kelsey* (1982) 74 Cr App R 213, CA, represents a controversial extension of the basic principle. In that case it was held that a witness may also refresh his memory from the contents of a document which was made by another at his dictation, but without direct supervision, provided that the maker of the statement read it back to the witness for

The most common case was where a police officer testified that his note-book contained a contemporaneous account of the events in question, and was then permitted to read his evidence more or less verbatim from his notes. A third safeguard is that copies of memory-refreshing documents must be given to opposing counsel, who may utilize them for cross-examination, and also place them before the trier of fact.

In the final decades of the twentieth century, the common law rules regulating memory-refreshing were progressively relaxed, in two ways. First, the class of legitimate memory-refreshing documents was expanded by taking a liberal view of the contemporaneity criterion.[31] Secondly, in certain circumstances witnesses were permitted to refer to documents that could not plausibly qualify as memory-refreshers even *after* they had commenced testifying. This was achieved without technically breaching the common law rules by allowing the witness to take a break during their testimony in order to consult the document before going back into the witness-box and resuming their evidence.[32] Whilst the formal common law distinction between memory-refreshing in the witness-box and statement reading out of it was thereby maintained, its substance was just as surely eroded. However, this greater flexibility was widely endorsed, on the basis that testifying in court – often many months or even years after the incidents in question actually took place – should not be a test of memory.[33] The Criminal Justice Act 2003 took its cue from these recent developments at common law, and further developed the trend.

Section 139(1) of the Criminal Justice Act 2003 states:

s.139 – Use of documents to refresh memory
(1) A person giving oral evidence in criminal proceedings about any matter may, at any stage in the course of doing so, refresh his memory of it from a document made or verified by him at an earlier time if—

(a) he states in his oral evidence that the document records his recollection of the matter at that earlier time, and

(b) his recollection of the matter is likely to have been significantly better at that time than it is at the time of his oral evidence.[34]

Section 139 introduced a simple, all-purpose, functional standard to replace the more complex common law rules governing memory-refreshing. So long as the witness says the document records his 'recollection' (part or all of the content of his testimony) more reliably than his surviving unaided memory at the time of the trial, the standard appears to be satisfied. Thus, a witness suffering from amnesia or one whose memory is limited by disability may apparently refresh his or her memory, on the authority of

---

confirmation. The problem here is that, without seeing and checking the document for himself, the witness is relying on the *maker's* oral description of the document's contents. This puts in issue the credibility of the writer, as well as the powers of perception and credibility of the witness.

[31] In fact this revived the older, more flexible common law tradition: *Doe d. Church and Phillips v Perkins* (1790) 3 T R 749.

[32] *R v DaSilva* [1990] 1 WLR 31, CA; *R v South Ribble Magistrates, ex p. Cochrane* [1996] 2 Cr App R 544, DC.

[33] See, e.g., Lord Justice Auld, *Review of the Criminal Courts of England and Wales*, ch 11, para.85: 'the only condition for a witness's use of a written statement for refreshing memory [should be] that there is good reason to believe that he would have been significantly better able to recall the events in question when he made or verified it than at the time of giving evidence'.

[34] Section 139(2) confers the same evidentiary status on a transcript of a video-recorded oral statement, provided that conditions (a) and (b) are also satisfied.

section 139, even if the witness retains no spontaneous memory of the incidents in question.[35] It seems that English law has decisively turned its back on the Wigmorean conceptual distinction between 'present recollections revived' and 'past recollections received'.

The Criminal Justice Act 2003 did not rest content with the significant liberalization of memory-refreshing effected by section 139. First, as we explain more fully below, subsections 120(4) and (6) create a dedicated exception to the rule against narrative for an out-of-court statement which was 'made by the witness when the matters stated were fresh in his memory but he does not remember them, and cannot reasonably be expected to remember them, well enough to give oral evidence of them in the proceedings'. This rule of admissibility does not even retain the pretence that the witness's memory is being 'refreshed'; provided that the witness is still prepared to endorse it from the witness-box, the document is admitted for the truth of its contents. Secondly, section 137 of the CJA 2003 makes provision for the admissibility of a video-recorded statement *by any witness*, not just those designated exceptionally 'vulnerable' or 'intimidated' and eligible for the 'special measures' we will describe in Chapter 10. At the time of writing section 137 has still not been brought into force, although this may have as much to do with the financial and technological obstacles to making appropriate recording equipment available to police forces as with the revolutionary implications of routinely receiving video-recorded testimony in criminal trials. It would be a major departure from traditional conceptions of orality if live examination-in-chief were to be replaced by prerecorded witness statements in the majority of cases, just as live examination-in-chief has virtually disappeared from modern civil litigation. Not for nothing does Di Birch describe section 137 as an 'explosive device...ticking merrily'.[36]

(c) HOSTILE WITNESSES[37]

The logic of adversarial trial procedure supplies two principal reasons why a party is generally forbidden from cross-examining or 'impeaching the credibility' of his own witness. First, if a party seriously believes that a potential witness will not provide reliable evidence, he should not call that person to testify in the first place and avoid wasting the court's time. This stricture applies with particular force to prosecutors, who are expected to be 'ministers of justice' as well as adversarial parties in criminal proceedings.[38] Parties to adversarial proceedings in a sense vouch for the credibility of the witnesses they present to the court, a responsibility which is the counterpart of a party-dominated adversary procedure.[39] Secondly, it seems unfair that a person should be required to testify, under threat of punishment for contempt of court should he refuse, only to have aspersions cast upon his credibility by the party demanding his presence in court. In certain situations,

---

[35] *DPP v R* [2007] EWHC 1842 (Admin).

[36] Di Birch, 'The Criminal Justice Act 2003: (4) Hearsay – Same Old Story, Same Old Song?' [2004] *Crim LR* 556, 527.

[37] See Rosemary Pattenden, 'The Hostile Witness' (1992) 56 *Journal of Criminal Law* 414.

[38] *Grant v R* [2007] 1 AC 1, [2006] UKPC 2, [25]–[26]; *R v Preston* [1994] 2 AC 130, 146–7, HL; *R v Russell-Jones* [1995] 3 All ER 239, [1995] Crim LR 832, CA.

[39] Party-dominated proceedings, as an 'incident of adversarialism', was discussed in Chapter 2. Also see, Mirjan R. Damaška, *Evidence Law Adrift* (Yale UP, 1997), ch 4.

however, adherence to this prohibition could itself become a source of unfairness and an obstruction to discovering the truth.[40]

A party is always at liberty to contradict the testimony of his own witness by eliciting further evidence from other witnesses: in this sense, neither prosecution nor defence is bound by unexpectedly unfavourable testimony.[41] Where a witness is reluctant or evasive to the point of refusing to comply with his duty to divulge relevant information, however, the party who called him requires some means of pressing his case. In such situations, where in the old terminology the witness stood 'mute of malice', the judge may declare the witness 'hostile' and allow cross-examination by the instructing party. The common law principles[42] were encapsulated in section 3 of the Criminal Procedure Act 1865, which provides that:

A party producing a witness shall not be allowed to impeach his credit by general evidence of bad character; but he may, in case the witness in the opinion of the judge prove adverse, contradict him by other evidence, or, by leave of the judge, prove that he has made at other times a statement inconsistent with his present testimony...

Whether or not the witness's responses evince sufficient hostility to justify cross-examination is something that the judge has to decide in the light of all the circumstances of the case and what has transpired in court. 'There will be borderline cases whether a witness is hostile or merely unfavourable,' the Court of Appeal recently acknowledged, '[b]ut this is quintessentially a decision for the judge who has heard the evidence and is best placed to assess the demeanour of the witness and his animus.'[43]

Even if the witness is declared hostile, contradiction and impeachment are significantly more constrained than cross-examination of an opponent's witness. Counsel may only cross-question a hostile witness in order to elicit information relevant to the issues in the case and – hopefully – favourable to her client. As section 3 of the 1865 Act expressly states, this may be done, with the leave of the judge, only by contradicting the witness with other evidence or by demonstrating that the witness has made a previous inconsistent statement.[44] Attacks on the witness's general credibility, calculated to besmirch his character and to demonstrate to the trier of fact that the witness is not a person to be believed on his oath, are never permitted. These more aggressive tactics are traditionally reserved for

---

[40] The drawbacks of a rigid rule forbidding a party from impeaching his own witness led to abrogation of the so-called 'voucher rule' in the United States: see Christopher B. Mueller and Laird C. Kirkpatrick, *Evidence* (Aspen, 2nd edn. 1999), §6.16–§6.18. Rule 607 of the Federal Rules of Evidence provides that: 'The credibility of a witness may be attacked by any party, including the party calling the witness'. English law's flexible approach is preferable in principle, both to an absolute prohibition and to unlimited license to impeach one's own witness. In the United States, however, an accused is allowed to cross-examine a witness who unexpectedly gives evidence capable of incriminating the accused: *Chambers* v *Mississippi*, 410 US 284 (1973). This is a better approach, placing a higher premium on the protection of innocence. In England it is not enough that the accused's own witness has given unfavourable evidence against him. Cross-examination is reserved for legally 'hostile,' i.e. deliberately evasive or lying, witnesses.

[41] *Greenough* v *Eccles* (1859) 5 CB(NS) 786, Common Pleas, reaffirming *Ewer* v *Ambrose* (1825) 3 B & C 746.

[42] *R* v *Thompson* (1976) 64 Cr App R 96, CA.   [43] *R* v *Greene* [2009] EWCA Crim 2282, [67].

[44] Criminal Procedure Act 1865, s.3. Like cross-examination itself, the use of previous statements is subject to judicial permission: see *R* v *Booth* (1982) 74 Cr App R 123, CA. At common law, previous inconsistent statements were admissible only to credit: *R* v *Thomas* [1985] Crim LR 445; *R* v *Khan* [2003] Crim LR 428. Pursuant to CJA 2003, s.119, they are now admissible for their truth: *R* v *Joyce and Joyce* [2005] EWCA Crim 1785. These developments are explained and critically evaluated in §8.5 and §8.6, below.

an opponent's witnesses, and even here, Parliament has recently intervened to curtail the more flamboyant and theatrical extremes of cross-examination – as we will see later in the chapter.

8.3 THE RULE AGAINST NARRATIVE

The legal doctrine we will call the 'rule against narrative' is also variously known as the rule against previous consistent statements, the rule against self-serving statements, and the rule prohibiting a party from bolstering the credit of his own witness through 'self-corroboration'.[45] However styled, the substance of the rule is that a party may not adduce evidence of his witness's out-of-court statements simply to demonstrate consistency with the witness's courtroom testimony. There is good reason to discourage proof or mere narrative consistency. First, in many instances previous consistent statements add little if any weight to the witness's testimony and are therefore superfluous and possibly irrelevant. As Mr Justice Humphreys explained in *Roberts*:[46]

a party is not permitted to make evidence for himself.... [Such] evidence is said to be inadmissible on the ground that it is irrelevant. It would not help the jury in this case in the least to be told that [the accused] said to a number of persons, whom he saw while he was waiting his trial... that his defence was this, or that or the other...

Secondly, the introduction of previous consistent statements will often raise unnecessary side issues leading to confusion and delay. Third (a different way of expressing their irrelevance), such statements may be used artificially to bolster the credibility of the witness and so mislead the fact-finder about the true probative value of her evidence, as if saying the same thing over and over again somehow made it commensurately more likely to be true.[47]

The common law recognized numerous exceptions to the rule against narrative. Although there is broad agreement about the number and scope of the core exceptions, courts and commentators have offered competing specifications of the full detailed list.[48] The task of identifying exceptions to the rule against narrative is complicated by its entanglement with the law of hearsay.[49] The underlying principle which common law doctrines attempted to put into effect, however, was that previous consistent statements should exceptionally be admissible *only in order to support the witness's credibility* where, for some identifiable circumstantial reason, proof of consistency was *not* merely (almost) irrelevant narrative, but had genuine probative value in determining disputed questions of fact. This might be because the witness was making an allegation regarded as inherently lacking

---

[45] Cf. *R* v *Turner* [1975] QB 834, 842, CA.

[46] *R* v *Roberts* [1942] 1 All ER 187, CCA.

[47] Previous statements specially designed for use in litigation are especially dubious: see *Fox* v *General Medical Council* [1960] 1 WLR 1017, PC; *Corke* v *Corke and Cook* [1958] P 93, CA.

[48] R. N. Gooderson, 'Previous Consistent Statements' [1968] *CLJ* 64.

[49] Certain doctrines sometimes included on the list of common law exceptions to the rule against narrative, such as *res gestae*, statements on being accused or confronted with incriminating articles, and mixed statements, are more appropriately regarded as exceptions to the hearsay rule, and will be dealt with under that rubric in Chapter 9.

in credibility or because the witness had been directly accused in cross-examination of fabricating their testimony, for example. It is controversial whether the common law rules were successful in differentiating previous consistent statements with probative value from mere narrative. There is a familiar pattern of rigid and restrictive nineteenth century doctrines gradually giving way, over the course of the twentieth century, to more flexible procedural standards calibrated towards truth-finding.

Common law exceptions to the rule against narrative were in large measure superseded by section 120 of the Criminal Justice Act 2003, which, despite its length, merits quotation in full:

s.120 – Other previous statements of witnesses

(1) This section applies where a person (the witness) is called to give evidence in criminal proceedings.

(2) If a previous statement by the witness is admitted as evidence to rebut a suggestion that his oral evidence has been fabricated, that statement is admissible as evidence of any matter stated of which oral evidence by the witness would be admissible.

(3) A statement made by the witness in a document—

    (a) which is used by him to refresh his memory while giving evidence,

    (b) on which he is cross-examined, and

    (c) which as a consequence is received in evidence in the proceedings, is admissible as evidence of any matter stated of which oral evidence by him would be admissible.

(4) A previous statement by the witness is admissible as evidence of any matter stated of which oral evidence by him would be admissible, if—

    (a) any of the following three conditions is satisfied, and

    (b) while giving evidence the witness indicates that to the best of his belief he made the statement, and that to the best of his belief it states the truth.

(5) The first condition is that the statement identifies or describes a person, object or place.

(6) The second condition is that the statement was made by the witness when the matters stated were fresh in his memory but he does not remember them, and cannot reasonably be expected to remember them, well enough to give oral evidence of them in the proceedings.

(7) The third condition is that—

    (a) the witness claims to be a person against whom an offence has been committed,

    (b) the offence is one to which the proceedings relate,

    (c) the statement consists of a complaint made by the witness (whether to a person in authority or not) about conduct which would, if proved, constitute the offence or part of the offence,

    (d) the complaint was made as soon as could reasonably be expected after the alleged conduct,

    (e) the complaint was not made as a result of a threat or a promise, and

    (f) before the statement is adduced the witness gives oral evidence in connection with its subject matter.

(8) For the purposes of subsection (7) the fact that the complaint was elicited (for example, by a leading question) is irrelevant unless a threat or a promise was involved.

Section 120 is modelled on and around the core common law exceptions to the rule against narrative, which it also refines and extends in significant ways. By virtue of section 120(1), it applies only to the out-of-court statements of witnesses who actually testify in the trial. It has no application to hearsay statements generally.[50] A threshold objection to the admissibility of all out-of-court statements is that they are hearsay if they are adduced for their truth. However, previous consistent (and previous *inconsistent*) statements are the mildest form of hearsay, to the extent that they are hearsay at all.[51] By definition, the witness is in court and can be cross-examined on his previous statements as well as on his courtroom testimony.[52]

Subsection 120(2) is drafted as a rule of use – a forensic reasoning rule[53] – rather than a rule of admissibility. It assumes the continued existence of the common law exception to the rule against narrative, which permits previous consistent statements to rebut allegations of recent fabrication (as opposed merely to rehabilitating a witness whose evidence was torn to shreds in cross-examination, which is not permitted).[54] If a cross-examiner puts it to the witness that they have invented their testimony, perhaps to fit in with subsequent events or to match what other witnesses might say, it would be helpful to the fact-finder to know (where this is the case) that the witness has consistently said the same thing, even *before* the witness is supposed to have concocted a story. In these circumstances, the previous consistent statement logically contradicts the allegation of fabrication and rehabilitates the credibility of the witness, perfectly illustrating the underlying rationale of all traditional exceptions to the rule against narrative. Since the exception is motivated by a desire to promote accurate fact-finding, its trigger is not the intentions of the cross-examiner but the impression that a particular line of questioning might convey to a reasonable jury. Indeed, the exception may be triggered even where counsel goes out of her way *to avoid* any direct allegation of recent fabrication, if the implicit thrust of cross-examination is that the witness is deliberately spinning a yarn.[55] Likewise, the notion of 'recent' fabrication refers not to the time of the trial or to the underlying incident, but to the point at which the cross-examiner is claiming or implying that the witness made up her evidence. So long as the previous consistent statement predates the alleged time of fabrication it logically rebuts the allegation or implication.[56]

The common law exception permits an out-of-court statement adduced to rebut allegations of recent fabrication (only) to lend weight to the credibility of the witness's courtroom

[50] Section 120 mirrors the common law in this respect: cf. *R v Wallwork* (1958) 42 Cr App R 153, CCA; *Sparks v R* [1964] AC 964, PC.   [51] See Chapter 9.

[52] For general discussion, see Lee Stuesser, 'Admitting Prior Inconsistent Statements for Their Truth' (1992) 71 *Canadian Bar Review* 48. Law Com No 245, *Evidence in Criminal Proceedings: Hearsay and Related Topics*, Cm 3670 (TSO, 1997), para.10.11, observes that '[t]he main justification for the hearsay rule, namely the impossibility of cross-examining the declarant, clearly has no force where the witness testifies and is available for cross-examination'.   [53] See Chapter 15.

[54] *R v Oyesiku* (1971) 56 Cr App R 240, CA; *R v Ali* [2004] 1 Cr App R 501, CA: cf. *R v Beattie* (1989) 89 Cr App R 302, 306–7, CA. For illuminating discussion of relevant considerations, see *National Defendant* v *Clements* (1961) 104 CLR 476.

[55] *R v Athwal (Bachan) and Athwal (Sukhdave)* [2009] 2 Cr App R 14; [2009] EWCA Crim 789; *R v Gregson* [2003] 2 Cr App R 34, [2003] EWCA Crim 1099.

[56] '[W]e do not consider that the common law label of recent fabrication is to be confined within a temporal straitjacket... "recent" is an elastic description, the purpose of which is to assist in the identification of circumstances in which the traditional rule against self-corroboration, sometimes referred to as the rule against narrative, should not extend to the exclusion of a previous consistent statement where there is a rational and potentially cogent basis for its use as a tool for deciding where the truth lies': *R v Athwal* [2009] 2 Cr App R 14, [58].

testimony. Section 120(2), by contrast, specifically states that such statements are 'admissible as evidence of any matter stated of which oral evidence by the witness would be admissible'. In other words, they go to the issue as well as to credit. The intended effect of section 120(2) was therefore to 'piggy-back' on the common law exception ('*If* a previous statement by the witness is admitted as evidence to rebut a suggestion that his oral evidence has been fabricated...'), transforming the evidentiary significance of such statements *if* and to the extent that they are admitted at common law. However, this analysis was considered and expressly rejected by the Court of Appeal in *Athwal*. According to the court, interpretation of the overall framework of the 2003 Act 'leads inexorably to the conclusion that a previous statement which is admitted to rebut a suggestion of fabrication is admitted as admissible hearsay under the regime of the 2003 Act'.[57] If the court is right, statements admitted under this or any other part of section 120 must also satisfy the detailed rules pertaining to hearsay statements, which are discussed in the next chapter. The ruling in *Athwal* is a dubious and jurisprudentially heretical piece of statutory interpretation which may not survive further judicial scrutiny. For the time being it is likely to cause problems in practice, not least in relation to the rules requiring parties to give advance notice of an intention to adduce hearsay statements.[58]

Section 120(3) relates to an old common law doctrine[59] ancillary to the rules governing memory-refreshing, which we have already explained. At common law, a statement used to refresh the witness's memory is not evidence in the case. The other party or parties to the litigation are normally allowed to inspect the memory-refreshing document, and may cross-examine the witness on it. So long as the cross-examination is confined to those matters on which the witness has already testified the document does not itself become evidence in the case. However, the document may become evidence on the election of the party calling the witness if the cross-examiner strays beyond the scope of the witness's evidence in-chief. Section 120(3) is drafted in parallel terms to section 120(2), as a rule of use, converting out-of-court statements adduced at common law to credit into 'evidence of any matter stated of which oral evidence by [the witness] would be admissible'. In *Pashmfouroush* the Court of Appeal endorsed the orthodox interpretation, that '[s]ection 120(3) does not provide for the circumstances in which a documentary statement may be received in evidence, but provides for the evidential status of a document where it is received in evidence. Whether it should be received in evidence in the first place is subject to the former common law rules.'[60] These remarks are plainly at odds with the reasoning in *Athwal*, and should, in our submission, be preferred to it.

Subsection 120(4) has two purposes. Firstly, and in contrast to subsections (2) and (3)'s implicit references to common law exceptions, subsection (4) explicitly creates three new rules of admissibility which supersede the common law. Secondly, it imposes a generic criterion applicable to all of these new statutory exceptions to the rule against narrative. In every case, 'while giving evidence the witness [must] indicate [] that to the best of his belief he made the statement, and that to the best of his belief it states the truth'.

The first new statutory exception to the rule against narrative, contained in subsection 120(5), unproblematically restates the common law rule. In view of the obvious probative

---

[57] ibid. [53].   [58] A practical difficulty acknowledged in *Athwal* itself, but brushed aside: ibid. [54].

[59] Restated and applied in *R v Britton* [1987] 1 WLR 539, CA.

[60] *R v Pashmfouroush and Pashmfouroush* [2006] EWCA Crim 2330, [25].

limitations and exaggerated theatricality of courtroom 'dock identifications',[61] the long-established practice is to elicit evidence of a witness's previous out-of-court identification before asking him whether he can now see that person present in court.[62] Although it has occasionally been the subject of rather strained applications,[63] the common law rule's underlying rationale is sound and its statutory re-enactment and extension to places and objects cannot be faulted.

The second new statutory exception, contained in subsection 120(6), has already been mentioned in relation to memory-refreshing. We can now appreciate why subsection (6) represents a more decisive break with the common law tradition of orality. Section 139 preserves the formal distinction that memory-refreshing documents are not evidence in the case, even if this is merely a fiction in some or even many instances where 'memory-refreshing' is in reality 'reading aloud'. Subsection 120(6) dispenses with these niceties. If the witness has forgotten details that he could not reasonably be expected to remember – perhaps the precise time of an incident, a telephone number, or vehicle registration-plate – an out-of-court document containing the witness's more complete recollections may be admissible in its own right, in which case it goes directly to the issue; necessarily so, because (by definition) the witness is unable to remember the details in question and therefore cannot testify to them. All the witness can, and for the purposes of admissibility must, do is affirm his belief that the document faithfully records his now-forgotten recollections. The witness's testimonial credibility is engaged only in relation to *that* auxiliary question. In terms of its substantive content, the document is allowed to speak for itself.

The third statutory exception elaborated in some detail by subsections 120(7) and (8) supersedes the common law doctrine of 'recent complaint', which permitted evidence of prior complaints made soon after the incident by victims of sexual assault to be adduced in support of the victim's testimony.[64] Such statements had to be sufficiently spontaneous, as well as roughly contemporaneous with the alleged assault,[65] to qualify for admissibility under the complainant rule. Section 120(7) is considerably broader than the old common law doctrine, particularly as it applies to *all* complainants not merely those alleging sexual offences. The complaint must still be spontaneous, in the sense of being uncoerced by threats or promises, but it does not matter if the complaint was elicited by a leading question. This is more or less what the common law already said.[66] The further requirement that a qualifying complaint must be 'recent' invites arbitrary line-drawing and has, quite predictably, attracted criticism. In *Birks*[67] the Court of Appeal confirmed that 'recent complaints' must be made 'within a reasonable time of the alleged offence' to be admissible

---

[61] *R* v *Cartwright* (1914) 10 Cr App R 219, CCA.   [62] *R* v *Christie* [1914] AC 545, HL.

[63] *R* v *McCay* [1990] 1 WLR 645, CA (evidence of positive out-of-court identification provided by a third party); *R* v *Cook* [1987] QB 417, CA (treating a 'sketch or photofit by a police officer making a graphic representation of a witness's memory as another form of the camera at work, albeit imperfectly and not produced contemporaneously with the material incident but soon or fairly soon afterwards').

[64] *R* v *Valentine* [1996] 2 Cr App R 213, CA; *R* v *Lillyman* [1896] 2 QB 167; *R* v *Osborne* [1905] 1 KB 551, CCR.

[65] Cf. *R* v *Y* [1995] Crim LR 155, CA, where the statement was contemporaneous with the event triggering the complaint (an unrelated assault on a third party at school), as opposed to being contemporaneous with the assault itself. Quashing the conviction, the Court of Appeal held that the statement should not have been admitted. The statement, being written *after* the complaint-triggering event, did not even go to rebut the allegation that the complainant had fabricated the allegation after witnessing the assault at school.

[66] *R* v *Norcott* [1917] 1 KB 347, CCA.

[67] *R* v *Birks* [2003] 2 Cr App R 122, [2002] EWCA Crim 3091.

at common law. However, Rix LJ added *per curiam* that it would be better to relax the traditional constraints on admissibility so that the jury would not be 'kept in the dark as to what has happened'. As originally drafted, section 120(7)(d) introduced the requirement that 'the complaint was made as soon as could reasonably be expected after the alleged conduct', which might be regarded as a substantially relaxed variation on common law recency. A complaint of, e.g., child sexual abuse might be disclosed months or even years after the assault, but still satisfy the test if delay is explicable in terms of the complainant's fear, distress, natural disinclination to incriminate a carer or sibling, etc.[68] But on reflection Parliament decided to press the matter even further. The Coroners and Justice Act 2009 deletes paragraph (d) from section 120(7), dispensing entirely with any recency criterion to regulate the admissibility of 'recent complaints'.[69]

The rationale for the common law exception to the rule against narrative for recent complainants in sex cases was always rather obscure. It is probably best understood as a partial concession to a class of complainants who in virtually every other respect were given a very hard time by criminal trial procedure, through demanding competence and corroboration requirements, a cultural tendency towards disbelief and aggressive cross-examination to credit. Section 120 severs the historical link to sexual offences and recency survives only as a logical precondition of reliable memory or rebutting allegations of fabrication. The law has been simplified in favour of admissibility, but one may legitimately ask what remains of the common law's traditional bar on narrative so far as it pertains to complainant-witnesses. Indeed, there are occasional hints that the Court of Appeal no longer takes the rule against narrative very seriously.[70]

In these circumstances, it may be unhelpful and potentially misleading to conceptualize narrative consistent statements as being subject to a hard-and-fast rule of exclusion with limited exceptions. Both the Law Commission[71] and the *Auld Review*[72] recommended that criminal trial procedure should be governed by general principles of admissibility, anchored in fairness and probative value. The time has long since passed when proposing a shift from rules to principles in regulating the course of the trial might be regarded as dangerous revolutionary thinking. Contextual judgments of relevance and discretionary exclusion are classically matters for the trial judge to determine on the facts. In practice, one would expect judges to continue to work with the default assumption that previous consistent statements lack probative value. Such statements usually are in fact literally – or almost literally – irrelevant and worthless, and are rightly excluded, often with no more than cursory consideration of their flimsy claims to admissibility. But trial judges should be prepared and empowered to reassess the situation where a plausible argument for admissibility is made out on the facts.

Section 120 of the CJA 2003 gives trial judges considerably more latitude to admit previous consistent statements than the old common law exceptions to the rule against

[68] *R v Peter K and Terence K* [2008] EWCA Crim 434.   [69] Coroners and Justice Act 2009, s.112.

[70] Cf. *R v Avery* [2007] EWCA Crim 1830, (objection that the complainant's previous statement failed to satisfy s.120 was 'technically good' but did not affect the safety of the conviction – even where the jury had been directed that it could rely on the (inadmissible) out-of-court complaints as evidence of their truth).

[71] Law Com No 245, *Evidence in Criminal Proceedings: Hearsay and Related Topics*, Cm 3670 (TSO, 1997), Part X and Recommendations 34–40.

[72] Lord Justice Auld, *Review of the Criminal Courts of England and Wales: Report* (TSO, 2001), ch 11, paras.86–92.

narrative. What is more, when received, previous consistent statements are admitted for their truth. It is conceivable that some genuinely probative out-of-court statements of (non-complainant) witnesses would still be excluded under these rules. However, there is no genuine lacuna in the law. As we will see in the next chapter, English law now has a general inclusionary discretion applicable to *all* hearsay statements, whether or not the declarant appears as a witness in the trial.[73] In other words, even if a previous statement could not technically be admitted by way of exception to the rule against narrative it could in principle be admitted directly by way of exception to the more fundamental hearsay prohibition. Flexibility in the admission of out-of-court statements has therefore been achieved as a matter of law, and responsibility for the success of this admissibility regime in practice consequently now rests with trial judges and counsel. Trial judges must strive to ensure that the jury has access to genuinely probative information, whilst filtering out the dross and directing the jury accordingly. Opposing counsel should be alert to impress upon the jury, in appropriate cases, that the fact that the witness has said the same thing before does not necessarily mean that either the witness's previous out-of-court statement or her courtroom testimony is true and reliable.

8.4 CROSS-EXAMINATION AND WITNESS CREDIBILITY

Cross-examination has long been regarded within legal circles as the most effective method for testing a witness's evidence, epitomized, as we saw in the last chapter, by Wigmore's encomium to the 'greatest legal engine...'[74] The cross-examiner employs tactics designed to extract disclosures which the witness is reluctant to make, to prompt contradiction, to undermine confidence, to cast doubt on honesty and reliability, and generally to try to detract from the value of the testimony which the witness has given in-chief. While such impeachment methods are useful for ascertaining the truth and demonstrating that serious allegations have been fairly and rigorously tested, adversarial cross-examination could easily be abused or become oppressive. Legal constraints consequently have to be put in place to keep cross-examination within the bounds of propriety and in the service of effective fact-finding. Our discussion will focus on two dimensions of this problem. First, in this section, we explore the legal and ethical boundaries of cross-examination specifically targeting the witness's credibility. The following section then examines legal rules which regulate the extent to which a witness's initial denials can be contradicted by other evidence.

The probative force of testimony rests on four analytically distinct factors: (i) the reliability of the witness's initial perceptions; (ii) the accuracy of the witness's memory; (iii) his truthfulness when testifying; and (iv) effective communication to the fact-finder. Cross-examination bears on all four factors, but is particularly associated with testing a witness's truthfulness or 'veracity'. Broadly speaking, advocates may adopt either one of two approaches, singly or in combination, to impugn the veracity of an opponent's witness. Most straightforwardly, the advocate might attempt to show that the witness has given

---

[73] CJA 2003, s.114(1)(d).   [74] §7.1(b).

false testimony on particular points, by extracting an admission from the witness that he has lied, for example, or by calling other witnesses to contradict his evidence. Alternatively, the cross-examiner could attack the witness's general character; in order to suggest that the witness is not the kind of person who can be believed on his oath. The choice, one might say, is between direct and indirect proof of mendacity. Whilst mendacious testimony might be exposed directly be showing that it is contradicted by accepted facts, indirect proof of mendacity completely bypasses the content of the witness's evidence-in-chief and concentrates instead on his general record for truth-telling. Common sense – and the fable of the little shepherd-boy who cried 'Wolf!' – tell us that the testimony of an habitual liar should carry less weight than the testimony of a person of average truthfulness, and much less than the testimony of a paragon of honesty. Both the direct and the indirect approaches are alike calculated to diminish the probative value of the witness's testimony, but each adopts a distinctive strategy in pursuit of that common goal.

There is, however, rather more to the evidential significance of cross-examination than a narrow conceptual or doctrinal analysis can convey. For a cross-examiner resorting to the second, indirect approach sometimes intends, not just to diminish the probative value of testimony, but to impugn the witness's entire moral character. In these circumstances the cross-examiner goes beyond merely showing that the witness's word should carry less weight with the fact-finder, to imply that the moral standing or virtue of the witness is so compromised that no verdict could properly be based on his testimony.[75] The narrowly factual dimensions of a witness's veracity might be termed his 'probative credibility', in contradistinction to his 'moral credibility' – the tendency of a witness's moral standing to impact on the fact-finder's evaluation of his evidence. This is meant to be a loosely-specified functional distinction. There is certainly no categorical assumption that a person of dubious moral character can never be a truthful and compelling witness in a criminal trial. Nonetheless, law and legal practice have traditionally embraced the notion that a witness's testimony may be partly or even wholly discounted on grounds of moral (in)credibility, whether or not evidence is also evaluated in terms of the witness's probative credibility, more narrowly tied to the facts of the case.

Moral credibility has always played its part in criminal trials. As we saw in the previous chapter,[76] the long-standing testimonial incompetence of non-Christians, though ostensibly a function of their inability to swear an oath on the New Testament, sprang partly from a contemporary popular association between religious or racial difference and moral inferiority.[77] Today our moral beliefs are, generally speaking, more rational and coherent, but it would be naïve to suppose that narrow-minded preconceptions and moral prejudice no longer influence criminal adjudication. Indeed, the intrusion of moral evaluation into forensic fact-finding is celebrated in certain contexts, for example in arguments advocating the jury's (contested) authority to return a verdict of not guilty against the weight of evidence.[78] The question is not whether moral appraisal can be purged from such an

---

[75] See Rosemary Pattenden, 'The Character of Victims and Third Parties in Criminal Proceedings Other than Rape Trials' [1986] *Crim LR* 367. On the American law, see Richard C. Wydick, 'Character Evidence: A Guided Tour of the Grotesque Structure' (1987) 21 *UC Davis LR* 123. [76] §7.2.

[77] Wigmore accounted for the disqualification of non-Christians in terms of a 'deep-rooted instinct to distrust the alien of another nation, – much more the alien of another creed or race or color': *Wigmore on Evidence* (3rd edn. 1940), vol. 2, §§515–516.

[78] So-called 'jury equity' or, in America, 'jury nullification': see §2.4.

inherently morally-loaded enterprise as criminal adjudication, but rather whether morally-principled judgments can be insulated from corruption through unfair discrimination and prejudice.

A rational system of adjudication must limit the extent to which moral credibility can be allowed to influence the judgment of the trier of fact and distract attention from a balanced assessment of probative credibility. Criminal trials cannot be allowed to descend to the level of beauty pageants or personal popularity contests. This concern is especially acute in relation to the moral character of the accused: any person with previous convictions or an otherwise disreputable character is potentially at risk of being condemned for his past life rather than being judged on the basis of evidence proving that he has committed the offence with which he currently stands charged. The detailed legal rules and principles regulating the admissibility of the accused's bad character are explored at length in Chapter 14. Here, our focus is confined to cross-examiners' attacks on the moral credibility of witnesses other than the accused.

Historically, the law conceded surprisingly broad leeway to impugn the moral credibility of an opponent's witnesses during cross-examination. The common law permitted any question relating to the general character or past conduct of a witness that might have a significant bearing on jurors' evaluation of that witness's evidence.[79] This generous standard invalidated only questions about very trivial matters or those remote in time, such as 20-year-old convictions of driving offences or an adult's childhood misbehaviour in the school playground.[80] Within these broad parameters, a witness could be challenged on just about any arguably discreditable character trait, preference, or incident in his past. The only additional practical constraint was that the opposing advocate must first have been supplied with the ammunition for cross-examination, in the case of defence counsel, usually by the accused or another defence witness but also through prosecution disclosure.[81] He was then armed 'to delve into a man's past and to drag up such dirt as [he] can find there'.[82]

No prospective witness in a criminal trial would relish the prospect of being ambushed by cross-examination on possibly long-forgotten incidents and subjected to what, by both experience and design, may amount to character assassination on matters which most people would regard as irrelevant to the proceedings. Shabby treatment of witnesses is objectionable *per se*, and may engage the state's duty of humane treatment if apparently tolerated and allowed to continue without restraint, sanction, or redress. It is also counterproductive in terms of criminal justice policy at a time when there is already serious

---

[79] *Hobbs* v *Tinling* [1929] 2 KB 1, CA, adopting principles laid down in Stephen's Indian Evidence Act 1872.

[80] *R* v *Sweet-Escott* (1971) 55 Cr App R 316, Western Circuit. Lawton J. suggested by way of illustration that it would *not* be permissible to cross-examine an elderly man about his having been caned at school for stealing from another boy's desk. Another restriction is that 'spent' convictions may only be referred to in criminal proceedings with the leave of the judge, since it would be inconsistent with the rehabilitative ethos of the Rehabilitation of Offenders Act 1974 to permit unconstrained reference to them: *Practice Direction (Crime: Spent Convictions)* [1975] 1 WLR 1065.

[81] Information that could be used to cross-examine prosecution witnesses and '[a]ny material that might go to the credibility of a prosecution witness' must normally be disclosed by the prosecution: see *Attorney General's Guidelines on Disclosure*, paras. 8–12, on-line at: www.attorneygeneral.gov.uk/Publications/Pages/AttorneyGeneralsGuidelines.aspx.

[82] *R* v *Sweet-Escott* (1971) 55 Cr App R 316, 320, *per* Lawton J.

concern that many people are reluctant to testify as witnesses in criminal trials.[83] Some groups have experienced particular difficulties. Perhaps the worst treatment has been meted out to complainants of rape and other sexual assaults, whose previous sexual history and other 'misconduct' has routinely been paraded before the court with the clear intention of undermining their moral standing in the eyes of the jury.[84] This strategy plays up to jurors' high-minded moralism, in the hope that they will discount the gravity of harms suffered by victims perceived as lacking virtue or merit as complainants. 'Perhaps she invited trouble,' jurors might think to themselves, 'but even if she *was* raped, it cannot be so bad for a promiscuous woman.' The specific issue of previous sexual history evidence has twice been addressed by the legislature in modern times, as we shall see in Chapter 10. But the root of the problem, viewed in broader perspective, is that English law has been too lax in accepting the relevance and admissibility of evidence purporting to bear on a witness's credibility. Judges should be alert to prevent cross-examiners from pursuing lines of questioning the sole or primary purpose of which is to damn the witness with moral prejudice.

The Law Commission concluded that cross-examination to credit should not be permitted unless the probative value of such questioning, in terms of the genuine light that it might throw on the value of the witness's testimony, was sufficient to offset any moral prejudice that might in consequence be suffered by the witness.[85] This policy recommendation was enacted by section 100 of the Criminal Justice Act 2003 in the following terms:

s.100 – Non-defendant's bad character

(1) In criminal proceedings evidence of the bad character of a person other than the defendant is admissible if and only if –

    (a) it is important explanatory evidence,

    (b) it has substantial probative value in relation to a matter which—

        (i) is a matter in issue in the proceedings, and

        (ii) is of substantial importance in the context of the case as a whole, or

    (c) all parties to the proceedings agree to the evidence being admissible.

'Important explanatory evidence' is further defined as evidence without which 'the court or jury would find it impossible or difficult properly to understand other evidence in the

---

[83] In one survey, only 76% of witnesses said that they would be happy to testify in another trial; and of those witnesses who were dissatisfied with their first experience, a mere 6% said that they would be happy to repeat it: Emmy Whitehead, *Witness Satisfaction: Findings from the Witness Satisfaction Survey 2000*, HORS 230 (Home Office RDS, 2001).

[84] These uncomfortable allegations are backed-up by empirical research: for data and discussion, see Jennifer Temkin, 'Prosecuting and Defending Rape: Perspectives from the Bar' (2000) 27 *Journal of Law and Society* 219; Jessica Harris and Sharon Grace, *A Question of Evidence? Investigating and Prosecuting Rape in the 1990s*, HORS Research Study No 196 (Home Office, 1999), ch 6; Louise Ellison, 'Cross-Examination in Rape Trials' [1998] *Crim LR* 605; Zsuzsanna Adler, *Rape on Trial* (Routledge, 1987); Gerry Chambers and Ann Millar, 'Proving Sexual Assault: Prosecuting the Offender or Persecuting the Victim?' in Pat Carlen and Anne Worrall (eds.), *Gender, Crime and Justice* (Open UP, 1987).

[85] Law Com No 273, *Evidence of Bad Character in Criminal Proceedings*. Cm 5257 (TSO, 2001), Part IX and Recommendations 3–6. The Commission's own formulation was that 'the test of enhanced relevance should be whether the evidence has substantial probative value in relation to a matter in issue which is itself of substantial importance in the context of the case as a whole': ibid. para.9.39. As well as invoking the conceptual solecism of 'enhanced relevance' (see §3.2), this is perhaps a somewhat convoluted way of expressing the idea of significant probative value.

case, and...its value for understanding the case as a whole is substantial'.[86] Judges must assess 'substantial probative value' for the purposes of section 100(1)(b) in accordance with a detailed list of factors set out in subsection 100(3) and pertaining to the nature and timing of extraneous events constituting bad character evidence and their asserted connection to disputed matters in the instant case. Notwithstanding its convoluted drafting, section 100's intention to establish a PV > PE standard for the admissibility of witnesses' bad character evidence is tolerably clear. Such evidence cannot now be given or elicited through cross-examination without the express leave of the court.[87] The Court of Appeal has emphasized that these provisions 'introduce new and careful restrictions to what had previously been hitherto regarded as "fair game" when a witness is called by the prosecution'.[88]

The common law arguably already provided sufficient principles and precedents to achieve a fair balance between vigorous probing of testimony and solicitous protection of the witness from moral character assassination, yet the history of judicial supervision of cross-examination has been notably undistinguished.[89] Part of the problem might be laid at the door of the vague and open-ended nature of common law standards, in 'an area where it is impossible and would be unwise to lay down hard and fast rules as to how the Court should exercise its discretion'.[90] Section 100 of the CJA 2003 has introduced a fairly elaborate regulatory framework, but paradoxically, its very detail might actually *expand* trial judges' discretion whilst providing them with little useful guidance on how to exercise it wisely. As we will explore at greater length in Chapter 14 in relation to the accused's bad character, for all its sometimes byzantine complexity, the CJA 2003 leaves its basic concepts – including the pivotal concept of 'bad character' – largely undefined. Early decisions on the Act betray considerable inconsistency in trial judges' assessments of the type of activity falling within the scope of section 100,[91] whilst the Court of Appeal has announced that it will not intervene with correctives unless such determinations are (in the minds of appellate judges) clearly indefensible.[92] This regime might well provide greater protection to some witnesses, but – if early indications are anything to go by – only on a rather selective and uneven basis. It is also somewhat ironic that (some) witnesses

---

[86] s.100(2).

[87] s.100(4); unless the evidence is adduced by consent of the parties pursuant to s.100(1)(c).

[88] R v *Lennon* [2008] EWCA Crim 3305, [9], *per* Moses LJ.

[89] Periodic moral panics over excessively aggressive and demeaning cross-examination date back to the eighteenth century: see Jill Hunter, 'Battling a Good Story: Cross-Examining the Failure of the Law of Evidence', in Paul Roberts and Mike Redmayne (eds.), *Innovations in Evidence and Proof* (Hart, 2007), 266–8; John H. Langbein, *The Origins of Adversary Criminal Trial* (OUP, 2003), 306–10; J. M. Beattie, 'Scales of Justice: Defense Counsel and the English Criminal Trial in the Eighteenth and Nineteenth Centuries' (1991) 9 *Law and History Review* 221; Albert W. Alschuler, 'How to Win the Trial of the Century: The Ethics of Lord Brougham and the O. J. Simpson Defense Team' (1998) 29 *McGeorge Law Review* 291

[90] R v *Edwards* (1991) 93 Cr App R 48, 56, CA.

[91] Compare, for example, R v *Highton* (Carp's appeal) [2006] 1 Cr App R 7; [2005] EWCA Crim 1985; with R v *Renda* (Razaq's appeal) [2006] 1 WLR 2948, [2005] EWCA Crim 2826). For general discussion, see James Goudkamp, 'Bad Character Evidence and Reprehensible Behaviour' (2008) 12 *E & P* 116; Roderick Munday, 'What Constitutes "Other Reprehensible Behaviour" under the Bad Character Provisions of the Criminal Justice Act 2003?' [2005] *Crim LR* 24.

[92] 'These decisions have always to be reached in a particular factual context. We lack what is sometimes described as the trial judge's "feel" for the case. We should therefore hesitate before interfering with his conclusion in a matter of judgment': R v *Renda* (Osbourne's appeal) [2006] 1 WLR 2948, [2005] EWCA Crim 2826, [57] (Sir Igor Judge P.).

may now be shielded from cross-examination on their records just at the moment when evidence of *the accused's* bad character has become more readily admissible under the CJA 2003. Viewed purely from the perspective of common sense relevance, sauce for the goose ought to be jelly for the gander. The extent to which the accused's extraneous misconduct may be adduced to his detriment under the 2003 Act is explored in Chapter 14.

A vital lesson to be drawn from recent reform efforts (not to mention the centuries of common law experience preceding them) is that regulating witness examination is not only, or even primarily, a question of designing the most appropriate rules of law and practice. Lawyers' habitual trial practice, the ethics of advocacy, and judicial cultures are the principal determinants of cross-examination styles and tactics.[93] The structural framework of adversarial proceedings is also important. The parties control the development of their respective cases, and trial judges have not traditionally been sufficiently well-informed about the issues in the case to intervene with confidence in order to close down speculative lines of questioning and keep counsel on the straight and narrow. Moreover, trial judges are understandably reluctant to interfere too much in the conduct of the defence case for fear of provoking appeals. More extensive pre-trial disclosure and the modern emphasis on active judicial case management are gradually changing the balance of power between advocates and trial judges, but how far this will impact on judicial control of witness examination during criminal trials remains to be seen. If section 100 of the CJA 2003 has reinvigorated the cause of protecting witnesses from unjustifiably aggressive and humiliating cross-examination and swept away some old common law dogmas,[94] the law's aspirations for criminal trial procedure ultimately rest with the conduct of counsel and trial judges in individual cases – as, in significant measure, they always must.

8.5 COLLATERAL-FINALITY

On first principles, any evidence may be adduced, or question asked in cross-examination, provided only that it is (1) relevant and (2) not subject to any applicable exclusionary rule.[95] Generally speaking, the same legal rules and principles governing the admissibility of evidence in-chief also regulate the scope of permissible questioning in cross-examination.[96] The main additional rule of exclusion specifically applicable to cross-examination is the doctrine of 'collateral-finality', according to which a witness's answers to questions on collateral matters cannot be rebutted by independent evidence, but must be accepted by the questioner as final. This does not mean that the cross-examiner is obliged to assent to what the witness has said in her testimony; only that the witness's answers cannot be contradicted directly by adducing further evidence on the disputed issue. Legal orthodoxy has it that such rebuttal evidence would not be relevant to any issue in the case, but only to the 'collateral' question of the witness's credibility, and is therefore, in general, inadmissible.

---

[93] To similar effect, see Jill Hunter, 'Battling a Good Story: Cross-Examining the Failure of the Law of Evidence', in Paul Roberts and Mike Redmayne (eds.), *Innovations in Evidence and Proof* (Hart, 2007).

[94] Like the notion that all previous convictions go to credit, even if they have no logical connection with testimonial dishonesty: cf. *Clifford* v *Clifford* [1961] 3 All ER 231, HC.   [95] §3.1.

[96] *R* v *Treacy* [1944] 2 All ER 229, CCA.

The collateral-finality rule depends for its smooth operation on the availability of a reasonably robust and comprehensible conceptual distinction between evidence or questions 'going to the issue' and evidence or questions that are 'merely collateral'. The classic legal test was articulated by Pollock CB in *A-G v Hitchcock*:

> The test of whether an inquiry is collateral or not is this: if the answer of a witness is a matter which you would be allowed on your part to prove in evidence – if it have such a connection with the issue, that you would be allowed to give it in evidence – then it is a matter on which you may contradict him.[97]

In due course it will be necessary to reconsider the juridical and moral credentials of the *Hitchcock* test, and to question its practical utility. Modern courts and legal commentators have increasingly expressed their dissatisfaction with it. But for now, let us first work through the logic of the collateral-finality rule.

Preparing questions for cross-examination should be approached as a two-stage process. At the first stage the advocate must consider: can this question be asked at all? If the question is relevant and not subject to any applicable exclusionary rules, such as the general doctrines of hearsay[98] or bad character evidence,[99] it may be asked, and the witness is obliged to answer.[100] Next, at the second stage, the cross-examiner must consider whether the question goes directly to the issues in the case, or only to a collateral matter, including, in particular, the credibility of the witness. If the question goes to the issue, the witness's answer may be challenged or contradicted by other evidence. But if the question pertains merely to a collateral matter, the witness's answer must be accepted as final. The relevance, admissibility, and issue/credit status of questions in cross-examination are all ultimately questions of law on which the trial judge may be called on to rule if an opposing party, or the court of its own motion, takes exception to a cross-examiner's line of questioning.

(a) RATIONALE RECONSIDERED

The basic rationale underpinning the collateral-finality rule is that it would waste time and money, and possibly confuse the issues, if the parties were at liberty to embroil the fact-finder in an infinite regress of collateral issues – if, for example, the parties could open up the question whether a (disputed) lie on a previous occasion, otherwise entirely unconnected with the current proceedings, shows that the witness is more likely to be lying on oath in the instant case. A common method of challenging a witness during cross-examination is to suggest to him that he has previously made statements out-of-court which are inconsistent with his testimony at trial. However, unrestricted licence to prove previous inconsistent statements could easily produce much avoidable confusion, time-wasting, and mistaken inferences. These risks are greatly exacerbated in the modern world of the 'information superhighway', in which vast quantities of what the law might regard as 'previous inconsistent statements' are stored in personal computers and mobile phones, in e-mail correspondence, texts, tweets, and on publicly accessible webpages. Most of this material is retained, effectively, forever, even if ostensibly 'deleted'. In

---

[97] (1847) 1 Ex 91, 99; 154 ER 38, 42.   [98] Chapter 9.   [99] Chapter 14.
[100] In accordance with the principle of compulsory process: see §7.3.

the absence of appropriate legal regulation, witnesses testifying in this epistemological environment[101] would need to be fastidiously consistent in their electronic communications or be blessed with extraordinarily good memories in order to avoid being surprised, if not caught out, by indelible examples of their supposed inaccuracy, inconsistency, or falsehood under searching cross-examination.[102]

Suppose that a prosecution witness identifies the accused as the perpetrator of the alleged crime. In the course of cross-examination the witness is asked by the defence whether he has previously admitted having misidentified the accused in unrelated proceedings and he denies ever making such an admission. May the defence adduce evidence to prove that the witness, contrary to his current testimony, has previously admitted to misidentifying the accused? To enable the trier of fact to draw any reliable inference from an inconsistent previous statement supposedly made by the witness, the prosecution must prove both (1) that the statement attributed to the witness was actually made; *and* (2) that the statement was in fact true – in this case, that the witness's previous identification was indeed mistaken, and not only that he later said it was (there is always the possibility of a *false* or just mistaken admission of error). Moreover, the circumstances of the previous misidentification must be at least roughly comparable to the circumstances of the identification now under consideration, otherwise proof of a previous mistake will merely reiterate to the jury a truism that is already perfectly well understood: that the witness, being fallible flesh-and-blood, sometimes makes mistakes. Every step in this elongated chain of inferences might be contested by the party calling the witness, spawning further matters of dispute in their turn – such as who said what to whom on previous occasions, and whether what was supposedly said was properly understood. Before long the subject-matter of the current litigation would be in jeopardy of being drowned out by the 'noise' of collateral issues.

Like so many other traditional doctrines of common law evidence, the collateral-finality rule is by no means devoid of a sensible rationale. The problem is rather that, in attempting to foreclose contextualized judgments of probative value on the facts, the rule over-reaches itself and consequently threatens to work injustice. Consider the Australian case of *Piddington* v *Bennett and Wood*,[103] which is often cited as a paradigmatic illustration of the collateral-finality rule – and its shortcomings – in operation. In a tort action arising from a road accident one of the claimant's witnesses asserted, during cross-examination, that he had seen the accident whilst making his way to the local branch of the Bank of New South Wales. The witness was hazy on the details of this errand, but insisted that his recollection of the sequence of events was broadly accurate. The defendant's advocate then called the manager of the relevant branch, who testified that there was no record of the witness having transacted any business at the Bank on the day in question. On appeal the

---

[101] Cf. Alvin I. Goldman, *Knowledge in a Social World* (OUP, 1999), ch 6.

[102] Real-world hypotheticals are not difficult to construct. Imagine that a first-year student is raped at a party by another student. The next morning she texts her best-friend, emails her personal tutor, skypes with her parents, and later in the day makes a formal statement to the police. Each communication contains different degrees of detail about the incident, expressed in slightly different ways, depending on the intended audience. Discrepancies are only to be expected – but the defence scoops a windfall of material for cross-examination which the prosecutor is obliged to disclose.

[103] (1940) 63 CLR 533. The controversial nature of this ruling is clearly flagged-up by the cogent dissenting opinions of Latham CJ and Starke J.

trial judge's decision to allow the jury to hear the bank-manager's evidence was criticized, and a new trial was ordered explicitly on the basis that the jury had been exposed to inadmissible information. The High Court of Australia ruled that the banking line of cross-examination went only to the witness's credibility, raising merely collateral issues, so that the witness's answers regarding his (claimed) visit to the bank should have been accepted as final for the purposes of the litigation. As Dixon J put it, 'The tendency to discredit him may make the question of the admissibility of the evidence important, but it does not make the evidence admissible'.[104]

Common sense rebels against the conclusion that 'important' evidence is inadmissible. The defendant had in his possession apparently reliable evidence that one of the claimant's main witnesses was either mistaken or lying about an issue which, though strictly 'collateral' in the abstract, might have had a significant bearing on the claimant's proof of his case. The story of the bank visit was contextual detail provided by the witness in order – consciously or subconsciously – to lend credibility to the main substance of his evidence, and yet the jury was not supposed to know that those very details lending light and shade to his testimony could well have been false! It is true, as the majority of the High Court of Australia pointed out, that the witness was *not* claiming that his errand that day gave him some special reason for having witnessed the accident, as where a witness says he stopped at the scene of a crash *because* the traffic light was red: in these circumstances, the colour of the traffic light would itself be a fact in issue in the case. In *Piddington* the fact – if it was a fact – that the witness was on his way to visit a particular branch of the Bank of New South Wales was only part of the explanation as to why the witness happened to be a witness, without advancing any explanation as to how or why the accident occurred. Nonetheless, Latham CJ's dissenting conclusion that 'the evidence was admissible as tending to disprove the explanation given by [the witness] Donellan of his presence at the scene, although it was weak'[105] seems more plausible than the majority's doctrinaire insistence that 'this fact has no natural tendency to show that Donellan was absent from the scene of the accident. All it does is to discredit the account he gave under cross-examination of his movements before the time of the accident.'[106]

No matter how sensible the rationale underpinning the collateral-finality rule as a general proposition, the rule's rather mechanical application in a case like *Piddington*, to demand exclusion of pertinent information already in the hands of one of the parties, seems almost perverse. Fortunately, when common law courts appear constrained to perpetrate obvious injustice by a technical rule of evidence it is not unusual for judges to find some imaginative way of circumventing the rule. Two well-worn strategies involve either whittling down the scope of the primary rule of exclusion, or, alternatively, the 'discovery' of new exceptions limiting the operation of the rule. We now review the development and doctrinal content of formal exceptions to collateral-finality, before turning, in conclusion, to a more fundamental issue. The conceptual distinction between questions going to the issue and questions going only to credit or other collateral matters is the foundation stone on which the doctrine of collateral-finality is built. In the final section we will show that these conceptual foundations are highly unstable and incapable of bearing the weight either of traditional evidentiary doctrine or its ethical justification in the principle of orality.

---

[104] ibid. 553.   [105] ibid. 547.   [106] ibid. 553 (Dixon J).

(b) FIVE EXCEPTIONS TO COLLATERAL FINALITY

There are five well-established exceptions to the collateral-finality rule, specifying matters on which a witness's denials *can* be rebutted by his opponent, notwithstanding the general prohibition.

The first exception relates to the witness's previous convictions, and is mandated by statute. Section 6 of the Criminal Procedure Act 1865 (as amended) provides that, if a witness denies during cross-examination that he has been convicted of a relevant criminal offence, his conviction may be proved.[107] The same statute authorizes a second exception, regarding proof of previous inconsistent statements 'relative to the subject-matter of the indictment'.[108] The witness must first be reminded of the statement and invited to confirm it, but if he chooses to deny having made the statement, it may be proved against him by independent evidence. A third, common law, exception allows the cross-examiner to prove that the witness is biased against his client,[109] especially where bias might not otherwise be suspected,[110] or that the witness is corrupt.[111] A fourth exception sanctions proof that the witness has a general reputation for untruthfulness.[112] Finally, a fifth exception permits expert testimony to establish that a witness suffers from a medical condition radically undermining his or her testimonial reliability – where, for example, the witness is a pathological liar or suffers paranoid delusions.[113]

All five categories of exception make provision for recurrent situations in which truth-finding might be hindered if a party were precluded from rebutting the denials of his opponent's witnesses. If proof of collateral matters were confined to just these five categories, however, much important information would still remain concealed from the fact-finder. Sir Rupert Cross thought that the collateral-finality rule should be regarded as subject to an open-ended list of exceptions,[114] a view that has also attracted judicial endorsement.[115] The idea would be to retain allegiance to the rule, while at the same time

---

[107] The wording of s.6 was amended by the CJA 2003 to emphasize that the question about the witness's previous conviction(s) must be legitimate in the first place: cf. *Watson* v *Chief Constable of Cleveland* [2001] EWCA Civ 1547.

[108] Criminal Procedure Act 1865, s.4 (statements generally, including oral statements) and s.5 (written statements). The words 'relative to the subject matter' pose interpretational difficulties (see, e.g., *R v Funderburk* (1990) 90 Cr App R 466, 476, CA), but this technical problem is largely subsumed within the instability of the underlying credit/issue distinction, as discussed in the next section.

[109] *R v Mendy* (1976) 64 Cr App R 4, CA.

[110] There is an obvious suspicion that spouses may be biased in favour of each other, for example, but where a concealed prior relationship is denied by the witness in cross-examination, it may be proved by other evidence: *Thomas* v *David* (1836) 7 C & P 350 (witness was the claimant's mistress).

[111] *A-G v Hitchcock* (1847) 1 Ex 91.

[112] *Toohey* v *Metropolitan Police Commissioner* [1965] AC 595, HL; *R v Bogie* [1992] Crim LR 301, CA.

[113] *Toohey* v *Metropolitan Police Commissioner* [1965] AC 595, HL. Also see *R v Pinfold and MacKenney* [2004] 2 Cr App R 32, CA, discussed by Paul Roberts, 'Towards the Principled Reception of Expert Evidence of Witness Credibility in Criminal Trials' (2004) 8 *E & P* 215; and further discussion in §11.4(b).

[114] *Cross on Evidence* (5th edn. 1979), 265. Wigmore preferred to leave the matter to the good judgment of the trial judge: *Wigmore on Evidence* (3rd edn. 1940), vol. 3, §1003; cf. Stephen, *Digest of the Law of Evidence* (12th edn. 1946), Arts 143–144.

[115] *R v Funderburk* [1990] 1 WLR 587, 599, CA, *per* Henry J: 'The reason that the court evolved those exceptions is that where it is found that rules designed to promote justice interfere in any given case with justice, then the court must look anxiously to see whether this is an exceptional category of case. It may be that the categories of exception…are not closed. It is impossible to tell the circumstances in which some problems may arise in the future.'

reserving sufficient flexibility to deviate from it whenever justice so requires. That would be a reasonable compromise. However, the distinction between saying that the rule must accommodate *ad hoc* exceptions in the interests of justice, and saying, simply, that collateral evidence should be admitted whenever the interests of justice would be served by doing so, is surely a difference of emphasis rather than substance.

It would be preferable to state the position in a way that offers guidance, both to the parties and to the trial judge, for the unusual (or 'exceptional') situation as well as for run-of-the-mill cases. Lord Pearce pointed the way in *Toohey* v *Metropolitan Police Commissioner*:

The only general principles which can be derived from the older cases are these. On the one hand, the courts have sought to prevent juries from being beguiled by evidence of witnesses who could be shown to be, through defect of character, wholly unworthy of belief. On the other hand, however, they have sought to prevent the trial of a case becoming clogged with a number of side issues, such as might arise if there could be an investigation of matters which had no relevance to the issue save in so far as they tended to show the veracity or falsity of the witness who was giving evidence which *was* relevant to the issue. Many controversies which might thus obliquely throw some light on the issues must in practice be discarded, because there is not an infinity of time, money and mental comprehension available to make use of them.[116]

In *Toohey* the accused and two friends were charged with assault with intent to rob one Madden. According to the accused, they had come across *M* drunk and hysterical, and were only helping him to get home safely. *M* maintained that these self-avowed good samaritans were muggers. The issue on appeal was whether *M*'s admitted state of hysteria was caused by his being assaulted, or whether the causal relationship ran in the opposite direction, that *M*'s hysteria had made him imagine an assault. The accused wished to ask a police surgeon, who had examined *M* shortly after the incident, whether in his medical opinion the hysteria was alcohol-induced and whether *M* had a tendency towards hysteria. The trial judge disallowed the question as being contrary to authority. Overruling this decision, the House of Lords held that it was 'allowable to call medical evidence of mental illness which makes a witness incapable of giving reliable evidence'.[117]

Another illustration of the courts' flexibility in determining the permissible scope of cross-examination is supplied by *Doosti*.[118] In answer to a charge of conspiracy to supply heroin, the accused contended that he was being framed by the police. *D* had previously been acquitted of a similar charge (but convicted on a second count of obstructing a police officer in the course of duty), and in both sets of proceedings the prosecution's main witness at trial was the investigating officer, Sergeant Muth. The trial judge ruled that *D*'s previous acquittal was irrelevant in the later proceedings, on the sound theory that the prosecution's failure to prove guilt beyond reasonable doubt has no bearing either way on the proof of subsequent charges. With this the Court of Appeal concurred, but went on to hold that *after* the prosecutor had cross-examined *D* to credit on his conviction of obstruction, *D* should *then* have been permitted to challenge Muth's credibility by informing the jury about the circumstances of the prior acquittal. Whilst the precise ground of admissibility is difficult to rationalize in terms of the traditional rules of evidence, this flexible,

[116] [1965] AC 595, 607.   [117] [1965] AC 595, 608.   [118] *R v Doosti* (1986) 82 Cr App R 181, CA.

'knock-for-knock' approach[119] can be seen to promote both fairness to the accused and effective fact-finding. It permits the jury to be supplied with pertinent additional information to complete the 'bigger picture' of the events under scrutiny in the trial.[120]

On closer inspection, therefore, the boundaries of the collateral-finality rule proclaimed in *Hitchcock*, which supposedly define in advance when evidence may be admitted to contradict a witness and when it may not, appear to shift and blur. Moreover, cases such as *Doosti* remind us that the underlying concept of relevance is itself flexible and dynamic. In practice, admissibility ultimately turns on whether the evidence in question can make sufficient contribution to the determination of the issue. If the judge concludes, after due consideration of the risks of confusion, time-wasting, and unfairness, that evidence on a collateral matter could have a significant bearing on fact-finding, such evidence ought to be admitted.

Where a witness's denials are rebutted by reference to a previous inconsistent statement, a further question arises as to the purposes for which the previous statement is admitted into the trial. How should the judge direct the jury in relation to the out-of-court statement? The common law rule paralleled the limited admissibility conceded to previous *consistent* statements admitted in-chief (or in re-examination) by way of exception to the rule against narrative. As Lord Taylor CJ explained in *Derby Magistrates*:

It is settled law... that when a previous inconsistent statement goes before the jury, it is not evidence of the truth of its contents: *Rex* v. *Birch* (1924) 18 Cr App R 26. Its effect is confined to discrediting the witness generally or, if the inconsistencies relate directly to the matters in issue, to rendering unreliable the witness's sworn evidence on those matters.[121]

Just as section 120 of the CJA 2003 makes previous consistent statements – received by virtue of the (reformed) exceptions to the rule against narrative – admissible for their truth, section 119 confers the same status on admissible previous *in*consistent statements (including those received by way of exception to collateral-finality):

s.119 – Inconsistent statements
(1) If in criminal proceedings a person gives oral evidence and –
    (a) he admits making a previous inconsistent statement, or
    (b) a previous inconsistent statement made by him is proved by virtue of section 3, 4 or 5 of the Criminal Procedure Act 1865 (c. 18),
the statement is admissible as evidence of any matter stated of which oral evidence by him would be admissible.

---

[119] Ewbank J. ibid. 185 seemed to be basing the Court's decision on a kind of knock-for-knock principle of fairness, reasoning as follows: 'Surely, it is said, if the prosecution can discredit the appellant by bringing up the conviction for obstruction as evidence of the appellant's unreliability, the defence in justice ought to be allowed to refer to the acquittal which took place at the same time as the conviction. We think there is force in this submission. The prosecution are not obliged to bring out the defendant's conviction. If they choose to do so they, in our judgment, incur the risk that in such circumstances as obtained in this case a defendant will be permitted to refer to an acquittal on another charge which may throw doubt on the reliability of a prosecution witness.'

[120] Cf. *R* v *Edwards* (1991) 93 Cr App R 48, CA, in which Lord Lane CJ was rather less predisposed to accept that police officers' conduct in previous investigations could be relevant to the issues in later proceedings. His Lordship's complex judgment is expertly dissected by Rosemary Pattenden, 'Evidence of Previous Malpractice by Police Witnesses and *R* v *Edwards*' [1992] *Crim LR* 549. Also now see *O'Brien* v *Chief Constable of South Wales Police* [2005] 2 AC 534, [2005] UKHL 26, [34]–[43], where Lord Phillips opined: 'Evidence which indicates that a police officer has fabricated admissions in a previous case is not evidence "as to credit alone", if it is alleged that the same officer has fabricated evidence in a subsequent case.'

[121] *R* v *Derby Magistrates' Court, ex p. B* [1996] AC 487, 499, HL.

Section 119 is exclusively a rule of use. In contrast to section 120, it does not purport to create *any* new rules of admissibility. 'The effect of s.119(1) is clear,' the Court of Appeal noted in *Billingham*: 'it renders previous inconsistent statements made by a witness evidence',[122] and not merely collateral proof of the witness's testimonial consistency. It does not follow that a trial judge must or should direct the jury that a previous inconsistent statement automatically merits the same, or greater, credibility than the witness's testimony in court. There may be reasons why an out-of-court statement might appear to warrant belief, because it was made spontaneously or without any obvious motive for fabrication, for example. On other hand, the principle of orality and the traditional hearsay probation explored in the next chapter are predicated on the many well-known infirmities of out-of-court statements that are not made on oath from the witness-box and subjected to searching cross-examination. It is consequently 'by no means easy to direct a jury on the effect of s.119 without causing confusion'.[123] The jury is now entitled to rely on the previous inconsistent statement even if the witness continues to deny it from the witness-box, which would not have been permitted at common law. However, the trial judge should ensure that the jury is fully appraised of the dangers before adopting this unorthodox course.

8.6 THE INCREDIBLE VANISHING CREDIT-ISSUE DISTINCTION

The formal juridical distinction between evidence or questions going to the issue, and evidence or questions going only to collateral matters (including witness credibility), has been a recurring theme of the foregoing discussion of evidentiary regulation of the course of the trial. It is time now to place that distinction under the microscope of critical analysis. One should begin by recognizing that the issue-credit dichotomy, though ultimately flawed, has an internal logical structure that sometimes translates well enough into practice.

In *Cargill*,[124] for example, the complainant denied in cross-examination that she was a prostitute, and the accused was prevented from disproving her denial. At that time, prostitution was regarded as being relevant to the issue of consent on a charge of rape,[125] so the collateral-finality rule would not have prevented an accused charged with rape from rebutting a denial of prostitution.[126] However, in *Cargill* the charge was not rape, but unlawful sexual intercourse with a minor, an offence not requiring proof of lack of consent. Consequently, the only possible relevance of the complainant's alleged prostitution was that it might be said to affect her credibility as a witness, a matter clearly collateral to the issues in the case. Once this is appreciated it seems unobjectionable that the accused was prevented from contradicting the complainant's denials (although this impression is doubtless reinforced because the underlying premiss – that witnesses of general bad

---

[122] *R v Billingham and Billingham* [2009] 2 Cr App R 20; [2009] EWCA Crim 19, [60].

[123] ibid. [62].   [124] *R v Cargill* (1913) 8 Cr App R 224, CCA.

[125] The contested relevance of 'previous sexual history evidence' is explored in Chapter 10.

[126] *R v Clarke* (1817) 2 Stark 241, 171 ER 633; cf. *R v Holmes and Furness* (1871) Cox CC 137, CCA (specific allegations of sexual contact with third parties go merely to credit, and therefore are subject to collateral-finality).

character are more likely to lie on oath – is probably misconceived and illegitimate from the outset).

In other cases, however, the supposed issue-credit dichotomy becomes tenuous in the extreme. *Funderburk*[127] was a modern near-rerun of *Cargill*, where it had to be determined whether the complainant's virginity went to the issues in the case or only to her credit as a witness. Henry J. remarked that 'where the disputed issue is a sexual one between two persons in private the difference between questions going to credit and questions going to the issue is reduced to vanishing point'. He continued:

The difficulty we have in applying that celebrated [collateral-finality] test is that it seems to us to be circular. If a fact is not collateral then clearly you can call evidence to contradict it, but the so-called test is silent on how you decide whether that fact is collateral. The utility of the test may lie in the fact that the answer is an instinctive one based on the prosecutor's and the court's sense of fair play rather than any philosophic or analytic process.[128]

Lord Justice Eveleigh expressed similar sentiments in *Busby*.[129] The trial judge in this case had prevented the accused from rebutting a police officer's denials when it was put to the officer in cross-examination that he had 'warned off' a potential defence witness. Reversing the judge's ruling on appeal, Eveleigh LJ conceded that '[i]t is not always easy to determine when a question relates to facts which are collateral only, and therefore to be treated as final, and when it is relevant to an issue which has to be proved'.[130]

Such candid judicial admissions of uncertainty reflect a profound instability, or radical indeterminacy, in the application of the collateral-finality rule. The conceptual root of the problem can be pinpointed by scrutinizing the facts-in-issue/collateral issues dichotomy in its most familiar, issue-credit form. Recall that, roughly speaking, all relevant evidence is admissible unless its contribution to ascertaining the truth is outweighed by considerations of fairness, rights or justice, or by the residual concern to pre-empt avoidable confusion, cost, and delay. Relevant evidence will not normally be rejected by the trial court unless some specific exclusionary rule applies. Witnesses, we have seen, must be treated with appropriate concern and respect in accordance with the principle of humane treatment and the state's duty of humanity owed to all participants in criminal proceedings.[131] But this threshold consideration aside, there are no additional policy considerations specifically dictating the exclusion of evidence adduced to contradict a witness. What, then, are the factual generalizations and forensic policies underpinning the collateral-finality rule? The supposition appears to be that evidence merely tending to discredit a witness is insufficiently probative to warrant its reception in the general run of cases. But herein lies the root of much mischief, for this supposition is unwarranted.

Consider a case of assault in which the only issue is the offender's identity, and the main prosecution evidence is the testimony of W, who claims to have observed the attack from a distance of thirty metres. The accused's advocate puts it to W that she cannot see beyond a distance of ten metres and is too vain to wear spectacles. Moreover, the advocate has the evidence in-hand to prove it. Yet on the standard interpretation of the collateral-finality rule, this further evidence is inadmissible because it only relates to the credit of the witness, and not (directly) to the issue of the perpetrator's identity. If W were prepared to face

---

[127] *R* v *Funderburk* [1990] 1 WLR 587, CA.   [128] ibid. 597, 598.
[129] *R* v *Busby* (1981) 75 Cr App R 79, CA.   [130] ibid. 82.   [131] §1.3.

down her questioner and deny that she was short-sighted, the defence would be obliged to treat her denials as the final word on her powers of perception – indubitably a collateral question of credibility – and the jury would be none the wiser. By contrast, evidence to show that the accused was a close friend of the victim would be admissible, because it is directly relevant to the issue: it is less probable that the accused would have harmed his friend. But, surely, this rather weak evidence of motive is far less significant in the circumstances of our hypothetical case than W's ten-metre eyesight. It would not be irrational for the trier of fact to accept that the accused truly was the victim's friend, and yet still conclude that the accused was guilty of assault on this occasion. It is hardly unknown for friends to harm or betray each other; indeed some crimes are actually *more common* between intimates than between strangers. However, if the trier of fact believed that W was physically incapable of having observed the offence as she claims, it follows as a matter of inexorable logic that her identification of the accused must be rejected as worthless.

Such hypothetical scenarios expose the fallacy of the contention that credibility is typically, as a general rule, less important than evidence which impinges directly on an issue in the case. The true probative significance of any piece of evidence can only be judged contextually, taking proper account of the remainder of the evidence and of the progress of proceedings as the case unfolds at trial. Since the distinction between relevance to credibility and relevance to the issue is not a reliable proxy for probative value, it follows that the credit-issue dichotomy cannot be expected, and consequently should not be relied upon, to ensure that admissibility determinations consistently promote the interests of justice.

One fact is relevant to another when it renders the existence of that other more, or less, probable by any appreciable degree.[132] The fact that the witness says, 'The man who committed the offence was the accused' is relevant (if it is) because it increases the probability that the accused was the offender (if it does). But notice that W's testimony achieves this effect only if it satisfies some minimum threshold of credibility.[133] If the testimony had no credibility whatsoever – for example, because it is the product of a delusional fantasy or the ravings of a madman[134] – it could safely be discounted as irrelevant. Credibility, we might say, is an essential link in the chain of reasoning between W's testimony and any inference that W's testimony may be taken to support in the trial. Credibility is not something separate – a different species of 'issue' – which is somehow suspended between the witness's statement and the facts to which W testifies. The relevance of a witness's testimony is predicated on that witness's testimonial credibility.[135] Thus, W's myopia cannot be detached from the relevance of her testimony. Proof that W cannot see beyond ten metres is part-and-parcel of her evidence of identification, and any evaluation of the totality of the evidence in the case would be seriously deficient without it.

---

[132] §3.2.

[133] The traditional way of filtering such evidence out of the process would be to declare the witness incompetent. But this is simply an alternative conceptual avenue to the same practical destination. Put another way, the witness is incompetent *because* her testimony is irrelevant (or immaterial).

[134] The same practical result could be achieved by treating the witness as incompetent: see §7.2 and §11.3(a).

[135] Note that a witness's testimony may be unreliable and consequently lacking testimonial credibility even if the witness is considered scrupulously honest. The fact-finder may conclude that the witness did not in reality see what the witness truly believes he saw. The problem of the honest but unreliable eyewitness is particularly acute in relation to identification evidence: see §15.4.

In what sense could it be contended, as a general proposition, that W's eyesight is *not* relevant to the issue? It is not *directly* relevant in the sense that W's range of vision either increases or decreases the probability that the accused committed the *actus reus* of the offence charged with the requisite *mens rea*. W's myopia has no immediate bearing on whether D applied unlawful force to V's body, for example, or did so with intent. But this is to conceptualize relevance in an abstract and artificial way, as though admissibility turned on the question: What is the probability that the accused committed the offence given that W cannot see beyond ten metres? A more pertinent question, paying attention to the constellation of known facts, would be: What is the probability that the accused is the offender given that W claims to have recognized the accused from a distance of thirty metres by the naked eye when W cannot see beyond ten metres without her glasses?

Suppose that a witness testifies: 'I saw the accused, but I am not sure'. Nobody would deny that the supplementary qualification is just as pertinent to the issue as the principal assertion. What if W testified instead: 'I cannot usually see beyond ten metres, but on this occasion I identified the accused from thirty metres'? It would be nonsensical to contend that only the words after the comma are relevant to the issue, whilst the prefatory qualification is merely collateral.[136] To be sure, the relevance of W's eyesight is contingent on W giving evidence: we only become interested in W's powers of perception when *and because* W testifies as a witness in the case. There is no (metaphysical? what other?) sense in which the quality of W's eyesight proves the accused's guilt or innocence in the abstract. However, this kind of contingency is a universal characteristic of evidential facts,[137] and therefore contributes nothing to the argument. Suppose the issue is whether the accused was in a certain place at a certain time. The fact that a car bearing a given registration number was observed at the scene of the crime is relevant to the accused's whereabouts only if that vehicle is registered to him, or if he is known to have driven it. Still, nobody would regard evidence of the registration number as anything other than relevant to the issue, just because its significance is dependent on other facts to be proved in evidence. This is merely to repeat the truism that relevance must be judged, not in abstraction, but contextually and relative to the rest of the evidence in the case. By the same token, evidence of W's eyesight is not possessed of a different kind of relevance merely because its admissibility is contingent on W's first proffering testimony in the witness-box.

In practice, of course, evidence that W was too short-sighted to have identified the accused from the distance claimed would never be withheld from the jury, at least not if such information were known to the parties. If necessary, the formal collateral-finality rule, as stated in *Hitchcock*, would be bent into conformity with the unmistakable imperatives of justice. Thus in *Toohey*, Lord Pearce insisted that:

when a witness through physical (in which I include mental) disease or abnormality is not capable of giving a true or reliable account to the jury, it must surely be allowable for medical science to reveal this vital hidden fact to them. If a witness purported to give evidence

136 As Lord Havers remarked in *R v Sharp* [1988] 1 All ER 65, 71, HL: 'a jury will make little of a direction that attempts to draw a distinction between evidence which is evidence of facts and evidence in the same statement which whilst not being evidence of facts is nevertheless evidentiary material of which they may make use in evaluating the evidence which is evidence of the facts'.

137 Evidential facts were explained in §4.2. Note that the relevance of constitutive facts is also contingent, not primarily on the other evidence in the case, but on whether the parties choose to contest particular points of substantive criminal liability.

of something which he believed that he had seen at a distance of 50 yards, it must surely be possible to call the evidence of an oculist to the effect that the witness could not possibly see anything at a greater distance than 20 yards, or the evidence of a surgeon who had removed a cataract from which the witness was suffering at the material time and which would have prevented him from seeing what he thought he saw.[138]

However, even Lord Pearce's confident assertion is susceptible to a narrow, legalistic interpretation, which would restrict rebuttal evidence to medical or other expert testimony. On that interpretation, a strict application of *Hitchcock* might prevent *W*'s husband, as a lay person with no medical qualifications, from testifying to his wife's acute short-sightedness around the house.

The deleterious consequences of an excessively mechanical, rule-bound approach to collateral-finality can be inferred from trial rulings in cases such as *Busby*,[139] where the accused was charged with offences of burglary and handling. The evidence against him consisted mainly of his own statements to the police, in which he was alleged to have offered to enter into a plea-bargain, and statements attributed to him by alleged accomplices and gaolbirds with whom he had shared a prison cell. *B* did not testify at trial, but his case was that all the statements attributed to him were either police fabrications or convicts' lies purchased by inducements. Defence counsel put it to the investigating police officers in cross-examination that they had exerted pressure on a defence witness to stop him testifying in *B*'s favour. When this witness later appeared for the defence, however, prosecuting counsel objected to his being asked in-chief about the behaviour of the police towards him. The trial judge agreed with prosecution counsel, that such questioning was legally inadmissible: 'I am quite satisfied that this evidence does not go to a fact in issue at all. It is nothing more nor less than an attack upon credit and if [prosecuting counsel] applies, as he does, that it should be excluded, I must exclude it.'[140]

The Court of Appeal took an altogether different view of the matter. Defence counsel's line of questioning should have been permitted, their Lordships held, because, '[if] true, it would have shown that the police were prepared to go to improper lengths in order to secure the accused's conviction':

It was the accused's case that the statement attributed to him had been fabricated, a suggestion which could not be accepted by the jury unless they thought that the officers concerned were prepared to go to improper lengths to secure a conviction.[141]

As a result of the trial judge's error in disallowing this line of questioning, convictions of six counts of burglary and four of handling were quashed. Yet it would be unfair to lay all the blame for this unsatisfactory outcome solely at the trial judge's door. For if trial judges are told that the course of the trial is governed by inflexible legal rules, they will naturally regard themselves bound by decisions interpreting or applying those rules.[142] For as long as the courts live in the shadow of *Hitchcock*-mandated collateral-finality, and

---

[138]   *Toohey* v *Metropolitan Police Commissioner* [1965] AC 595, 608, HL.

[139]   *R* v *Busby* (1982) 75 Cr App R 79, CA. See also *R* v *Marsh* (1986) 83 Cr App R 165, CA.

[140]   Quoted in *R* v *Busby* (1982) 75 Cr App R 79, 82, CA.   [141]   ibid.

[142]   In *Busby* itself the Court of Appeal suggested that the trial judge's mistake lay in his misapprehending the effect of a 46-year-old decision upon a precedent of 135 years' vintage. As it happens, *Busby* is consistent with *Hitchcock*, in which both Pollock CB and Alderson B said that where a witness denies having offered a bribe to another witness, the denial may be contradicted by other evidence.

legal doctrine continues to fetishize the distinction between relevance to credibility and relevance to the issue, trial judges will occasionally be led astray.

Section 120 of the CJA 2003 has effectively abolished the credit/issue distinction, as a criterion of admissibility,[143] in relation to a witness's previous consistent statements. However, section 119 operates only on the evidential status of otherwise admissible *incon*sistent statements, leaving the credit/issue distinction intact for the purposes of applying the primary collateral-finality standard. The mischievous notion that the admissibility of collateral facts is governed by definitive rules and their protean categories of exception continues to haunt the law of criminal evidence. It will always be a sensible working hypothesis that evidence called for the sole purpose of discrediting a witness is, at best, of marginal probative value, and it will often be appropriate to exclude it. But it is – or at any rate should be – incumbent on trial judges to exercise their critical faculties whenever this assumption is reasonably challenged in particular circumstances. Decided cases constitute a repository of experience and offer useful instruction in how judges have dealt with similar problems in the past. In the final analysis, however, admissibility must depend on the trial judge's assessment of the probative value of the evidence in question and the balance of advantage in receiving it. The role of appellate courts should be restricted to intervening in exceptional cases where, as in *Busby*, common sense factual analysis and the dictates of justice have been hoodwinked by an arid conceptualism.

---

[143] There may still be circumstances in which it is appropriate for trial judges to direct juries as to whether a previous consistent statement may be regarded as supporting the witness's testimony or as constituting evidence in its own right, or as performing both evidential functions simultaneously. However, the need for such analytically complex directions will presumably be confined to exceptional cases; and trial judges are at liberty to mould the content of their summing-up to the requirements of the instant case, subject only to 'light touch' appellate supervision under the *Wednesbury* standard.

9

HEARSAY

9.1 INTRODUCTION

The 'rule against hearsay' is one of the most characteristic features of common law evidentiary systems around the world. As formulated in Sir Rupert Cross's classic definition, the common law exclusionary rule mandates that 'a statement other than one made by a person while giving oral evidence in the proceedings is inadmissible as evidence of any fact stated'.[1] A key task for this chapter will be to examine and elucidate the concept of hearsay, which for the purposes of English law was translated into statutory language by the Criminal Justice Act 2003. The logic of the exclusionary rule can easily become twisted unless each of its components is properly understood: indeed, the common law rule frequently created mischief in practice, and its statutory incarnation appears to have embarked on a similar career. To be going along with, however, a simpler approximation will suffice. We can say that: the hearsay rule excludes (1) out-of-court statements (2) adduced for their truth, unless a well-established exception to the exclusionary rule applies.

Thus formulated, the intimate connection between hearsay exclusion and the principle of orality is readily apparent. The rule against hearsay can be regarded as the reflection of English law's positive ideological preference for live oral testimony. In a system of adjudication in which, for the reasons we have examined in the preceding two chapters, oral testimony delivered in court by percipient witnesses is regarded as the paradigm of judicial evidence, out-of-court statements that were not delivered on oath or subjected to cross-examination at trial will naturally be regarded as inferior sources of proof. By the time that the modern law of evidence was crystallizing in the mid-nineteenth century, English law had decided that hearsay was presumptively inadmissible. The qualification 'presumptively' is vital, because the scenarios thrown up in litigation amply demonstrated that certain kinds of hearsay ought to be received on grounds of necessity or reliability. Practically-minded judges were not about to divest themselves of relevant and potentially cogent evidence unless they were sufficiently persuaded of good reasons for doing so.

The hearsay rule was all but abolished for civil proceedings in England and Wales by the Civil Evidence Act 1995, and pressure for abolition has carried over to criminal litigation in recent times. The Law Commission conducted a thorough re-examination of the hearsay doctrine in the late 1990s, but its recommendations, which subsequently became the basis for the hearsay provisions of the Criminal Justice Act 2003, were less radical than some might have

---

[1] *Cross on Evidence* (Butterworths, 5th edn. 1979), 6 and 462. Also see s.1(2) of the Civil Evidence Act 1995, substantially reproducing this definition. Whilst Cross's definition was embraced in England and Wales, alternative definitions have been advocated in the United States: see Roger C. Park, '*McCormick on Evidence* and the Concept of Hearsay' (1980) 65 *Minnesota LR* 423.

hoped for and others had feared. The reforms introduced by the 2003 Act effectively re-enacted the common law hearsay rule with most of the pre-existing common law exceptions intact and some new statutory ones thrown in for good measure. Whether this new admissibility framework has succeeded in simplifying the law, which was a principal objective of reform, is a central question for any evaluation of its merits. We will see in the course of the following discussion that simplicity and clarity have proved elusive in the English law of hearsay.

Although the 2003 Act did not go as far as many would have wished in breaking with common law traditions, this legislation still represents the most thorough-going reform of the law of hearsay in criminal proceedings ever undertaken in England and Wales. Since the hearsay provisions of the CJA 2003 came into force on 4 April 2005 a jurisprudence of case-law interpretation has been rapidly accumulating and continues to grow. This is consequently a time of flux and fluidity in the English law of hearsay. New legislation always introduces elements of uncertainty into the law. Although courts are typically inclined to interpret statutory language in accordance with settled common law understandings, so that common law doctrine remains influential despite no longer enjoying the formal status of legal precedent, it cannot always be assumed that judges will opt for the conservative interpretation when a more radical alternative presents itself. A fair evaluation of the CJA 2003's hearsay reforms must allow time for the new provisions to bed-down properly. At this juncture, conclusive assessment would be premature. It can already be said, however, that initial judicial reactions to the legislation were sometimes witheringly critical, and the early case-law has set about knocking some corners off the statutory scheme as the Law Commission envisaged it, with potentially far-reaching implications. This may hint at structural, and possibly irremediable, defects in the legislative design.

Most of this chapter is naturally taken up with detailed examination of the CJA 2003's hearsay provisions and their interpretation in decided cases to-date. Before turning to doctrinal analysis, however, we need to explore at greater length more fundamental issues concerning underlying rationales. Why exclude hearsay at all? To what extent do the primary rationales for excluding hearsay also explain the existence of inclusionary exceptions to hearsay exclusion? And how closely in practice has English law tracked its supposed theoretical rationalizations? Investigating these issues will require us, not for the first time, to grapple with fundamental tensions between accurate fact-finding and the range of other values which criminal adjudication must respect if criminal justice is to be achieved. It will also provide another striking illustration of the growing influence of human rights law on English criminal procedure.

9.2 EXCLUSIONARY RATIONALES: WHAT'S WRONG WITH HEARSAY?[2]

In a well-known passage in the Privy Council case of *Teper* Lord Normand explained why hearsay evidence is presumptively inadmissible in English law:

It is not the best evidence and it is not delivered on oath. The truthfulness and accuracy of the person whose words are spoken to by another witness cannot be tested by cross-examination, and the light which his demeanour would throw on his testimony is lost.[3]

---

[2] Generally, see Andrew L.-T. Choo, *Hearsay and Confrontation in Criminal Trials* (OUP, 1996), ch 2.

[3] *Teper* v *R* [1952] AC 480, 486, PC.

Each element of this rationalization can be challenged on its own terms. First, it is entirely possible that hearsay could be the best available evidence on the facts of the case. Secondly, oaths are little credited today as guarantors of veracity,[4] and neither cross-examination nor inferences from a witness's demeanour can be accepted uncritically as effective strategies for truth-finding.[5] Nonetheless, there is a durable residuum of truth in the sometimes inflated rationales for hearsay exclusion. Everyday experience teaches that information generally becomes less reliable the further one moves away from its original source,[6] and it is a forensic commonplace that evidence is virtually always harder to test if it is provided to the court indirectly, at one or more removes from a witness who could vouch directly for the truth of the matter stated. It also seems unfair to the accused if he cannot effectively test the prosecution evidence against him, because the witness in court is a mere cipher relating what somebody else told him, whilst the originator of the evidence – the one who really knows the truth of the matter, if anybody does – is not available for further questioning. Even if cross-examination is not nearly as effective at winkling out the truth as lawyers have sometimes believed, depriving the accused of an opportunity to test evidence vigorously through cross-examination might still impact adversely on the fairness of proceedings, not least because people tend to trust in the efficacy of cross-examination, whatever behavioural science research might assert to the contrary. It is axiomatic that justice cannot fully be done unless justice is seen to be done, by the accused, by the witnesses, and by society at large.[7] Seeing justice done might well entail a fair opportunity for cross-examination, at least for as long as this procedure is popularly embraced as a feature of procedural justice.

The principle of hearsay exclusion is therefore *prima facie* supported both by instrumental considerations of truth-finding and by intrinsic arguments of fairness and justice.[8] Whilst truth-finding arguments have traditionally predominated, intrinsic rationales rooted in substantive (moral) conceptions of fair trial and due process have recently assumed much greater prominence.[9]

(a) HEARSAY EXCLUSION AS THE LOGIC OF PROOF

The mid-twentieth-century American scholar Edmund Morgan identified (1) misperception; (2) faulty memory; (3) insincerity; and (4) communication breakdown as the four 'hearsay dangers'.[10] The dangers are, in other words, that the maker of the statement

---

[4] §7.2.   [5] §7.1.

[6] Childhood whispering games will be familiar to most readers. A favourite example from the Great War runs something like this. Orders are dispatched from the frontline requesting headquarters to 'send reinforcements, we're going to advance'. But by the time the message has been passed along the trenches from one solider to another down the line, HQ is presented with the baffling instruction to 'send three-and four-'pence, we're going to a dance'! (That is, three shillings and four pence, in pre-decimalization currency.)

[7] See §1.2(c) and §2.3(b).

[8] See Choo, *Hearsay and Confrontation in Criminal Trials*, 13–16; Denis Galligan, 'More Scepticism about Scepticism' (1988) 8 *Oxford Journal of Legal Studies* 249, 255.

[9] Roger Park cautions that such arguments may be 'subtle and procedurally complex': Roger C. Park, 'A Subject Matter Approach to Hearsay Reform' (1987) 86 *Michigan LR* 51, 55 (providing an excellent general analysis).

[10] Edmund Morgan, 'Hearsay Dangers and the Application of the Hearsay Concept' (1948) 62 *Harvard LR* 177.

(conventionally, 'the declarant') may have mistaken or misunderstood what she originally perceived; forgotten crucial details; deliberately withheld information or told downright lies; or failed to communicate her meaning effectively to the witness who repeats the declarant's statement in court. Given that people tend to 'see' what they expect to see[11] and, anyway, have differing powers of perception and concentration, even the most punctilious declarant might make an honest mistake; and since meaning is so dependent on context, nuance, and shared cultural background, the scope for misunderstanding in communication is substantial.[12]

Most of these risks, it should be conceded, also attend direct testimonial evidence given orally in court. But hearsay involves one fundamental difference: when the declarant goes into the witness-box, his opponent can investigate the declarant's powers of perception, test his memory, and appraise his veracity directly through cross-examination, better enabling the trier of fact to assess the probative value of the witness's evidence. The unavailability of a hearsay declarant for cross-examination is the crux of hearsay exclusion. Where the declarant is unavailable, and the hearsay-relaying witness – not himself knowing any better – is effectively immune to the strictures of public cross-examination on oath, it is a fair assumption that hearsay evidence carries an enhanced risk of error in adjudication.

It does not necessarily follow that hearsay should be presumptively inadmissible, let alone automatically excluded from the trial. In ordinary affairs we may regard hearsay with suspicion but we hardly ever decline to rule it out of consideration altogether. Thus, in civil proceedings the rule against hearsay has effectively been abolished, so that – in conformity with a commonsensical approach – the acknowledged infirmities of hearsay evidence affect its weight, rather than its admissibility.[13] So why has the hearsay rule endured in criminal proceedings, even to the point of being reasserted and extended in major appellate court rulings throughout the twentieth century? One possibility is that hearsay evidence involves unacceptable risks of convicting the innocent, an outcome which English criminal procedure strives mightily to avoid, as we see time and again.

It is often argued that in the absence of cross-examination jurors are likely to overestimate the probative significance of hearsay statements.[14] This contention cannot be dismissed out of hand. Relying on hearsay reports in our everyday lives is normally epistemically warranted and there is often no real choice in the matter. On candid introspection, however, most of us would probably admit to undue susceptibility to hearsay, especially when it appears to confirm a pre-existing belief or flatter a firmly-held conviction or prejudice.

---

[11] See Choo, *Hearsay and Confrontation in Criminal Trials*, 22–5 (summarizing research by Allport and Postman (1947) in which subjects were briefly shown a picture of a crowded subway train featuring a black man with a tie talking to a white man holding a razor blade. Many subjects subsequently reported 'seeing' the razor blade in the black man's hand, and some even said he was 'brandishing it wildly' or 'threatening the white man with it').

[12] Cf. Eleanor Swift, 'Abolishing the Hearsay Rule' (1987) 75 *California LR* 495, 504.

[13] Section 1(1) of the Civil Evidence Act 1995, building on the more modest reforms introduced by the Civil Evidence Act 1968, provides that: 'In civil proceedings evidence shall not be excluded on the ground that it is hearsay.' A party seeking to adduce hearsay evidence must, however, serve advance notice on the other parties to the litigation, so that 'what used to be a rule of exclusion is now a rule of notice': see *Zuckerman on Civil Procedure*, §19.15, §19.39ff.

[14] Jack B. Weinstein, 'Probative Force of Hearsay' (1961) 46 *Iowa LR* 331.

Moreover, hearsay may be objectionable in criminal proceedings even when it would be perfectly serviceable for other purposes. Those accused of criminal wrongdoing should be tried on evidence produced in court, not on rumour, gossip, or careless off-the-cuff remarks uttered with no thought for the potential consequences.[15] The seductive notion that there can be 'no smoke without fire' might lend even to wholly unsubstantiated or maliciously-concocted rumour a probative significance it scarcely merits. The possibility that relaxation, or total abolition, of the hearsay rule might benefit the prosecution more than the defence is a further reason for reformers to contain their enthusiasm and proceed with caution.

As we will see in Chapter 12, the most significant type of prosecution hearsay evidence, namely the accused's confession, has always been freely admissible, historically by way of common law exception to the exclusionary rule, and after PACE 1984 on an independent statutory footing.[16] Nonetheless, it would clearly be a matter of grave concern if police officers were able to turn up to court and routinely testify to police canteen scuttlebutt or what informants may have allegedly told them on the basis of 'information received'.[17] Cynics would view such a system of proof as a standing invitation to police fabrication of evidence – a.k.a. 'pious perjury' or, in the USA, 'testilying' – and other, doubtless sporadic but nonetheless well-documented, investigative abuses. But even those with implicit trust and confidence in the police would have to concede that the accused would be very hard-pressed to mount an effective challenge to such evidence, conveyed to the court at second- (or third? or fourth? etc.) hand by a professional police witness. In those circumstances the trier of fact would effectively be presented with a stark choice between uncritical acceptance of police testimony, leading to almost automatic conviction, or a sceptical presumption of official foul-play demanding acquittal in every case in which the presumption could not be convincingly rebutted. Neither option is attractive, since both threaten to trivialize, if they do not entirely displace, the criminal trial's fundamental aspirations towards accurate fact-finding in the instant case.[18]

---

[15] These concerns overlap with the rationales underpinning the US Sixth Amendment right of confrontation and Article 6(3)(d) of the ECHR: see §9.2(b), below.

[16] PACE 1984, s.76. Also now see s.76A, in relation to evidence of admissions adduced by a co-accused, inserted by s.128 of the CJA 2003, which is discussed in §12.5.

[17] Cf. R v Rothwell (1994) 99 Cr App R 388, in which the Court of Appeal was astute to clamp down on such stratagems.

[18] Such protective considerations might, indeed, have partly motivated the majority's conceptually-confused approach to implied assertions in the pivotal House of Lords' decision in R v Kearley [1992] 2 AC 228, which is extensively discussed and criticized in §9.4(b), below. Tucked away at the end of Lord Ackner's speech one finds these little-noticed reflections: 'Professor Cross... stated that a further reason for justifying the hearsay rule was the danger that hearsay evidence might be concocted. He dismissed this as "simply one aspect of the great pathological dread of manufactured evidence which beset English lawyers of the late 18th and early 19th centuries". Some recent appeals, well known to your Lordships, regretfully demonstrate that currently that anxiety, rather than being unnecessarily morbid, is fully justified' (ibid. 258). The circumstances of Kearley's prosecution and conviction were hardly ideal. If the locality was teeming with Kearley's clientele, why could the police not procure one or more of these persons to testify at his trial? Because the callers were frightened or otherwise uncooperative? Or because junkies make poor witnesses, especially if their criminal records are as long as the track marks on their arms? Even those who find the suggestion of police impropriety too morbid to contemplate should concede that, especially in the murky world of drugs and vice prosecutions, it would be better if convictions rested on more than the unsubstantiated word of a policeman.

(b) HEARSAY EXCLUSION AS A PRINCIPLE OF FAIRNESS

The common law rule against hearsay has traditionally been justified on grounds intrinsic to the logic of proof, such as those just canvassed. The rule's advocates have claimed that systematically excluding hearsay evidence will achieve greater accuracy in fact-finding, at least in the longer run averaged out over all cases, compared with the wholesale admission of potentially misleading evidence infected with hearsay dangers. Hearsay exclusion might also be regarded as protecting the accused from wrongful conviction, although this rationalization, standing alone, plainly cannot account for the fact that the rule against hearsay applies to evidence adduced by the defence as well as to prosecution evidence.

The accuracy-promoting rationales are no longer universally accepted by courts and informed commentators. However, in the teeth of mounting criticism, the exclusionary rule has recently been reinvigorated by arguments linking the rejection of hearsay evidence to the demands of procedural fairness, and in particular to the idea of a 'right to confrontation'. This modified rationalization has secured a toehold in English law courtesy of Article 6(3)(d) of the European Convention on Human Rights (ECHR), which guarantees to the accused the rights 'to examine or have examined witnesses against him and to obtain the attendance and examination of witnesses on his behalf under the same conditions as witnesses against him'. Fairness-based arguments are not necessarily entirely distinct from instrumental truth-finding objectives, and these overlapping considerations frequently merge in judicial reasoning. But appeals to procedural rights and due process do contribute independent normative ballast to legal criticisms of hearsay. This is another area of criminal evidence on which the first decade of the Human Rights Act has made a tangible impact. Comparative common law jurisprudence and scholarship have also been influential.

In a sequence of articles, Richard Friedman has developed the argument that hearsay exclusion bolsters the 'Confrontation Clause' of the US Sixth Amendment. Requiring witnesses against the accused to testify in person, and in open court, is said to serve US federal law's constitutionally-mandated right to confront one's accuser.[19] The accused's right of confrontation can be traced historically through medieval jurisprudence, into Roman and other ancient systems of justice.[20] There would appear to be deep-rooted emotional attachment amongst human societies down the ages to the idea that an accuser should come forward and make his allegations face-to-face with the person whose conduct is being impugned. The kernel of this sentiment is reflected in the widely-felt conviction that, if people are going to say damaging or hurtful things about us – whether the accusation be true or false – it is better for them to say it directly in our presence, rather than spreading rumours about us behind our backs. In a related way, most people would like to think of themselves as the sort of person who 'looks people in the eye, and tells it straight', and

---

[19] Richard D. Friedman, 'Confrontation: The Search for Basic Principles' (1998) 86 *Georgetown LJ* 1011; 'Truth and Its Rivals in the Law of Hearsay and Confrontation' (1998) 49 *Hastings LJ* 545; 'Thoughts From Across the Water on Hearsay and Confrontation' [1998] *Crim LR* 697. Also see Charles R. Nesson and Yochai Benkler, 'Constitutional Hearsay: Requiring Foundational Testing and Corroboration Under the Confrontation Clause' (1995) 81 *Virginia LR* 149.

[20] Frank R. Herrmann and Brownlow M. Speer, 'Facing the Accuser: Ancient and Medieval Precursors of the Confrontation Clause' (1994) 34 *Virginia Journal of International Law* 481.

would not want to be regarded as weaselly gossip-mongers who only criticize people who are out of earshot. Criminal proceedings have regularly provided dramatic contexts for the play of such sentiments, none more frequently retold than the infamous denial of a right of confrontation to Sir Walter Raleigh.

Raleigh was convicted of treason, and executed, in 1603 on the basis of out-of-court testimonials secured from his alleged accomplice, Lord Cobham. It is sometimes contended that the right of confrontation derives from the significance of allowing the accused to cross-examine prosecution witnesses, relegating confrontation to an instrumental means of securing an opportunity for cross-examination. But the right of confrontation can also be rationalized and promoted in more purist terms, as an independent, intrinsic feature of legitimate criminal process. Raleigh, it seems, did not ask to cross-examine Cobham, or even to have him questioned in court by the judges, but only that he be produced: '[L]et Cobham be here, let him speak it. Call my accuser before my face, and I have done.' The judges were apparently fearful that the mere sight of Raleigh would induce Cobham to change his story: '[T]o save you, his old friend, it may be that he will deny all that which he hath said.' Boiled down to its essence, the right of confrontation does not even claim any such power to induce spontaneous retractions. It can be justified, without any reference whatsoever to effective fact-finding or other instrumental considerations, on the unadulterated basis that face-to-face confrontation is simply part of what a society owes to each of its citizens – as thinking, feeling, rational creatures with the capacity to give and receive justice – before it can legitimately convict them of a serious criminal offence and impose just punishment. The right to confrontation, on this view, is a legal and moral extrapolation from the ultimate precept of respect for human dignity, which in turn informs and underscores the foundational principles of criminal evidence identified in Chapter 1.[21]

Confrontation-based arguments advocating the exclusion of hearsay evidence have moved out of the jurisprudence classroom and into the courtroom in recent years. Four landmark decisions merit discussion. First, in *Crawford* v *Washington*[22] the US Supreme Court held that the Sixth Amendment right to confrontation exists independently of evidentiary hearsay doctrines. Thus, state courts and legislatures are obliged to respect the constitutional right of confrontation even if detailed rules of evidence are matters of democratic choice for individual states within the US federal legal system. The upshot is that an out-of-court statement must be excluded if the proponent wants to use it 'testimonially', that is, as proof of its truth in the manner proscribed by the hearsay rule, irrespective of state hearsay law. *Crawford* nicely illustrates that intrinsic or instrumental rationales for excluding out-of-court statements can be constructed entirely independently of conventional hearsay analysis and doctrines. It is a decision of high authority, albeit, of course, only persuasive for the purposes of English law.[23]

---

[21] See §1.3. The argument from dignity may be countered in its own terms where a 'right to eyeball' becomes a pretext for witness intimidation, especially if the witness is inherently vulnerable. Measures designed to address the needs and legitimate expectations of vulnerable or intimidated witnesses (VIWs) are discussed in Chapter 10.   [22] *Crawford* v *Washington*, 124 S Ct 1354, 541 US 36 (2004).

[23] For discussion, see Richard D. Friedman, '"Face to Face": Rediscovering the Right to Confront Prosecution Witnesses' (2004) 8 *E & P* 1; H. L. Ho, 'Confrontation and Hearsay: A Critique of *Crawford*' (2004) 8 *E & P* 147; William E. O'Brian Jr, 'The Right of Confrontation: US and European Perspectives' (2005) 121 *LQR* 481; Michael S. Pardo, 'Testimony' (2007) 82 *Tulane Law Review* 119.

Our second landmark case is unquestionably authoritative. The issue in *Davis*,[24] as we saw in Chapter 7,[25] was whether a conviction of murder could be sustained exclusively on the basis of evidence from eyewitnesses who testified anonymously from behind screens and utilizing voice-altering technology to disguise their identities. The Court of Appeal ruled that, in a situation where witnesses were in genuine fear of reprisals, these procedural modifications were acceptable at common law and in compliance with Article 6(3)(d) of the ECHR. Sensationally, the House of Lords unanimously allowed the accused's appeal. According to Lord Bingham, 'It is a long-established principle of the English common law that, subject to certain exceptions and statutory qualifications, the defendant in a criminal trial should be confronted by his accusers in order that he may cross-examine them and challenge their evidence'.[26] Although English law is no stranger to procedural modifications designed to protect vulnerable witnesses from intimidation,[27] none of these measures– their Lordships insisted – has ever been permitted to undermine the fairness of a criminal trial. The particular difficulty here was that the accused could not effectively challenge the evidence against him without knowing the identity of the eye witnesses who claimed to be able to identify him as the gunman who fired the fatal shot. As Lord Mance explained:

[I]n all such cases the problem exists that the concealment of identity means that the defendant cannot himself check, investigate or (save by guesswork) give directly any relevant information about the character, motives or reliability of the witness. The defence is to that extent potentially hampered both in cross-examination and in relation to any positive case and evidence which it can adduce. In many cases, particularly cases where credibility is in issue, identification will be essential to effective cross-examination.[28]

The immediate impact of the *Davis* ruling in halting all prosecutions based exclusively on anonymous witness evidence was promptly reversed by statute.[29] However, the broader significance of the case, for our purposes, lies in the House of Lords' unanimous endorsement of the right to confrontation at English common law. Hearsay exclusion is mandated, at least in part, by fair trial principles, albeit that Lord Bingham and Lord Mance seemed primarily concerned with preserving the instrumental effectiveness of cross-examination. Anticipating partial reversal by statute, Lord Brown of Eaton-under-Heywood declared, somewhat more expansively, that 'the creeping emasculation of the common law principle must be not only halted but reversed. It is the integrity of the judicial process that is at stake here. This must be safeguarded and vindicated whatever the cost.'[30]

---

[24] *R v Davis* [2008] 1 AC 1128, [2008] UKHL 36.   [25] §7.5(b).

[26] *R v Davis* [2008] 1 AC 1128, [5].

[27] For example, in *R v Smellie* (1919)14 Cr App R 128, CCA, it was held that the accused could be required to keep himself out-of-sight whilst a potentially intimidated witness was in court, providing that the accused could still *hear* the witness's testimony and follow the proceedings. Criminal accused have no strong common law right to observe, or be observed by, witnesses testifying against them: *R v X, Y and Z* (1990) 91 Cr App R 36, CA (endorsing Judge Pigot's use of physical screens to prevent child witnesses from having to see the accused in court). Generally, see Chapter 10.

[28] *R v Davis* [2008] 1 AC 1128, [2008] UKHL 36, [71]–[72].

[29] In the first instance, by means of a temporary legislative stop-gap in the form of the Criminal Evidence (Witness Anonymity) Act 2008. Now see Coroners and Justice (C&J) Act 2009, ss.86–97, discussed in §7.5(b).   [30] *R v Davis* [2008] 1 AC 1128, [2008] UKHL 36, [66].

The radical potential of ECHR Article 6(3)(d) to re-engineer the English law of hearsay was even more dramatically demonstrated by the European Court of Human Rights itself, in the third of our quartet of landmark cases, *Al-Khawaja and Tahery* v *UK*.[31] In these two conjoined proceedings the applicants separately made what were in substance identical complaints, viz. that they had been convicted of serious crimes in contravention of their right to a fair trial because the prosecution had relied on witness evidence that the defence had had no direct opportunity to test or challenge. Al-Khawaja had been convicted of sexual assault on the basis of a witness statement made to the police by a complainant who subsequently committed suicide prior to the accused's trial. Tahery had been convicted of wounding with intent on the strength of statements from witnesses who refused to testify in person through fear of reprisals. In both cases, the Court of Appeal had upheld the trial judge's ruling to admit the evidence in the interests of justice under the then-applicable hearsay exceptions covering the evidence of absent witnesses.[32] In Al-Khawaja's case, for example, the Court of Appeal held that:

Where a witness who is the sole witness of a crime has made a statement to be used in its prosecution and has since died, there may be a strong public interest in the admission of the statement in evidence so that the prosecution may proceed. That was the case here. That public interest must not be allowed to override the requirement that the defendant have a fair trial.... This was not a case where the witness had absented himself, whether through fear or otherwise, or had required anonymity, or had exercised a right to keep silent. The reason was death, which has a finality which brings in considerations of its own...[33]

Yet these considerations did not impress the European Court of Human Rights. The principle established in Strasbourg jurisprudence mandates that:

where a conviction is based *solely or to a decisive degree* on depositions that have been made by a person whom the accused has had no opportunity to examine or to have examined, whether during the investigation or at the trial, the rights of the defence are restricted to an extent that is incompatible with the guarantees provided by Article 6.[34]

The Strasbourg Court concluded that neither Al-Khawaja nor Tahery had been afforded a fair trial when assessed against the European standard. Neither the balancing of interests conducted by the domestic English courts nor any judicial warning designed to alert the jury to the disadvantages experienced by the defence in trying to counter the evidence of an absent witness was considered an Article 6-compliant surrogate for direct examination. Indeed, the Strasbourg Court expressly doubted 'whether any counterbalancing factors would be sufficient to justify the introduction in evidence of an untested statement which was the sole or decisive basis for the conviction of an applicant'.[35]

English criminal courts and practitioners predictably regarded *Al-Khawaja and Tahery* v *UK* as an unexpected and troubling decision of doubtful authority and wisdom.[36]

---

[31] *Al-Khawaja and Tahery* v *United Kingdom* (2009) 49 EHRR 1.

[32] In Al-Khawaja's case, Criminal Justice Act 1988, s.23, now superseded by CJA 2003, s.116 (which was applied to admit the evidence in Tahery's case): see §9.5(a), below.

[33] *R* v *Al-Khawaja* [2005] EWCA Crim 2697, *The Times*, 15 November 2005, [26].

[34] *Lucà* v *Italy* (2003) 36 EHRR 46, [40] (emphasis supplied).

[35] *Al-Khawaja and Tahery* v *UK*, [37].

[36] For further initial reactions, see Editorial (Ian Dennis) [2009] *Crim LR* 311; Andrew Ashworth [2009] *Crim LR* 353.

In sweeping terms, the European Court of Human Rights had apparently rejected English law's settled approach to the reception of hearsay evidence from legitimately absent witnesses – an approach which was very recently confirmed by Parliament when enacting CJA 2003, section 116,[37] and in relation to deceased witnesses, in particular, implements a long-standing common law preference for allowing the claims of the dead to be heard in court.[38] The British government promptly referred the decision for re-hearing by the Grand Chamber of the European Court of Human Rights. In the meantime, domestic English courts, were soon called upon to perform a damage-limitation exercise.

In *Horncastle*,[39] the Court of Appeal and then, on further appeal, the fledgling UK Supreme Court presented a united home front in rejecting the apparent implications of *Al-Khawaja*. Their Lordships ruled that English law complies with Article 6 without the need to adopt a categorical 'sole or decisive' evidence criterion for the exclusion of hearsay. Lord Phillips PSC, writing for a unanimous Supreme Court, doubted that existing Strasbourg jurisprudence actually supported a 'sole or decisive' rule, but in any event, a rigid test of admissibility incorporating this criterion would be unjustifiable in theory and a liability in practice. 'In the case of a jury trial,' Lord Phillips observed, 'a direction to the jury that they can have regard to a witness statement as supporting evidence but not as decisive evidence would involve them in mental gymnastics that few would be equipped to perform'.[40] Any putative 'sole or decisive' test would consequently have to be policed by judicial determinations of admissibility. But in that event, '[i]f "decisive" means capable of making the difference between a finding of guilt and innocence, then all hearsay evidence will have to be excluded'. Their Lordships did not deny the importance of subjecting hearsay evidence to strict scrutiny, especially where it forms a central plank of the prosecution's case. However, the ECtHR was regarded as having underestimated or misunderstood English law's democratically-mandated procedural mechanisms for regulating hearsay and assessing its epistemic credentials:

[T]he justification for the sole or decisive test would appear to be that the risk of an unsafe conviction based solely or decisively on anonymous or hearsay evidence is so great that such a conviction can never be permitted. Parliament has concluded that there are alternative ways of protecting against that risk that are less draconian, as set out in the 1988 and 2003 Acts... When the Strasbourg decisions are analysed it is apparent that these alternative safeguards would have precluded convictions in most of the cases where a violation of article 6(1)(3)(d) was found. In particular the legislation does not permit the admission of the statement of a witness who is neither present nor identified.... The cases suggest that in general our rules of admissibility provide the defendant with at least equal protection to that provided under the continental system.[41]

It remains to be seen whether the Grand Chamber of the ECtHR will be prepared to accept the broad thrust of the UK Supreme Court's analysis in *Horncastle*. The argument must

---

[37] See §9.5(a), below.

[38] See, e.g., *R v Woodcock* (1789) 1 Leach 500; *R v Bedingfield* (1879) 14 Cox CC 341, Assizes; *Nembhard v R* (1982) 74 Cr App R 144, 146, PC: '[I]t is important in the interests of justice that a person implicated in a killing should be obliged to meet in court the dying accusation of the victim...'

[39] *R v Horncastle* [2009] UKSC 14, [2010] 2 WLR 47 (for [2009] EWCA Crim 964) and 94 (SC). The Supreme Court expressly endorsed and sanctified the authority of the Court of Appeal's judgment below.

[40] ibid. [90].   [41] ibid. [92]–[93].

be that the hearsay provisions of the CJA 2003, as implemented through the institutional framework of criminal adjudication in England and Wales,[42] fall within an acceptable domestic 'margin of appreciation' compatible with Article 6. Generally speaking, the Strasbourg Court assesses Article 6 fairness in the round and refuses to be drawn into the minutiae of states parties' procedural law.[43] Strictly speaking, *Al-Khawaja and Tahery* v *UK* is not a case about the English law of hearsay as such, but rather a decision specifying pan-European minimum requirements of fairness in a contested criminal trial. A trial cannot be fair if the accused was denied a fair opportunity to test key prosecution evidence. Whilst the application of that standard to particular facts is eminently contestable (after all, the ECtHR reached a different conclusion to the domestic English courts in the cases of both Al-Khawaja *and* Tahery), the general style of argument suggests an independent rationale for excluding hearsay statements which does not rely on traditional hearsay analysis or appeal directly to circumstantial criteria of reliability. In its pristine form, the objection from confrontation implies that the fairness of the trial is compromised whenever the accused is denied the opportunity of challenging key evidence, *even if unconfronted evidence is true and reliable.* The question then becomes whether this procedural defect is serious enough to derail trial proceedings[44] or to undermine the safety of a conviction on appeal.[45] '[T]he fairness of a trial has to be assessed on a case by case basis, viewing each trial as a whole', the UK Supreme Court concluded in *Horncastle*. Consequently, 'an inability on the part of a defendant to cross-examine the maker of a statement that is admitted in evidence will not *necessarily* render the trial unfair'.[46]

Arguments appealing to confrontation or other fair trial rights are plainly not plausible rationalizations of the historical evolution of the rule against hearsay at common law. For one thing, such considerations extend only to prosecution evidence in criminal proceedings,[47] whereas the traditional common law exclusionary rule applied generally to all parties, plaintiffs, prosecution or defence, in civil as well as criminal litigation. Only considerations of reliability – actual or perceived – can account for the doctrinal development over several centuries of a general exclusionary rule of this extensive scope. However, arguments from confrontation and fair trial are not advanced as revisionist legal history, but rather as normative criteria of justice by which to evaluate existing legal developments and potentially stimulate further procedural reform. This is the dimension along which such rationalizations should be assessed. Arguments from confrontation and fair trial now take their place alongside more traditional rationales for hearsay exclusion predicated on the logic of proof. Notably, the conception of defence rights endorsed by the European Court of Human Rights under Article 6(3)(d), and crystallized in a reinvigorated right to confrontation at English common law, must also somehow accommodate the rights of victims and witnesses to an effective and humane criminal process.[48]

---

[42] Sketched in Chapter 2.

[43] Cf. *Schenk* v *Switzerland* (1991) 13 EHRR 242, [46]: 'While Article 6 of the Convention guarantees the right to a fair trial, it does not lay down any rules on the admissibility of evidence as such, which is therefore primarily a matter for regulation under national law. The Court therefore cannot exclude as a matter of principle and in the abstract that unlawfully obtained evidence... may be admissible'.   [44] §2.5(c).

[45] §2.5(e).   [46] *R* v *Horncastle* [2009] UKSC 14, [74] (emphasis supplied).

[47] With a possible limited extension to the evidence of one co-accused directly implicating another.

[48] *Doorson* v *The Netherlands* (1996) 22 EHRR 330. The principle of humane treatment was introduced in §1.3 as another – in this context, competing – foundational principle of criminal evidence.

(c) RATIONALIZING HEARSAY REFORM

There are plainly good reasons to be cautious about receiving hearsay evidence in criminal trials. Moreover, as we have just seen, arguments internal to the logic of proof have lately been reinforced by intrinsic considerations of fairness and confrontation rights. The pertinent question is whether any given formulation of the exclusionary rule operates as an effective servant of the objectives and values it is supposed to promote. The hearsay rule might be well-intentioned and aimed at appropriate targets, but how has it measured up in practice? Could any conceivable refinement of the exclusionary rule enhance its efficacy?

The common law rule attracted criticism because it mandated exclusion even when hearsay represented the best available source of information. There are situations in which hearsay, far from being inferior to direct oral testimony, is actually *more* trustworthy than any evidence that a witness could present in person at trial, yet the rule operated mechanically to exclude all hearsay (subject to inclusionary exceptions) irrespective of its probative value, and regardless of whether the declarant also testified in court.

The decision of the House of Lords in *Myers* v *DPP*[49] represents the high-water mark, or dreary depths, of a formalistic approach to hearsay exclusion, wholly divorced from common sense reasoning and the underlying rationales for rejecting hearsay. Myers was involved in a classic car-ringing scam. He would buy scrapped Austin cars, complete with their logbooks, then steal similar newer cars, and finally pass the stolen cars off as rebuilds of the old wrecks by switching their registration plates and chassis numbers. The only clue to the true identity of the stolen cars was another number stamped indelibly into the engine block of each vehicle. At trial, the prosecution adduced the Austin factory's records of these unique engine block numbers, by then reduced to microfilm but originally compiled by individual workers on the production line, to prove that Myers was selling stolen cars with falsified registration details. Though Myers' conviction was ultimately upheld on other evidence, the House of Lords ruled by a narrow 3–2 majority that the records of engine block numbers were hearsay and should not have been admitted in that form. The prosecution should have called the individual workers who first made the records to testify to each number directly.

From a common sense perspective, this ruling seems perverse. There could be no better evidence of the numbers than the Morris factory's records. Even if the individual production line workers had been traced, they would not have been able to remember the engine block numbers of particular vehicles, hundreds or even thousands of which it had been their job, day in and day out, to record. Their Lordships noted that individual workers would have been permitted to 'refresh their memories' from the records whilst testifying, but this, too, was a transparent fiction.[50] All that the workers could have done was to read out the numbers from the factory's records and, assuming that they were confident in the accuracy of their own work at the time and of the integrity of the factory's record-keeping since, to confirm that the relevant numbers were in all likelihood correct. The workers would not in any sense be testifying to their present recollections of past events. They would instead be relying on the accuracy and integrity of the records, just like the employee responsible for record-keeping who actually testified at Myers' trial. Calling the individual workers in these circumstances would have been an elaborate and wasteful

---

[49] *Myers* v *DPP* [1965] AC 1001, HL.   [50] Memory refreshing was discussed in §8.2(b).

charade. And yet that, said a majority of the House of Lords, was exactly what the common law of hearsay required.

Their Lordships were fully aware that the decision in *Myers* flouted common sense. Lord Reid, who (it is worth emphasizing) was in the majority, remarked that 'the law regarding hearsay is technical, and I would say absurdly technical', and concluded:

it is quite unreasonable to refuse to accept as *prima facie* evidence a record obviously well kept by public officers and proved never to have been discovered to contain a wrong entry though frequently consulted by officials… But that is the settled law.[51]

Myers decided that the hearsay rule at common law was a rigid exclusionary doctrine which could not be tempered by the exercise of judicial discretion. Indeed, the majority went further by indicating that the judges no longer retained the common law power, freely exercised in former times, to create *ad hoc* exceptions to hearsay exclusion. Reform must in future come from Parliament, if it were to come at all. Such judicial passivity was vigorously contested by Lord Pearce, who wrote in dissent:

[J]ustice and common sense have in the past demanded various exceptions if the general rule was to be acceptable at all. That the court should be slow to introduce or further adapt exceptions is reasonable. That the court should debar itself forever from introducing further exceptions or adapting them under any circumstances, however unforeseen or unforesee-able, would be unreasonable.[52]

But this pragmatic appeal fell on deaf ears (just as similar sentiments expressed by Lord Griffiths in *Kearley* would do nearly thirty years later).[53] *Myers* ever afterwards stood for the proposition that there could be no new common law exceptions to the hearsay rule. Ostensibly at least, the iron logic of hearsay exclusion could not be bent to match the contours of common sense fact-finding.

In this isolated instance, Parliament acted uncharacteristically swiftly, enacting the Criminal Evidence Act 1965 specifically to reverse *Myers* by creating a dedicated statutory exception to the hearsay rule for business documents.[54] But the legislature seldom turned its attention to reforming technical rules of criminal evidence, until the twilight years of the twentieth century. In the meantime, *Myers* exerted a profoundly conservative influence on the application and development of the hearsay rule, and presented judges, into the bargain, with a highly convenient means of passing the buck when the law appeared to take its leave of common sense. This is what transpired in *Blastland*, when the House of Lords was exhorted to recognize an exception for relevant defence evidence of third party confessions. Lord Bridge firmly declined, with the alibi that *Myers* had 'established the principle, never since challenged, that it is for the legislature, not the judiciary, to create new exceptions to the hearsay rule'.[55]

The loss of relevant evidence is not necessarily a conclusive objection to an automatic rule of exclusion. Rules are categorical generalizations which by their very nature are

---

[51] [1965] AC 1001, 1019, 1023.   [52] ibid. 1038.

[53] The (still) important decision in *R v Kearley* [1992] 2 AC 228, HL, is dissected in §9.4(b), below.

[54] The statutory exception for business documents subsequently went through several incarnations, before finding its current home in s.117 of the CJA 2003: see §9.5(b), below.

[55] *R v Blastland* [1986] 1 AC 41, 52, HL.

nearly always both under- and over-inclusive to some extent.[56] The question is whether a rule that indiscriminately excludes both probative and potentially misleading evidence offers a better strategy for minimizing the risk of error in truth-finding, or better safeguards other intrinsic criminal justice values and instrumental objectives, than a particularistic strategy of evaluating the potential strengths and weaknesses of hearsay evidence on a case-by-case basis. Untrammelled judicial discretion would probably be insufficiently robust to contain the potential shortcomings of hearsay evidence. A rigid exclusionary rule, it might plausibly be contended, is not only a more reliable mechanism for preventing poor quality information from contaminating the forensic process, but also saves time and reduces uncertainty for the parties in preparing for trial.

Risk-reduction, efficiency, and predictability are indubitably valuable in criminal adjudication,[57] but the argument for an inflexible rule of exclusion can only succeed in practice if two further conditions are met: first, the rule prohibiting hearsay must produce results broadly in conformity with common sense and foundational principles of justice; and, secondly, the rule must be reasonably determinate and certain in its application. Unless the first condition is satisfied, the benefits of exclusion will be outweighed by the loss of too much valuable evidence, producing an intolerable level of erroneous verdicts and increased risks of injustice, including wrongful convictions. This in turn would be liable to precipitate potentially catastrophic loss of public confidence in the administration of criminal justice.[58] If the second condition is not fulfilled the promised benefits of predictability, clarity, and consistent and straightforward application will not materialize. To the extent that a 'rule' could still meaningfully be said to exist in such depleted circumstances, it would afford little if any practical advantage over free-ranging judicial discretion.

The common law rule against hearsay was vulnerable on both flanks. The risk of injustice was presented most directly when the rule operated to exclude potentially exculpatory hearsay evidence tendered by the defence. In *Sparks* v *R*,[59] for example, the accused was convicted of indecently assaulting a four-year-old girl. The defence proposed to ask the victim's mother whether the girl had not said, shortly after the incident, that 'it was a coloured boy' who perpetrated the assault. This would have been highly pertinent evidence for the defence, since the accused was white. The victim was not called to testify in person: such a young child would not at that time have been regarded as a competent witness.[60] Yet the trial judge refused to compensate for the victim's absence by allowing her statement to be elicited through cross-examination of the mother, on the ground that this line of questioning called for hearsay; and his ruling was upheld by the Privy Council. As luck would have it, in this instance, the conviction was quashed on other grounds, but the risk of serious injustice posed by hearsay exclusion in a case like *Sparks* is manifest. Andrew Choo observes that, 'if there was ever a case in which defence hearsay evidence should clearly have been admitted, *Sparks* was that case'.[61] Yet the accused's plea for individualized justice on the merits left Lord Morris cold:

The cause of justice is ... best served by adherence to rules which have long been recognised and settled. If the girl had made a remark to her mother (not in the presence of the appellant) to the effect that it was the appellant who had assaulted her and if the girl was not to

---

[56] Frederick Schauer, *Playing by the Rules: A Philosophical Examination of Rule-Based Decision-Making in Law and in Life* (OUP, 1991), ch 2.   [57] §1.2(c).

[58] §3.2(b).   [59] *Sparks* v *R* [1964] AC 965, PC.   [60] §7.2.

[61] Choo, *Hearsay and Confrontation in Criminal Trials*, 66.

be a witness at the trial, evidence as to what she had said would be the merest hearsay. In such circumstances it would be the defence who would wish to challenge a contention, if advanced, that it would be 'manifestly unjust' for the jury not to know that the girl had given a clue to the identity of her assailant. If it is said that hearsay evidence should freely be admitted and that there should be concentration in any particular case upon deciding as to its value or weight it is sufficient to say that our law has not been evolved upon such lines but is firmly based upon the view that it is wiser and better that hearsay should be excluded save in certain well defined and rather exceptional circumstances.[62]

Further examples of potentially exculpatory defence evidence falling foul of hearsay exclusion include cases involving third party confessions[63] or statements apparently incriminating another person,[64] in circumstances where the involvement of a second suspect would logically exonerate the accused.

Turing to the second practical pre-condition for effective categorical exclusion, the rule of law virtues extolled by the law of hearsay were compromised by a catalogue of formally prescribed and informally cultivated quasi-exceptions, the latter aptly styled 'hearsay fiddles' by Di Birch.[65] Hearsay-fiddles were perpetrated by manipulating the definition of hearsay, adopting indulgent interpretations of recognized categories of exception, treating particular types of evidence (including confessions, scientific evidence, and real evidence) as though they were exempt from the normal rules, and utilizing procedural devices like 'memory-refreshing' to outflank meaningful hearsay exclusion and thereby reduce compliance with the letter of the law to a hollow ritual.[66] So the grand gesture of foreswearing new common law exceptions solemnly intoned in *Myers* was really rather misleading if taken in isolation, since *existing* exceptions to the hearsay rule were flexible and open to a certain amount of, possibly wilful, judicial manipulation. The tried, tested, and time-honoured way of circumventing *Myers'* injunction against the creation of new common law exceptions was to interpret the prohibition flexibly and wink at *de facto* exceptions, allowing courts to receive evidence on the basis of *ad hoc* assessments of reliability and probative value. Viewed in the round, therefore, the byzantine technicality of hearsay doctrine began to seem gratuitous as well as irritating. It could not even deliver the one set of normative virtues that was supposed to justify deliberate departures from common sense reasoning, the loss of much probative evidence, and enhanced risks of wrongful conviction – clarity, predictability, consistency, and legal certainty.

Prior to the advent of the Criminal Justice Act 2003, criticism of the law of hearsay had become so widespread and incessant that one could doubt whether the rule against hearsay would, or should, survive in any form in English criminal proceedings. Academic commentators argued that it would be preferable to abolish the general exclusionary rule outright,

---

[62] [1964] AC 965, 978.

[63] R v *Blastland* [1986] 1 AC 41, HL. Also see R v *Thompson* [1912] 3 KB 19, CCA; R v *Malcherek and Steel* (1981) 73 Cr App R 173, 185–6, CA.   [64] R v *Harry* (1986) 86 Cr App R 105, CA.

[65] D. J. Birch, 'Hearsay-logic and Hearsay-fiddles: *Blastland* Revisited', in Peter Smith (ed.) *Criminal Law: Essays in Honour of JC Smith* (1987), 25: 'The overall picture of the hearsay rule in criminal cases is one of hidden tension between the apparently inexorable hearsay-logic and the judicially unacknowledged but ever-present hearsay-fiddle'. Also see Choo, *Hearsay and Confrontation in Criminal Trials*, ch 3; Andrew Ashworth and Rosemary Pattenden, 'Reliability, Hearsay Evidence and the English Criminal Trial' (1986) 102 *LQR* 292.

[66] A fuller account of the various hearsay-fiddles was presented in the first edition: Roberts and Zuckerman, *Criminal Evidence* (OUP, 2004), 609–23.

leaving trial judges free to determine the merits of admitting proffered hearsay on a case-by-case basis.[67] The twin pillars of the abolitionist case were, first, that the rationales for hearsay exclusion could not withstand sustained critical scrutiny and, secondly, that the rule and its exceptions, as currently formulated, anyway failed to serve the stated rationales. Nobody was arguing that the prosecution (or, for that matter, the defence) should be able to dispense with calling its witnesses to testify in court whenever convenience or fancy might dictate. Cultural allegiance to English law's traditional commitment to orality remained strong. The argument was essentially that hearsay should be admissible whenever the party seeking to adduce it could demonstrate sufficient criteria of reliability and necessity to justify its admission. In short, hearsay should be admitted where it was the 'best available evidence'.[68]

Other voices favoured less radical, more gradualist reform.[69] The Law Commission began working in earnest on reform of the law of hearsay in the mid-1990s. Its consultation paper[70] and final report[71] featured extensive critique of the existing rules, but the Commission's ultimate recommendations to Parliament were relatively conservative. The main proposals were that the definition of hearsay should be restricted to intentionally assertive conduct, removing so-called 'implied assertions' from the ambit of the exclusionary rule;[72] and that judges should have an overriding residual discretion to admit any oral or documentary hearsay statement in the interests of justice.

Reform of the law of hearsay was subsequently taken up by the government as part of its aspiration to modernize and, ultimately, codify the law of criminal evidence.[73] The result is Chapter 2 of Part 11 of the CJA 2003, comprising sections 114–136, which came into force on 4 April 2005. It is time now to get to grips with the details of the statutory provisions. We begin by reviewing the overarching structural framework for regulating the admissibility of hearsay evidence created by the 2003 Act.

9.3 STRUCTURE OF THE CJA 2003'S HEARSAY PROVISIONS

The starting point for hearsay analysis in English criminal proceedings is now section 114 of the CJA 2003, entitled 'admissibility of hearsay evidence'. Subsection (1) merits citation in full:

s.114(1) – Admissibility of hearsay evidence
In criminal proceedings a statement not made in oral evidence in the proceedings is admissible as evidence of any matter stated if, but only if –

---

[67] See, e.g., John D. Jackson, 'Hearsay: the Sacred Cow that Won't be Slaughtered?' (1998) 2 *E & P* 166; Andrew L.-T. Choo, *Hearsay and Confrontation in Criminal Trials*, ch 8; A. A. S. Zuckerman, 'The Futility of Hearsay' [1996] *Crim LR* 4; J. R. Spencer, 'Hearsay Reform: A Bridge Not Far Enough?' [1996] *Crim LR* 29.

[68] J. R. Spencer, 'Hearsay Reform: A Bridge Not Far Enough?' [1996] *Crim LR* 29.

[69] Colin Tapper, 'Hearsay in Criminal Cases: An Overview of Law Commission Report No 245' [1997] *Crim LR* 771; P. B. Carter, 'Hearsay: Whether and Whither?' (1993) 109 *LQR* 573.

[70] LCCP No 138, *Evidence in Criminal Proceedings: Hearsay and Related Topics* (HMSO, 1995).

[71] Law Com No 245, *Evidence in Criminal Proceedings: Hearsay and Related Topics* (TSO, 1997).

[72] See §9.4(b), below.

[73] See CJS, *Justice for All*, Cm 5563 (TSO, 2002), paras.4.60–4.62; Home Office, *Criminal Justice: The Way Ahead*, Cm 5074 (2001), paras.3.44, 3.57–3.59; Lord Justice Auld, *Review of the Criminal Courts of England and Wales: Report* (2001), ch 1, paras.35–36 and ch 11, paras.95–104; Labour Party, *Ambitions for Britain: Labour's Manifesto 2001*, 33.

(a) any provision of this Chapter or any other statutory provision makes it admissible,
(b) any rule of law preserved by section 118 makes it admissible,
(c) all parties to the proceedings agree to it being admissible, or
(d) the court is satisfied that it is in the interests of justice for it to be admissible.

The effect of the 'if, but only if' formula in the operative part of subsection (1) is to estab-lish section 114 as the controlling provision. Henceforth, a hearsay statement can only be admitted if it can be brought under one of the paragraphs (a)–(d). It is not quite true to say that section 114 effects a statutory codification of the hearsay rule, however, because paragraph (b) operates by reference to preserve designated pre-existing common law exceptions. The legal basis for admitting the evidence becomes section 114(1)(b), but com-mon law definitions of the scope and content of individual exceptions continue to function in conjunction with section 118. These are examined in detail in §9.6, below.

The CJA 2003 proceeds to create two main heads of hearsay exception, pursuant to section 114(1)(a). First, section 116 lays down detailed rules governing the admissibility of hearsay statements made by people who are, for a range of designated reasons, unavaila-ble to testify as witnesses in the trial. The witness unavailability provisions are elucidated in §9.5(a) of this chapter. Secondly, section 117 creates a dedicated exception for business records and analogous statements in documents, which is analysed in §9.5(b). Sections 116 and 117 are modelled, respectively, on sections 23 and 24 of the Criminal Justice Act 1988, which the CJA 2003 supersedes and repeals.[74] An important distinction is that, whereas the 1988 Act's hearsay exceptions were restricted to statements in documents, section 116 of the CJA 2003 extends to oral as well as written hearsay. The extension is, however, subject to the further restriction created by section 121 of the CJA 2003, that hearsay statements of hearsay statements – 'second-hand' or 'multiple hearsay' – cannot be admitted under either section 116 or section 118 unless 'the court is satisfied that the value of the evidence in question, taking into account how reliable the statements appear to be, is so high that the interests of justice require the later statement to be admissible for that purpose'. Section 121 therefore sets up a presumption in favour of receiving only first-hand hearsay under sections 116 or 118, but multiple hearsay nonetheless remains potentially admissible if the judge is satisfied that its reception would serve the interests of justice.

Section 114(1)(d) creates a new inclusionary discretion of general application, which subsection 114(2) structures by enumerating factors to which 'the court must have regard' before receiving hearsay evidence in exercise of this discretion. The nine factors listed are:

(a) how much probative value the statement has (assuming it to be true) in relation to a matter in issue in the proceedings, or how valuable it is for the understanding of other evidence in the case;
(b) what other evidence has been, or can be, given on the matter or evidence mentioned in paragraph (a);
(c) how important the matter or evidence mentioned in paragraph (a) is in the context of the case as a whole;
(d) the circumstances in which the statement was made;

----

[74] s.136.

(e) how reliable the maker of the statement appears to be;

(f) how reliable the evidence of the making of the statement appears to be;

(g) whether oral evidence of the matter stated can be given and, if not, why it cannot;

(h) the amount of difficulty involved in challenging the statement;

(i) the extent to which that difficulty would be likely to prejudice the party facing it.

In Law Commission papers preceding the CJA 2003[75] and in the wider debates surrounding hearsay reform,[76] the idea of a residual inclusionary discretion was presented as a 'safety valve', a measure that could be invoked when all else failed, in order to secure the admissibility of reliably probative hearsay and thereby avoid judicial applications of hearsay doctrine that seemed to defy common sense. Models for a statutory 'safety valve' could be found in the inclusionary common law discretions developed by the Supreme Court of Canada and the High Court of Australia in the 1990s.[77] This understanding of section 114(1)(d) was reflected in some of the early judgments dealing with the hearsay provisions of the CJA 2003. In *Maher* v *DPP*, for example, Scott Baker LJ's described sections 114(1)(d) and 114(2) as 'the sweeping up provisions'.[78] In possibly the most important decision to-date on the hearsay aspects of the 2003 Act, however, the Court of Appeal rejected any gloss on the statutory wording.

In *R* v *Y* Lord Justice Hughes insisted that the language of section 114(1)(d) should be given its ordinary natural meaning, irrespective of its drafting history; and on a natural reading, hearsay was to be admitted if that would satisfy the interests of justice, unencumbered by pre-existing common law doctrines (such as, in this particular case, the rules relating to confession evidence). Section 114(1)(d) was capable of taking the lead in orchestrating the admissibility of hearsay under the CJA 2003 and was not confined to playing second fiddle to sub-paragraphs (a)–(c):

It follows that hearsay contained in a confession is, in law, as open to admission under sub-paragraph (d) as any other hearsay. There is no basis on which section 114(1) can be read so as to subordinate sub-paragraph (d) to (b). If that had been intended, the Act would have said so.... Explicit statutory provision prevails over the common law, not the other way round. The residual power to admit hearsay under section 114(1)(d), if the interests of justice genuinely require it, does indeed prevail over the general common law rule that hearsay is inadmissible, and thus it prevails over the particular common law rule that hearsay contained in a confession is inadmissible except against its maker.[79]

---

[75] Law Com No 245, paras.8.136, 8.143: '[O]ur purpose is to allow for the admission of reliable hearsay which could not otherwise be admitted, particularly to prevent a conviction which that evidence would render unsafe. We remain convinced that the safety-valve is needed. We recommend that there should be a limited discretion to admit hearsay evidence not falling within any other exception.... A party would only need to turn to the safety-valve when none of the other exceptions could be used.'

[76] See J. R. Spencer, *Hearsay Evidence in Criminal Proceedings* (Hart, 2008), §1.89 and ch 5: 'In its new and prominent position, the Law Commission's designation no longer seemed to fit: instead of being a "safety-valve", for use in emergency when all else fails, it now looked more like an alternative tap, which a court could open whenever it felt appropriate.'

[77] See Choo, *Hearsay and Confrontation in Criminal Trials*, ch 7; Carter, 'Hearsay: Whether and Whither?' (1993) 109 *LQR* 573.   [78] *Maher* v *DPP* [2006] EWHC 1271 (Admin), [15].

[79] *R* v *Y* [2008] 1 WLR 1683, [2008] EWCA Crim 10, [47]–[48]; applied in *R* v *Z* [2009] 1 Cr App R 34, [2009] EWCA Crim 20, [20], where the Court of Appeal added the significant proviso that 's.114(1)(d) is to be cautiously applied, since otherwise the conditions laid down by Parliament in s.116 would be circumvented'.

This was a bold ruling, and a striking departure from the technical logic-chopping with which the law of hearsay has traditionally been associated. It raises two obvious questions. First, if section 114(1)(d) is going to be allowed free rein, where does this leave the rest of the Law Commission's carefully-crafted admissibility framework which was predicated on section 114(1)(d) being kept tightly in harness? We will defer general evaluation of the CJA 2003's merits to this chapter's conclusion. A second question has greater immediate practical significance: can section 114(1)(d) be kept on the straight-and-narrow path signposted 'the interests of justice', or might it now cut a swathe through hearsay doctrine with little regard for its studied logic or refined intuitions?

Although troubling when extended to evidence tendered by the defence,[80] application of the hearsay prohibition to third party confessions is well-grounded in the rationales underpinning the exclusionary rule. It often happens that a suspect, whilst apparently confessing his own guilt, also implicates a co-accused, or deliberately attempts to minimize his own involvement by laying most of the blame on his erstwhile associates, or perhaps even sees an opportunity to settle a score with his enemies. There are clear incentives to fabricate false allegations in these situations, and the common law has sensibly pursued a policy of ignoring third party confessions or accusations unless and until the allegations are repeated in court and subjected to searching cross-examination. In principle, however, section 114(1)(d) has decisively rejected the exclusionary premiss. Sensing the danger, the Court of Appeal in *R v Y* was quick to add that no hearsay could be received under section 114(1)(d) unless it also satisfied the criteria for assessing the interests of justice specified in section 114(2). The court went out of its way to stress that it was *not* announcing a general amnesty for third party confessions in police stations regardless of circumstantial suspicions.[81] Whether trial judges, or indeed other compositions of the Court of Appeal, will be astute to hold this wavering line remains to be seen.

All the statutory bases for admitting hearsay evidence established by CJA 2003, sections 114–118, including section 114(1)(d)'s general inclusionary discretion, must be read in the light of section 126, dealing with exclusionary discretions. First, section 126(1) authorizes the court to refuse to admit any hearsay statement where 'the case for excluding the statement, taking account of the danger that to admit it would result in undue waste of time, substantially outweighs the case for admitting it, taking account of the value of the evidence'. This provision is clearly designed to protect the jury from hearsay evidence of marginal probative value that would probably be more trouble than it would be worth, in resolving disputed factual issues, if admitted into the trial. Section 126(2) proceeds to announce, secondly, that nothing in Chapter 11 of the CJA 2003 prejudices the operation of either section 78 of PACE or 'any other power of a court to exclude evidence at its discretion (whether by preventing questions from being put or otherwise)'.[82] A trial judge would therefore never be obliged to receive hearsay evidence unless she considers, taking everything into account including fairness to the accused and the moral integrity of the proceedings, that the jury ought to hear it.

---

[80] As in *R v Blastland* [1986] AC 41, 57–9, HL, discussed in §3.2.

[81] '[T]he existence of section 114(1)(d) does not make police interviews routinely admissible in the case of persons other than the interviewee, and…the reasons why they are ordinarily not admissible except in the case of the interviewee are likely to continue to mean that in the great majority of cases it will not be in the interests of justice to admit them in the case of any other person': *R v Y* [2008] 1 WLR 1683, [2008] EWCA Crim 10, [57].   [82] Section 126(2)(b).

What if it subsequently transpires, in the light of the way in which the trial unfolds, that hearsay evidence is unreliable and, with the benefit of hindsight, ought not to have been admitted in the first place? Parliament has foreseen and pre-empted this contingency, also. Section 125 provides that the trial judge must either direct an acquittal or order a retrial whenever the case against the accused rests 'wholly or partly' on a hearsay statement and 'the evidence provided by the statement is so unconvincing that, considering its importance to the case against the defendant, his conviction of the offence would be unsafe'.[83] Trial judges are thus empowered, pro-actively, to prevent hearsay evidence from leading to miscarriages of justice, rather than requiring the accused to argue on appeal, and after the fact, that the admission of hearsay at his trial rendered his conviction unsafe.

Although the CJA 2003 puts the English law of hearsay on a systematic statutory footing for the first time in its history, Parliament was not building from the ground up. Rather, the CJA 2003 was able to appropriate the successes, and learn from the mistakes, of more than a century of common law jurisprudence shaping modern hearsay doctrine, as well as drawing on the experience of previous attempts – none of them entirely satisfactory – to legislate in this field, including the ill-fated provisions of the Criminal Justice Act 1988. This chapter undertakes detailed analysis of sections 116–118 of the CJA 2003, in the light of their common law and statutory antecedents and their rapidly accumulating judicial interpretations in decided cases.

Before turning to detailed doctrinal analysis of particular hearsay exceptions, however, we need to become better acquainted with the definition of the hearsay rule, by exploring its conceptual scope and considering some concrete illustrations of its application in practice. Answering the question 'What is hearsay?' is logically prior to determining the admissibility of evidence so classified. Moreover, settling on and sticking with a serviceable definition of hearsay is easier said than done. The task confronts us with some thorny theoretical difficulties, which have also arisen in criminal litigation in recent years. So the following discussion will have immediate salience for legal practice as well as being educational in the broader sense. It is worth stressing at the outset that one must avoid slipping into the habit of thinking that 'all hearsay is inadmissible'. To the contrary, much evidence that falls squarely within the ambit of the exclusionary rule can still be admitted under one or more hearsay exceptions. Considering the admissibility of evidence that might potentially be classified as hearsay is therefore a three stage process (implementing the general legal framework introduced in §3.1):

1. Is the evidence relevant? (It greatly simplifies matters if the precise basis on which relevance is asserted is spelt out from the beginning.) If yes, then:

2. Does evidence proffered on that basis fall within the scope of hearsay exclusion? In short-hand, is it an out-of-court statement adduced for its truth? If yes, then:

3. Is this hearsay evidence nonetheless admissible under an applicable exception created by statute or at common law?

Relevance was discussed in Chapter 3, and inclusionary exceptions to the exclusionary rule are examined later, below. Focusing now on the second stage of the analysis takes us directly to the heart of the matter: what evidence is properly classified as hearsay in English law?

---

[83] Section 125(1)(b).

9.4 DEFINITION AND SCOPE OF THE
RULE AGAINST HEARSAY

Section 115 of the CJA 2003 defines a 'statement' for the purposes of the law of hearsay in broad terms as 'any representation of fact or opinion made by a person by whatever means', including in pictures.[84] Section 115(3) further limits the statutory definition of hearsay to that sub-class of statements where 'the purpose, or one of the purposes, of the person making the statement appears to the court to have been (a) to cause another person to believe the matter, or (b) to cause another person to act or a machine to operate on the basis that the matter is as stated'. Section 121(2) subsequently declares the meaning of 'hearsay statement' to be 'a statement, not made in oral evidence, that is relied on as evidence of a matter stated in it'.[85]

These definitions, when read in conjunction with section 114, substantially replicate the terminology and scope of the common law exclusionary rule, with one important revision or clarification (depending on one's view of the authentic common law position prior to the Act). The new statutory hearsay rule is expressly limited to out-of-court statements which were intended by the speaker to affect another person's beliefs or conduct, i.e. to 'propositional' or 'assertive' conduct. The intended effect of this formulation, which will be systematically appraised in §9.4(b), is to exclude so-called 'implied assertions' from the ambit of the hearsay prohibition. Before venturing into that seemingly interminable but mightily instructive controversy, however, we can get a firmer grip on the law of hearsay by investigating its application to paradigm cases. To this end, §9.4(a) reviews the basic definition and scope of the hearsay rule, with practical illustrations.

(a) THE CONCEPT OF HEARSAY

Cross's classic definition of the hearsay rule, quoted at the beginning of this chapter, has three basic components: (1) a statement; (2) not made orally in the proceedings; (3) tendered as evidence of some fact stated or asserted. The meaning of a 'statement' is now defined by section 115 of the CJA 2003, as we have just seen. Component (2) of Cross's definition entails that only oral testimony in the current trial evades the clutches of the hearsay prohibition: every other statement, whether made orally or in documentary form and including even testimony made under oath in different court proceedings, fell within the scope of the common law definition. The CJA 2003, in referring to 'a statement not made in oral evidence in the proceedings',[86] adopts an exactly equivalent formula. It is often convenient to refer more simply to 'out-of-court statements', which is harmless enough shorthand provided that it is understood that this is only a close approximation, rather than an absolutely faithful translation, of the real test. Even in-court statements can sometimes be hearsay, where the testimony in question does not form part of *the current* proceedings.

---

[84] Section 115(2). Photofit identifications are specifically mentioned as falling within the definition.

[85] Section 121(2) modestly defines the meaning of 'hearsay statement' only '[i]n this section'. However, this limitation probably indicates only that 'hearsay statement' is not a term of art when invoked elsewhere in the Act. The draftsman's caution should not be turned on its head, to imply that 'hearsay statement' ever means anything else when employed on other occasions.   [86] Sections 114 and 116.

In every case, however, component (3) of Cross's definition still had to be satisfied for a statement to constitute hearsay at common law, and the same pre-condition is retained under the CJA 2003 by use of the words 'of any matter stated' in the operative sections.[87] Crucially, this makes one of the defining features of hearsay *the purpose* for which the evidence is adduced in the trial. Evidence may be inadmissible hearsay if adduced for one (impermissible) purpose, but freely admissible and possibly highly probative if adduced for another (permitted) purpose. The operation of the hearsay rule depends on how evidence is actively presented within lawyers' trial strategies, a question of what lawyers *do*, rather than what they find.[88] In the abstract, this observation is no more difficult to grasp than to state, yet its neglect lies at the root of a great deal of the confusion and error with which the topic of hearsay has become associated over the years. The following mantra, if taken to heart, can serve as invaluable guidance, better even than Theseus' ball of string, when one finds oneself trapped in the labyrinth of hearsay: there is no such thing as hearsay *evidence*, only hearsay *uses*.

The best way of becoming thoroughly familiar with the concept of hearsay, so that it may be invoked almost by instinct in preparing witness statements or during the cut-and-thrust of a criminal trial, is to see how the rule has been applied to determine admissibility in contested cases. Previous decisions at common law are not, of course, strictly speaking precedents on the interpretation of the CJA 2003. However, since the CJA 2003 substantially adopts the common law's pre-existing definitions, the persuasive authority of much common law jurisprudence is barely diminished by the Act.

In the well-known nineteenth century case of *Gibson*,[89] where the charge was malicious wounding, the complainant testified that a bystander had said to him 'the man who threw the stone went in there,' and pointed to the accused's door. The Court for Crown Cases Reserved ruled that the evidence was inadmissible hearsay which should not have been given. Whilst the bystander was allegedly an eyewitness to the crime, the complainant was merely reporting to the court what the bystander had told him, rather than anything that the complainant had apprehended directly through his own senses. Furthermore, the bystander's assertion was being adduced in order to prove the truth of the matter stated, namely that the man who threw the stone really did go into the accused's house, where the accused was duly apprehended a short time later. This is classic hearsay, and *prima facie* inadmissible, unless the evidence could be brought within one of the recognized heads of exception that will be considered later in the chapter.

This first illustration suggests another handy, informal, test of hearsay. Imagine you are opposing counsel challenging a witness testifying in court with the clinching question: how do you know that? If the witness would reply 'I saw it', 'I heard it', 'I touched it', 'I felt it', or 'I smelt it' (taking care to define the 'it', the contested fact to which the witness purports to testify, with appropriate precision), this is non-hearsay testimonial evidence. Evidence of what the witness perceived with his or her own unaided senses, or in other words direct testimonial evidence, evades the clutches of the hearsay rule. But if the witness replies to the effect that 'so-and-so told me,' her testimony is hearsay and

---

[87] CJA 2003, ss.114, 116, 117, 118 (in various formulations), and 121(2).

[88] Another way of putting it: 'hearsay-ness' is not some mysterious, passive, evidentiary quality that inheres within speech, writing, or objects, and which lawyers have been specially trained to detect and ferret out. Hearsay evidence is made rather than found. [89] *R v Gibson* (1887) 18 QBD 537, CCR.

prima facie inadmissible to the extent that it is adduced for a hearsay purpose, i.e. for its truth content.

Gibson exemplifies a familiar scenario involving oral hearsay testimony. However, the common law exclusionary rule (anticipating CJA 2003, section 115's all-inclusive definition of 'statement') was by no means limited to the spoken word. Indeed, words as such were not required at all. Thus, in *Chandrasekera*[90] the complainant *in extremis* was prevented from speaking because her throat had been cut, but she managed to indicate using hand-signals that the accused was her assassin. The Privy Council confirmed that such non-verbal assertive conduct was caught squarely within the rule against hearsay (though in this case, fortunately, there was an appropriate exception under which the evidence could properly be admitted). The rule extended *a fortiori* to statements in documents, and to writing on objects, providing, of course, that the statement or writing was adduced for its truth.

In *Patel* v *Comptroller of Customs*[91] the accused was convicted of falsely declaring to customs officials that the country of origin of five bags of imported seed was India, when in fact the seed came from Morocco. The prosecution proved the seed's country of origin at trial by removing its outer packaging to reveal inner bags marked with the legend 'produce of Morocco'. This might seem, from a common sense perspective, pretty conclusive proof of the seed's origin. However, the Privy Council held that the markings were hearsay and should have been excluded, and this must be correct on a logical application of the hearsay rule. The words 'produce of Morocco' were being adduced to prove that the seed really was the produce of Morocco. Yet the bag itself could not vouch testimonially – by direct oral evidence – for the authenticity of this assertion. As Lord Hodson said:

Nothing here is known of when and by whom the markings on the bags were affixed and no evidence was called to prove any fact which tended to show that the goods in question in fact came from Morocco.[92]

What the prosecution needed was a witness who could come to court and testify that he, personally, could speak to the origin of the seed. Without such testimony, the prosecution was merely relying on second-hand assertions from an unknown source, in other words inadmissible hearsay, and the accused's appeal against conviction was allowed.

A telling contrast can be drawn with cases in which an out-of-court statement is being adduced, not for the truth of its propositional content, but for some other reason. Sometimes, the very fact that words were spoken is itself relevant to matters in dispute in the litigation. For example, it may be pertinent to show that the declarant is able to speak, speaks a particular language, or expresses himself in a particularly distinctive way.[93] Likewise, the utterance of a threat may be proved to demonstrate that the accused acted under duress without infringing the rule against hearsay.[94] To substantiate a criminal law defence of duress, it is unnecessary to prove that a threat – such as: 'Harm X, or I will kill you' – is genuine or likely to be carried out. Substantive criminal law requires only that the threat was made, that the accused believed it to be genuine, and that the will of a person of reasonable fortitude would have been overborne by the threat.[95] In short, an

---

[90] *Chandrasekera* v R [1937] AC 220, PC.   [91] *Patel* v *Comptroller of Customs* [1965] AC 356, PC.
[92] ibid. 365.   [93] *R* v *Voisin* [1918] KB 531, CCA.
[94] *Subramaniam* v *Public Prosecutor* [1956] 1 WLR 965, PC.
[95] *R* v *Howe* [1987] AC 417, HL; *R* v *Graham* (1982) 74 Cr App R 235, CA.

out-of-court statement containing a threat cannot be hearsay when the statement is not being adduced for its truth but, rather, for its impact on the hearer: *there is no such thing as hearsay evidence, only hearsay uses*. Notice that this result coheres nicely with the probative rationale for hearsay exclusion, because the hearer in this example is actually a first-hand, percipient witness to the fact that the statement was made (but not to the truth of its contents). The hearsay dangers do not arise in this scenario, and the rationale for excluding (some) hearsay falls away.

A trickier set of examples concerns what are sometimes characterized as 'legally operative words'. Where the very act of making an out-of-court statement may attract legal consequences,[96] such utterances may be proved – irrespective of the truth of their contents – without infringing the hearsay prohibition. In civil litigation, words constituting a contractual offer may be proved in order to establish the existence of a binding contract, just as evidence of defamatory writing can be adduced in a libel action. In the logic of hearsay, such 'legally operative words' are proved as original evidence, directly apprehended by the person to whom the offer, defamatory assertion, etc. was made. Such statements are not adduced as evidence of anything other than the fact that they were made.[97]

Notwithstanding their outward conformity with the logic of the rule against hearsay, however, the doctrine of legally operative words sometimes seems to shade into a hearsay-fiddle with attendant hearsay dangers. In *Woodhouse* v *Hall*[98] the accused was charged with managing a brothel. Police witnesses proposed to testify that, posing as clients, they had discussed the availability and price of sexual services with the accused and two of the masseuses employed by him. The magistrates ruled this evidence inadmissible hearsay, but the Divisional Court allowed the prosecutor's appeal by way of case stated, on the basis that:[99]

There is no question here of the hearsay rule arising at all. The relevant issue was did these ladies make these offers? The offers were oral and the police officers were entitled to give evidence of them.

Viewed from one perspective, this is impeccable hearsay logic. But the facts of *Woodhouse* v *Hall* can also be presented in a more troubling light.

The chain of factual inferences, running from the fact of what was allegedly said to the officers to the conclusion that the accused was running a brothel, contains several weak links. Evidence of the prices quoted to the officers for 'hand relief' and 'topless hand relief' was adduced to prove that such services were on offer, and would be performed for payment on demand. But a quotation is not a contract, nor in itself the subject of the charge. So in what sense were the words allegedly spoken legally operative? The prosecution was essentially advancing the contested statements as *de facto* admissions that prostitution was taking place on the premises. Yet this borders on, if it does not encroach into, hearsay

---

[96] That is, the statement is a constitutive fact, as explained in §4.2.

[97] Though cf. Roger C. Park, '*McCormick on Evidence* and the Concept of Hearsay' (1980) 65 *Minnesota LR* 423, 441.

[98] (1981) 72 Cr App R 39, DC. Cf. *Roberts* v *DPP* [1994] Crim LR 926, DC; *R* v *McIntosh* [1992] Crim LR 651, CA.

[99] (1981) 72 Cr App R 39, 42 (Donaldson LJ). Comyn J added, ibid. 42–3, 'we are not dealing with an exception to the hearsay rule. What we are here dealing with is a more fundamental question as to whether the evidence proffered by the prosecution, rejected by the justices, was hearsay at all... [T]his was never a question of hearsay evidence.'

territory: out-of-court statements, implicitly admitting on-going prostitution, tendered to prove that the accused's premises were operating as a brothel.

The hearsay rule excludes out-of-court statements adduced for their truth. On a literal interpretation, *false* statements which are advanced to prove that the declarant lied fall outside the ambit of hearsay exclusion. To adduce an out-of-court statement to establish a lie is the opposite of relying on it for its truth. In *Mawaz Khan v R*[100] the prosecution adduced out-of-court statements of the accused and his co-accused in order to show that they had jointly concocted a false alibi. This was challenged as hearsay on appeal, but the Privy Council held that the evidence had been properly admitted. The alibis were proved to be false by other independent evidence, so that no reliance was placed upon them for a hearsay purpose; nor, it might be added, did evidence of the false alibis present significant hearsay dangers.[101] The prosecution merely sought to establish that false statements had been made, and to invite the fact-finder to draw negative inferences against the accused from their failed attempt to lie their way out of trouble. In this instance, both hearsay logic and common sense fact-finding converge in supporting the judges' reasoning and conclusion.

Other cases of 'negative hearsay' are more dubious, however. The early 1980s produced a rash of appeals in which business records were adduced in order to support an inference from the absence of a relevant bookkeeping entry. This procedure was said to be acceptable, whereas evidence of positive entries in the records would clearly have been inadmissible at common law under *Myers*. In *Shone*,[102] for example, the accused was charged with stealing three car springs from a warehouse. The prosecution called the warehouse supervisor who testified that, had the springs been removed from the warehouse legitimately, there would have been an entry to that effect in the stock records. Since the records showed no such entry, the clear inference was that the springs must have been purloined. The Court of Appeal confirmed that the stock records were properly admitted, since they were 'not hearsay, but evidence from which the jury were entitled to draw the inference... that all three springs were stolen'.[103]

Fastening on negative inferences might have been a doctrinally convenient way of limiting the impact of *Myers*, but it is difficult to discern the basis for any defensible distinction in the logic of proof. In what material respect does drawing a negative inference from the absence of an entry in a stock record differ from drawing a positive inference from a completed record of sale, or, for that matter (recalling *Myers*), from a microfilm record of engine block numbers? An inference from the absence of an entry presupposes that the record is substantially complete, correct, and reliable – that the record does not lie when it is silent.[104] Whenever the record has been compiled by one or more individuals not called

---

[100] *Mawaz Khan and Amanat Khan v R* [1967] AC 454, PC.

[101] But for discussion of other, non-hearsay, dangers of drawing negative inferences from lies, see §15.3(b).   [102] *R v Shone* (1983) 76 Cr App R 72, CA.

[103] ibid. 76, developing *dicta* in *R v Patel* (1981) 73 Cr App R 117, CA. And see *R v Muir* (1984) 79 Cr App R 153, CA.

[104] Might it be said that the inference is drawn, not from the entries, but from the very existence of a record in which entries would be made in appropriate cases? Negative inferences could conceivably be drawn from a completely empty record. However, such inferences would only be reliable on the strength of some express or implied assurance that the record is accurate and complete. See, further, Michael H. Graham, '"Stickperson Hearsay": A Simplified Approach to Understanding the Rule Against Hearsay' [1982] *University of Illinois LR* 887; Stephen A. Saltzburg, 'A Special Aspect of Relevance: Countering Negative Inferences Associated with the Absence of Evidence' (1978) 66 *California LR* 1011.

as witnesses, the inference must run through an assumption, wholly unsubstantiated in evidence, that accurate and complete entries have in general been made by every person responsible for compiling the record. This is classic hearsay in English law, and should be inadmissible as evidence of the disputed fact.[105] It is, of course, irrelevant to the logic of hearsay that records are often the best evidence, and that it would typically be very inconvenient, if not impossible, to procure credible first-hand oral testimony describing how particular records were complied and maintained.

Cases like *Patel*, *Woodhouse v Hall*, and *Shone* (not to mention *Myers*) remind us that the operation of the rule against hearsay was not always sensible or convenient, even when it was arguably logical. However, the formal logic of hearsay itself came under serious strain after a landmark decision of the House of Lords in the early 1990s. This brings us, at least, face-to-face with the well-trailed conundrum of 'implied assertions'.

(b) IMPLIED ASSERTIONS AND THE LOGIC OF HEARSAY

The question whether so-called 'implied assertions' fall within the ambit of the hearsay rule is a long-standing controversy, with important implications for the concept and scope of hearsay in general. Until the 1990s authorities were few, antiquated, and in considerable disarray. However, in *Kearley*[106] the House of Lords authoritatively decided, albeit by a bare 3–2 majority, that implied assertions were indeed caught by the hearsay rule at common law, just as an explicit assertion to the same effect would be *prima facie* inadmissible. In ostensibly settling an outstanding point of legal doctrine, however, *Kearley* reignited deeper controversy surrounding the scope of the hearsay rule. Section 115 of the CJA 2003 was subsequently drafted with the express purpose of reversing *Kearley* on implied assertions. The intended effect has seemingly been achieved, though possibly not as completely or conclusively as legislators might have hoped. (We will work our way back to this thought, and amplify it, in the concluding paragraphs of this section.) At all events, it remains highly instructive to consider how the reasoning employed by the *Kearley* majority exposed the logic of hearsay exclusion to *reductio ad absurdum*,[107] even though *Kearley's* days as a formal legal precedent were short-lived.

Alan Robert Michael Kearley – 'Chippie' to his friends and business associates – was charged with drug-dealing. A small quantity of amphetamine was recovered from his house, but no more than might plausibly be kept for personal use. In order to establish that Kearley possessed this substance with intent to supply,[108] the prosecution called several police witnesses who testified that, whilst searching Kearley's abode, they had received some fifteen telephone calls from people wanting to buy drugs from 'Chippie'. Later, no less

---

[105] Otherwise *Myers* itself could have been argued on the basis that the factory records contained no entries corresponding to the combination of registration, chassis, and engine block numbers to be found on the accused's 're-builds'.

[106] *R v Kearley* [1992] 2 AC 228, HL. See Rosemary Pattenden, 'Conceptual Versus Pragmatic Approaches to Hearsay' (1993) 56 *MLR* 138; Michael Hirst, 'Conduct, Relevance and the Hearsay Rule' (1993) 13 *Legal Studies* 54; C. F. H. Tapper, 'Hearsay and Implied Assertions' (1992) 109 *LQR* 524; J. R. Spencer, 'Hearsay, Relevance and Implied Assertions' [1993] *CLJ* 40.

[107] The argument was anticipated by Stephen Guest, 'The Scope of the Hearsay Rule' (1985) 101 *LQR* 385; and Guest, 'Hearsay Revisited' [1988] *CLP* 33.

[108] Contrary to s.5(3) of the Misuse of Drugs Act 1971.

than seven callers (some of whom may also have previously telephoned) came in person to the house, several with cash in hand, to buy drugs. From a common sense viewpoint, this was damning evidence of drug-dealing, and it cannot have taken the jury long to find Chippie Kearley guilty as charged. Nor could the Court of Appeal find anything wrong with his conviction. But a majority of the House of Lords held that the callers' requests for drugs contained implied assertions that Kearley was a drug dealer, rendering the officers' evidence inadmissible hearsay. The callers could have testified directly to Kearley's drugs sales on the basis of their own personal experience, but the police officers were merely reporting information that they had gathered from somebody else. Absent any admissible evidence of intent to supply, Kearley's conviction had to be quashed.

Their Lordships' reasoning embraced and exuded a simple and seductive logic. If the callers had come right out and asserted that Kearley was selling them drugs, this would clearly have been caught by hearsay exclusion: it would have been an out-of-court statement adduced to prove the truth of the matter stated, namely that Kearley was dealing drugs. But, not surprisingly, the callers did not say, in so many words, that Kearley was a drug dealer, because there was no need for them to mention something that was an unstated – and crucial – premiss of their repeated transactions. Thinking themselves to be addressing Chippie Kearley, the telephone callers simply asked to be supplied with their 'usual', or variations on that theme. But surely, ran the majority's argument, there is in such requests, for 'the usual' and similar expressions, an implied assertion that Chippie will sell drugs on request, and it would be a sorry specimen of a rule that could be circumvented by the simple expedient of merely hinting at that which cannot be asserted directly. If a direct out-of-court assertion that Chippie was dealing drugs would be excluded by the hearsay rule, a verbal nod and a wink in the same direction must also be inadmissible by parity of reasoning. Or as Lord Ackner put it:

What is sought to be done is to use the oral assertion, even though it may be an implied assertion, as evidence of the truth of the proposition asserted. That the proposition is asserted by way of necessary implication rather than expressly cannot, to my mind, make any difference. The object of tendering the evidence would be to establish the truth of what is contained in the statement. That is precisely what the rule prohibits...[109]

In short, according to the *Kearley* majority, the common law hearsay rule must apply with equal vigour to implied, as to express, assertions.

The minority speeches took an altogether different tack. Lords Griffiths and Browne-Wilkinson emphasized the common sense inferences that could be, and were, drawn from the conduct of the callers, recounted at first-hand by the police officer witnesses who testified at Kearley's trial to what they had heard the callers say. Lord Griffiths was characteristically robust in his assessment of the officers' evidence:

It is hardly surprising that the jury convicted the appellant for as a matter of common sense it is difficult to think of much more convincing evidence of his activity as a drug dealer than customers constantly ringing his house to buy drugs and a stream of customers beating a path to his door for the same purpose.... The requests for drugs made by the callers were not hearsay as generally understood, namely an out-of-court narrative description of facts which have to be proved in evidence. The callers were neither describing the appellant as a drug

---

[109] [1992] 2 AC 228, 255.

dealer nor stating their opinion that he was a drug dealer. They were calling him up to visit him as customers, a fact revealed by the words they used in requesting drugs from him.[110]

On this view, *Kearley* presented no hearsay problem at all, but Lord Griffiths nonetheless added for good measure:

The hearsay rule was created by our judicial predecessors and if we find that it no longer serves to do justice in certain conditions then the judges of today should accept the responsibility of reviewing and adapting the rules of evidence to serve present society.[111]

Whether or not one sympathizes with Lord Griffiths' frontal assault on *Myers*, the *Kearley* majority's reasoning, to the effect that 'if it can't be said directly, it can't be said indirectly', is deeply flawed and all the more insidious for appearing eminently plausible. For the majority's approach, when systematically applied, collapses into the *reductio ad absurdum* of converting virtually all evidence into hearsay and thereby completely undermining the logic and practical utility of an exclusionary rule.[112] The argument proceeds through several incremental steps. It should first be stated unequivocally that true 'implied assertions' fall within the ambit of the exclusionary rule. This proposition is amply demonstrated by *Teper* v *R*,[113] where the accused was convicted of arson after burning down his own fully-stocked warehouse in order to make a fraudulent insurance claim. Teper appealed against the admission at his trial of a police officer's testimony to the effect that the officer had overheard an unidentified woman at the scene saying 'Your place burning, and you going away from the fire…'[114] The Privy Council ultimately ruled that this evidence was inadmissible hearsay, and the accused's conviction was quashed. Notice, however, that *Teper* really does involve an implied assertion. Though couched in allusive language, the speaker's intended meaning is quite obviously something like 'Isn't it fishy that you, the owner of the warehouse, are slipping into the night whilst behind you your livelihood is burning to the ground'. The intended tone of accusation infuses the words actually spoken. Inasmuch as the speaker meant to challenge the accused, or at least to bring suspicion on him, this was an out-of-court statement adduced to prove the truth of the fact stated, namely that the accused was implicated in the arson. It was, in other words, inadmissible hearsay at common law, as the Privy Council rightly concluded, and remains so under the CJA 2003's rubric of 'a statement, not made in oral evidence, that is relied on as evidence of a matter stated in it'.[115]

Cases like *Teper* illustrate the range of register, flexibility, and richness of language. Direct statements are only a small part of our linguistic repertoire. One's intended meaning may be communicated indirectly by allusion, suggestion, or implication. It is even possible, through inflexion or body language, to give words the exact opposite of their usual meaning, as when one is being ironic: 'Oh, what a lovely hat you are wearing!' Now, true implied assertions are no less susceptible to the classic dangers presented by hearsay evidence than direct statements.[116] It would therefore be foolish to insulate a statement

---

[110] ibid. 236, 238.   [111] ibid. 237.

[112] To similar effect, Mueller warns that under *Kearley* hearsay risks becoming 'the "pac-man" of trial rules, devouring inference after inference as it chews its way through common proof, exhausting courts and litigators': Christopher B. Mueller, 'Incoming Drug Calls and Performative Words: They're Not Just Talking About it, Baron Parke!' (1995) 16 *Mississippi College Law Review* 117.

[113] *Teper* v *R* [1952] AC 480, PC.   [114] Quoted ibid. 482.   [115] Section 121(2).

[116] Indeed, to the extent that they introduce additional elements of ambiguity and imprecision, implied assertions may often *increase* the danger of miscommunication and misunderstanding.

from hearsay exclusion just because the speaker chose to communicate her intentions indirectly, by allusion, euphemism, or intended implication. *Teper* has long stood for the proposition that English common law did not commit itself to this perversity.

Now for the second step in the argument: *Kearley* was not concerned with implied assertions of the genuine sort exemplified by *Teper*. The callers who asked Chippie for their usual did not mean to assert anything about Kearley's status as a drug dealer, not even indirectly. In the language of CJA 2003, section 115, they did *not* make 'any representation of fact or opinion' *in relation to Kearley's drug-dealing activities* (the matter for which the evidence was being adduced as proof) in order 'to cause another person to believe the matter, or to cause another person to act or a machine to operate on the basis that the matter is as stated'. It was simply an unspoken assumption of the callers that they were speaking to Chippie Kearley, and that he was going to sell them drugs. Conversely, the callers *did* represent to Kearley the fact that each caller wanted drugs, and intended Kearley to act on *that* representation. But the evidence was not being tendered to prove anything about callers' desires or beliefs *per se*: viewed in isolation, the desires and beliefs of the callers would have been irrelevant, as all of their Lordships agreed – including the dissentients.[117] In reality, when the *Kearley* majority spoke of 'implied assertions' in this context what their Lordships were really doing was *imputing* assertions to the callers, and this move is fatal to the logic of hearsay. The problem is that it is always possible to impute assertions to just about any evidence that could be adduced in a criminal trial, not only to out-of-court speech, but also to non-verbal conduct and even, remarkably, to inanimate objects and real evidence. This is the third and final step in the argument: if the logic of *Kearley* turns all evidence into hearsay, the logic of hearsay would render the exclusionary rule vapid and absurd.

This radical and startling conclusion demands further demonstration. How can it be maintained that *Kearley* logic makes everything hearsay, even real evidence like a DNA profile or the smoking gun? It is disconcertingly easy to tie oneself up in knots in the midst of this analysis, and courts and criminal practitioners are far from immune from the reasoning fallacies which sometimes ensnare scholars and students of the law of proof. Let us try to retrace our steps. The easy case, involving verbal communication, is demonstrated by *Kearley* itself. Speech is intelligent human conduct, to be differentiated from a verbal tick or involuntary scream or yelp of pain etc., which are things that the body does, just like a sneeze or a heart-attack, rather than things done by the person whose body it is. The hallmark of human conduct is that it is done for reasons, and these reasons in their turn reflect a person's beliefs, desires, and intentions.[118] With regard to that form of verbal conduct known as speech, it is always possible to infer, or at least to attempt to

---

[117] [1992] 2 AC 228, 238 (Lord Griffiths: 'The evidence is offered not for the purpose of inviting the jury to draw the inference that the customers believed they could obtain drugs but to prove as a fact that the telephone callers and visitors were acting as customers or potential customers which was a circumstance from which the jury could if so minded draw the inference that the appellant was trading as a drug dealer...The callers were neither describing the appellant as a drug dealer nor stating their opinion that he was a drug dealer. They were calling him up or visiting him as customers, a fact revealed by the words they used in requesting drugs from him'); and 279 (Lord Browne-Wilkinson: 'I accept that the opinions or beliefs of the callers were irrelevant and as such inadmissible').

[118] For a compact and accessible conceptual elaboration, see John Gardner and Timothy Macklem, 'Reasons', in Jules Coleman and Scott Shapiro (eds.), *The Oxford Handbook of Jurisprudence and Philosophy of Law* (OUP, 2002).

reconstruct, the beliefs, desires, and intentions that lie behind what a person has said. This is what the majority did in *Kearley*. The callers obviously wanted drugs and believed that Kearley would supply their demand. The *Kearley* majority took these desires and beliefs and reconstructed them into what their Lordships referred to as 'implied assertions', but which would more accurately be described as *imputed* assertions, because the callers never intended to assert anything, even impliedly, about Kearley's status or business.

The *Kearley* three-card-shuffle can easily be adapted to render any out-of-court speech or writing hearsay. An excellent illustration is *R v Lydon (Sean)*,[119] in which the accused was convicted of armed robbery of a post office, and the question on appeal concerned the admissibility of a piece of paper containing the words 'Sean rules 85'. This piece of paper was found near to the crime scene, together with the weapon used in the robbery, which bore traces of the ink probably used to write on the paper. The logical chain of inference therefore ran from the gun to the writing via the ink. Dismissing the accused's appeal against conviction, Woolf LJ (as he then was) gave the following pithy endorsement of the trial judge's admission of the piece of paper, as non-hearsay circumstantial evidence:

The inference that the jury could draw from the words written on the piece of paper is that the paper had been in the possession of someone who wished to write 'Sean rules,' and that person would presumably either be named Sean himself or at least be associated with such a person, and thus it creates an inferential link with the appellant. By itself it could not possibly satisfy the jury that the appellant was the other robber, but it could be circumstantial evidence which could help to satisfy the jury that the Crown's case was correct.... [A]lthough the name 'Sean' may be fairly common, it is still material to which the jury could have regard.[120]

Woolf LJ's analysis and conclusion follow from a logical application of the hearsay rule. The words 'Sean rules 85' were clearly not being adduced for their propositional truth content – the prosecution was not asserting that 'Sean rules 85', whatever that might mean! – but in order to suggest, as Woolf LJ explained, that the person who had dumped the gun used in the robbery could well have been called Sean.

Lydon was not doubted in *Kearley*, and to all intents and purposes remained good law. Moreover, the same style of analysis, upholding the admissibility of out-of-court writing as non-hearsay circumstantial evidence, was adopted by the Court of Appeal in post-*Kearley* cases.[121] Yet the *Kearley* majority's reasoning could easily be deployed to support a revisionist interpretation of cases like *Lydon*, producing the opposite result. All that it takes to render out-of-court writing inadmissible hearsay is to insist that the actual words or other explicit marks made on the paper contain a pertinent implied assertion. Little imagination is required, because the implied assertion must relate to some relevant issue in the case, which the evidence is being tendered to prove. 'Sean rules 85,' for example, might be construed to imply the assertion 'Sean woz ere on a particular day in 1985'.[122] Now, on the *Kearley* approach, if the prosecution tried to adduce the piece of paper to

---

[119] *R v Lydon (Sean)* (1987) 85 Cr App R 221, CA.   [120] ibid. 224–5.

[121] See, e.g., *R v Lilley* [2003] EWCA Crim 1789, where the contextual, fact-specific nature of such judgments was emphasized.

[122] It is no objection that Sean never meant to communicate the contents of the implied assertion imputed to him; neither did the callers in *Kearley*. Once it is accepted that implied assertions can be *imputed* the author's intentions no longer have any bearing on their scope or content.

prove that Sean was there, it appears to be blocked by the hearsay rule: the prosecution, on this view, is attempting to adduce an out-of-court statement, to the effect that Sean was there, for the purposes of establishing precisely that, that *Sean was there* (and whilst there deposited physical evidence linking him to the crime). Since a direct out-of-court statement to this effect would be barred by the hearsay rule, so (says *Kearley* logic) an indirect, implied assertion amounting to the same thing must also be inadmissible.

That the reasoning of the *Kearley* majority could be turned against apparently sound – and for trial courts, binding – decisions in previous and subsequently-decided cases might be thought a serious enough indictment. However, a more profound and corrosive threat to the logic of hearsay exclusion was that *Kearley's* rival conceptual logic lacked any inherent limitation. Suppose, for example, that an address-book or personalized key-fob is dropped by the offender at the scene of the crime. This is presumptively powerful evidence of the perpetrator's identity that detectives would seize on as a serendipitous discovery. Such personalized items would usually be admitted at trial without a murmur of objection as highly probative evidence that the accused was at least present at the scene. Yet, as with the paper in *Lydon*, an address-book or key-fob might be said to contain the implied assertion that 'I belong to the person named, who was here' which, when adduced for its truth, seems to fit the definition of hearsay. Even a fingerprint or blood sample recovered from a crime scene can be treated as 'saying' something like 'the person who matches me is the offender'. Just as a placard at the scene declaring that 'Bloggs is guilty' would be inadmissible hearsay if adduced to prove Bloggs' guilt, so fingerprints or genetic material identifying Bloggs as the culprit might logically have been excluded as implied assertions under *Kearley*.

Something has obviously gone seriously wrong with the logic of *Kearley* if it produces the absurd conclusion that forms of real evidence, which are daily admitted in criminal trials up and down the land, ought to be regarded as inadmissible hearsay and routinely withheld from triers of fact. Pragmatically, it might have been tempting to try to confine *Kearley* more or less narrowly to its facts – a special rule about telephone calls, perhaps – but it has to be said that the majority's ruling on implied assertions, and the underpinning logic of 'if it can't be said directly, it can't be said indirectly', were announced in perfectly general terms. Moreover, their Lordships expressly committed themselves to applying the hearsay rule to non-verbal conduct by endorsing Baron Parke's notorious remarks in *Wright* v *Tatham*.[123]

The question in *Wright* v *Tatham*, where the validity of a will was contested, was whether the testator's competence could be inferred from letters written to him by a number of persons, themselves since deceased, who were apparently addressing him in correspondence as though he were *compos mentis*. The answer is probably that the opinions of medically unqualified laymen were irrelevant on the question of testamentary competence,[124] though the judgments are a thicket of contradiction and indeterminacy form which no clear *ratio* emerges. The case is remembered, however, for its introduction of the following set of hypothetical examples, all of which, according to Baron Parke, involved inadmissible hearsay:

the supposed conduct of the family or relations of a testator, taking the same precautions in his absence as if he were a lunatic; his election, in his absence, to some high and responsible

---

[123] *Wright* v *Tatham* (1837) 7 Ad & Ell 313; 112 ER 488, Ex Cham.
[124] Competency requirements for expert witness are discussed in §11.3.

office; the conduct of a physician who permitted a will to be executed by a sick testator; the conduct of a deceased captain on a question of seaworthiness, who, after examining every part of a vessel, embarked in it with his family; all these, when deliberately considered, are, with reference to the matter in issue in each case, mere instances of hearsay evidence, mere statements, not on oath, but implied in or vouched by the actual conduct of persons by whose acts the litigant parties are not to be bound.[125]

Baron Parke's celebrated sea-captain hypothetical has, in particular, captured the imagination of succeeding generations. Yet it is difficult to see how such conduct could truly be brought within a sensibly delimited exclusionary rule. Of course, the sea-captain could have been mistaken about the sea-worthiness of his vessel, or engaged in some other secret business – an elaborate plot to drown himself and his family at sea, perhaps? But this merely restates a forensic truism. In every conceivable scenario there are always myriad possibilities, ranged across the entire spectrum of plausibility, and an infinite variety of more or less sound inferences to be drawn, as Lord Griffiths remarked in his *Kearley* dissent:

The obvious inference is that the appellant had established a market as a drug dealer by supplying or offering to supply drugs and was thus attracting customers. There are of course other possible explanations such as a mistaken belief or even a deliberate attempt to frame the appellant, but there are very few factual situations from which different inferences cannot be drawn and it is for the jury to decide which inference they believe they can safely draw.[126]

Juries (and lay magistrates) are part of the procedural architecture of English criminal adjudication precisely in order to resolve such contested questions of fact.[127] Though some out-of-court conduct may be, on reflection, either irrelevant to any live issue in the trial or so very equivocal and unreliable that it would only confuse or mislead the jury to hear about it, evidence that a qualified sea-captain has carefully examined 'every part of the vessel' prior to entrusting his own life and those of his family to its care on the high seas must, in logic and common sense, be probative evidence of the vessel's condition.[128] Anticipating the *Kearley* majority's argumentative strategy by more than a century-and-a-half, Baron Parke demonstrates that it is possible to conceptualize such evidence as an implied assertion by conduct, thus falling within the ambit of hearsay exclusion. Which is only to rehearse the fundamental truism, that *any* evidence of human conduct – including even an eyewitness account of an offence[129] – can be conceptualized in the alternative, either as conduct to which a witness who observed it can testify directly, or as an inadmissible implied (imputed) assertion.

Notwithstanding Parliament's decisive intervention in the CJA 2003, the Law Lords' speeches in *Kearley* deserve a long jurisprudential afterlife, as textbook expositions of the two opposing styles of argument and analysis that may be brought to bear on the

---

[125] *Wright* v *Tatham* (1837) 7 Ad & Ell 313, 388.   [126] [1992] 2 AC 228, 238.   [127] §2.4.

[128] Sir Rupert Cross suggested this compelling counter-example of admissible circumstantial evidence, *contra* Parke B: testimony that a doctor examined a patient and placed him in a mortuary van, adduced to prove that the patient was dead: *Cross on Evidence* (Butterworths, 5th edn. 1979), 473.

[129] *D* lunges at *V* with a knife and kills him. This conduct contains the implied assertion that *D* wishes to harm *V*. But a direct assertion to that effect would be hearsay (albeit admissible under the confessions exception). What cannot be said directly, cannot be said indirectly. *Ergo*, an eyewitness account tendered at *D*'s murder trial would be hearsay!

problem of 'implied assertions' and thereby delimit the scope of hearsay exclusion. The three members of the House of Lords comprising the majority propounded the 'inadmissible implied assertion' construction, where the two dissentients advocated the rival 'admissible circumstantial evidence' interpretation.[130] Section 115 of the CJA 2003 has undone the immediate damage of *Kearley* and put English law back on the right track, by re-establishing[131] the essential connection between the scope of hearsay exclusion and the declarant's intentions ('purpose') in making a statement. *Kearley* stands as an enduring jurisprudential monument to the perils of backsliding. It bears constant repetition, moreover, that an intentional assertion is not a 'matter stated' within the meaning of the 2003 Act unless it is adduced 'as evidence of any matter stated'. *There is no such thing as hearsay evidence, only hearsay uses.*

It would be premature to conclude that section 115 has 'solved' the implied assertions problem in the English law of hearsay. Instructive comparative guidance on this issue can be found in American law. The US Federal Rules of Evidence prefigure the legislative strategy adopted a quarter of a century later for England and Wales, by tying the concept of hearsay to the declarant's intention to assert.[132] As defined by Rule 801(c) FRE, the hearsay prohibition attaches to 'a statement, other than one made by the declarant while testifying at the trial... offered in evidence to prove the truth of the matter asserted'. However, the problem of implied assertions could not be laid to rest so easily. It still fascinates scholars and intermittently creates difficulties for US courts (and, presumably, for prosecutors and defence lawyers as well). The root of the problem lies beyond law; it is intertwined with how we understand and interpret language, which in turn mediates much of our daily experience and knowledge of the world.[133] As Craig Callen has explained, human communications are open to a spectrum of narrower or broader interpretations which map directly onto correspondingly narrower or broader definitions of the hearsay prohibition, ranging from directly intended assertions to any communicative conduct capable of inviting competing inferences (including Baron Parke's sea-captain hypothetical in *Wright* v

---

[130] Indeed, Lord Browne-Wilkinson, [1992] 2 AC 228, 280, briefly touched on the *reductio* argument: 'Any action involving human activity necessarily implies that the human being had reasons and beliefs on which his action was based. But the fact that his action (viz. asking for drugs or queuing for coffee) is capable of raising an inadmissible inference of irrelevant fact does not mean that evidence of that action cannot be admitted with a view to proving a relevant fact.'

[131] See, e.g., *Ratten* v *R* [1972] AC 378, 387, PC, *per* Lord Wilberforce: 'A question of hearsay only arises when the words are spoken "testimonially," i.e. as establishing some fact narrated by the words'. Also *Subramaniam* v *Public Prosecutor* [1956] 1 WLR 965, 970, PC: 'Evidence of a statement made to a witness by a person who is not himself called as a witness may or may not be hearsay. It is hearsay and inadmissible when the object of the evidence is to establish the truth of what is contained in the statement. It is not hearsay and is admissible when it is proposed to establish by the evidence, not the truth of the statement, but the fact that it was made.'

[132] The concept of 'assertion' is not further defined in the text of the FRE. It was initially attributed 'the connotation of a forceful or positive declaration': *US* v *Zenni*, 492 F Supp 464 (1980), 468. But this was subsequently glossed 'to include within the meaning of "assertion"... an expression of a fact, opinion, or condition that is implicit in the words of an utterance as long as the speaker intended to express that fact, opinion, or condition': *State* v *Kutz*, 671 NW 2d 660 (2003), 679. Also see *US* v *Long*, 905 F2d 1572 (1990); and Christopher B. Mueller and Laird C. Kirkpatrick, *Evidence* (Aspen, 2nd edn. 1999), §8.4 (arguing against a narrow conception of 'assertion' delimited by the speaker's chosen mode of expression, as opposed to what he intends to communicate).

[133] The thought encapsulated in Wittgenstein's aphorism that 'the limits of my language are the limits of my world'.

Tatham).[134] Language being more fundamental than law, the inherent ambiguities of human linguistic practices cannot be legislated out of existence by any legal definition of hearsay, no matter how sensibly drafted.

Consider, for example, the exclamation of a proud parent, 'That's my boy!' Although literally assertive, this statement should not be hearsay to prove identity or relationship under the test enacted by CJA 2003, section 115, unless spoken with the express intention of causing another person to believe some fact about identity or relationship. The approach advocated here demands a contextual analysis. The statement 'That's my boy' might well be hearsay when adduced to prove identity or relationship if the speaker was talking to a complete stranger, but not if the speaker was addressing a friend or relative who knew very well that the boy in question was the speaker's son and would not have needed the obvious fact of their relationship spelling out. Even when addressing a complete stranger, the exclamation 'That's my boy' would not be hearsay if adduced to prove that the speaker spoke of his child affectionately. The father's affection for his son, if manifested by his enthusiastic expostulation, is a matter on which the hearer might give direct testimonial evidence, having witnessed the father's evident pride and admiration with his own eyes and ears. As Callen shows, however, alternative interpretations, concentrating more centrally on the contextual dangers of mistaken inferences, remain possible.

To conform with section 115, the analysis would need to work back from perceived inferential risks to the conclusion that the speaker (more broadly, the person whose communicative conduct is in question) made the relevant utterance (did the act or made the omission) in order 'to cause another person to believe the matter, or to cause another person to act or a machine to operate on the basis that the matter is as stated'. This might well be an evidentially plausible approach in the circumstances of many cases. Perhaps even a close family friend might have mistakenly misidentified the boy's similarly-attired best friend or identical twin sister, without relying on the proud parent's exclamation, 'That's my boy' (read, according to context, as 'That's *my* boy'; or 'That's my *boy*', etc.). Thus, even if the basic concept of hearsay, now stabilized by section 115's statutory formulations, was always applied properly in practice (a manifestly implausible assumption for any avid readers of law reports), the inherent ambiguities of human communication would ensure that the problem of so-called 'implied assertions' will always live to fight another day. The argumentative styles and strategies exemplified by the *Kearley* majority and minority, respectively, are correspondingly timeless, even if the transient preoccupations of litigation may leave them temporarily out of fashion.

9.5 STATUTORY EXCEPTIONS TO THE RULE AGAINST HEARSAY

Wigmore espoused what later became the orthodox, truth-seeking rationale for excluding hearsay. He maintained that 'many possible sources of inaccuracy and untrustworthiness which may be underneath the bare untested assertion of a witness can best be brought to

---

[134] Craig R. Callen, 'Interdisciplinary and Comparative Perspectives on Hearsay and Confrontation', in Paul Roberts and Mike Redmayne (eds.), *Innovations in Evidence and Proof* (Hart, 2007).

light and exposed, if they exist, by the test of cross-examination'.[135] However, Wigmore also accepted that two countervailing considerations may trump the desirability of cross-examination in particular circumstances. The first countervailing consideration is necessity. Hearsay may be received if it provides the only available information on a particular point and its admission, even as hearsay, would be preferable to foregoing the information altogether. The second consideration is reliability. As Wigmore put it, where 'a statement has been made under such circumstances that even a skeptical caution would look upon it as trustworthy... in a high degree of probability, it would be pedantic to insist on a test whose chief object is already secured'.[136]

Wigmore's twin criteria of necessity and reliability have been invoked somewhat selectively and intermittently in English law, as *Myers*, *Kearley*, and other landmark decisions on the law of hearsay described in this chapter amply demonstrate. The common law's modern legacy was a plethora of judge-made exceptions to the hearsay rule. Some were already obsolete or obsolescent by the final decades of the twentieth century. Nearly all were hedged about with technical and often anachronistic qualifications, with which modern courts were obliged to grapple. Common law doctrines were subsequently augmented by important statutory exceptions, culminating in sections 23 and 24 of the CJA 1988 relating to documentary hearsay. Legislative intervention widened the ambit of admissible hearsay, and thus improved the flow of relevant information to the fact-finder, but also, on the downside, inflicted further technical difficulties and fresh anomalies on the law of hearsay. Since the provisions of the Criminal Justice Act 1988 were limited exclusively to statements in documents, moreover, the admissibility of oral hearsay remained hostage to the vagaries of the common law exceptions.

For a time, English lawyers consequently become accustomed to thinking of hearsay as an essentially common law doctrine with bolt-on statutory amendments. In placing the law of hearsay on a statutory footing and extending the ambit of existing exceptions, the CJA 2003 reversed this order of priority. Henceforth, English law characterizes the rule against hearsay as a creature of the CJA 2003, augmented by those aspects of common law doctrine which the 2003 Act expressly preserves. We will therefore begin our review of hearsay exceptions with the dedicated statutory exceptions carved out by sections 116 and 117 of the CJA 2003, before turning in §9.6 to consider the common law survivals preserved by section 118 of the 2003 Act.

(a) SECTION 116: ABSENT WITNESSES

Section 116 of the CJA 2003 permits hearsay statements to be admitted where the declarant is unavailable to testify as a witness for one or more of the five designated reasons specified by section 116(2), namely:

(a) death;

(b) physical or mental unfitness;

(c) absence from the UK, where 'it is not reasonably practicable to secure his attendance';

---

[135] *Wigmore on Evidence* (Chadbourn revision), vol. 5, §1420.   [136] ibid.

(d) disappearance, 'although such steps as it is reasonably practicable to take to find him have been taken'; or

(e) with the leave of the court, fear.

(i) Rationale

The rationale animating section 116 is obviously necessity: if the witness cannot, or will not, testify in court, then the legal process has a straight choice between admitting the witness's hearsay statement or doing without her evidence altogether. It would be highly inconvenient, and risk injustice, if probative evidence were lost to criminal proceedings whenever the declarant unfortunately happened to die, become incapacitated, leave the UK, or disappear before the trial.

The argument from necessity is reinforced by considerations of justice. A vulnerable victim '*prima facie* has a right to have her complaint placed before a jury and a right to have a jury assess whether they are sure that the complaint is established'.[137] The argument is even stronger where the accused himself is responsible for the witness's absence, through homicide, physical assault, or intimidation.[138] As we have seen, admissibility under section 116 (and, for that matter, under every other inclusionary exception to the hearsay prohibition) is subject to the requirements of a fair trial, as specified by the European Court of Human Rights in *Al-Khawaja and Tahery* v *UK*.[139] A criminal conviction may never rest 'solely or to a decisive degree' on the untested evidence of an absent witness. However, even the European Court might be prepared to make an exception where the witness's absence was deliberately engineered by or on behalf of the accused himself.[140]

Considerations of necessity, however pressing, plainly do not automatically reduce, much less eliminate, the probative dangers and other defects traditionally associated with hearsay evidence. An appropriate balance must be struck in a scheme of legislation between necessity, probative reliability, fairness to the parties, and the moral integrity of the proceedings. Admissibility under section 116 is consequently subject to various pre-conditions and balancing measures (in addition to European fair trial standards), some of which are expressly stated in the legislation itself whilst others are evidentiary principles of general application.

(ii) General pre-conditions to admissibility

There are three general pre-conditions applicable to all the absence conditions specified by section 116(2)(a)–(e). First, only evidence that the declarant himself could have given if he had been available to testify in the trial can be adduced.[141] Section 116 is designed to compensate for the unavoidable absence of a witness; it does not cure any non-hearsay defect in the evidence, and, in particular, it does not provide a basis for admitting evidence that (irrespective of the applicable section 116 condition) the witness would not have been

---

[137] *R* v *D (Video Testimony)* [2003] QB 90, [2002] EWCA Crim 990, [39], [3] (referring to an eighty-one-year-old complainant of rape and indecent assault with long-standing psychological problems and Alzheimer's disease, who 'will never be fit to give live evidence').

[138] *R* v *Sellick* [2005] 1 WLR 3257, [2005] EWCA Crim 65.

[139] *Al-Khawaja and Tahery* v *United Kingdom* (2009) 49 EHRR 1.   [140] ibid. [37].

[141] Section 116(1).

competent to give if called to testify in person at the trial.[142] For example, a witness suffering from dementia at the time of the trial may meet the absence condition specified by section 116(2)(b) – physical or mental infirmity – *provided that* the witness was *compos mentis* at the time she made her statement,[143] but not otherwise. If the witness was not legally competent when the relevant hearsay statement was made, section 116 cannot cure this fundamental evidentiary defect.

Secondly, the operation of section 116 is restricted to cases where 'the person who made the statement…is identified to the court's satisfaction'.[144] This is a significant safeguard, ensuring that only the statements of properly identified declarants may be adduced. In colloquial terms, section 116 admits 'hear-say' but not 'who-say?' An opponent has at least some opportunity of testing the evidence if he knows its source. It follows *a fortiori* that section 116 cannot be invoked successfully if the proponent of the evidence cannot even establish, to the court's satisfaction, that the alleged declarant actually exists.[145] Receiving evidence from an absent mystery-man would compound the vice of anonymous testimony condemned by the House of Lords in *Davis*.[146] On the defence side, the need to identify the declarant puts paid to shadowy alibi witnesses whom the defence claims to have made conveniently exculpatory hearsay statements in their favour, but whose existence cannot be verified.

Thirdly, section 116 does not operate if the proponent of the evidence is himself responsible for causing the witness's absence, either by his own actions or through the agency of a person acting on his behalf.[147] It is an elementary principle of justice that a person should not profit by his own wrongdoing. It does not lie in the mouth of a party who is responsible for a potential witness's absence or incapacitation to complain about the consequent loss of evidence at trial. Nor should the law present parties with perverse incentives to keep witnesses away from the courtroom whenever it would better suit a party's evidential strategy to adduce the witness's out-of-court statement rather than bring the witness to court, and expose her evidence to cross-examination. In addition, section 116 is, of course, subject to the overriding exclusionary discretions specified by section 126, and the court's general powers to direct an acquittal or order a retrial pursuant to section 125, which (as previously explained) constitute part of the basic structure of the CJA 2003's hearsay provisions.[148]

(iii) Achieving justice in fact-finding: factors in the balance

Absence condition (e) benefits from further statutory elucidation. Subsection 116(3) provides that '"fear" is to be widely construed and (for example) includes fear of the

---

[142] This restriction is reinforced by s.123 of the CJA 2003, which spells out that admissibility under s.116 is limited to the statements of declarants with 'the required capability', which is further defined by s.123(3) to mean the capability of '(a) understanding questions put to him abut the matters stated, and (b) giving answers to such questions which can be understood'. The test parallels the criteria of testimonial competence specified by YJCE Act 1999, s.53(3): see §7.2.

[143] *R v Cole; R v Keet* [2007] 1 WLR 2716, [2007] EWCA Crim 1924 (one of K's elderly victims was too confused to testify at trial, but had provided the police with a coherent account when first reporting the incident).

[144] Section 116(1)(c), adopting the judicial construction previously placed on CJA 1988, s. 23: *R v JP* [1999] Crim LR 401, CA.

[145] *R v Nkemayang* [2005] EWCA Crim 1937, [14] (a decision on CJA 1988, s.23(2)(b), which the Court of Appeal expressly contemplated would be extended to CJA 2003, s.116).

[146] *R v Davis* [2008] 1 AC 1128, [2008] UKHL 36, discussed in §9.2(b), above.   [147] Section 116(5).

[148] §9.3, above.

death or injury of another person or of financial loss'. Subsection 116(4) then elaborates on the additional leave requirement attaching to this absence condition. A court may only admit a hearsay statement on the basis that the declarant will not testify through fear, 'either at all or in connection with the subject matter of the statement',[149] where it considers 'that the statement ought to be admitted in the interests of justice', having regard to:

(a) the contents of the statement;

(b) the risk of unfairness to any party;

(c) the possibility (where appropriate) of making any special measures direction pursuant to section 19 of the Youth Justice and Criminal Evidence (YJCE) Act 1999;[150] and

(d) 'any other relevant circumstances'.

In contrast to the first four of section 116(2)'s absence conditions, fear is essentially subjective. A witness might potentially fake fear for tactical reasons, or claim to be frightened as an excuse not to have to go to the trouble and inconvenience of testifying in court. Section 116 is designed to secure the admissibility of probative information which would otherwise, through the mishap of a witness's unavailability, be lost to the trial process; not to pander to the convenience of readily available witnesses, which, indeed, would be likely to result in further loss of evidence, since potential witnesses might get the impression that their civic obligations have been fully discharged by providing a statement to the police.[151] Parliament has therefore erected an additional hurdle to admissibility in relation to fearful witnesses. A party will only succeed in adducing hearsay evidence under section 116(2)(e) if he can persuade the court, not only that his witness is genuinely in fear, but also that the interests of justice overall clearly favour the admission of the witness's out-of-court statement as evidence in the trial. ECHR Article 6 fair trial principles also, naturally, apply.

Whenever the court receives the hearsay statement of a person who does not testify in the trial,[152] the opposing party is deprived of the opportunity of cross-examining the maker of the statement. This remains true even where the balance of considerations overwhelmingly favours admitting the statement in the interests of justice. The magnitude of the opposing party's forensic disadvantage depends both on the particular hearsay statement's probative significance in the circumstances of the case, and on the general effectiveness of cross-examination as a truth-finding procedure – a contentious matter on which, as we have seen, reasonable minds may differ.[153] However, English law remains committed, for the time being at least, both to the primacy of oral witness testimony, and

---

[149] As s.116(2)(e) further specifies, authoritatively settling an issue that the corresponding provision in CJA 1988, s.23(3), failed to address; albeit that the literalist contention that s.23 ceased to apply as soon as the witness managed to get into the witness-box and started to speak, even if the witness then 'dried up' in midflow, did not find favour with the courts: *R v Waters* [1997] Crim LR 823, CA; *R v Ashford Magistrates' Court, ex p. Hilden* [1993] 96 Cr App R 92, DC; *R v Setz-Dempsey and Richardson* (1994) 98 Cr App R 23, CA.

[150] Special measures directions (SMDs) are discussed in §10.4.

[151] Recall that, in accordance with the principle of compulsory process, witnesses can be subpoenaed to testify against their will, and punished for contempt of court if they refuse to co-operate: §7.3.

[152] Strictly speaking, does not testify in the trial *in connection with the subject matter of his statement*, as s.124(1)(b) correctly specifies.   [153] See §7.1.

to cross-examination as the best means of testing a witness's veracity and reliability.[154] If English law was wavering on this point of principle, the House of Lords in *Davis* and the European Court of Human Rights in *Al-Khawaja* should have stiffened its resolve. The UK Supreme Court in *Horncastle*, whilst rejecting *Al-Khawaja*'s 'sole or decisive evidence' test as a criterion of admissibility, did not diminish the dangers of hearsay or question the need to treat hearsay evidence with appropriate circumspection when it is admitted in criminal trial proceedings.[155]

Section 124 of the CJA 2003 attempts to mitigate the consequences of admitting the hearsay statements of absent witnesses, by permitting the opposing party to adduce any evidence relevant to the credibility of the declarant that would have been admissible on ordinary principles to impeach the declarant's credit,[156] had the hearsay declarant testified as a witness in the trial in the normal way. This includes previous inconsistent statements and, with the leave of the court, other impeachment material that could only have been put to the witness in cross-examination, without necessarily being admissible for the opposing party in-chief.[157] Subsection 124(3) equips the court with a broad discretion to allow the proponent of a hearsay statement to respond to attacks on the credibility of his absent witness by adducing evidence to answer any allegation advanced under subsection 124(2), with a view to rehabilitating the credibility of his witness. The spectacle of parties to criminal litigation fiercely contesting the credibility of a witness who has not even appeared in court at any point during the trial has an air of unreality. But there is no reason of principle, if relevant material bearing on the credibility of an absent witness is to hand, why the parties should be precluded from adducing it, within the parameters specified by section 124.

Section 116 of the CJA 2003 was modelled on section 23 of the CJA 1988, which it superseded, with one major difference. Whereas section 116 applies to hearsay in any form, section 23 of the 1988 Act was restricted exclusively to documentary hearsay. Section 116's scheme of absence conditions, the possibility of admitting evidence bearing on the credibility of absent witnesses,[158] and the provision of an overriding, structured discretion empowering the trial judge to exclude hearsay evidence in the interests of justice[159] all derive from the CJA 1988. Pre-existing case-law interpreting relevant provisions of the 1988 legislation is obviously not, strictly speaking, binding in relation to corresponding

---

[154] See, in particular, §2.3(b), §7.1, §8.1, and §10.5.

[155] *R v Horncastle* [2009] UKSC 14, [2010] 2 WLR 94, [36], [38]: '[B]oth in the case of unavailable witnesses, and in the case of apparently reliable hearsay, the CJA 2003 contains a crafted code intended to ensure that evidence is admitted only when it is fair that it should be.... The principal safeguards designed to protect a defendant against unfair prejudice as a result of the admission of hearsay evidence...can be summarised as follows. (i) The trial judge acts as gatekeeper and has a duty to prevent the jury from receiving evidence that will have such an adverse effect on the fairness of the proceedings that it should not be received. (ii) Hearsay evidence is only admissible in strictly defined circumstances. In essence the judge has to be satisfied beyond reasonable doubt that the prosecution is not able to adduce the evidence by calling the witness. (iii) Once the prosecution case is closed, the judge must withdraw the case from the jury if it is based wholly or partly on hearsay evidence and that evidence is so unconvincing that, considering its importance, the defendant's conviction would be unsafe. (iv) The judge has to direct the jury on the dangers of relying on hearsay evidence. (v) The jury has to be satisfied of the defendant's guilt beyond reasonable doubt. (vi) The defendant can apply for permission to appeal against his conviction... [if] the admission of hearsay evidence contrary to the rules on its admissibility [renders the conviction unsafe].'   [156] See §8.4 and §8.5.

[157] CJA 2003, s.124(2)(b) and (c).   [158] Formerly governed by sch.II to the CJA 1988.

[159] CJA 1988, s.25 (now repealed).

sections of the CJA 2003. Nonetheless, the interpretational principles developed by the judges, over a period of some fifteen years, in working through the practical implications of the hearsay exceptions created by the 1988 Act were always likely to be extended *mutatis mutandis* to similar provisions in the new legislation. The first raft of cases on the CJA 2003 bears out this prediction. If only as a transitional expedient, therefore, it is still worthwhile consulting decided cases on sections 23–26 CJA 1988, especially on points which have not been fully ventilated on appeal since April 2005 when the hearsay provisions of the CJA 2003 entered into force.

The history of the CJA 1988's documentary hearsay provisions also contains some valuable lessons for law reformers. The drafting of section 23 was deficient in several important respects,[160] and its shortcomings were rapidly exposed in the crucible of litigation. In enacting section 116 of the CJA 2003, Parliament had the opportunity to learn from past legislative mistakes in reforming the law of hearsay, whilst retaining and consolidating existing provisions that had already proved their worth through practical experience.

One crucial question of legislative policy concerns the permissible degrees of hearsay – first-hand, second-hand, *n*th-hand – potentially admissible under the relevant statutory exception. Section 23 of the CJA 1988 was probably intended to be restricted to first-hand (documentary) hearsay (the shoulder-note accompanying the section said as much), but this was not quite achieved in practice. An unforeseen consequence of employing the test of 'evidence of any fact of which direct oral evidence by [the maker of the statement] would be admissible' as a proxy for first-degree hearsay was that second-hand (or, theoretically, third-hand etc.)[161] hearsay could be admitted under section 23 where a common law exception to the exclusionary rule, such as *res gestae* or dying declarations, applied.[162] A witness who merely recorded the original declarant's hearsay statement would apparently himself qualify as a person making a statement in a document within the terms of section 23. In addition to its patent complexity, this construction of the statute was rendered even more problematic by a drafting infelicity affecting cases of multiple hearsay. On a literal reading, section 23 appeared to apply the absence condition to the wrong person – to the person who 'made the statement in the document' rather than to the person who originally supplied the information contained in the statement. Common sense could only be restored by a highly creative, 'purposive' construction of the statutory language and at the cost of defining a 'statement' and the identity of its 'maker' in two different ways within the very same section of the Act.

Section 116 of the CJA 2003 deftly sidesteps the drafting problems that dogged its predecessor by abandoning section 23's ostensible restriction to first-hand hearsay entirely. Section 116 applies straightforwardly to any 'statement not made in oral evidence in the proceedings', and the focus of admissibility determinations remains fixed on that statement and its maker. Section 116(2)'s absence conditions correspondingly apply to the original declarant, designated by section 116(1)(b) as 'the relevant person'. No possibility of confounding the contested statement, or its maker, with the statement of another person who merely records or repeats the original statement should arise under the CJA 2003.

---

[160] As commentators noted from the outset: D. J. Birch, 'The Criminal Justice Act 1988: (2) The Evidence Provisions' [1989] *Crim LR* 15.

[161] Third-hand etc. hearsay was theoretically possible, as where *W2* overhears *W1*'s excited utterance of *V*'s dying declaration. In practice such cases were presumably exceedingly rare.

[162] The main common law exceptions are surveyed in §9.6, below.

Moreover, the analysis is further simplified because section 116 is not restricted to documentary hearsay – 'a statement in a document' – as was section 23 of the 1988 Act.

Yet the elegance of this solution to a pre-existing drafting problem simultaneously casts underlying issues of principle in sharper relief. The 'relevant person' for the purposes of section 116 CJA 2003 could be a witness who makes an admissible hearsay statement at one or more removes from the original source of the information contained in it. The witness or document produced in court might, for example, supply a hearsay report of *A*'s hearsay recollection of *B*'s original statement, in which case *A* – rather than *B* – would be the relevant person for the purposes of section 116. To be a bit more specific (without anticipating too much of the analysis still to come), suppose that PC *X* adduces *A*'s witness statement of *B*'s 'excited utterance' at the scene of the crime. *B*'s exclamation is found to satisfy the well-established *res gestae* exception to the hearsay prohibition.[163] For the purposes of applying section 116's absence conditions, *A* would be the 'relevant person', not *B*, the original statement-maker. And to repeat, this applies to oral as well as written hearsay in witness statements and other documents, carrying heightened risks of misperception, faulty memory, deliberate deception, or breakdowns in communication.

Here we should recall the additional safeguard to be found in section 121, which imposes a special leave requirement for multiple hearsay tendered under section 116 (or section 118, in relation to retained common law exceptions).[164] Does this go far enough in addressing the hearsay dangers? If an appropriate balance is to be struck between admitting probative evidence and upholding principles of justice, it is essential that, on every such occasion when the admissibility of multiple hearsay is contested, courts recognize that the quality of information, and its susceptibly to robust testing in a criminal trial, will often diminish as the evidence tendered in court gets further and further away from the original source of the information. Every additional link in the chain of informants increases the risk of informational degradation through the familiar hearsay dangers. It is submitted, moreover, that only in exceptional circumstances (e.g. where the probative value of the evidence is marginal and/or securing attendance of the witness would be especially difficult or burdensome) would it be appropriate for the court to admit hearsay evidence under section 116 where, although the 'relevant person' satisfies an absence condition, the person who originally supplied the information is available to appear as a witness in the trial. Why should the court be forced to make do with stable-lads' gossip, when it could hear the relevant information from the horse's mouth? These considerations must take their place, alongside all other pertinent factors, in judicial calculations of the interests of justice and the requirements of a fair trial whenever multiple hearsay is tendered for admission pursuant to sections 116 and 121 of the CJA 2003.

(iv) Judicial interpretation

Judicial interpretations of CJA 1988, section 23, also contribute valuable experience of applying the general absence conditions now contained in section 116(2)(a)–(e). The invariable starting point is that the proponent of the evidence must establish, through admissible evidence, that a particular absence condition is actually satisfied on the facts. Proving the absence condition, in other words, is a condition precedent to adducing the proffered hearsay statement. A death certificate would normally satisfy absence condition-(a), whilst

---

[163] §9.6(b), below.   [164] Section 121.

the infirmity of a witness within the terms of absence condition-(b) could be established by expert medical evidence. Absence conditions such as the declarant's fear or location overseas might conceivably be proved by evidence which is itself hearsay, provided that such evidence is independently admissible under a surviving common law or statutory exception to the exclusionary rule.[165]

The absence criteria were never treated by the courts as mere formalities. In order to demonstrate that it is not reasonably practicable for an extra-territorial witness to travel to the UK to give evidence in person, for example, it did not suffice under section 23 to make unsubstantiated claims of financial hardship, especially where there were unexplained counter-indications, such as a visit to the UK in the preceding three months.[166] In order to prove legitimate absence through illness it might be necessary to call to court the doctor who examined the witness so that his clinical diagnosis could be subjected to cross-examination.[167] Conversely, where the prosecution had made detailed arrangements to secure the attendance of a witness – including, in one case, a guarantee of immunity from prosecution and assurances that all travel costs would be reimbursed[168] – and yet the witness still refused to come, the Court of Appeal accepted that all reasonably practicable options had been exhausted, in satisfaction of the relevant absence condition.[169]

Predictably enough, this commonsensical, fact-sensitive approach has been extended to the absence conditions re-enacted in section 116. In one post-CJA 2003 case, the Court of Appeal was satisfied that the CPS had done enough to secure a teenage witness's attendance, and thus to have his video-recorded statement admitted under section 116, where prosecutors had telephoned the child's parents in the USA daily over a two-week period, and at one point had discussed the possibility of organizing a chaperon.[170] Section 116 was also successfully invoked to admit a hearsay statement where the witness had gone to Jamaica and his father was, apparently, refusing to allow his son to testify via live-link.[171] However, the flexible limits of section 116 were overstepped in R v Ishmael Adams.[172] In proceedings for possession of ecstasy and ketamine tablets with intent to supply, a key prosecution witness – the club bouncer who had allegedly caught Adams in the act – failed to turn up on the day of trial. The prosecution successfully applied to adduce the club bouncer's written statement under section 116(2)(d), on the basis that 'the relevant person cannot be found although such steps as it is reasonably practicable to take to find him have been taken'. The Court of Appeal condemned this lax approach. The witness had originally confirmed his willingness to testify at trial in September 2006, but had subsequently not been contacted by the prosecution until Friday, 12 January 2007 when the trial was due to begin on the following Monday. Half-hearted efforts to leave messages on the witness's answering service, without even attempting to verify that the witness had actually listened

---

[165] See, e.g., *Neill v North Antrim Magistrates' Court* [1992] 1 WLR 1220, HL; *R v Ashford Magistrates' Court, ex p. Hilden* [1993] 96 Cr App R 92, DC: cf. *R v Wood and Fitzsimmons* [1998] Crim LR 213, CA. For discussion, see Roderick Munday, 'The Proof of Fear' (1993) 143 *NLJ* 542 and 587.

[166] *R v Hurst* [1995] 1 Cr App R 82, CA. That this was an application by the accused perhaps explains the unsatisfactory state of the evidence. It also illustrates the particular difficulties that may be encountered by the defence in proving the existence of an absence condition.

[167] *R v Elliott* [2003] EWCA Crim 1695.   [168] *R v Gokal* [1997] 2 Cr App R 266, CA.

[169] Also see *R v Henry* [2003] EWCA Crim 1296 (police are not obliged to delay deportation of a person whom they had no reason to believe would be wanted as a defence witness).

[170] *R v Gyima* [2007] Crim LR 890, CA.   [171] *R v Bailey* [2008] EWCA Crim 817.

[172] *R v Adams (Ishmael)* [2008] 1 Cr App R 35, [2007] EWCA Crim 3025.

to his messages, left the Court of Appeal distinctly unimpressed: 'if…it is thought to be sufficient to leave a message the night before a witness is due to attend, we desire to say as emphatically as we can that it will not do … What happened in this case was a very long way short of what is in practice needed to get witnesses to come to court.'[173] In the view of the Court, the prosecution ought to have been better prepared in advance, and further-more, should have made more strenuous efforts to ascertain the witness's whereabouts after his absence was noticed on the day of trial. '[R]easonably practicable steps which ought to have been taken included a visit to his address and/or to his place of work or agency, or at least contact with those places, perhaps by telephone.'[174]

This was a welcome and even necessary intervention by the Court of Appeal (albeit a pyrrhic victory for the accused, since the Court of Appeal went on to hold that, on the particular facts and litigation history of the instant case, the evidence could properly have been admitted under section 114(1)(d)). Flexible though it is, section 116 cannot be allowed to function as a fail-safe for prosecutorial disorganization, as though the hearsay rule and the tradition of orality which stands behind it can now be abandoned for the sake of expe-diency. Absence condition-(d) is especially vulnerable to this kind of corruption, because, as *Adams* demonstrates, it could be all-too-easy for prosecutors and trial judges to latch on to the notion that there are no 'reasonably practicable' options to secure the attendance of an absent witness when a trial is just about to commence.

A final notable design feature in which the documentary hearsay provisions of the CJA 1988 anticipated the 2003 Act is the proliferation of judicial discretions. The CJA 1988 contained both an overriding exclusionary discretion[175] and a special leave requirement applicable in certain circumstances,[176] and the exercise of each power was further struc-tured by bespoke 'interests of justice' tests. The statutory discretions proved to be inte-gral, occasionally even decisive,[177] features of the admissibility framework established by the CJA 1988. This is significant, because the hearsay provisions of the CJA 2003 are equipped, or burdened, with even more discretionary standards than the legislation they replaced.

The Court of Appeal was disinclined to accept that any evidential or strategic considera-tion could ever amount to a conclusive, knock-down objection to the admission of docu-mentary hearsay under CJA 1988, section 23. In particular, the fact that the accused would probably be obliged to waive his privilege against self-incrimination[178] and testify in his own defence in order to mount an effective challenge to a hearsay statement was no general bar to its admissibility.[179] The impact of a hearsay statement on the accused's tactical choice to testify or remain silent was not judged to be a decisive factor in calculating the interests of justice.[180] Nor was major probative significance or centrality to the case an automatic barrier to receiving hearsay under the 1988 Act.[181] Determinations of admissibility were said to require contextual examination of each and every material factor bearing on the reliability of the evidence and its likely impact on the fairness and outcome of the trial.

---

[173] ibid. [12]–[13].   [174] ibid. [13].   [175] CJA 1988, s.25 (repealed).
[176] CJA 1988, s.26 (repealed).
[177] *R v Jennings and Miles* [1995] Crim LR 810, CA (conviction quashed, in part, because the trial court had erroneously applied CJA 1988, s.25, where it should have considered the more exacting leave require-ments imposed by s.26).   [178] See Chapter 13.
[179] *R v Cole* (1990) 90 Cr App R 478, CA.   [180] *R v Gokal* [1997] 2 Cr App R 266, CA.
[181] *R v Dragic* [1996] 2 Cr App R 232, CA; *R v Fairfax* [1995] Crim LR 949, CA.

Needlessly cumulative evidence,[182] or the written testimony of a witness whose credibility was seriously in doubt,[183] were normally to be excluded. But it was impossible categorically to rule out unusual forms of such evidence, or exceptional circumstances, where admissibility rather than exclusion would better serve the interests of justice.

So far as the exercise of judicial discretion is concerned, the Court of Appeal has picked up under the CJA 2003 exactly where it left off in its case-law interpreting CJA 1988, sections 23–26. In *Cole and Keet*[184] Lord Phillips CJ said that the test of unfairness specified by PACE 1984, section 78, which CJA 2003 section 126 extends to hearsay exclusion, in this context parallels the primary admissibility standard created by section 114(1)(d). This seems to imply that the factors specified in section 114(2) to structure the admissibility of hearsay statements might equally be invoked when assessing their discretionary exclusion. Furthermore, the Court of Appeal displayed no inclination to revise its previous stance on the relationship between the privilege against self-incrimination and discretionary hearsay exclusion, even though it entertained no illusions about the practical implications of this ruling for the accused:

It is sometimes argued that it is unfair to put in a statement if the defendant will have to go into the witness box to rebut it. This may be the case where the evidence is not strong, but we can see no unfairness on the facts of the present case. It would, of course, have been open to the appellant to decline to give oral evidence, leaving his counsel to do his best with the statements made to the police. The reality is, however, that where issues are as stark as in the present case, whether oral or statement evidence is adduced by the prosecution, the jury will expect to hear from the defendant.[185]

It would therefore appear to be settled law that the accused cannot invoke his privilege against self-incrimination as an all-purpose normative objection trumping the admissibility of hearsay evidence under section 116. Challenges seeking to establish the contextual unreliability or marginal probative value of the evidence, generally speaking, stand a better chance of success. English courts are constrained to hold that it can never be fair (section 126(2)) or in the interests of justice (section 114(1)(d)) to allow the prosecution to adduce and rely on hearsay evidence in circumstances incompatible with the accused's Article 6 right to a fair trial. However, as the UK Supreme Court explained in *Horncastle*, the application of the general fair trial standard 'has to be assessed on a case by case basis, viewing each trial as a whole.... [A]n inability on the part of a defendant to cross-examine the maker of a statement that is admitted in evidence will not necessarily render the trial unfair.'[186]

(b) SECTION 117: BUSINESS, ETC. DOCUMENTS

Section 117 of the CJA 2003 provides for the admissibility of statements contained in 'business and other documents' (to quote the section's title), which is further defined by section 117(2)(a) to encompass documents 'created or received by a person in the course of

---

[182] *R v Patel* [1993] Crim LR 291, CA.

[183] *R v Lockley and Corah* [1995] 2 Cr App R 554, CA (hearsay evidence of alleged confession to cellmate should not have been admitted under either CJA 1988, ss.23 or 24).

[184] *R v Cole; R v Keet* [2007] 1 WLR 2716, [2007] EWCA Crim 1924.   [185] ibid. [39].

[186] *R v Horncastle* [2009] UKSC 14, [2010] 2 WLR 94, [74].

a trade, business, profession or other occupation, or as the holder of a paid or unpaid office'. Admissibility is extended to all statements contained in a document, or part of a document, created or received in the course of business, broadly conceived, or by any office-holder, provided that 'the person who supplied the information contained in the statement (the relevant person) had or may reasonably be supposed to have had personal knowledge of the matters dealt with'.[187] In contrast to section 116 which applies to all forms of hearsay, only documentary hearsay – 'a statement contained in a document' – can be received under section 117. However, it is no bar to admissibility that the relevant information was communicated orally in the first instance, before subsequently being written down in a document created or received in the course of business or in the execution of an official duty.

(i) Statutory framework

Section 117 contemplates the information contained in the statement being passed along a chain of receivers and conduits of any length,[188] provided that every person constituting a link in the chain passed on the information, or created or received the document containing the statement, in the course of business or as an office-holder, as defined by section 117(2)(a). Where, for example, the dairy-maid tells the cook, and the cook informs the butler, and the butler writes a note for the queen, who pens a personal message for the king, the statement in the queen's message that there is no butter for the royal breakfast would be admissible under section 117 provided that dairy-maid, cook, butler, and queen all acted in the course of business or (more likely in this case) as office-holders performing their duties. Section 117, in other words, authorizes the court to receive hearsay of any degree – first-hand, second-hand, even nineteenth-hand hearsay – provided that the original source of the information can reasonably be supposed to have had personal knowledge of the relevant matters, and every person passing the information along the chain of custody was conducting themselves in the course of business or discharging their duties of office. The permissive formulation 'or may reasonably be supposed to have had personal knowledge' deliberately accommodates 'who-say?' in certain circumstances. However, all relevant parties must have been testimonially competent[189] at the time that they (as the case may be) created, received, or passed on the information contained in a hearsay statement, or else can reasonably be assumed to have been competent if their identities are unknown.[190]

We have seen that section 116 attempts to mitigate the impact of being obliged to respond to an absent witness's hearsay statement by allowing an opponent to adduce information bearing on the declarant's credibility that would otherwise have been admissible had the declarant testified in person in court. Subsection 124(4) extends the same compensating measure to every person who must either have supplied or received information, or made or received a document, for a statement in a document to be admissible under section 117.

---

[187] Section 117(2)(b).

[188] Section 121(1)(a) exempts s.117 from the additional, strongly-worded, requirement to secure judicial leave otherwise applicable to the admission of multiple hearsay, under ss.116 and 118.

[189] The statute refers to 'the required capability', which is further defined by s.123(3) to mean the capability of '(a) understanding questions put to him abut the matters stated, and (b) giving answers to such questions which can be understood'. The test parallels the criteria of testimonial competence specified by YJCE Act 1999, s.53(3): see §7.2.   [190] s.123(2).

This is a principled approach. Every person through whose hands the information has passed, or in whose custody the document ultimately containing the information has been kept, could have misunderstood what he was told, forgotten crucial details, mistranscribed the information, or introduced deliberate inaccuracies or omissions. In other words, the traditional hearsay dangers arise afresh, and are compounded, every time information passes from one individual to another. The opposing party should therefore be entitled to test the credibility of each human link in the chain. Live cross-examination in the court-room is impossible in relation to the hearsay statement of an absent witness, but when such a statement has been admitted under section 117, subsection 124(4) at least facilitates the next-best-thing.

In common with all the other hearsay provisions of the CJA 2003, section 117 is subject to the overriding exclusionary discretions mandated by section 126, and to the court's general power to direct an acquittal or order a retrial pursuant to section 125 of the Act. Parliament has nonetheless equipped section 117 with its own dedicated exclusionary discretion, which – it must be said, for no apparent reason – is phrased in terms of the court 'making a direction' not to admit a particular hearsay statement under that section.[191] Subsection 117(7) continues:

The court may make a direction under this subsection if satisfied that the statement's reliability as evidence for the purpose for which it is tendered is doubtful in view of –
(a) its contents,
(b) the source of the information contained in it,
(c) the way in which or the circumstances in which the information was supplied or received, or
(d) the way in which or the circumstances in which the document concerned was created or received.

Parliament's intention to create a structured exclusionary discretion is unmistakable; though this objective might have been achieved more economically by making section 117 subject to an overriding judicial duty to exclude 'business, etc.' documents whenever it would be contrary to the interests of justice to admit them, taking account of all relevant factors and circumstances.

A final, additional hurdle to admissibility is imposed on what we might call, for short-hand, 'criminal process statements'. Such statements are defined by subsection 117(4)(a) as those 'prepared for the purposes of pending or contemplated criminal proceedings, or for a criminal investigation'.[192] Before any criminal process statement can be admitted under section 117, it must also either satisfy one of the absence conditions specified by section 116(2) (briefly, that the declarant is dead, infirm, overseas, missing, or too frightened to testify in person), or it must be proved in accordance with subsection 117(5)(b) that:

the relevant person cannot reasonably be expected to have any recollection of the matters dealt with in the statement (having regard to the length of time since he supplied the information and all other circumstances).

---

[191] s.117(6).
[192] But s.117(4)(b) specifically exempts statements prepared for the purposes of international judicial co-operation, pursuant to s.7 of the Crime (International Co-operation) Act 2003 or sch.13, para.6, of the Criminal Justice Act 1988.

In short, a criminal process statement cannot be admitted under section 117 unless at least one of six further conditions (the five section 116(2) absence conditions, plus the extra one contained in section 117(5)(b)) justifying the declarant's absence from the witness-box is also satisfied.

(ii) Rationale

Section 117 is the latest version of a business documents exception to the hearsay rule first introduced into English law over forty years ago by the Criminal Evidence Act 1965, which was enacted for the explicit purpose of reversing *Myers* on its facts. The business documents exception subsequently went through several further legislative incarnations before assuming its current form. Section 117 is closely modelled on its immediate predecessor, CJA 1988, section 24. The basic structure of section 24, most of its terminology, and the central distinction, to be explored in a moment, between ordinary business documents and documents created for the purposes of criminal proceedings have all been retained by section 117. It is perhaps worth repeating that, whereas section 116 of the CJA 2003 applies to oral as well as documentary hearsay – a significant departure from its statutory predecessor, CJA 1988, section 23 – section 117 of the CJA 2003, like section 24 before it, is limited to *statements in documents* created or received in the circumstances envisaged.

It is a reasonable expectation, very broadly speaking, that statements in documents created in the course of 'a trade, business, profession or other occupation or as the holder of a paid or unpaid office' should be more reliable and trustworthy than other classes of statement, perhaps scribbled idly, in haste, temper, or amusement, in a personal document like a notebook, diary, letter, or email. If it is somebody's job to maintain an accurate record, for example, and there is no earthly reason – apart from inherent human fallibility – why they should have erred or falsified their record-keeping, then this document will often be the best evidence of the matters recorded that any fact-finder could ever hope to see. *Myers*, once more, supplies a telling illustration. Companies and other businesses are obliged to devise and operate elaborate systems for stock-checking, deliveries, payments and so forth, for legal (e.g. tax) as well as commercial reasons. Even a relatively junior employee in a small business is unlikely to keep his job if he cannot discharge his record-keeping duties effectively.

Provision for a dedicated statutory exception to admit business documents, under what is now CJA 2003, section 117, may therefore be regarded as a sensibly pragmatic response to the realities of information generation and storage in modern commercial enterprises.[193] Today, for example, it is commonplace for scores or even hundreds of an undertaking's employees to input information into computer databases, so that it would be impossible to say, months or years after the event, precisely which employee generated which pieces of data. Even if it were feasible to retrace the flow of information ultimately incorporated into a particular business record or databank, what would be the advantage in doing so? Surely not to test whether human employees have better memories than computers. Section 117 followed CJA 1988, section 24's lead, in skipping lightly through this potential evidentiary

---

[193] The business documents exception also caters for non-commercial, public documents created by office-holders. However, the pressure for a dedicated statutory exception was greatest in relation to private, commercial records, since many classes of public document were already admissible, at common law – either as recognized hearsay exceptions or under the guise of 'judicial notice' – or pursuant to specific statutory authorization: see §3.4(a) (proof by formalities) and §4.7 (judicial notice).

minefield. Provided that it can be shown that the relevant information, once received or generated, remained within an organization's data-processing (electronic or human) systems, a statement in a business document, though technically still hearsay, can be adduced at trial without requiring its proponent to produce percipient witnesses to every detail of the statement's provenance.

It is harder to see, however, why the mere *receipt* of a document in the course of business, etc. should vouch for the reliability of its contents, as section 117 implies. Commentators were quick to point out, in relation to identical wording in section 24 of the CJA 1988, that any letter sent to the Editor of *The Times* qualifies, literally, as a document received in the course of business, the business of running a daily newspaper.[194] It cannot really have been Parliament's intention to allow inadmissible hearsay to be laundered into admissible evidence simply by reducing information into the form of a letter and sending it to a newspaper editor, or even posting it through the mails to oneself,[195] and yet a literal reading of section 117, like CJA 1988, section 24 before it, would produce exactly that result. Indeed, the argument can be pressed much further, because every document tendered as evidence will already have been received in the course of business by a police officer, a prosecutor, a defence lawyer, or the court.[196] Yet if receipt by criminal justice professionals and office-holders were sufficient to satisfy the business documents exception, there would never be any need for a separate set of exceptions to cater for non-business documents or, for that matter, absent witnesses (because any oral statement can be written down in a document and produced as documentary evidence in court). Given that a literal reading of section 117 would displace section 116's absence conditions, the argument from literal construction is unlikely to recommend itself to judges interpreting the hearsay provisions of the CJA 2003 any more than it did in relation to CJA 1988, sections 23 and 24.[197] Indeed, the argument was implicitly rejected by the Administrative Court in *Maher*,[198] a case concerning a minor collision between a manoeuvring vehicle and a stationary vehicle in a supermarket car-park. A public-spirited citizen who witnessed the collision left a note on the windscreen of the stationary vehicle, informing its owner of the other vehicle's registration number. The Court ruled that the note could not be adduced under section 117, because the complainant car-owner did not receive it from the eyewitness whilst acting in the course of a trade or business or under any cognizable duty. The general civic duty of assisting the authorities to prosecute criminal wrongdoers is plainly deemed insufficient for these purposes.

The clinching consideration in favour of a purposive construction is that Parliament would not have gone to the trouble of setting out detailed provisions on the absence of witnesses, now listed in section 116(2)(a)–(e), if hearsay could always be tendered under section 117, regardless of the availability of the original declarant, simply by writing it down and giving the written statement to a police officer or lawyer. At all events, the scope

---

[194] See Di Birch, 'The Criminal Justice Act 1988: (2) The Evidence Provisions' [1989] *Crim LR* 15, 25 (attributing the example to Sir John Smith).

[195] Mark Ockelton, 'Documentary Hearsay in Criminal Cases' [1992] *Crim LR* 15.

[196] Donal McEvoy, 'Police Documents as Admissible Hearsay' [1993] *Crim LR* 480; J. C. Smith, 'Sections 23 and 24 of the Criminal Justice Act 1988: (1) Some Problems' [1994] Crim LR 426; Donal McEvoy, 'Sections 23 and 24 of the Criminal Justice Act 1988 (2): A Reply' [1994] *Crim LR* 430.

[197] *R* v *McGillivray* (1993) 97 Cr App R 232, CA, 236.

[198] *Maher* v *DPP* [2006] EWHC 1271 (Admin). The evidence was received under s.114(1)(d) instead.

for circumventing section 116's absence conditions is limited to documents not created in contemplation of criminal proceedings, since criminal process documents are subject to the expanded list of six absence conditions in every case, pursuant to subsections 117(4) and (5) of the CJA 2003.

(iii) Criminal process statements

The distinction between 'criminal process statements' and ordinary commercial records generated in the normal course of business taps into a significant source of hearsay dangers. Compared with the ordinary transactions of everyday life, personal and private as much as commercial or official, statements in documents created 'for the purposes of pending or contemplated criminal proceedings, or for a criminal investigation' inevitably raise suspicions about their authenticity, truthfulness, and reliability. Once criminal proceedings are on foot, witnesses and others may have new motives to be selective with the truth, and in any case experience unfamiliar institutional influences and pressures in the serial retelling of their stories. There is no police force in the world that does not occasionally succumb to the temptations of corner-cutting illegality, not to mention outright corruption. Even where neither private calculation nor official malpractice are suspected, moreover, there remain two important reasons for subjecting criminal process documents to especially searching forensic scrutiny: first, the selective process of case-construction[199] introduces well-documented risks of distortion or error into the production of witness statements and other evidence specially prepared for the purposes of criminal litigation;[200] and secondly, the opportunities for fraud, perjury, and every other manifestation of forensic impropriety should be reduced to the unavoidable minimum in order to establish a robust procedural system in which justice is done and, as the European Court of Human Rights expresses it, 'objectively' seen to be done.[201]

Criminal process statements were consequently made subject to more stringent admissibility requirements within the framework of the 1988 Act, and this evidential precept was carried over into the CJA 2003. In view of their differential admissibility, it is vital to be able to differentiate clearly and consistently between routine business documents and the more closely regulated 'criminal process' variety. In relation to CJA 1988 section 24, the courts developed a pragmatic, 'dominant purpose' test. Provided that the document had been created in the routine course of business, it would not be treated as containing a criminal process statement only because it formed part of a record with potential relevance for criminal litigation. This was a sound approach, which will presumably be extended to section 117 of the CJA 2003. A dominant purpose test correctly implies, to revisit a familiar example, that the record of engine block numbers in *Myers* would have been an ordinary business document, subject only to section 117's basic admissibility regime, even though such records have obvious forensic utility in the prosecution of auto-crime. Likewise, the paper instruments of commerce and

---

[199] See §2.3(a) and §4.2.

[200] Chapter 12 provides further detailed illustrations in relation to custodial confessions.

[201] Cf. *Borgers* v *Belgium* (1993) 15 EHRR 92, [46]: 'The existence of impartiality for the purposes of Article 6(1) must be determined according to a subjective test, that is on the basis of the personal conviction of a particular judge in a given case, and also according to an objective test, that is ascertaining whether the judge offered guarantees sufficient to exclude any legitimate doubt in this respect.' The value of open justice has already been emphasized on several occasions: see §1.2(c), §2.3(b), and §7.1(a).

finance, which are primarily the means and permanent record of business transactions and only secondarily evidence of fraud,[202] qualified as ordinary business documents under section 24, and should continue to do so under section 117. Conversely, a video-recorded police interview carried out with a key witness[203] and records stored on the police national computer (PNC)[204] are clearly instances of criminal process statements for the purposes of section 117.

The additional absence condition for criminal process statements in documents created or received in the course of business, now contained in section 117(5)(b) of the CJA 2003, originally appeared in section 24(4)(iii) of the 1988 Act. It posed some interpretative difficulties in its previous incarnation. On first acquaintance, the condition that the declarant cannot reasonably be expected 'to have any recollection of the matters dealt with in the statement' appears stringent – not to have *any* recollection *whatsoever* of the relevant matters. However, in their interpretations of section 24(4)(iii), the courts favoured a somewhat more relaxed standard, that the maker of the statement could not reasonably be expected to recall the material parts of the statement. For instance, a witness might well recall having written down the registration number of the getaway car, and might even also remember the model and colour of the vehicle, but (special circumstances aside) it would not generally be reasonable to expect spontaneous recall of a seven-character number-plate many months after the incident in question.[205] This pragmatic approach was predictably carried over to CJA 2003, section 117(5)(b). Thus, the Administrative Court ruled that a police officer could not be expected to remember the details of criminal aliases he had recently added to the PNC, because these were routine intelligence-gathering operations which officers would not generally commit to memory. 'The crucial fact,' according to the Court, 'is that alias names are not unusual. Police officers keep a record of alias names given by offenders as a matter of routine. Although it is possible that police officers will have a recollection of alias names given, these are not the kind of details of which police officers could reasonably be expected to retain a recollection.'[206]

The old section 24(4)(iii) was also afflicted by the drafting error, previously mentioned in relation to CJA 1988, section 23, which created a mismatch between the absence conditions and the person who originally supplied the information contained in a proffered hearsay statement.[207] Mimicking the elegant solution adopted by section 116, subsection 117(5) of the CJA 2003 applies its 'could-not-reasonably-be-expected-to-recollect' bonus absence condition to 'the relevant person', who is defined by subsection 117(2)(b) as 'the person who supplied the information contained in the statement' and who 'had or may reasonably be supposed to have had personal knowledge of the matters dealt with'. This careful drafting should ensure that a person who is merely an intermediate link in the chain along which information has been passed cannot be 'the relevant person' for the purposes of subsection 117(5).

---

[202] *R v Bedi and Bedi* (1992) 95 Cr App R 21, CA. Also see *R v Hinds* [1993] Crim LR 528, CA (forms to replace lost or stolen Post Office benefit books).   [203] *R v Bailey* [2008] EWCA Crim 817.

[204] *R (Pierre Wellington) v DPP* [2007] EWHC 1061 (Admin).

[205] *R v Carrington* (1994) 99 Cr App R 376, CA.

[206] *R (Pierre Wellington) v DPP* [2007] EWHC 1061 (Admin), [32].

[207] See *R v Derodra* [2000] 1 Cr App R 41, CA; *R v Carrington* (1994) 99 Cr App R 376, 380–1, CA; Sir John Smith, 'Documentary Evidence in Criminal Proceedings' [1999] *NLJ* 1550 (22 October).

(iv) Multiple discretions

In another respect, however, the CJA 2003 does perpetuate, and even compounds, a defect in the structure of admissibility bequeathed by the 1988 Act. The proliferation of overlapping structured discretions has already been mentioned in relation to section 116. In view of the basic rationale for admitting 'business, etc.' documents, section 117 is properly exempted from the leave requirement normally imposed on multiple hearsay by section 121(1)(c).[208] However, as if by way of compensation, section 117 contains its very own exclusionary discretion, which is triggered when the court judges that 'the statement's reliability as evidence for the purpose for which it is tendered is doubtful in view of (a) its contents, (b) the source of the information contained in it, (c) the way in which or the circumstances in which the information was supplied or received, or (d) the way in which or the circumstances in which the document concerned was created or received'. To draw these disparate threads together, a trial judge may,[209] in his discretion, exclude a hearsay statement otherwise admissible under section 117 if the judge has serious concerns about its reliability. This power is in addition to the judge's explicit authority to exclude any hearsay statement under section 126(1) on grounds of insufficient probative value. There is also the roving jurisdiction (explicitly preserved in this context by section 126(2)) to exclude unfair prosecution evidence under PACE 1984, section 78, which operates in tandem with any residual power at common law (also preserved by section 126(2)) to exclude evidence on a PV < PE basis. These exclusionary discretions are now informed and underpinned by Article 6 fair trial standards. Not forgetting, finally, the failsafe provided by CJA 2003, section 125, empowering trial judges to direct an acquittal or discharge the jury[210] where hearsay evidence that has been admitted in the trial turns out to be 'so unconvincing that, considering its importance to the case against the defendant, his conviction of the offence would be unsafe'.

It seems safe to conclude that a judge who is strongly minded to exclude hearsay evidence which she regards as problematic will not have to strain too hard to find a legal justification for doing so. One scenario in which judicial vigilance may be at a premium is where the prosecution attempts to utilize section 117 to introduce low-grade or disputed evidence of the accused's extraneous misconduct,[211] a forensic strategy deprecated by Lord Woolf CJ in *Humphris*,[212] even when pursued for laudable motives (here, to spare vulnerable complainants another court appearance). One is left to ponder why Parliament thought that judges need to be equipped (or perhaps, prodded and prompted) with a suite of intricately calibrated discretions, all of which share essentially the same purpose of keeping dubious documentary hearsay out of court.

---

[208] Section 121(1) provides that: 'A hearsay statement is not admissible to prove the fact that an earlier hearsay statement was made unless— (a) either of the statements is admissible under section 117...'

[209] The provision is permissive rather than mandatory. Although s.117(6) states that '[a] statement is not admissible under this section if the court makes a direction to that effect under subsection (7)', subsection (7) provides that '[t]he court *may* make a direction under this subsection if...' (emphasis supplied).

[210] An acquittal is final (at least unless and until quashed pursuant to CPIA 1996, ss.54–57, or CJA 2003, Part 10: see §2.5(f)), whereas discharging the jury results in a mistrial and the accused could be re-tried in appropriate circumstances.   [211] See Chapter 14.

[212] *R v Humphris* [2005] EWCA Crim 2030, (2005) 169 JPN 718.

9.6 COMMON LAW EXCEPTIONS
PRESERVED BY SECTION 118 OF THE CJA 2003

In contrast to sections 114, 116, and 117 of the CJA 2003, which create new, self-sufficient statutory bases for the admission of hearsay evidence, section 118 is a somewhat curious hybrid. Its prosaic title is 'Preservation of certain common law categories of admissibility', and this is precisely what section 118 achieves. It does not re-enact the old common law exceptions as new statutory provisions. Rather, section 118 merely describes pre-existing exceptions, which continue to subsist at common law, at least to the extent specifically preserved by the section. Subsection 118(2) proceeds to enact that, 'With the exception of the rules preserved by this section, the common law rules governing the admissibility of hearsay evidence in criminal proceedings are abolished'. We can at least infer, therefore, that common law exceptions to the hearsay rule survive the CJA 2003 only to the extent specifically preserved by section 118(1).

Eight groups of common law exception are retained, under the following numbered headings:

1. Public information etc.

2. Reputation as to character.

3. Reputation or family tradition.

4. *Res gestae.*

5. Confessions etc.

6. Admissions by agents etc.

7. Common enterprise.

8. Expert evidence.

This rag-bag list of 'special pleading' for particular kinds of hearsay is a relic of a time, long before *Myers*, when the judges were prepared to invent new exceptions to the exclusionary rule almost whenever probative value and convenience might dictate. Most entries on the list can be dealt with summarily.

Exception [1] relates primarily to published works, public documents, and official records,[213] which were previously mentioned in connection with the formalities of proof.[214] It does, however, also include 'evidence relating to a person's age or date or place of birth...given by a person without personal knowledge of the matter,' which is a helpful reiteration of a point that has sometimes caused difficulty.[215] A witness is generally

---

[213] '(a) published works dealing with matters of a public nature (such as histories, scientific works, dictionaries and maps) are admissible as evidence of facts of a public nature stated in them; (b) public documents (such as public registers, and returns made under public authority with respect to matters of public interest) are admissible as evidence of facts stated in them; (c) records (such as the records of certain courts, treaties, Crown grants, pardons and commissions) are admissible as evidence of facts stated in them; or (d) evidence relating to a person's age or date or place of birth may be given by a person without personal knowledge of the matter'.   [214] §.3.4(a).

[215] See, e.g., *R v Ward, Andrews and Broadley* [2001] Crim LR 316, CA.

permitted to give evidence of their name, age, and date and place of birth, even though such evidence must technically be hearsay: granted that we were all present at our own births and christenings (or other naming ceremony), none of us can actually remember these events! Section 118(1), Exception [1](d), usefully restates this principle in clear, modern language, as well as securing its preservation.

The two reputation exceptions are archaic, and can only have been retained for the sake of completeness. Exception [2] preserves the rule in *Rowton*,[216] which is explained in Chapter 14, according to which 'bad character' means reputation (not disposition or particularized conduct) at common law.[217] Exception [3] covers: '(a) pedigree or the existence of a marriage; (b) the existence of any public or general right; or (c) the identity of any person or thing'. The common law exception for disputed questions of pedigree or marriage harks back to Dickensian times, when babies born out of wedlock 'on the wrong side of the blanket' were given up for adoption, and only a gin-soaked midwife or kindly maiden aunt knew the truth of an 'orphan's' heritage. It is difficult to see why the overriding inclusionary discretion conferred by section 114(1)(d), if not sections 116 or 117, would not have been sufficient to restore Oliver Twist to his rightful fortune under the CJA 2003. But parts (b) and (c) of Exception [3] may be regarded, like Exception [1], as a useful restatement of common law principles.

Exceptions [2] and [3] are both subject to the rider, idiosyncratically described in the legislation as a 'Note', that: 'The rule is preserved only so far as it allows the court to treat such evidence as proving or disproving the matter concerned'. The meaning of this provision is obscure. The only obvious interpretation is that each exception is also limited by the threshold constraint of (logical) relevance,[218] but if that was Parliament's intention, the chosen wording barely implements it. The principal objection to these archaic evidentiary doctrines is precisely that, in certain circumstances, they may authorize the fact-finder to draw inferences that would not have been made through the application of ordinary common-sense reasoning. But the 'Note' appended to section 118(1), Exceptions [2] and [3], apparently accommodates evidence of reputation, even where these exceptions may authorize inferences at odds with common sense reasoning, so it is hard to see what this seemingly circular provision is supposed to have achieved.

Exception [5] preserves, '[a]ny rule of law relating to the admissibility of confessions or mixed statements in criminal proceedings'. Confessions and mixed statements are examined in Chapter 12. Exception [6] concerns narrowly-circumscribed, and relatively uncontroversial, principles of agency.[219] Exception [7] preserves a useful, wholly pragmatic, rule according to which 'a statement made by a party to a common enterprise is admissible against another party to the enterprise as evidence of any matter stated'. This rule was invented by the judges to make it easier to prosecute criminal conspiracies, which are often clandestine and consequently difficult to prove. Though its underlying rationales and probative reliability may be questioned, '[t]he common enterprise (or co-conspirators) exception to the hearsay rule is now so firmly established ... that it would take a doctrinal

---

[216] *R v Rowton* (1865) Le & Ca 520, 34 LJMC 57, 10 Cox CC 25, CCR.   [217] See §14.2.

[218] Different conceptions of relevance were discussed in §3.2.

[219] Exception [6] covers: 'Any rule of law under which in criminal proceedings: (a) an admission made by an agent of a defendant is admissible against the defendant as evidence of any matter stated; or (b) a statement made by a person to whom a defendant refers a person for information is admissible against the defendant as evidence of any matter stated'.

earthquake to expunge it'.[220] Accomplice evidence is often problematic, because erstwhile accomplices frequently have strong motivation and sufficient inside information to lie convincingly in order to shift the blame onto a co-conspirator. This is why accomplice evidence used to attract mandatory corroboration warnings.[221] Prosecution evidence tendered under section 118(1), Exception [7], may be challenged on similar grounds under section 126 of the CJA 2003 before its admission, or under section 125 where its infirmities emerge during the course of the trial.

This leaves only Exception [4], bearing the arcane description *res gestae*, and Exception [8] authorizing an expert witness to 'draw on the body of expertise relevant to his field'. These two retained common law exceptions merit more extended discussion. We first examine the relationship between hearsay and expert evidence, a matter of major practical significance which also reprises the fundamental issue of the scope of the accused's right to test the evidence adduced against him. The following section (b) gets to grips with the many-headed hydra that is *res gestae*. The principal authorities on *res gestae* are well worth knowing, in the first place because they remain good law by virtue of section 118(1), Exception [4], but also because their historical development sheds interesting light on modern hearsay reform and feeds into an overall evaluation of CJA 2003. Finally, the section (c) considers an historically significant common law exception that did not survive the 2003 Act: dying declarations. The common law power to receive hearsay evidence of a homicide victim's final words was only tenuously related to the hearsay dangers and its rigid formulation tended to produce anomalies in practice. Nobody will mourn its passing. Yet this solitary instance of thinning out deadwood prompts the question, whether Parliament might not have been bolder with its pruning-shears?

(a) EXPERT EVIDENCE

Scientific, medical, and other expert witnesses constantly rely on theories, concepts, and data produced by peers and colleagues. Science is by its very nature a collaborative enterprise. Whether one thinks of a textbook distilling and synthesizing the accumulated wisdom of a scientific specialism, or of contemporary experimental data generated by scores of research teams working in laboratories around the world, it is obvious that individual experts are directly responsible only for a tiny fraction of the knowledge-base of their discipline. Even medical examination and treatment, during which doctors have had direct access to patients, draw upon knowledge of physiology and employ diagnostic techniques which doctors simply accept at face-value as part of their professional training. If put on the spot whilst testifying in court, medical experts would not be able to vouch personally for a tenth of the information on which they rely in their daily medical practice, any more than professors of chemistry or forensic geneticists could vouch personally for data collected in their absence by laboratory technicians.

There can be no doubt, therefore, that it would be intolerably inconvenient for criminal litigation if the literal logic of the hearsay rule were to be applied to expert testimony.

---

[220] Keith Spencer, 'The Common Enterprise Exception to the Hearsay Rule' (2007) 11 *E & P* 106, 132.
[221] §15.2(b).

The nonchalance with which the hearsay rule was cast aside when the point arose in *Abadom*[222] is nonetheless revealing. The Court of Appeal simply announced that experts are entitled to incorporate information generated by others into their 'opinions', without the faintest trace of a suggestion that this might be contrary to *Myers'* injunction against the creation of new common law exceptions to the hearsay rule. This is the common law doctrine preserved by section 118(1), Exception [8].

The common law approach to hearsay in expert evidence is reinforced by two important statutory provisions. First, section 30 of the CJA 1988 provides that '[a]n expert report shall be admissible as evidence in criminal proceedings, whether or not the person making it attends to give oral evidence in those proceedings', and such reports are admitted for their truth.[223] If the expert does not testify in person, however, her report can only be admitted with the leave of the court.[224] Secondly, section 127 of the CJA 2003 created a new, dedicated, hearsay exception permitting experts to base their testimony on statements prepared by other persons, provided that notice requirements have been complied with and admissibility is in the interests of justice.[225] Section 127 covers test results, medical examination or post-mortem reports, scientific data, and other preparatory work undertaken by lab technicians and the like. Where a testifying expert relies on such a statement, the statement becomes evidence in the case.[226] Notice, however, that section 127 does not redefine such material as non-hearsay; rather, it makes certain classes of hearsay admissible in certain circumstances. Information adduced under section 127 consequently remains subject to the court's overriding powers to exclude hearsay evidence in the interests of justice[227] and to direct an acquittal or order a retrial where the case against the accused rests wholly or partly on unconvincing hearsay.[228]

It would be complacent to assume that expert testimony is always entirely free of hearsay dangers. To the contrary, the spurious authority of expertise may be invoked as an alibi for a multitude of evidentiary sins, through ignorance or deliberate sharp practice. In *Hurst*,[229] for example, a consultant psychiatrist's report was tendered by the defence in an attempt to establish that the accused had only participated in drug-smuggling under duress. The expert's report contained all manner of hearsay claims and assertions, about the accused's background, medical history, and alleged intimidation by 'sinister' Roger, a friend of a friend. Most of this information was supplied to the psychiatrist by the accused, but then repeated in his report as though it were established fact. In this instance, the Court of Appeal upheld the trial judge's firm ruling that both the psychiatrist's report and his intended testimony would be unhelpful speculation, and therefore failed the general test for the admissibility of expert evidence elaborated

---

[222] *R v Abadom* [1983] 1 WLR 126, CA. This case has already been discussed in §6.4(b), in relation to statistical evidence and the sufficiency of proof.   [223] CJA 1988, s.30(4).

[224] Section .30(2). In determining whether to grant leave, the trial judge should have regard: (a) to the contents of the report; (b) to the reasons why it is proposed that the person making the report shall not give oral evidence; (c) to any risk, having regard in particular to whether it is likely to be possible to controvert statements in the report if the person making it does not attend to give oral evidence in the proceedings, that its admission or exclusion will result in unfairness to the accused or, if there is more than one, to any of them; and (d) to any other circumstances that appear to the court to be relevant': s.30(3).

[225] s.127(4) and (5).   [226] s.127(3).   [227] s.126; PACE 1984, s.78.   [228] CJA 2003, s.125.

[229] *R v Hurst* [1995] 1 Cr App R 82, CA. See Paul Roberts, 'Will You Stand Up In Court? On the Admissibility of Psychiatric and Psychological Evidence' (1996) 7 *Journal of Forensic Psychiatry* 63.

in *Turner*.[230] But *Hurst* remains a vivid illustration of the need for judicial vigilance, lest untested and potentially unreliable hearsay should be smuggled into the trial under cover of expert testimony.[231] The courts should therefore continue to scrutinize information incorporated into an expert's report or testimony carefully, and make full use of their ample powers to exclude such evidence where the traditional hearsay dangers may be substantial.

The application, or more aptly *non*-application, of the hearsay rule to expert evidence is an object lesson in how easily traditional doctrines and principles of evidence law can be disparaged when they appear to conflict with administrative convenience. In 1993 (i.e. before CJA 2003, section 127 was enacted), the Runciman Royal Commission on Criminal Justice implied that it might be in breach of counsel's professional duty to the court to take a hearsay point against forensic science experts relying on data produced by their laboratory colleagues.[232] This flirts with the extraordinary proposition that it could be professional malpractice for counsel to take advantage of a point favouring her client just because the law happens to be very inconvenient for her opponent. The approach of the US Supreme Court, which recently confronted the same issue of the admissibility of reports from non-testifying experts, could hardly provide a more striking contrast. In *Melendez-Diaz* the Supreme Court ruled, by a 5–4 majority, that adducing the reports of drug analysts who did not testify in person at trial, in order to establish the identity of a narcotic (cocaine) found in the accused's possession, contravened the Sixth Amendment's Confrontation Clause.[233] Objections based on the inconvenience of requiring every laboratory analyst to testify in person (unless the accused was prepared to agree their evidence) could not override a basic point of principle. Writing for the majority, Justice Scalia insisted that the opportunity to cross-examine lab technicians and similar experts undertaking preparatory work for their colleagues was no mere formality, since so-called 'neutral scientific testing' may not, in reality, be quite as neutral or reliable as one might assume: 'Forensic evidence is not uniquely immune from the risk of manipulation...A forensic analyst responding to a request from a law enforcement official may feel pressure – or have an incentive – to alter the evidence in a manner favourable to the prosecution.'[234] If there were any credible suggestion of such factors operating in particular criminal proceedings in England and Wales, a trial judge might refuse to admit expert evidence that is hearsay, either in the form of a report under CJA 1988, section 30, or presented as preparatory work pursuant to CJA 2003, section 127.

---

[230] *R* v *Turner* [1975] 1 QB 835, CA. Generally, see Chapter 11.

[231] In *Turner*, ibid. 840, Lawton LJ remarked: 'It is not for this court to instruct psychiatrists how to draft their reports, but those who call psychiatrists as witnesses should remember that the facts upon which they base their opinions must be proved by admissible evidence. This elementary principle is frequently overlooked.' If cases like *Hurst* are anything to go by, some psychiatrists and their instructing lawyers do not always take the hint. For further discussion, see Mike Redmayne, *Expert Evidence and Criminal Justice* (OUP, 2001), 162–4; Rosemary Pattenden, 'Expert Opinion Evidence Based on Hearsay' [1982] *Crim LR* 85.

[232] Royal Commission on Criminal Justice, *Report* (HMSO, 1993), ch 9, para.78: 'Any unreasonable exploitation of the system should be met by sanctions against the counsel concerned if he or she is found to be responsible.'   [233] *Melendez-Diaz* v *Massachusetts*, 129 S Ct 2527 (2009).

[234] ibid. 2536.

(b) *RES GESTAE*: EXCITED UTTERANCES, PHYSICAL SENSATIONS, AND MENTAL STATES

A number of loosely-related common law exceptions to the hearsay rule are convention-ally grouped together under the rubric of *res gestae*.[235] This lapse into Latin is almost wholly uninformative and superfluous. According to *Phipson on Evidence*,[236] *res gestae* is a corruption of the phrase 'res gesta pars rei gestae,' meaning literally a specific thing which is part of things in general. In the Golden Age Latin of Cicero, *res gestae* meant 'great public events or exploits'. Translated for forensic purposes, it equates to something like 'the events at issue in the litigation', which does little more than replicate the basic evidentiary concepts of relevance and materiality discussed in Chapter 3.[237] *Res gestae* has therefore, unsurprisingly, never been a particularly helpful classification. It long ago outlived its jurisprudential usefulness, except as convenient shorthand for the *cognoscenti* and, more cynically, as a suitably obscure categorization facilitating the admission of tech-nically inadmissible hearsay.[238]

The parliamentary draftsmen has nonetheless dignified *res gestae* with statutory rec-ognition, as the title of common law Exception [4] preserved by section 118(1) of the CJA 2003. More specifically, Exception [4] preserves:

Any rule of law under which in criminal proceedings a statement is admissible as evidence of any matter stated if –

(a) the statement was made by a person so emotionally overpowered by an event that the possibility of concoction or distortion can be disregarded,

(b) the statement accompanied an act which can be properly evaluated as evidence only if considered in conjunction with the statement, or

(c) the statement relates to a physical sensation or a mental state (such as intention or emotion).

Paragraph (a) concerns what can conveniently be described as 'excited utterances', whilst paragraph (b) refers to the doctrine of 'composite acts'. These technical concepts are eluci-dated below. Paragraph (c) is sufficiently prosaic to speak for itself, but like excited utter-ances and composite acts statements relating to 'a physical sensation or a mental state (such as intention or emotion)' have been the subject-matter of sometimes convoluted case-law. Common law exceptions to the hearsay prohibition accumulated by accretion over the centuries. They are generally characterized by excessive technicality as well as by ancient pedigree, and the motley of *res gestae* exceptions preserved for posterity by section 118(1)'s Exception [4] are perfect specimens.

---

[235] For historical context, see Julius Stone, '*Res gestae reagitata*' (1939) 55 *LQR* 66; James Bradley Thayer, '*Bedingfield's Case*: Declarations as a Part of the *Res Gesta*' (1881) 15 *American LR* 1; *Wigmore on Evidence* (Chadbourn revision), vol. 5, §1767.   [236] (Sweet & Maxwell, 15th edn. 2000), 817.

[237] §3.2(d). The *OED* takes us no further: '*res gestæ*, (an account of) things done, achievements; an account of a person's career; events in the past; in Law, the facts of a case, used esp. with reference to evidence that includes spoken words'.

[238] Older authorities often treat *res gestae* as non-hearsay evidence, as opposed to hearsay admissible under an exception to the exclusionary rule: see R. W. Baker, *The Hearsay Rule* (Pitman, 1950), 160. This usage, as the cases quoted by Baker indicate, was often accompanied by an implausible claim that *res gestae* statements were not being relied upon for their truth.

(i) Excited utterances

At one time, the excited utterance exception was strictly confined to statements exactly contemporaneous with the events charged in the indictment. The extent of the law's sterile and pedantic formalism is demonstrated by the infamous decision in *Bedingfield*,[239] where the accused was charged with murdering a woman, and claimed in his defence that her death was suicide. The prosecution proposed to call evidence that the deceased had rushed out of the accused's room, moments after her throat had been cut, crying: 'Oh dear Aunt, see what Bedingfield has done to me.' She later died from her wounds. Evidence of the victim's declaration was ruled inadmissible on the exceedingly narrow ground that it was not an integral part of the same transaction as the murder/suicide, but rather a separate and severable incident forming part of its aftermath.[240] In Cockburn CJ's estimation, the deceased's words were 'something stated... after it was all over, whatever it was, and after the act was completed'.

Modern decisions, taking their lead from the Privy Council's landmark ruling in *Ratten* v *R*,[241] have cast off these formalistic shackles. In *Ratten* the accused was convicted of murdering his wife; he claimed it had all been a tragic accident. According to the accused, his shotgun had discharged unexpectedly whilst he was cleaning it, with fatal consequences. The accused, his wife, and their children were home alone on the day in question. Other evidence established conclusively that the shooting occurred between 1.12 pm and 1.20 pm. A telephone operator, called as a witness by the prosecution, testified that around 1.15 pm she had taken a call from a domestic telephone number, and heard a woman's voice on the other end of the line which sounded frightened and hysterical. The caller asked for the police but immediately hung up. The telephone call was traced to the accused's house, implying that his wife's death had been anything but a tragic accident.

On appeal, the defence objected that the telephonist's testimony was inadmissible hearsay. Rejecting this contention, the Privy Council held that the evidence did not infringe the hearsay rule because the telephone call and the caller's request for assistance, made at an evidentially significant time, were themselves relevant facts in the case. Lord Wilberforce elaborated:[242]

The mere fact that evidence of a witness includes evidence as to words spoken by another person who is not called, is no objection to its admissibility. Words spoken are facts just as much as any other action by a human being. If the speaking of the words is a relevant fact, a witness may give evidence that they were spoken. A question of hearsay only arises when the words spoken are relied on 'testimonially', i.e. as establishing some fact narrated by the words.

In this case, the fact that the call was made at a crucial moment, and that the caller was clearly distressed, tended to rebut the defence of accident. The telephonist was able to testify directly to those facts, since she had taken the call and heard the speaker's distress and plea for assistance herself.

---

[239] *R* v *Bedingfield* (1879) 14 Cox CC 341, Assizes.

[240] Note that the dying declaration exception was inapplicable because the deceased had not been labouring under a settled hopeless expectation of death at the time of her utterance. These points are elaborated in §9.6(c), below.   [241] *Ratten* v *R* [1972] AC 378, PC.

[242] ibid. 387.

In *Kearley* the House of Lords doubted that this was the true *ratio* of *Ratten*, despite Lord Wilberforce's unequivocal analysis and emphasis.[243] A second, alternative ground of admissibility suggested by the Privy Council in *Ratten*, was that the call, if hearsay,[244] was admissible as part of the *res gestae*. This would appear to represent the official, revisionist, orthodoxy post-*Kearley* (unless the enactment of CJA 2003, section 115, can be said by implication to have restored *Ratten's* authentic ground of decision). *Ratten* remains a jurisprudential landmark, nonetheless, in strongly endorsing probative value as the authentic test of admissibility for excited utterances, rather than entrusting the reliability of evidence to conformity with some technical legal definition. Lord Wilberforce continued:[245]

[H]earsay evidence may be admitted if the statement providing it is made in such conditions (always being those of approximate but not exact contemporaneity) of involvement or pressure as to exclude the possibility of concoction or distortion to the advantage of the maker or disadvantage of the accused.

Lord Wilberforce was consciously breaking with past approaches, whereby the court's 'concentration tends to be focused on the opaque or at least imprecise Latin phrase rather than upon the basic reason for excluding the type of evidence which this group of cases is concerned with'.[246]

The seal was placed on this overdue development by the House of Lords in *Andrews*.[247] Counsel for Andrews launched a direct assault on *Ratten*, inviting their Lordships to renounce the Privy Council's decision as an illegitimate extension of *Bedingfield* in flagrant breach of the Law Lords' promise in *Myers* to leave the creation of new hearsay exceptions in the exclusive care of Parliament. But on this occasion counsel's appeal to tradition and precedent was steadfastly rebuffed. Lord Ackner, speaking for a unanimous House of Lords, identified probative value, in terms of the reliability of the evidence in all the circumstances of the case, as the pre-eminent criterion of admissibility:[248]

The primary question which the judge must ask himself is: can the possibility of concoction or distortion be disregarded?... To answer that question the judge must first consider the circumstances in which the particular statement was made, in order to satisfy himself that the event was so unusual or startling or dramatic as to dominate the thoughts of the victim, so that his utterance was an instinctive reaction to that event, thus giving no real opportunity for reasoned reflection....Thus, the judge must be satisfied that the event, which provided the trigger mechanism for the statement, was still operative.

Andrews thus confirmed a significant shift in the basis of admissibility, from a fixed definition to a flexible, context-sensitive reliability standard. In broad terms, an eyewitness's hearsay statements are admissible as excited utterances if their reliability is indicated by intense and unselfconscious involvement in an event. In its sweeping generality and freedom from detailed doctrinal constraints, this test effectively made other common law exceptions redundant.[249]

---

[243] *R v Kearley* [1992] AC 228, 245–47 (Lord Bridge) and 257 (Lord Ackner); cf. *R v Blastland* [1986] AC 41, 57–9, HL.   [244] Presumably, an implied assertion under *Kearley*: see §9.4(b), above.
[245] [1972] AC 378, 391. The involvement of the declarant in the event in question has, of course, to be proved by evidence independent of the declaration.   [246] ibid. 389.
[247] *R v Andrews* [1987] AC 281, HL.   [248] ibid. 300–1.
[249] Including, in particular, the exception covering 'dying declarations' discussed below, §9.6(c).

Excited utterances are presumptively more reliable than the general run of out-of-court statements. The declarant is assumed to have had neither the time nor the inclination to concoct falsehoods, being fully immersed in the 'exciting' event in which she was caught up. The spontaneity and contemporaneity of the declarant's statement are the guarantors of its reliability. In *Andrews*, Lord Ackner was at pains to emphasize the importance of detailed factual inquiry into all the relevant circumstances. A highly dramatic event, like the homicidal attack suffered by the deceased in *Andrews*, is more likely to dominate the mind of the declarant, and for longer, than marginal involvement in an occurrence that is barely out of the ordinary.[250] The requisite degree of contemporaneity likewise turns upon the broader factual context. Post-*Andrews* case law confirmed the courts' rejection of a rigid, *Bedingfield*-style time limit, within which an out-of-court statement must be made in order to qualify for admissibility as an excited utterance.[251]

Factors weighing against admissibility must also be taken into account. Lord Ackner observed in *Andrews* that, whilst the specific risks of concoction and faulty memory may be diminished, excited utterances possibly carry increased dangers of misperception and miscommunication. If the declarant is highly agitated he may be especially prone to errors of perception; and the chances of the witness misinterpreting or misunderstanding what the declarant is trying to say must increase to the extent that the declarant is emotional, confused, incapacitated, or ailing.[252] Lord Ackner specifically mentioned two aspects of the instant case pointing in the direction of exclusion: the deceased had been on bad terms with Andrews, suggesting a motive for false accusation, and he had 'drunk to excess, well over double the permitted limit for driving a motor car'.[253] On the other hand, Andrews was well-known to the deceased – an instance of recognition, rather than stranger identification.[254] In the final analysis, taking all these countervailing considerations into account, the overwhelming drama of the event was regarded as clinching the argument in favour of admission. Although the notorious infirmities of eyewitness identification supply ample warning against exposing juries to excited utterances of every type and description,[255] the flexible, fact-focused, contextual approach to admissibility adopted by *Andrews* could be welcomed as a decisive break with past formalisms.

Finally, Lord Ackner went out of his way to stress a recurrent concern of the courts when admitting prosecution hearsay. The shift towards a reliability-based admissibility

---

[250] Cf. *Tobi v Nicholas* (1988) 86 Cr App R 323, DC, in which a minor road accident was insufficiently 'exciting' to justify the admissibility of an out-of-court identification some 20 minutes later. Glidewell LJ, ibid. 334, commented: 'Of course anyone whose vehicle has been damaged is annoyed about it, but there is a world of difference between such an unfortunately commonplace situation and the thoughts of someone who has been assaulted and stabbed.'

[251] An example is *R v Carnall* [1995] Crim LR 944, CA (delay of over an hour between the deceased victim's fatal stabbing and his identification of his assailant to the police did not prevent the victim's statement being adduced at trial as an excited utterance).

[252] Cf. Jack B. Weinstein, 'Some Difficulties in Devising Rules for Determining Truth in Judicial Trials' (1966) 66 *Columbia LR* 223, 232: 'The problem becomes more complex when the witness is not an objective spectator, but an observer involved in the event and subject to the distortion of his own heightened emotional and intellectual expectations and needs. The possibility of error in the trier's reconstruction of the event is compounded by the necessity of discounting what the trier believes to be the effect of such involvement on the witness's observation, memory and relation.'

[253] *R v Andrews* [1987] AC 281, 301.

[254] A distinction material to *Turnbull* warnings: see §15.4(b). [255] §15.4.

standard should not be treated as a convenient short-cut to save prosecutors the bother of having to prove the accused's guilt by adducing evidence in the normal way:[256]

[T]he doctrine admits hearsay statements, not only where the declarant is dead or otherwise not available but when he is called as a witness.... I would, however, strongly deprecate any attempt in criminal prosecutions to use the doctrine as a device to avoid calling, when he is available, the maker of the statement. Thus to deprive the defence of the opportunity to cross-examine him, would not be consistent with the fundamental duty of the prosecution to place all the relevant material facts before the court, so to ensure that justice is done.

Nonetheless, there is no categorical, formal requirement that a declarant must be unavailable before his out-of-court statement may be adduced as *res gestae*.[257] To this extent, the common law *res gestae* exception remains (at least in principle) more flexible than the statutory exception catering for absent witnesses now contained in CJA 2003, section 116.

(ii) Composite acts

Preserved common law Exception [4](b) covers statements accompanying conduct 'which can be properly evaluated as evidence only if considered in conjunction with the statement'. The rationale for admitting such statements is unmistakably pragmatic: where the conduct in question would not be fully intelligible if stripped of the words accompanying it, the law must take both together or benefit from neither. The admissibility of these so-called 'composite acts' is sometimes conceptualized as an extension of the doctrine of legally operative words to conduct which is *per se* evidentially significant in the trial. On this view, composite acts do not fall within the ambit of the hearsay prohibition at all. More commonly, however, composite acts are characterized as admissible hearsay under the rubric of *res gestae*, especially in older cases and commentary.[258] Thus in *Howe* v *Malkin* Grove J said:

Though you cannot give in evidence the declaration *per se*, yet when there is an act accompanied by a statement which is so mixed up with it as to become part of the *res gestae*, evidence of such statement may be given.[259]

Sensing, perhaps, that such a doctrine had the potential to hollow out the exclusionary rule to an empty husk, the judges kept composite acts strictly corralled. The statement had to relate to a relevant act with which it was roughly contemporaneous; be made by the actor himself; and was admissible only in order to prove the actor's purpose in performing the act. The contested statements in *Howe* v *Malkin* were made by a third party, and were accordingly ruled inadmissible.

If the composite act doctrine already had a rather antique feel by the second half of the twentieth century, this did not prevent modern courts from invoking it as necessity

---

[256] [1987] AC 281, 302.

[257] *Attorney General's Reference (No 1 of 2003)* [2003] 2 Cr App R 29, CA (confirming that *res gestae* evidence may be admitted even where the declarant is willing and able to testify in person at trial. There is no formal absence condition in relation to this hearsay exception).

[258] For example, G. D. Nokes, '*Res Gestae* as Hearsay' (1954) 70 *LQR* 370.

[259] *Howe* v *Malkin* (1878) 40 LT 196, applied by *R* v *McCay* (1990) 91 Cr App R 84, 87, CA.

appeared to dictate. In the Commonwealth[260] and the United States[261] it was held that, on a charge of running an illegal betting shop, the prosecution could adduce evidence that, while the police were raiding the premises, telephone calls were received in which unidentified callers tried to place bets. The words spoken could be treated as words accompanying and explaining the act of dialling and making the call, a unified composite act for doctrinal purposes. However, the interposition of a telephone line between declarant and witness hardly diminishes the hearsay dangers; risks of misperception, misapprehension, and insincerity may, indeed, be exacerbated to the extent that the caller remains wholly anonymous and quite possibly unidentifiable. There is surely no material distinction between saying face-to-face, 'Look here Mr Bookie, I wish to place a bet on Lucifer' and dialling Mr Bookie's number and saying into the telephone receiver, 'I wish to place a bet on Lucifer'. Accepting that there is none, but rejecting the composite act approach adopted by other common law courts, the House of Lords in *Kearley* decided that both are inadmissible hearsay. The composite act argument was raised and explicitly rejected on the facts.[262]

A significant modern application (or extension) of the composite act doctrine occurred in *McCay*,[263] where a pub licensee was a witness to a 'glassing' assault during a fracas on his premises. The publican later attended a formal identification parade, and picked out the accused from behind a two-way mirror. But by the time of the trial he could no longer remember whom he had picked out, or even where that person had stood in the line-up. A police officer was permitted to testify that the publican had said 'it's number eight', and that the accused had occupied the number eight position on the parade. The Court of Appeal was reluctant to say that the officer's evidence was hearsay at all, but if it was hearsay, the Court held, the evidence was nonetheless admissible as a statement accompanying and explaining the publican's act of identification.

Although *McCay* did not itself involve particularly pronounced hearsay dangers, the Court's reasoning was patently strained. The officer's evidence boiled down to the fact that the witness had asserted, otherwise than while giving evidence in court, that the accused was the offender – classic hearsay, if anything is. Notwithstanding the rigours of hearsay logic and the injunction prohibiting the creation of new common law exceptions laid down

---

[260] *McGregor v Stokes* [1952] VLR 347, cited with approval in *Ratten v R* [1972] AC 378, 388, PC, where Lord Wilberforce explained that: 'A telephone call is a composite act, made up of manual operations together with the utterance of words'. Also see *Police v Marchirus* [1977] 1 NZLR 288, NZCA; *Davidson v Quirke* [1923] NZLR 552, NZCA.

[261] *State v Tolisano*, 70 A 2d 118 (1949). Cross observed that, it 'is truly said that the evidence is only relevant if it is assumed that the unknown callers believed the premises in question to be a betting-shop, but they were acting on their beliefs by attempting to place bets and not merely making assertions about their states of mind. It is therefore arguable that the receipt of the calls is proved as circumstantial evidence of the conduct and not as a set of hearsay statements of the reasons for making them': *Cross on Evidence* (5th edn. 1979), 10. A similar approach was followed in a string of subsequent cases concerned with proof of drug-dealing: *US v Lewis*, 902 F 2d 1176 (5th Cir 1990); *US v Long*, 905 F 2d 1572 (DC Cir 1990); *US v Jackson*, 588 F 2d 1046 (1979). For critical commentary, see James M. Ulam, 'The Hearsay Rule: Are Telephone Calls Intercepted by Police Admissible to Prove the Truth of Matters Impliedly Asserted?' (1991) 11 *Mississippi College Law Review* 349. These authorities anticipated the House of Lords' landmark ruling on anonymous telephone calls and implied assertions in *Kearley*, discussed in §9.4(b), above.

[262] [1992] 2 AC 228, 247, HL, *per* Lord Bridge: 'While the admissibility of words which accompany an action may be derived from the relevance of the action itself, if an action considered apart from any accompanying words is not of any relevance, the action will be of ño assistance in establishing the admissibility of the accompanying words.'   [263] *R v McCay* [1990] 1 WLR 645, CA.

in *Myers*, decisions like those in *McCay* appear to be driven by *sub rosa* calculations of reliability, necessity, and convenience. A significant factor in *McCay* was presumably that all the relevant witnesses were available to testify in court and were subjected to cross-examination;[264] albeit that the cross-examiner's forensic weapons may be blunted by a witness who consistently and truthfully responds, 'I cannot recall'. The need for creative applications of concepts such as 'composite acts' or 'legally operative words' to rescue otherwise inadmissible hearsay has been substantially reduced, if not entirely pre-empted, by the advent of CJA 2003, section 114(1)(d). Parliament has nonetheless explicitly preserved composite acts as an authentic variety of *res gestae*, itself an act of conservation that can only be attributed to a superabundance of caution.

(iii) Declaration of physical sensation, state of mind, or intention

A third group of hearsay exceptions traditionally discussed under the rubric of *res gestae* concerns declarations of physical sensation, state of mind, or present intention to do something in the future. The old law is, as one quickly comes to expect, a thicket of technical criteria.

Contemporaneous declarations of physical sensation are the most straightforward case. The closer such exclamations get to involuntary grunts, groans, or shrieks of pain, the less they resemble any kind of 'statement', hearsay or otherwise. Physical things that the human body does, so to speak, of its own accord do not amount to purposive human conduct, let alone statements that could be adduced for the truth of the proposition they state. But even clearly hearsay assertions, like 'my head hurts' or 'I feel sick', are admissible under a well-established common law exception as evidence of the declarant's currently-experienced sensations.[265]

The exception can be justified on grounds of reliability. Somebody who cries out in anguish could be faking it, but is more likely to be vocalizing genuine discomfort. Especially where subsequent events appear to bear out the truth of an exclamation,[266] it will usually be safe to rely on its veracity. Historically, the exception was reinforced by cogent considerations of necessity. At a time when medical diagnosis was primitive, reliance was inevitably placed on a person's own stated feelings and expressions of their current state of health.

There is a further, overriding doctrinal limitation. Only that part of the declaration directly expressing a physical sensation can be adduced in a criminal trial; any incidental material, including the declarant's theories as to how he might have arrived at his current condition, remain inadmissible.[267] The distinction was highly salient in old poisoning cases[268] where the victim would typically say something like, 'I feel terrible. So-and-so must have poisoned me'. Only the first sentence, not the second, could be admitted under the declarations of physical sensation exception. Unless the declarant was at that time sufficiently convinced of his demise to trigger the dying declarations exception,[269] it would usually be impossible to adduce the second sentence containing the accusation in any

---

[264] Analogous to the admission of a witness's previous consistent statement by way of exception to the rule against narrative: §8.3. There are also close parallels – in practice, if not in theory – to the witness permitted to 'refresh memory': §8.2(b).   [265] *Gilbey* v *Great Western Railway Co* (1910) 102 LT 202, CA.

[266] As where a person complains of feeling sick and subsequently vomits; or in the late Spike Milligan's favourite epitaph – 'I told you I was ill'.   [267] *R* v *Nicholas* (1846) 2 Car & Kir 246.

[268] See, e.g., *R* v *Black* (1922) 16 Cr App R 118, CCA.   [269] §9.6(c), below.

subsequent trial, despite its patent probative significance. Poison was generally too slow-acting to bring the declaration within the *Bedingfield* conception of *res gestae*. In modern times, however, similar cases could easily be accommodated by regarding the whole of the deceased's statement as an excited utterance under *Andrews*.

Statements expressing the declarant's present state of mind are, by parity of reasoning, also admissible, to prove that state of mind. To this day, a declarant's statement is frequently valuable information, and sometimes the best evidence, of his state of mind; though it should not be overlooked that a person's conduct is also normally very good evidence of what they were thinking at the time.[270] The legal principle was pithily summarized by Lord Bridge in *Blastland*:

[S]tatements made to a witness by a third party are not excluded by the hearsay rule when they are put in evidence solely to prove the state of mind either of the maker of the statement or the person to whom it was made. What a person said or heard said may well be the best and most direct evidence of that person's state of mind. This principle can only apply, however, when the state of mind evidenced by the statement is either itself directly in issue at the trial or of direct and immediate relevance to an issue which arises at the trial.[271]

Lord Bridge's insistence on 'direct and immediate relevance'[272] hints at a potential difficulty with this exception. Some judges have worried that the state of mind exception could be extended to outflank the hearsay prohibition entirely. If the trier of fact were always permitted to infer the truth of fact-*x* from *W*'s belief in *x*, counsel could routinely circumvent the hearsay rule by asking the witness: 'what did you believe after the declarant had spoken?' as opposed to: 'what did the declarant say?' In the usual course of events the witness in court will be in no position to second-guess the declarant. Having no reason to doubt the truth of the declarant's assertion, the witness will therefore most likely respond that she believes *x*, from which the trier of fact will be invited to infer that *x* is true. This is precisely the reasoning that the hearsay rule forbids. Consequently, the exception is said to allow only the inference that *W* believed *x*, without sanctioning the further inference that *W*'s belief in *x* makes it more likely that *x* is true. For example, *W*'s statement that his bank account is overdrawn is admissible to prove that *W* believed his bank account to be overdrawn, but not to prove that the account was in fact overdrawn. Conversely, Mark's esoteric knowledge in *Blastland* and the callers' shared belief that 'Chippie' would supply them with drugs in *Kearley* were both ruled inadmissible on grounds of lack of relevance. In the one case, it was unclear how Mark had come by his knowledge of the murder;[273] and in the other, it was said by their Lordships comprising the majority, the beliefs of individual callers had no bearing on *Kearley's* willingness to supply them with drugs.[274]

Both decisions make a mockery of common sense reasoning, as the judges in the *Kearley* minority observed. Since the common law test of relevance is meant to be, precisely, one of

---

[270] Recalling Wittgenstein's powerful aphorism, that 'the human body is the best picture of the human soul': for illuminating discussion, see Roger A. Shiner, 'Intoxication and Responsibility' (1990) 13 *International Journal of Law and Psychiatry* 9.

[271] *R v Blastland* [1986] 1 AC 41, 54. See P. B. Carter, 'Hearsay, Relevance and Admissibility: Declarations as to State of Mind and Declarations Against Penal Interest' (1987) 103 *LQR* 106.

[272] Whatever that might mean: see the discussion of concepts of relevance in §3.2.

[273] *R v Blastland* [1986] 1 AC 41, 54.

[274] *R v Kearley* [1992] 2 AC 228, 243–5 (Lord Bridge), 254 (Lord Ackner), and 263, 273–4 (Lord Oliver).

'logic and common sense', it is difficult to see how such reasoning and conclusions could be good law, either. The way to prevent the state of mind exception from winnowing out the hearsay rule is to pay closer attention to contextual relevance and probative value. Unless counsel is deliberately employing a strategic ruse to short-circuit the hearsay rule, evidence of states of mind should be admitted to support whatever inferences they can logically bear, to the full extent of their probative significance. The aspiration to reduce flexible assessments of probative value to a determinate rule of law – so that a statement may prove a state of mind, but is supposedly incapable of supporting any factual inference implied by that state of mind – is a recipe for avoidable confusion and potential injustice.

A third type of statement involves declarations of intention as to future conduct. This is an area of considerable practical importance and longstanding legal controversy. English precedents are divided on the question of whether a declaration of intention can be admitted to prove that the intention was subsequently carried out.[275] For further illumination we must look to the decisions of common law courts in other jurisdictions.

In the celebrated American case of *Mutual Life Insurance Co* v *Hillmon*,[276] where a claim under a life insurance policy was contested, the question was whether a body found at Crooked Creek was that of the assured, Hillmon, or the remains of one Walters. The defendant insurance company contended that the deceased was Walters, and that he had been murdered by Hillmon. To prove their allegation, the defendants proposed to adduce certain letters, which had been written by Walters and sent to his relatives two weeks before the grisly discovery at Crooked Creek, in which Walters confided that he intended to leave Wichita in the company of Hillmon. The US Supreme Court held that the letters were admissible to prove Walters' intention to travel with Hillmon, and that such intention – if proved – made it more probable that Walters did go with Hillmon, than if no intention had ever been expressed.

The decision in *Hillmon's* case can be seen as a reasonable application of logic and common sense: why would Walters tell his family that he was preparing to travel with Hillmon unless it were true? Viewed through the lens of hearsay doctrine, however, the statement has obvious infirmities which cannot easily be tested through forensic process. Who knows what reasons Walters might have had for lying about his future plans? Maybe Walters was involved in troubles of his own and wanted to throw his family, and anybody who might subsequently recover his letters from them (as in fact the insurance company did), off the scent. Or perhaps he was simply mistaken in thinking that Hillmon would travel with him? Above all, there is the elementary objection that many intentions, no matter how considered and earnestly formed, are nonetheless never carried out. Any number of things, ranging from a simple change of heart to *force majeure*, could have intervened, between the writing of the letter and the departure for Wichita, to prevent Hillmon and Walters from embarking on the journey together.

In *Hillmon* the US Supreme Court opted to receive evidence of an expressed intention of future conduct, notwithstanding the attendant hearsay dangers, in preference to

---

[275] In *R* v *Buckley* (1873) 13 Cox CC 293, Assizes, the prosecution was permitted to adduce the deceased police officer's statement, that he was going to keep watch on the accused that night because he 'was at his old game of thieving again'. The statement was received as evidence connecting the accused with the officer's murder. But in the nearly contemporaneous case of *R* v *Wainwright* (1875) 13 Cox CC 171, CCC, where the deceased was an ordinary member of the public but the facts were in other material respects identical, the decision went the other way in favour of exclusion.   [276] 145 US 285 (1892).

depriving the fact-finder altogether of information which in common sense had some material bearing on the issues in the case. Walters' letter, even if an authentic record of a genuine intention, might still be regarded as quite flimsy evidence of what actually transpired; but, then again, the courts apparently had precious little else to go on (without the assistance of modern forensic science techniques) in their efforts to identity the deceased. In presenting his case to the fact-finder, Hillmon's counsel was at liberty to emphasize all of the uncertainties and contingencies attending the hearsay statements of future intention contained in Walters' correspondence.

The same preference for admissibility was displayed, almost a century later, by the High Court of Australia in *Walton*,[277] where the accused was charged with murdering his wife. The deceased had allegedly announced, upon receiving a telephone call, that the caller was her husband, and that she was going to meet him in the centre of town later that day. According to the High Court, the deceased's declared intention was nothing more exotic than admissible circumstantial evidence from which the jury was entitled, if it should choose, to draw the invited inference: that she had indeed kept the announced rendezvous with her husband later that day, making him the prime suspect for her murder. Of course the statement could just as easily have been characterized, in the fashion of *Kearley*, as an inadmissible implied assertion that the husband had asked the deceased to meet him. Once more, the rationale of these decisions is to be found in a 'policy choice' (i.e. moral and political judgment), rather than in the mechanical application of the hearsay rule's elusive logic. In *Walters*, as in *Hillmon*, the court sensibly chose admissibility as the superior evidentiary strategy, allowing the jury access to pertinent information and trusting them to make appropriate allowances for its vulnerability to the well-rehearsed hearsay dangers.

By expressly referring to intentions as an example of a relevant 'mental state', CJA 2003, section 118(1), Exception [4](c), seems to nudge English common law towards accepting that, even on the supposition that they are hearsay,[278] declared intentions of future conduct may be admissible under the capacious umbrella of *res gestae*. In any event, such statements could always be received under section 114(1)(d)'s catch-all 'safety-valve' inclusionary discretion, were a sufficiently meritorious case to present itself. The crucial determinant of admissibility, in either case, will be the trial judge's assessment of the probative value of a declarant's intention, set against considerations of potential unreliability and unfairness to the opposing party. Even where the balance of considerations favours admissibility and the evidence is duly received, we must never become complacent about the

---

[277] *Walton v R* (1989) 84 ALR 59, HCA.

[278] Roderick Munday suggests that, whatever might have been arguable at common law, statements of future intention will necessarily fall within the scope of the hearsay prohibition as defined by CJA 2003, ss.114(1)(b) and 115: 'Legislation that Would "Preserve" the Common Law: The Case of the Declaration of Intention' (2008) 124 *LQR* 46, 52–3. However, this confident conclusion may be premature. Statements of future intention are *not* adduced for their truth in any straightforward sense. Rather, they are adduced as evidence that the intention was subsequently carried out. One might argue that the material inference is predicated on the fact that the declarant *expressed* an intention ('if he said he was going to do it, that makes it more likely that he did do it') rather than on the evidentially elusive mental state of intention itself. In other words, the pertinent generalization is 'people usually/often/sometimes do what they say they are going to do', as opposed to 'people usually/often/sometimes do what they intend to do'. On that analysis, intention *per se* drops out of the picture and s.115 does not bite, since the only 'representation of fact or opinion' relates to the intention, and not to the deed.

dangers of relying on hearsay. Trial judges should strive fastidiously to draw to the jury's attention any circumstantial factors suggesting that even an authentic and genuinely-expressed intention might never in fact have been carried out.

(c) DYING DECLARATIONS RIP

Before leaving the topic of common law exceptions to the hearsay rule, it is worth marking the passing of one doctrine that the CJA 2003 killed off. Under the hearsay exception for 'dying declarations' the courts were permitted to receive the last words of a deceased witness, provided that certain technical preconditions to admissibility were satisfied. Necessity was obviously a major pressure towards admitting the out-of-court statements of permanently absent witnesses, but arguments of reliability were also traditionally advanced in favour of receiving dying declarations. The rise and demise of this superannuated doctrine presents an illuminating case study in the evolution of common law exceptions to the rule against hearsay, and their ultimate (partial) eclipse by the CJA 2003.

The mature exception for dying declarations was summarized by Cross in the following terms:[279]

[The] oral or written declaration of a deceased person is admissible evidence of the cause of his death at a trial for his murder or manslaughter provided he was under a settled hopeless expectation of death when the statement was made and provided he would have been a competent witness if called to give evidence at the trial.

Each substantive element of the test had to be satisfied to secure admissibility: (1) a declaration; (2) by a person since deceased; (3) who would otherwise have been a competent witness; (4) made under a 'settled hopeless expectation of death'; (5) and relating to the cause of death; (6) adduced on a charge of murder or manslaughter. The conventional rationale for receiving dying declarations, ostensibly supplanting the more prosaic consideration that the dead are simply unavailable to testify in person, was encapsulated in the following sombre *dictum* of Eyre CB, where dying declarations are characterized as statements *in extremis*:[280]

when the party is at the point of death, and when every hope of this world is gone; when every motive to falsehood is silenced, and the mind is induced by the most powerful considerations to speak the truth; a situation so solemn, and so awful, is considered by the law as creating an obligation equal to that which is imposed by a positive oath administered in a Court of Justice.

Being in the grip of a 'settled hopeless expectation of death'[281] was thus supposed to operate as a surrogate for swearing an oath, and thereby guarantee the reliability of the deceased witness's dying declaration. It followed that if the declarant entertained even a faint hope of recovery the exception could not be relied upon.[282] Yet the logic of this rationale was not consistently applied, making further restrictions on the availability of the exception appear arbitrary. Why, in particular, should admissibility have been confined to charges

---

[279] *Cross on Evidence* (Butterworths, 5th edn. 1979), 564.   [280] *R v Woodcock* (1789) 1 Leach 500.

[281] Memorized by generations of law students by posing the mnemonic question, was the witness in a SHED?   [282] *R v Perry* [1909] 2 KB 697, CCA; *R v Jenkins* (1869) LR 1 CCR 187.

of murder or manslaughter? Working through the logic of Eyre CB's rationalization, the determining factor ought to have been the declarant's convinced belief in his imminent demise at the material time, when the declaration was made. The prosecutor's subsequent choice of legal charge has no logical bearing on the reliability of the deceased's statement.[283] Why, again, was the declaration only admissible on the issue of the declarant's cause of death?[284] If the awe-inspiring prospect of meeting one's Maker is supposed to induce reflex veracity, why were the courts restricted to relying upon only one part of a dying declaration? Why, for that matter, did the exception cease to operate just because, contrary to all expectations, the declarant rallied and survived? If the rationale for receiving dying declarations was supposed to be their exceptional reliability, rather than the unavailability of the declarant, qualifying utterances should not have been regarded as any less reliable just because the declarant turned out, after all, to be available to testify in the trial. And why, above all, was the admissibility of a dying declaration confined to cases where the accused was charged with the homicide of the declarant himself? Surely, a presumptively reliable, material statement should have been no less worthy of belief in the trial of offences perpetrated against a different victim.

In modern times, an alternative, more coherent and appealing, rationale for the admission of dying declarations was suggested by Sir Owen Woodhouse in *Nembhard v R*: 'it is important in the interests of justice that a person implicated in a killing should be obliged to meet in court the dying accusation of the victim'.[285] This idea has considerable moral purchase, and chimes with the modern emphasis on increased concern and respect for victims of crime. It might also explain why the courts felt constrained to keep the exception strictly confined. Being a concession to moral sentiment, the law conceded the bare minimum.

Latterly, there were encouraging signs of growing judicial impatience with technical doctrinal restrictions on the availability of common law hearsay exceptions. Thus, in *Mills v R*[286] the Privy Council was prepared to look beyond the ancient language in which the dying declarations exception was couched, to reappraise the underlying reasons for admitting or excluding such evidence. Lord Steyn highlighted the following features of this case:[287]

[T]he deceased's last words were closely associated with that attack which triggered his statement. It was made in conditions of approximate contemporaneity. The dramatic occurrence, and the victim's grave wounds, would have dominated his thoughts. The inference was irresistible that the possibility of concoction or distortion could be disregarded.

The considerations mentioned by Lord Steyn consciously echo the criteria enunciated by the House of Lords in *Andrews*[288] to govern the admissibility of 'excited utterances'. Taken together, these lines of authority suggested a welcome trend towards more flexible

---

283 The anomaly would be especially stark where the accused was charged with an offence which is a functional equivalent of manslaughter, for example causing death by dangerous driving. Cf. *R v Jurtyn* (1958) OWN 335, where the Ontario Court of Appeal extended the dying declarations exception to a charge of causing death by criminal operation of a motor vehicle.   284 *R v Mead* (1824) 2 B & C 605.

285 *Nembhard v R* (1982) 74 Cr App R 144, 146, PC; though it was also maintained, in accordance with tradition, that: 'Nobody...would wish to die with a lie on his lips. So it is considered quite unlikely that a deliberate untruth would be told, let alone a false accusation of homicide, by a man who believed that he was face to face with his own impending death.'   286 *Mills v R* [1995] 1 WLR 511, PC.

287 ibid. 522.   288 [1987] AC 281.

interpretations of common law hearsay exceptions, without implying that the judges could afford to relax their guard against the admission of poor quality information which, in all the circumstances of the case, it would be better to withhold from the jury.[289]

In this instance, however, the CJA 2003 opted for revolution in preference to continued evolution. Dying declarations are not included within section 118(1)'s list of preserved common law exceptions, and are consequently abolished by operation of subsection 118(2). But there is no need to fear any contraction of the scope of admissibility for deceased persons' dying words; quite the reverse. One of the main reasons why the common law dying declarations exception continued to be significant in modern times was that section 23 of the CJA1988 applied only to written, documentary hearsay. This gap has now been plugged by CJA 2003, section 116, which is apt to secure the admissibility of any dying declaration previously admissible at common law because section 116(2)'s first absence condition – that the relevant person is dead – must *ex hypothesi* be satisfied. Whilst the judges deserve praise for gradually beginning to liberate the dying declarations exception from its doctrinal encrustations, Parliament must be congratulated for having disposed with all surviving formalistic restrictions on admissibility with one decisive flourish of the draftsman's pen.

9.7 BACK TO THE FUTURE: RECONSTRUCTING A PRINCIPLED LAW OF HEARSAY

In the period immediately prior to the enactment of the CJA 2003, it was a fair question whether the rule against hearsay, for all its ancient pedigree, had any future whatsoever in English criminal proceedings.[290] That question was emphatically answered in the affirmative by the CJA 2003. Parliament had never before enacted such a comprehensive reform of the law of hearsay, and it is exceedingly unlikely that this topic will qualify again for such sustained legislative attention for many, many years to come. In crudely instrumental terms, the hearsay provisions of the CJA 2003 'work', or can be made to do so. Whatever else it might have achieved or failed to achieve, the CJA 2003 entrusts trial judges with ample discretion to regulate the admissibility of hearsay evidence in broad compliance with the dictates of common sense and justice. The courts coped well enough with the documentary hearsay provisions of the CJA 1988, despite some lamentable drafting. Section for section, the CJA 2003 is at least the equal of its predecessor and prototype, and in numerous points of detail can be regarded as a clear improvement, as we have seen.

Many critics nonetheless regarded the 2003 Act as a missed opportunity for more systematic, root-and-branch reform. Lord Justice Auld's *Review of the Criminal Courts* had

---

[289] The deceased's last words in *Mills* were reported to be: 'Jules and him bwoy dem chop me up'. This strongly-accented exclamation apparently presents the hearsay danger of miscommunication, even if the dangers of misperception, loss of memory, and deliberate falsehood were sufficiently remote to be disregarded on the facts. However, given the evidential significance of V's denying accusation, the considerations weighing in favour of its admissibility were strong and, on balance, probably overwhelming.

[290] For discussion, see John D. Jackson, 'Hearsay: the Sacred Cow that Won't be Slaughtered?' (1998) 2 *E & P* 166; Andrew L.-T. Choo, *Hearsay and Confrontation in Criminal Trials* (OUP, 1996), ch 8; A. A. S. Zuckerman, 'The Futility of Hearsay' [1996] Crim LR 4; J. R. Spencer, 'Hearsay Reform: A Bridge Not Far Enough?' [1996] *Crim LR* 29.

advocated 'making hearsay generally admissible subject to the principle of best evidence, rather than generally inadmissible subject to specified exceptions'.[291] A general exception covering the oral (as well as written) hearsay of absent witnesses[292] and provision for an overriding inclusionary discretion[293] are significant innovations, but in other respects the CJA 2003 kept faith with the past. The technique of attempting to graft new law onto old necessarily further complicates the pre-existing admissibility regime, which was widely considered already too complex to justify its up-keep. It might well be asked, for example, why it was deemed necessary to retain the old categories of *res gestae* when a flexible safety value would surely facilitate the reception at trial of excited utterances and the like whenever circumstances favour their admissibility.[294] Gratuitous complexity tends to inflate the costs of litigation, increases the risk of error, and is a blight on the formal, rule-of-law qualities of procedural norms.

The conjunction of old and new legal rules is further deficient to the extent that it preserves existing anomalies and defects. Roderick Munday has pointed out that some of the old common law exceptions are of such doubtful scope that it is hard to know just what Parliament has actually 'preserved', or thought it was preserving, by enacting section 118.[295] Incremental reform does nothing to address the more substantive complaint that the existing common law and statutory exceptions are over- as well as under-inclusive, that they admit evidence of poor quality or untestable provenance that should not be influencing criminal adjudication. This might be considered no less regrettable than the mirror-image vice, of depriving fact-finders of valuable evidence which would have assisted them to return a true and just verdict.

At the heart of the dispute between proponents of limited hearsay reform, and those who would have welcomed more radical restructuring dictated less by historical convention and more by principles of logical fact-finding and justice, lies the age-old choice between rule-bound regimes of admissibility and more discretionary approaches calling for the exercise of judgment on the facts. No system of rules, no matter how carefully constructed, will ever successfully anticipate context-sensitive judgments of probative value in the unique circumstances of each individual case. This simple thought implies that common lawyers might have fallen into the habit of contemplating hearsay exclusion through the wrong end of the telescope. Rather than wasting so much precious time with technical definitions, complex exceptions, and proliferating exceptions to exceptions, it might have been preferable to hack away the doctrinal thickets completely in order to reinstate the purity of probative value. Certainly, it is no easier now to construct a coherent, systematic rationale for the scheme of hearsay exceptions created by the CJA 2003 than it was previously to rationalize the pre-existing plethora of common law and statutory exceptions. All attempts to encapsulate the essence of forensically valuable hearsay in a determinate rule of admissibility seem doomed to disappoint expectations. Even quite general criteria of 'reliability' and 'necessity' tend to cut across each other in particular circumstances.

---

[291] Lord Justice Auld, *Review of the Criminal Courts of England and Wales* (2001), ch 11, [95]–[104].

[292] Section 116.   [293] Section 114(1)(d).

[294] David Ormerod, 'Redundant Res Gestae?' [1998] *Crim LR* 301.

[295] Roderick Munday, 'Legislation that Would "Preserve" the Common Law: The Case of the Declaration of Intention' (2008) 124 *LQR* 46; Roderick Munday, '"Preservation" of the Common Law and the Perpetuation of Error: Section 118, r.4(b) of the Criminal Justice Act 2003' (2008) 172 *Justice of the Peace* 348.

In some situations, unreliability stands out as the most serious obstacle to admissibility. Here, removal of the main source of unreliability might well sufficiently neutralize any hearsay danger to justify an exception. Evaluating the extent to which a witness correctly understood an out-of-court statement is a serious and recurrent forensic challenge. Hence many common law, and later, statutory hearsay exceptions coalesced around evidence which could safely be relied upon once the risk of communication failure had been reduced to an acceptable level. Common law exceptions catering for published works and public records fit this description, as do the modern statutory exceptions for business and related documents that gradually superseded common law doctrines during the final third of the twentieth century. Issues of credibility and reliability still remain to be investigated, of course, but at least with documents of this kind we can be reasonably confident that the declarant conveyed what he meant to say and meant what he said.

Yet it would be complacent to assume that the elimination of one source of unreliability automatically answers all the objections to receiving hearsay in criminal trials. We have seen, for example, that excited utterances blurted out in circumstances allowing no time for concoction or loss of memory are generally regarded as reliable. Recalling the four traditionally-recognized 'hearsay dangers', however, excited utterances are immunized from only two sources of unreliability: mendacity and faulty recall. The other two hearsay dangers, mistaken perception and misinterpretation by the witness, remain undiminished. Indeed, it often transpires that the scope for misperception and communication breakdown increases in inverse proposition to diminished risks of concoction and forgetfulness. Pressure and excitement typically engender greater risks of misperception, where the declarant has no time to choose his words carefully or express himself with deliberation. If the person overhearing the exclamation is himself caught up in the 'exciting' event, experiencing stress or emotional disturbance impairing his faculties of perception, communication failure on both sides of the equation is all the more likely to result.

The related *res gestae* exception embracing contemporaneous exclamations of state of mind or physical sensation, which is also preserved by section 118 of the CJA 2003, can be deconstructed in similar fashion. The declarant is unlikely to mistake his own state of mind, nor is there much scope for forgetfulness, but there is considerable scope for misunderstanding and falsehood. People constantly lie about their intentions, desires, emotions, and attitudes. Much misrepresentation of this nature is socially acceptable, and even encouraged, for reasons of politeness, respect for another's feelings, protection of one's own privacy, and so forth (an array of special-pleading euphemisms has been invented – 'fibs', 'white lies', 'fudges', etc. – to differentiate such behaviour from the more unequivocally disreputable forms of deception). It is therefore naïve and unrealistic to suppose that statements concerning the speaker's state of mind are always a reliable form of hearsay for which an automatic inclusionary exception is entirely unproblematic.

'Necessity' fares no better than 'reliability' as a coherent rationalization of modern hearsay exceptions, before or after the CJA 2003. Necessity is fundamentally ambiguous as a test of admissibility, since the question, 'Is it necessary to admit this evidence?' could be judged relative to the remainder of the evidence in the case, or with respect to the particular source of information in question. On the first interpretation (call it 'issue-related necessity'), hearsay information might be regarded as indispensable to adjudication because there is literally no other evidence available to the court bearing on the relevant issue.[296] On this strict standard, for example, a prosecution would have to be abandoned if the evidence were ruled inadmissible. However, this interpretation is too exacting to account for the necessity-based hearsay exceptions which we actually encounter in English law. An alternative theory of 'declarant-related necessity' might imply that hearsay is admissible whenever the declarant's evidence would make a major probative contribution to resolving the issues in the trial, even where there is other admissible evidence addressing the same issue(s). This somewhat relaxed standard of 'necessity' offers a more promising rationalization of many current and historical hearsay exceptions, including, for example, the common law and statutory exceptions catering for deceased, incapacitated, or otherwise unavailable declarants. However, declarant-related necessity is not consistently reflected in English legal doctrine,[297] and as a normative rationalization it proves too much. An appeal to necessity implies that hearsay is essential for determining an issue in the trial: otherwise, why strain to create a special exception to secure its admission? But the very indispensability of hearsay, which is taken to justify its admission in such circumstances, also accentuates the notorious hearsay dangers that caused a general exclusionary rule to be devised and adopted in the first place. The more that hearsay comes to be relied upon as a basis for criminal adjudication, the greater the risk of mistaken verdicts and miscarriages of justice. Sustaining the integrity of criminal proceedings and upholding the legitimacy of verdicts becomes correspondingly more difficult as hearsay proliferates.

Criticism of the hearsay rule is as old as the rule itself. Bentham set about the task of normative demolition with his characteristic thoroughness and penchant for idiosyncratic terminology.[298] More than two centuries later the self-same fundamental dilemmas and inconsistencies still stalk the law. We appear to be perennially torn between, on the one hand, a rational mistrust of hearsay, and, on the other, our resistance to taking the hearsay rule, which expresses that mistrust, to its logical conclusion. The rule ordains exclusion, yet the plethora of exceptions, quasi-exceptions, and hearsay-fiddles devised by the judges and subsequently sanctified by statute betrays a manifest desire not to forego reliance on hearsay information, much of which remains vulnerable to the classic hearsay

---

[296] Or, if there is pertinent other evidence, it would be inferior, incomplete, or less convenient than receiving hearsay information. In this diluted sense a timetable is 'necessary' for ascertaining the departure time of a train, even though such information might be obtained from other, presumptively less reliable sources – perhaps an infrequently train-travelling neighbour's recommendation, or one's own, somewhat hazy, memories of a previous journey.

[297] As a matter of necessity, a deceased declarant obviously cannot attend court to say his piece. However, as we saw in relation to dying declarations, common law hearsay exceptions are generally rooted in considerations of (perceived) reliability, in addition to responding to circumstances of necessity. Something more than the mere unavailability of the declarant to testify as a witness at trial is usually required to secure admissibility. For instance, the family of arcane common law exceptions that, prior to the CJA 2003, permitted declarations against pecuniary or proprietary interest by deceased third parties to be adduced in criminal proceedings, was premised on the assumption that a person would not say something contrary to their own financial interests unless it were true. The scope of the exception was accordingly strictly confined by technical limitations: see *R* v *Rogers* [1995] 1 Cr App R 374, CA.

[298] Bentham, *Rationale of Judicial Evidence* (Hunt and Clarke, 1827), vol. 3, bk. 6, chs 2, 4, and 5. See George W. Keeton and O. R. Marshall, 'Bentham's Influence on the Law of Evidence', in George W. Keeton and Georg Schwarzenberger (eds.), *Jeremy Bentham and the Law: A Symposium* (Stevens, 1948), 79. Bentham accepted that hearsay was often inferior to direct oral testimony but maintained that hearsay should be excluded only when superior oral evidence was available; otherwise it should be admissible. He judged that systematic exclusion of hearsay was more productive of factual error than its routine reception.

vices. Compromise has been the inevitable outcome in Anglo-American jurisprudence. The hearsay prohibition has been tempered with common law exceptions, statutory exceptions, judicial inventiveness, and real or pretended ignorance of the more unpalatable consequences of the exclusionary rule. When opponents of reform have objected that a more discretionary approach to admissibility would introduce too much uncertainty into the law, they all-too-often appeared to be overlooking the fact that the status quo effectively concealed the reality of discretionary decision-making behind the facade of rule-based adjudication. The law dictated that the logic of hearsay should govern admissibility, irrespective of contextual judgments of probative value, but in reality determinations of admissibility were often strongly influenced by probative force. Judges were left to manage the disjunction between theory and practice as best they could in the circumstances of individual cases.

It would surely be preferable if judicial discretion were exercised more openly, promoting transparency and accountability in accordance with the foundational principles of criminal evidence and the requirements of international human rights law, as it now impinges on criminal proceedings in England and Wales via the Human Rights Act. A judge who believes that a piece of evidence should be admitted on the grounds that its usefulness outweighs the disadvantages of receiving it, should be able to say so plainly, and squarely face the consequences of criticism on appeal and censure before the tribunal of public opinion. One consequence of greater accountability might be that judges would be less inclined than they have been, in recent memory, to exclude hearsay proof of innocence.

Discretion may assume many guises.[299] The logical terminus of an expanding list of exceptional categories of admissible hearsay is exemplified by the US Federal Rules of Evidence, which prescribe a long and complex list of discrete exceptions topped-off by the following catch-all provision:

Rule 803 (24) *Other exceptions*
A statement not specifically covered by any of the foregoing exceptions but having equivalent circumstantial guarantees of trustworthiness, if the court determines that (A) the statement is offered as evidence of a material fact; (B) the statement is more probative on the point for which it is offered than any other evidence which the proponent can procure through reasonable efforts; and (C) the general purpose of these rules and the interests of justice will best be served by admission of the statement into evidence. However, a statement may not be admitted under this exception unless the proponent of it makes known to the adverse party sufficiently in advance of the trial or hearing to provide the adverse party with a fair opportunity to prepare to meet it, his intention to offer the statement and the particulars of it, including the name and address of the declarant.[300]

This remarkable provision might be mistaken for a parody of the law of hearsay. It is the exception catering for evidence that cannot be fitted into any of the other, articulated exceptions, manifesting 'circumstantial guarantees of trustworthiness' notionally 'equivalent' to an utterly disparate collection of exceptions variously justified by appeals to reliability and/or necessity! The controlling consideration in practice must surely be that

---

[299] The meaning of 'discretion' (or judgment) in law was discussed in §1.4(b).

[300] Rule 803 exceptions obtain irrespective of the declarant's availability. They are augmented by Rule 804's list of exceptions applicable where the declarant is unavailable, complete with its own residual exception equivalent to Rule 803(24).

'the interests of justice will best be served by admission of the statement into evidence'. For English lawyers, there are obvious parallels with the power introduced by CJA 2003, section 114(1)(d), to receive hearsay where 'the court is satisfied that it is in the interests of justice for it to be admissible'. This perhaps brings the parody closer to home.

The Court of Appeal has said that section 114(1)(d) should be given its ordinary, literal meaning, unvarnished by its legislative history.[301] This is not what the Law Commission envisaged when it proposed the creation of a 'safety value' inclusionary discretion, and the predictions of many commentators have been falsified.[302] Others more or less saw it coming. Di Birch mused that, '[i]n another twenty [years] we may be reflecting on how the inclusionary discretion has forever altered the landscape of criminal evidence'.[303] The midst of a revolution (if that is what English hearsay law is currently experiencing) is probably not the best vantage point from which to try to predict its long-term consequences or to pronounce conclusively on its merits.

John Spencer once characterized the modern miscellany of hearsay exceptions as 'over-complex, incoherent, devoid of any unifying principle, and in certain vital respects, simply arbitrary'.[304] The doctrinal analysis presented in this chapter refutes the proposition that the CJA 2003 has succeeded in simplifying English hearsay law. If anything, the new law of hearsay is more complex and uncertain than ever. Although relics like the dying declarations exception have been jettisoned, section 118 has 'preserved' most of the common law of hearsay in all its obscure and idiosyncratic glory, whilst sections 116 and 117 are crammed with legal terms of art and conceptual distinctions which are going to require further authoritative elucidation for many years to come. A paradoxical feature of this highly technical framework of admissibility is its provision for a raft of partially overlapping or coterminous judicial discretions, which the Court of Appeal has been quick to exploit. Colin Tapper suggests that early section 114(1)(d) jurisprudence betrays a disturbing tendency (also, in his view, infecting other chapters of the modern law of evidence) towards *ad hoc* improvisation and disregard for precedent which is antithetical to the rule of law.[305] Contrary to expectations, multiplying evidentiary rules may *expand* rather than confine the scope for discretionary judicial decision-making, inasmuch as each novel concept, term or standard creates new opportunities for legal classification, the more so where doctrinal rules overlap, compete or apparently conflict. One begins to suspect that the CJA 2003 may have fallen between two world-views and, thus conflicted, burdened the English law of hearsay with the worst of both: the uncertainty of an essentially discretionary focus on probative value, coupled with the excessive technical complexity of category-based exceptions to a presumptive exclusionary rule (which in turn

---

[301] *R* v *Y* [2008] 1 WLR 1683, [2008] EWCA Crim 10, [47]–[48].

[302] Including ours, when we suggested in the first edition of this book, (OUP, 2004), 662–3, that s.114(1)(d) 'is really nothing more than a modest, logical extension of the kind of flexible guidelines which the House of Lords and Privy Council began to elaborate in cases such as *Andrews* and *Mills*, and which the Court of Appeal has been developing in relation to documentary hearsay under sections 25 and 26 of the Criminal Justice Act 1988'. Also see Roderick Munday, 'The Judicial Discretion to Admit Hearsay Evidence' (2007) 171 *Justice of the Peace* 276 (21 April).

[303] Di Birch, 'Criminal Justice Act 2003: (4) Hearsay: Same Old Story, Same Old Song?' [2004] *Crim LR* 556, 573.

[304] J. R. Spencer, 'Orality and the Evidence of Absent Witnesses' [1994] *Crim LR* 628, 631.

[305] Colin Tapper, 'The Law of Evidence and the Rule of Law' (2009) 68 *Cambridge Law Journal* 67.

breeds further uncertainty).[306] If the scope for anomaly has been diminished through the provision of more flexible judicial discretions, the sheer volume and complexity of the law of hearsay – and therefore the scope for doctrinal error and confusion – has surely increased.

Our best chance of making progress with this perennial conundrum is to reassert the essentials of a principled approach to hearsay. Despite its ostensibly roving commission, section 114(1)(d) should not become a backdoor route for the routine admission of poor quality information, or a convenient mechanism for rescuing poorly-prepared prosecutions from directed verdicts of acquittal. It ought to require a convincing argument, securely-founded in considerations of probative value and justice, to persuade a judge that hearsay evidence which cannot be brought within any of the discrete exceptions created or preserved by the CJA 2003 should nonetheless be admitted in the interests of justice under section 114(1)(d). The Court of Appeal officially endorses this elementary presupposition, without which the entire superstructure of the CJA 2003's hearsay provisions would barely make any sense; though the clarity of the message is admittedly sometimes clouded by the Court's willingness to find alternative ways of receiving hearsay evidence afflicted with otherwise incurable defects.

Three further fixed points contributing towards a principled approach to regulating hearsay emerge from the preceding discussion. First, if the maker of the statement is available, he should normally be called as a witness. Recall that Lord Ackner 'strongly deprecat[ed] any attempt in criminal prosecutions to use the [res gestae] doctrine as a device to avoid calling, when he is available, the maker of the statement'.[307] Declarant availability is a factor that a court is specifically required to take into account in relation to section 114(1)(d)'s inclusionary discretion,[308] and, of course, governs the admissibility of the statements of absent witnesses under section 116. Where the declarant testifies, his previous statement will normally have insufficient probative value to merit admission as an independent supplement to his oral testimony, unless the previous statement reveals some inconsistency bearing on the declarant's credibility.[309] In most cases, therefore, the principle of orality[310] will continue to dictate the procedure for producing witness evidence with undiminished force. If this is to be more than an empty promise, the courts must police witness availability rigorously. There can be no question of relaxed standards of admissibility being used to compensate for prosecutorial laziness or incompetence. Courts must act decisively in rejecting hearsay evidence proffered by the prosecution if there is any serious suggestion of a ruse – e.g. in keeping witnesses with bad characters out

---

[306] Parliament took its lead from Law Com No 245, *Evidence in Criminal Proceedings: Hearsay and Related Topics*, Cm 3670 (TSO, 1997), which in turn was prefigured by the gradualist approach to reforming the law of hearsay advocated by the Criminal Law Revision Committee's Eleventh Report, *Evidence: General*, Cm 4991 (HMSO, 1972). It is noteworthy that earlier American proposals for root-and-branch hearsay reform, contained in the Model Code of Evidence (1942) and the Uniform Rules of Evidence (1953), were too radical to win over a conservative legal profession set in its ways: see Barton and Cowart, 'The Enigma of Hearsay' (1978) 49 *Mississippi LJ* 31, 33.   [307] §9.6(b)(i), above.

[308] s.114(2)(g): 'whether oral evidence of the matter stated can be given and, if not, why it cannot'.

[309] Hence, purely self-serving statements are prohibited by the rule against narrative, which is more a principle of relevance and probative value – such statements are often probatively next-to-worthless and therefore inadmissible on that ground – than hearsay exclusion: see §3.2. But to the extent that narrative statements may be admissible, they are now received for their truth, and not merely as evidence of consistency, pursuant to CJA 2003, s.120: see §8.3.   [310] §7.1.

of court – to put the accused at a tactical disadvantage in answering the charges brought against him.[311]

Secondly, advance notice of an intention to adduce hearsay evidence should be served on the opposing party or parties. This simple procedural guarantee goes a long way to ensuring that litigants have time and fair opportunity to respond effectively to their opponent's hearsay evidence, either by challenging its admissibility or by adducing additional evidence in rebuttal. A notice system applicable to hearsay evidence was first introduced into English civil litigation in 1968,[312] and was greatly expanded in 1995.[313] Notice requirements are also an established feature of American criminal proceedings. Section 132(3) of the CJA 2003 builds on this experience by authorizing rules of court to 'require a party proposing to tender [hearsay] evidence to serve on each party to the proceedings such notice, and such particulars of or relating to the evidence, as may be prescribed'. Notification of an intention to adduce hearsay is now governed by Rule 34.2 of the Criminal Procedure Rules 2010. Failure to serve notice in the prescribed form may lead to otherwise admissible hearsay evidence being excluded at trial, or to adverse inferences being drawn from a failure to give notice if the evidence is nonetheless still admitted.[314]

Notice requirements address the concern that a more overtly discretionary approach to the admission of hearsay will hamper the parties' trial preparation or expose the opponent of admissible hearsay to 'ambush' by the sudden appearance in court of untested information which is consequently immunized from the standard techniques of impeachment. The tactic of resorting to a procedural device to ameliorate a problem traditionally conceptualized as evidentiary comports with the broader trend in English criminal litigation towards more active judicial case management, of which the Criminal Procedure Rules are the most visible cipher and manifestation.[315] Thorough pre-trial preparation may contribute towards a rational system of adjudication in which accurate fact-finding is highly valued, but it cannot be an all-purpose remedy for the infirmities of hearsay. For one thing, courts are temperamentally disinclined to enforce notice requirements, especially where, given the evolutionary dynamics of litigation, the relevance of hearsay at trial could not easily have been predicted in advance. Even where defence counsel has deliberately flouted notice requirements, trial judges may think it unjust to burden the accused with the forensic consequences of their legal advisers' default. A parallel argument in favour of crime victims might resonate in some quarters. More fundamentally, no amount of pre-trial preparation can compensate for genuine informational deficits, or circumvent due process rights.

A third fixed point in a principled approach to hearsay was exemplified by the House of Lords in *Davis*,[316] by the European Court of Human Rights in *Al-Khawaja*, and by the US Supreme Court in *Crawford* and *Melendez-Diaz*. Rights-based objections to hearsay draw on intrinsic values as well as instrumental considerations of truth-finding. Adversarial trials will not produce legitimate outcomes if one party is denied a fair opportunity of testing his opponent's evidence or, more globally, if the evidence presented to the fact-finder

---

[311] This answers the objection that abolition of the exclusionary rule would automatically open the door to 'burden shifting' tactical ploys to avoid calling available witnesses: see, e.g., Eleanor Swift, 'Abolishing the Hearsay Rule' (1987) 75 *California LR* 495.   [312] Civil Evidence Act 1968, s.8(2).
[313] Civil Evidence Act 1995, s.2.   [314] Section 132(5).
[315] Criminal Procedure Rules 2010, Part 3.   [316] *R v Davis* [2008] 1 AC 1128, [2008] UKHL 36.

is qualitatively too inferior to supply adequate epistemic warrant for a verdict of guilty.[317] Instrumental truth-finding and intrinsic rationales for excluding hearsay, though analytically distinguishable,[318] become mutually reinforcing through the practice of criminal adjudication. Having floated the possibility that a chemical analyst's test results could conceivably be erroneous or falsified, Justice Scalia was quick to add that the Supreme Court majority's construction of the Sixth Amendment Confrontation Clause in *Melendez-Diaz* was *not* predicated on contextual calculations of probative reliability: 'we would reach the same conclusion if all analysts always possessed the scientific acumen of Mme. Curie and the veracity of Mother Theresa'.[319]

Like constitutional rights in US criminal jurisprudence, the right to a fair trial in English law is in principle non-negotiable. Yet this only defers the practical issue: what exactly does the right to a fair trial require in relation to the admission of hearsay evidence? In *Al-Khawaja*[320] the European Court of Human Rights built on its previous case law to spell out that Article 6 ECHR prohibits untested hearsay from constituting the sole or decisive evidential basis of a criminal conviction. The UK Supreme Court in *Horncastle*[321] replied that English criminal procedure is able to satisfy European fair trial standards without adopting a mechanical 'sole or decisive evidence' test, which it rejected. It remains to be seen whether the Strasbourg Court will endorse this analysis. Article 6 of the ECHR evidently accommodates the partly competing rights of complainants and witnesses in a way which the jurisprudentially more primitive US Bill of Rights does not. Appeals to confrontation or related due process rights are therefore, in and of themselves, insufficient to determine the scope of the English law of hearsay. This is further confirmation, if any were needed, that the perennial tension between discretionary and rule-based approaches to regulating the admissibility of hearsay evidence eludes any simple, peremptory, or comprehensive resolution. General rules are constantly reinterpreted (adapted, ignored, refined, subverted, transformed, etc.) through their particularistic applications.

Besides, getting to grips with hearsay evidence in criminal adjudication is not simply a question of designing and implementing appropriate exclusionary rules. It should always be remembered that the epistemic infirmities of hearsay typically remain *even when hearsay evidence is admissible and properly admitted in criminal trials*. In summing-up at the close of proceedings, trial judges should emphasize to juries the need to evaluate hearsay with care.[322] Jurors should be reminded, not only of the commonplace fallibilities of hearsay, but also that the opponent of hearsay evidence may have been forensically disadvantaged by having no opportunity to cross-examine the declarant in the witness-box. Unless hearsay is probatively marginal to the disputed issues in the case (and therefore better ignored altogether), a judicial direction incorporating these elements, and crafted to the instant facts, should be the normal expectation. Where hearsay evidence is adduced

---

[317] Hock Lai Ho, *A Philosophy of Evidence Law – Justice in the Search for Truth* (OUP, 2008), ch 5.
[318] §9.2, above.   [319] *Melendez-Diaz* v *Massachusetts*, 129 S Ct 2527 (2009), 2537, n.6.
[320] *Al-Khawaja and Tahery* v *United Kingdom* (2009) 49 EHRR 1.
[321] *R* v *Horncastle* [2009] UKSC 14.
[322] Cf. *R* v *Z* [2009] 1 Cr App R 34, [2009] EWCA Crim 20, [26], where 'the error made by the judge in allowing the evidence of *D*'s allegations to be admitted in evidence by hearsay was compounded by the lack of an appropriate and clear direction requiring the jury to be sure that those allegations were true before taking them into account'.

by the prosecution, moreover, an appropriate judicial warning drawing attention to the problems associated with hearsay evidence is a requirement of a fair trial under Article 6 of the ECHR and, one should think, at common law. This is one important manifestation of a more general trend in English criminal procedure, whereby flexible forensic reasoning rules come to perform some of the normative functions formerly discharged by evidentiary rules of admissibility and exclusion.[323]

---

[323] This observation is developed in §§15.3–15.5, and §16.3(a).

10

VULNERABLE WITNESSES AND THE PRINCIPLE OF ORALITY

10.1 IDENTIFYING TESTIMONIAL VULNERABILITY

All witnesses in criminal proceedings are 'vulnerable' in the senses we have seen in previous chapters: they are subject to compulsory process, must answer fully and truthfully on pain of imprisonment for contempt, and can be exposed to wide-ranging cross-examination which may be directed towards undermining their moral credibility, as well as probing the actual content of their testimony. When criminal justice policy-makers and evidence lawyers speak of 'vulnerable witnesses', however, they have traditionally had one or both of two groups in mind: adult complainants of sexual assault and child witnesses. In recent times, personal characteristics associated with vulnerability have been yoked together with circumstantially experienced intimidation, to produce a new class of intended beneficiaries of procedural reform, 'vulnerable and intimidated witnesses', typically abbreviated to VIWs.

The general concerns relating to adult and child witnesses are somewhat different (though of course some child witnesses are also complainants of sexual victimization). So far as adult complainants are concerned, the basic policy question is whether their treatment by the trial process is conducive to the successful prosecution of serious criminal offences such as rape and other sexual assaults. If complainants are badly treated in criminal litigation they will be dissuaded from testifying against their assailants, and perhaps even from coming forward to report the incident in the first place. Without the trust and co-operation of complainants, successful prosecutions will be unsustainable in most cases, and the criminal process will be failing in its primary objectives of doing justice and protecting the public.

Child witnesses may also be victims of crime, or witnesses to crimes against others. Court proceedings designed for adults are likely to be unsuitable for children, and the question is whether the standard processes and procedures of criminal trials should be adapted to meet the special needs of the child witness. As with adult complainants of sexual assault, however, the issue should be conceived in terms of designing a principled trial process that succeeds in combining effective fact-finding with humane treatment of witnesses and fairness to the accused. The Human Rights Act 1998, too, demands nothing less.

The treatment of vulnerable witnesses is a topic of obvious importance meriting attention in its own right. There have been repeated legislative interventions beginning in the

1980s and culminating in the Youth Justice and Criminal Evidence (YJCE) Act 1999, which has itself undergone further amendment. The provisions of the 1999 Act not only consolidated previous initiatives in this area, but also introduced radical new measures with the potential for further extension to witnesses generally. Legal provision for vulnerable witnesses consequently serves as a barometer of current official attitudes towards criminal trial procedure – and a weather-vane predicting the direction of possible future developments that may ultimately transform the adversarial tradition of oral evidence-taking and testing.

10.2 PREVIOUS SEXUAL HISTORY EVIDENCE

The legal system's treatment of adult complainants of rape and other serious sexual assaults has been a matter of acute concern since the 1970s when feminists and other researchers drew attention to appalling experiences endured by complainants in criminal proceedings. Much of the problem resulted from the callous, stereotyping attitudes of the police, at a time when police forces were wholly unprepared to cater for the needs and expectations of rape victims,[1] but the trial process also attracted its fair share of criticism.

At trial, the principal grievance was that complainants could be exposed under cross-examination to wide-ranging attacks on their moral credibility. In particular, a cross-examiner might spin out evidence of the complainant's previous sexual conduct in lurid and embarrassing detail.[2] The pretext was that evidence of promiscuity or other sexual 'misconduct' went to the issue of consent and/or to the complainant's credit as a witness, but in reality, more often than not, the objective was to upset the complainant and lower her moral standing in the eyes of the jury. Over the years some strange notions of relevance became embedded in the common law. For example, it was assumed that evidence of prostitution diminishes the credibility of a rape complainant and increases the probability that intercourse was consensual,[3] when, on a dispassionate appraisal, one might expect prostitutes to be the last people to make false allegations of rape, since sending customers to gaol can hardly be good for business. Equally, a promiscuous person is not the most likely to concoct a false accusation of rape in order to protect her reputation, nor would one particularly expect a sexually experienced person (as opposed to a shrinking violet with no previous sexual history to exploit) to be overcome by shame or remorse into falsely accusing her partners of rape.[4] All-too-frequently, it would appear, the real purpose

---

[1] See generally, Jennifer Temkin, *Rape and the Legal Process* (OUP, 2nd edn. 2002).

[2] Zsuzanna Adler, *Rape on Trial* (Routledge, 1989).

[3] Since evidence of prostitution was taken to go to the issue, the complainant's denials could always be rebutted by other evidence: *R v Holmes and Furness* (1871) 12 Cox CC 137, CCR; cf. *R v Cargill* (1913) 8 Cr App R 224, CCA (where consent was *not* in issue, the complainant's denial that she was a prostitute had to be accepted as final, since prostitution could logically only be relevant to the collateral matter of her credibility as a witness). Exceptions to collateral-finality were discussed in §8.5.

[4] For description and critique of these strategies, see Philip McNamara, 'Cross-examination of the Complainant in a Trial for Rape' (1981) 5 *Crim LJ* 25; D. W. Elliot, 'Rape Complainants' Sexual Experience with Third Parties' [1984] *Crim LR* 4; Jennifer Temkin, 'Regulating Sexual Evidence History Evidence: the Limits of Discretionary Legislation' (1984) 33 *ICLQ* 942; Susan Estrich, 'Rape' (1986) 95 *Yale LJ* 1087.

of such cross-examination was to suggest that the complainant was herself too morally flawed to deserve the court's sympathy or to justify punishing the accused.[5]

These troubling issues were investigated by the Heilbron Advisory Group on the Law of Rape, whose 1975 report concluded that 'unless there are some restrictions, questioning can take place which does not advance the cause of justice but in effect puts the woman on trial'.[6] Parliament responded by enacting section 2(1) of the Sexual Offences (Amendment) Act 1976, which implemented the basic policy, but not the full package of recommendations, proposed by Heilbron. Section 2(1) made all evidence and questions in cross-examination 'about any sexual experience of a complainant with a person other than the defendant' subject to the leave of the court. Section 2(2) further provided that the trial judge must not give leave unless he was 'satisfied that it would be unfair to that defendant to refuse to allow the evidence to be adduced or the question to be asked'. In essence, the admissibility of evidence in-chief and questions in cross-examination relating to the complainant's previous sexual history with third parties became subject to a judicial filter to regulate its salience in the interests of justice.

Prevailing wisdom amongst commentators,[7] and even according to senior members of the judiciary,[8] is that section 2(1) of the 1976 Act was an abject failure. Trial judges and the Court of Appeal, it was said, failed to rise to the challenge of exercising their discretion to provide adequate protection for vulnerable witnesses. In consequence, when section 41of the YJCE Act 1999 was enacted to replace section 2(1), it implemented a completely different legislative policy aimed at eliminating judicial discretion. Evidence or questions in cross-examination regarding 'any sexual behaviour of the complainant' (other than behaviour during the events that are the subject matter of the charge) are *prima facie* prohibited by section 41. Such information can be introduced into the trial only with the trial judge's express permission, and a judge may grant leave only if the evidence or question falls within one of a closed list of four exceptional 'gateways': (1) it does not relate to an issue of consent, but rather to the accused's belief in consent;[9] (2) the sexual behaviour 'is

---

[5] Cf. John Jackson, 'Questions of Fact and Questions of Law', in William Twining (ed.), *Facts in Law* (Franz Steiner, 1983), 98: 'One's moral criteria of what makes a good, honest witness will be difficult to distinguish from one's criteria of what makes a good, honest person, and, therefore, when a fact relating to what a witness did or did not do is in issue, judgments which are made on what kind of person the witness is for the purpose of assessing his credibility, will inevitably colour one's judgment of what kind of acts he committed or did not commit.'

[6] *Report of the Advisory Group on the Law of Rape*, Cm 6352 (HMSO, 1975), para.91.

[7] See, e.g., Neil Kibble, 'The Sexual History Provisions: Charting a Course Between Inflexible Legislative Rules and Wholly Untrammelled Judicial Discretion?' [2000] *Crim LR* 274, 275–6 ('An extensive body of literature indicates that the Act has not achieved its objective of controlling the illegitimate use of prior sexual history evidence in rape trials'); Jennifer Temkin, 'Sexual History Evidence – the Ravishment of Section 2' [1993] *Crim LR* 3; Aileen McColgan, 'Common Law and the Relevance of Sexual History Evidence' (1996) 16 *OJLS* 275. Cf. the more nuanced evaluation of Louise Ellison 'Cross-Examination in Rape Trials' [1998] *Crim LR* 605.

[8] In *R v A (No 2)* [2002] 1 AC 45, [2001] UKHL 25, [28], Lord Steyn declared that '[t]he statute did not achieve its object of preventing the illegitimate use of prior sexual experience in rape trials. In retrospect one can now see that the structure of this legislation was flawed.'

[9] s.41(3)(a). At common law, a genuine belief in consent negatived the *mens rea* for rape even if the belief was unreasonable: *DPP v Morgan* [1976] AC 182, HL. Sexual Offences Act 2003, s.1, replaced *Morgan* with a standard of reasonable belief. It remains the case, however, that a belief of the relevant kind is incompatible with criminal liability. The law of criminal evidence tracks the substantive law of rape, by permitting the accused to adduce evidence capable of supporting a liability-defeating belief.

alleged to have taken place at or about the same time as the event' underlying the charges;[10] (3) previous sexual behaviour is so similar to the complainant's alleged behaviour in the circumstances of the current charge 'that the similarity cannot reasonably be explained as a coincidence';[11] or (4) the evidence or question goes 'no further than is necessary to enable the evidence adduced by the prosecution to be rebutted or explained by or on behalf of the accused'.[12] In every case, 'the evidence or question must relate to a specific instance (or specific instances) of alleged sexual behaviour on the part of the complainant',[13] ruling out generalized allegations of prostitution, promiscuity and the like, which might have been regarded as legitimate 'reputation' evidence at common law.[14] For the avoidance of doubt, section 41(4) adds that for the purposes of these exceptions 'no evidence or question shall be regarded as relating to a relevant issue in the case if it appears to the court to be reasonable to assume that the purpose (or main purpose) for which it would be adduced or asked is to establish or elicit material for impugning the credibility of the complainant as a witness'.

Section 41 applies to all 'sexual behaviour', not only to 'rape offences' as did its statutory predecessor. Moreover, section 41 controversially extended the complainant's 'rape shield' to previous sexual behaviour involving the accused himself, not merely to conduct with third parties.

There are bound to have been cases when trial judges were insufficiently energetic or robust in their application of section 2(1) of the 1976 Act. However, it would be cavalier revisionism to write-off the entire exercise as an unmitigated disaster. The Court of Appeal cannot fairly be accused of failing to take section 2(1) seriously. In the leading case of *Viola*[15] Lord Lane CJ confirmed that trial judges should generally disallow questions going merely to credit. Conversely, questions 'relevant to an issue in the trial in the light of the way the case is being run' should normally be permitted, 'because to exclude a relevant question on an issue in the trial... will usually mean that the jury are being prevented from hearing something which, if they hear it, might cause them to change their minds about the evidence given by the complainant'.[16] This approach was followed through in cases such as *Brown*,[17] where the accused was prevented from showing that the complainant enjoyed 'casual sexual relations' (her description) with other men and had contracted venereal disease. This is exactly the short of probatively insignificant information, typically adduced to diminish the complainant's moral credibility, that section 2(1) was designed to pre-empt. It was also confirmed in *Brown* that admissibility under *Viola* was not simply a question of receiving evidence that *would* influence a jury, but evidence that might *reasonably* do so.[18] Properly understood, *Viola* did not merely pander to jurors'

---

[10] Section 41(3)(b).   [11] Section 41(3)(c).   [12] Section 41(5).   [13] Section 41(6).

[14] Cf. *R v White* [2004] EWCA Crim 946; *R v Pemberton* [2007] EWCA Crim 3201.

[15] *R v Viola* [1982] 1 WLR 1138, CA.   [16] ibid. 1143.

[17] *R v Brown* (1989) 89 Cr App R 97, CA. Also see *R v Barton* (1987) 85 Cr App R 5, CA, where the accused was similarly prevented from cross-examining the complainant on her alleged general promiscuity.

[18] *R v Brown* (1989) 89 Cr App R 97, 109, *per* May LJ: 'in the present climate of opinion a jury would be unlikely to be influenced, *nor should it be influenced*, when considering veracity by the mere fact that the complainant may have been promiscuous...' (emphasis supplied). Cf. *R v Lawrence* [1977] Crim LR 492, 493 *per* May J: 'before a judge is satisfied... that to refuse to allow a particular question or a series of questions in cross-examination would be unfair to a defendant he must take the view that it is more likely than not that the particular question or line of cross-examination, if allowed, might *reasonably* lead the jury, properly directed in the summing up, to take a different view of the complainant's evidence' (emphasis supplied).

prejudices. Finally, it is notable that the Court of Appeal was prepared to extend section 2(1), by analogy at common law, to offences not strictly covered by the legislation.[19]

Several of the cases in which the courts have attracted criticism for permitting cross-examination under section 2(1) actually involve plausible applications of *Viola*. If a complainant has previously made false allegations of rape;[20] or if she makes statements (or implications) in-chief about the events in question that can be contradicted by other evidence;[21] or if she is alleged to have made statements at the time of the incident bearing on her attitude towards and relationship with the accused:[22] then a trial judge's conclusion that a jury might reasonably be influenced by such evidence is not manifestly irrational. Though evidence of such matters will hardly ever, and perhaps never, be determinative, it is material which most jurors would understandably want to take into account in deciding whether the accused had been proved guilty beyond reasonable doubt.

We do not advocate resurrecting section 2(1) or suggest that it achieved a perfect balance between the needs of complainants, the rights of the accused, and the interests of justice. Most probably it did not.[23] The enduring lesson of section 2(1)'s unlamented demise is that judgments of relevance and probative value are highly contextual, depending on the facts of individual prosecutions and the way in which each party develops its case at trial. Any attempt to define in advance the situations in which it would be proper to adduce previous sexual history evidence is therefore bound to run into difficulties, because the infinite variety of circumstances cannot be exhaustively anticipated much less legislatively prescribed. Unfortunately, the architects of section 41 of the YJCE Act 1999 paid too little attention to the relevance of *legislative* history for devising and implementing effective law reform. Where significant evidence of the complainant's previous sexual behaviour could not be fitted into any of the four admissibility gateways prescribed by section 41, courts would have three basic options: either (i) stretch the categories of exception, with or without the assistance of the interpretative obligation under section 3 of the Human Rights Act; (ii) declare section 41 incompatible with Article 6 of the ECHR on the facts of the instant case; or (iii) uphold a conviction obtained in a trial at which significant evidence in the hands of the parties was concealed from the jury. None of these options is particularly attractive, and the second and third would merely defer the issue, respectively, to Parliament or Strasbourg. The House of Lords was soon faced with precisely this unpalatable menu in *R v A*.[24] Their Lordships chose option (i), pre-empting a constitutional imbroglio but in the process reintroducing the very judicial discretion that section 41 purported to banish from criminal trial proceedings.

This statement was endorsed in *R v Mills* (1978) 68 Cr App R 327, CA, and adopted in *R v Viola* [1982] 1 WLR 1138, CA, 1142.

[19] *R v Funderburk* [1990] 1 WLR 587, CA (unlawful sexual intercourse with a minor).

[20] *R v Barton* (1987) 85 Cr App R 5, CA; *R v Cox* (1987) 84 Cr App R 132, CA.

[21] *R v Riley* [1991] Crim LR 460, CA (where *V* said that she would never have had consensual intercourse with her baby in the room, accused was permitted to call witnesses who said that they had had sex with *V* whilst her baby was in the room); *R v C* [1996] Crim LR 37, CA (where the prosecution led medical evidence that *V* was not a virgin, cross-examination on letters suggesting that *V* had had sex with her boyfriend should have been permitted).   [22] *R v Said* [1992] Crim LR 433, CA.

[23] One example of a case where complainants' interests appear to have been undervalued is *R v Bogie* [1992] Crim LR 301, CA.

[24] *R v A (No 2)* [2002] 1 AC 45, [2001] UKHL 25. The Court of Appeal's ruling is reported sub nom *R v Y* [2001] Crim LR 389.

R v A involved an interlocutory appeal[25] against the trial judge's evidentiary ruling restricting the permissible scope of cross-examination under section 41. The accused wanted to cross-examine the complainant in relation to alleged previous sexual relations with the accused himself – the most controversial aspect of section 41's extension of the 'rape shield'. The trial judge was willing to allow the accused to ask the complainant about (alleged) sexual contact between them earlier on the day of the (alleged) assault, but refused to grant leave for questioning about their on-going relationship. According to the accused, he and the complainant had been conducting a clandestine affair without the knowledge of the complainant's boyfriend. Lord Slynn articulated the basic dilemma confronting a court ruling on the permissible scope of cross-examination under section 41 in circumstances such as these:

The need to protect women from harassment in the witness box is fundamental. It must not be lost sight of but I suspect that the man or woman in the street would find it strange that evidence that two young people who had lived together or regularly as part of a happy relationship had had sexual acts together, must be wholly excluded on the issue of consent unless it is immediately contemporaneous…. [I]t seems to me clear that these restrictions in section 41 *prima facie* are capable of preventing an accused person from putting forward relevant evidence which may be evidence critical to his defence, whether it is as to consent or to belief that the woman consented. If thus construed section 41 does prevent the accused from having a fair trial then it must be declared to be incompatible with the Convention.[26]

Their Lordships were unanimous in rejecting the stereotypes of the past. 'Ideas which may have seemed sound in the nineteenth century,' declared Lord Clyde, 'should be discarded in the face of the very different society in which we now live':

The respect which is due to women in society requires that a proper recognition should be given to their independence of mind and the autonomy which they undoubtedly should enjoy. General beliefs about the propensity of unchaste women to consent to intercourse or to be unworthy of credit which may have held sway in an age when the position of women in society bears little comparison with what it is today should now be seen as heresies and discarded as outmoded. Any general idea that because a woman has consented once she is likely to have consented on the occasion in dispute should be relegated to history.[27]

However, an important distinction needed to be drawn between previous sexual history with third parties, which section 41 rightly excluded as – at best – dubiously relevant material with which to attack a complainant's credibility,[28] and previous sexual relations between the two main protagonists in the trial, the accused and the complainant. Lord Steyn elaborated:

As a matter of common sense, a prior sexual relationship between the complainant and the accused may, depending on the circumstances, be relevant to the issue of consent. It is a species of prospectant evidence which may throw light on the complainant's state of mind. It cannot, of course, prove that she consented on the occasion in question. Relevance

---

[25] Pursuant to Criminal Procedure and Investigations Act 1996, s.35.

[26] *R v A (No 2)* [2002] 1 AC 45, [10].   [27] ibid. [124].

[28] 'Such matters are almost always irrelevant to the issue whether the complainant consented to sexual intercourse on the occasion alleged in the indictment or to her credibility. To that extent the scope of the reform of the law by the 1999 Act was justified': ibid. [30] (Lord Steyn).

and sufficiency of proof are different things…. It is true that each decision to engage in sexual activity is always made afresh. On the other hand, the mind does not usually blot out all memories. What one has been engaged on in the past may influence what choice one makes on a future occasion. Accordingly, a prior relationship between a complainant and an accused may sometimes be relevant to what decision was made on a particular occasion.[29]

In order to avoid 'the spectre of the possible need for a declaration of incompatibility',[30] four of their Lordships held, it was necessary court to 'subordinate the niceties of the language of section 41(3)(c), and in particular the touchstone of coincidence, to broader considerations of relevance judged by logical and common sense criteria of time and circumstances'. Parliament could not have intended 'to deny the right to an accused to put forward a full and complete defence by advancing truly probative material'. Consequently, section 41 should be read 'subject to the implied provision that evidence or questioning which is required to ensure a fair trial under article 6 of the Convention should not be treated as inadmissible'.[31] Lord Hope dissented from this reasoning, pointing out, with some justice, that the majority's approach achieved precisely the opposite of what Parliament had set out to accomplish in enacting section 41 as a replacement for section 2 of the 1976 Act.[32] All five Law Lords concurred in the ultimate, notably narrow, holding, that it had not been demonstrated that section 41 was necessarily incompatible with the accused's right to a fair trial. The problem was thus batted back to the trial judge to resolve through a contextual application of the law, as now clarified, to the facts of the case.

The decision in R v A was hailed as politically savvy, but criticized for being evasive and unprincipled.[33] At root, there remains a debilitating reluctance to grasp the nettle of relevance.[34] It is often said in the parliamentary and wider public debates surrounding rape shield laws that previous sexual history is 'irrelevant' to the issue of consent, but this proposition is often misleading when it is not simply false. Sometimes its proponents mean to say that prior sexual history does not *prove* consent. That is perfectly true, but beside the point, since the legal test of relevancy[35] asks whether the evidence makes consent more or less probable, not whether it settles the issue conclusively.

A better argument is that previous sexual history evidence lacks sufficient probative value to justify its admission, given that such evidence is likely to be distressing for complainants and may invite moral prejudice from the fact-finder. This would be enough in most cases to exclude sexual history evidence going only to credit, on the basis that, as *Viola* held, its probative value is outweighed by its potentially prejudicial effect (PV < PE). Section 41(4) of the YJCE Act 1999 enacted this generalization as a rule of law. Notice, however, that it is already implicit in this argument that the evidence *is* relevant (to credit),

---

[29] ibid. [31].   [30] ibid. [32] (Lord Steyn).   [31] ibid. [45] (Lord Steyn).

[32] ibid. [108]–[110]. Lord Hope concurred with Lords Slynn, Steyn, Clyde and Hutton in dismissing the appeal, on the basis that section 41 was not irremediably in conflict with ECHR Article 6. But Lord Hope's conclusion of compatibility employing only ordinary canons of statutory interpretation was a dissent in all but name.

[33] For discussion, see Di Birch, 'Rethinking Sexual History Evidence: Proposals for Fairer Trials' [2002] *Crim LR* 531; Jennifer Temkin, 'Sexual History Evidence – Beware the Backlash' [2003] *Crim LR* 217; Di Birch, 'Untangling Sexual History Evidence: A Rejoinder to Professor Temkin' [2003] *Crim LR* 370; Ian Dennis, 'Editorial: Sexual History Evidence' [2002] *Crim LR* 529; Jenny McEwan, 'The Rape Shield Askew? R v A' (2001) 5 *E & P* 257.

[34] For illuminating discussion, see Mike Redmayne, 'Myths, Relationships and Coincidences: The New Problems of Sexual History' (2003) 7 *E & P* 75.   [35] §3.2.

but excluded when the full range of pertinent considerations is factored into the admissibility equation. Moreover, it would be difficult on this basis to justify excluding any evidence that might reasonably have a significant bearing on the issue of consent, which previous sexual contact between the complainant and the accused frequently does or may do. If previous physical intimacy between the complainant and the accused *might* have a *significant* bearing on the issues in the case, it cannot simply be dismissed out-of-hand without careful consideration. How can the accused be said to have been afforded a fair trial if material evidence of innocence – or at least material that could raise a reasonable doubt about his guilt – was concealed from the fact-finder? It certainly looks as though withholding material evidence from the jury would be incompatible with the substantive conception of the presumption of innocence developed in Chapter 6.

No well-informed, fair-minded and sympathetic observer could fail to be troubled by an attrition rate in rape prosecutions variously estimated at 90% or greater,[36] or remain unmoved by the genuine anguish experienced in the witness-box by many complainants in sexual cases. But two questions must be confronted squarely in any good faith evaluation of the law's treatment of sexual history evidence: first, to what extent can alterations to evidentiary rules of admissibility alleviate complainants' plight without undermining the essential precepts of a fair trial? And secondly, does section 41 really improve on the old law, even on the assumption that the exercise of judicial discretion under section 2(1) was far from perfect?

In answering the first question, it needs to be borne in mind that rules of admissibility constitute only one dimension of a complainant's experience of the criminal trial, and are not necessarily the most influential factor. The treatment meted out to rape complainants is, up to a point, an inevitable incident of an adversarial system of justice in which any witness who is the linchpin of the prosecution's case is going to be subjected to vigorous and possibly aggressive cross-examination by the defence.[37] Empirical research has also emphasized the importance of legal – and especially barristers' – professional culture in contributing to complainants' experiences in criminal trials.[38] To the extent that stereotypical attitudes and beliefs continue to inform the behaviour of prosecuting

---

[36] Liz Kelly, Jo Lovett, and Linda Regan, *A Gap or a Chasm? Attrition in Reported Rape Cases*, Home Office Research Study 293 (Home Office RDS, 2005), on-line at: www.homeoffice.gov.uk/rds/pdfs05/hors293. pdf; Jessica Harris and Sharon Grace, *A Question of Evidence? Investigating and Prosecuting Rape in the 1990s*, HORS 196 (Home Office, 1999); Jeanne Gregory and Sue Lees, 'Attrition in Rape and Sexual Assault Cases' (1996) 36 *British Journal of Criminology* 1. Lord Steyn in *R v A (No 2)* [2002] 1 AC 45, [27], lamented 'absurdly low conviction rates in rape cases'. Whilst the general sentiment is easily appreciated, the notion of 'low' (let alone absurdly low) conviction rates does pose some difficult questions about how the ideal or appropriate or merely acceptable conviction rate might be calculated. Generally, see Jennifer Temkin and Barbara Krahé, *Sexual Assault and the Justice Gap: A Question of Attitude* (Hart, 2008); Paul Roberts and Candida Saunders, 'Pre-Trial Witness Interviews and "the Justice Gap": A Plea for Sophistication in Criminal Procedure Reform', http://ssrn.com/abstract=1486040.

[37] David Brereton, 'How Different are Rape Trials? A Comparison of the Cross-Examination of Complainants in Rape and Assault Trials' (1997) 37 *British Journal of Criminology* 242; Louise Ellison, 'Cross-Examination in Rape Trials' [1998] *Crim LR* 605.

[38] Jennifer Temkin, 'Prosecuting and Defending Rape: Perspectives from the Bar' (2000) 27 *Journal of Law and Society* 219. In relation to judicial culture, see Neil Kibble, 'Judicial Perspectives on the Operation of s.41 and the Relevance and Admissibility of Prior Sexual History Evidence: Four Scenarios' [2005] *Crim LR* 190; Kibble, 'Judicial Discretion and the Admissibility of Prior Sexual History Evidence under Section 41 of the Youth Justice and Criminal Evidence Act 1999: Sometimes Sticking to Your Guns Means Shooting Yourself in the Foot' [2005] *Crim LR* 263.

and defending counsel (many of whom, incidentally, are women), significant and lasting improvements in the treatment of rape complainants will not be achieved. This is a timely reminder that the attitudes and behaviour of the legal professionals who apply the rules are often as important in practice as the content of the rules themselves. Such attitudes and behaviour might be a more promising target for reformers keen to improve the lot of sexual assault complainants, rather than tinkering with technical evidentiary rules of admissibility which often appear unresponsive to reformers' best endeavours.

Rape complainants have benefited from a raft of ancillary procedural reforms in recent years. Progressive relaxation of the 'recent complaint' exception to the rule against narrative, culminating in Criminal Justice Act (CJA) 2003, s.120, was described in Chapter 8. In addition, offences triable only on indictment are now 'sent' directly to the Crown Court for trial,[39] so there is no longer any question of complainants being subjected to the 'baptism of fire' at 'old style' committal proceedings in the magistrates' court, and then having to testify again at the trial itself. And after several high-profile instances of abusive cross-examination by an accused conducting his own defence,[40] the right of accused persons to cross-examine rape complainants in person was removed by Parliament.[41] All cross-examination of sexual offence complainants will be conducted by professional advocates bound by the professional ethics of the Bar. An accused may still choose to defend himself in a rape case, but court-appointed special counsel now takes over the phases of the trial involving cross-examination of the complainant.[42] This arrangement presents some of the practical difficulties alluded to in Chapter 7's discussion of special advocates in PII hearings,[43] albeit in somewhat diluted form,[44] and therefore has direct implications for the accused's right to a fair trial. Nonetheless, complainants' interests now prevail to this extent. The prohibition on cross-examination by the accused in person may go some way to ameliorating the experience of rape complainants in the witness-box, without requiring relevant evidence to be excluded from the trial. In addition, rape complainants may be assisted by some of the 'special measures' afforded to 'vulnerable and intimidated witnesses' which are discussed in detail later in the chapter.[45]

---

[39] Crime and Disorder Act 1998, s.51. Oral evidence at committal proceedings had previously been abolished by s.47 and sch.1 to the Criminal Procedure and Investigations Act 1996.

[40] *R v Milton Brown* [1998] 2 Cr App R 364, CA; *R v Ralston Edwards* (1996), Central Criminal Court. See Joanna Bale, 'Rapist Who Quizzed Victim is Given Life', *The Times*, 10 October 1996; Nigel Morris, 'Probe Call on 6-Day Grilling – Politicians Demand Probe into Julie Mason's Rape Trial Ordeal', *Daily Mirror*, 24 August 1996; Don Mackay, 'It was Just Like Being Raped All Over Again – Mum tells of Court Hell', *Daily Record*, 23 August 1996; Emily Wilson *et al*, 'How Can They Allow It? Rape Victim's Anger at Rapist Court Ordeal', *Daily Mirror*, 23 August 1996.

[41] Youth Justice and Criminal Evidence Act 1999, s.34. Section 36 empowers the court to extend this restriction to any witness in *any* case, provided that the quality of the witness's evidence would thereby be improved and it is not contrary to the interests of justice to prevent the accused from cross-examining the witness in person. For discussion, see Diane Birch and Roger Leng, *Blackstone's Guide to the Youth Justice and Criminal Evidence Act 1999* (Blackstone, 2000), ch 6.

[42] Youth Justice and Criminal Evidence Act 1999, s.38.   [43] §7.5(c).

[44] The element of secrecy is removed, and there are no formal restrictions on discussions between counsel and the accused. Still, the accused has lost the right to conduct his own defence in relation to what may well be the only material witness in the case and he cannot be forced to co-operate with appointed counsel.

[45] §10.4, below.

The second reform-related question can be answered without equivocation: as an exercise in legislative drafting, section 41 is an inferior substitute for the old section 2(1). Interpreted as a political gesture of solidarity with rape complainants, section 41's radical restriction of judicial discretion may be applauded, but from an evidentiary perspective the strategy of a closed list of inclusionary exceptions to a general exclusionary rule was always calculated to fail. Probative value is too mercurial to be captured by inflexible evidentiary categories and too unpredictable to be defined in advance by legislation. On a critical view, it might be said that section 41, as glossed by the House of Lords in *R v A*, has achieved the worst of both worlds. It has introduced detailed rules of admissibility ripe for doctrinal nit-picking and a gift to defence counsel in search of arguable grounds for appeal, yet this bloated juridical superstructure is no more capable of controlling judicial discretion than its statutory predecessor, as interpreted in *Viola*.[46]

Section 41 has undoubtedly spawned novel problems of interpretation and fostered judicial errors and unmeritorious appeals, albeit some of these difficulties may be put down to teething troubles which invariably attend new legislation of any importance or complexity.[47] On-going points of doctrinal dispute include: the duration of 'at or about the same time' in section 41(3)(b);[48] the meaning of 'similarity [which] cannot reasonably be explained as a coincidence' in section 41(3)(c);[49] and the scope of 'a specific instance (or specific instances) of alleged sexual behaviour' specified by section 41(6). Significantly, the Court of Appeal has continued to insist that false allegations of rape are not 'sexual behaviour' within the scope of section 41, but rather lies directly relevant to a complainant's credibility as witness.[50] This is a logical position – falsely claiming to have walked on the moon, for example, would not generally be regarded as experience of moon-walking. However, critics of the old section 2 were exercised by the fact that its rape shield could easily be circumvented by alleging that the complainant had made false allegations of rape in the past. Section 41, for all its linguistic ju-jitsu, can still be bypassed in exactly the same way, provided that there is a proper evidential basis for attributing false accusations to the complainant.[51]

Going forward, section 41's prospects need not be anticipated quite so pessimistically. Increasing judicial familiarity with the new provision may be expected to foster greater confidence in its application. Taking its lead from the House of Lords in

---

[46] *R v Viola* [1982] 1 WLR 1138, CA.

[47] See, e.g., *R v T* [2004] 2 Cr App R 32, CA (trial judge directed jury on wrong admissibility gateway); *R v Bahador* [2005] EWCA Crim 396 (defence trial counsel argued wrong basis for admissibility); *R v C* [2008] 1 WLR 966, [2007] EWCA Crim 2581 (Parliament accidently repealed s.41 in relation to offences charged under the old Sexual Offences Act 1956, though the Court of Appeal found a way to hold otherwise).

[48] The House of Lords in *R v A (No 2)* [2002] 1 AC 45 indicated that the outer limits of this gateway must be measured in days rather than weeks. Lord Clyde, ibid. [132], considered that '[i]t would be undesirable to prescribe any test in terms of days or hours, but where the point of reference is to the time of the event it may be difficult to extend that to a period of several days'.

[49] 'Judgements on what is similar for the purposes of s.41 are not always easy': *R v Harris* [2009] EWCA Crim 434, [19].

[50] *R v T* [2002] 1 WLR 632, [2001] EWCA Crim 1877; *R v Garaxo* [2005] Crim LR 883, CA.

[51] *R v Abdelrahman (Samir)* [2005] EWCA Crim 1367.

R v A,[52] the Court of Appeal has repeatedly said that fact-specific determinations of the appropriate limits of cross-examination are primarily a matter for the trial judge; though this is properly characterized as an application of legal principle according to law rather than an exercise of 'judicial discretion' in the loose sense.[53] Section 41(4) prohibits cross-examination on previous sexual history *purely* to credit, but will not prevent otherwise legitimate cross-examination incidentally undermining the complainant's credibility. As with any other manifestation of the protean credit/issue distinction, '[i]ssues of consent and issues of credibility may well run so close to each other as almost to coincide. A very sharp knife may be required to separate what may be admitted from what may not.'[54] The accused should always be allowed to pursue any truly probative and not wholly disproportionate line of cross-examination, where this is required to ensure a fair trial, as R v A insisted. However, trial judges appear wise to disingenuous attempts to smear complainants with extraneous details about their sex lives lacking any real probative connection to disputed matters in the case, and the Court of Appeal has normally been prepared to endorse trial judges' instincts and contextual analysis.[55] Viewed in broader perspective, section 41's principal success may have been in providing a very clear signal to trial judges that 'credibility myths'[56] embedded in the common law have been consigned to the jurisprudential dustbin and replaced with common sense relevance infused with twenty-first-century sensibilities. Nonetheless, if section 41 is moulded over time into an appropriately flexible admissibility standard empowering trial judges to make contextual determinations of probative value and procedural justice, akin to the open-ended balancing test adopted not long ago in Scotland,[57] this will be in spite of section 41's undistinguished legislative drafting rather than because of its vaunted merits.

---

[52] '[B]eyond stating that the test is that of relevance, I think that it is not possible to state with precision where the dividing line is to be drawn—it will depend on the facts of the individual case as assessed by the trial judge': R v A *(No 2)* [2002] 1 AC 45, [152] (Lord Hutton).

[53] In R v F [2005] 2 Cr App R 13, [2005] 1 WLR 2848, [29], Judge LJ stated: 'It is sometimes loosely suggested that the operation of section 41 involves the exercise of judicial discretion. In reality, the trial judge is making a judgment whether to admit, or refuse to admit evidence which is relevant, or asserted by the defence to be relevant.... [T]he judge is required to ensure that a complainant is not unnecessarily humiliated or cross-examined with inappropriate aggression, or treated otherwise than with proper courtesy. All that is elementary, but his obligation to see that the complainant's interests are protected throughout the trial process does not permit him, by way of a general discretion, to prevent the proper deployment of evidence which falls within the ambit permitted by the statute merely because, as here, it comes in a stark, uncompromising form.'   [54] R v A *(No 2)* [2002] 1 AC 45, [138] (Lord Clyde).

[55] See, e.g., R v *Harris* [2009] EWCA Crim 434; R v *Kordasinksi* [2007] 1 Cr App R 17, CA; R v *Hamadi* [2007] EWCA Crim 3048, [2008] Crim LR 635; R v *Pemberton* [2007] EWCA Crim 3201; R v W [2006] EWCA Crim 1292. More problematically, the Court of Appeal has also sometimes upheld convictions where the trial judge's application of section 41 was found to be too restrictive of defence cross-examination: R v *Martin* [2004] 2 Cr App R 354, CA.

[56] Cf. R v A *(No 2)* [2002] 1 AC 45, [147] *per* Lord Hutton: 'The intent of section 41 is to counter what have been described as the two myths. One is that because a woman has had sexual intercourse in the past she is more likely to have consented to intercourse on the occasion in question. The other is that by reason of her sexual behaviour in the past she is less worthy of belief as a witness.'

[57] Sexual Offences (Procedure and Evidence) (Scotland) Act 2002, substituting Criminal Procedure (Scotland) Act 1995, ss.274 and 275. The key test is whether the 'probative value of the evidence sought to be admitted or elicited is significant and is likely to outweigh any risk of prejudice to the proper administration of justice arising from its being admitted or elicited'. See further, Ian Dennis, 'Editorial: Sexual History Evidence' [2002] *Crim LR* 529.

10.3 CHILDREN'S EVIDENCE

In 1987 Glanville Williams wrote:

From the point of view of the child victim, much the happiest outcome of a sexual offence generally is that the offender should not be caught. When he is not found, the child often makes a good recovery, her chief source of distress frequently being the agitation and disapproval of her parents when they come to know the facts. Long-term effects need not be serious even in cases of rape resulting in conception and the birth of illegitimate offspring. But if the offender is discovered and in the hands of the police, the consequent proceedings are often very disturbing to the victim.[58]

The extent of Williams' insight into the trauma of child sex abuse may be doubted, but his stinging indictment of the criminal justice system is unanswerable. At that time, no special provision[59] was made for child witnesses, who were obliged to contend with a trial process that many adults find traumatic and intimidating. Very young children were effectively excluded as incompetent,[60] and many older children and teenagers were unable to endure the rigours of testifying in open court about forms of victimization often experienced as shameful and humiliating as well as deeply hurtful. Worse, children had to negotiate *additional* legal hurdles before their evidence could be admitted at trial. Routine competence testing and a mandatory corroboration warning[61] reflected popularly held assumptions that children are especially suggestible, mendacious, and prone to fantasy, so that their evidence must be subject to especially stringent criteria of admissibility before it would be safe to allow a jury to hear it.

By the 1980s, however, a substantial body of behavioural science data had accumulated contradicting widespread assumptions about the innate deviousness, romancing, and unreliability of children.[62] This research confirmed that children are generally more suggestible than adults, and that their memories fade faster. Nonetheless, a sensitive questioner using age-appropriate language could still recover from a child as young as three years-of-age a sufficiently detailed and coherent account of her kidnapping and attempted

---

[58] Glanville Williams, 'Child Witnesses', in Peter Smith (ed.), *Criminal Law: Essays in Honour of J C Smith* (Butterworths, 1987), 192.

[59] Other than the very narrowly circumscribed provisions of the Children and Young Persons Act 1933, ss.42–43: where a medical practitioner certified that to require a child to testify in court 'would involve serious danger to his life or health', a magistrate was authorized to take a deposition from the child on oath, and that deposition could be admitted in evidence provided that the accused had been notified of the intention to depose the child, and had been afforded the opportunity of cross-examination.

[60] In R v *Wallwork* (1958) 42 Cr App R 153, CCA, where a five-year-old incest complainant was called to testify against her father, but was incapable of speaking once in the witness-box, Lord Goddard CJ fumed: 'The court deprecates the calling of a child of this age as a witness.... The jury could not attach any value to the evidence of a child of five; it is ridiculous to suppose that they could. Of course, the child could not be sworn.... [B]ut in any circumstances to call a little child of the age of five seems to us to be most undesirable, and I hope it will not occur again.'

[61] See §15.2(b). Specifically in relation to child witnesses, see Laura Hoyano and Caroline Keenan, *Child Abuse: Law and Policy Across Boundaries* (OUP, 2007), 690–8; Penney Lewis, *Delayed Prosecution for Childhood Sexual Abuse* (OUP, 2006), ch 6.

[62] For a thorough and illuminating review, see J. R. Spencer and Rhona Flin, *The Evidence of Children: The Law and the Psychology* (Blackstone, 2nd edn. 1993), ch 11.

murder to bring the assailant to justice.[63] Throughout the 1980s there was increasing awareness of the prevalence[64] of the physical and sexual abuse of children, including allegations of systematic, organized, and ritualistic abuse. The law's traditional attitude, that children should in general be neither seen nor heard in criminal proceedings, become utterly untenable in this social and political climate.

Reform occurred simultaneously on a number of fronts, at first piecemeal and uncoordinated, but soon as a concerted and systematic government policy.[65] The Criminal Justice Act 1988 abolished automatic corroboration warnings for children's evidence and made provision for child witnesses to testify via 'live-link' CCTV from outside the potentially intimidating atmosphere of the courtroom.[66] Competency requirements were reduced almost to vanishing point, as we saw in Chapter 7;[67] children were permitted to give evidence from behind a screen shielding them from direct eye-contact with the accused,[68] and to be accompanied by a social worker or other support person in the witness-box.[69] Wigs, gowns, and other formal courtroom attire could be dispensed with to make a child more at ease whilst giving evidence. The accused was prohibited from cross-examining child witnesses in person,[70] presaging a measure later extended (as we have seen) to adult complainants of sexual assault.[71] Efforts were also made to 'fast-track' child abuse prosecutions in order that the child's memory would be fresher at the time of the trial, and to allow therapeutic interventions to commence earlier.[72] The most radical reform was video-taped examination-in-chief, recorded by the police at the time of the original complaint and later admissible at trial *in lieu* of live testimony, which was introduced by the Criminal Justice Act 1991.[73] However, this was only half as radical as the reform package originally recommended by Judge Pigot's Advisory Committee on Video Evidence,[74] which favoured video-recorded pre-trial cross-examination, as well as examination in-chief.

The 1991 Act's 'half-Pigot' scheme[75] applied to children under 14 years-of-age testifying in relation to designated offences of violence, and to children under 17 years-of-age testifying in relation to designated sexual offences. A pre-recorded video could stand *in*

---

[63] David P. H. Jones, 'The Evidence of A Three-Year-Old Child' [1987] *Crim LR* 677.

[64] For a critical assessment of prevalence, see Elizabeth Birchall, 'The Frequency of Child Abuse – What Do We Really Know?' in Olive Stevenson (ed.), *Child Abuse: Public Policy and Professional Practice* (Harvester Wheatsheaf, 1989). Also see Spencer and Flin, *The Evidence of Children*, 9–11.

[65] See, in particular, Home Office, *Speaking Up for Justice* (June, 1998), ch 10. And see, for example, Julie A. Lipovsky, 'The Impact of Court on Children: Research Findings and Practical Recommendations' (1994) 9 *Journal of Interpersonal Violence* 238.   [66] CJA 1988, s.32.

[67] See YJCE Act 1999, s.53. For previous developments, see *R v Hampshire* [1995] 2 All ER 1019, CA; *R v Z* [1990] 2 QB 355, CA; Hoyano and Keenan, *Child Abuse*, 599–613; J. R. Spencer, 'Children as Witnesses: A Blunder Averted', *Archbold News*, 1 July 1994; Spencer and Flin, *The Evidence of Children*, ch 4.

[68] *R v X, Y and Z* (1990) 91 Cr App R 36, CA.   [69] *R v Smith* [1994] Crim LR 458, CA.

[70] CJA 1988, s.34A inserted by CJA 1991, s.55. Now see YJCE Act 1999, s.35. When in force, C&J Act 2009, s.105, will raise the age of protected child witnesses to seventeen and under.   [71] YJCE Act 1999, s.34.

[72] CJA 1991, s.53, replaced committal proceedings in child abuse cases with a streamlined notice of transfer procedure, but the overall impact of fast-tracking was found to be disappointing: Joyce Plotnikoff and Richard Woolfson, *Prosecuting Child Abuse: An Evaluation of the Government's Speedy Progress Policy* (Blackstone, 1995).

[73] CJA 1991, s.54, inserting CJA 1988, s.32A. See Spencer and Flin, *The Evidence of Children*, ch 7; D. J. Birch, 'Children's Evidence' [1992] *Crim LR* 262.

[74] *Report of the Advisory Group on Video Evidence* (Home Office, 1989).

[75] 'Half-Pigot' is convenient shorthand and fairly common currency in policy discussions, but this terminology is potentially misleading, as we explain *infra*. Also see Debbie Cooper, 'Pigot Unfulfilled: Video-

lieu of a child witness's examination in-chief, provided that the witness was available for cross-examination and the judge was satisfied that the video, as appropriately edited, did not have to be excluded in the interests of justice. Interviews conducted in accordance with the Home Office *Memorandum of Good Practice*[76] were presumptively fit to be admitted, but minor deviations from the 'model interview' did not automatically entail exclusion. The judge was obliged to tailor his overriding exclusionary discretion to the particular circumstances of each individual case.

Evaluations of the 1991 Act's scheme for the reception of pre-recorded video evidence pronounced it a major, though by no means unqualified, success.[77] The ability to capture a child's evidence on tape at the earliest opportunity affords prosecutors a considerable and sometimes decisive forensic advantage, in some cases prompting the accused to plead guilty and thereby altogether avoiding the delay, trauma and expense of a trial. Minor teething problems aside, half-Pigot, broadly speaking, attracted two groups of critics: those who thought that it already departed too radically from the traditional paradigm of live oral evidence at trial; and those on the other side of the argument who thought that it did not go far enough in accommodating the special needs of child witnesses. Members of the conservative camp ranged from 'ultra-traditionalist barrister peers',[78] who opposed video evidence in principle as an unacceptable erosion of the rights of the accused, to prosecutors who were broadly sympathetic to the aims of the legislation but felt that video and CCTV evidence had less impact on the jury than a complainant's live oral testimony, and therefore tended to dispense with the technology whenever a child was amenable to testifying 'live' in the courtroom. In fact the assumption that video evidence lacks impact on the fact-finder is largely unsubstantiated by research, but appears to be deeply rooted in the professional culture of prosecuting barristers. There was also some concern, especially amongst defence lawyers, that video evidence might make false allegations more difficult to expose.

On the reformist side of the debate, criticism focused on the fact that the child still had to undergo cross-examination, which, as we have seen, is the most stressful and potentially traumatic aspect of appearing as a witness in criminal proceedings. Moreover, the half-Pigot compromise is arguably much less than half a loaf. The child witness is still required to recall minute details of alleged offences many months or even years after the event. Nor can the child benefit from therapeutic rehabilitation until the trial is finally over and there is no longer any risk of – intentional or unconscious – 'witness-coaching' or contamination of testimony by therapists. In certain respects, testimony split between a pre-recorded examination-in-chief and a live cross-examination could prove to be more problematic for the prosecution than the traditional, entirely oral, procedure. Under the

Recorded Cross-Examination Under Section 28 of the Youth Justice and Criminal Evidence Act 1999' [2005] *Crim LR* 456.

[76] Jenny McEwan, 'Where the Prosecution Witness is a Child: The Memorandum of Good Practice' (1993) 5 *Journal of Child Law* 16; Ray Bull, 'Obtaining Evidence Expertly: The Reliability of Interviews with Child Witnesses' (1992) 1 *Expert Evidence* 5.

[77] Gwynn Davis, Laura Hoyano, Caroline Keenan, Lee Maitland, and Rod Morgan, *An Assessment of the Admissibility and Sufficiency of Evidence in Child Abuse Prosecutions* (Home Office, 1999); Amanda Wade, Anna Lawson, and Jan Aldridge, 'Stories in Court – Video-Taped Interviews and the Production of Children's Testimony' (1998) 10 *Child and Family Law Quarterly* 179; Graham Davies, Clare Wilson, Rebecca Mitchell, and John Milsom, *Videotaping Children's Evidence: An Evaluation* (Home Office, 1995).

[78] Spencer and Flin, *The Evidence of Children*, 90.

1991 Act scheme the child was thrown straight into cross-examination without the benefit of relatively gentle 'warm-up' questioning in-chief, and the defence were able to seize on small discrepancies between tape and testimony – in reality merely the inevitable traces of temporally discontinuous testimony – to suggest that the child was confused, mistaken, or lying. For some reformers, half-Pigot was a compromised muddle that neither delivered better evidence for the criminal justice system nor significantly improved the welfare of the child witness.

10.4 SPECIAL MEASURES FOR VULNERABLE OR INTIMIDATED WITNESSES

The Youth Justice and Criminal Evidence Act 1999 superseded and extended the provisions of the 1988 and 1991 Criminal Justice Acts. It took English law further away from the traditional paradigm of live oral evidence than any previous legislation, and can be regarded as marking a decisive conceptual shift from treating 'special measures' as a procedural response to *children's* special needs to be accommodated within an essentially adult trial process to a general system of procedural adjustments potentially available to *all* witnesses. As the categories of 'vulnerable or intimidated witness' (VIW) have progressively been expanded, so the number of witnesses testifying in the traditional way has correspondingly diminished. The extent to which ostensibly exceptional 'special measures' have become normalized in contemporary criminal adjudication is a theme which must be revisited in this chapter's conclusion, having first surveyed the statutory framework for assisting VIWs to give their best evidence introduced by the YJCE Act 1999.[79]

(a) THE STATUTORY FRAMEWORK

For the purposes of the 1999 Act, a witness is 'vulnerable' if he or she is:

A. under 17 years of age[80] at the time of the hearing; or

B. suffering from any mental disorder, impairment or physical disability likely to diminish the quality of the witness's evidence.[81]

A witness qualifies as 'intimidated' if he or she is:

C. experiencing fear or distress likely to diminish the quality of the witness's evidence.[82]

On application by a party or of its own motion, the court is obliged to determine the eligibility of every witness for assistance by special measures, and then, for any witness deemed either vulnerable or intimidated, to make a special measures direction (SMD)

---

[79] The primary legislation is accompanied by extensive practitioner guidance: see CJS, *Achieving Best Evidence in Criminal Proceedings: Guidance on Interviewing Victims and Witnesses, and Using Special Measures* (2007 revision), on-line at: www.cps.gov.uk/publications/docs/achieving_best_evidence_final.pdf.

[80] The age threshold will be raised to 18 years by the C&J Act 2009, s.98.   [81] Section 16.

[82] Section 17. The three categories of witness have been labelled A–C to correspond with the first part of Figure 10.1, below.

ordering provision for 'those measures (or combination of them) [which] would, in its opinion, be likely to maximize so far as practicable the quality of [the witness's] evidence'.[83] Vulnerable adult and child witnesses eligible for an SMD were intended to benefit, in appropriate cases, from any combination of the following special measures (subject to practical feasibility, e.g. a video can only be shown if one was actually made, etc.): screens; live-link CCTV; exclusion of members of the public from the courtroom; removal of the judge's and barristers' wigs and gowns; pre-recorded evidence in-chief; pre-recorded cross-examination ('full-Pigot'); and interpreters, intermediaries, and artificial communication aids.[84] Intimidated adult witnesses are eligible for the full range of special measures *with the exception of* interpreters, intermediaries, and artificial communication aids (which are presumptively inapplicable to their situation).[85] For adults, however, the judge must always take into account the witness's own wishes and the implications, if any, for effectively testing the witness's evidence before ordering any special measures.[86] Moreover, the pre-existing constraints on 'half-Pigot' continue to apply: the witness must be available for cross-examination, and the judge retains a broad discretion to exclude the video in the interests of justice.[87] If for any reason the judge decides not to admit a video of the witness's evidence in chief, video-recorded cross-examination is automatically precluded.[88] There can be no reverse-Pigot.

The legal definition of 'child witness' was further extended and subdivided. All child witnesses (including, for these purposes, young persons who were under 17 years-of-age at the time when a video of their evidence was made),[89] automatically qualify for an SMD with the presumption that they will: (1) give their evidence in-chief in the form of a pre-recorded video (if one has been made); and (2) present the remainder of their evidence via live-link (unless a pre-recorded cross-examination has also been undertaken).[90] This is the so-called 'primary rule'[91] for child witnesses. It is subject to the proviso that these measures are considered 'likely to maximise the quality of the witness's evidence'.[92] The judge also retains an overriding exclusionary discretion in the interests of justice.[93] However, a child witness in proceedings concerned with designated offences of sex or violence is deemed 'in need of special protection',[94] and in consequence qualifies automatically for pre-recorded evidence in-chief and CCTV live-link cross-examination *regardless of whether these special measures are considered likely to maximize the quality of the child's evidence*.[95] In other words, there is a legal presumption that the factual

---

[83] Section 19.

[84] Sections 18(1)(a) and 23–30. Another innovation, previously mentioned in n. 41 above, is that an accused charged with designated offences of sex or violence may not cross-examine a complainant or 'protected witness' in person, or any witness in any proceedings where the court so directs in the interests of justice: ss.34–36. Consequential arrangements have been made to appoint independent counsel to conduct cross-examination on behalf of an unrepresented accused, apparently even where the accused refuses to co-operate with appointed counsel if the interests of justice require cross-examination: s.38. The legislation is silent on how appointed counsel is supposed to conduct an effective cross-examination if the accused is un-cooperative.   [85] Section 18(1)(b).

[86] Section 19(3).   [87] Subsections 19(3)(b) and 27(2)–(4).

[88] Because cross-examination under s.28 is explicitly premissed on the admission of video-recorded evidence in-chief under s.27.

[89] These are 'qualifying witnesses' pursuant to s.22. The age threshold will be raised to 18 by the C&J Act 2009, s.98.   [90] Section 21(3).

[91] ibid.   [92] Section 21(4)(c).   [93] Subsections 21(4)(b) and 27(2).   [94] Section 21(1)(b).

[95] Section 21(5).

predicate (the quality of the child's evidence will be maximized) is satisfied in these cases.[96] Furthermore, in any *sex offence* case where an SMD directs that a child witness in need of special protection will give evidence in-chief via pre-recorded video, the SMD must also direct pre-recorded cross-examination.[97] As originally conceived then, full-Pigot presumptively applied to child witnesses in need of special protection in prosecutions of sex offences; half-Pigot to child witnesses in need of special protection in non-sexual assault proceedings.

Finally, in all cases and for all witnesses, adult or child, special measures are subject to: (a) the availability of particular measures at the relevant court centre, as designated by the Secretary of State;[98] and (b) the consent of the witness (other than in relation to the primary rule for child witnesses). Making the availability of particular measures subject to the designation of the Home Secretary[99] facilitated a policy of phased implementation which extended over five years form the introduction of the first tranche of special measures into Crown Court proceedings in 2002.[100] The Home Office's implementation schedule differentiated between vulnerable witnesses, eligible for special measures by virtue of youth or disability, and intimidated witnesses eligible on grounds of fear or distress at giving evidence; between adults and children; and also between three different trial venues, the Crown Court, magistrates' courts, and the Youth Court. Phased implementation of special measures was designed to allow time for piloting on an experimental basis and to organize appropriate training for criminal justice professionals, but an unfortunate consequence of these practical arrangements was that the availability of special measures was patchy and sometimes quite difficult to ascertain in the meantime. With the benefit of hindsight, the Court of Appeal was decidedly unimpressed by the complexity and constitutional credentials of the implementation schedule.[101] By 2007, however, all of the principal special measures had been introduced for all types of witness in all criminal proceedings, with one notable exception. In July 2004 it was announced that the Government had had second thoughts about section 28's provision for pre-recorded cross-examination ('full Pigot'),[102] and its introduction would be deferred pending another thoroughgoing review of the whole area of children's evidence.[103] In the light of this review and a further consultation process,[104] it now appears that section 28 will be implemented, after all, 'subject to

---

[96] The operation of legal presumptions of fact was explained in §6.2(b).

[97] Section 21(6).   [98] Subsection 18(2)–(5).

[99] Subsequently the Justice Secretary, following the creation of the Ministry of Justice in May 2007.

[100] Youth Justice and Criminal Evidence Act 1999 (Commencement No 7) Order, SI 2002/1739.

[101] *R v R (Video Recording: Admissibility)* [2008] 1 WLR 2044, [2008] EWCA Crim 678. Thomas LJ reviews the entire convoluted history of phased implementation, ibid. [21]–[27], concluding rather dryly, that '[a]ll Parliament was therefore doing was providing for what is known as "good administration"… Unfortunately, it would be difficult to apply that descriptive epithet to what actually happened in relation to the administrative arrangements in respect of the 1999 Act': ibid. [31].

[102] Partly in the light of CPS policy advice and a Home Office briefing prepared by Di Birch and Rhonda Powell, University of Nottingham School of Law: see Hoyano and Keenan, *Child Abuse*, 660–3.

[103] A review of children's evidence was formally launched on 1 December 2004: see Press Release, 'Giving Child Witnesses the Support They Need', on-line via www.cjsonline.gov.uk/. For further discussion, see Debbie Cooper, 'Pigot Unfulfilled: Video-recorded Cross-Examination under Section 28 of the Youth Justice and Criminal Evidence Act 1999' [2005] *Crim LR* 456.

[104] Office for Criminal Justice Reform, *Improving the Criminal Trial Process for Young Witnesses: A Consultation Paper* (2007), critically assessed by Laura C. H. Hoyano, 'The Child Witness Review: Much Ado about Too Little' [2007] *Crim LR* 849.

the successful development of rules of procedure and practitioner guidance'.[105] Scots law already provides a precedent, but there is limited practical experience to-date.[106]

These provisions are evidently detailed and complex (see Figure 10.1, below, for graphical summaries), and were rendered even more so by the uneven patchwork of piecemeal implementation which has characterized this legislation. The convoluted drafting of Part II of the YJCE Act 1999 was partly a consequence of extending the ambit of special measures originally devised for child witnesses to adults.[107] However, detail and complexity also reflected Parliament's determination to be more directive in policy terms and to reduce the scope for discretionary decision-making by police, prosecutors, and judges. Thus, it was a general policy of the 1999 Act that a witness's own preferences should be taken into account in deciding which, if any, special measures would enhance the witness's evidence and safeguard her wellbeing. The exception was that the primary rule in relation to child witnesses was *not* displaced by a child's preference for giving live testimony in court.

Experience had taught that, even where the trial judge is very supportive of pre-recorded video evidence, prosecutors may steer child complainants away from relying on their pre-recorded testimony in the belief that a child's evidence will make a greater impact on the jury if it is delivered orally in the courtroom. So Parliament removed this temptation by taking that option away. However, a mandatory directive was always likely to be regarded as anomalous by criminal justice professionals when other witnesses retained the option of live testimony. Moreover, the primary rule might be experienced as oppressive and unfair by particular child witnesses themselves who would have preferred to testify in person.[108] It is therefore not entirely surprising that section 100 of the Coroners and Justice Act 2009, when brought into force, will amend section 21 of the 1999 Act to allow trial judges to disapply the primary rule at the request of the witness. Although this will implement the policy of respecting witnesses' preferences more consistently, it does not necessarily address the concerns which originally motivated an inflexible primary rule. We glimpse here the more general challenges of constructing a statutory framework capable of mediating between a range of interests which may not be entirely compatible, and which contributes to the sense that efforts to reform criminal trial procedure in order to accommodate the needs of vulnerable and intimidated witnesses have a tendency to go round in circles. Achieving an appropriate balance between statutory imperatives and operational flexibility is something of an eternal preoccupation.

---

[105] Office for Criminal Justice Reform, *Government Response to the Improving the Criminal Trial Process for Young Witness[es] Consultation* (Ministry of Justice, 2009), 12.

[106] ibid. 10–11. The relevant Scottish provision is Criminal Procedure (Scotland) Act 1995, s.271I, inserted by the Vulnerable Witnesses (Scotland) Act 2004, authorizing the evidence of a child or vulnerable adult witness to be produced by pre-recorded video of a pre-trial hearing conducted by a commissioner appointed by the court.

[107] Thus, the category 'children in need of special protection' reflected the priority accorded to child witnesses testifying in connection with sexual and violent offences under the Criminal Justice Acts 1988 and 1991. This historical survival will be abolished by the Coroners and Justice Act 2009, s.100; albeit that the 2009 Act simultaneously creates some new distinctions in witness eligibility for special measures.

[108] Birch and Leng remarked that 'if it is thought that he would make a good witness, there does not seem any obvious reason for denying him this option': *Blackstone's Guide to the Youth Justice and Criminal Evidence Act 1999* (Blackstone, 2000), 51. Also see Hoyano and Keenan, *Child Abuse*, 687 (criticizing 'the rigidity of the primary rule which can thwart children's preferences as to how they will give evidence').

Fig. 10.1 Skeleton Key to Special Measures under the Youth Justice and Criminal Evidence Act 1999 [as amended by the Coroners and Justice Act 2009]

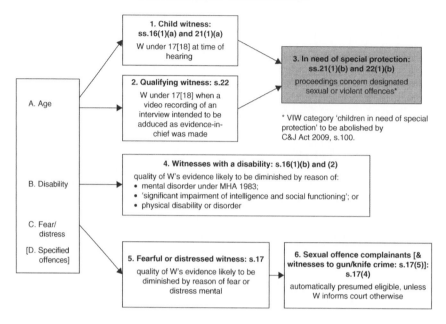

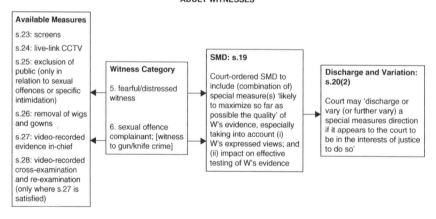

3: SPECIAL MEASURES APPLICABLE TO SECTION 16 WITNESSES

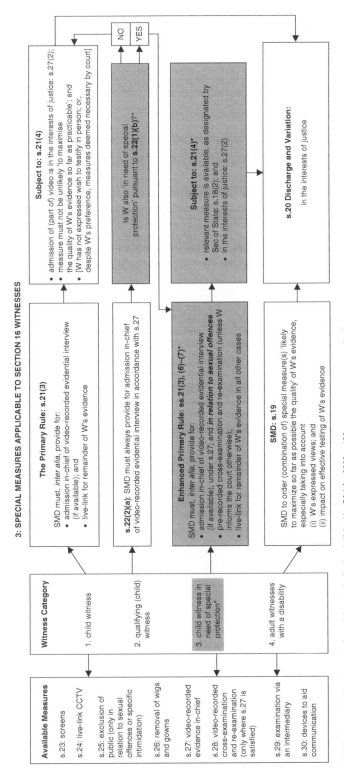

Available Measures

s.23: screens

s.24: live-link CCTV

s.25: exclusion of public (only in relation to sexual offences or specific intimidation)

s.26: removal of wigs and gowns

s.27: video-recorded evidence in-chief

s.28: video-recorded cross-examination and re-examination (only where s.27 is satisfied)

s.29: examination via an intermediary

s.30: devices to aid communication

Witness Category

1. child witness

2. qualifying (child) witness

3. child witness in need of special protection*

4. adult witnesses with a disability

The Primary Rule: s.21(3)

SMD must, *inter alia*, provide for:
- admission in-chief of video-recorded evidential interview (if available); and
- live-link for remainder of W's evidence

s.22(2)(a): SMD must always provide for admission in-chief of video-recorded evidential interview in accordance with s.27

Enhanced Primary Rule: ss.21(3), (6)—(7)*

SMD must, *inter alia*, provide for:
- admission in-chief of video-recorded evidential interview (if available), under s.27, and *in relation to sexual offences*, pre-recorded cross-examination and re-examination (unless W informs the court otherwise);
- live-link for remainder of W's evidence in all other cases

SMD: s.19

SMD to order (combination of) special measure(s) 'likely to maximize so far as possible the quality' of W's evidence, especially taking into account
(i) W's expressed views; and
(ii) impact on effective testing of W's evidence

Subject to: s.21(4)
- admission of (part of) video is in the interests of justice: s.27(2);
- measure must not be unlikely 'to maximise the quality of W's evidence so far as practicable'; and
- [W has not expressed wish to testify in person; or, despite W's preference, measures deemed necessary by court]

Is W also 'in need of special protection' pursuant to **s.22(1)(b)?***

NO   YES

Subject to: s.21(4)*
- relevant measure is available, as designated by Sec of State: s.18(2); and
- in the interests of justice: s.27(2)

s.20 Discharge and Variation:

in the interests of justice

* VIW category 'children in need of special protection' to be abolished by C&J Act 2009, s.100.

(b) EVALUATION

Leaving aside transitional issues (exacerbated, as we have seen, by the phased implementation of special measures), and deferring until later a more general assessment of their
impact on the principle of orality, evaluation of the framework of special measures for
vulnerable and intimidated witnesses introduced by the YJCE Act 1999 may be organized
around two central questions. First, are special measures 'working', in the sense of achieving their objective of helping VIWs to give their best evidence at trial? Secondly, do special
measures promote the interests of justice, compatibly with common law procedural standards and the right to a fair trial under the Human Rights Act?

Special measures have benefitted from comparatively extensive empirical evaluation
(albeit there is always room for more and better empirical data as a rational basis for legal
reform).[109] In round terms, they have achieved considerable success. Special measures
have always been popular with victims and witnesses themselves and with the police, and
over time they have gradually won over more prosecutors and judges, some of whom were
initially sceptical. There is no doubt that very large numbers of witnesses are now benefiting from special measures, particularly pre-recorded evidence admitted under section 27
and live TV links covering both examination-in-chief and cross-examination pursuant
to section 24.[110] The vast majority of measures which are applied for by the prosecution
are granted by trial judges.[111] Intermediaries and communication devices assist far fewer
VIWs in purely numerical terms, but the assistance they provide to particular individuals
is often vital in bringing to justice those who commit serious offences against the most vulnerable members of society.[112] The successful integration of special measures into criminal trial procedure is reflected in their further extension to *all* sexual offence complainants and to any (adult) witness to offences committed with an offensive weapon by the

---

[109] See Mandy Burton, Roger Evans, and Andrew Sanders, *Are Special Measures for Vulnerable
and Intimidated Witnesses Working? Evidence form the Criminal Justice Agencies,* Home Office Online
Report 01/06 (Home Office, 2006); Debbie Cooper and Paul Roberts, *Special Measures for Vulnerable and
Intimidated Witnesses: An Analysis of Crown Prosecution Service Monitoring Data* (CPS, 2005); Becky
Hamlyn, Andrew Phelps, Jenny Turtle, and Ghazala Sattar, *Are Special Measures Working? Evidence from
Surveys of Vulnerable and Intimidated Witnesses,* Home Office Research Study 283 (RDS, 2004); Joyce
Plotnikoff and Richard Woolfson, *In Their Own Words: The Experiences of 50 Young Witnesses in Criminal
Proceedings* (NSPCC, 2004). These empirical studies built upon a solid foundation of earlier research and
reports examining children's evidence: Graham Davies and Helen Westcott, *Interviewing Child Witnesses
under the Memorandum of Good Practice: A Research Review,* Police Research Series Report 115 (Home
Office, 1999); HMCPSI, *Thematic Review of Cases Involving Child Witnesses* (CPS Inspectorate, 1998);
Graham Davies, Claire Wilson, Rebecca Mitchell, and John Milsom, *Videotaping Children's Evidence: An
Evaluation* (Home Office, 1995); Graham Davies and Elizabeth Noon, *An Evaluation of the Live Link for
Child Witnesses* (London: Home Office, 1991).

[110] For example, CPS Monitoring Data for 2003/4 indicate that 6,064 VIWs were identified by the police
or by the CPS during that period, producing some 7,132 applications for individual special measures, 6,088
(85%) of which were actually presented in court: Cooper and Roberts, *Special Measures for Vulnerable and
Intimidated Witnesses,* Tables 2-A and 5-A and accompanying text.

[111] Paul Roberts, Debbie Cooper, and Sheelagh Judge, 'Monitoring Success, Accounting for Failure:
The Outcome of Prosecutors' Applications for Special Measures Directions Under the Youth Justice and
Criminal Evidence Act 1999' (2005) 9 *E & P* 269.

[112] Joyce Plotnikoff and Richard Woolfson, 'Making Best Use of the Intermediary Special Measure at
Trial' [2008] *Crim LR* 91; Louise Ellison, 'Cross-Examination and the Intermediary: Bridging the Language
Divide?' [2002] *Crim LR* 114.

Coroners and Justice Act 2009.[113] There is, naturally, always room for improvement. One area of on-going concern is that police and (to a lesser extent) prosecutors may be failing to identify the vulnerabilities of many witnesses.[114] Clearly, witnesses who are never recognized and subsequently classified as VIWs cannot benefit from special measures.

The normative credentials of special measures, and in particular their compatibility with Article 6 of the ECHR, were tested on several fronts. With the assistance of some further legislative tweaking by Parliament, special measures have emerged from this period of enhanced legal scrutiny unscathed. The automatic primary rule, dictating that child witnesses in need of special protection should normally give their evidence in-chief by pre-recorded video (if there is one) and be cross-examined by live TV link even where these measures might *not* maximize the quality of their evidence, was an obvious target for legal challenge. Initially, some Youth Courts appeared to believe that they retained a discretion to depart from the primary rule in the interests of justice, especially where the witness and the accused were of similar age. But the Divisional Court moved swiftly to correct any misapprehension in the lower courts. The primary rule in section 21(3)–(5) of the YJCE Act 1999 meant exactly what it says.[115] The point was placed beyond any doubt by the House of Lords in *Camberwell Green Youth Court.*[116] Baroness Hale explained that 'departures from the primary rules are clearly intended to be exceptional':

It is clear that, by enacting the primary rule and limiting the circumstances in which it may be disapplied, Parliament did not mean to allow defendants to challenge the use of a video recording or live link simply because it is a departure from the normal procedure in criminal trials…. Parliament has decided what is to be the norm when child witnesses give evidence. Hence there will have to be a special reason for departing from it. The fact that there is no particular reason to think that this particular child will be upset, traumatised or intimidated by giving evidence in court does not make it unjust for her to give it by live link and video if there is one…[117]

ECHR jurisprudence, it was pointed out, guarantees no absolute right of face-to-face confrontation, and emphasizes that the rights of the accused are compatible with appropriate concern for victims' interests. Live testimony and cross-examination are not necessarily indispensable to the conception of a fair trial enshrined in ECHR Article 6 and embedded in the procedural traditions of Council of Europe member states, the vast majority of which have a continental/civilian jurisprudential heritage which places far less emphasis on the principle of orality than common law trial systems.[118] The essence of the European

---

[113] C&J Act 2009, ss.99 and 101.

[114] Mandy Burton, Roger Evans, and Andrew Sanders, 'Implementing Special Measures for Vulnerable and Intimidated Witnesses: The Problem of Identification' [2006] *Crim LR* 229.

[115] *R (D)* v *Camberwell Green Youth Court* [2003] 2 Cr App R 257, DC. This result was anticipated by Laura C. H. Hoyano, 'Striking a Balance Between the Rights of Defendants and Vulnerable Witnesses: Will Special Measures Directions Contravene Guarantees of a Fair Trial?' [2001] *Crim LR* 948.

[116] *R* v *Camberwell Green Youth Court, ex p. D (a minor)* [2005] 1 WLR 393, [2005] UKHL 4.

[117] ibid. [37], [45].

[118] 'With minor qualifications…derivative information is readily available to Continental fact finders, especially in written form and in the form of hearsay remarks by firsthand witnesses': Mirjan R. Damaška, *Evidence Law Adrift* (Yale UP, 1997), 15–16. But one should also acknowledge the significance of the 'principle of immediacy' in the historical development of Continental criminal procedure, on which see Sarah J. Summers, *Fair Trials: The European Criminal Procedural Tradition and the European Court of Human Rights* (Hart, 2007), 47–58, 154–5.

principle is that the accused should enjoy 'equality of arms', which in this context means a fair opportunity to test the prosecution's evidence and roughly equivalent access to the state's witnesses as the prosecutor.[119] Full-Pigot envisages a mediated form of videotaped pre-trial cross-examination, in which the judge and opposing counsel sit in chambers with the witness, and the accused can observe the witness being questioned from behind a two-way mirror, instructing his counsel via an ear-piece. Some version of this arrangement is guaranteed by statute.[120] True, this is a long way removed from the traditional public cross-examination 'live' in court, which prior to 1988 the accused was always entitled to conduct in person. But radical procedural reform is precisely what the 1999 Act aims to implement and entrench. It is highly unlikely that full-Pigot would fail to pass muster under Article 6 of the ECHR.[121] Moreover, as Lord Rodger acknowledged in *Camberwell Green Youth Court*, '[s]ince the forms of trial have evolved... over the centuries, there is no reason to suppose that today's norm represents the ultimate state of perfection or that the procedures will not evolve further, as technology advances'.[122]

A second human rights-inspired objection to the 1999 Act's special measures regime alleged 'inequality of arms' in a different, more direct sense. In *R (S) v Waltham Forest Youth Court*,[123] for example, the accused *S* was 13 years old, and regarded by local authority social services as a 'vulnerable child' with serious learning difficulties. She was charged, along with three older co-accused, with a robbery of a mobile phone from two girls. *S* claimed to have received threats from her co-accused, and said that she was too scared to testify in their physical presence at court. An application was made to allow *S* to testify via live TV link, similar arrangements already having been made to receive the complainants' evidence remotely. But the trial judge ruled that the unambiguous terms of the 1999 Act precluded him from making any such order in favour of an accused, and this interpretation was upheld on appeal by the Divisional Court. In *Camberwell Green Youth Court*, however, their Lordships made no secret of the fact that they were sympathetic to the plight of young defendants like the accused in *Waltham Forest Youth Court*, and hinted that the Divisional Court's ruling might be reconsidered if the equality of arms point were to fall for their decision.[124]

---

[119] '[T]he principle of equality of arms – in the sense of a "fair balance" between the parties – requires that each party should be afforded a reasonable opportunity to present his case under conditions that do not place him at a substantial disadvantage vis-à-vis his opponent... The right to adversarial proceedings means that each party must be given the opportunity to have knowledge of and comment on the observations filed or evidence adduced by the other party': *Salov v Ukraine* (App. no. 65518/01), ECtHR Judgment, 6 September 2005, [87]. And see *Doorson v Netherlands* (1996) 22 EHRR 330; cf. *Mechelen v Netherlands* (1997) 25 EHRR 647. For discussion, see William E. O'Brian Jr, 'The Right of Confrontation: US and European Perspectives' (2005) 121 *LQR* 481; Richard D. Friedman, 'Thoughts from Across the Water on Hearsay and Confrontation' [1998] *Crim LR* 697; Annemarieke Beijer, Cathy Cobley, and André Klip, 'Witness Evidence, Article 6 of the European Convention on Human Rights and the Principle of Open Justice', in Phil Fennell, Christopher Harding, Nico Jörg, and Bert Swart (eds.), *Criminal Justice in Europe: A Comparative Study* (OUP, 1995).

[120] YJCE Act 1999, s.28(2).

[121] See, in particular, *SN v Sweden* (2004) 39 EHRR 13, [2002] Crim LR 831. For extended analysis arriving at the same conclusion, see Laura C. H. Hoyano, 'Striking a Balance Between the Rights of Defendants and Vulnerable Witnesses: Will Special Measures Directions Contravene Guarantees of a Fair Trial?' [2001] *Crim LR* 948.

[122] *R v Camberwell Green Youth Court, ex p. D (a minor)* [2005] 1 WLR 393, [9].

[123] *R (S) v Waltham Forest Youth Court* [2004] 2 Cr App R 335, [2004] EWHC Admin 715.

[124] *R v Camberwell Green Youth Court, ex p. D (a minor)* [2005] 1 WLR 393, [17] (Lord Rodger), [63] (Baroness Hale).

In the event, Parliament seized the initiative. Section 47 of the Police and Justice Act 2006[125] authorizes trial judges, on application by the accused, to give a 'live link direction' in relation to any youthful (under 18 years-of-age) or mentally disordered accused where 'live link would enable him to participate more effectively in the proceedings as a witness', and in accordance with the interests of justice. The same principled concern to promote equality of arms animates section 104 of the Coroners and Justice Act 2009,[126] which makes provision for the testimony of these two groups of defendants to be given through intermediaries in appropriate cases. Parliament's willingness to make special measures available to the accused as well as to complainants and witnesses, if somewhat belated, should serve to pre-empt any human rights challenge alleging inequality of arms. Indeed, it can fairly be regarded as a strength of the special measures regime in general that Parliament has been prepared to make minor adjustments to the 1999 Act's statutory framework on a rolling basis and in the light of experience.[127]

10.5 THE DEMISE OF ORALITY?

It might be tempting to conclude from the analysis presented in this and the preceding three chapters that the days of live oral testimony in criminal trials are numbered. The 'common sense' empirical assumptions about memory, credibility, and truth-finding, on which the traditional trial model appears to rest, have been undermined by behavioural scientists; and the traditional procedural values of due process, fairness, and defendants' rights have been challenged by critics of the status quo and advocates for the interests of victims and witnesses. The YJCE Act 1999 and the CJA 2003 may be viewed as the latest and certainly most comprehensive in a series of progressively more radical legislative interventions modifying the rules governing witness testimony, and they might not be the last. Perhaps the oral tradition is already in decline, and the seeds of its ultimate demise have been sown.

Before allowing oneself to get carried away with some of the more apocalyptic predictions, however, more sober counsels should prevail. Even if the oral tradition in criminal procedure is scientifically flawed, as the psychologists contend, it certainly does not follow that the legal paradigm must conform to some postulated scientific model of evidence-taking. Criminal adjudication aspires to legitimacy, and legitimacy is rooted in public confidence and trust in the integrity of state officials and institutions. From this perspective, the most significant behavioural science finding may be that people generally believe that they *can* gauge credibility from a witness's demeanour. The oral tradition will retain its attraction, and its ability to generate public confidence in criminal verdicts, for at least as long as this belief – and others

---

[125] Inserting YJCE Act 1999, ss.33A and 33B.   [126] Inserting YJCE Act 1999, ss.33BA and 33BB.

[127] Reference has already been made to modification of the primary rule to take account of the child witness's own wishes, effected by C&J Act 2009, s.100. Another problem with the scheme as originally enacted was that it prohibited supplementary examination-in-chief on any matter already covered by an admissible video-recording. This defect has been remedied by C&J Act 2009, s.103, modifying YJCE Act 1999, s.27(5)(b), so that supplementary examination-in-chief will be permissible with the leave of the court.

like it – endure. Moreover, the intuitive value of cross-examination as a forensic tool for interrogating witness testimony still resonates with the general public beyond the realms of criminal adjudication. Thus, the opening of the Chilcot Inquiry into the Iraq War was greeted by objections that the truth would never come out in the absence of cross-examination by lawyers.[128] Legal reform can, and often should, lead and educate public opinion, but it risks alienating its constituency if it runs too far and too fast beyond popular consensus. Wellborn concludes, after a wide-ranging review of the psychological literature:

It is probably more important that the results of litigation be accepted than that they be accurate. Accuracy is merely a factor, albeit a rather important factor, in acceptability. Live testimony may be essential to perceptions of fairness, regardless of the real relation between live testimony and accuracy of outcomes.[129]

With the addendum that acceptability should be *earned* through legitimacy, which in turn is partly predicated on the accuracy of verdicts, this conclusion seems entirely warranted. Why should the public have faith in a scientifically rational model of fact-finding that contradicts common sense beliefs and is beyond the intellectual grasp of ordinary citizens? Judging by the standard Bond-film plot, the misanthropic mad scientist with an H-bomb (to say nothing of a terrorist with a home-made chemistry lab) looms larger in the gallery of popular fears than traditional criminal trial procedure or adjudication by a lay jury of fellow citizens. Questions of social authority and deference to expertise will be explored in the next chapter.

For those of more rationalistic inclination, behavioural science data and conclusions are frequently vulnerable to challenge on their own scientific terms. Psychological experiments have well-documented methodological limitations:[130] they are often conducted with unrepresentative populations of college students; they seldom take account of the impact on behaviour of cultural factors or social changes over time; and, most significantly of all, the experience of being a juror who is responsible for determining the fate of an accused can never be replicated with complete authenticity in a laboratory experiment. This is not to say that all behavioural science data should be taken with a pinch of salt. To the contrary, the consistency of certain replicated findings is persuasive evidence that psychological evaluations of witness testimony contain more than a grain of truth.[131] But these methodological considerations do nonetheless recommend a healthy reciprocal scepticism of sceptical evaluations of the oral tradition. Furthermore, psychologists have discovered that certain behavioural cues really do signal credibility, so that a modest refinement of judicial directions, e.g. to encourage jurors to concentrate on

---

[128] See, e.g., Robert Verkaik, 'Chilcot inquiry must investigate abuse claims, say lawyers', *The Independent*, 24 November 2009; William Bowles, 'The Chilcot Inquiry: A Theatre of the Absurd', *Pacific Free Press*, 29 December 2009 ('Chilcot went out of his way to inform us that it wasn't a trial, there was to be no attempt to assign culpability or responsibility, no serious cross-examination. So what's the point?').

[129] Olin Guy Wellborn III, 'Demeanor' (1991) 76 *Cornell LR* 1075, 1092.

[130] For more systematic critical evaluation, see Roderick Bagshaw, 'Behavioural Science Data in Evidence Teaching and Scholarship', in Paul Roberts and Mike Redmayne (eds.), *Innovations in Evidence and Proof* (Hart, 2007).

[131] For balanced discussion, see Jenny McEwan, 'Reasoning, Relevance and Law Reform: The Influence of Empirical Research on Criminal Adjudication', in Paul Roberts and Mike Redmayne (eds.), *Innovations in Evidence and Proof* (Hart, 2007); Jenny McEwan, *The Verdict of the Court* (Hart, 2003), chs 4–5.

the right bits of body language, may be all that is required to deflect one prominent line of criticism.[132]

The normatively-inspired critique of the oral tradition is no more conclusive than its empirical science sibling. There is no doubt that trial procedure needed up-dating to accommodate the interests of complainants and witnesses, and to secure more valuable evidence for the court. Hoyano and Keenan nicely encapsulate the prevailing mood: 'The adversarial trial is no longer its own justification; it must adapt itself to the needs of witnesses, and not *vice versa*'.[133] Reform is on-going. Three further developments which we have described and, broadly speaking, endorsed in previous chapters are: (1) pronounced relaxation of competency requirements, which are now predicated on the (presumed) intelligibility of individual witnesses rather than specifying presumptively excluded categories of witness;[134] (2) firmer legal restrictions on the use of general character evidence to attack a witness's credibility;[135] and (3) a progressive shift away from categorical rules of exclusion and closed lists of exceptions, particularly in the law of hearsay[136] and the rule against narrative,[137] towards broad principles of admissibility adapted to the circumstances of particular cases. All three developments should serve to de-emphasize the formalistic dichotomy between evidence (or questions in cross-examination) going to the issue and evidence (or questions) on collateral matters. A domesticated credit/issue distinction, stripped of the power to mandate exclusion of probative evidence and to force judges to give directions that most jurors must find unintelligible, survives only as a harmless rule-of-thumb. Judges and lawyers may continue to invoke it as a shortcut to assessing relevance and probative value, but should remain at liberty to disregard a categorical approach to adducing evidence whenever the interests of justice clearly favour flexibility.

So far as other recent innovations are concerned, it would be inadvisable to rush to judgment before the provisions of the YJCE Act 1999 and the CJA 2003 have had time to bed-down properly. After more than a decade of practical experience, the implementation of video-recorded examination-in-chief for child witnesses under the Criminal Justice Act 1991 appears to have been a success, though inevitable teething-troubles took time to overcome and it remains unclear to what extent legal professionals have been fully converted to the cause.[138] The further step to full-Pigot and the extension of SMDs to adult witnesses will take at least as long to incorporate into the routines and expectations of criminal litigation, and progress will be impeded by at least as many practical and procedural obstacles along the way. There may be further scope, meanwhile, for extending such novelties as specially-appointed independent counsel to conduct particularly sensitive phases of criminal

---

[132] Jeremy A. Blumenthal, 'A Wipe of the Hands, A Lick of the Lips: The Validity of Demeanor Evidence in Assessing Witness Credibility' (1993) 72 *Nebraska LR* 115.

[133] Hoyano and Keenan, *Child Abuse*, 685.   [134] §7.2.   [135] §8.4.   [136] Chapter 9.

[137] §8.3.

[138] Some respondents to the Child Review consultation were still saying that live link 'is less "real" for the jury – they find it hard to judge the demeanour and body language of the witness': OCJR, *Government Response to the Improving the Criminal Trial Process for Young Witness[es] Consultation* (Ministry of Justice, 2009), 15. For evaluations of pre-YJCE Act 1999 special measures, see Gwynn Davis, Laura Hoyano, Caroline Keenan, Lee Maitland, and Rod Morgan, *An Assessment of the Admissibility and Sufficiency of Evidence in Child Abuse Prosecutions* (Home Office, 1999); Amanda Wade, Anna Lawson, and Jan Aldridge, 'Stories in Court – Video-Taped Interviews and the Production of Children's Testimony' (1998) 10 *Child and Family Law Quarterly* 179; Graham Davies, Clare Wilson, Rebecca Mitchell, and John Milsom, *Videotaping Children's Evidence: An Evaluation* (Home Office, 1995).

proceedings, like *ex parte* PII hearings or the cross-examination of vulnerable witnesses; though on-going concerns have been noted. Only time will tell where such innovations in the presentation of witness evidence might ultimately lead.

For all that, no contemporary development of common law principles or recent legislative enactment can be assumed to presage orality's inevitable demise.[139] Although video evidence and the like constitute a radical departure from traditional forms of evidence gathering and presentation, the traditional trial model is flexible enough to accommodate modern innovations whilst still retaining its essential characteristics, at least so long as special measures under the 1999 Act are justified as exceptional departures from the norm to assist vulnerable or intimidated witnesses. Only if the full range of 'exceptional' measures came to be utilized routinely for many or most adult witnesses might we suspect that the oral tradition was truly in terminal decline. In that event, we would need urgently to consider whether English criminal trials were still being conducted in accordance with the essential canons of fairness and due process, under the Human Rights Act and in principle.

Even modernized, more witness-friendly adversary trial is far from perfect.[140] Many witnesses will continue to feel that they have been ill-used in court, and the truth will often be a casualty of their treatment. But what realistic alternative would be superior? The traditional common law model of criminal trial may be reminiscent of Churchill's reputed assessment of democracy, as the worst form of government imaginable, apart from all the others. For the time being, at least, oral witness testimony seems here to stay.

---

[139] Cf. Linda Mulcahy, 'The Unbearable Lightness of Being? Shifts Towards the Virtual Trial' (2008) 35 *Journal of Law and Society* 464, 473, who misinterprets an open-ended question as positive endorsement of the normalization of special measures.

[140] Cf. Louise Ellison, *The Adversarial Process and the Vulnerable Witness* (OUP, 2001), 160, contending that 'the paradigmatic adversarial trial offers limited scope for the improved treatment of vulnerable and intimidated witnesses. An accommodation approach must be eschewed in favour of a fundamental re-assessment of key features of the adversarial trial process'. And see Mandy Burton, Roger Evans, and Andrew Sanders, 'Vulnerable and Intimidated Witnesses and the Adversarial Process in England and Wales' (2007) 11 *E & P* 1 (agreeing that adversarialism is the ultimate problem, but identifying greater practical scope for amelioration within the confines of the existing procedural system).

11

EXPERT EVIDENCE

11.1 THE SIGNIFICANCE OF EXPERT EVIDENCE

Expert evidence is conventionally discussed by the textbook writers under the general rubric of 'opinion evidence'.[1] However, this categorization is insufficiently precise or informative to do justice to the role of scientific expertise in criminal proceedings. It is more illuminating to see expert evidence as a topic organized around issues of epistemic authority, the transparency of the inferential process, and the durability of social trust in the legitimacy of criminal verdicts. These have been recurrent themes of the contextualized approach to evidence and proof developed throughout this book. The growing significance of forensic science at all levels and stages of criminal proceedings should anyway qualify expert evidence as a topic worthy of individualized attention. Yet common law Evidence textbooks, and presumably therefore also Evidence teaching, have tended to downplay its significance.

Expert evidence is an increasingly prominent feature of criminal litigation, whether communicated directly through an expert witness's live oral testimony or in the form of a written report adduced at trial.[2] The Runciman Royal Commission's *Crown Court Study* estimated that around one third of all contested trials on indictment involves scientific evidence.[3] Though by any reckoning a significant percentage, this still probably underestimates the true extent of scientific expertise in criminal litigation, since experts employed by the defence do not always testify at trial and their reports need not be disclosed either to the prosecution or to the court. These 'defence examiners' still nonetheless play an important role in an adversary system. They scrutinize the prosecution's evidence, carry out checks and further testing, brief defence lawyers about the strengths and

---

[1] See, e.g., Colin Tapper, *Cross and Tapper on Evidence* (OUP, 11th edn. 2007), ch 11; Adrian Keane, *The Modern Law of Evidence* (OUP, 7th edn. 2008), ch 18; Gregory Durston, *Evidence: Text and Materials* (OUP, 2008), ch 11; Ian Dennis, *The Law of Evidence* (Sweet & Maxwell, 3rd edn. 2007), ch 20 ('Opinion and Expert Evidence'); cf. A. A. S. Zuckerman, *The Principles of Criminal Evidence* (OUP, 1989), ch 5.

[2] Expert reports, which would otherwise be inadmissible hearsay, can be adduced under s.30 of the Criminal Justice Act 1988, but only with the leave of the court if the expert is not also going to testify in person.

[3] Michael Zander and Paul Henderson, *Crown Court Study* RCCJ Research Study No 19 (HMSO, 1993), 84–5. Scientific evidence was judged 'very important' in over 2/5ths of such cases, and 'fairly important' in one third of the remaining cases.

weaknesses of the prosecution's scientific evidence, and sometimes even advise counsel on the presentation of the defence case in court.[4]

New medical and scientific techniques are constantly being developed and adapted to forensic purposes, as knowledge and experience in general have become ever more specialist, compartmentalized, detailed, and complex in the technology-driven modern world. It is no exaggeration to regard DNA technology as the most revolutionary contribution to criminal investigation and forensic proof since the introduction of fingerprinting a century earlier. Less feted, but cumulatively no less important for the smooth operation of contemporary criminal investigations and prosecutions, are the armies of experts in medicine, dentistry, pathology, psychiatry, psychology, fingerprinting, toxicology, biological sciences (blood, hair, and bodily fluids analysis), genetics, ballistics, narcotics, trace-mark examination (paint, glass, fibres, toolmarks, and footprint inspection), and document and handwriting analysis, to mention only some of the fields of expertise most commonly encountered in modern criminal litigation.[5] A minority of complex or serious cases involves multiple forms of scientific evidence and a veritable procession of expert witnesses.

The long-standing relationship between law and science, like any partnership of enduring value,[6] is infused with a certain creative tension, and there have been some rough patches and the odd unsavoury incident. The reputation of forensic science has not entirely recovered from its association with several of the high profile miscarriages of justice that came to light in the late 1980s,[7] precipitating a Royal Commission to consider root-and-branch reform of the criminal justice system.[8] More recently, forensic science has featured in the convictions and subsequent exonerations of Sally Clark,[9] Sion Jenkins,[10] and Barry

---

[4] Paul Roberts, 'Science in the Criminal Process' (1994) 14 *OJLS* 469, 489ff.; Paul Roberts and Christine Willmore, *The Role of Forensic Science Evidence in Criminal Proceedings*, RCCJ Research Study No 11 (HMSO, 1993), ch 3.

[5] For accessible introductions and overviews, see Jim Fraser, *Forensic Science: A Very Short Introduction* (OUP, 2010); Jim Fraser and Robin Williams (eds.), *Handbook of Forensic Science* (Willan, 2009); National Research Council, *Strengthening Forensic Science in the United States: A Path Forward* (National Academies Press, 2009); Bernard Robertson and G. A. Vignaux, *Interpreting Evidence: Evaluating Forensic Science in the Courtroom* (Wiley, 1995); J. H. Phillips and J. K. Bowen, *Forensic Science and the Expert Witness* (Law Book Co, Sydney, 1985). More doctrinal treatments include Tristram Hodgkinson, *Expert Evidence: Law & Practice* (Sweet & Maxwell, 1990), Part D; and, from a US perspective but including copious detail on particular areas of expertise, Andre A. Moenssens, James E. Starrs, Carole E. Henderson, and Fred Inbau, *Scientific Evidence in Civil and Criminal Cases* (Foundation Press, 4th edn. 1995).

[6] Cf. Anita K. Y. Wonder, 'Science and Law, A Marriage of Opposites' (1989) 29 *Journal of the Forensic Science Society* 75.

[7] See Clive Walker and Russell Stockdale, 'Forensic Evidence', in Clive Walker and Keir Starmer (eds.), *Miscarriages of Justice: A Review of Justice in Error* (Blackstone, 1999); Carol A. G. Jones, *Expert Witnesses: Science, Medicine and the Practice of Law* (OUP, 1994), ch 10; Joshua Rozenburg, 'Miscarriages of Justice', in E. Stockdale and S. Casale (eds.), *Criminal Justice Under Stress* (Blackstone, 1992).

[8] For critical evaluation of what the Commission had to say about science and experts, see Paul Roberts, 'Forensic Science Evidence After Runciman' [1994] *Crim LR* 780; Peter Alldridge, 'Forensic Science and Expert Evidence' (1994) 21 *Journal of Law and Society* 136; Mike Redmayne, 'The Royal Commission's Proposals on Expert Evidence: A Critique' (1994) 2 *Expert Evidence* 157.

[9] *R v Clark* [2003] EWCA Crim 1020; Terry Kirby, 'Devoted mother's agonising wait to win freedom. After three years, two appeals and a huge legal bill, prosecution file no. 89 vindicates solicitor jailed for killing her babies', *The Independent*, 30 January 2003; Joshua Rozenberg, 'Pathologist misled appeal judges in Sally Clark case', *Daily Telegraph*, 12 April 2003.

[10] *R v Jenkins (Sion David)* [2004] EWCA Crim 2047; Jason Bennetto, 'Nine-year ordeal ends as jury acquits Sion Jenkins', *The Independent*, 10 February 2006; Sandra Laville, 'Sion Jenkins acquittal: Scientific evidence – case hinged on mist of blood found on clothes', *The Guardian*, 10 February 2006.

George.[11] Indeed, the association of forensic science and expert witness testimony with miscarriages of justice has a long history, and is today a commonplace of all legal systems that are willing to expose the evidential basis of criminal convictions to a modicum of critical scrutiny.

It is vital to retain a sense of proportion. The benefits of scientific, medical, and other expert evidence are manifest, in the detection of 'volume' crimes like burglary and car theft,[12] as well as in the prosecution of more serious offences including robbery, rape, wounding, and homicide.[13] Generally speaking, scientific evidence compares very favourably against the known infirmities of confessions,[14] eyewitness identification,[15] and other comparatively equivocal forms of evidence, which still nonetheless routinely supply the principal evidential pillar supporting a criminal conviction. Problems with expert evidence tend to materialize when people are seduced into thinking that science is an evidentiary panacea, devoid of blind-spots, limitations, or special demands of its own. The implication of scientific evidence in so many notorious miscarriages of justice ought to serve as a dramatic reminder of what can, and sometimes does, go wrong when courts are taken in by flaky expertise or place too much faith in the wrong kinds of science.

11.2 BEYOND EXPERT 'OPINION': EDUCATION OR DEFERENCE?

An expert is often called on to report facts observable or intelligible only to a trained eye (sometimes with the assistance of specialist equipment like an electronic microscope) and to draw conclusions from these direct observations. An expert might also, or instead, be invited to express a view on the basis of information supplied by others. For instance, a pathologist might state his opinion of the cause of death based on a police report describing the condition of the victim's body when first recovered. Or a toolmark examiner might work from photographs of the damaged window rather than drawing upon her own personal observations. Whether this 'distance' between expert and primary data affects the quality of the evidence, and if so how and to what degree, always depends on the type of expertise in question and the particular facts of the case. Forensic chemists and biologists, for example, regularly work with samples supplied to them by police scenes of crimes officers (SOCOs) and lab technicians without in principle diminishing the validity of their scientific conclusions, provided that the physical integrity of the evidence is properly maintained (e.g. by using 'tamper-proof' packaging to guard against accidental

---

[11] *R v George (Barry)* [2007] EWCA Crim 2722; Duncan Campbell, 'A whispered thank-you and Barry George walks free: Eccentric cleared of Dando murder after spending eight years in prison', *The Guardian*, 2 August 2008.

[12] Sarah-Anne Bradbury and Andy Feist, *The Use of Forensic Science in Volume Crime Investigations: A Review of the Research Literature*, Home Office Online Report 43/05 (RDS, 2005), www.homeoffice.gov. uk/rds/pdfs05/rdsolr4305.pdf. Cf. Carole McCartney, 'The DNA Expansion Programme and Criminal Investigation' (2006) 46 *British Journal of Criminology* 175.

[13] For general discussion, see Robin Williams and Paul Johnson, *Genetic Policing: The Use of DNA in Criminal Investigations* (Willan, 2008); *The Forensic Use of Bioinformation: Ethical Issues* (Nuffield Council on Bioethics, 2007); Carole McCartney, *Forensic Identification and Criminal Justice* (Willan, 2006).

[14] Chapter 12.   [15] §15.4.

cross-contamination) and continuity of the chain of evidence can be demonstrated. The probative value of other types of evidence is more likely to suffer if the expert is working from second-hand information supplied by others. Thus, a medical assessment of a victim's wounds or a psychiatrist's evaluation of the accused's mental health are bound to be less satisfactory in the absence of direct medical examination by the reporting expert.

The formal juridical distinction between 'facts' and 'opinions', which is usually assumed to differentiate expert evidence from other sources of information in criminal litigation, is impossible to sustain in practice. Consider, for example, a pathologist who testifies to the presence of bruising around the deceased's neck *and* to the likely cause of death being strangulation. Or a toolmark examiner who testifies that distinctive marks observed on a window damaged by a burglar in gaining entry match up sufficiently closely with a jemmy recovered from the accused's shed to allow one to conclude that the jemmy was probably used in the burglary. Just as we saw, in Chapter 4, that 'facts' and 'opinions' run together in the evidence of ordinary witnesses,[16] there is no self-evident way of distilling out the primitive 'factual' elements from the interpretative framework of 'opinion' in expert witness testimony.

The foregoing unexceptional examples of medical and forensic science hint at the complexities involved in assessing the probative value of expert evidence. The distinctive feature of expert evidence is not that it comes in the form of an 'opinion', but rather that it often blends together different types of fact. Matters of direct observation, like the temperature of a body or the condition of a window, are clearly facts. But so, too, are the factual generalizations comprising the accumulated knowledge of a scientific discipline. It is these generalizations on which experts draw, and which they weave together with their personal professional experience, in order to arrive at scientific conclusions. What really distinguishes different types of fact for forensic purposes is their relative testability and means of verification, rather than their position on the continuum between 'fact' and 'opinion'.

In principle, if not always in practice, primary evidential facts are open to relatively unmediated forms of proof. For example, the nature of bruising on the victim's neck or marks on a window frame can be verified by the testimony of the investigating police officers, and shown to the jury in photographs or even, these days, in a video-recording of the scene of the crime. Expert evidence, by contrast, seems more opaque, mediated, and impervious to standard forensic means of verification. If a pathologist testifies that, on the basis of a medical literature search and his personal involvement in scores of previous similar cases, the bruising found on the deceased's neck is indicative of strangulation, how is the jury supposed to evaluate the validity of this information? It would be possible, though extremely inconvenient, for jurors to work their way through the relevant literature on cases of strangulation in specialist medical journals. Yet even on the doubtful assumption that a lay person could pick up a specialist medical journal and make head or tail of its contents, jurors would still lack a qualified pathologist's training and experience. Even after a month in the library, it could not be said that jurors would be in a position to verify, or contest, the pathologist's diagnosis of strangulation in anything like the way in which a photograph of the deceased's neck would allow jurors to 'see for themselves' the nature of the bruising.

[16] §4.3.

The distinctive nature of the facts to which experts testify presents a fundamental choice in the reception of scientific evidence between juror education and juror deference. Traditional theory has it that the role of the expert is to furnish lay fact-finders with the specialist knowledge they require to return a well-informed, true verdict on the facts of the case. Expert witnesses are not supposed to pre-empt the jury's determinations, even on technical or scientific matters beyond lay knowledge or experience. When summing-up at the close of trial proceedings judges frequently instruct jurors that it is permissible for them to reject even uncontested expert testimony if, for some reason, the jury chooses not to accept it.[17] Conversely, a conviction may be quashed on appeal where the judge has improperly directed the jury that they must rely on the expert's findings and not seek to draw their own conclusions.[18]

The proper role of scientific experts was explained by Lord President Cooper in a Scottish case, *Davie* v *Edinburgh Magistrates*, which was subsequently adopted as the leading authority in England and Wales as well:

Their duty is to furnish the judge or jury with the necessary scientific criteria for testing the accuracy of their conclusions, so as to enable the judge or jury to form their own independent judgment by the application of these criteria to the facts proved in evidence.[19]

This approach is plainly animated by the desire to constrain experts' influence on the outcome of criminal trials. It implies some conception of juror instruction or education. Expert evidence must inform jurors on specialist topics so that the jury itself, as the designated fact-finder in contested criminal cases, will be able to form its own independent conclusions of fact, even on recondite questions of a scientific or technical nature. Yet, as our last pathologist hypothetical indicates, the aspiration to juror education is founded on a naïve understanding of the types of fact involved in forensic expertise.

Although there may be some limited scope for juror education at trial,[20] it is usually more realistic to characterize expert testimony as commanding juror *deference*. That is to say, jurors simply accept and adopt an expert's conclusions within the scope of the expert's specialist expertise as valid and reliable.[21] After all, the legal process calls upon scientific experts precisely because they are expected to be able to contribute to the administration

---

[17] *R* v *Byrne* [1960] 2 QB 396, 403–4; *R* v *Dietschmann* [2003] 1 AC 1209, HL. JSB Specimen Direction No 33 includes this advice to jurors: 'You should bear in mind that if, having given the matter careful consideration, you do not accept the evidence of the expert/s, you do not have to act upon it. [Indeed, you do not have to accept even the unchallenged evidence of an expert].' But cf. *R* v *Matheson* [1958] 1 WLR 474; *R* v *Bailey* (1978) 66 Cr App R 31, 32 (suggesting that, although 'of course juries are not bound by what the medical witnesses say', yet 'at the same time they must act on evidence, and if there is nothing before them, no facts and no circumstances shown before them which throw doubt on the medical evidence, then that is all that they are left with, and the jury, in those circumstances, must accept it').

[18] *R* v *Flynn and St John* [2008] 2 Cr App R 20, [2008] EWCA Crim 970.

[19] *Davie* v *Edinburgh Magistrates* [1953] SC 34, 40; applied, e.g., in *R* v *Gilfoyle* [2001] 2 Cr App R 57, 67, CA; *R* v *JP* [1999] Crim LR 401 (Transcript on LEXIS).

[20] See Edward J. Imwinkelreid, 'The Next Step in Conceptualizing the Presentation of Expert Evidence as Education: the Case for Didactic Trial Procedures' (1997) 1 *E & P* 128; Gary Edmond, 'The Next Step or Moonwalking? Expert Evidence, the Public Understanding of Science and the Case Against Imwinkelreid's Didactic Trial Procedures' (1998) 2 *E & P* 13; Imwinkelreid, 'Correspondence: Didactic Trial Procedures' (1998) 2 *E & P* 205. Cf. the Court of Appeal's dim view of attempts to educate jurors in the use of Bayes Theorem in the *Adams* litigation, recounted in §4.5(d).

[21] The argument is cogently developed by Ronald J. Allen, 'Expertise and the *Daubert* Decision' (1994) 84 *Journal of Criminal Law and Criminology* 1157.

of criminal justice knowledge or experience beyond the competence of lay fact-finders. Epistemic authority is a defining feature of expertise in general.[22] Even if in principle it might be possible to equip juries with the understanding attained by experts through long years of study and practical experience, by putting them through some kind of litigation crash-course in science for beginners, it would rarely be cost-effective to attempt to do so.

According to the juror deference model, expert evidence presents jurors with a simple choice: either accept what an expert says wholesale and at face-value, or reject the expert's evidence – or some part of it – on irrational grounds. This may be the most realistic account of the reception of expert evidence in English criminal trials, but the deference model is not free from dilemmas of its own, as Ron Allen perceptively observes:

> Jurors or judges who cannot understand the reasoning of a witness can only accept or reject the witness' conclusions, but neither acceptance nor rejection will occur rationally. The choice will not be made because a fact finder understands the reasoning and sees either its cogency or its flaws; it will be made for some other reason. And the set of 'some other reasons' is, from the point of view of the law's aspirations, filled with unsavory characters.[23]

Such 'unsavoury characters' include irrelevant considerations, like the eloquence or charisma of a particular expert witness, and prejudicial grounds for accepting or rejecting testimony, such as a juror's personal animus or lack of comprehension. The prospect of passive juror deference underlines the importance of ensuring, so far as possible, that expert evidence given in court is valid and reliable. Yet monitoring the validity and reliability of scientific evidence presents a stern challenge to the legal process. The traditional forensic tools for evaluating testimony – cross-examination and scrutiny of a witness's demeanour – are patently ill-suited to the job of testing expert evidence, even on the assumption (which, as we have seen, has been challenged) that these tools are effective in assessing the evidence of ordinary witnesses.[24]

The problem is especially acute, moreover, where there is disagreement between experts called by the parties. What should conscientious jurors do when *conflicting* scientific advice pre-empts the simple and relatively safe option of deference to expertise? In cases of genuine[25] conflict, accepting one expert's testimony necessarily implies rejecting the authority of another expert, but how is the jury to choose between them? Informed observers have contemplated this dilemma for over a century,[26] but there are seemingly no simple solutions to this perennial challenge. Ultimately, in cases of unresolved doubt, the jury should fall back on the burden and standard of proof to acquit the accused, unless there is other evidence in the case which is independently sufficient to establish the accused's guilt beyond reasonable doubt.

English law has relied chiefly on the traditional evidentiary tests of relevance and admissibility to shut out unreliable scientific evidence before it can reach the fact-finder.

---

[22] See Harry Collins and Robert Evans, *Rethinking Expertise* (Chicago UP, 2007); Alvin I. Goldman, *Pathways to Knowledge: Private and Public* (OUP, 2002), ch 7.

[23] Allen, 'Expertise and the *Daubert* Decision', 1175.   [24] §7.1(c).

[25] It is sometimes possible to suggest a reconciliation where the conflict is only apparent, where for example experts have built their theories or undertaken statistical analysis etc. on the basis of different factual scenarios supplied by the parties. In these cases the experts' results differ only because they began with different factual suppositions, not because of some deep *scientific* disagreement between them.

[26] Learned Hand, 'Historical and Practical Considerations Regarding Expert Testimony' (1901) 15 *Harvard LR* 40, 54–5.

Provided that expert testimony satisfies these threshold criteria, the orthodox method of ensuring its reliability is 'to subject the evidence to rigorous testing in the witness box'.[27] However, this strategy has not been wholly satisfactory, not least because the precise formulation of the rules applicable to expert evidence continues to be dogged by confusion and controversy. These rules will be examined in section four of this chapter, where 'helpfulness' will be advocated as the essential criterion of admissibility. Before considering the specific role of evidentiary rules in harnessing the power of science to the administration of criminal justice, however, we need to develop a deeper understanding of the precise nature of that challenge. In particular, we need to say more about the credentials of forensic 'expertise' and to explore the problem of the inept, corrupt, or 'biased' expert.

11.3 QUALIFIED EXPERTISE AND THE PROBLEM OF BIAS

English courts have for centuries gratefully received and relied on the evidence of experts in matters requiring specialized knowledge or training beyond the competence of ordinary judges and jurors. As long ago as the mid-sixteenth century, Saunders J declared in *Buckley* v *Rice Thomas*:

[I]f matters arise in our law which concern other sciences or faculties, we commonly apply for the aid of that science or faculty which it concerns. Which is an honourable and commendable thing in our law. For thereby it appears that we do not despise all other sciences but our own, but we approve of them and encourage them as things worthy of commendation... [I]n an appeal of mayhem the Judges of our law have used to be informed by surgeons whether it be a mayhem or not, because their knowledge and skill can best discern it.[28]

There are two essential elements of legitimate expert evidence: (i) a genuine expert, (ii) with expertise in a genuine science, technology, practical skill, or field of learning. Mixing and matching these elements, one could have a fake expert in a genuine science, like a 'doctor' who never went to medical school; or a genuine expert in a fake science, somebody learned in the lore of alchemy, palmistry, astrology, witchcraft, etc. Neither is a good combination for the law. Only genuine experts in genuine fields of expertise can supply or contribute towards the epistemic warrant for a legitimate verdict in a criminal trial.

The difficult task of identifying the departments and parameters of authentic scientific knowledge will be explored later in the chapter, after we have clarified the legal rules of admissibility specifically pertaining to expert evidence. This section examines the expert witness's credentials. We begin with the law's – notably liberal – normative standards for qualifying a witness as an 'expert', before moving on to consider the forensic challenges posed by incompetent or 'biased' experts.

---

[27] *R* v *Atkins* [2009] EWCA Crim 1876, [27]. For illuminating general discussion, see Stephen D. Easton, 'That is Not all There Is: Enhancing *Daubert* Exclusion by Applying "Ordinary" Witness Principles to Experts' (2006) 84 *Nebraska LR* 675.

[28] *Buckley* v *Rice Thomas* (1554) 1 Plowden 118, 124–5, CB. Also see *Folkes* v *Chadd* (1782) 3 Doug KB 157; W. M. Best, *The Principles of the Law of Evidence* (Sweet & Maxwell, 12th edn. 1922), 436; Learned Hand, 'Historical and Practical Considerations Regarding Expert Testimony' (1901) 15 *Harvard LR* 40; H. A. Hammelmann, 'Expert Evidence' (1947) 10 *MLR* 32.

(a) LEGAL QUALIFICATION

At the most basic level of analysis, expert qualification is conceptually (not merely contingently) related to *relevance*, the first hurdle of admissibility for all evidence adduced in criminal trials.[29] Fake experts, or exponents of fake sciences, cannot provide information pertinent to resolving matters at issue in a criminal trial because such testimony would, at best, be worthless. There is no logical or common sense reason why a fact-finder should place any reliance on what pseudo-scientists might say. A genuine expert in some fringe discipline like astrology or alchemy, which lacks any basis in validated scientific principles or methodology, can provide no more rational basis for judgment than an unqualified charlatan posing as an expert in an established science.[30] Likewise, it is on simple grounds of irrelevance that courts also reject the testimony of laymen on matters which call for special expertise. Clinical diagnosis of mental illness[31] and the comparison of handwriting samples[32] are examples of matters on which the courts long ago decided that only the testimony of a properly qualified expert can be received.

Expert qualification can also be conceptualized as a question of *competence* – the competence of an expert to supply information within her properly qualified sphere of expertise. Competence might be viewed as another way of expressing categorical judgments of relevance and irrelevance. Charlatan experts as a category are deemed incompetent to testify in criminal trials, and the presumptive irrelevance of anything they might say is the rationale for treating them as incompetent. Thinking about the issue in terms of witness competency places greater emphasis on the credibility of individual experts. However, it hardly meets the case to say that the charlatan expert lacks credibility – indeed, by conventional measures, the charlatan may appear highly credible and persuasive. This is precisely why he poses such a serious threat to justice. The problem with the out-and-out charlatan is that he is spouting scientific nonsense, and this goes much deeper than a mere failure of credibility. This radical epistemic shortcoming undermines *the validity* of scientific evidence. Pseudo-expert testimony that cannot be squared with any logical, rational, informed, genuinely scientific view of the world falls at the first hurdle of admissibility – to admit it would fly in the face of logic and common sense. The practical challenge for trial judges is to distinguish pseudo-science from the genuine article when ostensibly well-credentialled experts present themselves in court. Exposing artful fakery, needless to add, is easier said than done, the more so where individual experts are genuinely convinced of their own insight and infallibility.

In the final analysis it is largely a matter of linguistic convenience whether we say that charlatan experts are incompetent as witnesses or that their evidence is irrelevant or that they fail some notional 'expert qualification rule'. What must be stressed under any of these formulations is that English courts adopt a notably liberal and flexible approach to assessing the qualifications of expert witnesses. In practice, this doctrinal pre-condition adds little if anything to the basic test of relevance and generally promotes the reception of expert testimony.

---

[29] §3.2.

[30] It is true that many people habitually check 'their stars' in the daily papers. However, even if some readers consider astrology anything more than light entertainment, few if any would want to see issues in criminal trials determined by astrologers!   [31] R v *Loake* (1911) 7 Cr App R 71, CCA.

[32] R v *Rickard* (1918) 13 Cr App R 140, CCA.

There is no requirement of formal training or paper qualifications, relevant professional employment or experience, or even membership of a related organization or learned
society. The well-known case of *Silverlock*[33] decided that a witness's informal interest and
study were sufficient to qualify him as an expert in handwriting analysis. As Lord Russell
of Killowen CJ explained, the question is simply whether or not the witness possesses
expert knowledge relevant to an issue before the tribunal, irrespective of how he or she
might have acquired it:

It is true that the witness who is called upon to give evidence founded on a comparison of
handwritings must be *peritus*; he must be skilled in doing so; but we cannot say that he must
have become *peritus* in the way of his business or in any definite way. The question is, is he
peritus? Is he skilled? Has he an adequate knowledge? Looking at the matter practically, if a
witness is not skilled the judge will tell the jury to disregard his evidence. There is no decision which requires that the evidence of a man who is skilled in comparing handwriting,
and who has formed a reliable opinion from past experience, should be excluded because his
experience had not been gained in the way of his business.[34]

It is not difficult to find case-law illustrations of the courts' catholic conception of expertise. A drug user with no scientific training or knowledge has been permitted to identify a
substance in his possession as heroin,[35] and drug-squad officers may give expert testimony
on the street prices and routine commercial practices of the drugs trade.[36] In another
memorable case, membership of the Inner Circle of Magic qualified a witness as 'a highly
expert magician'.[37] In 1993 the Court of Appeal said that it was perfectly proper for an
artist to give 'facial mapping' evidence, even though he had 'no scientific qualifications,
no specific training, no professional body and no database'.[38] Sixteen years later, in a case
co-incidentally involving the same facial-mapping expert, the Court of Appeal reaffirmed
this position.[39]

Perhaps most revealing of all is the remarkable holding in *Clare and Peach*,[40] which
concerned acts of violent disorder at a football match. The court permitted a police officer
to testify that he recognized the accused from closed circuit video footage of the incident.
Although the images on the tape were indistinct, the officer claimed he could make a
positive identification because he had watched the tape many times over in preparation
for the trial. The Court of Appeal endorsed the trial judge's decision to admit the evidence, on the basis that the police officer had become an 'expert *ad hoc*' through his close
study of the videotape. The expert *ad hoc* is a controversial arrival on the English legal
scene, and *Clare and Peach* may have been wrongly decided.[41] More recently, the Court

---

[33] *R v Silverlock* [1894] 2 QB 766, CCR.

[34] ibid. 771. Mathew J thought the handwriting evidence 'clearly admissible', and Day, Vaughan Williams,
and Kennedy JJ all concurred in the judgment of the Lord Chief Justice.

[35] *R v Chatwood* [1980] 1 WLR 874, CA, *per* Forbes J: 'these drug abusers were expressing an opinion, and
an informed opinion, that, having so used the substance which they did use, it was indeed heroin, because
they were experienced in the effects of heroin'.   [36] *R v Hodges* [2003] 2 Cr App R 247, CA.

[37] *Moore* v *Medley, The Times*, 3 February 1955, cited by J. C. Smith, *Criminal Evidence* (Sweet & Maxwell,
1995), 113.   [38] *R v Stockwell* (1993) 97 Cr App R 260, 264, CA.

[39] *R v Atkins* [2009] EWCA Crim 1876.

[40] *R v Clare and Peach* [1995] Crim LR 947, CA. Also see *R v Oakley* [1979] RTR 417, CA.

[41] Having considered a *dictum* of Maule J in *Crouch* (1850) 4 Cox CC 163 and the Court of Criminal
Appeal's decision in *R v Rickard* (1918) 13 Cr App R 140, the Court of Appeal in *R v Robb* (1991) 93 Cr App
R 161, 168, expressed the view that '[t]he ratio of these cases is.... that a witness cannot qualify as an expert

of Appeal has warned that 'this description is unhelpful, since those who acquire the specialist knowledge cannot in our view properly be referred to as experts'.[42] This remark in turn invites the question why the legal concept of 'expertise' must exclude skills or knowledge acquired specifically for the task in hand; but there is little profit in pursuing such definitional perplexities. For our purposes, the significance of the 'expert *ad hoc*' is that only a legal test of expert competency closely approximating threshold relevance could have produced such an ambivalent character. In truth, the legal standard of expertise appears to be nothing more exotic than a particularized application to the testimony of experts of the first hurdle to admissibility which applies to all evidence adduced in criminal trials.

(b) FORENSIC BIAS

For as long as there have been expert witnesses in English criminal proceedings, there has also been the concomitant fear that people holding themselves out as *bona fide* experts might lack proper credentials, exhibit bias, or even be outright impostors and charlatans. People who make their living from providing expert evidence to the courts are inevitably motivated to some extent by financial considerations. Even those who view themselves as crusaders for justice, like solicitors of similar ilk, still have a business to run. Moreover, the risks of deliberate partisanship and unconscious bias are bound to be exacerbated in an adversarial system of criminal procedure in which experts are instructed, and paid for, directly by the prosecution and defence lawyers themselves.

Taylor's early-twentieth century *Treatise* addressed the problem of expert bias with a measure of tact and sophistication:

[I]t is often quite surprising to see with what facility, and to what an extent [expert witnesses'] views can be made to correspond with the wishes or the interests of the parties who call them. They do not, indeed, wilfully misrepresent what they think, but their judgments become so warped by regarding the subject in one point of view, that, even when conscientiously disposed, they are incapable of forming an independent opinion.[43]

With rather less delicacy, Lord Campbell declared in the *Tracy Peerage Case* that 'skilled witnesses come with such bias on their minds to support the case in which they are embarked that hardly any weight should be given to their evidence'.[44] Modern variations

---

entitled to give evidence of opinion by making an examination during and for the very purpose of the investigation in question. It prohibits policemen engaged in an investigation from putting themselves forward as instant experts in order to advance that investigation. To permit such evidence would conflict with the fundamental principle that a skill depending on education, training or experience beyond the range of the average man (which alone qualifies a witness to give his opinion as an expert) cannot be acquired on the instant.' And see Roderick Munday, 'Videotape Evidence and the Advent of the Expert *Ad Hoc*' (1995) 159 *Justice of the Peace* 547.

[42] *R v Flynn and St John* [2008] 2 Cr App R 20, [2008] EWCA Crim 970, [14] (Gage LJ).

[43] John Pitt Taylor, *Treatise on the Law of Evidence* (Sweet & Maxwell, 12th edn. 1931), 59. It is recognized that even lawyers, who are officers of the court, cannot help judging matters from their clients' point of view: *Columbia Picture Industries* v *Robinson* [1986] 3 All ER 338, 370, 375.

[44] *Tracy Peerage Case* (1843) 10 Cl & F 191, quoted by H. A. Hammelmann, 'Expert Evidence' (1947) 10 *MLR* 32, 39, who adds that this acidic evaluation 'still holds good to a large extent today'.

on this venerable theme continue to be recycled by commentators,[45] and do the rounds in practitioners' anecdotal tales of 'cowboys', 'hired guns', 'instant experts', and 'liars for hire'.[46]

Setting aside countless unverified war stories and some isolated instances of documented bad practice,[47] there is no evidence of systematic charlatanism or other abuses of expertise in modern English criminal proceedings. Every occupational barrel must inevitably contain a few rotten apples. But the employees of the Forensic Science Service (FSS), who undertake predominantly prosecution work, and the private firms of 'forensic examiners' with mainly defence practices, appear for the most part to be well-qualified experts displaying skill and integrity. Nor is English criminal litigation awash with 'junk science' – bogus theories and data masquerading as reliable scientific information – as the American tort system, for example, is said to be.[48]

There have been occasions when individual scientists overstated their cases, or were too wrapped up in a pet scientific theory to admit, or even notice, that they had made a crucial mistake. The names of Alan Clift in relation to the *Preece* Affair,[49] and of Dr Frank Skuse and his Home Office and RARDE[50] colleagues in relation to the *Birmingham Six*, *Maguire Seven*, and *Judith Ward* cases,[51] are amongst the most prominent entries in the rogues'

---

[45] 'Constructing the legal case may…be described as an exercise in competitive lying', according to Carol A. G. Jones, *Expert Witnesses: Science, Medicine, and the Practice of Law* (OUP, 1994), 165 (this quotation is taken from a chapter dealing with civil litigation, but criminal proceedings are not exempted from the general (theoretically-driven) indictment).

[46] See Roberts and Willmore, *The Role of Forensic Science Evidence in Criminal Proceedings*, 83. The standard fears, and some of the reasons for crediting them, are wittily surveyed by J. E. Starrs, 'In the Land of Agog: An Allegory for the Expert Witness' (1985) 30 *Journal of Forensic Sciences* 289.

[47] R. H. L. Disney, 'Fraudulent Forensic Scientists' (2002) 45 *Journal de Médecine Légale Droit Médical* 225; Zakaria Erzinçlioglu, 'British Forensic Science in the Dock' (1998) 392 *Nature* 859 (30 April). In *Lillie and Reed* v *Newcastle City Council* [2002] EWHC 1600 (QB), [393], an expert consultant paediatrician diagnosing child abuse was found to have been 'prepared to make up the deficiencies by throwing objectivity and scientific rigour to the winds in a highly emotional misrepresentation of the facts'.

[48] Peter W. Huber, *Galileo's Revenge: Junk Science in the Courtroom* (Basic Books, 1991). Huber, in his turn, has been condemned as a politically-motivated protagonist pedalling shoddy scholarship: Jeff L. Lewin, 'Calabresi's Revenge? Junk Science in the Work of Peter Huber' (1992) 21 *Hofstra LR* 183; Kenneth J. Chesebro, 'Galileo's Retort: Peter Huber's Junk Scholarship' (1993) 42 *American University LR* 1637. See further, Paul C. Giannelli, '"Junk Science": The Criminal Cases' (1993) 84 *Journal of Criminal Law and Criminology* 105; David E. Bernstein, 'Junk Science in the United States and the Commonwealth' (1996) 21 *Yale Journal of International Law* 123; Joseph Sanders, 'From Science to Evidence: The Testimony on Causation in the Bendectin Cases' (1993) 46 *Stanford LR* 1; Michael H. Graham, 'The *Daubert* Dilemma: At Last A Viable Solution' (1998) 2 *E & P* 211 (arguing for a more *liberal* approach to the admissibility of tort plaintiffs' expert evidence).

[49] *Preece* v *HM Advocate* [1981] Crim LR 783. See Parliamentary Commissioner for Administration, 4th Report, HC Paper 191, Session 1983–84; Phillips and Bowen, *Forensic Science and the Expert Witness*, ch 1; Mick Hamer, 'How A Forensic Scientist Fell Foul of the Law' (1981) 91 *New Scientist* 575; Jones, *Expert Witnesses*, 230–7.

[50] The former Royal Armament Research and Development Establishment, since superseded by the Defence Science and Technology Laboratory: www.dstl.gov.uk/.

[51] *R* v *McIlkenny* (1991) 93 Cr App R 287, CA; *R* v *Maguire* (1992) 94 Cr App R 133, CA; *R* v *Ward* (1993) 96 Cr App R 1, CA. The shortcomings of the scientific evidence relied on to convict the Maguires are painstakingly laid bare in the two reports of Sir John May's *Inquiry into the Circumstances Surrounding the Convictions Arising Out of the Bomb Attacks on Guildford and Woolwich in 1974*, HC Paper 556 (1990) and HC Paper 296 (1992). For commentary, see Mike Redmayne, 'Expert Evidence and Scientific Disagreement' (1997) 30 *UC Davis LR* 1027; Clive Walker and Russell Stockdale, 'Forensic Evidence and Terrorist Trials in

gallery of prosecution forensic scientists gone wrong. On the defence side, meanwhile, there are a handful of practitioners whose conduct is widely regarded as scientifically unsound or unethical by their scientific peers.[52] However, these are seemingly isolated instances; albeit that even occasional scientific malpractice may entail very serious consequences for those wrongly convicted.

A more systematic source of apparent bias arises from the way in which some police officers and lawyers selectively brief the experts they instruct about the factual background to the case, and then press 'their' experts to come up with definite conclusions in their scientific reports and courtroom testimony.[53] Such 'information management' may sometimes be a deliberate litigation strategy to slant an expert's conclusions in a particular direction favourable to the instructing party. But it could also arise from simple lack of communication and mutual misunderstanding between forensic scientists, police, and lawyers.

Prosecutors and defence lawyers look to science to provide clear and straightforward answers, preferably answers that support their side's version of events. If pressed, however, most criminal litigators would probably say that the overriding desideratum is a clear conclusion either way, so that case management and crucial decisions, including (for prosecutors) whether to discontinue proceedings and (for defence lawyers) whether to tender a guilty plea, can proceed on a surer evidential footing. Scientists, by contrast, are trained to think in terms of probabilities and to hedge their conclusions with qualifications.[54] The result of this clash of disciplinary methodologies may be exasperation on both sides, with justice the loser. Lawyers may perceive pedantic fastidiousness, excessive equivocation, and unhelpful stonewalling, whilst experts experience what they take to be untoward pressures to compromise the professional standards and integrity of their science. A significant part of the perceived problem of expert 'bias' might consequently be an artefact of adversarial criminal procedure. Scientific experts are lured or manoeuvred into adopting adversarial postures by lawyers looking for just a little bit more 'clarification' or certainty in the expression of an opinion. Expert witnesses occupy a precarious position in adversarial criminal proceedings, since they are constantly at risk of being criticized for failing to live up to the law's unrealistic demands for scientific impartiality and objectivity.

A related source of what might be regarded as 'charlatanism' in criminal trials is attributable to genuine experts testifying beyond the parameters of their legitimate expertise. On a purist view, it is hardly less discreditable for a genuine expert to trespass on a field of expertise beyond the ambit of his qualifications than for a person with no qualifications whatever to hold himself out as a *bona fide* expert. Both abuses present an identical danger, that the jury will deferentially adopt a proposition of fact lacking scientific validity. An opinion on a question of fact carries no special weight just because

the United Kingdom' (1995) 54 CLJ 69; Robert Kee, *Trial & Error* (Hamish Hamilton, 1986) ch 14; Jones, *Expert Witnesses*, ch 10; 'Ward Scientists Condemned', *The Guardian*, 5 June 1992.

[52] Cf. Roberts and Willmore, *The Role of Forensic Science Evidence*, 84; R. H. L. Disney, 'Fraudulent Forensic Scientists' (2002) 45 *Journal de Médecine Légale Droit Médical* 225.

[53] These phenomena are reported by Roberts and Willmore, *The Role of Forensic Science Evidence*, esp. §§2.3, 2.4, 2.6(b), 2.8, 3.5, 3.6, and chs 4–5.

[54] See, e.g., D. J. Gee, 'The Expert Witness in the Criminal Trial' [1987] *Crim LR* 307; H. J. Walls, 'What is "Reasonable Doubt"? A Forensic Scientist Looks at the Law' [1971] *Crim LR* 458.

it happens to be expressed by an expert qualified in a different field. But how is the jury supposed to be able to differentiate between expert opinion and the mere opinions of an expert?

Perhaps there are certain individuals whose celebrity status as a recognized expert witness has gone to their head, emboldening them to make *ex cathedra* pronouncements on a variety of subjects beyond the legitimate scope of their expertise.[55] For such *blaggeurs*, the cap of charlatanism fits well enough and they should rightly be made to wear it. But the problem of disciplinary over-reaching cannot be so easily dismissed as a vice of personal vanity. For one thing, many fields of expertise overlap in the forensic context, where science is by definition applied rather than pure. An important example is DNA evidence, which is underpinned by statistical calculations[56] as well as by the physical biology of genetics.[57] It is consequently very easy for a properly qualified biologist, for example, to stray into cognate fields, like population genetics or demography, in which a biologist may lack training and confidence. Moreover, adversarial trials tend to encourage expert witnesses to do just that. Put on the spot to elaborate on her conclusions, a biologist in the witness-box might be tempted to try to bluff her way through the statistical elements of her evidence, rather than admit to not being able to vouch for its statistical foundation. The dilemma for the expert is that if she concedes doubt about one part of her evidence, the fact-finder may infer that the whole of her testimony is unreliable and should be rejected, even though its biological component may be perfectly sound.

In reality, the problem is not so much one of the expert's own making, but rather stems from widespread public ignorance of the disciplinary divisions and subdivisions within modern science. The better course would be for counsel to ensure that they have assembled an appropriately qualified team of expert witnesses who are, in combination, competent to testify to every scientific aspect of the case. However, this would require lawyers to be much better informed about the disciplinary boundaries demarcating scientific expertise than, by all accounts, they currently are. More and more, the problem of expert qualification and the risks of biased scientific evidence appear to stem from the institutional limitations of criminal proceedings, rather than reflecting the inadequacies of scientific method or the failings of individual experts *per se*. This line of thought seems to run in the direction of more wide-ranging criminal procedure reform, a suggestion subjected to critical analysis in this chapter's concluding section.

---

[55] It is said of great figures of the early years of modern expert witnessing, like the renowned pathologist Sir Bernard Spilsbury, that their word in court was treated like holy writ, making both the temptation to embroidery and its consequent mischief all the greater: cf. Alec Bourne, 'I have the greatest respect for Sir Bernard when he speaks as a pathologist, but when he dares to give an opinion about the treatment of a living woman, I would regard it with contempt': quoted in K. Simpson, 'Medicine v The Law – Part Heard' (1971) 3 *Australian Journal of Forensic Sciences* 114, 118. On 'the rise of the medical detective', see Jones, *Expert Witnesses*, ch 5. [56] §4.5.

[57] See National Research Council, *The Evaluation of Forensic DNA Evidence* (National Academy Press, 1996), 25–30 and ch 4; Peter Donnelly and Richard D. Friedman, 'DNA Database Searches and the Legal Consumption of Scientific Evidence' (1999) 97 *Michigan LR* 931; Mike Redmayne, 'Doubts and Burdens: DNA Evidence, Probability and the Courts' [1995] *Crim LR* 464; Richard Lempert, 'Some Caveats Concerning DNA as Criminal Identification Evidence: With Thanks to the Reverend Bayes' (1991) 13 *Cardozo LR* 303.

11.4 RULES OF ADMISSIBILITY

Previous chapters have introduced and developed the idea that rules of admissibility are the law's primary technique for regulating the quality of information presented to the fact-finder at trial. The traditional common rule regulating the admissibility of expert evidence was recently reiterated by the Court of Appeal in *Atkins*:

Evidence of opinion is not ordinarily admissible. Opinion based upon identifiable expertise outside the experience of the jury is one exception. If objection be taken to admissibility (though not otherwise) it must be determined by the judge. It is for him who tenders such evidence to establish the exception, *viz* the expertise and that it is the foundation of the opinion. The power to rule on admissibility applies equally to Crown and defence.[58]

This conventional formulation is problematic, both in terms of what it does say and in terms of what it leaves unsaid. The rule supposedly restricting witness testimony to matters of fact and forbidding any expression of 'opinion' has already been criticized on both theoretical and practical grounds.[59] In any event, as the Court of Appeal observes in *Atkins*, the so-called opinion rule has no bearing on expert evidence, since experts are conventionally said to be exempt from its strictures. It has long been recognized that scientific facts are frequently expressed in the form of an expert's judgment, or 'opinion', about those facts, and the law has, generally speaking, striven to avoid placing artificial fetters on the help that it can receive from experts in settling questions of fact.

It is widely thought that the admissibility of expert evidence is subject to a raft of further doctrinal pre-conditions, which may be expressed as discrete components of a unified 'opinion rule' or as 'rules' of admissibility in their own right. In addition to 'the expert qualification rule' discussed in the previous section, commentators have discerned or imagined various normative standards supposedly regulating the admission of expert evidence in English criminal trials, including:

- the common knowledge rule;
- the abnormality rule;
- the ultimate issue rule; and
- the field of expertise rule.[60]

Each of these creatures of commentary contains more than a grain of truth about the courts' approach to expert testimony. As we will see in this section, however, whilst courts do intermittently refer to 'common knowledge', 'abnormality', and so forth in certain circumstances, elevating such criteria to the status of formal rules of exclusion mischaracterizes judicial practice. It also contributes to the false impression that English courts have

---

[58] *R v Atkins* [2009] EWCA Crim 1876, [9].   [59] §4.3.

[60] For a smattering of illustrations, see I. R. Freckelton, *The Trial of the Expert* (OUP, 1987), chs 3–5 (common knowledge, field of expertise, and ultimate issue); R. D. Mackay and Andrew M. Colman, 'Excluding Expert Evidence: A Tale of Ordinary Folk and Common Experience' [1991] *Crim LR* 800; David H. Sheldon and Malcolm D. MacLeod, 'From Normative to Positive Data: Expert Psychological Evidence Re-Examined' [1991] *Crim LR* 811 (discussing 'common knowledge', 'abnormality', and 'personality' interpretations of *Turner*); Peter Thornton, 'The Admissibility of Expert Psychiatric and Psychological Evidence – Judicial Training' (1995) 35 *Medicine, Science and the Law* 143 (abnormality rule).

constructed elaborate rules to exclude expert testimony, when in fact English law is notably liberal in its approach to the admissibility of expert evidence.

Confusion has arisen because certain judicial pronouncements, which in reality were meant only as contextual applications of settled principles, have been treated as though they laid down some novel precedent or hard-and-fast rule to regulate the reception of expert testimony in future proceedings. The leading case of *Turner*,[61] to where many of the phantom 'rules' trace their origin, has been especially vulnerable to misinterpretation. Fortunately, the law governing the admission of expert evidence can be reconstructed in a way which is not only coherent and reasonably robust in practice, but also greatly simplified.

(a) REAFFIRMING FIRST PRINCIPLES

Recall the basic evidentiary criteria of admissibility introduced in Chapter 3. On first principles, in order to be legally admissible at a criminal trial evidence must be:

1. relevant to a fact in issue; and

2. not rendered inadmissible by any of the generally applicable exclusionary rules, such as the rules excluding hearsay, extraneous misconduct, or unfairly prejudicial evidence (where PV < PE).

The relevance standard applies straightforwardly to expert evidence. No matter how reliable or powerful a particular scientific technique might be in the abstract, it has nothing to contribute to the resolution of criminal cases unless it is directed towards a live issue in the trial. DNA evidence provides an excellent illustration, since it is both reliable and powerful, but also restricted to proving certain types of issue. If, on a charge of rape, the accused puts up an alibi or claims mistaken identity, DNA evidence might provide extremely cogent proof of guilt or innocence. However, if the accused admits intercourse with the complainant and argues consent, DNA evidence has no bearing on the dispute between the parties and cannot be given, because – as a matter of logic and common sense – it is irrelevant to any contested issue in the trial.

Scientific evidence can throw up some tricky issues of relevance which are not always immediately apparent. Suppose that, on a charge of possessing cocaine with intent to supply, banknotes containing traces of cocaine are found in the accused's possession. On a common sense view, the cocaine-contaminated banknotes support the prosecution's case hypothesis that the accused has been dealing in cocaine. Tempting as this inference may be, it is far too quick. We are told that the prevalence of cocaine in the UK today is such that almost all banknotes are impregnated with trace amounts of the drug.[62] The contamination of banknotes by cocaine powder is so widespread that the banknotes currently in your wallet or purse will be just as likely to test positive for trace amounts of cocaine as

---

[61] *R v Turner* [1975] 1 QB 834, CA.

[62] 'More than 99% of the banknotes in circulation in London are tainted with cocaine, according to a study. And one in 20 of the notes show levels high enough to indicate they have been handled by dealers or used to snort the drug': 'UK Banknotes "tainted with cocaine"', BBC News, 4 October 1999, http://news.bbc.co.uk/1/hi/uk/464200.stm; and see Ed Pilkington, 'Traces of cocaine found on up to 90% of dollar bills in American cities', *The Guardian*, 17 August 2009.

banknotes in the possession of a suspected drug-dealer. At this tipping point, banknote evidence *is literally irrelevant* and therefore, on first principles, inadmissible. The prosecution's hypothesis that the contaminated banknotes support the accused's guilt has exactly the same probability as the defence hypothesis that contaminated banknotes could be found in the possession of an entirely innocent person. Where the probability of evidence is exactly the same on both the prosecution and defence hypotheses it cannot rationally alter the overall probability of the accused's guilt or innocence. This is just another, more mathematically rigorous, way of saying that the evidence is irrelevant.[63]

Exactly this scenario arose in the case of Barry George, who in July 2001 was convicted of murdering the TV personality Jill Dando, who was shot to death outside her London home. Part of the evidence at trial was a firearms discharge residue (FDR) particle recovered from the pocket of George's coat, which the prosecution advanced as proof that George had recently fired a gun. In relation to this evidence, the trial judge directed the jury that they must be sure that innocent contamination could be ruled out before treating the particle as probative, but that the prosecution's case would be considerably weakened without the FDR particle evidence. In 2006 the Forensic Science Service (FSS) adopted new analytical protocols, under which evidence of a single particle of FDR was to be reported as 'inconclusive' and entirely lacking in probative value. The risks of secondary transfer and background contamination were now judged to be too great to place any positive interpretation on a single particle of FDR. On a reference back to the Court of Appeal from the Criminal Cases Review Commission, George's conviction was quashed.[64] Lord Phillips CJ explained how the significance of the FDR evidence adduced at trial had been completely transformed on appeal:

A single particle of FDR had been found in the pocket of the appellant's coat. According to the evidence that [the FSS scientist] gave to us, this was an equally unlikely event, whether it had come from the cartridge that killed Miss Dando, or from some innocent source. There was an even chance that it had resulted from innocent contamination. In these circumstances it was not correct for him [at trial] to dismiss as 'most unlikely' the possibility that it had resulted from such contamination.... [W]hen considered objectively that evidence conveyed the impression that the Crown's scientists considered that innocent contamination was unlikely and that, effectively in consequence, it was likely that the source of the single particle was the gun that killed Miss Dando. In that respect their evidence at the trial was in marked conflict with the evidence that they have given to this court with the result that the jury did not have the benefit of a direction that the possibility that the FDR had come from the gun that killed Miss Dando was equally as remote as all other possibilities and thus, on its own, entirely inconclusive. In the light of the way in which [the FSS scientist] now puts the matter, we have no doubt that the jury were misled upon this issue.[65]

The Court of Appeal concluded that the safety of George's conviction had been undermined by the direction given by the trial judge in summing up on the FDR evidence. Their

---

[63] Applying the precepts previously explained in §3.2 and §4.5(c). Trace evidence of cocaine on banknotes could still be relevant to proving drug-dealing if the *level* or *location* of contamination were significant. Also, the prosecution would naturally be permitted to adduce evidence of contamination in rebuttal of any attempt by the defence to suggest that the prosecution's failure to adduce the banknote evidence in the first instance supported the (false) inference that the accused's money was *un*contaminated.

[64] *R v George (Barry)* [2007] EWCA Crim 2722.   [65] ibid. [38], [51].

Lordships' focus possibly reflects the fact that the FDR evidence had already been adduced in the trial, and then the question became what the judge should have told the jury about it in summing-up. However, if the FDR evidence was truly 'neutral' (as it was later described on appeal) then it is difficult to see how it could have been relevant in the first place. In theory, it should never have been adduced. Yet in practice these are not easy determinations, particularly because there is seldom an appropriate database from which rigorous probabilities of relevant events – the likelihood of a UK banknote being contaminated by cocaine; the likelihood of innocent contamination by FDR, etc. – can be calculated. In the absence of hard quantification, it is impossible to identify the tipping point at which relevant evidence with limited probative value becomes *ir*relevant evidence with no probative value. One solution, exemplified by the new FSS guidelines on FDR, is to err on the side of caution by reporting very small amounts of trace material as 'inconclusive' and incapable of supporting any positive inference. It is not so obvious that the same conservative standard of admissibility should be applied to ostensibly exculpatory evidence adduced by the accused. Be that as it may, the more general moral to be extracted from these examples is that assessing relevance, as the first hurdle to legal admissibility, is no mere formality in relation to scientific and other forms of expert evidence.

To overcome the second hurdle to admissibility, relevant evidence must also steer clear of criminal procedure's general exclusionary rules. We have already seen that expert evidence is sometimes rejected because it incorporates inadmissible hearsay evidence.[66] However, in keeping with English law's characteristically permissive approach to expert testimony, the courts have moulded hearsay doctrine in order to accommodate the standard working practices of the scientific community. Thus, experts are permitted to draw upon databases, test results, and academic literature that would normally be rejected as hearsay if relied upon by an ordinary witness of fact.[67] Section 127 of the Criminal Justice Act 2003 extends this indulgence to preparatory lab work conducted by scientific assistants and technicians.[68] At other times expert evidence must be rejected, or at least bowdlerized, because it reveals inadmissible evidence of the accused's bad character. Expert testimony might also be objectionable on occasion because it discloses an inadmissible confession, infringes the privilege against self-incrimination, or constitutes improperly obtained evidence within the scope of section 78 of PACE. Above all, it is the judge's overriding responsibility at common law to exclude prosecution evidence of any description where the probative value of the evidence is outweighed by its likely prejudicial effect (PV < PE).[69]

The two basic hurdles to admissibility are more than mere points of departure for understanding English law's approach to the admissibility of expert evidence. As a matter of positive law, they constitute the greater part of the analysis, though there is extensive

---

[66] §9.6(a): cf. *R* v *Hirst* [1995] 1 Cr App R 82, CA, discussed in Paul Roberts, 'Will You Stand Up in Court? On the Admissibility of Psychiatric and Psychological Evidence' (1996) 7 *Journal of Forensic Psychiatry* 63.

[67] *R* v *Abadom* [1983] 1 WLR 126, CA; *H* v *Schering Chemicals Ltd* [1983] 1 WLR 143, QBD. For general discussion, see Rosemary Pattenden, 'Expert Opinion Evidence Based on Hearsay' [1982] *Crim LR* 85; Paul R. Rice, 'Inadmissible Evidence as a Basis For Expert Opinion Testimony: A Response to Professor Carlson' (1987) 40 *Vanderbilt LR* 583.

[68] Cf. the US Supreme Court's very different approach to this issue in *Melendez-Diaz* v *Massachusetts*, 129 S Ct 2527 (2009), discussed in §9.6(a).

[69] *R* v *Sang* [1980] AC 402, HL; *R* v *Christie* [1914] AC 545, HL. See §2.5(a).

work to be done in stripping away superfluous accretions and restoring the rules to their authentic, uncluttered condition. We now set to work on that restoration project. Our first job, undertaken in subsection (b), is to explain the translation of the familiar PV/PE admissibility standard into a more localized question of the 'helpfulness' of expert evidence, a term which though not inaccurate does require further elucidation. It will be argued that 'helpfulness', as a concrete application of PV > PE, is the genuine test for admitting expert evidence in English criminal trials, whilst notional exclusionary rules based on 'common knowledge', 'abnormality', or foreign precedents are either inauthentic doppelgangers or inconsequential phantoms. Subsection (c) concludes this part of the discussion by briefly despatching the so-called 'ultimate issue rule' to the landfill site for worn out evidentiary concepts. We hold over the important and difficult topic of novel scientific evidence and its purported association with a notional 'field of expertise' rule to detailed analysis in the following section.

(b) HELPFULNESS – THE ONE AND ONLY AUTHENTIC CRITERION OF ADMISSIBILITY

In the leading case of *Turner*,[70] the question for the Court of Appeal was whether an accused charged with murdering his girlfriend could adduce psychiatric evidence to support a plea of provocation. In a much-cited passage Lawton LJ explained that the accused's psychiatric evidence had been properly rejected by the trial judge because it would not have assisted the jury's deliberations in the circumstances of this particular case:

An expert's opinion is admissible to furnish the court with scientific information which is likely to be outside the experience and knowledge of a judge or jury. If on the proven facts a judge or jury can form their own conclusions without help, then the opinion of an expert is unnecessary.... We all know that both men and women who are deeply in love can, and sometimes do, have outbursts of blind rage when discovering unexpected wantonness on the part of their loved ones; the wife taken in adultery is the classical example of the application of the defence of 'provocation': and when death or serious injury results, profound grief usually follows. Jurors do not need psychiatrists to tell them how ordinary folk who are not suffering from any mental illness are likely to react to the stresses and strains of life. It follows that the proposed evidence was not admissible to establish that the defendant was likely to have been provoked....[W]e are firmly of the opinion that psychiatry has not yet become a satisfactory substitute for the common sense of juries or magistrates on matters within their experience of life.[71]

This passage has been taken as authority for the existence of a 'common knowledge' rule, according to which expert evidence cannot be admitted if it concerns matters within the knowledge and experience of 'ordinary folk'.[72] Alternatively or in addition, it has been proposed that expert evidence may only be given of mental abnormality, as opposed to normal mental or psychological processes – an 'abnormality rule' of admissibility.[73] More

---

[70] *R v Turner* [1975] 1 QB 834, CA.   [71] ibid. 841–2, 843.

[72] See I. R. Freckelton, *The Trial of the Expert* (OUP, 1987), ch 3; R. D. Mackay and Andrew M. Colman, 'Excluding Expert Evidence: A Tale of Ordinary Folk and Common Experience' [1991] *Crim LR* 800.

[73] Discussed by, e.g., David H. Sheldon and Malcolm D. MacLeod, 'From Normative to Positive Data: Expert Psychological Evidence Re-Examined' [1991] *Crim LR* 811, 816–19; Peter Thornton, 'The Admissibility

expansively, Lawton LJ's observations are held up as a typical example of legal ignorance and hostility towards science in general, and mental health professionals in particular. However, even if these constructions can fairly be placed on Lawton LJ's *Turner* judgment (which is very much open to doubt), they grievously misrepresent judicial approaches to the admissibility of expert evidence in the general run of criminal trials.

Turner's critics rightly observe that expert testimony might still be helpful to jurors even if it concerns matters broadly within the sphere of general knowledge or questions of normal psychology. Jurors are unlikely to share an expert's detailed, systematic knowledge of specific aspects of normal psychological processes, for example. Where 'common sense' beliefs are a witches' brew of genuine knowledge and folkloric invention, an expert might be able to help jurors to disentangle fact from fiction and to evaluate the disputed evidence more objectively. It is for these sound reasons that the courts do *not* systematically apply any 'common knowledge' or 'abnormality' standard. Such criteria are never more than rough rules of thumb to guide the application of the helpfulness standard in particular cases. A clear illustration is *Stockwell*,[74] which concerned expert 'facial mapping' evidence identifying the accused from security camera footage of a robbery. Having quoted from the relevant passage in *Turner*, Lord Taylor continued:

It is to be noted that Lawton LJ there referred to a jury forming their own conclusions 'without help'. Where, for example, there is a clear photograph and no suggestion that the subject has changed his appearance, a jury could usually reach a conclusion without help. Where, as here, however, it is admitted that the appellant had grown a beard shortly before his arrest, and it is suggested further that the robber may have been wearing clear spectacles and a wig for disguise, a comparison of photograph and defendant may not be straightforward. In such circumstances we can see no reason why expert evidence, if it can provide the jury with information and assistance they would otherwise lack, should not be given. In each case it must be for the judge to decide whether the issue is one on which the jury could be assisted by expert evidence...[75]

If English law really did sponsor a 'common knowledge' rule, expert evidence of identification from a photograph could not have been received in *Stockwell*. Looking at photographs is hardly an arcane activity, yet the Court of Appeal endorsed the reception of expert evidence where it was felt that jurors would benefit from further assistance in a matter well within their everyday experience. The decision in *Stockwell* was recently emphatically reaffirmed in *Atkins*.[76] The existence of a 'common knowledge' rule is also directly contradicted by the case of *Clare and Peach*,[77] discussed in the previous section.

The so-called 'abnormality rule' is treated by the courts in the same flexible fashion as nothing more than an eminently defeasible presumption about the type of evidence jurors usually find helpful. Courts have received expert evidence of child psychology, for example, without any suggestion that children, as a class, are 'abnormal' or beyond the experience of ordinary people.[78] Helpfulness, however, is a composite standard incorporating negative as well as positive considerations, and this is something *Turner's* critics tend to

---

of Expert Psychiatric and Psychological Evidence – Judicial Training' (1995) 35 *Medicine, Science and the Law* 143.

[74] *R v Stockwell* (1993) 97 Cr App R 260, CA.   [75] ibid. 263–4.

[76] *R v Atkins* [2009] EWCA Crim 1876.   [77] *R v Clare and Peach* [1995] Crim LR 947, CA.

[78] *DPP v A and BC Chewing Gum Ltd* [1968] 1 QB 159, DC.

overlook. Perhaps it is a defining feature of all genuinely expert evidence that it informs lay jurors about things they did not already know. But even on that capacious conception of expertise, it does not follow that all expert evidence is by definition helpful and should automatically be admitted in a criminal trial.

The historical record of miscarriages of justice should be a constant reminder that expert evidence imports risks, as well as major benefits, into criminal litigation. Beyond the residual (and possibly ineradicable) risk that charlatan experts or bogus science might infect particular proceedings, even authentic expert evidence may be misinterpreted or misunderstood, divert jurors' attention into collateral issues, or waste time with cumulative proof of points already well-established by other evidence. Some forms of expert evidence may be especially prone to misinterpretation. It is widely believed, for example, that lay jurors have a poor grasp of statistical evidence, though there is disagreement about whether jurors are overawed by statistics or underestimate their true value.[79] The perils of statistical evidence were highlighted in the *Sally Clark* case, in which the accused – a solicitor of previously unblemished character – was convicted of serially murdering her first two infant sons, partly on the basis of expert testimony to the effect that the likelihood of two accidental cot-deaths occurring in the same family was 1-in-73 million. Sally Clark was subsequently exonerated by the Court of Appeal, at the second attempt and after spending over two years' in gaol, when it transpired that both deceased infants may have been suffering from potentially fatal viral infections.[80] The Court of Appeal added that the 1-in-73 million figure quoted at trial 'very likely ... grossly overstates the chance of two sudden deaths within the same family from unexplained but natural causes', and intimated that allowing statistical evidence to go to the jury in that naked form might have constituted an independent ground for allowing the appeal.[81]

Above all, it is feared that jurors will be overly deferential to expert evidence, to the point where the expert is effectively usurping the jury's role as fact-finder. This is a serious and complex problem for modern criminal litigation, which is nowhere more acute than when experts proffer evaluations of the credibility of other witnesses. Clinical psychologists, amongst others, are sometimes only too willing to comment on witness credibility, without necessarily realizing that they are trespassing on the province of the jury. Sensing what amounts to a challenge, intended or unwitting, to the basic procedural architecture of criminal litigation, trial judges can generally be counted upon to insist that experts must not encroach on the jury's evaluation of witness credibility, in sympathy with Lawton LJ's uncompromising remarks in *Turner*:

The jury had to decide what reliance they could put upon the defendant's evidence. He had to be judged as someone who was not mentally disordered. This is what juries are empanelled to do. The law assumes they can perform their duties properly. The jury in this case did not need, and should not have been offered, the evidence of a psychiatrist to help them decide whether the defendant's evidence was truthful.... If any such rule was applied in our courts,

---

[79] For empirical evidence of the power of statistics to beguile, see Jonathan L. Koehler, 'The Psychology of Numbers in the Courtroom: How to Make DNA-Match Statistics Seem Impressive or Insufficient' (2001) 74 *Southern California LR* 1275.

[80] *R v Clark* [2003] EWCA Crim 1020; cf. *R v Clark* (2000), Transcript on LEXIS.

[81] *R v Clark* [2003] EWCA Crim 1020, [178], [180].

trial by psychiatrists would be likely to take the place of trial by jury and magistrates. We do not find that prospect attractive and the law does not at present provide for it.[82]

Similar sentiments continue to be expressed by senior judges. In *R v Davies* Swinton Thomas LJ remarked that it was 'fundamental that experts must not usurp the functions of the jury in a criminal trial. Save in particular circumstances, it is the task of the jury to make judgments on the questions of reliability and truthfulness'.[83] These *dicta* were quoted with approval by the Divisional Court in *G v DPP*,[84] where the accused in answer to a charge of indecent assault on a child wanted to adduce an expert psychologist's report purporting to establish that the allegations against him were fabrications. Phillips LJ pulled no punches in rejecting the accused's appeal and upholding his conviction of indecent assault:

[T]his exercise was misconceived, inappropriate and a complete waste of, no doubt, considerable money. The test of whether a child is capable of giving intelligible evidence does not require any input from an expert. It is a simple test well within the capacity of a judge or magistrate..... The report of Dr Shepherd encroaches far beyond the boundaries mapped out by Swinton Thomas LJ. In meticulous detail, applying a graphic technique called THEMA (Thematic Emergence of Anomaly), he traces the process which leads the children's evidence to become what he describes as 'comprehensive exercises in confabulation'. It may be that the time will come when this technique is recognised as a better means for evaluating truth and determining guilt or innocence than trial by judge and jury, or magistrate, for Dr Shepherd almost wholly usurps that function of the court, but that time is not yet come.[85]

Notice that Phillips LJ did *not* say that Dr Shepherd's evidence was inadmissible because it concerned a matter of 'common knowledge' or normal psychology, or even that the magistrates would not have been informed by Dr Shepherd's advice or learnt something useful from his THEMA technique. Experts proffering assessments of witness credibility, like Dr Shepherd, are in essence claiming to be able to resolve forensic disputes in superior fashion to the traditional methods of the courts. Judges can never accept that type of claim, not – as some would have it[86] – because they are jealous guardians of their own power, but because they rightly interpret their duty as requiring them first and foremost to ensure that the existing trial system of lay adjudication operates fairly and effectively. This is incompatible with wholesale capitulation to alternative forms of forensic process. If society ever did decide that it would prefer trial by scientific expert, or any other radical realignment of criminal trial procedure, the changes would have to be wrought by legislative enactment. Judges simply lack the legal or political authority to make fundamental alterations to the basic procedural architecture of criminal litigation.

Expert testimony regarding witness credibility has consequently hitherto been strictly confined. Experts are allowed to inform a judge in a competency hearing on the *voir dire*,[87]

---

[82] *R v Turner* [1975] 1 QB 834, 841–2, CA.   [83] *R v Davies*, 3 November 1995, unreported.

[84] *G v DPP* [1997] 2 All ER 755, 759, DC.   [85] ibid. 759, 760.

[86] Cf. Jones, *Expert Witnesses*, 96: 'The need to structure expert evidence stemmed from the real possibility that experts would usurp the judicial role, and the fear that science would displace law as the touchstone of social order.'

[87] At common law, competence hearings had to be conducted in the jury's absence so that jurors were not improperly influenced by expert evidence of testimonial competence: *R v Deakin* [1995] 1 Cr App R 471, CA. The common law principle was given statutory formulation by the Youth Justice and Criminal Evidence (YJCE) Act 1999, subss.54(4)–(5).

or the jury in a trial, that a witness suffers from an illness which *prevents* him or her from telling the truth,[88] or which 'substantially affect[s] the witness's capacity to give reliable evidence',[89] but it has never been permissible to call psychiatric evidence 'with a view to warning a jury about a witness who is capable of giving reliable evidence, but who may well choose not to do so'.[90] In the light of experience in other common law jurisdictions, however, English judges' resolve in this regard will probably be increasingly tested. Novel forms of expert testimony, regarding such matters as Post Traumatic Stress Disorder (PTSD), Battered Women Syndrome (BWS), Child Abuse Accommodation Syndrome (CAAS), Recovered Memories, and a host of other psycho-acronyms, have become a regular feature of criminal litigation in North America and elsewhere,[91] and are likely to be proffered in English proceedings with greater frequency in the coming years. While keeping faith with their traditional liberal approach to receiving helpful expert witness testimony, English judges should nonetheless continue to scrutinize novel forms of behavioural science evidence with a critical eye, the more so where experts purport to pronounce on issues of witness credibility – the traditional province of the jury.[92]

(c) ULTIMATE ISSUES

Behavioural science evidence bearing on the credibility of lay witnesses illustrates a more general challenge which expert evidence potentially poses for the procedural structures and foundational assumptions of common law criminal adjudication. According to the 'ultimate issue rule', an expert witness may not testify directly to the existence or non-existence of a constitutive fact[93] such as an 'intention to kill' in murder or the fact of 'entry' in burglary. The animating notion is that no expert witness, no matter how knowledgeable or eminent, should be allowed to express a conclusion on the very facts at issue – the 'ultimate' issue(s) – in the trial which the jury is being called upon to resolve. The ultimate issue rule is related to the *Davie* principle discussed earlier in the chapter,[94] which entails that decisions on questions of fact are always ultimately matters for the jury even on uncontested points of expert evidence. However, the putative ultimate issue rule clearly goes beyond *Davie*, which only mandates juror education over juror deference as the ultimate

---

[88]　*Toohey* v *Metropolitan Police Commissioner* [1965] AC 595, 608, HL, previously discussed in §8.5(b).

[89]　*R* v *MacKenney and Pinfold* (1983) 76 Cr App R 271, 276, CA, *per* Ackner LJ.

[90]　ibid. And see *R* v *Smith (Allen)* [2002] EWCA Crim 2074.

[91]　For general discussion, see Erica Beecher-Monas, *Evaluating Scientific Evidence: An Interdisciplinary Framework for Intellectual Due Process* (CUP, 2007); Fiona E. Raitt and M. Suzanne Zeedyk, 'Rape Trauma Syndrome: Its Corroborative and Educational Roles' (1997) 24 *Journal of Law and Society* 552; Robert P. Mosteller, 'Syndromes and Politics in Criminal Trials and Evidence Law' (1996) 46 *Duke Law Journal* 461; Ian Freckelton, 'Repressed Memory Syndrome: Counterintuitive or Counterproductive?' (1996) 20 *Criminal Law Journal* 7; Marie Fox, 'Legal Responses to Battered Women who Kill', in Jo Bridgeman and Susan Millns (eds.), *Law and Body Politics: Regulating the Female Body* (Dartmouth, 1995); Ian Freckelton, 'Contemporary Comment: When Plight Makes Right – The Forensic Abuse Syndrome' (1994) 18 *Criminal Law Journal* 29; David L. Faigman, 'The Battered Woman Syndrome and Self-Defense: A Legal and Empirical Dissent' (1986) 72 *Virginia LR* 619.

[92]　A somewhat less restrictive approach to expert evidence bearing on witness credibility was signalled in *R* v *Pinfold and MacKenney* [2004] 2 Cr App R 32, CA. See Paul Roberts, 'Towards the Principled Reception of Expert Evidence of Witness Credibility in Criminal Trials' (2004) 8 *E & P* 215.

[93]　i.e., the facts constituting offence elements (*actus reus* and *mens rea*) or any pertinent excuse or justification: see §4.2.　　　　　　　　　　　　　　　　　　　　　　[94]　§11.2.

authority for criminal verdicts. *Davie* does not stipulate anything about the means by which experts may set about educating jurors in their specialist areas of expertise. In particular, *Davie* does not forbid experts from expressing conclusions on constitute facts in issue. That is the peculiar office of the ultimate issue rule.

It is doubtful, however, whether any such rule has ever fully been recognized,[95] and its current status as a formal rule of admissibility is extremely tenuous. It *Atkins*, the Court of Appeal mentioned the ultimate issue rule in the past tense and flatly denied its continued existence in English law.[96] Nonetheless, there are good reasons, related to English law's traditional hostility towards expert evidence of witness credibility, why courts should be cautious in permitting experts to testify on the elements of the offence charged. Suppose that the required element of *mens rea* is an intention to kill, and the issue in the case is whether the accused fired his gun intentionally. If a psychiatrist were allowed to testify, on the basis of his expert evaluation of the accused's character and emotional make-up, that the gun was fired intentionally, this might convey the impression that the determinative finding of fact was made, not so much by the jury, as by the psychiatrist.

Expert testimony addressing the elements of the offence is sometimes rightly said to amount to a usurpation of the court's, and more particularly of the jury's, fact-finding jurisdiction. This is not because there is any general objection to disputed issues effectively being settled by the testimony of one witness, which often happens in criminal trials. As we will see in Chapter 15, there is no general formal requirement in English law for witness testimony to be corroborated. The real problem posed by expert testimony is that final judgment might not be reached according to normative standards determined by the jury.[97] The danger of usurpation is especially pronounced where common sense expectations and specialist expertise diverge. It is always ultimately a question of political morality whether expert technical standards should take precedence over community norms, as represented in the courtroom by lay jurors. This is a further dimension of the pervasive tension between common sense fact-finding and juror deference to expertise in criminal trials to which we have already drawn attention.[98]

In *Stamford*,[99] the issue was whether an article was 'indecent or obscene'. The court rejected an application by the defence to call an expert witness to explain the meaning of these words. The expression 'indecent or obscene' connotes moral judgment, a matter clearly entrusted to the jury rather than to experts, as Lord Morris elaborated:

Even if accepted public standards may to some extent vary from generation to generation, current standards are in the keeping of juries, who can be trusted to maintain the corporate good sense of the community and to discern attacks upon values that must be preserved.

A contrasting approach was taken in the earlier case of *DPP v A and BC Chewing Gum Ltd*,[100] where the accused was charged with publishing allegedly obscene bubble-gum cards, depicting battle scenes, contrary to section 2 of the Obscene Publications Act 1959.

---

[95] Cases purportedly establishing the ultimate issue rule are often explicable on alternative grounds: see *Wigmore on Evidence* (Chadbourn revision), vol. 7, §1921.

[96] *R v Atkins* [2009] EWCA Crim 1876, [14].

[97] It is no mere historical accident that, in the very case establishing the sovereignty of the jury to acquit according to jurors' own lights, Vaughan CJ declared that a witness's role is confined to testifying to facts, leaving the jury to draw further inferences: *Bushell's case* (1671) Vaugh 135.   [98] §11.2, above.

[99] *R v Stamford* [1972] 2 QB 391, CA.   [100] [1968] 1 QB 159, DC.

The Divisional Court, reversing the holding of the magistrates below, ruled that the prose-cution should be allowed to tender evidence from child psychiatrists to establish the prob-able impact of violent images on the psyche of bubble-gum eating children.[101] According to the Divisional Court, lay fact-finders do not understand the workings of a child's mind like they understand the mind of an adult, and it followed that 'when dealing... with chil-dren from five upwards, any jury and any justices need all the help they can get'.[102]

It may be doubted, however, whether psychiatry can provide a superior benchmark for determining what might 'deprave and corrupt'[103] young children than ordinary common sense and experience of life. The central point at issue in this case, as in *Stamford*, was a question of moral judgment. *A and BC Chewing Gum Ltd* has subsequently been side-lined.[104] As Lord Dilhorne remarked in *DPP v Jordan*:

If an article is not manifestly obscene as tending to deprave or corrupt, it seems to me some-what odd that a person should be liable to conviction for publishing obscene matter if the evidence of experts in psychiatry is required to establish its obscenity.[105]

A judge deciding whether expert evidence should be the arbiter of particular standards in litigation will naturally try to anticipate social attitudes and meet popular expectations. If the community has come to defer to certain professionals in particular spheres of life, the courts will normally follow suit. Medical evidence is admissible on questions of injury and illness because it is normal, in our culture, to accept the authority of the medical pro-fession in matters of health-care. Psychiatry does not yet inspire quite the same degree of public confidence, however, and the various branches of psychology are further down the hierarchy of social trust and authority, though substantially more respected than com-pletely untrustworthy pseudo-sciences. Courts' intermittent rejection of proffered psy-chiatric or psychological expert evidence[106] is best explained by trial judges' – sometimes faltering – attempts to satisfy public expectations, rather than by the existence of any sup-posed evidentiary rule limiting expert testimony to 'abnormal' psychology.[107] An element of inconsistency in judicial decision-making is only to be expected for as long as society in

---

[101] Section 4(2) of the 1959 Act provides that 'It is hereby declared that the opinion of experts as to the literary, artistic, scientific or other merits of an article may be admitted in any proceedings under this Act either to establish or to negative [a 'public good' defence of artistic merit]'.

[102] *DPP v A and BC Chewing Gum Ltd* [1968] 1 QB 159, 165, DC (Lord Parker CJ).

[103] The test of obscenity given in s.1 of the Obscene Publications Act 1959.

[104] See *R v Stamford* [1972] 2 QB 391, CA; *R v Anderson* [1972] 1 QB 304, CA.

[105] *DPP v Jordan* [1977] AC 699, 722, HL.

[106] In addition to *Turner* itself, see for example, *R v Gilfoyle* [2001] 2 Cr App R 57, CA; *R v Hurst* [1995] 1 Cr App R 82, CA; *R v Robinson* (1994) 98 Cr App R 370, CA; *R v Weightman* (1991) 92 Cr App R 291, CA; *R v Mackenney and Pinfold* (1983) 76 Cr App R 271, CA; *R v Chard* (1972) 56 Cr App R 268, CA; But cf. *R v Clark (Nigel Paul)* [2006] EWCA Crim 231; *R v Pinfold and MacKenney* [2004] 2 Cr App R 32, CA; *R v Ward* (1993) 96 Cr App R 1, 66, CA; *R v Toner* (1991) 93 Cr App R 382, CA; *R v Smith* (1979) 69 Cr App R 378, CA; *Lowery v R* [1974] AC 85, PC.

[107] For further discussion, see David Ormerod, 'The Evidential Implications of Psychological Profiling' [1996] *Crim LR* 863; R. D. Mackay and Andrew M. Colman, 'Equivocal Rulings on Expert Psychological and Psychiatric Evidence: Turning a Muddle into a Nonsense' [1996] *Crim LR* 88; Paul Roberts, 'Will You Stand Up in Court? On the Admissibility of Psychiatric and Psychological Evidence' (1996) 7 *Journal of Forensic Psychiatry* 63; David E. Bernstein, 'The Science of Forensic Psychiatry and Psychology' (1995) 2 *Psychiatry, Psychology and Law* 75; David H. Sheldon and Malcolm D. MacLeod, 'From Normative to Positive Data: Expert Psychological Evidence Re-Examined' [1991] *Crim LR* 811; JUSTICE (Chair: Judge Oddie), *Science and the Administration of Justice* (Justice, 1991), chs 9–10; Freckelton, *The Trial of the Expert,*

general is uncertain or ambivalent about the extent to which particular branches of science inspire confidence and merit respect.

The policy of maintaining jury standards in criminal adjudication does not, however, require a formal rule of admissibility forbidding expert evidence going to the elements of the offence. It merely recommends judicial vigilance against allowing expert evidence, regarding offence elements or any other issues in criminal adjudication (including witness credibility), to trespass beyond the limits of a community's deep-seated values, social expectations, and faith in the epistemic authority of science and experts. Appropriately, the modern trend in common law jurisdictions has been towards repudiating the existence of a formal ultimate issue rule.[108] In *Stockwell* Lord Taylor CJ declared:

> The rationale behind the supposed prohibition is that the expert should not usurp the functions of the jury. But since counsel can bring the witness so close to opining on the ultimate issue that the inference as to his view is obvious, the rule can only be...a matter of form rather than substance. In our view an expert is called to give his opinion and he should be allowed to do so. It is, however, important that the judge should make clear to the jury that they are not bound by the expert's opinion, and that the issue is for them to decide.[109]

Whilst reasserting the underling policy, these *dicta* appear to have administered the last rites to a formal ultimate issue prohibition in English law, confirming commentators' long-standing predications of its imminent obsolescence.[110]

11.5 NOVEL SCIENCE AND 'FIELD OF EXPERTISE'

To this point we have argued that the admissibility of expert evidence in English law is determined in accordance with familiar general principles. Expert evidence must be relevant, and not subject to an applicable exclusionary rule. An expert witness must be competent, that is to say a genuine expert, otherwise the expert's evidence would not be worth receiving in a criminal trial, and at the limit it would not even pass the threshold relevance standard. Beyond that, the only additional criterion of admissibility specifically applicable to expert testimony is *Turner* helpfulness. This is the best post-hoc rationalization of English law. It is simple, elegant, and explains the vast majority of decided cases, certainly

ch 10; Rosemary Pattenden, 'Conflicting Approaches to Psychiatric Evidence in Criminal Trials: England, Canada and Australia' [1986] *Crim LR* 92.

[108] The rule is moribund in Canada: see *R v Burns* [1994] 1 SCR 656, SCC; *R v R (D)* (1996) 136 DLR (4th) 525, SCC; *Graat v R* (1982) 144 DLR (3d) 267; *MacDonald v Taubner* [2010] CarswellAlta 162, [323] (Alb QB) ('The "ultimate issue" rule, is no longer a "rule" but rather a caution against turning trials into contests of experts who might be seen to be usurping the functions of the trier of fact'). In New South Wales, s.80 of the Evidence Act 1995 (NSW) now provides that 'Evidence of an opinion is not inadmissible only because it is about – (a) a fact in issue or an ultimate issue'; confirming the direction in which Australian common law was moving in any event: *Murphy v R* (1989) 167 CLR 94, HC; *Dodd v Tamigi* [2007] WASC 42, [16]–[17]. As long ago as 1976, Rule 704 of the US Federal Rules of Evidence established that 'testimony in the form of an opinion or inference otherwise admissible is not objectionable because it embraces an ultimate issue'.

[109] *R v Stockwell* (1993) 97 Cr App R 260, 265–6, CA; reaffirmed in *R v Atkins* [2009] EWCA Crim 1876, [14].

[110] See Tristram Hodgkinson, *Expert Evidence: Law and Practice* (Sweet & Maxwell, 1990), 150–4; Freckelton, *The Trial of the Expert*, ch 5; J. D. Jackson, 'The Ultimate Issue Rule: One Rule Too Many' [1984] *Crim LR* 75.

better than any rival theory of admissibility. The *Turner* standard encounters some of its sternest challenges in its application to novel forms of expertise and new scientific discoveries and their technological applications.

Criminal proceedings are obliged to stand back and distance themselves somewhat from the precipitous cutting-edge of science. If juries are going to make decisions resulting in citizens being sent to gaol for twenty years or more they cannot afford to be swayed by today's latest scientific fad, which might turn out to have been ill-conceived and wrong-headed tomorrow. But at the same time, prosecutors and defence lawyers are naturally keen to exploit forensic applications of recent scientific discoveries, DNA profiling being an obvious – and especially potent – contemporary illustration. This tension poses the more general question of how law should respond to the constant process of discovery and innovation that is the hallmark of modern science.

One answer that has commended itself to some judges and jurists is that expert evidence in general, or perhaps just those forms of expert evidence which are regarded as relying on novel ideas, discoveries or applications, should be subject to an additional criterion of admissibility calculated to ensure the validity of the underlying science and the reliability of the expert's conclusions. This additional criterion can be formulated in different ways, but the kernel of the idea is that novel science should have been tested, validated, and institutionalized (in the broadest sense) so that it is possible to speak of its constituting an accepted technique, disciplinary specialism, or field of inquiry. The so-called 'field of expertise rule' is associated with two non-English common law precedents, *Frye* v *US*[111] and, more recently, *Bonython*.[112] We will argue that although degrees of institutionalization and acceptance amongst knowledgeable professional communities may be significant factors in assessing the relevance and potential helpfulness of proffered expert testimony, there is no formal 'field of expertise rule' governing the admissibility of scientific evidence, novel or otherwise, in English law.

(a) COMMUNITY ACCEPTANCE IN COMPARATIVE JURISPRUDENCE

The celebrated American case of *Frye* v *US* formulated the following test for the admission of novel scientific evidence in criminal proceedings:

Just when a scientific principle or discovery crosses the line between the experimental and demonstrable stages is difficult to define. Somewhere in this twilight zone the evidential force of the principle must be recognized, and while courts will go a long way in admitting expert testimony deduced from a well-recognized scientific principle or discovery, the thing from which the deduction is made must be sufficiently established to have gained general acceptance in the particular field to which it belongs.[113]

For seventy years, the *Frye* 'general acceptance' test was American judges' primary point of reference in assessing the admissibility of expert evidence based on novel scientific theories, data, or techniques. *Frye* has been cited (though rarely explicitly adopted) throughout

---

[111] *Frye* v *US* 54 App DC 46; 293 F 1013 (1923).   [112] *R* v *Bonython* (1984) 38 SASR 45.
[113] *Frye* v *US* 54 App DC 46, 47; 293 F 1013, 1014 (1923).

the Commonwealth,[114] and has occasionally even elicited favourable judicial comment in England and Wales.[115]

In 1993 the US Supreme Court issued what became the leading authority on the admissibility of expert evidence in all US federal courts and the majority of state jurisdictions. *Daubert* v *Merrell Dow*,[116] a civil torts action, reconsidered the status of *Frye*'s 'general acceptance' test for novel scientific evidence in the light of FRE Rule 702, which provides that '[i]f scientific, technical, or other specialized knowledge will assist the trier of fact to understand the evidence or to determine a fact in issue, a witness qualified as an expert by knowledge, skill, experience, training, or education, may testify thereto in the form of an opinion or otherwise'. In *Daubert* the Supreme Court reasoned that, since there is no mention of 'general acceptance' being a pre-requisite of admissibility either in Rule 702 itself or anywhere else in the Federal Rules, *Frye* must be regarded as impliedly overruled. The Court went on to hold (Rehnquist CJ and Stevens J dissenting in part) that, in order to be received in court, expert evidence must be both reliable and relevant, and that a trial judge should pay particular regard to four, non-exhaustive, criteria when determining its admissibility: (1) whether the theory or technique underpinning the evidence has undergone testing and withstood the scientific process of falsifiability; (2) whether it has been subjected to peer review and publication in refereed journals; (3) its known or potential error rate; and (4) whether the theory or technique enjoys the support of some relevant scientific community or communities.

The US Supreme Court's *Daubert* ruling, as befits a decision of such major theoretical and practical significance,[117] provoked extensive discussion and a deluge of academic commentary, much of it quite critical of the Court's reasoning and allegedly tenuous grasp of scientific methodology.[118] The Court was obliged to hear two further appeals in fairly

---

[114] *Frye* was ultimately rejected in Canada: *R* v *Béland* [1987] 2 SCR 398, SCC; *R* v *Johnston* (1992) 12 CR (4th) 99; 69 CCC (3d) 395, Ontario Gen Div; *Grant* v *Dube* (1992) 73 BCLR (2d) 288, British Columbia Sup Ct. Australian state courts, however, have been more receptive to the *Frye* test: *R* v *Karger* (2001) 83 SASR 1; [2001] SASC 64, Sup Ct of South Australia; *R* v *J (No 2)* (1994) 75 A Crim R 522, Sup Ct of Victoria; *R* v *Jarrett* (1994) 62 SASR 443, Sup Ct of South Australia. But cf. *Lakatoi Universal Pty Ltd* v *Walker* [1999] NSWSC 1336, Sup Ct of New South Wales (s.79 of the Evidence Act 1995 (NSW) amounts to a direct rejection of *Frye*). For discussion, see Paul Roberts, 'Expert Evidence in Canadian Criminal Proceedings: More Lessons from North America', in Helen Reece (ed.), *Law and Science* (OUP, 1998); David E. Bernstein, 'Junk Science in the United States and the Commonwealth' (1996) 21 *Yale Journal of International Law* 123; Stephen J. Odgers and James T. Richardson, 'Keeping Bad Science Out of the Courtroom – Changes in American and Australian Expert Evidence Law' (1995) 18 *University of New South Wales Law Journal* 108.

[115] See *R* v *Gilfoyle* [2001] 2 Cr App R 57, CA, [25]; but cf. *R* v *Dallagher* [2002] EWCA Crim 1903, [29].

[116] *Daubert* v *Merrell Dow* 125 L Ed 2d 469; 113 S Ct 2786 (1993).

[117] Paul C. Giannelli, '*Daubert* "Unbound"' (2002) 17 (Fall) *Criminal Justice* 55 (pronouncing *Daubert* 'perhaps the most important evidence case ever decided').

[118] See, e.g., Erica Beecher-Monas, *Evaluating Scientific Evidence* (CUP, 2007), ch 1; Joëlle Anne Moreno, 'Eyes Wide Shut: Hidden Problems and Future Consequences of the Fact-Based Validity Standard' (2003) 34 *Seton Hall Law Review* 89; Michael H. Graham, 'The *Daubert* Dilemma: At Last a Viable Solution' (1998) 2 *E & P* 211; Gary Edmond and David Mercer, 'Keeping "Junk" History, Philosophy and Sociology of Science Out of the Courtroom: Problems with the Reception of *Daubert* v *Merrell Dow Pharmaceuticals Inc*' (1997) 20 *University of New South Wales Law Journal* 48; Martin L. C. Feldman, 'May I Have the Next Dance, Mrs *Frye*?' (1995) 69 *Tulane LR* 793; James T. Richardson, Gerald P. Ginsburg, Sophia Gatowski and Shirley Dobbin, 'The Problems of Applying *Daubert* to Psychological Syndrome Evidence' (1995) 79 *Judicature* 10; Ronald J. Allen, 'Expertise and the *Daubert* Decision' (1994) 84 *Journal of Criminal Law and Criminology* 1157. For more positive evaluations, see Bert Black, Francisco J. Ayala, and Carol Saffran-Brinks, 'Science and the Law in the Wake of *Daubert*: A New Search for Scientific Knowledge' (1994) 72 *Texas LR* 715; David

quick succession in order to clarify the implications of its *Daubert* holding,[119] though the position subsequently appears to have stabilized at the Supreme Court level. FRE Rule 702 was redrafted to focus trial judges' admissibility inquiries directly on issues of scientific reliability.[120] For present purposes, the most salient feature of the *Daubert* admissibility standard is the Supreme Court's fourth criterion of validity, which effectively preserves the *Frye* general acceptance test – albeit now reinterpreted as part of a flexible, multi-factorial, assessment of evidentiary reliability, rather than a free-standing test of admissibility in its own right. It should also be noted that a minority of US state jurisdictions has continued to prefer *Frye* over *Daubert*, including legal heavyweights such as New York, Florida, Illinois, and California.

In *Gilfoyle*, where the defence was attempting to adduce a 'psychological autopsy' purporting to show that the deceased might have committed suicide rather than being murdered by the accused, Lord Justice Rose observed: 'The guiding principle in the United States appears to be (as stated in *Frye* v *United States*…) that evidence based on a developing new brand of science or medicine is not admissible until accepted by the scientific community as being able to provide accurate and reliable opinion. This accords with the English approach.'[121] However, the most influential 'field of expertise' authority in English law has not been either *Frye* or *Daubert*, but, somewhat curiously, the decision of the South Australian Supreme Court in *Bonython*.[122] In that case King CJ stated:

Before admitting the opinion of a witness into evidence as expert testimony, the Judge must consider and decide two questions. The first is whether the subject matter of the opinion falls within the class of subjects upon which expert testimony is permissible. This first question may be divided into two parts: (a) whether the subject matter of the opinion is such that a person without instruction or experience in the area of knowledge or human experience would be able to form a sound judgment on the matter without the assistance of witnesses possessing special knowledge or experience in the area; and (b) whether the subject matter of the opinion forms part of a body of knowledge or experience which is sufficiently organised or recognised to be accepted as a reliable body of knowledge or experience, a special acquaintance with which of the witness would render his opinion of assistance to the court. The second question is whether the witness has acquired by study or experience sufficient knowledge of the subject to render his opinion of value in resolving the issue before the court.[123]

E. Bernstein, 'The Admissibility of Scientific Evidence After *Daubert* v *Merrell Dow Pharmaceuticals, Inc*' (1994) 15 *Cardozo LR* 2139; James T. Richardson, 'Dramatic Changes in American Expert Evidence Law' (1994) 2 *Judicial Review* 13; Paul Roberts, 'The Admissibility of Expert Evidence: Lessons from America' (1996) 4 *Expert Evidence* 93.

[119] *Kumho Tire Co* v *Carmichael*, 119 S Ct 1167 (1999); *General Electric* v *Joiner*, 118 S Ct 512 (1997). See further, Mara L. Merlino *et al*, 'Meeting the Challenges of the *Daubert* Trilogy: Refining and Redefining the Reliability of Forensic Evidence' (2007) 43 *Tulsa Law Review* 417; Margaret A. Berger, 'The Supreme Court's Trilogy on the Admissibility of Expert Testimony', in Federal Judicial Center, *Reference Manual on Scientific Evidence* (2nd edn. 2000), on-line via www.fjc.gov/; Paul Roberts, 'Tyres with a "Y": An English Perspective on *Kumho Tire* and Its Implications for the Admissibility of Expert Evidence' (1999) 1(2) *International Commentary on Evidence*, Article 5, www.bepress.com/ice/vol1/iss2/.

[120] FRE Rule 702 now states that scientific evidence may be admitted only: 'if (1) the testimony is based upon sufficient facts or data, (2) the testimony is the product of reliable principles and methods, and (3) the witness has applied the principles and methods reliably to the facts of the case'.

[121] *R* v *Gilfoyle* [2001] 2 Cr App R 57, CA, [25]. Cf. *R* v *Luttrell* [2004] 2 Cr App R 31, CA.

[122] *R* v *Bonython* (1984) 38 SASR 45.   [123] ibid. 46.

Plainly, *Bonython* is not strictly speaking a precedent in English law. However, it is said to be 'a judgment which has often been quoted in this jurisdiction'[124] and which 'correctly states the position in criminal cases'.[125] According to the Law Commission, 'three factors, which are also part of the common law in England and Wales... were conveniently summarized by King CJ in... *Bonython*'.[126]

The better view is that *Bonython* does not state English law, nor is King CJ's statement of relevant principles especially helpful or illuminating. King CJ's Question 1(a) is a restatement of the *Turner* principle couched in language unfortunately reminiscent of the discredited 'common knowledge' rule. Question 2 addresses the expert witness's competence in accordance with *Silverlock*. Question 1(b) states the 'field of expertise' rule, but in terms of 'opinions' rather the expert testimony in general and repeating the helpfulness criterion. It does not assist comprehension to have to extract this kernel from the surrounding pulp, having discarded its superfluous husk – the obscure proposition that there is a 'class of subjects upon which expert testimony is permissible' (and therefore, presumably, a complementary class of subjects on which expert testimony is not admissible). If judges were intent on augmenting existing English law with a field of expertise rule they would be better off adopting the more elegant and explicit *Frye* standard.

However, there are well-known problems besetting all versions of the putative field of expertise rule, including the *Frye* standard, which is why the majority of US legal jurisdictions have replaced *Frye* with *Daubert*.[127] Pragmatically, it is sometimes difficult to gauge what the relevant 'field' is and which experts comprise it. Whether there is 'general' acceptance sufficient to satisfy *Frye* may depend on which and how many other practitioners are asked for their evaluations. More fundamentally, 'general acceptance' is only a very rough proxy for scientific validity. Scientific pioneers like Galileo, Darwin, and Einstein were mavericks who disdained the orthodoxies of their day. Conversely, the fact that forensic disciplines like bite mark analysis[128] or even fingerprinting[129] are well-established with hundreds of current practitioners does not necessarily mean that their results deliver everything that paid-up members of the guild claim for their testimony. These intractable limitations entail that field of expertise is better treated as a flexible rule of thumb

---

[124] *Doughty* v *Ely Magistrates' Court* [2008] EWHC 522 (Admin), [6].

[125] *Leo Sawrij Ltd* v *North Cumbria Magistrates' Court* [2009] EWHC 2823 (Admin), [16].

[126] Law Commission Consultation Paper No 190, *The Admissibility of Expert Evidence in Criminal Proceedings in England and Wales* (TSO, 2009), para.1.2. Also see Andrew Roberts, 'Drawing on Expertise: Legal Decision-Making and the Reception of Expert Evidence' [2008] *Crim LR* 443, 453 ('The frequency with which it is cited and approved as authority for the principles governing the reception of expert evidence in English proceedings suggests that it has secured rather more than a foothold in this jurisdiction').

[127] For critical evaluation of *Frye*, see Freckelton, *Trial of the Expert*, ch 4; Paul C. Giannelli, 'The Admissibility of Novel Scientific Evidence: *Frye* v *United States*, a Half-Century Later' (1980) 80 *Columbia LR* 1197; David L. Faigman, Elise Porter, and Michael J. Saks, 'Check Your Crystal Ball at the Courthouse Door, Please: Exploring the Past, Understanding the Present, and Worrying About the Future of Scientific Evidence' (1994) 15 *Cardozo LR* 1799.

[128] Erica Beecher-Monas, 'Reality Bites: The Illusion of Science in Bite-Mark Evidence' (2009) 30 *Cardozo Law Review* 1369.

[129] Erica Beecher-Monas, *Evaluating Scientific Evidence: An Interdisciplinary Framework for Intellectual Due Process* (CUP, 2007), 104–9; Carole McCartney, *Forensic Identification and Criminal Justice: Forensic Science, Justice and Risk* (Willan, 2006), 82–92; Robert Epstein, 'Fingerprints Meet *Daubert*: The Myth of Fingerprint "Science" is Revealed' (2002) 75 *Southern California Law Review* 605; Jennifer L. Mnookin, 'Fingerprint Evidence in an Age of DNA Profiling' (2001) 67 *Brooklyn Law Review* 13.

rather than a formal rule of admissibility, i.e. *Daubert* rather than *Frye*. Recognizing that 'it would be wrong to deny to the law of evidence the advances to be gained from new techniques and new advances in science',[130] this is, for the most part, exactly how English law proceeds.

(b) ENGLISH LAW'S RECEPTIVE APPROACH TO NOVEL SCIENCE

Suggestions to the contrary notwithstanding,[131] there does not appear to be any specific rule of English law restricting the scope of expert testimony to recognized branches of science, institutionalized disciplines, or authenticated fields of knowledge or research. All that the court requires is some guarantee that proffered scientific evidence is valid, relevant, and likely, on balance, to be helpful to the fact-finder. Whilst a particular expert's authority might be rooted in his or her membership of an established scientific discipline, it need not be. As Bingham LJ explained in *Robb*:

The old-established, academically-based sciences such as medicine, geology or metallurgy, and the established professions such as architecture, quantity surveying or engineering, present no problem. The field will be regarded as one in which expertise may exist and any properly qualified member will be accepted without question as an expert. Expert evidence is not, however, limited to those core areas. Expert evidence of finger-prints, hand-writing and accident reconstruction is regularly given. Opinions may be given of the market value of land, ships, pictures or rights. Expert opinions may be given of the quality of commodities, or on the literary, artistic, scientific or other merit of works alleged to be obscene (Obscene Publications Act 1959, s.4(2)). Some of these fields are far removed from anything which could be called a formal scientific discipline. Yet while receiving this evidence the courts would not accept the evidence of an astrologer, a soothsayer, a witch-doctor or an amateur psychologist and might hesitate to receive evidence of attributed authorship based on stylometric analysis.[132]

Why are the courts not interested in hearing from astrologers, soothsayers, or witchdoctors? Simply because, in our culture, the 'knowledge' possessed by these experts is considered to be incredible and unreliable, and therefore virtually[133] always irrelevant to legal proceedings.

---

[130] *R v Clarke* [1995] 2 Cr App R 425, 429, CA.

[131] Colin Tapper suggests that, '[a]t one time a conservative approach requiring the field of expertise to have become generally accepted was widely adopted. This is now regarded as too stultifying.... The better, and now more widely accepted, view is that, so long as a field is sufficiently well established to pass the ordinary tests of relevance and reliability, then no enhanced test of admissibility should be applied': *Cross and Tapper on Evidence*, 581–2 (footnotes omitted). Yet no authority is cited for this proposition, and it may be doubted whether anything resembling the US *Frye* 'general acceptance' test has ever been applied in England and Wales.

[132] *R v Robb* (1991) 93 Cr App R 161, 164, CA. For further discussion of stylometric evidence, see Bernard Robertson, G. A. Vignaux and Isobel Egerton, 'Stylometric Evidence' [1994] *Crim LR* 645.

[133] This qualification is necessary chiefly because English criminal law incorporates many subjective *mens rea* requirements which frame the accused's liability in terms of what he truly (even if unreasonably) believed: see Andrew Ashworth, *Principles of Criminal Law* (OUP, 6th edn. 2009), 154–6. Expert evidence on *any* subject might therefore in principle be admissible, as evidence of what the accused believed (e.g. 'as a senior member of Cult X, I can confirm that this accused, like all obedient Cult members, truly believes Prophesy Y'), even though the rest of us might think that these beliefs are superstitious claptrap.

The issue on appeal in *Robb* concerned evidence of voice-identification. Dr Baldwin had listened to tape-recordings of ransom demands made over the telephone and concluded that there was a precise match between the accused's voice and the man speaking on the tape. Whilst strongly hinting that this was a borderline case, the Court of Appeal nonetheless endorsed the trial judge's decision to admit Dr Baldwin's evidence, even though this expert witness's exclusive reliance on auditory techniques – basically just careful repeated listening unaided by quantitative analysis of speech patterns – appeared to be highly unorthodox:

The great weight of informed opinion, including the world leaders in the field, was to the effect that auditory techniques unless supplemented and verified by acoustic analysis were an unreliable basis of speaker identification.... A unit recently established in Germany under a respected director rejected identification based on auditory techniques alone. Other Western European countries did not receive such evidence. There were only a handful of others, and they were in this country, who shared Dr Baldwin's opinion. He had published no material which would allow his methods to be tested or his results checked. He had conducted no experiments or tests on the accuracy of his own conclusions. Despite all this, Dr Baldwin's opinion remained that acoustic analysis itself called for interpretation. Voice identification was not an exact science. While accepting that he could be wrong, Dr Baldwin was led by his experience and training to believe that his conclusions were reliable. Acoustic analysis was a possible, but not in his view a necessary, supplement. If he thought otherwise he would adopt that technique also, but he did not. His opinion remained that the voice on the disputed tapes and the control tape was the same.... Dr Baldwin's reliance on the auditory technique must, on the evidence, be regarded as representing a minority view in his profession but he had reasons for his preference and on the facts of this case he was not shown to be wrong.[134]

The Northern Ireland Court of Appeal subsequently held in *O'Doherty* that cases resting substantially on auditory voice identification should not generally be brought to trial.[135] However, contrary to many people's expectations,[136] the English Court of Appeal has stood by *Robb*, and in *Flynn*[137] specifically declined to follow *O'Doherty*. Although '[t]here can be no doubt that the admission of voice recognition evidence is controversial, perhaps highly controversial', the English court thought it 'neither possible nor desirable to go as far as the Northern Ireland Court... which ruled that auditory analysis evidence given by experts in this field was inadmissible unless supported by expert evidence of acoustic analysis'.[138]

The Court of Appeal's own explanation of its decision in *Robb* runs together considerations of expert qualification and field of expertise (as did King CJ in *Bonython*). Yet there was no real dispute in *Robb* about Dr Baldwin's credentials: the accused was objecting to the particular technique employed by Dr Baldwin rather than to his status as a *bona fide* expert.[139] Put another way, the accused was contending that exclusive reliance on auditory

---

134 (1991) 93 Cr App R 161, 165, 166. 135 *R v O'Doherty* [2002] Crim LR 761, CA(NI).

136 The first edition of this book floated the possibility that 'English courts might...distance themselves from the specific holding in *Robb*': *Criminal Evidence* (OUP, 2004), 317. For further discussion, see David Ormerod, 'Sounding Out Expert Voice Identification' [2002] *Crim LR* 771; David Ormerod, 'Sounds Familiar? – Voice Identification Evidence' [2001] *Crim LR* 595.

137 *R v Flynn and St John* [2008] 2 Cr App R 20, [2008] EWCA Crim 970. 138 ibid. [13], [62].

139 The Court recited Dr Baldwin's impressive credentials: 'Dr Baldwin was and had for many years been a lecturer in phonetics in the department of phonetics and linguistics at University College London. He had gained a B.A. in modern languages, an M.A. in general linguistics and phonetics and a Ph.D. in phonetics.

analysis as a basis for a conclusive identification placed Dr Baldwin beyond the pale of legitimate forensic practice. The court effectively replied that, once it was established that Dr Baldwin was properly qualified in anything that might plausibly be called a scientific discipline, his choice of technique was a matter of professional judgment which the court would not presume to query or second-guess. Relevance is once more the key to admissibility, and only notoriously bogus 'sciences' like alchemy, astrology, or phrenology are conclusively presumed to be invalid and therefore irrelevant for the purposes of criminal proceedings.

Robb is emblematic of a long and remarkably consistent line of appellate authority implicitly rejecting 'field of expertise' as an independent factor regulating the admissibility of expert evidence in English criminal trials. The cases involve such diverse forms of expertise as interpretation of photographs[140] and videos,[141] the effects of weather and lighting conditions on visual identification,[142] stylometric analysis of handwriting,[143] lip-reading from CCTV images,[144] and identification by ear-prints.[145] In *Kempster*,[146] the accused's appeal against conviction was allowed, at the second attempt, but only because his ear was not a perfect match with the crime-scene print at the level of minutiae and the experts disagreed on whether the discrepancies could satisfactorily be accounted for by movement or changes of pressure when the original print was left on the window of the burgled house. The Court of Appeal still maintained that positive identifications could in principle be made solely on the basis of gross characteristics, even whilst acknowledging that ear-print identification is a new and relatively untested science and that some experts doubt the reliability of matches based exclusively on gross characteristics. Indeed, the only scenarios in which the Court of Appeal is prepared to say that expert evidence should have been excluded typically involve scientific theories that have been wholly discredited[147] or conflicts of expert testimony leading the court to conclude that proof beyond reasonable doubt could not be established on the facts.[148]

Rejecting a formal 'field of expertise' rule is entirely in keeping with English law's liberal approach to the admissibility of expert evidence. There is no better illustration of the merits of a completely flexible admissibility inquiry than the way in which DNA evidence was accepted by English criminal courts as a legitimate form of forensic proof, promptly,

---

He had been engaged in phonetic studies for 30 years. He had given expert evidence in court on some 25 occasions, on each of which the court's decision had been consistent with his opinion': *R* v *Robb* (1991) 93 Cr App R 161, 165.

[140] *R* v *Clarke* [1995] 2 Cr App R 425, CA; *R* v *Stockwell* (1993) 97 Cr App R 260, CA.

[141] *R* v *Clare and Peach* [1995] Crim LR 947, CA.   [142] *R* v *Latte* [1996] 2 *Archbold News* 1, CA.

[143] *R* v *McCrossen*, 10 July 1991, CA, criticized by Bernard Robertson, G. A. Vignaux and Isobel Egerton, 'Stylometric Evidence' [1994] *Crim LR* 645; and in 'Editorial Introduction: Some Legal Issues Affecting Novel Forms of Expert Evidence' (1992) 1 *Expert Evidence* 79. *McCrossen* itself does not appear ever to have been reported, but was discussed in a related appeal: *R* v *Clemmett*, 21 October 1992, Transcript on LEXIS.

[144] *R* v *Luttrell* [2004] 2 Cr App R 31, CA.

[145] *R* v *Dallagher* [2002] EWCA Crim 1903, [2002] Crim LR 821, CA.

[146] *R* v *Kempster (No.2)* [2008] 2 Cr App R 19, [2008] EWCA Crim 975.

[147] *R* v *Harris* [2006] 1 Cr App R 5, [2005] EWCA Crim 1980.

[148] *R* v *Cannings* [2004] 1 WLR 2607, CA. Here, the conclusion is not really one of inadmissibility, but rather that the prosecution has failed to establish a case to answer. In *Cannings* itself, Lord Justice Judge advised that 'if the outcome of the trial depends exclusively or almost exclusively on a serious disagreement between distinguished and reputable experts, it will often be unwise, and therefore unsafe, to proceed': ibid. [178].

smoothly, and without the need for explicit statutory authorization.[149] At the same time, there is no denying that the unvarnished *Turner* 'helpfulness' standard entails a degree of vulnerability to untried and untested novel scientific discoveries, which ultimately might not stand the test of time. In cases such as *Robb, Luttrell* and *Kempster,* fact-finders appear to have been exposed to the eccentricities of individual expert witnesses. In the final analysis, this may be an inescapable occupational hazard of a trial system built on the principle of factual adjudication by lay jurors and magistrates. Nonetheless, many commentators have lately come around to thinking that English law's approach to regulating the admissibility of scientific evidence is insufficiently rigorous and robust, and the Law Commission now also shares this view.[150]

Although 'helpfulness' has been advocated in this chapter as the guiding principle of admissibility, it must be conceded that the common law rules applicable to expert evidence remain to a surprising extent uncertain and controversial, which in turn generates unpredictability and inconsistency in judicial decisions to admit or exclude expert witness testimony at trial. The unsatisfactory state of the law is exemplified by *Gilfoyle,*[151] in which the Court of Appeal identified no less than six grounds on which evidence of a 'psychological autopsy' proffered by the defence was held to have been properly ruled inadmissible at trial: (1) the witness was a *bona fide* expert, but had never previously undertaken a similar exercise; (2) there was no database or academic literature against which the court could test the expert's conclusions; (3) the expert's report was based on one-sided factual information; (4) human happiness is not something outwith the experience of a jury on which expert instruction is required; (5) psychological profiles have been rejected in other jurisdictions, and would not satisfy the *Frye* test which 'accords with the English approach';[152] and (6) if such evidence were admitted for the defence it would also have to be admissible for the prosecution, and 'the roads of enquiry thus opened up would be unending and of little or no help to a jury'.[153] It is not that these factors are irrelevant to an assessment of admissibility, or even that they could not for the most part[154] be brought under the umbrella of the helpfulness test. The problem lies in the unsystematic and unpredictable fashion in which the court goes about its task. An approach to the admissibility of expert evidence that might be characterized as 'when in doubt, make a list!' gives the appearance of 'throwing in the kitchen sink'.

Not surprisingly, practitioners and commentators complain that, when it comes to assessing the reliability of scientific evidence, 'English law might be considered, at best,

---

[149] *R v Gordon* [1995] 1 Cr App R 290, CA; *R v Reed and Reed* [2009] EWCA Crim 2698. This is not to imply that DNA evidence is always entirely problem-free, only that the basic technologies were easily assimilated into criminal adjudication despite their startling novelty: cf. *R v Gray* [2005] EWCA Crim 3564; *R v Bates* [2006] EWCA Crim 1395.

[150] Law Commission Consultation Paper No 190, *The Admissibility of Expert Evidence in Criminal Proceedings in England and Wales* (TSO, 2009), para.2.12: [T]here is a real, ongoing problem which demands an urgent solution. In short, it would appear that expert evidence is sometimes admitted too readily and that, notwithstanding a number of successful and highly publicised appeals concerning the reliability of expert opinion evidence, there continues to be a "pressing danger" [David Ormerod and Andrew Roberts, 'Expert Evidence: Where Now? What Next?' [2006] 5 *Archbold News* 5] of wrongful convictions (and, no doubt, wrongful acquittals).' Also see House of Commons Science and Technology Committee, *Forensic Science on Trial – Seventh Report of Session 2004–05*, HC 96-I (TSO, 29 March 2005), [173].

[151] *R v Gilfoyle* [2001] 2 Cr App R 57, CA.   [152] ibid. [25].   [153] ibid.

[154] Cf. the Court of Appeal's apparent endorsement of *dicta* in *Davie* v *Edinburgh Magistrates* [1953] SC 34, 40.

rather vague, and at worst incoherent and inconsistent';[155] that it is 'difficult to predict where the law in the United Kingdom is heading';[156] and even that the courts have succeeded only in 'turning a muddle into a nonsense'.[157] Taking its cue from this rising chorus of criticism, the concluding section of this chapter briefly reviews our main arguments and canvasses options for reform.

11.6 THE FUTURE OF EXPERT EVIDENCE

Scientific and other forms of expert evidence already play an enormously influential role in today's criminal proceedings, and their influence is only likely to grow for the foreseeable future. Damaška detects in scientific evidence the potential for epistemic revolution in criminal adjudication:

Let there be no mistake. As science continues to change the social world, great transformations of factual inquiry lie ahead for all justice systems. These transformations could turn out to be as momentous as those that occurred in the twilight of the Middle Ages, when magical forms of proof retreated before the prototypes of our present evidentiary technology.[158]

In the sphere of criminal justice, as in everything else in modern life, it is tempting to believe that science *is* the future, though, of course, this is an exceptionally naïve, and potentially very dangerous, conceit. Against the dazzling mirage of science and technology as the saviour of human civilization, it is worth recalling that science fiction contains few utopias.[159]

The key themes of this chapter have been the power of science to settle disputed questions of fact and to generate social trust in the legitimacy of criminal verdicts, the preservation of the jury's standard-setting role in matters of moral judgment, and the balance between deference and education in the reception of expert evidence in criminal trials. These themes articulate perennial challenges for criminal adjudication. Striking an appropriate balance between juror-education and juror-deference to scientific evidence is not an objective that can be achieved conclusively, once and for all, but rather demands constant judicial attention. Negotiating their way around popular cultural ambivalence towards all things scientific, the courts must strive to construct a compromise between blind faith and pathological scepticism which is capable, for the time being, of satisfying public demands for an effective trial system delivering factually reliable, socially credible, and morally legitimate verdicts. The immediate operational goal is to harness the awesome power of science to the administration of criminal justice.

---

[155] Andrew Roberts, 'Drawing on Expertise: Legal Decision-Making and the Reception of Expert Evidence' [2008] *Crim LR* 443, 448.

[156] William E. O'Brian Jr, 'Court Scrutiny of Expert Evidence: Recent Decisions Highlight the Tensions' (2003) 7 *E & P* 172, 173.

[157] R. D. Mackay and Andrew M. Colman, 'Equivocal Rulings on Expert Psychological and Psychiatric Evidence: Turning a Muddle into a Nonsense' [1996] *Crim LR* 88.

[158] Mirjan R. Damaška, *Evidence Law Adrift* (Yale UP, 1997), 151. And see Mirjan R. Damaška, 'Rational and Irrational Proof Revisited' (1997) 5 *Cardozo Journal of International and Comparative Law* 25.

[159] For some, perhaps surprising, connections between science fiction and criminal justice policy, see Mike Nellis, 'News Media, Popular Culture and the Electronic Monitoring of Offenders in England and Wales' (2003) 42 *Howard Journal of Criminal Justice* 1.

We have seen that English law adopts a liberal – according to one commentator, 'incredibly liberal'[160] – approach to the reception of novel forms of scientific expertise. There are no special rules, over and above the threshold criteria of relevance and 'helpfulness' specified by the leading case of *Turner*. A flexible and undemanding approach to admissibility ensures that the law is able to enlist the services of the very latest cutting-edge science, but there are obvious risks in over-reliance on theories, techniques, or data that have not (yet) stood the test of time. Public confidence in the truth and legitimacy of verdicts in criminal trials needs to be maintained for a substantial duration, if not literally forever, then at least for the lifetimes of the people directly involved as victims and perpetrators of crime and their immediate families and supporters. This elementary demand of justice is a significant force for conservatism in criminal procedure, which the volatile, unstable, conjectural nature of knowledge on the cutting edge of scientific discovery and technology transfer does little to placate.[161]

The question of which rules should govern the admissibility of expert evidence in criminal trials has never been systematically addressed, either by the legislature or at the highest judicial level. Trial judges are consequently left with no choice but to muddle along as best as they can, by eliciting such guidance as may found in equivocal, and in certain respects contradictory, pronouncements of the Court of Appeal to determine the admissibility of contested expert evidence on a case-by-case basis. In this regard English law might be thought to have fallen behind the pace of modern requirements, whilst developments in other common law jurisdictions have led the way. Reference has already been made to the tests propounded by common law courts in *Frye*, *Daubert*, and *Bonython*, all of which – in their different ways, and with varying levels of success – attempted to provide more concrete guidance for trial judges faced with the difficult task of assessing the reliability of expert evidence incorporating novel theories, recent scientific discoveries, or technological innovation. In New South Wales, the admissibility of expert evidence is now governed by statute as part of the comprehensive codification of the law of evidence undertaken in that jurisdiction.[162] For the benefit of those Australian states where the common law still prevails, the High Court of Australia has elaborated on the basic *Turner* standard in an attempt to give more detailed guidance to trial judges on the admissibility of expert evidence.[163] The Supreme Court of Canada has undertaken a similar exercise to assist Canadian trial judges and legal practitioners.[164]

---

[160] David Ormerod, 'Sounding Out Expert Voice Identification' [2002] *Crim LR* 771, 777.

[161] For general discussion, see Andre A. Moenssens, 'Novel Scientific Evidence in Criminal Cases: Some Words of Caution' (1993) 84 *Journal of Criminal Law and Criminology* 1; Peter Alldridge, 'Recognizing Novel Scientific Techniques: DNA as a Test Case' [1992] *Crim LR* 687; 'Editorial Introduction: Some Legal Issues Affecting Novel Forms of Expert Evidence' (1992) 1 *Expert Evidence* 79.

[162] Section 79 of the Evidence Act 1995 (NSW and Cth) provides that 'If a person has specialised knowledge based on the person's training, study or experience, the opinion rule does not apply to evidence of an opinion of that person that is wholly or substantially based on that knowledge'. On the broader codification project, see Ian Dennis, 'Codification and Reform of Evidence Law in Australia' [1996] *Crim LR* 477.

[163] *Murphy* v *R* (1989) 167 CLR 94, HCA, up-dating *Clark* v *Ryan* (1960) 103 CLR 486, HCA. See Stephen J. Odgers and James T. Richardson, 'Keeping Bad Science Out of the Courtroom – Changes in American and Australian Expert Evidence Law' (1995) 18 *University of New South Wales Law Journal* 108.

[164] *R* v *Mohan* (1994) 114 DLR (4th) 419, SCC. See Paul Roberts, 'Expert Evidence in Canadian Criminal Proceedings: More Lessons from North America', in Helen Reece (ed.), *Law and Science* (OUP, 1998).

Needless to say, we do not advocate the naïve (indeed, strictly speaking impossible)[165] wholesale transplantation of foreign legal reforms into English law. Comparative research nonetheless supplies a library of alternative possibilities demonstrating that the perils of common law pragmatism are not entirely beyond amelioration. The Law Commission has provisionally proposed enacting a series of admissibility criteria, inspired by *Daubert* and designed to ensure the reliability of all scientific and other expert evidence adduced in criminal trials.[166] The trial judge's new statutory 'gatekeeping' duty would extend to all expert evidence, not just to novel science;[167] but an inquiry into the validity of proffered scientific evidence would not normally be required unless another party to the litigation provokes it by challenging the evidence.[168] One might quibble with particular aspects of the Commission's initial proposals,[169] but their overall thrust seems sound, if only for the reasons that codification of criminal procedure law (if done well) is always a good idea in principle. However, the Law Commission is wise to caution that 'reforming the law governing the admissibility of expert evidence would not provide a panacea'[170] for all the problems associated with expert testimony. Indeed, research on the limited impact of *Daubert* on US trial proceedings should make sobering reading for law reformers. Changing the formal rule of admissibility does not necessarily alter judicial culture or practice, or to the extent that it does, the changes may not be exactly what reformers had in mind.[171] This is not an argument against reforming rules of admissibility, only an admonition against thinking that this can ever be a silver bullet. As the Commission insists, doctrinal reform must be viewed as only one part of a comprehensive procedural package,[172] which might conceivably include more radical elements designed to compensate for the shortcomings of adversarial criminal proceedings.

The most obvious way of mitigating the distorting influence of adversarial procedure on scientific evidence would be to move to a system of court-appointed experts, whereby an appropriate expert, chosen from a court-approved list of suitably qualified practitioners, would be instructed directly by the judge and testify as an independent witness of the court. Judicially-appointed experts are the norm in continental jurisdictions,[173] and are a

---

[165] Law is always also *transformed* at the moment that it is transplanted: see, e.g., Máximo Langer, 'From Legal Transplants to Legal Translations: The Globalization of Plea Bargaining and the Americanization Thesis in Criminal Procedure' (2004) 45 *Harvard International Law Journal* 1.

[166] Law Commission Consultation Paper No 190, *The Admissibility of Expert Evidence in Criminal Proceedings in England and Wales* (TSO, 2009), Part 6.   [167] ibid. paras.4.35–4.38, 6.4–6.15.

[168] ibid. paras.6.17, 6.54.

[169] A number of telling objections are entered by Andrew Roberts, 'Rejecting General Acceptance, Confounding the Gate-keeper: The Law Commission and Expert Evidence' [2009] *Crim LR* 551.

[170] LCCP No 190, para.1.13. For the avoidance of doubt, the Commission adds that '[i]t is fair to say … that the problems associated with expert evidence can never be entirely resolved': ibid. para.1.17.

[171] See, e.g., D. Michael Risinger, 'Goodbye To All That, Or A Fool's Errand, By One of the Fools: How I Stopped Worrying about Court Responses to Handwriting Identification (and "Forensic Science" in General) and Learned to Love Misinterpretations of *Kumho Tire* v *Carmichael*' (2007) 43 *Tulsa Law Review* 447; Sophia I. Gatowski *et al*, 'Asking the Gatekeepers: A National Survey of Judges on Judging Expert Evidence in a Post-*Daubert* World' (2001) 25 *Law and Human Behavior* 433.   [172] LCCP No 190, para.1.14.

[173] For comparative analysis, see Peter Alldridge, 'Scientific Expertise and Comparative Criminal Procedure' (1999) 3 *E & P* 141; Petra van Kampen, *Expert Evidence Compared: Rules and Practices in the Dutch and American Criminal Justice System* (Intersentia, 1998); For a comparative inventory of formal judicial powers to appoint experts, see Nigel Osner, Anne Quinn and Giles Crown (eds.), *Criminal Justice Systems in Other Jurisdictions*, Royal Commission on Criminal Justice (HMSO, 1993), Part 2 (*Australia* – court-appointment limited to South Australia, and rarely used), Part 3 (*Belgium* – experts appointed by

growing force in post-Woolf English civil litigation.[174] Commentators such as John Spencer have long argued that English criminal procedure should follow suit, by making provision for court-appointed experts in criminal proceedings as well.[175] The Law Commission is attracted to this idea, but declined to make concrete proposals before putting the suggestion out to further consultation.[176]

The sticking point, of course, is that court-appointed experts challenge the autonomy of the parties over the collection and presentation of evidence, which is not only a hallmark of adversarial process but has also become a basic expectation of fair and legitimate procedure in English criminal trials. The compilation of a 'court-approved' list of forensic practitioners, let alone the choice of experts in particular cases, would inevitably be contentious, and it is far from clear how, or by whom, such a task might be undertaken. Judges themselves are clearly unqualified for the job, and would inevitably need to call upon experts for advice as to which of their fellow experts should be included on the list. At which point we should be asking, with Juvenal, *sed quis custodiet ipsos custodes*? The practical obstacles to implementing this suggestion parallel the limitations of *Frye's* 'community acceptance' standard of admissibility. Even the most well-qualified and experienced medical and scientific experts sometimes disagree with one another, nor are they completely immune from the personal vanities, jealousies, and old boys' networks that operate in all the established professions.[177] The problem of accreditation is particularly acute because forensic science comprises an exceptionally diverse array of disciplines and sub-disciplines, extending from core variations on physics, chemistry, biology, and medicine, to a multitude of 'small ologies'[178] on the periphery, including forensic entomology, forensic archaeology, forensic odontology, facial mapping, psychological profiling, and countless other exotica. It is an open question whether any individual or group of practitioners within these minor disciplines would have the scientific credentials to pass judgment on the competence of their peers, who might actually be arch-rivals promoting competing scientific theories. One might wonder whether *any* card-carrying exponent of

examining magistrate and defence), Part 4 (*Canada* – judicial appointment power exists, but little used), Part 5 (*Denmark* – court-appointed experts plus party experts), Part 6 (*France* – examining magistrate, plus rarely defence experts), Part 7 (*Germany* – court-appointed experts, plus rarely defence experts), Part 10 (*Italy* – court and party experts), Part 11 (*The Netherlands* – court, examining magistrate, and defence experts), Part 13 (*Spain* – examining magistrate and party experts), Part 14 (*Sweden* – party experts, plus rarely court-appointees), and Part 15 (USA – FRE Rule 706 authorizes court-appointed experts, but rarely invoked).

[174] See Déirdre Dwyer, 'Changing Approaches to Expert Evidence in England and Italy' (2003) 1(2) *International Commentary on Evidence*, Article 4, www.bepress.com/ice/vol1/iss2/art4.

[175] J. R. Spencer, 'Court Experts and Expert Witnesses: Have we a Lesson to Learn from the French?' [1992] *CLP* 213; J. R. Spencer, 'The Neutral Expert: An Implausible Bogey' [1991] *Crim LR* 106. And see JUSTICE (Chair: Judge Oddie), *Science and the Administration of Justice* (Justice, 1991), ch 7; Tristram Hodgkinson, *Expert Evidence: Law and Practice* (Sweet & Maxwell, 1990), ch 3; I. R. Freckelton, *The Trial of the Expert* (OUP, 1987), ch 11; A. Kenny 'The Expert in Court' (1983) 99 *LQR* 197; John Basten, 'The Court Expert in Civil Trials' (1977) 40 *MLR* 175.   [176] LCCP No 190, paras.6.65–6.71.

[177] Cf. M. N. Howard QC, 'The Neutral Expert: A Plausible Threat to Justice' [1991] *Crim LR* 98, 101, observing that: 'It is slightly mysterious that it should be thought that experts are venal mountebanks when engaged by the parties but transformed into paragons of objectivity when employed by the court', and warning against 'the usual cabal of log-rollers, time-servers, self-publicists and people with friends'.

[178] Corinne Duhig, 'The Need for an Independent Institute: A View from One Small "Ology"', paper to the Solon Institute conference on *Independence and Objectivity in Forensic Science: Problems and Solutions*, Cambridge, 9–12 July 2003.

a newly-emerging or otherwise controversial discipline should be trusted by the courts to vouch for their own or their fellow practitioners' scientific credentials.

The challenge of expert accreditation is endemic to any system for incorporating scientific expertise into criminal proceedings. It must ultimately be addressed pragmatically on a case-by-case basis. For decades, English lawyers were obliged to rely on lists of experts compiled by learned societies and certain commercial organizations, which were patchy in coverage and of dubious reliability. A succession of august bodies made recommendations,[179] and the nettle of expert witness accreditation was finally grasped with the creation of the Council for the Registration of Forensic Practitioners (CRFP).[180] Unfortunately, after a promising start the CRFP experiment failed, apparently for lack of resources, and the baton has now passed to the Forensic Science Regulator[181] assisted by the Forensic Science Advisory Council.[182] The Regulator is more directly concerned with developing quality standards for forensic science services and monitoring compliance with them as opposed to accrediting individual forensic practitioners. The scale of the task is daunting and it is unclear how much progress can be made in the short-term, especially in an austere financial climate. Novel scientific advances and evolving disciplinary specialization will subject even the most comprehensive and elaborate system of regulatory standards and expert qualification to demands for regular updating, and the enterprise of accrediting some would-be forensic practitioners and rejecting others will never be entirely uncontroversial.

A more fundamental dilemma for any system of court-appointed expert witnesses stems precisely from the fact that the court, rather than the parties, is entrusted with so many potentially crucial strategic decisions. Convictions resting mainly on (circumstantial) scientific evidence are already viewed with suspicion by many observers, but at least it can currently be said (where it can in fact be said)[183] that the accused had the opportunity to instruct his own experts to check the work of the prosecution's scientists and, if the defence should choose, to call scientific evidence in rebuttal of the prosecution's case at trial. Procedural fairness in securing access to scientific expertise thus contributes to the public acceptability and moral legitimacy of the jury's verdict. To the extent that these aspects of the accused's autonomy to mount a defence were withdrawn, by empowering the court to impose a particular expert – and therefore particular scientific conclusions – on the accused and on the fact-finder, this dimension of legitimacy in criminal proceedings would be undermined.

---

[179] See Royal Commission on Criminal Justice (Chair: Viscount Runciman), *Report* Cm 2263 (HMSO, 1993), ch 9; House of Lords Select Committee on Science and Technology, Session 1992–93, 5th Report (Chairman: Lord Dainton), *Forensic Science*, HL Paper 24, (HMSO, 1993). For discussion, see Paul Roberts, 'What Price a Free Market in Forensic Science Services? The Organization and Regulation of Science in the Criminal Process' (1996) 36 *British Journal of Criminology* 37.

[180] Cf. www.forensic-access.co.uk/forensic-access-publications/benchmark-newsletter/crfp.htm.

[181] Forensic Science Regulator, *Annual Report* (2009); http://police.homeoffice.gov.uk/operational-policing/forensic-science-regulator/.

[182] http://police.homeoffice.gov.uk/operational-policing/forensic-science-regulator/forensic-advisory-council/.

[183] We need to inquire about the reality of defence access to scientific expertise in particular cases, which raises a host of further issues including (1) the competence of defence lawyers to locate and instruct appropriate experts; and (2) the availability of public funding to pay for defence examiners. For further discussion, see Roberts and Willmore, *The Role of Forensic Science Evidence*, ch 3; Paul Roberts, 'Obtaining Defence Experts in Criminal Proceedings: Pragmatism and the Impossible Dream' (1993) 42 *The Criminal Lawyer* 1; Paul Roberts, 'Expert Systems?' (1993) *Solicitors Journal*, Expert Witnesses Supplement, 37 (3 December).

Furthermore, although it is undeniable that scientific truth is sometimes a casualty of courtroom 'battles of experts', it should not be overlooked that defence experts actively promote truth-finding in criminal litigation. Defence examiners may expose gaps or errors in prosecution scientific evidence, propose alternative interpretations of agreed primary facts, or draw the fact-finder's attention to points of genuine scientific disagreement. Although a second scientific viewpoint in a sense makes the fact-finder's task more difficult, it is surely preferable to be honest and open at trial about the limitations of scientific proof than to KISS[184] the jury for the sake of smoothing the path to criminal convictions.[185] Earlier in the process, defence examiners may pre-empt miscarriages of justice by ferreting out previously undisclosed material, the significance of which will not always be appreciated by scientists instructed by the prosecution who are working to a different 'theory of the case'. Moving to an exclusive system of court-appointed experts would therefore increase the risk of convicting the innocent, as well as fuelling perceptions of injustice. In light of these considerations and the long-standing association between scientific evidence and miscarriages of justice, it is difficult to see how preventing the parties from instructing their own expert witnesses could be justified as a progressive procedural reform in England and Wales.

Another possibility would be to provide for court-appointed experts *in addition* to any expert witnesses instructed by the parties. At first blush, this proposal might appear to strike a sensible compromise between party autonomy and the court's desire for a more formal means of quality control over expert testimony. However, any perceived advantage of this 'mixed economy' of forensic expertise is largely illusory. First and foremost, the proposal relinquishes the court-appointed expert's greatest asset: unchallenged authority to dictate the scientific facts of the case. A mixed economy system would not pre-empt battles of expertise. It might instead exacerbate the jury's confusion by inviting them to choose between three, rather than just two, competing scientific conclusions. Besides, it is unclear what jurors should be expected to infer from the fact that one expert bears the imprimatur of the court, whilst the others are called by the parties. If jurors are supposed to accord special weight to the testimony of the court's expert just in virtue of the fact that he is not a presumptively 'biased' party-instructed expert, this might appear to imply that the evidence of the court-appointed expert is *de facto* determinative whilst the parties' experts are merely going through the motions. Conversely, if being instructed by the court carries no special status, it is unclear what the purpose of the exercise is supposed to be and uncertain whether instructing court experts could be an efficient use of scarce judicial resources.[186] There may be greater scope for experts to play a more limited role as court

---

[184] Disreputable advice for presenters scornful of the intelligence of their audience: Keep It Simple and Stupid.

[185] Cf. Sir Roger Ormrod [1968] *Crim LR* 240, 245–6: 'Indifferent scientific advice given into the court's ear is much worse than the worst expert evidence given from the witness-box.'

[186] It is instructive to observe how the Court of Appeal dances around this issue in *R v Clark* [2003] EWCA Crim 1020, [40]: 'The Family Court charged with the responsibility of making these decisions [concerning the welfare of the appellant's third child] had thought it right to approach an independent expert of its own to review the case. That expert was Professor David. He came, therefore, to the case with a completely independent stance. It was only when his conclusions were favourable to the defence that they sought to rely upon his evidence. Recording these matters is not in any way to suggest that the other experts did not do their best to give evidence which was independent of the side that instructed them but the value of an expert free from any influence, however innocently manifesting itself, cannot be discounted.'

advisers or 'assessors' on the model now familiar in civil litigation.[187] Court-appointed advisers might assist the trial judge to understand expert evidence adduced by the parties and to formulate appropriate directions to the jury. Be that as it may, most commentators who advocate the introduction of court-appointed experts in English criminal adjudication appear to have something more substantial in mind.

These objections do not establish that court-appointed experts could *never* make a positive contribution to criminal litigation, but they do seriously question whether judicial intervention would satisfactorily resolve the problem of securing reliable scientific evidence in the general run of criminal cases. The desirability of instructing a court-appointed expert in particular circumstances might be better gauged by the trial judge on a case-by-case basis. Implementing a system of supplementary court experts would not require major procedural reform, since trial judges arguably already posses the authority to instruct scientific experts as part of their basic common law duty of ensuring a fair trial.[188] By convention this residual judicial authority is seldom invoked in criminal proceedings, partly out of deference to party autonomy, but also because trial judges currently lack the structural opportunity and institutional resources to set about instructing expert witnesses of their own motion. Were it felt that court-appointed experts should play a greater role in English criminal litigation than has traditionally been the case, the way forward lies in training trial judges to discern when circumstances call for supplementary scientific expertise and equipping them to know which experts to consult, and for what purposes.[189]

If radical solutions like an exclusive system of court-appointed experts only flatter to deceive, we must concentrate instead on making existing adversarial procedures perform better in accommodating scientific evidence. There is genuine scope for improvement in such matters as pre-trial disclosure and agreement of scientific evidence,[190] as well as in the seemingly mundane but actually very important sphere of educating lawyers about science, and scientists about criminal justice. It is platitudinous to say that lawyers would be more effective in their preparation and presentation of forensic science evidence if they cultivated a better understanding of scientific methodologies, and that scientists would be more effective expert witnesses if they improved their grasp of the basic aspirations and assumptions of English criminal trials. But sometimes the best law reform solutions are simple and prosaic.

It should by now be apparent why problems surrounding expert qualification and the threat of 'bias' are much deeper and more enduring than the periodic, almost ritualistic,

---

[187] See *Zuckerman on Civil Procedure*, §20.85ff.

[188] This seemingly follows from the trial judge's general residual discretion to call any witness of fact in the interests of justice: *R v Roberts* (1985) 80 Cr App R 89, CA; *R v Cleghorn* [1967] 2 QB 584, CA. In former times court-appointed experts were the norm, though modern authority for the continued existence of a residual judicial power to instruct court-appointed experts is admittedly sparse: e.g. *R v Holden* (1838) 8 Car & P 606, 173 ER 638.

[189] Debates surrounding scientific literacy, judicial training and the provision of 'bench books'/instruction manuals are comparatively well-advanced in the USA: see Federal Judicial Center, *Reference Manual on Scientific Evidence* (Federal Judicial Center, 1994; 2nd edn. 2000); Laurens Walker and John Monahan, '*Daubert* and the *Reference Manual*: An Essay on the Future of Science in Law' (1996) 82 *Virginia LR* 837; Sheila Jasanoff, 'What Judges Should Know about the Sociology of Science' (1993) 77 *Judicature* 77.

[190] Now see Criminal Procedure Rules (CrimPR) 2010, Rule 33.7 (power of court to direct single joint expert). This is not a new idea: Paul Roberts, 'Forensic Science Evidence After Runciman' [1994] *Crim LR* 780, 783–8; Roberts and Willmore, *The Role of Forensic Science Evidence*, §3.1.

denunciation of individual rogue experts in the courts and in the media might lead one to believe. The Court of Appeal never tires of saying that the professional duties of expert witnesses are 'owed to the court and override any obligation to the person from whom the expert has received instructions or by whom the expert is paid. It is hardly necessary to say that experts should maintain professional objectivity and impartiality at all times.'[191] These are impeccable normative ideals, but experts who have been exposed to the direct and more subtle pressures of adversarial criminal proceedings might be forgiven for experiencing, if not total bewilderment, at least mild cognitive dissonance. Legal process is only too happy in principle to offload responsibility for findings of fact by deferring to pertinent scientific expertise. Yet in the very act of deference lies the possibility of being duped by a charlatan, or taken for a ride by counterfeit junk science; and seemingly the only recourse is to rely on the evaluations of other scientists, whose credentials may in turn be disputed. At some point the law is obliged to trust, but it does so grudgingly. An unshakeable institutional attachment to an abstract conception of objective and impartial science is combined with regulation scepticism for individual flesh-and-blood experts, who are frequently found wanting when measured against the unattainable ideal.

The law's schizoid attitude to scientific evidence is hardly surprising, since it merely replicates society's general ambivalence about the merits of science – an ambivalence given cultural expression in classic tales of mad scientists, from Dr Frankenstein to Dr Strangelove. Whether the topic is climate change and global warming, BSE/mad cow disease, combined-MMR jabs, or the existence of weapons of mass destruction in Iraq, experts are simultaneously feted for their privileged access to the truth and pilloried for their supposed incompetence, equivocation, and duplicity.[192] Forensic science evidence receives special treatment only to the extent that pervasive social tensions are played out within a distinctive institutional framework of principles of criminal justice. In England and Wales, this implies, in particular, that expert evidence must conform to the fundamental precepts of adversarial criminal procedure.[193]

---

[191] *R v B(T)* [2006] 2 Cr App R 3, [2006] EWCA Crim 417, [176]. And see CrimPR 2010, Rule 33.2: 'Expert's duty to the court'.

[192] For discussions of science in its broader social context, see David Nelken, 'A Just Measure of Science', in Michael Freeman and Helen Reece (eds.), *Science in Court* (Ashgate, 1998); Sheila Jasanoff, *Science at the Bar: Law, Science and Technology in America* (Harvard UP, 1997); Peter H. Schuck, 'Multi-Culturalism Redux: Science, Law and Politics' (1993) 11 *Yale Law and Policy Review* 1; Roger Smith and Brian Wynne (eds.), *Expert Evidence: Interpreting Science in the Law* (Routledge, 1989).

[193] See further, Paul Roberts, 'Science, Experts and Criminal Justice', in Mike McConville and Geoffrey Wilson (eds.), *The Handbook of the Criminal Justice Process* (OUP, 2002).

12

CONFESSIONS

12.1 SELF-INCRIMINATING EVIDENCE

Confessions are freighted with enormous social and cultural significance. The confessional is central to the western Christian tradition, Protestants and Catholics differing only on liturgical details such as whether confession should be a public incantation by the congregation or a private interview between priest and penitent. The confession is also a staple of the western literary canon, from the *Confessions* of Augustine,[1] Montaigne,[2] Rousseau,[3] and De Quincey[4] to (indubitably at the other end of the literary spectrum) *Confessions of a Window Cleaner*[5] and *Confessions of a Shopaholic*.[6] Contemporary society is characterized by an almost compulsive desire to reveal all to therapists, support groups, internet blogs, and talk-show hosts. It should hardly be surprising if some of these associations also attach to legal evidence and proof. What, after all, could be more compelling proof of guilt as a basis for criminal conviction than to hear the accused condemn himself out of his own mouth? In France confessions are known as *la reine des preuves* – the queen of proofs. In common with other western legal traditions, confession evidence has since time immemorial been afforded special attention in English criminal trials.[7]

The accused is always at liberty to plead guilty in adversarial criminal proceedings and thereby unilaterally conclude a contested criminal trial. This might be regarded as the most comprehensive species of 'confession', and it is certainly the most conclusive in the eyes of the law. It is normally very difficult to reopen the tactical decision to plead guilty on appeal.[8] When considering 'confession evidence' in the context of criminal adjudication, however, we are usually referring to a situation in which the accused has confessed, or is alleged to have done so, but has since retracted and is now pleading 'not guilty'. This might well involve an attempt to have the (alleged) confession excluded as inadmissible

---

[1] James J. O'Donnell (ed.), *Augustine: Confessions* (OUP, 1992 [AD 397]), on-line at: www.stoa.org/hippo/.   [2] *Montaigne: Essays*, trans. John M. Cohen (Penguin, 1993 [1580–95]).

[3] *The Confessions of Jean-Jacques Rousseau*, trans. J. Cohen (Penguin, 2005 [1781]).

[4] Thomas De Quincey, *The Confessions of an English Opium-Eater: And Other Writings* (OUP, 2008 [1821]).

[5] (Columbia Pictures, 1974). This series of 'British sex comedies', starring Robin Askwith, also included such instantly forgettable titles as *Confessions of a Pop Performer*, *Confessions of a Driving Instructor* and *Confessions from a Holiday Camp*.

[6] (Touchstone Pictures, 2009) ('All she ever wanted was a little credit...A new job? Hopefully. A new man? Possibly. A new handbag? Absolutely!')

[7] John Langbein, *The Origins of Adversary Criminal Trial* (OUP, 2003), 218–21, dates the emergence of a special rule of admissibility for confessions to around 1740. Confessions were presumably routinely received in evidence before that time.   [8] *R v Chalkley* [1998] QB 848, CA.

evidence. Failing that, where a confession does go before the jury, the accused will seek to reinterpret its apparent meaning or to undermine its reliability or both – knowing full well that a confession is likely to be treated by the jury as damning evidence of guilt, unless its probative impact can be neutralized by a plausible explanation capable, at the least, of raising a reasonable doubt. The undeniable power of confession evidence also explains its long association with miscarriages of justice.[9] This troubled relationship forms the backdrop to the evolution of the modern procedural framework described in this chapter, which was designed with the express purpose of reducing the risk of wrongful conviction arising from false confessions.[10]

The accused might be condemned as much by what he does *not* say as by what he positively confesses. Guilty silence parallels guilty words as potentially incriminating conduct. If the accused fails to provide a satisfactory explanation when confronted with an accusation, and even more so if the accused subsequently declines to testify in his own defence at trial, the jury may easily conclude that silence implies the absence of anything positive to be said by way of exculpation. In the context of a criminal trial in which the accused stands in peril of condemnation and punishment for serious wrongdoing, the normal expectation would be that if the accused is not guilty, or guilty only of a lesser charge, he would be keen to take advantage of any reasonable opportunity to say so. Whilst English law has readily admitted and relied upon evidence of confessions, however, it has traditionally been sceptical of the supposed evidential value of silence. The accused's 'privilege against self-incrimination' and the closely related 'right to silence' have generally been regarded as cornerstones of common law criminal procedure, which have prevented prosecutors and judges from inviting juries to draw adverse inferences from the accused's silence in or out of court. We will see in the next chapter that the legal status of the privilege against self-incrimination is problematic, not only because it has been diluted by legislation and case-law in recent decades but also, more fundamentally, because it is surprisingly difficult to ground the privilege in a convincing justificatory rationale. Before grappling with modern English law's attitude towards the probative significance of silence, however, we first need to deal with the comparatively more straightforward topic of confessions as evidence. What is a 'confession'? When are confessions admissible, and how is this determined? What are the procedural rights of detainees during the period of police interrogation? How should trial judges direct juries in relation to confessions? Is there special provision for particularly vulnerable suspects, such as children and adults with mental disability? To what extent can the accused rely upon the confession of a co-accused? These are the principal doctrinal questions addressed in this chapter.

In orthodox textbook treatments of the subject, confessions are presented as one amongst a long and arcane list of hearsay exceptions[11] whilst the accused's privilege

---

[9] See, generally, Clive Walker, 'Miscarriages of Justice in Principle and Practice', in Clive Walker and Keir Starmer (eds.), *Miscarriages of Justice: A Review of Justice in Error* (Blackstone, 1999); I. H. Dennis, 'Miscarriages of Justice and the Law of Confessions: Evidentiary Issues and Solutions' [1993] *Public Law* 291.

[10] Royal Commission on Criminal Justice, *Report*. Cm.2263 (HMSO, 1993), ch 4; Royal Commission on Criminal Procedure, *Report*. Cmnd. 8092 (HMSO, 1981), ch 4.

[11] The orthodox common law position was that a voluntary out-of-court confession was admissible as an exception to the hearsay rule (though the historical accuracy of this doctrinal basis for admissibility is disputed by Peter Mirfield, *Silence, Confessions and Improperly Obtained Evidence* (OUP, 1997), 54–5). Now also see Criminal Justice Act 2003, s.118, discussed in §9.6.

against self-incrimination is submerged under the general rubric of 'Privilege'. This may have suited an undifferentiated Law of Evidence in its formative years, but it makes little sense today, for two important reasons. First, confessions and the right to silence have assumed unprecedented importance in modern criminal proceedings, and their legal significance has been further enhanced by the advent of the Human Rights Act. It is high time that these topics came in from the cold and were afforded the headline-billing they deserve in dedicated chapters of their own.[12] When the spotlight shifts in this way, a second methodological principle is thrown into sharper relief. Neither confessions nor the right to silence can be properly understood unless doctrinal rules of evidence are placed in their broader procedural context. In striving to cram novel juridical forms into the pre-packaged taxonomies of a unified Law of Evidence, traditional treatments have driven a distorting wedge between the law of criminal evidence and the law and practice of criminal procedure. In this chapter and the next, we endeavour to put evidence and procedure back together again, and to situate them both within the broader institutional framework and socio-legal realities of criminal adjudication.

12.2 THE LAW AND PRACTICE OF CUSTODIAL INTERROGATION

The state is not only the principal prosecutor, but also the primary investigator, of most serious crime. To facilitate such investigation the police and other investigative authorities are entrusted with considerable powers to search person and premises, place citizens under arrest, confiscate contraband and evidence, and detain suspects for interrogation.[13] To preserve our freedom from excessive state interference such powers must be strictly delimited by law and their exercise assiduously supervised. Constitutional principles and human rights law provide most of the instruments for that purpose, but the law of criminal evidence is also concerned with some aspects of the broader constitutional structure.

Custodial interrogation exposes the suspect to two broad types of risk for which legal protection is required: (1) the risk that a detainee's person or dignity will be abused; and (2) the risk that a detainee's statements will be distorted or misinterpreted or even possibly concocted, in order to generate incriminating evidence against him. So far as the first type of risk is concerned, it is accepted in every enlightened society that no person should be subjected to physical violence, unless bodily restraint is necessary in order to prevent a detainee from harming others or himself. The police suspect and the convicted prisoner enjoy the same fundamental rights not to be killed, injured, or physically abused as any other member of the community. Physical torture during interrogation is forbidden, not by virtue of special provisions of criminal procedure, but by ordinary criminal law and

---

[12] Now also see Andrew L.-T. Choo, Evidence (OUP, 2nd edn. 2009), chs 4–5; I. H. Dennis, *The Law of Evidence* (Sweet & Maxwell, 3rd edn. 2007), chs 5–6. cf. Colin Tapper, *Cross & Tapper on Evidence* (OUP, 11th edn. 2007), chs 9 and 14; Peter Murphy, *Murphy on Evidence* (OUP, 10th edn. 2008), chs 9 and 14.

[13] For an overview, see Paul Roberts, 'Law and Criminal Investigation', in Tim Newburn, Tom Williamson, and Alan Wright (eds.), *Handbook of Criminal Investigation* (Willan, 2007).

human rights standards.[14] The common law's emphatic rejection of evidence tainted by torture was reiterated in *A v Home Secretary (No 2)*, as we saw in Chapter 5.[15]

Torture and other forms of physical or mental abuse in the course of an official investigation degrade the system of justice as well as harming the individual suspect. Though torture would sometimes doubtless be an effective way of getting at the truth, there is no deep conflict between the need to protect citizens from crime and the policy of rejecting the evidential fruits of torture or degrading treatment. Convictions procured through these methods would defeat the aims of the administration of justice, by reducing police investigations themselves to a form of criminality and consequently undermining the moral legitimacy of criminal proceedings. Abuses falling short of criminal offences, such as insulting or degrading treatment of the suspect, also threaten to undermine the moral legitimacy of the criminal process.[16] Such investigative practices contradict foundational principles of criminal evidence, especially the principle of upholding the moral integrity of the verdict and the principle of humane treatment.[17]

Physical maltreatment and other substantive rights violations aside, police station detainees are also vulnerable to their statements being distorted or manipulated, so as to implicate them in a crime they did not commit. This type of forensic risk is especially difficult to reduce. Questioning in the police station typically occurs in a tense atmosphere and under conditions of relatively low visibility limiting opportunities for external scrutiny. Suspects under investigation often experience considerable strain even when they are innocent: just being suspected or accused may induce guilty feelings, as nearly everybody experiences when a police car draws up behind us or the store detective looks our way. Those who genuinely do have something to hide or fear, meanwhile, may be doubly susceptible to confusion and manipulation. If one adds to this the natural tendency of the investigator to manipulate the suspect's responses and interpret them in a way that confirms his own suspicions, the scope for generating unreliable confessions is manifest.[18]

If the reliability of confessions could be guaranteed, only the guilty would be convicted on their confession. From a practical point of view, however, false or misleading confessions do present the courts with a serious problem. In the common law tradition the interrogation of suspects is carried out by police officers with minimal outside supervision. The police have an obvious motive for concealing any breach of the suspect's rights or procedural irregularity for which fellow officers are responsible, whilst suspects themselves

---

[14] Torture is an international crime and its prohibition is a *jus cogens* norm of customary international law: see Robert Cryer *et al*, *An Introduction to International Criminal Law and Procedure* (CUP, 2007), 294.

[15] *A v Secretary of State for the Home Department (No 2)* [2006] 2 AC 221, [2005] UKHL 71, discussed in §5.4(c).

[16] Verbal abuse of another does not generally constitute a criminal offence because the victim can usually spare himself any harm or indignity by walking away from the abuser. But a suspect under arrest is not free to do so, hence his abuse by insults and degradation is offensive to our sense of justice.   [17] §1.3.

[18] See Andrew Sanders and Richard Young, *Criminal Justice* (Butterworths, 3rd edn. 2007), 269–73; Andrew Ashworth and Mike Redmayne, *The Criminal Process* (OUP, 3rd edn. 2005), ch 4; Gisli H. Gudjonsson, 'Investigative Interviewing', in Tim Newburn, Tom Williamson, and Alan Wright (eds.), *Handbook of Criminal Investigation* (Willan, 2007); Gisli Gudjonsson, *The Psychology of Interrogations and Confessions* (Wiley, 2003); Robert Kee, *Trial and Error* (Penguin, 2nd edn. 1989); Laurence S. Wrightsman and Saul M. Kassin, *Confessions in the Courtroom* (Sage, 1993); Jerome H. Skolnick, *Justice Without Trial: Law Enforcement in Democratic Society* (Wiley NY, 2nd edn. 1966), 182.

have an equally obvious self-interest in fabricating stories of malpractice in order to have a true confession excluded at trial. Before the days of tape-recording, when most or all of the information about the interrogation came from presumptively biased sources, the courts were bound to have great difficulty in ascertaining what really transpired in the interview room in order to assess the reliability of a custodial confession. Major reforms have been implemented since then. The procedural landscape of criminal investigations in England and Wales was transformed by the Police and Criminal Evidence Act (PACE) 1984, which came into force nationwide on 1 January 1986.

Threats to the proper administration of criminal justice arising from oppressive inter-rogation or unreliable confessions are now addressed directly by section 76 of PACE 1984 (and indirectly by section 78, where police impropriety would make it unfair to adduce a contested confession).[19] Section 76 will be examined in detail later in the chapter. However, the specifically *evidentiary* response to the problem of unreliable confessions is activated only at the trial-end of a long investigative and prosecution process, by which time legal intervention might be regarded as too little and too late in many cases. Anticipating these concerns, PACE 1984 introduced a number of important measures designed to safeguard suspects' interests and assist the courts to supervise custodial interrogation effectively.[20] To understand and evaluate the law of criminal evidence relating to confessions and the evidential value of silence during police questioning, we first need to review, at least in outline, the legal framework and institutional context structuring custodial inter-rogation, beginning with the elementary question: when can a suspect be detained for questioning?

(a) POLICE POWERS TO DETAIN SUSPECTS FOR QUESTIONING

The common law has traditionally viewed police officers as 'citizens in uniform' with exactly the same legal powers and duties as ordinary members of the public.[21] Whilst this quaint conception of policing became increasingly anachronistic with the development of professionalized police forces over the course of the twentieth century, it does help to explain why the legality of police detention for questioning was not settled at common law until as recently as the early 1980s.[22] If ordinary citizens cannot detain suspects for ques-tioning – indeed this might constitute the offence of false imprisonment – neither could 'citizens in uniform'. In reality, at least by mid-century police officers were in fact routinely

---

[19] *R v Mason* [1988] 1 WLR 139, CA.

[20] For overviews and detailed analysis, see Sanders and Young, *Criminal Justice*, ch 4; Michael Zander, *The Police and Criminal Evidence Act 1984* (Sweet & Maxwell, 5th edn. 2006); Ed Cape and Richard Young (eds.), *Regulating Policing: The Police and Criminal Evidence Act 1984 – Past, Present and Future* (Hart, 2008); Mike Maguire, 'Regulating the Police Station: The Case of the Police and Criminal Evidence Act 1984', in Mike McConville and Geoffrey Wilson (eds.), *The Handbook of the Criminal Justice Process* (OUP, 2002); Andrew Sanders, 'Rights, Remedies, and the Police and Criminal Evidence Act' [1988] *Crim LR* 802.

[21] See, e.g, Stephen Skinner, 'Citizens in Uniform: Public Defence, Reasonableness and Human Rights' [2000] *Public Law* 266; Helen Beynon, 'The Ideal Civic Condition' [1986] *Crim LR* 580 (ascribing the phrase to J. F. Stephen). This idea is closely linked with the notion that British policing is effectively community self-policing or 'policing by consent'. For more nuanced histories, see David Dixon, *Law in Policing* (OUP, 1997), ch 2; Clive Emsley, 'The Birth and Development of the Police', in Tim Newburn (ed.), *Handbook of Policing* (Willan, 2nd edn. 2008); Robert Reiner, *The Politics of the Police* (OUP, 3rd edn. 2000), ch 1.

[22] *Holgate-Mohammed* v *Duke* [1984] AC 437, HL.

detaining suspects for questioning, on the euphemistic pretext that suspects were 'helping the police with their inquiries'.[23] This created a most undesirable situation in which suspects were held in police stations in a kind of legal limbo, without any proper legal framework to regulate their detention or to safeguard their procedural rights. It was a system of studied non-regulation ripe for abuse.

PACE 1984 was enacted with the express purpose of regularizing police detention and subjecting it to the rule of law. Section 37 authorizes detention where a 'custody officer has reasonable grounds for believing that [the suspect's] detention without being charged is necessary... to obtain... evidence by questioning him'.[24] This confirmed a decisive shift in English law's conception of the legitimate purposes of custodial interrogation, as Wolchover and Heaton-Armstrong comment:

PACE embodied the philosophy of encouraging the use of detention as an instrument for the obtaining of evidence by questioning. Thus, the very reason why 98 per cent of defendants who are charged are arrested is in order that they can be interrogated.[25]

At the same time, PACE mandated that custodial interrogation would henceforth be strictly delimited and supervised. Section 37 requires that investigative questioning in relation to any particular offence must cease as soon as there is sufficient evidence to support a formal criminal charge. Questioning may continue in relation to other alleged or suspected offences, but the police are prohibited from using custodial interrogation to build up a case beyond the charging threshold.[26]

Police interviews and the duration and conditions of detention are regulated in minute detail by PACE Code of Practice C governing 'Detention, Treatment and Questioning', the 'DTQ Code'.[27] In brief, suspects may be detained without charge on the authorization of police officers for up to 36 hours,[28] but this period can be extended on application to

---

[23] David Wolchover and Anthony Heaton-Armstrong, *Confession Evidence* (Sweet & Maxwell, 1996), 619; David Dixon, *Law in Policing* (OUP, 1997), ch 4. The 1964 Judges' Rules may in fact have conferred *ex post facto* legitimacy on practices of detention for questioning already well-entrenched by the 1950s. Dixon, ibid. 135–6, observes: 'The first of the 1964 rules gave explicit approval to the questioning of arrested suspects before charge. In retrospect, this was an extraordinary use of administrative rule-making power... In the 1980s, there was considerable criticism that PACE legalized police malpractice: in fact, the 1964 Judges' Rules were a better example of doing so.' Also see David Dixon, 'Authorise and Regulate: A Comparative Perspective on the Rise and Fall of a Regulatory Strategy', in Ed Cape and Richard Young (eds.), *Regulating Policing* (Hart, 2008).

[24] Section 37(2). The need for further questioning is also a ground for extending the period of detention: ss.42(1)(a) and 43(4)(a).   [25] Wolchover and Heaton-Armstrong, *Confession Evidence*, 137.

[26] Post-charge questioning has, however, been mooted in relation to detainees suspected of involvement in terrorism or organized crime: see Clive Walker, 'Post-Charge Questioning of Suspects' [2008] *Crim LR* 509.

[27] PACE Code C, *Code of Practice for the Detention, Treatment and Questioning of Persons by Police Officers* (2008 Edition). Also see PACE Code H, *Code of Practice in Connection with the Detention, Treatment and Questioning by Police Officers of Persons under Section 41 of, and Schedule 8 to, the Terrorism Act 2000* (2006). The DTQ Code is one of eight PACE Codes of Practice, designated A–H, issued by the Home Secretary pursuant to sections 66 and 60A of PACE 1984: see http://police.homeoffice.gov.uk/operational-policing/powers-pace-codes/pace-code-intro/. PACE 1984, s.67(10), provides that, 'A failure on the part... of a police officer to comply with any provision of such a code... shall not of itself render him liable to any criminal or civil proceedings'. However, by subsection (11): 'In all criminal and civil proceedings any such code shall be admissible in evidence; and if any provision of such a code appears to the court or tribunal conducting the proceedings to be relevant to any question arising in the proceedings it shall be taken into account in determining that question'.   [28] PACE 1984, ss.41(1) and 42(1)

a magistrate for a maximum of 96 hours,[29] that is, four days in the police cells without charge. Those held on terrorism charges can be detained for substantially longer periods.[30] Vulnerable, confused, or intimidated suspects have been known to make false confessions after very much shorter periods of custodial detention than four days. The duration and conditions of detention are subject to periodic reviews by the appointed custody officer[31] – a police officer of at least the rank of sergeant who is not otherwise involved in the relevant criminal investigation[32] – who is tasked with monitoring the treatment of detainees and ensuring their welfare.[33]

The accused is not obliged to say anything when interviewed by the police. As we will explore in the next chapter, 'the principle against self-incrimination…is a long recognized principle of the common law'.[34] However, although paragraph 1.1 of PACE Code C unambiguously states that '[a]ll persons in custody must be dealt with expeditiously, and released as soon as the need for detention no longer applies', there is no indication, either in PACE itself or in the accompanying Codes of Practice, that the accused's prerogative to refuse to answer questions implies that the police cannot continue to press him for answers. Clearly, the 'right to silence' in the police station is not to be confused with an immunity form being questioned under PACE. One of the advantages of arrest and interrogation for investigators is precisely the opportunity to break down the accused's natural inhibitions against making a confession, partly through the inherently coercive nature of custodial detention. The Royal Commission on Criminal Procedure, on whose recommendations the PACE detention regime was based, nonetheless acknowledged that 'in psychological terms custody in itself and questioning in custody develop forces upon many suspects which…so affect their minds that their wills crumble and they speak when they would have stayed silent'.[35] Here we glimpse the acute tension between the practical demands of effective criminal investigation and normative legal requirements, which still remains substantially unresolved.

(b) DETAINEES' RIGHTS

Having provided for the lawful detention and questioning of suspects in the police station, PACE 1984 proceeds to specify detainees' rights. The most important right afforded

---

[29] Sections 43–44. The overall time-limit is set by s.44(3).

[30] Terrorism Act 2006, s.23(7), amending the Terrorism Act 2000, sch.8. The maximum period of detention without charge for terrorist suspects has repeatedly been extended in recent years, from 7 days to 14 days to the current limit of 28 days (the government having been unsuccessful in its serial attempts to persuade Parliament to authorize 90 days', 60 days', or 42 days' detention without charge).

[31] Section 40 and Code C, Part 15.

[32] PACE 1984, s.36. Custody officers are duty-bound 'to ensure: (a) that all persons in police detention at [their police] station are treated in accordance with this Act and any code of practice issued under it and relating to the treatment of persons in police detention; and (b) that all matters relating to such persons which are required by this Act or by such codes of practice to be recorded are recorded in the custody records relating to such persons': PACE 1984, s.39(1).   [33] Section 39(1) and Code C, para.1.1A and Part 2.

[34] *Wizzard* v R [2007] UKPC 21, [37] (Lord Phillips).

[35] *Report*, Cm.8092 (HMSO, 1981), paras.3.66 and 4.74. Indeed, the Commission concluded that the 'rarity of complete silence may not be altogether surprising in view of the psychological pressures that custody in the police station generates': ibid. para. 4.46. The US Supreme Court made similar observations in *Miranda* v *Arizona* 384 US 436, 457, 467 (1966).

to suspects in police detention is undoubtedly the right to custodial legal advice, which is guaranteed by primary legislation. Section 58(1) of PACE provides:

A person arrested and held in custody in a police station…shall be entitled, if he so requests, to consult a solicitor privately at any time.[36]

Suspects also have a flanking statutory right not to be held incommunicado. Section 56 of PACE guarantees detainees the right to have someone informed of their arrest (the fabled 'one phone call') and of their place of detention. This right is calculated to lessen the fear and psychological pressures associated with isolated confinement.

These enumerated statutory rights are underpinned and extended by detailed provisions of PACE Code of Practice C. Paragraph 3.1 of Code C requires the custody officer to notify detainees on their arrival at the police of their rights: to have someone informed of their detention; to consult privately with a solicitor; and to be provided with copies of the PACE codes of practice for consultation. The suspect must also be given written notification of these key rights.[37] If the suspect does not know any solicitor, he must be advised of the availability of duty solicitors whose services are provided free of charge.[38] Subject to limited exceptions,[39] a suspect who asks for legal advice may not be interviewed until he has received it, either in person or by telephone. Moreover, suspects are entitled to be accompanied by their legal adviser during the police interview itself,[40] which ought to be a highly significant procedural protection in an adversarial system of justice.

To facilitate judicial supervision of the treatment of suspects in custody, PACE made detailed provision for keeping a written record of the progress of a suspect's detention. The police are now obliged to state their reasons for continuing to detain a suspect,[41] and must record and justify their decision-making in the course of the investigation, particularly in relation to evidentially significant matters like responding to a suspect's request for legal advice,[42] conducting an interrogation,[43] or holding a particular type of identification procedure.[44] Suspects must be reminded of their legal rights, including their right to remain silent, at every significant stage during their detention, such as at the beginning or resumption of formal interviews.[45] Each time the caution is administered a record of it must be made in the custody record together with a note of the suspect's replies, if any.[46]

---

[36] Both these important rights, to have someone informed of one's arrest and to legal advice, can be delayed or denied in limited circumstances: see PACE 1984, ss.56(5)–(5A) and 58(8)–(8A).

[37] PACE Code C, para.3.2.   [38] PACE Code C, para.6.1 and Notes 6B and 6J.

[39] Essentially where delay might risk harm to persons, loss of evidence, or unreasonable obstruction to the conduct of the investigation (e.g. where the solicitor requested will take an excessively long time to arrive, or refuses to attend altogether): PACE Code C, para.6.6 and Annex B.

[40] PACE Code C, para.6.8. The solicitor can only be required to leave if 'their conduct is such that the interviewer is unable properly to put questions to the suspect': ibid. paras.6.9–6.11 and Notes 6D and 6E.

[41] PACE 1984, ss.34, 37(4), 38(3), and 42(5)(b), and Code of Practice C, para.15.

[42] PACE Code C, paras.6.5, 6.6, 6.15–6.17, and Annex B paras.4, 6–7. Also see Note 6E, providing that: 'In a case where an officer takes the decision to exclude a solicitor [from an interview], he must be in a position to satisfy the court that the decision was properly made. In order to do this he may need to witness what is happening himself.'   [43] PACE Code C, para.12.9.

[44] PACE Code D, paras.2.11, 3.25–3.27.   [45] PACE Code C, Part 10.

[46] PACE Code of Practice C, para.12.13 and Annex D. By PACE Code of Practice C, para.11.7: 'An accurate record must be made of each interview, whether or not the interview takes place at a police station…The record must be made during the course of the interview, unless in the investigating officer's view this would not be practicable or would interfere with conduct of the interview, and must constitute either a verbatim record of what has been said or, failing this, an account of the interview which adequately and accurately

Most significant of all for present purposes, PACE introduced routine tape-recording of all interviews with suspects, which is now governed by Code of Practice E.[47] With limited exceptions, it is mandatory to record interviews with suspects in relation to indictable offences triable in the Crown Court, whilst interviews relating to summary offences may be recorded at investigators' discretion.[48] It bears repetition that these safeguards were devised in the light of pre-PACE experience, when detention and questioning in police stations lacked effective regulation, leading to unchecked abuses and miscarriages of justice.

(c) CUSTODIAL LEGAL ADVICE, IN THEORY AND PRACTICE

Police station detainees' notional right under the old Judges' Rules to consult with a solicitor was a paper tiger that interviewing detectives routinely scorned or ignored.[49] The only practical authority to which officers needed to appeal was the (fictional) 'Ways and Means Act'. In creating an express statutory right to custodial legal advice, section 58 of PACE marked a major advance on the pre-PACE position. Still, it must not be assumed that because suspects have a *legal right* to custodial legal advice that they always want or are able to exercise that right in practice. Nor should it be assumed that custodial advice is always appropriately helpful to suspects who actually receive it.

We saw in Chapter 5, in the context of applications under section 78 of PACE to exclude confessions obtained in breach of section 58,[50] that the Court of Appeal has not been entirely consistent in its expressed attitudes towards suspects' right to custodial legal advice. In *Samuel*[51] the Court of Appeal described this as 'one of the most important and fundamental rights of a citizen',[52] a sentiment which the European Court of Human Rights wholly endorses.[53] In *Alladice*,[54] by contrast, the Court of Appeal held that breaches of section 58, for example through unreasonable delay or dubious refusals of a suspect's request to see a solicitor, would not necessarily lead to automatic exclusion of any admissions that the suspect might subsequently make during interrogation. Absent deliberate bad faith, it was 'not possible to say in advance what would or would not be fair'.[55] In

---

summarises it.' Paragraph 11.8 adds that: 'If a written record is not made during the interview it must be made as soon as practicable after its completion'.

[47] PACE Code E, *Code of Practice on Audio Recording Interviews with Suspects* (2008 Edition). Interviews with terrorist suspects detained pursuant to s.41 or sch.7 of the Terrorism Act 2000 are governed by a separate Code of Practice. Also see PACE Code F, *Code of Practice on Visual Recording with Sound of Interviews with Suspects* (2005 Edition), extending Code E *mutatis mutandis* to video-recording.

[48] PACE Code of Practice E, paras.3.1 and 3.3 and Note for Guidance 3A.

[49] A serving chief constable recalls: 'Judges Rules were commonly flouted and some detainees kept in custody for much longer than was necessary and without access to the legal advice to which they were entitled. Many supervisors turned a blind eye to this': Barbara Wilding, 'Tipping the Scales of Justice? A Review of the Impact of PACE on the Police, Due Process and the Search for Truth 1984–2006', in Ed Cape and Richard Young (eds.), *Regulating Policing* (Hart, 2008).   [50] §5.4(b).

[51] *R v Samuel* [1988] QB 615, CA.

[52] ibid. 630; recently endorsed by *R v James (David)* [2008] EWCA Crim 1869, [35]–[36].

[53] The European Court of Human Rights has said that 'in order for the right to a fair trial to remain sufficiently "practical and effective" Article 6(1) requires that, as a rule, access to a lawyer should be provided as from the first interrogation of a suspect by the police, unless it is demonstrated in the light of the particular circumstances of each case that there are compelling reasons to restrict this right': *Salduz v Turkey* (2009) 49 EHRR 19, [55].   [54] *R v Alladice* (1988) 87 Cr App R 380, CA.

[55] ibid. 386.

Alladice itself the Court of Appeal agreed with the trial judge's case-specific assessment. Alladice was regarded as a professional criminal who 'knew the score' and was perfectly capable of exercising his rights without the benefit of professional legal advice. 'Had the solicitor been present,' Lord Lane CJ concluded, 'his advice would have added nothing to the knowledge of his rights which the appellant already had.... This is therefore a case where a clear breach of section 58 nevertheless does not require the Court to rule inadmissible subsequent statements by the defendant.'[56]

Regardless of Mr Alladice's supposed competence as a barrack-room lawyer, such 'harmless error' analysis is always distorted by the hollow ring of insincerity and possible abuse of hindsight. Who can confidently say, after the fact, whether the presence of a solicitor would have changed the course of events? Lord Lane's remarks, moreover, imply an unrealistically narrow conception of the role of the solicitor during police interrogation. As well as providing general legal advice – including, of course, advice as to whether the suspect should answer questions or remain silent – the presence of a defence legal representative in the police station brings reassurance and emotional support to suspects who may be frightened or disorientated. For many detainees, police stations are an unfamiliar environment with a daunting atmosphere. In situations perceived as coercive or threatening it must be reassuring for any detainee to know that somebody is 'on my side', a confidante and champion who will look out for one's interests and ensure proper treatment and fair play. The presence during interrogation of a criminal justice professional independent of the police also serves the fact-finder as an additional unbiased source of information about the conduct of the interview. This remains a significant function even after the advent of routine tape-recording for all formal police interviews in the 1990s. Incidents and interactions can occur before or after the tape is switched on, a reason for caution that applies with equal force to experiments with video-recording.[57] Meanwhile, audio-only tape-recording is restricted to capturing the verbal part of communication, whereas the true meaning of speech is sometimes embedded within the physical, including especially facial, gestures accompanying the spoken word.[58]

Criminal suspects in England and Wales benefit from what must be the most liberal and generous duty solicitor scheme to be found anywhere in the world. All detainees are entitled to free legal advice regardless of means, at a cost of nearly £200 million *per annum*,[59] and the police are obliged to make this known to suspects. PACE Code of Practice C even requires a poster advertising the duty solicitor scheme to be placed prominently in all police station charging areas, no effort being too great or any detail too trivial in the drive to ensure that the availability of free legal advice is communicated effectively to suspects.[60] Moreover, in contrast to most other European jurisdictions, solicitors are entitled to advise their clients during the police interrogation itself. Yet, for all that, it

---

[56] ibid. 387.

[57] Experiments which have proved revealing in several respects: see Mike McConville, 'Videotaping Interrogations: Police Behaviour On and Off Camera' [1992] *Crim LR* 532; Margaret S. Barnes, 'One Experience of Video Recorded Interviews' [1993] *Crim LR* 444.

[58] On the scope for evading PACE protections, see Helen Fenwick, 'Confessions, Recording Rules and Miscarriages of Justice' [1993] *Crim LR* 174.

[59] Legal Services Commission, *Annual Report and Accounts 2008/09* (TSO, 2009), 22.

[60] PACE Code C, para.6.3. Guidance Note 6H further directs that '[i]n addition to a poster in English, a poster or posters containing translations into Welsh, the main ethnic minority languages and the principal European languages should be displayed wherever they are likely to be helpful and it is practicable to do so'.

remains the case that no more than around half, and possibly as little as one third, of police station detainees actually contacts a solicitor.[61] This is a substantial improvement on the pre-PACE position and the advice rate appears to be gradually increasing over time.[62] But there remains a large percentage of suspects who decline the offer of free legal advice, which on the face of it is puzzling.[63] Why refuse free expert help in a tight spot? Empirical research reveals that suspects decline legal advice for a variety of personal reasons and contextual factors, but one recurrent influence is the various 'ploys' devised by police officers to persuade suspects to be interviewed before the duty solicitor arrives, or to forego legal advice altogether.[64] By inducing suspects into 'voluntary' waivers of their right to see a solicitor the police have been able in practice to neutralize section 58 whilst notionally still 'going by the book'.

Empirical data on the performance of advisers who do attend police stations and sit through interviews present no less cause for concern. The first thing to note is that, although advisers may work for solicitors' firms, they are not necessarily themselves trained and admitted solicitors, but rather 'law clerks' or solicitors' assistants. This poses the question whether such individuals are appropriately qualified to be advising suspects during interview on such matters as, for example, whether the facts of the case satisfy legal offence definitions or criteria of exculpation. There are documented cases of 'advisers' being manifestly incompetent and woefully inept.[65] But the issue is not simply one of competence. There is also a major question-mark hanging over the appropriate role and performance of police station legal advisers. Contrary to expectations of combativeness and 'zealous advocacy' in an adversarial process, empirical research has shown that defence legal advisers are often passive, compliant, and reliant upon the police for information about the suspect's situation.[66] Whilst it is fair to point out that a confrontational approach will not always be in a client's best interests,[67] researchers have branded defence legal advisers 'pusillanimous'[68] and found them 'prepared to sit passively through interrogations conducted in a hostile atmosphere and where there were open attempts to intimidate or belittle the suspect'.[69] These data suggest that defence practices castigated by the

---

[61] Zander and Henderson's *Crown Court Study*, para.1.3.3, found that legal advice in person or by telephone, or both, was provided to some 53% (according to the police) or 56% (according to the accused themselves) of police station detainees. These estimates may be on the high side.

[62] A recent study reports an advice rate of 55%: Layla Skinns, '"Let's Get it Over With": Early Findings on the Factors Affecting Detainees' Access to Custodial Legal Advice' (2009) 19 *Policing & Society* 58.

[63] David Brown, *PACE Ten Years On: A Review of the Research*, Home Office Research Study No 155 (HMSO, 1997) suggests an advice rate of 33%. An attendance rate of 25% was reported by Jacqueline Hodgson, 'Tipping the Scales of Justice: The Suspect's Right to Legal Advice' [1992] *Crim LR* 854. Research conducted in the late 1980s estimated the advice rate to be less than 20%.

[64] Such 'ploys' have been found to include: reading the suspect's rights incompletely or incomprehensibly; delaying tactics; misinformation about whether a solicitor will attend, or how long it will take, and so on. See A. Sanders, L. Bridges, A. Mulvaney, and G. Crozier, *Advice and Assistance at Police Stations and the 24 Hour Solicitor Scheme* (LCD, 1989); Sanders and Young, *Criminal Justice*, ch 4.

[65] In the most egregious cases, the office typist or a student on vacation placement has been sent to advise a suspect.

[66] John Baldwin, 'Legal Advice in the Police Station' [1992] *NLJ* 1762 (December 18); Michael McConville, Jacqueline Hodgson, Lee Bridges, and Anita Pavlovic, *Standing Accused* (OUP, 1994), ch 5.

[67] David Roberts, 'Questioning the Suspect: The Solicitor's Role' [1993] *Crim LR* 368.

[68] John Baldwin, 'Legal Advice at the Police Station' [1993] *Crim LR* 371.

[69] McConville *et al*, *Standing Accused*, 113.

Court of Appeal in *Paris, Miller and Abdullahi*,[70] the case of 'the Cardiff Three', might only be the tip of a mostly submerged iceberg.

Stephen Miller was one of three accused convicted of murdering his girlfriend. During a period of interrogation lasting some 13 hours he denied any involvement in the murder no less than 300 times before finally making a confession. Having listened to the interview tapes, Lord Taylor CJ exclaimed that 'each member of this Court was horrified. Miller was bullied and hectored. The officers...were not questioning him so much as shouting at him what they wanted him to say. Short of physical violence, it is hard to conceive of a more hostile and intimidating approach by officers to a suspect.'[71] Resort to such interrogation tactics reinforces the importance of providing advice and support for suspects for the duration of their detention and questioning at the police station. Astonishingly, however, Miller was one of the fortunate minority of suspects actually to have had the benefit (dubious though it was in his case) of a solicitor's presence during the greater part of his interrogation. The Court of Appeal deplored the fact that 'the solicitor appears to have been gravely at fault for sitting through this travesty of an interview'. Hodgson's trenchant conclusion is a reasonable headline-summary of the empirical data on the provision of custodial legal advice in the late 1980s and early 1990s:

The empirical reality of custodial legal advice is that it does not occupy a central role in an adversarial process, but has been redefined by solicitors in essentially non-adversarial terms. The division of labour within criminal defence practices is such that it is never contemplated that the suspect will receive legal advice, competent advice, or, indeed, anything which could properly be called 'advice'.[72]

Since that time, concerted efforts have been made to tighten up the Codes of Practice and secure higher standards of service from defence legal advisers, through more rigorous schemes of training and accreditation, latterly within the framework of franchises awarded by the Legal Services Commission and the introduction of salaried public defenders.[73] The symbiotic relationship between practice and regulation is constantly evolving, and real improvements doubtless continue to be made – though it should be added that the criminal legal aid budget is perennially squeezed (quite apart from the fallout from the current global financial crisis) and some solicitors' firms claim that criminal legal aid work has ceased to be economically viable.[74] Besides, there are limits to what can be achieved simply by changing the rules, because working practices and process outcomes are significantly influenced by the institutional and procedural contexts, occupational cultures, and professional ideologies of police officers and defence legal advisers. The lesson for law reformers is that change must be carried forward on several fronts and at various levels if lasting improvements are to be made. Working to

---

[70] *R v Paris, Miller and Abdullahi* (1993) 97 Cr App R 99, CA.   [71] ibid. 103.

[72] Hodgson, 'Tipping the Scales of Justice', 861. Also see Hodgson, 'Adding Injury to Injustice: The Suspect at the Police Station' (1994) 21 *Journal of Law and Society* 85.

[73] See Ed Cape, 'Assisting and Advising Defendants before Trial', and Lee Bridges, 'The Right To Representation and Legal Aid', both in Mike McConville and Geoffrey Wilson (eds.), *The Handbook of the Criminal Justice Process* (OUP, 2002); Lee Bridges and Jacqueline Hodgson, 'Improving Custodial Legal Advice' [1995] *Crim LR* 101.

[74] A gloomy prognosis is canvassed by Ed Cape, 'The Rise (and Fall?) of a Criminal Defence Profession' [2004] *Crim LR* 401.

promote greater professionalism in police interviewing and respect for law and ethical standards,[75] for example, is at least as important as putting up informational posters in custody suites.[76]

12.3 EVIDENTIARY REGULATION: THE ADMISSIBILITY OF CONFESSIONS

Viewed in historical perspective, English criminal procedure law can be seen to have evolved a two-pronged approach to the forensic risks associated with custodial interrogation. The first prong was constituted by rules to regulate the treatment of suspects in custody. These standards were originally set down as 'rules of practice' in successive editions of the court-issued Judges' Rules, but were subsequently subsumed within the comprehensive statutory framework introduced by PACE 1984, as we have just seen. The second prong comprised a legal rule of admissibility for extra-judicial confessions, technically known as 'informal admissions' (to differentiate them form formal admissions at trial).[77] As Lord Griffiths pithily summarized in *Lam Chi-ming* v *R*:

[T]he rejection of an improperly obtained confession is not dependent only upon possible unreliability but also upon the principle that a man cannot be compelled to incriminate himself and upon the importance that attaches in a civilised society to proper behaviour by the police towards those in their custody.[78]

Thus, informal admissions were admissible at common law only if the accused's confession was made 'voluntarily'. The meaning of a 'voluntary' confession was explained by the Privy Council in *Ibrahim* v *R*,[79] in terms later incorporated into the Judges' Rules:[80]

It is a fundamental condition of the admissibility in evidence against any person, equally of any answer given by that person to a question put by a police officer and of any statement made by that person, that it shall have been voluntary, in the sense that it has not been obtained from him by fear of prejudice or hope of advantage exercised or held out by a person in authority, or by oppression.

Although confessions procured by threats or inducements were notionally inadmissible at common law, English criminal procedure has always evinced a strong sense of the legitimacy and practical utility of confession evidence, just as confessions have always exerted a peculiar hold over the popular imagination. Only four years after *Ibrahim*, Darling J remarked, with no hint of equivocation or embarrassment, that, '[i]t would be a lamentable thing if the police were not allowed to make inquiries, and if statements

---

[75] Seumas Miller, John Blackler, and Andrew Alexandra, *Police Ethics* (Waterside Press, 2006).

[76] See further, A. A. S. Zuckerman, 'Miscarriage of Justice – A Root Treatment' [1992] *Crim LR* 323.

[77] Now pursuant to CJA 1967, s.10, discussed in 3.4(b).

[78] *Lam Chi-ming* v *R* [1991] 2 AC 212, 220, PC.

[79] *Ibrahim* v *R* [1914] AC 599, 609–10, PC, *per* Lord Sumner: 'It has long been established as a positive rule of English criminal law, that no statement by an accused is admissible in evidence against him unless it is shewn by the prosecution to have been a voluntary statement, in the sense that it has not been obtained from him either by fear of prejudice or hope of advantage exercised or held out by a person in authority. The principle is as old as Lord Hale.' For a survey of the pre-PACE common law see Peter Mirfield, *Confessions* (Sweet & Maxwell, 1985), 42.   [80] Principle (e) of the Judges' Rules 1964.

made by prisoners were excluded because of a shadowy notion that if the prisoners were left to themselves they would not have made them'.[81] Confessions were regularly adduced in evidence at trial which had been made in circumstances that any fair-minded person might regard as coercive or involving an inducement. By and large, the appellate courts refused to intervene, regarding applications of the test of 'voluntariness' as a question of fact for the trial judge.[82] The Royal Commission on Criminal Procedure expressed concern that psychologically coercive features of custodial interrogation capable of inducing false confessions 'do not fall within the legal definition of factors that would render a confession involuntary and therefore unreliable. In other words, legal and psychological "voluntariness" do not match.'[83] The time was ripe for replacing the discredited common law test with a statutory framework to regulate the admissibility of extra-judicial confessions.

From 1 January 1986, the old common law test of voluntariness was duly superseded and replaced by section 76 of PACE. Section 76(1) provides that:

In any proceedings a confession made by an accused person may be given in evidence against him in so far as it is relevant to any matter in issue in the proceedings and is not excluded by the court in pursuance of this section.

The principal grounds of exclusion are then adumbrated by section 76(2):

If, in any proceedings where the prosecution proposes to give in evidence a confession made by an accused person, it is represented to the court that the confession was or may have been obtained –
   (a) by oppression of the person who made it; or
   (b) in consequence of anything said or done which was likely, in the circumstances existing at the time, to render unreliable any confession which might be made by him in consequence thereof,
the court shall not allow the confession to be given in evidence against him except in so far as the prosecution proves to the court beyond reasonable doubt that the confession (notwithstanding that it may be true) was not obtained as aforesaid.

It is a measure of how seriously Parliament takes the responsibility of monitoring the quality of confession evidence that the onus is placed squarely on the prosecution to disprove beyond reasonable doubt any objection to the admissibility of a confession under either paragraph (a) or (b) of subsection (2).[84] Section 76 of PACE created an independent doctrinal basis for the admission and exclusion of confession evidence, so that continued reference to concepts and doctrines from the law of hearsay is neither necessary nor desirable when assessing the admissibility of confessions.[85]

---

[81] *R* v *Cook* (1918) 34 TLR 515, 516.

[82] 'A whole body of case law seems to have been conjured out of what are essentially decisions on questions of fact': *DPP* v *Ping Lin* [1976] AC 574, 606, HL, *per* Lord Salmon. See also *Report of the Commission to consider legal procedures to deal with terrorist activities in Northern Ireland* ('the Diplock Report'), Cm.5185 (HMSO, 1972), paras.59, 80ff.

[83] *Report*, Cm.8092 (HMSO, 1981), para.4.73. The quoted passage elides admissibility and reliability, but the main point is unaffected. Also see the Diplock Report (1972), para.84.

[84] The court is also empowered to raise the issue of its own motion: s.76(3).

[85] But see CJA 2003, s.118, discussed in §9.6, which still treats confessions as a common law hearsay exception.

There is, however, no general 'fruit of the poisoned tree' doctrine in English law mandating exclusion of evidence obtained through a tainted confession.[86] Consequently, evidence discovered during an interrogation breaching section 76 does not automatically become inadmissible when the original confession is excluded. Subsection 76(4)(a) of PACE provides that, '[t]he fact that a confession is wholly or partly excluded in pursuance of this section shall not affect the admissibility in evidence...of any facts discovered as a result of the confession'.[87] Subsection 76(5) adds the crucial proviso that reference must not be made to any part of an excluded confession when adducing evidence resulting from it. To illustrate, if the police bully a suspect into confessing where the murder weapon is hidden, the weapon itself would still be admissible even if the confession were excluded under section 76(2) *provided that the weapon could be linked to the accused without referring to the inadmissible confession.* Thus, the murder weapon would be admissible in its own right if it were recovered from the suspect's tool-shed or bore his fingerprints, etc., but not if it were found in the middle of a field and could not be connected to the suspect in any other way than through his knowledge of its location – which *ex hypothesi* cannot be revealed to the jury. The operation of subsections 76(4)–(5) remains subject to section 78's overriding test of procedural fairness discussed in Chapter 5.

(a) ASSESSING ADMISSIBILITY ON THE *VOIR DIRE*

The admissibility of contested confessions is determined by the trial judge, in the absence of the jury, at a *voir dire* hearing,[88] colloquially known as a 'trial within a trial'. Evidence for and against admissibility is called by the parties in the normal way. The question for the trial judge is simply whether the prosecution has proved, beyond reasonable doubt, that the confession was not obtained in contravention of section 76(2). A majority of the Privy Council has said that the accused may not even be cross-examined on the truth of his confession on the *voir dire*,[89] because the truth of the confession is not strictly speaking in issue, only its admissibility. The logic of that proposition may be doubted: as we discuss in relation to section 76(2)(b), below, issues of veracity and procedural propriety are difficult to disentangle, as a matter of logic and common sense.[90] It is, in any case, an established practice in England and Wales that, where a confession is admitted by the trial judge, the jury is not informed that the confession has already successfully overcome a defence

---

[86] 'As for the rule that we do not necessarily exclude the "fruit of the poisoned tree", but admit relevant evidence discovered in consequence of inadmissible confessions, this is the way we strike a necessary balance between preserving the integrity of the judicial process and the public interest in convicting the guilty': *A v Home Secretary (No 2)* [2006] 2 AC 221, [2005] UKHL 71, [88] (Lord Hoffmann); 'The "fruits of the poisoned tree" are not inadmissible in a criminal trial in this country. Accordingly, even if the prospect that such evidence would be deployed at the appellant's trial in the USA were satisfactorily established, it could not be said to be an abuse of process for the appellant to be extradited to another jurisdiction where, like our own, such evidence would, in principle, be admissible': *Mustafa Kamel Mustafa (Abu Hamza) v USA* [2008] EWHC 1357 (Admin), [48].

[87] Section 76(4)(b) likewise preserves the admissibility, 'where the confession is relevant as showing that the accused speaks, writes or expresses himself in a particular way, of so much of the confession as is necessary to show that he does so'.

[88] Sometimes rendered with an optional extra 'e': *voire dire*.

[89] *Wong Kam-ming v R* [1980] AC 247, PC, disapproving *R v Hammond* [1941] 3 All ER 318, CCA (Humphreys J).

[90] Cf. Lord Hailsham's dissent in *Wong Kam-ming v R* [1980] AC 247, 262–4, PC.

challenge on the *voir dire*. As Lord Steyn explained in *Mitchell*,[91] an appeal before the Privy Council originating from the Bahamas:

The principle that the judge must not inform the jury of his decision to reject such a submission is therefore squarely based on the need to avoid the risk of prejudice to a defendant.... The decision on the admissibility of a confession after a *voire dire* is the sole responsibility of the judge. There is no logical reason why the jury should know about the decision of the judge. It is irrelevant to the consideration by the jury of the issues whether the confession was made and, if so, whether it is true. There is also no practical reason why the jury need to be informed of the judge's decision. This is underlined by the fact that in modern English practice the judge's decision after a *voire dire* is never revealed to the jury. Moreover, if the judge reveals his decision to the jury, the risk of unfair prejudice to a defendant is created.

The accused is entitled to renew his challenge to the truth or authenticity[92] of his alleged confession before the jury,[93] and in assessing these issues the jury should not be influenced by any decision made by the judge on the *voir dire*. '[T]he advantages of that system for a defendant,' Lord Rodger observed in *Mushtaq*, 'are not in doubt':

The *voire dire* system allows him to give his evidence on this limited but important matter as to the admissibility of the confession, without infringing his right to elect not to give evidence in the trial of the general issue... Moreover, even where the confession is admitted, the circumstances can be explored again in evidence before the jury who can be invited to take them into account in deciding the weight and value to be attached to the statement. To that extent, at least, the defendant gets a second bite at the cherry.[94]

Testimony given by the accused on the *voir dire* is inadmissible in the main trial, regardless of whether the confession is subsequently admitted or excluded; though if the confession is admitted, the accused's testimony may be used by the prosecution as material for cross-examination – for example, as a previous inconsistent statement – if the accused later elects to testify in his own defence.[95] In an appropriate case, the defence may call expert psychiatric or psychological evidence to substantiate the contention that the accused's confession cannot be relied upon as proof of his guilt, notwithstanding that the confession has been adduced as evidence in the trial.[96]

---

[91] *Mitchell* v R [1998] AC 695, 703, PC. Also *Thompson* v R [1998] AC 811, 842–4, PC.

[92] This used to be a hotly-contested issue, with the accused frequently asserting that admissions ('verbals') had been falsely attributed to them by the police: see Royal Commission on Criminal Procedure, *Report* (1981), para.4.2; Mirfield, *Confessions*, ch 1. The tape-recording requirements introduced by PACE have largely resolved the question of authenticity with regard to formal interviews conducted in the police station, though disputes can still arise in relation to 'spontaneous' statements allegedly made by a suspect prior to a formal interview being held. Also see *Wizzard* v R [2007] UKPC 21, where the issue was whether the accused had been coerced into signing a confession as opposed to the reliability of the confession itself (to the extent that these two issues can be differentiated).

[93] Including making the same arguments and repeating the cross-examination of witnesses that proved unsuccessful on the *voir dire*: R v *Murray* [1951] 1 KB 391, CCA.

[94] R v *Mushtaq* [2005] 1 WLR 1513, [2005] UKHL 25, [38].

[95] *Wong Kam-ming* v R [1980] AC 247, PC.

[96] R v *Fell* [2001] EWCA Crim 696; R v *Ward* [1993] 1 WLR 619, CA; R v *MacKenzie* (1992) 96 Cr App R 98, CA; *Silcott, Raghip and Braithwaite*, *The Times*, 9 December 1991, discussed by Peter Mirfield, 'Expert Evidence and Unreliable Confessions' (1992) 108 *LQR* 528.

In summing-up at the close of trial proceedings, the judge must give a clear direction to the jury that the weight to be attached to a confession is entirely a matter for them, bearing in mind the circumstances in which it was obtained.[97] For a time, it was standard practice for trial judges to direct juries that they should, of course, ignore a confession if they were not sure about its reliability, but that if they were sure it was true and reliable a confession could support a verdict of guilty even if it might have been obtained by oppression.[98] This approach was rejected by the House of Lords (Lord Hutton dissenting) in *Mushtaq* on the basis that it is incompatible both with PACE 1984, s.76(2), and with Article 6[99] of the European Convention on Human Rights to invite the jury to rely upon a confession that was, or may have been, obtained by oppression:

The evidence is excluded because…Parliament considers that it should not play any part in the jury's verdict. It flies in the face of that policy to say that a jury are entitled to rely on a confession even though, as the ultimate arbiters of all matters of fact, they properly consider that it was, or may have been, obtained by oppression or any other improper means…[T]herefore, the logic of section 76(2) of PACE really requires that the jury should be directed that, if they consider that the confession was, or may have been, obtained by oppression or in consequence of anything said or done which was likely to render it unreliable, they should disregard it.[100]

The JSB Specimen Direction was amended accordingly.[101] The situation envisaged in *Mushtaq* will materialize only very rarely (and did not arise, their Lordships unanimously agreed, on the instant facts). One has to imagine a scenario in which the prosecution has proved to the judge on the *voir dire* beyond reasonable doubt that the confession was *not* obtained in violation of section 76(2), and yet after hearing the evidence presented at trial the jury is inclined to think that it might have been and yet still believes beyond reasonable doubt that the confession is true and reliable. It seems distinctly artificial to try to draw a firm distinction between oppression and reliability in this way. In most trials, it will be sufficient for the judge to tell the jury simply that if they are sure the confession is true (taking account of the circumstances in which it was made) they can rely on it, but must otherwise disregard it. The ruling in *Mushtaq* nonetheless retains symbolic importance, in reaffirming English law's commitment to due process and moral legitimacy in criminal adjudication. The procedural fault criticized by the House of Lords in *Mushtaq* was not that the jury might have convicted on the basis of an unreliable confession or that the trial judge must always tell the jury to disregard confessions that might have been obtained by oppression, but rather that the jury had been expressly invited 'to act in a way that was

---

[97] And see *R v Burgess* [1968] 2 QB 112, CA.

[98] *Chan Wei Keung v R* [1967] 2 AC 160, PC; *R v Burgess* [1968] 2 QB 112, CA. The JSB Specimen Direction on confession evidence included the instruction to jurors: 'It is for you to assess what weight should be given to the confession. If you are not sure, for whatever reason, that the confession is true you must disregard it. If, on the other hand, you are sure that it is true you may rely on it.'

[99] Lord Carswell thought that the majority's conclusion could be reached only with the assistance of Article 6 and the Human Rights Act.

[100] *R v Mushtaq* [2005] 1 WLR 1513, [2005] UKHL 25, [46]–[47] (Lord Rodger).

[101] Specimen Direction No 25 now reads: 'If you think that the confession was or might have been obtained by [something said or done which was likely to render it unreliable] you must disregard it…even if you think that it was or may have been true. If, however, you are sure that the confession was not obtained in this way, and that it was true, you may take it into account when considering your verdict.'

incompatible with the appellant's right against self-incrimination under Article 6(1). As such, the direction was itself incompatible with that right.'[102] *Mushtaq*, in other words, did not hold that juries must always be directed not to rely on confessions that might have been obtained by oppression. Rather, it decided that juries must never be told, in terms, that the law sanctions reliance on involuntary confessions.[103]

(b) THE MEANING OF 'CONFESSION'

In the popular imagination a 'confession' is a full, frank, and florid admission of guilt, completely wrapping up the case and leaving no loose ends untied. Such satisfyingly dispositive confessions occasionally appear in real life,[104] but are more likely to be encountered in episodes of *Inspector Morse* or an Agatha Christie novel. Section 82(1) of PACE stipulates a far more inclusive definition of 'confession', being 'any statement wholly or partly adverse to the person who made it'. An adverse statement can be made in words or by non-verbal conduct,[105] such as a nod of the head or holding up one's hands.[106] In addition to the central case of an unvarnished admission, a partly self-serving 'mixed statement'[107] can also constitute an admission under PACE, as where the accused confesses: 'yes I stabbed him, but he attacked me first' (self-defence); or 'yes I shot him, but only because X made me do it' (duress); or 'yes I took the video recorder, because X said I could have it' (lawful authority); and so forth.

A definitional issue which has proved troublesome in practice poses the question whether a statement has to be 'adverse' on its face to qualify as a confession. What if, for example, the suspect gives a false alibi which is later conclusively shown to have been a lie? In retrospect the alibi now appears 'adverse' to the accused. Should it therefore come within the admissibility rules for confessions? One might think that even a proven lie should be inadmissible if it was procured in circumstances that would have led to a confession being excluded at trial. Presenting such material to the jury is, by definition, detrimental to the accused in either scenario. Why should the accused be exposed to forensic disadvantage arising from wrongful treatment in the one instance, but not in the other?[108] It is difficult to see why a false alibi advanced during coercive interrogation should be admissible when any more directly incriminating statement procured in these circumstances would be excluded. And the same might be said for 'significant silences', as we discuss in the next chapter.

Acknowledging the force of these arguments, the Court of Appeal held in Z[109] that even apparently exculpatory extra-judicial admissions must still satisfy section 76 before they

---

[102] *R* v *Mushtaq* [2005] 1 WLR 1513, [53].

[103] *R* v *Pham (Minu)* [2008] EWCA Crim 3182; *Wizzard* v *R* [2007] UKPC 21.

[104] In Zander and Henderson's *Crown Court Study*, para.1.5.2, around one-in-four suspects made undisputed admissions or confessions, but the methodology of the research was too imprecise to assess the frequency of 'full' confessions.

[105] PACE 1984, s.82(1). The old common law requirement that the confession be made to a 'person in authority' (usually a police officer) was abandoned.

[106] Police-organized video-taped re-enactments at the crime-scene are another interesting possibility, as in *Lam Chi-ming* v *R* [1991] 2 AC 212, PC (accused re-enacted throwing murder weapon into the sea).

[107] *R* v *Aziz* [1996] 1 AC 41, HL, reaffirming *R* v *Sharp* [1988] 1 WLR 7, HL.

[108] The argument was accepted by the Supreme Court of Canada in *Piche* v *R* [1971] SCR 23; 11 DLR (3d) 700, as well as by the US Supreme Court in *Miranda* v *Arizona* 384 US 436 (1966). It was a pity that the Court of Appeal in *Sat-Bhambra* saw fit to brush these well considered opinions aside.

[109] *R* v *Z* [2003] 1 WLR 1489, CA.

can be admitted at trial as prosecution evidence against the accused. Rix LJ conceded the logical implication of his own rhetorical question:[110]

If...an accused is driven to make adverse statements by reason of oppression, why should he lose the protection of section 76(2) just because, although he may have sought to exculpate himself, in fact he damned himself?

On further appeal to the House of Lords, however, the more orthodox common law position was restored: in order to constitute an 'admission' within the meaning of section 82(1) a statement must be incriminating on its face and from the moment it is uttered.[111] The House of Lords felt that this conclusion was compelled by the literal wording of the section read in the light of the overall structure of the relevant parts of PACE 1984. '[I]t is wholly implausible,' Lord Steyn insisted, 'that the draftsman would have made express reference only to wholly or partly adverse statements if he also had in mind covering under the definition of "confession" wholly exculpatory statements. There is no support in the preceding case law for such a view.... The plain meaning of the statute is against such a strange interpretation.'[112] Their Lordships were reinforced in this conclusion by the fact that the admissibility of *ex facie* exculpatory statements subsequently deployed as prosecution evidence is still regulated by section 78 of PACE, as well as by the residual common law PV > PE discretion[113] expressly preserved by the statute.[114] In formal legal terms, this analysis is undoubtedly correct, although commentators who regard section 78 as a rather unpredictable and unreliable servant of procedural integrity might not be wholly persuaded. Rix LJ's question in the Court of Appeal retains its rhetorical purchase. Why should the accused who may have been subjected to improper pressures be denied the additional protection afforded by section 76? The circumstances would have to be rather unusual, but it is not impossible to imagine a scenario in which even the outright denial 'I did not do it' might later return to haunt the accused at his trial. If the accused's expostulation was procured by oppression or in circumstances likely to diminish its reliability, why should section 76(2)'s admissibility tests be side-stepped by a restrictive technical conception of 'adverse statement'?[115]

(c) SECTION 76(2)(a): EXCLUSION ON GROUNDS OF OPPRESSION

The first ground of exclusion, specified by section 76(2)(a), is that a tendered confession was obtained by oppression of the accused. This was previously part of the common law test of voluntariness, as we have seen. Section 76(8) contains a partial definition, explicitly stated to be non-exhaustive, which echoes the language of ECHR Article 3:

'oppression' includes torture, inhuman or degrading treatment, and the use or threat of violence (whether or not amounting to torture).

Associations with torture imply rather extreme connotations, but in the light of the common law's traditional understanding of involuntariness and the widespread public

---

[110] ibid. 1500.

[111] sub nom *R v Hasan* [2005] 2 AC 467, [2005] UKHL 22, rehabilitating *R v Park* (1993) 99 Cr App R 270, CA; and *R v Sat-Bhambra* (1988) 88 Cr App R 55, CA.   [112] *R v Hasan* [2005] 2 AC 467, [56].

[113] §2.5(a).   [114] PACE 1984, s.82(3).

[115] For further discussion, see Roderick Munday, 'Adverse Denial and Purposive Confession' [2003] *Crim LR* 850; Mirfield, *Silence, Confessions and Improperly Obtained Evidence*, 57–8.

concerns about false confessions which preceded the enactment of PACE, Parliament must surely have intended that virtually all physical and most psychological ill-treatment of suspects should be regarded as intolerably oppressive for the purposes of assessing the admissibility of extra-judicial confessions. Torture is merely paradigmatic of the tactics to which a liberal rights-respecting polity ought never to resort: '[t]he use of torture is dishonourable. It corrupts and degrades the state which uses it and the legal system which accepts it.'[116] Section 76(2)(a) deliberately makes no reference to the truth or falsity of the confession. The point is that oppression, let alone torture, is an unacceptable means of enforcing the criminal law even if it might sometimes be an efficient way of securing admissions. A state cannot maintain its liberal credentials if its standard repertoire of investigative techniques includes the routine physical or psychological brutalization of criminal suspects.[117] Interrogation tactics falling well short of torture should come within the proscribed sphere of 'oppression'; though it must be conceded that the appropriate boundaries of *psychological* pressure are difficult to stipulate with confidence, not least because the psychological characteristics of individual suspects are infinitely variable.

The Court of Appeal's early decision in *Fulling*[118] remains one of the leading judicial pronouncements on the meaning of 'oppression' under section 76(2)(a) of PACE. At trial, the accused contended that she had eventually confessed, having initially refused to cooperate with the police, only because she was told by her interrogators that her partner was having an affair with the woman being held in the next-door cell. This revelation, the accused later contended in court, was so upsetting to her, and close proximity to her rival so unbearable, that she felt compelled to confess in order to escape from the police station. The trial judge, and then the Court of Appeal, found it unnecessary to investigate the truth of this allegation. Even on the assumption that the accused was telling the truth, it was held, the conduct of the police could not be regarded as constituting 'oppression'. According to Lord Lane CJ, section 76(2)(a)'s concept of oppression bears its ordinary dictionary meaning:

The Oxford English Dictionary as its third definition of the word runs as follows: 'exercise of authority or power in a burdensome, harsh, or wrongful manner; unjust or cruel treatment of subjects, inferiors, etc., or the imposition of unreasonable or unjust burdens'. One of the quotations given under that paragraph runs as follows: 'There is not a word in our language which expresses more detestable wickedness than oppression'.[119]

Lord Lane CJ added that 'it is hard to envisage any circumstances in which such oppression would not entail some impropriety on the part of the interrogator'.[120]

The Court of Appeal must be correct in holding that 'oppression' involves something over and above the inherently coercive nature of custodial interrogation, since PACE plainly anticipates admissible custodial confessions arising from lawful detention for

---

[116] *A v Secretary of State for the Home Department (No 2)* [2006] 2 AC 221, [2005] UKHL 71, [82], *per* Lord Hoffmann.

[117] It is interesting to observe that the Israeli Supreme Court took refuge in the euphemism 'moderate physical pressure' rather than openly admit to endorsing police torture of suspects. This demonstrates a perverse kind of respect for the anti-oppression norm, even whilst it was routinely being breached. The Court has since ruled that even moderate physical pressure is unacceptable: see Andreas Laursen, 'Israel's Supreme Court and International Human Rights Law: The Judgement on "Moderate Physical Pressure"' (2000) 69 *Nordic Journal of International Law* 413.   [118] *R v Fulling* [1987] QB 426, CA.

[119] ibid. 432.   [120] ibid.

questioning.[121] However, Lord Lane's more expansive remarks are problematic. Perfunctory reference to dictionary entries hardly provides the police with much concrete guidance on the conduct of interrogation, and equating oppression with 'detestable wickedness' surely goes too far. Indeed, the *OED* mentions alternative definitions that seem more appropriate, including 'the feeling of being oppressed or weighed down; bodily or mental uneasiness or distress'. These alternatives were ignored by the Court.[122] Even if the Court's restrictive definition were correct, it remains unclear why the conduct of the investigating officers in *Fulling* was not 'unjust or cruel treatment' and involved no impropriety, since the police were obviously trying to manipulate the accused through emotional pressure. Nor does the Court pause to consider whether this tactic amounted to an illegitimate undermining of the accused's common law privilege against self-incrimination.

Subsequent authorities have interpreted section 76(2)(a) somewhat less restrictively, albeit that the Court of Appeal's analysis is often highly contextualized and fact-specific, and therefore provides limited guidance for future proceedings. Amongst the most important decisions is *Paris, Miller and Abdullahi*,[123] the case of the 'Cardiff Three' convicted of murdering Miller's former girlfriend, to which reference has already been made in relation to suspects' access to custodial legal advice. Miller, it will be recalled, was interrogated over some 13 hours, during which time he denied the murder no less than 300 times, before he finally confessed. Lord Taylor CJ seemed genuinely shocked by the audio-taped record of the interview, exclaiming that '[s]hort of physical violence, it is hard to conceive of a more hostile and intimidating approach by officers to a suspect'.[124]

Paris, Miller and Abdullahi established that protracted verbal aggression, not amounting to overt threats of violence, can constitute 'oppression', though it must be stressed that the Court characterized this as an extreme case. At the other end of the spectrum, an officer's isolated shouting, swearing, or fleeting loss of temper would not amount to oppression,[125] nor does every police impropriety automatically trigger exclusion.[126] The maturity, mental stability, and physical health of the suspect,[127] as well as the conduct of the interviewing officers themselves, must all be taken into account in arriving at an intensively fact-sensitive judgment. This approach has the considerable merit of flexibility, but it does rely on proactive enforcement by vigilant defence lawyers and robust trial judges.

Finally, before leaving the first exclusionary limb of section 76(2), it should be noted that conduct falling short of oppression might nonetheless lead to exclusion under section 78 of PACE or at common law on grounds of unfairness, illegality, or forced self-incrimination.[128] These evidentiary doctrines were discussed in Chapter 5. Here it is sufficient to

---

[121] PACE 1984, s.37(2), discussed in §12.2(a).

[122] It is possible that the Court was distracted by the *OED's* characterization of this meaning as late Middle English. However, the same definition is included without qualification in more modern dictionaries like *Chambers Twentieth Century Dictionary* and the *Longman Pocket English Dictionary*.

[123] *R v Paris, Miller and Abdullahi* (1993) 97 Cr App R 99, CA.   [124] ibid. 103.

[125] *R v Emmerson* (1990) 92 Cr App R 284, CA; *R v Heaton* [1993] Crim LR 593, CA.

[126] *R v Parker* [1995] Crim LR 233, CA; a specific application of the more general principle established in cases such as *R v Keenan* [1990] 2 QB 54, CA: see §5.4(a), above.

[127] See, e.g., *R v Seelig* [1992] 1 WLR 148, CA; *R v Smith (Wallace Duncan)* (1994) 99 Cr App R 233, CA.

[128] *Lam Chi-ming v R* [1991] 2 AC 212, 220, PC. Also see *R v Sang* [1980] AC 402, 456–7, HL (Lord Scarman); *R v Barker* [1941] 2 KB 381, DC.

recall that a police ruse or trick, though not readily described as 'oppressive', might still be a strong candidate for discretionary exclusion under section 78.[129]

(d) SECTION 76(2)(b): EXCLUSION ON GROUNDS OF POTENTIAL UNRELIABILITY

At first blush, section 76(2)'s second exclusionary limb appears to be a straightforward test of reliability: what could be more logical than a rule that said that reliable confessions may be admitted, but unreliable confessions are to be excluded? However, the law's approach to potentially unreliable confessions is more nuanced than might appear from a superficial reading of the statute.

Closer examination of the language of section 76(2)(b) reveals that the admissibility test it prescribes is actually hypothetical, and therefore normative in two senses. The test requires the court to determine, not whether *this* particular confession is reliable, but rather whether the conditions under which the confession was obtained are, in general, conducive to unreliability. This interpretation is confirmed by the final clause of section 76(2), which states explicitly that a contested confession will still be excluded 'notwithstanding that it may be true' unless the prosecution proves that neither paragraph (a) nor (b) of the subsection is applicable. Section 76(2)(b) is predicated on the assumption that a categorical rule of exclusion will promote the reliability of confession evidence on aggregate and over time, in preference to allowing the admissibility of confessions to turn on case-specific inquiries and *ad hoc* exceptions.

Even when section 76(2) operates in the instant case to exclude a confession that appears to be true, the court can still be said to be promoting reliability in future cases. If the court were tempted to make *ad hoc* exceptions for apparently reliable confessions procured in dubious circumstances, on the other hand, the police might then routinely ignore legal constraints on interviewing practice in the hope that the courts would continue to make further *ad hoc* exceptions in their favour for 'obviously' reliable confessions. Following the rule will not infallibly distinguish reliable from unreliable confessions in every individual case, but it might produce the best achievable results over the long run of cases.

Assessments of a confession's reliability in the instant case, and beliefs about the general conditions in which unreliable confessions are likely to be made, are bound to be closely related. It is natural to think, especially from the vantage point of hindsight, that apparently reliable confessions must have been obtained in conditions consistent with their reliability, and *vice versa*.[130] Under section 76(2)(b), however, the court may have regard to the

---

[129] A classic illustration is *R v Mason* [1988] 1 WLR 139, CA, in which a police lie about the nature of the evidence in their possession was aggravated by having deceived the suspect's lawyer, as well as the suspect himself. Watkins LJ, ibid. 144, deprecated 'the deceit practised upon the appellant's solicitor' and expressed the hope 'never again to hear of deceit such as this being practised on the accused person, and more particularly possibly on a solicitor whose duty it is to advise him, unfettered by false information from the police'. For general discussion, see Andrew Ashworth, 'Should the Police Be Allowed to Use Deceptive Practices?' (1998) 114 *LQR* 108.

[130] This connection was previously made in the CLRC's Eleventh Report, *Evidence: General*, Cm.4991 (HMSO, 1972), para.44, recommending reform of the common law voluntariness test: 'although the fact that a particular confession seems clearly to be true will not make it admissible if the threat or inducement was of a sort likely to cause the accused to make an unreliable confession, yet evidence of the terms of the confession may throw light on the facts concerning interrogation'.

truth or falsity of a contested confession only if this can be shown to have a bearing on the reliability of confessions in general. The reliability of particular admissions is not treated as a criterion of admissibility in its own right.[131] In the absence of trustworthy criteria for predicting the impact of particular interrogation tactics or conditions of detention on the reliability of custodial confessions, ethical considerations inevitably inform the analysis. Do we say, for example, that detainees must have meal breaks, warmth, proper ventilation, and adequate sleep because they will otherwise be prone to making false admissions, or simply because these are basic requirements of humane custodial interrogation? The obvious response is that both sets of considerations are important; or else to dismiss the question as presupposing an artificial and unrealistic dichotomy. Either reaction exposes the fallacy of regarding the two exclusionary limbs of section 76(2) as entirely unrelated, when they must necessarily overlap. We have already encountered this point in relation to *Mushtaq*[132] directions. It is fallacious to view section 76(2)(b) as specifying an exclusively instrumental and empirically verifiable test of admissibility, over-exaggerating the contrast with section 76(2)(a)'s more overtly normative standard.

Whilst such conceptual and philosophical issues lurk in the background, in practice the courts have been more immediately preoccupied with doctrinal aspects of section 76(2)(b). There is a jurisprudential drift towards narrowing down the scope of the exclusionary rule; though it should again be recalled that section 78 and the common law discretion constitute an exclusionary safety-net for confessional evidence that slips through the cracks of section 76(2).[133]

The familiar indicia of unreliability, drawing on pre-PACE jurisprudence,[134] are threats, promises, and inducements. Clear examples include threats to withhold bail, charge more serious offences, or switch attention to the suspect's family members if he fails to co-operate; and promises of immediate release, reduced charges, or a lighter sentence in exchange for a confession. The frowned-upon practice of offering inducements is now addressed directly by PACE Code C.[135] The courts have, however, insisted that there must be a causal connection between potential unreliability and something 'said or done' by a person other than the accused. Thus, for example, the mere fact that a drug addict is experiencing 'cold turkey', and is therefore liable to say just about anything in order to secure his release and find another fix, affords no basis for excluding a confession under section 76(2)(b).[136]

In such retreats into formalistic interpretations of section 76, the courts demonstrate their continued reluctance to undertake a more proactive and systematic screening of the

---

[131] *R v Kenny* [1994] Crim LR 284, CA. A useful analogy is suggested by the distinction in the substantive criminal law of rape, between consent in fact and the accused's belief in consent. Consent in fact is linked evidentially with the accused's belief in consent, but is analytically quite distinct.

[132] *R v Mushtaq* [2005] 1 WLR 1513, [2005] UKHL 25.

[133] *R v Howden-Simpson* [1991] Crim LR 49, CA.

[134] Which may be treated as a guide to the interpretation of section 76(2): see, e.g., *R v Phillips* (1988) 86 Cr App R 18, CA. For a thorough review of the pre-PACE cases, see Peter Mirfield, *Confessions* (Sweet & Maxwell, 1985), ch 4.

[135] PACE Code C, para.11.5 directs that: 'no interviewer shall indicate, except to answer a direct question, what action will be taken by the police if the person being questioned answers questions, makes a statement or refuses to do either. If the person asks directly what action will be taken if they answer questions, make a statement or refuse to do either, the interviewer may inform them what action the police propose to take provided that action is itself proper and warranted.'

[136] *R v Crampton* (1991) 92 Cr App R 369, CA; *R v Goldenberg* (1988) 88 Cr App R 285, CA.

threshold reliability of confession evidence. Yet it is in these very circumstances, where suspects may be at their most vulnerable, that interrogation practices call for especially stringent scrutiny. If this is true of adults in full possession of their faculties, moreover, the risk of wrongful conviction can only increase where the suspect's age, personality or circumstances disclose additional vulnerabilities. The peculiar vulnerability of juvenile detainees or suspects with learning difficulties, mental disorder, or mental illness is a factor to be taken into account in applying the test of unreliability under section 76(2)(b).[137]

12.4 VULNERABLE SUSPECTS

By the late 1970s it was already well-known that certain vulnerable individuals are more than usually susceptible to making false confessions, especially in an inherently coercive situation like a custodial police interview. Indeed, the Philips Royal Commission on Criminal Procedure was preceded by a *cause célèbre* involving dubious admissions by vulnerable juveniles.[138] PACE Code C consequently makes further dedicated provision for vulnerable detainees, who should normally be accompanied during interview by a parent, guardian, social worker, or other 'appropriate adult'.[139] But what if these safeguards are not respected in any particular case? Parliament might have decided that it was simply too risky to allow a vulnerable suspect's confession to be put before a jury in such circumstances. PACE in fact adopts a less radical approach, preserving the admissibility of the evidence but subjecting it to a specially crafted judicial warning. Section 77(1) provides:[140]

Without prejudice to the general duty of the court at a trial on indictment with a jury to direct the jury on any matter on which it appears to the court appropriate to do so, where at such a trial –

    (a)   the case against the accused depends wholly or substantially on a confession by him; and

---

[137] *R* v *Walker* [1998] Crim LR 211, CA; *R* v *Everett* [1988] Crim LR 826, CA. Cf. the pre-PACE case of *R* v *Miller* [1986] 3 All ER 119, CA, in which the confession of a paranoid schizophrenic who later claimed not to have been his 'full self' after a period of 24 hours in custodial detention was nonetheless held to have been properly admitted.

[138] Sir Henry Fisher, *Report of the inquiry into the circumstances leading to the trial of Ronald Leighton, Colin Lattimore and Ahmet Salih on charges arising out of the death of Maxwell Confait and the fire at 27 Doggett Road, London, SE6* (HMSO, 1977).

[139] By PACE Code C, para.1.7, an 'appropriate adult' is a parent, guardian or carer, a social worker or medical professional, or 'failing these, some other responsible adult aged 18 or over who is not a police officer or employed by the police'. PACE Code C, para.11.15, directs that, subject to limited exceptions: 'A juvenile or a person who is mentally disordered or mentally vulnerable must not be interviewed regarding their involvement or suspected involvement in a criminal offence or offences, or asked to provide or sign a written statement under caution or record of interview, in the absence of the appropriate adult…' Note for Guidance 11C adds: 'Although juveniles or people who are mentally disordered or otherwise mentally vulnerable are often capable of providing reliable evidence, they may, without knowing or wishing to do so, be particularly prone in certain circumstances to provide information that may be unreliable, misleading or self-incriminating. Special care should always be taken when questioning such a person, and the appropriate adult should be involved if there is any doubt about a person's age, mental state or capacity. Because of the risk of unreliable evidence it is also important to obtain corroboration of any facts admitted whenever possible.'

[140] Subsections 77(2) and (2A) extend the same principle to, respectively, summary trials before the magistrates and trials on indictment tried by judges without a jury, who must then 'treat the case as one in which there is a special need for caution before convicting the accused on his confession'.

(b) the court is satisfied –
    (i) that he is mentally handicapped; and
    (ii) that the confession was not made in the presence of an independent person,
the court shall warn the jury that there is special need for caution before convicting the accused in reliance on the confession, and shall explain that the need arises because of the circumstances mentioned in paragraphs (a) and (b) above.

Section 77 is an exemplar of a generic evidentiary technique, discussed in Chapter 15, which may be characterized as 'forensic reasoning rules'. The trial judge's duty in the present context was further elaborated in *Bailey*,[141] where the Court of Appeal explained:

What is required of a judge in a summing up in such cases…is a full and proper statement of the mentally handicapped defendant's case against the confessions being accepted by the jury as true and accurate. Because the defendant is significantly mentally handicapped, this duty will include a duty to see that points made on the defendant's behalf and other points which appear to the judge to be appropriate to his defence that the confessions are unreliable or untrue, are placed before the jury.[142]

The factors which the trial judge ought specifically to mention, in an appropriate case, include the role that an independent adult might have played, had one been present, in protecting the accused's interests, and general observations about the propensity of 'mentally handicapped' persons to make false admissions, as well as matters pertaining directly to the accused's personal vulnerabilities.[143] There is no canonical form of words, but it would usually be wise for the judge to warn the jury quite explicitly of the 'special need for caution' in any case where section 77 applies.[144]

    The practical scope for activating the judicial direction mandated by section 77 is narrowed considerably by other applicable evidentiary rules. A confession obtained from a mentally handicapped suspect in the absence of an independent support person would normally be a strong candidate for exclusion under section 76(2)(b); indeed, in *MacKenzie*,[145] the Court of Appeal stressed that it would often be appropriate for the trial judge to rule that there was no case to answer, under the *Galbraith*[146] test, if the prosecution case rested on an inherently flawed confession of this nature. But there might still be rare cases – perhaps involving limited admissions during an urgent or very short interview – in which a mentally impaired suspect's confession would remain admissible, despite the absence of an independent adult, and would consequently attract a judicial warning on the special need for caution under section 77.[147]

---

[141] *R v Bailey* [1995] 2 Cr App R 262, CA.   [142] ibid. 275.

[143] The statutory concept now seems rather unfortunately anachronistic. We might today prefer to make provision for suspects with a mental disability or learning difficulties.

[144] *R v Campbell* [1995] 1 Cr App R 522, CA. The JSB Specimen Direction reads: 'In this case you should approach the evidence of the defendant's confession with special caution before convicting him on it. I say this for three reasons. Firstly, because the case against him depends [wholly/substantially] on that confession. Secondly, because he is a mentally handicapped person. Thirdly, because no independent person was present when he made it – that is, someone other than the investigator or other person to whom it was made.'   [145] *R v MacKenzie* (1992) 96 Cr App R 98, CA, applied in *R v Wood* [1994] Crim LR 222, CA.

[146] [1981] 1 WLR 1039, CA, discussed in §2.5(c), above.

[147] Cf. *R v Moss* (1990) 91 Cr App R 371, CA; *R v Lamont* [1989] Crim LR 813, CA.

12.5 CONFESSIONS OF CO-ACCUSED

Rules of evidence that function perfectly satisfactorily when a single accused is on trial have a tendency to work less well, or barely at all, in trials involving multiple co-accused with competing forensic interests. The problem is nowhere more acute than in relation to confessions, since evidence incriminating *D1* can often, depending on all the circumstances of the case, be regarded as exculpating *D2* to some extent – inviting a cut-throat defence.[148] Simply put, the question is: should *D2* ever be able to adduce *D1*'s confession where that confession has been ruled inadmissible for the prosecution? Or, put another way with different emphasis, why should *D2* ever be prevented from adducing relevant evidence of *D1*'s confession, which helps *D2*'s defence, just because the prosecution is not entitled to adduce *D1*'s confession?

In principle, *D2* should be free to defend himself with any relevant evidence at his disposal. This might suggest a distinction based on the doctrinal rationale for excluding a confession tendered by the prosecution under section 76(2). If *D1*'s confession is utterly unreliable, because, for example, the circumstances of his interrogation completely undermine any confidence in his confession, then there is a strong case for excluding the confession from the trial *tout court* and irrespective of the party seeking to adduce it. At some point along the spectrum of unreliability, the probative value of *D1*'s confession becomes so attenuated as to shade into irrelevance, regardless of whether the confession is tendered by the prosecution or by *D2*. But what if the confession is excluded on grounds of police impropriety, in order to safeguard the integrity of the proceedings, even though it appears to be perfectly reliable? It is one thing to prevent the prosecution, as a manifestation of the state, from adducing such a confession, quite another to tell *D2* that he may not adduce what from his perspective is exculpatory evidence, in the name of procedural propriety.

Rather than confronting these issues of principle directly, the courts became embroiled in common law technicalities. As a starting point, section 76(2) was clearly intended by Parliament to apply only to prosecution evidence, since it is expressly framed in terms of 'the prosecution prov[ing] to the court beyond reasonable doubt that the confession (notwithstanding that it may be true) was not obtained as aforesaid'. On first principles, a party is entitled to adduce any evidence that is both (i) relevant to the issues in the case, and (ii) not rendered inadmissible by any applicable exclusionary rule.[149] Extra-judicial confessions are hearsay at common law, but the admissions of an accused (as opposed to a third party to the litigation)[150] are admissible for their truth by way of long-standing exception.[151] It should follow that *D2* is free to adduce *D1*'s confession whenever *D1*'s confession is relevant to *D2*'s case. Thus, in several cases the courts disavowed the existence of any judicial discretion to fetter 'a defendant's absolute right,

---

[148] Which often also give rise to evidentiary and procedural issues concerning bad character evidence, cross-admissibility, and applications for severance: see §14.5, below.   [149] §3.1.

[150] *R v Blastland* [1986] 1 AC 41, HL. Note that 'third parties' for these purposes include erstwhile accomplices not charged in the same proceedings, or who have already been convicted or acquitted and are therefore no longer co-accused: see Colin Tapper, 'Use of Third Party Confessions: *R v Finch*' (2007) 11 *E & P* 318.   [151] Now see CJA 2003, s.118, discussed in §9.6.

subject to considerations of relevance, to deploy his case asserting his innocence as he thinks fit'.[152]

However, the Court of Appeal held in *Beckford and Daley* that *D2* cannot adduce *D1*'s confession if that confession has already been ruled inadmissible for the prosecution under section 76(2).[153] As Di Birch remarked at the time,[154] this comes uncomfortably close to 'applying' section 76 to co-accused, and the fact that *D1*'s confession remains available to *D2* as material with which to cross-examine *D1*[155] is barely adequate compensation for *D2*'s loss of evidence going to the issues in the case. Quite apart from the potentially reduced impact of evidence restricted to credibility, this will not generally improve *D2*'s position at all if *D1* chooses not to testify in his own defence.[156]

In *Melanie Myers*[157] the House of Lords was presented with an opportunity of resolving, if not strictly speaking a conflict in the authorities, then at least a deep ambiguity at the level of legal principle. Unfortunately, the opportunity was lost. Their Lordships were content to leave any apparent conflict between *Beckford and Daley* and *Campbell and Williams* unresolved, on the basis that the confession in *Myers* would have been admissible for the prosecution in any event, had the prosecutor chosen to adduce it. The status of an inadmissible confession did not therefore arise on the facts.[158] At which point in the saga, Parliament intervened.

Adopting a recommendation of the Law Commission,[159] section 128 of the Criminal Justice Act 2003 inserted a new section 76A into PACE, creating a tailor-made version of section 76 applying specifically to co-accused. Section 76A unequivocally states that '[i]n any proceedings a confession made by an accused person may be given in evidence for another person charged in the same proceedings (a co-accused) in so far as it is relevant to any matter in issue in the proceedings and is not excluded by the court in pursuance of this section'. The meaning of 'confession' is governed by section 82(1), just as it is in relation to admissions adduced by the prosecution under section 76. This extends to partly incriminating, partly exculpatory 'mixed statements' as previously discussed.[160] However, whenever the admissibility of *D1*'s confession is contested, *D2* is now obliged to prove, albeit to the lesser balance of probabilities standard, that *D1*'s confession was not obtained by oppression or in circumstances conducive to unreliability, in accordance with section

---

[152] *Lobban v R* [1995] 2 Cr App R 573, 586, PC (Lord Steyn); *R v Campbell and Williams* [1993] Crim LR 448, CA.

[153] *R v Beckford and Daley* [1991] Crim LR 833, CA, discussed by Peter Mirfield, '*Blastland* Extended' (1992) 108 *LQR* 34.

[154] Case-commentary on *R v Campbell and Williams* [1993] Crim LR 448, CA.

[155] *Lui Mei Lin v R* [1989] AC 288, PC; *R v Rowson* [1986] QB 174, CA.

[156] *R v Knutton and England* [1993] Crim LR 208, CA. But for unusual circumstances in which *D1*'s confession may become relevant to *D2*'s credibility even if *D1* does *not* testify, see *R v Thompson, Sinclair and Maver* [1995] 2 Cr App R 589, CA; *R v Bracewell* (1978) 68 Cr App R 44, CA.

[157] *R v Myers (Melanie)* [1998] AC 124, HL.

[158] John Hartshorne and Andrew L.-T. Choo, '"Hearsay-Fiddles" in the House of Lords' (1999) 62 *MLR* 290, while endorsing the outcome, branded the reasoning in *Myers* a fiddle. But their Lordships reasoning is simply a straightforward application of the common law rules governing the admissibility of a confession by a party to the litigation. The problem with *Myers* is not what was said, but what went unsaid – a deafening silence, perhaps, but not a hearsay-fiddle.

[159] Law Com No 245, *Evidence in Criminal Proceedings: Hearsay and Related Topics*, Cm.3670 (TSO, 1997), paras.8.95–8.96 and Recommendation 19.

[160] Confirmed in relation to s.76A in *R v Nazir* [2009] EWCA Crim 213, [23].

76A(2)(a) and (b). This certainly clarifies the situation, though whether it represents an improvement is open to debate. It is pertinent to inquire, where is *D2* supposed to get his information from? The circumstances of *D1*'s interrogation would presumably have to be fully disclosed by the police and prosecution. On a principled view, section 76A may be regarded as a triumph for legality and procedural propriety, inasmuch as confessions procured after egregious breaches of PACE or other abuses are no longer admissible at trial for any party. The downside is that *D2* might in future be prevented from adducing apparently reliable exculpatory evidence because the constable has blundered in taking *D1*'s confession.

13

THE ACCUSED'S PRIVILEGE
AGAINST SELF-INCRIMINATION

13.1 INTRODUCTION: ENGLISH
COMMON LAW'S PRIVILEGE

The privilege against self-incrimination is a venerable common law institution dating from at least the seventeenth century.[1] The Lord Chief Justice recently observed that '[t]he privilege against self-incrimination is deeply rooted in the common law',[2] and a judge of the European Court of Human Rights even maintains that 'the formula "*nemo tenetur seipsum prodere*" goes back to the very origins of western legal tradition'.[3] However, the precise origins of the privilege remain obscure.[4] Its exalted status in modern legal thinking doubtless owes something to the unpopularity of the Elizabethan and Stuart courts of Star Chamber and High Commission. These tribunals were empowered to investigate allegations of treason and heresy by requiring suspects to answer questions under oath.[5] Recalcitrant individuals were occasionally tortured in order to extract statements of faith, which would then form the basis of their conviction at trial. What today is known – not always helpfully – as the suspect's 'right to silence' (or 'right of silence') is thus bound up historically with a rejection of authoritarian, 'foreign', methods of criminal investigation, and consequently stands for the victory of freedom and justice over tyranny and despotism.

In order to understand the modern legal status and contemporary function of the privilege against self-incrimination in English criminal proceedings, it is necessary to set these

---

[1] For historical exegesis, see John H. Wigmore, 'Nemo Tenetur Seipsum Prodere' (1891) 5 *Harvard LR* 71; E. M. Morgan, 'The Privilege Against Self-incrimination' (1949) 34 *Minnesota LR* 1; John A. Kemp, 'The Background of the Fifth Amendment in English Law: A Study of its Historical Implications' (1958) 1 *William & Mary LR* 247; Leonard W. Levy, *Origins of the Fifth Amendment: The Right Against Self-Incrimination* (OUP, NY, 1968); John H. Langbein, *The Origins of Adversary Criminal Trial* (OUP, 2003), 277–84; Jeremy Bentham, *Rationale of Judicial Evidence* (Hunt and Clarke, 1827), vol. 5, 250.

[2] *R v S (F)* [2009] 1 WLR 1489, [2008] EWCA Crim 2177, [16] (Lord Judge CJ).

[3] Judge Zupančič, concurring in *Jalloh v Germany* (2007) 44 EHRR 32, O-II1. And see Boštjan Zupančič, 'The Privilege Against Self-Incrimination' [1981] *Arizona State Law Journal* 1.

[4] Even the connection between the privilege and the accused's right not to testify is unclear. The privilege obviously antedates the Criminal Evidence Act 1898, when for the first time the accused became generally competent to testify in his own defence. This aspect of the modern privilege was therefore largely redundant prior to 1898.

[5] *Rationale of Judicial Evidence* (1827), vol. 5, 241. For discussion, see Michael A. Menlowe, 'Bentham, Self-incrimination and the Law of Evidence' (1988) 104 *LQR* 286; William Twining, *Theories of Evidence: Bentham & Wigmore* (Weidenfeld, 1985), ch 2.

awe-inspiring historical associations to one side, for they are apt to mislead. The first issue we must tackle is one of definition. The 'privilege against self-incrimination' is often invoked loosely and has a tendency to become confused with the overlapping notion of the 'right to silence'. These juridical concepts need to be disentangled and kept distinct if we are to make any analytical progress. However, conceptual clarification is only the first step towards resolving enduring puzzles surrounding the privilege against self-incrimination. When we examine its recent legal history, we find that common law courts, in England and Wales and elsewhere, have not been as enthusiastic or vigorous in its defence as the privilege's illustrious pedigree might lead one to expect. Indeed, English judges have sometimes carped and sniped at the privilege against self-incrimination. Do the privilege's judicial detractors and academic critics betray their common law heritage? Or does the fault lie with the privilege itself? Does the privilege, in other words, truly deserve its glittering reputation?

The second section of this chapter undertakes a systematic inquiry into the principal justificatory rationales thought to underpin the privilege against self-incrimination. With an unavoidable element of reductionism, we organize the plethora of overlapping and competing rationales into three groups according to their primary structural characteristic: intrinsic, conceptual, or instrumental. Each approach has its attractions and adherents, but we will argue that none of them establishes a particularly compelling case for preventing juries form drawing common-sense inferences from silence in appropriate circumstances. This discussion of underlying rationales provides a platform for critical analysis of recent developments in English law. The third section of the chapter describes the important changes made to the privilege against self-incrimination by the Criminal Justice and Public Order Act 1994 and considers the impact of Article 6 of the ECHR and the Human Rights Act 1998. Reconceptualizsing the privilege against self-incrimination as a human right has implications for the legitimacy of statutory obligations to divulge information as well as redefining the acceptable scope of evidence and proof in criminal adjudication. Here again, however, the protection afforded by the privilege is more limited than many would expect or hope to discover. The solution to the puzzle of English law's ambivalence towards the privilege against self-incrimination is to be found, we suggest, in its shaky theoretical and moral foundations.

(a) CONCEPTUAL CLARIFICATIONS

In *R* v *Director of Serious Fraud Office ex p. Smith* Lord Mustill observed that '"the right of silence"…arouses strong but unfocused feelings. In truth it does not denote any single right, but rather refers to a disparate group of immunities, which differ in nature, origin, incidence and importance, and also as to the extent to which they have already been encroached upon by statute.'[6] Lord Mustill proceeded to identify six discrete immunities associated with the right to silence:

(1) A general immunity, possessed by all persons and bodies, from being compelled on pain of punishment to answer questions posed by other persons or bodies.

(2) A general immunity, possessed by all persons and bodies, from being compelled on pain of punishment to answer questions the answers to which may incriminate them.

---

[6] *R* v *Director of Serious Fraud Office, ex p. Smith* [1993] AC 1, 30–1, HL.

(3) A specific immunity, possessed by all persons under suspicion of criminal responsibility whilst being interviewed by police officers or others in similar positions of authority, from being compelled on pain of punishment to answer questions of any kind.

(4) A specific immunity, possessed by accused persons undergoing trial, from being compelled to give evidence, and from being compelled to answer questions put to them in the dock.

(5) A specific immunity, possessed by persons who have been charged with a criminal offence, from having questions material to the offence addressed to them by police officers or persons in a similar position of authority.

(6) A specific immunity (at least in certain circumstances, which it is unnecessary to explore), possessed by accused persons undergoing trial, from having adverse comment made on any failure (a) to answer questions before the trial, or (b) to give evidence at the trial.[7]

Though some might see fit to quibble with particular details of this taxonomy, Lord Mustill's list is an important reminder that both the 'right of silence' and the 'privilege against self-incrimination' can be defined and disaggregated in different ways. All of Lord Mustill's immunities expect (5) will figure prominently in this chapter's discussion of the privilege against self-incrimination, with particular emphasis on (3), (4), and (6).

Specific immunity from compulsory legal process is what distinguishes the privilege against self-incrimination, more narrowly defined, from the general freedom that citizens enjoy to refuse to answer questions or provide information (Lord Mustill's first immunity). Just as citizens are generally entitled to freedom of expression,[8] so they are, in counterpart, at liberty to decline to speak in most situations. It is a bedrock political principle in liberal societies that a person approached for information by the police, or any other authority or person, is free to withhold their co-operation, and cannot literally be compelled to respond. In modern liberal democracies, however, a general freedom to remain silent and withhold information must be balanced against a variety of weighty public interests across a diverse range of activities. Personal liberty is always constrained by the liberty of others, and by social and moral responsibility.[9] Thus, legal obligations to provide information are many and varied: the duty to make tax returns, to fill out periodic electoral register and census forms, to present one's motoring documents at a police station on request, to disclose relevant previous convictions in a job application, to register a company name, to disclose the location of one's assets in response to a freezing order,[10] to notify the authorities of a change in car ownership, and countless others. In most European countries citizens have an obligation to carry an identity card and to show it to a police officer on request. An identity card scheme for the United Kingdom has been a serious talking point since the world-changing events of 11 September 2001.[11] For our purposes, the most significant public interest in obtaining information is concerned with establishing the truth in legal proceedings in order to enforce the criminal law.

---

[7] ibid.

[8] Expressly enshrined in ECHR Article 10: see Alastair Mowbray, *Cases and Materials on the European Convention on Human Rights* (OUP, 2nd edn. 2007), ch 12.

[9] An important illustration being the 'harm principle' in criminal law: see A. P. Simester and G. R. Sullivan, *Criminal Law Theory and Doctrine* (Hart, 3rd edn. 2007), §16.1; Andrew Ashworth, *Principles of Criminal Law* (OUP, 6th edn. 2009), §2.3.

[10] Civil Procedure Rules 25.1(1)(f)–(g): see *Zuckerman on Civil Procedure*, §9.158ff.

[11] Home Office, *Identity Cards: The Next Steps*, Cm 6020 (TSO, 2003).

The general witness privilege against self-incrimination was outlined in Chapter 7.[12] This chapter is concerned with the privilege enjoyed exclusively by suspects and the accused in criminal proceedings to refuse to answer potentially incriminating questions or to provide potentially incriminating information under threat of penal sanctions.[13] The accused is exempted from that compulsory process of law which binds all other witnesses in English criminal proceedings.[14]

It is essential to appreciate that contemporary debates surrounding the privilege against self-incrimination and the right to silence are not *directly* concerned with the exemption of suspects and the accused from testimonial obligations. Though judicial torture – and worse besides – is part of the dim and dark distant history of criminal investigation, nobody today is seriously suggesting that suspects should be forced, by actual or meta-phorical 'arm-twisting', to respond to police questioning or that accused persons should be dragged kicking and screaming into the witness-box and forced to speak up for them-selves at trial. Physical or severe emotional compulsion can no longer be countenanced at any stage of criminal proceedings, and are now proscribed *per se* by Article 3 of the ECHR and at common law.[15] Any incriminating statements procured through oppressive inter-rogation would be excluded under PACE 1984, section 76(2), as we saw in the last chapter.

Determining the proper scope of the accused's privilege against self-incrimination in modern English law is largely a question of regulating the forensic implications, if any, of silence in the face of an accusation. Lord Mustill's sixth immunity encapsulates the salient question. When the accused chooses to exercise what is his undoubted right, to stay silent in the police station or at court, should he suffer any adverse evidential consequences? Silence might be costly for the accused, either because it triggers legal rules operating to his detriment, or, in a more diffuse and informal sense, if fact-finders adopt the commonly-held view that, whereas innocence loudly proclaims itself, silence is guilty. An alternative way of formulating the central question would be to ask whether silence should be allowed to carry its ordinary probative force in criminal adjudication? Which in turn prompts sup-plementary questions requiring careful consideration: what exactly *is* the probative force of silence, and how should judges direct juries in relation to it? If untutored common sense reasoning regularly produces mistaken inferences, rules of evidence might be deployed to try to neutralize our natural tendency to equate silence with guilt.

On the face of it, the privilege against self-incrimination and the objective of convict-ing the guilty are at loggerheads. Truth-finding is best served by securing access to all information relevant to the issues in the case. Any privilege to withhold information will almost inevitably detract from effective truth-finding, the more so when the holder of the privilege is typically peculiarly well-placed to know the truth of the matters under investigation.[16] Generally speaking, it will profit the guilty not to co-operate with police

---

[12] §7.4(a).

[13] This is Lord Mustill's second, general, immunity. On a narrower conception, the privilege against self-incrimination might be said to prohibit self-incriminating disclosure under threat of penalty only where the information disclosed subsequently forms the basis for a criminal charge against the person forced to disclose it. On this conception, the privilege is not infringed unless and until compelled self-incriminating information is actually *used* to prosecute the accused: see §13.3(a), below.

[14] §7.3. Subject to isolated pockets of non-compellability and testimonial privilege: see §7.4

[15] *A v Secretary of State for the Home Department (No 2)* [2006] 2 AC 221, [2005] UKHL 71.

[16] Cases of false accusation or genuine mistaken identity aside, even accused who are legally innocent of the crime charged are usually in some way connected to the events of the trial and could provide the court with useful information.

investigators, to refuse to answer questions, to withhold information, and to decline to testify, because the more they expose themselves to probing enquiries, the greater volume of incriminating evidence is likely to emerge. However, even if evidentiary rules operate to reduce the ordinary probative significance of silence, and to that extent make it more likely that the guilty will evade conviction and punishment, this might still be regarded as an unavoidable, if regrettable, side-effect of faithfully serving competing values and principles. It is not enough for critics to show that the privilege against self-incrimination is costly, in terms of lost evidence and pre-empted convictions. The policy question is always whether the costs imposed by the privilege must be borne with fortitude, in the light of whatever positive benefits it is thought to confer.

(b) EVOLUTION OF THE ACCUSED'S COMMON LAW PRIVILEGE, IN THEORY AND PRACTICE

We saw in Chapter 7 that witnesses summoned to testify in criminal trials are duty-bound to disclose information relevant to the issue, under threat of arrest and possibly even committal to prison for contempt of court if they refuse.[17] The witness privilege against self-incrimination entitles ordinary witnesses called to testify in a criminal trial to refuse to answer any question which might expose the witness personally to criminal liability, or other penalty or forfeiture, if a truthful answer were given.[18] But the accused is no ordinary witness. Quite apart from the peculiar vulnerability of being *on trial* and at peril of conviction and punishment, it would be normatively incoherent and self-defeating to treat the accused as an ordinary witness subject to compulsory process but armed with the witness privilege against self-incrimination. As a structured inquiry into the accused's guilt or innocence, virtually every question that prosecuting counsel might want to ask the accused in the witness-box would activate the privilege. The result would be a pointless ritual, whereby the accused would be forced into the witness-box, on pain of penalty for contempt, only to stone-wall the prosecutor's every question by constantly invoking the privilege against self-incrimination. The choice is therefore clear: either force the accused to testify stripped of the privilege against self-incrimination afforded to all other witnesses, or release the accused from compulsory testimonial duty altogether.

When accused persons first became generally competent in their own defence in 1898, English law took the latter course: the accused is wholly exempt from compulsory process, but enjoys no witness privilege against self-incrimination if he elects to testify in his own defence.[19] There are two dimensions to the accused's exemption. First, there is an absolute prohibition on the prosecution calling the accused to testify, effected indirectly by the rules governing witness competency. By statute, the accused is never competent as a witness for the prosecution.[20] Secondly, the accused is free to decline to testify as a witness for the defence in his own trial.

In addition to its important role in criminal trials, the privilege against self-incrimination also operates in favour of suspects in the pre-trial stages of criminal proceedings. In

---

[17] §7.3.

[18] *Blunt* v *Park Lane Hotel Ltd* [1942] 2 KB 253, CA; Civil Evidence Act 1968, s.14: see §7.4(a).

[19] The privilege is explicitly withheld from those accused who choose to testify by s.1(2) of the Criminal Evidence Act 1898.   [20] Youth Justice and Criminal Evidence Act 1999, s.53(4).

particular, as originally conceived, the common law privilege entitled suspects to decline to answer questions during police investigations and interrogations without exposing themselves to adverse comment at trial. However, as we saw in the last chapter, the right to remain silent did not prevent the police from detaining and questioning suspects in an attempt to get a confession.[21] The privilege against self-incrimination confers a measure of control over the generation of admissible evidence, but it does not equip suspects with any veto over the conduct of criminal investigations.

The law of the privilege against self-incrimination needs to be set against the pragmatic realities of custodial interrogation.[22] This is one of those areas where 'the law in the books' and 'the law in action' tend to diverge. In practice, it has always been difficult for a suspect to invoke his privilege in the police station. Bentham observed that simply being questioned by a person in authority exerts pressure on the suspect to comply: 'Silence…on the part of the affrighted culprit, seems to his ear to call for vengeance; confession holds out a chance for indulgence.'[23] Even if the suspect intended to give nothing away, the mental and emotional pressures generated by police interrogation and the fear that silence will be construed as an admission of guilt are powerful incentives to start talking. These situational pressures are overlaid by a more diffuse social expectation, to which few suspects would be entirely impervious, that those under suspicion or accused of a criminal offence should account for themselves, and rebut the accusation if they can.[24] When put on the spot to respond to an allegation, it is a natural human reaction to proffer a denial or explanation. Broadly speaking, it is perfectly proper to respond to the promptings of conscience by co-operating with such inquiries, even though there is no general legal duty to be a model citizen when the policeman comes knocking. There are, after all, many legal rights which, from a broader moral perspective, one ought not to insist on exercising at every opportunity, and which one sometimes ought to waive.[25] It is a moral failing, and in this context also a derogation of civic responsibility, always to stand on the strict letter of one's legal rights.

We saw in the last chapter, however, that when the police detain suspects for questioning, the authorities are in a position to exploit powerful moral and social pressures to induce the suspect to says things against his better judgment that he might later have cause to regret.[26] It is therefore not surprising that few detainees consistently exercise their right to silence throughout an interview or series of interviews.[27] The situational pressure to speak can only have been ratcheted up by the Criminal Justice and Public Order Act 1994,

---

[21] PACE 1984, s.37, discussed in §12.2(a).

[22] The law and practice of custodial interrogation were described in §12.2.

[23] *Rationale of Judicial Evidence* (1827), vol. 5, 134; and see Michael A. Menlowe, 'Bentham, Self-incrimination and the Law of Evidence' (1988) 104 *LQR* 286.

[24] Antony Duff has developed an entire theory of criminal law and criminal adjudication from the core intuition that criminal wrongdoers should be called to account in a public trial: see R. A. Duff, *Answering for Crime: Responsibility and Liability in the Criminal Law* (Hart, 2007); Antony Duff, Lindsay Farmer, Sandra Marshall, and Victor Tadros, *The Trial on Trial Volume Three: Towards a Normative Theory of the Criminal Trial* (Hart, 2007).

[25] See Donagan, 'The Right Not to Incriminate Oneself', in Ellen Frankel Paul, Jeffrey Paul, and Fred D. Miller Jr. (eds.), *Human Rights* (Blackwell, 1984), 137.   [26] §12.2.

[27] An important finding of empirical research on post-PACE policing is that consent requirements are easily circumvented unless steps are taken to ensure that consent is genuine and fully-informed. People tend to assume that they have no choice but to comply when a police officer asks them to agree to something in order to facilitate police investigations: see David Dixon, *Law in Policing* (OUP, 1997), ch 3.

which imposed additional forensic penalties on silence. A minority of guilty individuals doubtless calculated that their best chance was to respond to police questioning with a consistent 'no comment', and it is not disputed that defence lawyers have always advised silence under certain conditions.[28] But the received wisdom in police and policymaking circles that, prior to the 1994 Act's intervention, silence frequently stymied police investigations or that legal advisers routinely instructed suspects to keep their mouths shut and give nothing away, were never substantiated by empirical research.[29]

In circumstances where police interrogators are free to exploit moral and social pressure to procure admissions from suspects detained in the police station, the pre-trial privilege against self-incrimination would not amount to much if adverse inferences could later freely be drawn from a suspect's silence. Likewise, if failure to testify at trial were widely interpreted as an admission of guilt, it could hardly be said that accused persons enjoyed an effective privilege against self-incrimination. The common law's response was to say that adverse inferences must not be drawn either from the accused's silence during police questioning[30] or from his refusal to testify in his own defence at trial, and the jury should be directed accordingly. The classic police caution informed suspects that 'You do not have to say anything, but anything you do say may be taken down and used in evidence', and these words were propagated by films and TV police dramas into a catchphrase of popular culture. The reality of criminal investigations was more mundane. As we saw in the last chapter, prior to the PACE revolution in English criminal procedure the notional guarantees of suspects' rights contained in the Judges' Rules were largely symbolic, and rarely enforced through evidentiary exclusion. If suspects were actually 'read their rights' at all, this might be done in a perfunctory manner, leaving them in no doubt that they were expected to speak up for themselves or face the consequences – which might be a criminal charge or even a 'verbal' (falsified confession).[31] Although the general position of police detainees improved dramatically after 1 January 1986 when PACE 1984 came into force nationwide, empirical research conducted for the Runciman Royal Commission in the early 1990s clearly showed that the incidence of suspects remaining silent during police interrogation still remained low.[32]

---

[28] Zander and Henderson's *Crown Court Study*, para.1.2.3, found that '[i]n close to 80 per cent of cases . . . legal advice did not lead to silence – either the suspect had been silent prior to receiving legal advice (17%), or the suspect was not silent even after receiving the advice (62%) . . . . [A] little over one-quarter (26%) of those [suspects] who saw or spoke to a solicitor said they were advised to answer no questions and just under another quarter (23%) were advised to be selective about the questions they answered. On the other hand, in over a third of cases (36%) solicitors (or their representatives) were advising clients to answer all questions.'

[29] David Dixon, *Law in Policing*, 29, concurs that '[c]ritics of the right to silence had to face the difficulty that the image which they invoked (of professional criminals escaping conviction in increasing numbers by using the right to silence) found little support in the research literature'.

[30] An accused's failure to deny informal allegations could be taken as an admission by conduct only where the accuser confronted the accused 'on even terms', i.e. was not a police officer or other person in authority: *R v Norton* [1910] 2 KB 496, CCA; *R v Christie* [1914] AC 545, HL.

[31] See Royal Commission on Criminal Procedure, *Report* (1981), para.4.2; Mirfield, *Confessions*, ch 1. The scourge of 'verballing' was largely eradicated by compulsory tape-recording of formal PACE interviews, as explained in §12.2(b)–(c).

[32] In Roger Leng's carefully-designed study, less than 5% of suspects stayed silent, and about half of this group were anyway subsequently convicted, suggesting that remaining silent may have been the last refuge of the hopeless as often as it provided a 'get-out-of-gaol-free' card to the wily professional criminal: Roger Leng, *The Right to Silence in Police Interrogation: A Study of Some of the Issues Underlying the Debate*, RCCJ

The history of the privilege against self-incrimination in English law is characterized by deep ambivalence. Officially, the pre-1994 Act law was committed to the proposition that adverse inferences should not generally be drawn from the accused's pre-trial silence during police interviews, whether or not the formal caution had been administered.[33] Prosecutorial comment on the accused's decision to stay out of the witness-box at trial was expressly forbidden by statute,[34] and judicial comment, though permitted,[35] must be circumspect. The jury were to be directed that the non-testifying accused was per-fectly entitled to 'sit back and see if the prosecution have proved their case, and that while the jury have been deprived of the opportunity of hearing his story tested in cross-examination, the one thing they must not do is to assume that he is guilty because he has not gone into the witness box'.[36] At the same time, appellate courts sometimes made no effort to conceal their impatience with mandatory judicial directions that could appear to contradict common sense fact-finding in certain situations.[37] Stronger judicial comment on courtroom silence was permitted, even at common law, where the defence case hinged on an explanation that the jury might have expected to hear directly from the horse's mouth.[38] It was possible, for example, to point out that the accused's failure to provide an exculpatory explanation before the start of the trial had deprived the police of any opportunity of conducting further investigations to see whether the accused's story could be verified.[39] The fact that the accused had responded selectively to police questioning, answering some questions but refusing to answer others, might also emerge during the course of the trial.[40] In addition, failure to provide the police with certain forms of real evidence on demand, such as a hair sample, could be the subject of an adverse inference,

---

Research Study No 10 (HMSO, 1993), 20. A range of 11–13% refusing to answer any police questions during interview, and a further 9–17% partially silent, was reported by Michael Zander and Paul Henderson, *Crown Court Study*, RCCJ Research Study No 19 (HMSO, 1993), para.1.2. The highest estimates came from the police, suggesting – alongside Zander and Henderson's own reference to 'Mickey Mouse answers' – that the concept of 'remaining silent' is less clear-cut than might be imagined. Also see McConville and Hodgson, *Custodial Legal Advice and the Right to Silence*, ch 11.

[33]   *R v Chandler* [1976] 1 WLR 585, CA; *Parkes v R* [1976] 1 WLR 1251, PC; *Hall v R* [1971] 1 WLR 298, PC.

[34]   Criminal Evidence Act 1898, s.1(b) (now repealed).

[35]   *R v Rhodes* [1899] 1 QB 77, CCR: 'There is nothing in the [1898] Act that takes away or even purports to take away the right of the Court to comment on the evidence in the case, and the manner in which the case has been conducted.... There are some cases in which it would be unwise to make any such comment at all; there are others in which it would be absolutely necessary in the interests of justice that such comments should be made. That is a question entirely for the discretion of the judge; and it is only necessary now to say that that discretion is in no way affected by the provisions of the Criminal Evidence Act 1898.'

[36]   *R v Bathurst* [1968] 2 QB 99, 107–8, CA. Also *R v Mutch* (1973) 57 Cr App R 196, CA.

[37]   In *R v Gilbert* (1977) 66 Cr App R 237, 243, CA, for example, Viscount Dilhorne exclaimed: 'As the law now stands, although it may appear obvious to the jury in the exercise of their common sense that an inno-cent man would speak and not be silent, they must be told that they must not draw the inference of guilt from his silence.... Nevertheless the law as it now is must be applied even though in some cases its application seems inconsistent with the exercise of common sense.'

[38]   *R v Martinez-Tobon* [1994] 1 WLR 388, CA; *R v Chandler* [1976] 1 WLR 585, 589, *per* Lawton LJ: 'The law has long accepted that an accused person is not bound to incriminate himself; but it does not follow that a failure to answer an accusation or question when an answer could reasonably be expected may not provide some evidence in support of an accusation. Whether it does will depend upon the circumstances.'

[39]   *R v Raviraj* (1987) 85 Cr App R 93, CA.

[40]   As in *R v Mann* (1972) 56 Cr App R 750, CA, where it was held that the whole interview may be admit-ted in evidence where the accused answered selectively, thus drawing the jury's attention to the unanswered questions.

both at common law[41] and subsequently under PACE.[42] Whether or not such judicial directions actually serve to emphasize the strength of the case against the accused or, to the contrary, tend to fortify jurors against allowing their 'common sense' inferences to run riot is a matter of tactical calculation for trial counsel as well as enduring jurisprudential speculation.[43]

The ambivalence of judicial attitudes towards the privilege against self-incrimination was only one symptom of a more pervasive conflict between realizing suspects' rights and effective law enforcement permeating English criminal procedure. If English law had been serious about enforcing the privilege, the obvious solution would have been to insulate suspects from deliberately coercive interrogation tactics designed to persuade, cajole, or entice suspects to confess. Invocation of the privilege would then have pre-empted detention for questioning, or concluded an on-going interview. Of course, English law did not evolve in that direction, and the reason is not hard to find. If the rules were strictly enforced, the Diplock Commission mused, 'they would have the effect of rendering inadmissible any statement made by the accused after his arrest unless it was volunteered by him upon his own initiative without any pressure or encouragement by anyone in authority. Guilty men do not usually do this. If left to themselves they would prefer to remain silent.'[44] Consequently, detectives must not be obstructed in their efforts to persuade suspects to waive their privilege against self-incrimination as a prelude to making damaging admissions; and even if suspects do remain silent, it has always been quite likely that the jury will get to hear about it and draw their own conclusions,[45] whatever the trial judge might say about it when summing-up at the close of proceedings. The realities of custodial interrogation coupled with the seemingly indomitable logic of common sense inference led many commentators to conclude that the privilege against self-incrimination was a broken reed. Indeed, to the extent that it obscured the truth about the coercive pressures precipitating custodial confessions and deflected attention away from more worthwhile reforms, the privilege might be suspected of doing more harm than good.[46]

It is surely more than mere coincidence that the historical evolution of the privilege against self-incrimination in US constitutional law has shared a similar fate. With great fanfare in *Miranda v Arizona*[47] the US Supreme Court extended the Fifth Amendment

---

[41] *R v Smith (Robert William)* (1985) 81 Cr App R 286, CA.

[42] PACE 1984, s.62(10). Hair samples can now be plucked without the suspect's consent, pursuant to PACE 1984, ss.63(3A)–(3C) and 65, as amended.

[43] Prior to the 1994 Act it was not uncommon for *defence counsel* to ask trial judges to direct juries regarding the accused's right to stay out of the witness-box, in order to pre-empt any more damning common sense inference that jurors might otherwise draw against the accused: see, e.g., *R v Harris* (1987) 84 Cr App R 75, CA.

[44] Diplock Report, Cm.5185 (1972), paras.81–82.

[45] In Zander and Henderson's *Crown Court Study* for the Runciman Commission, the jury learned of the accused's silence during police interview in around 80% of cases in which the privilege against self-incrimination had been invoked in the police station: (HMSO, 1993), para.1.2.5.

[46] Commentators adopting this perspective were dubbed 'exchange-abolitionists'. For discussion, see Steven Greer and Rod Morgan (eds.), *The Right to Silence Debate* (University of Bristol, 1990).

[47] *Miranda v Arizona*, 384 US 436, 444–5 (1966) laid down the following minimal procedural requirements: 'Prior to any questioning the person must be warned that he has a right to remain silent, that any statement he does make may be used as evidence against him, and that he has a right to the presence of an attorney, either retained or appointed. The defendant may waive any of these rights, provided the waiver is made voluntarily, knowingly and intelligently. If, however, he indicates in any manner and at any stage of the process that he wishes to consult with an attorney before speaking there can be no questioning. Likewise, if

privilege against self-incrimination to the right of silence and legal representation during police interrogation.[48] *Miranda* ranks alongside decisions on school desegregation[49] and abortion[50] as amongst the US Supreme Court's best-known jurisprudence, by turns lauded and reviled across the political spectrum. Yet the political controversies ignited by *Miranda* are undercut by a prosaic but frequently overlooked reality. Almost from the day on which the decision was handed down, US federal courts have busied themselves creating exceptions[51] and whittling down its ambit[52] until it has become hard to say what all the fuss was really about. The US Supreme Court has clearly found it inexpedient to remain faithful to *Miranda*'s animating philosophy. Meanwhile, American police officers remained at liberty to persuade suspects to waive their rights to silence and to an attorney, just as British detectives are freely able to question suspects within the framework of PACE 1984 unimpeded by the common law privilege against self-incrimination. Once again, the pragmatic imperatives of effective law enforcement seemingly win out over the principled defence of suspects' rights.[53] From a comparative law perspective, the familiarity of this story lends further impetus to the case for reconsidering, and reassessing, the rationales purportedly justifying the privilege against self-incrimination. If the privilege has been built on shaky theoretical foundations, is it any wonder that its doctrinal constructions have suffered storm damage in an increasingly hostile political climate?

13.2 RATIONALES RE-EXAMINED

We have seen that the privilege against self-incrimination may be asserted in two different phases of the criminal process: during police interrogation ('the right to silence') and at trial. Although particular rationalizations of the privilege are sometimes directed

---

the individual is alone and indicates in any manner that he does not wish to be interrogated, the police may not question him.'

[48] The Fifth Amendment to the US Constitution guarantees that, 'No person...shall be compelled in any criminal case to be a witness against himself'. For discussion, see Joshua Dressler, *Understanding Criminal Procedure* (Matthew Bender, 2nd edn. 1997), chs 23, 24, and 26; Akhil Reed Amar and Renée B. Lettow, 'Fifth Amendment First Principles: The Self-Incrimination Clause' (1995) 93 *Michigan LR* 857; Peter Arenella, '*Schmerber* and the Privilege Against Self-incrimination: A Reappraisal' (1982) *American Criminal LR* 31; Robert Heidt, 'The Conjurer's Circle – The Fifth Amendment Privilege in Civil Cases' (1982) 91 *Yale LJ* 1062; Henry J. Friendly, 'The Fifth Amendment Tomorrow: A Case For A Constitutional Change' (1968) 37 *University of Cincinnati LR* 671.   [49] *Brown v Board of Education*, 347 US 483, 74 S Ct 686 (1954).

[50] *Roe v Wade*, 410 US 113, 93 S Ct 705 (1973).

[51] See, e.g., *Nix v Williams*, 467 US 431 (1984) ('inevitable discovery'); *Rhode Island v Innis*, 446 US 291 (1980) (public safety).

[52] See, e.g., *Michigan v Harvey*, 494 US 344 (1990); *Berkemer v McCarty*, 468 US 420 (1984); *Oregon v Mathiason*, 429 US 492 (1977); *Harris v New York*, 401 US 222 (1971).

[53] On the practical impact of *Miranda*, see Joshua Dressler, *Understanding Criminal Procedure* (Matthew Bender, 2nd edn. 1997), ch 24; Stephen J. Schulhofer, 'Miranda's Practical Effect: Substantial Benefits and Vanishingly Small Social Costs' (1996) 90 *Northwestern University LR* 500; Paul G. Cassell, 'All Benefits, No Costs: The Grand Illusion of Miranda's Defenders' (1996) 90 *Northwestern University LR* 1084; Richard A. Leo, 'The Impact of *Miranda* Revisited' (1996) 86 *Journal of Criminal Law and Criminology* 621; The Honorable Edwin Meese III, 'Promoting Truth in the Courtroom' (1987) 40 *Vanderbilt LR* 271; Harold E. Pepinsky, 'A Theory of Police Reaction to *Miranda v. Arizona*' (1970) 16 *Crime and Delinquency* 379.

predominantly to one institutional context or the other, core themes are generic and can usefully be explored in tandem without fastidiously distinguishing between pre-trial silence and silence at trial. The disputed issue, it must be remembered, is not literal compulsion to speak or testify, but the propriety of drawing adverse inferences from the accused's silence in the police station or at court.

Jeremy Bentham was the first to subject the privilege against self-incrimination to sys-tematic critical examination in the late eighteenth century. Bentham was no reactionary apologist for judicial torture,[54] but he did believe that abuses in criminal investigations should be targeted directly, rather than in the roundabout fashion of adopting evidentiary rules capable of thwarting good laws and practices as well as curbing undesirable ones. The privilege against self-incrimination was an obvious target for Bentham's utilitarian critique, since it appeared to him to undermine the efficacy of all criminal investigations for little or no practical gain.

Modern scholars have built on, extended, and sought to answer Bentham's critique of the privilege. Broadly speaking, three types of argument have been advanced as justifica-tory rationales for the privilege. The first strategy involves ascribing some intrinsic value to the privilege. It might be contended, for example, that compelled self-incrimination is inherently degrading, or involves unwarranted state intrusion into the private thoughts of citizens. On this view, the privilege against self-incrimination may be regarded as an extension of human rights to dignity, privacy, or personal autonomy. A second strategy purports to derive the privilege against self-incrimination from conceptual analysis of other well-established features of criminal proceedings. Thus, it might be claimed that the privilege is an inherent feature of adversarial criminal procedure, or that it is implied by the presumption of innocence, or that it follows logically from the right to a fair trial. Finally, instrumental rationales justify the privilege, not in terms of its inherent qualities or conceptual logic, but because respect for the privilege is said to produce desirable con-sequences. Advocates of instrumental rationales contend that the privilege leads to more and better evidence being produced in court, for example, or that it works to protect the innocent from wrongful conviction.

Countless rationales for the privilege against self-incrimination have been put forward over the years, with ingenious and sophisticated variations and myriad subtle inflexions on the central themes. A comprehensive survey is beyond the scope of this chapter.[55] What follows, instead, is an overview of the principal claims and counter-arguments developed by advocates and critics of the privilege.

---

[54] Bentham was driven by a progressive liberal concern to curb penal excess, but his utilitarian approach nonetheless committed him to endorsing the use of torture where to do so would produce an aggregate social balance of pleasure over pain: see Rod Morgan, 'The Utilitarian Justification of Torture: Denial, Desert and Disinformation' (2000) 2 *Punishment & Society* 181; W. L. Twining and P. E. Twining, 'Bentham on Torture' (1973) 24 *Northern Ireland Legal Quarterly* 305. A modern reworking of the Benthamite argument is pre-sented by Mirko Bagaric and Julie Clarke, 'Not Enough Official Torture in the World? The Circumstances in Which Torture is Morally Justifiable' (2005) 39 *University of San Francisco LR* 581.

[55] Generally, see Ronald J. Allen, 'Theorizing About Self-Incrimination' (2008) 30 *Cardozo Law Review* 729; Mike Redmayne, 'Rethinking the Privilege Against Self-Incrimination' (2007) 27 *OJLS* 209; Ian Dennis, 'Instrumental Protection, Human Right or Functional Necessity? Reassessing the Privilege Against Self-Incrimination' (1995) 54 *Cambridge Law Journal* 342; John T. McNaughton, 'The Privilege Against Self-incrimination: Its Constitutional Affectation, Raison d'Etre and Miscellaneous Implications' (1960) 51 *Journal of Criminal Law, Criminology and Police Science* 138.

(a) INTRINSIC RATIONALES: HARDSHIP, DILEMMA, AND PRIVACY

Bentham identified a number of possible justifications for the privilege, all of which serve as literary aunt sallies satirized with comic epithets. This is Bentham's 'old woman's reason':

The essence of this reason is contained in the word *hard*: 'tis hard upon a man to be obliged to criminate himself.[56]

For Bentham, the hardness of compelled self-incrimination lay not so much in being put under pressure to make incriminating statements, as in the judicial punishment to which an admission of guilt might lead after trial and conviction. In this form, the hardship objection is reduced to little more than a squeamish loss of nerve in executing the demands of justice. Given that society declares its intention to inflict proportionally hard treatment on convicted criminals, Bentham rightly considered it pusillanimous to recoil from the lesser hardship of questioning criminal suspects and the accused and giving their silence whatever probative value it might merit.

In a more substantial modern version of the argument, a different form of hardship is regarded as inherently objectionable. The privilege against self-incrimination is said to spare the accused the 'dilemma' of the choice between testifying truthfully and contributing to his own conviction, or committing perjury in order to escape punishment. In some – mostly American – variations, this hateful choice becomes 'the cruel trilemma': confession, perjury, or contempt.[57] And in yet a further variant on the theme of tough choices, Bill Stuntz suggests, by analogy to substantive criminal law excuses like duress and provocation,[58] that the privilege against self-incrimination is a mechanism for making allowances for human frailty. In contrast to justification defences, such as self-defence and necessity which apply to conduct that is morally appropriate or at least permitted,[59] excuse defences relate to conduct that is indubitably wrong but understandable on account of recognizable human failings, and to that extent (partly) excusable. Stuntz suggests that the privilege against self-incrimination can be understood along similar lines. Whilst honesty may be, morally speaking, the best policy, the fact is that people are tempted to lie to save their skins, especially if they feel cornered and there is seemingly no other way out. On this excuse interpretation of the hardship rationale, the privilege spares the accused from having to tell wrongful, but excusable, lies that would expose him to the risk of prosecution for perjury. Stuntz contends:

Anglo-American criminal law has a tradition of acquitting some categories of offenders even while acknowledging that their conduct was both criminal and wrong. That tradition may help explain why as a society we wish people would confess to their crimes, but are unwilling to force them to do so.[60]

---

[56] *Rationale of Judicial Evidence* (1827), vol. 5, 230.

[57] Cf. *Brannigan v Davison* [1997] AC 238, 249, PC, *per* Lord Nicholls, quoting Goldberg J. in *Murphy v Waterfront Commission of New York Harbor*, 378 US 52, 55, (1964) on 'the cruel trilemma of self-accusation, perjury or contempt'.

[58] William J. Stuntz, 'Self-Incrimination and Excuse' (1988) 88 *Columbia LR* 1227.

[59] Justification defences have been aptly described as 'contextual permissions': see E. Colvin, 'Exculpatory Defences in Criminal Law' (1990) 10 *OJLS* 381.   [60] Stuntz, 'Self-Incrimination and Excuse', 1242.

So we do not draw the common sense inference against the silent suspect essentially out of compassion.

Modern rationales emphasizing the hardship of compelled self-incrimination have their particular attractions, but none of them satisfactorily neutralizes Bentham's original critique of the privilege against self-incrimination. On sustained reflection can it really be said that the accused's *n*-lemma is intolerably harsh? In reality, perjury charges are hardly ever brought against accused persons who lie in their own defence, partly for pragmatic reasons,[61] and partly because such a prosecution, conveying the impression of state victimization of the accused, would be vulnerable to being stayed as an abuse of process.[62] Those who stand trial on substantive charges are, practically speaking, virtually immune to prosecution for perjury, though self-serving lies in court must be commonplace. After all, accused persons who testify in their own defence are routinely convicted. Such individuals are either unfortunate innocents wrongly convicted, or liars as well as felons.

If the sanction for perjury were regarded as the principal stumbling-block it could easily be removed, and without incurring the loss of relevant evidence exacted by the privilege against self-incrimination. In most continental European jurisdictions the accused is not sworn as a witness when speaking in court, so no question of perjury can arise. The accused is free to speak – indeed, he is strongly encouraged and expected to address the court, and most accused gratefully accept this opportunity to put their side of the story.[63] It is taken as read that false defences might be advanced, but there is no additional legal penalty for the accused who attempts to lie his way out of trouble. Besides, when all is said and done, fear of conviction is likely to be the dominant factor when an accused confronts the 'cruel dilemma' of truth or perjury in English criminal proceedings. For if prosecution for perjury is barely a remote prospect, the testimonial oath no longer carries a credible threat of eternal damnation, as it once did,[64] and can hardly be counted on to motivate the majority of accused persons to think twice before perjuring themselves.

Another objection to hardship-based rationales is that ordinary witnesses are routinely faced with no less agonizing choices in criminal proceedings. For example, a parent might find the prospect of testifying against a son or daughter no less awful then compelled self-incrimination, whilst doctors and priests and other confidantes may have very strong ethical inhibitions against breaching professional confidences. It is sometimes harder to

---

[61] If the accused is convicted of the substantive charge there is little practical point in bringing further proceedings against her for lying, unsuccessfully, on oath. If the accused is acquitted, on the other hand, it is likely to be difficult to prove that she has lied.

[62] But cf. *DPP* v *Humphrys* [1977] AC 1, in which the House of Lords reaffirmed the independent basis of a perjury charge, and definitively ruled that the civil law doctrine of issue estoppel has no application to English criminal proceedings. For criticism, see Peter Mirfield, 'Shedding a Tear for Issue Estoppel' [1980] *Crim LR* 336.

[63] See Gordon van Kessel, 'European Perspectives on the Accused as a Source of Testimonial Evidence' (1998) 100 *West Virginia LR* 799; Jeffrey K. Walker, 'A Comparative Discussion of the Privilege Against Self-Incrimination' (1993) 14 *New York Law School Journal of International and Comparative Law* 1; Bron McKillop, 'Anatomy of a French Murder Case' (1997) 45 *American Journal of Comparative Law* 527, 575–78; Mirjan Damaška, 'Evidentiary Barriers to Conviction and Two Models of Criminal Procedure: A Comparative Study' (1973) 121 *University of Pennsylvania LR* 506, 527: 'In contrast to the common law concept of the privilege, the continental defendant is not free to decide whether to take the stand and submit to the interrogation process. Questions can always be asked of him .... Thus, it should occasion no surprise that almost all continental defendants choose to testify.'   [64] See §7.2, above.

betray a significant other than to give oneself up – which, indeed, can be a kind of release. Yet English law concedes no quarter. As we saw in Chapter 7, ordinary witnesses enjoy no general immunity from having to make the choice between damaging a valued relationship, or laying themselves open to proceedings for perjury or contempt. The general civic duty to contribute to law-enforcement by speaking the truth in court, is taken, in England and Wales,[65] to override competing values and interests.[66]

Finally, rationales promoting the privilege against self-incrimination as a response to the cruel dilemma/trilemma can be refuted directly by denying that the accused's choice involves any objectionable harshness at all. Critics such as Ron Allen bluntly reply that an innocent person only has to tell the truth, whilst the guilty accused is morally obligated to confess in any event: 'the morally correct view, even if pragmatically implausible, is that people should co-operate and should be encouraged to co-operate rather than encouraged to stymie legitimate governmental investigations of serious criminality'.[67] Sir Rupert Cross was of similar mind. Perhaps, he suggested, the emotive language of 'privilege' has become an obstacle to clear-headed and dry-eyed appreciation of what is truly at stake in drawing adverse inferences from an accused's silence?

If for the loaded phrase 'self accusation' we were to substitute 'liability for cross-examination', the defendant at a criminal trial would be confronted with the choice between giving the court his version of the facts with the possibility of a cross-examination which might or might not be unpleasant, and running the risk of adverse inferences being drawn from his failure to testify, a risk the magnitude of which would vary considerably from case to case. If...an accused with a criminal record is adequately protected from cross-examination on that subject, I fail to see how the choice can realistically be described as a cruel one.[68]

Setting supposed hardships and cruelties to one side, an alternative strategy for infusing the privilege against self-incrimination with intrinsic value is to relate it to the accused's interests in privacy and personal autonomy. The liberty to go about one's lawful business without molestation, and in particular without the snooping or interference of government, is a cherished right in liberal societies. A right to privacy can be justified in terms of its distinctive contribution to personal autonomy,[69] and the privilege against self-incrimination has obvious affinities with the right to privacy. The privilege permits the accused to keep his knowledge, as well as his private thoughts, to himself. Perhaps it could be reconceptualized as an essential dimension of freedom of thought and conscience, as well as constituting an important safeguard against state oppression.

However, the right to privacy is subject to numerous qualifications and limitations.[70] Witnesses called to testify in criminal proceedings are denied the freedom to withhold

---

[65] Testimonial privileges are generally broader in continental jurisdictions, evincing a different order of priorities. In this respect, at least, these jurisdictions appear to place a higher value on the sanctity of personal relationships, and correspondingly less importance on the effective detection and punishment of crime.   [66] §7.3.

[67] Ronald J Allen, 'The Simpson Affair, Reform of the Criminal Justice Process, and Magic Bullets' (1996) 67 *University of Colorado LR* 989, 1021.

[68] Rupert Cross, *An Attempt to Update the Law of Evidence*, 19th Lionel Cohen Lectures (1973).

[69] Paul Roberts, 'Privacy, Autonomy and Criminal Justice Rights: Philosophical Preliminaries', in Peter Alldridge and Chrisje Brants (eds.), *Personal Autonomy, the Private Sphere and Criminal Law* (Hart, 2001).

[70] This is clearly flagged in ECHR Article 8(2), permitting violations of the right to respect for private life on grounds of 'national security, public safety or the economic well-being of the country, for the prevention

information simply because it is private. Community interests in the effective administration of justice frequently override the right to privacy. Police surveillance and investigation are justified where there is reasonable suspicion of criminal activity.[71] Although
people should be left alone with their private thoughts if there is no good reason to demand
public confession, it is not oppressive, where material suspicions of offending are aroused,
to invite citizens to respond to accusations or to account for apparently incriminating
circumstances. This, after all, is what criminal trials do.[72] And unless there are particular
reasons for withholding co-operation during police interrogation, such as a pre-emptive
collateral challenge to the legality of an arrest, the right to privacy is no more persuasive
justification for silence in the police station than at court. This is Ron Allen's uncompromising conclusion:

The historical justifications for the self-incrimination clause are a dead letter in every
respect.... We can talk about the ethic of individualism until we are blue in the face, but it
remains the case that civilization requires an enormous amount of cooperative effort. I do
not think it plausible that we entered into society in order to have rights of the accused: they
are obviously instrumental to something else. [The accused's interest in choosing to confess
or remain silent] is seriously detrimental to the effort to construct and maintain civil society
and not worthy of respect.[73]

If the argument from privacy were taken to its logical extreme, no criminal investigation
would be possible without the suspect's agreement because modern criminal investigations and prosecutions involve all manner of privacy invasions, which in many – though
certainly not all – instances are fully justifiable. If the police had a machine for looking
into suspects' heads and reading their thoughts defenders of civil liberties would rightly
be alarmed. But given the practical realities of modern criminal investigations, which do
involve extensive surveillance and undercover operations but do *not* make use of non-
existent thought-reading machines, it is difficult to see how drawing adverse inferences
from silence somehow damages a special interest in privacy that is uniquely protected by
the privilege against self-incrimination.

(b) CONCEPTUALIST RATIONALES: ADVERSARY PROCEDURE, THE PRESUMPTION OF INNOCENCE, AND FAIR TRIAL

Rather than arguing that the privilege against self-incrimination has intrinsic value,
a second group of rationales claims that the privilege is conceptually implied by other
well-established features of criminal procedure. On the most general version of this
argument, the privilege is vindicated by the adversarial structure of English criminal
proceedings. In a party-dominated procedural system organized around a contest

---

of disorder or crime, for the protection of health or morals, or for the protection of the rights and freedoms
of others'. Generally, see R. Kent Greenawalt, 'Silence as a Moral and Constitutional Right' (1981) 23 *William
and Mary LR* 15; Stuntz, 'Self-Incrimination and Excuse', 1232–7.

[71] Similar considerations arose in our discussion of the jurisprudence of s.78 of PACE: see §5.4, above.

[72] Cf. R. A. Duff, *Answering for Crime* (Hart, 2007); Duff *et al*, *The Trial on Trial Volume Three: Towards
a Normative Theory of the Criminal Trial* (Hart, 2007).

[73] Ronald J. Allen, 'The Simpson Affair, Reform of the Criminal Justice Process, and Magic Bullets' (1996)
67 *University of Colorado LR* 989, 1016, 1021.

between competing adversaries,[74] neither party (so the argument goes) should be compelled to assist his opponent. As we observed in Chapter 2, the prosecution commands the law enforcement resources of the state, and consequently enjoys significant structural advantages over the defence in the preparation and presentation of its case. On what basis can it be contended that the accused should be dragooned into helping the prosecutor assemble proof of the accused's own guilt? A strange game this, it might be thought, if the weaker of the two parties, on top of all his other disadvantages, is also obliged to score own-goals.

The appearance of the sporting metaphor to characterize criminal proceedings is frequently an ominous sign that rhetoric is about to impersonate reasoned argument, and this adversarial rationale for the privilege against self-incrimination does not disappoint. It posits an unrealistically purist conception of adversarial process which is difficult to justify in principle, and in practice never encountered. For decades, parties to civil litigation have been under comprehensive mutual disclosure duties,[75] but this does not mean that the English civil trial has transmogrified into an entirely different procedural species. Despite even greater emphasis on 'cards on the table' disclosure following Lord Woolf's reforms, civil litigation remains a recognizably common law, adversary system in its history, institutions, and culture. In criminal proceedings, too, there is considerable pre-trial disclosure[76] and most suspects in fact make statements to the police and testify at trial in their own defence. Yet it remains perfectly intelligible to characterize English criminal process as 'adversarial' in contradistinction to the 'inquisitorial' systems of continental Europe, South America, and parts of Africa and Asia. In reality, all modern systems of criminal procedure combine elements from both major European traditions. It is consequently fallacious to infer detailed evidentiary rules and principles from 'pure' – for which, read 'naïvely unsophisticated' – models of adversarial or inquisitorial process. As we explained in Chapter 2, procedural models are ideal-types constructed for the purpose of analysis, rather than accurate descriptive accounts of real systems.[77]

Lurking behind the invocation of adversarial values, one suspects, is the sentimental attachment to 'fair play' that Bentham derided as the 'fox hunter's reason':

This consists in introducing upon the carpet of legal procedure the idea of *fairness*, in the sense in which the word is used by sportsmen. The fox is to have a fair chance for his life: he must have (so close is the analogy) what is called *law*: leave to run a certain length of way, for the express purpose of giving him a chance for escape.[78]

Fox-hunting evokes rather different associations for modern sensibilities than in Bentham's day, but we can be sure that the analogy was not intended to cast the law of criminal procedure in a favourable light. Adversarial process is not an abstract end in itself, but a means to the end of convicting the guilty and protecting the innocent. Particular forms of criminal adjudication may boast their own internal procedural logic and institutional

---

[74] §2.2.   [75] See *Zuckerman on Civil Procedure*, §§10.25–10.29 and ch 14.

[76] As briefly described in §2.3(c)(ii), above.

[77] See further, Paul Roberts, 'Faces of Justice Adrift? Damaška's Comparative Method and the Future of Common Law Evidence', in John Jackson, Maximo Langer, and Peter Tillers (eds.), *Crime, Procedure and Evidence in A Comparative and International Context – Essays in Honour of Professor Mirjan Damaska* (Hart, 2008).   [78] *Rationale of Judicial Evidence* (1827), vol. 5, 238–9.

moral virtue,[79] but this valuation only makes sense as part of the broader enterprise of achieving justice. And justice is not a field sport, any more than getting married or having children is a game of chess. Specific features of adversarial procedure should ultimately be judged by reference to their contribution to effective fact-finding, in the light of the other foundational principles of criminal evidence. Which is to say that, rather than deriving the privilege against self-incrimination from a conceptual analysis of adversarial procedure, adversarial features of criminal proceedings themselves require moral justification, just like the privilege.

Another common conceptualist strategy for defending the privilege against self-incrimination is to contend that it follows by necessary implication from the presumption of innocence. The two ideas have frequently been linked, usually to the advantage of the privilege, since – as we saw in Chapter 6 – the presumption of innocence is rightly regarded as a cornerstone of legitimate criminal procedure. But conceptual analysis can never be an adequate surrogate for moral argument in rationalizing aspects of criminal procedure. In seeking to side-step the moral issue, none of the following conceptualist arguments yields a convincing rationale for the privilege.

According to one conception of the presumption of innocence, removing the privilege against self-incrimination would diminish the prosecution's duty to prove guilt beyond reasonable doubt. However, this contention rests on an elementary fallacy: it confuses a normative standard of sufficiency of proof with the type of evidence capable of satisfying that standard. Where silence is evidentially probative it may contribute towards discharging the prosecutor's burden of proof without in any way diluting the traditional standard of proof. Confession evidence has always been a prominent feature of English criminal proceedings, as we saw in the last chapter, but it is not suggested that the standard of proof is being lowered when the prosecutor adduces evidence of the accused's admissions. It is true that the availability of silence as a piece of evidence may make the prosecutor's task easier in some cases. But there is no more justification for preventing the prosecutor from relying on probative silence, than for discounting other apparently incriminating evidence, such as, for example, evidence that the suspect was seen fleeing from the scene of the crime.

Alternatively, it may be asserted that the privilege is a component of the accused's right not to be troubled to defend himself unless the prosecution first establishes a *prima facie* case. An important function of the presumption of innocence is to protect the accused from having to respond to criminal charges unless and until the prosecution adduces sufficient evidence to justify a reasonable jury in returning a verdict of guilty. However, the removal of the privilege against self-incrimination would not diminish citizens' liberty in this regard. Even if the privilege were abolished the prosecution should still continue to bear the burden of establishing a *prima facie* case before the accused is required to defend himself. Procedural rules governing prosecutorial decision-making and submissions of 'no case to answer'[80] give practical effect to this aspect of the presumption of innocence in English law. Silence in court might *contribute* to a *prima facie* case, but could never

---

[79] See further, Hock Lai Ho, *A Philosophy of Evidence Law – Justice in the Search for Truth* (OUP, 2008); Duff *et al, The Trial on Trial Volume Three: Towards a Normative Theory of the Criminal Trial* (Hart, 2007); Robert S. Summers, 'Evaluating and Improving Legal Processes – A Plea for "Process Values"' (1974) 60 *Cornell LR* 1; Lon L. Fuller, *The Morality of Law* (Yale UP, 1969).   [80] §2.5(c).

constitute a case to answer. Silence, that is to say, is only ever probative in the context of other incriminating evidence.

Pushing the argument further back into the initial stages of criminal proceedings, it might be contended that the presumption of innocence is greatly weakened if accused persons are required to account for themselves during police interrogation. The prosecution might then rely either on incriminating statements or, where suspects clammed up, 'suspicious silences' in order to establish a *prima facie* case at trial. This prospect is all the more perplexing to the extent that the police are not obliged to disclose information to the suspect prior to an interrogation, beyond the bare fact that he is suspected of particular offences.[81] If the police were empowered to interrogate citizens without justifiable cause, furthermore, this might encourage officers to make random arrests on the off-chance that some detainees would divulge incriminating information. Such dragnet police tactics would be intolerable in a free society, where state interference in citizens' liberty requires some explicit justification, such as reasonable suspicion of incipient or consummated criminality. The presumption of innocence is truly a bulwark of autonomy, a cipher of justice, and a servant of democratic accountability in liberal societies. The difficulty lies in understanding how the privilege against self-incrimination is supposed to contribute to any of these noble objectives.

Police powers of arrest, detention, and interrogation are defined in the law of criminal procedure completely independently of the privilege.[82] Moreover, a suspect who initially refuses to co-operate with police investigations may be arrested and detained with a view to securing his waiver of the privilege, whereupon interrogation may proceed without legal objection (subject, of course, to the custody time-limits on pre-charge detention and the legal regulation of interrogation techniques detailed in the last chapter). The privilege against self-incrimination itself consequently does little to safeguard the citizen from the perils of arrest, detention, and police interrogation. In the final analysis, the only reliable guarantor of citizens' liberty and freedom from arbitrary arrest and detention is a liberal democratic culture and sympathetic political administration under the rule of law. The familiar social and institutional manifestations of liberal democracy are what ultimately circumscribe police powers and sustain the framework of legal checks and balances, ideally to pre-empt abuses of state power by officials before they occur, but at a minimum providing effective remedies to aggrieved citizens whose rights have been infringed.

Despite their inherent weakness in seeking to supplant moral argument with conceptual logic, one further variation on the conceptualist gambit merits brief mention, because it might derive some credibility from the Article 6 jurisprudence of the European Court of Human Rights. The privilege against self-incrimination is not mentioned in the text of the ECHR, presumably because the Convention was something of an international human right law prototype and the privilege was overlooked.[83] In a sequence of important

---

[81] PACE 1984, s.28(3) requires that a person placed under arrest be 'informed of the ground for the arrest at the time of, or as soon as is practicable after, the arrest'. Section 37(5) imposes a corresponding duty on the custody officer to explain to suspects why they are being detained at the police station. And see PACE Code C, paras.10.5A–10.5C (special warnings in anticipation of drawing adverse inferences from a suspect's silence under the Criminal Justice and Public Order Act 1994). [82] PACE 1984, Part III.

[83] Every subsequent relevant international instrument specifies the privilege against self-incrimination as part of the human right to a fair trial, including Article 14(3)(g) of the International Covenant on Civil and Political Rights.

judgments the Court boldly held that the privilege is anyway implied by the notion of a fair trial under Article 6 of the Convention. It is now well-established that:

Although not specifically mentioned in Article 6 of the Convention, there can be no doubt that the right to remain silent under police questioning and the privilege against self-incrimination are generally recognised international standards which lie at the heart of the notion of a fair procedure under Article 6.[84]

Such statements invite conceptualist interpretations, whatever the Strasbourg Court itself may have intended. In its judgment in *Saunders v UK*[85] the Court directly linked the privilege against self-incrimination to the presumption of innocence, though in other cases greater reliance seems to be placed on instrumental rationales for the privilege.[86] Whilst instrumental rationales merit further critical scrutiny, conceptualist arguments always run into the sand. A secure moral foundation for the privilege against self-incrimination will not be generated by meditations on the concept of a fair trial, any more than conceptual approaches to adversary proceedings or the presumption of innocence have succeeded in what is an inescapably *moral* enterprise of rationalization.

(c) INSTRUMENTAL RATIONALES: PROMOTING FACT-FINDING AND PROTECTING THE INNOCENT

According to instrumental rationales, the privilege against self-incrimination is justified, not on the grounds of its intrinsic merit or conceptual entailment by other features of criminal proceedings, but because it serves, as an 'instrument', to promote some other value or desirable outcome. Instrumental rationales are as numerous as the objectives and values which the privilege might be claimed to serve, with many subtle and overlapping iterations. They are not infrequently run together and sometimes confused, with each other and with overt or implicit appeals to intrinsic values. As before, a survey of the most prominent variants will suffice.

The most general and straightforward instrumental argument for the privilege is that it increases the amount of evidence available to the fact-finder, or improves the quality of the evidence presented at trial, and in either case promotes the overriding aims of truth-finding and effective adjudication. On the face of it, these are paradoxical claims, for surely, it might be thought, the privilege operates to withhold information from the jury (guilty suspects and accused are permitted to remain silent without their silence counting against them), rather than providing the court with more or better evidence. However, various ingenious arguments have been devised to turn this common sense logic on its head.

On one analysis, the privilege protects the courts from an avalanche of perjury and lies, which guilty accused would inevitably fabricate if they were forced to speak or suffer adverse evidential consequences from their silence. Without the accused's privilege against self-incrimination, it is said, the jury would become mired in deceit and distraction, to the inevitable detriment of accurate fact-finding. This argument is closely related to another contention that we will consider more carefully in a moment: that the privilege protects

---

[84] *Murray v UK* (1996) 22 EHRR 29, [45].   [85] *Saunders v UK* (1996) 23 EHRR 313, [68]–[69].

[86] As in *Murray v UK* (1996) 22 EHRR 29, [45], where the Court explained that '[b]y providing the accused with protection against improper compulsion by the authorities these immunities contribute to avoiding miscarriages of justice and to securing the aims of Article 6'.

the innocent from wrongful conviction. But observe, for now, that even if the privilege does spare the courts from an appreciable volume of potentially misleading lies, this gain must be offset against the routine loss of probative silence as evidence. Moreover, untruthful or evasive testimony itself often eases the path to conviction, since proven lies and manifest evasion can betray the offender just as effectively as any other circumstantially incriminating evidence.[87] Most accused testify in their own defence.[88] Since the majority are convicted it appears that juries are not routinely taken in by the accused's false testimony. When a full accounting of factors on both sides of the evidential balance-sheet is made, it would not be surprising if the privilege against self-incrimination imposed a net *loss* in the total stock of reliable evidence available to fact-finders. Admittedly, these calculations are all rather speculative, but this only underscores the difficulty of justifying the privilege against self-incrimination in terms of its putatively positive contribution to fact-finding.

A different spin on the 'more-and-better-evidence' rationale exploits the perverse incentives incidental to over-reliance on the suspect as a source of evidence. Where procedural rules tend to foster such reliance, investigators might regularly eschew alternative, and potentially superior, sources of information and lines of inquiry, and instead fall into the lazy habit of treating the suspect's confession as conclusive of guilt. Without the privilege, it might be argued, police officers would be disinclined to expend limited resources searching for confirmatory evidence. It is nearly always going to be more cost-effective to question suspects until they make damaging admissions and then rely on their confession as proof of guilt at trial. The net result would be a reduction in the quantity and quality of relevant information in criminal trials, and the effectiveness of criminal adjudication would be correspondingly diminished, to the detriment of justice.

One should not be too dogmatic in responding to this contention. In the absence of detailed empirical information about the context, motivations, and routine conduct of criminal investigations, the significance of the suspect's right to silence in shaping police investigative strategies is difficult to assess. That said, the existence in England and Wales of a more extensive common law privilege prior to 1995[89] did not appear to provide much incentive for the police to go to additional lengths in obtaining evidence independent of the accused. The Royal Commission on Criminal Procedure found that interviewing suspects for their confession was police officers' routine and entirely legitimate investigative strategy, concluding that 'there can be no adequate substitute for police questioning in the investigation and, ultimately, in the prosecution of crime'.[90] Even if it is regarded as lazy policing to rely on suspects to confess under interrogation, the privilege against self-incrimination can hardly be credited with having helped police investigators in England and Wales to kick the habit.

---

[87] Albeit that the probative value of lies may be prone to over-estimation, and the law consequently requires a cautionary judicial direction pursuant to *R* v *Lucas* [1981] QB 720, CA, discussed in §15.3(b).

[88] Some 70–74% testified in their own defence in Zander and Henderson's *Crown Court Study* (1993), para.4.5, around half of whom were convicted.

[89] When the relevant provisions of the CJ&PO Act 1994 came into force: see §13.3, below.

[90] Royal Commission on Criminal Procedure, *Report*, Cm.8092 (HMSO, 1981), para.4.1. The Commission observed, ibid. para. 2.12, that only a small proportion of offences was discovered as a consequence of police detection. And see Michael Zander, 'The Investigation of Crime: A Study of Cases Tried at the Old Bailey' [1979] *Crim LR* 203.

A more sympathetic appraisal of police work should acknowledge that the course of a criminal investigation is shaped by the dynamic relationship between national and local policing priorities and individual officers' appreciation of situational constraints and opportunities as they present themselves in the circumstances of a particular investigation. Frequently, there may be no additional evidence to find; and, in any event, searching for confirmatory evidence consumes police resources that might be deployed more effectively elsewhere, to advance investigations in cases where a suspect has not already admitted the offence. Police officers know that most prosecutions end with a guilty plea, in which case the strength of the prosecution's evidence is never actually tested in court. To the extent that policing practice is influenced by strategic calculations, the guilty plea culture of English criminal proceedings[91] is likely to be far more influential than the existence or extent of any testimonial privilege against self-incrimination. Of course, the likelihood of the accused pleading guilty may be increased by removing the privilege.

Forensic applications of novel scientific techniques are opening up new investigative possibilities which do not require the accused's consent or active co-operation. Video surveillance tapes and DNA identification evidence are important examples already widely in use. These technological developments might conceivably offset detectives' historical reliance on confessions as proof of guilt. But new scientific techniques will advance only certain kinds of investigation, and there are always cost implications. Investigators might decide not to send crime-scene samples for DNA analysis or leave video surveillance footage unwatched, in the hope that the suspect will anyway confess and save everybody the trouble. Additional sources of proof might not actively be sought unless and until they become necessary; and the very existence of new forensic technologies may increase the pressure to confess. The more possibility of DNA profiling evidence coming to light, for example, may induce fatalism in suspects. Whatever the future holds for the shape of criminal investigation, there is no reason to expect that the privilege against self-incrimination will ever be more than a marginal influence on investigators' conduct or that it could materially enhance the nature or quality of evidence available at trial.

If general claims to the evidence-enhancing properties of the privilege are found unconvincing, what of more narrowly-focused, particularistic rationales? According to an enduring, and rhetorically powerful, tradition of argument the privilege against self-incrimination's ultimate justification is that it functions to protect the innocent from wrongful conviction. Bentham thought it preposterous that the privilege could be regarded as a mechanism for protecting the innocent:

Can it be supposed that the rule in question has been established with the intention of protecting them? They are the only persons to whom it can never be useful.... What is [the innocent accused's] highest interest, and his most ardent wish? To dissipate the cloud which surrounds his conduct, and give every explanation which may set it in its true light; to provoke questions, to answer them, and to defy his accusers.[92]

---

[91] See, in particular, Mike McConville, 'Plea Bargaining', in Mike McConville and Geoffrey Wilson (eds.), *The Handbook of the Criminal Justice Process* (OUP, 2002), 376, describing plea-bargaining as 'the most virulent virus ever to have invaded the criminal justice system's body. It has left no part of the process untouched. It has altered the language of the law.'   [92] *Judicial Evidence* (1825, Dumont ed.), 241.

However, there must be innocent accused who, on account of being inarticulate or possessing an unfortunate manner, will make unconvincing witnesses and are therefore more likely to be convicted if they are exposed to cross-examination in the witness-box.[93] Whether this is a widespread problem is difficult to assess. Behavioural science research tends to confirm the common sense suspicion that juries can be biased against personalities they find unsympathetic;[94] but the revelation of potentially prejudicial background information is anyway often permitted by rules governing the admissibility of the accused's bad character, regardless of whether the accused testifies or invokes his privilege to remain silent in court. Even supposing that there are innocent accused who might sabotage their own defences by an incompetent performance in the witness-box, this must be viewed in light of the fact that, pragmatically speaking, an accused who passes up the opportunity of testifying in his own defence is always likely to create a negative impression with the jury. Invoking the privilege against self-incrimination is a double-edged sword for any accused, because jurors will suspect that a person who declines to argue his case doesn't really have a case to argue. Besides, the law of criminal evidence should cater directly for the needs of all witnesses, not just those who are especially vulnerable. Foundational principles of humane treatment and effective fact-finding are mutually reinforcing in their demands that neither the accused, nor any other witness, should be subjected to cross-examination which is calculated to confuse, manipulate, or demean.[95]

Glanville Williams emphatically reasserted the Benthamite position for a modern readership:

The crux of the matter is that immunity from being questioned is a rule which by its nature can protect the guilty only. It is not a rule that may operate to acquit some guilty for fear of convicting some innocent.[96]

Yet this overstates the case. In the light of modern psychological research, and with growing experience of miscarriages of justice, we have come to realize that the slightest pressure is sufficient to induce some vulnerable or disturbed individuals to make false admissions. Police stations are inherently coercive, and, for many, frightening places: suspects may feel confused and intimidated even if their interrogators behave impeccably. We also know that an alarmingly large percentage of police station detainees exhibit psychological symptoms, from serious personality disorders to mild intoxication with drink or drugs.[97] In these circumstances, it is not fanciful to imagine that an innocent person could make incriminating statements, or even a full confession, which would later be difficult to

[93] Alfred C. Clapp, 'Privilege Against Self-Incrimination' (1956) 10 *Rutgers LR* 541, 548. The self-same objection was raised against the 1898 Act reforms by which accused persons, generally, became competent witnesses in their own trials: *Wigmore on Evidence* (3rd edn. 1940), vol. 2, para.579.

[94] See Sally Lloyd-Bostock, 'The Effects on Juries of Hearing About the Defendant's Previous Criminal Record: A Simulation Study' [2000] *Crim LR* 734. Issues relating to evidence of the accused's (bad) character are investigated at length in Chapter 14.   [95] §1.3; §10.5.

[96] *The Proof of Guilt* (Stevens, 3rd edn. 1963), 53.

[97] In one small-scale study in two police stations conducted for the Runciman Royal Commission, no less than 'one third (35 per cent) of subjects were in some way judged to have problems which might interfere with their functioning or coping ability during police interviewing.... Twelve subjects (7 per cent) were judged to be mentally ill...': Gisli Gudjonsson, Isabel Clare, Susan Rutter, and John Pearse, *Persons at Risk During Interviews in Police Custody: The Identification of Vulnerabilities*, RCCJ Research Study No 12 (HMSO, 1993), 15. Previous research had estimated the percentage of police-station interviewees suffering from mental disturbance in the broad range 9%–42%: see Barrie Irving and Ian K McKenzie, *Police*

withdraw and could conceivably result in a mistaken conviction. An argument can therefore be made that the privilege safeguards innocence *at the police station*, if not at trial. The right to remain silent, it might be said, gives the suspect an important procedural protection against the manufacture of false, or at any rate misleading, evidence against him.

This argument has a superficial plausibility, but crumbles under closer examination. How exactly is a legal right to silence supposed to safeguard police-station detainees from abuse, manipulation, or false confessions? After all, every suspect, however vulnerable to suggestive interrogation, remains at liberty to waive his privilege and submit to police questioning. Any incriminating statements that he makes will be admissible at trial, even if the suspect later recants and claims to have been pressured or tricked into a confession. Far from equipping police-station detainees with a robust practical immunity form insistent questioning, the privilege against self-incrimination may amount to little more than a mild inconvenience to investigators, who are obliged, in the first instance, to secure the suspect's waiver of privilege. Thereafter, interrogation may proceed with the law's unambiguous blessing.

The brutal reality is that custodial interrogation puts suspects under almost irresistible pressures to answer police questions.[98] Any notional legal entitlement conflicting with this reality is unlikely to be an effective instrument for realizing desired practical objectives. The suspects most in need of protection in the police station are those who are vulnerable to psychological pressure or who are suggestible. Yet the vulnerable are the least likely to have the fortitude to assert their privilege in the face of determined police questioning. Vulnerable suspects will remain silent in practice only with effective legal assistance. Optional access to a lawyer is insufficient, because vulnerable suspects will predictably be persuaded to waive the right to legal assistance, just as they have always waived the right to silence. Only a comprehensive duty solicitor scheme, requiring all suspects to accept custodial legal representation, whether or not they request it – indeed, whether or not they want it – could resolve this conundrum. Even if such a scheme were economically viable and politically credible,[99] however, one should still ask whether the problem of oppressive, manipulative, or distorting interrogation is best addressed by employing an army of lawyers to attend on suspects in police stations at massive public expense. A more sensible approach might be to attack the roots of the problem directly, by searching for ways to correct improper police practices and to improve interrogation techniques.

Despite these fundamental objections, instrumental rationales for the privilege against self-incrimination continue to be advanced. A notably sophisticated version of the claim that the privilege protects the innocent has recently been advanced by Daniel Seidmann and Alex Stein, who adopt a 'game-theoretic' analysis of criminal adjudication as a general practice rather than examining the impact of the right to silence in individual cases.[100] As

---

Interrogation: The Effects of the Police and Criminal Evidence Act (Police Foundation, 1989); Barrie Irving, *Police Interrogation: A Case Study of Current Practice* (HMSO, 1980).

[98] See §12.2.

[99] The duty solicitor scheme for custodial legal advice boasts impressive geographical coverage, but such expenditures are not obvious vote-winners. The idea of spending public money to force lawyers on recalcitrant suspects who deny wanting or needing legal representation is, presumably, a political non-starter.

[100] Daniel J. Seidmann and Alex Stein, 'The Right to Silence Helps the Innocent: A Game-Theoretic Analysis of the Fifth Amendment Privilege' (2000) 114 *Harvard LR* 431. And see Alex Stein, 'The Right to Silence Helps the Innocent: A Response to Critics' (2008) 30 *Cardozo Law Review* 1115.

well as answering Bentham's contention that the privilege is nothing more than a refuge for scoundrels from which the innocent never benefit, this argument also contradicts the prevailing orthodoxy amongst courts and legal commentators in America that *Miranda's* interpretation of the Fifth Amendment privilege has succeeded only in allowing more guilty people to evade justice.

The Seidmann-Stein thesis proposes that accused persons effectively 'signal' their guilt by remaining silent. Innocent people, by contrast, are keen to tell the truth and dispel any suspicion against them. So far, Bentham – and most other commentators since – would agree. But what would happen, ask these authors, if the right to silence were removed? At least some of those guilty suspects who would otherwise remain silent would now tell exculpatory lies. They would, in the game-theoretic language, 'pool' with innocent suspects who also give exculpatory replies, which in their case are truthful. The problem for criminal adjudication, of course, is that neither the police nor the jury know who is telling the truth. Faced with this pooling of true and false accounts, a rational fact-finder must apply a credibility discount to *all* exculpatory stories to reflect the fact that, in the absence of a right to silence, a greater proportion of suspects' statements will be lies than would have been the case under a legal regime in which guilty suspects were offered the penalty-free option of remaining silent. Bentham and his followers focused only on individual cases, and from this perspective it is indeed difficult to see how any innocent person derives any instrumental advantage from the privilege against self-incrimination. Seidmann and Stein's approach, by contrast, concentrates on aggregate flows of cases through the system and hypothesizes the impact of suspects' decisions on other sub-groups of suspects and on the accused at trial. From this perspective it can be argued that innocent suspects, as a group, would be adversely affected by the removal of the privilege. In economists' terminology, lies impose 'negative externalities' on innocent accused. If the removal of the privilege produced a greater volume of false statements in criminal proceedings across the board, innocent suspects would suffer from the fall-out. Fewer truthful stories would be believed, and more innocent people would in consequence endure wrongful conviction.

Seidmann and Stein present a logical model rather than an empirically demonstrated thesis; though they do proceed to argue that their model is compatible with US constitutional jurisprudence on the Fifth Amendment privilege, and consistent with such limited empirical data as exist on the effects of removing the privilege in England, Northern Ireland, and Singapore. Game-theoretic modelling is based on controversial assumptions concerning the rationality of human decision-making. Treating individual suspects as competent rational maximizers of their own welfare is clearly a greatly simplified, if not grossly distorting, account of the complex way in which human beings make decisions about how to act or what to do. The authors rightly concede the artificiality of these assumptions, however, and rest content by observing that the framework assumptions of game theory are no more vulnerable to objection (albeit for different reasons) than the preconceptions of any rival or alternative methodology. Structural objections aside, there appear to be two principal pressure points in this ingenious thesis.

First, Seidmann and Stein make cumulative concessions that various types of scenario involving suspects' lies are excluded from their analysis. Given that their total relevant population is the small group of detainees who actually exercise the right to remain silent during interrogation, it is unclear whether many additional convictions of the innocent could, or would, be risked by abolishing the privilege. Even if the authors' argument is basically correct, how would the abolition of the right of silence further weaken the general plausibility of exculpatory statements? If guilty suspects believe they can spin a good story and get away with it, will they not go ahead and try to lie their way out of trouble irrespective of whether they could have invoked a formal right of silence? Silence is rarely the best policy at the police station. As we have observed, most suspects choose to waive their privilege and submit to interrogation, and many of them are subsequently convicted. So, in terms of the Seidmann-Stein thesis, the guilty are already pooling themselves with innocent suspects in considerable numbers. It seems dubious to suggest that withdrawing a rule that, in current practice, affects the behaviour of only a small percentage of suspects – those few who do choose to remain silent – might or should appreciably reduce the credibility of truthful statements to the police in the eyes of the fact-finder.[101]

A second pressure point concerns the social and institutional mechanics 'signalling', a crucial, but largely unexplored, dimension of the authors' thesis. The assumption is that by taking away the right to silence jurors will be induced to apply a proportionate discount to suspects' self-serving statements in every case. But the socio-psychological dynamics of this process are obscure. To begin with, it is a fair assumption that most jurors are already quite sceptical about suspects' self-serving statements, whether or not suspects are factually guilty. How much *more* sceptical could they be, in an inference permissive regime? Does it even make any sense to talk about quantities of suspicion in this way? Secondly, and in addition, even supposing that a discount should theoretically be applied, how will jurors get to know that suspects' self-serving statements are now x-less believable than formerly? Juries are one-shot players lacking relevant institutional knowledge. Are we to assume that the message is somehow carried by the usual political and culture modes of transmission, including the media? If so, it would have to be a very muffled and fuzzy – and predictably confused and often misleading – message, and this generates a third problem.

The authors think that non-criminal proceedings can be hermetically sealed-off from the pooling effects they are concerned to avoid. But how plausible is this? Is there not a risk that the message potential jurors will receive, from the media or general common sense experience, is something like 'all litigants advance self-serving lies', without distinguishing criminal litigation from, say, family law disputes concerning divorce or custody of children, landlord and tenant matters, commercial litigation, or bankruptcy proceedings. In this way, the fallout from non-criminal litigation could mirror the pooling effect in criminal cases, unless there is some way of signalling to jurors that the existence of the right to silence in criminal proceedings exerts a unique influence on the behaviour of the

---

[101] It could be said that what matters here is not how often suspects in fact choose to remain silent, but how often jurors *think that* suspects choose to remain silent. Jurors might place a premium on all exculpatory statements in the mistaken belief that the innocent would usually give an explanation, whilst the guilty generally remain silent. But then the argument would have to be that 'the privilege protects the innocent, just insofar as jurors remain ignorant of its infrequent use'. This is hardly a defensible position in a democratic society committed to transparency and accountability in the administration of criminal justice. It would also mean that the guilty gain an undeserved probative advantage by lying in the police station, and this fact in itself, if it became widely known, should logically encourage more lies to be told in police interviews by guilty suspects – which is the very behaviour that the privilege, according to this rationale, is supposed to prevent.

parties in that context. If so, we might expect to see some institutional traces of this kind of thinking. It might be reflected, for example, in jury instructions advising that because the accused might have remained silent but chose to speak, his explanation is *pro tanto* more believable. But such institutional traces are nowhere to be found in England and Wales, either in criminal trials or in any broader cultural manifestation.

Seidmann and Stein's hypothesis is not amenable to systematic empirical testing. By the same token, it cannot be conclusively refuted. The argument presents an impressive logical structure, but its realism and practical significance are questionable – even if sound in theory. There are, in any case, too many gaps in the analysis and unanswered questions to persuade sceptics. Finally, one could accept every last detail of Seidmann and Stein's analysis, and yet still insist that the privilege's contribution to avoiding wrongful conviction is marginal in comparison to other procedural safeguards for innocent suspects and the accused, whether already now in existence or aspirational blueprints for future reforms.

13.3 THEORY INTO PRACTICE: LEGISLATIVE TRANSFORMATIONS OF THE PRIVILEGE AGAINST SELF-INCRIMINATION

Readers hoping that systematic investigation of underlying rationales might yield a firm theoretical foundation on which to build a resilient legal privilege against self-incrimination will be disappointed by the foregoing discussion. It turns out, to the contrary, that the theoretical weakness of the standard rationales might go some way to explaining why the privilege has attracted such half-hearted judicial allegiance and equivocal common law precedents, despite its popular historical associations and rhetorical purchase. This is not to say that an effective privilege against self-incrimination could never be devised or implemented, only that the arguments for doing so have failed to convince judges and policy-makers that the price is worth the cost.

Reform of the privilege against self-incrimination in English law was first placed firmly on the policy-making agenda by the Criminal Law Revision Committee's influential Eleventh Report on *Evidence* published in 1972.[102] Notwithstanding the vocal endorsement of its most prominent Evidence scholar-member, Sir Rupert Cross,[103] the CLRC's recommendations for curtailing the right to silence provoked a defensive backlash from academic and practising criminal lawyers who instinctively rallied to the defence of the traditional common law privilege against self-incrimination.[104] The first assault on the citadel had been repulsed. Over time, however, policymakers' opposition to the privilege hardened, and by the late 1980s it was clear that the Conservative administration

---

[102] CLRC Eleventh Report, *Evidence: General*, Cm.4991 (HMSO, 1972), paras.28–52; discussed by A. A. S. Zuckerman, 'Criminal Law Revision Committee 11th Report – Right of Silence' (1973) 36 *MLR* 509.

[103] Rupert Cross, 'A Very Wicked Animal Defends the 11th Report of the Criminal Law Revision Committee' [1973] *Crim LR* 329; Rupert Cross, 'The Right to Silence and the Presumption of Innocence – Sacred Cows or Safeguards of Liberty?' (1970) 11 *Journal of the Society of Public Teachers of Law* 66.

[104] A flavour of critical reactions is given by C. J. Miller, 'Silence and Confessions – What Are They Worth?' [1973] *Crim LR* 343, 348–50.

of the day was determined to push through legislation to curtail the privilege.[105] Not for the first or last time, a controversial reform of criminal procedure was road-tested first in Northern Ireland.[106] Having sponsored a substantial programme of new empirical research in order to establish an informed basis for assessing reform options, the Runciman Royal Commission on Criminal Justice, which reported in 1993, concluded that the right to silence and the privilege against self-incrimination should be retained in their existing forms.[107] Undeterred, Home Secretary Michael Howard assured the Conservative Party conference later that year that '[t]he so-called right to silence is ruthlessly exploited by terrorists. What fools they must think we are. It's time to call a halt to this charade. The so-called right to silence will be abolished.'[108] The promised legislation duly materialized in the form of sections 34–38 of the Criminal Justice and Public Order Act 1994, which entered into force on 10 April 1995. Michael Zander, a former member of the Runciman Commission, branded this legislation almost unconstitutional, since the historic right to silence had been restricted in the teeth of contrary advice from two Royal Commissions and in the absence of any empirical evidence to substantiate the government's claims of widespread abuse by terrorists and professional criminals. Received wisdom about the crime control costs exacted by the right to silence was indeed mostly contradicted by the empirical data generated by the Royal Commission's research studies.[109] However, the privilege against self-incrimination's unimpressive underlying rationales may well have contributed to its vulnerability in the face of determined governmental opposition.

Modern English law on the privilege against self-incrimination addresses two distinct questions, which this section will explore in turn. First, when, if ever, may the prosecution in a criminal trial rely on information which the accused has been forced to divulge under threat of a penalty for non-disclosure? Or to put it more bluntly, in what situations, if any, can the privilege against self-incrimination be circumvented, disapplied, or overridden? The second question is: when, if ever, may the fact-finder lawfully draw negative inferences from the accused's silence during pre-trial police questioning or at trial? Under this rubric, there is no independent legal punishment or sanction for non-disclosure but silence may carry a forensic cost, in the sense that the accused is more likely to be found guilty of the offences or offences for which he is on trial. We will see in this section that both dimensions of the privilege against self-incrimination in modern English law reflect the growing influence of ECHR jurisprudence as mediated by the Human Rights Act 1998. The reforms implemented by the 1994 Act focus on the second, forensic, question, and are therefore aptly described as curtailing the right to silence. The first question concerns more direct and potentially far-reaching derogations from the privilege against self-incrimination.

---

[105] Home Office, *Report of the Working Group on the Right to Silence* (Home Office, 1989), discussed by A. A. S. Zuckerman, 'Trial by Unfair Means' [1989] *Crim LR* 855.

[106] Criminal Evidence (Northern Ireland) Order 1988; see J. D. Jackson, 'Interpreting the Silence Provisions: The Northern Ireland Cases' [1995] *Crim LR* 587.

[107] See Michael Zander, 'Abolition of the Right to Silence, 1972–1994', in David Morgan and Geoffrey Stephenson (eds.), *Suspicion & Silence* (Blackstone, 1994). Runciman was following the lead of the Philips Royal Commission on Criminal Procedure (1981), which had previously considered, and rejected, the CLRC's proposals for extending the range of permissible comment on silence.

[108] Quoted by Michael Zander, ibid. 145.   [109] See RCCJ Research Studies cited n.32, above.

(a) DELIMITING THE PRIVILEGE AGAINST SELF-INCRIMINATION

As previously observed,[110] neither the right to silence nor the privilege against self-incrimination is specifically mentioned in the ECHR, but the European Court of Human Rights has declared that both right and privilege 'are generally recognised international standards which lie at the heart of the notion of a fair procedure under Article 6'.[111] English law contains many statutory provisions requiring the accused to provide potentially incriminating information under a penalty for refusal.[112] The technique is particularly common in regulatory contexts where compelled information is regarded as essential to assist the police or a dedicated regulatory agency, like the Financial Services Authority, H. M. Revenue and Customs, the Health and Safety Executive, or the Environmental Protection Agency, to perform their duties in the public interest. It is clear that using compelled information as proof of the accused's guilt in his subsequent criminal trial could in principle breach Article 6. However, despite some sweeping *dicta* in *Saunders* implying otherwise, it is equally clear that the privilege against self-incrimination is a limited, rather than an absolute, privilege in international human rights law. Moreover, infringement of the privilege can be justified if government action is limited to proportionate measures designed to achieve a legitimate objective.

The first significant test-case exploring the scope of the privilege against self-incrimination under the Human Rights Act concerned section 172 of the Road Traffic Act 1988, which requires car-owners to divulge the identity of the person who was driving their car at a particular time and place, subject on refusal to a maximum fine of £1,000, automatic endorsement of their licence, and possible disqualification from driving. This type of provision is utilized in many European legal systems to prove speeding offences detected by automatic speed cameras. In *Brown* v *Stott*,[113] however, it was the accused's apparent state of inebriation that prompted police officers, pursuant to section 172, to demand information about the identity of the person who had recently been driving a now stationary vehicle. The Scottish High Court, applying what it took to be the ruling in *Saunders* v *UK*, held that *B*'s admission that she was the driver could not subsequently be relied upon by the prosecution on a charge of driving with excess alcohol, because that admission had been compelled under penalty in contravention of the privilege against self-incrimination. However, the Privy Council, allowing the prosecutor's appeal, said that the High Court had mistakenly treated Article 6(1)'s privilege against self-incrimination as absolute, when in fact proportionate restrictions on the privilege in pursuit of a legitimate objective are permitted. Here, the accused was only required to provide limited factual information, and the objective of helping investigators to identify drivers suspected of road traffic offences in order to promote road safety was unquestionably a legitimate

---

[110] §13.2(b), above.

[111] *Saunders* v *UK* (1996) 23 EHRR 313, [68]; *Funke* v *France* (1993) 16 EHRR 297; *IJL, GMR and AKP* v *UK* [2001] Crim LR 133.

[112] See the lists of such provisions collected in Hodge M. Malek *et al*, *Phipson on Evidence* (Sweet & Maxwell, 17th edn. 2009), para.24. and *Blackstone's Criminal Practice 2009*, F9.25–F9.26. The pre-Human Rights Act situation is discussed by Susan Nash and Mark Furse, 'Self-Incrimination, Corporate Misconduct, and the Convention on Human Rights' [1995] *Crim LR* 854; and *Cross and Tapper on Evidence* (Butterworths, 9th edn. 1999), 432–5.

[113] *Brown (Margaret)* v *Stott* [2003] 1 AC 681, PC (Scotland); applied in England and Wales in *DPP* v *Wilson* [2001] EWHC Admin 198, [2002] RTR 6.

statutory purpose. Section 172 was therefore a proportionate infringement of the privilege against self-incrimination and perfectly compatible with both the ECHR and the Human Rights Act.

Subsequent cases have emphasized that the privilege against self-incrimination operates to prevent *the use* of compelled information in later criminal proceedings.[114] Provisions requiring the accused to provide information under penalty as part of a statutory scheme of regulation are not *per se* objectionable. Financial penalties for non-compliance can be imposed if the accused refuses to provide requested information without engaging any human rights issue. This distinction has been reinforced by a number of legislative amendments to pre-existing statutory duties to provide information, introduced in response to the European Court's *Saunders* judgment.[115] Generally speaking, information compelled under the relevant statutory duties is no longer admissible as evidence to prove a substantive charge in subsequent criminal proceedings. The scope for challenge under the Human Rights Act is correspondingly substantially reduced.

Even if compelled information *is* later used against the accused in a subsequent criminal prosecution this will not necessarily constitute an actionable violation of Article 6. In its most recent decisions, the European Court of Human Rights appears to have rowed back from some of its earlier, more adventurous pronouncements on the scope of the privilege against self-incrimination under the ECHR. In *O'Halloran and Francis* v *UK*[116] the applicants directly challenged section 172 of the Road Traffic Act 1988 before the Strasbourg court, contending that a provision expressly designed to require car owners to disclose information that would then often be used by the authorities to mount a criminal prosecution against them could not be compatible with the privilege against self-incrimination. Rather than bringing English law into line with Article 6 standards, the Grand Chamber of the European Court of Human Rights, quoting liberally from the judgment of the Privy Council in *Brown* v *Stott*, rejected the applicants' complaints. The Court identified as decisive considerations 'the nature and degree of compulsion used to obtain the evidence, the existence of any relevant safeguards in the procedure, and the use to which any material so obtained was put'.[117] In this context, there was a weighty public interest in promoting road safety, car owners voluntarily accepted a regulatory framework by choosing to drive on public roads, the demand for information was narrowly limited to the identity of the driver on a particular occasion, the remainder of the relevant road traffic offence – which were not strict liability crimes – had to be proved by the prosecution to the criminal standard, and the penalties for non-compliance were modest and non-custodial. This balancing of interests is perfectly defensible, and if the European Court had come right out and said that the privilege against self-incrimination does not extend to the information demanded of car owners pursuant to section 172 it would have been difficult to object to this pragmatic limitation of the privilege. But the Court seemed to want to have its cake and eat it, declaring that 'the essence of the applicants' right to remain silent and their privilege against

---

[114] See, e.g., *R* v *Hertfordshire CC, ex p. Green Environmental Industries Ltd* [2000] 2 AC 412, HL, discussed by Haydn Davies and Beverley Hopkins, 'Environmental Crime and the Privilege Against Self-Incrimination' (2000) 4 *E & P* 177; *R* v *Kearns* [2002] 1 WLR 2815, [2002] EWCA Crim 748.

[115] Youth Justice and Criminal Evidence Act 1999, s.59 and sch.3, which were brought into force on 14 April 2000.   [116] *O'Halloran and Francis* v *UK* (2008) 46 EHRR 21.

[117] ibid. [55].

self-incrimination has not been destroyed'.[118] This is a perplexing conclusion. In what sense does section 172 preserve 'the essence' of the privilege against self-incrimination? For Judge Pavlovschi, dissenting, it was 'perfectly obvious that for an individual to state that he was the driver of a car which was speeding illegally is tantamount to a confession that he was in breach of the speed regulations'.[119] Whilst the actual decision in *O'Halloran and Francis* may be sound, the analysis used to support it concedes major hostages to future. The Grand Chamber's approach seems to expose the privilege against self-incrimination to unconstrained policy 'balancing', which still permits the court to say that the privilege against self-incrimination is being preserved even as individuals' interests are subordinated to the public good – surely the very antithesis of rights protection.

O'Halloran and Francis was preceded by the Grand Chamber's decision in *Jalloh v Germany*,[120] which on the face of it presents a very different story. Jalloh was suspected of drug dealing by undercover police officers. When the officers attempted to apprehend him, Jalloh swallowed his remaining drugs. He was taken to a local hospital and forced to regurgitate the drugs through the administration of an emetic through a nasogastric tube. Most suspects who undergo this procedure in Germany apparently consent, but Jalloh refused to co-operate and had to be held down by four officers whilst the tube was inserted and the solution poured into his stomach. He later complained of serious temporary and more long-lasting health effects. The German courts nonetheless found that the administration of an emetic to recover suspected illegal narcotics was a lawful means of criminal investigation properly implemented by a qualified doctor. Although the officers might have waited for nature to take its course, this would have interfered with the progress of the investigation. Resort to forced regurgitation had been a reasonable and proportionate response in the circumstances. The European Court of Human Rights disagreed. The procedure had violated Article 3 in constituting inhuman and degrading treatment (though it did not reach the threshold necessary for torture). In addition, in the circumstances of this case, the use of evidence procured in this manner at Jalloh's subsequent trial for drug trafficking violated Article 6. The integrity of criminal proceedings, a ten-member majority of the Grand Chamber held, would always be compromised if evidence obtained by torture were admitted in a criminal trial, and breaches of Article 3 falling short of torture might also – as here – fatally compromise the fairness of a trial in which tainted evidence was adduced. So far, this was a fairly straightforward (albeit controversial) application of the concept of a fair trial elucidated in Chapter 5. However, the Court then went on to say that Jalloh's Article 6 privilege against self-incrimination had also been violated by forced administration of an emetic. This conclusion is more difficult to swallow.

Article 6 case-law since *Saunders* has gradually cemented the orthodoxy that '[t]he right not incriminate oneself is primarily concerned...with respecting the will of an accused person to remain silent'.[121] One logical implication of this rationale is that artefacts and 'real evidence' which exist independently of the will of the accused are not covered by the privilege. Thus, 'documents acquired pursuant to a warrant, breath, blood and urine samples and bodily tissue for the purpose of DNA testing' were all instanced in *Saunders* as illustrations of material routinely collected from the accused during crimi-

---

[118] ibid. [62].   [119] ibid. [O-II50].   [120] *Jalloh v Germany* (2007) 44 EHRR 32.
[121] *Saunders v United Kingdom* (1996) 23 EHRR 313, [69].

nal investigations which do not engage the privilege against self-incrimination, even if taken by force.

It might have been thought that the drugs recovered from Jalloh would similarly qualify as material existing independently of the will of the accused and therefore outside the ambit of the privilege. Yet a majority of the Grand Chamber concluded otherwise. Having regard to 'the nature and degree of compulsion used to obtain the evidence; the weight of the public interest in the investigation and punishment of the offence at issue; the existence of any relevant safeguards in the procedure; and the use to which any material so obtained is put',[122] the Strasbourg judges concluded that Jalloh's privilege against self-incrimination had been violated. The procedures involved were far more invasive than routine investigative measures like fingerprinting and mouth swabbing. Introducing an emetic into a suspect's body involved 'the administration of a substance so as to provoke a pathological reaction',[123] posing tangible health risks. Moreover, it was a wholly disproportionate measure to apply to a low level street dealer when the drugs he had swallowed could have been recovered in due course without resorting to such extreme means. *Jalloh* superficially extends the privilege against self-incrimination – after all, the applicant won the argument – but in reality tends to undermine it. The balancing approach pioneered in *Jalloh*, directly pitting individual rights against various types of public interest, paved the way to the opposite result in *O'Halloran and Francis*. Moreover, extending the privilege to real evidence like swallowed narcotics demonstrates that the European Court of Human Rights has no coherent concept of the privilege against self-incrimination or its underlying rationales. A protean privilege lacking either determine boundaries or clearly identifiable objectives is unlikely to provide much real protection for individual rights. It will be vulnerable to being carried along on the prevailing tides of *ad hoc* balancing in individual cases.

The following general principles were helpfully synthesized from the pre-*Jalloh* jurisprudence of the European Court of Human Rights (EctHR) by the Court of Appeal in *Kearns*:[124]

(1) Article 6 is concerned with the fairness of a judicial trial where there is an 'adjudication'. It is not concerned with extra-judicial enquiries as such..

(2) The rights to silence and not to incriminate oneself are implicit in Article 6. The rationale for the implication of those rights in criminal cases is that (a) an accused should be protected against improper compulsion by the authorities, which would militate against a fair procedure; and (b) the prosecution should prove their case against the accused without using evidence obtained through methods of coercion or oppression in defiance of the will of the accused...

(3) The rights to silence and not to incriminate oneself are not absolute, but can be qualified and restricted. A law which qualifies or restricts those rights is compatible with Article 6 if there is an identifiable social or economic problem that the law is intended to deal with and the qualification or restriction on the rights is proportionate to the problem under consideration.

(4) There is a distinction between the compulsory production of documents or other material which had an existence independent of the will of the suspect or accused person

---

[122] *Jalloh v Germany* (2007) 44 EHRR 32, [117].   [123] ibid. [114].
[124] *R v Kearns* [2002] 1 WLR 2815, [2002] EWCA Crim 748, [53].

and statements that he has had to make under compulsion. In the former case there was no infringement of the right to silence and the right not to incriminate oneself. In the latter case there could be, depending on the circumstances.

(5) A law will not be likely to infringe the right to silence or not to incriminate oneself if it demands the production of information for an administrative purpose or in the course of an extra-judicial enquiry. However if the information so produced is or could be used in subsequent judicial proceedings, whether criminal or civil, then the use of the information in such proceedings could breach those rights and so make that trial unfair.

(6) Whether that is the case will depend on all the circumstances of the case, but in particular (a) whether the information demanded is factual or an admission of guilt, and (b) whether the demand for the information and its subsequent use in proceedings is proportionate to the particular social or economic problem that the relevant law is intended to address.

These are broadly speaking sound principles, but they are also notably open-ended and susceptible to different interpretations in various combinations. As with the domestic reception of Article 6(2)'s presumption of innocence,[125] there is scope for proliferating litigation in relation to each individual statutory provision requiring the accused to provide information to the authorities under threat of a legal penalty for non-compliance.

The question of the application of the privilege against self-incrimination to real evidence was addressed by the Court of Appeal in *R v S*.[126] The accused was charged with conspiracy to assist a third party to evade a control order imposed under the Prevention of Terrorism Act 2005. In connection with these proceedings, he was issued with a notice pursuant to section 53 of the Regulation of Investigatory Powers Act 2000 to supply the police with encryption keys to allow them to access data in their possession which had been seized from the accused's computers. Having considered what was said by the ECtHR in *Saunders* and *Jalloh*, the Court of Appeal observed that the encryption keys, just like ordinary physical keys to a locked filing cabinet, had an existence independent of the accused's will. Moreover, this remained so even if the accused had originally willed the encryption keys into being, and even if they were contained in the accused's memory and nowhere else. The keys themselves could not be incriminating. However, the data to which the keys would facilitate access might be incriminating; and consequently, the accused's *knowledge* of the keys could be incriminating by extension if the data were, in due course, to prove incriminating (as the prosecution clearly expected).

Strictly speaking, then, the privilege against self-incrimination *was* engaged by a section 53 notice. However, this was really beside the point. If the means by which the data were procured were unfair or improper, the data would be excluded under PACE 1984, sections 76 or 78, or failing that at common law. But if the means of securing the data were unobjectionable there would no grounds on which to contest their admissibility. 'Accordingly,' the Court of Appeal concluded, 'the extent to which the privilege against self-incrimination may be engaged is indeed very limited.'[127] This analysis would also cover all real evidence, without getting into the conceptual knots in which the European Court tied itself in *Jalloh*. Between illegitimate means of evidence-gathering, resulting

---

[125] §6.5(c) and §6.6.   [126] *R v S(F)* [2009] 1 WLR 1489, [2008] EWCA Crim 2177.
[127] ibid. [24].

directly in exclusion, and legitimate investigative measures producing untainted evidence, the privilege against self-incrimination simply drops out of the picture.

(b) CURTAILING THE RIGHT TO SILENCE: CRIMINAL JUSTICE AND PUBLIC ORDER ACT 1994, SECTIONS 34–38

Sections 34–38 of the Criminal Justice and Public Order Act 1994 made significant legislative inroads on the common law privilege against self-incrimination by expanding the range of legally permissible inferences from the accused's silence in the police station or at court. The prosecution as well as the judge was authorized to comment on pre-trial silence where the accused fails to mention when questioned under caution, or at the time of being charged, some fact that he later relies on at trial,[128] or when questioned after arrest about incriminating articles in his possession or marks on his clothing[129] or about his presence at the scene of the crime.[130] The police caution was amended accordingly, to inform the suspect that pre-trial silence, when questioned, 'may harm your defence'.[131]

In court, the procedure introduced by section 35 of the Act is as follows. The judge must ask the accused's counsel in open court whether the accused has been fully informed of his right to testify, and that the point in the trial has now been reached when he should exercise that right if he wishes to do so, or run the risk of adverse inferences being drawn against him if he declines.[132] The effect, of course, is to emphasize to the jury that the accused who does not testify has consciously chosen to remain silent and deliberately passed up the opportunity of defending himself in person in the witness-box. It is a public admonition that any adverse evidential consequences that might flow from this reticence are entirely on the accused's own head. Section 35 has not produced the same volume of case-law as the provisions addressing pre-trial silence, especially section 34 which we will discuss in a moment, but several difficult points have arisen. One question concerns the status of the accused who stays out of the witness-box in order to forestall cross-examination on his previous record and extraneous 'bad character'.[133] The House of Lords has confirmed the line taken by the Court of Appeal, which is that section 35 inferences may still be drawn.[134] However, this places the accused in a rather invidious position: the reason that he declines to go into the witness-box may *not* be that he has no defence to offer (or none that would stand up to cross-examination), but the reason for his reticence is the very thing he wishes to conceal from the jury. A second problematic scenario concerns the accused suffering from mental disorder or disability. Section 35(1)(b) of the CJPO Act 1994 specifies that

---

[128] Section 34.   [129] Section 36.   [130] Section 37.

[131] PACE Code C, para.10.5, contains the new caution: 'You do not have to say anything. But it may harm your defence if you do not mention when questioned something which you later rely on in court. Anything you do say may be given in evidence.' This was an essential concomitant of legislative reform, as US experience also demonstrates. The old caution informed suspects of their right not to speak, which implies – as the US Supreme Court recognized in *Doyle* v *Ohio*, 426 US 610 (1976) – an assurance that silence will carry no penalty. The phrase 'but what you say may be given in evidence' plainly implied, as the other side of the coin, that no evidential significance would be attached to anything *not* said.

[132] *R* v *Cowan* [1996] QB 373, [1996] 1 Cr App R 1, CA; JSB Specimen Direction No 38; *Practice Direction (Crown Court: Defendant's Evidence)* [1995] 1 WLR 657.   [133] See Chapter 14.

[134] *R* v *Becouarn* [2006] 1 Cr App R 2, [2005] UKHL 55, affirming *R* v *Cowan* [1996] QB 373 and *R* v *Taylor* [1999] Crim LR 77.

factfinders may not draw adverse inferences from the accused's failure to testify where 'it appears to the court that the physical or mental condition of the accused makes it undesirable for him to give evidence'. Consequently, the trial judge might consider it appropriate not to give the standard section 35 direction where the accused, though by definition deemed fit to stand trial, may be suffering from physical ailments or lack of full mental capacity[135] and should not prevent the defence from adducing medical evidence intended to establish this fact, even if the evidence was served late in the proceedings.[136]

On first acquaintance, the most striking feature of sections 34–38 is their complexity. Judicial Studies Board (JSB) Specimen Direction No 40 addressing the 'Defendant's Failure to Mention Facts when Questioned or Charged – Section 34, CJPOA 1994' is easily one of the most lengthy and complicated sets of judicial instructions in the entire *Crown Court Bench Book*. First of all, certain procedural pre-conditions must be satisfied before the sections are triggered. Section 34 requires that the accused has been questioned under caution or charged, and then subsequently relies in court on a fact[137] that he should reasonably have been expected to mention to the police when questioned or cautioned;[138] for sections 36 and 37 to operate the accused must have been placed under arrest before being questioned about incriminating possessions or marks or his presence at the crime scene; and in all cases there must be sufficient other evidence to constitute a *prima facie* case to answer without placing any reliance on the accused's failure to answer questions or refusal to testify in his own defence.[139] Only if the relevant pre-conditions have all been satisfied can jurors then be instructed by the judge that they may draw 'such inferences from the failure or refusal as appear proper'. An accused who provided his police interviewers with a full prepared statement outlining his defence at trial, for example, has *not* failed to mention facts he later relies on in court and no inference can be drawn under section 34.[140] Where all the pre-conditions are satisfied, only 'proper' inferences are permitted, that is to say, inferences warranted by logical deduction and common sense

---

[135] JSB Specimen Direction 39, n.10, advises trial judges: 'If it is contended that the physical or mental condition of the accused makes it undesirable for him to give evidence, that question has to be decided by the court (see section 35(1)(b) of the 1994 Act). If the court decides in his favour, then the jury must be directed not to draw any adverse inference.' Also see *R* v *Friend (No 2)* [2004] EWCA Crim 2661; cf. *R* v *Friend* [1997] 2 All ER 1011, CA.   [136] *R* v *Anwoir* [2008] 2 Cr App R 36, [2008] EWCA Crim 1354.

[137] 'Since the object of s.34 is to bring the law back into line with common sense . . . "fact" should be given a broad and not a narrow or pedantic meaning. The word covers any alleged fact which is in issue and is put forward as part of the defence case . . . [A] defendant relies on a fact or matter in his defence not only when he gives or adduces evidence of it but also when counsel, acting on his instructions, puts a specific and positive case to prosecution witnesses, as opposed to asking questions intended to probe or test the prosecution case': *R* v *Webber* [2004] 1 Cr App R 40, [2004] UKHL 1, [33]–[34].

[138] These pre-conditions were fully spelt out in *R* v *Argent* [1997] 2 Cr App R 27, 32–3, CA. What should count as a 'fact' not mentioned, and when the accused can properly be said to have relied on such a fact in his defence, have generated significant case law: see Ian Dennis, 'Silence in the Police Station: The Marginalisation of Section 34' [2002] *Crim LR* 25; Stephen Seabrooke, 'More Caution Needed on s.34 of the Criminal Justice and Public Order Act' (1999) 3 *E & P* 209.

[139] Silence can only ever serve as evidence corroborating other evidence, by virtue of subs.38(3) providing that: 'A person shall not have the proceedings against him transferred to the Crown Court for trial, have a case to answer or be convicted of an offence solely on an inference drawn from such a failure or refusal . . .' However, after some initial prevarication, the Court of Appeal went further, insisting that silence cannot be afforded any evidential value at all until a *prima facie* case of guilt has been made out: *R* v *Gill* [2001] 1 Cr App R 160, CA; *R* v *Milford* [2001] Crim LR 330, CA: cf. *R* v *Daniel* [1998] 2 Cr App R 373, CA.

[140] *R* v *Knight* [2004] 1 Cr App R 9, [2003] EWCA Crim 1977. Cf. *R* v *Syrus* [2005] EWCA Crim 1776.

inductive reasoning. The avowed intention of the 1994 Act was to give common sense freer rein in criminal adjudication, not to shore-up flimsy prosecution cases incapable of establishing proof beyond reasonable doubt on their merits. Trial judges must take great care to cover all the essential points without introducing errors when summing-up on the evidential implications of silence, for as Di Birch observes, 'the complexities of section 34 continue to provide pitfalls for the anything-less-than perfect direction'.[141] Lord Justice Dyson has described section 34 as a 'notorious minefield' where any misstep could spell disaster.[142] However, a misdirection on section 34 will not automatically render a conviction unsafe.[143] Everything depends on the facts of the case.

On a very strict construction, sections 34, 36, and 37 – the pre-trial silence provisions – might have been treated as little more than structured codifications of the pre-existing common law. The Court of Appeal soon scotched the idea that nothing had really changed: the objectives of the 1994 Act were well known, and the sections should not be interpreted in a way that would completely undermine their intended impact.[144] In several subsequent decisions, however, the Court of Appeal appeared more guarded, insisting that since these legislative provisions 'restrict rights recognized at common law as appropriate to protect defendants against the risk of injustice, they should not be construed more widely than the statutory language requires'.[145] The House of Lords has also stressed the importance, 'if the statutory provisions are not to be an instrument of unfairness or abuse, that the statutory safeguards are strictly observed, that jury directions are carefully framed and, in cases under section 34, that care is taken to identify the specific facts relied on at trial which were not mentioned during questioning'.[146]

Particularly after the introduction of the Human Rights Act, a pressing question was whether the silence provisions of the 1994 Act were compatible with the ECHR Article 6. The first relevant Strasbourg case concerned the provisions of the Criminal Evidence (Northern Ireland) Order 1988, a broadly equivalent precursor to the 1994 English legislation.[147] In *John Murray* v *UK*[148] the European Court took a balanced approach to inferences from silence. The importance of the right to silence and the privilege against self-incrimination were reaffirmed in principle, the Court pronouncing it 'self-evident that it is incompatible with the immunities under consideration to base a conviction solely or mainly on the accused's silence or on a refusal to answer questions or to give evidence himself'.[149] On the other hand, the right to silence was by no means absolute. In particular, Article 6 did not preclude a fact-finder from drawing common sense inferences from silence, even 'very strong inferences', where incriminating facts clearly called for an explanation. So the ECHR was not *per se* an obstacle to affording evidential value to silence; and this is hardly a

---

[141] Case-commentary on *R* v *Milford* [2001] *Crim LR* 330, 331.

[142] *R* v *B (Kenneth)* [2003] EWCA Crim 3080, [20].

[143] *R* v *Boyle and Ford* [2006] EWCA Crim 2101.

[144] It has been suggested that the tenor of earlier decisions reflected Lord Taylor CJ's personal support for the legislation: see Rosemary Pattenden, 'Silence: Lord Taylor's Legacy' (1998) 2 *E & P* 141. Also see Rosemary Pattenden, 'Inferences from Silence' [1995] *Crim LR* 602 (anticipating the ways in which the Act would go further than the common law in permitting adverse inferences from silence).

[145] *R* v *Bowden* [1999] 2 Cr App R 176, 181, CA, *per* Lord Bingham CJ.

[146] *R* v *Webber* [2004] 1 Cr App R 40, [27].

[147] Generally, see J. D. Jackson, 'Interpreting the Silence Provisions: The Northern Ireland Cases' [1995] *Crim LR* 587.   [148] (1996) 22 EHRR 29.

[149] ibid. [47].

surprising conclusion, since the majority of continental European jurisdictions have always treated silence in the face of an accusation as confirmation of guilt. However, as commentators noted,[150] it weighed heavily in the Strasbourg Court's reasoning that Murray had been tried in a judge-only 'Diplock court' and that the evidential basis of his conviction had been fully set out in a reasoned judgment.[151] It therefore remained an open question whether drawing adverse inferences from an accused's silence in an English jury trial would be compatible with Article 6. The ECtHR subsequently held that it was, but added that important safeguards must be observed in order to comply with the accused's right to a fair trial.

Condron v *UK*[152] involved a direct challenge to section 34 of the 1994 Act. The European Court refused to lay down hard-and-fast rules as to when adverse inferences would be inappropriate, but it did say that when the trier of fact is a jury, rather than an experienced judge as in *Murray*, it is especially important for the judge to direct the jury with care about the uses to which silence can properly be put. On the facts of this case, the applicants' Article 6(1) right to a fair trial had been violated because:

as a matter of fairness, the jury should have been directed that it could only draw an adverse inference if satisfied that the applicants' silence at the police interview could only sensibly be attributed to their having no answer or none that would stand up to cross-examination.[153]

Remaining silent in the face of an allegation or indictment is typically quite equivocal behaviour, potentially supporting a broad spectrum of inferences about a person's beliefs, motivations, and past conduct. In the context of criminal adjudication it might be all too easy to jump to the wrong conclusion, especially when silence is viewed retrospectively by a jury weighing up how and why the accused came to be standing in the dock. There is ample common law authority reflecting on the ambivalence of silence, including a line of cases in which the courts poured cold water on the notion that failure to respond to an accusation always betokens guilt. As Bowen LJ exclaimed:

It would be a monstrous thing if it were the law that the mere fact of a man not answering a letter charging him with some offence, or making some claim against him, would necessarily and in all circumstances be evidence of admission of the truth of the charge or statement contained in the letter. There must be some limit placed upon such a proposition to make it consonant with common sense.... [S]ilence upon the receipt of a letter cannot be taken as evidence of admission of the truth of its contents, unless there are some circumstances in the case which would render it probable that the person receiving the letter, who dissented from the statements, would answer it and deny them...[154]

Juries should always be warned about the dangers of too easily equating silence with guilt whenever there is a real risk that they may be tempted to do so. However, the direction mandated by the European Court in *Condron* v *UK* is not strictly warranted by the logic of

---

[150] Roderick Munday, 'Inferences from Silence and European Human Rights Law' [1996] Crim LR 370.

[151] *John Murray* v *UK* (1996) 22 EHRR 29, [51].   [152] *Condron* v *UK* (2001) 31 EHRR 1.

[153] This quotation is taken directly from the Transcript hosted by the ECtHR's website. Cf. (2001) 31 EHRR 1, [61], where the text appears to have become corrupted.

[154] *Weidemann* v *Walpole* [1891] 2 QB 534, CA (as reported at 60 LJQB 762, extracted in P. B. Carter, *Cases and Statues on Evidence* (Sweet & Maxwell, 2nd edn. 1990), 336–7. The official Law Report is couched in slightly less conversational language). Cf. *Bessela* v *Stern* (1877) 46 LJCP 467, CA (defendant's silence in the face of an accusation, accompanied by his offer of money if the plaintiff would go away, taken to be an admission of breach of promise to marry on the facts).

inference,[155] nor is it dictated by the language of the statute. 'Significant silences', as they have come to be known, might logically support the prosecution's case even where the jury cannot be sure that 'silence at the police interview could only sensibly be attributed to [the accused] having no answer or none that would stand up to cross-examination'. English appellate judges nonetheless anticipated the ECtHR's ruling. From its earliest decisions on the 1994 legislation, the Court of Appeal has insisted that the jury must be directed in these restrictive terms.[156] Thus, the settled JSB Specimen Direction on section 34 admonishes jurors that they may draw an adverse inference from the accused's failure to mention relevant facts in police interview 'only if you think it is a fair and proper conclusion, and you are satisfied about three things':

first, that when he was interviewed he could reasonably have been expected to mention the facts on which he now relies; second, that the only sensible explanation for his failure to do so is that he had no answer at the time or none that would stand up to scrutiny...; third, that apart from his failure to mention those facts, the prosecution's case against him is so strong that it clearly calls for an answer by him.

This is a notably protective interpretation, in deference to the realization that there are often many plausible reasons for silence, some of which would be just as consistent with innocence as with guilt. In consequence, even under the 1994 Act's more permissive regime, the jury remains forbidden from holding the accused's silence against him unless every innocent explanation for his reticence can reasonably be discounted. The criminal standard of proof beyond reasonable doubt effectively attaches to the discrete issue of drawing adverse inferences from silence.

The principal elements of a section 34 direction were summarized by the Court of Appeal in *Petkar and Farquhar*:[157]

(i)   The facts which the accused failed to mention but which are relied on in his defence should be identified...in a common-sense way.

(ii)   The inferences (or conclusions, as they are called in the [JSB] direction) which it is suggested might be drawn from failure to mention such facts should be identified....

(iii) The jury should be told that, if an inference is drawn, they should not convict 'wholly or mainly on the strength of it'...

(iv)   The jury should be told that an inference should be drawn 'only if you think it is a fair and proper conclusion'... This is not stated in the statute, but is perhaps inherent in that part of it...glossed...as requiring a jury 'not arbitrarily to draw adverse inferences'.

(v)   An inference should be drawn 'only if...the only sensible explanation for his failure' is that he had no answer or none that would stand up to scrutiny.... In other words the inference canvassed should only be drawn if there is no other sensible explanation for the failure...

---

[155] Mike Redmayne, 'Analysing Evidence Case Law', in Paul Roberts and Mike Redmayne (eds.), *Innovations in Evidence and Proof* (Hart, 2007), 130.

[156] *R v Cowan* [1996] 1 Cr App R 1, CA (in relation to s.35); *R v Condron* [1997] 1 WLR 827, CA; *R v Betts and Hall* [2001] 2 Cr App R 16, CA (regarding s.34).

[157] *R v Petkar and Farquhar* [2004] 1 Cr App R 22, [2003] EWCA Crim 2668, [51].

(vi) An inference should only be drawn if, apart from the defendant's failure to mention facts later relied on in his defence, the prosecution case is 'so strong that it clearly calls for an answer by him'... This is a striking way to put the need... for a case to answer...

(vii) The jury should be reminded of the evidence on the basis of which the jury are invited not to draw any conclusion from the defendant's silence... This goes with point (iv) above, because it is only after a jury has considered the defendant's explanation for his failure that they can conclude that there is no other sensible explanation for it.

(viii) A special direction should be given where the explanation for silence of which evidence has been given is that the defendant was advised by his solicitor to remain silent...

The full direction will normally have to be given in every case. It has been said that there can be no legal 'no man's land' in which jurors become aware of the accused's silence in interview but are left without judicial guidance to assist them in interpreting its evidential significance. If an adverse inference is not permissible on the facts, e.g. because the statutory pre-conditions are not satisfied, the judge should spell this out to the jury.[158] However, the trial judge's overriding duty is to ensure that the summing-up fairly reflects the respective cases advanced by prosecution and defence and the state of the evidence at the end of the trial. A proposed direction should be discussed with counsel in advance, and the trial judge should, in appropriate cases, accede to defence counsel's preference that no direction on silence be given. Sometimes, a 'low key' approach may be best.[159] Instructing jurors that they may not draw an adverse inferences may be counterproductive, from the defence perspective, if it only serves to underline the fact that the accused has advanced a late defence at trial.

The suspect remaining silent in the police station on legal advice has presented the most enduring difficulties for section 34. Fearing complete emasculation of the pre-trial silence provisions, the Court of Appeal was quick to dispel the notion that an accused might immunize himself from adverse inferences simply by claiming to have remained silent on legal advice.[160] Yet this comes perilously close to imposing a penalty on a suspect for good faith reliance on legal advice whenever the court subsequently deems that advice to have been ill-founded or unreasonable. As Ed Cape fairly pointed out:[161]

If defendants can never be sure that they are acting reasonably in relying on the advice of their lawyer, then they can never be sure that they should accept their lawyer's advice. If they cannot be sure about that, then it raises the fundamental question of the utility of legal advice at the police station.

We saw in the last chapter that access to legal advice, from the first moment of custodial interrogation, is regarded as an essential component of the right to a fair trial guaranteed by ECHR Article 6.[162] More specifically, the European Court has emphasized the importance of access to custodial legal advice if suspects are to make an informed choice whether

---

[158] *R* v *McGarry* [1999] 1 Cr App R 377, CA.   [159] *R* v *Abdalla* [2007] EWCA Crim 2495.

[160] *R* v *Condron* [1997] 1 WLR 827, CA; *R* v *Roble* [1997] Crim LR 449, CA; *R* v *Bowden* [1999] 1 WLR 832, CA.

[161] Ed Cape, 'Sidelining Defence Lawyers: Police Station Advice After *Condron*' (1997) 1 *E & P* 386, 402. Also see Desmond Wright, 'The Solicitor in the Witness Box' [1998] *Crim LR* 44.

[162] *Salduz* v *Turkey* (2009) 49 EHRR 19, discussed in §12.2(c).

to speak or remain silent in the police station. This is recognized to be a crucial decision in the context of a legal regime where silence, as well as positive admissions, can later work to the detriment of an accused.[163] The CJPO Act 1994 was subsequently amended, in direct response to Strasbourg rulings, in order to prevent trial courts from drawing any adverse inference from the accused's silence during police interview unless first given the opportunity to receive legal advice.[164] This does not mean, however, that inferences are limited to cases in which a suspect actually receives custodial legal advice, for as we saw in the last chapter, very many suspects refuse the offer of a solicitor or receive only telephone advice. Scope remains for doubting whether English law's approach to ascribing evidential significance to the accused's silence is fully compatible with the ECHR,[165] or that it will continue to survive post-Human Rights Act domestic criminal litigation entirely unscathed.

Partly under the influence of Strasbourg jurisprudence, the Court of Appeal has been obliged to reconsider the significance of legal advice to remain silent during police interrogation on a number of subsequent occasions. In *Betts and Hall* the question for the jury was said to be whether the accused truly relied on legal advice in remaining silent – essentially a causal test – rather than merely invoking legal advice as a smokescreen to conceal his lack of any innocent explanation.[166] On this view, the accused is not expected to be able to evaluate the quality of the legal advice he received, but advice will insulate him from adverse inferences only if the jury believes that the advice might actually have influenced the accused in choosing to remain silent. This was indubitably an improvement on what was said in *Condron* and *Argent*.[167] In *Howell*[168] and *Beckles*,[169] however, the Court of Appeal propounded a more exacting standard, according to which legally-advised silence in the police station will pre-empt adverse inferences only if it was based on *reasonable* grounds. Laws LJ spelt out the new thinking in *Howell*:

We do not consider, *pace* the reasoning in *Betts & Hall*, that once it is shown that the advice (of whatever quality) has genuinely been relied on as the reason for the suspect's remaining silent, adverse comment is thereby disallowed. The premise of such a position is that in such circumstances it is in principle not reasonable to expect the suspect to mention the facts in question. We do not believe that is so. What is reasonable depends on all the circumstances.... The kind of circumstance which may most likely justify silence will be such matters as the suspect's condition (ill-health, in particular mental disability; confusion; intoxication; shock, and so forth – of course we are not laying down an authoritative

---

[163] *Beckles v UK* (2003) 36 EHRR 13; *Averill v UK* (2001) 31 EHRR 36, [58]; *John Murray v UK* (1996) 22 EHRR 29, [66].

[164] Subsections 34(2A), 36(4A), and 37(3A), as inserted by the Youth Justice and Criminal Evidence Act 1999, s.58 (in force from 1 April 2003), all have the effect of blocking any adverse inference from the accused's silence '[w]here the accused was at an authorised place of detention at the time of the failure... if he had not been allowed an opportunity to consult a solicitor prior to being questioned, charged or informed' of the relevant matter. See Diane Birch and Roger Leng, *Blackstone's Guide to the Youth Justice & Criminal Evidence Act 1999* (Blackstone, 2000), ch 10.

[165] Anthony Jennings, Andrew Ashworth, and Ben Emmerson, 'Silence and Safety: The Impact of Human Rights Law' [2000] *Crim LR* 879.

[166] *R v Betts and Hall* [2001] 2 Cr App R 16, CA; *R v Robinson* [2003] EWCA Crim 2219.

[167] *R v Argent* [1997] 2 Cr App R 27, CA (approving the direction: 'You should consider whether or not he is able to decide for himself what he should do or having asked for a solicitor to advise him he would not challenge that advice').   [168] *R v Howell* [2005] 1 Cr App R 1; [2003] EWCA Crim 1.

[169] *R v Beckles* [2005] 1 Cr App R 23, [2004] EWCA Crim 2766. And see *R v Knight* [2004] 1 Cr App R 9, [17]; *R v Hoare and Pierce* [2005] 1 WLR 1804, [2004] EWCA Crim 784.

list), or his inability genuinely to recollect events without reference to documents which are not to hand, or communication with other persons who may be able to assist his recollection. There must always be soundly based objective reasons for silence, sufficiently cogent and telling to weigh in the balance against the clear public interest in an account being given by the suspect to the police. Solicitors bearing the important responsibility of giving advice to suspects at police stations must always have that in mind.[170]

In *Beckles*, Lord Woolf CJ acknowledged that '[w]here the reason put forward by a defendant for not answering questions is that he is acting on legal advice, the position is singularly delicate', but still concluded, in keeping with *Howell*, that '[i]f the jury consider that the defendant genuinely relied on the advice, that is not necessarily the end of the matter. It may still not have been reasonable for him to rely on the advice, or the advice may not have been the true explanation for his silence.'[171] The suspicion remains that English law expects some suspects to be better lawyers than their lawyers, fuelling commentators' doubts about the section 34's compatibility with ECHR Article 6 where the suspect is silent on legal advice.[172] In this as in many other contexts, reliance on legal advice is no excuse.

13.4 CONCLUSIONS

The privilege against self-incrimination is a creature of the broader procedural – and, indeed, social, political, and cultural – environment in which it operates. The historical development of the privilege in England and Wales (as well as in other common law jurisdictions) is a story of grand rhetorical appeals and deflated expectations. The common law privilege never delivered all it promised, not least because jurors have always been able to draw common sense inferences from failures to respond to accusations whenever pre-trial silence is drawn to their attention, as it often was even at common law; and common sense, as Bentham insisted two centuries ago, anticipates that innocence will loudly proclaim itself whereas 'guilty' is one of the adjectives most closely associated with 'silence'.

The common law privilege was further curtailed by the Criminal Justice and Public Order Act 1994, largely on the basis of political conviction rather than any empirically demonstrated need for reform. The silence provisions of the 1994 Act are problematic in various ways, and few commentators have had many kinds words to say about them. Di Birch[173] and John Jackson[174] have both argued that outright repeal remains the best

---

[170] *R v Howell* [2005] 1 Cr App R 1, [23].   [171] *R v Beckles* [2005] 1 Cr App R 23, [43], [46].

[172] Simon Cooper, 'Legal Advice and Pre-trial Silence – Unreasonable Developments' (2006) 10 *E & P* 60; Andrew L.-T. Choo and Anthony F. Jennings, 'Silence on Legal Advice Revisited: *R v Howell*' (2003) 7 *E & P* 185; Roger Leng, 'Silence Pre-trial, Reasonable Expectations, and the Normative Distortion of Fact-finding' (2001) 5 *E & P* 240; Anthony Jennings, Andrew Ashworth, and Ben Emmerson, 'Silence and Safety: The Impact of Human Rights Law' [2000] *Crim LR* 879.

[173] Di Birch, 'Suffering in Silence: A Cost-Benefit Analysis of Section 34 of the Criminal Justice and Public Order Act 1994' [1999] *Crim LR* 769.

[174] John D. Jackson, 'Silence and Proof: Extending the Boundaries of Criminal Proceedings in the United Kingdom' (2001) 5 *E & P* 145 (silence provisions should be abolished unless pre-trial procedure undergoes more extensive reform); J. D. Jackson, 'Interpreting the Silence Provisions: The Northern Ireland Cases' [1995] *Crim LR* 587.

option for remedying this legislation's defects. Ian Dennis demurred only to the extent
that, in his view, judicial interpretation of the silence provisions had already effectively
relegated them to the margins of fact-finding.[175] He subsequently concluded that section 34 'ought to be repealed as a matter of principle'.[176] Mike Redmayne cautions comparative lawyers against importing section 34 as a model for local reform.[177] Aside from
the sheer complexity of the legislation, the most serious unresolved issue of principle is
undoubtedly the potential for adverse inferences from silence to undermine the value
of suspects' access to custodial legal advice. Conversely, the courts have considerably
narrowed down the scope for adverse inferences from silence by fortifying the specified
statutory pre-conditions with the additional requirement that the jury must first satisfy
itself that the accused's silence cannot be interpreted in any other, non-incriminating,
way. The effect of this judicially-created restriction comes close to reinstating the pre-Act
common law on the scope of judicial comment in many cases.

Empirical investigation in England and Northern Ireland suggests that the 1994 Act *did*
exert some influence on the interview situation: suspects are now somewhat less likely to
remain silent in the police station, and somewhat more likely to testify at trial, than they
were under the old common law regimes.[178] But it must be remembered that the incidence
of silence prior to Parliament's intervention was already low, so that – even on the most
optimistic predictions – there was only limited scope for the 1994 Act to influence the conduct of criminal investigations or the outcome of trials in the round. A percentage of those
who now speak where they would formerly have kept silent, furthermore, are apparently
telling the police and the courts 'a pack of lies',[179] which some would regard as a greater
threat to justice than pre-trial silence.[180] Certainly, there has been no demonstrable effect
on either the charging or the conviction rate, and this is hardly surprising, given the statistical unlikelihood of a suspect's remaining silent and pleading not guilty.

Reflecting more general trends in the law of criminal evidence and procedure, the privilege against self-incrimination (incorporating the pre-trial right to silence) has been reconceptualized as a component of the right to a fair trial under the ECHR and the Human
Rights Act. It is interesting to note, however, that the modern human rights revolution has
not had the same impact on the privilege against self-incrimination as it has exerted on
other aspects of criminal procedure law and practice discussed in this book. If anything,
juridical influence has run in the opposite direction: restrictive decisions on the scope of
the privilege in UK law, notably *Brown* v *Stott*,[181] have contributed towards a retrench-
ment in Strasbourg, stressing that Article 6's privilege against self-incrimination is not
absolute and can be overridden by other considerations, including public safety. The most
recent decisions of the ECtHR appear to expose the privilege against self-incrimination

---

[175] Ian Dennis, 'Silence in the Police Station: the Marginalisation of Section 34' [2002] *Crim LR* 25.

[176] Ian Dennis, *The Law of Evidence* (Sweet & Maxwell, 3rd edn. 2007), 206.

[177] Mike Redmayne, 'English Warnings' (2008) 30 *Cardozo Law Review* 1047.

[178] John D. Jackson, 'Silence and Proof: Extending the Boundaries of Criminal Proceedings in the United
Kingdom' (2001) 5 *E & P* 145; Tom Bucke, Robert Street, and David Brown, *The Right of Silence: The Impact
of the Criminal Justice and Public Order Act 1994*, Home Office Research Study No 199 (Home Office RDS,
2000).   [179] Buck *et al*, *The Right of Silence*, 35.

[180] Daniel J. Seidmann and Alex Stein, 'The Right to Silence Helps the Innocent: A Game-Theoretic
Analysis of the Fifth Amendment Privilege' (2000) 114 *Harvard Law Review* 431.

[181] *Brown (Margaret)* v *Stott* [2003] 1 AC 681, PC (Scotland).

to the hazards of no-holds-barred policy balancing.[182] Meanwhile, continental/civilian jurisprudence has never found any difficulty in condoning common sense inferences from silence.

The central argument of this chapter has been that the gap between rhetoric and reality haunting English law's privilege against self-incrimination is attributable in no small part to fundamental inadequacies in the justificatory rationales supposedly underpinning the privilege. Three distinctive (but not necessarily mutually exclusive) theoretical strategies for rationalizing the privilege, by appealing to intrinsic, conceptual, or instrumental considerations, were examined in §13.2. Variants of these strategies have their past and current defenders, but none of them, individually or in combination, strikes us as especially compelling. The interests of suspects in the police station, and of the accused at trial, are more fairly and effectively protected by tailor-made procedural safeguards, such as those set out in minute detail by PACE 1984 and its associated Codes of Practice. Whilst there is never any warrant for complacency in a matter so vital for individual liberty and the proper administration of criminal justice, the position of the suspect in the police station has undeniably improved under PACE compared with the all-too-often illusory protection offered by a notional 'right to silence' at common law.

To give practical effect to the privilege against self-incrimination in the police station would require the creation of a procedural environment in which suspects are genuinely free to choose, without experiencing any police pressure, whether or not to submit to an interrogation. If the only ground for arresting a suspect was the desire to interrogate him, the suspect should be informed that he cannot be detained and interrogated without his consent and asked whether he agrees to custodial interrogation. Likewise, where a suspect has been arrested on other grounds, the police should not be allowed to have any discussion with him regarding the matters under investigation before the suspect has been informed, in the presence of his solicitor or support person, that he may not be interrogated without his consent. Provided that mechanisms were in place to ensure that consent to interrogation was genuine, this type of procedural arrangement would undoubtedly guarantee suspects' freedom from compelled self-incrimination; but it would also put an end to much fruitful police questioning and effective criminal investigation, defy historical experience, and lack all credibility with democratic politicians and electorates.

English law continues to grapple with the tension between the suspect's – now somewhat deflated – legal privilege against self-incrimination and society's need to interrogate persons against whom there is a well-founded suspicion of criminality. The possibility of prosecutorial or judicial comment should not become an instrument in the hands of the police to force people to speak whenever a policeman has an unverified hunch that somebody might possibly have done something illegal. A suspect who is told nothing about the case against him, except that the police suspect him of having committed an offence, should be entitled, even encouraged, to refuse to account for himself. Inferences from silence are legitimate only where the police had a sufficiently strong case against the suspect to necessitate a response and had informed the suspect of the evidential basis for their suspicions. Genuine opportunity to receive custodial legal advice has been erected into a formal pre-condition of drawing adverse inferences from pre-trial silence, partly at the behest of Strasbourg. It might also be desirable to legislate that the suspect's pre-trial

---

[182] *O'Halloran and Francis v UK* (2008) 46 EHRR 21; *Jalloh v Germany* (2007) 44 EHRR 32.

silence may be revealed to the jury only if he was properly informed of the case and the evidence against him and has had a reasonable opportunity to make well-informed choices. Suspects should not be harried or chivvied into making precipitate decisions that are likely to seal their fate, forensically speaking. If the accused is expected to put his cards on the table in the police station, deliberate police deception to mislead a suspect or his solicitor about the state of the evidence should not be tolerated.

So far as the accused's decision not to testify at trial is concerned, all that would ever really be necessary is for the judge to inform the jury, at the end of the trial,[183] that the accused had the opportunity of testifying under oath and rebutting the charges levelled against him, but that he declined to do so. It is unlikely that this information would surprise the majority of jurors; and it barely modifies the common law position prior to the implementation of the silence provisions of the Criminal Justice and Public Order Act 1994. To forestall the possibility of hasty or over-confident inferences from silence, the trial judge should make the jury understand that an accused person is entitled to remain silent at trial, that refusal to testify is not tantamount to an admission of guilt, and that the accused's failure does not discharge jurors from their primary duty to weigh carefully all the evidence presented by both prosecution and defence before arriving at their verdict. This is essentially what *Cowan* now demands of conscientious trial judges and juries.

---

[183] Section 35 of the 1994 Act is slightly more dramatic, in requiring this information to be imparted during the trial itself, but not nearly so theatrical as other proposals that have been suggested, involving the accused being 'called upon' to testify and having to state his refusal in open court: see Martin Wasik and Richard Taylor, *Blackstone's Guide to the Criminal Justice & Public Order Act 1994* (Blackstone, 1995), para.3.17.

14

THE ACCUSED'S CHARACTER
AND EXTRANEOUS
MISCONDUCT

14.1 INTRODUCTION – A REFORMED
CHARACTER?

Chapter 9 described how the law of hearsay in English criminal proceedings was transformed by the Criminal Justice Act 2003. If anything, the impact of the 2003 Act on the law of character evidence was even more far-reaching. The character evidence provisions of the CJA 2003 are located in sections 98–113, which were brought into force on 15 December 2004[1] and apply to all subsequent criminal trials[2] (including trials relating to charges or indictments preceding the commencement date[3]). Several of the methodological curiosities previously noted in relation to hearsay evidence also characterize Parliament's approach to reforming the law of bad character. On first acquaintance, one seems to encounter systematic, sweeping reform. The Court of Appeal has said that 'the Criminal Justice Act 2003 introduces a wholly new scheme for the admission of evidence of bad character. The previously existing common law and statutory rules are abolished. The correct approach is not to start with what the old law would have been, but to address the law as it is set out in the new Act.'[4] First appearances, however, can be deceptive. As we saw in relation to hearsay, on closer inspection it turns out that significant aspects of the common law have survived the statutory cull, and what is more, common law authorities remain a rich source of illustrations, practical experience, and critical commentary.

The old law of character evidence was highly technical and complex, sometimes almost absurdly. It had three principal sources: (i) common law rules relating to the character of all witnesses; (ii) the common law 'similar facts' rule, regulating the admissibility in-chief of evidence of the accused's extraneous misconduct; and (iii) statutory rules governing cross-examination of the accused (if he elected to testify) contained in the Criminal Evidence Act 1898. Each of these primary sources, but especially the second and third, accumulated a massive case-law over the course of more than a century. By creating a more unified structure to regulate the admissibility of character evidence and

---

[1] Section 113 and sch.6, relating to the armed forces, came into force on 1 January 2005.

[2] Section 141.

[3] *R v Bradley* [2005] EWCA Crim 20; (2005) 169 JP 73, [34]; *R v Sukadave Singh* [2006] 1 WLR 1564, [2006] EWCA Crim 660, [10].   [4] *R v Lawson* [2007] 1 WLR 1191, [2006] EWCA Crim 2572, [23].

simultaneously jettisoning old precedents, the CJA 2003 signals a new beginning. We have already considered the admissibility and uses of character evidence relating to witnesses (including complainants) other than the accused,[5] for which the starting point is now section 100 of the CJA 2003. This chapter focuses on the character of the accused, in particular on his *bad* character or 'extraneous misconduct' (both terms requiring elucidation in due course).

Traditionally, the common law has set its face against receiving evidence of the accused's general bad character, previous convictions, disposition, or reputation. Lord Sankey LC once described this precept as 'one of the most deeply rooted and jealously guarded principles of our criminal law' which is 'fundamental in the law of evidence as conceived in this country'.[6] Strict observance of this rule was earlier proclaimed 'sacred in our Courts'.[7] In the next section we will carefully examine the underlying rationales that could have inspired such judicial reverence. Here, we need only stress that a formal rule of inadmissibility must not be equated with blanket exclusion in practice. In fact, the accused's bad character has routinely been revealed to the fact-finder in contemporary criminal trials, often in accordance with the rules, but sometimes in defiance of them.

The *Crown Court Study* conducted by Zander and Henderson for the Runciman Royal Commission on Criminal Justice in the early 1990s found that previous convictions became known to the jury in some 20% of cases in which the accused had a criminal record (such cases comprising 77% of the total sample of over 650 cases).[8] More often than not, revelation of the accused's record was made voluntarily *by the defence*, typically in order to show that, having 'paid his debt to society' for previous offending, the accused had subsequently 'gone straight' and renounced all criminal activity. Zander and Henderson also surveyed jurors' opinions on whether juries *ought* to be informed of the accused's criminal record before reaching a verdict. Forty-two per cent did indeed want juries to know about an accused's previous offences. Contrary to what might have been expected in the increasingly intolerant penal climate of the 1990s, however, a majority of 58% of jurors supported a general policy of inadmissibility.[9]

A second, more significant, reason why juries often found out about the accused's previous convictions and other general bad character was that the rules themselves did not create absolute prohibitions on admissibility. To the contrary, much of the old law on character evidence was devoted to specifying exceptional circumstances in which the general prohibitions could be defeated. Nowhere better is this exemplified than by Lord Herschell's LC's classic (and beguiling) statement of what successive generations of lawyers came to know as the 'similar facts' rule in the infamous case of *Makin*.[10]

Enduring fascination with *Makin* doubtless stems in part from its memorable, appallingly grisly facts. Mr and Mrs Makin were convicted of the murder of a tiny infant, Horace Amber Murray, who was just a few weeks old when they had agreed to adopt him for the sum of £3. The baby's body was later discovered buried in the garden of the Makins' former residence, along with the remains of three other children. Further investigations produced seven more children's corpses from the garden of the Makins' current abode, and a further

---

[5] §8.4.   [6] *Maxwell v DPP* [1935] AC 309, 317, 320, HL.

[7] *R v Bond* [1906] 2 KB 389, 398, CCR.

[8] Michael Zander and Paul Henderson, *Crown Court Study*, RCCJ Research Study No 19 (HMSO, 1993), para.4.6.6.   [9] ibid. para.8.2.7.

[10] *Makin v AG for New South Wales* [1894] AC 57, PC.

two sets of bones from a house previously rented by the Makins, making thirteen bodies in all. The prosecution contended that the Makins were 'baby farmers', accepting infants into their care to be systematically murdered so that the Makins could pocket the money provided by desperate parents for the up-keep of children they were not able to look after themselves. At their trial, however, the Makins were formally charged only with one murder, that of the infant Horace. They replied that they had only ever received one child to nurse at 10 shillings a week, who was subsequently returned safely to its parents. They denied all knowledge of Horace Amber Murray and of the other twelve deceased infants whose remains had been found on their current and former properties.

On appeal, the Makins objected to admission at their trial of the evidence of five women who, like Horace's mother, had testified that they had surrendered their children into the Makins' care, for a fee, and that their babies were never seen or heard of again. Rejecting the Makins' appeals, Lord Herschell LC gave the following classic rendition of the common law 'similar facts' rule:

It is undoubtedly not competent for the prosecution to adduce evidence tending to shew that the accused has been guilty of criminal acts other than those covered by the indictment, for the purpose of leading to the conclusion that the accused is a person likely from his criminal conduct or character to have committed the offence for which he is being tried. On the other hand, the mere fact that the evidence adduced tends to shew the commission of other crimes does not render it inadmissible if it be relevant to an issue before the jury, and it may be so relevant if it bears upon the question whether the acts alleged to constitute the crime charged in the indictment were designed or accidental, or to rebut a defence which would otherwise be open to the accused.[11]

It will be observed that the first half of this canonical passage resoundingly endorses the common law prohibition on extraneous bad character ('It is undoubtedly not competent...'), whilst the second half of the passage ('On the other hand...') proceeds to identify situations in which such evidence *can* be adduced, notwithstanding. Later, the essence of the common law prohibition was thought to be encapsulated in catchphrases such as 'striking similarity'[12] (hence, 'similar fact evidence'), until, in its mature form, the rule was reduced to a simple, all-purpose, balancing formula, as explained by Lord Mackay LC in the common law's ultimately leading case, *DPP* v *P*:

[T]he essential feature of evidence which is to be admitted is that its probative force in support of the allegation that an accused person committed a crime is sufficiently great to make it just to admit the evidence, notwithstanding that it is prejudicial to the accused in tending to show that he was guilty of another crime.... Whether the evidence has sufficient probative value to outweigh its prejudicial effect must in each case be a question of degree.[13]

The test, in short, was that evidence of the accused's extraneous misconduct could only be admitted if its probative value outweighed its likely prejudicial effect: in our symbolic shorthand, PV > PE. Although the 'similar facts' exclusionary rule had always busied itself as much

---

[11] ibid. 65.

[12] '[P]robative force is derived, if at all, from the circumstance that the facts testified to by the several witnesses bear to each other such a striking similarity that they must, when judged by experience and common sense, either all be true, or have arisen from a cause common to the witnesses or from pure coincidence': *DPP* v *Boardman* [1975] AC 421, 444, HL, *per* Lord Wilberforce.   [13] *DPP* v *P* [1991] 2 AC 447, 460–1, HL.

with identifying *admissible* evidence as material to be excluded,[14] there was a general sense, after a century of jurisprudential development from *Makin* to *DPP* v *P*, that the rule was no longer as robust in practice as it once had been when judges waxed lyrical on its virtues.

The rules contained in the Criminal Evidence Act 1898 regulating cross-examination of the accused on his bad character were, in many respects, even less reliable servants of the common law prohibition. Some of their problematic features have been carried over into the scheme of admissibility created by the CJA 2003 and will be examined in detail later in the chapter. It is enough to know, by way of introduction, that the 1898 Act purported to protect the accused with a 'shield' (as it became known) against cross-examination on his extraneous misconduct, but the shield could be forfeited in many circumstances, often through no fault of the accused. This could produce irregular and unplanned disclosures of the accused's criminal record and general bad character with little regard to proportionality, almost as if the law had been designed to create maximum prejudice to the accused. The effect was compounded by some of the most strained statutory interpretation to be found in the annals of English law,[15] mandating judicial directions to the jury which – as the Court of Appeal itself intermittently confessed – invited jurors to undertake 'difficult feats of intellectual acrobatics'.[16] Even if jurors were not left bemused by the entire performance (as many surely were), it is difficult to see how they were supposed to understand the common law's tangled policy towards evidence of the accused's bad character; and jurors could not be expected to appreciate or to apply sympathetically what they could not hope to understand.

The law of character was evidently ripe for reform. However, it was not until the early 1990s that systematic rethinking was seriously contemplated in policy circles.[17] Briefly noting the unsatisfactory state of the law, the Runciman Royal Commission on Criminal Justice referred the topic of bad character evidence to the Law Commission,[18] which produced a detailed consultation paper[19] and final report recommending major new legislation.[20] Further impetus was supplied by Lord Justice Auld's wide-ranging review of the criminal courts.[21] Although the existing law of character was blighted by many serious

---

[14] 'Similar facts', after all, describes the *inclusionary exception* to the common law's general exclusionary prohibition on character evidence.

[15] Perhaps the most notorious instance is *Jones* v *DPP* [1962] AC 635, HL, which was extensively discussed in the first edition of this work: *Criminal Evidence* (OUP, 2004), 546–51. Also see Colin Tapper, 'The Meaning of s.1(f)(i) of the Criminal Evidence Act 1898', in C. F. H. Tapper (ed.), *Crime, Proof and Punishment* (Butterworths, 1981).

[16] *R* v *Watts* (1983) 77 Cr App R 126, 129. As the Law Commission justly observed, 'giving juries directions which they will find bizarre or incomprehensible, or which require them to engage in mental gymnastics, does no credit to the law': Law Com No 273, *Evidence of Bad Character in Criminal Proceedings*. Cm. 5257 (TSO, 2001), para.14.35.

[17] Earlier proposals were put forward in the Criminal Law Revision Committee's *Eleventh Report – Evidence: General*. Cm. 4991 (HMSO, 1972); summarized by Colin Tapper, 'Criminal Law Revision Committee 11th Report: Character Evidence' (1973) 36 *MLR* 56 and 167.

[18] Royal Commission on Criminal Justice (Chairman: Viscount Runciman of Doxford), *Report*, Cm. 2263 (HMSO, 1993), ch 8, para.30.

[19] LCCP No 144, *Previous Misconduct of a Defendant* (HMSO, 1996).

[20] Law Com No 273, *Evidence of Bad Character in Criminal Proceedings*. Cm. 5257 (TSO, 2001). For commentary see Peter Mirfield, 'Bad Character and the Law Commission' (2002) 6 *E & P* 141; Jenny McEwan, 'Previous Misconduct at the Crossroads: Which "Way Ahead"?' [2002] *Crim LR* 180.

[21] Lord Justice Auld, *Review of the Criminal Courts of England and Wales* (2001), 563–8. Sir Robin candidly recorded his 'long held resistance, both at the Bar and as a judge, to putting the defendant's previous

technical defects for which remedies needed to found, the principal motivation driving reform was the perception, apparently widespread amongst policymakers, that the law was conspiring to deprive juries of relevant information about the accused's bad character and that recidivist offenders were consequently evading justice. The official rationale for reforming the law of bad character was set out in the government's white paper, *Justice for All*:

The current rules of evidence...are difficult to understand and complex to apply in practice. There has been growing public concern that evidence relevant to the search for truth is being wrongly excluded.... We favour an approach that entrusts relevant information to those determining the case as far as possible. It should be for the judge to decide whether previous convictions are sufficiently relevant to the case, bearing in mind the prejudicial effect, to be heard by the jury and for the jury to decide what weight should be given to that information in all the circumstances of the case.... Under this approach, where a defendant's previous convictions, or other misconduct, are relevant to an issue in the case, then unless the court considers that the information will have a disproportionate effect, they should be allowed to know about it. It will be for the judge to decide whether the probative value of introducing this information is outweighed by its prejudicial effect. These safeguards will be set out in legislation. This will reform the current haphazard collection of exclusionary rules.[22]

The white paper clearly flagged a fundamental shift in legal thinking, which was subsequently carried over into the CJA 2003's legislative scheme, from an approach assuming that evidence of the accused's bad character is *prima facie* inadmissible, to an initial presumption of admissibility subject to exclusion on grounds of disproportionate prejudice. This was said to be warranted by 'growing public concern' about the loss of 'evidence relevant to the search for truth' which was being 'wrongly excluded' from criminal trials. The white paper did not present any reasoned critique of traditional common law theories advocating the exclusion of bad character evidence, or consider recent jurisprudential developments, including the House of Lords' important decision in *DPP* v *P*, promoting more relaxed standards of admissibility. It did not explain how the concerned public had arrived at its conclusion that relevant evidence was being 'wrongly' excluded from criminal trials.

On the face of it, CJA 2003, ss. 98–113 ('Evidence of Bad Character') implement the white paper's radical agenda. Section 99(1), entitled 'Abolition of common law rules', boldly announces that:

The common law rules governing the admissibility of evidence of bad character in criminal proceedings are abolished.

We have already noted that the CJA 2003 does not, despite initial impressions, achieve systematic statutory codification of the law of character evidence. Common law precedents

---

convictions before a jury', but was persuaded, largely for the pragmatic reason that the current rules in reality often fail to conceal the accused's record from the jury, that 'there is much to be said for a more radical view...placing more trust in the fact finders and for introducing some reality into this complex corner of the law': ibid. 564, 567.

[22] CJS, *Justice for All*, Cm. 5563 (TSO, 2002), paras.4.52, 4.56, and 4.57. Also see Home Office, *Criminal Justice: The Way Ahead*. Cm. 5074 (2001), paras.3.50–3.52; Labour Party, *Ambitions for Britain: Labour's Manifesto 2001*, 33.

survive *qua* precedents in relation to aspects of character *other than* 'rules governing the admissibility of evidence of bad character'. In relation to those rules expressly abolished by section 99 of the CJA 2003, cases decided at common law have been stripped of their status as formal precedents, but (as we also observed in relation to hearsay) they might still be consulted as helpful illustrations of recurring factual scenarios, exemplars of forensic logic and inferential reasoning, and guides to the calculus of probative value and prejudicial effect.

There is a second, more profound, reason why the CJA 2003 did not simply kill off the common law of bad character evidence. English law's suspicion of bad character and extraneous misconduct evidence has been cultivated over many centuries. It is deeply embedded in English judicial culture and institutions, and has frequently been actively propounded and celebrated. It is more like a cherished heirloom than old junk in the attic. In a moment we will test the heirloom's mettle, and try to ascertain whether it is genuine twenty-four carat or only fools' gold. But as a sociological observation about legal culture, it is safe to assume that deep-seated attitudes are not going to be changed simply by reversing the polarity of judicial supervision, replacing presumptive exclusion at common law with a statutory rule of presumptive admissibility. Extraneous evidence of bad character will continue to be regarded as a decrepit species of proof after the CJA 2003 more or less as it was before. Thus, in one of the first – and still leading – decisions on the 2003 Act, we find the Court of Appeal issuing this admonition to prosecuting counsel and trial judges:

The starting point should be for judges and practitioners to bear in mind that Parliament's purpose in the legislation, as we divine it from the terms of the Act, was to assist in the evidence based conviction of the guilty, without putting those who are not guilty at risk of conviction by prejudice. It is accordingly to be hoped that prosecution applications to adduce such evidence will not be made routinely, simply because a defendant has previous convictions, but will be based on the particular circumstances of each case.[23]

The CJA 2003 demands that we reorganize and reappraise our common law heritage, but its complete abandonment cannot seriously be contemplated.

14.2 CHARACTER, PROOF, AND PREJUDICE

What is supposed to be objectionable about bad character evidence? Here, as elsewhere in evidentiary theory and doctrine, common law tradition reaches for the well-worn concepts of 'probative value' and 'prejudice'.

The probative value, or weight, of character evidence is a function of common sense inferences, which in turn depend on the precise meaning or meanings ascribed to 'character' and the purposes for which the evidence is adduced. English law does not supply unequivocal or determinate answers to these questions, as we will see in the first section of this chapter. The centrality of assessments of probative value in determining the admissibility of bad character evidence makes the judicial task highly contextual and fact-sensitive. As Lord Hoffmann, writing extra-judicially, once put it, '[t]he same similar fact evidence may be admissible in one context and inadmissible in another; the slightest movement of the

---

[23] *R v Hanson, Gilmore and Pickstone* [2005] 1 WLR 316, [2005] EWCA Crim 824, [4], (Rose VP).

kaleidoscope of facts creates a new pattern which must be examined afresh'.[24] That same contextual quality that makes this, for students and teachers of criminal evidence, a highly educational topic for exploring ideas and illustrations of relevance, inference, and fact-finding, in the real world of criminal litigation frequently creates practical difficulties. As Lord Herschell LC warned long ago in *Makin* (a judicial admonition repeated countless times ever since) '[t]he statement of these general principles is easy, but it is obvious that it may often be very difficult to draw the line and to decide whether a particular piece of evidence is on the one side or the other'.[25]

Common lawyers are similarly eclectic in their references to 'prejudice'. Etymologically, prejudice is contrary to the interests of justice. In the context of bad character evidence, this is often translated as contrary to the interests of the accused, although it can also imply a detriment to accurate fact-finding. As we will see later in this section, 'prejudice' has acquired some technical meanings in English law and legal commentary on character evidence and its reform. A noteworthy general feature of this usage is that 'prejudice' is capable of straddling the divide between instrumental and intrinsic rationales for rules of evidence. Sometimes it is said that bad character evidence is prejudicial because it encourages mistaken inferences and faulty fact-finding. On other occasions the prejudice of bad character is located in some intrinsic feature which is found to conflict with basic precepts of fair trial and legitimate adjudication. These distinctive rationalizations are not necessarily mutually exclusive. There could be cumulative grounds for rejecting evidence of the accused's extraneous misconduct.

No less than at common law, the CJA 2003 contemplates judicial balancing of probative value and prejudicial effect, and in key respects predicates admissibility on satisfaction of the PV > PE standard. Contrary to a freely circulating misconception, this exercise does not propose an incoherent calculus of 'incommensurables'. Probative value and prejudicial effect are to be assessed in terms of their relative contribution to the objectives and values of criminal proceedings, and in particular, in this context, to accurate fact-finding and protection of the innocent. In the same way that 'apples and oranges' can be compared and contrasted by reference to fruit-relative criteria, such as sweetness or vitamin C content, probative value and prejudicial effect can be set against each other by reference to the formative ideals of criminal adjudication.[26]

Things have to stand in an intelligible relationship to one another in order to make meaningful comparisons between them. This threshold criterion is satisfied by English criminal procedure law's adaptable PV > PE test, which involves neither linguistic nor moral incommensurability. Accurate fact-finding and protecting the accused from prejudice are both equally indispensable components of a single, integrated objective – to dispense justice in criminal trials. This is not to say that practical applications of the PV > PE

---

[24] L. H. Hoffmann, 'Similar Facts After *Boardman*' (1975) 91 *LQR* 193, 204.

[25] *Makin v AG for New South Wales* [1894] AC 57, 65, PC.

[26] A genuine example of linguistic incommensurability might involve an attempt to compare 'apples and Thursdays'. For most purposes, like asking 'How many apples make Thursday?' or 'Which is the better of the two to eat?' such an enterprise would not just be difficult, but nonsensical. Somebody who thought that such questions made sense would not be a competent user of the words 'apple' or 'Thursday'. More realistic instances of moral incommensurability might involve attempted comparisons between whole lives or entire cultures. Is it 'best' (in what sense *best*?) to be a fireman, a nurse, or a lawyer? Is it 'better' (in what sense *better*?) to be a twenty-first century law professor, a nineteenth century denizen of the Amazon rainforest, or a Roman centurion?

test are always straightforward or uncontroversial. Fine-grained analyses of the facts of individual cases coupled with contextual, and necessarily somewhat speculative, evaluations of potential prejudice might conceivably lead reasonable minds to divergent conclusions. The weight of responsibility for policing the admissibility of bad character evidence consequently devolves to trial judges. Appellate tribunals are unlikely to be inclined to second-guess first instance determinations of admissibility which appear to have been arrived at conscientiously on the basis of relevant considerations.

(a) THE PROBATIVE VALUE OF CHARACTER EVIDENCE

To expound the logic of the law pertaining to character evidence one must begin by re-examining the basic relationship between character and proof. How is character evidence supposed to be *relevant* to proving any fact in issue? What is its probative value? The answers to these questions must depend in part on what one means by evidence of 'character'. English common law simultaneously worked with three different meanings of 'character', a lack of conceptual consistency immediately courting further confusion and misunderstanding. The CJA 2003 defines 'bad character' as 'misconduct',[27] which at the level of fundamental theorization barely takes us any further.

The first common law meaning of 'character', traceable to *Rowton*,[28] is the oldest and weakest. It equates character with *reputation*, which is patently problematic. One's reputation *might* be a sound guide to one's past or future behaviour, but then again, reputation might equally well be a figment of malicious gossip, rumour, or ill-informed tittle-tattle. Today, reputation seems ludicrously weak material on which to base a criminal conviction. Its evidentiary significance is best explained in historical terms. At the time when *Rowton* was decided the accused was generally disqualified from testifying in his own defence and the modern sciences of personality were yet to be born. Moreover, people lived in relatively small, static communities where everybody more or less knew everybody else's business. Perhaps in these circumstances, and in the absence of anything better, reputation could be taken as a reliable guide to character and conduct. In the modern period, and particularly after the accused was made generally competent in his own defence by the Criminal Evidence Act 1898, alternative sources of information revealing the accused's character have become available. The reliability of reputation as a proxy for information about a person's behaviour has simultaneously declined as a function of the growing anonymity of modern urban existence. Yet *Rowton* has never formally been overruled, and was specifically retained as a common law hearsay exception by the CJA 2003.[29] Strange to say, to this day 'character' still means 'reputation' at common law, though the formal *Rowton* doctrine is rarely invoked in contemporary criminal trials.

---

[27] CJA 2003, s.98, defines 'bad character' evidence as 'evidence of, or of a disposition towards, misconduct'. Section 112(1) adds that '"misconduct" means the commission of an offence or other reprehensible behaviour'.

[28] *R v Rowton* (1865) Le & Ca 520, 34 LJMC 57, 10 Cox CC 25, CCR. But cf. *R v Del-Valle* [2004] EWCA Crim 1013, [11] ('In many respects the law has moved well beyond *Rowton* and evidence of particular opinions and acts are routinely admitted, as is evidence of good character based on the absence of convictions. Indeed it is rare for evidence of general character founded on general reputation to be adduced in a modern criminal trial'); *R v Colwill* [2002] EWCA Crim 1320, [12] (doubting 'whether a modern jury would be assisted by evidence of opinion by a witness the basis of which is not in any way particularised').

[29] Section 118(1), Exception [2]; see §9.6.

A second legal meaning of 'character', closer to common modern usage, refers to relatively stable behavioural traits, dispositions, or propensities. Thus, for example, a person may be described as being of generous, courageous, spiteful, timid, miserly, out-going, or introverted character or disposition. A propensity to be generous, courageous, spiteful, etc., on any given occasion is partly constitutive of one's character, since people are, in significant respects, what they do, have done, or would do given the opportunity. Legal jargon refers compendiously to a person of 'good character' or 'bad character'. More generally, one may speak of a person acting 'in' or 'out of' character according to whether that person's behaviour on a particular occasion matches his or her usual – or, as we say 'characteristic' – personality traits. When character is understood in this second sense its relationship with probative evidence is clear. All things being equal, it is more likely that a person acted 'in' character than out of character; in accordance with, rather than contrary to, their settled dispositions and propensities. People are not pre-programmed machines with absolutely predictable patterns of conduct, but in general people behave how, knowing them – that is to say, knowing their *character* – we would expect them to behave. This is often more than enough to satisfy the low threshold of evidentiary relevance. Sometimes character is highly probative evidence within the context of a particular case.

In a third evidentiary guise 'character' is equated with particularized acts or other specific conduct, and especially with previous convictions. At common law, all previous convictions go to testimonial credibility, even if the conviction(s) in question have no logical bearing on a person's general veracity (let alone disposition to lie under oath).[30] As a matter of ordinary language, this legal convention seems exorbitant: in the same way that one swallow does not make a summer, one instance of (bad) behaviour will not usually[31] constitute one's character. Particular events may be character-*forming*, or may be *evidence* of a settled character-trait, but that would be to revert to the second established meaning. Be that as it may, however, this peculiar usage became settled in English law, and certain pre-CJA 2003 statutory provisions[32] could not sensibly be interpreted in any other way.

Linguistic niceties aside, it makes probative good sense for fact-finders to infer an individual's conduct in relation to disputed issues in the trial from that person's specific acts on other comparable occasions. The inference may be drawn directly, or proceed through an intermediate inference of propensity or disposition. There is a strong common sense relationship between past conduct and future conduct, inasmuch as 'nothing predicts behaviour like behaviour'. In other words, people who have done something before – including committing criminal offences – are more likely, all else being equal, to have done it again. This proposition also draws some support from modern social psychological evidence, though one must be very careful not to over-generalize from limited experiments or equivocal data.

When lawyers casually refer to a person of 'good' character they usually mean that someone has no previous convictions, in contrast to a person of 'bad' character with a

---

[30] See, e.g., *Clifford* v *Clifford* [1961] 1 WLR 1274, 1276, HC (PD&A), where Cairns J remarked that, 'it has never…been doubted that a conviction for any offence could be put to a witness by way of cross-examination as to credit, even though the offence was not one of dishonesty'.

[31] One should not be too dogmatic here. Certain conduct may be so dramatic, decisive, or memorable that it does serve to define a character (or a life). Perhaps a single gold medal performance is enough to define an athlete as 'an Olympic champion'; perhaps a single murder is enough to constitute a murderer, etc.

[32] Especially CEA 1898, s.1(f)(ii) (now repealed).

criminal record. Of course, people with blank police files may in reality be thoroughly unsavoury characters; they might even be career criminals whose crimes have thus far evaded detection. Conversely, even the nicest people sometimes lapse into breaking the criminal law. Criminologists estimate that more than one third of adult males have a criminal conviction by the time they turn forty,[33] but this cannot mean that one-in-three men is a definitively 'bad character'! The essential point to remember is that ordinary language conventions and understandings are not always a reliable guide to lawyers' technical use of 'character' in English criminal proceedings. One must be alive to the particular sense or senses of character being invoked in particular contexts.

(b) FORMS OF PREJUDICE IN CHARACTER

Although the ghost of English law's traditional hostility to character evidence can also be traced in doctrinal rules and principles applicable to witnesses generally, like the collateral-finality rule,[34] evidence of the *accused's* extraneous misconduct is particularly frowned upon as being unfairly *prejudicial*. It must be stressed that bad character evidence is not rejected on grounds of *irrelevance*. That would have been an erroneous basis on which to justify its exclusion, for the reasons we have just established. Rather, bad character evidence is ruled inadmissible notwithstanding its acknowledged relevance to ascertaining facts disputed at trial. More specifically, bad character evidence is excluded on the basis that it is *insufficiently* probative to justify its admission in view of its concomitant potential for prejudice.

According to standard rationalizations, there are at least two (possibly three) senses in which bad character evidence is considered unfairly prejudicial to the accused. Prejudice in this context has conventionally been discussed under the rubrics of 'reasoning prejudice' and 'moral prejudice'.[35] However, for reasons of conceptual clarity as well as better syntax, we will refer to 'prejudicial reasoning' and 'moral prejudice'. Prejudicial reasoning involves faulty inferential logic which detracts from accurate fact-finding. If bad character evidence encourages prejudicial reasoning this supports an instrumental, truth-orientated rationale for excluding it. Moral prejudice might also engender inferential errors, but alternatively or in addition could supply an intrinsic rationale for excluding bad character evidence. To succeed, such arguments need to show that bad character evidence is (sometimes) intrinsically objectionable because reliance on it is incompatible with fundamental principles of criminal adjudication, if not with even more deeply cherished values of liberal legality such as human dignity, personal autonomy, and democratic accountability.

---

[33] 'Research shows that a very large proportion of people, especially males, are known to have been offenders at some time during their lives; for example, over one-third of males have at least one conviction for an offence on the standard list before the age of 40': *Digest 4: Information on the Criminal Justice System in England and Wales* (RDS, 1999), 12, www.homeoffice.gov.uk/rds/digest41.html. In fact, the actual rate of *offending* (as opposed to conviction) is far higher: see David J. Smith, 'Crime and the Life Course', in Mike Maguire, Rod Morgan, and Robert Reiner (eds.), *The Oxford Handbook of Criminology* (OUP, 4th edn. 2007). [34] See §8.5.

[35] See, for example, I. H. Dennis, *The Law of Evidence* (Sweet & Maxwell, 3rd edn. 2007), 756–8; Paul Roberts, 'All the Usual Suspects: A Critical Appraisal of Law Commission Consultation Paper No 141' [1997] *Crim LR* 75, 80; LCCP No 144, *Previous Misconduct of a Defendant* (HMSO, 1996), Part VII.

(i) Prejudicial reasoning

Prejudicial reasoning occurs when fact-finders give too much weight to bad character evidence. Jurors might say to themselves, for example: 'Oh, if the accused has this and that previous conviction, he *must have* done it this time, too'. Notice that objection is *not* taken to jurors ascribing probative value to bad character evidence. To the contrary, if character evidence had no probative value whatsoever, it would *ex hypothesi* be irrelevant, and should be excluded from the trial on first principles of admissibility. Rather, the objection is to jurors according *too much* weight to bad character evidence, and thereby committing a reasoning fallacy also sometimes known as 'excess probative value prejudice'.

Prejudicial reasoning is easy enough to explain as a theoretical construct, but it has a will o' the wisp, intangible, quality at the level of practical adjudication. Just how much weight *should be* accorded to an accused's previous misconduct in deciding whether the current charges against him have been proved to the criminal standard? Reasonable people might give rather different answers to this question. Social psychology offers many interesting hypotheses and some insights but no clear guidance for policy-makers or fact-finders. Of one thing we can be sure, however: the probative value of bad character evidence varies enormously depending on the facts of the case. Fine-grained, contextual, careful, analysis is therefore always required. From an institutional perspective, appeal courts will not be inclined to intervene provided that a trial judge has approached the admissibility of bad character evidence in accordance with appropriate criteria and reached a conclusion within the bounds of reasonableness.

A second variant of prejudicial reasoning is characterized by premature, as opposed to probatively extravagant, inferences. Engrossed in weighing the truth of allegations of extraneous misconduct, the jury may become distracted, to the point where conscientious adjudication of the current charges is short-circuited by a displacement of focus and inferential effort. Having agonized at length over whether the witness really did see D commit an earlier assault, for example, the jury says to itself: 'We conclude that D did indeed commit the earlier assault, and *therefore* we find him guilty of the current charge'. Whether juries ever do reason in this precipitously defective manner, leaving out the crucial step between proof of the previous incident and assessing its probative value in relation to the present charge, is unknown. But there is no doubting the existence of a logical fallacy into which juries could potentially be drawn. The source of the fallacy might be dubbed 'diversion prejudice', though additional terminology is not strictly necessary to describe what is really only a particular variant of prejudicial reasoning. There would be no pressing need to create a dedicated exclusionary rule to deal with this type of prejudice, since prosecution evidence which would be unfairly misleading, time-consuming, or superfluous in the proceedings is already inadmissible at common law as part of the judge's general background discretion to ensure a fair trial.[36]

Some judges and commentators argue that fears of prejudicial reasoning are groundless or exaggerated, and at all events insufficient to justify withholding material information from the jury. To press the point, it might be added that the argument implicitly treats jurors like morons who are incapable of interpreting evidence of the accused's bad character sensibly. The common law system of adjudication exalts trial by lay jury as one of its

---

[36] See §2.5(a) and §3.2.

crowning glories. It is therefore hypocritical as well as disrespectful to install lay juries as the arbiters of fact in criminal adjudication and then treat them in way which implies that they are not up to the job. This line of thinking easily feeds into a manifesto for 'free proof', nicely encapsulated by Lord Griffiths in *R v H*:

In the past when jurors were often uneducated and illiterate and the penal laws were of harsh severity, when children could be transported, and men were hanged for stealing a shilling and could not be heard in their own defence, the judges began to fashion rules of evidence to protect the accused from a conviction that they feared might be based on emotion or prejudice rather than a fair evaluation of the facts of the case against him. The judges did not trust the jury to evaluate all the relevant material and evolved many restrictive rules which they deemed necessary to ensure that the accused had a fair trial in the climate of those times. Today with better educated and more literate juries the value of those old restrictive rules of evidence is being re-evaluated and many are being discarded or modified.... This seems to me to be a wholly desirable development of law. The basic reason why criminal cases are heard by juries rather than by a judge alone is that our society prefers to trust the collective judgment of 12 men and women drawn from different backgrounds to decide the facts of the case rather than accept the view of a single professional judge. Deciding the facts requires the jury in all cases to decide whose evidence they find credible and what inferences they are prepared to draw from the facts as they find them. I would therefore resist any attempt to remove this essential role from the jury for to do so seems to me to strike root and branch at the very reason we have jury trial.[37]

Does excluding (some) evidence of bad character 'strike root and branch at the very reason we have jury trial'? Does it insult jurors' cognitive capacities and maturity and trivialize their role in criminal adjudication? None of these depressing conclusions necessarily follows from the common law prohibition on extraneous misconduct evidence. One need only postulate that jurors are human beings with the flaws, blind-spots, and susceptibility to temptation characteristic of our species to provide a legitimate basis for withholding certain sorts of potentially prejudicial information from criminal trials – especially where that information's potential for prejudice is out of all proportion to its marginal or supplementary probative value. This is being realistic rather than disrespectful. There are many social situations in which people would 'prefer not to know' certain facts, lest that information should improperly – albeit perhaps involuntarily – influence one's judgments. Reflecting extra-judicially on his experience of trying criminal cases without a jury in Kenya, Mr Justice Schofield confided that:

if I cannot write a satisfactory judgment in which previous convictions have probative force, then I cannot reasonably expect a jury, which does not give its reasons to anyone, to deal satisfactorily with evidence of previous convictions where they are not of particular relevance to the *offence* in the indictment[38]

If a High Court judge struggled to put bad character evidence to legitimate probative work, it should not be regarded as a slur on lay jurors that they might experience similar difficulties. This rebuttal is reinforced by the prospect that bad character evidence might be inherently toxic on grounds of moral prejudice.

---

[37] *R v H* [1995] 2 AC 596, 613, HL.
[38] Schofield J, 'Should Juries Know of a Defendant's Convictions?' [1992] *NLJ* 1499, 1500 (30 October).

(ii) Moral prejudice

Moral prejudice is conceived as a free-standing vice in criminal adjudication. Although moral prejudice has several discrete strands, and somewhat overlaps with prejudicial reasoning, there is a clear conceptual distinction between them. Prejudicial reasoning occurs when fact-finders perform their allotted role defectively, by committing logical fallacies or overestimating probative value. The fount of moral prejudice, by contrast, is the jury's inclination to abandon its oath to return a verdict according to the evidence, and instead to declare the accused guilty notwithstanding – perhaps even irrespective of – the absence of proof beyond reasonable doubt.

The danger arises where, on hearing of the accused's extraneous misconduct, the jury forms the belief that he is a 'bad man' who deserves to be punished regardless of the evidence on the current charge (hence one version of moral prejudice is 'bad man prejudice'). Perhaps the accused's past crimes (for which he may have already been punished) are so sickening and abhorrent to ordinary people that the task of evaluating the evidence on the current charge appears trivial compared with the 'imperative' of putting a dangerous offender behind bars. Alternatively, the jury might allow itself to be satisfied with a lower standard of proof, where jurors reassure themselves that, after all, the accused is a confirmed criminal with previous convictions. The jury might salve its collective conscience with the thought that it would not be so bad for a criminal, as opposed to a 'truly innocent' person, to be wrongly convicted of another offence. Further variations blend moral prejudice into prejudicial reasoning. Thus, the jury might convict an accused with a criminal record on the basis that 'he might not actually have done this crime, but there are probably many others that he has so far managed to get away with, so we will punish him for those undetected or uncharged offences'. Or the jury might hastily conclude, on learning of the accused's previous crimes, that a person with those previous convictions is 'bound to be lying' and summarily reject out of hand any defence that the accused might advance.

The common law's traditional fear of moral prejudice rested largely on untested armchair speculations. It is a plausible suspicion that jurors may be tempted to damn the accused by moral prejudice, and not much of a stretch of the imagination to contemplate jurors falling prey to such temptations (even if we are all piously resistant to the idea that, given the opportunity, we might indulge in moral prejudice ourselves). In an increasingly punitive penal climate, which is both cause and effect of historically unprecedented crime-rates and widespread feelings of insecurity, it is all the more likely that jurors will project their fear and anger into scapegoating 'criminals' for all the ills of society. Less anecdotally, a Law Commission-sponsored 'mock-jury' experiment[39] found that jurors were less likely to believe an accused's testimony, and more likely to convict him, if they were told that he had a previous conviction of indecent assault on a child *irrespective of the nature of the current charge*. Indeed, an accused with this criminal record was regarded by mock jurors with suspicion across a range of forensically-significant evaluative criteria:

When participants were told the defendant had a previous conviction for indecently assaulting a child his testimony was least believed, and he was perceived as most likely to commit the kind of crime he was on trial for (which in no cases was indecent assault on a child), least

---

[39] Sally Lloyd-Bostock, 'The Effects on Juries of Hearing About the Defendant's Previous Criminal Record: A Simulation Study' [2000] *Crim LR* 734.

trustworthy, most deserving of punishment, most likely to have committed crimes he has got away with, and most definitely not given a job where he would look after children; as well as most likely to tell lies in courts.[40]

This finding suggests that mock jurors' evaluations of extraneous misconduct evidence were infected by moral prejudice, and also possibly distorted by prejudicial reasoning (though it must be conceded that the methodological limitations of this type of research caution against reading too much into its findings). There is no obvious, logical, reason why a person with a previous conviction for indecent assault should in general make a less credible witness than any other accused. Nor are there any very cogent grounds for thinking that an habitual child-abuser – let alone an individual with a single previous conviction of indecent assault – would be more likely to handle stolen goods, indecently assault adult women, or physically assault adult males,[41] which were the three alternative current charges employed in the study. The study concluded that, 'the results clearly confirm that evidence of previous convictions can have a prejudicial effect, especially where there is a recent previous conviction for a similar offence'. Moreover, the experimental parameters of the research tended to imply that the impact of moral prejudice could potentially be much greater in real cases with aggregating features:[42]

Significant effects were found even though no information about the previous conviction other than the offence was provided, and where there was only one previous conviction. It may well be that greater effects would be found for a longer criminal record, especially one including several similar previous convictions. The findings concerning the effects of a previous conviction for indecent assault on a child in particular show the potential for such convictions to be highly prejudicial.... Very thin information about a previous conviction (the name of the offence) is evidently sufficient to evoke a quite rich stereotype, so that a similar recent conviction (especially for sexual abuse of a child) is potentially damaging for no reason that the law permits.... If we assume that, amongst defendants with similar previous convictions, some are innocent of the current offence, we have good grounds to infer that routinely revealing previous convictions would indeed increase the risk of convicting an innocent man.

Though certainly suggestive, this study is far from conclusive. Other research findings are counterintuitive, including the surprising proposition that an accused with a previous conviction *dissimilar* to the current charge is more likely to be acquitted than an accused with no previous convictions – a person 'of good character' in the eyes of the law. More predictably, mock jurors' assessments of credibility were, generally speaking, *not* affected by knowledge of the accused's previous convictions, even if they included dishonesty offences. This finding is consistent with modern psychological

[40] ibid. 748.

[41] One argument might be that, once a person has 'crossed the Rubicon' into criminality by committing any criminal offence, they are more likely to commit other offences than a person with a clean record. But that seems doubtful as a general proposition, not least because many offenders appear to commit only certain types of offences. Somebody who specializes in fraud, for example, may be *less likely* to resort to violence than a person chosen at random from the general public. Why, then, should the stereotypical child-abuser, who preys on the weak and defenceless, be regarded as a likely candidate for assaulting adults (which requires greater courage) or handling stolen goods (which requires different know-how)?

[42] Sally Lloyd-Bostock, 'The Effects on Juries of Hearing About the Defendant's Previous Criminal Record: A Simulation Study' [2000] *Crim LR* 734, 753, 754–5.

research showing that (dis)honesty is highly contextual, rather than constituting a predictable and consistent personal character trait.[43] That is to say, whether an accused or other witness will tell the truth, and the whole truth, depends more on the nature of the question and that person's assessment of its significance, for their own welfare and in the context of the trial as a whole, than on enduring characteristics of truthfulness or mendacity. Real people are not like the young George Washington who famously 'could never tell a lie' or the fabled Cretan who never told the truth. Moreover, it seems that jurors, as well as behavioural scientists, are generally speaking well aware of this fact.

A pervasive difficulty with the Law Commission study is that it appears to assume that reasoning from propensity to guilt is always inappropriate. From the perspective of drawing common sense inferences, it is not.[44] To the extent that previous convictions are genuinely probative of guilt, where criminal behaviour really does predict further criminal behaviour, there is no logical objection to the jury using this information, along with the rest of the evidence in the case, to arrive at a verdict. Bad character evidence that is 'properly prejudicial' (a paradoxical notion, which occasionally turns up in decided cases)[45] presents no epistemic problems, so long as its probative value is correctly assessed. The common law's traditional prohibition on bad character evidence is intended to quarantine information that could be *unfairly* prejudicial, utilizing rules of admissibility and inference to neutralize that threat.

(c) PROOF, PREJUDICE, AND PRINCIPLES OF PROCEDURAL JUSTICE

Notwithstanding its methodological shortcomings, the Law Commission's pioneering research supplies an empirical foundation for believing that traditional fears of prejudicial reasoning and moral prejudice arising from evidence of bad character are not mere phantoms. The law of criminal evidence should be informed by the best empirical knowledge available. In the final analysis, however, the content and design of evidentiary rules and doctrines must answer to normative moral and political principles, including, of course, the foundational principles of criminal evidence described in Chapter 1.[46]

The strongest moral claim that has been levelled against bad character evidence is that admitting it in a criminal trial is incompatible with respecting the accused's personal or moral autonomy. For example, Wasserman contends that we object to the inference of guilt from extraneous misconduct 'because it ignores the defendant's capacity to diverge

---

[43] For a useful summaries of the research, see LCCP No 141, *Previous Misconduct of A Defendant* (HMSO, 1996), Part VI; Roderick Munday, 'The Paradox of Cross-Examination to Credit – Simply Too Close for Comfort?' (1994) 53 *CLJ* 303.

[44] For a cogently-argued reminder of this essential point, see Mike Redmayne, 'The Relevance of Bad Character' (2002) 61 *CLJ* 684.

[45] See, for example, *R v Wilmot* (1989) 89 Cr App R 341, 348, CA, *per* Glidewell LJ: 'the prejudice of course may be perfectly proper prejudice in the sense that if the jury knows and becomes convinced that he has committed one series of offences, and the details of that series of offences are strikingly similar to another series of offences, it will indeed assist them to reach the conclusion that the defendant is indeed guilty of the second series. That is prejudicial to him too, but it is properly prejudicial.' [46] §1.3.

from his associates or from his past, thereby demeaning his individuality and autonomy'.[47] Ho develops the argument:[48]

Respect for the accused requires that the court must not be dismissive of his capacity to revise, or act against, his bad character. This is best interpreted as the point of the ban... It prohibits the court from drawing any probability of guilt, however slight, simply and imme-diately from his discreditable life history. His past, standing on its own, should not be used directly against him on the assumption of probability that he is still the evil man or the moral weakling that he was.... [T]he rule is grounded in the moral imperative of respect for personal autonomy.

The charge could hardly be graver, since the entire corpus of western liberal legality – not merely the English law of criminal evidence – is predicated on respect for individuals' human dignity and moral autonomy. According to this argument, convicting the accused on his record or extraneous misconduct is tantamount to treating him as though he were some kind of automaton incapable of making rational choices about his conduct. The accused, it is said, is implicitly regarded as a prisoner of his past behaviour, a slave to his bad character who is incapable of *not* re-offending when presented with the opportunity. Criminality is conceived as a Pavlovian reaction. Not only does this attitude renounce basic precepts of liberal political morality; it is also incompatible with prevailing theories of culpability embedded in substantive criminal law offences and defences, which assume that offenders have the capacity and choice to live law-abiding lives.

A related objection to bad character evidence is that it effectively punishes the accused twice for the same offence, thereby infringing one aspect of the fundamental legal prohibi-tion on 'double jeopardy'. In respect of previous convictions, the accused has already 'paid his debt to society' and should not be subjected to double punishment. As well as being wrong in principle, double punishment is also incompatible with penal law's aspirations to reform or rehabilitate offenders. Misconduct not capable of constituting a criminal offence should not be exposed to criminal censure and sanctions at all, since this would be tanta-mount to a surreptitious extension of the criminal law and a violation of the *nullum cri-men sine lege* principle.[49] Even misconduct involving uncharged crimes is not a legitimate object of criminal punishment, because the accused has not been formally charged with those offences, depriving him of proper notification and a fair opportunity to defend him-self against those particular allegations.

---

[47] David T. Wasserman, 'The Morality of Statistical Proof and the Risk of Mistaken Liability' (1991) 13 *Cardozo Law Review* 935, 943; critically reappraised by Amit Pundik, 'Statistical Evidence and Individual Litigants: A Reconsideration of Wasserman's Argument from Autonomy' (2008) 12 *E & P* 303.

[48] Hock Lai Ho, *A Philosophy of Evidence Law – Justice in the Search for Truth* (OUP, 2008), 300–1, 337.

[49] 'No crime without law': criminal prohibitions must be clearly specified and properly legislated in advance, ruling out retrospective criminalization. 'There are two guiding principles: no one should be pun-ished under a law unless it is sufficiently clear and certain to enable him to know what conduct is forbidden before he does it; and no one should be punished for any act which was not clearly and ascertainably punish-able when the act was done': *R v Rimmington* [2006] 1 AC 459, [2005] UKHL 63, [33] (Lord Bingham). Cf. Bentham's critique of 'dog law', quoted ibid.: 'When your dog does anything you want to break him of, you wait till he does it, and then beat him for it. This is the way you make laws for your dog: and this is the way the judges make law for you and me. They won't tell a man beforehand what it is he should not do – they won't so much as allow of his being told: they lie by till he has done something which they say he should not have done, and then they hang him for it'. Also see ECHR Article 7.

Both the moral autonomy and double jeopardy objections to bad character evidence tap into significant intuitions suggesting why extraneous misconduct may be a suspect or decrepit form of criminal proof. However, both objections are seriously question-begging as currently stated. Why does it deny a person's autonomy to regard their past behaviour as a guide to their subsequent conduct? As an unqualified assertion, the moral autonomy objection risks slipping into a radical scepticism about individual character and personality. It is hard to see how people could even be thought to have 'character' or 'personality' unless their relevant attitudes and conduct are reasonably stable over time and in different places. If these characteristics are stable, then they provide a logical basis for drawing factual inferences. People are morally autonomous, but moral agents are also somewhat constrained by their past history, choices, and environment. As Mike Redmayne fairly concludes, 'there does not seem anything wrong, or disrespectful, in treating the defendant as less than fully free.... Incomplete autonomy has got to be the realistic starting point for any theory which values autonomy.'[50] Wasserman, it should be emphasized, is primarily concerned with inferences from 'naked statistical evidence',[51] which do present particularly strong and troubling examples in which the accused's past is being, in a sense, used against him.[52] But even here, the logic of the appropriate inference is not so much that the accused *could* not have acted differently, but that he *did* not break with his past. Even if we concede the objection in relation to naked statistical evidence, this would not prevent bad character evidence from being credited with whatever probative value it truly merits. Jurors might then take bad character into account in the light of all the other evidence in the case, incriminating and exculpatory, without in any way denying the accused's moral autonomy or capacity for choice and change.[53]

The answer to the double jeopardy objection runs along similar lines.[54] If the accused *were* being punished for his past convicted or uncharged crimes, or for his non-criminal misconduct, this would indeed be deeply objectionable for the reasons suggested. However, the admissibility of bad character evidence is not predicated on these objectives. Bad character evidence is supposed to serve a purely *epistemic* function, in helping

---

[50] Mike Redmayne, 'The Ethics of Character Evidence' (2008) 61 *Current Legal Problems* 371, 387.

[51] Previously discussed in §4.5(b).

[52] Wasserman's most powerful illustrations involve inferences from 'group base-rates', i.e. naked statistics generated from *other people's* past behaviour. As he explains, 'the reliance on group base-rates to impose liability triggers very strong self-protective reflexes. In rejecting the use of group base-rates to impose liability, we defend our conception of ourselves as autonomous individuals whose fates should depend on our own choices and conduct, and on our own mental and physical endowment': David T. Wasserman, 'The Morality of Statistical Proof and the Risk of Mistaken Liability' (1991) 13 *Cardozo Law Review* 935, 949.

[53] Ho elucidates a similar distinction: 'the probative value of the accused's disposition depends on the availability of evidence, not only of its existence and precise nature, but also of the presence of conditions in the circumstances of the case that would activate the first-order desire to act in the alleged manner.... The demand that the evidence must have enough of the relevant details, and the motivational account be sensitive to the multi-dimensionality of character, is arguably how we should read the law's insistence that similar fact evidence must have sufficiently high probative value.... On the present view, similar fact evidence supports the inference of guilt only *indirectly* by offering an *explanation* for the alleged action that is grounded in the situation of the crime and in the *reasons* which motivated the agent': Hock Lai Ho, *A Philosophy of Evidence Law – Justice in the Search for Truth* (OUP, 2008), 304–5 (original emphasis, footnotes omitted).

[54] Mike Redmayne undertakes a more extensive reconsideration of 'criminal justice' rationales for the bad character prohibition, and finds them entirely unpersuasive: 'The Ethics of Character Evidence' (2008) 61 *Current Legal Problems* 371.

the jury to decide whether or not the accused is guilty of the offences *charged*, and only them. Extraneous misconduct is not supposed to expand the scope of the indictment on which the accused strands trial, although it may increase the factual issues in dispute in the proceedings.[55] On closer examination, the double jeopardy objection anticipates the adverse consequences when processes of proof go awry, that is, when the admission of bad character evidence leads to prejudicial reasoning or moral prejudice.

We can try to reformulate the autonomy and double jeopardy objections to bad character evidence in a way which retains their core intuitions whilst grounding them more securely in a conception of legitimate criminal adjudication. Two salient principles of procedural justice are already implicit in the preceding discussion of proof and prejudice. First, the 'principle of full proof' asserts that offenders must only be convicted on the basis of reliable evidence constituting proof of guilt beyond reasonable doubt, and nothing less. The principle of full proof is another way of expressing the law's commitment to the presumption of innocence and its functional extension into the burden and standard of proof in *Woolmington*'s case.[56] Behind these doctrinal commitments stand two of our foundational principles of criminal evidence: the principle of accurate fact-finding and the principle of protecting the innocent from wrongful conviction.[57] Given the various forms of prejudice to which it is manifestly susceptible, bad character evidence should not automatically be admitted in criminal trials simply because it is relevant. This is the enduring wisdom of the common law's traditional suspicion of extraneous misconduct evidence. Such evidence should be excluded where its probative value is too slight to justify its associated risks of prejudice.

Over-reliance on bad character evidence would also risk further repercussions for criminal proceedings. If bad character were an acceptable make-weight for evidentially weak prosecution cases, police officers might be disinclined to look for more reliable evidence and prosecutors might be prepared to bring weaker cases to trial. Indeed, citizens with previous convictions might be targeted by law enforcement (even more than they are at present), since their criminal records would in themselves already constitute partial proof of guilt. In this way, the law of criminal evidence would be in danger of generating mutually reinforcing perverse incentives in the administration of criminal justice, with predictably deleterious consequences. These include: additional wrongful convictions; misplaced focus of law enforcement efforts, possibly allowing more serious offenders to escape detection; and a pervasive corruption of the processes of proof, allowing citizens (guilty and innocent) to be condemned on an evidential basis that, objectively considered in the light of the *Woolmington* standard, is insufficiently robust to support the burden of criminal censure and punishment.

A second core principle of procedural justice in common law jurisdictions[58] is that the accused is entitled to be tried exclusively on the charges preferred against him, not

---

[55] This analysis applies even to previous offences of which the accused has been acquitted: see Paul Roberts, 'Acquitted Misconduct Evidence and Double Jeopardy Principles, From *Sambasivam* to *Z*' [2000] *Crim LR* 952.   [56] Previously discussed in Chapter 6.

[57] §1.3.

[58] Cf. the continental preference for trying 'the whole man', drawing freely on evidence of character and disposition. See, further, Stewart Field, 'State, Citizen, and Character in French Criminal Process' (2006) 33 *Journal of Law and Society* 522; Mirjan R Damaška, 'Propensity Evidence in Continental Legal Systems' (1994) 70 *Chicago-Kent LR* 55. However, the contrast should not be overdrawn. Hock Lai Ho finds

on vague suspicions of uncharged offences, still less on his general moral character as a whole. Criminal proceedings involve specific, particularized criminal charges, specified and communicated sufficiently in advance of trial to allow the accused a fair opportunity to mount a defence. They are not wide-ranging examinations of the moral quality of the accused's life or personality, which in our culture would be thought an intolerable intrusion into personal privacy and a careless invitation to totalitarian government. Criminal justice is a political as well as a moral enterprise. Empowering the authorities to require the accused to answer at large for his entire existence and moral character would not be compatible with liberal conceptions of limited government. What we might call the 'principle of confining verdicts to the charge' encapsulates this essential restriction on the scope of criminal trial proceedings in England and Wales.

To the extent that evidence of the accused's misconduct may lead, through prejudicial reasoning or moral prejudice, to a *de facto* reduction in the standard of proof or to punishment for 'bad character' at large, these formative principles of criminal justice are imperilled. But that is not all. We observed in Chapter 1 that criminal justice in the full sense is not achieved unless justice is done and manifestly *seen to be done*.[59] It follows that the quality of justice is *pro tanto* diminished whenever a jury *might have* reached its verdict through unfair prejudice, even if neither prejudicial reasoning nor moral prejudice entered into the jury's deliberations in the instant case. Of course, once the accused's bad character has been revealed in the trial, we can never know for sure either way: the appearance of injustice will not be dispelled for as long as juries deliberate in secret and return unreasoned general verdicts.[60] Fundamental considerations of justice therefore account for English law's traditional disdain for evidence of the accused's extraneous misconduct.

Of course, the absence of explicit evidence of the accused's bad character does not prevent jurors from speculating that if an accused is not put forward by his barrister as a person 'of good character' he almost certainly has previous convictions. Some jurors might already be wise to this legal convention – arguably criminal procedure's worst kept secret – particularly if this is not their first trial. And it only takes one well-informed juror to spill the beans to the other eleven. Two thirds of the Law Commission study mock jurors who were given no information about previous record nonetheless speculated that the accused had 'at least one or two' previous convictions.[61] Similar speculation is likely to be even more prevalent in summary proceedings, in which magistrates, as semi-professional 'repeat players' in criminal adjudication, will be finely attuned to what the evidence may imply about the accused's antecedents.[62] For all that, speculations about jurors' speculations do not amount to an argument for routinely supplying fact-finders with the accused's

'no substantial disagreement between common law and civilian law on the injustice of assuming guilt simply from the accused's previous bad record; the moral sensibility of the two traditions is not as different as one might think': *A Philosophy of Evidence Law – Justice in the Search for Truth* (OUP, 2008), 312.

[59] §1.2(c); §2.3(b); §7.1(a).   [60] §2.4.

[61] Sally Lloyd-Bostock, 'The Effects of Hearing About the Defendant's Previous Criminal Record' [2000] *Crim LR* 734, 753.

[62] In some localities, it is said, the mere mention of the surname of a notorious 'problem family' is enough to have the magistrates tut-tutting to themselves and assuming the worst, even supposing that the accused himself is not personally already all-too-well-known to the bench. See Penny Darbyshire, 'Previous Misconduct and Magistrates' Courts – Some Tales from the Real World' [1997] *Crim LR* 105; Martin Wasik, 'Magistrates: Knowledge of Previous Convictions' [1996] *Crim LR* 851.

criminal record in defiance of the attendant dangers of prejudicial reasoning and moral prejudice. Juries and magistrates should be encouraged not to speculate in the absence of information. This is best achieved, not by denigrating fact-finders' humanity and cognitive abilities, but by helping them to understand the principled basis on which bad character evidence is excluded from criminal trials (when it is) in accordance with the presumption of innocence.[63] The principle of full proof and the principle of confining verdicts to the charge are embedded features of English criminal jurisprudence. We might say that these two principles have helped to forge the character of procedural justice in England and Wales and continue, in part, to define it. The enduring popular appeal of these principles was, perhaps, intuitively grasped by the 58% of real jurors who informed Zander and Henderson's *Crown Court Study* that they would prefer *not* to be told about the accused's criminal record.[64]

14.3 SCOPE AND STRUCTURE OF THE CJA 2003'S BAD CHARACTER PROVISIONS

The CJA 2003 restructures the topic of bad character evidence by providing a comprehensive new statutory framework of admissibility to replace the pre-existing amalgam of common law rules and statutory provisions. Although many of the Act's substantive provisions have the appearance of updated restatements of the pre-existing law, the new structure is already changing the way in which lawyers think about adducing bad character evidence and reshaping judicial approaches to determining its admissibility. Before examining particular aspects of the new admissibility framework in detail, it is first necessary to clarify the scope and structure of the CJA 2003's bad character provisions.

(a) SCOPE – THE MEANING OF 'BAD CHARACTER'

The CJA 2003 deals comprehensively with the admissibility of bad character evidence, in relation to ordinary witnesses (including complainants[65]) as well as evidence of the accused's misconduct. Section 99 abolishes *all* 'common law rules governing the admissibility of evidence of bad character in criminal proceedings'. Section 100, addressing 'evidence of the bad character of a person other than the defendant', was considered in §8.4. The remaining provisions are concerned with the accused's bad character.

The CJA 2003's scope of coverage rightly implies that the same basic principles of relevance and admissibility should apply to all forms of bad character evidence. The old law was deficient, excessively complex, and confusing in this regard. However, it is important not to lose sight of the accused's exceptional vulnerability in general discussions of the prejudice generated by bad character evidence. Ordinary witnesses may be held up

---

[63] §6.4(b).

[64] Michael Zander and Paul Henderson, *Crown Court Study*, RCCJ Research Study No 19 (HMSO, 1993), para.8.2.7.

[65] Additional rules may apply to certain categories of complainant, e.g. limitations on the admissibility of evidence of sexual assault complainants' previous sexual history (regarded as 'bad character' at common law) imposed by Youth Justice and Criminal Evidence Act 1999, s.41: see §10.2.

to ridicule and vilification in the witness-box, whilst complainants of violent and sexual crimes, in particular, are at risk of being severely traumatized by the experience of cross-examination. Witnesses in criminal trials may suffer serious injustice, which defeats the public interest as well as harming particular individuals. Still, only the accused is at risk of suffering the profound injustice of wrongful censure and punishment, a risk which is exacerbated by potentially prejudicial bad character evidence.

Sections 98–113 of the CJA 2003 are expressly limited to 'evidence of *bad* character'.[66] The Act does not purport to say anything about the meaning of 'character' in general, or about 'good character' in particular.[67] These remain creatures of the common law. Secondly, section 98 specifically excludes from the statutory definition of 'bad character' 'evidence which (a) has to do with the alleged facts of the offence with which the defendant is charged, or (b) is evidence of misconduct in connection with the investigation or prosecution of that offence'. By implication, any common law rules relating to (a) or (b) have survived the Act. Thirdly, it should not be overlooked that section 99's abolition of the common law is limited to 'rules governing the admissibility of evidence'. Common law rules governing matters other than admissibility, such as the terms in which a jury should be directed about the probative value or dangers of particular evidence, apparently remain unaffected.

The CJA 2003 does not purport to offer a comprehensive statutory definition of 'bad character', but it does provide several additional hints of what Parliament had in mind. The starting point is section 98, which states that '[r]eferences...to evidence of a person's "bad character" are to evidence of, or of a disposition towards, misconduct on his part'. Section 112(1) elaborates that '..."misconduct" means the commission of an offence or other reprehensible behaviour'. So 'bad character' for the purposes of the CJA 2003 means 'reprehensible behaviour' including, but evidently not limited to, previous convictions. Commentators were quick to observe that the 2003 Act's concept of bad character evidence is completely open-ended and potentially very broad. Roderick Munday composed the following colourful list of illustrations, loosely divided between 'episodic misconduct', 'general character traits', and 'slightly shifty' forms of employment 'on the fringes of legality':[68]

What does one say of public figures who regularly consort with common vice girls, or of clergymen who abandon their livings to elope with married parishioners? What of a senior female police officer whose personal website lists as one of her interests 'getting wasted'? Is it reprehensible for parents to condone their children's truancy? What of wife-swappers, breadwinners who gamble away the family income on scratchcards, officers in military intelligence who indulge in secret bondage sessions with 'Miss Whiplash', or professional sportsmen who engage in a spot of recreational 'dogging'? Is it 'reprehensible' to go through a form of same-sex marriage in a jurisdiction where such things are permissible? Does the law share the tabloids' indignation and dub 'reprehensible' the behaviour of women who have innumerable children by different fathers and brazenly live off state hand-outs? Is it considered reprehensible to admire Hitler and to collect Nazi memorabilia, to refuse to bathe, to

---

[66] Sections 98 and 99 (emphasis supplied).

[67] The law pertaining to good character is explained in §14.4(c), below.

[68] Roderick Munday, 'What Constitutes "Other Reprehensible Behaviour" under the Bad Character Provisions of the Criminal Justice Act 2003?' [2005] *Crim LR* 24, 38–9.

practise Christian Science and thereby deny one's children healthcare, or to lecture on the virtues of slavery, cannibalism, Satanism, foot fetishism, incest or the routine destruction of infants with birth defects? Is it reprehensible to have withheld assistance from someone whose life one could all so easily have saved, or to fail to have warned someone of risks they ran? .... [C]ould the following types reasonably be described as 'reprehensible': the shameless sponger or the congenital miser, the vainglorious boaster or the kind of Flash Harry who frequents pubs that are known thieves' kitchens, who sports ostentatious gold jewellery and who consorts with noted villains? What of the deepdyed liar, the profligate, those given to wanton promiscuity, confirmed misogynists, pathological social mountaineers, the highly irascible, or the sort of poseurs who would pass themselves off as old Etonians or papal nuncios. Again, might the reprehensibility of one's behaviour relate to one's choice of calling? .... One might consider here prostitutes, escorts, masseuses, pole-dancers, strip-club proprietors – and their sleazy paddlers, mercenaries, gang-masters, breeders of pit-bulls, debt collectors, trainers of prize-fighters, travellers and beggars, paparazzi, the more sordidly exploitative television hosts, and almost anyone employed in the porn industry or by the Inland Revenue.

In *Tirnaveanu* the Court of Appeal observed that sections 98 and 112(1) create 'a very far-reaching definition' of bad character.[69] The Court of Appeal has also said, reasonably enough, that 'as a matter of ordinary language, the word "reprehensible" carries with it some element of culpability or blameworthiness'.[70] On one view the notion of 'reprehensibility' might be taken to imply serious wrongdoing, but then again, could almost just as easily describe trivial violations of etiquette.

Linguistic awkwardness and amusing hypotheticals aside, what is at stake in framing such a broad concept of 'bad character' for evidentiary purposes? The answer depends on whose bad character one has in mind, and also, relatedly, on who is asking the question. From the accused's perspective, there are clear advantages in having his own 'bad character' construed broadly. Any evidence so designated must satisfy additional hurdles to admissibility and, if admitted, should attract further scrutiny in the form of judicial comment and warnings to the jury against its improper use. From the prosecution's or a co-accused's perspective, of course, evidence qualifying as 'bad character' presents corresponding difficulties of admissibility and proof. Conversely, a broad definition of 'bad character' may work to the accused's strategic disadvantage when the bad character in question relates to a prosecution witness or co-accused. Now it is the accused who must overcome procedural obstacles to using this information. Even where the bad character of a prosecution witness or co-accused is ruled admissible, adducing it may have adverse procedural consequences for the accused – and the wider the definition of 'bad character', the greater the risk of forensic blowback. There is no assumption that the accused, a co-accused, and the prosecution should all be subject to exactly the same evidentiary regime for adducing evidence of somebody else's bad character. To the contrary, we will see that English law insists on some important distinctions depending on the party seeking to adduce the evidence. However, it would be rather odd if the basic concept of 'bad character' meant one thing in relation to the accused, and something else in relation to the complainant, a prosecution witness, or a co-accused. The CJA 2003 makes no such

---

[69] *R v Tirnaveanu* [2007] 1 WLR 3049, [2007] EWCA Crim 1239, [17].
[70] *R v Renda* [2006] 1 WLR 2948, [2005] EWCA Crim 2826, [24].

suggestion, and appellate courts have striven to avoid unnecessary definitional complexity or duplication when interpreting relevant provisions of the Act.

A core doctrine of the Court of Appeal's early jurisprudence on the CJA 2003 is that 'bad character', 'misconduct', and related statutory concepts are intended to convey their ordinary, common sense meanings. Although section 112(1) specifically mentions convictions, the misconduct constituting bad character evidence need not previously have been the subject of criminal proceedings or any other formal inquiry. Reprehensible behaviour does not cease to be evidence of bad character simply because it has not previously come to the attention of the authorities.[71] Indeed, the definition plainly extends to behaviour which is unethical but not in itself unlawful, such as a priest striking up improper relationships with members of his congregation[72] or generalized allegations of promiscuity.[73] A fortiori, conduct leading to criminal proceedings that did not result in conviction may nonetheless constitute bad character where the non-conviction outcome still clearly imports blame – for example, where the individual in question received a formal police caution (which could only have been administered if the offence was admitted)[74] or was found unfit to plead in circumstances where the jury had made adverse findings of fact.[75] Even previously charged conduct resulting in an *acquittal* can constitute bad character evidence in subsequent criminal proceedings, if the party seeking to adduce the evidence is prepared to argue that the earlier verdict of acquittal was factually erroneous.[76] The vital ingredient is relevance. Conversely, some information may be inadmissible, not because it is evidence of bad character, but because it is *irrelevant*. A mere arrest is not evidence of bad character, because suspicion could conceivably fall upon anybody and being arrested and questioned by the police, without further action or consequences, establishes nothing.[77] Likewise, mere proximity to public order disturbances or presence at the scene of a crime is not *per se* 'bad character', unless the party seeking to adduce the evidence wishes to assert, and can prove, the relevant individual's culpable participation.[78]

Any juridical concept of 'bad character', no matter how generously capacious, will still leave room for argument at the margins. In *Manister*,[79] for example, the accused, who was thirty-nine years-of-age, was convicted of sexually assaulting a thirteen-year old girl. The

---

71 *R v Ngyuen* [2008] EWCA 585, [2008] Crim LR 547; *R v Tirnaveanu* [2007] 1 WLR 3049, [2007] EWCA Crim 1239, [19]–[20]; *R v Renda (Osbourne's* case) [2006] 1 WLR 2948, [2005] EWCA Crim 2826. There are pre-Act common law authorities to similar effect, e.g. *R v Butler* (1987) 84 Cr App R 12, CA; *R v Bishop* [1975] 1 QB 274, CA.   72 *R v Weir (Somanathan's* case) [2006] 1 WLR 1885, [2005] EWCA Crim 2866.

73 *R v Renda (Ball's* case) [2006] 1 WLR 2948, [2005] EWCA Crim 2826 (B made an attack on the complainant's character, triggering s.101(1)(g), when he informed the police in interview that the complainant was 'a bag really, you know what I mean, a slag'.)

74 *R v Weir (Yaxley-Lennon's* case) [2006] 1 WLR 1885, [2005] EWCA Crim 2866.

75 *R v Renda* [2006] 1 WLR 2948, [2005] EWCA Crim 2826.

76 *R v O'Dowd* [2009] EWCA Crim 905; *R v Ngyuen* [2008] EWCA 585, [2008] Crim LR 547; *R v Edwards and Rowlands (Smith's* case) [2006] 2 Cr App R 4, [2005] EWCA Crim 3244. These decisions confirm the continued post-CJA 2003 application of *R v Z (Prior Acquittal)* [2000] 2 AC 483, HL. Quite right, too: the 2003 Act cannot and does not dictate the contextual relevance of previously acquitted misconduct. For further discussion, see Paul Roberts, 'Acquitted Misconduct Evidence and Double Jeopardy Principles, From *Sambasivam* to *Z*' [2000] *Crim LR* 952.

77 *R v Mohammed Yousaf* [2009] EWCA Crim 435, [13] (an arrest is 'mere unsubstantiated assertion').

78 *R v Weir (Hong's* case) [2006] 1 WLR 1885, [2005] EWCA Crim 2866, [120]; *R v Mohammed Yousaf* [2009] EWCA Crim 435, [14].

79 *R v Weir (Manister's* case) [2006] 1 WLR 1885, [2005] EWCA Crim 2866.

trial judge ruled that evidence that five years earlier the accused had had a sexual relationship with a sixteen-year-old teenager was 'bad character' under the CJA 2003. The Court of
Appeal demurred: absent any indication of 'grooming' or the like, the fact that the accused
had had a perfectly lawful sexual relationship with a much younger girl was not 'misconduct' in the relevant sense. A second contested item of evidence alleged that the accused
had had a sexually-charged conversation with the complainant's fifteen-year-old sister, in
which he sighed, 'if only you were a bit older and I a bit younger…'. On this, the Court of
Appeal agreed with the trial judge's analysis that the conversation was not evidence of bad
character, but rather straightforwardly admissible as part of the general background to the
case. The Court of Appeal said that the first item of evidence about the accused's previous
relationship should have been handled in the same way, without any need to satisfy the
rules relating to bad character evidence.

There is doubtless considerable diversity in social attitudes towards the propriety of a
sexual relationship between a sixteen-year-old girl and a man more than twice her age.
Misconduct here is somewhat in the eye of the beholder. Besides, the essential point to
grasp is that quibbling over the exact parameters of an open-ended statutory concept is a
perilous diversion. The real issue is that it is not hard to imagine *some* jurors being prejudiced against the accused on hearing this information. In fact, the point is even clearer in
relation to the second item of evidence. If the accused did in fact say what he was alleged
to have said (which he denied), this evidence, taken literally, was logically exculpatory. He
was telling the complainant's sister that he was too old for her, and that she was not old
enough to be in a relationship of that kind with him. Expressions of this conventional sexual morality are not, it might be thought, evidence of a propensity to assault even younger
girls. Yet, by the courts' own admission, the only conceivable relevance of such information was to demonstrate the accused's 'sexual interest in early or mid-teenage girls, much
younger than [himself]',[80] and this was certainly a predilection liable to diminish the
accused in the eyes of some jurors. The moral is this: even if information falls outside the
proper scope of the statutory definition of 'bad character', trial judges should still be on
their mettle to ensure that jurors do not slip into prejudicial forms of thinking and reasoning. Potentially prejudicial information does not cease to be potentially prejudicial just
because it is also admissible and properly admitted in the trial. So whether or not the information is formally 'bad character', trial judges should in every pertinent instance deliver
appropriately-formulated judicial directions aimed at neutralizing foreseeable threats of
prejudice.

Commentators in search of definitive appellate guidance on the meaning of 'bad character' under the CJA 2003 are likely to be disappointed.[81] The reason is partly conceptual,
and partly institutional. If the meaning of 'bad character' is essentially a matter of common sense, as the Court of Appeal keeps insisting, then it is not realistic to expect appeal
courts to provide exhaustive or definitive guidance, beyond reiterating the circular injunction that bad character is misconduct, and misconduct is exactly what it says (as any juror
should recognize). Another way of expressing this *impasse* is to emphasize that primary

---

[80] ibid. [95].

[81] Cf. James Goudkamp, 'Bad Character Evidence and Reprehensible Behaviour' (2008) 12 *E & P* 116;
Roderick Munday, 'What Constitutes "Other Reprehensible Behaviour" under the Bad Character Provisions
of the Criminal Justice Act 2003?' [2005] *Crim LR* 24.

responsibility for dealing with potentially prejudicial extraneous misconduct evidence lies with trial judges; and herein lies the institutional constraint. The Court of Appeal cannot afford to get drawn into second-guessing finely balanced judgments that only really make sense within the context of the trial as a whole, and which are therefore quintessentially matters for determination by the trial judge. As Sir Igor Judge P. explained in *Renda*, '[t]hese decisions have always to be reached in a particular factual context. We lack what is sometimes described as the trial judge's "feel" for the case. We should therefore hesitate before interfering.'[82] Nor should the Court of Appeal treat every minor linguistic slip or divergence of opinion as grounds for declaring a conviction unsafe. It would be an intolerable strain on trial judges, and almost certainly completely counterproductive, for appellate tribunals to pore over every word and phrase of the judge's summing-up in search of minor deviations form the script which, at counsel's insistent prompting, could be lifted out of context and blown out of proportion. What is required is effective communication to the jury and substantial justice overall.

The downside of this sensible judicial policy, however, is that appellate supervision will inevitably appear to lack clarity or consistency. The Court of Appeal will not necessarily intervene just because it disagrees with the trial judge's determinations, and it certainly will not treat every minor error or disagreement as good grounds for allowing the appeal. Often, the best person to correct a trial judge's missteps in relation to bad character evidence will be the trial judge him- or herself. In *Yaxley-Lennon*, for example, the trial judge acceded to the prosecution's request, pursuant to CJA 2003, section 100, to cross-examine a defence witness on her previous police caution for cocaine possession.[83] By the trial's completion the judge had evidently reconsidered, and had this to say about the witness's caution in his summing-up to the jury:

You have heard about it. Can I ask you to disregard it completely? It has got about as much to do with this case as the price of tomatoes.... It has got really no issue, no bearing on any issue in this case...I am directing you to disregard her previous caution completely because it cannot help you decide what happened in the street that night...In fairness please just disregard that completely.

The Court of Appeal held that the original ruling on admissibility had been in error, because the caution was not capable of satisfying section 100 on the facts of this case. However, the trial judge's curative direction had averted any lasting damage and preserved the safety of the conviction.[84] As Sir Igor Judge summarized the position in *Renda*, '[c]ontext therefore is vital. The creation and subsequent citation from a vast body of so-called "authority", in reality representing no more than observations on a fact-specific decision of the judge in the Crown Court, is unnecessary and may well be counter-productive.'[85] If it is taking lawyers and trial judges a little time to process and fully assimilate the implications of a common sense approach to bad character evidence, this may in part reflect the novelty of the new dispensation.

The CJA 2003's concept of bad character poses a different set of issues arising from what it expressly excludes. Recall that section 98 exempts from the statutory definition

---

[82] *R* v *Renda* [2006] 1 WLR 2948, [2005] EWCA Crim 2826, [57].
[83] *R* v *Weir* (*Yaxley-Lennon*'s case) [2006] 1 WLR 1885, [2005] EWCA Crim 2866.   [84] ibid. [75].
[85] *R* v *Renda* [2006] 1 WLR 2948, [2005] EWCA Crim 2826, [3].

'evidence which (a) has to do with the alleged facts of the offence with which the defendant is charged, or (b) is evidence of misconduct in connection with the investigation or pros-ecution of that offence'. The motivation driving these exclusions is clear. Reprehensible conduct forming part-and-parcel of the offences charged in the indictment should not be singled out as 'bad character' evidence and subjected to a special scheme of admissibility, because it is not *extraneous* in the relevant sense. Suppose that the accused shouts abuse at his victim before robbing or raping her; or that he drives recklessly for five miles before knocking down a pedestrian on a zebra crossing; or that he tries the door-handles of ten cars without success before, at the eleventh attempt, finding one which the owner has been careless enough to leave unlocked. It would be ridiculous if, in each case, the precursor ver-bal abuse, reckless driving, or attempted car thefts had to be classified as 'bad character', forcing the prosecution to go through a special procedure to admit the evidence, just to be able to present its basic narrative to the fact-finder. This procedure would also be pointless, because in every such case the judge would surely be obliged to admit the evidence on pain of withholding essential background material from the jury. Section 98(a) pre-emptively solves the problem by ensuring that misconduct leading up to the offence(s) charged in the indictment does not qualify as 'bad character' under the CJA 2003. Section 98(b) per-forms a parallel function in relation to misconduct which is part-and-parcel of the current criminal prosecution or the investigation preceding it, as where the accused resists arrest, tells lies during police interview, threatens the complainant with reprisals, or attempts to suborn perjury from a witness.

The success of this legislative strategy turns on section 98's notably loose and non-tech-nical pivotal concept 'has to do with'. In *Tirnaveanu*[86] prosecution counsel argued that 'has to do with' equated to 'is central to the prosecution's case'. This interpretation would have seriously compromised the CJA 2003's bad character provisions, because evidence which is plainly of extraneous misconduct is sometimes also central to the prosecution's case. The Court of Appeal saw the danger and rejected prosecution counsel's submission. Instead, the Court ruled that 'the exclusion must be related to evidence where there is some nexus in time between the offence with which the defendant is charged and the evi-dence of misconduct which the prosecution seek to adduce', adding that 'the application of section 98 is a fact-specific exercise involving the interpretation of ordinary words'.[87] Like the meaning of 'misconduct' and 'reprehensible behaviour', the scope of section 98's 'exclusions' – i.e. paragraphs (a) and (b) – can therefore only be determined contextually within the broad parameters of a temporal connection.

The problem of potentially prejudicial 'background information' was well-known at common law prior to the advent of the CJA 2003, and we will have more to say about it in the next section. For now, we need only draw attention to two general kinds of prob-lems, which are effectively the mirror-image of each other. The first problem is that evi-dence falling within section 98's exclusions might still be open to prejudicial uses, yet it will not attract any of the CJA 2003's supervisory provisions because, by definition, it is not 'bad character' under the Act. The answer ought to be that, in that event, the evidence is still subject to the common law PV > PE exclusionary discretion[88] – which is

---

[86] *R v Tirnaveanu* [2007] 1 WLR 3049, [2007] EWCA Crim 1239.   [87] ibid. [23].

[88] *Noor Mohamed* v *R* [1949] AC 182, PC. Though open to dispute, the better view is that the common law discretion continued to coexist alongside the mature similar fact exclusionary rule.

untouched by section 99's abolition of rules relating to 'bad character', which can only mean 'bad character' as defined by the Act. Despite some loose *dicta* in one early case,[89] the preponderance of authority supports this general proposition: prosecution evidence falling within paragraphs (a) or (b) of section 98 is still subject to exclusion on grounds of unfairness under PACE 1984, s.78,[90] if not at common law as well. Besides representing a principled approach to the admissibility of potentially prejudicial misconduct evidence, fairness scrutiny under section 78 should help to ensure compliance with Article 6 of the ECHR.[91]

The mirror-image problem arises in relation to evidence that *does* seem to be part-and-parcel of the prosecution's (or other party's) narrative but which *cannot* be brought within section 98's exclusions. The problem was intimated in *Tirnaveanu*,[92] in which *T* was charged with various offences relating to illegal immigration including forging passports and identity papers on behalf of third parties seeking to settle in the UK. It was part of the prosecution's case that *T* – who had no relevant qualifications or experience – was posing as a solicitor offering various services to illegal immigrants, including a '24-hour helpline' for those detained at ports of entry. Posing as a bogus solicitor in order to facilitate illegal immigration is plainly 'misconduct' by any common sense standard. However, *T* was not being charged specifically with this deception; rather, the prosecution sought to establish that *T* was falsely holding himself out as a solicitor experienced in immigration matters as part of the general background to the particularized offences of forgery and obtaining property by deception for which he was prosecuted. The question for the trial judge, and later for the Court of Appeal, was whether evidence of telephone calls and a business card adduced to establish *T*'s bogus legal practice 'had to do with' the specific charges on the indictment. On the facts of this case, the Court of Appeal ruled that the required 'nexus in time' had not been shown. Consequently, general evidence of *T*'s conduct as a 'solicitor' was 'bad character' evidence within the meaning of sections 98 and 112(1) of the CJA 2003.

The Court of Appeal's interpretation of section 98 created no practical difficulties in *Tirnaveanu* itself, as the contested bad character evidence was plainly admissible in any event. The more difficult case is illustrated by *Wallace*,[93] in which the accused was charged with planning and, in some cases, participating in four robberies of commercial premises all perpetrated in the Nottingham area within the space of about three weeks. The case against *W* was entirely circumstantial and, in relation to each individual robbery looked at in isolation, not particularly compelling. The prosecution nonetheless contended that, when viewed holistically, the evidence demonstrated that all the robberies had been perpetrated by the same 'team' on a prolonged spree, and that *W* was its planning mastermind, or one of them. In technical parlance, this scenario presents issues of 'cross-admissibility',

[89] In *R v Edwards and Rowlands* [2006] 2 Cr App R 4, [2005] EWCA Crim 3244, [1], Scott Baker LJ indicated that, '[w]here the exclusions in s.98 are applicable the evidence will be admissible without more ado'. However, it is clear from the context that his Lordship was primarily making the point that misconduct evidence could be admissible without necessarily satisfying the s.101 gateways (discussed below). These *dicta* have been confined to their context in subsequent cases.

[90] *R v Tirnaveanu* [2007] 1 WLR 3049, [2007] EWCA Crim 1239, [27]–[29]; *R v O'Dowd* [2009] EWCA Crim 905, [31]; *R v Weir* (*Somanathan's* case) [2006] 1 WLR 1885, [2005] EWCA Crim 2866.

[91] *R v Highton* [2006] 1 Cr App R 7; [2005] EWCA Crim 1985, [13]–[14].

[92] *R v Tirnaveanu* [2007] 1 WLR 3049, [2007] EWCA Crim 1239.

[93] *R v Wallace* [2008] 1 WLR 572, [2007] EWCA Crim 1760.

that is to say, is the evidence pertaining to one count on the indictment also admissible in relation to the other count(s) on the indictment, and *vice versa*? So, on the facts of *Wallace*, could evidence specifically relating to robbery #1 also be used as partial proof of robberies #2–#4; and evidence specifically relating to robbery #2 also be used to prove robberies #1, #3, and #4; and so on? Assuming that the minimal threshold test of relevance is satisfied in each case, as it presumably is,[94] the issue resolves itself into the question whether there are any additional evidentiary impediments to cross-admissibility?

The simplest way of answering this question, in the negative, would be to say that once evidence 'has to do with' one count in the indictment it 'has to do with' them all. Such evidence would definitively be excluded from the statutory meaning of 'bad character' so long as it 'had to do with' at least one count in the indictment. That conclusion would faithfully reflect the logic of drawing inferences from a mass of circumstantial evidence. Unfortunately, as the Court of Appeal recognized in *Wallace*, it is precluded by the express language of section 112(2) of the CJA 2003, which provides that:

Where a defendant is charged with two or more offences in the same criminal proceedings, this Chapter [i.e. the bad character provisions contained in ss.98–113] (except section 101(3)) has effect as if each offence were charged in separate proceedings; and references to the offence with which the defendant is charged are to be read accordingly.[95]

The plain meaning of subsection 112(2) is that each count in a multi-count indictment must be analysed separately for the purposes of determining the admissibility of bad character evidence, and this includes issues of cross-admissibility between individual counts. On appeal in *Wallace*, prosecuting counsel sought to argue that, in reality, no issue of bad character was raised at all, because circumstantial evidence supporting unproved allegations would not *per se* demonstrate any actual misconduct on the part of *W* unless and until the jury found him guilty of the relevant count(s) of robbery, which for cross-admissibility purposes were to be regarded as mutually extraneous. The evidence was not 'bad character', it was said, but 'indirect[ly] relevant circumstantial evidence'.[96] This is another version of an argument we have already encountered, which attempts to drive an illusory wedge between relevance and bad character. As always, the argument fails because there is no middle ground on which it can be defended. If the evidence was relevant, it was because it showed that *W* had committed other burglaries, which is patently evidence of bad character as defined by section 112(1); if the evidence did not show that *W* had committed other burglaries, it would be irrelevant and inadmissible on elementary principles. Firmly, if reluctantly, the Court of Appeal rejected this argument, also.

---

[94] The inferential logic seems straightforward and reasonably robust. If *W* participated in one robbery perpetrated by a local 'team', then he is more likely to have participated in (some of) that team's other robberies. The more robberies ascribed to *W*, the stronger becomes the inference that he is a member of the team of robbers responsible, supplying further grounds for inferring *W*'s participation in more, if not all, of the team's series of robberies. Likewise, linking more robberies to this same team simultaneously implicates *W* in further offending via his team-membership. (This thumbnail sketch of the patterns of logical inference is a reminder that extraneous bad character is problematic because it may be prejudicial, not because it is *irrelevant* or necessarily lacks substantial probative value.)

[95] The exemption of s.101(3) means that the court can take an holistic view of the potentially prejudicial effect of multiple counts, rather than being restricted to considering just two at a time.

[96] *R v Wallace* [2008] 1 WLR 572, [2007] EWCA Crim 1760, [35].

The inescapable conclusion is that circumstantial evidence of misconduct, such as that presented by the prosecution in *Wallace*, must indeed be regarded as extraneous bad character for the purposes of judicial rulings on cross-admissibility and related directions to the jury when summing-up at the close of proceedings. As a matter of linguistic construction, that conclusion seems strained, as the Court of Appeal reflected:[97]

In our view, the important matter in issue was not whether the defendant had a propensity to commit offences or to be untruthful but whether the circumstantial evidence linking him to the robberies, when viewed as a whole, pointed to his participation in and guilt of each offence.... Although technically within the definition of bad character, the purpose of the admission of the evidence was not to prove that the defendant was of bad character in the sense that that expression is commonly understood. Once before the jury the evidence was relevant for what it tended to prove, namely that when viewed as a whole the defendant was guilty of each of the offences.

When basic legal concepts are invested with strained or counterintuitive meanings practical difficulties are almost guaranteed to follow. It never occurred to anybody at Wallace's trial that the evidence of each robbery was 'bad character' in relation to the other counts on the indictment, and so issues of cross-admissibility were never directly addressed. The Court of Appeal – perhaps rather too blithely – asserted that the oversight made no difference in this case, because the evidence would certainly have been ruled admissible if anybody had thought to ask the question.[98] Will similar failures to consider the admissibility of evidence always be so easily remediable on appeal? On the positive side, it can at least be said that the interpretation of section 98 confirmed in *Wallace* should encourage closer judicial scrutiny of potentially prejudicial evidence in cases involving issues of cross-admissibility.

(b) STRUCTURING ADMISSIBILITY – GATEWAYS THROUGH ROOM 101

The CJA 2003 created a framework of rules to regulate the admissibility of evidence of the accused's extraneous misconduct which meets the statutory definition of 'bad character'. The controlling provision is section 101(1), which specifies seven statutory 'gateways' to admissibility:

In criminal proceedings evidence of the defendant's bad character is admissible if, but only if –
   (a) all parties to the proceedings agree to the evidence being admissible,
   (b) the evidence is adduced by the defendant himself or is given in answer to a question asked by him in cross-examination and intended to elicit it,
   (c) it is important explanatory evidence,
   (d) it is relevant to an important matter in issue between the defendant and the prosecution,
   (e) it has substantial probative value in relation to an important matter in issue between the defendant and a co-defendant,
   (f) it is evidence to correct a false impression given by the defendant, or
   (g) the defendant has made an attack on another person's character.

---

[97] ibid. [39].   [98] ibid. [40].

Subsection 101(2) explains that sections 102–106 supplement subsection (1). This they do by further elucidating and augmenting the admissibility criteria specified by section 101(1)'s gateways (c)–(g). Section 101(3) then enters the following vital qualification:

The court must not admit evidence under subsection (1)(d) or (g) if, on an application by the defendant to exclude it, it appears to the court that the admission of the evidence would have such an adverse effect on the fairness of the proceedings that the court ought not to admit it.

Subsection (4) further specifies that, on hearing a defence application to exclude bad character evidence under subsection (3), 'the court must have regard, in particular, to the length of time between the matters to which that evidence relates and the matters which form the subject of the offence charged'. The clear implication is that stale bad character evidence, in particular, may lack sufficient probative value to be admitted.

Section 101(3) effectively turns gateway (d) into a version of the common law PV > PE 'similar facts' rule, with the important distinction that relevant bad character evidence is now presumptively admissible but subject to a mandatory exclusionary rule ('The court *must not* admit…'). The CJA 2003 thereby reverses the polarity of the common law, which declared extraneous misconduct evidence presumptively *in*admissible. This was confirmed by Kennedy LJ in *Somananthan*, emphatically rejecting defence counsel's suggestion that section 101 effectively codified the pre-existing common law: 'The 2003 Act completely reverses the pre-existing general rule. Evidence of bad character is now admissible if it satisfies certain criteria (see section 101(1)), and the approach is no longer one of inadmissibility subject to exceptions'.[99] Without the qualification imposed by section 101(3), however, admissibility through gateway (d) would have been a straightforward question of relevance, and almost[100] all remaining vestiges of the common law similar fact rule would have been abandoned.

Paragraphs (a)–(g) of section 101(1) are the only bases on which evidence of the accused's 'bad character', as defined in the Act, may be adduced at his trial ('…admissible if, but only if…'). There are consequently seven possible gateways to admissibility.

The first two gateways, specified by paragraphs (a) and (b), are reasonably self-explanatory and replicate the pre-existing common law position. The interested parties may admit bad character evidence by agreement under paragraph (a); and by virtue of paragraph (b) the accused is permitted to make pre-emptive revelations of his own bad character, either as a way of admitting stale convictions in order to suggest to the jury that he has since turned over a new leaf, or as a damage limitation exercise before the prosecutor wades in. Paragraphs (a) and (b) do not contain an explicit relevance requirement, with the implication that these gateways could be invoked to admit irrelevant bad character evidence, contrary to the basic precepts of evidence. In theory, this seems wrong in principle. Relevance is a function of logic and common sense, which cannot be dictated by the parties. However, this quibble may be purely theoretical, because it is difficult to imagine why the accused (in relation to paragraph (b)) or all the parties to the proceedings (in relation to

---

[99] *R v Weir* (*Somanathan*'s case) [2006] 1 WLR 1885, [2005] EWCA Crim 2866, [35].

[100] There may be some scope at the margins for arguing that particular instances of bad character do not go to 'an important matter'. But this minimal requirement will virtually always be satisfied by relevant evidence of the accused's bad character.

paragraph (a)) would ever get into their heads to try to introduce irrelevant bad character evidence into the trial. Nothing more need be said about gateways (a) and (b).

The core of section 101(1) is constituted by paragraphs (c), (d), (f), and (g), which specify the gateways most likely to be utilized by the prosecution in seeking to adduce evidence of the accused's extraneous bad character. All of these gateways have precursors in the pre-CJA 2003 law, but the Act introduced some important modifications. These four prosecution gateways are considered in detail in §14.4. Paragraph (e) relates to bad character evidence with 'substantial probative value in relation to an important matter in issue between the defendant and a co-defendant'. Bad character evidence battles pitting accused against co-accused raise somewhat different issues, which are considered on their own merits in §14.5, below.

Two further considerations affecting the general structure of admissibility under section 101 need to be mentioned before turning to detailed consideration of the individual gateways. First, there is the question of multiple admissibility through two or more gateways. The old law governing cross-examination of the accused under the Criminal Evidence Act 1898 was quite strict in this regard. Evidence could generally be used only for the precise purpose for which it had been adduced, and the jury had to be directed to disregard it for all other purposes. The law became highly technical, and judicial directions to juries could appear unrealistic. The Court of Appeal moved promptly to ensure that these artificial rigidities would not be replicated under the CJA 2003. In *Highton*, Lord Woolf CJ laid down the following *dictum*, which quickly became established orthodoxy:[101]

[T]he width of the definition in s.98 of what is evidence as to bad character suggests that, wherever such evidence is admitted, it can be admitted for any purpose for which it is relevant in the case in which it is being admitted. We therefore conclude that a distinction must be drawn between the admissibility of evidence of bad character, which depends upon it getting through one of the gateways, and the use to which it may be put once it is admitted. The use to which it may be put depends upon the matters to which it is relevant rather than upon the gateway through which it was admitted.

It is worth emphasizing that, although the uses of bad character evidence are not restricted to the gateway(s) through which the evidence was formally admitted, relevance remains the vital criterion. Bad character evidence, like any other species or category of evidence, is admissible only if, and to the extent that, it is relevant. Moreover, in summing-up the case to the jury, the trial judge must clearly explain the potential relevance of bad character evidence, indicating the issue or issues on which it is capable of shedding some light, and warn jurors against the seductions of prejudicial reasoning. The precept established by Lord Woolf in *Highton* is therefore not quite as sweeping as might be imagined, and it certainly does not invite jurors to utilize bad character evidence irresponsibly, as Rose V-P spelt out in *Edwards*:[102]

What the summing-up must contain is a clear warning to the jury against placing undue reliance on previous convictions, which cannot, by themselves, prove guilt. It should be explained why the jury has heard the evidence and the ways in which it is relevant to and may help their decision, bearing in mind that the relevance will depend primarily, though

---

[101] R v *Highton* [2006] 1 Cr App R 7; [2005] EWCA Crim 1985, [9]–[10].
[102] R v *Edwards* [2006] 1 Cr App R 3; [2005] EWCA Crim 1813, [3].

not always exclusively, on the gateway in s.101(1) of the Criminal Justice Act 2003, through which the evidence has been admitted.

Secondly, we need to reiterate and expound upon a point already made in relation to section 98 and the definition of 'bad character'. We have seen that an application to exclude bad character evidence on grounds of unfairness under section 101(3) is expressly restricted to just two gateways, (d) and (g). Although the Court of Appeal has said that it is incumbent upon the accused to initiate such an application,[103] the Court has also advised, with somewhat greater circumspection, that 'bearing in mind the provisions of Article 6 of the European Convention on Human Rights, we consider it important that a judge should if necessary encourage the making of such an application whenever it appears that the admission of the evidence may have such a adverse effect on the fairness of the proceedings that the court ought not to admit it'.[104] Much more importantly, the Court of Appeal has said that, to be on the safe side,[105] trial judges should apply PACE 1984, section 78, (and possibly the common law PV > PE test as well, if there is any difference of substance between them) to *all* bad character evidence adduced by the prosecution, regardless of the gateway(s) authorizing its admissibility.[106] Furthermore, the Court of Appeal has pooh-poohed the suggestion that section 101(3) creates a more robust admissibility standard than section 78, in view of the fact that section 101(3) is drafted in mandatory language ('The court *must not* admit...') whereas section 78 adopts a permissive formula ('...the court *may* refuse to allow evidence...').[107] Whilst the courts have been known to accede to far more pedantically formalistic arguments in the past, this new attitude is all of apiece with the modern, especially post-Criminal Procedure Rules, philosophy that substance should normally predominate over form. The upshot in this context is that Parliament's restriction of section 101(3) to gateways (d) and (g) hardly seems to matter, as least in relation to evidence adduced by the prosecution,[108] because 'there is no difference between that section and section 78(1) of PACE and the guidance should be the same'.[109]

In summary, the Court of Appeal in *Tirnaveanu* helpfully identified the following list of six questions, which we here paraphrase, as a logical way of structuring inquiries into the admissibility of evidence that is, or could be, 'bad character' evidence under the CJA 2003:

1. Is the evidence relevant? (If not, it cannot be admissible under any circumstances).

2. Is it 'bad character' evidence within the 'very far-reaching definition'[110] provided by sections 98 and 112(1)?

---

[103] *R v Renda (Razaq's case)* [2006] 1 WLR 2948, [2005] EWCA Crim 2826, [77].

[104] *R v Weir (Somanathan's case)* [2006] 1 WLR 1885, [2005] EWCA Crim 2866, [38].

[105] Lord Woolf CJ advised that 'judges may consider that it is a sensible precaution, when making rulings as to the use of evidence of bad character, to apply the provisions of s.78 and exclude evidence where it would be appropriate to do so under section 78, pending a definitive ruling to the contrary. Adopting this course will avoid any risk of injustice to the defendant': *R v Highton* [2006] 1 Cr App R 7, [2005] EWCA Crim 1985, [13].

[106] *R v O'Dowd* [2009] EWCA Crim 905, [31]; *R v Weir (Somanathan's case)* [2006] 1 WLR 1885, [2005] EWCA Crim 2866.   [107] *R v Tirnaveanu* [2007] 1 WLR 3049, [2007] EWCA Crim 1239, [27]–[29].

[108] Gateway (e), regulating the admission of evidence between co-accused, is a different matter: see §14.5, below.   [109] *R v Tirnaveanu* [2007] 1 WLR 3049, [2007] EWCA Crim 1239, [29].

[110] ibid. [17].

3. Is the evidence 'to do with the alleged facts of the offence' or its investigation or prosecution? (If so, the evidence falls into section 98's exceptions, and cannot be 'bad character' under the Act.)

4. Is the evidence admissible under one of the section 101 gateways? (This assessment obviously requires contextual application of the relevant gateway(s) to the facts of the instant case.)

5. Would the evidence have such an adverse effect on the fairness of the proceedings that it ought not to be admitted (under CJA 2003, section 101(3) and/or PACE 1984, section 78, and/or at common law, as the case may be)?

6. Does the jury need help in the summing-up as to how to use this evidence? (It almost certainly will, because '[w]here evidence of bad character is admitted, the judge's direction is likely to be of the first importance.... In an appropriate case, the judge's direction may need to underline that, given the course taken by the trial, the evidence of bad character is by then of very little weight indeed'[111].)

(c) PROCEDURAL REQUIREMENTS

The structure of the CJA 2003's character evidence provisions is completed by a series of procedural requirements. First, where the prosecution (or a co-accused) intends to adduce evidence of bad character, it must serve notice to this effect on the court and to all other parties to the proceedings.[112] We have already met the notice technique in relation to hearsay evidence. Advance notification is intended to allow contested issues of bad character evidence to be resolved in an orderly fashion during the pre-trial process, and to pre-empt 'ambush' at trial. This is sensible in principle but can give rise to difficulties in practice, partly because admissibility issues cannot always be foreseen, let alone resolved, in advance of trial; and partly because courts are naturally reluctant to impose anything resembling evidential sanctions in response to a procedural failure to comply with notice requirements.[113] On one view, procedural requirements such as timely notice merely specify legal pre-conditions to admissibility and a party can hardly complain if he is precluded from adducing evidence because he failed to comply with those pre-conditions. Excluding the evidence in these circumstances is not so much a 'sanction' for non-compliance as the logical implication of a party's failure to follow established court procedure. However, the introduction of notice requirements (as part of the broader package

---

[111] *R v Edwards and Rowlands* [2006] 2 Cr App R 4, [2005] EWCA Crim 3244, [1].

[112] The power to create rules of court to regulate the production of bad character evidence was conferred by CJA 2003, s.111. Subsection 111(2) states that, '[t]he rules may, and, where the party in question is the prosecution, must, contain provision requiring 'a party who (a) proposes to adduce evidence of a defendant's bad character, or (b) proposes to cross-examine a witness with a view to eliciting such evidence, to serve on the defendant such notice, and such particulars of or relating to the evidence, as may be prescribed'. The required procedure is specified by CrimPR 2010, Part 35. Some practical difficulties are noted by Roderick L. Denyer QC, 'Proving Bad Character' [2009] *Crim LR* 562.

[113] Explicit statutory reference to sanctions for non-compliance is limited to s.111(4), providing that '[i]n considering the exercise of its powers with respect to costs, the court may take into account any failure by a party to comply with a requirement imposed by virtue of subsection (2)...' Cf. CJA 2003, s.132(5), in relation to hearsay evidence (also authorizing inadmissibility and adverse inferences as sanctions for non-compliance with notice requirements).

of measures implementing proactive judicial trial management) in practice has to contend with entrenched professional habits and the prosaic realities of criminal litigation, which frequently fall short of the ideal. Depending on the reasons for failure to give timely, or any, notice in individual cases, the ultimate evidential consequence – outright exclusion – may sometimes appear disproportionate in relation to the prosecution and entirely inappropriate in relation to evidence proffered by a co-defendant.[114] It will be a bold trial judge who tells an accused that he cannot adduce material evidence of innocence because notice requirements were not satisfied. Yet, in the absence of meaningful sanctions for non-compliance, the efficacy of notice requirements rests entirely on the goodwill of the parties, particularly, in this context, the practice of the Crown Prosecution Service, which is responsible for the vast majority of applications to adduce evidence of the accused's extraneous bad character.

A second procedural requirement is specified by section 109, which sets up an 'assumption' (really, a *pre*sumption) 'of truth in assessment of relevance or probative value':

CJA 2003, s.109

(1) Subject to subsection (2), a reference in this Chapter to the relevance or probative value of evidence is a reference to its relevance or probative value on the assumption that it is true.

Extraneous misconduct evidence is logically probative against the accused only if, in fact, the accused actually behaved in the ways alleged. Bad character may be probative if the accused does indeed have a bad character (in the technical legal sense), but mere allegations of bad character do not establish that he does. The allegations could be unfounded. Even when bad character is constituted by previous convictions, which are accepted as *prima facie* proof of the underlying criminality,[115] the accused is at liberty to challenge the soundness of his previous convictions in subsequent proceedings and so deny the foundational premise of adducing extraneous misconduct as part of the prosecution's[116] evidence on the instant charge. On the face of it, section 109(1) is therefore a rather curious provision, because it instructs the court, for the purposes of determining admissibility, to assume that the prosecution's factual assertions regarding the accused's bad character are true. This is subject to the proviso entered by subsection 109(2), that 'a court need not assume that the evidence is true if it appears, on the basis of any material before the court (including any evidence it decides to hear on the matter), that no court or jury could reasonably find it to be true'. In other words, the court is not obliged to assume the truth of evidence that is patently false; and nobody could argue with that, even if one might be slightly taken aback to encounter this pearl of wisdom spelt out in a statute.

The point at issue had in fact recently become controversial at common law. The older authorities tended to assume that, if the accused challenged the authenticity of extraneous misconduct evidence proffered by the prosecution, the matter would have to be thoroughly

---

[114] But cf. *R v Musone* [2007] 1 WLR 2467, [2007] EWCA Crim 1237, [56], [60], where the Court of Appeal found that 'the judge was entitled to exclude that evidence in circumstances where he concluded that the defendant had deliberately manipulated the trial process so as to give his co-defendant no opportunity of dealing properly with the allegation'. It was cautioned that '[a] court should be most reluctant to exclude evidence of that quality by reason of a breach of the procedural code. None the less, there will be cases, of which the instant appeal is an example, where the only way in which the court can ensure fairness is by excluding evidence, even when it reaches the quality described in section 101(1)(e).'

[115] PACE 1984, s.74, discussed in §3.4(a).

[116] Section 109(1) also applies to extraneous misconduct evidence tendered by a co-accused.

investigated on the *voir dire* in order to allow the trial judge to make an informed ruling on admissibility.[117] This was a logical and principled approach. Evidence is not admissible unless it is relevant; and bad character evidence cannot be relevant if it does not, in fact, establish that the accused has a bad character in the pertinent legal sense. However, this manner of proceeding could also be highly inconvenient. It could potentially involve protracted inquiries into (by definition) collateral issues, almost turning the *voir dire* into a form of satellite litigation and requiring witnesses to testify twice on the same issues if the evidence were in due course ruled admissible and presented to the jury. Even then, the whole *voir dire* proceeding could take on an artificial quality, since it is impossible fully to anticipate the relevance and probative value of bad character evidence, which might well fluctuate in the light of the parties' evolving litigation strategies and what actually occurs at trial.

In *R* v *H*,[118] the House of Lords opted for a pragmatic solution to this problem, ruling that the trial judge should assume that extraneous misconduct evidence is true unless, exceptionally, no 'reasonable jury could be sure that the evidence was not contaminated'.[119] This general approach was subsequently endorsed by the Law Commission,[120] and in substance duly enacted by section 109. The net effect is to transform an issue pertaining to admissibility into a question of weight for the determination of the jury. Although some commentators were highly critical of the decision in *R* v *H*,[121] section 109 may be regarded as an acceptable compromise to a genuinely awkward practical problem. As always, however, the practical significance of legislative provisions is ultimately a function of their implementation. Trial judges must not become complacent and allow section 109 to award a 'free pass' to any low-grade evidence of extraneous misconduct to which the prosecution happens to take a shine. Subsection 109(2) is there to be used in appropriate circumstances, and a measure of judicial activism in calling upon the prosecution to substantiate its allegations may sometimes be in order. Finally, it is necessary to acknowledge a particularly striking oddity produced by section 109. Where the prosecution is seeking to rely on previously acquitted extraneous misconduct as proof of the accused's propensity or *modus operandi* on the instant charge,[122] section 109 obliges the trial judge to assume that the accused must have been guilty of offence(s) for which he was previously tried and acquitted. If this is a derogation from the presumption of innocence, it is one which English law is committed to tolerating in the name of pragmatism.

The scenario in *R* v *H* presented the especially acute issue of cross-admissibility between evidence relating to separate counts in the indictment. In cases of familial child abuse, serial rape, and gang-related violence (amongst other crimes) it is not unusual for there to be multiple complainants each making similar allegations against the accused. In these recurrent scenarios, bad character evidence is 'extraneous' not in the sense of relating to uncharged misconduct, but in the sense that each complainant is testifying directly only

---

[117] *R* v *W* (1994) 99 Cr App R 185, CA (Lord Taylor CJ); *R* v *Ananthanarayanan* (1994) 98 Cr App R 1, CA (Laws J). But cf. *R* v *H* (1994) 99 Cr App R 178, CA (Russell LJ).   [118] *R* v *H* [1995] 2 AC 596, HL.

[119] ibid. 609 (Lord Mackay LC).

[120] Law Com No 273, *Evidence of Bad Character in Criminal Proceedings*. Cm. 5257 (TSO, 2001), Part XV.

[121] It is condemned as 'draconian' by Colin Tapper, 'The Criminal Justice Act 2003: (3) Evidence of Bad Character' [2004] *Crim LR* 533, 547.

[122] As in *R* v *Z (Prior Acquittal)* [2000] 2 AC 483, HL, discussed by Paul Roberts, 'Acquitted Misconduct Evidence and Double Jeopardy Principles, From *Sambasivam* to *Z*' [2000] *Crim LR* 952.

in relation to their own victimization. This reprises the question of cross-admissibility, which we have already met in relation to the scope of section 98: can the evidence of *V1* be used in relation to the counts relating to *V2* (and *V3*, etc.), and *vice versa*? The logical basis for cross-admissibility is the common sense thought that the more people who are making the same allegation, the more likely it is that all the allegations are true. One complainant might be mistaken or motivated to lie, but two, or three, or twenty? How could two (or more) complainants be making up very similar allegations against the same accused, unless all of them are speaking the truth?

A possible answer is that the witnesses have put their heads together and concocted a story, or else unconsciously influenced each others' accounts through 'innocent contamination'. We saw in §7.1 that contemporary psychology regards memory as a work of construction which is progressively 'fixed', and modified, through periods of reflection and successive narration. Witnesses who have discussed their experiences together (which in the context of familial offences, for example, could be virtually inevitable) might produce what is effectively a jointly-authored narrative, through a process psychologists call 'confabulation', without realizing that the integrity of their recollections has been compromised. In these situations, the mutual corroboration that each complainant's account appears to provide to the other(s) is entirely spurious. However, this may not be readily apparent to the fact-finder. The common law consequently evinced the concern that contaminated testimony might lead to miscarriages of justice. In one of the leading common law authorities, *DPP v Boardman*, Lord Wilberforce observed:

[P]robative force is derived, if at all, from the circumstance that the facts testified to by the several witnesses bear to each other such a striking similarity that they must, when judged by experience and common sense, either all be true, or have arisen from a cause common to the witnesses or from pure coincidence. The jury may, therefore, properly be asked to judge whether the right conclusion is that all are true, so that each story is supported by the other(s).

I use the words 'a cause common to the witnesses' to include not only (as in *R v Sims* [1946] KB 531) the possibility that the witnesses may have invented a story in concert but also the possibility that a similar story may have arisen by a process of infection from media of publicity or simply from fashion. In the sexual field, and in others, this may be a real possibility: something much more than mere similarity and absence of proved conspiracy is needed if this evidence is to be allowed.[123]

The cautious approach to potential risks of contamination advocated by Lord Wilberforce was rejected by the House of Lords in *R v H*, and section 109 of the CJA 2003 subsequently cemented that rejection. The trial judge is to assume the truth of multiple allegations for the purposes of ruling on their cross-admissibility, just as the truth of all extraneous misconduct is to be assumed at the admissibility stage (unless manifestly unreliable within the

---

[123] *DPP v Boardman* [1975] AC 421, 444, HL. To similar effect, Lord Cross stated, ibid. 459: 'the first question which arises is obviously whether his accusers may not have put their heads together to concoct false evidence and if there is any real chance of this having occurred the similar fact evidence must be excluded.... But even if collaboration is out of the way it remains possible that the charge made by the complainant is false and that it is simply a coincidence that others should be making or should have made independently allegations of a similar character against the accused. The likelihood of such a coincidence obviously becomes less and less the more people there are who make the similar allegations and the more striking are the similarities in the various stories. In the end...it is a question of degree.'

terms of subsection 109(2)). However, again taking its lead from the Law Commission,[124] Parliament did create a further safeguard. Section 107 of the CJA 2003 provides that, where evidence of the accused's bad character has been admitted into the trial under section 101(1) paragraphs (c)–(g), and the court is satisfied at any time after the close of the prosecution's case that (i) that evidence is contaminated such that (ii) a conviction would be unsafe, 'the court must either direct the jury to acquit the defendant of the offence or, if it considers that there ought to be a retrial, discharge the jury'.[125] Either way, proceedings will not be allowed to continue if it emerges during the course of the trial that material evidence of bad character has been contaminated. Section 107(5) defines 'contamination' broadly to include innocent confabulation as well as deliberate concoction or conspiracy. Further counts charged in the indictment and lesser included charges must also be abandoned if convictions of those offences would be unsafe as well, in light of the discovery of contamination.[126]

In cases allowed to proceed to a verdict, the judge should spell out to the jury any weaknesses in the evidence, including, as appropriate, his misgivings about whether particular evidence can be believed, as well as warning jurors about the dangers of prejudicial reasoning and moral prejudice. All in all, sections 107 and 109 of the CJA 2003 may be regarded as codifying the pre-existing common law. These procedural provisions probably represent the best achievable compromise if very serious offences are to be prosecuted successfully without excessive delay or unconscionably traumatizing witnesses and complainants.[127] The law of criminal procedure has nonetheless seemingly travelled quite a long way, in a comparatively short time, from the more fastidious approach advocated by Lord Wilberforce in *DPP* v *Boardman*.

In theory, another possible solution to the contamination problem would have been to order separate trials whenever there was a genuine risk that the accused might suffer unfair prejudice from the jury's hearing evidence lacking cross-admissibility between separate counts in the indictment. Lord Cross observed in *Boardman* that, although severance of counts in an indictment (or ordering separate trials for co-accused) would be administratively inconvenient, indictments should nonetheless be severed in appropriate cases if the courts were going to take the common law 'similar facts' doctrine seriously: 'so long as there is that general rule the courts ought to strive to give effect to it loyally and not, while paying lip service to it, in effect let in the inadmissible evidence by trying

---

[124] 'If evidence has been admitted which is highly prejudicial, and a direction from the judge may not adequately guard against prejudice, then protection for the accused from an unsafe conviction requires intervention to withdraw the case from that jury': Law Com No 273, *Evidence of Bad Character in Criminal Proceedings*. Cm. 5257 (TSO, 2001), para.15.36.

[125] Section 107 seemingly runs in parallel with the pre-existing common law power to discharge the jury in these circumstances. Section 99(1) abolishes only those common law rules 'governing the *admissibility* of evidence of bad character'. Procedural rules governing matters other than admissibility remain intact.

[126] Section 107(2).

[127] Cf. *R* v *Johannsen* (1977) 65 Cr App R 101, 105, CA, where Lawton LJ spelt out some of the practicalities of the situation: 'In the cases of this class which are the most common, namely those against schoolmasters and others who have dealings with the young, the depositions will almost certainly reveal that the alleged victims knew each other. Is the judge to infer in every such case that acquaintance with one another may have resulted in a conspiracy to give false evidence? If he is, many sexual molesters of the young will go free.' And see Peter Mirfield, 'Proof and Prejudice in the House of Lords' (1996) 112 *LQR* 1, 8, opining that 'the House believes that prejudice to the accused ... is a price worth paying in the fight against sexual abuse'.

all the charges together'.[128] In reality, however, joinder of counts has long been the norm, irrespective of cross-admissibility.

What is now Rule 14.2 of the CrimPR 2010[129] provides (in material part) that '[a]n indictment may contain more than one count if all the offences charged (a) are founded on the same facts; or (b) form or are a part of a series of offences of the same or a similar character'. In the leading case of *Ludlow*[130] the accused was charged with attempted theft from one pub and violent robbery from another, neighbouring pub committed some two weeks later. Although the evidence regarding one offence was, at common law, clearly inadmissible regarding the other, the House of Lords felt that the offences were sufficiently related in time, geographical proximity and broad similarity to approve joinder in a single indictment. Prosecuting both offences in the same trial was bound to suggest to the jury that Ludlow was a serial and – especially when inebriated – violent thief and robber who targeted public houses. Lord Pearson nonetheless brushed aside the risk of prejudice, maintaining that modern juries 'could be relied upon in any ordinary case not to infer that, because the accused is proved to have committed one of the offences charged against him, therefore he must have committed the others as well'.[131] In the absence of cross-admissibility, the trial judge would have to direct the jury that they must not use evidence relating to one charge as proof of any other, but must instead strictly confine the testimony of each witness to the specific relevant charge. Even supposing that jurors could understand and be motivated to follow such convoluted judicial directions, it seems psychologically naïve, to put it no higher, that relevant information could be neatly compartmentalized and utilized only in accordance with the strict rules of evidence.

Despite its potential in practice to undermine the presumptive exclusion of extraneous bad character at common law,[132] *Ludlow*'s pragmatic approach prevailed.[133] The permissive rule endorsed by the House of Lords could easily be satisfied in the absence of cross-admissibility:[134]

The judge has no duty to direct separate trials... unless in his opinion there is some special feature of the case which would make a joint trial of the several counts prejudicial or embarrassing to the accused and separate trials are required in the interests of justice.

The pressures towards joinder of related counts in a single trial cannot be explained entirely by considerations of administrative convenience or economic efficiency, or even by the legitimate concern to spare witnesses the trauma of multiple trials and repeat testimony. We saw in Chapter 1 that the criminal trial serves *inter alia* as a forum for expressing society's disapproval of crime and for reinforcing public confidence in the

---

[128] *DPP v Boardman* [1975] AC 421, 459, HL. Lord Cross continued: 'If the charges relating to different offences are tried together it is inevitable that the jurors will be influenced, consciously or unconsciously, by the fact that the accused is being charged not with a single offence against one person but with three separate offences against three persons'.   [129] Re-enacting Rule 9 of the Indictment Rules 1971.

[130] *Ludlow* v *MPC* [1971] AC 29, HL.   [131] ibid. 41.

[132] Occasionally acknowledged by courts preferring a stricter approach: see *R v Novac* (1977) 65 Cr App R 107, 111, CA: cf. *R v Mansfield* (1977) 65 Cr App R 276, 279–80, CA; *R v Rance and Herron* (1976) 62 Cr App R 118, 121, CA.

[133] *R v Christou* [1997] AC 117, HL; *R v Cannan* (1991) 92 Cr App R 16, CA; *R v West* [1996] 2 Cr App R 374, CA; *R v McGlinchey* (1984) 78 Cr App R 282, 287–8, CA.

[134] *Ludlow* v *MPC* [1971] AC 29, 41, HL.

administration of criminal justice.[135] Separate trials of associated offences or accused who are linked together in the popular imagination might fail to satisfy public expectations of seeing justice done, especially if inconsistent verdicts are subsequently returned by different juries in linked proceedings. A further, particularly acute, practical problem is that witnesses and defendants (especially if they are erstwhile accomplices[136]) may trim their evidence to suit the exigencies of different trials, potentially thwarting justice by preventing the prosecution from proving guilt beyond reasonable doubt against any one accused in any single trial.

Consider, for example, the gangland murders trial of the notorious Kray twins.[137] The Court of Appeal recognized that joinder of two separate counts of murder involved 'inevitable prejudice', yet went on to say that since these homicide offences were 'committed in cold blood and… bore the stamp of a gang leader asserting his authority by killing in the presence of witnesses whose silence could be assured by that authority' it was 'desirable *in the public interest* that these two unusual cases should be examined together'.[138] For similar reasons, in the recent Soham murders case it was unthinkable that Maxine Carr should have been tried separately from Ian Huntley, even though the scale of Carr's involvement, reflected in the charges against her of perverting the course of justice and helping an offender, was trivial compared to Huntley's terrible crimes. Given the intense media interest surrounding the Soham murders, and equally intense and widespread public loathing for the perpetrators, Carr was at serious risk of suffering moral prejudice through her association with Huntley,[139] but a full accounting of these tragic events seemed to require nothing less than their joint trial and public examination. As it turned out, Carr's defence was apparently assisted by being able to make a great show of distancing herself from Huntley, crying out in the courtroom that Huntley was inhuman.[140] Joint trials thus add to the theatre and symbolism of a trial, as well as facilitating effective fact-finding in criminal adjudication. Even apparently inconsistent verdicts are likely to have greater legitimacy if they have been produced in the same proceedings, where it cannot be said that the inconsistency arose from an artificial process of parcelling out the accused and the evidence of their guilt between separate trials.

---

[135] §1.2(c).   [136] See further §14.5(c), below.

[137] *R v Kray (Ronald); R v Kray (Reginald) and others* [1970] 1 QB 125, CA.

[138] ibid. 131 (emphasis supplied). A similar argument could be extended to the well-known case of *Makin v A-G for New South Wales* [1894] AC 57, PC, discussed in §14.1, above.

[139] Reflected in remarks to the press that they should be both be hanged. The following short letter from one W. H. James of Alum Rock, published in the Birmingham *Evening Mail* on 1 January 2004, captures the tone: 'I like many others think it's disgusting that Ian Huntley, who murdered those little girls Holly and Jessica, is living in luxury in prison. That swine and his fancy woman should have been hanged by the neck until dead for the evil deed they did.' Cf. Bruce Anderson, 'We Should be Offering Mercy to Carr and Exacting Retribution on Huntley', *The Independent*, 22 December 2003.

[140] As reported in the *Sunday Mirror*, 21 December 2003: 'Maxine Carr erupted in anger at Ian Huntley, shouting at her former lover: "You should f*****g hang, you bastard." Carr, 26, yelled obscenities in a dramatic outburst when she and child killer Huntley were being taken from the dock during their trial. Carr left Huntley stunned as she screamed at him below The Old Bailey's Court One after Day 23 of their trial. It was the day when Carr electrified the court as she pointed at Huntley and shouted: "I am not going to be blamed for what that thing in the box has done to me or those children." As the pair, both handcuffed and escorted by guards, reached the bottom of the stairs below the historic court-room, she screamed at him again.'

The CJA 2003 did not formally alter the procedural rules governing joinder of counts and joint trials, but it might well have reduced the apparent dissonance between the Indictment Rules and the law of criminal evidence – by weakening the common law prohibition on extraneous misconduct evidence. Overall evaluation of the impact of the CJA 2003 on character evidence must await detailed examination of the admissibility gateways, which is undertaken in the next two sections. For now, it is worth underlining the symbiotic relationship between rules of criminal evidence and their broader procedural context. Sometimes evidentiary and procedural rules work in harmony, but on other occasions they may be in tension. In relation to extraneous bad character, what the law of criminal evidence gives with one hand, the rules on joinder and severance may effectively take away with the other.

A fourth, and final, procedural requirement is contained in section 110 of the CJA 2003, which imposes a duty on trial judges to give reasons in relation to a 'relevant ruling'. Relevant ruling is further defined by subsection 110(2) to mean, '(a) a ruling on whether an item of evidence is evidence of a person's bad character; (b) a ruling on whether an item of such evidence is admissible under section 100 or 101 (including a ruling on an application under section 101(3)); [and] (c) a ruling under section 107'. Providing reasons for decisions is generally regarded as promoting rationality in decision-making: if the grounds for a decision cannot be articulated and publicly defended, the decision itself may be indefensible.[141] Reason-giving is also a feature of good governance, long recognized by English law as an aspect of natural justice[142] and nowadays regarded as part of the notion of a fair trial under ECHR Article 6.[143] It is noteworthy that section 110 requires trial judges to articulate their reasoning in relation to the threshold conceptual question of what constitutes 'bad character', as well as explaining their subsequent decisions on admissibility, exclusion on grounds of unfairness, and remedial interventions to neutralize contamination.

Imposing duties to give reasons on trial judges should, in principle, facilitate effective appellate supervision and guidance, and in the long run promote more rational, consistent, and predictable first instance rulings on the admissibility of bad character evidence. Whether or not these potential benefits will be realized in practice depends on the ability of the Court of Appeal to provide consistent guidance firmly rooted in evidence doctrine's underlying philosophies, and on the willingness of trial judges to accept and follow it. Albeit still relatively early days for the CJA 2003, the courts' track-record to-date in this regard is not especially encouraging.[144]

---

[141] H. L. Ho, 'The Judicial Duty to Give Reasons' (2000) 20 *Legal Studies* 42; D. J. Galligan, *Discretionary Powers: A Legal Study of Official Discretion* (OUP, 1990), esp. ch 6; cf. Rosemary Pattenden, *Judicial Discretion and Criminal Litigation* (OUP, 2nd edn. 1990), 395 (noting the difficulty of challenging decisions for which no reasons are given).   [142] Galligan, *Discretionary Powers*, ch 7.

[143] Hence the – albeit easily satisfied – post-Human Rights Act duty on magistrates to give reasons for their decisions: see *R v Brent Justices, ex p. McGowan* [2001] EWHC Admin 814; [2002] Crim LR 412, applying *Helle v Finland* (1998) 26 EHRR 159, [55]; *R (Pierre Wellington) v DPP* [2007] EWHC 1061 (Admin); *Filmer v Director of Public Prosecutions* [2006] EWHC 3450 (Admin).

[144] Some critics have been much harsher: see, e.g., Colin Tapper, 'The Law of Evidence and the Rule of Law' (2009) 68 *Cambridge Law Journal* 67 (suggesting that much recent jurisprudence on the CJA 2003 runs counter to the rule of law).

14.4 THE FOUR PROSECUTION GATEWAYS

We turn now to examine, in detail, the four admissibility gateways most likely to be utilized by the prosecution in order to adduce evidence of the accused's bad character. To recap, they are: gateway (c), covering 'important explanatory evidence'; gateway (d), where bad character evidence is 'relevant to an important matter in issue between the defendant and the prosecution' and it would not be unfair to admit it; gateway (f), where bad character evidence is adduced 'to correct a false impression given by the defendant'; and gateway (g), where the accused has 'made an attack on another person's character'.

Although it means taking the paragraphs out of the order in which they appear in the statute, gateway (d) is in fact the central provision, and consequently the logical place for our detailed examination of the admissibility gateways to begin.

(a) GATEWAY (d): FAIR RELEVANCE TO A MATTER IN ISSUE

Prosecution[145] evidence of the accused's bad character is admissible pursuant to paragraph (d) of section 101(1), where 'it is relevant to an important matter in issue between the defendant and the prosecution'. This simple test of relevance, as we have seen, is subject to the additional fairness criterion contained in section 101(3), which in turn was modelled on section 78 of PACE 1984.[146] For shorthand, then, we might call this the 'fair relevance' gateway. When trial judges ask themselves whether bad character evidence 'would have such an adverse effect on the fairness of the proceedings that the court ought not to admit it', they will naturally be influenced by how the PV > PE test might have applied at common law, and still applies in other contexts. If evidence of the accused's extraneous misconduct would be more prejudicial than probative at common law under *DPP* v *P*, then it will quite possibly be too unfair to admit under section 101(1)(d) as well. The conservative influence of judicial culture and practice should not be underestimated, especially in the short term before the new provisions have fully bedded down, even though the language of the CJA 2003 plainly takes precedence over the old common law, and the Court of Appeal in *Somanathan* unequivocally administered the last rites to the 'similar facts' exclusionary rule:[147]

The Act does not say anything about 'enhanced probative value' or 'enhanced relevance'... If the evidence of a defendant's bad character is relevant to an important issue between the prosecution and the defence (section 101(1)(d)), then, unless there is an application to exclude the evidence, it is admissible. Leave is not required. So the pre-existing one stage test which balanced probative value against prejudicial effect is obsolete...

Gateway (d) is supplemented by section 103, making further prescriptions specifically in relation to propensity evidence. At common law it was disputed whether a direct

---

[145] Paragraph (d) is expressly limited to prosecution evidence by s.103(6).   [146] See Chapter 5.

[147] *R* v *Weir* (*Somanathan*'s case) [2006] 1 WLR 1885, [2005] EWCA Crim 2866, [36]. Also see, e.g., *R* v *Lawson* [2007] 1 WLR 1191, [2006] EWCA Crim 2572, [23]: 'As this court has had occasion to say before, the Criminal Justice Act 2003 introduces a wholly new scheme for the admission of evidence of bad character. The previously existing common law and statutory rules are abolished. The correct approach is not to start with what the old law would have been, but to address the law as it is set out in the new Act.'

'propensity inference', inferring the accused's guilt directly from his criminal propensities, was ever permitted. In *Boardman* Lord Hailsham characterized inferences from propensity as 'the inadmissible chain of reasoning' and 'the forbidden reasoning'.[148] This is
also one plausible interpretation of Lord Herschell's celebrated *dictum* in *Makin*, according to which extraneous misconduct is inadmissible when tendered 'for the purpose of
leading to the conclusion that the accused is a person likely from his criminal conduct
or character to have committed the offence for which he is being tried'.[149] However, this
was a minority view – not least because a number of equally well-known common law
authorities clearly implied that propensity inferences *were* permissible, at least in certain
circumstances.[150]

Section 103 clears up any lingering ambiguity about the threshold permissibility of propensity inferences, by stating in terms that 'the matters in issue between the defendant and
the prosecution' include, '(a) the question whether the defendant has a propensity to commit offences of the kind with which he is charged, except where his having such a propensity makes it no more likely that he is guilty of the offence'; and '(b) the question whether
the defendant has a propensity to be untruthful, except where it is not suggested that the
defendant's case is untruthful in any respect'.[151] In other words, propensity inferences are
to be regarded as legitimate, whether going to the issue or to the accused's credibility as a
witness (or to both), provided that the stated inferential conclusion is relevant on ordinary
evidentiary principles.

Subsections 103(2)–(5) elaborate on the ways in which propensity may be proved, where
such proof is allowed. Subsection 103(2) states that the accused's propensity going to the
issue may be proved, *inter alia*,[152] by his previous convictions of offences which are (a) of
'the same description', or (b) of 'the same category' as the offences currently charged.
Subsection 103(4) further defines these new terms of art:

For the purposes of subsection (2)—
    (a) two offences are of the same description as each other if the statement of the offence in
a written charge or indictment would, in each case, be in the same terms;
    (b) two offences are of the same category as each other if they belong to the same category
of offences prescribed for the purposes of this section by an order made by the Secretary of
State.

---

[148] According to Lord Hailsham, '[i]f the inadmissible chain of reasoning is the *only* purpose for which
the evidence is adduced, as a matter of law the evidence itself is not admissible. If there is some other relevant,
probative purpose than for the forbidden type of reasoning, the evidence is admitted, but it should be made
subject to a warning from the judge that the jury must eschew the forbidden reasoning': *DPP* v *Boardman*
[1975] AC 421, 453, HL.   [149] *Makin* v *AG for New South Wales* [1894] AC 57, 65, PC.
    [150] They include *R* v *Ball* [1911] AC 47, HL (evidence of previously lawful incestuous intercourse between
brother and sister adduced to establish their continued 'guilty passion towards each other' after sibling
incest had been redefined as a criminal offence); *Thompson* v *R* [1918] AC 221, 234–5, HL (evidence of possession of powder puffs and indecent photographs of boys adduced to establish 'the habitual gratification of a
particular propensity. The [accused], as his possession of the photographs tends to show, is a person with the
same propensity. Indeed, he went to the place of the appointment with some of the outfit, and he had the rest
of it at home'); *R* v *Sims* [1946] KB 531, CCA (evidence of sexual preference as proof of propensity to commit
offences involving homosexual acts).   [151] Section 103(1)(a) and (b).
    [152] Since these elaborations are merely illustrative, a previous conviction may still be capable of going
to propensity under s.103(2) even if it does not satisfy either limb of s.103(4): *R* v *Weir* [2006] 1 WLR 1885,
[2005] EWCA Crim 2866, [7]–[8].

Subsection 103(5) additionally stipulates that '[a] category prescribed by an order under subsection (4)(b) must consist of offences of the same type'. Part of the purpose of these rather convoluted provisions appears to have been to empower the Home Secretary to dictate certain aspects of the logic of propensity inferences. This was a curious aspiration. Thus far, two categories of offences have been stipulated for the purposes of section 103(2)(b), the 'theft category' and the 'sexual offences (persons under the age of sixteen) category'.[153] It is unclear what this adds to the ordinary canons of common sense relevance and logical inference that the courts would have identified for themselves. At all events, '[s]ubsection (2) does not apply in the case of a particular defendant if the court is satisfied, by reason of the length of time since the conviction or for any other reason, that it would be unjust for it to apply in his case'.[154]

The complexity and novelty of the considerations introduced by section 103 should not blind us to the fact that the fulcrum of gateway (d) is relevance and probative value superintended by fundamental fairness. In essence this replicates the mature common law test for the admissibility of 'similar fact' evidence. One of the great lessons of the accretion of this bulky jurisprudence over the course of more than a century was that assessments of relevance and probative value are intensely contextual and fact-specific. As Lord Mackay LC admonished in *DPP* v *P*, they cannot be reduced to a single, all-purpose formula:[155]

Once the principle is recognised, that what has to be assessed is the probative force of the evidence in question, the infinite variety of circumstances in which the question arises, demonstrates that there is no single manner in which this can be achieved. Whether the evidence has sufficient probative value to outweigh its prejudicial effect must in each case be a question of degree.

The force of these observations has in no way been diminished by the passage of the CJA 2003. The old decided cases have as much – and frequently much more – to teach about the logic of factual inference and proof, as they do about doctrinal rules of admissibility.

In the early jurisprudence on gateway (d) one sees the Court of Appeal walking a fine line between obediently implementing the legislative policies motivating the CJA 2003's bad character provisions, and fidelity to the common law's traditional, long-cultivated suspicions of potentially prejudicial extraneous misconduct evidence. Rose V-P set the tone in *Hanson*,[156] which was the first major decision on these provisions of the 2003 Act and remains one of the leading cases. His Lordship sought to square the circle by suggesting that Parliament's intention must have been to facilitate conviction of the guilty,

---

[153] See Criminal Justice Act 2003 (Categories of Offences) Order 2004, SI 2004/3346 (15 December 2004). The 'theft category' includes robbery, burglary, taking a motor vehicle without consent ('TWOCing'), handling, going equipped, making off without payment, and related inchoate and secondary participation offences; the 'sexual offences (persons under the age of 16) category' includes rape on under 16s, unlawful sexual intercourse (USI), incest, buggery, indecency between men on under 16s, sexual assaults on under 16s, sexual intercourse with mental health patients, indecency with children, and related incitement and abuse of trust offences, particularly all the newly individuated offences relating to minors created by the Sexual Offences Act 2003.   [154] Section 103(3).

[155] *DPP* v *P* [1991] 2 AC 447, 460–1, HL. Lord Hailsham LC had previously remarked, to similar effect, that '[t]he permutations are almost indefinite…. [T]hey cannot in fact be closed by categorisation. The rules of logic and common sense are not susceptible of exact codification when applied to the actual facts of life in its infinite variety': *DPP* v *Boardman* [1975] AC 421, 452, HL.

[156] *R* v *Hanson* [2005] 2 Cr App R 21, [2005] EWCA Crim 824.

without, however, increasing the risks of wrongful conviction. A cautious approach was therefore required:[157]

The starting point should be for judges and practitioners to bear in mind that Parliament's purpose in the legislation, as we divine it from the terms of the Act, was to assist in the evidence based conviction of the guilty, without putting those who are not guilty at risk of conviction by prejudice. It is accordingly to be hoped that prosecution applications to adduce such evidence will not be made routinely, simply because a defendant has previous convictions, but will be based on the particular circumstances of each case.

The Court refused to lay down any hard-and-fast rules about the circumstances in which bad character evidence would properly be admitted, or how many previous convictions would be required to establish a relevant propensity, since everything turns on the facts of the case, the previous conviction(s), and the particular propensity in question. 'A single previous conviction for an offence of the same description or category will often not show propensity,' the Court explained, '[b]ut it may do so.' By way of illustration, Rose V-P continued: 'Child sexual abuse or fire setting are comparatively clear examples of such unusual behaviour but we attempt no exhaustive list.'[158] Significantly, the Court stressed that previous convictions are capable of establishing a propensity to lie on oath only if the convictions truly support that inference as a matter of logic and common sense. This would normally imply that previous conviction(s) the accused had made an admissible out-of-court statement or given testimony in court which the jury had clearly disbelieved. *Hanson* therefore appeared to disavow the old common law doctrine that all previous convictions, irrespective of their subject-matter or circumstances, go to credit.[159] Rose V-P went on to stress the importance of the judge's dealing adequately with bad character evidence in his summing-up to the jury, and issued this resounding warning:[160]

Evidence of bad character cannot be used simply to bolster a weak case, or to prejudice the minds of a jury against a defendant. In particular, the jury should be directed; that they should not conclude that the defendant is guilty or untruthful merely because he has these convictions. That, although the convictions may show a propensity, this does not mean that he has committed this offence or been untruthful in this case; that whether they in fact show a propensity is for them to decide; that they must take into account what the defendant has said about his previous convictions; and that, although they are entitled, if they find propensity as shown, to take this into account when determining guilt, propensity is only one relevant factor and they must assess its significance in the light of all the other evidence in the case.

However, the force of these strictures was somewhat diminished by the Court of Appeal's announcement that it would not interfere with a trial judge's decisions in relation to bad character evidence 'unless the judge's judgment as to the capacity of prior events to establish propensity is plainly wrong, or discretion has been exercised unreasonably in

---

[157] ibid. [4].   [158] ibid. [9].

[159] *Clifford* v *Clifford* [1961] 1 WLR 1274, HC (PD&A). Trial judges nonetheless retained a discretion to limit the ambit of cross-examination to those previous convictions properly regarded as relevant to credibility: *R* v *Lawrence* [1995] Crim LR 815, CA; *R* v *Sweet-Escott (Robin Patrick Bickham)* (1971) 55 Cr App R 316, Derby Assizes; *Watson* v *Chief Constable of Cleveland* [2001] EWCA Civ 1547.

[160] *R* v *Hanson* [2005] 2 Cr App R 21, [2005] EWCA Crim 824, [18].

the *Wednesbury* sense'.[161] The Court of Appeal has largely, if not always consistently,[162] followed this self-imposed policy of restraint in subsequent appeals on points of bad character.

The principled, relevance-based approach to propensity signalled in *Hanson* was reaffirmed and further entrenched, specifically in relation to testimonial credibility, by the Court of Appeal in *Campbell*.[163] The accused in this case was convicted of false imprisonment and assault occasioning actual bodily harm on a woman with whom he sometimes took drugs and apparently had an on-off sexual relationship. C had a long list of previous convictions for violence and dishonesty offences, but the trial judge permitted the prosecution to refer to only two of these previous convictions under gateway (d) – both of which involved broadly similar assaults on previous 'girlfriends' in which C had pulled their hair, grabbed them around the throat and started to throttle them, as he was alleged to have done again to the complainant in the instant case. The Court of Appeal reiterated that the CJA 2003 had ushered in a new era for bad character evidence. Anticipating the prevailing mood, defence counsel did not even attempt to reprise the argument contesting the admissibility of C's bad character which had previously been urged on the trial judge. Admissibility under gateway (d) was simply conceded on appeal. Instead, defence counsel took issue with the way in which the trial judge had dealt with C's bad character in summing-up the case to the jury. The Court of Appeal took this opportunity to issue general guidance on the nature of the trial judge's responsibility in discharging this important function.

The overriding consideration, Lord Phillips CJ explained, is that the trial judge should give directions that would be maximally helpful to the jury, in the light of the way in which the case had been run and presented at trial. The old law had been excessively technical and complex, but there was to be no going back to that 'lamentable state of affairs' which had 'kept the Court of Appeal and, not infrequently, the House of Lords, busy with appeals against jury directions in respect of character'.[164] Henceforth, common sense relevance would be the one true guide:[165]

The change in the law relating to character evidence introduced by the 2003 Act should be the occasion for simplifying the directions to juries in relation to such evidence. Decisions in this field before the relevant provisions of the 2003 Act came into force are unhelpful and should not be cited. Where evidence of bad character is introduced the jury should be given assistance as to its relevance that is tailored to the facts of the individual case. Relevance can normally be deduced by the application of common sense. The summing up that assists the jury with the relevance of bad character evidence will accord with common sense and assist them to avoid prejudice that is at odds with this.

With common sense its touchstone, the Court of Appeal could not accede to counsel's submission that the uses of bad character evidence should be restricted to the gateway(s) through which it was formally admitted. This would amount to backsliding into the bad old days, when courts felt constrained to give 'unrealistic' directions categorically

---

[161] ibid. [15].

[162] An impressive roster of inconsistencies is compiled by Colin Tapper, 'The Law of Evidence and the Rule of Law' (2009) 68 *Cambridge Law Journal* 67.

[163] *R v Campbell (Kenneth)* [2007] 1 WLR 2798, [2007] EWCA Crim 1472.   [164] ibid. [22].

[165] ibid. [24].

differentiating between propensity to offend and testimonial credibility. It should now be candidly acknowledged that, '[i]f the jury learn that a defendant has shown a propensity to commit criminal acts they may well at one and the same time conclude that it is more likely that he is guilty and that he is less likely to be telling the truth when he says that he is not'.[166] So far, this was a scrupulously 'on-message' rendition of the new bad character orthodoxy under the CJA 2003. But then the Court of Appeal added this:[167]

The question of whether a defendant has a propensity for being untruthful will not normally be capable of being described as an important matter in issue between the defendant and the prosecution. A propensity for untruthfulness will not, of itself, go very far to establishing the commission of a criminal offence. To suggest that a propensity for untruthfulness makes it more likely that a defendant has lied to the jury is not likely to help them. If they apply common sense they will conclude that a defendant who has committed a criminal offence may well be prepared to lie about it, even if he has not shown a propensity for lying whereas a defendant who has not committed the offence charged will be likely to tell the truth, even if he has shown a propensity for telling lies. In short, whether or not a defendant is telling the truth to the jury is likely to depend simply on whether or not he committed the offence charged. The jury should focus on the latter question rather than on whether or not he has a propensity for telling lies. For these reasons, the only circumstance in which there is likely to be an *important* issue as to whether a defendant has a propensity to tell lies is where telling lies is an element of the offence charged. Even then, the propensity to tell lies is only likely to be significant if the lying is in the context of committing criminal offences, in which case the evidence is likely to be admissible under section 103(1)(a).

It plainly follows that trial judges should not routinely encumber their summings-up with abstruse boilerplate, such as this meditation: 'you may take bad character into account when deciding whether or not the defendant's evidence to you was truthful. A person with a bad character may be less likely to tell the truth, but it does not follow that he is incapable of doing so.' These lines originally formed part of the Judicial Studies Board's post-CJA 2003 Specimen Direction on bad character, which the trial judge faithfully repeated in *Campbell*. The Court of Appeal condemned this passage, not because its contents are false, but – to the contrary – because they are truistic and therefore, without some attempt at contextualization, completely unhelpful. The JSB Specimen Direction had to be rewritten.[168] However, the significance of *Campbell* is not limited to precipitating this tangible procedural reform. The tenor of Lord Phillips CJ's analysis of the logic of propensity inferences would seem to be that propensity to be untruthful will hardly ever qualify as an 'important matter in issue between the defendant and the prosecution' within the terms of admissibility gateway (d), whatever section 103(1)(b) might appear to imply. It remains to be seen whether the courts will systematically extend this approach to every situation in which bad character evidence might bear upon the credibility of the accused, co-accused, complainants, or witnesses.[169] Once again, successful implementation chiefly depends on the awareness and attitudes of trial judges, because the Court of Appeal has made it clear that it will not routinely step in to correct minor errors that are not thought to imperil the safety of a conviction.

---

[166] ibid. [28].   [167] ibid. [30]–[31] (original emphasis).

[168] JSB Specimen Direction No 24 (October 2008).

[169] The discussion is taken up by Peter Mirfield, 'Character and Credibility' [2009] *Crim LR* 135.

Characteristically, in *Campbell* itself the appeal was dismissed, notwithstanding the Court of Appeal's unsparing critique of the trial judge's directions on bad character (and, by extension, of the original JSB Specimen Direction which the trial judge had followed).

Given that the legitimacy of *ever* drawing propensity inferences was controversial at common law, it is somewhat ironic that the post-CJA 2003 jurisprudence on bad character has been dominated by propensity-related issues. What is now commonly known as the 'Hanson direction' focuses on propensity. *Campbell* purports to finesse the relevance of propensity to testimonial credibility. Both the continuity and the differences between the old, common law similar facts rule and the new, statutory gateway (d) are well illustrated by *Chopra*,[170] which involved a classic propensity-evidence scenario. C, a dentist, was accused of molesting three of his young female patients during the course of routine dental examinations. The three allegations spanned a decade and were entirely separate, with minimal scope for collusion or contamination between the complainants' accounts. The Court of Appeal found no difficulty in confirming the trial judge's ruling that the evidence of each complainant was cross-admissible[171] under gateway (d) and that section 101(3) was comfortably satisfied on the facts. The question was fundamentally one of logical relevance, as it had always been, but the admissibility of propensity evidence 'is not necessarily the same as it would have been before the common law rules of admissibility were abolished by section 99. The test now is the simple test of relevance [pursuant to] section 101(1)(d)'.[172]

The idea that 'striking similarity' was a precondition of admissibility at common law was scotched by *DPP* v *P*.[173] Cases in which cross-admissibility was rejected because the evidence was taken to show only 'the common coin of evidence in cases of father-daughter incest'[174] or 'the stock-in-trade of the seducer of small boys'[175] were expressly disavowed. However, the CJA 2003 goes still further in authorizing the admission under gateway (g) of 'mere propensity' evidence, so that 'reasoning simply from *DPP* v *P* and from a supposed requirement for enhanced probative value in evidence of this kind do not give effect to the plain language of the statute'.[176] The situation in *Chopra* was that three of the accused's young female patients had independently complained that he had groped them during a dental check-up. All three were quite certain that they each had experienced deliberate groping rather than accidental physical contact. There was no conceivable medical explanation for such behaviour.[177] Nor was the court at all perturbed by defence counsel's suggestion that, if the allegations had been true, C's local health authority employer ought to have been able to come up with more than three complainants in ten years, when C must have treated thousands of patients over the relevant period. The argument was that C had a propensity occasionally to grope his pubescent female patients, not that he was doing so

170 *R* v *Chopra* [2007] 1 Cr App R 16, [2006] EWCA Crim 2133.

171 Applying s.112(2), discussed in §14.3(a), above.

172 *R* v *Chopra* [2007] 1 Cr App R 16, [2006] EWCA Crim 2133, [16].

173 *DPP* v *P* [1991] 2 AC 447, HL.   174 *R* v *Brooks* (1990) 92 Cr App R 36, 43, CA.

175 *R* v *Inder* (1977) 67 Cr App R 143, 149, CA.

176 *R* v *Chopra* [2007] 1 Cr App R 16, [2006] EWCA Crim 2133, [17]. Also see *R* v *Weir* (*Somanathan*'s case) [2006] 1 WLR 1885, [2005] EWCA Crim 2866, [35].

177 Cf. the pre-CJA 2003 case of *R* v *Cowie* [2003] EWCA Crim 3522, which the *Chopra* court contrasted on its facts.

whenever the opportunity presented itself. Contextual relevance is key, as the court's own summary reiterated:[178]

There was, as it seems to us, sufficient connection and similarity between the allegations which were made to make them cross-admissible under the new Act. Put simply, if three girls, or for that matter two girls, said this it did make it more likely that it was true than if only one of them said it. That, as it seems to us, remains so notwithstanding that there were countless opportunities to commit such offences which there was no evidence whatever that the defendant had taken. Nor, as it seems to us, could it possibly be contended that the proceedings would be made unfair by the admission of this evidence.... In saying what we have, we are not to be taken to hold that all evidence of other alleged offending is necessarily admissible under s.101(1)(d). That is very far from the case... [T]here must in each case be an examination of whether the evidence really does tend to establish the relevant propensity. There will have to be sufficient similarity to make it more likely that each allegation is true. The likelihood or unlikelihood of innocent coincidence will, we are sure, continue to be a relevant and sometimes critical test.

The prominence of propensity-based arguments since the CJA 2003 came into force has been such that the Court of Appeal has occasionally had to remind counsel and trial judges that, whilst gateway (d) plainly encompasses propensity, it is certainly not exhausted by it.[179] Inferences to and from propensity are only one pattern of reasoning by which the fair relevance necessary to satisfy gateway (d) and section 101(3) can be established. For example, the four robberies in the *Wallace* case[180] discussed in the last section did not establish *W*'s 'propensity' to commit certain kinds of raids on commercial premises. The issue there was identity, partly established through a recognizable 'm.o.' – the offender's signature *modus operandi*. Decisions at common law still afford classic illustrations. As well as the Sydney 'baby-farmers' Mr and Mrs Makin,[181] there is the 'brides in the bath' murderer George Smith[182] and the notorious Broadmoor escapee Straffen,[183] not forgetting Lord Hailsham's entertaining hypotheticals in *Boardman*.[184] It was also firmly established at

---

[178] *R v Chopra* [2007] 1 Cr App R 16, [2006] EWCA Crim 2133, [22], [24].

[179] See, e.g., *R v Freeman*; *R v Crawford* [2009] 1 Cr App R 11, [2008] EWCA Crim 1863. The Court suggests that *Chopra* is best viewed as a case of mutually corroborating complaints rather than propensity to offend in a particular fashion. When directing juries it might well be preferable to avoid the term 'propensity' altogether whenever possible. Conceptually, however, the two analyses are perfectly compatible: i.e. the complainants in *Chopra* gave mutually corroborative evidence of *C*'s propensity to be a groper.

[180] *R v Wallace* [2008] 1 WLR 572, [2007] EWCA Crim 1760. For illuminating discussion of the common law authorities, see Rosemary Pattenden, 'Similar Fact Evidence and Proof of Identity' (1996) 112 *LQR* 446.

[181] *Makin v AG for New South Wales* [1894] AC 57, PC.

[182] *R v Smith (George Joseph)* (1916) 11 Cr App R 229, CCA.

[183] *R v Straffen* [1952] 2 QB 911, 916–17, CCA: 'Abnormal propensity is a means of identification.... It is an abnormal propensity to strangle young girls and to do so without any apparent motive, without any attempt at sexual interference, and to leave their bodies where they could be seen and where, presumably, their deaths would be detected.... [T]hat evidence was admissible because it tended to identify the person who murdered Linda Bowyer with the person who confessed in his statement to having murdered the other two girls a year before, in exactly similar circumstances.'

[184] '[W]hilst it would certainly not be enough to identify the culprit in a series of burglaries that he climbed in through a ground floor window, the fact that he left the same humorous limerick on the walls of the sitting room, or an esoteric symbol written in lipstick on the mirror, might well be enough. In a sex case,... whilst a repeated homosexual act by itself might be quite insufficient to admit the evidence as confirmatory of identity or design, the fact that it was alleged to have been performed wearing the ceremonial

common law that even a single previous incident may be enough, when logically interpreted, to rebut the accused's plea of ignorance or similar *mens rea*-defeating contention.[185] Parallel logic underpins certain statutory provisions.[186] Continued awareness of this heritage should help to fortify the courts against continual re-inventing of the wheel under the CJA 2003.

In *Hanson* Rose VP suggested that the details of extraneous bad character evidence would normally be settled by agreement between counsel, so that extensive factual inquiries on the *voir dire* to determine admissibility would be unnecessary.[187] This may be a reasonable expectation in relation to most[188] previous *convictions*, but the situation is entirely different where the allegations in question have never been tested by a court or were the subject of earlier proceedings resulting in an acquittal or some other non-conviction disposal, such as a stay for abuse of process. Here it is eminently foreseeable that the accused will contest the factual basis of the allegations, and defence counsel would be falling down on the job if they failed to challenge the admissibility of any allegation that might not, on closer examination, satisfy the threshold standard demanded by section 109(2). The Court of Appeal had warned prosecuting counsel against packing out the evidence with flimsy unproved allegations on several previous occasions,[189] before the matter eventually came to a head in *O'Dowd*.[190]

O'Dowd was convicted of rape, false imprisonment, making threats to kill, and attempting to poison his girlfriend, apparently in an attempt to make it look as though she had committed suicide. The prosecution case was that O was an exceptionally violent and dangerous individual who repeatedly preyed on vulnerable, drug-using women in this fashion. In order to establish this pattern of conduct – and doubtless anticipating, correctly, that the complainant's credibility would be sorely tested in cross-examination – the prosecution adduced evidence of three previous assaults on other former 'girlfriends', one of which had resulted in a conviction of rape, the second produced an acquittal (though O was subsequently convicted of perjury for presenting forged evidence in securing that acquittal), and the third case was stayed for abuse of process on the basis that the complainant's testimony had been contaminated by her knowledge of O's previous conviction of rape. In these circumstances, defence counsel naturally vehemently contested the facts surrounding the unproved allegations. The trial judge undertook conscientious enquiries on the *voir dire*, devoting 16 out of the 42 trial hearing days (38% of the trial) to resolving these contested issues of admissibility. At the close of proceedings, bad character points took up a staggering 148 pages (out of a total of 434) of the judge's summing-up to the jury.

The Court of Appeal was sympathetic to the trial judge's predicament, but felt that he had allowed the trial to run away from him. In the end, trial proceedings dragged on for 6½

head-dress of a Red Indian chief or other eccentric garb might well in appropriate circumstances suffice': *DPP* v *Boardman* [1975] AC 421, 454, HL.

[185] *R* v *Rance and Herron* (1975) 62 Cr App R 118, CA; *R* v *Francis* (1874) LR 2 CCR 128.

[186] See, e.g., Official Secrets Act 1911, s.1(2); Theft Act 1968, s.27(3), discussed in *R* v *Hacker* [1994] 1 WLR 1695, HL.   [187] *R* v *Hanson* [2005] 2 Cr App R 21; [2005] EWCA Crim 824, [17].

[188] Even in relation to previous convictions, the accused might want to contest circumstantial details or even dispute that the recorded convictions are his: cf. *R* v *Burns* [2006] 1 WLR 1273, [2006] EWCA Crim 617.

[189] See, e.g., *R* v *K (Peter) and K (Terence)* [2008] EWCA Crim 434, [67]; *R* v *Hanson* [2005] 2 Cr App R 21; [2005] EWCA Crim 824, [12]: 'Where past events are disputed the judge must take care not to permit the trial unreasonably to be diverted into an investigation of matters not charged on the indictment.'

[190] *R* v *O'Dowd* [2009] EWCA Crim 905.

months, which the Court of Appeal found totally unacceptable: 'For a trial involving just one defendant and the relatively simple issues that the jury had to decide to have lasted for this length of time with the consequent vast cost to the public is not only disproportionate but a serious blot on the administration of justice.'[191] Many factors had contributed to the delays – from the accused's ill-health and ill-advisedly sacking his counsel, to Christmas and Easter recesses – but the diversion of the trial into questions of extraneous misconduct was one significant, and in the eyes of the Court of Appeal avoidable, source of complexity and procrastination. The judge should have been much stricter in forcing the prosecution to narrow down its factual claims, and 'consideration should have been given to directing the Crown to pick the best of the three allegations and only to consider whether to admit that evidence'.[192] As events had transpired, the Court of Appeal was driven to the conclusion that 'the intensive investigation of satellite issues combined with the numerous interruptions to the trial and its overall length made it very difficult for the jury to keep its eye on the ball'.[193] With evident reluctance, the appeal was allowed, the Court of Appeal remarking ruefully that, '[i]f ever there is a case to illustrate the dangers of satellite litigation through the introduction of bad character evidence this is it'.[194]

   O'Dowd crystallizes the difficult strategic choices facing prosecutors when preparing for trial. If extensive evidence of 'system' or 'pattern' is to-hand, it must be tempting to try to present it all, so that the jury can be left in no doubt about the accused's wicked behaviour. However, the Court of Appeal has now clearly signalled that a blunderbuss approach will not be tolerated. Trial judges, for their part, must keep a firm grip on trial management and the overall timetable, and take appropriate measures to narrow down the issues or, where the parties are amenable, to implement procedural shortcuts, such as formal proof by PACE 1984, sections 73 and 74,[195] or consensual admissibility under gateways (a) or (b). One of the errors that the trial judge was found to have made in *O'Dowd* was that, although he had carefully considered the admissibility of each individual extraneous allegation under gateway (d) and section 101(3), he 'did not or did not adequately consider the cumulative effect of the introduction of three separate contested issues into the trial on its overall length and on the jury, or how the evidence might be timetabled or truncated'.[196] A different kind of error led to the accused's conviction being quashed in *Bullen*,[197] where B was charged with homicide after a late-night brawl at a taxi-rank. B originally indicated that he would argue self-defence, and on this basis the trial judge ruled that B's long record of violent crime was admissible to demonstrate a propensity for violence. By the commencement of the trial, however, B was admitting that he had unlawfully killed the deceased and the only contested issue was whether he had done so with malice aforethought, i.e. whether it was murder or only manslaughter. The trial judge went wrong, said the Court of Appeal, because he failed to consider the impact of this change of plea on the prosecution's case. Whilst a general propensity for violence might undermine a claim of self-defence, it was not sufficiently discriminating to help the jury decide whether B had the necessary 'specific intent' for murder. So B's previous convictions did not go to

---

[191] ibid. [1].   [192] ibid. [71].   [193] ibid. [84].   [194] ibid. [2].

[195] These formalities provisions were discussed in §3.4(a). Foreign convictions may be proved pursuant to the Evidence Act 1851, s.7: see *R v Kordasinksi* [2007] 1 Cr App R 17, [2006] EWCA Crim 2984.

[196] *R v O'Dowd* [2009] EWCA Crim 905, [61].

[197] *R v Bullen* [2008] 2 Cr App R 25, [2008] EWCA Crim 4.

an important matter in issue within the meaning of gateway (d), and on this analysis the evidence could not possibly have satisfied section 101(3) either.

Bullen demonstrates that trial judges need to keep their rulings on admissibility through the section 101 gateways under continuous review, and to be prepared to revisit questions of admissibility in the light of changes in the matters in issue, which in turn reflect the evidence actually led or the way in which the case is being run at trial. If the trial judge in *Bullen* had thought carefully about the matter (which, the Court of Appeal found, he did not), he might have been able to fashion a direction to the jury that could have neutralized the threat of prejudice arising from the admission of *B*'s criminal record – perhaps to the point of instructing the jury to ignore it altogether, as the trial judge in *Yaxley-Lennon* (quoted above) did.[198] Yet hindsight is a wonderful thing, and the judge's remedial options are relatively limited after the evidence has already been admitted and revealed to the jury, as the Court of Appeal acknowledged in *O'Dowd*.[199] With the benefit of a little experience, it is apparent that issues pertaining to the proof and admissibility of (unconvicted) extraneous misconduct evidence are rather more complex, time-consuming and potentially disruptive than the Court of Appeal originally intimated in *Hanson*.[200]

(b) GATEWAY (c): IMPORTANT EXPLANATORY EVIDENCE

Section 101(1)(c) of the CJA 2003 renders prosecution evidence of the accused's bad character admissible where 'it is important explanatory evidence'. By section 102, evidence qualifies as important explanatory evidence if '(a) without it, the court or jury would find it impossible or difficult properly to understand other evidence in the case, and (b) its value for understanding the case as a whole is substantial'. These provisions deal with what was known at common law as 'background evidence',[201] which has already featured in our earlier discussion of the scope of section 98 and the meaning of 'bad character'. This is where the limitation of the common law 'similar facts' rule to the accused's *extraneous* misconduct was especially salient, and a parallel set of issues arises under the CJA 2003 – even though gateway (c) has not figured prominently in post-Act jurisprudence, possibly owing to the acknowledged the overlap with section 98. As the Court of Appeal pointed out in *Tirnaveanu*, 'such evidence could be admitted either as "to do" with the offence or as important explanatory evidence under section 101(1)(c) of the CJA 2003'.[202]

The key conceptual distinction is between evidence that is part-and-parcel of the events forming the basis of the charge, and evidence which might be relevant to prove the current charges, but is not an integral aspect of the events themselves or their inseparable background and context. Suppose that D is charged with V's murder. Evidence that in

---

[198] *R v Weir* (*Yaxley-Lennon*'s case) [2006] 1 WLR 1885, [2005] EWCA Crim 2866, [66].

[199] *R v O'Dowd* [2009] EWCA Crim 905, [60]: 'It is incumbent upon a judge considering the application to try to project forward to see the problems which might later arise in the trial as a result of the disputed bad character evidence being admitted before ruling on the application. This is because, once the evidence is admitted, unless it has been contaminated (and section 107 applies) the question is of its weight. The judge will then only have limited remedies open to deal with problems that arise thereafter'.

[200] *R v Hanson* [2005] 2 Cr App R 21; [2005] EWCA Crim 824, [17].

[201] *R v Davis* [2009] 2 Cr App R 17, [2008] EWCA Crim 1156, [33]: 'Gateway (c), important explanatory evidence, no doubt reflects the common law rule which permitted background or explanatory material where the account otherwise to be placed before the court would be incomplete and incomprehensible...'

[202] *R v Tirnaveanu* [2007] 1 WLR 3049, [2007] EWCA Crim 1239, [24].

the week prior to the murder *D* threatened to kill *V* is clearly direct evidence of a murderous intent. Though a temporally distinct instance of the accused's misconduct, evidence of the threat is not extraneous to the proceedings, and consequently did not fall within the scope of the exclusionary rule at common law. Evidence that *D* made death threats, or killed other people, on previous occasions could also be relevant to prove the accused murdered *V*. However, in contrast to threats uttered against the deceased himself, threats against others or incidents of violence not directed towards *V* would usually be extraneous to the current charge, and therefore squarely within the purview of the common law exclusionary rule.[203]

The conceptual distinction between evidence going to the issue and evidence of 'extraneous' bad character can be grasped easily enough as a theoretical proposition. Indeed, without some loose operational sense of that distinction the common law rule would have dissolved into *reductio ad absurdum*, inasmuch as each and every act leading up to a crime (buying the knife; ascertaining the victim's whereabouts; approaching the victim; brandishing the weapon, etc.) could be individuated as a separate instance of the accused's misconduct and presented as a candidate for exclusion. Of course, such applications were never made. It was implicitly understood that the common law exclusionary rule had no application to evidence of the very events disputed in the trial. This is now spelt out by section 98 of the CJA 2003, which (as we have seen[204]) excludes evidence which 'has to do with the alleged facts of the offence with which the defendant is charged, or…is evidence of misconduct in connection with the investigation or prosecution of that offence' from the governing statutory definition of 'bad character'.

The pristine conceptual distinction between facts in issue and 'background' evidence did not always translate smoothly into practice. In *R* v *M* the Court of Appeal formulated the following statement of principle to govern the scope of the common law exclusionary rule:[205]

Where it is necessary to place before the jury evidence of part of a continual background of history relevant to the offence charged in the indictment and without the totality of which the account placed before the jury would be incomplete or incomprehensible, then the fact that the whole account involves including evidence establishing the commission of an offence with which the accused is not charged is not of itself a ground for excluding the evidence.

The Court of Appeal's test clearly anticipated the language of CJA 2003, section 102; indeed, both contain a major equivocation. It is one thing to say that without the disputed bad character evidence the case would be 'incomprehensible' (at common law) or 'impossible…to understand' (under section 102); quite another that without the disputed evidence the case would be 'incomplete' (common law) or 'difficult properly to understand' (section 102). The first limb of each test is very much more stringent than its second, back-up limb. What is fundamentally at issue here is whether the prosecution may be permitted to adduce evidence of the accused's bad character which is more prejudicial than probative. The common law authorities supply some illuminating case-studies but little in the way of principled guidance.

---

[203] It is necessary to say *usually*, because it is always possible that threats against or harm to others could be in issue on the facts – for example, where *D* has previously uttered racially-motivated insults against others and *V*'s murder may have been racially-motivated.   [204] §14.3(a), above.

[205] *R* v *M* [2000] 1 All ER 148, 152–3, CA.

In *O'Leary*, for example, details of the accused's violent attacks on various third parties during an all-day 'drunken orgy' were held to have been properly admitted at his murder trial because, concluded the High Court of Australia, this sequence of assaults constituted 'a connected series of events…which should be considered as one transaction'.[206] This rationalization has been explained as an application of the ubiquitous doctrine of *res gestae*,[207] which is more commonly associated with the law of hearsay.[208] A more recent English illustration is *Fulcher*,[209] where the accused was convicted of murdering his baby boy. The infant had suffered a fatal skull fracture, sustained in all probability by being thrown head-first against a wall. One point contested on appeal was the admissibility of evidence that the accused was often irascible towards his child, and that the child had sustained other injuries in the weeks preceding his death. The Court of Appeal ruled that the evidence fell outside the ambit of the common law prohibition on extraneous misconduct evidence and had been properly admitted at trial; though it was added that the court retained a residual common law discretion to exclude evidence if its probative value was exceeded by its likely prejudicial effect.[210] Examples of less meticulous judicial approaches can also be found. During Rosemary West's high-profile trial in the 25 Cromwell Street 'House of Horror' case,[211] leading to her conviction of 10 counts of murder, witnesses testified at great length and in lurid detail to husband Fred and Rose's sexual deviancy, prostitution, and violent and sexual abuse of their daughters and other victims. The Court of Appeal rebuffed all objections to this evidence, including prejudicial revelations of the accused's lesbianism which the Court of Appeal conceded were strictly irrelevant.[212] A parallel might be drawn with the admission of evidence of multiple instances of the accused's mistreatment of Jewish prisoners in the contemporary English war crimes prosecution of *Sawoniuk*.[213] Once again, the Court of Appeal condoned the presentation of wide-ranging misconduct evidence to the jury, but on this occasion suggested that its admissibility rested on the 'broader basis' of background evidence rather than qualifying as evidence of 'similar facts'. Finally in *Mackie*, where the accused was charged with the manslaughter of his step-son, the Court of Appeal asserted that the trial judge was perfectly entitled, in his discretion, to admit evidence of the accused's misconduct even where the 'prejudicial effect of the evidence admitted

---

[206]   *O'Leary* v *R* (1946) 73 CLR 566, 577, HCA (Dixon J).

[207]   See, e.g., *Phipson on Evidence* (15th edn. 2000), ch 34; P. B. Carter, *Cases and Statutes on Evidence* (Sweet & Maxwell, 2nd edn. 1990), 354.

[208]   The doctrine of *res gestae* was discussed in §9.6(b).

[209]   *R* v *Fulcher* [1995] 2 Cr App R 251, CA.

[210]   'It went to the *actus reus* and the *mens rea*. It was not intended as evidence of similar facts, and any objection to it on the basis that it was similar fact evidence would have been misconceived … Of course, a court always has power to exclude evidence which it finds to be more prejudicial than probative': ibid. 257, 258.

[211]   See, e.g., Alex Bellos, 'The House of Horror Vanishes,' *The Guardian*, 8 October 1996; Cheryl Stonehouse, So Ordinary Yet So Evil; Beyond Belief… The Depraved Web of Rose West House of Horror: Verdict – Ordinary But Evil Rosemary West Guilty on all 10 Charges of Murder,' *Daily Mirror*, 23 November 1995. One of the Wests' victims was Martin Amis's cousin, Lucy Partington. Amis weaves this family tragedy into his memoir *Experience* (Vintage, 2001).

[212]   Cf. Richard Duce, 'West "was convicted on non-existent evidence"', *The Times*, 19 March 1996.

[213]   *R* v *Sawoniuk* [2000] 2 Cr App R 220, CA, previously discussed (in relation to a different point) in §3.4(c). For a detailed account of the trial, see David Hirsch, *Law Against Genocide: Cosmopolitan Trials* (Glasshouse, 2003), ch 6.

was enormous and far outweighed its value in proving that the child was frightened of the defendant'.[214]

Rather than focusing squarely on the substantive balance of probative value and prejudicial effect, the old common law authorities sometimes dissipated their energies in debating the proper scope of legal classifications or in quibbling over technicalities, such as whether the prohibition on extraneous misconduct evidence was properly characterized as a rule of admissibility or merely as a judicial 'discretion'. Common law experience also demonstrates the importance of considering the *uses* that the jury might make of probative misconduct evidence *after it has been admitted into the trial*. The task of neutralizing risks of unfair prejudice in such circumstances rests partly on the judge's direction to the jury, explaining how jurors should incorporate misconduct evidence into their deliberations.[215] This is best achieved, not by lecturing the jury like naughty schoolchildren, but by helping jurors to appreciate the values animating criminal adjudication and to fortify themselves against the temptations of prejudice. As the respected American Evidence scholar Judge Jack Weinstein observed many years ago:[216]

The rules of evidence can do little, by themselves, to prevent conscious distortions by the trier. They should, however, permit all possible relevant evidence and argument to be brought to bear on the trier so that he will at least be forced to bare his soul to himself and to consciously, though silently, justify his actions.

Conversely, jurors will not be disposed to defer to a legal standard which they either cannot comprehend or which fails to engage their sympathies by appearing to contradict common sense reasoning. This hard-won wisdom should continue to inform the law of bad character evidence under the CJA 2003. Questions of admissibility may recede in importance to the extent that alternative procedural tools and evidentiary mechanisms are developed for counteracting prejudice.[217]

Given the laxity of the pre-existing common law, gateway (c) might plausibly be regarded as retaining or even raising the bar to admissibility for background evidence. Although subsection 101(3)'s general fairness criterion does not apply to gateway (c), section 102 does specify that bad character evidence must have 'substantial' value 'for understanding the case as a whole', which presumably rules out bad character evidence with marginal probative value. Allowing[218] that any residual exclusionary discretion at common law has been abolished by

---

[214] *R v Mackie* (1973) 57 Cr App R 453, 464, CA. The authority of this *dictum* was always doubtful, and it was implicitly rejected in subsequent cases such as *R v Fulcher* [1995] 2 Cr App R 251, CA.

[215] See, to similar effect, Rajiv Nair, 'Weighing Similar Fact and Avoiding Prejudice' (1996) 112 *LQR* 262.

[216] Jack B. Weinstein, 'Some Difficulties in Devising Rules for Determining Truth in Judicial Trials,' (1966) 66 *Columbia LR* 223, 238.

[217] Also note the prosecuting counsel's professional duty to eschew unnecessarily emotive language which might 'excite sympathy for the victim or prejudice against the accused in the minds of the jury': *R v Francis (Hassana)*, CA Trans. 2000/2901/25, 8 November 2000, [52], quoting *Archbold*. Prosecuting counsel should regard themselves as ministers of justice: see *R v Banks* (1916) 12 Cr App R 74, 76, CCA; and discussion in §2.3(c)(iv).

[218] This concession is not inevitable, because s.99 refers to 'common law *rules* governing the *admissibility* of evidence', as opposed to exclusionary judicial *discretions*. But the Court of Appeal has, in general, deprecated technical, logic-chopping interpretations of the CJA 2003, preferring instead broadly-based, 'common sense' interpretations orientated towards the interests of justice, which appear to exclude 'technical' defence arguments perceived as lacking substantive merit: see, e.g., *R v Adams (Ishmael)* [2008] 1 Cr App R 35, [2007] EWCA Crim 3025.

section 99 of the CJA 2003, section 78 of PACE 1984 still applies to any evidence, including evidence of bad character, on which the prosecution 'proposes to rely'; and beyond that, a fair trial-based argument is not inconceivable where egregiously prejudicial bad character evidence has been admitted into the trial.[219] To the extent that the problem of background evidence at common law concerned information 'having to do with' the facts of the instant case, gateway (c) might not be apposite to the extent that such information does not even qualify as 'bad character' within section 98's controlling definition. It follows (albeit perhaps somewhat paradoxically) that section 99 cannot possibly have abolished the residual common law discretion announced in cases such as *Fulcher* which applies to this species of background evidence.

The CJA 2003 in no way restricts the freedom of the trial judge to spell out to the jury the dangers of prejudicial reasoning and moral prejudice in relation to admissible evidence of the accused's misconduct. Explicit articulation of the risks might also help trial judges to resist their own visceral reactions to the accused's bad character, and would contribute towards satisfying principles of open justice and accountability, reinforcing the particularized duties to give reasons imposed by section 110. Whenever potentially prejudicial information is before the jury, whether it emerged unexpectedly in the course of the trial or only after searching judicial scrutiny following a challenge to its admissibility, appropriately formulated judicial directions to the jury remain an essential legal instrument for taming the scourge of prejudice in criminal adjudication.

(c) GATEWAY (f): EVIDENCE TO CORRECT A FALSE IMPRESSION

Paragraph (f) of section 101 of the CJA 2003 authorizes the admission of prosecution[220] evidence of the accused's bad character where 'it is evidence to correct a false impression given by the defendant'. Gateway (f) is amplified by section 105.

Section 105 states, first of all, that a defendant gives a false impression 'if he is responsible for the making of an express or implied assertion which is apt to give the court or jury a false or misleading impression about the defendant'.[221] Crucially, then, gateway (f) is concerned with false impressions that the accused gives *about himself*, not deception at large (which would have given gateway (f) a vastly expanded potential field of application). Secondly, 'evidence to correct such an impression is evidence which has probative value in correcting it'[222] and 'goes no further than is necessary to correct the false impression'.[223] Subsection 105(2) lists the following circumstances in which the accused is to be treated as 'being responsible for making an assertion' giving a false impression:

(a) the assertion is made by the defendant in the proceedings (whether or not in evidence given by him),

(b) the assertion was made by the defendant—

    (i) on being questioned under caution, before charge, about the offence with which he is charged, or

    (ii) on being charged with the offence or officially informed that he might be prosecuted for it,

and evidence of the assertion is given in the proceedings,

---

[219] Cf. *R v A (No 2)* [2002] 1 AC 45, HL.

[220] Subsection 105(7) provides that, '[o]nly prosecution evidence is admissible under section 101(1)(f)'.

[221] Section 105(1)(a).   [222] Section 105(1)(b).   [223] Section 105(6).

(c) the assertion is made by a witness called by the defendant,

(d) the assertion is made by any witness in cross-examination in response to a question asked by the defendant that is intended to elicit it, or is likely to do so, or

(e) the assertion was made by any person out of court, and the defendant adduces evidence of it in the proceedings.

Moreover, '[w]here it appears to the court that a defendant, by means of his conduct (other than the giving of evidence) in the proceedings, is seeking to give the court or jury an impression about himself that is false or misleading, the court may if it appears just to do so treat the defendant as being responsible for the making of an assertion which is apt to give that impression'.[224] 'Conduct' for these purposes 'includes appearance or dress'.[225] In every case, however, the accused must have the opportunity explicitly to disavow or disown the false impression and pre-empt any rebuttal by the prosecution. Subsection 105(3) provides that, '[a] defendant who would otherwise be treated as responsible for the making of an assertion shall not be so treated if, or to the extent that, he withdraws it or disassociates himself from it'.

Gateway (f) largely replicates, though in some incidental ways also extends and improves upon, the pre-existing law of bad character. The paradigmatic forensic illustration of giving 'a false or misleading impression' is fraudulent evidence of the accused's 'good character', which the prosecution is now entitled to rebut under gateway (f), as amplified by section 105. Since the CJA 2003's character evidence provisions are expressly limited to evidence of *bad* character, it is still necessary to consult the common law in order to make sense of gateway (f).

(i) Good character at common law

Counsel are not normally allowed to lead evidence bolstering the credit of their own witnesses.[226] However, by way of a special exception (or indulgence) stretching back at least into the seventeenth century and possibly much further, an accused has been permitted to lead evidence of 'good character' and call 'character witnesses' to testify to his general moral virtues.[227] In modern times this means that an accused is entitled to a judicial direction informing the jury of his good character whenever the accused has a clean police record.

An obvious interpretation of good character evidence is that it supports the accused's credibility as a witness in his own defence. The accused is presenting himself to the jury as, literally, 'a good character' (a 'good egg'; a 'sterling chap', etc.), whose testimony merits additional weight on that account. But credibility cannot logically have been at the historical root of good character evidence, which was permitted before those standing trial generally became competent witnesses in their own defence pursuant to the Criminal Evidence Act 1898.[228] It follows that good character evidence must originally have gone

---

[224] Section 105(4).   [225] Section 105(5).

[226] *R v Turner* [1975] QB 834, CA; an alternative formulation of the rule against narrative: see §8.3.

[227] A modern example is *R v Ananthanarayanan* (1994) 98 Cr App R 1, CA, where the accused called no less than seven consultants, a nursing manager, a matron in a private home, a professor of psychiatry, four nurses, two occupational therapists, a clinical psychologist and a senior probation officer, all of whom testified to his professionalism, personal integrity, and courteous behaviour towards women.

[228] The practice was already well-established by the time that the Court for Crown Cases Reserved delivered its well-known decision in *R v Rowton* (1865) 34 LJMC 57, 10 Cox CC 25. James Fitzjames Stephen

directly to the issue, not to credit. It must, in other words, have been taken to show that an accused of good character was *eo ipso* less likely to have committed the offence with which he was charged than a person of lesser moral credentials.

The evidential significance of good character was debated throughout the twentieth century. There was high judicial authority that good character evidence goes directly to the issue of guilt or innocence,[229] but this was doubted on other occasions. The point was reconsidered by Lord Taylor CJ in *Vye*,[230] where it was established that a good character direction has two components: first, the jury must be told that an accused of good character is less likely to have committed the offence charged because he has no known propensity to offend; secondly, in any case where the accused testifies or has made an admissible out-of-court statement, the jury must also be told that the accused's testimony or statement is more likely to be true because he is a person of good character. In other words, evidence of good character goes to the issue *and* to credit, whenever the accused's testimonial credibility is in issue in the trial.

Judges are well aware, of course, that the fact that the accused has no previous convictions does not literally mean that he is a good person with admirable character traits. It does not even necessarily prove that he is not a professional criminal; only that he has never previously been caught. But in formal legal terms it is now settled[231] that a good character direction has two limbs, both of which must be spelt out for the benefit of the jury: good character is evidence suggesting lack of criminal propensity in every case, and in addition enhances the accused's credibility whenever he testifies or adduces any out-of-court statement. Trial judges are free to depart from this stricture only where a direction in these terms would be absurd, for example where the accused has already admitted a lesser offence in the proceedings and can no longer claim never to have broken the law, even though he has no prior police record.[232] The Court of Appeal has recently reiterated that, '[t]he good character direction is appropriate to those who are, or who the judge rules may be treated as if they are, those without known bad character of any kind. It does not extend automatically also to those whose bad character exists, but is not of sufficient probative value or relevance to be admitted against them. Still less does it extend to those whose bad character is excluded as a matter of discretion.'[233]

---

identified *Colonel Turner's case* (1664) 6 How St Tr 565, 613, as the first recorded example; cited by Viscount Simon LC in *Stirland* v *DPP* [1944] AC 315, 325, HL.

[229] In *Maxwell* v *DPP* [1935] AC 309, 319, HL, Viscount Sankey LC stated that an accused who calls evidence of good character does so 'for the purpose of showing that it is unlikely that he committed the offence charged'. Also see *R* v *Naudeer* (1985) 80 Cr App R 9, CA.

[230] *R* v *Vye; Wise; Stephenson* (1993) 97 Cr App R 134, CA, approved by *R* v *Aziz* [1996] 1 AC 41, HL.

[231] In *R* v *Vye* (1993) 97 Cr App R 134, 139, CA, Lord Taylor CJ dropped the following heavy hint that the Court of Appeal would not be well-disposed to a flood of appeals based on supposed defects in good character directions: 'Provided that the judge indicates to the jury the two respects in which good character may be relevant, i.e. credibility and propensity, this court will be slow to criticise any qualifying remarks he may make based on the facts of the individual case.'

[232] *R* v *Teasdale* (1994) 99 Cr App R 80, CA; *R* v *Challenger* [1994] Crim LR 202, CA. It is no objection in multi-party trials that a good character direction in favour of one accused will have an adverse impact on a co-accused with previous convictions, about whose character the judge remains silent and leaves the jury to draw its own conclusions: *R* v *Cain* [1994] 1 WLR 1449, CA.

[233] *R* v *Lawson* [2007] 1 WLR 1191, [2006] EWCA Crim 2572, [40]. Also see *R* v *Doncaster* [2008] EWCA Crim 5, [2008] Crim LR 709. For general discussion, see Roderick Munday, 'Judicial Studies Board Specimen

A third possible function of good character evidence, running beyond its relevance to propensity and credibility, has attracted a modicum of academic commentary[234] but remains virtually invisible in formal legal terms. In adducing good character evidence the accused might be regarded as inviting the jury to consider, in a rather loose and wide-ranging sense, his general moral character and standing in the community, to judge, as it were, the person rather than the offence before condemning him as a criminal. In this register, proof of good character constitutes a plea for recognition, clemency, or deliverance. It might even be conceptualized as a direct appeal to jury equity or 'nullification', at least by those who regard temporary suspension of the criminal law as a legitimate, if residual, aspect of trial by jury.[235]

Affording such an expansive significance to evidence of good character, however, is plainly in tension with the principle of confining the evidence to the charge. It is far from clear whether this forensic strategy should be open to an accused at all. Pleas in mitigation are conventionally confined to the sentencing stage, after issues of legal guilt and innocence have already been determined, but the point at issue runs deeper than formal compliance with orthodox procedural arrangements. An accused who invokes the general moral calculus exposes himself to the risk of an unfavourable accounting. Yet convictions resting substantially on evidence of general bad character are incompatible with the foundational principles of criminal evidence, even if the instigator of the moral contest is the accused himself. Conscientious jurors should strive towards a dispassionate evaluation of the evidence adduced in the trial, and refuse to convict unless the charge is proved beyond reasonable doubt on the basis of reliable evidence. Judicial directions on good character should be fashioned accordingly, with their emphasis on probative value.

(ii) Rebutting good character evidence under the CJA 2003

Section 105 of the CJA 2003 was drafted with the benefit of previous experience, good and bad. Like all highly contextual, multi-factorial decision-making, the question whether the accused has put his character in issue ought to be determined by the trial judge's exercise of judgment rather than by application of mechanical general rules. The legal regime for correcting false impressions introduced by the CJA 2003 is appropriately open-ended, and free of the interpretational baggage accumulated by its statutory predecessor.[236]

Section 105 prescribes that a false impression may be given by conduct as well as through testimony.[237] This covers situations in which good character is effectively asserted by implication, as where the accused appears in the dock in military uniform – with or without his medals for bravery – or wearing a vicar's dog collar[238] or mayoral chain of office, and clearly intending to convey the air of an upright pillar of the community. In Renda,[239] the accused told the jury that he had sustained a serious head injury, leading to long-term brain damage, whilst serving in Her Majesty's Armed Forces. Whilst this was

---

Directions and the Enforcement of Orthodoxy: A Modest Case Study' (2002) 66 *Journal of Criminal Law* 158; Roderick Munday, 'What Constitutes a Good Character?' [1997] *Crim LR* 247.

[234] Going back at least to William Wills, *Theory and Practice of the Law of Evidence* (Stevens, 1894), 56–7.

[235] Jury equity was discussed in §2.4.

[236] Proviso (f)(ii) of the Criminal Evidence Act 1898 (now repealed).   [237] Section 105(4) and (5).

[238] Cf. *R v Ferguson* (1909) 2 Cr App R 250, CCA (good character implicitly asserted by professions of religious piety, e.g. regular attendance at mass).

[239] *R v Renda* [2006] 1 WLR 2948, [2005] EWCA Crim 2826.

all true, technically speaking, it was also misleading, because the head injury had been sustained in a car accident whilst the accused was on holiday, rather than whilst serving Queen and country on active service as his testimony appeared to imply. The Court of Appeal found that the accused was 'plainly seeking to convey that he was a man of positive good character'.[240] Conversely, the accused should not be taken to imply that he has no relevant previous convictions simply because he denies the current charge or positively asserts that the complaint against him is malicious.[241] To proceed otherwise would be tantamount to treating a plea of 'not guilty' as an assertion of good character, with the further implication that the accused's record would be revealed to the jury automatically in virtually every case. The situation is different again in the more complex scenarios thrown up by cut-throat defences, where allegations against a co-accused might well be interpreted, on the facts, as assertions of good character by implication. If *D1* adduces *D2*'s previous convictions of burglary in their current joint trial for burglary, she could be taken to be asserting '*D2* is the burglar, not me!', thus triggering admissibility of her own burglary-related record through gateway (f).[242]

Under section 105(3) the accused may withdraw or dissociate himself from any assertion for which he would otherwise be held responsible. This was a welcome statutory innovation, providing an elegant solution for the problem of unintentional assertions of good character, which sometimes slip out, for example, in the testimony of a well-meaning but misinformed defence witness.[243] Rather than making the accused suffer for a forensic accident, the accused can simply say that he never meant to convey the contested impression, and the matter ends there without creating any additional risk of prejudice. However, the Court of Appeal has said that the disavowal must be voluntary and unambiguous.[244] Having the truth wrung out of him on cross-examination did not save the accused in *Renda* from having previous incidents of violence adduced through gateway (f), where his subsequent concessions had been grudging and incomplete. Sir Igor Judge P. warned that, '[a] concession extracted in cross-examination that the defendant was not telling the truth in part of his examination-in-chief will not normally amount to a withdrawal or dissociation from the original assertion for the purposes of section 105(3)'.[245]

A potentially more troubling innovation was the extension of gateway (f) to the accused's pre-trial assertions during police questioning under caution or on being charged with the offence.[246] This provision has the effect of extending the forensic contest deep into pre-trial proceedings, to a procedural stage where the accused (then merely a suspect) may lack adequate legal advice. A careless boast or half-truth uttered to police officers could

---

[240] ibid. [19].   [241] *R v Hanson* (*Pickstone*'s case) [2005] 2 Cr App R 21, [2005] EWCA Crim 824.

[242] The validity of this line of reasoning was acknowledged in *R v Bovell* (*Dowds*' case) [2005] EWCA Crim 1091, [32]. Its logic was anticipated by the pre-CJA 2003 decision in *R v Bracewell* (1978) 68 Cr App R 44, CA.

[243] There was no penalty under the CEA 1898 if the witness merely spontaneously volunteered his favourable opinion of the accused: *R v Redd* [1923] 1 KB 104, CCA. Similarly, allusion to one conviction does not imply the absence of others, and is not evidence of good character at common law: *R v Thompson* [1966] 1 WLR 405, CCA.   [244] *R v Renda* [2006] 1 WLR 2948, [2005] EWCA Crim 2826, [21].

[245] ibid. [21].

[246] Section 105(2)(b). A further condition is that evidence of the assertion must be given in the proceedings, though this is anyway implicit in the notion of an assertion 'which is apt to give the court or jury a false or misleading impression about the defendant'. The jury cannot be misled by an assertion of which it is wholly ignorant.

later come back to bite the accused in court. Part of the answer may be that the accused would be well advised to refrain from repeating misleading assertions during the trial, but that is an incomplete response. The accused's pre-trial comments could be adduced by the prosecution in the form of a 'mixed statement',[247] for example, or by a co-accused. In that event, however, the accused still has the option of disassociating himself from any misleading impression.

What if, for some reason, the accused is unable or unwilling to dissociate himself from misleading impressions? Perhaps he disputes the premiss, has different standards of 'good' character, or simply prefers to try to brazen it out. This is where the CJA 2003 made one of its most valuable, if modest, contributions to law reform. At common law, character was regarded as 'indivisible'.[248] This meant that, as soon as the accused's bad character became admissible (for example, where the accused lost his 'shield' under the Criminal Evidence Act 1898), his entire police record became fair game for cross-examination. The net effect could be wholly disproportionate and unjustifiably punitive to the defence.[249] On charges of sexual assault, for example, the accused's previous convictions of sexual offences which everyone agreed were not admissible as 'similar facts' in-chief under *Boardman*[250] or *DPP* v *P*[251] could subsequently become admissible during cross-examination of the accused, ostensibly as material going primarily[252] to his credibility as a witness. By limiting rebuttal evidence under gateway (f) to information that 'goes no further than is necessary to correct the false impression'[253] the CJA 2003 brought the curtain down on this legal playacting. If the accused tries to present himself as something he is not, that specific misrepresentation can be corrected and the record set straight, but evidence of good character no longer presents the prosecution with unlimited licence to damn the accused for his past misdeeds.

With character now divisible, trial judges may restrict admissibility to those aspects of the accused's extraneous misconduct with probative value in correcting a false impression. This is consistent with the new, post-CJA 2003 emphasis on logical relevance as a precondition of the admissibility of bad character evidence announced by the Court of Appeal in *Hanson*[254] and emphatically reiterated in *Campbell*.[255] If the accused claims that he would never behave dishonestly, for example, the prosecution should be allowed to show that he has previous convictions of theft or other dishonesty offences, but not

---

[247] Mixed statements were explained in §12.3(b).

[248] *R v Winfield* [1939] 4 All ER 164, 165, CCA, *per* Humphreys J: 'there is no such thing known to our procedure as putting half a prisoner's character in issue and leaving out the other half. A prisoner, who has a bad character for dishonesty, is not entitled to say that he has never acted indecently towards women and claim that he has not put the rest of his character in issue.'

[249] Trial judges did, however, retain a discretion to restrain cross-examination which might be utilized to prevent prosecutorial overkill in responding to assertions of good character: *Maxwell* v *DPP* [1935] AC 309, HL.   [250] *DPP* v *Boardman* [1975] AC 421, HL.

[251] *DPP* v *P* [1991] 2 AC 447, HL.

[252] The precise effect of evidence rebutting good character, whether it went only to credibility as the prevailing orthodoxy maintained or – more logically, in the light of *Rowton* – to the issues as well, was never conclusively settled at common law: see, e.g., *R v Richardson and Longman* [1969] 1 QB 299, CA; cf. *R v Samuel* (1956) 40 Cr App R 8, 12; *R v Inder* (1977) 67 Cr App R 143, 146, CA; and generally, Rosemary Pattenden, 'The Purpose of Cross-Examination Under Section 1(f) of the Criminal Evidence Act 1898' [1982] *Crim LR* 707.   [253] Section 105(6).

[254] *R v Hanson* [2005] 2 Cr App R 21, [2005] EWCA Crim 824.

[255] *R v Campbell (Kenneth)* [2007] 1 WLR 2798, [2007] EWCA Crim 1472.

that he has been convicted of cruelty to animals or dangerous driving. Other cases may require more fine-grained contextual analysis of what, exactly, is required to correct particular false impressions. Once the accused has opened up an issue, the trial judge may well decide to allow the prosecution to lay the entire matter before the jury, and the defence will not necessarily be able to confine further related revelations to its best strategic advantage.[256] In this more restricted sense, the accused risks incurring a forensic penalty by giving the jury a false impression about himself. Whilst section 101(3) plainly does not apply to gateway (f), the clear preponderance of Court of Appeal authority states that gateway (f) is subject to PACE 1984, s.78,[257] so this may well be a formal distinction without a difference. Though admitting corrective evidence through gateway (f) will still inevitably expose the accused to an increased risk of unfair prejudice, inasmuch as bad character evidence always carries this implication, the risk is justified where information about his antecedents would be significantly probative on the current charge, in light of the way in which the case is being run. Rather than withholding this information from the jury and allowing the accused to benefit illegitimately from a false impression the remedy is to admit the evidence subject to appropriate judicial instructions on its proper, and improper, uses.

(d) GATEWAY (g): TIT-FOR-TAT RETALIATION FOR AN ATTACK ON ANOTHER PERSON'S CHARACTER

Gateway (g) authorizes the admission of bad character evidence adduced by the prosecution[258] where 'the defendant has made an attack on another person's character'.[259] Section 106(1) of the CJA 2003 provides further elucidation:

For the purposes of section 101(1)(g) a defendant makes an attack on another person's character if –
  (a) he adduces evidence attacking the other person's character,
  (b) he … asks questions in cross-examination that are intended to elicit such evidence, or are likely to do so, or
  (c) evidence is given of an imputation about the other person made by the defendant –
      (i)   on being questioned under caution, before charge, about the offence with which he is charged, or
      (ii) on being charged with the offence or officially informed that he might be prosecuted for it.

Attacking another person's character is further defined by section 106(2) to mean alleging that another person has committed any criminal offence or 'has behaved, or is disposed to behave, in a reprehensible way'. This clearly echoes the 2003 Act's definition (to the extent that it gives one) of 'bad character'.[260] In contrast to gateway (f), gateway (g) does not contain a dedicated proportionality criterion restricting the scope of rebuttal evidence. Section 101(1)(g) is, however, subject to the fairness test brought into play by a

---

[256] R v Weir (*Somanathan's* case) [2006] 1 WLR 1885, [2005] EWCA Crim 2866, [43].

[257] See, e.g., ibid. [44]: 'we see no reason to doubt that section 78 of the 1984 Act should be considered where section 101(1)(f) is relied upon…'.

[258] Gateway (g) is limited to prosecution evidence: s.106(3).   [259] Section 101(1)(g).

[260] Sections 98 and 112(1).

defence application under section 101(3), which (as we have seen) replicates the language of section 78 of PACE 1984.

Gateway (g) is closely modelled on a parallel provision of the Criminal Evidence Act 1898, which was triggered by an 'imputation' on the character of the complainant, a prosecution witness, or the deceased victim of the offence.[261] After the CJA 2003 we must speak primarily of 'attacks on character' rather than 'imputations',[262] but the essential idea remains the same. Loss of the accused's character shield for casting an imputation on the character of a prosecution witness was one of the most controversial aspects of the old law of character evidence, and the retention of this doctrine is one of the least satisfactory aspects of the CJA 2003. Indeed, in one significant respect the CJA 2003 has made matters much worse. Before examining its operation in practice, we first need to consider what, exactly, gateway (g) is supposed to achieve.

(i) Two rationales: tit-for-tat vs. no-stymie

There are, in essence, two competing rationales for revealing the accused's bad character in response to his attacks on the character of prosecution witnesses. The first, more respectable, rationale emphasizes evidential completeness and transparency of proof. On this view, the jury should be informed of the character of a person making an imputation in order to assess the merits of that person's attack on the credit of another witness. In deciding whom to believe, it might be said, the jury must undertake a comparative assessment of the relative moral probity of the witness (or complainant or deceased victim) and the accused who makes the attack. Thus, Stephen Seabrooke argued that if 'the accused attacks the character of a prosecution witness and there is no tit-for-tat response by the prosecution, the net effect will often be the creation of a false impression in the mind of a juror'.[263]

The argument is at its most convincing where the accused himself goes into the witnessbox and personally assaults the credit of a prosecution witness. In these circumstances one might infer that the accused is effectively seeking to bolster his own testimony by suggesting that the evidence of a witness with bad character is less believable by comparison. If the accused's own character is bad, however, the prosecution ought to be entitled to bring this out, at least to the extent necessary to 'set the record straight' regarding the character of the person casting aspersions on others.

A second, less respectable but nonetheless pervasively and almost insidiously influential, rationale boils down to retaliatory tit-for-tat. Bluntly, if the accused decides to start slinging mud at a witness he deserves to have the same treatment meted out to him, in spades. Additionally, the threat of retaliation in kind might be regarded as a deterrent to gratuitous and insulting imputations on the character of complainants or prosecution witnesses. Perhaps the best that can be said for the tit-for-tat argument is that feelings

---

[261] This provision will always be known as the second limb of s.1(f)(ii) to the CEA 1898, although it was technically – briefly and entirely pointlessly – re-designated s.1(3)(ii) by the Youth Justice and Criminal Evidence Act 1999, s.67(1) and sch.4, s.1. The words 'or the deceased victim of the alleged crime' were inserted into s.1(f)(ii) by the Criminal Justice and Public Order Act 1994, s.31: see Roderick Munday, 'One Example of Law-Making' [1995] *NLJ* 855 and 895 (9 and 16 June).

[262] Although subss.106(1)(c) and (2) still refer to 'imputation', possibly out of nostalgia.

[263] Stephen Seabrooke, 'Closing the Credibility Gap: A New Approach to Section 1(f)(ii) of the Criminal Evidence Act 1898' [1987] *Crim LR* 231, 232.

of righteous indignation are entirely understandable when an accused with an appalling criminal history and vicious character sets out to blacken the reputation of a witness or complainant who is in every respect his moral superior. Why this should have any bearing on the trial of the issue is more puzzling, however. By attacking the credibility of a prosecution witness the accused is not necessarily inviting judgment on his general moral character almost irrespective of the evidence in the case, as might sometimes be inferred when the accused adduces evidence of his own good character. On a less indulgent interpretation, the tit-for-tat rationale regresses to the 'talionic "justice" of the playground (you bash me, I bash you back)'.[264]

Tit-for-tat is especially objectionable when it encroaches upon what Peter Mirfield conveniently christened the 'no-stymie principle'.[265] No-stymie holds that all the parties to criminal proceedings, prosecution as well as defence, should be allowed to present any evidence crucial to their respective case 'stories' free of any unreasonable impediment or disincentive and without incurring any procedural penalty. This principle reflects the criminal trial's fundamental aspiration to factually accurate verdicts, with the further implication that any gratuitous interference with effective truth-finding should be eliminated. More precisely, the no-stymie principle implies a functional distinction between 'general' and 'specific' credibility – the latter relating directly to the contents of the witness's testimony in the current proceedings. Under a no-stymie regime, the accused would be allowed to attack a prosecution witness's 'specific credibility' with impunity, for example by alleging that the witness has framed the accused in order to claim reward money or to cover up the witness's own involvement in the crime. Imputations on a witness's 'general credibility', exemplified by cross-examination regarding the witness's extraneous bad character or criminal antecedents to establish general lack of veracity, would be the only kind of imputation capable of triggering a tit-for-tat response.

The significance of an imputation is not simply a function of the words spoken. An allegation such as 'the witness is a thief' may vary in significance depending on the facts of the case and the course of the trial. A particularistic, contextual inquiry is consequently required in order to differentiate legitimate developments of the defence case from strategically gratuitous attacks on the character of prosecution witnesses. Imagine that a prosecution witness has testified that he observed the accused committing the crime from a distance of thirty yards. If the accused testifies that the witness has defective eyesight and cannot see clearly at that distance, the accused is not impugning the witness's entire moral credibility and no question of retaliatory cross-examination should arise. Suppose now that the accused goes on the offensive by claiming that the witness has testified falsely to satisfy a grudge. Although an allegation of malicious perjury indubitably impugns the character of an opposing witness, it should not signal 'open season' on the accused's entire record. Cross-examination should in principle be limited to investigating the accused's specific allegation of a grudge, which may or may not implicate his antecedents, or some of them, depending on the material facts. To the extent that this investigation might incidentally reveal the accused's previous convictions or extraneous bad character, the accused has no real grounds for complaint, having chosen to raise the issue himself. The

---

[264] Paul Roberts, 'All the Usual Suspects: A Critical Appraisal of Law Commission Consultation Paper No 141' [1997] *Crim LR* 75, 91.

[265] Peter Mirfield 'The Argument from Consistency for Overruling *Selvey*' (1991) 50 *CLJ* 490.

no-stymie principle insists that the prosecution must be allowed to put its case, which includes probing any line of defence put forward by the accused. But unlimited, tit-for-tat cross-examination to credit would only serve to damn the accused with prejudicial bad character evidence that might well be, and prior to the CJA 2003 would have been, inadmissible for the prosecution in-chief.

What if the accused raises the stakes even higher, by attacking the witness's general moral standing as well as her particularized probative credibility? The accused now invites the jury to conclude that the witness is such a venal or depraved character that they cannot credit a word she says. A no-holds-barred moral contest between witness and accused should nonetheless still be avoided if at all possible. The principle of confining the evidence to the charge mandates that a criminal trial should not be a free-ranging contest of comparative virtue – a medieval 'swearing match', pitting oath against oath – but a trial of specific charges that the prosecution must prove beyond reasonable doubt. To the extent that the moral character of a prosecution witness is put in issue in the proceedings, the witness's character could be judged on its own merits without automatically making the accused's relative moral standing a factor in the equation. Admittedly, there are certain situations in which it is difficult, in practice, to maintain sharp distinctions between general and specific credibility, or between a witness's moral character and that of the accused. Cases of 'one person's word against another's', such as the depressingly familiar 'date rape' scenario, immediately spring to mind. Even here, however, the trial should not be allowed to degenerate into a general moral contest unless, at the least, it is abundantly clear that the accused has chosen to take the fight beyond the realms of the strictly probative, so that, having put his own moral character on the line through a deliberate forensic strategy of attacking a prosecution witness's moral character, it is necessary to ventilate the accused's extraneous misconduct in order to set the moral record straight.[266]

The no-stymie principle received implicit recognition in several old common law authorities,[267] and attracted strong endorsement from law reformers, including the Law Commission, in more recent times.[268] However, the House of Lords expressly rejected it in *Selvey*,[269] on the basis that a consistent principled distinction could not be drawn between permissible and impressible imputations, at least not without affording the accused an excessively generous sphere of immunity which, it was said, would be unfair to the prosecution. Lord Pearce feared that 'there would be no limit to the amount of mud which could be thrown against an unshielded prosecutor [i.e. complainant] while the accused could

---

[266] The Court of Appeal came close to adopting this rationale in *R v St Louis and Fitzroy* (1984) 79 Cr App R 53.

[267] In *R v Preston* [1909] 1 KB 568, 575, CCA, Channell J said that, 'if the defence is so conducted... as to involve the proposition that the jury ought not to believe the prosecutor or one of the witnesses for the prosecution upon the ground that his conduct – *not his evidence in the case, but his conduct outside the evidence given by him* – makes him an unreliable witness, then the jury ought also to know the character of the prisoner who either gives that evidence or makes that charge...' (emphasis supplied). Sir Rupert Cross viewed this *dictum* as authoritative: *Cross on Evidence* (Butterworths, 5th edn. 1979), 433.

[268] Law Com No 273, *Evidence of Bad Character in Criminal Proceedings*. Cm. 5257 (TSO, 2001), paras.7.4–7.7 and 8.20–8.28. The CLRC's 'necessity' test ('was it *necessary* for the defendant to make the imputation as an incidental part of his defence?') and the Runciman Royal Commission's 'centrality' test can also be understood as attempts to extend the no-stymie principle to defence imputations on a prosecution witness: see CLRC Eleventh Report, *Evidence: General*. Cm. 4991 (HMSO, 1972); Royal Commission on Criminal Justice (Chairman: Viscount Runciman of Doxford), *Report*, Cm.2263 (HMSO, 1993), Chapter 8, para.33.

[269] *Selvey* v *DPP* [1970] AC 304, HL.

still crouch behind his own shield'.[270] Prosecution witnesses were, apparently, to be protected from disparaging imputations by threatening the accused with trial by bad character should he have the temerity to make, by definition relevant,[271] objections to the conduct or character of an opposing witness. The upshot was that the accused would expose himself to wide-ranging cross-examination on his entire police record and general bad character whenever his defence involved making counter-claims against the complainant, as in *Selvey* itself where, on a charge of buggery, the accused testified that the complainant had propositioned *him* by offering sex for a £1. The same result followed whenever the defence case included allegations of impropriety in the conduct of the proceedings, as where the accused claimed that his confession, or parts of it, had been fabricated by the police.[272] The accused's only protection was a residual exclusionary discretion, expressly preserved by the House of Lords,[273] but in practice seldom exercised in the accused's favour.[274]

The ruling in *Selvey* placed any accused person with previous convictions in an invidious position, since even a truthful defence necessarily involving imputations could amount to forensic suicide. Besides its adverse impact on the fairness of the trial, this arrangement was a standing invitation for corrupt police officers to cook up or embellish confessions, safe in the knowledge that an accused with previous convictions would not be able to mount an effective challenge unless he testified at his trial and submitted to cross-examination on his record.[275]

An important, countervailing restriction is implicit in this critical summary of the pre-CJA 2003 law. The accused did not lose his character shield under the 1898 Act, and so become subject to cross-examination on his record, *unless he elected to testify in his own defence*. If imputations were directly suggested to prosecution witnesses by defence counsel during their cross-examination, or otherwise elicited through the testimony of defence witnesses, the accused was insulated from any retaliatory action. Nor was this merely a legislative oversight or procedural lacuna. For as the Court of Criminal Appeal explained in *Butterwasser*,[276] impeaching the credit of a prosecution witness puts *her* character in issue, but has no necessary bearing on the character of the accused. Defence counsel is saying to the jury, for example: 'don't believe this witness because she is a criminal and

---

[270] ibid. 355. 'Prosecutor' is the old term for 'complainant', a legacy of the common law tradition of private prosecutions run by the victims of crime themselves.

[271] Irrelevant imputations are anyway inadmissible, on elementary evidentiary principles: §3.1.

[272] *R v Britzmann* (1983) 76 Cr App R 134, CA. Loss of the character shield could not be avoided through circumspect or euphemistic language, as Lawton LJ elaborated, ibid. 138: 'The jury had to decide whether these officers had made up what they alleged had been said. If in any case that is the reality of the position and would be seen by a jury to be so, there is no room for drawing a distinction between a defence which is so conducted as to make specific allegations of fabrication and one in which the allegation arises by way of necessary and reasonable implication'. Also see *R v Tanner* (1977) 66 Cr App R 56, CA; *R v McGee and Cassidy* (1979) 70 Cr App R 247, CA.

[273] Confirming *R v Cook* [1959] 2 QB 340, CCA; *R v Watson* (1913) 8 Cr App R 249, CCA.

[274] A rare sighting is *R v Morris* [2002] EWCA Crim 2968, [16], where Mitchell J insisted that 'a measure of proportionality must prevail, the balance must be maintained'. Although '[t]he fact that this court would have exercised its discretion differently is not a basis for interfering with the trial judge's discretion', in this particular instance '[n]ot one member of this court would have acceded to the application. The imputation arose only out of a denial of a single allegation and that allegation related to an extremely short-lived incident.'

[275] The scourge of police 'verbals' was ameliorated, if not entirely resolved, by the advent of tape-recording police interviews with suspects in accordance with PACE Codes C and E: see §12.2.

[276] *R v Butterwasser* [1948] 1 KB 4, CCA.

has previous convictions to prove it'; not 'don't believe this witness because my client, the accused, asks you not to'. The accused electing not to testify is merely putting the prosecution to proof, no matter what his counsel might say to prosecution witnesses in order to test *their* evidence in cross-examination.

The impeccable logic of *Butterwasser* did not fully compensate for the House of Lords' rejection of the no-stymie principle in *Selvey*, but it did at least introduce a measure of damage-limitation whenever the defence case could feasibly be presented without relying on the accused's own courtroom testimony. *Butterwasser* stood as a bulwark against unfair prejudice, until the tidal wave of reform unleashed by the CJA 2003 swept it clean away.

(ii) The CJA 2003's uninhibited retaliation

There can be no ambiguity about the rationale informing section 101(1)(g) of the CJA 2003. Since the objective of correcting a false impression is already expressly catered for by gateway (f); gateway (g) must, by process of elimination, be predicated on tit-for-tat retaliation, possibly coupled with deterrence. This was soon implicitly confirmed in *Pickstone*,[277] where the accused claimed that his step-daughter had maliciously concocted allegations of rape and sexual assault against him. The Court of Appeal endorsed the trial judge's ruling that this defence was free of any misleading impression capable of triggering gateway (f), but it easily satisfied gateway (g), notwithstanding the passage of time since the accused's 1993 conviction of indecent assault on another minor.

Furthermore, the CJA 2003 traduced the logic of *Butterwasser*, which had become the target of much criticism for allowing the accused (so it was said) to attack prosecution witnesses with impunity. Electing not to testify, and thereby pre-empting retaliatory cross-examination on the accused's own bad character, was viewed by critics as a strategic ruse,[278] rather than as a legitimate exercise of the accused's privilege against self-incrimination and a logical implication of the presumption of innocence. As enacted, the operation of gateway (g) is entirely independent of the accused's status as a witness in the trial, with the clear and deliberate implication that his bad character could become admissible even where the accused's testimonial credibility is not in any sense in issue in the proceedings. The accused's credibility arguably *is* in issue where the accused's own pre-trial imputation is admitted pursuant to section 106(1)(c), even if the accused does not actually testify in his own defence at trial. However, the accused need not have made *any* admissible testimonial statement to launch an attack in the ways identified by section 106(1)(a) or (b).

The probative logic of these arrangements remains obscure. Since the CJA 2003 did not introduce any compensating measures to protect the no-stymie principle, moreover, the scope for naked tit-for-tat retaliation is even greater than it was before. In *Singh*,[279] the Court of Appeal refused to place any limitations on the purposes for which the accused's previous convictions (or, presumably, his other, unconvicted, extraneous misconduct)

---

[277] *R v Hanson* (*Pickstone's* case) [2005] 2 Cr App R 21; [2005] EWCA Crim 824.

[278] The Law Commission was amongst those ultimately persuaded by this dubious argument: Law Com No 273, *Evidence of Bad Character in Criminal Proceedings.* Cm. 5257. (TSO, 2001), paras.4.60–4.65, 14.28–14.30. Prior to that, the Runciman Royal Commission on Criminal Justice had expressed the view that '[i]t does not seem to us to be reasonable that a defendant can avoid the consequences of the present rule by the simple expedient of staying out of the witness box': *Report*, Cm. 2263 (HMSO, 1993), Chapter 8, para.34.

[279] *R v Singh (James Paul)* [2007] EWCA Crim 2140.

could in principle be adduced under gateway (g). In this case, *S*'s previous convictions were treated as relevant to his credibility, not only specifically in relation to the allegations constituting his attack on the complainant, but also on the current charges of robbery and assault, even though none of his previous convictions were for offences of dishonesty and despite the fact that he had always previously pleaded guilty. According to the Court of Appeal:[280]

When the jury was assessing the evidence of the two main parties to this trial it was judging the complainant's credibility against that of the accused. The attack having been made, it was entitled to have regard to the source from which came the accusations which might affect the jury's judgment of the complainant. It would be wholly artificial to say that this information about the appellant went to whether he was to be believed in what he said about the complainant being a user of crack cocaine and not to whether he was believed in what he said about how the complainant came to be parted from his chain and his mobile phone. We think that it is perfectly plain that, once admitted under gateway g, bad character evidence does go to the credibility of the witness in question. That accords with common experience.... [P]ersons of bad character may of course tell the truth and often do, but it is ordinary human experience that their word may be worth less than that of those who have led exemplary lives.

This reasoning sits uneasily with the emphasis placed on logical relevance in *Hanson*,[281] less comfortably still with the Court of Appeal's rigorous analysis of testimonial credibility in *Campbell*.[282] True, there is a popular sense in which an accused who chooses to fight dirty on the terrain of credibility can only expect a response in kind; and there would certainly be little public sympathy for an accused who attempted to save his own hide by smearing a complainant with false allegations that may be embarrassing, if not hurtful and distressing, for a complainant to endure. It may feel like a kind of poetic justice if the mudslinger ends up covered in mud himself, just as the burglar who cuts himself on the window he smashed to gain entry may evoke a certain sense of *schadenfreude*. The problem for this rationale of gateway (g) is that criminal trials are meant to be realms of actual rather than poetic justice, which aspire to high standards of procedural rectitude in accordance with the foundational principles of criminal evidence.[283] Yet revealing the accused's bad character in these circumstances smacks of a reversion to talionic tit-for-tat, shamefacedly masquerading as the argument from comparative credibility. Considerations of justice and proportionality are left to hinge on judicial exercises of the power to exclude bad character evidence on grounds of unfairness under section 101(3); and the Court of Appeal will not intervene, applying the *Wednesbury* review standard, unless 'the judge has either misdirected himself or…arrived at a conclusion which is outside the legitimate band of decisions available to him'.[284] It would be far better, from the point of view of justice, if the accused were prevented in the first instance from smearing complainants and other witnesses with false or otherwise gratuitous attacks on their character. Section 100 of the CJA 2003 may go some way towards securing this end.[285]

When interpreting the now-repealed provisions of the Criminal Evidence Act 1898, the courts tied themselves up in knots trying to specify the purpose or purposes for which

---

280 ibid. [10].   281 *R v Hanson* [2005] 2 Cr App R 21, [2005] EWCA Crim 824.
282 *R v Campbell (Kenneth)* [2007] 1 WLR 2798, [2007] EWCA Crim 1472.   283 §1.3.
284 *R v Singh (James Paul)* [2007] EWCA Crim 2140, [10].   285 §8.4.

bad character evidence presented in reaction to defence imputations could be adduced.[286] At least in some moods and constitutions, the Court of Appeal has been anxious not to repeat this mistake in relation to the CJA 2003. Relevance and probative value ostensibly have replaced sterile formalism as the controlling considerations. In *Highton* Lord Woolf CJ went so far as to hold that 'a distinction must be drawn between the *admissibility* of evidence of bad character, which depends upon it getting through one of the gateways, and the *use* to which it may be put once it is admitted. The use to which it may be put depends upon the matters to which it is relevant rather than upon the gateway through which it was admitted.'[287] These *dicta* are not always followed, however, and are potentially misleading if quoted out of context. Simple relevance will not guarantee cross-admissibility between separate counts (or co-accused),[288] or automatic admissibility to credit where bad character evidence was adduced, explicitly, for its relevance to guilt.[289] Whilst the Court of Appeal's back-to-basics emphasis on relevance is generally to be welcomed, the absence of additional normative constraints underlines the importance of the jury's receiving very clear judicial directions on the nature of the bad character evidence they have heard and the inferences which it might legitimately support should the jury choose to believe it.

Turning now to gateway (g)'s specified 'triggering conditions' for admitting bad character evidence against the accused, the concept of 'making an attack an another person's character' appears to convey a more deliberate sense of purpose than casting an imputation, which might be done almost accidentally. However, the Court of Appeal has indicated that the situation should be judged objectively, so that an attack occurs when the effect is to inflict forensic harm on another person even if the accused was not (or claims not to have been) motivated to achieve that outcome; and subsection 101(3) will not generally invalidate that interpretation.[290] One can certainly maintain that the accused intends an attack even though he does not desire it or make it his primary purpose, inasmuch as a person who wills the end also wills the means chosen to achieve it. But an incidental side-effect of a legitimate defence ought not to be treated as an attack. Prior to the CJA 2003, an 'emphatic denial' was not regarded as an imputation.[291] Now, pursuant to section 106, a relevant 'attack' is made whenever questioning is 'likely'[292] to elicit evidence of another person's criminal record or reprehensible behaviour or disposition.[293] Alleging that

---

[286] See, e.g., *R v Powell* (1986) 82 Cr App R 165, CA; *R v Burke* (1986) 82 Cr App R 156, CA; *R v Owen* (1986) 83 Cr App R 100, CA; *R v McLeod* [1995] 1 Cr App R 591, CA; *R v Mallett* [2001] EWCA Crim 1032. Cf. *R v Watts* (1983) 77 Cr App R 126, 129–30, CA, where Lord Lane CJ could no longer keep up the charade: '[I]t would have been extremely difficult, if not practically impossible, for the jury to have done what the learned judge was suggesting…The jury in the present case was charged with deciding the guilt or innocence of a man against whom an allegation of indecent assault on a woman has been made. They were told that he had previous convictions for indecent assaults of a more serious kind on young girls. They were warned that such evidence was not to be taken as making it more likely that he was guilty of the offence charged, which it seems it plainly did, but only as affecting his credibility, which it almost certainly did not.'

[287] *R v Highton* [2006] 1 Cr App R 7; [2005] EWCA Crim 1985, [10] (original emphasis).

[288] Rudi Fortson and David Ormerod, 'Bad Character Evidence and Cross-Admissibility' [2009] *Crim LR* 313, 332: 'the general proposition in *Highton* was overbroad and failed to respect the legislative intention that bad character is no longer to be regarded as indivisible'.

[289] *R v McDonald* [2007] EWCA Crim 1194; Peter Mirfield, 'Character and Credibility' [2009] *Crim LR* 135, 140.   [290] *R v Bovell* (*Dowds'* case) [2005] EWCA Crim 1091, [32].

[291] *R v Rouse* [1904] 1 KB 104, CCR.   [292] Section 106(1)(b).   [293] Section 106(2).

complainants have fabricated the allegations[294] or lied to the police in their statements,[295] or were the ones truly at fault in initiating or provoking criminal conduct[296] will almost certainly amount to an attack in the relevant sense. But character assault need not be defence counsel's direct objective, nor does any such attempt have to succeed, to satisfy gateway (g). Still, even though section 106 does not respect the no-stymie principle, it must be assumed that emphatic denials remain unfettered. It would be an abuse of language, as well as an audacious outflanking manoeuvre on the presumption of innocence and the principle limiting the evidence to the charge, if the accused's criminal record were to be revealed every time the defence case necessitates contradicting the evidence of a prosecution witness.

Paralleling gateway (f) in this regard, gateway (g) extends to imputations adduced in evidence which were made during police interview or when being formally charged with the offence.[297] It was previously observed, when discussing gateway (f), that the accused (suspect) may not have access to appropriate legal advice at these early stages of criminal proceedings. The sweeping purview of gateway (g) is well illustrated by *Ball*,[298] in which the accused was charged with raping a women with whom he was having an on-off casual relationship. He denied the allegations in police interview, and casually informing the interviewing officers – apparently by way of explanation – that the complainant was 'a bag really, you know what I mean, a slag'. In the circumstances of the alleged rape, this was taken to be a confession, effectively demonstrating that the accused neither knew nor cared whether the complainant was actually consenting at the material time. As such, though casually bigoted and presumably ill-considered hearsay, the statement was admissible – with the further consequence that the accused's extensive record immediately became admissible against him under gateway (g). Notice that section 106(1)(c) requires only that 'evidence is given of an imputation', not that the accused himself must be the one to adduce it. And of course, with *Butterwasser* dead and buried, the accused's record will be admissible under gateway (g) regardless of whether he chooses to testify in his own defence or not. Nor is there any formal damage-limiting option for the accused to dissociate himself from the imputation, or any logical relationship with the accused's forensic strategy delimiting the scope or extent of the prosecution's retaliation, as there is in relation to false impressions potentially triggering gateway (f).[299] The accused's only recourse in opposing admissibility lies with section 101(3), and the Court of Appeal's jurisprudence to-date evinces little inclination for holding trial judges to an exacting proportionality standard.

The extent to which the accused may adduce evidence of another person's bad character was restricted by the CJA 2003, section 100, to information with substantial probative value. This effectively closes down any leeway there might have been in the old law for the accused to provoke a moral credibility contest with a complainant or other witness unrelated to the issues in the case. If inadmissible evidence of bad character starts to leak

---

[294] *R v Weir* (*Somanathan's* case) [2006] 1 WLR 1885, [2005] EWCA Crim 2866; *R v Hanson* (*Pickstone's* case) [2005] 2 Cr App R 21; [2005] EWCA Crim 824.

[295] *R v Highton* [2006] 1 Cr App R 7; [2005] EWCA Crim 1985.

[296] *R v Renda* (*Razaq's* case) [2006] 1 WLR 2948, [2005] EWCA Crim 2826; *R v Highton* (*Carp's* case) [2006] 1 Cr App R 7; [2005] EWCA Crim 1985.   [297] Section 106(1)(c).

[298] *R v Renda* (*Ball's* case) [2006] 1 WLR 2948, [2005] EWCA Crim 2826.

[299] A contrast noted by the Court of Appeal in *R v Weir* (*Somanathan's* case) [2006] 1 WLR 1885, [2005] EWCA Crim 2866, [45].

out in the forensic cut-and-thrust of the trial, the judge should intervene to put an end to the offensive line of questioning and warn the jury to disregard entirely what it has already improperly heard. So far as evidence of a witness's extraneous bad character or general credibility is concerned, therefore, the accused will by definition be adducing information with an important bearing on disputed issues of fact. But still gateway (g) will be triggered, and the full extent of the accused's own bad character will be revealed to the jury, unless section 101(3) imposes a measure of restraint and discipline. On this legislative version of tit-for-tat, the accused could be repaid with interest.

An allegation of misconduct relating to the offence charged or its investigation or prosecution is not evidence of 'bad character' within CJA 2003, section 98's threshold definition. Section 100, covering 'the bad character of a person other than the defendant',[300] consequently does not apply to allegations of fabricating confessions or suborning perjury such as those which cropped up in a number of the old authorities on the 1898 Act. But such allegations will nevertheless still virtually always constitute 'an attack on another person's character' for the purposes of gateway (g), read in conjunction with section 106, because section 106 is concerned with attacks on 'character' *simpliciter* and makes no reference to 'bad character'. This superficially trivial deviation is actually pivotal in the scheme of the CJA 2003's character evidence provisions. If section 106 had defined an 'attack on character' for the purposes of gateway (g) in terms of introducing evidence of a witness's bad character, the accused would have been free within the bounds of common law relevance to challenge the specific credibility of prosecution witnesses, for example by alleging that a confession attributed to him had been concocted, without exposing himself to tit-for-tat retaliation. Where imputations on the character of a prosecution witness might be regarded as conveying a misleading impression to the jury, evidence of the accused's bad character would then become admissible under gateway (f), but only to the extent strictly necessary to correct any false impression.[301] The no-stymie principle would otherwise have been preserved.

In fact, the CJA 2003 implements an all-together different policy. Gateway (g) authorizes the introduction of the accused's bad character in response to an imputation which is central to the defence case, without any dedicated proportionality constraint and in the absence of any conceivable probative purpose other than trial by prejudice. Section 101(1)(g) does not so much forsake the no-stymie principle, as spit on its grave. This might be popular politics in punitive times, but it is difficult to see how it is supposed to promote justice. Section 101(3)'s fairness test is the last line of defence. Although the career of its common law predecessor was undistinguished, two factors strengthen the trial judge's hand under the CJA 2003. First, gateways (a)–(f) spell out alternative grounds for admitting evidence of the accused's bad character, making gateway (g)'s punitive rationale more transparent, and undeniable, than ever before. Secondly, it must at least be arguable, before English courts under the Human Rights Act if not before the European Court in Strasbourg, that a conviction secured after the revelation of highly prejudicial *and logically irrelevant* evidence of the accused's extraneous misconduct is incompatible with the right to a fair trial guaranteed by Article 6 ECHR. In an ideal world, trial judges would use their section 101(3) fairness discretion to exclude *all* evidence of the accused's bad character proffered under gateway (g), on the basis that, if the evidence cannot legitimately be channelled

----

[300] §8.4.   [301] Section 105(6).

through any of the alternative gateways (a)–(f), it ought not to be admitted at all. Of course, that cannot have been what Parliament intended; but sometimes the interests of justice may need to be rescued from the clutches of political opportunism.

14.5 BAD CHARACTER IN ISSUE BETWEEN ACCUSED AND CO-ACCUSED

Section 101(1)(e) of the CJA 2003 authorizes the admission of evidence of the accused's bad character where 'it has substantial probative value in relation to an important matter in issue between the defendant and a co-defendant'. Section 104(1) adds the further condition that:

Evidence which is relevant to the question whether the defendant has a propensity to be untruthful is admissible on that basis under section 101(1)(e) only if the nature or conduct of his defence is such as to undermine the co-defendant's defence.

Only a co-accused can rely on section 101(1)(e);[302] the prosecution is not permitted to 'step into the shoes' of a co-accused,[303] but must instead confine its attempts to adduce contested evidence of the accused's bad character to gateways (c), (d), (f), and (g). The foregoing analysis of these four, capacious prosecution gateways suggests that the prosecutor will hardly be much inconvenienced by this restriction.

Gateway (e), as elucidated by section 104, is partly modelled on an earlier, now repealed, provision of the Criminal Evidence Act 1898.[304] However, the CJA 2003 also introduced some potentially important changes to the way in which the law regulates bad character evidence adduced by a co-accused, prompting one commentator to anticipate 'a sea change in the dynamics of joint trials'.[305] In order to understand the rationale and assess the implications of gateway (e) it is first necessary to appreciate the common law's traditional approach to regulating character battles between co-accused running 'cut-throat' defences.

(a) THE TRADITIONAL COMMON LAW APPROACH TO CUT-THROAT DEFENCES

The common law has traditionally striven to interfere as little as possible in the forensic strategies pursued by co-accused running mutually destructive, 'cut-throat' defences. There are sound reasons for this policy of abstention. First, it is regarded as an elementary principle of justice that an accused should be able to run his case in any way he chooses, within the broad parameters of the law and adversarial ethics. Where there are two or more co-accused in a

---

[302] Section 104(2).

[303] In certain, quite rare, circumstances it was arguably appropriate, under the corresponding provisions of the Criminal Evidence Act 1898, for the prosecutor to 'step into D2's shoes' in order to cross-examine D1 on his record: see *Murdoch v Taylor* [1965] AC 574, 593, HL; *R v Seigley* (1911) 6 Cr App R 106, CCA. For further discussion, see Roderick Munday, 'The Wilder Permutations of Section 1(f) of the Criminal Evidence Act 1898' (1987) 7 *Legal Studies* 137.   [304] Proviso (f)(iii).

[305] Roderick Munday, 'Cut-throat Defences and the "Propensity to be Untruthful" under s.104 of the Criminal Justice Act 2003' [2005] *Crim LR* 624, 631.

joint trial, the same latitude should be granted to all. Secondly, any attempt by the judge to mediate between co-accused will necessarily benefit one and disadvantage the other (or others), and this might easily give the appearance of favouritism or hostility, depending on one's perspective. Abstention therefore reinforces judicial impartiality and, no less importantly, preserves the appearance of even-handed, 'umpireal' judging. A third consideration is rather less lofty, but may exert pragmatic influence. Left to their own devices, guilty co-accused are quite likely to damn each other with incriminating evidence and mutual recriminations, enabling the jury to convict all of them. The common law's policy of abstention might then seem no less attractive to prosecutors, and to the public interest, than to trial judges.

In keeping with this overriding policy, the common law 'similar facts' rule did not apply to evidence adduced by co-accused tried in the same proceedings. Any co-accused (hereafter, D2) was free to elicit evidence of D1's bad character, either in-chief or through cross-examination of any witness other than D1 himself, subject only to the threshold criterion of (logical) relevance.[306] If D1 chose to testify in his own defence, his 'bad character shield' furnished by the Criminal Evidence Act 1898 protected him from character-based cross-examination by D2, just as it protected him from prosecution cross-examination, unless and until D1 had 'given evidence against any other person charged in the same proceedings'. As soon as D1 tripped this forensic switch, however, the character shield was forfeit, and he became liable to cross-examination on his record by D2 to the full extent of its relevance. Moreover, the prevailing judicial philosophy entailed that D2's freedom to cross-examine D1 on his record was not subject to any overriding judicial discretion to ensure balance and fairness, such as (supposedly) limited cross-examination by the prosecution under the Criminal Evidence Act 1898.[307] As Lord Donovan explained in *Murdoch v Taylor*, 'when it is the co-accused who seeks to exercise the right conferred by proviso (f) (iii)...[h]e seeks to defend himself; to say to the jury that the man who is giving evidence against him is unworthy of belief; and to support that assertion by proof of bad character. The right to do this cannot, in my opinion, be fettered in any way.'[308]

Albeit grounded in a perfectly defensible rationale, in the absence of any proportionality criterion an unremittingly inflexible policy of judicial abstention could produce dubious outcomes redolent of injustice. For one thing, D1 was denied even the vestigial remnants of no-stymie protection vis-à-vis D2. Where D1 opted to run the classic 'cutthroat' defence,[309] by testifying that D2 was solely responsible for the offences charged, the accused with a criminal record would almost inevitably expose himself to potentially prejudicial cross-examination on his criminal antecedents. In the words of Lord Reid, 'an accused person with previous convictions, whose story contradicts in any material respect the story of a co-accused ... will find it almost impossible to defend himself, and if he elects not to give evidence his plight will be just as bad'.[310] The situation was compounded where

---

[306] *R v Miller* (1952) 36 Cr App R 169, Winchester Assizes (Devlin J); *R v Kracher* [1995] Crim LR 819, CA. But cf. *R v Neale* (1977) 65 Cr App R 304, 307, CA, where there is some – probably heretical – suggestion of a relevance-plus standard, in terms of the need for 'a positive probative link'.

[307] *Selvey v DPP* [1970] AC 304, HL.   [308] *Murdoch v Taylor* [1965] AC 574, 393, HL.

[309] Generally, see D. W. Elliott, 'Cut Throat Tactics: the Freedom of an Accused to Prejudice a Co-Accused' [1991] *Crim LR* 5.

[310] *Murdoch v Taylor* [1965] AC 574, 583, HL. Sections 34–37 of the Criminal Justice and Public Order Act 1994, permitting adverse inferences from silence, made D1's predicament even worse than Lord Reid envisaged: see 13.3(b).

the damage done to *D1*'s case by being exposed to cross-examination on his record was out of all proportion to the adverse impact of his evidence affecting *D2*. A mild incursion into *D2*'s forensic territory, quite possibly motivated by self-preservation rather than any overt hostile intent, could result in nuclear retaliation, placing *D1*'s antecedents before the jury in a very prejudicial light. To cap it all, *D1* would not necessarily be able to launch a parallel strike against *D2*'s character, because *D2* did not automatically expose himself to cross-examination on his own record by attacking *D1*'s credit. The test of 'giving evidence against' a co-accused operated like a legal light-switch to determine whether the jury would see the accused's character in glorious technicolor or be kept entirely in the dark. It could be all or nothing in certain circumstances, and technical rules of evidence rather than the inferential logic of fact-finding made all the difference. Distracted by formalism, the Criminal Evidence Act 1898's character shield framework failed to guarantee reciprocity, as well as lacking proportionality, in the way it regulated – or rather, declined to regulate – the competing forensic interests of co-accused.

The vice of these arrangements was that they fetishized *D2*'s freedom to establish his innocence unfettered by artificial legal constraints to the point where all other considerations of fairness and justice were cast aside. Proportionality, no-stymie, the risks of prejudice and trial by character rather than by evidence were all side-lined. Legal principle demands a more balanced and nuanced approach. *D2* should certainly always be free to attack *D1*'s testimonial credibility through cross-examination. But if *D1* has stuck to the issues in the case, without attempting any blunderbuss assault on *D2*'s general moral character, there is no compelling reason why *D2* should be at liberty to pillory *D1*'s moral standing where doing so would have no significant bearing on the probative value of *D1*'s testimony. Unless *D1* has chosen to open up the proceedings to a no-holds-barred contest of character, trial judges should strive to contain the scope of the dispute within reasonable bounds. The judge's overriding duty to ensure a fair trial is incompatible with passively condoning a mud-slinging match between co-accused, which would be calculated to retard rather than to promote effective fact-finding and risks bringing the criminal trial process itself into disrepute. Once mud starts to fly, it is likely that everybody involved will get dirty.

Trial judges occasionally responded to the intuitive unfairness of the strict letter of the law, but the only legitimate legal avenue available to them to alleviate the situation was to exploit the inherent ambiguity of the notion of 'giving evidence against' a co-accused.[311] If *D1*'s forensic strategy could be characterized as advancing his own case without adducing evidence 'against' *D2* his character shield would remain intact. Whilst potentially effective on an *ad hoc* basis in individual cases, this creative judicial approach was neither a transparent nor, consequently, a systematic or reliable way of mediating between the interests of co-accused. Orthodox legality drove trial judges to disguise their calculations of fairness in the illusory language of 'direct' and 'strict' relevance.[312]

---

[311] Cf. *Murdoch v Taylor* [1965] AC 574, 591, HL, *per* Lord Donovan: '[W]hat is "evidence against" a co-accused is perhaps the most difficult part of the case. At one end of the scale is evidence which does no more than contradict something which a co-accused has said without further advancing the prosecution's case in any significant degree.... [T]his is not the kind of evidence contemplated by proviso (f)(iii). At the other end of the scale is evidence which, if the jury believes it, would establish the co-accused's guilt.'

[312] *R v Thompson, Sinclair, and Maver* [1995] 2 Cr App R 589, CA; *R v Bracewell* (1978) 68 Cr App R 44, CA.

Resort to the procedural remedy of ordering separate trials is always a theoretical possibility in cases in which co-accused might foreseeably damn each other with prejudice if tried together in the same proceedings. However, the principled and pragmatic objections to severing joint-trials of accomplices are even more formidable than the obstacles to solving problems of cross-admissibility by severing multiple counts against a single accused.[313] Where the prosecution alleges that co-accused acted in concert, it is crucial that the 'full picture' of the disputed event is placed before the jury and that cut-throat defences can be tested properly without presenting individual accused with a golden opportunity of shifting the blame onto third parties who are not charged in the proceedings and, likely as not, are absent from the courtroom and beyond the jury's ken. As Lawton LJ once remarked, 'in the majority of cases where men are charged jointly, it is clearly in the interests of justice and the ascertainment of truth that all the men so charged should be tried together'. The probative case against severance is often further reinforced by the entirely well-motivated desire to spare complainants and other witnesses the trauma of appearing in multiple trials. These are generally regarded as decisive considerations favouring joint-trials of accomplices, even if it may be doubted that the public interest in efficient criminal process always outweighs the risks of unfair prejudice in every case.[314]

(b) A PARTIAL RE-BALANCING OF INTERESTS BY THE CJA 2003

Section 101(1)(e) of the CJA 2003 has the potential to re-establish judicial regulation of bad character issues between co-accused on a more principled footing. Gateway (e) overcomes a major limitation of the previous arrangements, by uncoupling judicial scrutiny of admissibility from a restrictive focus on *D1*'s cross-examination. If evidence of *D1*'s bad character has 'substantial probative value in relation to an important matter in issue' between *D1* and *D2* it is admissible by any lawful means, including cross-examination of *D1* if he elects to testify. The new standard of admissibility is at once both easier and harder to satisfy than the old law.

Gateway (e) lowered the threshold to admissibility inasmuch as there is no additional general requirement that *D1* has 'has given evidence against' *D2*. Of course, if cross-examined on his record, *D1* himself may well prove uncooperative, but *D2*'s counsel can at least pose the pertinent questions in cross-examination and invite the jury to scrutinize *D1*'s reactions for tell-tale signs of evasion or dissembling. Also, as we saw in Chapter 8, previous convictions are an exception to the collateral-finality rule, so that if *D1* attempts to deny his record it can be proved against him. Once admitted in this way, previous convictions go to the issue as well as to credit by virtue of CJA 2003, section 119. The only further restriction is imposed by section 104 specifically in relation to bad character evidence adduced to show *D1*'s propensity to lie. In this case only, the conduct or nature of *D1*'s defence must be such as to 'undermine' *D2*'s defence before propensity evidence adduced for this purpose can be admitted through gateway (e).

Gateway (e) simultaneously *raises* the threshold to admissibility by requiring 'substantial' probative value in relation to an 'important matter in issue', which obviously applies

---

[313] §14.3(c), above.

[314] Robert O. Dawson, 'Joint Trials of Defendants in Criminal Cases: an Analysis of Efficiencies and Prejudices' (1979) 77 *Michigan LR* 1379.

to all evidence of *D1*'s bad character adduced through this gateway, including evidence which would have been admitted on a simple test of relevance prior to the CJA 2003. (A parallel point can be made in relation to bad character adduced by *D2* under gateway (c), which stipulates that 'explanatory evidence' must be 'important' as a precondition of its admissibility.) Trial judges are now effectively required to undertake proportionality review. Evidence of *D1*'s bad character, though admittedly relevant and quite irrespective of *D1*'s forensic strategy, will still not be admissible for *D2* if its probative value is not sufficiently 'substantial' to satisfy gateway (e) (or alternatively, insufficiently 'important' to satisfy gateway (c)). These new admissibility thresholds open up doctrinal spaces for trial judges to try to achieve a fairer balancing of interests between co-accused, providing that they are prepared to embrace the challenge.

The framework of admissibility erected by the CJA 2003 ought to be capable of protecting *D1* from revelations of bad character which would have only a marginal bearing on *D2*'s case but which could be highly prejudicial to *D1*'s prospects of receiving a fair trial. At the same time, switching to *D2*'s perspective, the no-stymie principle is substantially honoured by gateway (e). *D2* is only prevented from adducing relevant evidence of *D1*'s bad character where the impact on *D1* would be wholly disproportionate to the benefit that *D2*'s case might derive from the evidence. *D2* should be able to count on statutory permission to adduce all significant or important evidence of *D1*'s bad character going either to the issues in the case or to *D1*'s specific credibility. Such protection that *D1* might derive from section 101(1)(e) has therefore been secured with little or no detriment to *D2*'s right to make a defence, in accordance with the dictates of the no-stymie principle.

The Court of Appeal has considered gateway (e) on a number of occasions since the bad character provisions of the CJA 2003 came into force. In *Edwards and Rowlands*, where the co-accused ran mutual cut-throat defences on drug-dealing charges, several elementary points of interpretation were confirmed.[315] First, gateway (e) is not a mere formality; although applications to adduce bad character evidence lodged by a co-accused 'may well be difficult to refuse', the trial judge must not accede to such applications unless the requirement for 'substantial probative value' is satisfied. Secondly, whether particular evidence relates to an issue between co-accused 'will inevitably turn on the facts of the individual case'. Thirdly, whether or not the evidence in question rises to the level of substantial probative value on an important issue 'is ultimately a question for the judge on his "feel" of the case'.[316] Fourthly, although subsections 101(3) and (4) do not directly apply to gateway (e), the fact that previous convictions or other bad character occurred a long time in the past might be something that the trial judge ought to draw to the attention of the jury in summing-up.[317] As in case-law addressing section 101's other admissibility gateways, the 'first importance' of a careful judicial direction on the salience and potential probative value of bad character evidence was stressed. Finally, fifth, in view of the importance of the trial judge's familiarity with the facts and 'feel' for the case, the Court of Appeal would be reluctant to second-guess the trial judge's determinations on the admissibility of bad character evidence through gateway (e), and 'will only interfere when the conviction is unsafe'.[318]

---

[315] *R v Edwards and Rowlands* [2006] 2 Cr App R 4, [2005] EWCA Crim 3244, [1] (v) and (vii).
[316] ibid. [27].   [317] ibid. [26].   [318] ibid. [1](viii).

The decision in *Edwards and Rowlands* itself well illustrates these propositions. The trial judge had ruled *R*'s – mostly stale – previous convictions admissible for *E* under gateways (e) and (g). The ruling on gateway (g) was plainly erroneous, because the statute specifically says that only the prosecution can make use of it.[319] The Court of Appeal was also 'very doubtful' whether *R*'s previous convictions satisfied the admissibility threshold for gateway (e), and even remarked that it was 'difficult to see how any of them could possibly have had any relevance in the case except possibly the handling'.[320] *R*'s appeal was nonetheless dismissed, because the Court of Appeal was satisfied that the trial judge's summing-up, which seemed to come 'very close to advising the jury to ignore the previous convictions',[321] was an adequate corrective to preserve the safety of *R*'s conviction. Right or wrong, the judge's ruling on gateway (e) was regarded as irrelevant to the substantive outcome.

Section 104 remains something of an enigma.[322] It is expressly limited to bad character adduced as proof of a co-accused's propensity to be untruthful, and therefore does not apply to direct proof of propensity to offend, which, when advanced by a co-accused, is subject only to the general requirements of gateway (e).[323] The provision potentially retains the light-switch quality of the old character shield, inasmuch as the conduct of *D1*'s case could be the trigger to allowing *D2* to expose the full extent of *D1*'s bad character to the jury. The Court of Appeal's explicit disavowal in *Somanathan*[324] of the common law doctrine of the 'indivisibility of character' ought to go some way to pre-empting that eventuality. More generally, the practical impact of section 104 hinges as much on judicial understandings of what evidence is (logically) capable of establishing a 'propensity to be untruthful' as on authentic legal interpretations of the pivotal statutory concept of 'undermining the codefendant's defence'. The idea of 'undermining' *D2*'s defence is surely intended to establish a more exacting criterion than its statutory predecessor, which required only 'giving evidence against'. Although the boundaries of 'undermining' are not necessarily any more determinate than the contours of giving evidence 'against', which proved itself a potentially troublesome concept, the scope of section 104 is relatively narrow and judicial practice could conceivably make it narrower still. If the restricted, strictly relevance-based understanding of propensity to lie on oath propounded by the Court of Appeal in *Hanson*[325] and *Campbell*[326] were consistently followed, the interpretational issues posed by section 104 could be 'solved' by making the section virtually redundant.

However, in *Lawson*[327] the Court of Appeal took a different line. *L* was involved in an incident with two others, *Q* and *K*, in which a man with serve mental disabilities was pushed into a lake and drowned. *Q*, who was *L*'s cousin, eventually admitted to being the one who had actually pushed the victim to his death, and pleaded guilty to manslaughter. The joint trial of *L* and *K* focused on their respective behaviour in the build-up to the drowning,

---

[319]   Section 106(3).

[320]   *R v Edwards and Rowlands* [2006] 2 Cr App R 4, [2005] EWCA Crim 3244, [27], [20].

[321]   ibid. [29].

[322]   Some of the puzzles are explored by Roderick Munday, 'Cut-throat Defences and the "Propensity to be Untruthful" under s.104 of the Criminal Justice Act 2003' [2005] *Crim LR* 624.

[323]   *R v Edwards and Rowlands* (*McLean*'s case) [2006] 2 Cr App R 4, [2005] EWCA Crim 3244.

[324]   *R v Weir* (*Somanathan*'s case) [2006] 1 WLR 1885, [2005] EWCA Crim 2866, [43], rejecting *R v Winfield* [1939] 4 All ER 164, CCA.   [325]   *R v Hanson* [2005] 2 Cr App R 21, [2005] EWCA Crim 824.

[326]   *R v Campbell (Kenneth)* [2007] 1 WLR 2798, [2007] EWCA Crim 1472.

[327]   *R v Lawson* [2007] 1 WLR 1191, [2006] EWCA Crim 2572.

much of which had been captured on CCTV. *K* maintained that he had only been trying to look out for the victim's safety. *L* painted *K* as an instigator, asserting that *K* had originally been the one to boast that he was going to push the deceased into the lake but had subsequently 'bottled it', requiring *Q* to step in. *L* and *K* were both convicted, after a contested trial, as accessories to manslaughter. On appeal, *L* took objection to the fact that the trial judge had permitted *K*'s counsel to cross-examine him on a recent conviction of unlawful wounding, which, the judge ruled, went to *L*'s testimonial credibility. The Court of Appeal was highly critical of *K*'s trial counsel for launching into this line of cross-examination without first signaling his intentions to *L*'s counsel and to the judge (much less complying with the notice requirements under section 111 and the CrimPR) which was 'contrary to every good practice of advocacy, as it has been understood for generations'.[328] Proceeding in this haphazard fashion deprived the trial judge of an ordered opportunity to consider the admissibility of the proposed line of questioning, and consequently risked provoking a mistrial which would squander public funds and greatly inconvenience all concerned. On the underlying question of admissibility, however, the Court of Appeal endorsed the trial judge's approach.

The conclusion that *L* had 'undermined' *K*'s defence within the meaning of section 104 is eminently plausible on the facts. The Court of Appeal identified this central conflict of evidence in the trial:[329]

It was an important part of *K*'s defence that he had never contemplated touching [the deceased], that he had only gone near out of curiosity, that he had done no more than offer him the kindness of a cigarette and that it was Lawson who had spoken of pushing him in whilst he, *K*, was simply an innocent bystander. If accepted, Lawson's evidence, however qualified, that King had made the remark alleged undermined that defence.

Although from this application it would appear that 'undermining' is not to be glossed as '*completely* undermining', the Court of Appeal's interpretation of this aspect of section 104 seems unexceptional. Far more troubling is the Court of Appeal's understanding of 'propensity to be untruthful', implicit in the following passage:[330]

A defendant who is defending himself against the evidence of a person whose history of criminal behaviour or other misconduct is such as to be capable of showing him to be unscrupulous and/or otherwise unreliable should be enabled to present that history before the jury for its evaluation of the evidence of the witness. Such suggested unreliability may be capable of being shown by conduct which does not involve an offence of untruthfulness; it may be capable of being shown by widely differing conduct, ranging from large scale drug or people trafficking via housebreaking to criminal violence. Whether in a particular case it is in fact capable of having substantive probative value in relation to the witness's reliability is for the trial judge to determine on all the facts of the case.

The court did add, by way of partial qualification, that 'not every past conviction or other episode of bad character on the part of a witness whose truthfulness or credibility is in issue will be capable of having substantial probative value on that question'.[331] So *Winfield* indivisibility of character has not quite been resurrected for the purposes of gateway (e), even though treating a conviction of violence or other 'unscrupulous and/or otherwise

---

[328] ibid. [17].   [329] ibid. [30].   [330] ibid. [34]   [331] ibid. [39].

unreliable' misconduct as relevant to testimonial credibility can only be regarded as significantly resiling from the principled analysis advertised in *Hanson* and *Campbell*. The fact that in the latter cases the Court of Appeal was dealing with prosecution gateways (d), (f), and (g), but in *Lawson* with the co-accused gateway (e), should not make any difference to the *logical relevance* (or irrelevance) of extraneous misconduct to testimonial credibility.

The CJA 2003 stops short of equipping trial judges with a general discretion to achieve fairness between co-accused in the admission of bad character evidence. Section 101(3) does not apply to gateway (e), and – of course – PACE 1984, section 78, has no application to evidence adduced by an accused.[332] In the past, the passive discretion to stand well back from dog-and-cat-fights between co-accused has been regarded as the better part of judicial valour. Was Parliament, in the final analysis, hidebound by traditional thinking, or perhaps lacking in confidence that trial judges would exercise such a discretion appropriately? The text of the CJA 2003 is capable of being interpreted to equip trial judges with all the juridical tools they require to mediate fairly between the interests of co-accused in relation to bad character evidence, without needing to invoke any novel residual exclusionary discretion. However, so long as the Court of Appeal prefers the artificial rationalizations of *Lawson* to the inferential logic championed by *Hanson* and simultaneously refuses to correct trial judges' errors unless the circumstances are regarded as truly egregious, the potential for co-accused to be damned by disproportionately prejudicial bad character evidence admitted through gateway (e) will remain more than merely theoretical.

14.6 THE CHARACTER OF CRIMINAL EVIDENCE

The English law of bad character evidence has always been a byword for proliferating case-law and technical learning. Since sections 98–113 of the Criminal Justice Act 2003 came into force on 15 December 2004, however, these character traits have been greatly amplified. Westlaw already[333] lists 233 appellate decisions citing section 101 alone, almost one new case bearing on that section every single week since section 101 became effective. The law of bad character evidence is plainly a rapidly moving target. Much confusion and uncertainty currently surrounds the topic, and any general conclusions about the impact of the 2003 Act must necessarily be rather tentative and provisional.

The broad consensus amongst commentators is that the CJA 2003's bad character provisions were a poorly executed reform driven by the ideological politics of 'victims' rights'. Tapper wrote that they were 'based upon a misconception of the old law, and represent an illiberal reaction to the problems it presented. If they really are an attempt at simplicity, they hardly seem to have achieved it, since anomalies and vagueness have been exacerbated rather than eliminated'.[334] Characterizing the legislative methodology as 'demented dentistry' and 'Polyfilla law', Munday seriously contemplated the possibility that 'no matter how hard the courts endeavour to steady the ship, the Criminal Justice Act 2003 will

---

[332] *R v Lawson* [2007] 1 WLR 1191, [2006] EWCA Crim 2572, [31]; *R v Musone* [2007] 1 WLR 2467, [2007] EWCA Crim 1237, [47]. The Court of Appeal, ibid. [51], also rejected any scope for an exclusionary discretion derived from ECHR Article 6.   [333] March 2010.

[334] Colin Tapper, 'The Criminal Justice Act 2003: (3) Evidence of Bad Character' [2004] *Crim LR* 553, 554.

prove a nightmare of interpretation'.[335] Commentators are in the business of criticism, and can generally be counted on to find fault with new legislation. The hostility of senior judges to the provisions, however, was something entirely unexpected. One of the earliest decisions on the Act contains the following extraordinary judicial outburst:[336]

It is in the public interest that the criminal law and its procedures, so far as possible, be clear and straightforward so that all those directly affected, in particular, defendants, victims, the police, the probation service, jurors, lawyers for defence or prosecution, judges and magistrates, professional and lay, should be readily able to understand it. Sadly the provisions of the Criminal Justice Act 2003 ... are, as is apparent, conspicuously unclear in circumstance where clarity could easily have been achieved. It is not this Court's function to identify whether the government, Parliament or Parliamentary draftsmen are responsible for this perplexing legislation. It is this Court's duty loyally to glean from the statutory language, if it can, Parliament's intention and this we have sought to do in the face of obfuscatory language. The public is entitled to know of the difficulties which such legislation creates for all concerned....

It is more than a decade since the late Lord Taylor of Gosforth CJ called for a reduction in the torrent of legislation affecting criminal justice. Regrettably, that call has gone unheeded by successive governments. Indeed, the quantity of such legislation has increased and its quality has, if anything, diminished. The 2003 Act has 339 sections and 38 schedules and runs to 453 pages. It is, in pre-metric terms, an inch thick. The provisions which we have considered have been brought into force prematurely, before appropriate training could be given by the Judicial Studies Board or otherwise to approximately 2,000 Crown Court and Supreme Court judges and 30,000 magistrates. In the meantime, the judiciary and, no doubt, the many criminal justice agencies for which this Court cannot speak, must, in the phrase familiar during the Second World War 'make do and mend'. That is what we have been obliged to do in the present appeal and it has been an unsatisfactory activity, wasteful of scarce resources in public money and judicial time.

It must be remembered, however, that the pre-existing common law was barely a paragon of jurisprudential virtue. Despite its evident shortcomings, the CJA 2003 deserves some credit for dispensing with the CEA 1898's obscurely drafted statutory framework, which formerly regulated cross-examination of the accused on his extraneous bad character, together with its excruciatingly convoluted case-law encrustations. In other respects, too, the CJA 2003 purged the law of excessive technicalities and brought trial procedure into closer conformity with common sense reasoning and expectations.

The CJA 2003's bad character provisions evidently did not enjoy a very favourable start in life. Their early years have witnessed uneven development. The Court of Appeal has faithfully received the policy message 'that Parliament intended that evidence of bad character would be put before juries more frequently than had hitherto been the case',[337] and in view of the notoriety of this aspect of the government's law reform programme it is difficult to see how the judges could have done otherwise. Yet the common law's traditional suspicion of extraneous misconduct evidence has not been entirely jettisoned. In

---

[335] Roderick Munday, 'What Constitutes "Other Reprehensible Behaviour" under the Bad Character Provisions of the Criminal Justice Act 2003?' [2005] *Crim LR* 24, 41, 43.

[336] *R v Bradley* [2005] 1 Cr App R 24, [2005] EWCA Crim 20, (2005) 169 JP 73, [38]–[39].

[337] *R v Edwards and Rowlands* [2006] 2 Cr App R 4, [2005] EWCA Crim 3244, [1](iii).

Hanson[338] the Court of Appeal insisted that prosecutors must not get carried away by overloading the trial with bad character evidence or using it as a makeweight for an otherwise flimsy case. After several pointed warnings went unheeded in some quarters, the Court of Appeal's patience ran out in *O'Dowd*.[339] There have been many earnest declarations to the effect that logical relevance must henceforth be treated seriously as the first criterion of admissibility. The high point of this new orthodoxy was *Campbell*;[340] yet as we have just seen, the Court of Appeal was apparently incapable of sustaining the logic of common sense inferences in *Lawson*.[341]

To be fair to the courts, some of the difficulties they are encountering are inherent to the legislation. The bad character provisions of the CJA 2003 are complex and susceptible to anomalies, real or apparent. Admissibility gateway (g), coupled with the ideologically-motivated mugging of *Butterwasser*, is the worst offender. Lacking any obvious legitimate purpose, this legislative intervention can only succeed in accentuating the risks of moral prejudice and prejudicial reasoning. In terms of the evidentiary principles discussed in this chapter, gateway (g) licenses the prosecution to 'fight fire with fire', turning a trial of the issue into a competitive 'swearing match' or comparative credibility battle, allowing the evidence to stray beyond the confines of the charge, and diminishing the practical significance of the standard of proof to the detriment of the *Woolmington* principle.[342] Proactive and creative judicial applications of section 101(3) offer the best hope for amelioration, but there is so far little sign of those. Although victims' rights are a worthy and timely cause (and are underpinned by our principle of humane treatment), measures to assist complainants and witnesses should not require the accused to be exposed to unfair risks of prejudice. No matter how badly a witness is treated, or may feel mistreated, in the course of criminal proceedings, she does not stand in peril of criminal conviction and punishment (unless of course she perjures herself). Only the accused runs the risk of wrongful conviction, a risk which criminal procedure is committed to reducing to a tolerable minimum in the interests of justice. As the courts struggle to 'make do and mend' provisions like section 101(1)(g), they may experience the wisdom of another of our grandparents' wise proverbs about silk purses and sows' ears.

The most significant jurisprudential development in the English law of bad character evidence since the relevant provisions of the CJA 2003 came into force on 15 December 2004 has been the pronounced shift in focus from admissibility to judicial directions as the principal institutional mechanism for neutralizing potential prejudice. The Court of Appeal has said, time and again, that the trial judge's summing-up is vitally important in explaining to jurors, on the one hand, the risks associated with bad character evidence, and on the other, the inferences which it might legitimately support if jurors are persuaded that the evidence is reliable. In this respect, the law of bad character may be a weathervane for the English law of evidence in general. Practitioners must grasp and fully appreciate that '"admissibility" and "use" give rise to different questions'.[343] Trial judges must not be lulled by the JSB's Specimen Direction into repeating rote phrases as if they were magical charms. The Court of Appeal expects that judicial directions will be carefully tailored

---

[338] *R v Hanson* [2005] 2 Cr App R 21; [2005] EWCA Crim 824, [4].
[339] *R v O'Dowd* [2009] EWCA Crim 905.
[340] *R v Campbell (Kenneth)* [2007] 1 WLR 2798, [2007] EWCA Crim 1472.
[341] *R v Lawson* [2007] 1 WLR 1191, [2006] EWCA Crim 2572.   [342] §6.3.
[343] *R v Edwards and Rowlands* [2006] 2 Cr App R 4, [2005] EWCA Crim 3244, [1](viii).

to the facts of particular cases, as well as containing the standard advice and warnings expressed in language that jurors can understand. Crucially, however, the Court of Appeal has also plainly signalled that it will not get dragged into raking over the language of judicial directions with a fine-toothed comb. Trial judges' summings-up will be considered in the round, and the safety of convictions assessed holistically. Minor errors will be judged harmless and left to stand so far as the instant case is concerned, although critical assessments of trial judges' performance should still provide guidance for the future.

The vulnerabilities of this approach will be apparent to any lawyer. A *Wednesbury* review standard tolerant of deviation, idiosyncrasy, and even straightforward mistakes by trial judges is likely to breed inconsistency, lack of clarity, uncertainty, and confusion, not to mention leaving possible rights violations and injustices un-remedied – all of which might easily be regarded as bringing the law into disrepute.[344] But what are the viable alternatives to trusting trial judges in these detailed matters of trial management and jury instruction? It is simply unrealistic to imagine that the Court of Appeal is going to intervene in more than a faction of cases. If appellate judges gave the impression of being more interventionist in the cases reaching them, the Court of Appeal would soon be overwhelmed with countless more appeals along similar lines: for it would be a sorry indictment of contemporary standards of legal representation if defence counsel could not virtually *always* find *something* to complain about in judicial directions which typically run to scores or even hundreds of transcript pages. Given the post-CJA 2003 legal framework that is beginning to take shape, emphasizing the appropriate uses of evidence over questions of admissibility, the prospects of achieving justice rest with proper legal training and instruction for trial judges – which the Court of Appeal can best encourage by consistently endorsing the primacy of logical inference and continually highlighting the risks of prejudice.

One should not pretend, however, that this conclusion is entirely satisfactory. Chief amongst the reasons why academic researchers and policy-makers ought to feel frustration is that, in the absence of well-designed empirical studies, nobody really knows what is currently happening at the trial level with bad character evidence. The cases reaching the Court of Appeal might well be an entirely unrepresentative sample; and circulating anecdotes are no substitute for systematic research. It can only be hoped that academic researchers, senior policymakers, and criminal justice agencies and professionals, working collaboratively can do something to remedy this gaping hole in our knowledge of criminal proceedings.

---

[344] Colin Tapper, 'The Law of Evidence and the Rule of Law' (2009) 68 *Cambridge Law Journal* 67.

15

CORROBORATION AND FORENSIC REASONING RULES

15.1 THE MEANING OF CORROBORATION

To the extent that corroboration imposes 'quantitative' constraints on the process of proof, it has always occupied something of a marginal position in English criminal adjudication. In contrast to most continental legal systems (and also, intriguingly, Scotland),[1] there is no general corroboration requirement in English criminal law. Even very serious offences like murder, robbery, and rape are capable of being proved by the testimony of a single witness or, in theory at least,[2] entirely by damning circumstantial evidence. Most common law rules of evidence are concerned with regulating the *quality* of evidence admitted into the trial. A preoccupation with evidential quality is reinforced by the tendency in common law jurisprudential thought and practice to treat *rules of admissibility* as being virtually synonymous with the rules of evidence. Rules of admissibility stand as custodians at the courtroom door, barring the way to sub-standard evidence deemed to fall short of the quality threshold on grounds of irrelevance, unreliability, insufficient probative value, illegality, or moral impropriety. Once evidence is before the fact-finder, the only question is whether the appropriate standard of proof has been met.[3] Jurors in England and Wales, for the most part, are not required to calibrate their verdicts to quantitative evidentiary standards.

The topic of corroboration exemplifies many of this book's central themes. Until quite recently, corroboration was a byword for arcane technical law and inflexible evidentiary rules. Most of this old learning has now been swept aside and replaced with flexible standards for evaluating evidence. We have already encountered exemplars of this new breed of 'forensic reasoning rules', e.g. in relation to inferences from silence.[4] Forensic reasoning rules have two complementary components: the reasoning standard that the jury ought to apply in its deliberations, and the procedural rule requiring trial judges to direct jurors in relation to that standard. In this chapter we will explore more systematically the ways in which forensic reasoning rules emerged from and improved upon the moribund law of

---

[1] This is one respect in which Scots criminal procedure reveals its mixed common law/civilian heritage.

[2] For many types of offences, the circumstances would have to be quite unusual to facilitate proof beyond reasonable doubt without resort to *any* witness testimony. For example, it will not usually be possible to prove absence of consent on a charge of rape without relying on the complainant's testimony or, exceptionally, the testimony of an eyewitness. In practice, such prosecutions would rarely be brought: but cf. Louise Ellison, 'Prosecuting Domestic Violence Without Victim Participation' (2002) 65 *MLR* 834.   [3] §6.4.

[4] §13.3(b)

corroboration. The discussion encompasses topics of major practical significance such as identification evidence, 'turn-coat' accomplice testimony, and the probative value of lies.

Given that most of the technical law of corroboration has been abolished, leaving behind only a handful of disparate statutory remnants, it might be tempting to conclude that corroboration *tout court* can safely be entrusted to the legal antiquarians. Nothing could be further from the truth. Corroboration is fundamentally an epistemic rather than a legal matter.[5] Fact-finding in legal adjudication utilizes – and sometimes adapts – the ways we ordinarily think about combining pieces of evidence and assessing their cumulative probative value; just as the law borrows its criteria of relevance from logic and common sense.[6] This is why lawyers and other criminal justice professionals continue to speak and think in terms of 'corroboration', for the most part employing the notion of 'corroborating evidence' in its non-technical, everyday sense.[7] Abolishing the law of corroboration no more dispenses with epistemic standards for assessing evidential support than abolishing the law of hearsay would cure the inherent infirmities of second-hand evidence.

Corroboration is one of the very few evidentiary topics that has required the courts to give detailed attention to the jury's approach to fact-finding. In contrast to rules of admissibility, which are the exclusive concern of the judge in deciding to admit or exclude contested evidence, corroboration rules are instructions to the judge on *how to instruct the jury* to think about evidence and proof. The jurisprudence of corroboration consequently sheds light on neglected features and functions of the law of criminal evidence, usefully extending our discussion of relevance, inference, and fact-finding in Chapters 3 and 4. The old rules encapsulated, however imperfectly, a forensic library of factual generalizations some of which remain sound guides to fact-finding in criminal adjudication. The new, more flexible, forensic reasoning rules which have lately emerged from the shadow of doctrinal corroboration, can build upon these tried-and-tested foundations, whilst rightly eschewing the baroque excesses of past juridical follies.

(a) QUALITY OR QUANTITY?

In rejecting any general corroboration requirement, English common law diverges from nearly all systems of criminal procedure, ancient or modern. Quantitative 'corroboration' requirements feature in most modern European criminal trials, just as they were integral to historical systems of criminal procedure stretching back through the medieval Roman-canon period and into antiquity.

In its literal non-technical sense, 'corroboration' simply denotes 'supporting evidence'. Legal corroboration requirements reflect the assumption that it is too risky to rely on a single piece of evidence, or the testimony of merely one witness, as the basis for a determination of guilt that could cost the accused his reputation, livelihood, liberty, or even – in different times and places – his life. After all, no evidence can be absolutely unequivocal

---

[5] See Terence Anderson, David Schum, and William Twining, *Analysis of Evidence* (CUP, 2nd edn. 2005), 103ff; and for a diverse range of illustrations, William Twining and Iain Hampsher-Monk (eds.), *Evidence and Inference in History and Law* (Northwestern UP, 2003).   [6] §3.2.

[7] See, e.g., Paul Roberts and Candida Saunders 'Piloting PTWI—A Socio-Legal Window on Prosecutors' Assessments of Evidence and Witness Credibility' (2010) 30 *OJLS* 101, esp.112–18.

proof of guilt: confessions may be coerced; real evidence might have been planted or tampered with; a witness could be mistaken, confused, or deliberately untruthful. At the limit, the call for corroboration becomes nothing more than the common sense demand for sufficiency of proof. In criminal proceedings we should be as sure of guilt as circumstances permit before we damn the accused with penal censure and sanction, and this means gathering as much evidence as we can to substantiate the material facts whilst simultaneously exhausting the evidential possibilities of any potential avenues of innocence, excuse, or justification.

Corroboration requirements are not, however, mere epistemic rules-of-thumb benignly promoting sufficiency of proof. In modern legal systems retaining a general law of corroboration, the accused cannot be convicted on the basis of uncorroborated evidence. It is not difficult to imagine situations in which such a rule could operate harshly on crime victims and to the detriment of the public interest in deterring and punishing crime. Sexual offences, for example, are typically perpetrated in intimate circumstances where the only witness to the crime, apart from the perpetrator himself, is the victim. A rule that said that a complainant's testimony must be corroborated by other evidence might make rape and sexual assault very difficult to prosecute successfully. Jurisdictions maintaining quantitative proof requirements in reality tend to relax the legal meaning of 'corroboration'. In Scotland, for example, an accused's confession can supply the necessary corroboration if it displays 'special knowledge' corresponding to other evidence of the crime.[8] Nonetheless, a mandatory law of corroboration inevitably presents the risk that a complainant's entirely truthful, reliable, and persuasive testimony may be inadequate to secure a conviction because formal legal requirements cannot be satisfied.[9]

The risk of injustice is compounded by the tendency of corroboration requirements to accrete formidable legal technicality, divorcing the practical operation of the rules from their underlying epistemic rationale. An extreme medieval illustration is offered up by a mid-ninth century document known as the *False Decretals*:

A bishop should not be condemned except with seventy-two witnesses... a cardinal priest should not be condemned except with forty-four witnesses, a cardinal deacon of the city of Rome without thirty-six witnesses, a subdeacon, acolyte, exorcist, lector or doorkeeper except with seven witnesses.[10]

Apart from demonstrating how the Church endeavoured to take care of its own in the age of Inquisition, this remarkable passage reveals two characteristics of quantitative evidentiary standards which have survived into the modern period. Long after the mechanical Roman-canon system of pseudo-mathematical 'proofs' had been rejected in favour of

---

[8] *Wilson* v *HM Advocate* 1987 SCCR 217; *MacDonald* v *HM Advocate* 1987 SCCR 581; *McLaughlin* v *Clark* 2002 SLT 332, 2002 SCCR 335. This line of cases has been criticized, however, for unreasonably diluting the general corroboration requirement. Generally, see David Sheldon, *Evidence: Cases and Materials* (W. Green, 1996).

[9] Consider, e.g., Scottish cases such as *Lockwood* v *Walker* 1909 2 SLT 400 and *McCourt* v *HM Advocate* 1913 SC 6, discussed by Fiona Raitt, *Evidence* (W. Green, 3rd edn. 2001), 143–4. Failure of prosecutions for want of corroboration is not merely of antiquarian interest in the Scottish context: *Lockwood* v *Walker* was applied in *Paton* v *Wilson* 1988 SLT 634.

[10] The text is reproduced from James Franklin, *The Science of Conjecture: Evidence and Probability before Pascal* (Johns Hopkins UP, 2001), 13 (describing the *False Decretals* as 'an influential mixture of old papal letters, quotations taken out of context, and outright forgeries').

more naturalistic approaches to forensic reasoning, we still encounter both the legalistic aspiration to state precise and inflexible rules; and hierarchies of credibility founded on dubious, if not downright odious, assumptions about what sorts of people are worthy of belief, and by how much. According to the *False Decretals*, even the word of a lowly acolyte, exorcist, or doorkeeper trumped the testimony of six ordinary citizens. Modern corroboration requirements in English law have targeted forms of evidence like accomplice testimony and eyewitness identifications, which truly do merit enhanced scrutiny, but also types of witness, including children and complainants of sexual offences, where it is the law itself rather than the witness or her evidence which appears distinctly suspect.

(b) CORROBORATION IN LAW

On the face of it, legal rules requiring corroboration, or encouraging the jury not to return a guilty verdict without it, stipulate no more than what common sense dictates: a search for confirmatory evidence to satisfy sufficiency of proof. Over the course of the twentieth century, however, the English rules on corroboration degenerated into a web of technicalities which frequently impeded justice. The judge was obliged to give directions which would in all probability only confuse the jury and distract their attention from the genuine infirmities of suspect evidence. Furthermore, the rules became so complex that judges might easily misstate or overlook crucial parts of them, rendering perfectly sound convictions vulnerable to being quashed on appeal.

The meaning of 'corroboration' in English law was authoritatively expounded by Lord Reading CJ in *Baskerville*:

[E]vidence in corroboration must be independent testimony which affects the accused by connecting or tending to connect him with the crime... [I]t must be evidence which implicates him, that is, which confirms in some material particulars not only the evidence that the crime has been committed, but also that the prisoner committed it.[11]

Baskerville considered and rejected a competing theory of corroboration, according to which corroborating evidence need only provide independent confirmation of any aspect of a witness's testimony. This less rigorous approach was disfavoured because, it was observed, proof of a crime's having been committed does not dispel the principal doubt, that the accused might not have been the perpetrator and the witness could be implicating an innocent person.[12] However, the *Baskerville* test might be thought to over-compensate for this inadequacy, in both extension and rigidity.

It is true that evidence merely showing that the alleged offence has been committed does not necessarily make it safe to rely on, for example, an accomplice's testimony identifying the accused as the perpetrator. However, this limitation is a contingent feature of particular types of 'suspect' evidence, rather than an inherent feature of the concept of corroboration. Accomplices have 'inside knowledge' of the offence and are therefore in a

---

[11] *R v Baskerville* [1916] 2 KB 658, 667, CCA, *per* Lord Reading CJ.

[12] *R v Farler* (1837) 8 C & P 106, *per* Lord Abinger: 'The corroboration ought to consist in some circumstance that affects the identity of the party accused'; *R v Birkett* (1839) 8 C & P 732; *R v Mullins* (1848) 3 Cox CC 526, 531, *per* Maule J: 'The confirmation of an accomplice as to the mere fact of a crime having been committed, or even the particulars of it, is immaterial, unless the fact of the prisoner being connected with it is so [confirmed]'; *Tumahole Bereng v R* [1949] AC 253, 265, PC.

good position to spin an outwardly convincing yarn shifting their share of the blame onto the accused. In this situation, it is prudent not to be overly impressed by an accomplice's testimony accurately relating circumstantial details of a crime, unless the accomplice's story is confirmed by independent evidence specifically implicating the accused. But if testimony is considered suspect for different reasons, such as the witness's mental instability or personal animus towards the accused, precautions which are sensible in relation to accomplices may be wholly inapposite.

From a common sense perspective, independent evidence implicating the accused is not the *one and only* type of evidence capable of confirming an allegation in every situation. The fallacy of thinking otherwise was exposed by Joy CB, writing extra-judicially in the mid-nineteenth century,[13] and later reiterated by Wigmore:

> We are assuming that the accomplice is not to be trusted in the case in hand; his credit is an entire thing, not a separate one; therefore, whatever restores our trust in him personally restores it as a whole; if we find that he is desiring and intending to tell the true story, we shall believe one part of his story as well as another; whenever, then, by any means, that trust is restored, our object is accomplished, and it cannot matter whether the efficient circumstance related to the accused's identity or any other matter. The important thing is, not *how* our trust is restored, but whether it *is* restored at all.[14]

Wigmore's point applies with equal force to all categories of 'suspect' witness, not merely accomplices. Assessments of the nature and sufficiency of supporting evidence are highly contextual, depending on all the circumstances of the case. Such contextual assessments are in principle not reducible to mechanical legal tests of corroboration. Yet over the years English judges, in thrall to a mechanical approach, have struggled mightily with the concept of evidential 'independence'. The law became burdened with a variety of artificial fetters on common sense reasoning. Eventually, it was hard to say how, if at all, 'independence' remained a pre-condition of corroborating evidence.[15] The application of the independence requirement in particular cases was rendered more, not less, obscure by successive judicial pronouncements.[16]

A further doctrinal constraint, with no foundation in logical reasoning, was the rule that a witness requiring corroboration could not in turn corroborate the testimony of any other witness.[17] In *DPP* v *Kilbourne*[18] the House of Lords endeavoured to resolve the problem of 'mutual corroboration' in favour of a permissive commonsensical approach (albeit that the message took time to filter down through the Court of Appeal to trial judges steeped in the technical law of corroboration).[19] Lord Hailsham led the charge back to basics:

The word 'corroboration' by itself means no more than evidence tending to confirm other evidence. In my opinion, evidence which is (a) admissible and (b) relevant to the evi-

---

[13] Chief Baron Joy, *On the Evidence of Accomplices* (Milliken & Son, 1844).

[14] *Wigmore on Evidence* (Chadbourn revision), vol. 7, §2059.

[15] Compare *R* v *Beck* [1982] 1 WLR 461, CA, with *R* v *Donat* (1986) 82 Cr App R 173, 178, CA. Also see *R* v *Hills* (1988) 86 Cr App R 26, CA.

[16] For a pair of cases supposedly applying the same rule, yet reaching opposite conclusions on materially similar facts, see *R* v *McInnes* (1990) 90 Cr App R 99, CA; *R* v *Willoughby* (1989) 88 Cr App R 91, CA.

[17] *R* v *Noakes* (1832) 5 C & P 326, 328; *R* v *Gay* (1909) 2 Cr App R 327; *R* v *Baskerville* [1916] 2 KB 658, 664, CCA.   [18] *DPP* v *Kilbourne* [1973] AC 729, HL.

[19] See, e.g., *R* v *Hills* (1988) 86 Cr App R 26, CA.

dence requiring corroboration, and, if believed, confirming it in the required particulars, is capable of being corroboration of that evidence and, when believed, is in fact such corroboration.[20]

In similar vein, Lord Reid insisted that there was 'nothing technical in the idea of corroboration';[21] which at the time sounded more like wishful thinking than an accurate statement of English law. Yet the new alignment of law with logic and common sense reasoning was reiterated more than a decade later by the Privy Council in *Wong Muk-ping*:

When in the ordinary affairs of life one is doubtful whether or not to believe a particular statement [T]one naturally looks to see whether it fits in with other statements or circumstances relating to the particular matter; the better it fits in, the more one is inclined to believe it. The doubted statement is corroborated to a greater or lesser extent by the other statements or circumstances with which it fits in.[22]

We will see as the chapter unfolds that English judges today have no incentive to resurrect a highly technical legal concept of corroboration, and few opportunities to apply it were they ever so inclined. However, the travails of English law's concept of 'corroboration' teach an important lesson with enduring significance. The law of corroboration has always been a well-intentioned attempt to police the sufficiency of evidence in criminal adjudication. The project came unstuck when plausible factual inferences and generalizations were plucked from their original context and applied mechanically in future proceedings, as though the variety and spice of life could be reduced to an inflexible standardized recipe. The inevitable result, as Wigmore forewarned,[23] was that evidentiary standards designed to promote accurate fact-finding became estranged from logical and common sense reasoning, invariably to the detriment of justice.

15.2 CORROBORATION AND WARNINGS

Genuine corroboration requirements have always been few and far between in English criminal law. However, even in a system of proof traditionally so hostile to quantitative standards, English legislators have occasionally felt the need to utilize corroboration

---

[20] *DPP* v *Kilbourne* [1973] AC 729, 741, HL.

[21] ibid. 750. Also see *R* v *Turner* (1975) 61 Cr App R 67, 83, CA (James LJ); *R* v *Spencer* [1987] AC 128, 135, HL, *per* Lord Hailsham: 'the modern cases, quite correctly in my view, are reluctant to insist on any magic formula or incantation, and stress instead the need that each summing up should be tailor-made to suit the requirements of the individual case...Speaking for myself, I even dislike the expression "categories" as applied to the cases. They are simply classes of case where the experience of the courts has gradually hardened into rules of practice, owing, as my noble and learned friend points out, partly to the inherent dangers involved, and partly to the fact that the danger is not necessarily obvious to a lay mind. The less juries are confused by superfluous learning and the more their minds are directed to the particular issues relevant to the case before them, the more likely they are, in my view, to arrive at a just verdict.'

[22] *Attorney-General of Hong Kong* v *Wong Muk-ping* [1987] AC 501, 511, PC (Lord Bridge), quoting Lord Reid in *DPP* v *Kilbourne* [1973] AC 729, 750, HL.

[23] '[T]he requirement of corroboration leads to many rulings as to sufficiency, based wholly upon the evidence in each case; from these no additional development of principle can profitably be gathered. As recorded precedents of supreme courts, they are mere useless chaff, ground out by the vain labor of able minds mistaking the true material for their energies': *Wigmore on Evidence* (Chad revision), vol. 7, §2059.

requirements. A disparate residuum of statutory provisions still employs this evidentiary technique.[24] We must proceed by considering each corroboration requirement on its own specific merits.

Judges have also contributed to the quantitative corpus, by developing common law 'corroboration warnings' in relation to accomplices, children, and complainants of sexual offences. For a time, these judicial warnings were of far greater practical significance than the ragbag of random statutes imposing full corroboration requirements. Corroboration warnings were progressively abolished by statute in the late 1980s and 1990s. In retrospect, we can now see them as the unreconstructed ancestors of contemporary forensic reasoning rules.

(a) CORROBORATION STATUTES

Section 1 of the Treason Act 1795 stipulates that proof of treason offences requires a minimum of two witnesses. This provision typifies the miscellany of statutes imposing corroboration requirements in modern English criminal proceedings. Stipulating the minimum number of witnesses required to prove a criminal charge is a legislative technique at least as old as Judaism.[25] As the passage previously quoted from the *False Decretals* nicely illustrates, it was honed to a fine art by medieval Roman-canon lawyers. To its credit, modern English law has not followed suit in seeking 'safety in numbers' to any significant extent.[26] The contemporary statute book contains only a tiny number of disparate provisions emulating the Treason Act.[27]

Section 13 of the Perjury Act 1911 provides that no person shall be convicted of perjury 'upon the evidence of one witness'. One might attempt to rationalize this corroboration requirement by saying that a person should not be condemned as a perjurer when it is only a contest of oath against oath. Yet this line of argument would prove far too much, because the same could be said of any criminal charge prosecuted on the strength of a single witness's testimony. An alternative explanation is that potential witnesses might be deterred from coming forward to testify in legal proceedings if perjury were too easily alleged.[28] However, there are alternative procedural techniques for shielding an accused from groundless or vexatious allegations of perjury.[29] Moreover, criminal litigation was

---

[24] A clutch of historic corroboration requirements, which managed to survive into the last quarter of the twentieth century, were finally killed off in the late 1980s and 1990s: see Criminal Justice Act 1988, s.34(2) (in relation to children's evidence); Criminal Justice and Public Order Act 1994, s.33 (in relation to miscellaneous sexual offences).

[25] For biblical authority see Deuteronomy 19:15 (King James Version): 'One witness shall not rise up against a man for any iniquity, or for any sin, in any sin that he sinneth: at the mouth of two witnesses, or at the mouth of three witnesses, shall the matter be established.' Bentham mocked: 'In the multitude of counsellors, says the proverb, there is safety; in the multitude of witnesses there may be some sort of safety, but nothing more, it is by weight, full as much as by tale, that witnesses are to be judged': *Rationale of Judicial Evidence*, vol. 5, 467.   [26] *Wigmore on Evidence* (Chadbourn Revision), vol. 7, §2032.

[27] In addition to the two examples discussed *infra*, also see: Road Traffic Regulation Act 1984, s.88(7) (breaching temporary speed limits); Criminal Attempts Act 1981, s.2(2)(g) (general application to attempts).   [28] CLRC Eleventh Report, *Evidence: General*, Cm 4991 (1972), para.190.

[29] One procedural option is to make particular prosecutions subject to the consent of the Director of Public Prosecutions. Recent examples of this legislative technique include: Coroners and Justice Act 2009, s.62; Borders, Citizenship and Immigration Act 2009, s.18; Criminal Justice and Immigration Act 2008, s.63; Corporate Manslaughter and Corporate Homicide Act 2007, s.17. But cf. Law Com No 255, *Consents to Prosecution*, HC 1085 (TSO, 1998) (recommending the abolition of most consent requirements).

transformed by the creation of a national Crown Prosecution Service in the mid-1980s,[30] introducing an independent legal check and additional quality filter on all police and private criminal prosecutions. The CPS can even take over a private prosecution and discontinue it.[31] Thus, whilst section 13 of the 1911 Act might originally have been justified as a prophylactic against witness intimidation or manipulation, these fears no longer convincingly support a continuing demand for corroboration in modern prosecutions of perjury.

Not all surviving corroboration provisions are necessarily antiquated or objectionable. For example, section 89(2) of the Road Traffic Regulation Act 1984 provides that, 'A person prosecuted for [a speeding] offence shall not be liable to be convicted solely on the evidence of one witness to the effect that, in the opinion of the witness, the person prosecuted was driving the vehicle at a speed exceeding a specified limit'. Estimates of a moving vehicle's speed are notoriously subjective and approximate: most people can tell the difference between a car travelling at 30mph in a built-up area and a car speeding at 50mph on the same stretch of road, but few could accurately distinguish 69mph from 75mph on the motorway. It would consequently be risky to convict someone of speeding purely on the say-so of a single observer, even on the assumption that the observer is an astute judge of speed (and many will not be).

Now, it might be thought that the risk of factual error in estimating vehicle speeds is so obvious that a formal corroboration requirement is unnecessary; and it must be conceded that a witness's estimate of speed is bound to be a central, rigorously scrutinized, and evaluated piece of evidence in any prosecution for speeding. But it does not follow that a legal corroboration requirement is therefore entirely superfluous. By imposing an additional quantitative threshold on the proof of speeding offences, Parliament has helped to ensure that motorists are not unnecessarily intimidated or inconvenienced by a criminal charge or the threat of prosecution and public trial unless there is hard evidence of wrongdoing. This sends a clear signal to police investigators and prosecutors about the type, and amount, of evidence that must be secured before criminal proceedings can be initiated. In this way, corroboration requirements can be said to enlarge the liberty of the citizen and keep public power in check. So far as speeding prosecutions are concerned, the courts have successfully buttressed legislative purpose by confining section 89(2)'s corroboration requirement within sensible limits.[32] This example demonstrates how requiring corroboration remains, in principle, a useful and legitimate legislative option, albeit one which is seldom chosen in English law, past or present.

Novel corroboration requirements continue to be championed from time to time by criminal justice reformers. For example, the suggestion that a conviction should never be based solely on an uncorroborated confession attracted considerable attention in the late 1980s and early 90s following a spate of damaging revelations of miscarriages of justice involving false, coerced, or tainted confessions.[33] Research for the Runciman

---

[30] Prosecution of Offences Act 1985, s.1; see www.cps.gov.uk/.

[31] Prosecution of Offences Act 1985, ss.6(2) and 23.

[32] As we saw in §4.3, mechanical speed-detectors, speedometers, speed trap devices, and the like, are not the 'opinion' of a witness, and consequently do not require corroboration under s.89(2): *Castle* v *Cross* [1984] 1 WLR 1372, DC. Nor do the professional judgments of appropriately qualified experts: *Crossland* v *DPP* [1988] 3 All ER 712, DC.

[33] For discussion, see Rosemary Pattenden, 'Should Confessions be Corroborated?' (1991) 107 *LQR* 317; Andrew L.-T. Choo, 'Confessions and Corroboration: A Comparative Perspective' [1991] *Crim LR* 867;

Royal Commission on Criminal Justice indicated that the introduction of a corroboration requirement for all confession evidence would not dramatically harm the conviction rate, contrary to the dire warnings of the police and other critics, but would reduce
the risks of wrongful conviction.[34] However, the proposal failed to achieve any traction
with policymakers and momentum soon dissipated, as the temporary focus on remedying
miscarriages of justice predictably gave way to the more routine imperatives of 'cracking
down on crime' and 'rebalancing the criminal justice system in favour of the law-abiding
majority'.[35]

   Whether a formal rule requiring all confessions to be corroborated would promote, or
retard, the interests of justice is debatable and the question would benefit from further
empirical investigation. Quite apart form the marginality of *all* corroboration requirements in English law, this particular proposal must grapple with the talismanic status of
confessions in criminal litigation and popular culture.[36] Regardless of the immediate prospects for reform, however, the proposal in relation to confessions is illuminating on several
fronts. It reminds us that corroboration requirements must be evaluated on their own
individual merits. If some of English law's traditional corroboration requirements have
been rooted in false assumptions and discriminatory stereotypes, these vices are certainly
not conceptual features of corroboration. Any particular corroboration requirement can
only be as good as the factual generalizations on which it rests and the forensic objectives
it was designed to achieve. Sound factual generalizations, such as the proposition that it
is difficult for eyewitnesses to estimate the speed of a moving vehicle accurately and reliably, are a necessary pre-condition of defensible corroboration requirements; but they are
never a sufficient condition in a legal system that, for the most part, eschews quantitative
constraints on fact-finding and proof.

(b) CORROBORATION WARNINGS

Corroboration warnings, like many other modern rules of evidence, were originally stated
to be informal matters of 'practice'. However, by the mid-twentieth century the circumstances, as well as the terms, in which a corroboration warning had to be given were strictly
mandated by law. The practice which later evolved into hard-and-fast rules required the
trial judge to direct the jury that it was 'dangerous' to convict solely on the basis of certain classes of evidence in the absence of corroboration. These classes of evidence were
regarded as forensically *suspect*, and consequently attracted special evidentiary strictures.
But judicial warnings were not corroboration *requirements* in the full legal sense, requiring

Michael McConville, *Corroboration and Confessions: The Impact of a Rule Requiring that No Conviction can
be Sustained on the Basis of Confession Evidence Alone*, RCCJ Research Study No 13 (HMSO, 1993).

[34] McConville, *Corroboration and Confessions*, 85, 87, concluded that 'only a fraction of all prosecutions
and convictions would be adversely affected by a corroboration rule to the extent that non-prosecution or
an acquittal would be the inevitable or likely outcome.... [T]he unqualified assumption that the introduction of a corroboration requirement means "lost convictions" is unsustainable; rather, such a rule would,
among other consequences, merely confirm the result in cases which collapse under existing (lower) evidence thresholds and would additionally lead to the avoidance of some convictions based upon dubious
foundations.'

[35] *Rebalancing the Criminal Justice System in Favour of the Law-abiding Majority – Cutting Crime,
Reducing Reoffending and Protecting the Public* (Home Office, July 2006), www.homeoffice.gov.uk/docu-
ments/CJS-review.pdf/.   [36] §12.1.

the accused to be acquitted in the absence of corroboration. The trial judge delivering a corroboration warning, having solemnly sermonized on the dangers of convicting on uncorroborated testimony, was required to add that jurors were entitled to do just that if, having reflected carefully on the matter, they were prepared to accept the witness's uncorroborated testimony as sufficient proof of the accused's guilt.

In the modern law, it was established that a trial judge must issue a corroboration warning in relation to three classes of 'suspect' witness: (i) accomplices; (ii) complainants in sexual cases; and (iii) children. The substance of the warning, as previously stated, was that the jury should consider it 'dangerous' to arrive at a guilty verdict solely on the uncorroborated testimony of any accomplice, sex-offence complainant, or child, but nonetheless remained at liberty to convict in the absence of corroborative evidence. Corroboration warnings relating to children's testimony were abrogated by section 34(2) of the Criminal Justice Act 1988, though for a time child complainants of sexual abuse still continued to attract the sex crimes corroboration warning equally applicable to adults. The remaining two warning requirements were finally abolished by section 32 of the Criminal Justice and Public Order Act 1994, to the widespread approbation of legal reformers and commentators.[37] Before consigning corroboration warnings to the dustbin of legal history, it will repay us to examine the distinctive, and at times plausible, rationalizations underpinning each type of warning. This inquiry will help to clarify the process by which corroboration warnings evolved into a new generation of forensic reasoning rules.

Corroboration warnings for children's evidence took their cue from popular beliefs and assumptions that child witnesses, as a class, have limited powers of perception and memory, are susceptible to suggestion and manipulation by adults, and may be prone to confusing fact with fantasy or even to making mendacious complaints ('telling stories') without necessarily appreciating the serious implications of their allegations. In our earlier discussion of competency requirements,[38] we observed that such beliefs and assumptions have been systematically re-examined under the critical microscope of behavioural science research, in the light of which most of them must now be modified significantly or rejected altogether. Once its load-bearing factual buttresses had been fatally undermined, the mandatory corroboration warning for children's evidence, like the old and now discredited competency rules, became an intolerable embarrassment to a rational system of criminal procedure, and for much the same reasons.

The second type of corroboration warning attached to (female or male) victims' testimony in sex crime prosecutions.[39] In trials for sexual offences, the judge was obliged, adopting the standard formula, to warn the jury that it was unsafe to convict on the uncorroborated testimony of the complainant; but that it remained open to jurors to convict in the absence of corroboration, if satisfied that the complainant's testimony was true. This species of warning reflected two assumptions: first, that sex-offence complainants frequently make false accusations, perhaps due to neurotic fantasy, from spite, or out of

---

[37] Law Com No 202, *Criminal Law: Corroboration of Evidence in Criminal Trials* (HMSO, 1991) recommended outright abolition without replacement. The Commission was 'impressed by the almost unanimous view on consultation that the present obligation to give a corroboration warning should be abolished': ibid. para.2.20. For a more cautious assessment of the merits of abolition, see Peter Mirfield, 'An Alternative Future for Corroboration Warnings' (1991) 107 *LQR* 450.   [38] §7.2.

[39] See Ian Dennis, 'Corroboration Requirements Reconsidered' [1984] *Crim LR* 316.

shame or regret at having consented to sex with the accused;[40] secondly, that it is especially difficult in such cases for a jury to detect false allegations. The complainant may appear sincere and plausible and there is often little, if any, other evidence in the case to settle a direct conflict of testimony. Such cases often boil down to one person's word against another's. Moreover, the circumstances of the charges, especially where the alleged victim is a child, may generate strong prejudice and hostility towards the accused purely because of the nature of the offence, potentially eroding the presumption of innocence.

In their heyday, corroboration warnings in sex cases were not devoid of supporters within the legal fraternity. Glanville Williams was amongst their number.[41] Yet such warnings were seriously flawed, on several counts. To begin with, sexual offences are rarely easy to prove, in the absence of independent witnesses. Physical evidence may be available to establish sexual contact with the alleged perpetrator, but unless the attack was violent or conformed to the stereotypical but statistically unusual pattern of 'stranger rape' this will not help to prove lack of consent. As the problematic 'attrition rate'[42] in rape and sexual assault prosecutions became more widely recognized as a problem for justice, the idea that rape charges are too easy to bring and sustain became progressively more implausible. Rape victims appeared to be having quite enough trouble negotiating the considerable practical, psychological, and emotional barriers to taking their violators to court, without having, in addition, to confront artificial evidentiary hurdles to the successful prosecution of sexual assaults.

Nor should assumptions about the prevalence of false accusations go unchallenged. Sexual morality has come a long way since adultery, and even 'fornication', were widely considered sinful. It is no longer the norm in British society for unmarried mothers to be forced to give up their babies for secret adoption in order to avoid social ostracism and preserve the family name from indelible disgrace. As the social consequences of extra-marital sex and unwanted pregnancy have diminished, so the motivation for making false accusations of rape must correspondingly be weakened; albeit that one can only guess how often potential opportunities actually motivate false complaints. It remains conceivable that a woman or man might cry 'rape' in order to conceal sexual indiscretions from their spouses or partners, or in an attempt to blackmail the accused. False allegations against marital partners are sometimes suspected in the context of child custody disputes ('to get the man out of the house'), and it may even sometimes happen that a complainant is pressured by others into making an allegation of rape against her or his inclinations.[43] However, these conceivable scenarios hardly necessitate an automatic corroboration warning in each and every prosecution for rape or sexual assault. Although the risk of false accusation can never be eliminated entirely,[44] there is no reason to suppose that groundless allegations

[40] Cf. CLRC Eleventh Report, *Evidence: General*. Cm. 4991 (HMSO, 1972), para. 186.

[41] Glanville Williams, 'Corroboration: Sexual Cases' [1962] *Crim LR* 662.

[42] The rate at which cases are lost to the system through victim non-reporting, police 'no-criming', prosecution discontinuance, or failure of proof at trial: see: Liz Kelly, Jo Lovett, and Linda Regan, *A Gap or a Chasm? Attrition in Reported Rape Cases*, Home Office Research Study 293 (RDS, 2005), www.homeoffice.gov.uk/rds/pdfs05/hors293.pdf; CJS Framework Document, *Narrowing the Justice Gap* (2002); Home Office, *Digest 4: Information on the Criminal Justice System in England and Wales* (RDS Directorate, October 1999), 29.

[43] An illustration is reported by Roberts and Saunders, 'Piloting PTWI', 114

[44] One high-profile example involved false allegations of sexual assault levelled against the disgraced former Tory MP Neil Hamilton and his politician's-wife-turned-media-personality, Christine. Perhaps the main lesson of this episode, however, was that the allegations were soon exposed as fabrications. American

are either widespread or, generally speaking, credible enough to produce wrongful convictions on the rare occasions that they arise. It seems more likely that the complainant corroboration warning reflected sexist stereotyping of – predominantly, female – sexual assault complainants,[45] rather than well-founded assessments of complainants' testimonial unreliability.[46]

Moreover, even on the entirely unrealistic assumption of widespread false allegations, corroboration warnings were impotent to help the jury expose a complainant's, *ex hypothesi* often undetectable, mendacity. The law presented jurors with a straightforward choice: either credit the complainant's testimony and convict the accused, notwithstanding the advertised infirmities of suspect evidence, or take refuge in the asymmetric standard of proof[47] and acquit on the basis of reasonable doubt. In neither case could a corroboration warning contribute to rational deliberation and adjudication in the manner envisaged. The warning, in other words, was either superfluous (where the complaint's unreliability was manifest) or useless (in the case of the accomplished, convincing liar).[48] The complainant warning was worse than useless, however, because its technicalities could catch trial judges out in minor errors producing unmeritorious appeals. And the symbolism of the warning was an affront to justice and a public relations disaster for the law. It implicitly communicated the legitimacy-sapping impression that rape complainants suffered institutionalized discrimination in English criminal proceedings.

The final nail in the coffin was the realization that, although the complainant corroboration warning was obviously designed to protect the accused, in practice it could operate to his detriment. The warning had to be given in all cases, whether or not the circumstances called for it. Yet, at the Court of Appeal recognized in *Chance*:

[T]here will inevitably be occasions when the direction would be inappropriate on the facts. Juries are quick to spot such anomalies, and will understandably view the anomaly, and often, as a result, the rest of the directions, with suspicion, thus undermining the judge's purpose.[49]

examples include the curious case of *People* v *Dotson*, 424 NE 2d 1319 (1981), discussed by Sharon Cobb, 'Gary Dotson as Victim: the Legal Response to Recanting Testimony' (1986) 35 *Emory LJ* 969; Edwin Black, 'Why Judge Samuels Sent Gary Dotson Back to Prison' (1985) 71 *ABA Journal* 56.

[45] Cf. Wigmore's belief that '[t]he unchaste (let us call it) mentality finds incidental but direct expression in the narration of imaginary sex-incidents of which the narrator is the heroine or the victim. On the surface the narration is straightforward and convincing. The real victim, however, too often in such cases is the innocent man; for the respect and sympathy naturally felt by any tribunal for a wronged female helps to give easy credit to such a plausible tale': *Wigmore on Evidence* (Chadbourn revision), vol. 3A, §924a. For judicial remarks to similar effect, see *R* v *Henry and Manning* (1968) 53 Cr App R 150, 153, CA; *R* v *Mandley* [1988] Crim LR 688, CA.

[46] Generally, see Jennifer Temkin, *Rape and the Legal Process* (OUP, 2nd edn. 2003); Susan Estrich, 'Rape' (1986) 95 *Yale LJ* 1087. Cf. D. J. Birch, 'Corroboration in Criminal Trials: A Review of the Proposals of the Law Commission's Working Paper' [1990] *Crim LR* 667, 678–9: 'Like everyone else involved in the practice and teaching of criminal law, I have heard worrying tales of false complaints, particularly in rape cases. Police officers whose views I respect have suggested to me that the majority of complaints of rape are unfounded'.

[47] §6.3(b) and §6.4(b).

[48] Such considerations prompted Wigmore to advocate subjecting complainants to a battery of psychological tests: *Wigmore on Evidence* (Chadbourn revision), vol. 3A, §924a. However, as Glanville Williams, 'Corroboration: Sexual Cases' [1962] *Crim LR* 662, 663, retorted, the effectiveness of such tests is doubtful and, furthermore, may involve unacceptable indignities for complainants.

[49] *R* v *Chance* [1988] QB 932, 941, CA. Also see *R* v *Atkinson* (1988) 86 Cr App R 359, CA; but cf. *R* v *Mandley* [1988] Crim LR 688, CA.

The complainant corroboration warning required the trial judge to work systematically through the evidence presented at the trial, painstakingly explaining to the jury which testimony would benefit from corroboration and which evidence was capable of providing it. In many cases, the practical effect of this rigmarole must have been to fix in jurors' minds the most damning aspects of the prosecution's case against the accused, and this immediately prior to the jury's retiring to consider its verdict.[50]

Accomplices were the third category of witness attracting a compulsory corroboration warning, prior to the abolition of all such warnings by the 1994 Act. The leading case was *Davies v DPP*, in which the House of Lords expounded the following classic statement of the rule:

In a criminal trial where a person who is an accomplice gives evidence on behalf of the prosecution, it is the duty of the judge to warn the jury that, although they may convict upon his evidence, it is dangerous to do so unless it is corroborated. This rule, although a rule of practice, now has the force of a rule of law. Where the judge fails to warn the jury in accordance with this rule, the conviction will be quashed, even if, in fact, there be ample corroboration of the evidence of the accomplice...[51]

In contrast to the warnings formerly attaching to children's evidence and to the testimony of sexual assault complaints, the accomplice rule did not rest upon stereotypical assumptions of unreliability. Nor have the rationales underpinning the accomplice warning been undermined by new behavioural science research. To the contrary, the reasons for treating accomplice evidence with circumspection marshalled by Heydon[52] almost forty years ago still retain their epistemic validity. An accomplice may wish to exculpate himself or to purchase leniency by helping the prosecution obtain the conviction of other participants in the crime,[53] and in doing so may be tempted to exaggerate their culpability relative to his, or even to frame innocent people. An accomplice may inculpate another out of spite or revenge; and since the accomplice is familiar with the facts of the crime he can easily concoct a false account of another's involvement which would be difficult to discredit. Finally, an accomplice is, after all, a confessed criminal, whose credibility must at least be open to question.

Adopting the recommendations of the Law Commission, Parliament opted for the tidier solution of outright abolition of all remaining corroboration warnings, including the accomplice warning. However, it is worth considering whether the accomplice rule, or something like it, might not have been retained. It is not necessary to endorse every

---

[50] This may go some way towards explaining the Law Commission's (on the face of it, rather surprising) report that, although nearly all respondents to the Commission's consultation exercise favoured abolition of corroboration warnings, some thought that warnings were too generous to the accused, whilst others argued that they were detrimental to his interests! See Law Com No 202, *Criminal Law: Corroboration of Evidence in Criminal Trials*, paras.2.17–2.18; D. J. Birch, 'Corroboration in Criminal Trials: A Review of the Proposals of the Law Commission's Working Paper' [1990] *Crim LR* 667.

[51] *Davies v DPP* [1954] AC 378, 399, HL, *per* Lord Simonds LC (adopting propositions advanced in argument by counsel).

[52] J. D. Heydon, 'The Corroboration of Accomplices' [1973] *Crim LR* 264. Also see Glanville Williams, 'Corroboration: Accomplices' [1962] *Crim LR* 588; CLRC Eleventh Report, *Evidence: General*. Cm 4991 (HMSO, 1972), para.183.

[53] This ever-green prosecutorial tactic is now even sanctified by legislation: see Serious Organised Crime and Police Act 2005, ss.71–74.

technical encrustation on *Davies* in order to appreciate the wisdom of the accomplice warning's underlying factual generalizations.

Of the old accomplice warning's many doctrinal complexities, we need mention only one. *Davies* recast the concept of an 'accomplice' as a term of art, limited to: (i) principal offenders and common law accessories; (ii) thieves and their handlers; and (iii) parties to the accused's extraneous crimes, when adduced in the trial as evidence of 'similar facts'.[54] Although *Davies* went beyond the standard criminal law meaning of 'accomplice,' it was still too narrow to catch every witness connected with the crime, who might have the motive and sufficient 'inside knowledge' to frame an innocent accused by presenting false, but superficially colourable, testimony to the court.

Davies itself provides an illustration. The accused was convicted of murder by stabbing during an affray, partly on the evidence of another participant in the incident who testified for the prosecution. The House of Lords ruled that no corroboration warning was necessary, because the witness, whom it was accepted had never contemplated an attack with a knife, could not in law be an accomplice to murder (at most, his *mens rea* would stretch to manslaughter).[55] Yet surely the witness had a strong motive to deny any knowledge of the knife, in order to avoid implicating himself in a murder; and once outside the technical jurisdiction of the accomplice rule, he was free to use his insider-knowledge of the incident to damn the accused, in exactly the fashion that corroboration warnings were supposed to address. Again, where an offence must have been committed either by the accused or by the prosecution's chief witness acting alone, the danger of undetected perjury leading to wrongful conviction is every bit as great as it would be if the witness were an accomplice, yet the warning requirement did not apply.[56] It is easy to imagine many other scenarios in which a witness who could not be an 'accomplice' under *Davies*, and therefore failed to attract a corroboration warning, might nonetheless have both the motive to lie and the insider-knowledge to do it convincingly.[57]

It is hardly surprising that the concept of an 'accomplice', which was designed for the purposes of assigning criminal liability rather than for any evidentiary purpose, proved to be an unreliable trigger for corroboration warnings.[58] Given that substantive criminal law is generally unconcerned with the reliability of testimony, it was predictable that the courts' preoccupation with the subtleties of the law of complicity would turn out to be a

---

[54] But no warning was given where the accomplice was a co-accused testifying in his own defence, since to impugn the co-accused's credibility in these circumstances would have impinged on the presumption of innocence: *R v Bagley* [1980] Crim LR 572, CA; *R v Loveridge* (1983) 76 Cr App R 125, CA.

[55] On the applicable substantive law of complicity, see A. P. Simester and G. R. Sullivan, *Criminal Law Theory and Doctrine* (Hart, 3rd edn. 2007), 233–5.

[56] Cf. *R v Whitaker* (1976) 63 Cr App R 193, CA. A notorious example is the case of *Timothy Evans*, in which the accused was wrongly convicted of murdering his baby (and, by implication, his wife as well). The real perpetrator of this grisly double-murder was the Evans' neighbour, John Christie, who testified for the prosecution at the trial, thus helping to send the hapless, and utterly innocent, Evans to the gallows. Christie was subsequently exposed as a mass murderer, and Evans – for all the good it did him – was granted a posthumous pardon: see Ludovic Kennedy, *10 Rillington Place* (Grafton, 1971 [1961]), esp. chs 8–10.

[57] For further discussion, see J. D. Heydon, 'The Corroboration of Accomplices' [1973] *Crim LR* 264, 270–6.

[58] The House of Lords implicitly conceded as much in *Davies v DPP* [1954] AC 378, by stretching the normal definition of 'accomplice' designed to delimit the liability of parties to crime, to cover two additional categories for evidentiary purposes: receivers who testify against 'their' thieves; and participants in crimes other than the offence(s) charged.

misleading distraction.[59] The real question has always been whether additional procedural precautions should be taken to address the peculiar risks of unreliability posed by certain types of testimony. This is an epistemic problem in search of technical procedural solutions, an evidential (fact-finding) rather than an evidentiary (doctrinal) issue *per se*. We can see this much more clearly now that corroboration warnings have been completely abolished.

15.3 FORENSIC REASONING RULES

When confronted with suspect evidence which could not be fitted into any of the three established corroboration warnings, trial judges and appellate courts had three basic options. They could: (1) declare a new category of corroboration warning; (2) leave the matter to be resolved through the normal forensic processes for presenting and testing evidence; or (3) develop new techniques for bringing evidential infirmities to the attention of the fact-finder without elevating these instructions to the formal status of corroboration warnings. As frustrations mounted with an excessively technical law of corroboration, and with an eye to pre-empting unmeritorious appeals, the third option became increasingly attractive to trial judges. If suspect evidence might otherwise remain impervious to the ordinary course of forensic examination and potentially bamboozle jurors' common sense, the judge could issue an appropriately phrased note of caution tailored to the facts of the case. After all, this was only a modest extension of the trial judge's general duty to sum-up the evidence for the jury's benefit and explain the law applied to the facts of the case.[60]

In the era before old-style corroboration warnings were abolished by the 1994 Act, the new breed of flexible forensic reasoning rules might have been taken for a kind of second-class poor relation, with less stringent criteria and more muted legal consequences than their better nourished and more muscular corroboration cousins. But in a reversal of fortune of Dickensian proportions, the newcomers overtook and then superseded orthodox corroboration warnings, and today forensic reasoning rules proliferate throughout the modern law of criminal evidence.

(a) EVOLUTION: FROM COMMON LAW TO COMMON SENSE

In *Prater* Edmund Davies J. remarked, in relation to a witness not qualifying as a *Davies*-accomplice, that 'in practice it is desirable that a warning should be given that the witness, whether he comes from the dock, as in this case, or whether he be a Crown witness, may be a witness with some purpose of his own to serve'.[61] Five years later in *Stannard* the

---

[59] Cf. *Wigmore on Evidence*, (Chadbourn revision), vol. 7, §2060: 'From the point of view of safeguarding the accused against false tales of an associate, and of estimating the credit to be given to such testimony, all the foregoing rulings are a sheer waste of time, as generalities. It is difficult enough to determine who is lying; but we do not find it out by any of these technical niceties.' [60] §2.5(d).

[61] *R v Prater* [1960] 2 QB 464, 466, CCA; approved by the House of Lords in *DPP v Kilbourne* [1973] AC 729, 740, *per* Lord Hailsham LC: 'A judge is almost certainly wise to give a similar warning about the evidence of any principal witness for the Crown where the witness can reasonably be suggested to have some purpose of his own to serve in giving false evidence…'.

Court of Appeal was at pains to stress that this *dictum* was 'no more than an expression of what is desirable and what, it is to be hoped, will more usually than not be adopted... where it seems to be appropriate to the learned judge'.[62] The Court refused to treat *Prater* as extending the formal categories of corroboration warning, not because it believed that the risk posed by witnesses falling outside the traditional categories was invariably of lesser magnitude,[63] but because it wanted to liberate trial judges from the doctrinal straitjacket of corroboration warnings. As Ackner LJ subsequently elaborated in *Beck*:

[T]he burden upon the trial judge of the summing up is a heavy one. It would be a totally unjustifiable addition to require him, not only fairly to put before the jury the defence's contention that a witness was suspect, because he had an axe to grind, but also to evaluate the weight of that axe and oblige him... to give an accomplice warning with the appropriate direction as to the meaning of corroboration together with the identification of the potential corroborative material.[64]

What are now sometimes called 'Beck warnings' or directions relate to a witness 'with a purpose of their own to serve' or a witness 'with an axe to grind'. The *Beck* direction was further expounded and authoritatively endorsed by the House of Lords in *Spencer*,[65] where the accused were male nurses in a special hospital who were charged with mistreating mentally ill prisoners in their care. In view of the fact that the case against the nurses rested entirely on the testimony of mentally disturbed detainees, the trial judge, in summing-up, admonished the jury to approach the complainants' evidence with great care. The jury was reminded that the complainants were implicated in criminality, mentally unstable, and harbouring grudges against the accused. The judge also emphasized the absence of independent corroboration. On appeal against their convictions, the accused took the narrow point that the judge had omitted the word 'dangerous' (as in the old corroboration warning's standard formula, 'it would be dangerous to convict...') from his summing-up. The House of Lords was suitably unimpressed, declaring that 'the obligation to warn the jury does not involve some legalistic ritual to be automatically recited by the judge, or that some particular form of words or incantation has to be used and, if not used, the summing-up is faulty and the conviction must be quashed'.[66] Lord Ackner (as he by then was) seized the opportunity to reiterate the Court of Appeal's holding in *Beck* with enhanced legal authority:

[I]n a case which does not fall into the three established categories and where there exists potential corroborative material, the extent to which the trial judge should make reference to that material depends upon the facts of each case. The overriding rule is that he must put the defence fairly and adequately.[67]

Trial judges were entrusted with the task of adapting their directions to accommodate the demands of the current proceedings, in order to facilitate jurors' evaluation of problematic forms of testimony. Ritualistic incantations and formal legal mantras, which

---

[62] *R v Stannard* [1965] 2 QB 1, 14, CCA (Winn J). Also see *R v Whitaker* (1976) 63 Cr App R 193, 196, CA; *R v Knowlden* (1983) 77 Cr App R 94, CA.

[63] The facts of *R v Whitaker* (1976) 63 Cr App R 193, CA, and *R v Beck* [1982] 1 WLR 461, CA, scotch any such notion.　　　　　　　　　　　　　　　　　　　　　　　　　[64] *R v Beck* [1982] 1 WLR 461, 467, CA.

[65] *R v Spencer* [1987] AC 128, HL.

[66] ibid. 141 (Lord Ackner). Also see *R v Chance* [1988] QB 932, CA.　　　[67] ibid. 142.

would often be meaningless if not mystifying in the circumstances of particular cases, were a thing of the past.

The legislative provisions abolishing mandatory corroboration warnings left the trial judge's primary duty of ensuring a fair trial – by summing-up to the jury in a way that is simultaneously helpful, comprehensible, and fair to the parties – intact and unfettered. Parliament declined on this occasion to follow the path taken elsewhere,[68] of positively prohibiting certain judicial remarks about particular witnesses.[69] This remains an option for future legislative interventions; albeit that efforts to legislate against the grain of common sense reasoning have a very poor track record. Another possibility was that the judge, whilst now free to decline to give any warning at all, might still be bound by the old legal formulas defining the meaning and scope of 'corroboration' whenever he did choose to give a warning. Such a reactionary interpretation would have bucked the prevailing trend towards greater informality and judicial discretion resoundingly endorsed by the House of Lords in *Spencer*.[70] In the event, the Court of Appeal took an early opportunity, in *Makanjuola*,[71] to squash any notion that the old rules of corroboration might somehow live on in a kind of legal shadowland, waiting to answer a trial judge's necromantic invocation. Lord Taylor CJ administered the last rites without ceremony or sentimentality:

[I]t is clear that to carry on giving 'discretionary' warnings generally and in the same terms as were previously obligatory would be contrary to the policy and purpose of the [1994] Act. Whether, as a matter of discretion, a judge should give any warning and if so its strength and terms must depend upon the content and manner of the witness's evidence, the circumstances of the case and the issues raised. The judge will often consider that no special warning is required at all.... [J]udges are not required to conform to any formula and this court would be slow to interfere with the exercise of discretion by a trial judge who has the advantage of assessing the manner of a witness's evidence as well as its content.[72]

Trial judges were free at last from the curse of technical rules of corroboration, and English law was brought into line with the flexible approach to judicial warnings by now well-established in Commonwealth jurisdictions.[73]

---

[68] Cf. Canadian Criminal Code, s.274, providing that: '[i]f an accused is charged with [a designated sexual offence]...no corroboration is required for a conviction *and the judge shall not instruct the jury that it is unsafe to find the accused guilty in the absence of corroboration*' (emphasis supplied). In *R v Boss* (1988) 46 CCC (3d) 523, 531 (Ont CA), Cory JA explained: 'It is apparent that the section removes any legal requirement for corroboration with respect to the offences which it enumerates. Further, a trial judge is prohibited from instructing a jury that it is unsafe to convict an accused in the absence of corroboration. However, there is nothing in the section which would prohibit a judge from exercising his or her discretion when reviewing the factual issues with the jury.'

[69] For example, Parliament might have enacted a rule forbidding judges from pointing out (where this is the case) that a rape allegation rests on the unsupported word of the complainant.

[70] See Diane Birch, 'Corroboration: Goodbye to All That?' [1995] *Crim LR* 524.

[71] *R v Makanjuola* [1995] 1 WLR 1348, CA.   [72] ibid. 1351.

[73] From the early 1970s onwards, the trend in Commonwealth jurisdictions had been towards abrogating technical rules of corroboration altogether, as achieved by the Supreme Court of Canada in *Vetrovec v R* [1982] 1 SCR 811, or at least to mitigate the consequences of minor breaches of the rules. Thus, in Australia, failure to administer a warning no longer meant a conviction had to be quashed if the suspect evidence was in fact corroborated: *Kelleher v R* (1974) 131 CLR 534. For discussion, see Jill Hunter, Camille Cameron, and Terese Henning, *Litigation II: Evidence and Criminal Process* (Butterworths, Sydney, 7th edn. 2005), 903ff; Andrew B. Clarke, 'Corroboration in Sexual Cases' [1980] *Crim LR* 362.

(b) COMMON LAW WARNINGS

Beck-warnings, as clarified in *Spencer* and *Makanjuola*, became a prototype for judicial directions in relation to a wide variety of different forms of 'suspect' evidence. A direct and important extension of the concern with witnesses 'with a purpose of their own to serve' is to 'gaol cell confessions' to fellow inmates. Such confessions are notoriously suspect. The witness who testifies to the confession is himself an offender, or at least being held on remand pending trial, and has an obvious incentive to curry favour with the authorities. The alleged confession is typically unrecorded and its terms may be difficult to pin down precisely. English law has not gone down the road of categorically excluding such dubious evidence, on the assumption that gaol cell confessions are sometimes true despite their evidential infirmities. It is plausible that prisoners awaiting trial may boast about their crimes to other inmates or let incriminating details slip inadvertently. The compromise is that evidence of gaol cell confessions, though in principle potentially admissible, attracts a stiff judicial warning whenever it is adduced in a criminal trial. In *Pringle* the Privy Council advised:

It is not possible to lay down any fixed rules about the directions which the judge should give to a jury about the evidence which one prisoner gives against another prisoner about things done or said while they are both together in custody. There may be cases where the correct approach will be to treat the prisoner simply as an ordinary witness about whose evidence nothing out of the usual need be said. Examples of that situation are where the prisoner is a witness to an assault on another prisoner or a prison officer or is a witness to a drugs trans-action which has taken place in the place where he is being held. But a judge must always be alert to the possibility that the evidence by one prisoner against another is tainted by an improper motive. The possibility that this may be so has to be regarded with particular care where...a prisoner who has yet to face trial gives evidence that the other prisoner has confessed to the very crime for which he is being held in custody. It is common knowledge that, for various reasons, a prisoner may wish to ingratiate himself with the authorities in the hope that he will receive favourable treatment from them.... Where such indications are present, the judge should draw the jury's attention to these indications and their pos-sible significance. He should then advise them to be cautious before accepting the prisoner's evidence.[74]

In this case the trial judge had failed to give an adequate warning because he had not spelt out the reasons why this particular gaol cell confession needed to be approached with particular caution. This flawed direction was one of several defects in the trial leading to Pringle's conviction of capital murder being quashed. Specifically, the judge should have pointed out that the witness 'was an untried prisoner, that it is not unknown for persons in his position to wish to ingratiate themselves with the police and that to give them information that the appellant had confessed to the crime for which he was being held by them in custody was a convenient and obvious way of doing so'. The trial judge 'ought then to have given an express direction to the jury that they should be cautious before they accepted this witness's evidence'.[75] However, the Court of Appeal has resisted any backsliding into formulaic incantations, reiterating on several occasions that 'no specific

---

[74] *Pringle* v R (Appeal No. 17/2002, PC (Jam)), 27 January 2003, [30]–[31] (Lord Hope).
[75] ibid. [33].

formulation is required by a trial judge. It is for the trial judge to tailor his direction to fit the facts of this case'.[76]

Further examples of potentially 'suspect' evidence attracting special judicial warnings are legion. We have already encountered a good many of them in previous chapters, including hostile witnesses,[77] certain kinds of expert testimony,[78] and evidence of the accused's extraneous misconduct.[79] Tailored warnings may also be required in relation to the testimony of 'mentally disturbed' witnesses[80] and in cases of alleged historic childhood abuse involving long delays or 'recovered memories'.[81] Eyewitness identification evidence has spawned its own extensive jurisprudence meriting separate treatment later in the chapter.[82] The jury may also require further directions regarding events that have occurred during the course of the trial. Where, for example, the trial judge accedes to the jury's mid-deliberation request to be reminded of the complainant's testimony he should warn jurors 'not to give the complainant's evidence in that form disproportionate weight simply because it is repeated well after all the other evidence and to bear in mind the other evidence in the case'. Failure to issue an appropriate direction contextualizing the evidence may produce 'an unbalanced state of affairs' leading to a conviction being quashed.[83]

In each case in which a judicial warning is required, the trial judge must explain to the jury why particular items of 'suspect' evidence should be approached with circumspection spelling out their particular epistemic infirmities. Typically, the judge also needs to explain how that evidence might be combined with other evidence in the case in order to arrive at a holistic verdict, of guilty or not guilty. Discrete forensic reasoning rules thus merge into the trial judge's general duty to direct the jury on the facts and the law. One area presenting acute inferential difficulties that we have already examined in some detail is the minefield of drawing adverse inferences from silence.[84] Another illuminating illustra-

---

[76] *R v Nudds* [2008] EWCA Crim 148, [45]; cf. *Labrador v R* [2003] 2 Cr App R 390, PC.

[77] *R v Hulme* [2007] 1 Cr App R 26, [2006] EWCA Crim 2899.

[78] *R v Flynn and St John* [2008] 2 Cr App R 20, [2008] EWCA Crim 970; *R v Luttrell* [2004] 2 Cr App R 31; [2004] EWCA Crim 1344, [42], [44]: '[A] "special warning" is necessary if experience, research or common sense has indicated that there is a difficulty with a certain type of evidence that requires giving the jury a warning of its dangers and the need for caution, tailored to meet the needs of the case. This will often be the case where jurors may be unaware of the difficulty, or may insufficiently understand it ... We have no doubt that lip reading evidence requires a warning from the judge as to its limitations and the concomitant risk of error, not least because it will usually be introduced through an expert who may not be completely accurate... As with any "special warning", its precise terms will be fact-dependent, but in most, if not all cases, the judge should spell out to the jury the risk of mistakes as to the words that the lip reader believes were spoken; the reasons why the witness may be mistaken; and the way in which a convincing, authoritative and truthful witness may yet be a mistaken witness. Furthermore, the judge should deal with the particular strengths and weaknesses of the material in the instant case ...'

[79] *R v Campbell (Kenneth)* [2007] 1 WLR 2798, [2007] EWCA Crim 1472; *R v Edwards* [2006] 1 Cr App R 3; [2005] EWCA Crim 1813, [3]: 'What the summing-up must contain is a clear warning to the jury against placing undue reliance on previous convictions, which cannot, by themselves, prove guilt'. Generally, see Chapter 14.   [80] *R v Adams* [1997] 1 Cr App R 369, CA; *R v Spencer* [1987] AC 128, HL.

[81] Penney Lewis and Alastair Mullis, 'Delayed Criminal Prosecutions for Childhood Sexual Abuse: Ensuring a Fair Trial' (1999) 115 *LQR* 265; Mike Redmayne, 'A Corroboration Approach to Recovered Memories of Sexual Abuse: A Note of Caution' (2000) 116 *LQR* 147; Penney Lewis and Alastair Mullis, 'Supporting Evidence and Illusory Double-Counting: Recovered Memory and Beyond' (2001) 5 *E & P* 111; Mike Redmayne, 'Another Note of Caution' (2001) 5 *E & P* 121.   [82] §15.4, below.

[83] *R v McQuiston* [1998] 1 Cr App R 139, 141–2, CA.   [84] §13.3(b).

tion of forensic reasoning rules in action, which regularly crops up in criminal litigation, concerns the evidential significance of lies.

Lies are suspicious. A liar is someone whose word cannot be trusted, and a witness exposed as a liar in court lacks credibility. But lies told by the accused are also 'suspect' evidence in the extended, formal sense, signalling the risk that the jury might attribute more significance to an accused's lies than it should. Where the accused is caught out in a lie, whether told in court under oath or at some point in the pre-trial process (typically in police interview), the jury might easily conclude that the accused is obviously guilty. 'Why tell lies if you are innocent?' is the common-sense rhetorical challenge to the lying accused. However, there are many reasons, of varying merits, why people tell lies, and it does not necessarily follow that they are guilty of the offences with which they are charged. Indeed, it does not even follow from the fact that the accused *thinks* he is guilty that he *is in fact* guilty, since few accused have expert knowledge of the ingredients of criminal offences and some people feel morally guilty even when they are not legally culpable. The risk is that, when it comes to evaluating lies, popular beliefs and preconceptions will overwhelm the niceties of rigorous inferential reasoning, propelling the fact-finder to leap with one enthusiastic bound the logical chasm between evidence and proof. This tendency makes lies an ideal candidate for a special judicial direction.[85]

Authoritative appellate guidance on the appropriate warning was given in *Lucas*,[86] and subsequently reiterated in *Goodway*.[87] What is now known as a '*Lucas*-direction' was originally devised in order to explain to juries that an accused's lies could ever amount to corroboration of other incriminating evidence only if the following four criteria were satisfied:

(i) the lie must have been *deliberate*, as opposed to being a product of the accused's misapprehension or faulty expression (this is actually a conceptual predicate of lying: one can unintentionally mislead, but a lie, by definition, must involve deliberate falsehood);

(ii) the lie must relate to a material issue in the trial;

(iii) the motive for the lie must be shown to have been the accused's realization of guilt or fear of the truth, and the jury should specifically be directed that there could be other, more innocent motives for telling a deliberate lie; and

(iv) the lie must be proved *by independent evidence* to have been a deliberate falsehood.

In *Goodway* the Court of Appeal held that, notwithstanding the demise of corroboration warnings, the trial judge should continue to direct the jury on the significance of the accused's lies, except in the relatively unusual situation where proof of the lie is also logically proof of guilt (for example where the lie constitutes 'deception' for the purposes of theft, fraud, and related offences). Lord Taylor CJ confirmed that 'a *Lucas* direction should be given, save where it is otiose... whenever lies are, or may be, relied upon as supporting

---

[85] Cf. *Broadhurst v R* [1964] AC 441, 457, PC, *per* Lord Devlin: 'It is very important that a jury should be carefully directed on the effect of a conclusion, if they reach it, that the accused is lying. There is a natural tendency for a jury to think that if an accused is lying, it must be because he is guilty and accordingly to convict him without more ado. It is the duty of the judge to make it clear to them that this is not so.'

[86] *R v Lucas* [1981] QB 720, CA.   [87] *R v Goodway* (1994) 98 Cr App R 11, CA.

evidence of the defendant's guilt'.[88] This ruling clearly evinces the Court of Appeal's recognition that, even after the old rules on corroboration have been dispensed with, the problems of inference and fact-finding to which quantitative standards have always been directed remain undiminished.[89]

Forensic reasoning rules are designed to help fact-finders steer clear of logical fallacies and other reasoning errors when assessing the evidence presented at trial. The most blatant lie-related reasoning fallacy would be to conclude that the accused's testimony in court is false, and to use *that* conclusion itself as further evidence of the accused's guilt. This is a form of evidentiary boot-strapping, whereby factual inferences drawn from evidence are treated in themselves as independent pieces of evidence proving guilt. Such inferences-upon-inferences are like a house of cards built on a single evidentiary point of contact with the ground: pull away the foundation and the entire inferential superstructure would come crashing down. Whatever evidence the fact-finder uses to conclude that the accused is lying in court cannot then be 'double-counted' as a proven lie contributing further independent evidence of guilt. Condition (iv) of the *Lucas/Goodway* direction, requiring that a lie be proven by independent evidence to be a deliberate falsehood, is designed to prevent such evidentiary double-counting. Conversely, there is no need for a special direction on lies where the question is simply whether the jury believes the accused's explanations and protestations of innocence and there is no discrete evidence of 'a lie' *per se*, meaning an independently proven fact from which further inferences might legitimately be drawn.[90]

Other commonplace reasoning fallacies are all, essentially, variations on the theme of jumping to premature conclusions. Since we more or less expect offenders to try to lie their way out of trouble if they can,[91] proof of a lie might all too easily be taken as cast-iron proof of guilt. On more measured reflection, however, everyone knows that people sometimes lie, and even falsely confess to crimes, to protect a loved one or to conceal some other more shameful conduct (which might or might not be the subject of extraneous criminal charges). Sometimes the motivation for lying is just banal.

In *Wood*[92] the accused was convicted of burglary on the evidence of a taxi driver who said that he saw four men, including the accused, rummaging inside a recently broken shop window. Wood initially told the police that nobody was rummaging inside the shop window, but later admitted that this was a lie. His defence at trial was that he had been walking home at night, the worse for drink, and had stopped to cadge a cigarette from one of the three men who were already standing in a group outside the shop. The Court of Appeal accepted Wood's argument that a *Lucas* direction should have been given, and

---

[88] ibid. 17.   [89] Also see *R v Richens* (1994) 98 Cr App R 43, 50ff, CA.

[90] *R v Middleton* [2001] Crim LR 251, CA; *R v Barnett* [2002] Crim LR 489, CA. A troubling feature of *Barnett*, however, is that the accused had offered *mutually inconsistent* explanations for the discovery of a stolen painting under his bed. If the jury were bound to infer that B had lied, it might be thought that a *Lucas* direction should have been given. On the other hand, there was no independent proof as to *which* explanation was false, and perhaps the only reasonable inference to be drawn from B's serial story-telling was that he was guilty as charged.

[91] Of course, there are exceptions: some forms of criminality, including political protest and other expressive crimes, may even require flagrant offending and public avowals of guilt. But the average burglar or drug-dealer is trying to make crime pay by getting away with it, and lying is a time-honoured strategy for anyone in a tight corner.   [92] *R v Wood* [1995] Crim LR 154, CA.

quashed his conviction.[93] Whether or not one is inclined to believe Wood's revised story, it is, generally speaking, quite plausible that a person accidentally caught up in a compromising situation might inadvisably blurt out embellished denials that he is later obliged to retract. Even innocent people might be tempted to embroider the truth if things look bad for them;[94] and in *Wood* it is worth mentioning that the taxi driver's evidence was consistent with Wood's own insistence that the burglary had nothing to do with him. The *Lucas* direction, and especially condition (iii) drawing attention to the motivation behind a proven lie, is designed to encourage jurors to deliberate methodically and avoid jumping to premature conclusions. Jurors are to be forewarned against the lure of tempting, but possibly erroneous, inferential short-cuts capable of precipitating miscarriages of justice. The *Lucas* direction, in other words, is a paradigmatic illustration of a modern forensic reasoning rule.

Lies present one concrete manifestation of a more general problem of fact-finding and proof which common lawyers typically discuss in terms of 'prejudice' or prejudicial reasoning. It is not that the accused's lies are *irrelevant* to the question of his guilt. If lies were irrelevant they would be inadmissible for all purposes,[95] and there would be no evidentiary problem. Rather, lies can indeed be relevant but their admission in evidence turns on certain conditions being satisfied before their true probative value can reliably be assessed. Those logical pre-conditions are replicated in the *Lucas/Goodway* direction, reminding the jury that probative evidence of guilt does not necessarily add up to proof beyond reasonable doubt. The basic reasoning fallacy, which the direction seeks to pre-empt, involves jumping to the conclusion that the accused *must* be guilty of the offence(s) charged if he has told a lie about his involvement in the offence, rather than carefully considering how, if at all, a particular apparent falsehood affects the probability that the accused is guilty, taking proper account of all the other evidence in the case and any explanations consistent with innocence.[96]

(c) STATUTORY WARNINGS

Whilst forensic reasoning rules are predominantly judicial creations at common law, Parliament has also increasingly got in on the act, playing a supporting role in the development of judicial warnings. We have already encountered one example in relation to confession evidence.[97] Section 77(1) of PACE 1984 provides that:

Without prejudice to the general duty of the court at a trial on indictment to direct the jury on any matter on which it appears to the court appropriate to do so, where at such a trial

  (a) the case against the accused depends wholly or substantially on a confession by him; and

---

[93] Note, however, that the trial judge's omission of a *Lucas* direction will not automatically lead to a conviction being quashed, if the evidence is otherwise 'overwhelming': *R v Downey* [1995] 1 Cr App R 547, 558, CA.

[94] There is a parallel with the corrupt police practice of 'gilding the lily' by fabricating additional evidence against suspects the officers 'know' to be guilty. One important distinction, however, is that innocent accused who lie to bolster their protestations of innocence generally know they are truly innocent, whereas police officers can only surmise that guilty suspects are guilty.   [95] §3.1.

[96] Recall that one interpretation of the criminal standard of proof requires the jury to eliminate all plausible explanations consistent with innocence: §6.4(b).   [97] §12.4.

(b) the court is satisfied
    (i)   that he is mentally handicapped; and
    (ii)   that the confession was not made in the presence of an independent person,
the court shall warn the jury that there is special need for caution before convicting the accused in reliance on the confession, and shall explain that the need arises because of the circumstances mentioned in paragraphs (a) and (b) above.

Obviously, if the prosecution case rests 'wholly' on the confession of a mentally handicapped accused made in the absence of an independent adult, the trial judge will not be able to draw the jury's attention to potentially corroborating evidence of guilt – by definition, there is no other evidence. But in those circumstances the confession would most probably be excluded, as oppressive or unreliable, under section 76 of PACE[98] in any event.[99] Where the prosecution relies 'substantially' on such a confession, however, the Court of Appeal has emphasized the importance of a full summing-up covering all material aspects of the evidence.[100] In these circumstances, section 77 effectively operates as a statutory forensic reasoning rule.

    Parliament has reprised this legislative technique on a number of subsequent occasions. Legislation authorizing modifications to normal trial procedure, typically in order to ameliorate the courtroom experiences of vulnerable or intimidated witnesses and secure their best evidence,[101] has often included provision for mandatory judicial warnings whenever the modification in question might conceivably incite jurors to draw adverse inferences against the accused. Thus, the use of special measures such as physical screens or Live Link CCTV may attract a special warning;[102] and in relation to the minority of accused who conduct their own defence, the jury may be instructed, if the trial judge thinks it necessary to safeguard against unfair prejudice, not to read anything sinister into the fact that the accused is not permitted to cross-examine a child or sexual offence complainant in person.[103] The Coroners and Justice Act 2009 has added witness anonymity orders to the list of special measures which may require the trial judge to issue pre-emptive directions.[104] In each scenario, the accused would be exposed to unfair prejudice if the jury were to infer that special measures had been adopted because the man in the dock was too dangerous or frightening to allow the witness to testify in the normal way. The universal procedural remedy is to instruct the jury that the measures in question are now routine practice for particular types of witness and that they should not read any more into it than that. In all other respects, statutory forensic reasoning rules can be expected to conform with the general principles governing judicial warnings developed at common law.

15.4 EYEWITNESS IDENTIFICATION EVIDENCE

Identification of the perpetrator by an eyewitness to the crime frequently exerts a major influence on the course and outcome of criminal proceedings. The early stages of a criminal investigation are often shaped around descriptions of the offender's physical appearance,

---

[98] §12.3.   [99] R v MacKenzie (1992) 96 Cr App R 98, CA; R v Moss (1990) 91 Cr App R 371, CA.
[100] R v Bailey [1995] 2 Cr App R 262, CA.   [101] §10.4.
[102] Youth Justice and Criminal Evidence Act 1999, s.32 ('such warning (if any) as the judge considers necessary').   [103] YJCE Act 1999, s.39.
[104] Coroners and Justice Act 2009, s.90.

clothing, accent, or distinctive mannerisms, supplied to the police by the complainant him- or herself or by a witness who by chance happened to observe the commission or immediate aftermath of the offence. At the culmination of proceedings, in a case where the accused puts up an alibi or otherwise claims that the authorities have prosecuted the wrong man, eyewitness identification evidence may become the evidential fulcrum of the trial, its acceptance or rejection by the fact-finder effectively dictating whether the jury's verdict swings to conviction or acquittal.

However, eyewitness identification evidence has a chequered history of association with miscarriages of justice. A strong parallel might be drawn with confession evidence in this regard. But whereas coerced or fabricated confessions were the 'hot topic' for the Runciman Royal Commission in the early 1990s, mistaken identifications had by then already been producing *cause célèbres* for well over a century. Indeed, the extraordinary case of *Adolf Beck* was instrumental in generating sufficient public concern and reformist momentum to force through the creation of the Court of Criminal Appeal in 1907, in the teeth of long-standing judicial opposition.[105]

(a) IDENTIFICATION EVIDENCE AND MISCARRIAGES OF JUSTICE

In 1896 Beck was convicted of multiple counts of defrauding women of their jewellery, having been positively identified as the perpetrator by no less than eight complainants who testified for the prosecution at his trial. A retired policeman also testified that Beck was the man, going under the alias of Thomas Smith, whom he had arrested and successfully prosecuted for similar crimes several years earlier. Beck served five years' imprisonment for this latest spate of jewellery fraud. The Home Office was impervious to his protestations of innocence, and he remained in gaol even after it was discovered from prison records that Smith was a circumcised Jew, whereas Beck was an uncut gentile. Remarkably, just three years after his release from prison in 1901, Beck was once again misidentified as a jewellery fraudster and convicted after a contested trial! But fortunately, this time, the trial judge smelt a rat, and upon making further enquiries, discovered that the real Thomas Smith had been apprehended attempting to pawn a stolen ring and had confessed to all the frauds. Beck was duly granted two free pardons, and paid £5,000 compensation for his trouble.

It is tempting to dismiss cases like *Beck* as one-off aberrations, on the basis that Adolf Beck was just terribly unlucky to bear an uncanny visual resemblance to a confidence trickster operating in the vicinity. But this complacent rationalization cannot withstand serious scrutiny. Proven wrongful convictions resting on mistaken eyewitness identification so commonly recur throughout the modern history of criminal proceedings that the only plausible explanations must point to the inherent, systemic weaknesses of identification evidence in our system of criminal adjudication. Today, we can draw on extensive behavioural science research, conducted over the last four decades, which has amply demonstrated the shortcomings of eyewitness identification evidence.[106] An important

---

105 See Rosemary Pattenden, *English Criminal Appeals 1844–1994* (OUP, 1999), ch 1 (esp. at 28–30).

106 Jenny McEwan, *The Verdict of the Court: Passing Judgment in Law and Psychology* (Hart, 2003), ch 8; Andreas Kapardis, Psychology and Law (CUP, 1997), chs 2–3; Gary L. Wells and Elizabeth F. Loftus (eds.), *Eyewitness Testimony: Psychological Perspectives* (CUP, 1984).

finding is that an eyewitness's confidence in making an identification bears no strong correlation to accuracy or reliability.[107] In other words, an honest and very confident witness could well be mistaken, whilst, conversely, a hesitant, equivocal witness might nonetheless be identifying the real culprit. This conclusion has serious implications for a trial system resting on the notion that the strength and reliability of evidence may be gauged by observing a witness's demeanour whilst testifying in court.[108] Difficulties are further compounded by the modern scientific understanding of memories as active constructions rather than mental photographs stored in the brain.[109] If remembering is a creative and consciously-willed activity, then the risk arises that an eyewitness might be recalling the features of the person they first saw in police custody or in 'mugshot' photographs and transposing the image of this suspect onto their, now half-forgotten – and possibly always faulty – recollection of the original incident. To the extent that these mental processes of memory construction and reconstruction operate subconsciously, it is useless for lawyers to subject the witness to vigorous cross-examination, since, as far as the witness is concerned, their memory is clear and accurate. Indeed, seeking to undermine the grounds for the witness's recollection may only be counterproductive, provoking the witness into reasserting a positive identification with exaggerated conviction.

Lord Devlin's *Committee on Evidence of Identification* produced its influential report in 1976, rekindling interest in this topic amongst new generations of behavioural science researchers.[110] This landmark official inquiry into errors of identification in criminal proceedings was prompted, predictably, by another wave of high-profile miscarriages of justice, of which the case of Laszlo Virag is the most celebrated, or infamous. In 1969 Virag was convicted of thefts from parking meters in Bristol and Liverpool, and of unlawfully wounding a police constable with a firearm whilst attempting to resist arrest.[111] He was sentenced to ten years' imprisonment, but released early in 1974 and granted a free pardon, after the perpetrator of strikingly similar offences was linked by physical evidence (a previously unmatched fingerprint on a coin-box and his possession of a distinctive antique French pistol) to the Bristol and Liverpool thefts of which Virag had been convicted. The Devlin Committee pinpointed various flaws in the original police investigation and prosecution of Virag, including a botched alibi defence and selective pre-trial disclosure by the prosecution. But the most troubling feature of the case was that Virag was identified as the perpetrator in three different identification parades by *eight* eyewitnesses, including several of the police officers who had attempted to catch the thief *in flagrante*. Most impressive of all was PC Smith, the officer wounded in the Bristol raid, who testified in court, in accordance with his previous statement, that Virag's face was 'imprinted on my brain'.[112]

Persuaded of the very real dangers and infirmities of identification evidence, Devlin recommended that a criminal conviction should not normally rest on the uncorroborated

---

[107] Summarizing the findings of thirty-one previous studies, Gary L. Wells and Donna M. Murray, 'Eyewitness Confidence', in Wells and Loftus (eds.), *Eyewitness Testimony*, concluded unequivocally that 'eyewitness confidence is not useful as a predictor of eyewitness accuracy in actual criminal cases'.

[108] §7.1.   [109] ibid.

[110] Lord Devlin, *Report to the Secretary of State for the Home Department of the Departmental Committee on Evidence of Identification in Criminal Cases*. HC 338 (HMSO, 1976).

[111] The story is fully recounted, ibid. ch 3.   [112] ibid. para.3.56.

identification of a single eyewitness.[113] Although one eyewitness identification might be enough to sustain a conviction in exceptional circumstances – such as clear recognition in good light of a family member, work colleague, or close associate[114] – Devlin concluded that 'substantial' supporting evidence should be required in the normal run of cases. In the event (and presaging the fate of similarly-motivated proposals in the 1990s for a rule requiring confessions to be corroborated), Devlin's advocacy of a quantitative filter on identification evidence failed to attract parliamentary support and was never translated into legislation. However, the harvest of Lord Devlin's inquiry into identification evidence was not entirely barren. It bore fruit indirectly by fertilizing the common law.

(b) *TURNBULL* WARNINGS

In *Turnbull*[115] a specially convened full court of the Court of Appeal, comprising five judges led by Lord Chief Justice Widgery, seized the opportunity presented by the Devlin inquiry to lay down authoritative guidelines for trial judges summing-up in cases involving contested identification evidence. It is worth quoting at length from the operative parts of the Court of Appeal's judgment delivered by Widgery CJ. As well as rehearsing the essential components of what we know today as the '*Turnbull* warning', the following passages also provide another extended illustration of the law's attempt to facilitate lay fact-finding by developing evidentiary guidance, in the form of forensic reasoning rules, which incorporate factual generalizations distilled from previous experience of criminal proceedings:

In our judgment the danger of miscarriages of justice occurring can be much reduced if trial judges sum up to juries in the way indicated in this judgment. First, whenever the case against an accused depends wholly or substantially on the correctness of one or more identifications of the accused which the defence alleges to be mistaken, the judge should warn the jury of the special need for caution before convicting the accused in reliance on the

---

[113] ibid. para.8.4: 'in our opinion it is only in exceptional cases that identification evidence is by itself sufficiently reliable to exclude a reasonable doubt about guilt. We recommend that the trial judge should be required by statute...to direct the jury that it is not safe to convict upon eye-witness evidence unless the circumstances of the identification are exceptional or the eyewitness evidence is supported by substantial evidence of another sort.'

[114] An inflexible, categorical rule would certainly have been inappropriate if it failed to allow for the kinds of cases hypothesized by the Court of Appeal in *R v Turnbull* [1977] QB 224, 229: '*A* had been kidnapped and held to ransom over many days. His captor stayed with him all the time. At last he was released but he did not know the identity of his kidnapper nor where he had been kept. Months later the police arrested *X* for robbery and as a result of what they had been told by an informer they suspected him of the kidnapping. They had no other evidence. They arranged for *A* to attend an identity parade. He picked out *X* without hesitation. At *X*'s trial, is the trial judge to rule at the end of the prosecution's case that *X* must be acquitted? This is another example. Over a period of a week two police officers, *B* and *C*, kept observation in turn on a house which was suspected of being a distribution centre for drugs. A suspected supplier, *Y*, visited it from time to time. On the last day of the observation *B* saw *Y* enter the house. He at once signalled to other waiting police officers, who had a search warrant to enter. They did so; but by the time they got in, *Y* had escaped by a back window. Six months later *C* saw *Y* in the street and arrested him. *Y* at once alleged that *C* had mistaken him for someone else. At an identity parade he was picked out by *B*. Would it really be right and in the interests of justice for a judge to direct *Y*'s acquittal at the end of the prosecution's case? A rule such as the one under consideration would gravely impede the police in their work and would make the conviction of street offenders such as pickpockets, car thieves and the disorderly very difficult. But it would not only be the police who might be aggrieved by such a rule.'   [115] *R v Turnbull* [1977] QB 224, CA.

correctness of the identification or identifications. In addition he should instruct them as to the reason for the need for such a warning and should make some reference to the possibility that a mistaken witness can be a convincing one and that a number of such witnesses can all be mistaken. Provided this is done in clear terms the judge need not use any particular form of words.

Secondly, the judge should direct the jury to examine closely the circumstances in which the identification by each witness came to be made. How long did the witness have the accused under observation? At what distance? In what light? Was the observation impeded in any way, as for example by passing traffic or a press of people? Had the witness ever seen the accused before? How often? If only occasionally, had he any special reason for remembering the accused? How long elapsed between the original observation and the subsequent identification to the police? Was there any material discrepancy between the description of the accused given to the police by the witness when first seen by them and his actual appearance? . . . .

Finally, [the judge] should remind the jury of any specific weaknesses which had appeared in the identification evidence. Recognition may be more reliable than identification of a stranger; but even when the witness is purporting to recognise someone whom he knows, the jury should be reminded that mistakes in recognition of close relatives and friends are sometimes made. All these matters go to the quality of the identification evidence. If the quality is good and remains good at the close of the accused's case, the danger of a mistaken identification is lessened, but the poorer the quality, the greater danger. In our judgment when the quality is good, as for example when the identification is made after a long period of observation, or in satisfactory conditions by a relative, a neighbour, a close friend, a workmate and the like, the jury can safely be left to assess the value of the identifying evidence even though there is no other evidence to support it: provided always, however, that an adequate warning has been given about the special need for caution. Were the courts to adjudge otherwise, affronts to justice would frequently occur.

When, in the judgment of the trial judge, the quality of the identifying evidence is poor, as for example when it depends solely on a fleeting glance or on a longer observation made in difficult conditions, the situation is very different. The judge should then withdraw the case from the jury and direct an acquittal unless there is other evidence which goes to support the correctness of the identification. This may be corroboration in the sense lawyers use that word; but it need not be so if its effect is to make the jury sure that there has been no mistaken identification . . . [116]

Turnbull thus contributed not one, but two quantitative rules to the evidentiary corpus, both of which need to be considered 'whenever the case against an accused depends wholly or substantially on the correctness of one or more identifications of the accused which the defence alleges to be mistaken'. The first rule states that if contested identification evidence is 'poor', the case should be withdrawn from the jury altogether, unless supporting evidence is available to confirm the identification.[117] The Court of Appeal apparently envisaged that prosecutions resting exclusively on flimsy identification evidence would be relatively rare, and this should certainly be so now that evidential sufficiency is regulated by the Code for Crown Prosecutors.[118] In the remaining cases in which identification

---

[116] ibid. 228–9, 229–30.   [117] *Daley* v *R* [1994] 1 AC 117, PC.

[118] A high-profile example is the still-unsolved murder of Stephen Lawrence. Senior crown prosecutors refused to continue with proceedings precisely because they judged the equivocal identification evidence of

evidence satisfies the quality threshold, or where poor identification evidence is supported by other evidence confirming the identification, a second forensic reasoning rule requires trial judges to direct juries on 'the special need for caution' when evaluating eyewitness identifications of the accused as the offender.

Turnbull warnings exemplify forensic reasoning rules and were a significant strand in their historical development. There is no formal corroboration requirement in the old technical sense, since supporting evidence is not a legal prerequisite of proof beyond reasonable doubt. Anticipating by a decade later developments in the general law of corroboration, *Turnbull* disavowed technical legal formulae and emphasized the substance of the warnings over the particular language in which they are couched. The factors identified by Widgery CJ as bearing on the quality of identification evidence combine common sense generalizations,[119] the accumulated wisdom of forensic experience, and contemporary behavioural science research (which the Court of Appeal gleaned from the Devlin Committee's report).[120] Even though the effects of such factors as poor lighting and obscured line of sight are patently obvious, the risk of misidentification is deemed sufficiently serious to warrant drawing the implications of each potentially confounding variable to the jury's attention. Nor is the trial judge's duty discharged simply by rehearsing what is now received wisdom about the infirmities of eyewitness identification in general. Instead, the judge should work systematically through all the evidence presented at trial, emphasizing any circumstances of the offence or of its investigation which might have affected the quality – and therefore the reliability – of a contested identification. In 'fleeting glance' cases with sufficient supporting evidence to proceed, '[t]he trial judge should identify to the jury the evidence which he adjudges is capable of supporting the evidence of identification. If there is any evidence or circumstances which the jury might think was supporting when it did not have this quality, the judge should say so.'[121] Finally, the Court of Appeal signalled its determination to enforce the *Turnbull* guidelines:

A failure to follow these guidelines is likely to result in a conviction being quashed and will do so if in the judgment of this court on all the evidence the verdict is... unsafe.[122]

Turnbull warnings do not purport to have completely eliminated the risk that mistaken eyewitness identifications will lead to wrongful convictions. The epistemological conundrum presented by the absolutely certain and unimpeachably honest, yet still mistaken,

---

Duwayne Brooks to be insufficient to establish a reasonable prospect of conviction. The CPS judgment was later vindicated when the trial judge threw out the Lawrence family's private prosecution, on the ground that Brooks' partly self-contradictory testimony and contaminated parade identifications could not be relied upon: see *The Stephen Lawrence Inquiry – Report of an Inquiry by Sir William Macpherson of Cluny*. Cm. 4262-I (HMSO, 1999), ch 41.

[119] §4.4 and §4.6.

[120] Cf. *Report to the Secretary of State for the Home Department of the Departmental Committee on Evidence of Identification in Criminal Cases*. HC 338 (HMSO, 1976), paras.4.12–4.15. Devlin concluded that 'the stage seems not yet to have been reached at which the conclusions of psychological research are sufficiently widely accepted or tailored to the needs of the judicial process to become the basis for procedural change', but advocated further inter-disciplinary research 'directed to establishing ways in which the insights of psychology could be brought to bear on the conduct of identification parades and the practice of the courts in all matters relating to evidence of identification'. This call to arms has been enthusiastically answered by expanding cohorts of behavioural scientists during the ensuing decades.

[121] *R v Turnbull* [1977] QB 224, 230.   [122] ibid. 231.

eyewitness is ultimately intractable. Behavioural science research has identified further factors that ratchet up the effect. These include the propensity for multiple witnesses to replicate the same errors of misidentification, lending shared illusion the outward appearance of corroborated fact (as in poor Adolf Beck's case),[123] and the particular fallibility of inter-racial identifications. However, in terms of evidentiary reform *Turnbull* has probably achieved all that can reasonably be expected without fundamentally rethinking the basic adversarial structure of English criminal procedure and trial practice. Common lawyers have long doubted the evidential value of theatrical 'dock identifications' of the accused in the courtroom.[124] More recent efforts to enhance the quality and reliability of identification evidence have centred on improving identification procedures organized by the police, which are now minutely regulated by PACE Code of Practice D. Identification evidence procured in breach of Code D is liable to be excluded under section 78 of PACE.[125]

Post-*Turnbull* jurisprudence has staunchly defended the line staked out by Widgery CJ. *Turnbull* warnings are not to be extended by mechanical analogy to cases in which the risks of misidentification do not really arise.[126] Nor is there any canonical form of words,[127] or set 'order of service',[128] which trial judges must slavishly parrot. On the other hand, it is incumbent upon trial judges to take the trouble of applying, and where necessary modifying, the general criteria of good and bad identification evidence to the facts of the instant case.[129] A conviction resting on seriously defective eyewitness testimony is quite likely to be quashed on appeal.[130] In all of these doctrinal particulars, *Turnbull* warnings exemplify English law's expanding corpus of flexible, 'post-corroboration', forensic reasoning rules. *Turnbull* warnings have recently been extended *mutatis mutandis* to voice identification evidence,[131] which is seemingly even more error-prone than eyewitness identifications.

15.5 CORROBORATION AND FAIR TRIALS

This chapter has charted the rise of flexible forensic reasoning rules from the ashes of the old technical law of corroboration. English common law has always displayed a marked preference for qualitative over quantitative standards of fact-finding and proof. For a time, where, exceptionally, corroboration was required, the law fell prey to a sterile formalism, from which – with Parliament's helping hand – it has lately freed itself. Residual statutory provisions aside, most of the old law of corroboration has gone, including the largely unlamented 'corroboration warnings'. They have been replaced by a raft of judicial directions

---

[123] Cf. *R v Weeder* (1980) 71 Cr App R 228, CA (independent eyewitnesses can be mutually corroborating, provided that the judge reminds the jury that even several honest witnesses might all be mistaken).

[124] *R v Cartwright* (1914) 10 Cr App R 219, CCA.

[125] *R v Forbes* [2001] 1 Cr App R 430, HL. PACE Code D has undergone successive revisions. For critical commentary, see Andrew Roberts and Sarah Clover, 'Managerialism and Myopia: The Government's Consultation Draft on PACE – Code D' [2002] *Crim LR* 873.

[126] *R v Oakwell* [1978] 1 WLR 32, CA (issue was whether police officer witness was mistaken in singling out the accused from a group of young people as the one who assaulted him, and nothing to do with 'the ghastly risk run in cases of fleeting encounters').

[127] *Mills v R* [1995] 3 All ER 865, 872, PC (Lord Steyn).   [128] *R v Barnes* [1995] 2 Cr App R 491, CA.

[129] *R v Fergus* (1994) 98 Cr App R 313, CA.   [130] *Daley v R* (1994) 98 Cr App R 447, PC.

[131] *R v Flynn and St John* [2008] 2 Cr App R 20, [2008] EWCA Crim 970.

designed to assist jurors to evaluate various types of 'suspect' evidence. These flexible forensic reasoning rules enable jurors to benefit from the accumulated wisdom of litigation practice augmented, as appropriate, by empirical data. Today's accent is on genuine assistance and contextual application. This chapter of criminal evidence has emphatically renounced its ill-considered dalliance with the cult of legal formalism and dedicated itself to common sense reasoning with all the zeal of the convert.

Corroboration in the broad, non-technical sense, raises epistemic rather than doctrinal questions. Is testimony or other evidence reliable? How should it be combined with other evidence in the case? Does the testimony or other evidence, viewed in isolation or taken in combination with supporting or confirmatory information, satisfy the applicable standard of proof? The demise of the old technical law of corroboration consequently cannot be the last word on quantitative evidentiary standards in English law. Unlimited licence to give or withhold directions concerning 'suspect' evidence, and in whatever form takes the trial judge's fancy, would not serve the ends of justice. The common law's failed experiment with hair-splitting technical rules of corroboration cautions against excessive formalism and rigidity, but leaving trial judges entirely to their own devices without principled guidance from the Court of Appeal threatens to produce an anarchy of inconsistent, unpredictable, and possibly capricious decisions and directions that might be equally unattractive. Between the polar extremes of inflexible rule-worship and untrammelled judicial discretion, a happy medium should entrust trial judges with the flexibility of tailoring their directions to the facts of particulars case within a principled framework of appellate guidance.[132] This is what the trial judge's overriding duty to ensure the fairness of the trial demands, and by and large what English law has achieved through the legislation, appellate decisions, and Judicial Studies Board Specimen Directions discussed in this chapter.

Corroboration has a somewhat different relationship to the fairness of trials in the Article 6 jurisprudence of the European Court of Human Rights (EctHR). Most of the Strasbourg judges were schooled in the civilian legal tradition (or its Soviet variations) and can be expected to be comfortable with the non-technical concept of corroboration, meaning simply 'supporting evidence'. Sure enough, the ECtHR frequently refers to the existence or non-existence of supporting evidence when assessing overall fairness in the light of potential violations of Article 6's specifically enumerated rights. Thus, the Strasbourg judges have *not* said (translating into common lawyers' terminology) that hearsay evidence is *inadmissible* in a fair trial, only that untested hearsay evidence would require support from other evidence in order to generate a Convention-compliant conviction.[133] Hearsay evidence from anonymous witnesses is especially frowned upon, as we have seen.[134] A similar approach was evident in *Teixeira de Castro*, where the Court stressed the absence of any additional evidence 'to support the Government's argument

---

132 Quoted with approval by the Supreme Court of Canada in *R v Khela* [2009] SCC 4, [29] (Fish J.).

133 *Kostovski v The Netherlands* (1989) 12 EHRR 434; *Delta v France* (1990) 16 EHRR 574; *Unterpertinger v Austria* (1986) 13 EHRR 175. Indeed, a conviction based almost exclusively on what English lawyers would regard as hearsay evidence can still satisfy Article 6 if adequate provision is made to allow the accused or his legal advisers to put questions to prosecution witnesses in pre-trial proceedings: *SN v Sweden* (2004) 39 EHRR 13, [2002] Crim LR 831; *Doorson v The Netherlands* (1996) 22 EHRR 330.

134 *Visser v The Netherlands* [2002] Crim LR 495; *Van Mechelen v The Netherlands* (1997) 25 EHRR 647.

that the applicant was predisposed to commit [drug-dealing] offences'.[135] A third Article 6 example is that, although an accused's silence can in appropriate circumstances be used as evidence of guilt, 'it would be incompatible with the right to silence to base a conviction solely or mainly on the accused's silence or on a refusal to answer questions or to give evidence himself'.[136] Silence, in other words, requires corroboration as proof of guilt for a criminal conviction to withstand scrutiny under the Convention. On the other hand, the conviction in *Khan*[137] was found to be compliant with Article 6 even though the only, uncorroborated, evidence of the accused's guilt had been obtained in breach of Article 8.

In view of the ECtHR's insistence that Article 6 'does not lay down any rules on the admissibility of evidence as such, which is therefore primarily a matter for regulation under national law',[138] specifying the remit and content of forensic reasoning rules is likely to remain a predominantly domestic affair.[139] Ultimately, judicial instructions to the jury to 'take special care' cannot provide a definitive solution to the epistemic challenges of suspect evidence. Erstwhile accomplices might be entirely plausible liars; mentally ill witnesses or those with a mental disability will still sometimes strike lay-people as confused when they are being truthful, whilst appearing for all the world to be reliable when they are hopelessly confused; mistaken eyewitnesses could be absolutely convinced, and consequently utterly convincing, in their identification of the accused as the perpetrator; and the truth may be rendered more, not less, obscure to lay fact-finders by the interventions of scientific experts – including, these days, experts commenting on the testimonial reliability of other witnesses.[140] To the extent that the efficacy of forensic reasoning rules is inevitably circumscribed by the ordinary common sense and epistemic competence of lay fact-finders, it may be necessary to place renewed emphasis on pre-trial procedures for improving the quality and reliability of suspect evidence. Criminal proceedings in England and Wales have experienced significant procedural innovations in relation to identification procedures,[141] scientific evidence,[142] and pre-trial witness

---

[135] *Teixeira de Castro* v *Portugal* (1998) 28 EHRR 101. Cf. *Schenk* v *Switzerland* (1991) 13 EHRR 242, [48], where the prosecution's reliance on evidence procured through an unlawful telephone tap was held not to contravene Article 6(1), in part because 'the [Swiss] criminal court took account of a combination of evidential elements before reaching its opinion'.   [136] *Condron* v *UK* (2001) 31 EHRR 1, [56].

[137] *Khan* v *UK* (2001) 31 EHRR 45, discussed in §5.4(c).

[138] *Teixeira de Castro* v *Portugal* (1998) 28 EHRR 101, [34]. Also see *Schenk* v *Switzerland* (1991) 13 EHRR 242, [46]: 'While Article 6 of the Convention guarantees the right to a fair trial, it does not lay down any rules on the admissibility of evidence as such, which is therefore primarily a matter for regulation under national law. The Court therefore cannot exclude as a matter of principle and in the abstract that unlawfully obtained evidence… may be admissible.'

[139] Albeit that inferences from silence are a significant counterexample: §13.3(b).   [140] §11.4(b).

[141] PACE Code D, *Code of Practice for the Identification of Persons by Police Officers* (2008 Edition). A persuasive argument for 'virtual parades' by video-recording is made by Yvette Tinsley, 'Even Better than the Real Thing? The Case for Reform of Identification Procedures' (2001) 5 *E & P* 99; cf. Samuel R. Gross, 'Loss of Innocence: Eyewitness Identification and Proof of Guilt' (1987) 16 *Journal of Legal Studies* 395, 449 (conceding that it 'cuts against the grain to argue that prosecutors and police officers should have primary responsibility for protecting innocent defendants' but concluding that there is no genuine alternative).

[142] CrimPR 2010, Part 33. Expert scientific evidence is especially vulnerable to corruption and distortion through adversary process, and would often benefit from appropriately-structured opportunities for opposing experts to 'compare notes' with a view to refining the issues and isolating any genuine points of disagreement between them in anticipation of the trial: see Paul Roberts, 'Forensic Science Evidence After Runciman' [1994] *Crim LR* 780, 783–8.

interviewing,[143] amongst other on-going reforms. These targeted measures have been introduced against a more general backdrop of expanding and partly mutual pre-trial disclosure of evidence,[144] increasingly interventionist judicial case management,[145] and a discernible trend to replace traditional common law rules of admissibility with flexible judicial directions elucidating epistemic standards – forensic reasoning rules – for evaluating evidence.

---

[143] See Paul Roberts and Candida Saunders, 'Introducing Pre-Trial Witness Interviews – A Flexible New Fixture in the Crown Prosecutor's Toolkit' [2008] *Crim LR* 831.   [144] §2.3(c)(ii).
[145] CrimPR 2010, Part 3. And see §16.3(a).

16

CRIMINAL EVIDENCE – RETROSPECTIVE AND PROSPECTS

16.1 METHOD AND CONTEXT

This book proceeds from the methodological conviction that the law of evidence must be understood *contextually*, which on our account entails that legal rules, doctrines, and principles must be viewed from at least three major overlapping and reciprocally influential perspectives. First, there is the normative context of moral ideals and values. Criminal procedure is an applied field of moral and political philosophy.[1] Then there is the social and institutional context of criminal proceedings, the routine processes of criminal investigations, prosecutions, and trials.[2] This calls for socio-legal analysis of criminal justice practices and cultures and a sense of the pragmatic demands of criminal litigation. Finally, there is the epistemic context of criminal adjudication, the uses of information as a basis for drawing inferences and resolving disputed questions of fact.[3] Legal adjudication is organized around inquiries into past events. What happened? How do we know?[4] Are we sure enough to decide?[5] These questions supply the epistemic framework for those concerned with the management of 'information in litigation',[6] as students, practitioners, or scholars.

Fact-finding is plainly not unique to the law; and fact-finding just as obviously takes place in a wide variety of legal settings, from inquests, planning inquiries, and administrative hearings, through small claims courts, immigration proceedings, High Court civil actions, maritime disputes, and international commercial arbitration, to summary trials in the magistrates' courts and jury trials in the most serious criminal cases. Even within a single type of legal proceeding, such as Crown Court trials on indictment, there may be distinct phases and contexts of fact-finding: evidentiary rulings at a pre-trial hearing or on the *voir dire*;[7] jury deliberations and verdicts; sentencing hearings; new evidence on appeal; decisions to quash an acquittal[8] or to refer a conviction back to the Court of Appeal following re-investigation by the Criminal Cases Review Commission, etc.[9] Of course, fact-finding in legal and non-legal settings shares many features in common. To

---

[1] §1.2–§1.3.   [2] Chapter 2.   [3] Chapter 4.   [4] §4.4–§4.6.   [5] §6.3–§6.4.
[6] Cf. William Twining, *Rethinking Evidence: Exploratory Essays* (CUP, 2nd edn. 2006), ch 7; Terrence Anderson, David Schum, and William Twining, *Analysis of Evidence: Second Edition* (CUP, 2005).
[7] §12.3(a).   [8] §2.5(f).   [9] §2.5(e).

the extent that, in each and every one of these contexts, fact-finding is being performed by human beings with their impressive but far from unlimited cognitive capacities and their predictable biases and foibles, the continuities of 'common sense' inference and fact-finding across diverse social settings should occasion no surprise.[10] However, the ideals, objectives, and values motivating fact-finding are much more variable and distinctive of particular contexts, as are the institutions, practices, and conventions which structure different types of factual inquiry. To say that, for example, the historian, the journalist, and the criminal juror are 'doing the same thing' would be to purchase epistemological continuity at the exorbitant cost of obscuring very important differences in their respective institutional, normative, and practical situations. Even within the law, there are major differences distinguishing different types of legal process, action, and setting.

Criminal law is typically viewed as *sui generis*, not only by scholars and legal theorists but also by the public at large. Being found guilty of a crime is qualitatively different from, say, being sued for breach of contract or incurring a penalty for late payment of taxes. It is not merely that criminal convictions normally entail punishment, including imprisonment for the most serious offences. More fundamentally, a criminal conviction communicates censure for moral wrongdoing[11] of a type that demands a public accounting and accountability to the political community.[12] This is what lies behind the retributive sentiment,[13] that a good society will not suffer criminal wrongdoing to go unchecked and unpunished. No other form of normative regulation performs this unique public function in quite the same way.

It was in recognition of the unique role and status of criminal law that we chose to break with common law tradition, by focusing exclusively on *criminal* evidence rather than trying to distil a generic law of evidence from a diversity of institutionalized inquiries. Indeed, our principal focus has been even narrower than criminal adjudication in general, centring on jury trials on indictment in the Crown Court. It has been our contention that *criminal evidence* can truly be known only through its own distinctive normative and institutional contexts, that is, in terms of the ideals, objectives, values, and processes characteristic of criminal adjudication. This narrowing of topical focus is compensated by a broadening of contextual perspective. Evidence law should not be treated merely as a succession of doctrinal tableaux populated by a case-law cast of thousands. We have tried to indicate how the values and objectives of criminal evidence are derived from broader conceptions of political morality. The connection is most obvious when evidentiary reform acquires a political charge, as it has done, for example, in relation to 'rape shield' laws[14] and special measures for vulnerable witnesses.[15] But in reality, the political dimension of criminal adjudication is pervasive.

We also endeavoured to show how the rules of evidence often only really make sense, and then can properly be evaluated, by taking account of the practical contexts in which they operate. The practicalities of criminal adjudication are shaped by many intersecting

---

[10] §4.4–§4.6.

[11] Andrew von Hirsch, *Censure and Sanctions* (OUP, 1993); Andrew von Hirsch and Andrew Ashworth, *Proportionate Sentencing: Exploring the Principles* (OUP, 2005), esp. ch 2 and Appendix 2.

[12] R. A. Duff, *Answering for Crime: Responsibility and Liability in the Criminal Law* (Hart, 2007); Antony Duff, Lindsay Farmer, Sandra Marshall, and Victor Tadros, *The Trial on Trial Volume Three: Towards a Normative Theory of the Criminal Trial* (Hart, 2007).   [13] §1.2(a).

[14] §10.2.   [15] §10.4.

and overlapping influences, including social conventions, legal cultures, institutionalized working practices, technology, the built environment, representations of the administration of criminal justice in media and popular culture, and governments' willingness to fund state legal aid, in addition to formal legal rules and professional ethical standards. Empirical data documenting the specifically evidentiary aspects of first instance criminal trials are regrettably patchy and very incomplete. We have drawn on the available stock of socio-legal research on English criminal litigation, such as it is, to contribute light and shade to a more realistic picture of evidence and proof in criminal trials. In similar vein, we treated the blurry distinction between 'evidence' and 'procedure' as a convenient way of highlighting pertinent contrasts, rather than an invitation to entrench arbitrary conceptual taxonomies or an alibi for exhaustively elucidating 'evidence' whilst completely ignoring 'procedure'.

Every focus is selective in one way or another. Whilst the analytical spotlight illuminates one corner of the world the rest is cast in shade or darkness. Unified accounts of the law of evidence might claim some advantage in describing the epistemic continuities between different institutional contexts of fact-finding in and beyond the law, but they are seriously distorting from a normative or institutional perspective. The law of criminal evidence has evolved into a discrete subject in its own right, characterized by a distinctive set of ideals, objectives, institutions, juridical sources, processes, practices, and legal procedures. It is tempting to conclude, on the strength of this book's contents, that the common lawyer's traditional conception of a unified Law of Evidence has had its day. Less contentiously, there is a compelling case for Criminal Evidence and Civil Procedure[16] to take their places alongside orthodox conceptions of the Law of Evidence in the common law disciplinary canon.

16.2 PRINCIPLES OF CRIMINAL EVIDENCE

The greater part of this book has been devoted to identifying and elucidating the *principles* of criminal evidence. Principles are more enduring than mere legal rules and doctrines, which come and go with every statutory reform or innovative common law precedent. Legal principles provide a bridge between technical rules of law and the foundational normative commitments of political morality which are expressed and implemented through criminal proceedings. They help us to appreciate how evidentiary doctrines promote – or as the case may be, retard – liberty, security, personal autonomy, privacy, democratic accountability, and retributive justice. More prosaically, criminal litigation simply could not operate without resort to evidentiary principles, which are the oil preventing the machine from seizing up or exploding under the pressure of incessant demands and rising expectations.

Many procedural rules are open-ended and invite 'discretionary' decision-making by police officers, prosecutors, and trial judges. Discretion best serves justice when it is

---

[16] The switch from 'Evidence' to 'Procedure' is merely a linguistic convention, intended to reflect the relative distribution of 'evidentiary' and 'procedural' norms across the criminal/civil divide. Whereas the law of criminal evidence continues to thrive, the greater part of traditional civil evidence has either been abolished or subsumed within a reformed law of civil procedure. At any rate, nothing of substance is meant to turn on the suggested disciplinary labels.

exercised according to principle, and this is precisely what English law demands.[17] The guidance afforded by evidentiary principles is also indispensable to criminal practitioners on account of the sheer volume of evidentiary rules, statutory provisions, and case-law precedents, which continues to grow exponentially and almost daily. There is, quite simply, too much law for anybody to know and assimilate successfully. Technology is partly to blame, of course, most graphically in virtually obliterating what only a decade ago was a formative juridical distinction between 'reported' and 'unreported' cases. The only way in which this sprawling unruly mass of institutional materials can be tamed, purged of inconsistencies, and fashioned into a reasonably coherent normative system is by appealing to underlying principles and using them as an arbiter of doctrinal pedigree, preserving the wheat and discarding the chaff.

Principles may be specified at varying levels of generality. In the broadest terms we might say, taking our cue from Rule 1.1 of the Criminal Procedure Rules 2010, that the overriding objective of criminal adjudication is that 'criminal cases be dealt with justly'.[18] This is a promising point of departure, inasmuch as it rightly subordinates instrumental epistemic objectives to normative criteria of justice. However, this does not take us very far. It invites the obvious follow-up question, what exactly does it mean to deal with criminal cases *justly*? A parallel observation might be made in relation to the ubiquitous evidentiary principle of promoting fair trials, which was explored in Chapter 5. To insist without further elaboration that trials must be 'fair' is not to say much more than that criminal cases must be dealt with justly. Hence, legislative instruments such as Article 6 of the European Convention on Human Rights endeavour to spell out the meaning of a 'right to a fair trial' in greater detail, which is then further elucidated through the interpretational jurisprudence of the Strasbourg court. Yet another way of framing the primary question, this time with a more overtly penal theory twist, would be: what does retributive justice require of criminal adjudication?

We begin to provide meaningful answers to these questions by articulating principles of criminal evidence in concrete and progressively more fine-grained specifications. Chapter 1 introduced five general principles of criminal evidence designated as foundational: accurate fact-finding; protecting the innocent from wrongful conviction; minimum state intervention ('the liberty principle'); humane treatment of all trial participants; and procedural moral integrity. The legitimacy of criminal verdicts, in both the normative and sociological senses of 'legitimacy', is predicated on judges and other criminal justice professionals protecting and respecting these foundational principles. Further waves of progressively more concrete, refined, and particularistic principles can be derived from these foundational normative commitments.

The procedural framework of English criminal adjudication surveyed in Chapter 2 embodies a number of additional principles characterizing the common law adversarial tradition. These include: the principle of party control over evidence gathering, presentation, and testing; the corresponding principle of judicial independence, neutrality, and relative passivity; the principle of open justice; the principle of appellate review of the safety of convictions and the prohibition on 'double jeopardy'; and the principle of lay fact-finding in accordance with ordinary inferential reasoning. Each of these principles is

---

[17] '[D]iscretion must be exercised judicially': *R v Hubbard* [2002] EWCA Crim 1159, [10]. See §1.4(b).

[18] www.justice.gov.uk/criminal/procrules_fin/rulesmenu.htm.

closely associated with political liberalism and its characteristic virtues of personal freedom and autonomy, limited government, public participation, and democratic accountability, all of which sustain and are sustained by the principle of minimum state intervention
in individuals' lives and liberties.

Accurate fact-finding animates the two most elementary principles of admissibility
introduced in Chapter 3: the principle that only relevant (and material) evidence may be
adduced in the trial; and the principle that relevant evidence will be admitted unless it is
subject to an applicable exclusionary rule. Since exclusionary rules *ex hypothesi* deprive
the fact-finder of relevant information they require explicit justification. The justification
for excluding relevant evidence may be found in considerations of reliability or in appeals
to intrinsic moral values or competing rights, or in some overlapping and, ideally, integrated and mutually reinforcing combination of epistemic and normative criteria.

The preceding chapters have described and critically evaluated exclusionary doctrines
which, when liberated from the conceptual distortions of orthodox evidentiary theory
and shorn of case-law detritus, can be seen to derive from the foundational principles of
criminal evidence. We saw in Chapter 5, for example, that English law has settled on a
flexible and open-ended standard of fairness for assessing the admissibility of unlawfully
or improperly obtained evidence. The first doctrinal point of reference is the common law
principle that such evidence should be admitted only if its probative value outweighs its
prejudicial effect (PV > PE). This capacious general standard generates more determinate
sub-principles applicable to particular kinds of evidence and methods of criminal investigation. In relation to police undercover operations and defence claims of 'entrapment',
for example, the guiding principle is that the police must go no further than providing an
unexceptional opportunity for a willing offender to 'apply the trick to himself'.[19] Where
evidence has been obtained in violation of statutory rules such as PACE 1984 and its associated Codes of Practice, the principle is that exclusion is warranted only where police
transgressions can properly be characterized as 'significant and substantial'.[20]

Rules and principles of admissibility are central to criminal evidence, but they are not
its exclusive preoccupation. This book also explored the principles of proof structuring
fact-finding in criminal adjudication. Chapter 6, for example, elucidated the *Woolmington*
principle, English law's interpretation of the presumption of innocence. *Woolmington* has
two limbs: the principle that the burden of proof lies on the prosecution and the accused
is entitled simply to deny the allegation and call upon the prosecution to prove its case;
and the principle that the standard of proof in criminal proceedings should be steeply
asymmetric, which has traditionally been expressed as requiring 'proof beyond reasonable doubt'; though the preferred formulation is now that the jury should be 'sure' of guilt
before it convicts.[21] The two limbs of the *Woolmington* principle are direct applications
of the principle of protecting the innocent from wrongful conviction. They also incidentally buttress the principle of minimum state intervention and the principle of upholding
procedural integrity. Subsequent chapters extended this style of analysis to other familiar
evidentiary topics, including: compulsory process, privilege, and the principles regulating
access to information; the procedural rules and principles governing witness examination;

---

[19] *R v Christou and Wright* (1992) 95 Cr App R 264, 269, CA; *R v Looseley; Attorney-General's Reference
(No 3 of 2000)* [2001] 1 WLR 2060, [2001] UKHL 53.   [20] *R v Keenan* [1990] 2 QB 54, CA. See §5.4(a).
      [21] §6.4(a).

hearsay and the principle of orality; special measures for vulnerable or intimidated witnesses; the epistemic challenges of expert evidence and principles of lay fact-finding; the voluntariness principle in the law of confessions; principles delimiting the scope of the privilege against self-incrimination; and the law of bad character and its associated principles of confining the evidence to the charge(s) and protecting the accused from unfair prejudice.

To be sure, there are alternative ways of bundling and describing evidentiary principles and procedural rights. For example, the European Court of Human Rights sometimes invokes the principle of 'equality of arms' to encapsulate the thought that the accused must be given a fair opportunity and the means to defend himself against a criminal accusation prosecuted by the state. John Jackson suggests that it is more illuminating to conceptualize the procedural guarantees enumerated in ECHR Article 6(3) as aspects of a general right to participate effectively in the criminal trial process.[22] Drawing on and rearranging the institutional materials presented in previous chapters, it would be possible to construct alternative conceptualizations of criminal evidence that might be equally valid – neither better nor worse as descriptions – than the account developed in this book. The same could equally be said of any rival interpretations.

In expounding the main principles of criminal evidence it is essential to achieve an effective balance between coverage and comprehensibility. Ten principles would be too few to describe all the major landmarks and points of special interest which invest criminal evidence with its unique style and character. Yet a hundred (let alone five hundred) principles would overburden the reader with too many incidental details and distracting detours. We have tried to identify the irreducibly foundational principles of criminal evidence and to indicate how further tiers or waves of progressively more particularistic principles can be derived from them. This mosaic of principles forms a dynamic but mutually stabilizing institutional framework of law and practice. Foundational principles supply the normative rationales to develop and justify more fine-grained evidentiary principles, rules, and doctrines, whilst these applied procedural standards repay the compliment by confirming (to the extent that they do) the wisdom and justice of the foundational principles which inspired them. Ideally, this process should result in a virtuous dialectic of principle. It is our conviction that focusing on underlying principles in this way is the key to developing a deeper and more comprehensive, integrated, and critical understanding of the English law of criminal evidence than, say, reading, the next fifty evidence-related judgments of the Court of Appeal (Criminal Division), or possibly the next five hundred.

16.3 CURRENT TRENDS

The difficulty of making a reliable roadmap to English criminal evidence is increased immeasurably by the fact that procedural law and practice are currently in the grip of far-reaching reconsideration, reform, and normative realignment. Recent changes to the law are cumulative and concatenated but only partially coordinated, somewhat unpredictable, and already without modern precedent in their scale and innovation. This is a time

---

[22] John D. Jackson, 'The Effect of Human Rights on Criminal Evidentiary Processes: Towards Convergence, Divergence or Realignment?' (2005) 68 *MLR* 737.

of historic transformations in criminal adjudication in England and Wales. Attempting to document all of this frenetic legislative and judicial activity and to assess its meaning and significance at any given point in time forcefully brings to mind Zhou En-lai's quip about evaluating the impact of the French Revolution – it is far too early to tell.

In a world with few reliably fixed points from which to take our bearings, three dynamic vectors of change merit emphasis and further reflection: (a) choice of procedural mechanisms to regulate fact-finding; (b) the nature of cognizable legal sources; and (c) the variable normative significance of evidentiary principles, rules, and doctrines.

(a) PROCEDURAL MECHANISMS REGULATING FACT-FINDING

Admissibility is the common lawyer's evidentiary technique *par excellence* for regulating the flow and uses of information in legal adjudication. It is therefore entirely understandable that traditional common law treatments of the Law of Evidence, like the moth to its flame, became fascinated with rules of admissibility and exclusion. Over a period of time, however, English law has softened or entirely abandoned its traditional exclusionary rules, a process set in train by the judges but greatly accelerated by Parliament. The Criminal Justice Act 2003 exemplifies this trend in relation to two of the common law's exclusionary stalwarts, bad character evidence and hearsay. One must not overstate the case for the sake of rhetorical impact. Admissibility determinations remain highly significant in criminal litigation, and they are sometimes effectively dispositive. Yet the power of exclusionary rules is not what it once was and their sphere of influence is constantly being eroded.

As exclusionary doctrines have declined, forensic reasoning rules have been recast and reconditioned to take up some of the adjudicative strain. If probatively dubious or potentially prejudicial evidence is now being adduced in criminal trials where formerly it would have been excluded, evidence law must refocus its regulatory attentions on how and for what purposes the jury might use that information. So forensic reasoning rules become the paradigmatic evidentiary technique of our day. Chapter 15 told the story of how the pedantically technical and often irrational law of corroboration was gradually superseded by flexible judicial warnings tailored to provide maximum assistance to jurors in getting to grips with particular types of 'suspect' evidence. The jury is expected to utilize its powers of ordinary common sense reasoning in order to discharge its forensic duties, but it is not required to fly blind. The judge is there to provide assistance. Where experience teaches that, e.g. 'fleeting glimpse' eyewitness identifications[23] or gaol-cell confessions to fellow inmates,[24] suffer from predictable evidential weaknesses, the judge should draw these infirmities to the jury's attention and point out, where appropriate, the types of evidence which might be capable of providing confirmatory support. Whilst the majority of these forensic reasoning rules were developed by the judges at common law, there are now a significant and growing number of statutory provisions which also require some kind of warning to be given, particularly in relation to procedural adjustments (such as the use of special measures or witness anonymity) which might otherwise be misread by

---

[23] *R v Turnbull* [1977] QB 224, CA.

[24] *R v Nudds* [2008] EWCA Crim 148; *Pringle v R* [2003] UKPC 9 (Jam), extending the general principle formulated in *R v Beck* [1982] 1 WLR 461, CA.

fact-finders as implicitly reflecting badly on the accused.[25] Some forensic reasoning rules evince a quantitative orientation insofar as they instruct fact-finders about the desirability of 'corroborating' (i.e. supporting) evidence and where to look for it. Others focus exclusively on particular kinds of inference and warn against notorious inferential traps and fallacies. The details of such warnings are spelt out in the Judicial Studies Board's compendious Specimen Directions.[26] For the student of criminal evidence, rules of admissibility are no longer the only game in town (if they ever were).

A second general institutional technique for regulating evidence is active judicial case management, which in turn is linked to a trend towards more thorough and consequential case preparation in the pre-trial phases of criminal litigation.[27] The English criminal trial used to be a discrete event. Although the course of the trial has always inevitably been shaped by the investigation and formal charges which preceded it, the trial itself represented a juridically self-sufficient and temporally continuous forensic inquiry.[28] At the start of a traditional common law trial, the judge and jury have no prior knowledge of the case and counsel project their carefully crafted forensic narratives onto a clean slate. The verdict of the jury and, in the event of a conviction, sentencing by the judge brings trial proceedings proper to a close. Appeals and post-conviction processes are tightly circumscribed and regarded as incidental to the adjudicative focal point.

English criminal trials have progressively drifted away from this orthodox common law model.[29] There is now extensive pre-trial disclosure of evidence and other relevant information; even the defence bears increasing responsibilities in this regard.[30] Notice must be served on the other parties and to the court in order to adduce certain kinds of evidence, including hearsay and bad character.[31] Once information has been disclosed it can be managed. Judges have been tasked with taking a more active role in pre-trial case management, primarily with a view to promoting the efficiency of criminal litigation and avoiding costly adjournments and late guilty pleas ('cracked trials'). Legislative provision was made for pre-trial reviews[32] and plea and case management hearings (PCMHs)[33] to ensure that cases are properly prepared, to narrow down the issues for trial to those matters truly in dispute, and to encourage early guilty pleas. Whilst measures such as these have been tried before, the truly innovative feature is that decisions and agreements in these preparatory phases now bind the parties at trial. Pre-trial evidentiary rulings are definitive unless there is a material change of circumstances.[34] This partly explains why it was also necessary to introduce interlocutory appeals on points of evidence,[35] a complete novelty in

---

[25] §15.3(c).

[26] See Judicial Studies Board, *Crown Court Bench Book: Specimen Directions*, Part III 'Evidence': www. jsboard.co.uk/criminal_law/cbb/index.htm.

[27] HHJ Roderick Denyer QC, *Case Management in the Crown Court* (Hart, 2008).   [28] §1.2(b).

[29] Mirjan R. Damaška, *Evidence Law Adrift* (Yale UP, 1997).

[30] Criminal Procedure and Investigations Act 1996, ss.5–6E. The defence has been obliged to serve notice of alibi witnesses since the enactment of the Criminal Justice Act 1967, s.11. For investigations commenced after 1 April 1997, the controlling provision is now CPIA 1996, s.5.

[31] CrimPR 2010, Parts 34 and 35, implementing CJA 2003, ss.111 and 132.

[32] CPIA 1996, Part III; Crime and Disorder Act 1998, s.51. Also see the *Consolidated Criminal Practice Direction*, Part IV.41: www.justice.gov.uk/criminal/procrules_fin/.

[33] CrimPR 2010, Rule 3.8; *Plea and Case Management Hearing Form: Guidance Notes* (2009).

[34] CPIA 1996, s.40.   [35] CJA 2003, ss.58 and 63 (when brought into force); CPIA 1996, ss.35–36.

English criminal proceedings. The defence runs a real risk of provoking adverse inferences if it reneges on a pre-trial statement or undertaking. The Criminal Procedure Rules 2010 encourage trial judges to take a firm hand in pre-trial case management, and should leave the parties in no doubt that traditional expectations of party control over the course of litigation require significant adjustment in modern English criminal proceedings.[36]

The net effect of these important procedural innovations is to de-centre the trial and make it more continuous with the pre-trial process. Perhaps the most striking illustration of this temporal stretching of 'trial' proceedings is the transformed status of custodial police interviews in modern English criminal procedure. In retrospect, PACE 1984, s.58, and Code of Practice C might be viewed as presaging this sea-change, but the effect was intensified and became much more evident as a consequence of the limitations on the right to silence introduced by the Criminal Justice and Public Order Act 1994. Now that adverse inferences may be drawn from any 'significant silence' in the police station defence legal advisers must formulate an appropriate legal strategy without delay (with indecent haste, some would say), and preferably before their client is interviewed by the police. To the extent that potential evidence is actively being managed and indeed *created* from that moment onwards, it is hardly much of an exaggeration to say that many criminal trials begin in the police station.[37] Thereafter, if charges are filed and pursued a pre-trial judge (preferably, but not always, the designated trial judge) will orchestrate negotiations between the parties and play an interventionist role in ensuring that the case is well prepared for trial.[38]

The wider implications of active judicial case management extend far beyond the scope of the present discussion. For our purposes, the essential point is that evidence is now being scrutinized and its preparation and presentation actively managed by the court long before the point at which admissibility determinations have traditionally been made.

(b) JURIDICAL SOURCES

Evidence is regarded as a quintessentially case-based common law subject. The law of evidence evolved from rules of practice developed by the common law courts. It is judge-made law, and there is an enormous amount of it. One could cheerfully spend the entirety of one's professional life reading cases on points of evidence and the well would never run dry.

Today, the ingrained disciplinary conception of Evidence as a case-law subject is massively distorting. If one were forced to choose sides in a foolish dispute, it would be more accurate to say that the English law of criminal evidence is based on statutes. Miscellaneous enactments[39] and incidental amendments aside, the main statutory provisions discussed in this

---

[36] Cf. CrimPR 2010, Rule 3.2: 'The court must further the overriding objective by actively managing the case'. English civil proceedings have undergone similar and already more pronounced modifications: see Adrian Zuckerman, *Zuckerman on Civil Procedure: Principles of Practice* (Sweet & Maxwell, 2nd edn. 2006), chs 1 and 10.

[37] Another significant illustration of the trial's temporal extension is that gateway (g) of CJA 2003, s.101, is capable of being triggered by what the accused said during police interview: see §14.4(d).

[38] CrimPR 2010, Part 3.

[39] Including the scores of statutes containing reverse onus provisions (see Chapter 6) or ensuring compliance with the privilege against self-incrimination (see Chapter 13). Exclusion form the main list of statutes

book are contained in the Criminal Procedure Act 1865; the Criminal Evidence Act 1898; the Police and Criminal Evidence Act 1984; the Criminal Justice Act 1988; the Criminal Justice and Public Order Act 1994; the Criminal Procedure and Investigations Act 1996; the Youth Justice and Criminal Evidence Act 1999; the Regulation of Investigatory Powers Act 2000; the Criminal Justice Act 2003; and the Coroners and Justice Act 2009 (incorporating and superseding the Criminal Evidence (Witness Anonymity) Act 2008). Even simply listing these evidence-related enactments is sufficient to bring home the extent to which criminal litigation is now regulated by statute. Such an obvious development staring us right in the face can be overlooked only if we allow ourselves to be hoodwinked by a blinkered orthodoxy still insisting or assuming that Evidence is a case-law subject, distinct from 'procedure', which is devoted to elucidating generic common law rules applicable to civil as well as criminal proceedings.

The growing importance of statutes to the modern law of criminal evidence does not entail that case-law ceases to be significant: quite the reverse. Every new statutory provision spawns its own interpretative canon. Even good quality legislation may require extensive judicial interpretation. Poor quality legislation infected with internal drafting anomalies, inconsistent or in conflict with related statutory provisions, and posing evident risks of injustice requires still greater judicial fine-tuning. The Court of Appeal informs us that English criminal procedure law has been blighted by legislation of the latter sort in recent years,[40] and it is difficult to disagree. There is consequently more case-law than ever before. The difference lies in the fact that judicial reasoning on points of evidence now typically begins with a statutory provision or must at least contend with overlapping statutory concepts or language. The authority of many case-law precedents becomes contingent on statutory interpretation, which in turn limits the extent to which judicial pronouncements can take secure root in the law. The statute itself might later be amended or repealed, or an alternative judicial interpretation of the original provision may subsequently be proclaimed authentic. The upshot is that modern criminal evidence law contains a mixture of statutes and cases and case-law interpretations of statutory provisions, pre-empting serious debate about whether Criminal Evidence is really a statutory *or* a case-law subject. It is evidently a fusion or melange of legislation and common law precedents.

The emergence of legislation is only one part of a more complex story of diversification in the juridical sources of criminal evidence. We are, in fact, witnessing a period of radical pluralization in which the institutional sources of law are extending, as it were, upwards and downwards and outwards. Looking upwards, we encounter European human rights law and beyond that European law, international human rights law and public international law more generally. The pervasive and continually expanding influence of ECHR jurisprudence on English criminal procedure makes its presence felt in almost every chapter of this book. Looking downwards, we cannot fail to notice a proliferation of delegated legislation, administrative regulations, and informal but hardworking 'soft law' norms which have featured prominently in these pages. The most important informal sources of procedural standards for our purposes are undoubtedly the Criminal Procedure Rules,

---

is emphatically not intended to imply that scattered 'miscellaneous' provisions are unimportant in criminal adjudication.

[40] See, e.g., *R v Bradley* [2005] EWCA Crim 20, (2005) 169 JP 73, [38]–[39]; *R v R (Video Recording: Admissibility)* [2008] 1 WLR 2044, [2008] EWCA Crim 678.

the JSB's Specimen Directions, and the PACE Codes of Practice – though a variety of others might have been added to the list, not forgetting rules of professional practice like the Bar's *Code of Conduct*. It misrepresents the practical influence of these norms to describe them, in the conventional almost patronizing idiom, as 'soft law'. For most judges and criminal practitioners most of the time, these informal standards dictate the reality – they are 'the law' – of modern English criminal procedure. Finally, looking outwards, there is a discernable trend towards legislators, policymakers, and judges drawing upon comparative models and precedents in developing English law. In recent judgments of the House of Lords and now the Supreme Court, for example, it is not unusual to encounter citations to foreign law, and these are not limited to common law precedents (a well-established concomitant of judicial reasoning in England and Wales) but also sometimes extended to Continental/civilian jurisprudence and the pronouncements of international criminal courts. If there was ever a time when domestic appellate judgments exhausted the legal sources of criminal evidence in England and Wales, those days are long gone.

The Human Rights Act is part-and-parcel of an emergent legal cosmopolitanism[41] with further potential implications for the law of criminal evidence. Many of the ECHR's key concepts are borrowed from national legal systems, and their subsequent development has drawn inspiration from international treaties, regional legal orders (especially the EU, with which it overlaps), a nascent common law of international human rights,[42] national constitutions and municipal domestic laws. An imaginative and modestly expansionist jurisprudence might easily regard a diverse range of international, comparative, and foreign law materials as having been incorporated by reference into sources of English law under the Human Rights Act. It is right to say that English Evidence lawyers have always been mild comparativists, inasmuch as Australian, New Zealand, Canadian, Caribbean Commonwealth (Privy Council), and even occasionally US judgments are familiar sources of inspiration and auxiliary authority in English legal reasoning. However, confining one's comparative gaze to a handful of Anglophone municipal jurisdictions is beginning to appear anachronistic, if not faintly chauvinist. Only time will tell where this will all ultimately lead, but several potentially momentous developments can already be identified.

The advent of international criminal trials, from the *ad hoc* tribunals for the former Yugoslavia and Rwanda created in the 1990s[43] to the historic ratification of the Rome Statute for an International Criminal Court (ICC) in April 2002,[44] has taken criminal procedure into previously uncharted territory. Meanwhile, the European Union's formal competence in penal affairs has been considerably expanded, and now boasts a significant

---

[41] See further, Paul Roberts, 'Faces of Justice Adrift? Damaška's Comparative Method and the Future of Common Law Evidence', in John Jackson, Maximo Langer, and Peter Tillers (eds.), *Crime, Procedure and Evidence in A Comparative and International Context – Essays in Honour of Professor Mirjan Damaska* (Hart, 2008); Paul Roberts, 'Comparative Law for International Criminal Justice', in Esin Örücü and David Nelken (eds.), *Comparative Law – A Handbook* (Hart, 2007).

[42] Christopher McCrudden, 'A Common Law of Human Rights?: Transnational Judicial Conversations on Constitutional Rights' (2000) 20 *OJLS* 499.

[43] The ICTY and ICTR maintain excellent web-sites containing full transcripts of all (open) trial proceedings: www.icty.org; www.ictr.org.

[44] For concise introductions to the ICC regime, see Robert Cryer *et al*, *An Introduction to International Criminal Law and Procedure* (CUP, 2007), ch 8; Dominic McGoldrick, 'The Permanent International Criminal Court: An End to the Culture of Impunity?' [1999] *Crim LR* 627.

procedural dimension.[45] Though supra-national tribunals are institutionally and normatively *sui generis*, fashioning their law and practice from unique combinations of municipal
and international norms, it is evident that the UN's *ad hoc* tribunals base themselves on a
recognizably Anglo-American model of evidence law, and the ICC is developing its own
procedural hybrid incorporating common law elements.[46] The potential scope for Evidence
scholars to make major contributions to the theory and practice of the emergent discipline
of International Criminal Justice is immense. Conversely, students of criminal evidence
and procedure surely have much to learn from observing the attempts of the international
community to get to grips with traditional problems of evidence and proof in novel and
exceptionally challenging supra-national settings.[47] In these experimental judicial fora
conventional forensic strategies and assumptions are routinely tested to breaking point.

(c) NORMATIVE HIERARCHIES

The pluralization of legal sources poses insistent questions of normative hierarchy. On the
orthodox account to which English law still pays lip-service, parliamentary sovereignty is
unlimited, statutes trump cases, and administrative action is subject to common law judicial review. In the modern world of legal cosmopolitanism this is an increasingly qualified
and sometimes tenuous approximation of reality.

Membership of the European Union has recast the UK's political sovereignty, but this
transformation has not – yet – made much of an impact on the law of criminal evidence.
For our purposes, the ECHR is more significant. The statutory framework for translating
ECHR rights into English law established by the Human Rights Act 1998, we now know,
sometimes authorizes senior judges to rewrite statutes where this is deemed necessary
to avoid a declaration of incompatibility.[48] In theory, judicial authority still derives from
the will of Parliament, as expressed in the Human Rights Act, but this degree of interpretational latitude is entirely novel. As Humpty Dumpty instructed Alice, we are playing
a different kind of game when words can mean whatever we say they mean.[49] The UK is
presumably not yet politically ready for substantive judicial review of legislation and genuine separation of powers on the US constitutional model, but history will show that the
first steps down this road have already been taken. The recent creation of an independent

---

[45] Estella Baker, 'The European Union's "Area of Freedom, Security and (Criminal) Justice" Ten Years
On' [2009] *Crim LR* 833; Evan Bell, 'A European DPP to Prosecute Euro-Fraud?' [2000] *Crim LR* 154.

[46] Generally, see Peter Murphy, 'Excluding Justice or Facilitating Justice? International Criminal Law
Would Benefit from Rules of Evidence' (2008) 12 *E & P* 1; 'Special Issue: Fairness and Evidence in War Crimes
Trials' (2006) 4(1) *International Commentary on Evidence*, www.bepress.com/ice/vol4/iss1/; Richard May
et al (eds.), *Essays on ICTY Procedure and Evidence in Honour of Gabrielle Kirk McDonald* (The Hague, 2001);
Patricia M. Wald, 'To "Establish Incredible Events by Credible Evidence": the Use of Affidavit Testimony in
Yugoslavia War Crimes Tribunal Proceedings' (2001) 42 *Harvard International Law Journal* 535; Patrick
L. Robinson, 'Ensuring Fair and Expeditious Trials at the International Criminal Tribunal for the Former
Yugoslavia' (2000) 11 *European Journal of International Law* 569; Richard May and Marieke Wierda, 'Trends
in International Criminal Evidence: Nuremberg, Tokyo, the Hague and Arusha' (1999) 37 *Columbia Journal
of Transnational Law* 725; Rod Dixon, 'Developing International Rules of Evidence for the Yugoslav and
Rwanda Tribunals' (1997) 7 *Transnational Law and Contemporary Problems* 81.

[47] Paul Roberts, 'Why International Criminal Evidence?', in Paul Roberts and Mike Redmayne (eds.),
Innovations in Evidence and Proof: Integrating Theory, Research and Teaching (Hart, 2007).

[48] See *R* v *A (No 2)* [2002] 1 AC 45, [2001] UKHL 25, discussed in §10.2.

[49] Cf. *Liversidge* v *Anderson* [1942] AC 206, 245, HL (Lord Atkin, dissenting).

UK Supreme Court,[50] housed in its own premises outside the Houses of Parliament, will further institutionalize a reconstituted division of governmental labour and, in time, embolden the senior judiciary to fulfil its democratic constitutional destiny.

Meanwhile, the pluralization of legal sources presents criminal courts with a succession of jurisprudential puzzles. Which foreign laws, judgments, or other sources should be extracted from the dazzling cosmopolitan array of potential 'precedents'? How do these sources rank against one another in the hierarchy of legal authority? What is their precise bearing on the instant case? These questions pose challenges of information management no less than jurisprudential analysis. Sometimes, the answer is relatively straightforward (even if the question is not). For example, the House of Lords decreed that English courts should normally defer to the European Court of Human Rights' own interpretations of the text of the ECHR.[51] Applying this *dictum* is not necessarily straightforward, however, since English courts may be confronted with the argument that ECHR jurisprudence is not directly in point. Beyond this, complexities multiply. Which is more authoritative, a judgment of the International Criminal Tribunal for the Former Yugoslavia on the fair trial provisions of its Statute (which replicate ECHR Article 6) or a judgment of the South African Constitutional Court on identical wording in the South African Constitution? Or how about the status of a judgment of the German Federal Constitutional Court elucidating a German law concept[52] which was used as the basis for an EU or ECHR norm which also applies in the UK? What if the European Court of Justice were to produce an interpretation of EU fundamental rights[53] seemingly at odds with the ECtHR's interpretation of an overlapping provision of the ECHR? Needless to add, the English courts will have to make up their own minds on these questions as a matter of English law, but in order to render judgment on a principled and consistent basis English courts will be obliged to appraise the comparative jurisprudential merits and status of a diverse range of cosmopolitan legal standards and sources.

A final juridical development worth highlighting in these concluding paragraphs is the elevation of selected evidentiary norms to the status of constitutional principles. The partial constitutionalization of criminal procedure is closely related to the expanding influence of the ECHR on English law. Most of the substantive content of the ECHR, including the Articles bearing directly on criminal proceedings (Articles 3, 5, 6, and 8),[54] is already part of the constitutional law of other domestic legal systems. The UK has no comparable tradition of constitutional rights being specified in positive law, but the Human Rights Act was a decisive intervention and constitutionalism is now in the atmosphere.

In the absence of a written criminal procedure code with anything approaching constitutional status, common law judges have occasionally stepped into the breach. As long ago as 1979 the House of Lords declared compulsory process, secured through the

---

[50] www.supremecourt.gov.uk/.

[51] *R (Ullah)* v *Special Adjudicator* [2004] 2 AC 323, [2004] UKHL 26, which must now be read subject to *R* v *Horncastle* [2009] UKSC 14, [2010] 2 WLR 94, [11]. See §1.5(a).

[52] For a helpful English-language summary of the sources, normative hierarchy, and basic concepts of German criminal law, see Michael Bohlander, *Principles of German Criminal Law* (Hart, 2009), chs 1–2.

[53] See *Consolidated Versions of the Treaty on European Union and the Treaty on the Functioning of the European Union* (2008/C 115/01), Art 6 TEU; and *Charter of Fundamental Rights of the European Union* (2007/C 303/01): both on-line: http://eur-lex.europa.eu/en/treaties/index.htm.

[54] Though specifically addressing penal matters, Article 7 concerns substantive criminal law as opposed to criminal process.

compellability of witness testimony, to be a constitutional principle.[55] Subsequently, the absolute nature of legal professional privilege[56] and the categorical exclusion of evidence that was, or may have been, obtained by torture of any person were explicitly singled out for their constitutional pedigree.[57] These may be isolated judgments, but their significance cannot be doubted. The progressive constitutionalization of English criminal procedure goes hand-in-hand with the advancing pluralization of legal sources, including increasing resort to foreign constitutional law and international human rights standards. Common law constitutionalization also informs the expanding array of evidentiary techniques regulating evidence and proof in criminal trials. Determining whether particular evidence should be admitted in the first place, and then deciding how to direct the jury in relation to evidence ruled admissible, are tasks demanding contextualized applications of judicial discretion that ought to be informed by relevant constitutional standards.

16.4 FUTURE DIRECTIONS FOR CRIMINAL EVIDENCE

Sir Rupert Cross, the greatest English evidence law scholar of the twentieth century, provocatively declared in the heat of debate that he was working towards the day when his (and our) subject would be abolished.[58] Taken at face value, the statement is preposterous – and not merely in the ironic sense intended by Marx when he described capitalists as their own grave-diggers. Evidence is information; information is the epistemic fulcrum of criminal adjudication; and information management, regulation, analysis, and evaluation in criminal proceedings are the subject matter of Criminal Evidence. Only by narrowly equating the Law of Evidence with rules of admissibility and formulaic jury directions is it even intelligible to talk about abolishing the subject. For as long as criminal adjudication continues in something resembling its current form, the law of criminal evidence will remain an important and rewarding field of legal study and an indispensable component of professional legal practice.

Predicting the future shape and content of the law of criminal evidence in anything more than faint and blurry outlines is another matter entirely. The safest predictions might begin with continuing and doubtless increasingly rapid change. The current trends identified in the last section seem likely to intensify. Forensic reasoning rules will become more numerous and influential relative to rules of admissibility, and active judicial case management will continue to de-centre the traditional common law criminal trial and stretch its temporal duration. The sources of criminal evidence law will continue to expand upwards, downwards and outwards, becoming progressively more pluralistic and

---

[55] *Hoskyn v MPC* [1979] AC 474, 484, HL (Lord Wilberforce).

[56] *R v Derby Magistrates' Court, ex p. B* [1996] 1 AC 487, HL.

[57] *A v Secretary of State for the Home Department (No 2)* [2006] 2 AC 221, [2005] UKHL 71.

[58] According to William Twining, *Rethinking Evidence: Exploratory Essays* (CUP, 2nd edn. 2006), 1. Cross's immediate objective was systematic law reform which would 'spare the judge from talking gibberish to the jury, the conscientious magistrate from directing himself in imbecile terms and the writer on the law of evidence from drawing distinctions absurd enough to bring a blush to the most hardened academic face': Rupert Cross, 'The Evidence Report: Sense or Nonsense – A Very Wicked Animal Defends the 11th Report of the Criminal Law Revision Committee' [1973] *Crim LR* 329, 333.

cosmopolitan. The sheer bulk of evidentiary sources will grow exponentially, posing significant challenges of information management. More attention will need to be devoted to constructing normative hierarchies. Additional evidentiary norms may be promoted into the pantheon of constitutional principles, whilst the status of human rights in criminal proceedings will require further delineation and on-going adjustment to prevailing social needs and expectations.

The preoccupations of courts, legislatures, and policymakers should inform (without dictating) the agenda for evidence law teaching, research, and scholarship. Major tasks for Criminal Evidence teachers and scholars in the immediate future include:[59] developing the epistemology of forensic fact-finding and proof (particularly in relation to scientific evidence and other expert testimony, which are increasingly influential in all spheres of modern life); exploring the normative philosophical foundations of evidentiary doctrines and assessing the adequacy of their justificatory rationales; devising and refining explanatory models, taxonomies, and classifications of procedural norms; and contributing towards the evolution of a truly cosmopolitan jurisprudence of criminal evidence and procedure. This book is intended to contribute to each of these intersecting and mutually reinforcing intellectual and practical projects. Whilst the account of Criminal Evidence elaborated in these pages describes subsisting English law and identifies emergent trends, it is certain that future developments in the law and practice of criminal adjudication will require constant readjustments and refinements to our model, if not radical rethinking. The uncertainties of the future, no less than the jurisprudential demands of the present, can be viewed with greater equanimity from the vantage point of principle.

---

[59] Also see Paul Roberts and Mike Redmayne (eds.), *Innovations in Evidence and Proof* (Hart, 2007); Paul Roberts, 'Rethinking the Law of Evidence: A Twenty-First Century Agenda for Teaching and Research' (2002) 55 *CLP* 297.

INDEX

References specifying a range of consecutive pages (e.g."178–9") indicate (not necessarily continuous) discussion of a topic across several pages. Wherever possible, references to repeatedly occurring topics have either been divided into sub-headings or restricted to the most significant discussions. Thus, information regarding 'criminal evidence' and a handful of other basic concepts which recur throughout the book will be found under the corresponding detailed sub-headings.